GATES ON EVIDENCE
Zambian Theory and Practice

VOLUME 3

GATES ON EVIDENCE

Zambian theory and Practice

By

Reagan Blankfein Gates, PG Dip Business Management (USW), LL. M (UNISA), LL. B (UNZA), AHCZ

Founding and Managing Partner
Reagan Blankfein Gates Legal Practitioners

Formerly Assistant Senior Research Advocate
Judiciary of Zambia

Formerly Lecturer of International Investment, Contract and Company Law
Cavendish University Zambia

Formerly Lecturer of Pension Law (UG), Insurance Law (PG), Legal Aspects of International Finance (PG)
ZCAS University

First edition published 2023
by Thankerton Publishing Limited
Plot No 30107, Off Manchinchi Road, Olympia Park Lusaka, Zambia

Thankerton Publishing is an imprint of Thankerton Publishing Limited. It has as its objectives, the furtherance of learning, scholarship and edification and enabling authors to bring their work to the masses by leveraging its publication capabilities.

First edition published by Thankerton Publishing Limited 2022

National Archives of Zambia Cataloguing in Publication Data
A catalogue record for this book is available from the National Archives of Zambia

Reagan Blankfein Gates, author.

Gates on Evidence: Zambian Theory and Practice / Reagan Blankfein Gates — First edition.
Evidence (Law)—Zambia.

Typeset in Palatino Linotype by Mwanida Banda: bmwanida@gmail.com

Printed by Amazon Kindle Direct Publishing, USA.

For further information on this and other works by this author and updates generally, visit our homepage: http://thankertonpublishing.com.

In memory of my late daughter
Olivia Kaitlyn Gates
who died during her birth on 4 September 2020

CONTENTS SUMMARY

DETAILED CONTENTS

FOREWORD

By the Hon. Mr. Chief Justice Ernest L. Sakala (Rtd)

At its most elementary characterisation, the practice of law in general and mastering the rules of evidence (and their skillful deployment prior to and during trial) in particular, encompasses conducting research to find pertinent rules of law and then applying those same rules to the specific set of facts and circumstances for which counsel has been hired by the layperson. However, in the Zambian Law of Evidence which is primarily premised on English common law, the legal rules applicable to different sets of circumstances are derived from and premised on numerous sources, including the Constitution, statutory law, the common law and writings of jurists, among others. This complicates what is already an extensive branch of the law which encompasses civil and criminal law on the one hand, and adjectival law on the other.

This book, *Gates on Evidence: Zambian Theory and Practice* introduces first-time readers in the law of evidence, law lecturers, would-be practitioners, legal practitioners as well as magistrates and judges of the Superior Courts, and I dare say, policy-makers to not only what the law has been and is, but also where it should be headed in keeping with contemporary trends in the commonwealth and civil jurisdictions as well as other international fora.

The book also seeks to demystify this somewhat enigmatic branch of the law by employing a pithy style complete with decided cases from this jurisdiction and cases from other jurisdictions which still continue to influence the development of Zambian jurisprudence. Finally, the text illustrates how the different pieces come together and can be used in practice by students, litigants, practitioners and judges as the case may be.

I must conclude this foreword by pointing out that the author has vast work history from several law firms and the public sector where he worked previously. He has experience in corporate, commercial, criminal and civil litigation. From 2013 to 2016 he worked in, the Judiciary of Zambia as a Senior Research Advocate. Some of his duties included drafting opinions on rulings and judgments, conducting general and specific research into legal questions arising from cases before the court, statutory interpretation and general case management. In the end, he established his own law practice, Reagan Blankfein Gates Legal Practitioners in 2018 where he currently serves as Managing Partner.

I, therefore warmly welcome *Gates Evidence: Zambian Theory and Practice* and unreservedly recommend it to all who seek an easy-to-read but detailed text that arguably leaves no stone unturned and caters to the needs of students, lecturers, legal practitioners and judges alike. I do not doubt that it will be a valuable resource to those interested in appreciating the minutiaeof the theory and practice of the law of evidence within the Zambian context.

The Hon. Chief Justice Ernest L. Sakala (Rtd)
Lusaka, July 2022

PREFACE

The law of evidence is at the core of the practice of law leading to litigation. It, therefore, cannot be emphasised enough that a thorough understanding of the subject specifically the rules of admissibility, weight and relevance ought to underpin any practice. It is a truism that cases are won or lost because of a profound appreciation of evidence or lack thereof and the skilful and well-timed deployment thereof and not so much the substantive law or facts that may inform a cause. For an advocate who seeks to make a success of his litigation practice, a working knowledge of the rules and law of evidence is a *sine qua non* to this goal.

Unlike most branches of law, the law of evidence is experienced in real-time during trial and its sometimes-fatal consequences are brought to bear at once. This is because at trial, evidential questions or disputations will arise without warning and without any preparation for them, indeed, *ex improviso*, and must be addressed and determined as and when they arise and not later. Thus, when there is an attempt to introduce objectionable evidence, this must be objected to immediately. Failure to do so at the precise moment when the attempt is made may mean that fatal evidence which would otherwise not have been admissible is admitted. In the same analogy, objections that are raised during trial must be dealt with whether well-founded or not. Courts will listen to the objection in real time and ask counsel on the other side to respond before making a ruling. A failure to effectively deal with evidential issues which arise, as said in the preface to the first edition of *Murphy on Evidence* or more correctly, *A Practical Approach to Evidence*, 'ex improviso, [and] which no human ingenuity could foresee,' may also prove fatal. Whether counsel has the wherewithal to deal with evidentiary issues at trial is a skill that requires to be developed, fined tune and deployed so frequently that it becomes second nature. It must equip counsel with the instinct to immediately detect what is right, that is, what is admissible, relevant and has weight while at the same time, that which is inadmissible irrelevant and lacking in weight based on the common law and statutory rules of the law of evidence as circumscribed by rules of practice and where relevant, substantive law. The significance of the foregoing should not be lost on students, lecturers, legal practitioners and judges.

I would be remiss in my duties if I did not take the time to pay tribute to those that mustered the courage and took on the unenviable task of, prior to this work, authoring texts in the law of evidence from a Zambian vantage point. Professors Hatchard and Ndulo' s text, *The Law of Evidence in Zambia: Cases and Materials* was the first text of its kind to address the subject from a Zambian perspective. This text remains in print today and in many respects continues to be relevant. It stands atop the hill of knowledge as a pioneering work in the sphere law relating to Zambian evidence and explains the rules of evidence by employing the case method. It is without question a ground-breaking piece. It is a text I have relied on in writing this text to continue the journey started by those pioneering learned authors. My learned Colleague, Brian J Mwanza has written and published *Passing the Bar Made Easy: Evidence and Procedure* and deserves commendation for producing a work specifically geared at examination preparation for bar students. It is a text I recommend for this purpose. In the year 2022, my other learned colleague, Bright Chilufya Kaluba, published his work entitled *Evidence Law Practice and Procedure in Zambia*. The significance of this achievement cannot be overemphasised. Given the complexity of the subject, through its rather wide-ranging nature, and practical eminence, Mr. Kaluba has accomplished several things: (i) he has, in so far as authorship in this esoteric branch of the law is concerned, singlehandedly brought scholarship in the Zambian Law of Evidence into the 21st Century, when in the years following the publication by Hatchard and Ndulo, no other text had been published by a Zambian author for well over 37 years; (ii) he has skilfully managed to meld the rules of evidence with the general rules of practice in a manner that makes his text a 'one-stop shop' for the application of rules of evidence within the context of the rules of court much as that other text, by erstwhile Judge Dr Patrick Matibini, SC entitled *Zambian Civil Procedure*, does from a civil procedure perspective; and (iii) he has managed to deploy our most recent jurisprudence not only from our superior courts but from selected commonwealth jurisdictions. In that sense, his work is a *tour de force* in the rarefied field of the Zambian law of evidence. It too is a text to which I have made several references principally because of the last point here made and as such, is deserving of a space in your library.

This first edition of *Gates on Evidence: Zambian Theory and Practice* is an attempt not only to add to the body of knowledge in this respect but also to present this rather complex subject in terms of the theories that underpin and inform the considerations of practice in our courts by whatever name called. To this end, I have endeavoured to supply students, lecturers, legal practitioners, and judges with that which I hope will be considered a repository of the Zambian law of evidence at present and in future. The structure of the text has been designed to help the reader to grasp the core concepts of the subject with ease and serenity. The information is presented in a logical structure with an accessible explanation of concepts in a clear and precise format tinged with the necessary level of detail and background where this is called for. Though the text may go further than most in several respects, and appear dense, it still manages to lay an excellent foundation for learning the law of evidence within the Zambian context irrespective of the reader's motivation for its study. In saying the preceding, I am alive to the fact that the needs of students and lecturers on the one hand and candidates for the Legal Practitioners Qualifying Examinations Course (offered by the Zambia Institute of Advanced Legal Education (ZIALE)), practitioners and judges on the other, may be varied. Even so, this work, it is hoped, will sit in the middle of the needs of the various sets of audiences at whom it is aimed. A great effort has been made to present the work not only in terms of the thoughts of the author and those of other scholars, but also through the interpretation of the law of evidence as can be evidenced through judicial pronouncements by our courts or put another way, by reference to the *ipsissma verba* of judges. Therefore, the book brings the practical realities of substantive law as taught at university and procedural law as inculcated at ZIALE by including, among other things, cases, extracts from other jurists and contemporary discussion.

While every effort has been made to acknowledge sources in keeping with good academic practice, I apologise if I inadvertently left unacknowledged any sources used in this publication and will gladly take any required measures at the first opportunity.

The law, it is hoped, is as stated on 30 June 2022, though it has been possible to include changes to the law brought about by the enactment of the Children's Code, Act No 12 of 2022. Finally, I take full responsibility for any errors and omissions.

RBG
Lusaka, July 2022

ACKNOWLEDGEMENTS

This book has been under 'construction' for the better part of the last 4 years. During that time, I have become indebted to so many people directly or indirectly. Having started writing the text less than a year after setting up my law practice it became clear to me that this text would demand more than any works I had done previously. The team at Reagan Blankfein Gates Legal Practitioners (RBGLP), past and present have been helpful in this regard by working on instructions that would have been mine to work on otherwise, and in that regard gave me time to dedicate to this project. In this regard I would like to thank Annalise, Melody, Mwima, David, Mary, Tafwakose, Musendeka, Emmanuel, Precious, Martha, Jethro, Andrew, Brighton, Elizabeth, Chileshe, Chansa, Theresa, Bodwell, Hastings and Sinikiwe. I could not ask for a better team. Iam incredibly thankful to Chabala Chilufya our erstwhile office manager at RBGLP who took on, under extreme pressure and my time-bound demands, the unenviable task of type source material on which this work was based. I am further thankful to the erstwhile Chief Justice of Zambia, Mr. Justice Ernest L. Sakala for accepting to write the foreword to this text, Dr. Munyonzwe Hamalengwa for reviewing the entire text and giving helpful suggestions a good number, of which have been taken on board to strengthen the text and for having saved me from some rather obvious and glaring errors. I recognise Diana Musunga Mwewa's comments on chapter one and her helpful suggestions in that regard. The indefatigable and inimitable Mwanida Banda took on the uninviting task of having to typeset this work as she has done with my other previous projects. I am grateful for her attendance to the task in a limited space of time. Jehaph James Nkhata was a great help in ensuring that I did not lose the manuscript in its digital format. I acknowledge without reserve, the moral support I have received from fellow advocates and authors, Brian J Mwanza and Joseph Chirwa in word and deed. I am further grateful to the team at Thankerton Publishing for ensuring that this work saw the light of day. I am also indebted to the many works, including various law reports from several jurisdictions and electronic sites with case summaries, that I have had to rely on and which have been accordingly acknowledged, and some of which have been included in the select bibliography towards the end of this text. Finally, and as always, I am sincerely grateful to Mushota my wife for her support and patience during the subsistence of this project.

LAW REPORT ABBREVIATIONS

ACSR	Australian Corporations and Securities Report
All ER Rep	All England Reports Reprint
All ER (D)	All England Reports
All ER	All England Reports
ALR	Administrative Law Reports
App Cas	Appeal Cases
B & Ad	Barnwell & Adolphus' King's Bench Reports
B & CR	Reports of Bankruptcy & Companies Winding up Cases
BCC	British Company Law and Practice
BCLC	Butterworths Company Law Cases
Ch app	Law Reports Chancery appeals
Ch/D	Law Reports Chancery Division
CLR	Commonwealth Law Reports
Com Cas	Commercial Cases
Comp Cas Mad	Company Cases Madras (India)
Con LR	Construction Law Reports (UK)
CP Law	Reports Common Pleas
CPD	Law Reports Common Pleas Division
DLR	Directors Law Reports
DLR(2d)	Dominion Law Reports Second Series
Dr & Sm	Drewly and Smale's Vice-Chancellor's Reports
EB & E	Ellis, Blackburn & Ellis' Queen's Bench Reports
ER	English Reports
Eq	Equity Cases
Eq Cas Abr	Equity Cases Abridged
EWCA	England and Wales Court of Appeal
EWHC	High Court of England and Wales Reports
Ex Law	Reports Exchequer Division
F	Federal Reporter (USA); Fraser's Court of Session Cases
Fam	Family Law Reports
HCA	Hong Kong Court of Appeal
H Ct of Australia	High Court of Australia
H & M	Henning and Munford's Reports
HK	Ndola High Court Registry (Zambia)
HP	Lusaka High Court, Principal Registry (Zambia)
HPC	High Court for Zambia, Commercial Division
Hare	Hare Law Reports
IRLB	Industrial Relations Law Bulletin
IRLR	Irish Law Reports
JBL	Journal of Business Law
Jur	Juridical Review
KB/D	Kings Bench Division
LSG	Law Society Gazette
LJPC	Law Journal Privy Council
LJQB	Law Journal Queens Bench

LR	Law Reports
LR app Cas	Law Reports appeal Cases
LR Eq	Law Reports Equity
Lloyd's	Lloyd's Law Reports
LS Gaz	Law Society Gazette
Macq	Macqueen's Scotch Appeal Cases
Meg	Megone's Companies Act Cases
NE	North Eastern Reporter
NI/NILR	Northern Ireland Law Reports
NIJB	Northern Ireland Judgments Bulletin
NLJ	New Law Journal
NZCA	New Zealand Court of Appeal
NZLR	New Zealand Law Report
PCC	Palmer's Company Cases
P. Wms	Peere Williams' Reports
QB/D	Queens Bench
QdR/QR	Queensland Reports
Qd Sup Ct	Queensland Supreme Court
R	The Reports in all the Courts
SCLR	Scottish Civil Law Reports
SE	South Eastern Reporter (United States)
SJ	Solicitor's Journal
SLR	Scottish Law Reports
SLT	Scottish Law Reports
SN	Session Notes
Sol Jo	Solicitor's Journal and Reporter
TC	Tax Cases (United Kingdom)
The Times	The Times Reports
TLR	Times Law Reports
UKSC	United Kingdom Supreme Court
VLR	Victorian Law Report
WLR	Weekly Law Reports
WN	Weekly Notes
WR	Weekly Reporter
CAZ	Zambian Court of Appeal (Neutral Citation)
ZMHC	Zambian High Court (Neutral Citation)
ZMSC	Zambian Supreme Court (Neutral Citation)
ZR	Zambia Law Report

TABLE OF CASES

XX

TABLE OF STATUTES

Foreign legislation

England

TABLE OF STATUTORY INSTRUMENTS

TABLE OF PRACTICE DIRECTIONS

22

ESTOPPEL

22.1 Introduction

An estoppel may be defined as 'a disability whereby a party is precluded from alleging or proving in legal proceedings that a fact is otherwise than it is made to appear by the matter giving rise to that disability.'[1] Thus, an estoppel is said to exist against a party when such a party is not permitted to speak to the truthfulness of a particular statement whether the said fact is true or not. Thus:[2]

> Where a person has by words or conduct made to another a clear and unequivocal representation of fact, either with knowledge of its falsehood or with intention that it shall be acted upon, or has so conducted himself with another who, as a reasonable man, understands that a certain representation of fact was intended to be acted on, and that the other has acted on the representation and thereby altered his position to his prejudice, an estoppel arises against the party who made the representation and he is not allowed to aver that a fact is otherwise than he represented it to be.

In *H.C. Sitanga v The Attorney-General*,[3] the plaintiff was employed on permanent and pensionable staff in the Prisons Department. On the 19th December, 1974, he was prematurely retired by the Commissioner of Prisons for the purpose of the re-organisation of the Prison Service. The plaintiff asked for a declaration that the retirement was null and void. The defendant contended that the Commissioner of Prisons had power to retire the plaintiff; he argued also that the plaintiff having accepted terminal benefits was estopped from challenging the validity of the retirement. In *inter alia* rejecting the contention of estoppel against the plaintiff, Desai J as he then was, observed that there was no evidence that the defendant had acted unilaterally to retire the plaintiff. Further, that there was no evidence to suggest that the defendant (as is required to prove estoppel against a party as shown below) had acted on any representation of fact made by the plaintiff. Said the judge, '[t]here is no conduct on the part of the plaintiff which made a clear and unequivocal representation of fact, either

---

[1] *H.C. Sitanga v The Attorney-General* [1977] ZR 258 (HC).
[2] Halsbury's Laws of England 4th edn, vol. 16 para 1505.
[3] [1977] ZR 258 (HC).

with knowledge of its falsehood or with the intention that it be so acted upon, upon which the defendant has acted and thereby altered his position to his prejudice.'

An mportant, fact every advocate must be aware of in drafting pleadings, is that *facts* relied on to establish an estoppel of any kind (including estoppels in *pais*[4]) should be pleaded in any case in which it is intended to rely upon it.[5] In *Sitanga*,[6] the defence had not pleaded the facts relied on to establish an estoppel. As such, said the Court, it was not available to them. It is also important to remember that forbearance not to exercise a right will not automatically estop a party from making a claim; and trying to enforce such a claim once reasonable notice is given for the defendant to make good on his part of the contract.[7]

22.2   A rule of substantive law or a rule of evidence?

Whether estoppel is a rule of substantive law or a rule of evidence is, as a survey of cases below will demonstrate, a matter of great contention. In *Low v Bouverie*,[8] Bowen LJ took the following view: '[e]stoppel is only a rule of evidence; you cannot found an action upon estoppel. Estoppel is only important as being one step in the progress towards relief on the hypothesis that the defendant is estopped from denying the truth of something, he has said.' In *Sitanga*,[9] Desai J quoted with approval the principles set out in *Dawson's Bank Ltd v Japan Cotton Trading Co Ltd*[10] to the effect that estoppel is a rule of evidence which comes into operation if (a) a statement of the existence of a fact has been made by the defendant to the plaintiff, (b) with the intention that the plaintiff should act upon the faith of the statement, and (c) the plaintiff does act upon the faith of the statement. However, in *Mills v Cooper*[11] Diplock LJ was of the view that '[w]hatever may be said of other rules of law to which the label of 'estoppel' is attached, 'issue estoppel'[12] is not a rule of evidence [....]' In *Amalgamated Investment and Property Co Ltd v Texas Commerce International Bank Ltd*[13] it was held as follows: '[...] the true proposition of law, that, while a party cannot in terms found a cause of action on an estoppel, he may, as a result of being able

[4]'An estoppel in pais refers to an estoppel which does not spring from a record, or a deed. It is made to appear to the jury by competent evidence. By an estoppel in pais a party is prevented by his/or her own conduct from obtaining the enforcement of a right which would operate to the detriment of another who justifiably relied on such conduct. Courts adopt estoppel in pais when a contradictory stance stands unfair to another person who relied on the original position:' https://definitions.uslegal.com/e/estoppel-in-pais/ retrieved on 2/2/23.
[5]Halsbury's Laws of England 4th edn, vol. 16 para 1515.
[6][1977] ZR 258 (HC).
[7]*Tool Metal Manufacturing Co Ltd v Tungsten Electric Co Ltd* [1955] 2 Alle ER 657.
[8][1891] 3 Ch 82 at 105.
[9][1977] ZR 258 (HC).
[10][1955] 2 All ER 657 quoted with approval in *Nurdin Bandali v Lombank Tanganyika Ltd* [1963] EA 304.
[11][1967] 2 All ER 100 at 104i-105a, *per* Diplock LJ.
[12]In *Thoday v Thoday* [1964] 1 All ER 341, Diplock LJ explained the distinction between 'issue estoppel' on the one hand and 'case of action estoppel' and 'fact estoppel' on the other. See discussion below.
[13][1981] 3 All ER 577.

to rely on an estoppel, succeed on a cause of action on which, without being able to rely on that estoppel, he would necessarily have failed.'[14]

What significance has to be attached to whether estoppel is a "rule of evidence" or a rule of "substantive law" while an interesting subject of serious academic, even juristic debate, is rather hollow when one considers the realities of the theatre of the trial in which it may be deployed from time to time. Perhaps a good place to start would be to mention, even though we will return to this issue later in this chapter, the fact that estoppel arises in three instances which are as follows:

(i)   *Record*: When facts are treated as a matter of record with respect to court judgments;

(ii) *Deed*: When facts in question are stated in a *deed*; and

(iii) *Conduct*: A clear representation has arisen thanks to a party's own behaviour.

As with presumptions,[15] which work on the premise that proof of a tributary fact A entails proof of the existence of principal fact B, estoppel must be seen as a method of proof. Thus, when the issue at play involves a *deed*, proof of the secondary fact, i.e., that the defendant executed the *deed* in question ordinarily proves the existence of principal fact B, a state of affairs, which the court will presume as in fact being in existence and will not permit evidence to rebut such a 'presumption.' The foregoing demonstrates how estoppel under the circumstances discussed above, engenders an evidentiary process as regards the method of establishing facts. If said facts are established, it falls to the substantive law (contract, tort, the criminal law, land law etc) to dictate the rights and obligations of the parties concerned.[16] As a corollary to the foregoing, it is the rules encased in the substantive law that will determine the facts in issue to be proved. Thus, by a party adducing evidence based on any of the three instances in which it may arise, that is to say, of a *court judgment* or/and a *deed* or/and *conduct* relevant to the matter at hand, he, by device of estoppel irrefutably proves a fact in issue. 'It may well be that estoppel has the effect of a rule of substantive law or a rule of evidence according to the type of estoppel under consideration.'[17]

22.3   Estoppel and the general law[18]

The general rule is that there can be no estoppel against the general law. This has been demonstrated in several cases. In *R Leslie Ltd v Sheill*,[19] the defendant, an infant, borrowed money from the plaintiff company by misrepresenting himself as an adult. The plaintiff claimed damages for the tort of deceit. It

---

[14] [1981] 3 All ER 577 at 591h, *per* Brandon LJ; see also *Zambia Revenue Authority v Professional Insurance Corporation Zambia* (Appeal 34 of 2017) [2020] ZMSC 87.

[15] See chapter 24 below.

[16] See the case of *Central London Property Trust Ltd v High Trees House Ltd* [1947] KB 130; *Kelsen v Imperial Tobacco Co (of Great Britain and Ireland) Ltd* [1957] 2 All ER 343; *Re Parent Trust & Finance Company Ltd* [1937] 4 All ER 396; *Wilson v Wilson* [1963] 2 All ER 447.

[17] Hatchard J and Ndulo M, *The Law of Evidence* 67.

[18] See *Phipson on Evidence*, 9th edn 705.

[19] [1914] 3 KB 607.

was held that the misrepresentation did not estop the minor from pleading contractual incapacity. The court held the plaintiff's action to be an attempt to enforce an unenforceable contract.[20] In this jurisdiction, a liquidator is, according to s 127 of the Corporate Insolvency Act,[21] under obligation to follow the pecking order thereunder 'in so far as payment of debts in a winding-up'[22] is concerned. This was the position taken in the case of *Re Exchange Securities and Commodities Ltd.*[23] Having held that the liquidator was under statutory obligation to distribute assets of the company amongst its creditors, it went on to hold that estoppel being only a rule of evidence was not conclusive as regards the distribution of the statutory estate in winding-up proceedings or indeed personal bankruptcies. Finally, it has been held in *Nahar Investments v Grindlays Bank (Z) Limited*[24] that '[l]itigation must come to an end and it is highly undesirable that respondents should be kept in suspense because of dilatory conduct on the part of appellants.' If it be said as was held by Diplock LJ in *Mills v Cooper,*[25] that the estoppel doctrine is but an application of public policy in so far as finality in litigation[26] is concerned, then the foregoing authorities demonstrate this fact quite clearly.[27]

22.4   Classes of estoppel

HM Malek,[28] postulates that in contemporary law, the term "estoppel" is used to define an assortment of devices, some of which simply have the consequence of preventing a party from refuting a certain fact, or supposition. The old-style cataloguing of legal estoppels is that they fall into one of three classes; first, estoppel by record; second, estoppel by deed; and third, estoppel in *pais* or by conduct. In summary, there are three recognised types of estoppels, namely:
    (i)   Estoppel by record
    (ii)   Estoppel by deed; and
    (iii) Estoppel in *pais* or by conduct

We now discuss them in turn and in greater detail below.

22.4.1   Estoppel by record

Estoppels by record only come into being where a judgment of a court of competent jurisdiction exits. '[E]stoppels by record originally principally

---

[20] See general application of principles in this case in *Lo Kwong Lam and Lo Kwong Hin, (late an infant but now of full age) v Li Koon Chun and Kan Tang Po* [1927] HKCU 5.

[21] No 9 of 2017.

[22] Gates RB, *Gates on Understanding Zambian Corporate Insolvency Law* (Reagan Blankfein Gates 2019).

[23] [1987] 2 All ER 272.

[24] [1984] ZR 81.

[25] [1967] 2 All ER 100 at 104i-105a, *per* Diplock LJ.

[26] *Wilson Masauso Zulu v Avondale Housing Project Limited* [1982] ZR 175.

[27] See further, *O'Connell v Plymouth City Council* (unreported March 12, 1999 (CA).

[28] Malek HM, *Phipson on Evidence* (17th edn Thomson Reuters (Legal) Limited, 2010), para 5-01 at 100; cited and quoted by Matibini J, as he then was, in *North-Western Energy Company Limited v Energy Regulations Board* 2010/HP/786.

comprised judgments the conclusiveness of which is considered in conjunction with their admissibility. However, the modern tendency is to refer to estoppels based on judgments as estoppels by *res judicata*.'[29] Further,[30]

> A final adjudication of a legal dispute is conclusive as between the parties to the litigation and their privies as to the matters necessarily determined, and the conclusions on these matters cannot be challenged in subsequent litigation between them. This principle applies absolutely to a conclusion that a cause of action does not exist, but it will not apply to other issues necessarily determined if there are special circumstances.[31]

Finally,[32]

> The principle that estoppel arise from a judgment in previous litigation between the same parties applies in general to all civil litigation, including arbitrations and civil proceedings in Courts of summary jurisdiction. A cause of action estoppel operates to prevent a party relitigating a claim he has lost, even if he is now able to show that the earlier decision was wrong.

It plausibly follows that judgment-based estoppels have the contemporary reference to *res judicata*. In this text we will use these terms interchangeably. The essence of the doctrine of estoppel by *res judicata*, is that as between the parties to the dispute, a final judgment of a dispute is conclusive. Thus, the parties in question are prevented from attempting to re-litigate claims they may have lost. This is so even in instances where they can show the error in the earlier decision. By "parties" is meant not only those that were actively involved in the suit now impugned by way of their names being on the record, but also those who had opportunity to join the proceedings but did not.[33]

The foregoing begs the question at what juncture a matter is deemed to have been determined definitively, and thus *res judicata*. The question has arisen in several authorities the upshot of which is that a matter is deemed to have been heard when all issues in dispute have been determined on the merits, as they ought to be under law, rendering the court that presided over

---

[29] Hodge M. Malek, *Phipson on Evidence* (17th edn Thomson Reuters (Legal) Limited, 2010) para 5-08 at 112, quoted with approval by Matibini J in *Clementina Banda Emmanuel Njanje v Boniface Mudimba* 2010/HP/A39; *Res judicata* means "the thing has been decided" and is derived from the tenet *"interest reipublicae ut sit finis litium"*: Literally, 'it is for the good of the Commonwealth that there be a terminus to litigation.'

[30] Malek HM, *Phipson on Evidence* para 43-23 at 1433.

[31] See *Clementina Banda Emmanuel Njanje v Boniface Mudimba* (2010/HP/A39).

[32] Malek HM, *Phipson on Evidence* para 43-24 at 1433.

[33] See *Evans v Norton* [1983] 1 Ch 252 at 264; *Wakefield v Cooke* [1904] AC 31 at 36.

the proceedings *functus officio*.[34] Thus, it has been held in *Zambia Industrial and Mining Corporation Ltd v Muuka*[35] that '[t]here can be no *res judicata* if there has been no adjudication. This will apply where parties are clearly not litigating the same issues. Thus, '[n]either issue estoppel nor *res judicata* [can be] successfully raised or pleaded by either party in the one action to defeat the claims in the other.'

22.4.1.1   General

Quite apart from the preceding aspect, estoppel by record may arise in instances where there is a grant of *Letters Patent*[36] by the president, for example, constituting an individual to be judge in the following terms:

REPUBLIC OF ZAMBIA

LETTERS PATENT

CONSTITUTING

[NAME OF PERSON], Esquire,

To be judge of the High Court for Zambia

[NAME OF PRESIDENT], President in and over the Republic of Zambia

To [NAME OF PERSON], Esquire, GEETINGS

*WHEREAS, I am well satisfied of the loyalty, integrity and ability of
[NAME OF PERSON], Esquire,*

---

[34] See *Stanley Mwambazi v Morester Farms Ltd* [1977] ZR 108; *Wilson Masauso Zulu v Avondale Housing Project Limited* [1982] ZR 172; *Tata Zambia Ltd v Shilling Zinka* [1986] ZR 51 (SC); *John Mugala and Kenneth Kabenga v The Attorney-General* [1988 – 1989] ZR 171 (SC); *Zambia Revenue Authority v Jayesh Shah* [2001] ZR 60; *Mohammed and Others v Mohammed and Another* [2012] 2 ZR 522; *Gaedonic Automotive Ltd and Another v CEEC* (SCZ Judgment No 39 of 2014); *Elizabeth Catherine Cooke v Moses Mpundu, and Joseph Musonda* (Appeal No 207 of 2015); *Sanat v Shaileshkumar Suryakant Amin* (CAZ Appeal 146 of 2017); *DSS Design Limited v CPL Limited* Appeal No 236 of 2020.

[35] (SCZ Judgment No 1 of 1998).

[36] Letter patents (Latin: *litterae patentes* (patents) (always in the plural) are a kind of legal instrument, usually in the form of written orders issued by an emperor, president or other head of office. , Correctly, provides a monopoly. Title, or status of an individual or organization. Letter patents can be used to create corporations or government offices or to grant city status or a coat of arms. Letter patents are issued to appoint Crown representatives, such as the Governor and the Governor-General of the Commonwealth, as well as to appoint the Royal Commission. In the United Kingdom, they are also issued for the creation of peers.

NOW KNOW YE THEREFORE that I [NAME OF PRESIDENT], in exercise of the powers conferred upon me in that behalf by the Constitution do by these Presents constitute and appoint the said [NAME OF PERSON] Esquire, to be a judge of the High Court for Zambia, and to have, hold and exercise the office , trust and employment of a judge of the said Court with all jurisdiction, authority, powers, rights, privileges, emoluments and advantages whatsoever to that office belonging, or in anywise incident to or concerning the same.

AND I do hereby command all and singular officers and subjects in the said Republic, and all others whom it may concern, to take due notice thereof and to govern themselves accordingly.

IN WITNESS WHEREOF I have hereunto set my hand and the Public seal of the Republic at Lusaka this First day of March, in the year two thousand and twenty.

[President's signature]
BY THE PRESIDENT'S COMMAND

The existence of a judgment is conclusive evidence in any subsequent litigation estopping the parties[37] to proceedings that birthed the judgment in question from denying the facts on which the judgment is founded.

In *Musakanya Valentine Shula and Edward Jack Shamwana v Attorney General*,[38] a preliminary issue was raised on behalf of the State in both petitions to the effect that these petitions were barred on the doctrine of *res judicata*. The undisputed facts as regards the petitioner Edward Jack Shamwana were that the same matter was brought before the High Court by way of notice of motion supported by an affidavit. This was heard by Chaila J, who delivered his judgment dismissing the petitioner's application. With regard to petitioner Valentine Shula Musakanya, the undisputed facts were that he brought an application for a writ of habeas corpus and the matter was heard by Chaila J, again he delivered his judgment dismissing the application. Counsel for Mr Musakanya submitted that the doctrine of *res judicata* was not an absolute rule of law. That the courts had discretion and there were exceptions to the general rule; that since the application before Court was in the nature of an ordinary bail in a criminal matter, an applicant could, if unsuccessful, move from one judge to another in habeas corpus proceedings and that being the case, the proceedings of habeas corpus by petitioner Musakanya were no bar to the proceedings before court. Mr Shamwana on his own behalf in addition to endorsing what had been submitted by counsel for petitioner Musakanya as applying to him, argued, *inter alia*, that *res judicata* applied only to facts and not to the law and that the proceedings before court related to the law. Rejecting the

---

[37] And those, termed privies, whose title stems from the prior party or have commonality of interest in blood, estate or/and law.

[38] [1981] ZR 221 (HC).

foregoing arguments, Chirwa J, as he then was, held *inter alia* that *res judicata* was a strict [and not flexible/relative] rule of law and the parties were bound by any decision made by a competent court.[39] Further, that if facts were the same, the law should be the same. If from a given set of accepted facts a court pronounced the law, it could not be gainsaid that, only facts would bind the parties thereto and not the law.

In *ANZ Grindlays Bank (Z) Limited v Kaoma*,[40] the Supreme Court held that in order for the defence of *res judicata* to succeed, it is necessary to show not only that the cause of action was the same, but also that the plaintiff has had no opportunity of recovering in the first action that which he hopes to recover in the second.' We must, however, note that as was held by Grey CJ in *The Duchess of Kingston's Case*,[41] 'although a person who was a party to legal proceedings in which a judgment was given is estopped from denying the facts on which the judgment was based, the judgment was not binding on any third party.' In this particular instance, the Crown had not been a party to the proceedings in the Consistory Court and as such, could not be prevented from contradicting the facts on which the judgment in question was predicated. The second point to note is the one exemplified in *Sphere Drake Insurance plc & Another v The Orion Insurance Co plc*,[42] which is to the effect that estoppel on record will not be invoked where the judgment in question was predicated on fraud and all judicial acts, where fraud is shown to have been present, are thereby vitiated.

22.4.1.2   The basis of estoppel on record

Two principles form the basis of estoppel on record which we discuss below.

(i)   Interest rei publicae ut sit finis litium[43]

The first principle is, as shown in *Bank of Zambia v Tembo and Others*,[44] *Interest rei publicae ut sit finis litium*. It is in the public interest for there to be finality to litigation. Counsel for the respondent raised a preliminary objection to the hearing on the ground that it is *res judicata*. Counsel said that he would rely on the judgments of the court between the same parties made on 30 October, 1997 and 4 February, 2002, in SCZ appeal No 32 of 1997. Counsel for the respondents indicated that the appeal was against the judgment of the Industrial Relations Court made on 28 July, 1995. Counsel for the appellant conceded that there was no appeal against the Judgment of the Industrial Relations Court delivered on

---

[39] See with respect to non-availability of application to stay Rulings/judgments of the Supreme Court and related matters, see generally, Kaluba BC, *Evidence Law* at 649 – 650 and the cases cited thereunder: *Mohamed Muazu v Attorney General* [1988-1989] ZR (SC); *Trinity Engineering (PVT) Ltd v Zambia National Commercial Bank Ltd SCZ* (Judgment No 4 of 1997); *Cephas Kufamiti and Benjamin Banda v The People* (SCZ Judgment No 2 of 2002); *Benjamin Yoram Mwila v Victor John Bradbury* (SCZ Judgment No 18 of 2013); *Law Association of Zambia v The Attorney General, Ngosa Simbyakula and Others* (2016/CC/0010).

[40] (SCZ Judgment No 12 of 1995 (unreported)); See *Kandala v Zambia National Commercial Bank Plc* (HPC 766 of 2010) [2011] ZMHC 16.

[41] (1776) 20 St. Tr. 355.

[42] The Times, March 17, 2000 (CA).

[43] Literally, 'it is for the good of the Commonwealth that there be a terminus to litigation.'

[44] [2002] ZR 103; *Guest and Another v Makinga and Another* [2011] 1 ZR 370.

28 July, 1995, and that the appellants were bound by that Judgment. Counsel for the respondent pointed out that the issues that formed the same subject of the current appeal had already been determined in the previous judgment and are therefore *res judicata*. The court adopted a passage from Halsbury's Laws of England on the matter of *re judicata*:[45]

> In order that a defence of *res judicata* may succeed it is necessary to show that not only the cause of action was the same, but also that the plaintiff has had an opportunity of recovering, and but for his own fault might have recovered in the first action that which he seeks to recover in the second. A plea of *res judicata* must show either an actual merger, or that the same point had been actually decided between the same parties. Where the former judgment has been for the defendant, the conditions necessary to conclude the plaintiff are not less stringent. It is not enough that the matter alleged to be concluded might have been put in issue, or that the relief sought might have been claimed. It is necessary to show that it actually was so put in issue or claimed.

In upholding the preliminary objection, and thereby dismissing the appeal, the Court invoked the legal maxim *Interest rei publicae ut sit finis litium*[46] meaning that it is in the public interest that there should be an end to litigation. There are, however, instances when the doctrine may not be invoked. It has been held in *Attorney-General v EB Jones Machinists Limited*[47] that the doctrine of estoppel may not be invoked to render valid a transaction which the legislature has on grounds of general public policy, enacted is to be invalid, or to give the court a jurisdiction which is denied to it by statute or to oust the courts statutory jurisdiction under an enactment which precludes the parties from contracting out of its provisions. Where a statute enacted for the benefit of a section of the public imposes a duty of a positive kind the person charged with the performance of the duty cannot by estoppel be prevented from exercising his statutory powers.

Interest rei publicae ut sit finis litium applies to courts too but only in so far as they do not see it fit to inquire into facts in the public interest. As exemplified in *Wilson Masauso Zulu v Avondale Housing Project Limited*,[48] 'the trial court

---

[45] Halsbury's Laws of England vol. 16, of the 4th edn. In particular paragraph 1528 which deals with the essentials of *res judicata*.

[46] 'The public interest of a matter so that a litigation should end." An alternative phrase is *Expedit rei publicae ut sit finis litium*: '"It is advantageous to the public that there be an end to lawsuits." A maxim meaning that protracted litigation puts a strain on the judicial system and undermines the law's role in dispute resolution, and so the public interest requires that disputes be resolved in some final form rather than continuing indefinitely to drain the resources of courts and the parties.'- https://www.oxfordreference.com/search?q=Expedit+rei+publicae+ut+&searchBtn=Search&isQuickSearch=true. Retrieved on 25/12/202.

[47] (SCZ Judgment No 26 of 2000) [2000] ZMSC 30 (29 June 2000); *Hayward v Hayward* (1961) P. 152.

[48] [1982] ZR 175 quoted with approval in *The Attorney General v Aboubacar Tall and Zambia Airways Corporation Ltd* (SCZ Appeal No 77 of 1994); In *Zambia Telecommunications Company Limited (Zamtel) v Aaron Mweene Mulwanda Paul Ngandwe* SCZ Judgment No 7 of 2012, it was held regarding that the general rule as to the amendment and setting aside of judgments or orders after a judgment or order has been drawn up is as follows: Except by way of appeal, no Court, judge or master has power to rehear, review, alter or vary any judgment or order after it has been drawn up, either in application made in the original action or matter, or in fresh action brought to review such judgment or order. The object of this rule is to bring litigation to a finality.

has a duty to adjudicate upon every aspect of the suit between the parties so that every matter in controversy is determined in finality.' It has also been applied to arbitral proceedings. In *Martin Misheck Simpemba Rose Domingo Kakompe v Nonde Mukanta Zambia Industrial Minerals Limited*,[49] although the plaintiffs launched their action in the High Court, on 24 November, 2005, the agreement between the parties provided for an arbitration clause as follows: '[a]ny dispute between the parties shall be referred to the arbitration under the Arbitration Act of Zambia, and the Chairman of the Law Association of Zambia or his nominee will be the sole arbitrator. 'Thus, the matter was referred to arbitration sometime in 2007. After the arbitration was conducted, an award was rendered in favour of the plaintiff on 31 December, 2007. On 17 March, 2008, the defendants filed originating summons in the High Court to set aside the arbitral award pursuant to s 17(2)(b)(ii) of the Arbitration Act.[50] The gravamen of the application was that the award rendered on 31 December, 2007, ought to be set aside on the ground that the award in question was in conflict with public policy, and offensive to the relevant provisions of the Mines and Mineral Act. Matibini J, as he then was, held *inter alia*:

> At the substantive level, it must be noticed that the Courts aim at upholding arbitration awards. On application to set aside awards, arbitration awards are not approached with a view to discern the legal weaknesses, inconsistencies, or faults in the application of the law. The task of Court is not to upset, or frustrate the arbitral process. Rather the objective is to read an award in a reasonable and commercial sense assuming that there is no fundamental, or substantial procedural, or substantive error in the making of the award. *The defence of public policy is narrowly construed in a bid to preserve, and recognise the goal of finality in all arbitrations. Thus, an arbitral award is not liable to be struck down on allegations that it is premised on incorrect grounds whether of fact or law. An award will not be contrary to public policy merely because the reasoning, or conclusions of the arbitrator are wrong in fact or law.* This is so because an application to set aside an award is not an appeal on the merits. And the application should not be considered in the same way as the Court would consider the findings of a body over whom it had appellate jurisdiction (emphasis added).

(a)   Review of rulings or orders or judgments

Once the Court has rendered its ruling or order or judgment, it becomes *functus officio*.[51] As such, it is impermissible for such a court to attempt to cure omissions or mistakes by altering or varying its own order, ruling or judgment on its own motion.[52] Be that as it may, it is perhaps important to briefly consider the power of the court, the preceding notwithstanding, to vary or vacate its own

---

[49] 2008/HP/268.

[50] No 19 of 2000.

[51] *Functus officio* derives from "fungere": to perform, end or expire. It is similar to the commonplace English term "defunct."

[52] *Zamtel v Aaron Mweene Mulwanda and Paul Ngwane* (SCZ Judgment No 7 of 2012).

rulings/ orders/ judgments. The starting point is of course Order XXXIX of the HCR. [53] Order XXXIX r 1, HCR provides as follows:

> Any Judge may, upon such grounds as he shall consider sufficient, review any judgment or decision given by him (except where either party shall have obtained leave to appeal, and such appeal is not withdrawn), and, upon such review it shall be lawful for him to open and rehear the case wholly or in part, and to take fresh evidence, and to reverse, vary or confirm his previous judgment or decision. [54]

Accordingly, [55]

> [a]n action will lie to rescind a judgment on the ground of discovery of new evidence which would have had a material effect upon the decision of the court. It must be shown that such evidence is a discovery of something material in the sense that it would be a reason for setting aside the judgment, if it were established by proof that the discovery is new and that it would not with reasonable diligence have been discovered before. A mere suspicion of fresh evidence is not sufficient.

It has been held in *Walusiko Lisulo v Patricia Anne Lisulo*, [56] which was an appeal against the High Court's refusal to review a judgment on appeal from the Deputy Registrar on assessment relating to maintenance regarding the respondent that:

    (i)   The power to review under Order 39, Rule 1, is discretionary for the judge and there must be sufficient grounds to exercise that discretion.

    (ii)   Order 39, Rule 1, of the High Court Rules is not designed for parties to have a second bite at the cherry.

    (iii)   Litigation must come to an end, and successful parties must enjoy the fruits of their judgments.

The Court further observed that within the circumstances of this case, '[l]ooking at the reasons for asking for review, it [was] obvious that the new evidence [was] not new [nor] that [it] came to light later which no proper and reasonable diligence could earlier have secured.'

The power to review a court's own order or judgment raises the question of whether the court may, in doing so, take into consideration facts not in existence at the time the judgment or order or ruling now impugned, was delivered, but which subsequently came into being. The question arose and was considered in *Roy Chikata Ranching Company Limited* [57] where in Commissioner Dare opined as follows:

---

[53] Chapter 27 of the Laws of Zambia.

[54] See application in *Christian Diedricks v Konkola Copper Mines Plc* (HN 28 of 2010) [2011] ZMHC.

[55] Halsbury's Laws of England 3rd edn vol. 22 791 para 1670; *Lackson Mwabi Mwanza v Kangwa Simpasa and Another* [2012] 1 ZR 144 (HC).

[56] [1998] ZR 75 (SC); cited by Chali J in *Pakeza Bakery Limited Divine Foods Take Away and Butchery Limited v Aetos Tranfarm Limited Stillianos Geroge Koukoudis* 2004/HK/331.

[57] [1980] ZR 198.

> As a matter of basic principle, I have come to the conclusion that one can never take into account events which occur for the first time after the delivery of the judgment as grounds for judicial review of a judgment. If it were otherwise, there would never be an end to any litigation. The losing party would in most cases find something happening after he had lost which would enable him to ask from a second bite at the cherry.

Review of rulings/orders/judgments in accordance with Order XXXIX, HCR then 'does not exist to afford a dissatisfied litigant the chance to argue for an alteration to bring about a result considered more acceptable [....]'[58]

It is important to note that the application '[...] for review of any judgment or decision must be made not later than fourteen days after such judgment or decision. After the expiration of fourteen days, an application for review shall not be admitted, except by special leave of the Judge on such terms as seem just.'[59] Further, '[t]he application shall not of itself operate as a stay of execution[60] unless the Judge so orders, and such order may be made, upon such terms as to security for performance of the judgment or decision or otherwise as the Judge may consider necessary.[61] Any money in court in the suit shall be retained to abide the result of the motion or the further order of the Judge.'[62] A party will have to make a separate application for stay pending review of such order or judgment against which the application for review is made.

(b)   The slip rule

As discussed above, the rendering of a judgment denotes the end of a judge's work on a matter. Once a court has rendered judgment concerning all matters

---

[58] *Lackson Mwabi Mwanza v Kangwa Simpasa and Another* [2012] 1 ZR 144 (HC) *per* Matibini J, as he then was.

[59] Order XXXIX r 2, HCR, Chapter 27 of the Laws of Zambia; See also *Akashambatwa Mbikusita Lewanika and Others v Frederick Jacob Titus Chiluba* [1998] ZR 79; *Jamas Milling Company Ltd v Imex International Pty* (SCZ 20 of 2002), [2002] ZMSC 57; *Investrust Bank Plc v Chick Masters Ltd and Another* (HPC 13 of 2009), 2011 ZMHC 30; *Kalusha Bwalya v Chardore Properties Ltd and Another* (2009/HPC/0294).

[60] Order XXXIX r 3; *John Kunda v Keren Motors (Z) Ltd* (SCZ Judgment No 14 of 2012); *Ndola City Council v Charles Mwansa* (SCZ Judgment 15 of 1994), [1994] ZMSC 131; See also *Akashambatwa Mbikusita Lewanika and Others v Frederick Jacob Titus Chiluba* [1998] ZR 79; *Jamas Milling Company Ltd v Imex International Pty* (SCZ 20 of 2002), [2002] ZMSC 57; *Investrust Bank Plc v Chick Masters Ltd and Another* (HPC 13 of 2009), 2011 ZMHC 30; *Kalusha Bwalya v Chardore Properties Ltd and Another* (2009/HPC/0294); The provisions of the Order and its application as demonstrated in the foregoing authorities is similar to the principle based on Order 51, RSC, in *Ndola City Council v Charles Mwansa* (SCZ Judgment No 78 of 1994) that '[a]n appeal does not operate as stay of execution, it must be applied for and the decision is discretionary.' Order 51, RSC provides as follows: '[a]n appeal shall not operate as a stay of execution or of proceedings under the decision appealed from unless the [Court of Appeal] or the Court so orders and no intermediate act or proceeding shall be invalidated except so far as the Court may direct.' The criminal procedure equivalent is Rule 29(1), RSC which provides as follows: '[s]ubject to the provisions of section eighteen of the Act no appeal shall operate as a stay of execution, but the High Court or the Court may stay execution on any judgment, pending appeal, on such terms as to security for the payment of any money or the performance or non-performance of any act or the suffering of any punishment ordered by or in such judgment, as to such Court may seem reasonable.'

[61] *Michael Chilufya Sata v Chanda Chimba and Others* (HP 1282 of 2010), [2011] ZMHC 74.

[62] Order XXXIX r 2 of the HCR, Chapter 27 of the Laws of Zambia.

in controversy between the disputants, the court no longer has jurisdiction over the said matter and is thus rendered *functus officio*.[63] It has thus been observed in *Zamtel v Aaron Mweene Mulwanda and Paul Ngwane*[64] that 'a judgment is not supposed to be interpreted. It should be thorough, exhaustive, and clear on all issues.' Be that as it may, it is permissible for the court to make corrections pertaining to the judgment in question such as accidental slips or omissions in the judgment or order concerned.[65] The aim of this jurisdiction is not to upend the two principles mentioned earlier: (i) *Interest rei publicae ut sit finis litium* and (ii) double jeopardy. Rather, it is, as has been held in *Bristol Myers Squibb Company v Baker Norton Pharmaceuticals Inc (Costs)*,[66] to ensure that the formal text comprising the court's order/judgment is reflective of the court's manifest intent and decision in order to forestore the need for the court to reassess its verdict. As has been shown in *Abby Oy v Luanshya Copper Mines plc*,[67] the slip rule is not intended to permit the court to correct any mistakes, however apparent, as regards the interpretation of the law. That the discretion to exercise its power under this rule not only includes the discretion not to vary its judgment or order on the basis of the rule in instances where third parties intervene; but when exercising the discretion would be inequitable and/or inexpedient. Thus, where the judgment is a correct reflection of the manifest intent and verdict of the court, no variation is permissible, nor is it permissible under the rule to alter the operative and/or substantive portions of the judgment, if only to correct legal or factual errors by the court. *Abby Oy*[68] is also authority for the position that the court cannot vary a judgment on the basis of evidence that was absent from the pleadings during trial or matters not brought to the court's attention by counsel prior to it rendering its judgment.[69]

As regards the question whether the slip rule which is specifically provided for under Rule 78 of the Supreme Court Rules (SCR) in the following terms: '[c]lerical errors by the Court or a judge thereof in documents or process, or in any judgment, or errors therein arising from any accidental slip or omission, may at any time be corrected by the Court or a judge thereof' applies to the High Court whose rules appear not to have an equivalent rule, the Supreme Court

---

[63] According to Duhaim's Law Dictionary, 'Functus officio refers to an officer or agency whose mandate has expired, due to either the arrival of an expiry date or an agency having accomplished the purpose for which it was created:' http://www.duhaime.org/LegalDictionary/F/FunctusOfficio.aspx; The term is also used in a legal sense. It has been held in *Chandler v Alberta Association of Architects* 1989 CanLII 41 (SCC) [1989] 2 SCR 848 that 'the underlying rationale for the doctrine is clearly more fundamental: that for the due and proper administration of justice, there must be finality to a proceeding to ensure procedural fairness and the integrity of the judicial system.'

[64] Judgment No 7 of 2012.

[65] *Trinity Engineering (Pvt) Limited v Zambia National Commercial Bank Limited* [1995-1997] ZR 166 (SC); *Attorney General and Development Bank of Zambia v Gershom Moses Burton Mumba* [2006] ZR 77 (SC).

[66] [221] EWCA Civ 414.

[67] SCZ Judgment No 7 of 2015.

[68] SCZ Judgment No 7 of 2015.

[69] See *Tibles v SIG (T/a Asphaltic Roofing Supplies)* [2012] EWCA Civ 518.

came to the conclusion in *Abby Oy*[70] that the High Court does indeed have such power under Order 20 r 11 RSC.[71] That Order provides as follows: '[c]lerical mistakes in judgments or orders, or errors arising therein from any accidental slip or omission, may at any time be corrected by the Court on motion or summons without an appeal.' Thus, the High Court, may under Order 20 r 11 RSC correct clerical errors and/or omissions in, or vary a judgment or order for purposes of giving the intent and meaning of the court. Such power, said the court, was also inherent.

That the slip rule cannot be invoked by a court to change the substance of its judgment but simply to give effect to its intention by correcting accidental slips or omissions that may include typographical errors, arithmetic error or disambiguation or otherwise errors that are quite patent, is demonstrable in the way the Supreme Court dispatched the motion brought before it under rules 48(5) and 78 of the Supreme Court Rules (SCR) in *Chibote Limited and Others v Meridien BIAO Bank (Zambia) Limited (In Liq).*[72] The application sought for an order to correct a judgment delivered by the Supreme Court on 31st July, 2002, by setting aside the order for a new trial and instead to order that the appeal be dismissed and that the judgment and the orders claimed in the counter claim be granted to the applicant/respondent. It was held firstly, that an appeal determined by the Supreme Court will only be reopened where a party, through no fault of its own has been subjected to an unfair procedure and will not be varied or rescinded merely because a decision is subsequently thought to be wrong. Sakala CJ, as he then was, opined as follows: '[t]here was no error, omission or slip in the judgment. As we see it, the applicant was simply dissatisfied with the judgment and sought the Supreme Court to vary the judgment so as to bring about a result more acceptable.' Finally, *Limpic v Mawere and Others*[73] is authority for the position that the central element to variation and/or correction of an order or judgment impugned is not the satisfaction by way of enabling a party to have a second bite at the cherry through the slip rule but to serve interests of justice.

(ii)   Double jeopardy

The second principle is that no one should be sued/prosecuted more than once on the same grounds.

---

[70] SCZ Judgment No 7 of 2015.
[71] The High Court's Slip Rule.
[72] [2003] ZR 76 (SC).
[73] [2014] vol. 2 ZR 303.

(a)   Civil matters

The principle is demonstrated in the leading case of *Development Bank of Zambia and Another v Sunvest Limited and Another*.[74] The case concerned the grant of an injunction to restrain the appointment of a receiver and Manager. The facts revealed in the case showed that in an action numbered 1995/HN/307 the appellant bank had sued the respondents to recover certain monies which had been lent by the bank to the respondents. Among the claims endorsed in that action, was one for the repayment of the loan with interest and in default a claim that the bank be at liberty to repossess the plant and machinery charged to the plaintiff bank on a specific charge dated 14 November, 1994. The facts further disclosed that while that action was pending the bank appointed the Manager and Receiver in exercise or purported exercise of powers claimed by the bank under the loan agreement and under statute. The borrowers who were the respondents in this action commenced an action numbered 1995/HN/1394 in which they applied for an injunction to restrain the bank appointing the Receiver. This is the action that came up to the court on appeal. In dealing with the application the learned judge in the court below found that the step taken by the bank of commencing an action in court and then at the same time adopting a measure of self-redress was one to be deprecated. The learned trial judge viewed very dimly and with disapproval the appointment of a Receiver and Manager after the litigation had already been commenced and while such litigation was pending in the earlier action for the recovery of the same money by litigation. The Court opined as follows:

> We listened to the arguments in this appeal; and would like to immediately affirm the judge on his disapproval of the action taken in this matter whereby one action is pending and some other steps are being pursued. We also disapprove of parties commencing a multiplicity of procedures and proceedings and indeed a multiplicity of actions over the same subject matter. The objection raised by the borrowers in this action to the bank pursuing the remedy of self-redress in this action, that an action was pending, applies with equal force to the whole idea of the borrowers commencing a fresh action when there is already another one pending in the court with the

---

[74] [1995-1997] ZR 187; s 4 of the High Court Act Chapter 27 of the Laws of Zambia provides as follows: '[s] ubject to any express statutory provision to the contrary, all the Judges shall have and may exercise, in all respects, equal power, authority and jurisdiction, and, subject as aforesaid, any Judge may exercise all or any part of the jurisdiction by this Act or otherwise vested in the Court, and, for such purpose, shall be and form a Court.' *Musakanya and Others v The Attorney General* [1981] ZR 221 at 227; *Zambezi Portland Cement Limited and Another v Stanbic Bank Zambia Limited* [2012] 2 ZR 17; For egregious forms of forum shopping, see *Mukumbuta Mukumbuta Sam Mukamamba Kweleka Mubita Mooto Mooto and Kandumba Munganga v Nkwilimba Choobana Lubinda Richard Mbikusita Munyinda Rosalyn Mukelabai and Mongu Meat Corporation Ltd* (SCZ Judgment No 8 of 2003): Counsel was ordered to bear costs personally; *Kelvin Hang'andu and Company (A Firm) v Webby Mulubisha* (SCZ Judgment No 39 of 2008): According to the Court, this was a proper case to be referred to the Disciplinary Committee of the Law Association of Zambia for further investigations into the conduct of counsel to determine whether his conduct amounted to professional misconduct; *The Registered Trustees of The Archdiocese of Lusaka v Office Machine Services Limited* (SCA Judgment No 18 of 2007); *Muimui v Chanda* (SCZ Judgment No 50 of 2000).

result that various courts may end up making various conflicting and contradictory decisions because the parties have started another action in the courts. It follows therefore that we disapprove completely of the steps taken by the borrowers in commencing action No. 1995/HN/1394 when they could have made all the applications in the earlier action No 307. We also disapprove of the multiplicity of actions between the same parties involving carious issues proposed to be raised in the new action which as we said we disapprove of.

(b) Criminal matters

In criminal matters a plea of *autrefois convict* and *autrefois acquit* corresponds to estoppel: s 138 of the Criminal procedure Code[75] in line with Article 18(5) of the Constitution provides as follows: '[a] person who has been once tried by a court of competent jurisdiction for an offence, and convicted or acquitted of such offence, shall, while such conviction or acquittal remains in force, not be liable to be tried again on the same facts for the same offence.' Article 18(5) of the Constitution provides as follows:

> A person who shows that he has been tried by a competent court for a criminal offence and either convicted or acquitted shall not again be tried for that offence or for any other criminal offence of which he could have been convicted at the trial for that offence, except upon the order of a superior court in the course of appeal or review proceedings relating to the conviction or acquittal.

In fact, in consonance with Article 18(5), s 277 of the Criminal Procedure Code[76] provides the procedure to be followed in a case where s 138 of the Criminal procedure Code[77] is at play i.e., to say a plea of *autrefois acquit* and *autrefois convict* is made by the accused:

(1) Any accused person against whom an information is filed may plead-
    (a) that he has been previously convicted or acquitted, as the case may be, of the same offence; or
    (b) that he has been granted a pardon for his offence.
(2) If either of such pleas are pleaded in any case and denied to be true in fact, the court shall try whether such plea is true in fact or not.
(3) If the court holds that the facts alleged by the accused do not prove the plea, or if it finds that it is false in fact, the accused shall be required to plead to the information.[78]

---

[75] Chapter 88 of the laws of Zambia.
[76] Chapter 88 of the laws of Zambia.
[77] Chapter 88 of the laws of Zambia.
[78] As amended by G.N. No 303 of 1964.

The case of *Moses Sachigogo v The People*[79] demonstrates the importance of adhering to the procedure under s 277. The accused was tried by the Subordinate Court of the First Class in Kitwe and convicted of two offences: (1) obtaining goods by false pretences and (2) impersonating a public officer. He was sentenced to a total of two years' imprisonment. The appellant appealed to set aside the conviction and sentence on the ground that prior to his conviction by the court below he had been prosecuted before the senior resident magistrate who had acquitted him of the charges. It was found that this plea was taken by the accused in court below and even though there was evidence of his trial before the senior resident magistrate the issue was not properly tried and determined. It was held that the procedure applicable in High Court under s [277] of the Criminal Procedure Code[80] when *autrefois acquit* is pleaded is applicable in the subordinate court when the same is pleaded. Failure to observe the procedure renders the proceedings a nullity.

In *Fluckson Mwandila v The People,*[81] the appellant was convicted on three counts of causing death by dangerous driving and was sentenced to eighteen months' imprisonment with hard labour on each count, to run concurrently. The information against the appellant contained five counts of causing death by dangerous driving, in each of which it was alleged that, on the same occasion, he caused the death of five different persons. Counsel for the defence raised an objection to the form of the charge in that, as the deaths of all five persons mentioned were caused by one single act, it was oppressive to charge the appellant with a number of separate counts. The trial Commissioner considered that he was bound by the decision of the Court of Appeal in which it was held that where an accused was charged and convicted with causing the death of two persons by dangerous driving and both deaths were laid in one count, the count would be defective. It was held, *inter alia*, that the law relating to duplicity of charges is intended to avoid subjecting an accused person to an unfair trial and to enable him to know the case against him, so that he may in future plead autrefois convict or acquit.

(c)   Two distinguishable facets of a judgment

Taking the preceding discussion forward, we must now turn to the judgment itself and the two facets thereof that ought to be discerned:

(i)   Judgments are conclusive as respects the legal status of matters on which they are premised. Once a judgment is rendered, no person in the world will be allowed to adduce evidence denying the result.

(ii)   As against parties and/or their privies, judgments and the facts on which they are based can be conclusive. The parties to the proceedings upon the facts of which the judgment is predicated are precluded from adducing evidence gainsaying the basis on which the judgment

---

[79] [1971] ZR 139 (HC).
[80] Chapter 88 of the Laws of Zambia.
[81] [1979] ZR 174 (SC).

was rendered. The foregoing should not be misconstrued to mean that conclusiveness as to legal status entails a judgment's conclusiveness as to facts, at least with regard to third or non-parties to the suit and judgment concerned in any subsequent proceedings. The preceding may be demonstrated using the following examples:

(a) *Green v New River Co*[82] is authority for the position that where an ex-employer sues to recover damages from an ex-employee subsequent to the same being awarded, what is contestable is the negligence on which the judgment was based but not the amount awarded and received by the plaintiff.

(b) Where there is an acquittal in criminal proceedings, the record is only conclusive only as regards the acquittal, should that be in issue, but not the question whether the plaintiff in a subsequent malicious prosecution suit against the Attorney General committed the offence with which he was charged and from which he was subsequently acquitted. It follows therefore that while the Attorney General is estopped from adducing evidence contradicting the acquittal, he is not precluded from adducing evidence that the plaintiff had, despite his acquittal, in fact committed the offence.

22.4.1.3 *Cause of action estoppel and issue estoppel*

In *Thoday v Thoday*,[83] Diplock LJ discussed the variance between cause of action estoppel on the one hand and issue estoppel on the other. In the discussion that follows, we focus on the meaning and effect of these two classes of estoppel under the aegis of estoppel by record.

(i) Cause of action estoppel

As a general rule, parties to a cause of action are required and expected to bring before court their entire case at the initial hearing and are precluded from engaging in piecemeal litigation whereby a party is repeatedly hauled before various courts over the same dispute. As has been shown in *Muyawa Liuwa v Attorney General*,[84] courts take a dim view of litigants whom, when

---

[82] (1792) 4 Term. Rep. 589.

[83] [1964] 1 All ER 341 *per* Diplock LJ; cited in the following cases: *Good Challenger Navegante S A v Metalexportimport SA* [2004] 1 Lloyd's Rep 67; *Blackburn Chemicals Ltd v Bim Kemi Ab* [2004] EWCA Civ 1490; *Hormel Foods Corporation v Antilles Landscape Investments NV* [2006] 3 All ER 1029; *Special Effects Ltd v L'Oreal Sa and Another* [2007] EWCA Civ 1; *Fraser v HLMAD Limited* [2007] 1 All ER 383; *Campbell v Leeds United Association Football* [2009] EW Misc 4 (EWCC); *Schellenberg v British Broadcasting Corporation* [2000] EMLR 296; *Bank of Scotland v Hussain and Another* [2010] EWHC 2812 (Ch); *Coke-Wallis, Regina (on The Application of) v Institute of Chartered Accountants In England and Wales* [2011] 2 All ER 1; *Sarwar v The Royal Bank of Scotland plc (Rev 1)* [2011] EWHC 2233 (Ch)); *Virgin Atlantic Airways Ltd v Zodiac Seats UK Ltd* [2013] 4 All ER 715.

[84] [2014] 2 ZR 404 (SC).

dissatisfied with a judgment deploy mechanisms to compel the court *inter alia*, to reconsider the matter in question, modify the judgment, order or ruling or otherwise change its mind if only for the dissatisfied party to have a second bite at the cherry.[85] The proper course to take therefore is to launch an appeal to a higher court when dissatisfied with a lower court's decision.

The preceding is so because generally speaking, when, as discussed earlier, a court issues a judgment, it is rendered *functus officio*. In this sense then, the concept of *functus officio* is inextricably linked to another concept discussed elsewhere in this text: *res judicata*.[86] *Res judicata* stops the court, tribunal or other statutory actor from reviving a matter in which it issued a final decision otherwise without statutory authority to so do.[87] The foregoing link notwithstanding; the concepts of *res judicata* and *functus officio* should not be confused: A simple way to avoid the confusion is to think of *res judicata* as referring to the end of a case (which it does but *functus officio* does not), and *functus officio* as referring to the expiration of an office (which it does but *res judicata* does not).

A Zambian conceptual and jurisdictive inscription on the concept of *functus officio* is scant. The origin of the concept of *functus officio* may, however, be traced to the case *In re St. Nazaire Co.*[88] Fundamentally, no court has authority to re-open, revisit or change its mind as regards its final decision in a matter except in the following instances:[89] (1) where a 'slip' has occurred in the crafting of the judgment in question, or (2) where there has been a fault in articulating the obvious connotation of the court in the judgment in question. In *Chandler v Alberta Association of Architects*, Sopinka J, as he then was, reiterated the foregoing position on the doctrine of *functus officio* in the following terms: '[t]he general rule (is) that a final decision of a court cannot be reopened [...] the rule [applies] only after the formal judgment [has] been drawn up, issued and entered, and [is] subject to two exceptions: where there had been a slip in drawing it up, and where there was an error in expressing the manifest intention of the court.'

Diplock LJ has defined the concept of action estoppel in *Thoday*[90] as follows:[91]

'cause of action estoppel,' is that which prevents a party to an action from asserting or denying, as against the other party, the existence

---

[85] Zuckerman AA, *Zuckerman on Civil Procedure: Principles of Practice* 1066.

[86] Interchangeably used with the term issue estoppel in this text, and so used by Chirwa J in *Musakanya Valentine Shula and Edward Jack Shamwana v Attorney General* [1981] ZR 221 (HC).

[87] Therefore, where a statute authorises a variation of an initial verdict, the court in question may revisit the decision now impugned. Examples include but are not limited to family law proceedings, parole board hearings and legal competency hearings.

[88] (1879) 12 Ch D 88.

[89] see *In re Swire* (1885) 30 Ch D 239 (CA); *Paper Machinery Ltd v JO Ross Engineering Corp* 1934 CanLII 1 (SCC) [1934] SCR 186.

[90] [1964] 1 All ER 341 *per* Diplock LJ.

[91] Excerpted from summary at https://swarb.co.uk/thoday-v-thoday-ca-1964/.

of a particular cause of action, the non-existence or existence of which has been determined by a court of competent jurisdiction in previous litigation between the same parties. If the cause of action was determined to exist, i.e., judgment was given upon it, it is said to be merged in the judgment, or, for those who prefer Latin, transit in *rem judicatam.*[92] If it was determined not to exist, the unsuccessful plaintiff can no longer assert that it does; he is estopped per *rem judicatam.* This is simply an application of the rule of public policy expressed in the Latin maxim *'Nemo debet bis vexari pro una et eadem causa.'*[93] In this application of the maxim 'causa' bears its literal Latin meaning.

The *locus classicus*[94] regarding cause of action estoppel or this aspect of *res judicata* is the judgment of Wigram V-C in *Henderson v Henderson:*[95]

> […] where a given matter becomes the subject of litigation in, and of adjudication by, a Court of competent jurisdiction, the Court requires the parties to that litigation to bring forward the whole case, and will not, except under special circumstances, permit the same parties to open the same subject of litigation in respect of a matter which might have been brought forward as part of the subject in contest, but which was not brought forward, only because they have from negligence, inadvertence, or even accident omitted part of their case. The plea of *res judicata* applies, except in exceptional cases, not only to points upon which the Court was actually required by the parties to form an opinion and pronounce a judgment, but to every point which the parties, exercising reasonable diligence, might have brought forward at the time.

Mr. Justice Jack has observed in a recent case[96] that '[…] if a party could properly have raised an issue in proceedings, but does not, he will not be permitted to do so subsequently.' In so holding, Jack J was following not only *Henderson*[97] but also *Yat Tung Investment Company Limited v Dao Heng Bank*[98] wherein it had been held as follows: '[b]ut there is a wider sense in which the doctrine may be appealed to, so that it becomes an abuse of process to raise matters which could and therefore should have been litigated in earlier proceedings.' It has been suggested in approving the dicta in *Henderson*[99] by the House of Lords in *Arnold v National Westminster Bank plc*[100] that as regards the concept of cause of

---

[92] See *Hayward v Hayward* (1961) P. 152.

[93] No one shall be harassed twice for the same cause.

[94] NOUN: a passage considered to be the best known or most authoritative on a particular subject:' https://www.bing.com/search?q=locus+classicus+&qs=n&form=QBRE&sp=-1&pq=locus+classicus+&sc=516&sk=&cvid=187BC90CA3134F31A73413F99D5C728D.

[95] [1843-60] ER ALL 378; (1843) 3 Hare 100 at 114, *per* Wigram VC.

[96] *Aaron v Shelton* [2004] 3 ALL ER 560.

[97] [1843-60] ER ALL 378; (1843) 3 Hare 100 at 114, *per* Wigram VC.

[98] [1975] AC 581.

[99] [1843-60] ER ALL 378; (1843) 3 Hare 100 at 114, *per* Wigram VC.

[100] [1991] 3 ER ALL 41.

action estoppel, 'the bar is absolute in relation to all points decided unless fraud or collusion is alleged, such as to justify setting aside the earlier judgment. The discovery of new factual matter which could not have been found out by reasonable diligence for use in the earlier proceedings does not, according to the law of England, permit the latter to be re-opened.'[101]

In the leading case in this jurisdiction, that of *BP Zambia Plc v Interland Motors*,[102] the Supreme Court stated as follows:

> [A]s a general rule, it will be regarded as an abuse of the process if the same parties re-litigate the same subject matter from one action to another or from judge to judge […] In conformity with the Courts inherent power to prevent abuse of its process, a party in dispute with another over a particular subject should not be allowed to deploy his grievance piecemeal in scattered litigation and keep on hauling the same opponent over the same matter before various Courts. The administration of justice would be brought into disrepute if a party managed to get conflicting decisions, or decisions which undermine each other from two or more judges over the same subject matter.

A party seeking to rely on a cause of action estoppel to thwart a plaintiff from commencing a successive suit, will need to sufficiently show, to the satisfaction of the court, that the court in the first case did in fact determine the absence of the cause of action.[103]

(ii)   Cause of action estoppel in criminal matters

In criminal matters a plea of *autrefois convict* and *autrefois acquit* corresponds to estoppel: s 138 of the Criminal procedure Code[104] provides as follows: '[a] person who has been once tried by a court of competent jurisdiction for an offence, and convicted or acquitted of such offence, shall, while such conviction or acquittal remains in force, not be liable to be tried again on the same facts for the same offence.' Also known as double jeopardy, the concept takes on a fundamental rights orientation as it is provided for in the Constitution under Article 18(5) which provides as follows:

> '[a] person who shows that he has been tried by a competent court for a criminal offence and either convicted or acquitted shall not again be tried for that offence or for any other criminal offence of which he could have been convicted at the trial for that offence, except upon the

---

[101] See further, *Port of Melbourne Authority v Anshun Pty Ltd* (No 2) (1981) 147 CLR 589 at 602-604; *Talbot v Berkshire County Council* [1993] 4 All ER 9.

[102] [2001] ZR 37; affirmed in *Muyawa Liuwa v Attorney General* [2014] 2 Z 404 (SC); see also *Bradford and Bingley Building Society v Seddon* (1994) 4 All ER 217 *per* Auld LJ; *Johnson v Gore Wood & Co* [2001] 1 All ER 481 AT 499a-e, *per* Lord Bingham: *Johnson* speaks to a flexible approach employed by the House of Lords even as it laid down a general and justifiable principle regarding estoppel and abuse of process-doctrines that preclude litigants from pursuing claims in court, a significant aspect of the right to a fair trial.

[103] Hodge M. Malek, *Phipson on Evidence* para 43-30 at 1440.

[104] Chapter 88 of the laws of Zambia.

order of a superior court in the course of appeal or review proceedings relating to the conviction or acquittal.'

A brief analysis of the foregoing is perhaps appropriate. This is because of what is stated under s 181(1)(2) of the Criminal Procedure Code[105] which provides as follows:

(1) When a person is charged with an offence consisting of several particulars, a combination of some only of which constitutes a complete minor offence, and such combination is proved but the remaining particulars are not proved, he may be convicted of the minor offence although he was not charged with it.

(2) When a person is charged with an offence and facts are proved which reduce it to a minor offence, he may be convicted of the minor offence although he was not charged with it.

A careful reading of s 138 of the Criminal Procedure Code[106] appears to suggest that a person can only be tried and convicted of and/or acquitted of the offence in the indictment and nothing more. This is because it provides additionally, that '[…] while such conviction or acquittal remains in force,' such a person 'shall not be liable to be tried again on the same facts for the same offence.' This restrictive framing of the section, it would appear, was premised on the idea that, as provided by Article 18(2)(a-c):

(2) Every person who is charged with a criminal offence-
   (a) shall be presumed to be innocent until he is proved or has pleaded guilty;
   (b) shall be informed as soon as reasonably practicable, in a language that he understands and in detail, of the nature of the offence charged;
   (c) shall be given adequate time and facilities for the preparation of his defence [….]

The idea of an accused being presumed innocent as provided for under Article 18(2)(a) of the Constitution and being treated as such is fundamental to the concept of a free trial. It is a human right guaranteed under the Constitution. It is clear from Article 18(2)(a-c) above that the reason that s 138 of the Criminal Procedure Code[107] refers to 'an offence' and then to 'the same offence' is to ensure that it is in keeping with Article 18(2)(b-c) which mandates the arresting officer and the entire judicial apparatus to ensure that the accused person is 'informed as soon as reasonably practicable, in a language that he understands and in detail, of the *nature of the offence charged*; and is 'given adequate time and facilities for the preparation of his defence.' That an accused person

---

[105] Chapter 88 of the laws of Zambia; see "Convicting of a Lesser Offence: An examination of s 181 of the Criminal Procedure Code" Hatchard J 1981 *Zambia LR 75*.

[106] Chapter 88 of the laws of Zambia.

[107] Chapter 88 of the laws of Zambia.

should know the charge he has to answer to enable him confront his accuser, is a fundamental facet of due process. As has been said in *Robert Ndecho and Another v R*,[108] '[i]t would be a denial of natural justice that [the accused] should be burdened with the fear that during the course of his trial he might have to defend himself against other offences disclosed by the evidence of which he had received no notice and no particulars.'

The crafting of Article 18(5) of the Constitution is quite clearly more encompassing. Not only does it make reference to a person showing that he has been 'tried by a competent court for a criminal offence and either convicted or acquitted', it provides that such a person 'shall not again be tried for that offence [....]' At this point, Article 18 which is a higher plane provision compared to s 138 of the Criminal Procedure Code[109] by virtue of it being a Constitutional establishment, gives sufficient predication and validity to s 138 of the Criminal Procedure Code[110] and speaks the same language as does the latter provision. Like s 138 of the Criminal Procedure Code,[111] it restricts acquittal or conviction to an offence or offences on the indictment. It is the other part of Article 18(5) that seems to expand the purview of conviction to that beyond what the accused may have been charged with to an offence that becomes apparent during or at the end of trial. This is clear from the words '[…] or for any other criminal offence of which he could have been convicted at the trial for that offence [....]'

The foregoing is significant in many ways. For starters, it is a constitutional provision and as such, cannot be deemed 'unconstitutional or as contradicting the constitution.' It cannot be struck down by judicial action. Once one reads this part of the Constitution, it becomes easy to appreciate s 181 of the Criminal Procedure Code,[112] quoted above whose provisions are only subject to an 'order of a superior court in the course of appeal or review proceedings relating to the conviction or acquittal.' Section 181 of the Criminal Procedure Code,[113] permits a court in criminal proceedings to, convict an accused person of a '[…] minor offence although he was not charged with it.'[114] Further, it provides that even in situations where an accused person is charged with an offence and his guilt is not proved in so far as the charge for which he prepared a defence is concerned, if during trial or by the end of it, 'facts are proved which reduce it to a minor offence, he may be convicted of the minor offence although he was not charged with it.'[115] This was quite a departure from English common law norms which had always held that an accused person 'could not be convicted of an offence of an entirely different character from that charged in the indictment.'

---

[108] 18 E.A. App R Vol viii 171.
[109] Chapter 88 of the laws of Zambia.
[110] Chapter 88 of the laws of Zambia.
[111] Chapter 88 of the laws of Zambia.
[112] Chapter 88 of the laws of Zambia.
[113] Chapter 88 of the laws of Zambia.
[114] Section 181(1).
[115] "Convicting of a Lesser Offence: An examination of s 181 of the Criminal Procedure Code" Hatchard J 1981 *Zambia LR 75* in Hatchard & Ndulo, *The Law of Evidence in Zambia* 72.

The meaning, intent and practical application of s 181[116] was considered in the case of *Phiri (Charles) v The people*.[117] The appellant was charged with three counts of forgery and three counts of uttering a false document. He was found not guilty on the three counts of uttering; he appealed against the convictions for forgery to what was then the Court of Appeal for Zambia. The Court reviewed preceding authorities on s 181 and clarified the law by disapproving in part the interpretation given to s 181 by some previous authorities.[118]

The particulars of the offences are identical save for the amounts involved. In each case the appellant is alleged to have forged a payment voucher of the Ministry of Finance purporting to show that a certain Government officer was entitled to payment of housing allowance arrears when in fact he was not. The magistrate found, as he was fully entitled - and indeed bound - to find on the evidence, that the appellant had himself made out these vouchers, and on the strength of them he obtained cheques from the authorised officers in the ministry made payable to the person to whom the vouchers referred. There was thus a deliberate and calculated course of conduct to defraud the Government of the moneys in question and it must be said at the outset that morally there is no merit whatever in the appeal. It does however raise important questions of law.

The magistrate when dealing with the question of forgery said this:

> Quite clearly, on the evidence before the court, these completed forms were false documents since it has been shown to the court that Christopher Mwela was not entitled to these payments of housing allowance arrears [....] S 342 of the Penal Code[119] defines forgery as: '[…] the making of a false document with intent to defraud or deceive."

Section 344 states, *inter alia*, that a person makes a false document who: '(a) makes a document purporting to be what in fact it is not.' [....] [The documents] were false documents purporting to show on the face of the documents information which was not in fact true.'

The definition cited by the magistrate is a statement of the common law definition of forgery in England expounded by Blackburn J in *Ex Parte Windsor*.[120] In that case Blackburn J went on to say: '[Forgery] is not the making of an instrument which purports to be what it really is, but which contains false statements. Telling a lie does not become forgery because it is reduced into writing.'

---

[116] of the Criminal Procedure Code, Chapter 88 of the laws of Zambia.

[117] [1973] ZR 168 (CA); [1973] ZR 168 (CA); Cases cited: *Ex Parte Windsor* (1865) 10 Cox CC 118; *R v Mancinelli* 6 NRLR 19; *Ndecho and Anor v R* 18 EACA 171; *R v Justin* 1962 R & N 614; *Sikombo and Anor v The People* SCZ 19 of 1973; Cases disapproved in part: *R v Mancinelli* 6 NRLR 19, and *R v Justin* 1962 R & N 614; Legislation referred to: Penal Code, Chapter 146, ss 26(4), 157, 158, 309, 342, 344(a), 347; Court of Appeal for Zambia Act, Cap 52, s 15(2); Criminal Procedure Code, Chapter 160, s 181.

[118] In, among others, and more significantly, *R v Mancinelli* 6 NRLR 19.

[119] Chapter 87 of the Laws of Zambia.

[120] (1865) 10 Cox CC 118.

The matter is put thus by the learned author of the eighteenth edition of Kenny's Outlines of Criminal Law at page 375:

> The simplest and most effective phrase by which to express this rule is to state that for the purposes of the law of forgery, the writing must tell a lie about itself. Hence a conveyance which contains false recitals or states incorrectly the price paid is not thereby 'false'. And a letter or telegram sent to a newspaper containing false news is not a forged document: although it would be if it were sent falsely in the name of one (e.g., an official reporter) who did not send or authorise the sending of it, for in such a case it would purport to be his message, which it is not. So also, if a cashier or foreman makes out a pay sheet so as to receive A greater amount of money from his employer than he has to disperse to subordinate members of the staff, this is not forgery, for, although it tells a lie about the men, it does not tell a lie about itself, since it is a pay sheet which that man has prepared and rendered.

This passage, and particularly the last example given therein, makes it clear that the vouchers made out by the appellant were not forgeries; they contained false statements but they did not tell lies about themselves It follows that the convictions for forgery were bad.

However, this does not end the matter. Section 15(2) of the Court of Appeal for Zambia Act reads:

> Where an appellant has been convicted of an offence and the trial court could on the information, or charge, have found him guilty of some other offence, and on the findings of the trial court it appears to the Court that the trial court must have been satisfied of the facts which proved him guilty of that other offence, the Court may, instead of allowing or dismissing the appeal, substitute for the judgment of the trial court a judgment of guilty of that other offence and pass such sentence in substitution for the sentence passed at the trial as may be warranted in law for that other offence, not being a sentence of greater severity.

However, the powers of this court under that subsection depend on whether the trial court could, on the charge, have found the appellant guilty of some other offence. This would be so only if the matter falls within the provisions of s181 of the Criminal Procedure Code[121] which reads:

> (1)   When a person is charged with an offence consisting of several particulars, a combination of some only of which constitutes a complete minor offence, and such combination is proved but the remaining particulars are not proved, he may be convicted of the minor offence although he was not charged with it.

---

[121] Chapter 88 of the Laws of Zambia.

(2)   When a person is charged with an offence and facts are proved which reduce it to a minor offence, he may be convicted of the minor offence although he was not charged with it.

There is no definition of "minor offence" in our legislation, but the expression has been considered in a number of cases. In *R v Mancinelli*[122] the accused was charged with indecently assaulting a boy under the age of fourteen years contrary to a section of the Penal Code[123] corresponding to the present s 157. The age of the boy was not satisfactorily proved and it was held that the accused could be convicted of an offence under the section corresponding to the present s 158 which relates to indecent practices between males. S 168 of the Criminal Procedure Code[124] at that time was identical in terms with the present s 181 and in the course of the consideration of the question whether or not an offence under the section dealing with indecent practices was a minor offence as compared with the offence of indecently assaulting a boy under the age of fourteen years, Bell CJ said this:

> No offence can be a 'minor offence' within the meaning of that subsection unless it carries a lesser penalty than the offence with which the accused person is originally charged and unless it is cognate to the offence originally charged, that is to say is of the same genusor species, (*Robert Ndecho and Another v R*[125]), and comes within the ambit of s 168(1) of the Criminal Procedure Code.[126]

This dictum was cited with approval by Blagden J, as he then was, in *R v Justin*.[127]

The dictum of Bell CJ, would appear to hold that for an offence to be a minor offence for the purposes of s 181(2) of the Criminal Procedure Code, three conditions must be satisfied: first, that the other offence carries a lesser penalty than the offence with which the accused was originally charged; second, that it is cognate to the offence originally charged; and third, that it comes within the ambit of s181(1). We will deal first with the last of these requirements. With the greatest respect to Bell CJ, we are unable to see how it can be a necessary requirement that a matter falling under sub-s (2) must also fall within the ambit of sub-s (1); if that had been the intention of the legislature the section would have been framed quite differently and in such a way as to make it clear that in every case not only must the facts constituting a minor offence be proved but also the particulars of such minor offence must be contained as part of the particulars of the offence charged. It is difficult to see in such circumstances

---

[122] 6 NRLR 19.
[123] Chapter 87 of the Laws of Zambia.
[124] Chapter 88 of the Laws of Zambia.
[125] 18 EACA 171.
[126] Chapter 88 of the Laws of Zambia.
[127] 1962 R & N 614.

why subsection (2) would be necessary at all. The two subsections seem to us to contemplate two different cases. The first is where the offence consists of several particulars and some of these particulars constituting another offence are proved; the second is where none of the particulars of the offence charged is proved but facts are proved which disclose another offence. We must therefore with respect disapprove of that portion of the judgment in *Mancinelli*,[128] and disapprove also of the judgment in *Justin*[129] to the extent that it appears to adopt the earlier dictum.

In support of the second of the foregoing requirements, namely that the minor offence must be cognate to the offence charged, Bell CJ, relied on *Ndecho and Alan v R*.[130] However, what the court said in that case was [as follows]:

> […] where an accused person is charged with an offence he may be convicted of a minor offence although not charged with it, if that minor offence is of a cognate character, that is to say of the same genus or species. Furthermore, we point out that the wording of s 181(2) is permissible only […] The test the Court should apply when exercising its discretion is whether the accused person can reasonably be said to have had a fair opportunity of making his defence to the alternative.

This is not quite the same thing as saying that for an offence to be a minor offence for the purposes of s 181 it must be cognate to the offence charged; it is simply saying that a person may not be convicted of such minor offence unless it is cognate to the offence charged. On the first approach, the question of the cognateness or otherwise of the alternative offence is an aspect of the definition of "minor offence," whereas on the second approach it is a factor to be taken into account by the court in exercising its discretion whether or not to convict of the minor offence.

This distinction, far from being a matter of semantics, is of [great] importance. The expression "minor offence" appears in both subsections of s 181 and it would be absurd to think that the legislature intended the same expression to have one meaning in the first subsection and another in the second. Yet it is abundantly clear that for the purposes of sub-s (1), so long as the particulars comprising the minor offence have been included in the particulars of the offence charged, the accused may be convicted of the minor offence even though it was of a different species from the original offence charged. For instance, the essence of the offence of robbery is theft, the violence being merely something employed for the purpose of effecting such theft; the essence of assault is the violence itself. Robbery and assault could not therefore be said to be offences of the same *genus or species*, but on the clear wording of s 181(1) a conviction for assault is competent on a charge of aggravated robbery or robbery, and this court has recently so held in the case of *Sikombo and Anor v The People*.[131] S 181(2)

---

[128] 6 NRLR 19.
[129] R & N 614.
[130] 18 EACA 171.
[131] SCZ 19 of 1973.

however contemplates a different case, namely one where the particulars of the minor offence have at no time been expressed in the offence charged. The reason why the courts have held that before a conviction for the minor offence can be entered the offence must be cognate to the original offence is that, without this requirement, an accused would not have had a fair opportunity of making his defence to the alternative. As the court said in *Ndecho and Anor v R*[132] at 174:

> It would be a denial of natural justice that he should be burdened with the fear that during the course of his trial he might have to defend himself against other offences disclosed by the evidence of which he had received no notice and no particulars. Such a departure from the basic principles of the English common law will have to receive express legislative sanction before this court will countenance it.

This passage pinpoints the fundamental difference between the two sub-sections of section 181; under the first an accused will have received notice and particulars of the alternative, and consequently there will normally have been a fair opportunity for the accused to make his defence to that alternative.

We stress what was said in *Ndecho*,[133] namely that s 181 is permissive only and that the test the court should apply when exercising its discretion is whether the accused can reasonably be said to have had a fair opportunity to meet the alternative charge. The fact that the alternative is or is not cognate to the offence originally charged will be one of the factors to be taken into account by the court.

It remains to consider what is meant by a "lesser penalty", this being the first of the conditions postulated by BellCJ. At one stage in the history of the English common law it was axiomatic that a misdemeanour carried a lesser penalty than a felony, but with the passage of time the distinction between these two categories of crime has lost most of its importance. The codification of the criminal law in many of the former British colonies has further reduced the relevance of such a distinction. However, the definition is not entirely irrelevant; s26(4) of the Penal Code[134] provides that a person convicted of a misdemeanour may be sentenced to pay a fine in addition to or instead of imprisonment. Hence where a particular felony carries a maximum sentence of, say, five years, imprisonment with hard labour and a misdemeanour is expressed to card the seine maximum, the question is whether the misdemeanour is a minor offence. In one sense the permissible penalty which may be imposed in the case of misdemeanour is actually greater than that which may be imposed in the case of a felony, since it is conceivable that the court will impose the maximum sentence of imprisonment plus a fine. However, we are in no doubt that this is purely a theoretical possibility; the considerations to be taken into account when sentencing for a misdemeanour are well known and, for instance,

---

[132] 18 EACA 171.

[133] 18 EACA 171.

[134] Chapter 87 of the Laws of Zambia.

first offenders will normally be fined rather than imprisoned unless, in the circumstances, the court considers that a fine is not appropriate even in the case of a first offender. In our view, therefore, where the two offences under consideration are a felony and a misdemeanour and each is expressed to carry the same maximum sentence of imprisonment, the misdemeanour is a minor offence for the purposes of s 181.

Applying the principles enunciated above to the facts of the present case the first question is whether there is an alternative offence to the charge of forgery which carries a lesser penalty. The section under which the appellant was charged was s347 which defines the offence as a felony and prescribes a punishment of imprisonment for three years, s309 creates the misdemeanour of obtaining by false pretences and prescribes a punishment of imprisonment for three years. Consequently, obtaining by false pretences is, in accordance with what we have said above, an offence which carries a lesser penalty than that prescribed for forgery.

There are unquestionably great similarities between forgery and uttering on the one hand and obtaining by false pretences on the other, and had the appellant in the present case not been acquitted on the charges of uttering we would have had little hesitation in holding that he could have been convicted of obtaining by false pretences by virtue of the provisions of s 181. However, the appellant was acquitted on the facts on the three charges of uttering; these facts were essential to any conviction of obtaining by false pretences, and since the appellant was in peril in the court below of being convicted of this alternative offence he cannot now be convicted of that offence. For these reasons we have no alternative but to allow this appeal and to set aside the convictions and sentences.

Distillable from the foregoing case are the following principles:

(i)   A document purporting to be what in fact it is, but which contains a false statement, is not false within the meaning of s 344(c) of the Penal Code;[135] to be a false document it must tell a lie about itself.

(ii)   Section 181 of the Criminal Procedure Code is permissive only; the test the court should apply when exercising its discretion is whether the accused can reasonably be said to have had a fair opportunity to meet the alternative charge.

(iii) In cases falling within s 181(1) the accused will have received notice and particulars of the alternative, and consequently there will normally have been a fair opportunity to make his defence to that alternative even where it is of a different species from the original offence charged.

(iv)   In all cases falling under s 181, the question of the cognateness or otherwise of the alternative offence is not an aspect of the definition of "minor offence" but a factor to be taken into account by the court in exercising its discretion whether or not to convict of the minor offence.

---

[135] Chapter 87 of the Laws of Zambia.

Despite the relative clarity of *Phiri (Charles) v The People*,[136] concerns still remain regarding s 181.[137] What is quite clear from s 181(1) is that the premise for convicting an accused person on an offence, termed a lessor offence is that 'the particulars comprising the minor offence have been included in the particulars of the offence charged,'. It follows that the new offence on which the accused is convicted need not be similar/cognate to the original offence charged. For instance, the essence of the offence of robbery is theft, the violence being merely something employed for the purpose of effecting such theft; the essence of assault is the violence itself. Robbery and assault could not therefore be said to be offences of the same genusor species, but on the clear wording of s 181(1) a conviction for assault is competent on a charge of aggravated robbery or robbery.[138]

According to the Court, s 181(2) has in contemplation a different case, specifically, one where the particulars of the minor offence have at no time been expressed in the offence charged. The reason why the courts have held that before a conviction for the minor offence can be entered the offence must be cognate to the original offence is to give the accused a fair opportunity of making his defence to the alternative offence. The test set in *Ndecho*[139] is still good law and the bedrock of a fair criminal trial. The Court of Appeal, as it existed then, said as much in *Phiri (Charles) v The People*,[140] quoting from *Ndecho and Anor v R*:[141] '[i]t would be a denial of natural justice that he should be burdened with the fear that during the course of his trial he might have to defend himself against other offences disclosed by the evidence of which he had received no notice and no particulars.' Said the Court, '[t]his passage pinpoints the fundamental difference between the two sub-ss of s 181; under the first an accused will have received notice and particulars of the alternative, and consequently there will normally have been a fair opportunity for the accused to make his defence to that alternative.' It must be added that under s 181(2), no such notice and particulars of the alternative charge are availed to the accused thus giving the accused no fair opportunity for the accused to

---

[136] [1973] ZR 168 (CA); Cases cited: *Ex Parte Windsor* (1865) 10 Cox CC 118; *R v Mancinelli* 6 NRLR 19; *Ndecho and Anor v R* 18 EACA 171; *R v Justin* 1962 R & N 614; *Sikombo and Anor v The People* SCZ 19 of 1973; Cases disapproved in part: *R v Mancinelli* 6 NRLR 19, and *R v Justin* 1962 R & N 614; Legislation referred to: Penal Code, Chapter 146, ss 26(4), 157, 158, 309, 342, 344(a), 347; Court of Appeal for Zambia Act, Cap 52, s 15(2); Criminal Procedure Code, Chapter 160, s 181.

[137] Compare s 6(3) of the Criminal Law Act 1967 which is the equivalent of s 181(1) of the Criminal Procedure Code and provides as follows: '[w]here, on a person's trial on indictment for any offence except treason or murder, the jury find him not guilty of the offence specifically charged in the indictment, but the allegations in the indictment amount to or include (expressly or by implication) an allegation of another offence falling within the jurisdiction of the court of trial, the jury may find him guilty of that other offence.' There is no England & Wales equivalent for s 181(2) of our Criminal Procedure Code.

[138] See *Sikombo and Anor v The People* SCZ Judgment No 19 of 1973.

[139] 18 EACA 171.

[140] [1973] ZR 168 (CA); Cases cited: *Ex Parte Windsor* (1865) 10 Cox CC 118; *R v Mancinelli* 6 NRLR 19; *Ndecho and Anor v R* 18 EACA 171; *R v Justin* 1962 R & N 614; *Sikombo and Anor v The People* SCZ 19 of 1973; Cases disapproved in part: *R v Mancinelli* 6 NRLR 19, and *R v Justin* 1962 R & N 614; Legislation referred to: Penal Code, Chapter 146, ss 26(4), 157, 158, 309, 342, 344(a), 347; Court of Appeal for Zambia Act, Cap 52, s 15(2); Criminal Procedure Code, Chapter 160, s 181.

[141] 18 EACA 171 at 174.

make his defence to the alternative charge. This happened in *Haonga and Others v The People*.[142] This appears to fly in the face of the constitutional right to a fair trial in general and the *Ndecho*[143] test in particular.

Probably with the foregoing in mind the Court stressed what was said in *Ndecho*,[144]

> […] namely that [s] 181 is permissive only and that the test the court should apply when exercising its discretion is whether the accused can reasonably be said to have had a fair opportunity to meet the alternative charge. The fact that the alternative is or is not cognate to the offence originally charged will be one of the factors to be taken into account by the court.

It has been noted[145] that the wide-ranging nature of s 181 means that the court is not restricted from convicting the accused for another offence in cases where the accused is charged with murder. In *Haonga and Others v The People*,[146] the appellants were convicted of the murder of a farmer, who was shot and killed during an armed robbery carried out by five men. The appellants were identified by one witness as the occupants of a car which had been involved in an accident some three hours before the time of the murder; two of the appellants were identified, each by one witness, as having been among the five robbers, and a third was found some weeks later in possession of a firearm from which the fatal shots were proved to have been fired. The evidence as to who fired the shots was conflicting and the prosecution conceded that the case must proceed on the basis that it was not known who fired them.

The second, third, fourth and fifth appellants were alleged to have made confessions, to which objection was taken. The statement of the second appellant was excluded by the trial judge on the ground that it was extracted by beatings, but those of the other three, taken by substantially the same "team", were ruled to have been freely and voluntarily made and were admitted in evidence. It was argued by the prosecution that even if the statements be excluded there was sufficient evidence to support the findings that the five robbers were the same men as the five occupants of the car involved in an accident three hours earlier; it was argued further that the trial judge was right in holding that the five robbers were shown to have a common purpose involving the carrying of a firearm, or alternatively that they were guilty of murder because they were engaged together in the commission of a felony in the course of which someone was killed. It was held, *inter alia*: (i) An accused person may

---

[142] [1976] ZR 200; see discussion below.

[143] 18 EACA 171.

[144] 18 EACA 171 at 174.

[145] "Convicting of a Lesser Offence: An examination of s 181 of the Criminal Procedure Code" Hatchard J 1981 *Zambia LR 75* in Hatchard & Ndulo, *The Law of Evidence in Zambia* 72.

[146] [1976] ZR 200.

be convicted of a minor offence in terms of s 181(2) of the Criminal Procedure Code[147] provided he can reasonably be said to have had fair opportunity to meet the alternative charge; the question of cognateness or otherwise is not an aspect of the definition of the expression "minor offence" but a factor to be taken into account by the court in exercising its discretion. (ii) The court's discretion should not be exercised lightly; in particular person facing a charge of murder should not have his defence complicated by the possibility of a conviction for some other offence. But if the accused has quite clearly had a full opportunity to meet the other charge the court must not shirk its duty simply because the indictment is murder. Whether or not an accused has had Air opportunity to meet another charge will always depend on the facts of the particular case. (iii) On a charge of "capital aggravated robbery", i.e., under s 294(2) of the Penal Code[148] the onus is on the accused to satisfy the court as to the matters therein set out, whereas on a charge of murder the onus is on the prosecution throughout, including the onus to establish common purpose where this is in issue. Hence on a charge of murder an accused has never been called upon to discharge the onus under s 294(2) and he cannot therefore have had a fair opportunity to meet charge under that section.

Can it then be gainsaid that s 181 is too widely framed as to give the courts unfettered power in its interpretation, erroneous application and unjust consequences for the accused? While the provisions of s 181(1) as explained in *Phiri*[149] restrict the application of that section, in convicting for lessor offences which ordinarily a court should have power to do, the same cannot be said of s 181(2). While a theoretical possibility, it is difficult to see how in practice an accused person may reasonably be said to have had fair opportunity to meet the alternative charge as envisaged under s 181(2), no matter how generous the court may be in ensuring that this is so. As shown in *Haonga*,[150] 'cognateness or otherwise is not an aspect of the definition of the expression "minor offence" but a factor to be taken into account by the court in exercising its discretion.' This is too much latitude to give to a court in a section that, before *Phiri*[151] caused construction problems that were so consequential as to cause injustice to the accused and to bring the criminal justice system into disrepute. As has been observed by John Hatchard,[152]

> [...] it may well be that s 181(2) does give the courts an [unnecessarily] wide power as it may appear to the accused that the court is using every means to convict him of some offence even if the prosecution has failed to prove the offence with which he was charged. There must also be concern that a conviction for a lesser offence can be entered in cases where the original offence charged carries the [life] sentence. The strain which a trial for this type of offence inevitably inflicts on

---

[147] Chapter 88 of the Laws of Zambia.

[148] Chapter 88 of the Laws of Zambia.

[149] [1973] ZR 168.

[150] [1976] ZR 200.

[151] [1973] ZR 168.

[152] Hatchard & Ndulo, *The Law of Evidence in Zambia* 75.

an accused should not be compounded by the knowledge that there is still a chance of his being convicted of a different offence even if the capital charge is not proved.[153]

A case that illustrates the problem inherent in how s 181[154] is couched and the need to be cautious in determining the correct charge(s) is *Juma Zakalia v The People*:[155]

The applicant and another man were convicted of unlawful wounding the allegation being that they assaulted the complainant and inflicted injuries on him with bar. There is evidence that they interfered with a juke box in the tavern and which juke complainant was a watchman, but there is no evidence that anything was actually stolen.

In addition to the complainant himself the applicant was identified by a business man who saw two people running away from the tavern. This witness had been awakened at 03:00 hours in the morning and he saw the two men bit the lights of the tavern. He told the court that he knew both accused persons before, that he was only about ten metres away, and specifically in relation to the present applicant he said in cross-examination that he knew all the applicant's family and that he saw him clearly in the lights. The complainant also said that he knew both the accused persons very well and saw them clearly in the lights. There was thus ample evidence on which the learned trial magistrate was entitled to come to the conclusion that the applicant had been satisfactorily identified and there is no basis on which this court can interfere.

However, the accused persons were charged with unlawful wounding and convicted. This court has had occasion to consider this point more than once in the past and we refer for instance to *Lengwe v The People*[156] in which we followed an earlier decision of the same court in the case of *N'gambi v The People*.[157] In *Lengwe*[158] we quoted the following passage from *N'gambi*,[159] and since it appears that those responsible for prosecutions have overlooked these decisions we must, at the risk of labouring the matter, cite the passage again.

> 'wound' is defined in [s 4] of the Penal Code as 'any incision or puncture which divides or pierces any exterior membrane of the body'. A laceration inflicted by a blow with a stick which breaks the skin is not a wound within this definition. The meanings of the words 'incision' and 'puncture' make it clear that such a wound can be inflected only by a weapon with a cutting edge or point. Of course, this cutting edge or point need not be that of a metal object such as a

---

[153] It has been suggested that based on the foregoing, the decision in *Haonga and Others v The People* [1976] ZR 200 must be revisited: Hatchard & Ndulo, *The Law of Evidence in Zambia* 75.

[154] Of the Criminal Procedure Code Chapter 88 of the Laws of Zambia.

[155] [1978] ZR 149 (SC); following *Lengwe v The People* [1976] ZR 127 and approving *N'gambi v The People* [1975] ZR 97; Legislation referred to: ss 247, 248, 295 of the Penal Code, Chapter 87 of the Laws of Zambia.

[156] [1976] ZR 127.

[157] [1975] ZR 97.

[158] [1976] ZR 127.

[159] [1975] ZR 97.

> knife or spear, or indeed a bullet; a wound can equally be inflicted by
> a sharpened stone or stick.

In *Lengwe*[160] we held that injuries inflected with a hammer and spanner were not wounds within the definition; the same reasoning is entirely in point in the present case. As Mr Kinariwala very properly concedes, the conviction for unlawful wounding cannot therefore stand.

On the facts of this case the accused persons could well have been charged with aggravated assault contrary to s 295 of the Penal Code,[161] and certainly should have been charged at the very least with assault occasioning actual bodily harm contrary to s 248 of the Penal Code.[162] It is not however open to this court to substitute convictions under either of these sections in place of the incorrect conviction for unlawful wounding because both those other offences are more serious than the offence of which the applicant was convicted. The case of *Lengwe*[163] dealt with that point also; we said in precisely similar circumstances that the only conviction possible by way of substitution was one for common assault. It is with the greatest regret that we are forced to this conclusion, because this was a very serious offence and the maximum penalty for common assault, is quite inadequate.

The application so far as it relates to both conviction and sentence is allowed and the hearing will he treated as the hearing of the appeal. The conviction for unlawful wounding is set aside and a conviction for common assault contrary to s 247 of the Penal Code[164] is substituted. The sentence is also set aside and, in its place, there will be substituted the maximum sentence under the section, namely, one year's imprisonment with hard labour from the date of conviction, the 18 May, 1977.

(b)   Tainted acquittals

Acquittals that are tainted are liable to being set aside on appeal. This is the case in instances where it can be shown for example that an acquittal has been procured by the intimidation of witnesses; fraud or otherwise by illegal means. Therefore, where it can be shown that the trial judge was bribed or intimidated, the appellate court ought to quash the acquittal.

(c)   Fresh evidence in serious cases

The taking of fresh evidence may be dealt with on appeal under Order 39, RSC which provides for the Supreme Court to receive additional evidence and report from the Court below. Order 39, RSC, provides as follows:

---

[160] [1976] ZR 127.
[161] Chapter 87 of the Laws of Zambia.
[162] Chapter 87 of the Laws of Zambia.
[163] [1976] ZR 127.
[164] Chapter 87 of the Laws of Zambia.

(1) In dealing with any appeal the Court may, if it thinks additional evidence to be necessary, either take such evidence itself or direct it to be taken by the trial court or by the Master or by some other person as commissioner.

(2) When additional evidence is taken by the trial court it shall certify such evidence, with a statement of its opinion as to the credibility of the witness or witnesses giving such additional evidence, to the Court. When additional evidence is taken by the Master or a commissioner, he shall certify such evidence to the Court. The Court shall thereupon proceed in either case to dispose of the appeal.

(3) The parties to the appeal shall be entitled to be present when such additional evidence is taken, but such evidence shall not be taken in the presence of a jury or assessors.

(4) In dealing with any appeal the Court may also, if it thinks fit, call for and receive from the trial court a report on any matter connected with the trial, and in dealing with any second appeal, the Court may in addition, if it thinks fit, call for and receive from the High Court a report on any matter connected with the appeal proceedings before it.

The foregoing may enable the court to set aside acquittals or quash convictions in serious cases such as murder or aggravated robbery, where apparently good, compelling and reliable evidence emerges; which evidence may not have been available to the court or may have been ignored by the court below.

(iii) Issue estoppel

Issue estoppel applies to situations where an issue has been raised during proceedings and is distinctly determined by a court of competent jurisdiction. Under such circumstances neither of the parties to such suit will be permitted to contend on that issue ever again. They are effectively estopped from doing so on the basis of issue estoppel. In *Thoday v Thoday*[165] Diplock LJ[166] put it thus:

> [...] 'issue estoppel', is an extension of the same rule of public policy. There are many causes of action which can only be established by proving that two or more different conditions are fulfilled. Such causes of action involve as many separate issues between the parties as there are conditions to be fulfilled by the plaintiff in order to establish his

---

[165] [1964] 1 All ER 341 *per* Diplock LJ; cited in the following cases: *Good Challenger Navegante S A v Metalexportimport SA* [2004] 1 Lloyd's Rep 67; *Blackburn Chemicals Ltd v Bim Kemi Ab* [2004] EWCA Civ 1490; *Hormel Foods Corporation v Antilles Landscape Investments NV* [2006] 3 All ER 1029; *Special Effects Ltd v L'Oreal Sa and Another* [2007] EWCA Civ 1; *Fraser v HLMAD Limited* [2007] 1 All ER 383; *Campbell v Leeds United Association Football* [2009] EW Misc 4 (EWCC); *Schellenberg v British Broadcasting Corporation* [2000] EMLR 296; *Bank of Scotland v Hussain and Another* [2010] EWHC 2812 (Ch); *Coke-Wallis, Regina (on The Application of) v Institute of Chartered Accountants In England and Wales* [2011] 2 All ER 1; *Sarwar v The Royal Bank of Scotland Plc (Rev 1)* [2011] EWHC 2233 (Ch)); *Virgin Atlantic Airways Ltd v Zodiac Seats UK Ltd* [2013] 4 All ER 715.

[166] In *Mills v Cooper* [1967] 2 All ER 100 at 104g-105c, Diplock J traced the genesis of issue estoppel to the case of *Hoystead v Taxation Commissioners* [1926] AC 155.

cause of action; and there may be cases where the fulfilment of an identical condition is a requirement common to two or more different causes of action. If in litigation upon one such cause of action any of such separate issues as to whether a particular condition has been fulfilled is determined by a court of competent jurisdiction, either upon evidence or upon admission by a party to the litigation, neither party can, in subsequent litigation between one another upon any cause of action which depends upon the fulfilment of the identical condition, assert that the condition was fulfilled if the court in the first litigation determined that it was not, or deny that it was fulfilled if the court in the first litigation determined that it was.[167]

Referring with approval to the foregoing, Lord Denning opined in *Fidelitas Shipping v V/O Exportchles*:[168]

The umpire held in his interim award (subject to the opinion of the court) that the claim was not excluded. The court took a different view and held that the claim was excluded by the cesser clause. That issue having been decided by the court, can it be re-opened before the umpire? I think not. It is a case of 'issue estoppel' [....] The law as I understand it, is this if one party brings an action against another for a particular cause and judgment is given on it, there is a strict rule of law that he cannot bring another action against the same party for the same cause. Transit in *re-judicatam*. But within one cause of action there may be several issues raised which are necessary for the determination of the whole case, the rule then is that, once an issue has been raised and distinctly determined between the parties, then, as a general rule neither party can be allowed to fight that issue all over again. The same issue cannot be raised by either of them again in the same or subsequent proceedings except in special circumstances.

In *Mills v Cooper*[169] Diplock J, as he then was, discussed the doctrine of issue estoppel as it relates to civil as well as criminal proceedings. We analyse his *dicta* below:

(c)   Issue estoppel in civil matters

As far as civil proceedings go, the concept of issue estoppel is not only a recent invention but one that has had a somewhat sporadic development.[170] In *Mills v Cooper*,[171] Diplock J traced the genesis of issue estoppel to the case of

---

[167] Excerpted from summary at https://swarb.co.uk/thoday-v-thoday-ca-1964/.

[168] [1955] 2 All ER 4, 8; quoted with approval by Chirwa J, as he then was, in *Musakanya Valentine Shula and Edward Jack Shamwana v Attorney General* [1981] ZR 221 (HC).

[169] [1967] 2 All ER 100.

[170] *Mills v Cooper* [1967] 2 All ER 100, *per* Lord Diplock at 104g.

[171] [1967] 2 All ER 100.

Hoystead v Taxation Commission.[172] The concept, so far as it affects civil proceedings, can be stated as follows:

> a party to civil proceedings is not entitled to make, as against the other party, an assertion, whether of fact or of the legal consequences of facts, the correctness of which is an essential element in his cause of action or defence, if the same assertion was an essential element in his previous cause of action or defence in previous civil proceedings between the same parties or their predecessors intitle, and was found by a court of competent jurisdiction in such previous proceedings to be incorrect, unless further material which is relevant to the correctness or incorrectness of the assertion and could not by reasonable diligence have been adduced by that party in the previous proceedings has since been available to him.

(d)   Issue estoppel in criminal matters?

The doctrine of issue estoppel is applicable in the sense of the rule against double jeopardy in criminal proceedings as already discussed elsewhere in this text. As suggested therefore, a plea of *autrefois convict* and *autrefois acquit* corresponds to issue estoppel in terms of s 138 of the Criminal procedure Code[173] and in accordance with Article 18(5) of the Constitution. Says Article 18(5), '[a] person who has been once tried by a court of competent jurisdiction for an offence, and convicted or acquitted of such offence, shall, while such conviction or acquittal remains in force, not be liable to be tried again on the same facts for the same offence.' According to Lord Diplock,[174] however, 'the rule against double jeopardy also applies in circumstances in which those ancient pleas are not strictly available.' He criticised the use of the term issue estoppel both in criminal[175] and civil matters as being rather unhelpful as it sows confusion principally because 'there are obvious differences-lack of mutuality is but one-between the application of the rule against double jeopardy in criminal cases, and the rule that there should be finality in civil litigation.'[176]

The views of Lord Diplock about the need to distinguish issue estoppel as developed in civil matters from the analogous but distinct concept of double jeopardy applicable to criminal matters was followed in *DPP v Humphrys.*[177] In June 1973 the respondent was tried on a charge which alleged that on 18 July 1972 he had driven a motor cycle while disqualified. The respondent admitted that on 18 July he was disqualified but denied that he was the person driving the motor cycle on that particular date. At the trial a police constable testified that he had stopped the respondent while he was driving a motor cycle on that date. The respondent testified that he had not driven a motor vehicle at all during the

---

[172] [1926] AC 155.

[173] Chapter 88 of the laws of Zambia.

[174] *Mills v Cooper* [1967] 2 All ER 100, *per* Lord Diplock at 104g-105c.

[175] See the Australian High Court decisions in *Wilkes* (1948) 77 CLR 511; Mraz (No 2) (1956) 96 CLR 62.

[176] *Mills v Cooper* [1967] 2 All ER 100, *per* Lord Diplock at 104g-105c.

[177] [1976] 2 All ER 497 at 523d – 523g *per* Lord Hailsham.

year 1972 and gave evidence which suggested that the person stopped by the police constable was someone else. The respondent was acquitted. Subsequent enquiries made by the police disclosed evidence that the respondent was in fact the driver stopped by the police constable on 18 July 1972. The respondent was subsequently charged with perjury in that during the course of his trial in June 1973 he had wilfully made a false statement material in those proceedings, namely that he had not driven any motor vehicle during the year 1972. At the respondent's trial the Crown adduced evidence of several witnesses which tended to show that the respondent had driven a motor cycle during 1972. In addition, the same police constable who had given evidence at the respondent's trial in June 1973 was called to give exactly the same evidence that he had given at the earlier trial, i.e., that the respondent had been driving a motor cycle on 18 July 1972. The respondent was convicted of perjury. On appeal, the Court of Appeal, Criminal Division,[178] quashed the respondent's conviction on the ground that the doctrine of issue estoppel applied to charges of perjury and that, as the jury at the first trial had determined the question whether the respondent had been the driver of the motor cycle on 18 July 1972 in the respondent's favour, the evidence of the police constable that the respondent was the driver on that date was inadmissible in support of the charge that the respondent had falsely sworn that he had not driven a vehicle in 1972. The Crown appealed. It was held on appeal that the doctrine of issue estoppel had no application to criminal proceedings and in any event could not apply to prevent a charge of perjury being brought against a person who had been acquitted of another offence in respect of evidence given by him at the trial for that offence. Even if the doctrine did apply, the Crown was not precluded from relying on the police constable's evidence at the respondent's trial for perjury, since that evidence was not directed to proving that the respondent had been guilty of driving while disqualified but to the issue whether he had ridden a motor cycle in 1972 contrary to his sworn evidence. Accordingly, the appeal would be allowed and the respondent's conviction for perjury restored[179]

Based on the foregoing it is safe to draw the following conclusions which speak the more relaxed requirements regarding issue estoppel compared to the much stricter ones relating to cause of action estoppel:[180]

---

[178] [1975] 2 All ER 1023.

[179] Dictum of Diplock LJ in *Mills v Cooper* [1967] 2 All ER at 104, 105 and *HM Advocate v Cairns* 1969 SLT 167 applied; *Sambasivam v Public Prosecutor, Federation of Malaya* [1950] AC 485 and *Connelly v Director of Public Prosecutions* [1964] 2 All ER 401 explained; *R v Hogan* [1974] 2 All ER 142 overruled; *per* Lord Salmon and Lord Edmund-Davies (Viscount Dilhorne dissenting). A judge of a superior court has an inherent power to decline to allow a prosecution to proceed if he is satisfied that it is oppressive and vexatious and an abuse of the process of the court; dictum of Lord Parker CJ in *Mills v Cooper* [1967] 2 All ER at 104 applied; dicta of Lord Goddard CJ in *R v Middlesex Justices, ex parte Director of Public Prosecutions* [1952] 2 All ER at 313 and in *R v London Quarter Sessions (Chairman), ex parte Downes* [1953] 2 All ER at 752 explained; Decision of the Court of Appeal, Criminal Division [1975] 2 All ER 1023 reversed; For issue estoppel in criminal proceedings, see 11 Halsbury's Laws (4th Edn) para 245 and 16 ibid para 1531.

[180] Uglow S, *Evidence: Text and Materials* 730.

a)   it is only those issues that are in fact raised in the previous proceedings that are subject to an estoppel: the *Henderson*[181] principles relating to cause of action estoppel do not apply to issue estoppel which therefore does not extend to those issues which a party exercising due diligence could have raised.

b)   issue estoppel does not apply where significant fresh evidence is available or where the justice of the case requires re-litigation.[182] The test is that the new evidence must be such as "entirely changes the aspect of the case … and was not and could not by reasonable diligence have been ascertained before."[183]

(d)   Necessary conditions for invoking issue estoppel[184]

The rather relaxed framework within which issue estoppel can be invoked and exceptions which can be successfully raised means that the doctrine permits re-litigation in certain instances. This is likely to happen 'where there has become available to a party further material relevant to the correct determination of a point involved in the earlier proceedings, whether or not that point was specifically raised and decided, being material, which could not by reasonable diligence have been adduced in those proceedings [….]'[185] Having said that, this species of estoppel can only be invoked where the following five basic conditions discussed in brief detail here under, are present:[186]

(i)   There must be in existence a final judgment on the merits by a court of competent jurisdiction

The first condition to be satisfied to invoke issue estoppel is a two-part requirement of there being (a) a final judgment on the merits in existence; and (b) that the court that delivered the said final judgments on the merits was of competent jurisdiction. We will discuss these two requirements in turn.

(a)   The judgment must be final

As a necessary predicate for invoking issue estoppel the judgment impugned must be final i.e., determined on the merits following a full trial in terms of rules of court. As to the meaning of a final judgment, Lord Diplock has opined in *DSV Silo und Veraltungsgesellschaft mbH v Owners of the Sennar:*[187]

---

[181] [1843-60] ALL ER 378; (1843) 3 Hare 100 at 114.

[182] *Anold v National Westminster Bank plc* [1991] 3 All ER 41 wherein it was held that a subsequent change in the law can sufficient to bring a case within the exception to issue estoppel which is that 'in the special circumstance that there has become available to a party further material relevant to the correct determination of a point involved in the earlier proceedings, whether or not that point was specifically raised and decided, being material which could not by reasonable diligence have been adduced in those proceedings [….]'

[183] *Phosphate Sewage Co v Molleson* (1879) 4 App Cas 801 at 814 *per* Earl Cairns LC; approved in *Hunter v Chief Constable of West Midlands* [1981] 3 All ER 727 at 736c *per* Diplock LJ.

[184] See generally, Uglow S, *Evidence: Text and Materials* 730-41.

[185] *Anold v National Westminster Bank plc* [1991] 3 All ER 41.

[186] See generally, Uglow S, *Evidence: Text and Materials* 730-41 and the authorities quoted thereunder.

[187] [1985] 2 All ER 104 at 106g-h.

> What it means in the context of judgment delivered by courts of justice is that the court has held that it has jurisdiction to adjudicate on an issue raised in the cause of action to which the particular set of facts give rise, and that its judgment on that cause of action is one that cannot be varied, reopened or set aside by the court that delivered it or any other court of co-ordinate jurisdiction although it may be subject to appeal to a court of higher jurisdiction.

It follows from the foregoing that if a suit has been discontinued, dismissed, struck off the cause list or otherwise terminated short of a hearing on the evidence,[188] the said matter cannot be said to have been heard on the merits. The question that would remain for discussion is what place a judgment in default occupies in the grand scheme of things within the context of issue estoppel. It has been held that '[...] when an issue has been decided by a competent court against a party in an earlier proceeding, it should only be regarded as final if he has had a full and fair opportunity of defending himself therein and circumstances are such that it would not be fair or just to allow him to re-open it in subsequent proceedings.'[189] Thus, in *New Brunswick Rail Co v British and French Trust Corporation Ltd*[190] '[a] judgment by default is only an estoppel in respect of the matter directly decided, and the court should, as far as possible, only make declarations as to the construction of documents when the matter has been argued by counsel on each side.'

In this jurisdiction, courts have, for reasons that follow, consistently shown a disinclination to sustain default judgments or otherwise permit invocation of issue estoppel in this regard. The first is that Order 20 r 15, HCR permits a defendant to apply for the setting aside of a default judgment in the following terms: '[a]ny judgment by default, whether under this Order or under any other of these Rules, may be set aside by the court or a Judge, upon such terms as to costs or otherwise as such court or Judge may think fit.' The second reason is to avoid a scenario where issue estoppel is raised in a matter that was never heard on the merits. In essence, a denial of a person's right to have their day in court; and/or a denial of their right to trial. This would run counter to Article 118(2)(e) of the Constitution which provides that 'justice shall be administered without undue regard to procedural technicalities.' It has been held in the leading case of *Mwambazi v Morrester Farms Limited*[191] as follows:

> [...] it is the practice in dealing with *bona fide* interlocutory applications for courts to allow triable issues to come to trial despite the default of the parties. The situation is different from that which obtains when there has been a trial and there is default in connection with a proposed appeal because then it cannot be said that the parties have been denied the right to a trial. Where a party is in default, he may be

---

[188] *Mwambazi v Morester Farms Limited* (1977) ZR 108; *Water Wells Limited v Jackson* [1984] ZR 98; *Ladup Ltd v Siu* (The Times, Thursday November, 24, 1983).

[189] *Hunter v Chief Constable of West Midlands* [1980] 2 All ER 227 at 238 J, *per* Lord Denning.

[190] [1938] 4 All ER 747.

[191] [1977] ZR 108; *Fanny Muliango and Samson Muliango v Namdou Magasa and Muruja Transport & Farming Company Limited* (1988 - 1989) ZR 209 (SC).

ordered to pay costs, but it is not in the interests of justice to deny him the right to have his case heard.

However, Gardner JS, as he then was, held that the application to set aside a judgment in default will not be given as a matter of course. He stressed that 'for the court to set aside a default judgment, 'there must be no unreasonable delay, no male fides and no improper conduct of the action on the part of the applicant.' In the event that the foregoing conditions are not met, the judgment will not be set aside and if not, it will be enforceable against the party whom it is entered against.

The case of *Water Wells Limited v Jackson*[192] was an appeal against a refusal by the High Court to set aside a judgment in default of defence. Ngulube DCJ, as he then was, held as follows:

> Indeed, the Court of Appeal in England has held to similar effect in *Ladup v Siu*,[193] when they said that, although it is usual on an application to set aside a default judgment, not only to show a defence on the merits but also to give an explanation of the default, it is the defence on the merits which is the more important point to consider. We agree with them that, it is wrong to regard the explanation for the default, instead of the arguable defence as the primary consideration. If the plaintiff would not be prejudiced by allowing the defendant to defend the claim, then the action should be allowed to go on trial.

Turning briefly to the matter of decisions at *voire dire* which we have encountered already in this text, as they relate to admissibility, the position of the law is that a party will be estopped from raising, for example, a confession, if same was decided against the person who seeks to raise it in subsequent proceedings.[194]

(f)   Court of competent jurisdiction

By definition, court of competent jurisdiction means a court in the constitutional system of courts, that is, a superior court which otherwise has jurisdiction of the subject matter and the parties, or a lower court which otherwise has such jurisdiction provided for it in an Act of Parliament creating it pursuant to Article 120(1)(d). In *Godfrey Miyanda v The High Court*,[195] the applicant was a plaintiff litigant in a civil suit which was pending in the High Court in which, it was alleged, the reserved judgment had been pending for eight or more months. Being dissatisfied with the alleged delay or failure in the disposal of his action by the High Court, the applicant applied to the Supreme Court for leave to apply for an order of mandamus to compel the learned High Court judge seised of the suit to determine the action and deliver a judgment. The application was made, *ex parte*, to a single judge for such leave, but as a

---

[192] [1984] ZR 98; Approving *Mwambazi v Morester Farms Limited* [1977] ZR 108.

[193] (The Times, Thursday November, 24, 1983).

[194] See *Hunter v Chief Constable of West Midlands* [1980] 2 All ER 227 at 238J, *per* Lord Denning.

[195] [1984] ZR 62 at 64.

preliminary issue, Ngulube DCJ, as he then was, raised with the applicant the question whether the Supreme Court of Zambia had any original jurisdiction to entertain an application for an order of mandamus directed against the High Court.

The applicant had argued that the Supreme Court had jurisdiction to entertain the matter as framed. The applicant's submission could be summarised as follows:

(a) The Supreme Court had an inherent jurisdiction to control or to supervise the High Court.

(b) That it was logical and proper that the Supreme Court should exercise a supervisory jurisdiction over the High Court when no other court would be appropriate to entertain a complaint against the High Court itself.

(c) That jurisdiction should be assumed on the footing that, should the High Court fail to perform its duties, parties ought to have recourse to a superior court which must be able to control the court below.

Ngulube DCJ opined as follows:

> In the view that I have taken, the submission and the arguments to which I have referred in fact resolve themselves into a single assertion that this court has, or can assume, an original jurisdiction in mandamus and that the High Court would be amenable to such jurisdiction. The term "jurisdiction" should first be understood. In one sense, it is the authority which a court has to decide matters that are litigated before it; in another sense, it is the authority which a court has to take cognisance of matters presented in a formal way for its decision.

Confronted with an analogous query of jurisdiction, Tredgold CJ, as he then was, warned in *Codron v Macintyre and Shaw*[196] '[i]t is important to bear in mind the distinction between the right to relief and the procedure by which such relief is obtained. The former is a matter of substantive law, the later of adjective or procedural law.'

In discussing the issue of competent jurisdiction hereunder, it is perhaps important to advert to constitutional provisions having a general bearing on the issue. 'The limits of authority of each of the courts in Zambia are stated in the appropriate legislation. Such limits may relate to the kind and nature of the actions and matters of which the particular court has cognisance or to the area over which the jurisdiction extends, or both.'[197] The starting point therefore, are constitutional provisions as they relate to the matter of jurisdiction of each court and therefore their competence to hear a matter. As every legal practitioner

[196] [1960] R & N 418.
[197] *Godfrey Miyanda v The High Court* [1984] ZR 62 at 64.

ought to know: 'forum goes to jurisdiction.'[198] No amount of good evidence in the world will be entertained in the wrong forum, that is to say, a court in want of jurisdiction. This is exemplified in the words of Ngulube DCJ in *Godfrey Miyanda v The High Court:*[199]

> For the avoidance of doubt, I must say at the outset that this ruling does not decide that the applicants have no valid case in their complaints against the elections and/or that the elections were fairly and properly conducted. These are not issues for this forum but for the Supreme Court when it sits to hear any presidential election petition. The Supreme Court is the Court with jurisdiction in these matters.

The wrong mode of commencement will also rob a court of its jurisdiction and thus, its competence to entertain a matter brought before it let alone determine it on the merits.[200] It has been held in *Chikuta v Chipata Rural Council*[201] that '[w]here any matter is brought to the High Court by means of an originating summons when it should have been commenced by writ, the Court has no jurisdiction to make any declarations.' In *New Plast Industries v Commissioner of Lands and Another:*[202] '[w]e therefore hold that this matter having been brought to the High Court by way of Judicial Review, when it should have been commenced by the way of an appeal, the court had no jurisdiction to make the reliefs sought.' However, the foregoing must be seen within context. In *Zambia National Holdings Limited and the United National Independence Party v Attorney General,*[203] the Supreme Court endorsed Briggs, FJ's observation in *Codron v Macintyre and Shaw* that '[c]onfusion may arise from two different meanings of the word "jurisdiction." On an application for mandamus in England the King's Bench division may, because of a certain fact proved say "[t]here is no jurisdiction to grant mandamus in a case of this kind." That refers to an obstacle of substantive or procedural law which prevents the success of the application, but not any limits on the general jurisdiction of the court to hear and determine the application.'

(v)   Our system of courts

The starting point is what constitutes the judiciary. The courts are ranked as follows:

(a)   The Supreme Court and Constitutional Court rank equivalently.

(b)   The Court of Appeal

(c)   The High Court

---

[198] *Wynter Munacaambwa Kabimba (Suing in His Capacity as Secretary-General of The Patriotic Front) v Attorney-General Richard Kachingwe (Sued in His Capacity as National Secretary of The Movement for Multiparty Democracy) Electoral Commission of Zambia* 2011/HP/744; *Godfrey Miyand v The High Court* [1984] ZR 62.

[199] [1984] ZR 62 at 64.

[200] *Gilbert Muthiya & 30 Others v Universal Mining and Chemical [Ltd]* Appeal 175/2020, CAZ.

[201] [1974] ZR 241.

[202] [2001] ZR 51.

[203] [1993-1994] ZR 115 (SC).

(d)   Subordinate Courts;

(e)   small claims courts;

(f)   local courts; and

(g)   such lower courts, as may be prescribed by an Act of Parliament.

(vi)   Jurisdiction of the various courts

(h)   The Supreme Court

The Supreme Court which is established under Article 124 of the Constitution is, in terms of Article 125(1), the final court of appeal.[204] The Supreme Court has—(a) appellate jurisdiction to hear appeals from the Court of Appeal; and (b) jurisdiction conferred on it by other laws.[205] Perhaps the most interesting decision of recent times on this issue, and a divisive one both for the Supreme Court and the legal fraternity came in form of a tax dispute. In *Zambia Revenue Authority v Professional Insurance Corporation*,[206] the Court was faced with the significant issue of *jurisdiction ratione materiae*.[207] At 71 pages, main judgment and dissentient judgment included, this is a long read but one of crucial importance weakened only by the fact that it was delivered by a divided court. In view of the foregoing, our attempt here is to simply distill the salient points relevant to our discussion and not to author a treatise within a work of the law of evidence such as this one.[208]

A divided Supreme Court held by majority that it had, by virtue of Article 125(2)(b), jurisdiction 'conferred on it by other laws' jurisdiction to hear matters directly from the Tax Appeals Tribunal without such appeals being made to the Court of Appeal first, thereby bypassing the latter Court. The Court's decision was also predicated on its combined reading of Article 125(2)(b) and s 15(1) of Tax Appeals Tribunal Act.[209] The latter provides as follows: '[a] party to an appeal to the Tribunal may appeal to the Supreme Court from the decision of the Tribunal on a question of law or question of mixed law and fact but not on a question of fact alone.' Both the majority judgment by Malila JS with which Wood J concurred, and that by the dissentient, Mutuna JS

---

[204] Subject to Article 128.

[205] Article 125(2).

[206] Appeal No 34 of 2017; by dint of coincidence, Malila JS authored the majority decision; Mutuna JS dissented; approving *Richard Nsofu Mandona v Total Aviation and Export Limited and 3 Others* [Appeal No 82/2009].

[207] 'Otherwise known as subject-matter jurisdiction refers to the court's authority to decide a particular case. It is the jurisdiction over the nature of the case and the type of relief sought; the extent to which a court can rule on the conduct of persons or the status of things.' - definitions.uslegal.com/j/jurisdiction-ratione-materiae/ retrieved on 29 December 2020.

[208] A more extensive analysis is found in RB Gates, "Jurisdiction ratione materiae and 'leapfrog' appeals: The case of Zambia Revenue Authority v Professional Insurance Corporation Appeal No 34 of 2017 [....];" see also, Mbewe E, "An examination of the Zambian Supreme Court's majority ruling in the case of Zambia Revenue Authority v Professional Insurance Corporation Appeal No. 34/2017 (the "Zambia Revenue Authority v Professional Insurance Corporation (2020) case")": https://www.linkedin.com/pulse/examination-zambian-supreme-courts-majority-ruling-case-edwin-mbewe/?trackingId=cE%2F1NiaBRAu11b1RWlJGrw%3D%3D retrieved on 30 December 2020.

[209] No 1 of 2015.

came to their divergent opinions after taking into account, among others, the relevant provisions of the Constitution,[210] Court of Appeal Act[211] and the Tax Appeals Tribunal Act.[212]

In terms of Article 125(3), the Supreme Court is bound by its decisions, except in the interest of justice and development of jurisprudence.[213] For legal practitioners, it is important to be alive to provisions under s 25 of the Supreme Court Act[214] and rule 72 of the Supreme Court Rules (SCR). The former provides for receipt of further evidence by the Court in appropriate cases while the latter provides that '[a]ppeals to the Court shall be by way of re-hearing on the record and any further evidence received under [s 25] of the Act.' The Court of Appeal for Zambia (not to be confused with the current Court of Appeal of Zambia) which became the Supreme Court of Zambia highlighted the role of the Supreme Court in *Nkhata and Others v The Attorney General of Zambia*[215] as follows:

> A trial judge sitting alone without a jury can only be reversed on questions of fact if (1) the judge erred in accepting evidence, or (2) the judge erred in assessing and evaluating the evidence by taking into account some matter which he should have ignored or failing to take into account something which he should have considered, or (3) the judge did not take proper advantage of having seen and heard the witnesses, (4) external evidence demonstrates that the judge erred in assessing manner and demeanour of witnesses.

We may end this discussion by quoting from Ngulube DCJ's observation in *Godfrey Miyanda v The High Court*[216] as regards the Supreme Court's original jurisdiction in civil matters:

> The original civil jurisdiction of the Supreme Court is very limited indeed,[217] and would appear to cover such matters the granting of injunctions pending appeal, the making of orders to extend time, or for leave to appeal, or as to costs, or security for the costs of appeals. The Supreme Court would also have original jurisdiction, like the Court of Appeal in England, to make orders requiring the fulfilment of an undertaking given to it and an inherent jurisdiction to strike out an incompetent appeal. I would go so far as to assert that the Supreme Court has an inherent jurisdiction to prevent abuses of process and to protect its authority and dignity. What emerges, however, is that

---

[210] As amended by Act No 2 of 2016.

[211] No 7 of 2016.

[212] No 1 of 2015.

[213] *Hakainde Hichilema v Attorney-General* Appeal No 4/2019.

[214] Chapter 25 of the Laws of Zambia.

[215] [1966] ZR 124, 125 (CAZ).

[216] [1984] ZR 62 at 64.

[217] Halsbury's Laws of England, 65 4th edn, Vol 10 para 899.

this limited original jurisdiction arises either in connection with some matter pending in the courts below or some matter preliminary to, or during, incidental to, some proceedings before the court.

Based on the foregoing, Ngulube DCJ, as he then was, declined, 'in so far as the question of procedural law [was] concerned,' to assume jurisdiction to entertain an original application for mandamus because the Supreme Court had no jurisdiction to do so.

(i) The Constitutional Court

The Constitutional Court which is established under Article 127 of the Constitution, has, in terms of Article 128(1) but subject to subject to Article 28, original and final jurisdiction to hear—

(a) a matter relating to the interpretation of this Constitution;

(b) a matter relating to a violation or contravention of [the] Constitution;

(c) a matter relating to the President, Vice-President or an election of a President;

(d) appeals relating to election of Members of Parliament and councillors; and

(e) whether or not a matter falls within the jurisdiction of the Constitutional Court.

Further, in terms of Article 128(2), subject to Article 28 (2), where a question relating to the Constitution arises in a court, the person presiding in that court shall refer the question to the Constitutional Court. In terms of Article 128(3), subject to Article 28, a person who alleges that—(a) an Act of Parliament or statutory instrument; (b) an action, measure or decision taken under law; or (c) an act, omission, measure or decision by a person or an authority; contravenes this Constitution, may petition the Constitutional Court for redress. Finally, according to Article 128(4) a decision of the Constitutional Court is not appealable to the Supreme Court.[218]

The intent and effect of Article 128 as regards the apparent exclusive jurisdiction of the Constitutional Court in interpreting the Constitution came into sharp focus in *Henry M Kapoko v The People:*[219]

> [...] it is the responsibility of this Court to provide interpretation of the Constitution by virtue of Article 128(1)(a) of the Constitution as amended. This Court is also empowered to strike down any statutory provisions that contradict the Constitution under Article 128(1)(b) upon the application of any aggrieved person under Article 128(3)(a) [....] The Constitution as amended makes it clear in Article 128 as a whole that interpretation of any provisions of the Constitution other than the Bill of Rights is the preserve of this Court [....]

---

[218] See *Hakainde Hichilema v Attorney-General* Appeal No 4/2019.
[219] [2016/CC/0023].

Malila[220] has postulated that although the Constitutional Court has the final word on the interpretation of the Constitution, it cannot be gainsaid that this jurisdiction granted to the Constitutional Court under Article 128 and as construed by the said Court in *Kapoko*[221] entails a monopoly of interpreting Constitutional provisions at every turn. He contends that this is because the judicial process is much more than an application of common law norms and statutory provisions to the facts of a case before a court. He advances this argument by proposing that the interpretation of individual statutory provisions by judges irrespective, is at the same time a continual process of testing such provisions against the Constitution. Where a scenario arises, as it will from time to time, which requires a judge to test the common law or indeed statutory law against a constitutional provision(s), '[…] the judge in the ordinary court will have to come up with the initial answer as to whether the law in question is constitutional or not.' Malila further takes the view that 'in this sense it is not just the Constitutional Court, but also such other ordinary court that interprets, in that very limited sense, the Constitution.'[222]

There is another reason, according to Malila that the Constitutional Court may, despite, as he admits, having the last word on the interpretation and/ or application of the Constitution, not claim exclusivity regarding the Constitution's interpretation at every turn. As he sees it, ordinary courts such as the Supreme Court, the Court of Appeal, the High Court, the Subordinate Courts among others, have what he terms 'the inherent power of review.' In so saying, Malila is referring to an almost everyday occurrence where in judges will not apply a norm be it customary or common law or a statutory legal provision which is overtly and decidedly unconstitutional. He concludes: 'I think that a judge who is in doubt as to the unconstitutionality of a statutory provision or a principle of common law or customary law, has the power to proceed to decide the case without deferring the decision to the Constitutional Court.'[223]

That the view taken by Malila is correct is perhaps distillable from a recent case decided by the Supreme Court which touched on constitutional issues that at first glance appeared to fall into the *Kapoko*[224] test for matters within the purview of the Constitutional Court but which upon a careful analysis, appear, to have come within 'the inherent power of review' of the Supreme Court. In *Richard Nsofu Mandona v Total Aviation and Export Limited and 3 Others*,[225] following the dismissal of his appeal, the appellant filed a motion contending inter alia that the Supreme Court had no jurisdiction to dismiss his appeal in the manner it did (without hearing both parties) which was, it was argued, contrary to Article 18(9) of the Constitution which mandate any court before

---

[220] Mumba Malila, *The Contours of a Developing Jurisprudence of the Zambian Supreme Court* 372-385.

[221] [2016/CC/0023].

[222] Mumba Malila, *The Contours of a Developing Jurisprudence of the Zambian Supreme Court* 376-377.

[223] Mumba Malila, *The Contours of a Developing Jurisprudence of the Zambian Supreme Court* 377.

[224] [2016/CC/0023].

[225] [Appeal No 82/2009]; approved in *Zambia Revenue Authority v Professional Insurance Corporation* Appeal No 34/2017.

which proceedings are brought to give such a case 'a fair hearing within a reasonable time.' Essentially, this means that a court ought to generally allow parties to present their cases without rushing to dismiss them due to defaults or any technicalities. Further, it was contended by the appellant that the Supreme Court had failed, in dismissing his appeal, to take into account Article 118(2), Article 18(9) and Article 118(2)(e) of the Constitution. The Supreme Court held *inter alia*:

> To us, the argument made by the applicant regarding jurisdiction is crucial from at least two stand points. The broader, and perhaps more significant of these two questions is whether, in view of the creation by the Amended Constitution of the Constitutional Court, this court any longer has jurisdiction to deal with 'serious constitutional issue,' to use the words of the learned counsel for the applicant. The narrower issue is whether the Supreme Court could still determine an issue on the basis of procedural rules where a constitutional question is raised. We are fully alive to the provision of Article 128(2) of the Amended Constitution which states that: "[s]ubject to Article 28(2), where a question relating to this Constitution arises in a court, the person presiding in that court shall refer the question to the Constitutional Court."
>
> Article 28(1) on the other hand provides that: "Subject to clause (5), if any person alleges that any of the provisions of Articles 11 to 28 inclusive has been, is being or is likely to be contravened in relation to him, then, without prejudice to any other action with respect to the same matter which is lawfully available, that person may apply for redress to the High Court which shall-
>
> (a) hear and determine any such application;
>
> (b) determine any question arising in the case of any person which is referred to in pursuance of clause
>
> Granted that matters dealing with the bill of rights are constitutionally still very much within the jurisdictional ambit of the High Court to determine at first instance, with appeals on any such matters determined by the High Court lying to the Supreme Court under Article 28(l)(b), we are in no doubt that this court has jurisdiction to determine any issue raised touching on the bill of rights in the Constitution provided, of course, it comes to us by way of appeal from the High Court. This is so, notwithstanding the provisions of article 28(1) of the Amended Constitution. Where, however, a matter arises whose substance is primarily interpretation of a provision of the Constitution, this court would be obliged to refer such matter to the Constitutional Court in terms of Article 28(1) to which we have alluded. This does not in any case mean that every time the Constitution is mentioned in arguments made before this court, we shall close our records of appeal and rise until the Constitutional Court determines any such arguments. Making observations on obvious constitutional provisions as we determine disputes of a non-constitutional nature, is not, in our view, necessarily averse to the letter and spirit of the Constitution nor would

it encroach or usurp the jurisdiction of the Constitutional Court. This court, as any other superior court for that matter, is made up of judges of note, capable in their own way of understanding and interpreting the Constitution.

However, even if we do have the jurisdiction to interpret the constitution in regard to the bill of rights and generally to refer to the constitution when dealing with matters of a non-constitutional nature, we do not have original jurisdiction to do so.

An allegation that a provision of the bill of rights has been violated is redressable through a petition in the High Court. It is not in the province of this court to deal with issues arising from the bill of rights at first instance through motions such as the one before us.

More significantly perhaps, we see that the issues raised in the motion are ones that hinge purely on the rules of procedure. Their interpretation, therefore, is hardly one that should take us into the realm of constitutional interpretation. For good measure, we can do no better than repeat what we said in the case of *Access Bank (Z) Ltd v Group Five/ZCON Business Park Joint Venture*[226] that: "the Constitution never means to oust the obligations of litigants to comply with procedural imperatives as they seek justice from the courts."

(j)   The Court of Appeal

The Court of Appeal which is established under Article 130 of the Constitution, has, according to Article 131(1) of the Constitution, jurisdiction[227] to hear appeals from—(a) the High Court; (b) other courts, except for matters under the exclusive jurisdiction of the Constitutional Court;[228] and (c) quasi-judicial bodies, except a local government elections tribunal. An appeal from a decision of the Court of Appeal shall be made to the Supreme Court[229] with leave of the Court of Appeal.[230] The requirement for leave means the right to appeal is restricted. It is not and will not be granted, almost as a matter of right. Firstly, the application for leave must be made within 14 days, but even when this is complied with, the Court may grant leave to appeal where it considers that— (a) the appeal raises a point of law of public importance; (b) it is desirable and in the public interest that an appeal by the person convicted should be determined by the Supreme Court; (c) the appeal would have a reasonable prospect of success; or (d) there is some other compelling reason for the appeal to be heard.[231] In the recent *cause célèbre* that is *Savenda Management Services*

---

[226] SCZ/852/2014; see *Hakainde Hichilema v Attorney-General* Appeal No 4/2019.

[227] See s 4 of the Court of Appeal Act No 7 of 2016; *Zambia Revenue Authority v Professional Insurance Corporation* Appeal No 34 of 2017.

[228] Thus, according to s 4(2) of the Court of Appeal Act No 7 of 2016, 'where a question relating to the Constitution arises before the Court, the Court shall refer that question to the Constitutional Court.'

[229] s 13(1) of the Court of Appeal Act No 7 of 2016, is similarly couched. It provides that '[a]n appeal from a judgment of the Court shall lie to the Supreme Court with leave of the Court [of the Court of Appeal].'

[230] By Article 131(2); see Article 132 as to constitution of the Court of Appeal.

[231] Here again, the principle that leave to appeal shall not operate as a stay of execution of a judgment is codified in Article 131(4); See *Ndola City Council v Charles Mwansa* (SCZ Judgment No 78 of 1994).

v Stanbic Bank Zambia Ltd,[232] the Zambian Supreme Court had occasion to give guidance on the intent and effect of s 131(2), specifically on what kind of matters were befitting of an appeal to the Supreme Court and in what manner those appeals should come about. Reading the judgment of the Court, Mutuna, JS observed thus:

> We note that this is the first appeal we have dealt with emanating from a decision of the Court of Appeal. It comes before us by virtue of leave to appeal granted by the at the end of its judgment couched in the following terms, "leave to appeal granted." In so doing the Court of Appeal did not explain the reason why it felt that the dispute between the parties should be escalated to the apex court and neither was it moved by either of the parties prior to making the order. This omission by the Court of Appeal is important to us because, whilst there is a constitutional right of appeal to our Court by virtue of [s] 131(2) of the Constitution (as amended) such appeal is only with leave of the Court of Appeal on limited grounds which are set out in [s] 13(3) of the Court of Appeal, unlike the High Court, is not obliged to pronounce itself at the end of a judgment as to whether leave to appeal has been granted or not and give reasons for such grant or refusal.
>
> The Court of Appeal must wait for a party to move it after it has delivered its judgment, seeking leave to appeal, and if it is satisfied that one of the grounds for granting leave has been satisfied, it must grant the leave. If not, it must refuse the leave.
>
> The permissible grounds for the grant of leave to appeal in civil matters are set out in sections 13(3)(a), (c) and (d). These are where: the appeal raises a point of law of public importance; the appeal would have reasonable prospect of success; or, there is some compelling reason for the appeal to be heard.
>
> The rationale for the foregoing is an acknowledgement of the fact that the resources of the courts are overstretched and if it were otherwise, the doors to justice would be open to busy bodies whose only aim is to delay the inevitable execution of a judgment. We are of the firm view that this Court should only be open to a litigant who has moved the Court of Appeal and met the threshold set out in [s] 13(3).

(k) The High Court

The High Court is established under Article 133(1) is said, in terms of Article 134, to have, subject to Article 128—(a) unlimited and original jurisdiction in civil and criminal matters; (b) appellate and supervisory jurisdiction, as prescribed; and (c) jurisdiction to review decisions, as prescribed. We have to add that according to Article 135, the High Court shall be constituted by one judge or such other number of judges as the Chief Justice may determine. In *Irwin v The People*[233] the Supreme Court held as follows: '[t]he question of the jurisdiction of the High Court is of course irrelevant. Although Article [134]

---

[232] SCZ judgment No 10 of 2018 J152 – J155, para 213 – 217.
[233] [1993-1994] ZR 7 at 16.

of the Constitution gives the High Court unlimited jurisdiction that court is bound by all the laws which govern the exercise of such jurisdiction.'

In *Zambia National Holdings Limited and the United National Independence Party v Attorney General*,[234] the Supreme was, among other things, confronted with the question the meaning and effect of the words 'unlimited and original jurisdiction in civil and criminal matters' in Article 134(a) which then appeared in what was then Article 94(1) of the Constitution of 1991. Ngulube CJ as he then was made the following observations:

> In order to place the word "unlimited" in Article [134(a)] in its proper perspective, the jurisdiction of the High Court should be contrasted with then of lesser tribunals and courts whose jurisdiction in a cumulative sense is limited in a variety of ways. For example, the Industrial Relations Court is limited to cases under a single enactment over which the High Court has been denied any original jurisdiction. The Local Courts and Subordinate Courts are limited as to geographical area of operation, types and sizes of aware and penalties, nature of causes they can entertain, and so on. The jurisdiction of the High court on the other hand is not so limited; it is unlimited but not limitless since the court must exercise its jurisdiction in accordance with the law. Indeed, Article 94(1) must be read as a whole including phrases like "under any law and such jurisdiction and powers as may be conferred on it by this constitution or any other law." It is inadmissible to construe the word "unlimited" in vacuum and then to proceed to find that a law allegedly limiting the powers of the court is unconstitutional. The expression "unlimited jurisdiction" should not be confused with the powers of the High Court under the various laws. As a general rule, no cause is beyond the competence and authority of the High Court; no restriction applies as to type of cause and other matters as would apply to lesser courts. However, the High Court is not exempt from adjudicating in accordance with the law including complying with procedural requirements as well as substantive limitations such as those one finds in mandatory sentences or other specification of available penalties or, in civil matters, the types of choice of relief or remedy available to litigants under the various laws or causes of action.

(l)   Subordinate Courts

(i)   Criminal matters

As regards jurisdiction in criminal matters, s 19 of the Subordinate Courts Act[235] provides that '[i]n the exercise of their criminal jurisdiction, Subordinate Courts shall have all the powers and jurisdiction conferred on them by the Criminal Procedure Code,[236] this Act or any other law for the time being in force.'

---

[234] [1993-1994] ZR 115 (SC).
[235] Chapter 28 of the Laws of Zambia.
[236] Chapter 88 of the Laws of Zambia.

(ii)   Civil matters

Civil jurisdiction of the Subordinate Courts is to be found in ss 20 – 24 reproduced here below for ease of reference:

(iii)   Civil jurisdiction of Subordinate Courts of the first class

The jurisdiction of the Subordinate Courts of the first class are set out in terms of s 20(1),

> In civil causes and matters a Subordinate Court of the first class shall, subject to this Act and in addition to any jurisdiction which it may have under any other written law, within the territorial limits of its jurisdiction, have jurisdiction-
>
> (a)   in all personal suits, whether arising from contract, or from tort or from both, where the value of the property, debt or damage claimed, whether as balance of accounts or otherwise is-
>
>> (i)   where the court is presided over by a principal resident magistrate, not more than thirty million kwacha;
>>
>> (ii)   where the court is presided over by a senior resident magistrate, not more than twenty-five million kwacha;
>>
>> (iii) where the court is presided over by a resident magistrate, not more than twenty million kwacha; and
>>
>> (iv)   where the court is presided over by a magistrate of the first class, not more than ten million kwacha;
>
> (b)   to enforce by attachment any order made by the court;
>
> (c)   to hear and determine any action for the recovery of land where the value of the land in question or the rent payable per annum is, in case of a Subordinate Court presided over by-
>
>> (i)   a magistrate of the first class a value of up to five million kwacha or rent for one million, two hundred thousand kwacha;
>>
>> (ii)   a resident magistrate, a value of up to twenty million kwacha or rent for four million kwacha;
>>
>> (iii) a senior magistrate, a value of up to twenty-five million kwacha or rent for five million kwacha; or
>>
>> (iv)   a principal resident magistrate, a value of up to thirty million kwacha or rent for six million kwacha
>
> (d)   to make any order which may be made by a court of summary jurisdiction under the Summary Jurisdiction (Separation and Maintenance) Acts, 1895 to 1925 and section eleven of the Matrimonial Causes Act, 1937, of the United Kingdom:
> Provided that for the purposes of this section-
>
>> (i)   paragraph (c) of section five of the Summary Jurisdiction (Married Women) Act, 1895, of the

United Kingdom shall be read as if for the expression "such weekly sum not exceeding one thousand kwacha or such monthly sum not exceeding four thousand kwacha" there were substituted the expression "such weekly sum not exceeding twenty thousand kwacha or monthly sum not exceeding one hundred thousand kwacha"; and

(ii)   any reference to the term "married woman" or "wife" in the Summary Jurisdiction (Separation and Maintenance) Acts, 1895 to 1925, Matrimonial Causes Act, 1937, and Married Women Maintenance Act, 1920 shall be read as a reference to "spouse";

Provided further, that the allowance payable in respect of the spouse may be increased by fifty per centum of the amount by which the earnings or other income of the other spouse exceed two hundred thousand kwacha per month so that the total allowance shall not in any event exceed one hundred thousand kwacha per month:

Provided that a Subordinate Court of the first class shall not have jurisdiction in or cognizance of any suit or matter of the nature following, that is to say where:

(i)   the title to any right, duty or office is in question;

(ii)   the validity of any will or other testamentary writing or of any bequest or limitation under any will or settlement is in question;

(iii)   the legitimacy of any person is in question; or

(iv)   the validity or dissolution of any marriage is in question.

(2)   In addition to the jurisdiction conferred by subsection (1), a Subordinate Court presided over by a senior resident magistrate or a resident magistrate shall, within the local limits of its jurisdiction, have jurisdiction to enforce any judgment of the High Court for the payment of any money to a person where such judgment or order has been transferred by the High Court to such court as if it were a judgment of such court, and the provisions relating to the execution of judgments in Subordinate Courts (including the provisions relating to the staying of execution) shall have effect accordingly.

(iv)   Civil jurisdiction of Subordinate Courts of second class

The civil jurisdiction of Subordinate Courts of second class is set out in s 21[237] in the following terms:

---

[237] As amended by Act No 11 of 1990, No 41 of 1994 and No 25 of 1998.

In civil causes and matters, a Subordinate Court of the second class shall, within the territorial limits of its jurisdiction, have all the jurisdiction conferred by section twenty upon a Subordinate Court of the first class, subject to the limitations contained in that Section:

Provided that in personal suits whether arising from contract or from tort, or from both, the value of the property, debt or damage claimed whether as a balance of account or otherwise, shall not be more than one million kwacha.

(vi)   Civil jurisdiction of Subordinate Courts of third class

The civil jurisdiction of Subordinate Courts of second class is set out in s 22[238] in the following terms:

In civil causes and matters, a Subordinate Court of the third class shall, subject to the provisions hereinafter contained, and in addition to any jurisdiction which it may have under any other written law, within the territorial limits of its jurisdiction, have jurisdiction-

(a)   in all personal suits, whether arising from contract or from tort or from both, where the value of property or the debt or damage claimed, whether as balance of account or otherwise, is not more than four million kwacha.

(b)   to appoint guardians of infants and to make orders for the custody of infants;

(c)   to enforce by attachment any order made by the court:
      Provided that a Subordinate Court of the third class shall not have jurisdiction in or cognisance of any suit or matter of the nature following, that is to say:

      (i)   wherein the title to any right, duty or office is in question; or

      (ii)   wherein the validity of any will or other testamentary writing or of any bequest or limitation under any will or settlement is in question; or

      (iii) where the legitimacy of any person is in question; or

      (iv)   wherein the validity or dissolution of any marriage (other than a polygamous marriage contracted under African customary law) is in question.

(vii)   Where question of title to land is in issue

In terms of s 23 '[i]f, in any civil cause or matter before a Subordinate Court, the title to any land is disputed, or the question of the ownership thereto arises, the court may adjudicate thereon, if all parties interested consent; but, if they do not all consent, the presiding magistrate shall apply to the High Court to transfer such cause or matter to itself.' In *Phiri, Chisenga, Tembo v Mpata Hill*

---

[238] As amended by No 58 of 1966, 11 of 1990, No 41 of 1994 and No 25 of 1998.

Mining Company Limited; Thendelian Mining Company Limited; Michael Misepo[239] the meaning and effect of s 23 of the Subordinate Courts Act[240] was considered. This was a ruling that related to a preliminary issue in which the appellants contended that the respondents as a limited liability companies could not commence or carry-on proceedings in person.[241] Mulongoti J held as follows:

(i)   According to s 23 of the Subordinate Court Act, where a matter involves a dispute to the title or ownership to land, the Subordinate Court can only hear the matter when all the parties consent otherwise the magistrate is obliged to transfer the matter to the High Court;

(ii)   There was no evidence on record, that the consent of the parties was obtained before the magistrate proceeded to hear the matter.

(iii) The proceedings were therefore a nullity

(viii) Extension of jurisdiction

According to s 24,[242] '[t]he Chief Justice may, by order under his hand and the seal of the High Court, authorise an increased jurisdiction in civil causes and matters to be exercised by the magistrate named in the order, within the [d]istrict prescribed in the order, and to the extent specified in the order. Such order may, at any time, be revoked by the Chief Justice by an instrument under his hand and the seal of the High Court.

(m)   Small Claims Courts

The Small Claims Court is established under Article 120(1)(b) of the Constitution and the Small Claims Act[243] under s 3 which provides as follows: '[t]here is hereby established small claims courts which shall be situated in such areas as the Chief Justice may consider necessary, having regard to the needs of a particular area.' The jurisdiction of the Court is set out in s 5 as follows:

(1)   The jurisdiction of a Small Claims Court shall be limited to liquidated claims that do not exceed such sum as the Chief Justice may, by statutory instrument, specify

(2)   Notwithstanding the generality of Subsection (1), a small claims court shall have jurisdiction in respect of the following causes of action:

　　(a)   proceedings for the delivery of movable or immovable property whose value does not exceed the amount specified;

---

[239] [2012] Vol 3 ZR 562; *Yamfwa Enterprises Limited v Mechanised Mining Solutions Limited* 2011/HK/330 (unreported).

[240] Chapter 28 of the Laws of Zambia.

[241] See Order 5/6/2, RSC; *Workers Development Corporation Limited v Mkandawire* [1999] ZR 12.

[242] As amended by Act No 16 of 1937, GN No 444 of 1964 and No 28 of 1965.

[243] Chapter 47 of the Laws of Zambia.

(b)   proceedings for debts that are due and payable;

(c)   proceedings for rentals that are due and payable in respect of any premises;

(d)   proceedings for possess against the occupier of any premises where the right of occupation per month does not exceed the sum that the Chief Justice may, by statutory instrument, specify;

(e)   proceedings relating to or arising out of a cheque or an acknowledgement of debt signed by a debtor; and

(f)   Counterclaims in respect of any proceedings mentioned in paragraphs (a), (b), (c), (d) or (e).

(3)   A claim for interest or costs shall not be taken into account in determining whether a claim falls within the jurisdiction of a small claims court.

(4)   A small claims court shall not have jurisdiction in respect of-

(a)   a claim made under customary law;

(b)   an action which is beyond the jurisdiction of the court; notwithstanding any agreement of the parties thereto;

(c)   claims for divorce, custody or maintenance other than arrears in maintenance;

(d)   cases involving the validity of a will;

(e)   a matter in which an injunction is sought;

(f)   matter in which damages are sought for-

(i)   defamation;

(ii)   malicious prosecution or wrongful imprisonment or arrest; or

(iii) adultery or seduction;

(g)   an action against a consular officer;[244] or

(h)   An action against a foreign State.

5A.   Any provision in an agreement purporting to exclude the jurisdiction of a small claims court shall be of no effect.

(n)   Local Courts

Local Courts are the lowest form of courts in our judicial pecking order. They are established by the Constitution under Article 120(1)(c) and under s 4(1) under the Local Courts Act.[245] The jurisdiction of the Local Courts appears intertwined with their grading as set out in s 5(1) and a denial of jurisdiction as set out in the proviso to s 5(1) as follows:

Local courts shall be of such different grades as may be prescribed, and local courts of each grade shall exercise jurisdiction only within the limits prescribed for such grade:[246]

[244] In terms of s 5(5), [...] "consular officer" means any person appointed as consul general, consul, vice consul or consular agent by a foreign State and holding a valid exequatur or other authorization to act in Zambia in that capacity.

[245] Chapter 29 of the Laws of Zambia.

[246] In terms of s 5(2), the court warrant of any local court shall specify the grade to which such court belongs (as amended by Acts No 8 of 1991 and No 13 of 1994).

Provided that no local court shall be given jurisdiction-
- (i) to determine civil claims, other than matrimonial or inheritance claims, of a value greater than one hundred and twenty fee units; or
- (ii) to impose fines exceeding forty penalty units; or
- (iii) to order probation or imprisonment for a period exceeding two years; or
- (iv) to order corporal punishment in excess of twelve strokes of the cane.

Part III of the Local Courts Act provides for, among other things, jurisdiction. The extent of local Courts jurisdiction is set out in ss 8 – 11 of the Local Courts Act[247] briefly discussed below:

(i) Civil jurisdiction of Local Courts[248]

According to s 8, subject to the provisions of the Local Courts Act,[249] a local court shall have and may exercise, within the territorial limits set out in its court warrant, such jurisdiction as may be prescribed for the grade of court to which it belongs, over the hearing, trial and determination of any civil cause or matter in which the defendant is ordinarily resident within the area of jurisdiction of such court or in which the cause of action has arisen within such area: Provided that civil proceedings relating to real property shall be taken in the local court within the area of jurisdiction in which the property is situate.[250]

(ii) Criminal jurisdiction of local courts

According to s 9, subject to the provisions of the Local Courts Act,[251] a local court shall have and may exercise jurisdiction, to such extent as may be prescribed for the grade of court to which it belongs, over the hearing, trial and determination of any criminal charge or matter in which the accused is charged with having wholly or in part within the area of jurisdiction of such court, committed, or been accessory to the commission of an offence.

(iii) Preservation of jurisdiction

According to s 10, subject to the provisions of the Local Courts Act,[252] no local court shall be precluded from trying an offence under the Local Government Act by reason of the fact that such offence was a breach of a by-law or rule issued or made-

---

[247] Chapter 29 of the Laws of Zambia.
[248] Chapter 29 of the Laws of Zambia.
[249] Chapter 29 of the Laws of Zambia.
[250] As amended by No. 21 of 1976.
[251] Chapter 29 of the Laws of Zambia.
[252] Chapter 29 of the Laws of Zambia.

(a)   by a council, members of which are also members of such local court; or

(b)   by a member of such local court as a member of a council.

(iv)   Cases excluded from jurisdiction

According to s 11,[253] subject to any express provision of any other written law conferring jurisdiction, no Local Court shall have jurisdiction to try any case in which a person is charged with an offence in consequence of which death is alleged to have occurred or which is punishable by imprisonment for life.[254] Nor do Local Courts' jurisdiction, as shown in *Banda v Banda and Another*,[255] extend to foreign written laws.

It may be asked whether the procedure under s 221 of the Criminal Procedure Code[256] which provides that '[p]ayment by accused persons of fines which may be imposed for minor offences without appearing in court,' can be equated to a decision by a court of competent jurisdiction. It cannot. This is because if the offence for which the accused has been warned and cautioned falls under s 221(1)(b), sign and deliver to the prescribed officer an "Admission of Guilt Form"[257] admitting that he is guilty of the offence charged. As long as he complies with the conditions under s 221(1)(c)(i)(ii), that is, by paying the requisite fine 'which may be imposed by the court or such lesser sum as may be fixed by such officer; or furnishes to the prescribed officer such security, by way of deposit of property, as may be approved by such officer for the payment within one month of any fine which may be imposed by the court, such person shall not be required to appear in court to answer the charge made against him unless the court, for reasons to be recorded in writing, shall otherwise order.'

The foregoing is buttressed by the fact that a trial[258] which raises the issue of estoppel bar will ordinarily happen if in terms of s 221(3), a person who has signed and delivered an Admission of Guilt Form may, at any time before the fixed day, transmits to the clerk of the court - (a) an intimation in writing purporting to be given by him or on his behalf that he wishes to withdraw the Admission of Guilt Form aforesaid; or (b) in writing, any submission which he wishes to be brought to the attention of the court with a view to mitigation of sentence. Only then can there be said to have been trial and a decision of the court against which issue estoppel would arise.

In *Abraham v Metropolitan Commissioner*,[259] the plaintiff who had been arrested for the breach of the peace offence accepted a warn and caution statement from the police which required her to admit to committing the offence (in terms similar to those provided for under s 221 of our Criminal Procedure Code[260]).

---

[253] Chapter 29 of the Laws of Zambia.

[254] See Acts No 22 & 23 of 2022.

[255] [1968] ZR 123.

[256] Chapter 88 of the Laws of Zambia.

[257] Form 1(Section 221(1)(B)): Section 221 - Forms Prescribed for Admission of Guilt Procedure - Notice to Defendant and Statement of Facts, Criminal Procedure Code Chapter 88 of the Laws of Zambia.

[258] See s 221(5)(6).

[259] [2001] 1 WLR 1257.

[260] Chapter 88 of the Laws of Zambia.

She later sued claiming damages for unlawful arrest. On the defence's claim that the plaintiff was estopped from so claiming, Mantell LJ observed that even though the characteristics inherent in a formal caution are shared with those in a criminal conviction, the two cannot be said to be the same. A fundamental distinction lies in the fact that a formal admission procedure under s 221 of our Criminal Procedure Code[261] is not a decision of a court of law. He added inter alia that public policy, such as those attaching to a judgment for the court does not arise in an admission of guilt to a police officer. Mantell LJ added:

> [...] an attack on the admission to a police officer does not involve an attack on a court of co-ordinate jurisdiction; secondly, that the plea of guilty entered in a criminal court is open to public view and scrutiny and is subject to the supervision of a magistrate or a judge; thirdly, I would say that a conviction based upon a plea of guilty is nonetheless reviewable upon appeal if entered on a false basis or incorrect advice, whereas the only challenge to a formal caution lies by way of judicial review [....]

(v)   There must be mutuality of parties

Mutuality of parties is indispensable to issue estoppel being invoked. Put another way, the parties to the initial proceedings should be the same as the parties to subsequent proceedings for there to be sufficient predication to invoke issue estoppel. As Denning LJ has opined in *Fidelitas Shipping v V/O Exportchles*,[262] 'if one party brings an action against another for a particular cause and judgment is given on it, there is a strict rule of law that he cannot bring another action against the same party for the same cause.' In *Musakanya Valentine Shula and Edward Jack Shamwana v A-G*,[263] a preliminary issue was on behalf of the state in both petitions to the effect that these petitions were barred on the doctrine of *res judicata* (issue estoppel). The undisputed facts on this preliminary issue were that with regards to petitioner Edward Jack Shamwana same matter was brought before the High Court by way of notice of motion supported by an affidavit under this court's case number 1980/HP/1656. This was heard by my brother Chaila J, on 5 January, 1981 and on 14 January, 1981, he delivered his judgment dismissing the petitioner's application. Among other prayers prayed for in that motion was a prayer in the following words:

> be released from Lusaka Central Prison where he is being held in detention either unconditionally or upon reasonable conditions, including in particular such conditions as are reasonably necessary to ensure that the said Edward Jack Shamwana appears at later date for trial or proceedings preliminary to trial as the court or judge shall deem fit.

---

[261] Chapter 88 of the Laws of Zambia.

[262] [1955] 2 All ER 4, 8; quoted with approval by Chirwa J, as he then was, in *Musakanya Valentine Shula And Edward Jack Shamwana v Attorney General* [1981] ZR 221 (HC).

[263] [1981] ZR 221 (HC).

In his latest petition, the petitioner's prayer was in the same words:

> humble petitioner be released frown detention [...] either unconditionally or upon reasonable conditions, including in particular such conditions as are reasonably necessary to ensure that your lordship's humble petitioner will appear at a later date for trial or for proceedings preliminary to trial if any.

With regards to petitioner Valentine Shula Musakanya, the undisputed facts were that he brought an application for a writ of habeas corpus and the matter was heard by Chaila J, again, on 6 January, 1981, and at the hearing counsel for petitioner Mr Mwanakatwe obtained leave to argue an additional issue that if the court held the petitioner's detention lawful, the court should release him under Article 15(3)(b) of the Constitution. Chaila J, delivered his judgment on 20 January, 1981 and the petitioner's application was dismissed. The latest prayer in the petitioner's petition was also on a relief based on Article 15 (3) (b) of the Constitution.

Quoting *Fidelitas Shipping*[264] with approval, mutuality of parties was held to be a bar to the petitioners raising the same issues they had raised before the High Court albeit before another judge. Said Chirwa J, '[r]es judicata is a strict rule of law and the parties are bound by any decision made by' a court of competent jurisdiction.' While the proper course to take in *Musakanya & Shamwana*[265] ought to have been an appeal against the decisions of Chaila J, one may have sympathy for counsel's arguments predicated on the assertion that the procedure being used was different from that employed in the earlier unsuccessful proceedings. Ultimately though, the facts, and more importantly, the parties were the same, and for this reason, they were estopped from seeking their freedom through subsequent proceedings whatever the mode of commencement. What was untenable was the argument that the Court hearing this matter was different from the earlier one. In so far as the presiding judge was concerned, this was true, but in terms of the law it was quite misleading. Section 4 of the High Court Act[266] provides that '[s]ubject to any express statutory provisions to the contrary, all the judges shall have and may exercise, in all respects, equal power, authority and jurisdiction, and, subject as aforesaid, any judge may exercise all or any part of the jurisdiction by this Act or otherwise vested in the court, and, for such purposes, shall be and form a court.'

As Chirwa J, held therefore, his was not 'a special court.' The powers which he could exercise over this matter had, in terms of s 4 of the High Court Act,[267] been already exercised by Chaila J. The approach by the petitioners amounted to an abuse of process or in a sense, a collateral attack on original decisions of the High Court. In this, he cannot be faulted. Lord Upjohn has observed as follows in *Carl-Zeiss-Stiftung v Rayner and Keeler Ltd (No 2)*:[268]

---

[264] [1955] 2 All ER 4.

[265] [1981] ZR 221 (HC).

[266] Chapter 27 of the Laws of Zambia.

[267] Chapter 27 of the Laws of Zambia.

[268] [1966] 2 All ER 536 at 570, *per* Lord Upjohn.

It is clear that a party relying on such a plea must at least prove that the earlier proceedings were determinative of the issues arising in the second proceedings; that the same parties or their privies are common to both proceedings and that the earlier proceedings were within the jurisdiction of the court and were final and conclusive of the relevant issues.

Thus, as already noted, if there was any dissatisfaction with that decision, the proper remedy lay in an appeal to a higher court.

It appears though that courts may need to employ a more pragmatic approach to the issue as suggested by Goff LJ in his dissent in *Hunter v Chief Constable of West Midlands*[269] wherein the plaintiffs were estopped from contending that they had been assaulted by the police as the matter had apparently been determined by the original criminal court. The preceding is so because a strict unbending adherence as suggested by Chirwa J in *Musakanya and Shamwana*[270] may, in some cases, lead to absurd results.[271] *Townsend v Bishop*[272] is a demonstration of a rather narrow approach to the question of identities of parties concerned in so far as issue estoppel is concerned. The Court accepted that a son who had sued for damages relating to his injuries suffered by him from an accident caused by the defendant; but which ultimately was said to have been a case of contributory negligence in a suit brought by his father against the same defendant in an initial suit, was not estopped from denying the contributory negligence having not been a party to the initial action.

(vi)   The parties to the initial proceedings must be acting in the same capacity

That the parties to the initial proceedings must be acting in the same capacity as they did in the initial proceedings for issue estoppel to hold is demonstrated in several authorities[273] we have already considered in this text. *Musakanya and Shamwana*[274] presents a scenario where rather creative arguments were made on the matter of capacity of parties:

> Mr Shamwana, on his own behalf, in addition to endorsing what had been submitted by Mr Mwanakatwe on behalf of petitioner Musakanya

---

[269] [1980] 2 All ER 227; the case is reported as *McIlkenny v Chief Constable of West Midlands Police Force*. The House of Lords judgment is at [1981] 3 All ER 727, approving *Carl-Zeiss-Stiftung v Rayner and Keeler Ltd (No 2)* [1966] 2 All ER 536 at 570, *per* Lord Upjohn.

[270] [1981] ZR 221 (HC).

[271] *Petrie v Nuttall* (1856) 11 Ex 569.

[272] [1939] 1 All ER 805.

[273] *Development Bank of Zambia and Another v Sunvest Limited and Another* [1995-1997] ZR 187; *Musakanya and Others v The Attorney General* [1981] ZR 221 at 227; *Zambezi Portland Cement Limited and Another v Stanbic Bank Zambia Limited* [2012] 2 ZR 17; *Mukumbuta Mukumbuta Sam Mukamamba Kweleka Mubita Mooto Mooto and Kandumba Munganga v Nkwilimba Choobana Lubinda Richard Mbikusita Munyinda Rosalyn Mukelabai and Mongu Meat Corporation Ltd* (SCZ Judgment No 8 of 2003); *Kelvin Hang'andu and Company (A Firm) v Webby Mulubisha* (SCZ Judgment No 39 of 2008); *The Registered Trustees of The Archdiocese of Lusaka v Office Machine Services Limited* (SCA Judgment No 18 of 2007); *Muimui v Chanda* (SCZ Judgment No 50 of 2000).

[274] [1981] ZR 221 (HC).

as applying to him, submitted further that although the parties are the same and issues are similar, the petitioners are not suing in the similar capacities. He said both are now petitioners whereas in the previous proceedings he was plaintiff and the Attorney-General was defendant. Equally Mr Musakanya was applicant and the Attorney-General was respondent. These capacities are different from the present ones. To complete the plea of *res judicata*, the parties should not only be the same but must sue in same capacity.

Categorically rejecting the foregoing, Chirwa J reasoned as follows:

> The argument advanced by Mr Shamwana that the parties in the present proceedings are not of similar capacities is fascinating to say the least. He has not shown that he is presenting the present petition under any other capacity other than that he is the victim of the infringement of his constitutional rights. To me "petitioner" "applicant" "plaintiff" are titles and in no way show capacity. It is a question of playing with semantics which do not help us much. To be a petitioner is just wearing another title in place of applicant. I refuse to accept that the parties hereto have different capacities, they are the same. This ground for objecting the plea fails.

A case of particular interest in demonstrating the hair-splitting exercise that the court might need to engage in on the matter of sameness of capacity is *Marginson v Blackburn Borough Council*.[275] The plaintiff sued the defendants for damages in respect of injuries received by his daughter and himself, and in respect of the death of his wife, arising out of a collision between a car driven by the plaintiff's wife and a motor omnibus driven by the defendants' servant. Prior to the commencement of this action, 3 persons whose premises had been damaged as a result of this accident had, in a county court, sued both the present plaintiff and the present defendants, each of whom then served upon the other a third-party notice claiming indemnity and contribution in respect of any sum which the plaintiffs in the county court action might recover. In addition, the present defendants had claimed damages against the present plaintiff in respect of damage to their omnibus. In this prior action, judgment was given against the present plaintiff and present defendants jointly and severally, and it was ordered that they should be liable for the sum and costs in equal shares. With regard to the claim relating to the omnibus, it was also found that both parties were to blame, the judge treating the claim as a separate action. The defendants contended that, by reason of the judgment in the county court, the plaintiff was estopped from proceeding in the present action, which was on the same facts as was the action in the county court. The defendants' contention was argued as a preliminary point. It was held[276] as follows: (i) the plaintiff was estopped from bringing a personal claim for damages, as that point had

---

[275] [1939] 1 All ER 273.
[276] Varying decision of Lewis J ([1938] 2 All ER 539).

been decided in the earlier litigation; (ii) the plaintiff was not estopped from bringing his other claims, as he was making them in a representative capacity, whereas the third-party claims against him in the earlier case were against him in his personal capacity only; and (iii) in deciding the plea of *res judicata*, the court is entitled to look at the judge's reasons for his decision, and is not restricted to the record.

(vii) The same issues in the initial action must be involved in the subsequent action

Invoking issue estoppel also means that the subsequent action must involve the same issues involved in the initial action. The approach is not 'whether the issues are formally legally identical but whether they are substantially the same with regard to the issues of fact, the evidence to support them and the legal arguments.'[277]

In *Bell v Holmes*[278] On 26 March 1955, a collision occurred between two motor vehicles driven by B and H respectively, and on 18 August 1955, B commenced the present action in which he claimed damages against H for personal injuries suffered as a result of the collision. H counterclaimed for his own injuries. On 7 October 1955, a passenger in H's vehicle at the time of the collision instituted proceedings against both B and H in the county court in respect of injuries received by her in the collision. This action was heard and determined on 17 February 1956, when the passenger was awarded damages against both B and H. No formal notice claiming contribution was served by either of the defendants in that action on the other, but the county court judge was requested to deal with the matter of apportionment between B and H and adjudged that B should contribute five-sixths of the damages and H one-sixth thereof. Both B and H paid the damages awarded against them. In the present action the allegations of negligence between B and H were substantially the same as in the county court action, and H, the defendant, claimed that, by reason of the judgment in the county court proceedings, B, the plaintiff, ought not to be admitted to say that he was other than five-sixths to blame for the collision. It was held that (i) despite the absence of a notice claiming contribution in the county court proceedings, the county court judge had jurisdiction to apportion the damages;[279] and, even if a contribution notice were necessary in the first place, the fact that B had raised no objection to the county court judge dealing with the matter of contribution amounted to a waiver of the necessity for the notice; and (ii) estoppel by *res judicata* could arise although the judgment in the county court was not pronounced until after the commencement of the present action.[280]

---

[277] Uglow, *Evidence* 734.

[278] [1956] 3 All ER 449.

[279] *Croston v Vaughan* [1937] 4 All ER 249, followed.

[280] *The Delta, The Erminia Foscolo* (1876), 1 PD 393 and *Houstoun v Sligo (Marquis)* (1885), 29 Ch D 448, considered, and, since the issues of fact that the evidence to support them were identical with those in the county court, H's plea of estoppel succeeded; Dicta of Lush J in *Ord v Ord* [1923] 2 KB at 439, 443 applied.

In so far as approaches go, it would appear that the broader approach favoured in *Wall v Radford*[281] by Popplewell J and by Drake J in *North West Water v Binnie & Partners*[282] as regards same issues being involved in the initial as well as the subsequent matter is preferable to the narrow approach taken in *Randolph v Tuck.*[283]

(viii) Estoppel must be explicitly pleaded

It is clear from several authorities considered thus far in this text that estoppel must be specifically pleaded or it will not succeed. This is distillable from the case of *Bank of Zambia v Tembo and Others*[284] wherein the Court was referred to the fact that '[…] *a plea of res judicata* must show either an actual merger, or that the same point had been actually declared between the same parties where the former judgment has been for the defendant, the conditions necessary to conduct the plaintiff are not less stringent (emphasis added).[285] Similarly, in *Amber Louise Guest Milan Trbonic v Beatrice Mulako Mukinga, Attorney General*[286] Matibini J, as he then was, observed that in order for a plea of *res judicata* to succeed, it must be demonstrated that a judgment should have earlier on been pronounced between the parties (emphasis added). The consequences of not specifically pleading *res judicata*/issue estoppel in bar is demonstrated in *Vooght v Winch*[287] where a judge at first instance rejected the assertion that a judgment relating to an earlier action between the same parties for the same cause of action proffered in evidence by the defendant acted as an estoppel. In upholding the judgment on appeal, Abbott CJ, held *inter alia:*

> I am of the opinion that the verdict and judgment obtained for the defendant in the former action was not conclusive evidence against the plaintiff upon the plea of not guilty. It would indeed have been conclusive if pleaded in bar to the action by way of estoppel. In that case the plaintiff would not be allowed to discuss the case with the defendant, and for the second time to disturb and vex him by agitation of the same question. But the defendant has pleaded not guilty, and has thereby elected to submit his case to a jurisdiction […] It appears to me, however, that the party, by not pleading the former judgment in bar, consents that the whole matter shall go to the [judge], and leaves it open to [the judge] to inquire into the same upon evidence, and [the judge is] to give [his] verdict upon the whole evidence then submitted to [him].

---

[281] [1991] 2 All ER 741 at 750j -751b.

[282] [1990] 3 All ER 547 at 561c -d.

[283] [1961] 1 All ER 814; but see *Wall v Radford* [1971] 2 All ER 741.

[284] [2002] ZR 103; See *Guest and Another v Makinga and Another* [2011] 1 ZR 370.

[285] para 1254 of Halsbury Laws of England, Vol. 16.

[286] 2010/HP/0344.

[287] [1819] 2 B. & Ald. 662 at 668, *per* Abbott CJ.

We must conclude this discussion by briefly exploring the need to specifically plead issue estoppel within the context of the following:

(i)   criminal matters; and

(ii)   matrimonial causes

(xi)   Criminal matters

We have already discussed issue estoppel and whether as developed in civil cases, it applies in the same sense to criminal matters. We saw that even though it has been used by some both in civil matters and criminal matters,[288] the concept analogous to issue estoppel which is applicable to criminal matters is a plea of *autrefois convict* and *autrefois acquit*. That concept is provided for under s 138 of the Criminal procedure Code[289] and in accordance with Article 18(5) of the Constitution. Lord Diplock,[290] has, as we saw earlier, criticised the use of the term issue estoppel both in criminal[291] and civil matters as being rather unhelpful as it sows confusion principally because 'there are obvious differences-lack of mutuality is but one- between the application of the rule against double jeopardy in criminal cases, and the rule that there should be finality in civil litigation.'[292] The views of Lord Diplock about the need to extricate issue estoppel as established in civil matters from the comparable but discrete notion of double jeopardy pertinent to criminal matters was shadowed in *DPP v Humphrys*[293] where it was held on appeal that the doctrine of issue estoppel had no application to criminal proceedings; and in any event; could not apply to prevent a charge of perjury being brought against a person who had been acquitted of another offence in respect of evidence given by him at the trial for that offence.

We may just add to that discussion a few more authorities for consideration. The first is *Sabasivam v Malaya Federation Public Prosecutor*[294] which though supported by the EWCA in *Hay*,[295] must, in view of the decisions of the House of Lords, in among others, *R v Ollis*,[296] *DPP v Humphrys*[297] and more significantly, *R v Z*[298] be confined to being illustrative of a scenario of true jeopardy where the prosecution attempted to re-litigate the facts. The upshot of the foregoing cases is to the effect that the prosecution is, as it was in *G (an infant) v Coltart*,[299] estopped from launching collateral attacks on the acquittal of the accused by suggesting that he was in fact guilty.

---

[288] *Sabasivam v Malaya Federation Public Prosecutor* [1950] AC 458 at 479, *per* Lord MacDermott, modified in *R v Z* [2000] 3 All ER 385 at 403e-j, *per* Lord Hutton.

[289] Chapter 88 of the laws of Zambia.

[290] *Mills v Cooper* [1967] 2 All ER 100, *per* Lord Diplock at 104g-105c.

[291] See the Australian High Court decisions in *Wilkes* (1948) 77 CLR 511; Mraz (No 2) (1956) 96 CLR 62.

[292] *Mills v Cooper* [1967] 2 All ER 100, *per* Lord Diplock at 104g-105c.

[293] [1976] 2 All ER 497 AT 523D – 523G, *per* Lord Hailsham.

[294] [1950] AC 458 at 479, *per* Lord MacDermott.

[295] [1983] Crim.L.R. 390.

[296] [1900–3] All ER Rep 733.

[297] [1976] 2 All ER 497 AT 523D – 523G, *per* Lord Hailsham.

[298] [2000] 3 All ER 385 at 403e-j, *per* Lord Hutton.

[299] [1967] 1 All ER 271.

To what extent the prosecution may employ elements probative of their contentions from an earlier acquittal was considered and determined in *R v Ollis*.[300] The accused was acquitted on 5 July of an offence that involved bespeaking a dud cheque to one Ramsey. In his defence, he asserted that he had believed that there would be sufficient funds to ensure that the cheque in question was not dishonoured. However, on the 24 and 26 of June and also on the 6 July, the accused was again charged with similar offences. The Court for Crown Cases Reserved took the view that this did not amount to re-opening the issue of guilt but that the testimony offered by Ramsey, as he had done at the initial trial, showed what the accused's knowledge had been of the state of his bank account.

The principle adumbrated in *R v Ollis*,[301] came before and was reviewed by the House of Lords in *R v Z*.[302] In defence to a charge of rape, the defendant alleged that the complainant had consented to intercourse or, alternatively, that he believed she had consented. In order to rebut that defence, the prosecution wished to adduce the testimony of four women who had made previous complaints of rape against the defendant. Each of those complaints had been the subject of a separate trial, but in three of them the defendant had been acquitted. At a preparatory hearing, the judge ruled that the evidence of all four previous complainants came within the ambit of the similar facts rule. However, he excluded as inadmissible the evidence of the three complainants in the cases in which the defendant had been acquitted, holding, on the basis of previous authority, that a verdict of acquittal pronounced by a competent court on a lawful charge after a lawful trial was binding and conclusive in all subsequent proceedings between the parties to the adjudication. His decision was affirmed by the Court of Appeal, and the prosecution appealed to the House of Lords. It was held as follows: The principle of double jeopardy did not render inadmissible relevant evidence merely because that evidence showed or tended to show that the defendant was, in fact, guilty of an offence of which he had earlier been acquitted. That principle operated to cause a criminal court, in the exercise of its discretion, to stop a prosecution where the defendant was being prosecuted on the same facts or substantially the same facts as had given rise to an earlier prosecution which had resulted in his acquittal (or conviction). Thus, it would not be infringed by the prosecutor seeking to lead evidence which had been led at a previous trial, not for the purpose of punishing the accused in any way for the offence of which he had been acquitted, but in order to prove that he was guilty of a subsequent offence which had not been before the court in that previous trial. It also followed that there was no distinction between evidence which showed that the defendant was guilty of an earlier offence of which he had been acquitted and evidence which merely tended to show such guilt or which appeared to relate to one distinct issue rather than to

[300] [1900–3] All ER Rep 733.
[301] [1900–3] All ER Rep 733.
[302] [2000] 3 All ER 385 at 403e-j, *per* Lord Hutton.

the issue of guilt of such an offence. In the instant case the defendant had not been placed in double jeopardy because the facts giving rise to the prosecution were different to those which had given rise to the earlier prosecutions. The evidence of the earlier complainants was relevant, came within the ambit of the similar facts rule and thus was not rendered inadmissible simply because it showed that the defendant was, in fact, guilty of the offences of rape of which he had earlier been acquitted. Accordingly, the appeal would be allowed.[303]

(x)   Matrimonial causes

Matrimonial causes present a rather interesting challenge when it comes to dealing with the device of issue estoppel and the related legal maxim *Interest rei publicae ut sit finis litium*. Unlike the general approach taken in other cases, courts are compelled, given the very nature of matrimonial causes, to inquire into facts pertaining to the matrimonial cause in question. This apparent modification of principles of estoppel lends itself to the philosophy that while issue estoppel binds the parties, it does not bind the court or estop it from inquiring into the facts in order to do justice. In *Re B*,[304] care proceedings brought by a local authority in respect of two children were transferred to the High Court for the determination by a judge of the Family Division of the preliminary issue as to whether, in the proceedings so transferred, the respondent father was bound by a finding of sexual abuse in previous proceedings relating to two other children from another union, one of which was his own child. It was held as follows:

> Although the main rationale behind the doctrine of issue estoppel is the public policy rule that there should be finality in litigation, it is not appropriate to apply the doctrine strictly in cases involving care proceedings. In such cases the court has an inquisitorial rather than adversarial function, having regard to the paramount importance of the welfare of the child, and flexibility is an essential feature. However, the court is not bound to allow the parties to call evidence on each and every issue which may be relevant in the proceedings and its discretion to control the conduct of the hearing is an important feature of its investigative approach. In particular, the court will decide whether to allow any finding of fact which is relevant to a person's suitability to care for children to be tried afresh and in so doing will: (1) balance the underlying considerations of public policy with regard to (a) the public interest in an end to litigation, (b) the fact that any delay in determining the outcome of a case is likely to be prejudicial to the welfare of the individual child, (c) the fact that the welfare of the child is unlikely to be served by reliance on erroneous determinations

---

[303] *R v Ollis* [1900–3] All ER Rep 733 applied; dictum of Lord MacDermott in *Sambasivam v Public Prosecutor, Federation of Malaya* [1950] AC 458 at 479 considered; *G (an infant) v Coltart* [1967] 1 All ER 271 disapproved; for evidence challenging correctness of an acquittal and for similar fact evidence, see 11(2) Halsbury's Laws (4th edn reissue) paras 974, 1091.

[304] [1997] 2 All ER 29; approved in *Re F-K* [2005] EWCA Civ 155.

of fact and (d) the point that the court's discretion must be applied to work justice not injustice; (2) consider the importance of any previous findings on current proceedings; and (3) consider whether a rehearing will be likely to result in a different outcome.[305]

A further demonstration of the foregoing principles is to be found in *Thompson v Thompson*.[306] On the hearing in July, 1955, of a wife's application to the High Court for an order for maintenance under s 23 of the Matrimonial Causes Act, 1950, the divorce commissioner rejected the wife's charge of cruelty against the husband and accepted the evidence of the husband, but made no finding as to allegations of cruelty and desertion by the wife made by the husband in an affidavit refuting her charges. In November, 1955, the husband filed a petition for divorce on the ground of cruelty, in which he specified many instances of nagging and unreasonable complaints and other allegations, and charged the wife with testifying falsely in the maintenance proceedings that he had treated her with cruelty. In her answer denying cruelty and seeking a judicial separation, the wife denied the husband's charges in detail and charged him with cruelty, repeating allegations that she had made in the maintenance proceedings and reciting further incidents in detail. On an application by the husband to strike out the part of the answer relating to his alleged cruelty as *res judicata*, or as disclosing no reasonable cause of action or as being embarrassing, it was held as follows: The allegations in the wife's answer should not be struck out for the reasons stated below and, in the circumstances, the appropriate course was to direct the case to be tried by the commissioner who had heard the previous proceedings for maintenance. The reasons were as follows:

(i)   although the wife might herself be estopped from re-opening the issue of the husband's alleged cruelty which already had been determined by the Divorce Court, the court was not debarred by any estoppel between the parties from discharging its statutory duty[307] of inquiring into the truth of a petition or countercharge,[308] and

(ii)   in the present case the court, not being bound by any estoppel, should leave the wife's allegations open for trial because (a) the husband had charged her with making false allegations of cruelty in the maintenance proceedings and she should be allowed to defend herself against this charge,[309] and (b) the subject of litigation in the present case and the subject of litigation in the previous proceedings were not the same,[310] and

---

[305] Dictum of Lord Diplock in *Thoday v Thoday* [1964] 1 All ER 341 at 351, of Waite LJ in *Re S (discharge of care order)* [1995] 2 FLR 639 at 645, of Sir Stephen Brown P in *B v Derbyshire CC* [1992] 1 FLR 538 at 545 and of Lord Brandon in *DSV Silo- und Verwaltungsgesellschaft mbH v Sennar (owners), The Sennar* [1985] 2 All ER 104 at 110 applied.

[306] [1957] 1 All ER 161.

[307] Under s 4(1) of the Matrimonial Causes Act, 1950; see s of the Matrimonial Causes Act No 2007.

[308] *Harriman v Harriman* [1909] P 123, approved and applied.

[309] *Per* Denning and Morris LJJ.

[310] *Per* Hodson and Morris LJJ; *Winnan v Winnan* [1948] 2 All ER 862 adopted and applied; *Finney v Finney* (1868), LR 1 P & D 483, distinguished.

(iii)   although the pleadings infringed rules of pleading the defects of the answer had been invited by the similar defects of the petition.

Per Denning LJ:

> […] once an issue of a matrimonial offence has been litigated between the parties and decided by a competent court, neither party can claim as of right to re-open the issue and litigate it all over again if the other party objects; but the Divorce Court has the right, and indeed the duty in a proper case, to re-open the issue, or to allow either party to re-open it, despite the objection of the other party.[311]

22.4.2   *Estoppel by deed*

The general rule as regards estoppel by deed can be traced back to the case of *Bowman v Taylor*.[312] It is that where a person or entity is a party to a deed which avows a precise fact, that person or entity and any of his privies are estopped from refuting the truthfulness of the fact in question.[313] By deed, the plaintiff had granted the defendant a licence to use looms. The deed stated among other things, that the plaintiff was the inventor of certain improvements to the looms who had, *inter alia*, obtained letters patent for the same and caused a specification to be registered. It was held that the defendant was estopped from denying the foregoing matters. Lord Denman went so far as to hold that '[a]n estoppel operates because it concludeth a man to allege the truth by reason of the assertion of the party that that fact is true […] If a party has by his deed directly asserted a specific fact, it is impossible to say that he shall not be precluded from disputing that fact, thus solemnly admitted by him on the face of his deed [….]' Be that as it may, it has been shown in *Stroughill v Buck*[314] that the intentions of the parties will be an important factor in determining whether the said parties are indeed bound.

The importance of intention came up and was determined in *Greer v Kettle; Re Parent Trust & Finance Co Ltd*.[315] By a deed of guarantee for the repayment of a loan of £250,000 and interest, which recited that the lenders had, at the request of the guarantors, advanced to the borrowers £250,000, upon security

---

[311] See 165, letter e, post; Observations on pleading *per* Denning LJ with the concurrence of Morris LJ; see 169, letters b to f, and 176, letter h, post; Notes: The judgments touch on the question whether findings of magistrates in matrimonial proceedings before them give rise to an estoppel in subsequent proceedings in the High Court. At p 166, letter a, post, Denning LJ intimates that, in general, the rules of estoppel are not applied within the category of cases that he there discusses and that the High Court investigates the matter afresh; but Hodson LJ stresses that in principle the fact that the previous proceedings were before magistrates is not a ground of distinction excluding estoppel (see 170, letters g and h, post); Compare *per* Morris LJ at 175, letter i to 176, letter a, post; As to estoppel as a bar in divorce, see 12 Halsbury's Laws (3rd edn) 277, para 533, note (s), s 94, para 581, 15 Halsbury's Laws (34rd edn) 183, 184, para 356, and for cases on the subject, see 27 Digest (Repl 375, 376, 3089–3098.
[312] [1834] 4 LJKB 58.
[313] See *Greer v Kettle* [1938] AC 156 (discussed below); *John Kunda v Karen Motors (Z) Ltd* (2000/HPC/550); *Tropics Ltd v Ramaswamy Vaitheeswaran* (SCZ Judgment No 3 of 1996).
[314] (1850) 14 QB 781.
[315] [1937] 4 All ER 396; [1938] AC 156.

of a charge on certain shares, the guarantors covenanted, in the event of the borrowers failing to make the repayments provided for, forthwith to repay to the lenders the said sum of £250,000, with interest at the rate of 8 per cent per annum. The deed further provided that, whatever the position between the lenders and the borrowers, the guarantors should be liable for all moneys due as principal debtors, and that they were not to be released from liability by reason of time being given by the lenders, or by their taking no steps to protect their securities. The shares above-mentioned were at no time secured, and had not in fact been issued. Upon default in repayment of part of the loan, the liquidator of the guarantors rejected the proof by the liquidators of the lenders, contending that the security of the charge on the shares was a condition precedent to the guarantee. It was held that (i) upon a true construction of the deed of guarantee, the guarantors were not bound by the guarantee, as the security of the charge on the shares was a condition precedent to the guarantee; and (ii) the recital in the deed was not binding upon the guarantors, who were not estopped from setting up the facts, nor from asserting the non-existence of a charge on the shares.[316] Lord Maugham observed as follows:

> Estoppel by deed is a rule of evidence founded on the principle that a solemn and unambiguous statement or engagement in a deed must be taken as binding between the parties and privies, and therefore as not admitting any contradictory proof. It is important to observe that this is a rule of common law, though it may be noted that an exception arises when the deed is fraudulent or illegal [....][317]

It has, however, been shown in *Brooke v Haymes*[318] that estoppel by deed does not extend to fraudulent or deceptive acts as regards the document in question by the person who seeks to rely on the device, specifically, that '[a] party to a deed is not estopped in equity from averring against or offering evidence to controvert a recital therein contrary to the fact, which has been introduced into the deed by mistake of fact, and not through fraud or deception on his part.'

22.4.3 *Estoppel in pais or by conduct*

Estoppel in *pais* or by conduct is variously defined.[319] It is said to arise in instances where, a person or entity by words or their conduct leads another

---

[316] Order of Court of Appeal [1936] 3 All ER 432 affirmed; The House of Lords have adopted the views expressed in the Court of Appeal as to the existence of the charge on the shares being a condition precedent to the enforcement of the deed sued on. The decision on the estoppel point, in which a recital of the existence of the charge was relied on, is also affirmed by the House, it being held to be clearly established that a recital shown to be wrong in fact, and included by a mistake not induced by the party seeking to prove the true facts, does not estop that party from proving and relying upon the true facts; As to Estoppel by Recital, see Halsbury (Hailsham edn), Vol 13, pp 457–459, paras 514–518; and for Cases, see Digest, Vol 21, pp 252–266, Nos 769–856.

[317] [1937] 4 All ER 396 at 404a-f, *per* Lord Mugham.

[318] [1868] LR 6 Eq 25.

[319] See discussion and review of authorities by Mr. Justice Dr Matibini J in *North-Western Energy Company Limited v Energy Regulations Board* 2010/HP/786.

person to believe in; and rely on a given state of affairs; and thereby induces the innocent person to alter his legal position and act on that belief and reliance.[320] Thus, based on a party's previous conduct, the doctrine holds, it would be unconscionable to permit him to deny a fact.[321] The rule has been variously demarcated and/ or discussed in various cases:

It has been held in *Pickard v Sears*,[322] that '[w]here one by his words, or conduct wilfully causes another to believe the existence of a certain state of things, and induce him to act on that belief so as to alter his own previous position is concluded from averring against the latter a different state of things as existing at the same time.'

Blackburn J has described the concept in *Swan v North British Australian Company*[323] in the following terms:

> He omits to qualify it [the rule he has stated] by saying that the neglect must be in the transaction itself, and be the proximate cause of the leading the party into that mistake; and also as I think, that it must be the neglect of some duty that is owing to the person led into that belief, or what comes to the same things to the general public of which the person is one and not merely neglect of what would be prudent in respect to the party himself, or even of some duty owing to third persons, with whom those seeking to set up the estoppels are not privy.

In *Central Newbury Car Auctions Limited v Unity Finance Limited*,[324] Denning LJ has explained the doctrine as follows:

> Seeing that here we are considering the doctrine of estoppel by conduct, I would like to state the basis of it is this: you start with an innocent person who has been led to believe in a state of affairs which he takes to be correct (in this case the purchaser has been led to believe that the rogue was the owner of the car), and has acted on it. Then you ask yourself how has this innocent person been led into this belief? If it has been brought about by the conduct of another (in this case by the conduct of the original owner), who though not solely responsible, nevertheless has contributed so large a part to it that it would be unfair or unjust to allow him to depart from it, then he is not allowed to go back on it so as to prejudice the innocent person who has acted on it.

Further, that,

> In so stating the basis of estoppel by conduct, I am relying on the well-considered view by the Chief Justice of Australia, Sir Owen

---

[320] *North Western Energy Company Ltd v Energy Regulation Board* (2010/HP/786).

[321] *Phipson of Evidence*, at 118 para 5-18.

[322] [1837] 6A and E 469 at 474; cited in *Freeman v Cooke* (1848) 18 LJ Ex 114.

[323] [1863] 2H and C 175; applied in *Jacques Chisha Mwewa v Attorney-General,* IRC Comp No 95/08; *Galaunia Farms Ltd v National Milling Company Ltd* [2002] ZR 135.

[324] [1957] 1 QB 371 at 379.

Dixon (then Dixon J), in *Thompson v Palmer*[325] This formulation of the principle is the most satisfactory I know. As he points out, the basis of estoppel is that it would be unfair to allow a party to depart from a particular state of affairs which another has taken to be correct. But the law does not leave the question of fairness, or justice at large. It has defined with more, or less completeness the kind of participation by a party which will suffice to work an estoppel against him. There are to be found in the decided cases. Often it is a representation made by him which he is not allowed to controvert. But a representation is not the only basis of estoppel. Conduct too is a recognised head.

There are three types of estoppels by conduct:
  (i)   Estoppel by representation;
  (ii)   Estoppel by agreement; and
  (iii) Estoppel by negligence.

We discuss each in turn below:

(i)   Estoppel by representation

Estoppel by representation arises where a party makes a representation to an innocent party with the intent, real or supposed, of inducing the innocent party to alter his legal position and to, by way of reliance on said representation, act on the representation to the innocent party's detriment. We may proceed here by using the analogy of the banker customer relationship. 'It is well settled that a person has a duty to warn a banker if he knows or has reasonable ground for believing that a forged instrument, purporting to be his, is likely to be presented for payment.'[326] Further, that '[i]f a man knows or has reasonable ground for believing that his name has been forged on a bill or cheque and that it is about or likely to be presented for payment to a banker, he is bound with reasonable dispatch to warn the banker of the fact. If he does not, and the bank's position is thereby prejudiced, he adopts the bill or cheque.'[327] The position of the law is not any different when what is at play is the discovery of forgery only after the bank has paid on the instrument:[328]

> The prejudice or injury to the bank, resulting from the customer's or other person's silence, which will estop him from disputing his signature or constitute adoption by him of the bill or cheque, is not confined to payment thereof. The customer or other person will be equally bound if, by his silence, the bank [is] precluded from the opportunity of protecting themselves against subsequent forgeries, if any, by the same person, or lose the chance of taking proceedings, civil or criminal, against the forger, as by his escaping out of the jurisdiction in the interval.

---

[325] [1933] 49 CLR 507, 547.

[326] *Bank of Zambia v Attorney-General* [1974] ZR 24 (SC).

[327] *Paget's Law of Banking*, (6th edn Sweet & Maxwell, …) at 437.

[328] *Paget's Law of Banking* at 439.

Greenwood v Martins Bank Ltd[329] demonstrates the foregoing. Unbeknown to her husband, who was plaintiff in this matter, the wife had forged several cheques which were drawn on the defendant. He discovered this, confronted the wife about it with the result that the wife decided to take her own life. Despite the discovery, and a duty to disclose to the bank his wife's misfeasance, the plaintiff failed to do so. He sought to recover from the defendant the monies paid out on the sham cheques. His action failed. Lord Tomlin held *inter alia:*

> Mere silence cannot amount to a representation, but when there is a duty to disclose, deliberate silence may become significant and amount to representation [...] The appellant's silence, therefore, was deliberate and intended to produce the effect which it in fact produced-namely the leaving of the respondents in ignorance of the true facts so that no action might be taken by the against the appellant's wife. The deliberate abstention from speaking in those circumstances seems to me to amount to a representation to the respondents that the forged cheques were in fact in order, and assuming that detriment to the respondents followed, there were, it seems to me, present all the elements essential to estoppel.

The decision in *Taylor Fashions Ltd v Liverpool; Victoria Trustees Co Ltd*[330] expands on the notion of estoppel by representation, acquiescence, and unconscionability.[331] The second plaintiffs owned the freehold of commercial premises comprising two shops, each on five floors. In 1948 they leased one shop (no 22) to a third party for a term of 28 years with an option to renew for a further 14 years if, at his own expense, the tenant installed a lift. The option was not registered under the Land Charges Act 1925. Shortly after, the second plaintiffs sold the freehold of the premises to the defendants, who were adjoining owners, and took a lease back on the other shop (no 21) for a term of 42 years from 1948 subject to the defendants having the right to determine the lease of no 21 if the tenant of no 22 failed to exercise his option. The defendants were given notice of the terms of the lease to the third party and the option to renew. In 1958 the third party sold its lease of no 22 to the first plaintiffs, who installed a lift at a cost of £5,000 in expectation of their being entitled to exercise the option. The installation of the lift was known to and acquiesced in by the defendants. In 1963 the second plaintiffs wished to expand. They took a lease on an adjoining shop (no 20) from the defendants and spent some £12,000 altering the frontage and internal layout to combine nos 20 and 21 into a single shop. In order that the leases of both shops should coincide it was agreed that the lease of no 20 should be for 14 years with an option to renew for a further 14 years but subject to the defendants having the right to determine the lease if the tenant of no 22 failed to exercise his option. In 1976 the first plaintiffs served a notice exercising the option to renew the lease of no 22 but the defendants

---

[329] [1933] AC 51 at 57 – 58, per Lord Tomlin.
[330] [1981] 1 All ER 897.
[331] See *Beckingham v Hodges* (2003) EMLR 18.

claimed that it was void for want of registration and that the leases of nos 20 and 21 were also affected by that invalidity. The defendants accordingly served notices to quit on both plaintiffs who applied to the court for specific performance and declaratory relief. The plaintiffs contended (i) that the first plaintiffs' option was not void for want of registration, and (ii) that, even if it was, the defendants were estopped from relying on the invalidity, having regard to the expenditure in installing a lift made by the first plaintiffs with the defendants' concurrence and to the assertion of the existence of the option in the leases granted by the defendants to the second plaintiffs over nos 20 and 21. The defendants contended that the doctrine of estoppel did not apply because the estoppel alleged was proprietory estoppel or estoppel by acquiescence and, for such an estoppel to arise, it was an essential prerequisite that the representor knew what his rights were and that the representee was acting in the belief that those rights would not be enforced, and thus such an estoppel did not arise where both parties were acting under a mistake as to the representor's rights. Having decided that he was bound by authority to hold that the option was void as against the defendants for want of registration, the judge then considered the question whether the defendants were estopped from relying on the invalidity of the option. It was held as follows: (1) The doctrine of estoppel by acquiescence was not restricted to cases where the representor was aware both of what his strict rights were and that the representee was acting in the belief that those rights would not be enforced against him. Instead, the court was required to ascertain whether in the particular circumstances it would be unconscionable for a party to be permitted to deny that which, knowingly or unknowingly, he had allowed or encouraged another to assume to his detriment. Accordingly, the principle could apply where, at the time when the expectation was encouraged, both parties (and not just the representee) were acting under a mistake of law as to their rights. Whether the representor knew of the true position was merely one of the factors relevant to determining whether it would be unconscionable for him to be allowed to take advantage of the mistake.[332] (2) Although both the first plaintiffs and the defendants had mistakenly assumed that by installing the lift the first plaintiffs would then have been entitled to exercise the option to renew their lease, on the facts there was nothing to suggest that the defendants had in any way created or encouraged the first plaintiffs' mistaken belief, or that the first plaintiffs had installed the lift on the faith of their belief that they had a valid option, since they had not shown that they would not have installed the lift if they had known of the true position. The first plaintiffs' claim for specific performance therefore failed[333] (3) The defendants were, however, estopped from asserting the invalidity of the option against the second plaintiffs because the defendants were to be

---

[332] *Ramsden v Dyson* (1866) LR 1 HL 129; *Willmott v Barber* (1880) 15 Ch D 96; *Plimmer v Mayor of Wellington* (1884) 9 App Cas 699; *Sarat Chunder Dey v Gopal Chunder Lala* (1892) LR 19 Ind App 203; *Hopgood v Brown* [1955] 1 All ER 550; *Inwards v Baker* [1965] 1 All ER 446; *Ives Investments Ltd v High* [1967] 1 All ER 504; *Crabb v Arun District Council* [1975] 3 All ER 865; *Shaw v Applegate* [1978] 1 All ER 123 considered.

[333] Dicta of Lord Eldon LC in *Dann v Spurrier* (1802) 7 Ves at 235–236 and of Fry J in *Willmott v Barber* (1880) 15 Ch D at 106 applied.

taken as having represented both in 1948 and in 1963 in the leases offered to the second plaintiffs that the option granted to the first plaintiffs, and on which the second plaintiffs' prospects for renewal depended, was a valid option, and, further, the defendants had in 1963 encouraged the second plaintiffs to incur expenditure and alter their position irrevocably by taking additional premises on the faith of the supposition that the option was valid. In those circumstances it would be inequitable and unconscionable for the defendants to frustrate the second plaintiffs' expectation which the defendants had themselves created. The second plaintiffs were accordingly entitled to specific performance.[334]

(ii)   Estoppel by agreement

Estoppel by agreement arises in instances where parties have settled together to predicate their affiliation on a recognised state of affairs. The issue of estoppel by agreement, its effect and application were considered as early as 1792 in the case of *Cooke v Loxley*.[335] The landlord sued the tenant for use and occupation of the land. The tenant declined to yield arguing that the landlord had no title to the land in question to sue him for use and occupation of the said land. The court declined to accept the defendant's contentions or the evidence thereof. Lord Kenyon observed that '[…] in an action for use and occupation it ought not to be permitted to a tenant, who occupies land by the licence of another, to call upon that other to show the title under which he let the land.' According to his lordship, the foregoing position as escribed, was 'not a mere technical rule but is founded in public convenience and policy [….]' He deprecated the fact that the defendant, having being let onto the land in question by the plaintiff as a tenant then turned around and refused to fulfil his rental obligations towards the landlord, inspired by the deluded idea 'that he might contest the plaintiff's right [….]' Said Lord Kenyon, '[…] such an action as the present [did] not involve the question of title.'

Another situation in which estoppel by agreement can be invoked which is analogous to the triad of estoppel by representation or acquiescence nay the test of unconscionability as exemplified in *Taylor Fashions Ltd v Liverpool Victoria Trustees Co Ltd*[336] is one where an agent/principal; bailee/bailor relationship exists. The agent is estopped from denying the principal title as is the bailee that of the bailor.

(iii)   Estoppel by negligence

Estoppel by negligence arises, as the name suggests, in instances where the negligence of a party leads to an incorrect representation of a state of affairs as true when in fact not. Under such circumstances and given the correct set of facts in a proper case, the party responsible is estopped from denying the

---

[334] For estoppel by representation, see 21 Halsbury's Laws (4th edn) 72–74, 145–149, and for cases on the subject, see 21 Digest (Repl) 364–387, 1103–1195; For options to renew a lease, see 23 Halsbury's Laws (3rd edn) 473, para 1094, and for cases on the subject, see 31(1) Digest (Reissue) 278–282, 2301–2335; For the Land Charges Act 1925, see 27 Halsbury's Statutes (3rd edn) 685.

[335] (1972) 5 TR 4.

[336] [1981] 1 All ER 897.

truth of the said state of affairs.[337] Such a scenario arose in *Coventry, Sheppard & Co v Great Eastern Railway*[338] in which the defendant issued two delivery orders instead of one as respects a consignment of wheat. As a consequence of this negligent act or acts, two advances were obtained from the plaintiff by fraudulent individuals. As to whether the defendant was, as a result of this negligence, estopped from denying there being two consignments, Brett MR[339] held that '[t]he negligence of the defendants was to the prejudice of the plaintiffs and allowed the fraud to be perpetrated upon them. It seems to me, therefore, that the defendants are estopped as against the plaintiffs, their negligence having been the immediate cause of the advance [....]' It has been said that '[e]stoppel by negligence does require a breach of duty to the victim and might well be seen simply as part of the substantive law of negligence.'[340] In addition, it has been held, *inter alia*, in *Moorgate Mercantile Co Ltd v Twitchings*[341] that '[t]o constitute an estoppel [by negligence] a representation must be clear and must unequivocally state the fact which, ultimately, the maker is to be prevented from denying.'

It would appear that the matter of negligence such as would lead to a party being estopped from denying the truth of a state of affairs, is not so straight forward. A line of authorities seems to suggest that for estoppel by negligence to be invoked, the court ought to be satisfied that the negligence contended is not so distant or the carelessness alleged too remote to amount to conduct inducing an innocent party to fall prey to fraudulent schemes perpetrated as a result, for example, a bank being led to pay on a forged instrument such as a cheque. Thus, it has been said in *Bank of London v Vagliano Brothers*[342] that:

> [i]n order to make (these) cases... authorities in this case, it would be necessary to assume that the plaintiffs in those cases had by some voluntary act of their own given credit and the appearance of genuineness to the particular powers of attorney which were forged in those cases; and, if they had, I very much doubt whether the decision would have been what it was, but no such fact appeared; all that the parties whose negligence was relied on had done was to leave their seal carelessly in the custody of the person who abused the trust.

And in Bank of *Ireland v Evans Trustees*[343] it was held that:

> If there was negligence in the custody of the seal it was very remotely connected with the act of transfer. The transfer was not the necessary or ordinary or likely result of that negligence. It never would have

[337] See *Moorgate Mercantile Co Ltd v Twitchings* [1976] 2 All ER 641 at 659a-c, *per* Lord Edmund-Davies but see dissenting opinion *per* Lord Wilberforce at 648b-c.
[338] [1883] 11 QBD 776.
[339] *Coventry, Sheppard & Co v Great Eastern Railway* [1883] 11 QBD 776 at 780.
[340] Uglow Evidence, 743.
[341] [1976] 2 All ER.
[342] [1891-4] All ER 93 at 99 *per* Lord Halsbury, LC.
[343] 10 ER 950 5 HLC 389.

been but for the occurrence of a very extraordinary event, that persons should be found either so dishonest or so careless, as to testify on the face of the instrument that they had seen the seal duly affixed. It is quite impossible that the bankers could have maintained an action for the negligence of the trustees, and recovered the damages they had sustained by reason of their having made the transfer.

The foregoing authorities were quoted with approval in *Bank of Zambia* v *Attorney-General*.[344] The appellant paid on a cheque purporting to have been drawn by the Ministry of Health but which, as was conceded, was forged. The appellant argued that the respondent was negligent in its care of its cheque forms and stamps and in failing to discover that money had been paid on a forged cheque and for either of those reasons was estopped from denying the genuineness of the cheque. The appellant argued also there was no negligence on the part of the bank in paying on the forged cheque.

> The conduct which it is alleged induced the bank to pay on the forged cheque was the negligence in allowing the cheque to be stolen and allowing it to be completed on one of the machines in the machine room, and in failing to take adequate care of the "crossing cancelled" stamp with the result that such stamp was impressed on the cheque. The learned judge found that the respondent was not negligent in these respects, and on the evidence it cannot in my judgment be said that he was not justified in so finding. But the matter goes further; even assuming that the conduct of the Ministry amounted to gross carelessness it is impossible to say that this conduct was a proximate cause of the loss.

Going further and holding that the passages considered above in this text from *Bank of London v Vagliano Brothers*[345] and *Ireland v Evans Trustees*[346] were correct statements of the law, Baron DCJ, as he then was, opined that he was 'satisfied that even if it could be said that the Ministry was careless in the respects alleged, any such carelessness was too remote to amount to conduct inducing the bank to pay on the forged instrument.' He noted additionally, that '[w]here, however, a bank sets up conduct of its customer as supporting a defence of estoppel or ratification, it may be open to the customer to rely on negligence by the bank to meet such a defence.'[347] Further, that '[…] on any view the absence of negligence on the part of the bank can at best only be relevant if a prima facie case of estoppel or adoption has been made out against the customer.' The learned DCJ concluded thus:

---

[344] [1974] ZR 24.

[345] [1891-4] All ER 93 at 99 *per* Lord Halsbury, LC.

[346] 10 ER 950 5 HLC 389.

[347] Scrutton, LJ, in *Greenwood v Martin's Bank* [1933] AC 51 appears to have expressed misgivings concerning this proposition.

I will assume in favour of the bank, but without deciding, that negligence can be a ground for holding that a customer, because his conduct has deprived the bank of the opportunity of recovering from the forger, is estopped from denying the genuineness of a forged cheque [...] But there is totally inadequate evidence on which to hold that either the Ministry of Finance or the Ministry of Health has been negligent, and it is unnecessary therefore to consider what might have been the position had such negligence properly been found. I would dismiss this appeal.

22.5   Can there be an estoppel against a statute?

The law as confirmed in various decisions in this jurisdiction is that there can be no estoppel against a statute. Two authorities demonstrate this. In *Attorney General v EB Jones Machinists Ltd,*[348] the Supreme Court observed as follows: "[f]urther, the learned trial judge misdirected herself when she ruled that by conduct the Attorney – General could not rely on [s] 414 of the Sheriffs Act.[349] There cannot be an estoppel to a statute". In *City Express Service Limited v Southern Cross Motors Limited*[350] the Supreme Court employed similar wording: '[t]here can be no estoppels against a statute. A litigant can plead benefit of a statute at any stage.'[351]

---

[348] [2000] ZR 114.

[349] Chapter 37 of the Laws of Zambia.

[350] SCZ No 8/262/2006.

[351] *Embassy Supermarket v Union Bank Zambia Limited (In Liquidation)* SCZ Judgment No 25 of 2007.

23

JUDGMENTS AS EVIDENCE

23.1   Introduction

A judgment of the court is conclusive not only against the world as to the legal state of affairs but against the parties and their privies as to the facts on which the judgment in question was predicated. At common law therefore, a judgment and the facts leading to it are inadmissible in subsequent judicial proceedings that involve different parties who were not privy to the earlier proceedings or the resultant judgment. The reason is simple: no person or entity can, in the grand scheme of things, have rights awarded to, or obligations foisted upon them by proceedings in which they could not be heard or/and a subsequent judgment to which they were not a party. It has been held as follows in *The Case of the Duchess of Kingston*[1] (a case which we have already come across in this text):

> [...] as a general principle [...] a transaction between two parties in judicial proceedings ought not to be binding upon a third; for it would be unjust to bind any person who could not be admitted to make a defence, or to examine witnesses, or to appeal from a judgment he might think erroneous; and therefore the depositions of witnesses in another cause in proof of a fact, the verdict of the [judge] finding the fact, and the judgment of the court upon the facts found, although evidence against the parties and all claiming under them, are not, in general, to be used to the prejudice of strangers.

It follows, based on the foregoing holding, that at common law, it is not permissible for parties, in subsequent litigation to be bound by facts birthing the previous judgment. It is also not permissible for such parties to deploy the judgment of previous legal proceedings as evidence of the facts in subsequent legal proceedings.

23.2   The rule in *Hollington v F Hewthorn*[2]

The decision in *Hollington v F. Hewthorn & Company Limited*,[3] exemplifies the fact that parties to an earlier matter are not bound by the facts on which a previous judgment was premised even though unable to refute the legal state

---

[2] [1943] 2 All ER 35.
[3] (1776) 20 St Tr 355, col 538.

of affairs brought about by the decision in the judgment in question. The case is also demonstrative of the legal position that this is not limited to the parties not deploying facts relating to a previous judgment but that the judgment itself cannot be used as evidence of the facts by which they are not bound. The plaintiff's car was involved in a collision with a car owned by the defendants. The plaintiff's car was being driven by his son who had since died, though not as a result of the accident. The plaintiff brought an action for damage to his car and, as administrator, for personal injury sustained by his son. The defendants counterclaimed for negligence. At the close of the plaintiff's case, counsel for the defendants submitted that there was no case to answer and elected to call no evidence. Judgment was given for the plaintiff on both claim and counterclaim. The defendants appealed, and the plaintiff not only sought to uphold the judgment but contended that certain evidence tendered by him at the trial was wrongly rejected and, if the court should hold that there was no evidence to support the judgment, that there should be a new trial. The evidence which had been rejected at the trial was: (a) a certificate that the defendants' driver had been convicted of driving without due care and attention on the same day on which the accident occurred and in the same parish, and which, counsel contended, was admissible as prima facie evidence of negligence, and (b) a signed statement as to the cause of the collision made by the plaintiff's deceased driver to a police constable soon after the accident, and which, it was maintained, was admissible under the Evidence Act 1938, s 1(3). It was held as follows: (i) the damage to the cars was equally consistent with either car being at fault and the finding of negligence against the appellant could not be supported by the evidence; (ii) a certificate of a conviction cannot be tendered in evidence in civil proceedings and, in the present case, the certificate was rightly rejected. On a subsequent civil trial, the court should come to a decision on the facts before it without regard to the proceedings before another tribunal; and (iii) the statement made by the deceased driver to the police constable was made at a time when the deceased must have anticipated the likelihood of at least civil proceedings and, consequently, the statement was not admissible. *Per* Lord Goddard:

> In truth, the conviction is only proof that another court considered that the defendant was guilty of careless driving. Even were it proved that it was the accident that led to the prosecution, the conviction proves no more than what has just been stated. The court which has to try the claim for damages knows nothing of the evidence that was before the criminal court: it cannot know what arguments were addressed to it, or what influenced the court in arriving at its decision [...] It frequently happens that a bystander has a complete and full view of an accident; it is beyond question that while he may inform the court of everything that he saw, he may not express any opinion on whether either or both of the parties were negligent. The reason commonly assigned is that this is the precise question the court has to decide; but in truth it is because his opinion is not relevant. Any fact that

he can prove is relevant, but his opinion is not. The well-recognised exception in the case of scientific or expert witnesses depends on considerations which, for present purposes, are immaterial. So, on the trial of the issue in the civil court, the opinion of the criminal court is equally irrelevant.

Comment:[4] The judgment considers at full length the admissibility in evidence in civil proceedings of a conviction obtained in criminal proceedings. It was admitted that the conviction could not be tendered as conclusive evidence of the facts, but it was contended that it should be admitted as *prima facie* evidence. It was said that the objection to the admissibility of such evidence based on the maxim of *res inter alios acta*[5] was answered by the fact that the conviction, if it was only *prima facie* evidence, could be explained, but the EWCA was clear that the civil court must base its findings on the facts placed before it without any regard to the proceedings before another tribunal. Upon this point the EWCA has critically examined two cases: *In the estate of Crippen, Partington v Partington and Atkinson,*[6] and *O'Toole v O'Toole,*[7] and holds that these cases go beyond and are contrary to the authorities and ought not to be followed in future. The point raised on the Evidence Act 1938, turns entirely upon whether the statement was made with the likelihood of proceedings being taken in mind. It was held that the deceased must have anticipated that there would be such proceedings and the evidence is, therefore, inadmissible. Further, that it is not correct to say that *Robinson v Stern*[8] decided that a statement made to a police officer inquiring into a road accident is never admissible. The court must read the statement and draw from it such inference as is reasonable on the question whether the maker of the statement must have anticipated that proceedings were likely to be taken in respect of the accident.[9]

While the decision has never been overruled by the Supreme Court of the United Kingdom, it has, since it was delivered, been met with harsh, even caustic criticism.[10] Denning J who had argued against the decision taken by the court, as counsel at the time, would, when judge say, in *Goody v Odhams Press Ltd.*[11]

---

[4] *Hollington v F. Hewthorn & Company Limited* [1943] 2 All ER 35 - by editors at 35.

[5] In full, Res inter alios acta, aliis nec nocet nec prodest is Latin for "a thing done between others does not harm or benefit others." It is a legal doctrine which states that a contract cannot adversely affect the rights of a party not privy to the contract or indeed, a non-party. A common law meaning for "Res inter alios" is as follows: "[a] matter between others is not our business."

[6] [1911] P 108; 22 Digest 280, 2669, 80 LJP 47, 104 LT 224.

[7] (1926) 42 TLR 245; Digest Supp, 134 LT 542.

[8] [1939] 2 KB 260, [1939] 2 All ER 683; Digest Supp, 108 LJKB 665, 161 LT 3.

[9] As to Similar Facts, see Halsbury (Hailsham Edn), vol 13, pp 567–571, paras 639–641; and for Cases, see Digest, vol 22, pp 71–75, Nos 421–438; As to Necessity for Declaration to be *ante litem motam*, see Halsbury (Hailsham edn), vol 13, pp 592, 593, para 659; and for Cases, see Digest, vol 22, pp 121–123, Nos 965–982.

[10] See *Hunter v Chief Constable of the West Midlands* [1982] AC 529 at 543, *per* Lord Diplock; *Hall v Simons* [2002] 1 AC 615 at 702, *per* Lord Hoffmann; Law Reform Committee, Cmnd 3391, 1967; subsequent enactment of ss 11-13 of the Civil Evidence Act 1968 which partially reversed *Hollington*.

[11] [1966] 3 WLR 460 at 463.

It would not be sufficient to prove that he was convicted of the train robbery. The reason is because there is a strange rule of law which says that a conviction is no evidence of guilt, not even prima facie evidence. That was decided in *Hollington v F Hewthorn & Co., Ltd.*[12] I argued that case myself and did my best to persuade the court that a conviction was evidence of guilt. But they would not have it. I thought that the decision was wrong at the time. I still think that it was wrong. But in this court, we are bound by it.

Be that as it may, it has been treated as good law in such cases as *Hui Chi-Ming*[13] and recently in *Lincoln National Life Insurance v Sun Life Insurance.*[14] The use of the rule in *Hollington v Hewthorn*[15] in criminal matters has, however, led to the absurd situation that criminal convictions have been ignored in instances where conventional wisdom would have acknowledged their existence and considered their weight and relevance as regards matters before court. The case of *R v Spinks*[16] demonstrates this. F and the appellant were drinking in a public house when F heard that a friend of his had been involved in some trouble elsewhere. F decided to attack those whom he thought were responsible and, taking a knife with him, he left the public house with some friends while the appellant remained behind. F and his friends were involved in a fight with a rival group, some of whom received stab wounds. After the fight F returned to the public house and gave the knife to the appellant, who took it home and hid it. F and the appellant were subsequently arrested. F admitted to the police, in the absence of the appellant, that he had been responsible for one of the stabbings and made a written statement to that effect. The appellant told the police that when F gave him the knife to hide, he had known that there had been a fight but that he had not known that anyone had been stabbed. He also stated that there was no blood on the knife when he had received it. F was charged on indictment with wounding a person unknown with intent to do him grievous bodily harm, and the appellant was charged on the same indictment with doing, without lawful authority or reasonable excuse, an act (namely concealing a knife) with intent to impede the apprehension or prosecution of a person who had committed an arrestable offence, knowing or believing that person to be guilty of an arrestable offence, contrary to s 4(1)a of the Criminal Law Act 1967.[17] At his trial the appellant submitted that there was no case for him to answer because the only evidence that F had committed an arrestable offence came from F's own out of court admission to the police, which had been made in the absence of the appellant. The judge ruled that F's admission

---

[12] [1943] 1 KB 587.

[13] [1992] 1 AC 34.

[14] [2004] 1 Lloyd's Rep. 737, para.51 ff.

[15] [1943] 1 KB 587.

[16] [1982] 1 All ER 587.

[17] It provides: 'Where a person has committed an arrestable offence, any other person who, knowing or believing him to be guilty of the offence or of some other arrestable offence, does without lawful authority or reasonable excuse any act with intent to impede his apprehension or prosecution shall be guilty of an offence;' The Zambian Evidence Act Chapter 43 of the Laws of Zambia.

was 'evidence in the case' and that the jury could act on it when considering the case against the appellant. F and the appellant were convicted, and the appellant appealed. It was held that where a person charged with an arrestable offence and another person charged, under s 4(1) of the 1967 Act, with assisting him were tried together, the rule that out of court statements could not be used to provide evidence against a co-accused applied. It followed that the case against the appellant should have been withdrawn from the jury at the end of the prosecution case, since the only evidence of the commission of F's offence was his out of court statement. Accordingly, the appeal would be allowed and the conviction quashed. *Per* Russell J: [18]

> In the instant case it was conceded at the close of the case for the Crown that the only evidence that Fairey had stabbed anyone came from his own admissions to the police, made in the absence of the appellant. No one at the scene of the fracas had identified Fairey or indeed had witnessed the stabbing. The victims were unable to assist as to the identity of the assailants: hence the charge against Fairey was wounding a person unknown. The short point that is taken, therefore, is that the Crown had no admissible evidence as against the appellant to prove the first ingredient of the offence with which he was charged, namely as alleged in the particulars of offence, that Fairey had committed the arrestable offence of wounding. The only evidence of that fact came from an out of court admission of a co-defendant which was not admissible against the appellant.
>
> For the Crown it was argued that in some way the admission of Fairey was 'evidence in the case', and that the jury could act on it when considering the case of the appellant. But, as it seems to this court, the fallacy of that argument can be demonstrated in a number of ways. If Fairey had pleaded guilty and had not given evidence against the appellant, or if the appellant had been indicted and tried separately, could the Crown have relied on Fairey's conviction to prove the first ingredient of the offence? The answer must be in the negative. The appellant can be in no worse position because he was being tried alongside Fairey. In the judgment of this court the offence with which the appellant was charged and the means of establishing it do not provide any exception to the universal rule which excludes out of court admissions being used to provide evidence against a co-accused, whether indicted jointly or separately.

Despite absurd positions that *Hollington*[19] led to such as the one in *Spinks*[20] above, and its partial alteration in the UK as a result of ss 11-13 of the Civil Evidence Act 1968 and s 74 of the Police and Criminal Evidence Act 1984, it has, as we show below, continued to be good law in Zambia. As discussed below, though, there is no good reason to continue sustaining the position taken in

---

[18] [1982] 1 All ER 587 at 589b-e, *per* Russell J.
[19] [1943] 2 All ER 35.
[20] [1982] 1 All ER 587.

Kabwe Transport v Press Transport (1975) Limited[21] regarding the application of portions of *Hollington*[22] which are now considered bad law in England and Wales by virtue of legislative changes in those jurisdictions.

There had been an attempt to follow the rule in *Hollington v Hewthorn*[23] as altered by ss 11-13 of the Civil Evidence Act 1968 and s 74 of the Police and Criminal Evidence Act 1984, in *Sadi Siwingwa (being personal representative of deceased Yuna Namwalizi) v Phiri.*[24] It succeeded and would become the law for the next 5 years until the matter was raised and commented on *obiter* by the Supreme Court in *Kabwe Transport*[25] in 1984. This was an action for damages and consequential loss for the death of the deceased caused by the negligence of the defendant's servant or agent. A preliminary issue was raised as to whether the fact that the defendant's servant had been convicted of careless driving in relation to the fatal traffic accident which was now the subject of these civil proceedings was admissible in evidence. It was held as follows: (i) In the absence of any statutory or judicial authority in Zambia in matters relating to practice and procedure, s 10 of the High Court Act,[26] provides for the High Court to exercise jurisdiction on those matters in substantial conformity with the law and practice for the time being in force in England. (ii) In England a conviction is admissible in evidence under s 11 of the Civil Evidence Act of 1968. Zambia, following the law and practice observed in England, would follow the same procedure. (iii) The procedure concerning the admissibility of convictions is laid down under RSC Order 18 r 7A.

As Moodley J noted in *Siwinga*,[27] prior to the enactment of ss 11-13 of the Civil Evidence Act 1968 (and later, s 74 of the Police and Criminal Evidence Act 1984), the decision in *Hollington*[28] had, as we have noted above, been highly criticised. In *Hunter v Chief Constable of the West Midlands*[29] Lord Diplock expressed the view that *Hollington*[30] had been wrongly decided. Lord Hoffmann would, as late as 2002 in *Hall v Simons*,[31] post the decision in *Siwinga*[32] and *Kabwe Transport*,[33] opine that the EWCA had taken the technicalities of the matter too far in holding, *inter alia* that the conviction in question was *inter alios acta*.[34]

---

[21] [1984] ZR 43 which disapproved *Siwinga v Phiri* [1979] ZR 145 *obiter dicta,* and was followed in *Fanny Muliango and Samson Muliango v Namdou Magasa and Muruja Transport & Farming Company Limited* (1988-1989) ZR 209 (SC).

[22] [1943] 2 All ER 35.

[23] [1943] 2 All ER 35.

[24] [1979] ZR 145.

[25] [1984] ZR 43.

[26] Chapter 27 of the Laws of Zambia.

[27] [1979] ZR 145.

[28] [1943] 2 All ER 35.

[29] [1981] 3 All ER 727 at 736c *per* Diplock LJ.

[30] [1943] 2 All ER 35.

[31] [2002] 1 AC 615 at 702.

[32] [1979] ZR 145.

[33] [1984] ZR 43.

[34] In full, *res inter alios acta, aliis nec nocet nec prodest* is Latin for 'a thing done between others does not harm or benefit others.'

The consequence of this unrelenting criticism was the recommendation for alteration of the position in *Hollington*[35] in the Law Reform Committee,[36] and as a result, the enactment of ss 11-13 of the Civil Evidence Act 1968. Thus, when the issue came up once again in the case of *Stupple v Royal Insurance Company Limited*,[37] the EWCA held that the effect of s 11(2)(a) of the Civil Evidence Act 1968 was to shift the legal burden of proof. *Per* Lord Denning:[38]

> I think that the conviction does not merely shift the burden of proof. It is a weighty piece of evidence of itself. For instance, if a man is convicted of careless driving on the evidence of a witness, but that witness dies before civil action is heard; then the conviction itself tells in the scale in the civil action. It speaks as clearly as the witness should have done had he lived. It does not merely reverse the burden of proof. If that was all it did, the defendant might well give his own evidence negativing want of care and say: 'I have discharged the burden. I have given my evidence and it has not been contradicted.' In answer to the defendant's evidence, the plaintiff can say to him: 'But your evidence is contradicted. It is contradicted by the very fact of your conviction.' In addition, Mr Hawser sought as far as he could, to minimise the effect to shift the burden. In this, too, he did not succeed. The Act does not merely shift the evidential burden as it is called. It shifts the legal burden of proof. . . Take a running down case where a plaintiff claims damages for negligent driving by the defendant. If the defendant has not been convicted the legal burden is on the plaintiff throughout. But if the defendant has been convicted of careless driving, the legal burden is shifted. It is for the defendant himself. At the end of the day, if the Judge is left in doubt, the defendant fails because the defendant has not discharged the legal burden which is upon him. The burden is, no doubt, the civil burden. He must show, on the balance of probability that he was not negligent:[39] But he must show it nevertheless. Otherwise, he loses by the very force of the conviction.

Moodley J, then took the view that *Hollington*[40] had been reversed by the enactment of the Civil Evidence Act, 1968. This, it is submitted with respect, is incorrect. Section 11 of the Civil Evidence Act 1968 which Moodley J was referring to as having reversed the rule in *Hollington v Hewthorn*[41] provides as follows:

> (1)   In any civil proceedings the fact that a person has been convicted of an offence by or before any court in the United Kingdom

---

[35] [1943] 2 All ER 35.
[36] Cmnd 3391, 1967.
[37] [1970] 3 A ll ER 230.
[38] [1970] 3 A ll ER 230 at 223 and 224.
[39] See *Public Prosecutor v Yuvaraj* [1970] 2 WLR 226, 231, in the Privy Council quite recently.
[40] [1943] 2 All ER 35.
[41] [1943] 2 All ER 35.

or [of a service offence (anywhere)][42] shall (subject to subsection (3) below) be admissible in evidence for the purpose of proving, where to do so is relevant to any issue in those proceedings, that he committed that offence, whether he was so convicted upon a plea of guilty or otherwise and whether or not he is a party to the civil proceedings; but no conviction other than a subsisting one shall be admissible in evidence by virtue of this section.

(2)   In any civil proceedings in which by virtue of this section a person is proved to have been convicted of an offence by or before any court in the United Kingdom or [of a service offence][43] —

    (a)   he shall be taken to have committed that offence unless the contrary is proved; and

    (b)   without prejudice to the reception of any other admissible evidence for the purpose of identifying the facts on which the conviction was based, the contents of any document which is admissible as evidence of the conviction, and the contents of the information, complaint, indictment or charge-sheet on which the person in question was convicted, shall be admissible in evidence for that purpose.

(3)   Nothing in this section shall prejudice the operation of section 13 of this Act or any other enactment whereby a conviction or a finding of fact in any criminal proceedings is for the purposes of any other proceedings made conclusive evidence of any fact.

The better view is, it is submitted with great respect, as Moodley J himself opined in his judgment that the reversal of *Hollington*[44] by s 11 of the CEA 1968 is only to the extent that Courts in England and Wales are now legally bound 'to admit evidence of a conviction in civil proceedings.' Be that as it may a few points ought to be noted. The first is that CEA 1968 is an English Act that is inapplicable to Zambia. We will show why this is important below and humbly submit how both the High Court and Supreme Court could have better dealt with the issue when it came up for consideration. The second is that despite the vociferous criticism that *Hollington*[45] has received, it has not been overruled entirely by the UK Supreme Court even when opportunities to do so have arisen. This leads us to other points: s 11(1) of the CEA 1968's reference to 'the fact that a person has been convicted of an offence by or before any court in the United Kingdom' restricts the application of s 11(1) of the CEA 1968 to convictions within the United Kingdom. It therefore falls to reason that contrary to the somewhat blanket application Moodley J made

---

[42] Words in s. 11(1) substituted (28.3.2009 for certain purposes and otherwise 31.10.2009) by Armed Forces Act 2006 (c. 52), ss. 378(1), 383(2), Sch. 16 para. 51(2); S.I. 2009/812, art. 3 (with transitional provisions in S.I. 2009/1059); S.I. 2009/1167, art. 4.

[43] Words in s. 11(2) substituted (28.3.2009 for certain purposes and otherwise 31.10.2009) by Armed Forces Act 2006 (c. 52), ss. 378(1), 383(2), Sch. 16 para. 51(3); S.I. 2009/812, art. 3 (with transitional provisions in S.I. 2009/1059); S.I. 2009/1167, art. 4.

[44] [1943] 2 All ER 35.

[45] [1943] 2 All ER 35.

in *Sadi Siwingwa*[46] as regards the wholesale reversal of the rule in *Hollington v Hewthorn*, [47] the rule is still applicable to convictions by foreign courts (such as Zambian courts) and as such, based on the decision in *Union Carbide Corp v Naturin Ltd*,[48] such judgments and the facts on which they are based are inadmissible on account of irrelevance. Section 11 of CEA 1968 has also been held in *Thorpe v Chief Constable of Greater Manchester Police*[49] to be inapplicable to police disciplinary proceedings as regards adjudications of guilt. Nor does s 11(1) of CEA 1968 apply to convictions appealed against as it provides that 'no conviction other than a subsisting one shall be admissible in evidence by virtue of this section.' On the strength of *In Re Raphael (Decd)*,[50] all a court can do is to adjourn civil proceedings pending the determination of the criminal appeals. Recall too that the words 'convicted of an offence' in s 11(1) of CEA 1968 would appear to indicate that the section only permits the admissibility of evidence from previous criminal cases and not civil actions, the latter, it must follow logically, would under the rule in *Hollington v Hewthorn*[51] still remain inadmissible.

Two schools of thought appear to have emerged as regards the effect of s 11 of CEA 1968. The first is that a conviction merely operates to raise a presumption as to the truthfulness of the facts on which it was predicated. In this sense the conviction, as an item of evidence commands no weight to be attached to it. In the alternative, it has been suggested that the conviction is an item of evidence forming part of the evidence in totality against the defendant. The two schools of thought were considered in *Stupple v Royal; Insurance Co Ltd*.[52] Buckley LJ in support of the first school of thought opined as follows:

> It was suggested in argument that so to view s 11 [of CEA 1968] would result in the issues in the criminal proceedings being retried in the civil proceedings, and that this would be contrary to an intention on the part of the legislature to avoid this sort of duplication. I do not myself think that this would be the result in most cases, and I do not discern any such general intention in the section. If the fact of conviction were meant to carry some weight in determining whether the convicted man has successfully discharged the onus under s 11(2) (a) [of CEA 1968] of proving that he did not commit the offence, what weight should it carry? I cannot accept that this should depend on such considerations as, for instance, the status of the court which convicted, or whether the decision was a unanimous or a majority verdict of a jury. I cannot discover any measure of the weight which the unexplored fact of conviction should carry. Although the section has made proof of conviction admissible and has given proof of

---

[46] [1979] ZR 145.

[47] [1943] 2 All ER 35.

[48] [1987] FSR 538; see also *Calyon v Michailaidis* [2009] UKPC 34.

[49] [1989] 1 WLR 665.

[50] [1973] 1 WLR 998.

[51] [1943] 2 All ER 35.

[52] [1970] 3 All ER 230.

conviction a particular statutory effect under s 11(2)(a) [of CEA 1968], it remains, I think, as true today as before the Act that mere proof of conviction proves nothing relevant to the plaintiff's claim, and it clearly cannot be intended to shut out or, I think, to mitigate the effect of any evidence tending to show that the convicted person did not commit the offence. In my judgment, proof of conviction under this section gives rise to the statutory presumption laid down in s 11(2)(a) [of CEA 1968], which, like any other presumption, will give way to evidence establishing the contrary on the balance of probability, without itself affording any evidential weight to be taken into account in determining whether that onus has been discharged.

Lord Denning thought that the alternative school of thought was the better view, holding as follows:[53]

I think that the conviction does not merely shift the burden of proof. It is a weighty piece of evidence of itself. For instance, if a man is convicted of careless driving on the evidence of a witness, but that witness dies before civil action is heard;[54] then the conviction itself tells in the scale in the civil action. It speaks as clearly as the witness should have done had he lived. It does not merely reverse the burden of proof. If that was all it did, the defendant might well give his own evidence negativing want of care and say: 'I have discharged the burden. I have given my evidence and it has not been contradicted.' In answer to the defendant's evidence, the plaintiff can say to him: 'But your evidence is contradicted. It is contradicted by the very fact of your conviction.'

Based on the foregoing, Moodley J, could not see how it could be gainsaid that courts in this jurisdiction could not give effect; or that the courts in Zambia should not give effect to the law as it applies today in the United Kingdom. To buttress his position, he quoted s 10 of the High Court Act[55] which provides as follows:

The jurisdiction vested in the court shall, as regards practice and procedure, be exercised in the manner provided by this Act and the Criminal Procedure Code, or by any other written law, or by such rules, order or direction of the court as may be made under this Act, or the said Code, or such written law, and in default thereof in substantial conformity with the law and practice for the time being observed in England in the High Court of Justice.

As Moodley J saw it, and rightly so, [t]he operative terms were 'in substantial conformity with the law and practice for the time being observed in England in

---

[53] [1970] 3 All ER 230 at 223 and 224.
[54] As in *Hollington v Hewthorn* [1943] 1 KB 587.
[55] Chapter 27 of the Laws of Zambia.

the High Court of Justice.' He made reference to s 9(1) of the High Court Act,[56] which vests the High Court with all the jurisdiction, powers and authorities vested in the High Court of Justice in England. He thus concluded as follows:

> Now the law concerning the admissibility of a conviction as evidence in civil proceedings "for the time being observed in England" is that such evidence is admissible in terms of s 11 of the Civil Evidence Act of 1968. It follows therefore that in Zambia the High Court is bound to follow the "law and practice for the time being observed in England" and admit evidence concerning a conviction in civil proceedings.

As regards pleading, s 11 procedurally, that is to say, the rule of practice concerning the admissibility of convictions, Moodley J turned to Order 18 r 7A, RSC which provides as follows:

> If any action which is to be tried with pleadings any party intends, in reliance on section 11 of the Civil Evidence Act 1968 (convictions as evidence in civil proceedings) to adduce evidence that a person was convicted of an offence by or before a court in the United Kingdom or by a court martial there or elsewhere, he must include in his pleading a statement of his intention with particulars of (a) the conviction and the date thereof, (b) the court or court martial which made the conviction, and (c) the issue in the proceedings to which the conviction is relevant.

He further turned to Order 18/7A/2, RSC which provides as follows:

> If a party desires to rely on s 11 of the Civil Evidence Act 1968, his pleadings must comply with the following requirements, namely: (1) it must expressly state that he intends to adduce evidence at the trial that a person, whether or not a party to the proceedings, was convicted of a criminal offence, whether on plea of guilty or otherwise; and (2) it must give the specified particulars required.

He thus concluded by holding that 'subject to the provisions of RSC Order 18/7A, the plaintiff is entitled to adduce in these civil proceedings evidence concerning the conviction of the defendant's servant.' The foregoing would remain unchallenged until reference was, as noted above, made to it *obiter*, in *Kabwe Transport v Press Transport (1975) Limited*,[57] During the hearing of the appeal two specific issues were raised: (i) whether evidence of previous criminal proceedings could be admissible in civil proceedings; (ii) whether it was proper for a sketch plan produced in, court to contain data which the original sketch plan prepared at the scene of the accident did not contain. It was held as follows: (i) It is of the utmost importance that all details end

---

[56] Chapter 27 of the Laws of Zambia.

[57] [1984] ZR 43 which disapproved *Siwinga v Phiri* [1979] ZR 145 and was followed in *Fanny Muliango and Samson Muliango v Namdou Magasa and Muruja Transport & Farming Company Limited* (1988-1989) ZR 209 (SC).

measurements should be inserted in the sketch plan at the tinge of viewing the scene of the accident; *Per curium:* (ii) where there is a specific Act dealing with a matter of law, such as evidence, there is no default of legislation as envisaged by s 10 of the High Court Act and English practice and procedure does not apply.[58]

Per Gardner JS:

> A further point on a matter of law has been raised by Mr Jearey, that is whether it is improper in the courts of this country for evidence of previous criminal convictions to be produced. Mr Jearey has referred us to the case of *Hollington v F. Hewthorn & Company Limited*,[59] in which it was held that a certificate of a conviction cannot be tendered in evidence in civil proceedings. The ratio decidendi of that case was that the criminal proceedings were not relevant and that they were *"res alios inter acta"*. The case of *Siwingwa v Phiri*,[60] which was decided in this country by a High Court judge resulted in a ruling that the Civil Evidence Act 1968 applied in this country by virtue of [s 10] of the High Court Act,[61] which provides that the practice and procedure at present prevailing in the courts of England and Wales shall apply in this country. Mr Jearey argued that that provision can be called in aid in default of any legislation in Zambia. There is in fact in Zambia an Evidence Act,[62] in which there is no provision for the calling of evidence in criminal proceedings to assist a decision in civil proceedings. This Court has been asked to decide whether the provisions of [s 10] of the High Court Act enables courts in this country to decide that there is an absence of legislation when, in this specific instance, there is a definite act dealing with evidence. We have no hesitation in finding that, where there is a specific act dealing with a matter of law, such as evidence, in this country, there is no default of legislation as envisaged by [s 10] of the High Court Act. The result, therefore, is that there is no provision for convictions in criminal trial to be referred to and taken note of in a civil trial. For this reason, therefore, albeit that our remarks are *obiter dicta*, the decision in the case of *Siwingwa v Phiri*,[63] must incur the disapproval of this court.

It is important to remember that this was an appeal from a judgment of a judge of the High Court. The case arose out of a claim by the plaintiff against the defendant for negligent driving as a result of which damage was caused. Therefore, the *ratio decidendi* - the material facts and the decision which are

---

[58] *Siwingwa v Phiri* [1979] ZR 145 disapproved.
[59] [1943] 2 All ER 35.
[60] [1979] ZR 145.
[61] Chapter 27 of the Laws of Zambia.
[62] Chapter 43 of the Laws of Zambia.
[63] [1979] ZR 145.

binding on the lower courts is unfortunately not what *Kabwe Transport*[64] is known for. The reason for dismissing the appeal which is indeed the *ratio decidendi* of this case is that the Supreme Court essentially agreed with the finding of the Court below that there was not sufficient evidence for the said Court to decide which of the two drivers was to blame for the accident and as a result. Following *Baker v Market Harborough Industrial Co-op Society Limited*,[65] the judge found that he had no alternative but to find that both the plaintiff's driver and the defendant's driver were equally to blame for the accident. He thus awarded fifty percent damages on each side. As regards the criticism of the sketch map, the court quoted with approval *Chanda v The People*,[66] in which it said as follows:

> The "real" evidence (i.e., Skid or other tyre marks, the position of broken glass and dried mud droppings, the Position of the vehicles after the accident, the nature and lotion of damage to the vehicles and so on), will frequently enable the court to resolve conflicts between the evidence of eye witnesses, and should be carefully observed and recorded by the police officer who examines the scene."

The Court took the view that gaps in the sketch map was inconsequential to the eventual result of the appeal. It, however, agreed with Baron DCJ, 'that it is of the utmost importance that all details and measurements should be inserted in a sketch plan at the time of viewing the scene of the accident.' The Court made it clear that the Supreme Court agreed that the burden of proof in negligence cause lay on the plaintiff to and not the defendant to disprove it. The Court also showed that a court on appeal is quite constrained to overturn conclusions drawn by a court at trial because the judge at trial, unlike the court on appeal has 'the advantage of seeing the witnesses and was able to evaluate their evidence.' The foregoing is clearly the *ratio*, it is what forms precedent binding the courts below. It is the part of the case which possesses authority, the reason for the decision, as is the court's implied position that, it is the court and not the expert who makes the decision in the words '[t]he plaintiff's third witness, however, was not an expert in dynamics and his evidence on the facts before him, which could have been misinterpreted, was of no great assistance to the learned trial judge.'

The criticism levelled against the decision in *Sadi Siwingwa v Phiri*,[67] as the Court itself admitted, was made *obiter*. Thus, everything that was said in this respect was by the way, and strictly speaking, of no precedential value. We ought to thus discuss whether the criticism is binding on lower courts. Glanville Williams in discussing the concept of *obiter dicta* says the following:[68]

[64] [1984] ZR 43 which disapproved *Siwinga v Phiri* [1979] ZR 145 and was followed in *Fanny Muliango and Samson Muliango v Namdou Magasa and Muruja Transport & Farming Company Limited* (1988-1989) ZR 209 (SC).

[65] [1953] 1 WLR 1472.

[66] [1975] ZR 131.

[67] [1979] ZR 145.

[68] Williams G, *Learning the Law* (11th edn (Rep) Sweet & Maxwell/Universal Law Publishing Co, 2003) 77.

> In contrast with the *ratio decidendi* is the obiter dictum. The latter is a mere saying by the way, a chance remark, which is not binding upon future courts, though it may be respected according to the reputation of the judge[s], the eminence of the court, and the circumstances in which it came to be pronounced [....] The reason for not regarding an obiter dictum as binding is that it was probably made without a full consideration of the cases on the point, and that, if very broad in its terms, it was probably made without a full consideration of all the consequences that may follow from it; or the judge may not have expressed a concluded opinion.

Based on the foregoing, the Court's pronouncements in *Kabwe Transport*[69] cannot, *strictu sensu* be deemed binding on lower courts. The pronouncements, may, because of the position that the Supreme Court holds in our hierarchy of Courts be respected or said to be of considerable persuasive value. It is also the case that the three judges that presided over this matter namely, Silungwe CJ, Gardner and Muwo, JJS are some of the most revered judges to have ever risen to the Supreme Court bench. On that basis alone, the disapproval of *Sadi Siwinga*[70] by these eminent men appears to have taken on an aura of binding authority even though at law it does not bind lower courts who may distinguish it or simply state that the said pronouncements having been said *obiter* did not overrule *Sadi Simwinga*[71] and or are not binding on them. Even though this may sound like legal heresy to many, there are several reasons in support of this position based on the decisions in the two cases.

The sentiments with which we are concerned were stated in response to a question of law, as the Court put it. The Court took the view that the CEA 1968 could not be called in aid because our Parliament had enacted the Evidence Act.[72] At the same time, the Court held that the position in *Hollington*[73] which held that evidence in criminal proceedings could not be called on to assist a decision in civil proceedings was still good law in Zambia. This, according to the Court, was due to the fact that our Evidence Act[74] had no equivalent provision. There are several immediate problems that arise from this observation by the Court. The first is that the Court was insisting on upholding a portion of a case that was now bad law. How could something that no longer existed thanks to legislative action be a basis for a legal position? With the deepest respect, this quite clearly was an ill-considered stance. More to the point, the fact that *Sadi Siwinga*[75] had not been appealed against appears to have put the Court in the rather unenviable position of only being able to state their disapproval of the case *obiter*.

---

[69] [1984] ZR 43 which disapproved *Siwinga v Phiri* [1979] ZR 145 and was followed in *Fanny Muliango and Samson Muliango v Namdou Magasa and Muruja Transport & Farming Company Limited* (1988-1989) ZR 209 (SC).

[70] [1979] ZR 145.

[71] [1979] ZR 145.

[72] Chapter 43 of the Laws of Zambia.

[73] [1943] 1 KB 587.

[74] Chapter 43 of the Laws of Zambia.

[75] [1979] ZR 145.

The foregoing leads us to another problem. It is what professor Williams[76] has given as a reason for not considering such matters as the *Kabwe Transport*[77] *obiter* pronouncement as binding on the lower courts. The pronouncement, it is clear from a careful reading of the *Kabwe Transport*[78] judgment, 'was made without a full consideration of the cases on the point.' Quite apart from upholding a portion of the *Hollington*[79] decision that had been swept into the dustbin of history by s 11 of CEA 1968, the court failed to, as had done Moodley J in *Sadi Siwinga*,[80] consider the many decisions post *Hollington*.[81] As indicated earlier, the decision in *Hollington*[82] was highly criticised. In *Hunter v Chief Constable of the West Midlands*,[83] Diplock LJ took the view that *Hollington*[84] had been wrongly decided. Obviously the Supreme Court in *Kabwe Transport*[85] did not have the benefit of the 2002 decision in *Hall v Simons*,[86] where Lord Hoffmann observed that the Court of appeal had taken the technicalities of the matter too far in holding, *inter alia* that the conviction in question was *inter alios acta*.[87] The consequence of this unrelenting criticism was the recommendation for alteration of the position in *Hollington*[88] in the Law Reform Committee,[89] and as a result, the enactment of ss 11-13 of the Civil Evidence Act 1968. Thus, when the issue came up once again in the case of *Stupple v Royal Insurance Company Limited*,[90] the EWCA held, regarding the effect of s 11(2)(a) of CEA 1968:[91]

> I think that the conviction does not merely shift the burden of proof. It is a weighty piece of evidence of itself. For instance, if a man is convicted of careless driving on the evidence of a witness, but that witness dies before civil action is heard;[92] then the conviction itself tells in the scale in the civil action. It speaks as clearly as the witness should have done had he lived. It does not merely reverse the burden of proof.

---

[76] Williams G, *Learning the Law* (11th edn (Rep) Sweet & Maxwell/Universal Law Publishing Co, 2003) 77.

[77] [1984] ZR 43.

[78] [1984] ZR 43.

[79] [1943] 2 All ER 35.

[80] [1979] ZR 145.

[81] [1981] 3 All ER 727 at 736c *per* Diplock LJ.

[82] [1943] 2 All ER 35.

[83] [1980] 2 All ER 227.

[84] [1943] 2 All ER 35.

[85] [1984] ZR 43.

[86] [2002] 1 AC 615 at 702.

[87] In full, *res inter alios acta, aliis nec nocet nec prodest* is Latin for 'a thing done between others does not harm or benefit others.'

[88] [1943] 2 All ER 35.

[89] Cmnd 3391, 1967.

[90] [1970] 3 All ER 230.

[91] [1970] 3 All ER 230 at 223 and 224, *per* Lord Denning.

[92] As in *Hollington v Hewthorn* [1943] 1 KB 587.

In disproving *Sadi Siwinga*[93] out of hand, it appears that the Supreme Court, with respect, failed to show why, if the CEA 1968 could not be relied on, which position is correct; the common law decisions such as those discussed above; could not be relied on as the new position of the law, seeing as our Evidence Act, 1967 did not provide for the scenario that had arisen in *Sadi Siwinga*.[94] In this way, the Court could have sidestepped the use of a foreign statute, which in reality the CEA 1968 is; and premised the new position of the law on the considerable persuasive value of the decisions made in England and Wales following the enactment of s 11 of CEA 1968.

The sweeping remarks made *obiter* in *Kabwe Transport*[95] appear 'to [...] probably [have been] made without a full consideration of all the consequences that may follow from' them. As shown earlier, the use of the rule in *Hollington v Hewthorn*[96] in criminal matters has led to the absurd situation as demonstrated in *R v Spinks*[97] that criminal convictions have been ignored in instances where conventional wisdom would have acknowledged their existence and considered their weight and relevance as regards matters before court. With the deepest respect, to follow the *obiter dicta*, as it is suspected many courts may have done in this jurisdiction since the sentiments made in *Kabwe Transport*,[98] leads to injustice and makes a mockery of the judicial process. It may, if we may say so ourselves, be unconstitutional as Article 118(a)(b) and (c) of the Constitution provides as follows: '[i]n exercising judicial authority, the courts shall be guided by the following principles: (a) justice shall be done to all, without discrimination; (b) justice shall not be delayed; (c) justice shall be administered without undue regard to procedural technicalities.' Nothing said *obiter* in the *Kabwe Transport*,[99] it may be gainsaid, *can* be said to be consistent with Article 118(a)(b) and (c) of the Constitution.

We must now turn to the last issue fit for discussion. Section 10 of the High Court Act,[100] which was considered in the dicta in *Kabwe Transport*[101] and five years earlier, in *Sadi Siwinga*[102] provides, as it did at the material time, that the practice and procedure at present prevailing in the courts of England and Wales shall apply in this country. The Supreme Court rejected the argument that, that provision could be called in aid in default of any legislation in Zambia. It reasoned that since there was an Evidence Act,[103] and it had no provision for the calling of evidence in criminal proceedings to assist a decision in civil

---

[93] [1979] ZR 145.

[94] [1979] ZR 145.

[95] [1984] ZR 43.

[96] [1943] 1 KB 587.

[97] [1982] 1 All ER 587.

[98] [1984] ZR 43.

[99] [1984] ZR 43.

[100] Chapter 27 of the Laws of Zambia.

[101] [1984] ZR 43.

[102] [1979] ZR 145.

[103] Chapter 43 of the Laws of Zambia.

proceedings, s 10 of the High Court Act[104] could not, under the circumstances, be invoked by a Zambian court to decide that there is an absence of legislation. *Per Gardner* JS: 'We have no hesitation in finding that, where there is a specific act dealing with a matter of law, such as evidence, in this country, there is no default of legislation as envisaged by s 10 of the High Court Act.'[105] With the deepest respect, the Court appears to have missed the point here. The better view, it is submitted with respect, would have been to hold that in circumstances where there was no specific provision in an equivalent Act as was the situation in *Sadi Siwinga*,[106] there was default as respects that aspect, and s 10 of the High Court Act[107] could be invoked. The principle is used with procedural liberalism. If this be the case, one sees no point why it cannot apply substantively. If this be considered a usurpation of parliamentary authority to legislate, recourse may always be had to common law authorities that are more reflective of current legal trends.

Where the laws in Zambia do not provide for a situation such as in the instant case, the courts in this jurisdiction must, as they have routinely done procedurally speaking, have recourse to and abide by the decisions of the Superior Courts in England. Those decisions now show that the part of *Hollington*[108] held to be good law in *Kabwe Transport*[109] is bad law. For the foregoing reasons, it is submitted with deep respect, that the *obiter dicta* in *Kabwe Transport*[110] that there is no provision for convictions in criminal trial to be referred to and taken note of in a civil trial must be treated as bad law or at the very least, a by the way statement no longer fit for purpose. In any case, being *obiter*, it is not binding on the lower courts. It should be revisited because as Lord Denning has robustly stated in *Hunter v Chief Constable of the West Midlands Police Force*,[111] '[b]eyond doubt, *Hollington v Hewthorn*[112] was wrongly decided. It was done in ignorance of previous authorities. It was done *per incuriam*.'[113]

Before leaving this portion of our discussion, it is worth noting that by saying that '[…] where there is a specific Act dealing with a matter of law, such as evidence, in this country, there is no default of legislation as envisaged by s 10 of the High Court Act'[114] the Court was at the same time saying that where

---

[104] Chapter 27 of the Laws of Zambia.

[105] Chapter 27 of the Laws of Zambia.

[106] [1979] ZR 145.

[107] Chapter 27 of the Laws of Zambia.

[108] [1943] 1 KB 587.

[109] [1984] ZR 43.

[110] [1984] ZR 43.

[111] [1980] 2 All ER 227 at 237a.

[112] [1943] 2 All ER 35.

[113] It must be noted that this view did not receive support in the House of Lords and as such *Hollington v Hewthorn* [1943] 2 All ER 35 was not overruled and to the extent that it has not been reversed by ss 11-13 of CEA and s 74 of PACE, it remains good law in England and Wales. The principle from that case which was approved obiter in *Kabwe Transport* [1984] ZR 43 has also been reversed in s 91 of the Matrimonial causes Act No of 2007 and is thus inapplicable to matrimonial causes.

[114] Chapter 27 of the Laws of Zambia.

there is no specific Act dealing with a matter of law in this country, there is default of legislation as envisaged by s 10 of the High Court Act.[115] Under those circumstances then, the provisions of [s 10] of the High Court Act[116] would be construed to enable courts in this country to decide that there is an absence of legislation for want of specific legislation dealing with the particular issue before court. Logically, as Moodley J had opined in *Sadi Simwinga*,[117] and as said above, the courts in this jurisdiction must, as they have routinely done in the procedural space, have recourse to and abide, where necessity is laid upon them, by the decisions of the Superior Courts in England.

23.3   Admissibility of evidence of previous convictions in civil proceedings

We must unhappily begin with what, before the enactment of s 11 of the CEA 1968 in England and Wales, was the position as held in *Hollington*[118] that evidence that the person in question was convicted of an offence was inadmissible in civil proceedings.

23.3.1   General

Unfortunately, as we have shown above, the position taken in *Hollington*[119] as regards inadmissibility of evidence of a conviction in criminal proceedings in civil proceedings also appears to be the position in Zambia by virtue of the dicta in *Kabwe Transport*,[120] which it has been, and is again submitted with the deepest respect, is a position that needs revisiting. It is hoped that the contemporary positions taken in *Taylor v Taylor*;[121] *Stupple v Royal Insurance* (considered above) and *Hunter v Chief Constable of West Midlands Police*[122] or *J v Oyston*[123] all of which were decided after the enactment of s 11 of the CEA 1968 will one day be used to wean our courts of their rather curious and, with respect, archaic position that a portion of a case, namely *Hollington v Hewthorn*,[124] to the effect 'that there is no provision for convictions in criminal trial to be referred to and taken note of in a civil trial,' which position is now overturned in its jurisdiction by statute, should continue to be good law in this jurisdiction. It is an edifice without contemporary legal legs to stand on.

23.3.2   *Convictions for crimes to be evidence in matrimonial causes*

As noted in the discussion relating to estoppel in the preceding chapter, unlike the general approach taken in other cases, courts are compelled, given

---

[115] Chapter 27 of the Laws of Zambia.
[116] Chapter 27 of the Laws of Zambia.
[117] [1979] ZR 145.
[118] [1943] 2 All ER 35.
[119] [1943] 2 All ER 35.
[120] [1984] ZR 43.
[121] [1970] 2 All ER 609 at 613, *per* Davies LJ.
[122] [1980] 2 All ER 227.
[123] [1999] 1 WLR 694.
[124] [1943] 2 All ER 35.

the very nature of matrimonial causes,[125] to inquire into facts pertaining to the matrimonial cause in question. This apparent modification of principles of estoppel lends itself to the philosophy that while issue estoppel binds the parties, it does not bind the court or estop it from inquiring into the facts in order to do justice. The *dicta* in *Kabwe Transport*[126] predicated on an overturned portion of *Hollington v Hewthorn,*[127] to the effect 'that there is no provision for convictions in criminal trial to be referred to and taken note of in a civil trial,' is inapplicable in matrimonial cause by virtue of s 91 of the Matrimonial Causes Act[128] which provides as follows:

(1)   In any proceedings under this Act, evidence that a party to a marriage has been convicted, whether in Zambia or elsewhere, of a crime is evidence that the party did the acts or things constituting the crime.

(2)   In proceedings under this Act, a certificate of the conviction of a person of a crime by a court in Zambia or a court of any part of the Commonwealth, being a certificate purporting to be signed by the Registrar or other proper officer of that court, is evidence of the fact of the conviction and of any particulars of the crime or of the conviction, including the date on which the crime was committed, and of any sentence of imprisonment imposed, that are included in the certificate.

In *Re B,*[129] care proceedings brought by a local authority in respect of two children were transferred to the High Court for the determination by a judge of the Family Division of the preliminary issue as to whether, in the proceedings so transferred, the respondent father was bound by a finding of sexual abuse in previous proceedings relating to two other children from another union, one of which was his own child. It was held, *inter alia*, as follows:

Although the main rationale behind the doctrine of issue estoppel is the public policy rule that there should be finality in litigation, it is not appropriate to apply the doctrine strictly in cases involving care proceedings. In such cases the court has an inquisitorial rather than adversarial function, having regard to the paramount importance of the welfare of the child, and flexibility is an essential feature.

23.4   Admissibility of evidence of findings of paternity or adultery in civil proceedings

As we have already noted, matrimonial causes are generally treated differently when it comes to the concept of issue estoppel with the court playing

---

[125] See the Matrimonial Causes Act No 20 of 2007.
[126] [1984] ZR 43.
[127] [1943] 2 All ER 35; see s 11 of the CEA 1968.
[128] No 20 of 2007.
[129] [1997] 2 All ER 29; approved in *Re F-K* [2005] EWCA Civ 155.

an inquisitorial rather than an adversarial role. To that end, where, as is provided in s 119[130] of the Childrens Code,[131] a court of competent jurisdiction hears evidence relating to an application for an affiliation order in any of the instances provided for under ss 116, 117 and 118[132] of that Act, it would appear that if a person is adjudged to be the father of a child, as was the case in *Charity Oparaocha v Winfrida Murambiwa*,[133] where the Supreme Court held 'the documents on record' as 'clearly' showing that the deceased father to the children in question 'portrayed himself as the father of the children in the applications for passports and the children [appeared] to have claimed their status as Nigerian through the deceased,' and in the Court's view, found no basis to hold otherwise when 'the deceased duly acknowledged the children as his,' that fact will be admissible in evidence for purposes of proving, where such is a necessary predicate to proving any issue in the civil proceedings in question that he is/was the father of the child in question. If this be the case, the person adjudged to be a father of the child in question will ordinarily be taken to be the father of the child in question unless the contrary can be proved.[134] What this does, as exemplified in *R v Secretary of State for Social Security Ex p W*,[135] is to shift the burden of proof onto the denier of such a finding.

23.5 Defamation matters

The starting point is the fact that that a conviction will be conclusive as against the convict in subsequent defamation proceedings, and as such admissible evidence. For this reason, no person may be found liable for asserting that a person is guilty of an offence of which he was convicted. Further, it is not permissible for the convict to reopen the criminal proceedings, judgment or/ and indeed the conviction on the basis of a libel action even in circumstances where the defendant has knowledge of innocence regarding the plaintiff. In *Loughans v Odhams Press*,[136] the plaintiff brought an action in libel against the defendants following their publication of a statement that appeared to suggest that the plaintiff, despite having been acquitted, had committed murder some 20 years before. The defendants pleaded the defence of justification and

---

[130] Which replaces what was s 6 of the now repealed Affiliation and Maintenance of Children Act, chapter 64 of the Laws of Zambia.

[131] Act No 12 of 2022 which by s 297 repealed the Affiliation and Maintenance of Children Act, chapter 64 of the Laws of Zambia.

[132] Which replace what were ss 3,4 & 5 of the now repealed Affiliation and Maintenance of Children Act, chapter 64 of the Laws of Zambia.

[133] [2004] ZR 141.

[134] However see *Charity Oparaocha v Winfrida Murambiwa* [2004] ZR 141 which quoted s 15 of the Births and Deaths Registration Act Chapter 51 of the Laws of Zambia which states that "no person shall be bound as a father to give notice of the birth of an illegitimate child, and no person shall be registered as the father of such child except on the joint request of the mother and himself and upon his acknowledgement in writing to be the father of the child;' and Bromley PM, *Family Law*, (6th edn[...]) at 259 contends that '[...] entry of a man's name as that of the father on the registration of a child's birth will be prima facie evidence of paternity; if the child is illegitimate, however, this can be done only with his consent unless an affiliation order has been made against him.'

[135] [1999] 2 FLR 604.

[136] [1936] 1 QB 299.

proved that the plaintiff was, on a preponderance of probabilities, that he was indeed guilty. This was at variance with the verdict at the plaintiff's criminal prosecution at which the prosecution failed to prove their case against him beyond reasonable doubt.

23.6   Evidence of previous acquittals and subsequent civil proceedings

As a general rule, acquittals are not deemed as conclusive with respect to someone's innocence. In *R v Doosti*[137] the EWCA held a previous acquittal as being consistent only with the fact that court below was unsure that the prosecution had made out its case. Therefore, they will rarely be admitted into evidence in civil proceedings. In *R v Terry*[138] the prosecutor had alleged a conspiracy basing the charge on a conversation in a car. The court rejected the admissibility of evidence of a voice recognition expert, and the defendant was acquitted on direction. He then said that in the absence of a conviction on that count, the case against him on the other counts fell. The judge found that he was not entitled to lead that he was to be presumed not to have been in the car only because those present in the car were involved in a conspiracy of which he had been acquitted. It was held that the case of *Hay*[139] was inconsistent with *R v Z*,[140] where the test was said to be relevance, not conclusiveness. An acquittal was not conclusive evidence of innocence save in the restricted sense of innocence at law. *R v Z*[141] could not be limited to evidence of similar facts. A direction based on *R v Hay*[142] might be artificial and unsatisfactory. The judge had been correct and no unfairness followed.

It may be added that a fundamental reason for the preceding is the fact that the burden of proof in criminal matters which should be beyond reasonable doubt is different from that in civil matters which is on a preponderance of probabilities. It follows therefore that a defendant's acquittal in a criminal matter is irrelevant in a civil trial even if the civil matter is predicated on the same facts that the previous criminal trial birthing the defendant's acquittal was based on. The defendant's acquittal only signifies the fact that the prosecution failed to prove its case beyond reasonable doubt. It is therefore possible that the defendant may be found liable in a civil matter where the burden of proof is less strict, being on a preponderance of probabilities. To recap, an acquittal in a criminal matter has no effect on later civil proceedings. This is exemplified in *TD Radcliff and Co v National Farmers' Union Mutual Insurance*.[143] A director of the plaintiff company had been acquitted in a criminal case against him for arson of the insured property. Arising from the same facts, the plaintiff sued

---

[137] (1985) 82 Cr App R 181.

[138] [2004] EWCA Crim 3252, [2005] QB 996; summary taken from https://swarb.co.uk/regina-v-terry-cacd-21-dec-2004/ retrieved on 8/01/2021.

[139] CACD 1983.

[140] HL 22-Jun-2000.

[141] HL 22-Jun-2000.

[142] CACD 1983.

[143] [1993] CLY 708.

the defendant but the defendant asserted that it was not liable as the plaintiff, through its director and principal shareholder, was itself liable for the arson relating to the insured property. The court held that evidence of the director's earlier acquittal on a charge of arson arising from the same facts was irrelevant and therefore inadmissible.

The foregoing position has been supported by the European Court of Human Rights which has held in *Ringvold v Norway*[144] that the imposition of civil liabilities subsequent to an acquittal in a criminal trial does not infringe Article 6 of the ECHR. The position taken by the Law Reform Committee in 1967[145] is the antithesis of that taken by the European Court. It is also more in line with the public policy stance that those acquitted of a charge ought not to be 'twice vexed' over the same charge. It ought to follow, *a fortiori*, that they should be immune from further allegations that they committed the offence of which they have been acquitted. Specifically, that '[…] in defamation actions […] proof that [the plaintiff] was acquitted of that offence should be conclusive evidence of his innocence.'[146]

23.7   Non-judicial findings

The broad rationale of the ill-founded decision in *Hollington v F. Hewthorn & Company Limited*,[147] which the Supreme Court endorsed in its dicta in *Kabwe Transport*[148] is to the effect that a later court before which a matter that was heard in earlier court is brought ought not to receive as evidence, an earlier court's opinion relating to the facts. This raises the question whether this common law position extends to facts that were heard and determined in a political party's or basketball club's or indeed any association's disciplinary hearing, that is to say, the facts emanating from such non-judicial proceedings cannot be admitted as evidence in judicial proceedings proper before a competent court. There does not seem to be a legal basis in so far as the common law position is concerned, why the estoppel principle in *Hollington*[149] should not be applied to none-judicial proceedings such as the ones we have alluded to above. The practical implications of going this route, however, would be catastrophic and only lead to more absurdities such as excluding findings by all manner of inquiries or conclusions drawn by an expert. *Hill v Clifford*[150] demonstrates a sensible way around this issue. The plaintiff sought the dissolution of a dentist's partnership on grounds of professional misconduct by his partners. By majority, the EWCA held that '[a]n earlier decision of the [General Medical Council] striking the defendant off the register of dentists was *prima facie* evidence of the truth of the charges against him.'[151]

[144] Application No 34964/97, decision February 11, 2003.
[145] Law Reform Committee: 15th Report (1967) Cmnd. 3391.
[146] Law Reform Committee: 15th Report (1967) Cmnd. 3391, para 41.
[147] [1943] 2 All ER 35.
[148] [1984] ZR 43.
[149] [1943] 2 All ER 35.
[150] [1907] 2 Ch 236.
[151] https://swarb.co.uk/hill-v-clifford-ca-1907/ retrieved on 9/1/2020.

23.8   Evidence of previous acquittals and subsequent criminal proceedings

As already discussed above, the use of the rule in *Hollington v Hewthorn*[152] in criminal matters has led to the absurdity that criminal convictions have been ignored in instances where conventional wisdom would have acknowledged their existence and considered their weight and relevance as regards matters before court. A case in point is *R v Spinks*.[153] The appeal was allowed and the conviction quashed because as Russell J put it, *inter alia*: [154] 'In the judgment of this court the offence with which the appellant was charged and the means of establishing it do not provide any exception to the universal rule which excludes out of court admissions being used to provide evidence against a co-accused, whether indicted jointly or separately.' This absurdity was followed in other cases which included *R v Shepherd*[155] wherein the EWCA quashed a conviction of landlords who had been charged tenant harassment because the court below had permitted the use of a previous conviction for a similar case. According to the EWCA, the previous conviction did not come within the rules of evidence of similar facts and was unlikely to prejudice the court.[156] *R v Hassan*[157] is another case that bucked the trend of following the rule in *Hollington v Hewthorn*.[158] The accused who had been convicted of living off immoral earnings of a prostitute in a previous case had said prior conviction deemed inadmissible in the current case of living off immoral earnings of a prostitute. In *Hui Chi-Ming v The Queen*,[159] the defendant was charged with aiding and abetting a murder. A, carrying a length of water pipe and accompanied by the defendant and four other youths, seized a man and A hit him with the pipe, causing injuries from which he died. No witness saw the defendant hit the man, who was an innocent victim, or play any particular part in the assault. A was charged with murder, with three of the group. Two pleaded guilty to manslaughter and other was acquitted. The jury acquitted A of murder but convicted him of manslaughter. The defendant was later indicted for murder with another youth whose plea of guilty to manslaughter was accepted. The defendant refused an offer by the prosecution to accept a plea of guilty to manslaughter. He was prosecuted for murder as a party to a joint enterprise in which A had murdered the victim. The judge did not admit evidence of A's acquittal of murder and conviction of manslaughter only. The defendant was convicted of murder and sentenced to death. It was held that the conviction or acquittal of the principle was both irrelevant and inadmissible. A conviction for an aider and abettor was not dependent upon a conviction of the principal

---

[152] [1943] 1 KB 587.

[153] [1982] 1 All ER 587.

[154] [1982] 1 All ER 587 at 589b-e, *per* Russell J.

[155] [1980] Crim LR 428.

[156] But see *R v Ollis* [1900] 2 QB 758.

[157] [1970] 1 QB 423.

[158] [1943] 2 All ER 35.

[159] [1992] 1 AC 34; PC 5 Aug 1991; https://swarb.co.uk/hui-chi-ming-v-the-queen-pc-5-aug-1991/ retrieved on 9/1/2020; see *R v Turner* (1832) 1 Mood CC 347 where Lord Lowry held that the verdict of a different court at an earlier trial is irrelevant as it is no more than evidence of that court's opinion.

offender. In general, an acquittal upon a different charge in an earlier trial is irrelevant to the issues before the court in the second trial.

The absurd positions wrought by *Hollington*[160] in such cases as *Spinks*[161] above, led to the partial reversal of *Hollington*[162] in the UK as a result of ss 11-13 of the Civil Evidence Act 1968. All the decisions made in the wake of *Hollington*[163] as discussed above have now been overturned in the UK by s 74 of the Police and Criminal Evidence Act 1984.[164] The said Act, like the CEA, 1968 are of course inapplicable to Zambia. What would be more difficult to accept though, would be a position that the contemporary position that has issued out of the statutory changes in England and Wales as exemplified in common law positions is not of considerable persuasive value to courts in this jurisdiction unless a better way can be demonstrated.

We must conclude by stating that on the weight of English authorities, some of the most important of which we have considered in this chapter, a previous acquittal may be admissible. As was shown in *R v Cooke*,[165] it can be contended successfully that it has a bearing on the issues that the court is called upon to determine, or in some instances, where credibility is in issue. In *R v Deboussi*[166] the defence sought to adduce evidence of the acquittal of the accused on the basis that this went to the issue of credibility which was at the heart of the case before court. This was refused at first instance and the accused convicted. On appeal, the EWCA observed, approving the general rule in *Chi-Ming v The Queen*,[167] and the principle in *R v Cooke*,[168] observed that, where there is a clear inference from the verdict that the jury has rejected the witness's testimony, on the basis that they do not believe him (as opposed to thinking that he might be mistaken) and that witness's credibility is directly in issue in a subsequent trial, evidence of the outcome of the first trial is relevant. In *R v Doosti*,[169] where an acquittal was held to have become relevant because of the way police conducted its case, the court showed that in this particular instance not only had the conviction and acquittal resulted from the same trial, but the said trial was based on a charge and circumstances which were cognate. Finally, as in the initial case, the subsequent matter involved the same prosecution witness. *Per* Ewbank J: '[t]he prosecution is not obliged to bring

---

[160] [1943] 2 All ER 35.

[161] [1982] 1 All ER 587.

[162] [1943] 2 All ER 35.

[163] [1943] 2 All ER 35.

[164] See decisions in *R v Robertson* [1987] 3 All ER 231 at 237c, *per* Lord Lane CJ; *R v Golder* [1960] 1 WLR 1169; *R v Harris* [2001] Crim L R 227; *R v Shanks* [2003] EWCA Crim 689; *R v Dixon* [2001] Crim LR 126; *R v Hayter* [2005] 2 A ll ER 209; [2005] Crim LR 720; *R v Skinner* [1995]; Crim LR 805; *MH v UK* [1997] EHRLR 279; *R v Mattison* [1990] Crim LR 117.

[165] [1987] 84 Cr App R 286.

[166] [2007] EWCA Crim 684.

[167] [1992] 1 AC 34; PC 5 Aug 1991; https://swarb.co.uk/hui-chi-ming-v-the-queen-pc-5-aug-1991/ retrieved on 9/1/2020; see *R v Turner* (1832) 1 Mood CC 347 where Lord Lowry held that the verdict of a different court at an earlier trial is irrelevant as it is no more than evidence of that court's opinion.

[168] [1987] 84 Cr App R 286.

[169] (1985) 82 Cr App R 181.

out a defendant's conviction. If they choose to do so they, in our judgment, incur the risk that in such circumstances as obtained in this case a defendant will be permitted to refer to an acquittal on another charge which may throw doubt on the reliability of the prosecution witness.'[170]

---

[170] However, as shown in *R v Henri* [1990] Crim LR 51, an ambiguity tainted acquittal is inadmissible.

24

PRESUMPTIONS

24.1 Introduction

Central to any trial, whatever the system, is the proving or disproving of facts in issue. As seen elsewhere in this text, such proof of facts relevant to the case before court is generally done through judicial evidence in its several forms including real evidence, documentary evidence and oral testimony. It is also worth remembering that as already discussed in chapters preceding this one, the foregoing devices need not be used where the facts in issue can be proved through the concepts/doctrines of judicial notice, forms of estoppel and/or judgments as evidence. In this way, courts are able to determine facts relevant to the issue with economy of time without venturing on the winding road of employing real evidence, documentary evidence and oral testimony all of which will, at every turn be subject to myriad evidentiary rules of relevance, admissibility, weight to be attached, several case law rules, statutory provisions, hearsay, expert opinion, similar facts evidence, the niceties of the burden of proof and standard of proof among others.

In this chapter we consider presumptions as another one of the aforementioned devices catering to matters not necessitating full proof. 'Presumptions of fact are at best but mere arguments, and are to be judged by the common and received tests of the truth of propositions and the validity of arguments.'[1] In essence, a presumption will function in instances where even with the absence of full proof, certain facts may be presumed to exist. Thus, in situations where a party on whom the burden falls to prove a relevant fact is unable to do so through the conventional evidentiary devices of real evidence, documentary evidence and/or oral testimony, he may, under certain circumstances, be allowed to prove another fact from which proof of the relevant fact will be presumed. Let us illustrate: (i) Where a child is born during the subsistence of a marriage, the child is generally, unless the opposite is proved, presumed to be the legitimate child of the his 'lawfully married parents.' Thus, where it so happens that a claim brough before court is concerned with legitimacy, there will ordinarily be no need to prove by way of blood or DNA tests that the person in question is the legitimate child of his lawfully married parents; and (ii) Where a person has not been seen or heard from for at least seven years by those who ordinarily ought to have seen him or heard from him in the seven-year period preceding

---

[1] *Lawhorn v Carter*, 11 Bush. 7.

the relevant application as regards his status, he is presumed to be dead. It therefore follows that a party who seeks to prove that the person in question is dead need not prove that the said person is actually dead; but simply that during the seven years preceding the relevant matter relating to that person's state of being, no person or persons who could have seen him or heard from such a person has or have heard from or seen him.

Taking the argument further as regards the above illustrations, '[t]here is a basic fact ([the birth during wedlock], the seven-year absence) and a presumed fact (the person's death, the [plaintiff's] legitimacy).'[2] Presumptions are, with a few exceptions, generally rebuttable. It therefore follows that in the rebuttable presumptions that we have alluded to above; it is for the person negatively affected by the presumption to rebut the legitimacy of a child or indeed the death of the person in question and as such; prove same on a balance of probabilities. What is therefore patent is the fact that not only is the deployment of presumptions premised on the concept of risk allocation; but also the concept of burden of proof. As regards the latter point, it is worth pointing out that the complexities that are encountered in discussing the rather inextricable link between the concept of presumptions and that of burden of proof is predicated on the unavoidable fact that there can be and usually are distinctions in the allocation and nature of burden.

24.2   How presumptions arise

The concept of presumptions and how they arise has been the subject of both juristic authorship and judicial decisions. George W. Maxey J[3] illustrates it as follows:

> '[i]t is obvious that what are originally mere inferences may in time become presumptions of law. If, for example, "in the beginning," 100 human beings had been created, and sometime later 51% or more had died, there would then have arisen an inference that all men are mortal. Later in the course of time, with additional data all supporting the same inference, it would become a presumption of law that all men are mortal.'

It has been noted with concern in *Watkins v Prudential Ins Co*[4] that '[c]onsiderable confusion appears in judicial opinions as to the nature of presumptions and their function in the administration of justice.' George W. Maxey J notes though, that '[t]hey are not evidence and should not be substituted for evidence. Presumptions are generally grouped into two major classes: (1) of law; and (2) of fact. The former usually have the force of legal maxims and become rules of law, with definite procedural consequences.' It has been held

---

[2] Uglow S, *Evidence: Text and Materials* 760.

[3] *Watkins v Prudential Ins Co* (1934) 315 PA 497 (US); 173 A. 644 (Pa. 1934).

[4] (1934) 315 PA 497 (US); 173 A. 644 (Pa. 1934); see https://www.courtlistener.com/opinion/4088105/watkins-v-prudential-ins-co/ retrieved on 16/1/2021.

in *Tanner v Hughes and Kincaid*[5] that '[a] legal presumption is the conclusion of the law itself of the existence of one fact from others in proof, and is binding on the jury, prima facie till disproved, or conclusively, just as the law adopts the one or the other as the effect of proof.' Justice Agnew also making reference to other kind of presumption, Justice Agnew, opines that these are merely 'a natural probability,' that is to say, 'an inference of fact of the probability.'

As regards, the foregoing Professor Wigmore[6] observed as follows:

> The distinction between presumptions 'of law' and presumptions 'of fact' is in truth the difference between things that are in reality presumptions and things that are not presumptions at all. A presumption is in its characteristic feature a rule of law laid down by the judge, and attaching to one evidentiary fact certain procedural consequences as to the duty of production of other evidence by the opponent. It is based, in policy, upon the probative strength, as a matter of reasoning and inference, of the evidentiary fact; but the presumption is not the fact itself, nor the inference itself, but the legal consequence attached to it [....] A 'presumption of fact,' in the loose sense, is merely an improper term for the rational potency, or probative value, of the evidentiary fact, regarded as not having this necessary legal consequence. 'They are, in truth, but mere arguments,' and 'depend upon their own natural force and efficacy in generating belief or conviction in the mind.'[7] They have no significance so far as affects the duty of one or the other party to produce evidence, because there is no rule of law attached to them, and the jury may give to them whatever force or weight it thinks best [....] So long as the law attaches no legal consequences in the way of a duty upon the opponent to come forward with contrary evidence, there is no propriety in applying the term 'presumption' to such facts, however great their probative significance. The employment here of the term 'presumption' is due simply to historical usage, by which 'presumption' was originally a term equivalent, in one sense, to 'inference' [....] There is in truth but one kind of presumption; and the term 'presumption of fact' should be discarded as useless and confusing. Nevertheless, it must be kept in mind that the peculiar effect of a presumption 'of law' (that is, the real presumption) is merely to invoke a rule of law compelling the jury to reach the conclusion *in the absence of evidence to the contrary* from the opponent."

Wigmore says further:[8]

> In strictness, there cannot be such a thing as a 'conclusive presumption.' Wherever from one fact another is conclusively presumed, in the sense that the opponent is absolutely precluded from showing by any

---

[5] 53 Pa. 289.

[6] Wigmore on Evidence, 2nd edn, vol 5, section 2491.

[7] Greenleaf, Evidence, section 44.

[8] Wigmore on Evidence, 2nd edn, vol 5, section 2492.

evidence that the second fact does not exist, the rule really provides that, where the first fact is shown to exist, the second fact's existence is wholly immaterial for the purpose of the proponent's case; and to provide this is to make a rule of substantive law, and not a rule apportioning the burden of persuading as to certain propositions or varying the duty of coming forward with evidence. The term has no place in the principles of evidence (although the history of a 'conclusive presumption' often includes a genuine presumption as its earlier stage), and should be discarded.

Professor Thayer[9] in his Storrs Lectures, 1896, before the Law School of Yale University, said:

> By a loose habit of speech, the presumption is occasionally said to be, itself, evidence, and juries are told to put it on the scale and weigh it [....] A presumption itself contributes no evidence, and has no probative quality. It is sometimes said that the presumption will tip the scale when the evidence is balanced. But, in truth, nothing tips the scale but evidence, and a presumption — being a legal rule or a legal conclusion — is not evidence. It may represent and spring from certain evidential facts; and these facts may be put in the scale. But that is not putting in the presumption itself. A presumption may be called 'an instrument of proof,' in the sense that it determines from whom evidence shall come, and it may be called something 'in the nature of evidence,' for the same reason; or it may be called a substitute for evidence, and even 'evidence' — in the sense that it counts at the outset, for evidence enough to make a prima facie case. But the moment these conceptions give way to the perfectly distinct notion of evidence proper — i. e., probative matter, which may be a basis of inference, something capable of being weighed in the scales of reason and compared and estimated with other matter of the probative sort — so that we get to treating the presumption of innocence or any other presumption, as being evidence in this its true sense, then we have wandered into the region of shadows and phantoms.

It has been said in *Ward v Metropolitan Life Ins. Co.*,[10] that:

> The term 'presumption' is used to signify that which may be assumed without proof, or taken for granted [...] It is asserted as a self-evident result of human reason and experience. In its origin, every presumption is one of fact, and not of law. It may, in course of time, become a presumption of law, and even an indisputable one. Its truth may be so universally accepted as to elevate it to the position of a maxim of jurisprudence. Its convenience, as a rule of decision, may be so generally recognised as to place it in the rank of legal fictions. But, so long as it retains its original character as a presumption of fact, it has simply the force of an argument.[11]

---

[9] Professor Thayer in his Storrs Lectures, 1896, before the Law School of Yale University.

[10] 33 A. 902, 904, *per* Judge Baldwin of the Supreme Court of Errors of Connecticut.

[11] 1 Greenleaf, Evidence, section 44; Steph. Dig. Evidence 246.

It has been suggested[12] that '[n]otions, usually implicit rather than expressed, of social and economic policy incline the courts o [favour] one contention by giving it the benefit of a presumption, and correspondingly to handicap the [disfavoured] adversary.' By way of example, it is gainsaid that 'the presumption of ownership from possession [...] tends to [favour] the prior possessor and to make for the stability of estates.'

The question of how presumptions arise arose and was ably discussed in *Watkins v Prudential Ins Co.*[13] The question here was whether or not in an action on an insurance policy, the so-called "presumption against suicide" can take the place of evidence of accidental death in sustaining an averment of death "effected solely through external, violent and accidental means." On June 3, 1924, Norman C. Watkins obtained a policy of insurance from the appellant company in which the latter agreed to pay the insured's wife, Elizabeth M. Watkins, the sum of $20,000 upon receipt of due proof of the death of the insured during the continuance of the policy. It also agreed to pay the beneficiary "the further sum of $20,000 upon receipt of due proof that such death of the insured occurred during the continuance of said policy while there was no default in the payment of premium, as a result, directly and independently of all other causes, of bodily injuries, effected solely through external, violent and accidental means, of which, except in the case of drowning or of internal injuries revealed by an autopsy, there is a visible contusion or wound on the exterior of the body, and that such death occurred within sixty days of the accident, provided, however, that no accidental death benefit shall be payable if such death resulted from suicide — whether sane or insane; from having engaged in aviation or submarine operations [....] On March 19, 1928, Watkins obtained another policy from the same company providing for the payment of sixty monthly instalments of $200 each, upon the happening of the same contingencies as those specified in the first policy.

Plaintiff's statement sets forth that on April 16, 1931, "the insured, while engaged in his own pursuits in his garage, without intention on his part, but accidentally, inhaled carbon monoxide gas, as a result of which, directly and independently of all other causes, he died" on the same day. Defendant contested the suit on the ground that the inhalation was not accidental but intentional. The plaintiff claimed $20,000, being the amount of the accidental death benefit under the first policy, and also three instalments of $200 each due in April, May and June, 1931, under the second policy, making a total claim of $20,600 with interest. The case was tried before a jury and a verdict was returned for the plaintiff in the sum of $22,582.85. Defendant asked for a new trial. Upon refusal, this appeal followed. After considering various authorities and the facts, the Court held as follows:

1.   The operative facts of the insurance policy sued upon were "external, violent and accidental means" causing the insured's death, and any

---

[12] McCormick CT, *Handbook of the Law of Evidence* (Clearly *et al*, 1972).

[13] (1934) 315 PA 497 (US); 173 A. 644 (Pa. 1934); see https://www.courtlistener.com/opinion/4088105/watkins-v-prudential-ins-co/ retrieved on 16/1/2021.

evidence, whether direct or circumstantial, that tends to prove the operative facts, is admissible.

2. If there are in evidence credited facts or circumstances or both from which the jury may infer legitimately that the insured's death resulted from accidental means, plaintiff is entitled to recover. As to the test of submissibility of evidence to a jury.[14]

3. On plaintiff rests the burden of proving all the operative facts by a fair preponderance of the evidence. An even balancing of the evidence on the issue of death by accidental means or death by suicide denotes that plaintiff fails to sustain her burden of proof and the verdict should be for the defendant.

Causes of action are always set forth affirmatively and if they are to prevail, they must be supported either (1) by facts tending to prove directly the cause of action pleaded or (2) by legitimate inferences from circumstances which have met the tests of admissibility. Mere guesses and conjectures cannot be substituted for legal proof.

In the deliberations of the jury there are permissible inferences (sometimes miscalled "presumptions") rooted in general human experience and which have weight when the evidence, respectively, for and against a fact in issue leaves the jury in a "twilight zone" of doubt as to that fact. Such "presumptions may be looked upon as legally recognized phantoms of logic, flitting in the twilight, but disappearing in the sunshine of actual facts":[15]

Here plaintiff pleaded as her cause of action that the insured "without intention on his part, but accidentally, inhaled carbon monoxide gas, as a result of which he died." She proved that the death was caused by external and violent means, and the trial judge then said that this much being proved, "the law presumes that his [the insured's] death was not by suicide but was accidental" and that "this presumption has the same probative force and effect as direct evidence of accidental death." This was error, for, as already pointed out by us, plaintiff's invoking of a mere "presumption against suicide" (a presumption unsupported by relevant evidence) cannot serve, on the pivotal issue, as an adequate substitute for the proof the well-pleaded cause of action requires. *Per* George W. Maxey J:

> Presumptions arise as follows: They are either (1) a procedural expedient, or (2) a rule of proof production based upon the comparative availability of material evidence to the respective parties, or (3) a conclusion firmly based upon the generally known results of wide human experience, or (4) a combination of (1) and (3). The presumption as to the survivorship of husband-and-wife meeting death in a common disaster is a procedural expedient. It is not based upon extensive data arising from human experience. An unexplained absence for seven years raises the presumption of the death of the absentee upon the expiration of the last day of the period. This also is a

---

[14] see *Brown v Schock* 77 Pa. 471, at 479.

[15] *Mackowik v Kansas City*, St. J. C. B. R. Co. (Supreme Court of Missouri), 94 S.W. 256.

procedural expedient — an arbitrary but necessary rule for the solution of problems arising from unexplained absences of human beings. An example of (2) is the rule requiring persons on trial for doing certain acts which are illegal if done without a license to produce evidence that they belong to the class privileged by license.[16] The following are examples of (3): (a) an envelope properly addressed and stamped will reach the addressee if the latter is alive; (b) a child born during the wedlock of its parents is legitimate; (c) a person who drives across a railroad crossing will show due care. If the driver is killed at such a crossing, the presumption that he showed due care shifts the burden of proof to the party who defends the action on the ground of the victim's want of care. (In this example, the presumption of the victim's due care is merely the converse of the statement that the burden of proof rests on the asserter of the victim's negligence.) A presumption that a debt is paid after a lapse of a definite long period of time is both a procedural expedient (1) and a conclusion based on the results of wide human experience (3).

24.3   Different classes of presumptions

As a starting point, '[i]t is necessary to distinguish between different categories of presumptions, although only one of these categories, the rebuttable presumption, is a "true" presumption. The others merely reflect the different senses in which the word is used.'[17] Hereunder, we will discuss the following:

    (i)   Rebuttable presumptions;
    (ii)   Conclusive presumptions;
    (iii)   Presumptions as a method of stating the burden of proof; and
    (iv)   Presumptions as a factual inference.

24.3.1   *Rebuttable presumptions*

Unlike the other 'classes' of presumptions we are going to consider hereunder, the rebuttable presumption is the only one that is deemed to fit the bill of a true presumption.

24.3.1.1   *General*

While not evidence *per se*, the rebuttable presumption is employed as a method of dealing with evidence. Therefore, in the absence of evidence to the contrary, the proof of a basic fact entails that a further fact will be presumed to exist without more. As said already elsewhere in this text, the burden of proving otherwise or rebutting the presumption lies on the party adversely affected by such a presumption. To demonstrate the foregoing, we must again advert to the two examples we gave earlier.

---

[16] See *Com v Wenzel,* 24 Pa. Super. 467.
[17] Uglow S, *Evidence: Text and Materials* 760.

In the current discussion, it follows that once there has been proof, without affirmative evidence from persons who would ordinarily be expected to have heard from or seen the person in question; the burden of proving otherwise or rebutting the presumption of death will be on the party seeking to show that the person in question was alive or is alive at the material time. The foregoing is under the province of the evidential burden.[18] The persuasive burden will thus lie on the party that asserts that the person is dead.

As regards a situation where a party proves that either they or a person in question is legitimate by way of showing that they were born during the subsistence of a legal marriage between their parents; it will fall to the party disputing the legitimacy, the party imputing illegitimacy to satisfy the court on a balance of probabilities that the person in question is indeed illegitimate having born during the subsistence of a legal marriage but at a time when the alleged father was absent or/and was impotent. This is on a balance of probabilities.

24.3.1.2   *Specific presumptions at common law*

Most presumptions have as their origin, the common law but as we shall see below, they may also be codified. Thus, it is important to note the words of Lord Lyndhurst who in *Morris v Davies*[19] who stated that '[t]he presumption of law is not lightly to be repelled. It is not to be broken in upon or shaken by a mere balance of probability. The evidence for the purpose of repelling it must be strong, distinct, satisfactory and conclusive.' To this, Lord Cottenham added in *Piers v Piers*,[20] '[n]o doubt, every case must vary as to how far the evidence may be considered as 'satisfactory and conclusive;' but […] the presumption must prevail unless it is most satisfactorily repelled by the evidence in the cause appearing conclusive to those who have to decide upon that question.'

(i)   *Omnia paesumuntur rite esse acta*[21]

(a)   General

Referred to as the presumption of regularity,[22] *omnia paesumuntur rite esse acta* is an integral part of the law of evidence in England and the Commonwealth. A fuller expression is *omnia praesumuntur rite et solemniter esse acta donec probetur in contrarium*,[23] which may be shortened to *omnia praesumuntur rite et solemniter*

---

[18] In the American legal system (USA), in terms of Federal Rules of Evidence, r. 301, presumptions simply impose an evidential burden; see further *Mobile, J & K.C.R. Co v Turnspeed* 219 U.S. 35, 31 S.Ct. 136, 55 L.Ed. 78 (1910); *Western & Atlantic R. Co. v Henderson* 279 U.S. 639, 49 S.Ct. 445, 73 L.Ed. 884 (1929).

[19] (1837) 5 Cl & Fin at 265.

[20] (1849) 2 HL Cas 331.

[21] In its fuller form, the Latin maxim and presumption of law omnia praesumuntur rite et solemniter esse acta donec probetur in contrarium is loosely translated as '[a]ll things are presumed to have been rightly and duly performed until it is proved to the contrary.'

[22] See generally, Cooper S & Murphy P & Beaumont J, *Cases & Materials on Evidence* (4th edn Oxford University Press, 1994) 86.

[23] See generally, Archbold.

esse acta[24] or *omnia praesumuntur rite esse acta*.[25] Essentially, it means that where an official act is proved to have been done by a public official, it is presumed to have, in the absence of evidence to the contrary, been performed properly. Put another way, '[…] until the contrary is proved, it will be presumed, even in the case of murder, that a man who has acted in a public capacity or situation was duly appointed, and has properly discharged his official duties.'[26] Authorities on the foregoing are legion.[27] The reader is encouraged to consider them accordingly. We will just consider a few below. *Berryman v Wise*,[28] for example, is persuasive authority for the position that a legal practitioner need not prove that he is such by producing his practicing certificate issued by the Law Association of Zambia nor does a policeman, magistrate[29] or indeed a judge need to prove that he/she acted as such by producing documentation such as letter of engagement or in the case of a judge of a superior court, Letters Patent. The burden in the foregoing scenario seems to be an evidential one in that all the other party who may be adversely affected by the presumption needs to prove is that there is evidence to the contrary fit for consideration by the court.

Therefore, where, for example, genuine questions arise as to whether one who purports to be, and holds himself out to be counsel is not a qualified person in terms of the Legal Practitioners Act (LPA),[30] an appropriate question must be raised not only as to his qualification but also the invalidity of his acts within the course of the trial. Recall that s 35 of the LPA provides that '[i]t shall be the duty of the Association to issue, in accordance with the provisions of this Part, certificates in the prescribed form authorising the practitioners named therein to practice as advocates.' Accordingly, s 39(1) of the LPA provides that,

> '[a]ny list purporting to be published by authority of the Association and to contain the names of practitioners who have obtained practicing certificates for the current year before the 1st February in that year shall, until the contrary is proved, be evidence that the persons named therein as practitioners holding such certificates as aforesaid for the current year are practitioners holding such certificates.

---

[24] See generally, Cooper S & Murphy P & Beaumont J, *Cases & Materials on Evidence* 86.

[25] See generally, *Archbold Criminal Pleading, Evidence and Practice*, 1999, para 10-5 at 1130.

[26] *Archbold Criminal Pleading, Evidence and Practice*, 1997, para 10-5 at 1138.

[27] *R v Gordon* (1789) 1 Leach 515, (1789) 1 East PC 315; *R v Jones* (1806) 31 St Tr 251, (1806) 2 Camp 131; *R v Verelst* (1813) 3 Camp 432; *R v Catesby* (1824) 2 B & C 814, (1824) 4 Dow & Ry KB 434, (1824) 2 Dow & Ry MC 278; *R v Rees* (1834) 6 C & P 606; *R v Murphy* (1837) 8 C & P 297; *R v Townsend* (1841) C & Mar 178; *R v Newton* (1843) 1 C & K 469; *R v Manwaring* (1856) 26 LJMC 10, (1856) Dears & B 132, (1856) 7 Cox 192; *R v Cresswell* (1876) 1 QBD 446, (1876) 33 LT 760, (1876) 40 JP 536, (1876) 13 Cox 126; *R v Stewart* (1876) 13 Cox 296; *R v Roberts* (1878) 14 Cox 101, (1878) 42 JP 630, (1878) 38 LT 690, CCR; *Gibbins v Skinner* [1951] 2 K.B. 379, [1951] 1 All E.R. 1049, [1951] 1 T.L.R. 1159, (1951) 115 J.P. 360, 49 L.G.R. 713; *Campbell v Wallsend Shipway and Engineering Co Ltd* [1977] Crim LR 351, DC; *Dillon v R* [1982] AC 484, [1982] 2 WLR 538, [1982] 1 All ER 1017, 74 Cr App R 274, [1982] Crim LR 438, PC; *Gage v Jones* [1983] RTR 508, DC; *Kynaston v Director of Public Prosecutions*, 87 Cr App R 200, DC.

[28] (1791) 4 T.R. 366.

[29] *R v Roberts* (1878) 14 Cox 101 where the rule was applied to a county court judge.

[30] Chapter 33 of the Laws of Zambia.

Section 39(2) of the LPA also provides that,

> [t]he absence from such list of the name of any person shall, until the contrary is proved, be evidence that the person is not qualified to practice as a practitioner under a certificate for the current year, but in the case of any such person an extract from the register kept under the provisions of subsection (2) of section thirty-six certified as correct by the Association shall be evidence of the facts appearing in the extract.

With the increase in the number of legal practitioners in this jurisdiction such questions as these may be asked more and more, and legal practitioners and courts alike may require proof, as the presumption to act as a legal practitioner is a rebuttable one. In fact, s 41(1), provides that 'no person shall be qualified to act as an advocate within Zambia unless his name is on the Roll and he has in force a practicing certificate.' In terms of s 41(2), '[e]very person whose name is on the Roll and who has in force a practicing certificate or who is admitted to practice [under s 41(1)] shall be entitled to practice as an advocate in any court in Zambia other than a local court and shall be deemed to be an officer of the Court.'

According to s 42(1) of the LPA, '[n]o unqualified person shall act or practice, directly or indirectly, as an advocate or as such sue out any summons or other process, or commence, carry on or defend any action, suit or other proceeding in the name of any other person in any court of civil or criminal jurisdiction, or act as an advocate in any cause or matter, civil or criminal, or act as a Notary Public.' By s 42(2), [i]f any person contravenes the provisions of this section, he shall be guilty of an offence against this Act and of contempt of the court in which the action, suit, cause, matter or proceeding in relation to which he so acts is brought or taken and may be punished accordingly, and shall be incapable of maintaining any action for any costs in respect of anything done by him in the course of so acting, and shall, in addition to any other penalty or forfeiture and any disability to which he may be subject, be liable to a fine not exceeding two thousand penalty units or a period of imprisonment not exceeding six months. It is an offence, in terms of s 43 for an unqualified person to wilfully pretend to be, or takes or uses any name, title, addition or description implying that he is qualified or recognised by law as qualified to act as an advocate, or a Notary Public with the penalty of being liable on conviction to a fine not exceeding three thousand penalty units or to a term of imprisonment not exceeding two years, or to both.

It would appear from the foregoing that if a person contravened the sections here discussed, the prosecution may, in a trial against such a person, rely on this to establish relevant elements of the offence as stipulated in ss 42 and 43 of the LPA. This, it may be contended is because not only do the two sections state the offence, they also provide that once the qualification to practice is rebutted, a trial must follow, and if the accused is convicted, he must suffer the penalty as stipulated in ss 42 and 43 of the LPA.

The common law position as established in *R v Dillon*[31] appears to have taken a different approach from that in ss 42 and 43 of the LPA even though, it must be mentioned, the case involved the actions of a police officer who was charged with permitting prisoners who were lawfully detained to escape. On the question whether the prosecution could rely on the presumption of lawful detention/custody to avoid adducing evidence regarding the lawfulness of the detention, Lord Frazer opined as follows:[32]

> Their Lordships are of opinion that it was essential for the Crown to establish that the omission to do so was fatal to the conviction of the appellant [...] The lawfulness of the detention was a necessary precondition for the offence of permitting escape, and it is well established that the courts will not presume the existence of facts which are central to an offence [....] If there were to be a presumption that any person de facto in custody was there lawfully, the scales would be tipped in favour of the fait accompli in a way that might constitute a serious threat to liberty. It has to be remembered that, in every case where a police officer commits the offence of negligently permitting a prisoner to escape from lawful custody, the prisoner himself commits an offence by escaping, and it would be contrary to fundamental principles of law that the onus should be on a prisoner to rebut a presumption that he was being lawfully detained, which he could only do by the (notoriously difficult) process of proving a negative.

(b)   Business transactions

In instances where it can be shown to the satisfaction of the court, that is to say, proved that "necessary business transactions" have, as asserted, been made, the presumption, unless the contrary can be proved, will be that the transactions in question were carried out in the manner and pecking order, as the case may be, mandated.[33]

(c)   Mechanical contrivances

Where it has been shown to the satisfaction of the court that a mechanical contrivance or device is ordinarily in "good working order", it will be assumed/ presumed, until the contrary is proved, that the said contraption was in good working order at the relevant or material time in question.[34]

---

[31] [1982] 1 All ER 1017 at 1019 at 1019h-1020b, *per* Lord Fraser.
[32] [1982] 1 All ER 1017 at 1019 at 1019h-1020b, *per* Lord Fraser.
[33] *Eaglehill Ltd v J Needham (Builders) Ltd* [1973] AC 992, HL.
[34] See *Tingle Jacobs & Co v Kennedy* [1964] 1 WLR 638, CA.

(ii)   Presumption of marriage

The presumption of marriage may best be discussed by adverting to three specific presumptions relating to the subject of marriage. They are:

(a)   presumption of crucial validity;

(b)   presumption of formal validity; and

(c)   presumption of marriage from cohabitation/common law marriage.

It is important to note from the outset that while the first two may be considered to be presumptions in a proper case, the third has no place in Zambian legal jurisprudence. We will consider the specific presumptions in turn.

(a)   Presumption of crucial validity

The starting point should may be with the negative which is that in terms of s 32(1) of the Marriage Act[35] no marriage in Zambia shall be valid- (a) which if solemnised in England would, under the law relating to prohibited degrees of marriage for the time being in force in England, be null and void on the ground of kindred or affinity; (b) where either of the parties thereto at the time of the celebration of such marriage is married by African customary law to any person other than the person with whom such marriage is had.

It is to be noted that in terms of s 33(1),[36] a marriage between persons either of whom is under the age of sixteen years shall be void. There is a proviso to the foregoing which is that same shall not apply when a judge of the High Court has, on application being made, and on being satisfied that in the particular circumstances of the case it is not contrary to the public interest, given his consent to the marriage.[37]

The foregoing notwithstanding, it is to be remembered that given the common law/customary law dichotomy that this jurisdiction has to grapple with, s 34[38] provides that any person who is married under the Act or whose marriage is declared by the Act to be valid, shall be incapable during the continuance of such marriage of contracting a valid marriage under any African customary law, but, save as aforesaid, nothing in this Act contained shall affect the validity of any marriage contracted under or in accordance with any African customary law, or in any manner apply to marriages so contracted.[39]

It is therefore quite clear from the foregoing that a marriage will be void for incapacity due to any of the following reasons:

---

[35] Chapter 50 of the Laws of Zambia.

[36] Chapter 50 of the Laws of Zambia.

[37] An exemption of existing marriages is provided for under s 33(2), where it is provided '[…] that nothing in this section shall affect any marriage already solemnised or contracted before the 20th May, 1949 (No 12 of 1949 as amended by No 6 of 1955).

[38] Chapter 50 of the Laws of Zambia.

[39] No 48 of 1963.

(i)   Want of age (s 33(1)).[40]

(ii) Close consanguinity (s 32(1)(a));[41] or/and

(iii) Being already married whether customarily or under civil law (s 32(1)).[42]

(iv) Flouting any of the statutory requirements under s 32(2).[43]

Having said that, where it can be shown that a marriage ceremony took place, a presumption that the parties to the marriage had capacity to marry is raised.[44] Further, in terms of s 31,[45]

> Every certificate of marriage which shall have been filed in the office of the Registrar-General, or a copy thereof purporting to be signed and certified as a true copy by the Registrar-General for the time being, and every entry in a Marriage Register Book or copy thereof certified as aforesaid, shall be admissible as evidence of the marriage to which it relates in any court of justice or before any person now or hereafter having by law or consent of parties authority to hear, receive and examine evidence.

The legal burden to rebut the said presumption, predicated on the ordinary civil standard of balance of probabilities, is on the party seeking to have the marriage in question invalidated. In *Tweney v Tweney*,[46] the wife petitioned for dissolution of a second marriage, contracted in 1932, on the ground of desertion. Her husband by the previous marriage, contracted in 1920, had disappeared six months after that marriage and nothing had been heard of him again notwithstanding exhaustive inquiries. The question for determination was whether, in the absence of evidence that the previous husband was dead at the date of the second marriage, the court had jurisdiction to dissolve it as a valid marriage. It was held as follows: (i) The second marriage, being unexceptionable in form and duly consummated remained a valid marriage until evidence was adduced that it was in fact a nullity; (ii) the court ought to regard the petitioner as a married woman by that marriage until some evidence was given which led the court to doubt that fact; and (iii) desertion for three years and upwards before the presentation of the petition having been established, the petitioner was entitled to a decree.[47]

---

[40] Chapter 50 of the Laws of Zambia.

[41] Chapter 50 of the Laws of Zambia.

[42] Chapter 50 of the Laws of Zambia.

[43] Chapter 50 of the Laws of Zambia.

[44] *Spivack v Spivack* [1930] 99 LJP 52, though the case was said to refer to the validity of marriage and not capacity in *Re Peete v Crompton* [1952] 2 All ER 599.

[45] Chapter 50 of the Laws of Zambia.

[46] [1946] 1 All ER 564.

[47] *Parkinson v Parkinson* [1939] 3 All ER 108, [1939] P 346; Digest Supp; *Spurgeon v Spurgeon* (1930), 46 TLR 396, Digest Supp.

Re Peete v Crompton[48] was a case that concerned a woman who claimed to be the testator's widow. Evidence before court showed that sometime in 1919, she had undergone a marriage ceremony with the said testator. Additional evidence however showed that preceding her 'marriage' to the testator, she had married somebody else earlier in 1916. This latter evidence led to the presumption that she had validly been married in 1916 thus rebutting the presumption of a valid marriage in 1919. The woman's testimony failed to discharge the proper standard of proof regarding the question of capacity to marry.[49] 'Roxburgh J thus refused an application under the UK Inheritance (Family Provision) Act, 1938, on the ground that the applicant had failed to establish the death of her husband, her only evidence of that death being hearsay.'[50]

Two courses are open to a married spouse whose mate has disappeared, and who desires to marry again. The First is that he/she may proceed under s 24 of the Matrimonial Causes Act,[51] to petition for a decree of presumption of death and dissolution of marriage.[52] S 24 provides as follows:[53]

(1)   Any married person who alleges that reasonable grounds exist for supporting that the other party to the marriage is dead may present a petition to the Court to have it presumed that the other party is dead and to have the marriage dissolved, and the court, if satisfied that such reasonable grounds exist, may make a decree of presumption of death and dissolution of the marriage.

(2)   In such proceedings the fact that for a period of seven years or upwards the other party to the marriage has been continually absent from the petitioner, and the petitioner has no reason to believe that the party has been living within that time, shall be evidence that he or she is dead until the contrary is proved.

---

[48] [1952] 2 All ER 599.

[49] Cited with approval in *Re Watkins, Watkins v Watkins* ([1953] 2 All ER 1113 at p 1114) and *Chard v Chard* [1955] 3 All ER 721 at 724; [1956] P 259 at 266-267), which also related to capacity to marry.

[50] *Sammy-Joe v G P O Mount Pleasant Office and another* [1966] 3 All ER 924.

[51] Act No 20 of 2007 which must be read together with s 11 of the High Court Act and Rule 53 of the Non-Contentious Probate Rules 1987, SI No 2024; As to application to swear to the death of someone, see Order X R 3, HCR; As to requirement to prove the petitioner having been married to the person in question, see *Janet Nancy Mbewe v Andrew Mbewe* (2013/HPD158); As to application relating to production of Certificate of Marriage as evidence in such proceedings, see Rule 122(1) of the Matrimonial Causes Rules 1973.

[52] As to Presumption of Death Generally, see Halsbury, Hailsham Edn Vol 13 pp 629-634, para 701; and for Cases, see Digest, Vol 22, pp 165–170, Nos 1408–1460; and for Presumption of Death in Divorce Proceedings, see the Matrimonial Causes Act, 2007, s 24, Halsbury's Statutes Vol 30, p 340.

[53] However, as Sachs J has opined in *Chard v Chard* [1955] 3 All ER 721 at 728, 'in matters where no statute lays down an applicable rule, the issue whether a person is, or is not, to be presumed dead is, generally speaking, one of fact and not subject to a presumption of law.'

>   (3)   Part VII shall apply to a decree under this section as it applies to
>   a decree of dissolution of marriage.[54]

The statutory position is similar to the formulation elucidated by Sachs J in *Chard v Chard*.[55] In 1909 the husband married RML. RML was then eighteen years of age and an orphan with no known parents or other relations. Between October, 1909 and 1915, the husband was sentenced on six separate occasions to terms of imprisonment. In 1915 he saw RML on two occasions. In 1917 RML was known to be in Yorkshire. From October, 1917, until 23 April 1933, the husband was almost continuously in prison and did not hear of or from RML. On 15 May 1933, the husband went through a ceremony of marriage with the respondent. In 1954 inquiries were made concerning RML but no one was found who was likely to have heard from her and there was no trace of any death certificate concerning her. There was no evidence that in 1917 she was otherwise than in normal health with a normal expectation of life. The husband in his petition and the respondent in her answer prayed for a decree of nullity of their marriage on the ground that at the time of the ceremony in 1933, RML was still alive and that the husband's marriage with her was still subsisting. It was held as follows: (i) once the husband was shown to have contracted the marriage in 1909 the court was put on inquiry as to the validity of the marriage in 1933, and it was for the husband or the respondent to prove facts from which a cessation of the marriage in 1909 could be inferred;[56] in the present case there was no presumption of law either of the continuance of life of RML or of her having died, and since the correct inference from the known facts was that RML was alive on 15 May 1933, the marriage on that date

---

[54] In *Parkinson v Parkinson* [1939] 3 All ER 108, the petitioner and respondent were married in 1919, and in 1922 the respondent left her husband, saying that she was going to Blackpool and did not intend to return to him. Shortly afterwards the parties entered into a deed of separation in the usual form. Thereafter the petitioner once met his wife by accident during 1928, and had then a few minutes, casual conversation with her, but, from the time of that meeting, he neither saw her, nor had any news of her, although he made inquiries in Blackpool, and in other places where it was possible that she might be living. Advertisements as to her whereabouts were inserted in the Daily Telegraph and News Chronicle, but without result. The petitioner filed this petition asking for a decree of presumption of his wife's death and for dissolution of marriage. Affidavits were filed by two relations of the parties stating that they had not seen the respondent for over 8 years: — It was held as follows: (i) the fact that the respondent was continually absent from the petitioner under a deed of separation did not debar the petitioner from claiming the advantage of the Matrimonial Causes Act 1937, s 8(2). (ii) it was for the petitioner to satisfy the court that he had no reason to believe that his wife was living within the last 7 years. In this case the matter was one of pure speculation, and the court was entitled to hold that there was in fact no reason for the petitioner to believe that his wife was living within that time. (iii) the petitioner had brought himself within the subsection. There was no evidence that the respondent was alive, and the court on that evidence was satisfied that reasonable ground existed for supposing that she was dead. The petitioner was, therefore, entitled to a decree of presumption of death and a decree nisi; Editor's notes: This is the first case to be reported on the construction of the Matrimonial Causes Act 1937, s 8(2), which provides for the dissolution of 108 marriage on the ground of the presumed death of a spouse. The presumption of death may be made where the petitioner has no reason to believe that the other party has been living within a period of 7 years or upwards. The similar cases dealing with charges of bigamy are considered, the point mainly discussed being the burden of proof under the subsection; As to Decree of Presumption of Death and Dissolution of Marriage, see Halsbury (Hailsham Edn), Supp, Divorce, para 987A; and for the subsection, see Halsbury's Complete Statutes of England, Vol 30, p 340.

[55] [1955] 3 All ER 721.

[56] Dictum of Pilcher J in *Tweney v Tweney* [1946] 1 All ER at 565 applied.

was null; accordingly there would be a decree of nullity both on the petition and on the prayer in the respondent's answer, notwithstanding, in the case of the husband, his bigamy.[57] (ii) although where due inquiries had been made for an individual and he had not been traced as a result of them there was a presumption of law that, if he had not been heard of during seven years by persons who would have been likely to have heard of him if he had been alive, he had died at sometime within the seven years, yet that presumption did not apply in the present case as the husband would not have been likely to have heard of his first wife during the period between 1917 and his purported marriage in 1933.[58] Sachs J described the formulation for the common law presumption of death in the following terms:[59]

> By virtue of a long sequence of judicial statements, which either assert or assume such a rule, it appears accepted that there is a convenient presumption of law applicable to certain cases of seven years' absence where no statute applies. That presumption in its modern shape takes effect (without examining its terms too exactly) substantially as follows. Where as regards "A B" there is no acceptable affirmative evidence that he was alive at some time during a continuous period of seven years or more, then if it can be proved first, that there are persons who would be likely to have heard of him over that period, secondly, that those persons have not heard of him, and thirdly, that all due inquiries have been made appropriate to the circumstances, "A B" will be presumed to have died at sometime within that period. (Such a presumption would, of course, be one of law and could not be one of fact, because there can hardly be a logical inference from any particular set of facts that a man had not died within two thousand five hundred and fifty-five days but had died in two thousand five hundred and sixty.)

The second is for her to make 'all possible inquiries[60] [and thereafter] remarry, since the court, in any future proceedings, will regard a marriage contracted

---

[57] *Miles v Chilton (falsely calling herself Miles)* (1849) (1 Rob Eccl 684) applied.

[58] Principle stated by Lord Blackburn in *Prudential Assurance Co v Edmonds* (1877) (2 App Cas at p 509) applied; *Re Phené's Trusts* (1870) (5 Ch App 139) and *Chipchase v Chipchase* [1939] 3 All ER 895 explained; Editor's notes: As to there being no presumption of law in favour of the continuance of life, see 13 Halsbury's Laws (2nd Edn) 629, para 701; and for cases on the subject, see 22 Digest (Repl) 157–159, 1430–1443.

[59] [1955] 3 All ER 721 at 722; As to those likely to have seen the person in question see *Watson v England* (1844) 14 Sim 29; *Bowden v Henderson* (1854) 2 Sm and G 360; As regards the issue of the person in question not having been heard from, see *Prudential Assurance Co v Edmonds* (1877) 2 App Cas 487 at 512 but non-communication with the petitioner is immaterial: *Parkinson v Parkinson* [1939] 3 All ER 108; As regards what amounts to making due inquiries, see *Bullock v Bullock* (1960) 2 All ER 309; *Doe d. France v Andrews* (1850) 15 QB 756; As to time of death, see *Re Phene's Trusts* (1870) 2 App Cas 487.

[60] The requirement to make all possible inquiries has been shown to be doubly important in *Bradshaw v Bradshaw* [1939] P 391. The court upon the facts declined to accede to the plea that her husband be presumed dead by 1940 – where on the one hand, she had not then heard from him for 19 years, but on the other hand, had not made any and all possible inquiries during the period in question; see also *Prudential Assurance Co v Edmonds* [1877] 2 AC 487.

with proper formality as binding in the absence of evidence to the contrary.'[61]
It has been shown in *Spurgeon v Spurgeon*[62] as cited by Pilcher J in *Tweney v Tweney*,[63] that where '[…] the marriage between the petitioner and respondent was attended by all proper formalities, [t]he court ought to regard the petitioner, who comes before it and gives evidence of a validly contracted marriage, as a married woman, until some evidence is given which leads the court to doubt that fact.[64]

In *Monckton v Tarr*,[65] W1 married H1 in 1882, H1 then deserted W1 in 1887. W1 married H2 in 1895 on the strength of the fact that there was no evidence that H1 was alive at the time. H2 however left W1 and married W2 in 1913 knowing full well that W1 was still alive. Following H2's death, W2 made a claim for compensation as H2's widow. While the plaintiff can initially rely on the presumption in favour of the 1913 ceremony, this is rebutted by proof of the 1895 marriage and that W1 was still alive in 1913. This puts the burden of proof back onto the plaintiff who can only succeed by showing that the 1895 ceremony was a nullity and therefore that H2 was free to marry in 1913. In 1895 the first husband had been absent for seven years without contacting his wife and was thus presumed dead. W2 could only succeed by showing some evidence that H1 was alive at that time and this she was unable to do.

Incapacity to marry may render itself to the offence of bigamy[66] under s 38 of the Marriage Act[67] and s 166 of the Penal Code.[68] The former provision is framed as follows:

> Any person who-
> (a) contracts a marriage under this Act, being at the time married in accordance with African customary law to any person other than the person with whom such marriage is contracted;
> (b) having contracted a marriage under this Act, during the continuance of such marriage contracts a marriage in accordance with African customary law;
> shall be guilty of an offence and liable on conviction to imprisonment for a period not exceeding five years.
> Provided that this section shall not extend to any person who contracts a marriage during the life of a former husband or wife, if such husband or wife, at the time of the subsequent marriage, shall have been continually absent from such person for the space of seven

---

[61] Editor's notes to the decision in *Tweney v Tweney* [1946] 1 All ER 564; Dissolution of such a second marriage was granted by Bateson J in *Spurgeon v Spurgeon* [1930] 46 TLR 396.

[62] [1930] 46 TLR 396.

[63] [1946] 1 All ER 564 *per* Bateson J.

[64] *Parkinson v Parkinson* [1939] 3 All ER 108, [1939] P 346; Digest Supp.

[65] (1930) 23 B.W.C.C. 504; facts are presented partly as summarised in Uglow, *Evidence* 770.

[66] *The People v Chitambala* [1969] ZR 142 (HC); See the rather interesting case of *The People v Roxburgh* [1972] ZR 31 (HC) made even more amusing by Doyle CJ's caustic excoriation of the Magistrate Court's judgment in convicting the appellant whose conviction was ultimately quashed.

[67] Chapter 50 of the Laws of Zambia.

[68] Chapter 87 of the Laws of Zambia.

years, and shall not have been heard of by such person as being alive within that time.[69]

One school of thought which was advanced in *Fenias Mafemba v Ester Sitali*[70] which we discuss later in this text, is that since s 38 of the Marriage Act[71] does not prohibit the contracting of common law marriage whilst being married under the Act or under African customary, it follows that common law marriage is not recognised in Zambia; and that in terms of s 10 of the High Court Act,[72] the Marriage Act[73] has no *lacuna* in respect of how a marriage can be contracted but merely restricts the mode of contracting marriage to two namely, under the Marriage Act[74] or under African customary law. It was pointed out that there was no room to resort to the law and practice of England when the Marriage Act[75] sufficiently covers matrimonial law in Zambia in respect of how marriages are contracted. This position was not rejected in *Fenias Mafemba v Ester Sitali*[76] even though the arguments were considered irrelevant given the facts and circumstances of the case.

Section 166 of the Penal Code[77] provides as follows:

> Any person who, having a husband or wife living, goes through a ceremony of marriage which is void by reason of its taking place during the life of such husband or wife, is guilty of a felony and is liable to imprisonment for five years:
>
> Provided that this section shall not extend to any person whose marriage with such husband or wife has been declared void by a court of competent jurisdiction, nor to any person who contracts a marriage during the life of a former husband or wife, if such husband or wife, at the time of the subsequent marriage, shall have been continually absent from such person for the space of seven years, and shall not have been heard of by such person as being alive within that time.

The provisos common to s 38 of the Marriage Act[78] and s 166 of the Penal Code[79] may be read together with s 24 of the Matrimonial Causes Act[80] which provides for the law and procedure relating to the presumption of death of a spouse if he/she has not been seen or heard from by those who ordinarily should have

---

[69] No 48 of 1963.

[70] (SCZ Judgment No 24 of 2007).

[71] Chapter 50 of the laws of Zambia.

[72] Chapter 27 of the laws of Zambia.

[73] Chapter 50 of the laws of Zambia.

[74] Chapter 50 of the laws of Zambia.

[75] Chapter 50 of the laws of Zambia.

[76] (SCZ Judgment No 24 of 2007).

[77] Chapter 87 of the Laws of Zambia.

[78] Chapter 50 of the laws of Zambia.

[79] Chapter 87 of the Laws of Zambia.

[80] No 20 of 2007.

seen or heard from him/her. It has been held in *Re v Liddler Date*[81] that when a question arises regarding validity of a second marriage, the court ought to consider whether the first husband is to be presumed dead. To do so, the court can take into consideration the whole period down to the date of hearing and not limited to the facts as they existed at the date of second marriage.

The interplay between the two provisions was considered in *The People v Paul Nkhoma.*[82] The accused, who was charged with bigamy, had gone through a ceremony of marriage under the Marriage Act[83] when his first wife, whom he had married under customary law, was still living. In his defence he submitted that he had terminated his first customary marriage by a letter and he believed that the marriage had ended. The first marriage had not been validly dissolved. It was held as follows: (i) bigamy is committed if a person whose spouse is still living goes through a ceremony of marriage with another which, but for the earlier subsisting marriage, would have resulted in a valid marriage; (ii) a customary marriage is a valid marriage for the purposes of considering a second "Marriage Act" marriage as bigamous; and (iii) Mistake of fact is a defence to bigamy if, at the time of the second marriage, the offending spouse reasonably believed that his earlier marriage had been dissolved.[84]

The importance of discharging the burden of proof to rebut the presumption of validity is demonstrated in the case of *R v Willshire.*[85] The accused person was charged with bigamy for marrying B when in his lifetime marriage with A in 1864. The evidence shows that the accused had undergone four consecutive ceremonies with A, B, C, D. The accused person married D in his lifetime with C and was charge with bigamy. He was convicted. The EWCA quashed the conviction stating that the prosecution had failed to discharge the validity of the 1879 marriage i.e., they had failed to give rise to the presumption of validity in the 1879 marriage.

(b)   Presumption of formal validity

The presumption of formal validity is akin to the concept of *Omnia paesumuntur rite esse acta* or simply the presumption of rightness of official acts done in one's official capacity. To illustrate, s 32(2) of the Marriage Act[86] provides that a marriage shall be null and void if both parties knowingly and wilfully acquiesce in its solemnisation-

(a)   in any place other than the office of a Registrar or a licensed place of worship or a place authorised by the special licence; or

(b)   under a false name or names; or

---

[81] (1912) S 7 SJ 3.

[82] [1978] ZR 4 (HC) a decision at odds with that by Care J in *The People v Katongo* [1974] ZR 290 (HC) its treatment of customary marriage as a valid marriage.

[83] Chapter 50 of the Laws of Zambia.

[84] *Per* curium.

[85] (1881) 6QBD 366.

[86] Chapter 50 of the Laws of Zambia.

      (c)   without the Registrar's certificate of notice or special licence having been duly issued; or

      (d)   by a person not being a licensed minister of some religious denomination or body or a Registrar.[87]

According to the presumption of formality, the above statutory requirements notwithstanding, the burden of proof as regards the failure to observe such statutory requirements in s 32(2) [88] is on the person seeking to show that the marriage is invalid. There is no legal burden placed on two people that intend to get married and who go through a marriage ceremony to show that they complied with the requirements of s 32(2).[89] The legal proof is cast on the other party, as already mentioned, to prove otherwise. This is because the presumption is that the marriage in question is formally valid. The celebrated case of *Piers v Piers*[90] demonstrates the foregoing. In 1815 Sir John Piers went through a marriage ceremony in a foreign jurisdiction. It was later contended that the marriage was illegal as the ceremony had taken place at a private residence and no special licence for such a marriage had been obtained. The bishop, who had the responsibility of issuing such a licence, deposed that he had not granted any special licence. Upon returning home a second marriage was celebrated by the couple. It was held that the marriage that had taken place in 1815 was valid. Once there was proof the marriage ceremony, the marriage was, barring proof to the contrary, presumed to be valid.

As Lord Cottenham[91] quoting Lord Lyndhurst in *Morris v Davies*,[92] has opined, '[t]he presumption of law is not lightly to be repelled, and the evidence for repelling it must be strong, distinct, satisfactory and conclusive.'

The principle in *Piers v Piers*[93] is applicable to foreign marriage ceremonies as demonstrated in *Mahadervan v Mahadervan*.[94] On 16 July 1951, the husband and the wife, who were both born and domiciled in Malaya, went through a civil ceremony of marriage. On the evidence of the husband and the wife this took place at the wife's house in Ceylon before a registrar, who signed the marriage certificate subsequently in his office. The Ceylon marriage ordinance required the ceremony to take place at the registrar's office, although it could take place elsewhere by special licence. There was no evidence that a special licence had been granted in the present case. The Ceylon marriage ordinance also required the registrar to address the parties emphasising the monogamous nature of the union. There was no evidence that in the present case the registrar had fulfilled this requirement. However, the entry in the marriage register and the marriage certificate purported to show that the ceremony had been performed at the registrar's office. After the ceremony the parties returned to Malaya where

---

[87] As amended by No 11 of 1937, No 48 of 1963 and GN No 316 of 1964.

[88] Chapter 50 of the Laws of Zambia.

[89] Chapter 50 of the Laws of Zambia.

[90] (1849) 2 HL Cas 331.

[91] *Piers v Piers* ((1849) 2 HL Cas at p 362.

[92] (1837) 5 Cl & Fin 163.

[93] (1849) 2 HL Cas 331.

[94] [1964] P. 233; see further, *Chief Adjudication Officer v Bath* [2000] 1 FLR 8.

they lived together until February, 1952, when the husband went to Bombay; and in 1953 he came to England, where he had since resided. Between 1952 and 1954 the husband wrote affectionate letters to the wife signing himself "Your loving husband", and he signed a letter to his mother-in-law "Your affectionate son-in-law". In 1958 the husband went through a ceremony of marriage in England. In 1960 the wife came to England where she applied for a matrimonial order before a magistrate's court on her complaint that the husband had committed adultery. The husband contended that the ceremony in July, 1951, had not constituted a valid marriage because the proper formalities had not been observed. S 39 of the Ceylon marriage ordinance provided: "After any marriage shall have been registered under this ordinance it shall not be necessary, in support of such marriage, to give any proof [...] that the place [...] of marriage was the place [...] prescribed by this ordinance nor shall any evidence be given to prove the contrary in any suit or legal proceedings touching the validity of such marriage". The magistrates' court made an order in the wife's favour and the husband now appealed, contending that the performance of the civil ceremony at the wife's house instead of the registrar's office, and the failure by the registrar to address the parties, invalidated the marriage. It was held as follows: (i) s 39 of the Ceylon marriage ordinance, although it related to proof and evidence, was a matter of substantive law, not of adjective or procedural law, and, therefore, the marriage certificate was conclusive that the ceremony had been performed at the proper place.[95] (ii) even if s 3 were a matter of adjective law, the presumptions relating to the validity of a marriage, *viz, omnia praseumuntur rite esse acta* as regards the acts of the officials, and *omnia praseumuntur pro matrimonio*, which arose where a marriage ceremony was followed by cohabitation, had not been rebutted, for the evidence did not come up to the standard of proof required to displace the presumption.[96](iii) moreover even if the wife's evidence had been sufficient to establish that the marriage did not take place at the registrar's office, yet the presumption in favour of matrimony would oblige the court to infer that the marriage took place pursuant to a special licence.[97]

It is important to see the foregoing within the context of s 167 of the Penal Code[98] which provides that '[a]ny person who dishonestly or with a fraudulent intention goes through the ceremony of marriage, knowing that he is not thereby lawfully married, is guilty of a felony and is liable to imprisonment

---

[95] *Bodman v Bodman (orse Perry)* ((1913), 108 LT 383) and *Hill v Hibbit* ((1870), 25 LT 183) applied; *Leroux v Brown* ((1852), 12 CB 801) distinguished.

[96] *Piers v Piers* (1849) 2 HL Cas 331) applied; Where a ceremony of marriage is proved and is followed by cohabitation as man and wife, a presumption is raised which cannot be rebutted by evidence that merely goes to show on a balance of probability that there was no valid marriage; the evidence must be such as proves beyond reasonable doubt that there was no valid marriage (see p 1117, letters f and g, post).

[97] Editor's note: Quaere whether duress renders a marriage void or voidable: 12 Halsbury's Laws (3rd Edn) 225; *Parojcic (orse Ivetic) v Parojcic* ([1959] 1 All ER at p 3); As to the presumption of validity of marriage, see 19 Halsbury's Laws (3rd edn) 813, para 1324; and for cases on the subject, see 27 Digest (Repl) 69, 70, 469–484; As to the *lexi loci celebrationis* governing the forms and ceremonies of marriage, see 7 Halsbury's Laws (3rd Edn) 93, para 168, note (l); and for cases on the subject, see 11 Digest (Repl) 462–464, 953–971.

[98] Chapter 87 of the Laws of Zambia.

for five years.' While there appears to be no case that has been brought before any court in this jurisdiction, it would appear that the presumption of a lawful marriage would be rebutted if proof the burden of which is on the prosecution to prove such fraud is given to this effect. Consent of marriage obtained fraudulently leads to automatic invalidity. In *Bashford v Shabani*[99] the parties were married in accordance with Muslim law in Ontario Canada the petitioner being made to believe that the respondent was, at the time of the marriage ceremony, single. On arrival in Tanzania, the petitioner discovered that the respondent had, in fact, two other wives. The petitioner petitioned for a decree of nullity. It was held that where consent is obtained by fraud or force, a Muslim marriage is void unless ratified. On the facts, the petitioner's consent was obtained by fraud.

It is just as important to recall at this juncture that the foregoing authorities, in so far as they recognise common law marriage or marriage by co-habitation without anything more are inapplicable to Zambia which only recognises two types of marriage namely statutory/civil marriage and customary marriage.[100]

(c) Presumption of marriage from cohabitation/common law marriage

In England and Wales as shown in *Re Taplin*,[101] if a couple are shown to have lived together, they are, in the absence of evidence to the contrary presumed to be lawfully married. The starting point in Zambia is s 38 of the Marriage Act[102] which provides as follows:

> Any person who-
> (a) contracts a marriage under this Act, being at the time married in accordance with African customary law to any person other than the person with whom such marriage is contracted;
> (b) having contracted a marriage under this Act, during the continuance of such marriage contracts a marriage in accordance with African customary law;
> shall be guilty of an offence and liable on conviction to imprisonment for a period not exceeding five years [....]
>
> Provided that this section shall not extend to any person who contracts a marriage during the life of a former husband or wife, if such husband or wife, at the time of the subsequent marriage, shall have been continually absent from such person for the space of seven years, and shall not have been heard of by such person as being alive within that time.[103]

---

[99] EALR 1971.

[100] s 38 of the Marriage Act, Chapter 50 of the Laws of Zambia.

[101] [1981] 1 All ER 897; see also, *Al-Mudaris v Al-Mudaris* [2001] 2 FLR 6; *De Vire v De Vire* [2001] 1 FLR 460; *Chief Adjudication Officer v Bath* [2000] 1 FLR 8.

[102] Chapter 50 of the Laws of Zambia.

[103] No 48 of 1963.

Fenias Mafemba v Ester Sitali[104] was an appeal against the judgment of the High Court dated 31 August, 2005, allowing the respondent's appeal against the decision of the Subordinate Court which had upheld the Local Courts decision that the appellant was the widower and entitled to his deceased wife's estate. It was held on appeal that (1) the appellate judge was on firm ground when he held that the appellant was not a husband to the deceased despite the fact that the two had stayed together as husband and wife for 14 years and had two children; and that (2) the appellate judge was on firm ground when he ruled that the Local Court and the Subordinate Court should have restricted themselves to Lozi Customary law on marriage in defining the relationship between the appellant and the deceased.

In *Francina Milner Joan v Anthony George Hodgson*,[105] the defence and counter claim as pleaded was that the defendant was induced to enter into and execute the agreement referred to in the statement of claim by duress on the part of the plaintiff. Further, the defendant alleged that there was no consideration for the agreement or that there was only past consideration which was insufficient to support the agreement. In reply and defence to the counterclaim, the plaintiff claimed that there was a common law marriage between the parties, because the defendant held himself out as the plaintiff's husband and father to her children. The Court held inter alia: (i) the plaintiff was not entitled to compensation for having cohabited with the defendant; (ii) a common law marriage is reasonably presumed in a situation such as that of the plaintiff and defendant. However, there must be evidence that the parties celebrated the marriage; (iii) in the present case, there was no celebration of marriage and therefore, the parties could not be presumed to have been married under common law; and (iv) the plaintiff in the present case was trying to extort something from the defendant which she was not entitled to. *Per* Makungu J:

> Common law marriages are reasonably presumed in a situation such as that of the plaintiff and defendant. However, there must be evidence that the parties celebrated the marriage. In the text, *Family Law in Zambia: Cases and Material*,[106] the author states as follows:
>
>> Today a common law marriage is one where two people from different jurisdictions celebrate their marriage according to the law of the place of the marriage (lex loci celebrations), where formal requirements of a valid marriage according to English Law are not fulfilled, for instance celebrating a marriage without a priest, or a person with holy orders.
>
> In the present case there was no celebration of marriage at all. Therefore, the parties cannot be presumed to have been married under common law.

---

[104] (SCZ Judgment No 24 of 2007).

[105] 2007/HK/433.

[106] Mushota L, *Family Law in Zambia "Cases and Materials"* (UNZA Press, 2005) 69.

In the case of *Mafemba v Sitali*,[107] the facts in brief were that the parties had stayed together as husband and wife for 14 years and had two children. Since the case was initially filed in the Local Court the relationship was viewed as a customary law marriage. The Supreme Court upheld the High Court decision that Lozi customary law on marriage was not followed by the parties as there was no dowry paid. The Court held inter alia that: '[t]he appellate judge was on firm ground when he held that the appellant was not a husband to the deceased, despite the fact that the two had stayed together as husband and wife for 14, years and had two children.'

The differences between that case and the present case are that the Court dealt with Lozi customary law of marriage whilst in the present case the claim is that there was a common law marriage. In that case, the parties cohabited for 14 years and had two children. In the present case, the parties cohabited for 10 years and kept the plaintiff's two children. The two cases are similar in that the parties were not married under any law. Therefore, following that case, I find and hold that the parties hereto were not husband and wife.

It is perhaps important to remember that the circumstances relating to common law marriage which Makungu J referred to as appearing in the text, *Family Law in Zambia: Cases and Material*,[108] are actually taken from a leading case on common law marriage, *Taczanowska v Taczanowska*.[109] In July, 1946, the petitioner and the respondent went through a ceremony of marriage in Italy. The parties were both Polish nationals and were domiciled in Poland. The respondent was a member of the Polish forces allied with the United Kingdom and, at the date of the ceremony, was serving in the Polish 2nd Corps which was then part of the Allied armed forces in occupation of Italy prior to any peace treaty with Italy. After 14 February 1946, the Polish forces serving abroad were no longer recognised as part of the Polish army by the Polish ("Lublin") government, which had been recognised as the government of Poland by the British government in July, 1945. The ceremony of marriage was performed according to the rites of the Roman Catholic church by a Roman Catholic priest serving as a Polish army chaplain. The marriage was not valid by Italian law since certain articles of the Italian Civil Code were not read to the parties by the officiating priest, nor was the ceremony registered in the Italian civil register. Italian law would have recognised a ceremony of marriage performed in Italy between two foreigners to be valid if it were performed according to the law of their common nationality, but in 1946 by a decree of the Polish ("Lublin") government dated 25 September 1945, the only form of marriage valid by

---

[107] (SCZ Judgment No 24 of 2007).

[108] Mushota L, *Family Law in Zambia "Cases and Materials"* (UNZA Press, 2005); the author actually cites the authority in fn. 7 at 69.

[109] (1957) P 301; [1957] 2 All ER 563 which was cited in *Fenias Mafemba v Ester Sitali* (SCZ Judgment No 24 of 2007); but compare this to the Kenyan decisions in *Hontensia Wanjiku Yahweh v Public Trustee* CA No 13 of 1976; *In Re Estate of Patrick Kibunja Kamau* (2008) Eklr; *Phyllis Njoki Karamja and Another v Rosemary Mueni Karanja and Another* (2009) Eklr; *Veronica Rwamba Mbongo v Margaret Rachel Muthoni and Another* (Civil App No 311 of 2000) and other authorities which are analysed within the context of Fenias Mafemba in Kaluba BC, *Evidence Law* at 235-237.

Polish law was marriage before a civil registrar and the power of Polish army chaplains to perform valid marriages was revoked. There was no evidence that in 1946 the Allied forces in Italy were in any way subject to the laws of that country. From 1947 the parties had lived in England and claimed to be now domiciled in England. On a petition for nullity on the ground that the ceremony did not comply with the *lex loci celebrationis,* the respondent contended that the marriage was valid by English law (a) under the Foreign Marriage Act, 1892, s 22a; (b) because it was an act of "internal administration" within the meaning of the Polish Resettlement Act, 1947, s 9, and, therefore, validated by s 9(8) b of that Act; and (c) because the requirements of Italian law as to the form of the marriage did not apply, as the respondent was a member of a military force in belligerent occupation of Italy. It was held that the principle stated in *Scrimshire v Scrimshire,*[110] that the validity of a marriage depended on the *lex loci celebrationis,* did not apply in the case of a marriage in an occupied country by a member of the occupying forces,[111] and, as the ceremony of marriage between the parties fulfilled all the essentials of a common law marriage, it should be recognised as such, notwithstanding the foreign nationality and domicil of the parties at the date of the ceremony, since the common law conception of marriage knew no distinction of nationality, and, in the circumstances, it was unnecessary to look to the law of the domicil. *Per* Hodson LJ (Parker and Ormerod LJJ concurring):

(i) although the application of s 22 of the Foreign Marriage Act, 1892, was not limited in terms to marriage between parties of whom one at least was a British subject, the ceremony was not valid under that section because, on the evidence, the Polish 2nd Corps was an independent command, and, therefore, the chaplain who performed the ceremony was not "officiating under the orders of the commanding officer of a British army serving abroad", within s 22 (see p 568, letter b, post); the fact that the corps was under the operational command of an Allied army was too remote to justify the court in holding that the ceremony was valid under s 22, even though, by the time of the ceremony, the corps had been disowned by the Polish government (see p 568, letter c, post).

(ii) the ceremony was not rendered valid by English law by virtue of s 9(8) of the Polish Resettlement Act, 1947, as, although marriages by an army chaplain acting under the provisions of Polish law were matters of "internal administration" within s 9 of the Act of 1947, the powers conferred by the Allied Forces Act, 1940, were powers to be exercised within the United Kingdom (see p 569, letter a, post).[112]

---

[110] (1752), 2 Hag Con 395.

[111] Dicta of Lord Stowell in *Ruding v Smith* (1821), 2 Hag Con at p 380 *et seq* applied.

[112] Decision of Karminski J [1956] 3 All ER 457 reversed; Editor's notes: As to the *lex loci celebrationis* governing the forms and ceremonies of marriage, see 7 Halsbury's Laws (3rd Edn) 93, para 168, note (1); and for cases on the subject, see 11 Digest (Repl) 462–464, 953–971; As to the validity of a marriage at common law, see 7 Halsbury's Laws (3rd Edn) 94, para 170, note (r); For the Foreign Marriage Act, 1892, s 22, as originally enacted, see 11 Halsbury's Statutes (2nd Edn) 795, note; For the Allied Forces Act, 1940, s 1, see 22 Halsbury's Statutes (2nd Edn) 682; For the Polish Resettlement Act, 1947, s 9, see 22 Halsbury's Statutes (2nd Edn) 695.

(iii) Presumption of legitimacy

The presumption that children born during the subsistence of a marriage are the legitimate children of that marriage is a matter in the province of public policy. It is a rebuttable presumption which places the burden of proving illegitimacy squarely on the party seeking the contrary. The presumption is not any different for couples on separation, judicial or otherwise and those are divorced. In the latter case, however, it is easier to rebut the presumption than in a situation where the wife and husband still live or lived together at the material time. Even so, evidence that does to prove impotence; lack of sexual activity between husband and wife at the time of conception; blood type; infertility; co-habitation of woman with another; and admission by a woman of having conceived the child from another man other than her husband will, in a proper case, be sufficient to rebut the presumption. The modern day of dealing with legitimacy is to employ DNA testing. Still, as shown in *R v B*,[113] where a woman had hidden the fact of gravid state from her husband and family and put the baby up for adoption, the presumption still plays a role. The Court having determined that the woman had not rebutted the presumption that the baby in question was her husband's based on her testimony regarding the circumstances of the conception, granted the local authority's application for a care order and allowed service of proceedings on the woman's husband, over her opposition.

Whether the presumption should still have a role to play in our adversarial and evidentiary paradigm is one that has been considered by Thorpe LJ in *Re H*[114] wherein he opined as follows:

> […] I question the relevance of the presumption or justification for its application. In the nineteenth century, when science had nothing to offer and illegitimacy was a social stigma as well as a depriver of rights, the presumption was a necessary tool, the use which required no justification. That common law presumption, only rebuttable by proof beyond reasonable doubt, was modified by [s 26] of the Family Law Reform Act 1969[115] by enabling the presumption to be rebutted on the balance of probabilities. But as science has hastened on and as more and more children are born out of marriage it seems to me that the paternity of any child is to be established by science and not by legal presumption or inference.

(iv) *Doli incapax*

'*Doli incapax*' is Latin for 'incapability of committing a crime.' Thus, under s 14 of the Penal Code,[116] '[a] child under the age of twelve years is not criminally responsible for an act or omission.

---

[113] [2004] 1 FLR 527.

[114] [2002] 1 FLR 1145, *per* Thorpe LJ.

[115] Inapplicable to Zambia.

[116] Chapter 87 of the Laws of Zambia as amednded by Act No 13 of 2022.

An English case in which the presumptions similar to those under s 14 of the Penal Code[117] were considered is that of *C v Director of Public Prosecutions.*[118] The appellant, aged 12, and another boy were seen by police officers using a crowbar to tamper with a motor cycle in a private driveway. The appellant ran away but was caught and arrested. The motor cycle was found to be damaged and the appellant was charged with interfering with a motor vehicle with intention to commit theft, contrary to s 9(1) of the Criminal Attempts Act 1981. When the appellant was brought before the magistrates it was submitted on his behalf that he was *doli incapax* and that the prosecution had not rebutted the presumption that he did not know that his act was seriously wrong. The magistrates held that it was to be inferred from the fact that he had run away and that the motor cycle had been damaged that he knew that what he had done was seriously wrong. The appellant was convicted and fined. He appealed by way of case stated. The Divisional Court held, dismissing the appeal, that the presumption that a child aged between 10 and 14 who was charged with a criminal offence was *doli incapax* unless that presumption was rebutted by positive proof adduced by the prosecution that in fact, he knew that what he did was seriously wrong, was outdated and should be treated as being no longer good law. The appellant appealed to the House of Lords, contending that the Divisional Court, in holding that the presumption was no longer part of the law of England, had engaged in unjustified judicial law-making and was bound by authority to recognise and apply the presumption.

It was held that the presumption that a child between the ages of 10 and 14 was *doli incapax* and the rules that the presumption could only be rebutted by clear positive evidence that the child knew that his act was seriously wrong, and that evidence of the acts amounting to the offence itself was not sufficient to rebut the presumption, were still part of English law. Accordingly, the prosecution was required to prove, according to the criminal standard of proof, that a child defendant between the ages of 10 and 14 did the act charged and that when doing that act, he knew that it was a wrong act as distinct from an act of mere naughtiness or childish mischief, and the evidence to prove the defendant's guilty knowledge could not be mere proof of the doing of the act charged, however horrifying or obviously wrong that act might have been. It followed that the Divisional Court had been wrong not to apply the presumption. The appeal would therefore be allowed and the case remitted with a direction to dismiss the charge against the appellant.

Per Lord Jauncey, Lord Bridge, Lord Ackner and Lord Lowry. Having regard to the anomalies and even absurdities to which application of the presumption of *doli incapax* can give rise, Parliament should review the law as it now stands.

Per Lord Lowry. Judicial legislation should be approached by the courts on the following basis: (i) if the solution is doubtful, the judges should beware of imposing their own remedy; (ii) caution should prevail if Parliament has rejected opportunities of clearing up a known difficulty or has legislated while

---

[117] Chapter 87 of the Laws of Zambia.
[118] [1995] 2 All ER 43.

leaving the difficulty untouched; (iii) disputed matters of social policy are less suitable areas for judicial intervention than purely legal problems; (iv) fundamental legal doctrines should not be lightly set aside; (v) judges should not make a change unless they can achieve finality and certainty.[119]

(iv) Presumption of negligence

The presumption of negligence is mostly identified with the Latin maxim *res ipsa loquitur* which means 'the thing speaks for itself' or loosely, 'the accident tells its own story.' The presumption permits the plaintiff to successfully litigate on the basis of negligence without having to prove the cause of the accident by way of evidence or indeed whether the accident is attributable to the defendant. The principle was stated by Erle CJ in *Scott v London and St. Katherine Docks Co*[120] as follows:

> There must be reasonable evidence of negligence. But where the thing is shown to be under the management of the defendant or his servants, and the accident is such as in ordinary course of things does not happen if those who have the management use proper care, it affords reasonable evidence, in the absence of explanation by the defendants, that the accident arose from want of care.

The doctrine is applicable to criminal proceedings. In *Dobkins v R*,[121] Treadgold CJ observed as follows regarding the doctrine:

> In other words, the words indicate no more than this, that the circumstances of an occurrence may be such as, in the absence of explanation, to justify an inference of negligence. It is a matter of logical inference and not of presumption, and the danger in its use is that it may distract attention from what has to be proved in the case under consideration. In a criminal case the inference from the facts must be so strong as to exclude any other conclusions than that the accused is guilty.

In *Peter James Mullan v The People*,[122] Baron J (as he then was) held that '[t]he words "*res ipsa loquitur*" are a figure of speech indicating no more than that the circumstances of an occurrence may be such as, in the absence of explanation, to justify an inference of negligence. In a criminal case the inference sought to be drawn must be the only inference which can reasonably be drawn from the

---

[119] Decision of the Divisional Court of the Queen's Bench Division [1994] 3 All ER 190 reversed; Editor's notes: For the criminal capacity of children under 14, see 11(1) Halsbury's Laws (4th edn reissue) para 34, and for cases on the subject, see 14(1) Digest (2nd reissue) 91–92, 703–714; For the Criminal Attempts Act 1981, s 9, see 12 Halsbury's Statutes (4th edn) (1994 reissue) 787.

[120] (1865) 3 H & C 596 at 601.

[121] (1969) R 7 N 130.

[122] [1971] ZR 110 (HC).

facts.' In *Director of Public Prosecutions v Chilombo*,[123] it was held *inter alia* that it was an over-simplification, and misleading, to suggest that the doctrine of *res ipsa loquitur* had no application in the criminal law. The circumstances of an occurrence, the Court said, may be such as, in the absence of explanation, to justify an inference of negligence.

Emanating from the foregoing is the fact that the starting point is a reasonable basis for the presence of negligence in the act complained of. What logically must follow is that the cause of the accident must be the thing under the control of the defendant which, but for his negligence would not have caused the accident in question.

Considerable debate has ensued as regards the exact nature of *res ipsa loquitur*. Prominent among the contenders is the late P.S. Atiyah.[124] He postulates that there are two views regarding the purpose and effect of the maxim *res ipsa loquitur*. The first view is that *res ipsa loquitur* is not a rule of evidence in and of itself. It follows from this rule that the legal burden of proof in all cases of negligence is on the plaintiff. More than anything, *res ipsa loquitur* must be seen as nothing more than a swift way of describing a scenario in which it is permissible to infer from the facts and circumstances of the accident which raises the presumption that it was probably as a result of the defendant's negligence. Atiyah thus concludes: '[...] on this view, the inference of negligence is merely permissible (not obligatory) and if at the conclusion of the case the tribunal of fact is not satisfied that the accident was more probably than not caused by the negligence of the defendant, the plaintiff must fail.' There is support for this position. In *Lloyde v West Midlands Gas Board*[125] Megaw LJ, in a dictum that Atiyah cites, opined as follows:

> I doubt whether it is right to describe res ipsa loquitur as a 'doctrine'. I think that it is no more than an exotic, though convenient, phrase to describe what is in essence no more than a common-sense approach, not limited by technical rules, to the assessment of the effect of evidence in certain circumstances. It means that a plaintiff prima facie establishes negligence where: (i) it is not possible for him to prove precisely what was the relevant act or omission which set in train the events leading to the accident; but (ii) on the evidence as it stands at the relevant time it is more likely than not that the effective cause of the accident was some act or omission of the defendant or someone for whom the defendant is responsible, which act or omission constitutes a failure to take proper care for the plaintiff's safety.

The second view Atiyah advances is that *res ipsa loquitur* represents a rule of law (of evidence) in and of itself. This position entails, unlike the former, that

---

[123] [1975] ZR 248 (SC), disapproving *Chuzi v The People* [1967] ZR 100 (CA) on this point.
[124] Atiyah PS, 'Res Ipsa Loquitur in England and Australia' (1972) *35 MLR 337.*
[125] [1971] 2 All ER 1240 at 1246; see also *Henderson v Henry E. Jenkins & Sons* [1970] AC 282 at 301 *per* Lord Pearson of whose explanation of the difference between 'formal' and 'evidential' burdens of proof Goodhart (1970) 86 LQR 145, has said: 'it would be difficult to find elsewhere a clearer statement of the law on this point'; see also, *Ng Chun Pui v Lee Chuen Tat* [1988] RTR 298.

since a legal burden of proof may be placed on the defendant in a proper case with the relevant factual matrix and circumstances thereto, the maxim should be seen as setting an exception to the general rule of the burden of proof resting on the plaintiff throughout the course of negligence proceedings. Says Atiyah, '[o]n this view, once the maxim operates, the plaintiff is entitled to a verdict even though, at the conclusion of the evidence, the tribunal of fact remains in doubt whether the accident was more probably than caused by the defendant.' He of course admits that there could be no entitlement to a verdict in the plaintiff's favour 'unless the legal burden of disproving negligence is upon the defendant.'

The principle stated by Erle CJ in *Scott v London and St. Katherine Docks Co*[126] gives rise to additional issues as regards the impact of the maxim and its treatment. There are at least three ways to treat *res ipsa loquitur*:

    (a)   as inferential regarding facts;
    (b)   as persuasive so far as presumptions go; and
    (c)   as evidential so far as presumptions are concerned.

(a)   As inferential regarding facts

There is, when the presumption of *res ipsa loquitur* is raised, no need for the defendant to adduce evidence of reasonable care. The reason is that as Ngulube CJ, as he then was, opined in the case of *Mohamed v the Attorney General:*[127]

> An unqualified proposition that a plaintiff should succeed automatically whenever a defence has failed is unacceptable [....] A plaintiff must prove his case and if he fails to do so, the mere failure of the opponent's defence does not entitle him to judgment. I would not accept the proposition that even if a plaintiff's case has collapsed of its inanition or for some reason or other, judgment should nevertheless be given to him on the ground that defences set up by the opponent has also collapsed. Quite clearly a defendant in such circumstances would not even need a defence.

Be that as it may, this is a tactic to be sparingly used. As Langton J has opined in *The Kite,*[128]

> [...] what the defendants have to do [...] is not to prove that their negligence did not cause [the] accident. What they have to do is to give a reasonable explanation, which, if it be accepted, is an explanation showing that it happened without their negligence [....] If they give a reasonable explanation, which is equally consistent with the accident

---

[126] (1865) 3 H & C 596 at 601: '[...] where the thing is shown to be under the management of the defendant or his servants, and the accident is such as in the ordinary course of things, does not happen if those who have the management use proper care, it affords reasonable evidence, in the absence of explanation by the defendants that the accident arose from want of care.'

[127] [1982] ZR 49.

[128] (Probate, England, 1933).

happening without their negligence as with their negligence, they have again shifted the burden of proof back to the plaintiffs to show – as they always have to show from the beginning – that it was the negligence of the defendants that caused the accident [....]

(b)   Persuasive so far as presumptions go

By its very nature, *res ipsa loquitur* alters, where it is invoked, reverses the (evidential) burden of proof such that the defendant is called upon to adduce evidence to the effect that he was not negligent, specifically that the resulting accident is explainable by some other reason or cause other than the defendant's actions. In *Barkway v South Wales Transport Co Ltd*[129] the plaintiff sued in respect of the death of her husband, as a result of the defendant's bus running off the road. It was argued that the fact of the accident having happened was sufficient evidence of negligence. The defendant proved that the cause of the accident was the bursting of a tyre. The question then was, had the defendant displaced the inference arising from the unexplained accident. Asquith explained the law as follows:

> The position as to onus of proof in this case seems to me to be fairly summarised in the following short proposition: (i) If the defendants' omnibus leaves the road and falls down an embarkment, and this without more is proved, then res ipsa loquitur, there is a presumption that the event is caused by negligence on the part of the defendants, and the plaintiff succeeds unless the defendants can rebut this presumption. (ii) It is no rebuttal for the defendants to show, again without more, that the immediate cause of the omnibus leaving the road is a tyre-burst, since a tyre-burst per se is a neutral event consistent, and equally consistent, with negligence or due diligence on the part of the defendants. When a balance has been tilted one way, you cannot redress it by adding an equal weight to each scale. The depressed scale will remain down [...] (iii) To displace the presumption, the defendants must go further and prove (or it must emerge from the evidence as a whole) either (a) that the burst itself was due to a specific cause which does not connote negligence on their part but points to its absence as more probable, or (b), if they can point to no such specific cause, that they used all reasonable care in and about the management of their tyres [....]

(c)   As an evidential presumption

The presumption of negligence – *res ipsa loquitur* while altering the evidential burden thus necessitating the need for the defendant to adduce some evidence of reasonable diligence in the face of the presumption, does not alter the legal burden of proof. Lord Pearson observed as follows in *Henderson v Henry E. Jenkins & Sons*:[130]

---

[129] [1948] 2 All ER 460; *Henderson v H.E. Jenkins and Sons* (1870) AC 282.
[130] [1970] AC 282.

In an action for negligence the plaintiff must allege, and has the burden of proving, that the accident was caused by negligence on the part of the defendants. That is the issue throughout the trial, and in giving judgment at the end of the trial the judge has to decide whether he is satisfied on a balance of probability that the accident was caused by negligence on the part of the defendants, and if he is not so satisfied the plaintiff's action fails. The formal burden of proof does not shift. But if in the course of the trial there is proved a set of facts which raises a prima facie inference that the accident was caused by negligence on the part of the defendants, the issue will be decided in the plaintiff's favour unless the defendants by their evidence provide some answer which is adequate to displace the prima facie inference. In this situation there is said to be an evidential burden of proof resting on the defendants. I have some doubts whether it is strictly correct to use the expression 'burden of proof' with this meaning, as there is a risk of it being confused with the formal burden of proof, but it is a familiar and convenient usage [....]

Thus, in *Deutsch, Darling and Banda v Zambia Engineering and Construction Company Ltd*,[131] it was held *inter alia*, that '[i]f the doctrine of *res ipsa loquitur* is applicable, the burden of proof shifts from the plaintiff to the defendant; and the plaintiff will succeed unless the defendant refutes the probability that plaintiff's injury was caused by defendant's negligence.' As regards the application of the maxim, we must look to the decision in *Ng Chun Pui v Lee Chuen Tat*.[132] The first defendant was a coach driver. The second defendant was the first defendant's employer. The first defendant was driving a coach on the outer lane of a dual carriageway. Suddenly, he crossed the central reservation without warning. As a result, the coach collided with a bus in the inner lane of the eastbound carriageway. One person died, and several more were injured. The claimants, those injured and the estate of the person killed in the event, sued the defendants in negligence. The claimants relied on the doctrine of *res ipsa loquitur* to establish that the first defendant breached their duty of care. They argued that the fact the accident happened at all was sufficient evidence of breach. The first defendant blamed the accident on an unidentified car, which he claimed had cut in front of the coach and forced the first defendant to serve to avoid it. The trial judge concluded that the defendants were negligent. He argued that this was because the burden of proof had shifted to them after the claimant established *res ipsa loquitur*, and the defendants had failed to discharge that burden. The defendant appealed. The Court of Appeal of Hong Kong disagreed, reversing the decision and finding that the claimant had failed to establish negligence. The claimant appealed to the Privy Council. To the question what is the legal and evidential effect of establishing res ipsa loquitur? the Privy Council held in favour of the defendant. The defendant was not under a legal burden to disprove the claimant's case once *res ipsa*

---

[131] [1969] ZR 161 (HC).
[132] [1988] RTR 298.

loquitur is established. It was enough that they adduced evidence which made it no longer reasonable to presume negligence from the fact of the accident. The defendant had adduced evidence that they were acting reasonably in response to a serious emergency, which was enough. This Case is Authority for, among other things, the fact that *res ipsa loquitur* does not reverse the burden of proof. In appropriate cases it allows the claimant to establish a prima facie case by asking the court to infer from the fact the accident happened that the defendant must have been negligent.

If the defendant adduces no evidence, then the plaintiff will succeed.[133] This is not because the burden has shifted to the defendant, but because they will have failed to rebut the inference. However, if the defendant adduces evidence which makes it no longer reasonable to assume negligence purely from the fact that the accident occurred, the plaintiff no longer has a *prima facie* case.[134] The Privy Council in *Ng Chun Pui v Lee Chuen Tat*[135] stressed that a person in an emergency situation cannot be judged by too critical and exacting a standard.

Ultimately, the presumption as regards negligence – *res ipsa loquitur* - must be seen within the context of Barwick CJ's comments in *Government Insurance Office v Fredrichberg.*[136] He opined as follows:

> [...] the so-called 'doctrine' is no more than a process of logic by which an inference of negligence may be drawn from the circumstances of the occurrence itself where in the ordinary affairs of mankind such an occurrence is not likely to occur without lack of care towards the plaintiff on the part of a person in the position of the defendant; or perhaps, as it might more accurately, in my opinion, be expressed, where, in the opinion of the judge, the [judge] would be entitled to think that such an occurrence was not likely to occur in the ordinary experience of mankind without such a want of due care on the part of such a person.

(v)   Presumption of death

It is perhaps important to first consider what is termed the 'presumption of life' and whether the said presumption is one of law or fact. Sachs J has taken the

---

[133] See *Lyons Brooke Bond (Zambia) Limited v Zambia Tanzania Road Services Limited* [1977] ZR 317 (HC); *Zambia Electricity Supply Corporation Ltd v Readlines Haulage Ltd* [1992] SJ 52 (SC): 'The doctrine of *res ipsa loquitor* applies where the thing that inflicted the damage was under the sole management and control of the defendant, someone for whom he is responsible or when he has a right to control, where the occurrence is such that it would not have happened without negligence and where there must be no evidence as to why of how the occurrence took place;' *Eagle Charalambous Transport Ltd v Gideon Phiri* (SCZ Judgment No 8 of 1994): 'If a plaintiff knows the cause or alleges particulars of negligence it is inappropriate for him to plead *res ipsa loquitur* as well;' *Rosemary Bwalya v Zambia Consolidated Copper Mines Limited (Mufurila Division) Malcom Watson Hospital Dr. Y.C. Malik* [2005] ZR 1 (SC): 'the doctrine requires an unambiguous story for it to apply. The multiplicity of the potential explanations for the conception in the present case, ruled out its applicability.'

[134] *Lyons Brooke Bond (Zambia) Limited v Zambia Tanzania Road Services Limited* [1977] ZR 317 (HC): 'Liability for negligence may be effectively excluded if words are used which indicate that all damages, however caused, are to be comprehended within the exemption.'

[135] [1988] RTR 298.

[136] (1968) 118 CLR 403.

view in *Chard v Chard*[137] that such a presumption is one of fact and not law. This position is supported in *Rex v Lumley*[138] wherein Lush J held that '[t]he existence of the party at an antecedent period may or may not afford a reasonable inference that he was living at the subsequent date [....] The law makes no presumption either way.' Hodson J's observation in *MacDarmaid v Attorney General*[139] is more measured. He takes the view that '[t]here is no presumption of law as to continuance of life.' In this, he is in agreement with what is stated by certain juristic authors.[140] However, he also opines that '[...] each case must be determined on its own facts.' In the latter part of this observation, Hodson J leaves the door open for the presumption of the continuance of life to be one of law. In this, though not unconditionally, he is on the same page as other jurists who believe that the presumption of the continuance of life is one of law.[141]

As discussed elsewhere in this text, a party who wishes to predicate an action on the presumption of death ought to show that there is an absence of evidence in the affirmative that the person in question has been alive for a continuous period of seven years preceding the action; and that no person(s) who could have ordinarily seen or heard from him have done so. In *Prudential Assurance Co v Edmonds*[142] which was applied in *Chard v Chard*,[143] discussed below, there was a claim on a life insurance policy pertaining to one Robert Nutt. While he had not been heard of by his family, a certain niece did in her testimony, say that she had seen him in Melbourne but had not spoken to him, having lost him in the crowd. Was he dead? Lord Blackburn observed as follows:

> Supposing the jurymen had found as a fact that they thought she was mistaken, would or would not the grounds have existed upon which the presumption from a seven years' absence would arise that the man not heard of was dead? I think certainly they would. It seems to me that when she said, 'I have seen the man in the streets of Melbourne,' it upset the presumption arising from the relatives, including herself, never having seen or heard of him, and t turned the onus the other way. It was possible, however, that it might have been proved that the man she saw was not Robert Nutt, but somebody else. If that had been proved, it would have left the matter just as if she had never made the statement. When she said she thought she had seen him, and all the others had heard it from her, although that unexplained and uncontradicted statement affected the onus, yet, as soon as it was made out by satisfactory evidence that she was mistaken, the hearing from her was gone, and the presumption would remain as it was before [....]

---

[137] [1956] P. 259 AT 273, *per* Sachs J.

[138] [1869] LR 1 CCR 196 at 198.

[139] [1950] P 218, 221.

[140] *Phipson on the Law of Evidence* 702.

[141] *Taylor on Evidence* 12th edn para 196 *et seq.*

[142] (1877) 2 App Cas at 509.

[143] [1956] P 259; 5 Ch 139; [1955] 3 WLR 954; [1955] 3 All ER 721.

To this must added holdings by Sir Boyd Merriman P, who stated the following in *Chipchase v Chipchase*:[144] '[t]hat presumption – I am taking the statement of it from the judgment of Giffard LJ in *Re Phene's Trusts*[145] – is that the law presumes a person who has not been heard of for over seven years to be dead [....]' Henn Collins J opined in the same case as follows: '[a]s soon as it was established [...] that the former husband [...] had not been heard of for seven years, then undoubtedly there was evidence for their consideration that he was dead, and it was more than evidence because it was a presumption and conclusive evidence until rebutted by evidence which showed, in fact, that he was alive.' As Sachs J has observed in *Chard v Chard*,[146] '[i]n neither of these passages is there added after the words 'heard of' a phrase such as 'by persons who would naturally have heard of him, if alive.' He notes, however, that the passages hereinbefore quoted; were used based on the facts in the cases considered. He adds that the words 'heard of' as used by Blackburn J in *Prudential Assurance Co v Edmonds*[147] were so used in a particular sense which Lord Blackburn analysed in his speech. As such, Sachs J opines, *Chipchase v Chipchase*[148] and *Re Phene's Trusts*[149] ought to be construed on the foregoing footing.

Before going further, we must turn to a few points on the matter of presumption of death which, it is submitted, must be put on the same footing or understood to be based on the same legal reasoning as legal principles applicable to the presumption of life. It has been held in *re Watkins*,[150] as cited by Sachs J in *Chard v Chard*,[151] that, where no statute applies, there is no 'magic' in the mere fact of a period of seven years elapsing without there being positive evidence of a person being alive. It is, generally speaking, a matter in each case of taking the facts as a whole and of balancing, as a judge would, the respective probabilities of life continuing and having ceased. Based on the foregoing, the court upon the facts has, in *Bradshaw v Bradshaw*,[152] declined to accede to the plea that a woman's husband be presumed dead by 1940 – where on the one hand, she had not then heard from him for 19 years, but on the other hand, had not made any and all possible inquiries during the period in question. The foregoing would appear to be predicated on a principle laid down in *Prudential Assurance Co v Edmonds*[153] where Lord Blackburn opined as follows: '[i]n order to raise a presumption that a man is dead from not having been heard of for seven years, you must inquire amongst those who, if he was alive, would be likely to hear of him, and see whether or not there has been such an absence of hearing of him as would raise the presumption that he was dead.'

---

[144] [1939] P 391.

[145] [1870] 5 Ch 139.

[146] [1956] P 259.

[147] [1877] 2 AC 487 at 511; see below.

[148] [1939] P 391.

[149] [1870] 5 Ch 139.

[150] [1953] 2 Ad & El 540, 544.

[151] [1956] P 259.

[152] [1939] P 391; see also *Ivett v Ivett* [1930] 94' JP 237; *Hogton v Hogton* [1933] 50 TLR 18.

[153] [1877] 2 AC 487 at 511.

Distillable from the foregoing authorities is the now familiar point made elsewhere in the text which is that a seven-year absence creates a presumption of death which as we have said already, places an evidential burden on the party seeking to prove that the person in question, such As Mr. Nutt in *Prudential Assurance,* is still alive. Thus, the niece's testimony if accepted by the court would satisfy that burden. The onus would then revert to the person seeking to prove that the person in question is still alive to prove to the court on a balance of probability that he indeed is alive. Further, the lack of proof for the requirement that all apposite inquiries being made as expressed in *Bradshaw v Bradshaw,*[154] on the one hand and *Prudential Assurance Co v Edmonds*[155] on the other, may or may not be fatal depending on the facts and circumstances of each case;[156]and want of proof in this particular instance may be justifiable. However, proof of such inquiry being given may make proof of other factors irrelevant.

The foregoing is exemplified in *Bullock v Bullock.*[157] In 1921 the wife married one K. There were two children and in 1926 K deserted the wife. In 1929 the wife obtained an order in the magistrates' court for the payment by K of maintenance for herself and the children on the ground of K's desertion. In 1930, K being in arrears under the order, a committal order was made. A warrant was issued against K to the police but was not executed by them as K could not be found. The wife made no further inquiries about K and never heard of him again. In 1944, the wife describing herself as the widow of K, went through a ceremony of marriage with the husband. At the date of the marriage the husband knew all the circumstances concerning the wife's earlier marriage with K. In 1959 the wife applied by way of complaint in the magistrates' court for an order for the payment by the husband of maintenance for herself on the ground of his desertion. The husband contended that there was no jurisdiction to make any order since his marriage to the wife in 1944 was bigamous and void ab initio. As the lapse of time since K was last heard of was, now, thirty years and, in 1944, had been fourteen years, the magistrates inferred that K died before the wife's re-marriage in 1944 and made an order in the wife's favour. The husband appealed on the ground that, as the wife had made no inquiries about K, his death before her remarriage should not be inferred. It was held that the inference that K had died before the re-marriage in 1944 was rightly drawn because (i) of the lapse of time between the date when K was last heard of and the dates of the re-marriage (a period of fourteen years) and of the

---

[154] [1939] P 391.

[155] [1877] 2 AC 487 at 511.

[156] *Bullock v Bullock* [1960] 2 All ER 307.

[157] [1960] 2 All ER 307.

present proceedings (a period of thirty years), and (ii) of the fact that the police were unable in 1930 to execute the warrant against K issued to them, which met the objection that the wife had herself made no inquiries concerning K.[158]

The fulfilment of conditions for the presumption of death leads to additional questions one of which is at which point the person now presumed dead to all intents and purposes, be said to have died. The issue has arisen in two decided cases. The strict view taken in *Chipchase v Chipchase*[159] was that the person in question is only dead at the start of court proceedings relating the presumption relating to his death.

In *Re Phene's Trusts*,[160] is a case in which the testator who dies in January 1861 had left his estate to his nephews and nieces. One of these nephews who had deserted the Us Army in 1860, had not been heard of since that year. Upon a claim being launched for his share of the estate the court, ignoring the strong inference that the said nephew was likely to have continued to be alive from 1860, the year of his desertion to 1861 thereby surviving his uncle, determined that it could not presume that the nephew had survived his uncle.

In the leading case of *Chard v Chard*,[161] facts where that in 1909 the husband married RML. RML was then eighteen years of age and an orphan with no known parents or other relations. Between October, 1909 and 1915, the husband was sentenced on six separate occasions to terms of imprisonment. In 1915 he saw RML on two occasions. In 1917 RML was known to be in Yorkshire. From October, 1917, until 23 April 1933, the husband was almost continuously in prison and did not hear of or from RML. On 15 May 1933, the husband went through a ceremony of marriage with the respondent. In 1954 inquiries were made concerning RML but no one was found who was likely to have heard from her and there was no trace of any death certificate concerning her. There was no evidence that in 1917 she was otherwise than in normal health with a normal expectation of life.

The husband in his petition and the respondent in her answer prayed for a decree of nullity of their marriage on the ground that at the time of the ceremony in 1933, RML was still alive and that the husband's marriage with her was still subsisting. It was held as follows:

(i)   once the husband was shown to have contracted the marriage in 1909 the court was put on inquiry as to the validity of the marriage in 1933, and it was for the husband or the respondent to prove facts from which a cessation of the marriage in 1909 could be inferred;[162] in the present

---

[158] *Re Watkins, Watkins v Watkins* [1953] 2 All ER 1113 applied; Semble: there can be estoppel in *pais* preventing a party relying on a 307 plea that a marriage was void on the ground of bigamy (see p 309, letter i, and p 313, letter f, post); Observation of Lord Selborne LC in G v M ((1885), 10 App Cas at p 186) considered; Editor's notes: As to the presumption of death, see 15 Halsbury's Laws (3rd Edn) 345, para 623, notes (r)-(u); and for cases on the subject, see 22 Digest (Repl) 159, 160, 1446–1460. and Supplement; As to estoppel in suits for nullity, see 12 Halsbury's Laws (3rd Edn) 231, para 432, note (u); and for cases on the subject, see 27 Digest (Repl) 483, 4215, 4216.

[159] [1939] P. 391.

[160] [1870] 5 Ch 139.

[161] [1956] P 259; 5 Ch 139; [1955] 3 WLR 954; [1955] 3 All ER 721.

[162] Dictum of Pilcher J in *Tweney v Tweney* [1946] 1 All ER at p 565 applied.

case there was no presumption of law either of the continuance of life of RML or of her having died, and since the correct inference from the known facts was that RML was alive on 15 May 1933, the marriage on that date was null;[163] accordingly there would be a decree of nullity both on the petition and on the prayer in the respondent's answer, notwithstanding, in the case of the husband, his bigamy.[164]

(ii)   although where due inquiries had been made for an individual and he had not been traced as a result of them there was a presumption of law that, if he had not been heard of during seven years by persons who would have been likely to have heard of him if he had been alive, he had died at sometime within the seven years, yet that presumption did not apply in the present case as the husband would not have been likely to have heard of his first wife during the period between 1917 and his purported marriage in 1933.[165]

Per Sachs J:

> By virtue of a long sequence of judicial statements, which either assert or assume such a rule, it appears accepted that there is a convenient presumption of law applicable to certain cases of seven years' absence where no statute applies. That presumption in its modern shape takes effect (without examining its terms too exactly) substantially as follows. Where as regards "A B" there is no acceptable affirmative evidence that he was alive at some time during a continuous period of seven years or more, then if it can be proved first, that there are persons who would be likely to have heard of him over that period, secondly, that those persons have not heard of him, and thirdly, that all due inquiries have been made appropriate to the circumstances, "A B" will be presumed to have died at sometime within that period. (Such a presumption would, of course, be one of law and could not be one of fact, because there can hardly be a logical inference from any particular set of facts that a man had not died within two thousand five hundred and fifty-five days but had died in two thousand five hundred and sixty).

There are several statutory provisions that touch on the issue of presumption of death. We have already considered those under s 24 of the Matrimonial Causes Act;[166] on the one hand and the provisos to s 38 of the Marriage Act;[167] and s 166 of the Penal Code;[168] both of which provide a defence to the offence of bigamy where the spouse has been continually absent for a period of seven years and

---

[163] *MacDarmaid v A-G* [1950] 1 All ER 497 applied.

[164] *Miles v Chilton (falsely calling herself Miles)* (1849) (1 Rob Eccl 684) applied.

[165] Principle stated by Lord Blackburn in *Prudential Assurance Co v Edmonds* (1877) (2 App Cas at p 509) applied; *Re Phené's Trusts* (1870) (5 Ch App 139) and *Chipchase v Chipchase* ([1939] 3 All ER 895) explained.

[166] No 20 of 2007.

[167] Chapter 50 of the Laws of Zambia.

[168] Chapter 87 of the Laws of Zambia.

not been heard of by those who ordinarily must have, upon reasonable inquiry, have heard of such spouse. To them must be added s 16(12) of the Wills and Administration of Testate Estates Act[169] which provides as follows:

> Where a testator and a beneficiary under his will die in circumstances -
>
> (a) in which it appears that their deaths were simultaneous; or
> (b) rendering it uncertain which of them survived the other;
>
> *the beneficiary shall be deemed to have survived the testator*[170] for all purposes affecting the entitlement to property under the will of that testator; but for the purposes of the entitlement of that testator to that property under any will of the afore-mentioned beneficiary, that beneficiary shall be deemed to have survived the aforementioned testator, unless a contrary intention appears from the will.

This is referred to as *commorientes* (literally "simultaneous deaths"). The wording in s 16(12),[171] in so far as resolving instances of *commorientes* are concerned, is somewhat problematic in instances where the deceased die simultaneously in circumstances where it is uncertain which of them survived the other. Where the victims of such a death executed mutual wills, they are beneficiaries of each other's will. This leads to the ridiculous situation where both will, according to s 16(12),[172] be deemed to have predeceased each other for purposes of each will as the provision says: *'the beneficiary shall be deemed to have survived the testator.'* It would be interesting to see how the court would resolve this situation if it ever arose and came up for determination. However, s 40 of the Intestate Succession Act[173] resolves this problem somewhat for those that die intestate as follows:

> For the purpose of this Act where two or more persons have died in circumstances rendering it uncertain which of them survived the other or others, the deaths shall, for all purposes affecting rights in, to or over property, be presumed to have occurred in order of seniority, and accordingly *the younger shall be deemed to have survived the elder.*[174]

The doctrine of *commorientes* as provided for under s 16(12) of the Wills and Administration of Testate Estate Act[175] on the one hand and s 40 of the Intestate Succession Act[176] on the other, is applicable to people who die in the same car or house as well as to those who die in geographically distant places as long their

---

[169] Chapter 60 of the Laws of Zambia.
[170] Italics added for emphasis only.
[171] Chapter 60 of the Laws of Zambia.
[172] Chapter 60 of the Laws of Zambia.
[173] Chapter 59 of the Laws of Zambia.
[174] Italics added.
[175] Chapter 60 of the Laws of Zambia.
[176] Chapter 59 of the Laws of Zambia.

deaths occur simultaneously in circumstances where it is uncertain which of them survived the other or die 'in circumstances rendering it uncertain which of them survived the other or others.'

24.3.2   *Conclusive presumptions*

Conclusive or irrebuttable presumptions that like any other form presumptions outside 'the rebuttable kind' are not strictly speaking presumptions properly so called. They should be properly be seen and understood to be rules of substantive law built on the premise that upon proof of a basic fact; the presumed fact is deemed to have been established making any evidence to the contrary inadmissible to rebut the presumption (hence the term irrebuttable presumption). A statutory example is that which, prior to amendment was found in s 14 of the Penal Code.[177] The former s 14(1) provided that '[a] person under the age of eight years is not criminally responsible for any act or omission.' According to the now repealed s 14(3), '[a] male person under the age of twelve years [was] presumed to be incapable of having carnal knowledge.' Thus, dubiously, it appeared that a female person under the age of twelve years was presumed to be, by implication, capable of having carnal knowledge. This position which emanated from the common law as exemplified in cases such as *Groombride*[178] has been overturned in the UK by s 1 of the Sexual Offences Act 1993. A recent amendment to the Penal Code by s 2 of Act No 13 of 2022, has repealed the former s 14(1) – (3) with the above provisions; and now provides simply that '[a] child under the age of twelve years is not criminally responsible for an act or omission.'

Another area where conclusive presumptions have been held to exist is in the equitable doctrine of undue influence. This was exemplified in *Royal Bank of Scotland v Etridge* (No 2)[179] where in Lord Nicholls opined as follows:

> The evidential presumption […] is to be distinguished sharply from a different form of presumption which arises in some cases. The law has adopted a sternly protective attitude towards certain types of relationship in which one party acquires influence over another who is vulnerable and dependent and where, moreover, substantial gifts by the influenced or vulnerable person are not normally to be expected. Examples of relationships within this special class are parent and child, guardian and ward, trustee and beneficiary, solicitor and client, and medical advisor and patient. In these cases, the law presumes, irrebuttably, that one party had influence over the other. The complainant need not prove he actually reposed trust and confidence in the other party. It is sufficient for him to prove the existence of the type of relationship.

---

[177] Chapter 87 of the Laws of Zambia.

[178] (1836) 7 C. & P. 582; P, *Independent*, March 7, 1994.

[179] [2001] 4 All ER.

Worth considering too, may be the irretrievable presumption of malice aforethought discussed in *DPP v Smith*[180] which was to the effect that if a person would have predicted the grave consequences, specifically, injury, he must be presumed to have foreknown the similar result irrespective of divergent evidence. This position has now been overtaken by statutory provision in the UK under s 8 of the Criminal Justice Act 1967. Even so, it may be contended as have some[181] that '[…] since intent to cause serious harm is still regarded as sufficient *mens rea* for murder-*Cunningham*,'[182] irrebuttable presumptions still colour judicial views as regards malice aforethought. To that end, it may not be so much of a stretch to argue that the preceding is 'a hidden evidential presumption with intent to cause GBH being the basic fact and the intent to kill being the presumed fact.'[183]

24.3.3   *Presumptions as a method of stating the burden of proof*

This is not a presumption within the context of what we are discussing here. This is because there is no alteration in the allocation of risk as is the case with true presumptions. It is simply an alternative way of expressing the law as stated in *Woolmington v DPP*[184] that the burden of proof in criminal proceedings rests on the prosecution. Thus, provisions such as Article 8(2)(a) of the Constitution: 'every person is presumed to be innocent until he is proved guilty;' and s 11 of the Penal Code:[185] '[e]very person is presumed to be of sound mind, and to have been of sound mind at any time which comes into question, until the contrary is proven,' ought to be seen in the same light. As we have seen elsewhere in this text, if the prosecution fails to discharge this legal burden, the accused must be acquitted. Yet, it is the case that judges will loosely refer to what they may term 'presumptions of sanity, sobriety and volition' as did Lord Denning in *Bratty v Attorney-General for Northern Ireland*.[186] The accused killed a girl, with whom

---

[180] (1836) 7 C. & P. 582; P, Independent, March 7, 1994.

[181] Uglow S, Evidence 764.

[182] [1981] 2 All ER 863.

[183] Uglow S, Evidence 764.

[184] [1935] AC 462.

[185] Chapter 87 of the Laws of Zambia.

[186] [1961] 3 All ER 523; Editor's notes: Where the only cause alleged for an unconscious or involuntary act is defect of reason from disease of the mind within the M'Naghten rules and the jury reject a defence of insanity there is no room for the alternative defence of automatism (see p 528, letter f, p 529, letter a, p 533, letter c, and p 536, letter d, post); the fact, however, that a plea of insanity is rejected by the jury does not of itself always prevent the accused from raising the alternative defence of automatism (see p 528, letter h, p 537), letter f, post); If such a defence is to be left to the jury, a proper foundation must be laid for it by evidence emanating from the defence or prosecution from which the jury can reasonably infer that the accused acted in a state of automatism, such evidence not being evidence attributing the automatism solely to a disease of the mind (see p 530, letter a, p 535, letter c, p 536, letter d, p 537, letter d, post). Whether there is such evidence, proper to be left to the jury, is a question of law for the judge (see p 530, letter g, p 532, letter c, p 536, letter e, and p 537, letter e, post); Once a proper foundation for a defence of automatism is laid by evidence the proper direction to the jury is that, if the evidence leaves them in a state of real doubt whether the accused did or did not act in a state of automatism, they should acquit (see p 532, letters b and c, p 536, letter a, and p 537, letter b, post); Dicta of Devlin J in *Hill v Baxter* ([1958] 1 All ER at p 196) followed. Dicta of North J in *R v Cottle* ([1958] NZLR at p 1029) considered and explained; *Mancini v Director of Public Prosecutions* ([1941] 3 All ER 272) and *Woolmington v Director of Public Prosecutions* ([1935] All ER Rep 1) applied; see *Broadhurst v R* [1964] 1 All ER 111.

he was driving in his car on an errand. He took off her stocking and strangled her with it. He gave evidence that a "blackness" came over him and that "I didn't know what I was doing. I didn't realise anything." He also said that previously he had had "feelings of blackness" and headaches, and there was evidence of his odd behaviour at times, of his mental backwardness and his religious leanings. There was medical evidence that the accused might have been suffering from an attack of psychomotor epilepsy, which was a disease of the mind affecting the reason and which could cause ignorance of the nature and quality of acts done. No other pathological cause for the accused's acts, or a state of automatism on his part was assigned by medical evidence at the trial. The defences of automatism (i.e., unconscious involuntary action) and of insanity within the M'Naghten rules were raised at the trial. The trial judge refused to leave the defence of automatism to the jury, but left to them the defence of insanity, which the jury rejected. On appeal against conviction of murder, it was held that the trial judge was justified in not putting the defence of automatism to the jury since the evidence attributed any involuntariness in the appellant's act solely to a disease of the mind and there was no sufficient evidence of automatism, apart from insanity, to be left to the jury. The appeal was accordingly dismissed.[187] *Per* Lord Denning:[188]

> In the present case the defence raised both automatism and insanity. And herein lies the difficulty because of the burden of proof. If the accused says he did not know what he was doing, then, so far as the defence of automatism is concerned, the Crown must prove that the act was a voluntary act.[189] But so far as the defence of insanity is concerned, the defence must prove that the act was an involuntary act due to disease of the mind.[190] This apparent incongruity was noticed by Sir Owen Dixon, Chief Justice of the High Court of Australia, in an address which is to be found in *31 Australian Law Journal 255* and it needs to be resolved. The defence here say: Even though we have not proved that the act was involuntary, yet the Crown have not proved that it was a voluntary act: and that point at least should have been put to the jury.
>
> My Lords, I think that the difficulty is to be resolved by remembering that, *whilst the ultimate burden rests on the Crown of proving every element essential in the crime, nevertheless in order to prove that the act was a voluntary act, the Crown is entitled to rely on the presumption that every man has sufficient mental capacity to be responsible for his crimes: and that if the defence wish to displace that presumption they must give some evidence from which the contrary may reasonably be inferred. Thus, a drunken man is presumed to have the capacity to form the specific intent necessary to*

---

[187] Editor's notes: As to proof of murder, see 10 Halsbury's Laws (3rd Edn) 704, para 1349; as to the burden of proof, see ibid, 436, 437, paras 808–811; and for cases on the burden of proof, see 14 Digest (Repl) 493–495, 4767–4791.

[188] At 535a-b.

[189] See *Woolmington's case* [1935] All ER Rep at 8; [1935] AC at 482.

[190] See *M'Naghten's Case* (1843), 10 Cl & Fin at 210.

constitute the crime, unless evidence is given from which it can reasonably be inferred that he was incapable of forming it;[191] see the valuable judgment of the Court of Justiciary in Kennedy v HM Advocate[192] which was delivered by the Lord Justice-General (Lord Normand). So also, it seems to me that a man's act is presumed to be a voluntary act unless there is evidence from which it can reasonably be inferred that it was involuntary.[193] To use the words of Devlin J the defence of automatism "ought not to be considered at all until the defence has produced at least *prima facie* evidence,"[194] and the words of North J in New Zealand "unless a proper foundation is laid."[195] The necessity of laying this proper foundation is on the defence: and if it is not so laid, the defence of automatism need not be left to the jury, any more than the defences of drunkenness,[196] provocation[197] or self-defence[198] need be (Emphasis added).

Lord Denning's words as italicised above employ the presumption phraseology which, based on what we have discussed elsewhere in this text thus far, does nothing more than wring confusion. His loose usage of the presumptions phraseology is technical in character. This, as we soon show is untenable. There are good and compelling reasons for drawing this conclusion. For starters, it is a fact that once the accused is charged, he does, during trial have the responsibility to raise, where appropriate, such defences as self-defence, non-insane automatism insanity or/and provocation as the case may be. The goal is to persuade an equable tribunal that there is sufficient doubt to warrant an acquittal by discharging the evidential burden which is cast upon the accused under such circumstances. As the *Woolmington case*[199] and statutory provisions we have referred to in this text show, the burden of proof lies on the prosecution. The only exception is insanity in which the accused bears both the evidential and legal burden to prove that he is and was, at the material time, insane.

---

[191] For a Zambian take see s 13(4) of the Penal Code, Chapter 87 of the Laws of Zambia which provides as follows: 'Intoxication shall be taken into account for the purpose of determining whether the person charged had formed any intention, specific or otherwise, in the absence of which he would not be guilty of the offence;' On recent interpretation of this section, see: *Tembo v The People* [1972] ZR 220: 'Evidence of drinking, even heavy drinking, is not sufficient in itself, nor is evidence that an accused person was under the influence of drink in the sense that his co-ordination or reflexes were affected. To constitute 'evidence fit to be left to a [court]' for the purposes of s 13(4) [of the Penal Code, Chapter 87 of the Laws of Zambia] there must be evidence that an accused person's capacities may have been affected to the extent that he may not have been able to form the necessary intent;' On the difference between drunkenness as a defence and drunkenness as an extenuating circumstance, see *Elias Mukala & Major Shindanji v The People* Appeal No 219/2020 at J13 9.5 & 9.6; On the question whether drunkenness is an extenuating circumstance, see *Jose Antonio Golliadi v The People* SCZ Appeal No 26 of 2017.

[192] 1944 SC (J) at 177.

[193] Italics added.

[194] See *Hill v Baxter* [1958] 1 All ER at 196; [1958] 1 QB at 285.

[195] See *R v Cottle* [1958] NZLR at 1025.

[196] *Kennedy v HM Advocate* 1944 SC (J) at 177.

[197] *R v Gauthier* 29 Cr App Rep 113, 15 Digest (Repl) 938, 8986.

[198] *R v Lobell* [1957] 1 All ER 734, [1957] 1 QB 547, 41 Cr App Rep 100, [1957] 2 WLR 524, 3rd Digest Supp.

[199] [1935] All ER Rep at 8; [1935] AC at 482.

24.3.4 *Presumptions as a factual inference*

It is perhaps important to state here too that presumptions as to factual inferences are not in the true sense of the concept, true presumptions. This is because as the case is with presumptions as a method of stating the burden of proof; there is no alteration in the allocation of risk. To that end, our use of the presumption terminology should be understood within the context of the concept of inferential thought only. A person charged with an offence is provisionally taken to have contemplated the consequences of his actions. The case of *R v Steane*[200] exemplifies this. Before the war the appellant, a British subject, was employed as a film actor in Germany, where he resided with his wife and two children. At the outbreak of war, he was arrested and, according to his own evidence, his first interview on 11 September 1939, ended with the order: "Say Heil Hitler, you dirty swine," which he refused to obey. He was thereupon knocked down, losing several teeth, and was then interned. Just before Christmas, 1939, he was sent for by Goebbels who asked him to broadcast and, on his refusing to do so, was warned that he was in an enemy country and that they had methods of making people do things. Subsequently, hints were dropped by officials as to German methods of persuasion and in consequence he submitted to a voice test, trying to perform as badly as he could. Next day he was ordered to read news three times a day and continued to do so until Apr 1946, when he refused to do any more. "G men" called on him and said: "If you don't obey, your wife and children will be put in a concentration camp," and later he was badly beaten up by more "G men" one ear being partly torn off. He agreed to work for his old employers helping to produce films, but there was no evidence that the films were or could be of any assistance to the Germans or harmful to this country. He swore that he never had the slightest idea or intention of assisting the enemy, that what he did was done to save his wife and children and not to assist the enemy. On an appeal on the ground of misdirection against a conviction, under the Defence (General) Regulations, reg 2A, of doing an act likely to assist the enemy with intent to assist the enemy. It was held that the proper direction to the jury would have been that it was for the prosecution to prove the criminal intent, and that, while the jury would be entitled to presume that intent if they thought that the act was done as the result of the free, uncontrolled action of the accused, they would not be entitled to presume it if the circumstances showed that the act was done in subjection to the power of the enemy or was as equally consistent with an innocent intent as with a criminal intent, e.g., a desire to save his wife

---

[200] [1947] 1 All ER 813.

and family from a concentration camp, and that the jury should convict only if satisfied by the evidence that the act complained of was, in fact, done to assist the enemy.[201]

Distillable from the foregoing are the following points as summarised by the editors of the reported case:[202]

- That where the essence or a necessary constituent of an offence is a particular intent, that intent must be proved by the Crown just as much as any other fact necessary to constitute the offence, and the burden of proving that intent remains throughout on the prosecution.

- If the prosecution prove an act the natural consequences of which would be a certain result and no evidence or explanation is given, then the jury may, on a proper direction, find that the accused is guilty of doing the act with the intent alleged, but if on the totality of the evidence there is room for more than one view as to the intent of the accused, the jury should be directed that it is for the prosecution to prove the intent to the jury's satisfaction, and if, on a review of the whole evidence, they either think that the intent did not exist or are left in doubt as to the intent, the accused is entitled to be acquitted.

- Where acts are done by a person in subjection to the power of another, especially if that other be a brutal enemy, an inference that he intended the natural consequences of the acts must not be drawn merely from the fact that he did them. A guilty intent cannot be presumed and must be proved.

The House of Lords in establishing an objective test for intention ruled, in *DPP v Smith*,[203] that if a reasonable person in the same situation as the defendant, with the defendant's knowledge of the circumstances, would have foreseen that the victim would suffer death or grievous bodily harm as a probable consequence of the defendant's conduct, the jury may presume that the defendant possessed the sufficient *mens rea* for murder. Byrne LJ opined that, '[a]lthough [...] that is the inference which may be drawn, and on the facts in certain circumstances, must inevitably be drawn, yet if on all the facts of a particular case it is not the correct inference, then it should not be drawn.'

---

[201] Editor's notes: Lord Goddard CJ points out that where an intent is a necessary ingredient of the offence charged, the burden of proving that intent remains throughout on the prosecution. It would seem, however, that if prima facie proof of the intent be given and the defence wish to set up duress, the burden of proving duress would then shift to the defence. In many cases the facts constituting the res gestae must include those giving rise to the alleged duress, in which event the attempt of the prosecution to make out a prima facie case of intent may fail. The jury must say, on the whole of the facts, whether the act done was the free action of the accused or whether it was done in subjection to superior power; As to Criminal Intention, see Halsbury, Hailsham Edn, Vol 9, pp 10–16, paras 3–8; and for Cases, see Digest, Vol 14, pp 31–33, Nos 31–40.

[202] [1947] 1 All ER 813.

[203] [1960] 2 All ER 450; See summary this at https://lucidlaw.co.uk/criminal-law/homicide-murder/with-malice-aforethought/dpp-v-smith/#:~:text=The%20House%20of%20Lords%20ruled,may%20presume%20that%20the%20defendant retrieved on 25/1/21.

In *DPP v Smith*, [204] a police officer leapt onto the bonnet of a car to prevent the defendant from driving away with stolen goods. However, the defendant drove away at high speed, making zigzagging movements to dislodge the officer from his bonnet. The police officer was thrown into the path of an oncoming car and killed. The jury was given the following direction by the judge:

> If you are satisfied that [...] he must as a reasonable man have contemplated that grievous bodily harm was likely to result to that officer [...] and that such harm did happen and the officer died in consequence, then the accused is guilty of capital murder [...] On the other hand, if you are not satisfied that he intended to inflict grievous bodily harm upon the officer – in other words, if you think he could not as a reasonable man have contemplated that grievous bodily harm would result to the officer in consequence of his actions – well, then, the verdict would be guilty of manslaughter.'

The accused was convicted of the police officer's murder. The accused argued that the judge erred in his direction to the jury, arguing that the test of intention is subjective. He argued that he could not be guilty of murder as he did not possess the requisite intent to kill or cause GBH to the police officer. The EWCA accepted this argument and applied a subjective test of intention. They therefore substituted the accused's murder conviction for a manslaughter conviction. The prosecution appealed this point to the House of Lords. The issue facing the court was whether the *mens rea* for murder is a subjective or objective test. The House of Lords concluded the test for intention in murder is an objective test. Therefore, they agreed with the direction given by the trial judge and re-instated the accused's murder conviction. Therefore, the correct question for trier of fact was:

> Whether a reasonable person in the same situation as the defendant, with the defendant's knowledge of the circumstances, would have foreseen that the victim would suffer death or grievous bodily harm as a probable consequence of the defendant's conduct. If the answer to this question is yes, then the jury can presume that the defendant possessed the sufficient *mens rea* for murder.

Two more examples of factual inferences are deserving of consideration. The first exemplified in in *Rex v Lumley*[205] relates to the continuance of life. A woman married H in 1836, left him some 7 years later in 1843 and remarried in 1847. On the question of presumption of life, the court of first instance convicted the woman of bigamy holding that there was a presumption of law that the first husband was alive at the date of her second marriage. This was,

---

[204] [1960] 2 All ER 450; See summary this at https://lucidlaw.co.uk/criminal-law/homicide-murder/with-malice-aforethought/dpp-v-smith/#:~:text=The%20House%20of%20Lords%20ruled,may%20presume%20that%20the%20defendant retrieved on 25/1/21

[205] [1869] LR 1 CCR 196 at 198.

for reasons that are now obvious, including the fact that the law makes no such presumption, reversed. Lush J held that '[t]he existence of the party at an antecedent period may or may not afford a reasonable inference that he was living at the subsequent date [....] The law makes no presumption either way.' The second is proof of guilty knowledge which relates to the doctrine of recent possession.[206] The basic premise is that if an accused person is found in possession of goods known to have been recently stolen and no explanation is offered, the court is well within its rights to draw the inference that the accused is the thief. It has been observed by Gardner JS in *Kape v The People*[207] that '[w]hen a court purports to draw an inference of guilty [knowledge] in a case of recent possession of stolen property it is necessary to consider what other inferences might be drawn.' Further, it has been held in *George Chileshe v The People*,[208] that:

> [i]t is the duty of a trial court, in cases where recent possession of stolen property may lead to the conviction of the accused, to consider whether such recent possession may be the result of the receiving of stolen property as opposed to guilt of the major crime during the commission of which the stolen property was obtained.[209]

Even so, the burden of proof is, as shown in *R v Hepworth*,[210] on the prosecution and failure to discharge such a burden thus raising doubt in the mind of the court, entitles the accused to an acquittal:[211]

> [...] at the trial of a prisoner on a charge of receiving stolen property, where the prisoner has been found in possession of property recently stolen, it is particularly desirable that emphasis should be placed on the principle that it is for the prosecution to prove their case, because the prisoner will be entitled to be acquitted if the jury, after hearing his explanation, are left in any doubt whether he received the property dishonestly, knowing it to be stolen. Although there is no particular formula of words whose use is essential in order to express effectively the burden of proof which lies on the prosecution, and the words "you must feel sure of the prisoner's guilt" would suffice, yet a summing-up on a charge of receiving, in such circumstances as those indicated above, will not be satisfactory if the jury are told merely that they must feel satisfied, without qualification such as "completely satisfied," that the prosecution have proved their case.[212]

---

[206] *R v Schama* (1914) 11 Cr App R 45; *R v Garth* [1949] 1 All ER 773.

[207] [1977] ZR 192.

[208] [1977] ZR 176 (SC).

[209] *Per* Gardner JS on behalf of the Court.

[210] [1955] 2 All ER 918.

[211] [1955] 2 All ER 918.

[212] Observations in *R v Kritz* [1949] 2 All ER at p 410, and *R v Summers* [1952] 1 All ER 1059 confirmed.

In *George Nswana v The People*,[213] the application was found in possession of a car two days after it was stolen. The correct car number was etched on its windows and appeared on the licence disc but the vehicle carried a false number plate. When the applicant was apprehended, he produced a blue book which bore a false name of the purported owner. At his trial he said he was in possession of the car as a driver of his employer who had asked him to drive it. In an earlier explanation to the police, he said he had borrowed the car from the person he said in evidence was his employer. The trial magistrate found that as a prudent driver the applicant must have noticed the suspicious features surrounding the car and, that coupled with recent possession and that the applicant's explanation was not true, convicted him. In the Supreme Court he argued that the telling of lies does not necessarily indicate guilt and the magistrate's finding that the applicant did not obtain possession from another person should be rejected. It was held as follows: (i) the inference of guilt based on recent possession, particularly where no explanation is offered which might reasonably be true, rests on the absence of any reasonable likelihood that the goods might have changed hands in the meantime and the consequent high degree of probability that the person in recent possession himself obtained them and committed the offence. Where suspicious features surround the case that indicate that the applicant cannot reasonably claim to have been in innocent possession, the question remains whether the applicant, not being in innocent possession, was the thief or a guilty receiver or retainer (ii) The distinction is that a receiver receives with guilty knowledge at the time of receipt while the offence of retaining involves guilty knowledge of theft but acquired after the receipt of the property.

In *Zonde and Others v The People*,[214] the Supreme Court held that '[t]he doctrine of recent possession applies to a person *in the absence of any explanation* that might be true when found in possession of the complainant's property barely a few hours after the complainant had suffered an aggravated robbery.'[215] Put another way, the burden of proof is placed on the accused to prove his innocence which is a roundabout way of saying that the accused is presumed 'guilty' until he can prove otherwise by way of a satisfactory explanation.

In *Hahuti v The People*,[216] the facts of the case were, briefly, that the appellant was convicted of stock theft. The ox was stolen sometime in October 1972. It was next seen being sold by the appellant in May, 1973. Recent possession could not support such a case. A period of eight months could not be said to be recent possession as the ox could have changed hands during that period. The appellant was put on his defence and he gave evidence stating when he was in possession of the ox thus filling the gap in the prosecution evidence. After reviewing a number of cases, Doyle CJ (as he then was) observed as follows at 156 (lines 18-24):

---

[213] [1988 – 1989] ZR 174 (SC).

[214] (1980) ZR 337.

[215] See *George Nswana v The People* [1988 – 1989] ZR 174 (SC).

[216] [1974] ZR 154 (HC).

A man against whom there is no prima facie case at the close of the case for the prosecution is entitled to an acquittal. An error on the part of the trial court in thinking that there is prima facie case cannot alter that position. In my opinion section 206 of the CPC is mandatory, and means that if it appears to a court properly directed that the case is not made out, the accused is entitled to an acquittal. The appellant in this case should have been acquitted at the close of the prosecution case.

SELECT BIBLIOGRAPHY

Anderson T, Schum D and Twining W, *Analysis of Evidence* (2nd edn CUP, 2005)

Ashworth, A. and Blake, M. 'The presumption of innocence in English criminal law' [1998] Crim LR 306

Baki, N. and Agate, J. 'Too much, too little, too late? Draft CPS guidance on speaking to witnesses' [2015] Ent LR 155

Bennion, F. 'Statutory exceptions: a third knot in the golden thread' [1988] Crim LR 31

Birch, D. 'A better deal for vulnerable witnesses?' [2000] Crim LR 223

Birch, D. 'Children's evidence' [1992] Crim LR 262

Birch, D. 'Corroboration: Goodbye to All That?' [1995] Crim LR 524

Birch, D. 'Criminal Justice Act 2003: (4) Hearsay – same old story, same old song?' (2004) Crim LR, Jul, 556–573

Birch, D. 'Hunting the snark: the elusive statutory exception' [1988] Crim LR 221

Blom-Cooper QC, Sir L. 'Witness immunity: the argument against' (2006) 156 (7232) NLJ 1088–1089

Brabyn, J. 'A criminal defendant's spouse as a prosecution witness' [2011] Criminal Law Review 613

Branston, G. 'A reprehensible use of cautions as bad character evidence' [2015] Crim LR 594

Brennan, G. 'Sexual history evidence: The Youth Justice and Criminal Evidence Act 1999' (2002) 8 Queen Mary Law Journal 7

Brevis, B., Jackson, A. and Stockdale, M. 'Bad character evidence and potential satellite litigation' [2013] J Crim L 110

Brewis, B. and Stockdale, M. 'False allegations: the limitations of the "evidential basis" test' [2014] J Crim L 453

Bridge, C. 'Care Proceedings: burden of proof' [2012] Family Law 1074

Brown, S. 'Public interest immunity' (1994) PL, Win, 579–595

Buxton, R. 'Victims as witnesses in trials of sexual offences: towards equality of arms' [2015] Crim LR 679

Chippindall, A. 'Expert advice and legal professional privilege' (2003) JPI Law, Jan, 61–70

Chippindall, A.C. 'Expert evidence and legal professional privilege' (2003) JPI Law, Jan, 61–70

Choo, A. L. T. and Nash, S. 'Evidence law in England and Wales: the impact of the Human Rights Act 1998' (2003) 7(1) International Journal of Evidence and Proof 31–61

Civil Procedure Rules 1998: www.justice.gov.uk/courts/procedure-rules/civil/rules/part01

Coe, P. 'Justifying reverse burdens of proof: a tale of diminished responsibility and a tangled knot of authorities' [2013] J Crim L 360

Cooper, D. 'Pigot unfulfilled: video recorded evidence under section 28 of the YJCEA 1999' [2005] Crim LR 456

Cooper, P., Backen, P., and Marchant, R. 'Getting to grips with ground rules hearings: a checklist for judges, advocates and intermediaries to promote the fair treatment of vulnerable people in court' [2015] Crim LR 420

Cornish, W.R. and Sealy, A.P. 'Juries and the rules of evidence' [1973] Crim LR 208

Creaton, J. 'Competence to give evidence' [2007] Police Journal 356

Creighton, P. 'Spouse competence and compellability' [1990] Crim LR 34

Daniele, M. 'Testimony through a live link in the perspective of the right to confront witnesses' [2014] Crim LR 189

Dein, A. 'Police misconduct revisited' [2000] Crim LR 801

Dennis, I. 'Reverse onuses and the presumption of innocence: in search of principle' [2005] Crim LR 901

Dennis, I. 'Sexual history evidence: evaluating Section 41' [2006] Crim LR 869

Dennis I, *The Law of Evidence* (5th edn Sweet & Maxwell, 2013)

Dingwall, G. 'Statutory exceptions, burdens of proof and the Human Rights Act 1998' (2002) 65 MLR 450

Doak, J. and Huxley-Binns, R. 'Anonymous witnesses in England and Wales: charting a course from Strasbourg?' [2009] 73(6) 508

Douglas, G. 'Care Proceedings: medical evidence – burden and standard of proof' [2012] Family Law 936

Durston, G. 'Previous (in)consistent statements after the Criminal Justice Act 2003' [2005] Crim LR 206

Ellison, L. 'Cross-examination in rape trials' [1998] Crim LR 605

Ettinger, C. 'Case comment' (2005) JPI Law 3, C114–117

European Convention on Human Rights: www.echr.coe.int/Documents/Convention_ENG.pdf

Federal Rules of Evidence (2015) rules 801-807 at https://www.rulesofevidence.org/article-viii/ (accessed 1 July 2015)

Fitzpatrick, B. 'Reverse burden and Art 6(2) of the European Convention on Human Rights: official secrets' [2008] J Crim L 190

Gallanis, T.P. 'The rise of modern evidence law' (1999) 84 Iowa L Rev 499

Gillespie, A. 'Compellability of a child victim' (2000) (64)1 J Crim L 98

Gillespie, A. and Bettinson, V. 'Preventing secondary victimisation through anonymity' [2007] 70 MLR 114

Gooderham, P. 'Witness immunity: the argument in favour' (2006) 156 (7232), NLJ 1086–1087

Government Actuary's Department. Compensation for injury and death (Ogden tables): http://www.gad.gov.uk/services/Other%20Services/Compensation_for_injury_and_death.html

Hamer, D. 'Presumptions, standards and burdens: managing the cost of error' [2014] LP&R 221

Hamer, D. 'The presumption of innocence and reverse burdens: a balancing act' (2007) 66 CLJ 142

Hartshorne, J. 'Corroboration and care warnings after Makanjuola' (1998) 2 E & P (1) 1–12

Healey, P. 'Proof and policy: no golden threads' [1987] Crim LR 355

Henderson, E (2014) All the proper protections—the Court of Appeal rewrites the rules for the cross-examination of vulnerable witnesses. Crim LR 93–108.

Henderson, E. 'Bigger fish to fry: should the reform of cross-examination be expanded beyond vulnerable witnesses?' [2015] E&P 83

Henderson, E. 'Communicative competence? Judges, advocates and intermediaries discuss communication issues in the cross-examination of vulnerable witnesses' [2015] Crim LR 659

Henderson, E. 'Root or branch? Reforming the cross-examination of children' [2010] CLJ 460

Heydon JD, *Cross on Evidence* (10th edn Lexis Nexis, 2016)

Hjalmarsson, J. 'The standard of proof in civil cases: an insurance fraud perspective' [2013] E&P 47

Ho, H. 'Similar facts in civil cases' (2006) 26 Oxford Journal of Legal Studies 131

Hoffmann, L. 'Similar facts after Boardman' (1975) 91 LQR 193

Hoyano, L. 'Coroners and Justice Act 2009: special measures directions take two: entrenching unequal access to justice' [2010] Criminal Law Review 345

Hoyano, L. 'Reforming the adversarial trial for vulnerable witnesses and defendants' [2015] Crim LR 107

Hoyano, L. 'Striking a balance between the rights of defendants and vulnerable witnesses: will special measures directions contravene guarantees of a fair trial?' [2001] Crim LR 948

Hoyano, L. 'Variations on a theme by Pigot: special measures directions for child witnesses' [2000] Crim LR 250

Hoyano, L. 'Vulnerable witnesses: manner of cross-examination – witnesses young, female complainants' [2012] Crim LR 565

Jackson, J. 'Insufficiency of identification evidence based on personal impression' [1986] Crim LR 203

Jackson, J.D. 'The ultimate issue rule – one rule too many' [1984] Crim LR 75

James, J. 'Good character directions and blemished defendants' [1996] 2 Web JCLI

Jones, D. 'The evidence of a three-year-old child' [1987] Crim LR 677

Jones, I. 'A problem of the past? The politics of "relevance" in evidential reform' [2012] Contemporary Issues of Law 277

Justice website – Achieving Best Evidencewww.cps.gov.uk/publications/docs/best_evidence_in_criminal_proceedings.pdf

Kaluba BC, *Evidence Law: Practice and Procedure in Zambia* (Chribwa Publishers, 2022)

Keane, A. 'The collateral evidence rule: a sad forensic fable involving a circus, its sideshow, confusion, vanishing tricks and alchemy' [2015] E&P 100

Keane, A. 'Towards a principled approach to cross-examination of vulnerable witnesses' [2012] Crim LR 407

Keane, A. and Fortson, R. 'Leading questions – a critical analysis' [2011] Crim LR 280

Keane, A. and McKeown, P. (2012) The Modern Law of Evidence. Ninth edition.Oxford: Oxford University Press

Kibble, N. 'Judicial discretion and the admissibility of prior sexual history evidence' [2005] Crim LR 263

Kibble, N. 'Judicial perspectives on the operation of Section 41' [2005] Crim LR 190

Kibble, N. 'Sexual offences: whether a rape complainant's false complaint "misconduct" is the result of personality problems?' [2011] Crim LR 818

Law Commission (1997) Evidence in Criminal Proceedings: Hearsay and Related Topics, Law Com No 245

Law Commission Report, Law Com No 273 (2001) 'Evidence in criminal proceedings: previous misconduct of a defendant'

Lewis, P. 'The Human Rights Act 1998: shifting the burden' [2000] Crim LR 667

Lippke, R. 'Justifying the proof structure of criminal trials' [2013] E&P 323

Lloyd Bostock, S. 'The effects on juries of hearing about the defendant's previous criminal record: a simulation study' [2000] Crim LR 734

Mackie, J. 'A question of character' [2012] SJ 156(6), 7

Malek HM (Ed), *Phipson on Evidence* (16th edn Sweet & Maxwell, 2016)

Matibini, P (2017) Zambian Civil Procedure. London: Lexis Nexis

May, R and Powles, S. (2004) Criminal Evidence. Fifth edition. London: Sweet & Maxwell

Mirfi eld, P. (1998) Silence, Confessions and Improperly Obtained Evidence, Oxford Monographs on Criminal Law and Justice, Oxford University Press

Mirfi eld, P. 'Corroboration after the 1994 Act' [1995] Crim LR 448

Mirfield, P. 'Bad character and the Law Commission' (2002) 6 E&P 141

Mirfield, P. 'Character and credibility' [2009] Crim LR 135

Mirfield, P. 'Character, credibility and truthfulness' [2008] LQR 1

Mirfield, P. 'Human wrongs?' (2002) 118 LQR 20

Mirfield, P. 'The legacy of Hunt' [1988] Crim LR 19

Monaghan, N. 'Reconceptualising good character' [2015] E&P 190

Munday, R. (2011) The Law of Evidence. Sixth edition. Oxford: Oxford University Press

Munday, R. 'Adverse denial and purposive confession' (2003) Crim LR, Dec, 850–864

Munday, R. 'Athwal and all that: previous statements, narratives and the taxonomy of hearsay' (2010) 74 Crim JC L 415

Munday, R. 'Calling a hostile witness' [1989] Crim LR 866

Munday, R. 'Case management, similar fact evidence in civil cases, and a divided law of evidence' (2006) 10 International Journal of Evidence and Proof 81

Munday, R. 'Convicting on confessional evidence in the complete absence of a corpus delicti' (1993) 157 JPJo 275

Munday, R. 'Cut-throat defences and the "propensity to be untruthful" under Section 104 of the

Criminal Justice Act 2003' [2005] Crim LR 624

Munday, R. 'Misconduct that "has to do with the alleged facts of the offence with which the defendant is charged" . . . more or less' [2008] Crim L 214

Munday, R. 'Refreshing memory: previous statements that fail to revive witnesses' memories' [2012] CL&J 213

Munday, R. 'Sham marriages and spousal compellability' [2001] 65(4) J Crim L 336

Munday, R. 'Single-act propensity' [2010] J Crim L 128

Munday, R. 'The purposes of Gateway (g)' [2006] Crim LR 300

Munday, R. 'What constitutes "other reprehensible behaviour" under the bad character provisions of the Criminal Justice Act 2003?' [2005] Crim LR 24

Munday, R. 'What constitutes a good character?' [1997] Crim LR 247

Murphy P, *Murphy on Evidence* (12ᵗʰ edn OUP, 2005)

Mwanza BJ, *Passing The Bar Made Easy: Evidence and Procedure* (Brian J Mwanza, 2020).

Ormerod, D. 'Case Comment Evidence: hearsay - Criminal Justice Act 2003 s.116 - D C... Ali v Revenue and Customs Prosecutions Office [2008] EWCA Crim 1466.

Ormerod, D. 'Evidence: previous inconsistent statements – admissibility' [2007] Crim LR 887

Ormerod, D. 'Hostile witness maintaining contents of prior statement not true' [2009] Crim LR 197

Ormerod, D. 'Previous inconsistent statements: directing juries in relation to

Ormerod, D. 'R v Athwal: evidence – hearsay – previous consistent statement –admissibility – rebutting fabrication' [2009] Crim LR 726

Ormerod, D. 'Sounds familiar? Voice identifi cation evidence' [2001] Crim LR 595

Ormerod, D. and Birch, D. 'The evolution of the discretionary exclusion of evidence' [2004] Crim LR 767

Ormerod, D., Choo, A. and Easter, R. 'Coroners and Justice Act 2009: the witness anonymity and investigation anonymity provisions' [2010] Criminal Law Review 368

PACE 1984 Codes of Practice: www.homeoffi ce.gov.uk/police/powers/pace-codes

Padfield, N. 'The burden of proof unresolved' (2005) 64 CLJ 17

Pattenden, R. 'Evidence of previous malpractice by police witnesses and R v Edwards' [1992] Crim LR 549

Pattenden, R. 'The hostile witness' (1992) 56 J C L 414

Pattenden, R. 'The submission of no case – some recent developments' [1982] Crim LR 558

Picinali, F. 'The threshold lies in the method: instructing jurors about reasoning beyond reasonable doubt' [2015] E&P 139

Practice Direction 33 – Civil Evidence Act 1995 and Part 33 of the Civil Procedure Rules (Miscellaneous Rules About Evidence): http://www.justice.gov.uk/courts/procedure-rules/civil/rules/part33).

previous inconsistent statements in view of effect and application of s 119 of the Criminal Justice Act 2003' [2009] Crim LR 529

R v Delaney (1989) 88 Cr App R 338 – 'Case comment: evidence and the admissibility of a confession' (1989) Crim LR, Feb, 139–140

R v Goldenberg (1989) 88 Cr App R 285 – 'Case comment: admissions and confessions: words or acts of person making confession not included in matters affecting reliability'(1988) Crim LR, Oct, 678–679

Ragavan, S. 'The compellability rule in England and Wales: support for the spouse of the defendant' [2013] J Crim L 310

Redmayne, M. 'Recognising propensity' [2011] Crim LR 117

Redmayne, M. 'Rethinking the privilege against self-incrimination' (2007) 27(2) OJLS 209–232

Redmayne, M. 'The relevance of bad character' (2002) CLJ 684

Reforming the European Convention on Human Rights: Interlaken, Izmir, Brighton and beyond: http://www.coe.int/t/dghl/standardsetting/cddh/reformechr/Publications/Compilation%20ReformECHR2014_en.pdf

Roberts, A. 'Evidence – non-defendant's bad character' [2011] Crim LR 58

Roberts, A. 'Evidence: bad character of defendant – attack on prosecution witness – Criminal Justice Act 2003 s 101(1)(g) – test for admissibility' [2011] Crim LR 642

Roberts, P. 'Modernising police powers – again?' (2007) Crim LR, Dec, 934–948

Roberts, P. 'Taking the burden of proof seriously' [1995] Crim LR 783

Roberts, P. 'The presumption of innocence brought home/Kebilene deconstructed' (2002) 118 LQR 41

rules for the cross-examination of vulnerable witnesses' [2014] Crim LR 93

Rogers WVM, *Winfield & Jolowicz Tort* (18th edn Sweet & Maxwell, 2010).

Seabrooke, S. 'Current topic: the vanishing trick – blurring the line between credit and issue' [1999] Crim LR 387

Singh C and Ramjohn M, *Unlocking Evidence* (3rd edn Routledge, 2016).

Singh C, *Evidence: Question and Answers 2015–2016* (11th edn Routledge, 2015)

Singh, C. (2015). Quis custodiet ipsos custodies? Should Justice Beware: a review of the debate surrounding the reliability of voice identification evidence in light of advances in biometric voice identification technology. International Commentary on Evidence. Volume 11: 1–28. Germany and the USA: De Grutyer.

Smaller, E. 'Giving the vulnerable a voice' [2012] Counsel 25

Smith, E, and Stockdale, M. 'Bad character evidence as evidence of identity' [2015] J Crim L 12

Smith, J.C. 'The presumption of innocence' (1987) 38 NILQ 223

Spencer, J. 'Cautions as character evidence: a reply to Judge Branston' [2015] Crim LR 611

Spencer, J. 'Evidence of bad character – where we are today' [2014] Arch Rev 5

Spencer, J. 'Rape shields and the right to a fair trial' [2001] Cambridge Law Journal 452

Stapleton, J. 'Factual causation of mesothelioma and statistical validity' [2012] LQR 221

Stone, J. 'The rule of exclusion of similar fact evidence: England' (1932) 46 Harvard LR 954

Tapper C, *Cross & Tapper on Evidence* (11th edn, 2007)

Tapper, C. 'The Criminal Evidence Act 2003: evidence of bad character' [2004] Crim LR 533

Tavros, V. and Tierney, S. 'Presumption of innocence and the Human Rights Act' (2004) 67 MLR 402

The Crown Prosecution Service Website provides a useful summary of the law on hearsay at: www.cps.gov.uk/legal/h_to_k/hearsay/ (accessed 17 December 2012)

Twining W, *Rethinking Evidence: Exploratory Essays* (NUP, 1994)

Uglow S, *Evidence: Cases and Materials* (2nd edn Sweet & Maxwell, 1997)

Walchover, D. and Heaton-Armstrong, A. 'Reasonable doubt' (2010) 174 Criminal Law and Justice Weekly 484

Waterman, A. and Dempster, T. 'Bad character: feeling our way one year on' [2006] Crim LR 614

Williams, G. 'Evidential burdens on the defence' (1977) 127 NLJ 182

Williams, G. 'The evidential burden: some common misapprehensions' (1977) 127 NLJ 156

Worthern, T. 'Legislative comment: the hearsay provisions of the Criminal Justice Act 2003: so far, not so good?' (2008) 6 Crim LR 431–442

Wurtzel, D. 'The youngest witness in a murder trial: making it possible for very young children to give evidence' [2014] Crim LR 893

Zuckerman, A. 'The third exception to the Woolmington Rule' (1976) 92 LQR 402

APPENDIX

Select Statutes, rules of court and practice directions

CONSTITUTION OF THE REPUBLIC OF ZAMBIA
(As amended by Act No 18 of 1996 & No 2 of 2016)

PART III

PROTECTION OF THE FUNDAMENTAL RIGHTS AND FREEDOMS OF THE INDIVIDUAL

Fundamental rights and freedoms

11. It is recognised and declared that every person in Zambia has been and shall continue to be entitled to the fundamental rights and freedoms of the individual, that is to say, the right, whatever his race, place of origin, political opinions, colour, creed, sex or marital status, but subject to the limitations contained in this Part, to each and all of the following, namely:
    (a) life, liberty, security of the person and the protection of the law;
    (b) freedom of conscience, expression, assembly, movement and association;
    (c) protection of young persons from exploitation;
    (d) protection for the privacy of his home and other property and from deprivation of property without compensation; and the provisions of this Part shall have effect for the purpose of affording protection to those rights and freedoms subject to such limitations of that protection as are contained in this Part, being limitations designed to ensure that the enjoyment of the said rights and freedoms by any individual does not prejudice the rights and freedoms of others or the public interest.

Protection of right to life

12. (1) A person shall not be deprived of his life intentionally except in execution of the sentence of a court in respect of a criminal offence under the law in force in Zambia of which he has been convicted.
    (2) A person shall not deprive an unborn child of life by termination of pregnancy except in accordance with the conditions laid down by an Act of Parliament for that purpose.
    (3) Without prejudice to any liability for a contravention of any other law with respect to the use of force in such cases as are hereinafter mentioned, a person shall not be regarded as having been deprived of his life in contravention of this Article if he dies as a result of the use of force to such extent as is reasonably justifiable in the circumstances of the case-
        (a) for the defence of any person from violence or for the defence of property;
        (b) in order to effect a lawful arrest or to prevent the escape of a person lawfully detained;
        (c) for the purpose of suppressing a riot, insurrection, mutiny or if he dies as a result of a lawful act of war; or
        (d) in order to prevent the commission by that person of a criminal offence.

Protection of right to personal liberty

13. (1) A person shall not be deprived of his personal liberty except as may be authorised by law in any of the following cases:
        (a) in execution of a sentence or order of a court, whether established for Zambia or some other country, in respect of a criminal offence of which he has been convicted;
        (b) in execution of an order of a court of record punishing him for contempt of that court or of a court inferior to it;

161

(c) in execution of an order of a court made to secure the fulfillment of any obligation imposed on him by law;

(d) for the purpose of bringing him before a court in execution of an order of a court;

(e) upon reasonable suspicion of his having committed, or being about to commit, a criminal offence under the law in force in Zambia;

(f) under an order of a court or with the consent of his parent or guardian, for his education or welfare during any period ending not later than the date when he attains the age of eighteen years;

(g) for the purpose of preventing the spread of an infectious or contagious disease;

(h) in the case of a person who is, or is reasonably suspected to be, of unsound mind, addicted to drugs or alcohol or a vagrant, for the purpose of his care or treatment or the protection of the community;

(i) for the purpose of preventing the unlawful entry of that person into Zambia, or for the purpose of effecting the expulsion, extradition or other lawful removal of that person while he is being conveyed through Zambia in the course of his extradition or removal as a convicted prisoner from one country to another; or

(j) to such extent as may be necessary in the execution of a lawful order requiring that person to remain within a specified area within Zambia or prohibiting him from being within such area, or to such extent as may be reasonably justifiable for the taking of proceedings against that person relating to the making of any such order, or to such extent as may be reasonably justifiable for restraining that person during any visit that he is permitted to make to any part of Zambia in which, in consequence of any such order, his presence would otherwise be unlawful.

(2) Any person who is arrested or detained shall be informed as soon as reasonably practicable, in a language that he understands, of the reasons for his arrest or detention.

(3) Any person who is arrested or detained-

(a) for the purpose of bringing him before a court in execution of an order of a court; or

(b) upon reasonable suspicion of his having committed, or being about to commit, a criminal offence under the law in force in Zambia;

and who is not released, shall be brought without undue delay before a court; and if any person arrested or detained under paragraph (b) is not tried within a reasonable time, then, without prejudice to any further proceedings that may be brought against him, he shall be released either unconditionally or upon reasonable conditions, including in particular such conditions as are reasonably necessary to ensure that he appears at a later date for trial or for proceedings preliminary to trial.

(4) Any person who is unlawfully arrested or detained by any other person shall be entitled to compensation therefor from that other person.

Protection from slavery and forced labour

14. (1) A person shall not be held in slavery or servitude. Protection from slavery and forced labour

(2) A person shall not be required to perform forced labour.

(3) For the purpose of this Article, the expression "forced labour" does not include-

(a) any labour required in consequence of a sentence or order of a court;

(b) labour required of any person while he is lawfully detained that, though not required in consequence of a sentence or order of a court, is reasonably necessary in the interests of hygiene or for the maintenance of the place at which he is detained;

(c) any labour required of a member of a disciplined force in pursuance of his duties as such or, in the case of a person who has conscientious objections to service as a member of a naval, military or air force, any labour that that person is required by law to perform in place of such service;

(d) any labour required during any period when the Republic is at war or a declaration under Article 30 or 31 is in force or in the event of any other emergency or calamity that threatens the life and well-being of the community, to the extent that the requiring of such labour is reasonably justifiable in the circumstances of any situation arising or existing during that period, or as a result of that other emergency or calamity, for the purpose of dealing with that situation; or

(e) any labour reasonably required as part of reasonable and normal communal or other civic obligations.

Protection from inhuman treatment

15. A person shall not be subjected to torture, or to inhuman or degrading punishment or other like treatment.

Protection from deprivation of property

16. (1) Except as provided in this Article, property of any description shall not be compulsorily taken possession of, and interest in or right over property of any description shall not be compulsorily acquired, unless by or under the authority of an Act of Parliament which provides for payment of adequate compensation for the property or interest or right to be taken possession of or acquired.

    (2) Nothing contained in or done under the authority of any law shall be held to be inconsistent with or in contravention of clause (1) to the extent that it is shown that such law provides for the taking possession or acquisition of any property or interest therein or right thereover-

        (a) in satisfaction of any tax, rate or due;

        (b) by way of penalty for breach of any law, whether under civil process or after conviction of an offence;

        (c) in execution of judgments or orders of courts;

        (d) upon the attempted removal of the property in question out of or into Zambia in contravention of any law;

        (e) as an incident of contract including a lease, tenancy, mortgage, charge, pledge or bill of sale or of a title deed to land;

        (f) for the purpose of its administration, care or custody on behalf of and for the benefit of the person entitled to the beneficial interest therein;

        (g) by way of the vesting of enemy property or for the purpose of the administration of such property;

        (h) for the purpose of-

            (i) the administration of the property of a deceased person, a person of unsound mind or a person who has not attained the age of eighteen years, for the benefit of the persons entitled to the beneficial interest therein;

            (ii) the administration of the property of a person adjudged bankrupt or a body corporate in liquidation, for the benefit of the creditors of such bankrupt or body corporate and, subject thereto, for the benefit of other persons entitled to the beneficial interest in the property;

            (iii) the administration of the property of a person who has entered into a deed of arrangement for the benefit of his creditors; or

            (iv) vesting any property subject to a trust in persons appointed as trustees under the instrument creating the trust or by a court or, by order of a court, for the purpose of giving effect to the trust;

        (i) in consequence of any law relating to the limitation of actions;

        (j) in terms of any law relating to abandoned, unoccupied unutilised or undeveloped land, as defined in such law;

        (k) in terms of any law relating to absent or non-resident owners, as defined in such law, of any property;

        (l) in terms of any law relating to trusts or settlements;

        (m) by reason of a dangerous state or prejudicial to the health or safety of human beings, animals or plants.

        (n) as a condition in connection with the granting of permission for the utilisation of that or other property in any particular manner;

        (o) for the purpose of or in connection with the prospecting for, or exploitation of, minerals belonging to the Republic on terms which provide for the respective interests of the persons affected;

        (p) in pursuance of a provision for the marketing of property of that description in the common interests of the various persons otherwise entitled to dispose of that property;

        (q) by way of the taking of a sample for the purposes of any law;

        (r) by way of the acquisition of the shares, or a class of shares, in a body corporate on terms agreed to by the holders of not less than nine-tenths in value of those shares or that class of shares;

(s) where the property consists of an animal, upon its being found trespassing or straying;

(t) for so long as may be necessary for the purpose of any examination, investigation, trial or inquiry or, in the case of land, the carrying out thereon-

    (i) of work for the purpose of the conservation of natural resources of any description; or

    (ii) of agricultural development or improvement which the owner or occupier of the land has been required, and has without reasonable and lawful excuse refused or failed, to carry out;

(u) where the property consists of any licence or permit;

(v) where the property consists of wild animals existing in their natural habitat or the carcasses of wild animals;

(w) where the property, is held by a body corporate established by law for public purposes and in which no moneys have been invested other than moneys provided by Parliament;

(x) where the property is any mineral, mineral oil or natural gases or any rights accruing by virtue of any title or licence for the purpose of searching for or mining any mineral, mineral oil or natural gases-

    (i) upon failure to comply with any provision of such law relating to the title or licence or to the exercise of the rights accruing or to the development or exploitation of any mineral, mineral oil or natural gases; or

    (ii) terms of any law vesting any such property or rights in the President;

(y) for the purpose of the administration or disposition of such property or interest or right by the President in implementation of a comprehensive land policy or a policy designed to ensure that the statute law, the Common Law and the doctrines of equity relating to or affecting the interest in or rights over land, or any other interests or rights enjoyed by Chiefs and persons claiming through or under them, shall apply with substantial uniformity throughout Zambia;

(z) in terms of any law providing for the conversion of titles to land from freehold to leasehold and the imposition of any restriction on subdivision, assignment or sub-letting;

    (aa) in terms of any law relating to-

    (i) the forfeiture or confiscation of the property of a person who has left Zambia for the purpose or apparent purpose, of defeating the ends of justice;

    (ii) the imposition of a fine on, and the forfeiture or confiscation of the property of, a person who admits a contravention of any law relating to the imposition or collection of any duty or tax or to the prohibition or control of dealing or transactions in gold, currencies or securities.

(3) An Act of Parliament such as is referred to in clause (1) shall provide that in default of agreement, the amount of compensation shall be determined by a court of competent jurisdiction.

Protection for privacy of home and other property

17. (1) Except with his own consent, a person shall not be subjected to the search of his person or his property or the entry by others on his premises.

    (2) Nothing contained in or done under the authority of any law shall be held to be inconsistent with or in contravention of this Article to the extent that it is shown that the law in question makes provision-

    (a) that is reasonably required in the interests of defence, public safety, public order, public morality, public health, town and country planning, the development and utilisation of mineral resources, or in order to secure the development or utilisation of any property for a purpose beneficial to the community;

    (b) that is reasonably required for the purpose of protecting the rights or freedoms of other persons;

    (c) that authorises an officer or agent of the Government, a local government authority or a body corporate established by law for a public purpose to enter on the premises of any person in order to inspect those premises or anything thereon for the purpose of any tax, rate or due or in order to carry out work connected with any property that is lawfully on those premises and that belongs to the Government, authority or body corporate, as the case may be; or

164

(d) that authorises, for the purpose of enforcing the judgment or order of a court in any civil proceedings, the search of any person or property by order of a court or entry upon any premises by such order;

and except so far as that provision or, as the case may be, anything done under the authority thereof is shown not to be reasonably justifiable in a democratic society.

Provisions to secure protection of law

18. (1) If any person is charged with a criminal offence, then, unless the charge is withdrawn, the case shall be afforded a fair hearing within a reasonable time by an independent and impartial court established by law.

(2) Every person who is charged with a criminal offence-

    (a) shall be presumed to be innocent until he is proved or has pleaded guilty;

    (b) shall be informed as soon as reasonably practicable, in a language that he understands and in detail, of the nature of the offence charged;

    (c) shall be given adequate time and facilities for the preparation of his defence;

    (d) shall unless legal aid is granted to him in accordance with the law enacted by Parliament for such purpose be permitted to defend himself before the court in person, or at his own expense, by a legal representative of his own choice;

    (e) shall be afforded facilities to examine in person or by his legal representative the witnesses called by the prosecution before the court, and to obtain the attendance and carry out the examination of witnesses to testify on his behalf before the court on the same conditions as those applying to witnesses called by the prosecution; and

    (f) shall be permitted to have without payment the assistance of an interpreter if he cannot understand the language used at the trial of the charge;

and except with his own consent the trial shall not take place in his absence unless he so conducts himself as to render the continuance of the proceedings in his presence impracticable and the court has ordered him to be removed and the trial to proceed in his absence.

(3) When a person is tried for any criminal offence, the accused person or any person authorised by him in that behalf shall, if he so requires and subject to payment of such reasonable fee as may be prescribed by law, be given within a reasonable time after judgement a copy for the use of the accused person of any record of the proceedings made by or on behalf of the court.

(4) A person shall not be held to be guilty of a criminal offence on account of any act or omission that did not, at the time it took place, constitute such an offence, and a penalty shall not be imposed for any criminal offence that is severer in degree or description than the maximum penalty that might have been imposed for that offence at the time it was committed.

(5) A person who shows that he has been tried by a competent court for a criminal offence and either convicted or acquitted shall not again be tried for that offence or for any other criminal offence of which he could have been convicted at the trial for that offence, except upon the order of a superior court in the course of appeal or review proceedings relating to the conviction or acquittal.

(6) A person shall not be tried for a criminal offence if he shows that he has been pardoned for that offence.

(7) A person who is tried for a criminal offence shall not be compelled to give evidence at the trial.

(8) A person shall not be convicted of a criminal offence unless that offence is defined and the penalty is prescribed in a written law:

Provided that nothing in this clause shall prevent a court of record from punishing any person for contempt of itself notwithstanding that the act or omission constituting the contempt is not defined in a written law and the penalty therefore is not so prescribed.

(9) Any court or other adjudicating authority prescribed by law for determination of the existence or extent of any civil right or obligation shall be established by law and shall be independent and impartial; and where proceedings for such a determination are instituted by any person before such a court or other adjudicating authority, the case shall be given a fair hearing within a reasonable time.

(10) Except with the agreement of all the parties thereto, all proceedings of every court and proceedings for the determination of the existence or extent of any civil right or obligation before any other adjudicating authority, including the announcement of the decision of the court or other authority, shall be held in public.

(11)   Nothing in clause (10) shall prevent the court or other adjudicating authority from excluding from the proceedings persons other than the parties thereto and their legal representatives to such extent as the court or other authority-

   (a)   may consider necessary or expedient in circumstances where publicity would prejudice the interests of justice or in interlocutory proceedings; or

   (b)   may be empowered by law to do in the interest of defence, public safety, public order, public morality, the welfare of persons under the age of eighteen years or the protection of the private lives of persons concerned in the proceedings.

(12)   Nothing contained in or done under the authority of any law shall be held to be inconsistent with or in contravention of-

   (a)   paragraph (a) of clause (2) to the extent that it is shown that the law in question imposes upon any person charged with a criminal offence the burden of proving particular facts;

   (b)   paragraph (d) of clause (2) to the extent that it is shown that the law in question prohibits legal representation before a subordinate court in proceedings for an offence under Zambian customary law, being proceedings against any person who, under that law, is subject to that law;

   (c)   paragraph (e) of clause (2) to the extent that it is shown that the law in question imposes reasonable conditions that must be satisfied if witnesses called to testify on behalf of an accused person are to be paid their expenses out of public funds;

   (d)   clause (2) to the extent that it is shown that the law provides that-

      (i)   where the trial of any person for any offence prescribed by or under the law has been adjourned and the accused, having pleaded to the charge, fails to appear at the time fixed by the court for the resumption of his trial after the adjournment, the proceedings may continue notwithstanding the absence of the accused if the court, being satisfied that, having regard to all the circumstances of the case, it is just and reasonable so to do, so orders; and

      (ii)   the court shall set aside any conviction or sentence pronounced in the absence of the accused in respect of that offence if the accused satisfies the court without undue delay that the cause of his absence was reasonable and that he had a valid defence to the charge;

   (e)   clause (2) to the extent that it is shown that the law provides that the trial of a body corporate may take place in the absence of any representative of the body corporate upon a charge in respect of which a plea of not guilty has been entered by the court;

   (f)   clause (5) to the extent that it is shown that the law in question authorises a court to try a member of a disciplined force for a criminal offence notwithstanding any trial and conviction or acquittal of that member under the disciplinary law of that force, so, however, that any court so trying such a member and convicting him shall in sentencing him to any punishment take into account any punishment awarded him under that disciplinary law.

(13)   In the case of any person who is held in lawful detention, clause (1), paragraphs (d) and (e) of clause (3) shall not apply in relation to his trial for a criminal offence under the law regulating the discipline of persons held in such detention.

(14)   In its application to a body corporate clause (2) shall have effect as if words "in person or" were omitted from paragraph (d) and (e).

(15)   In this Article "criminal offence" means a criminal offence under the law in force in Zambia.

Protection of freedom of conscience

19.   (1)   Except with his own consent, a person shall not be hindered in the enjoyment of his freedom of conscience, and for the purposes of this Article the said freedom includes freedom of thought and religion, freedom to change his religion or belief, and freedom, either alone or in community with others, and both in public and in private, to manifest and propagate his religion or belief in worship, teaching, practice and observance.

   (2)   Except with his own consent, or, if he is a minor, the consent of his guardian, a person attending any place of education shall not be required to receive religious instruction or to take part in or attend any religious ceremony or observance if that instruction, ceremony or observance relates to a religion other than his own.

(3) A religious community or denomination shall not be prevented from providing religious instruction for persons of that community or denomination in the course of any education provided by that community or denomination or from establishing and maintaining instructions to provide social services for such persons.

(4) A person shall not be compelled to take any oath which is contrary to his religion or belief or to take any oath in a manner which is contrary to his religion or belief.

(5) Nothing contained in or done under the authority of any law shall be held to be inconsistent with or in contravention of this Article to the extent that it is shown that the law in question makes provision which is reasonably required-

    (a) in the interests of defence, public safety, public order, public morality or public health; or

    (b) for the purpose of protecting the rights and freedoms of other persons, including the right to observe and practice any religion without the unsolicited intervention of members of any other religion;

and except so far as that provision or, the thing done under the authority thereof as the case may be, is shown not to be reasonably justifiable in a democratic society.

Protection of freedom of expression

20. (1) Except with his own consent, a person shall not be hindered in the enjoyment of his freedom of expression, that is to say, freedom to hold opinions without interference, freedom to receive ideas and information without interference, freedom to impart and communicate ideas and information without interference, whether the communication be to the public generally or to any person or class of persons, and freedom from interference with his correspondence.

(2) Subject to the provisions of this Constitution, a law shall not make any provision that derogates from freedom of the press.

(3) Nothing contained in or done under the authority of any law shall be held to be inconsistent with or in contravention of this Article to the extent that it is shown that the law in question makes provision-

    (a) that is reasonably required in the interests of defence, public safety, public order, public morality or public health; or

    (b) that is reasonably required for the purpose of protecting the reputations, rights and freedoms of other persons or the private lives of persons concerned in legal proceedings, preventing the disclosure of information received in confidence, maintaining the authority and independence of the courts, regulating educational institutions in the interests of persons receiving instruction therein, or the registration of, or regulating the technical administration or the technical operation of, newspapers and other publications, telephony, telegraphy, posts, wireless broadcasting or television; or

    (c) that imposes restrictions upon public officers;

and except so far as that provision or, the thing done under the authority thereof as the case may be, is shown not to be reasonably justifiable in a democratic society.

Protection of freedom of assembly and association

21. (1) Except with his own consent a person shall not be hindered in the enjoyment of his freedom of assembly and association, that is to say, his right to assemble freely and associate with other persons and in particular to form or belong to any political party, trade union or other association for the protection of his interests.

(2) Nothing contained in or done under the authority of any law shall be held to be inconsistent with or in contravention of this Article to the extent that it is shown that the law in question makes provision-

    (a) that is reasonably required in the interests of defence, public safety, public order, public morality or public health;

    (b) that is reasonably required for the purpose of protecting the rights or freedoms of other persons;

    (c) that imposes restrictions upon public officers; or

    (d) for the registration of political parties or trade unions in a register established by or under a law and for imposing reasonable conditions relating to the procedure for entry on such a register including conditions as to the minimum number of persons necessary to constitute a trade union qualified for registration;

and except so far as that provision or, the thing done under the authority thereof as the case may be, is shown not to be reasonably justifiable in a democratic society.

Protection of freedom of movement

22. (1) Subject to the other provisions of this Article and except in accordance with any written law, a citizen shall not be deprived of his freedom of movement, and for the purposes of this Article freedom of movement means-
    - (a) the right to move freely throughout Zambia;
    - (b) the right to reside in any part of Zambia; and
    - (c) the right to leave Zambia and to return to Zambia.

    (2) Any restrictions on a person's freedom of movement that relates to his lawful detention shall not be held to be inconsistent with or in contravention of this Article.

    (3) Nothing contained in or done under the authority of any law shall be held to be inconsistent with or in contravention of this Article to the extent that it is shown that the law in question makes provision-
    - (a) for the imposition of restrictions that are reasonably required in the interests of defence, public safety, public order, public morality or public health or the imposition of restrictions on the acquisition or use by any person of land or other property in Zambia, and except so far as that provision or, the thing done under the authority thereof as the case may be, is shown not to be reasonably justifiable in a democratic society;
    - (b) for the imposition of restrictions on the freedom of movement of any person who is not a citizen of Zambia;
    - (c) for the imposition of restrictions upon the movement or residence within Zambia of public officers; or
    - (d) for the removal of a person from Zambia to be tried outside Zambia for a criminal offence or to undergo imprisonment in some other country in execution of the sentence of a court in respect of a criminal offence under the law in force in Zambia of which he has been convicted.

Protection from discrimination on the ground of race, etc.

23. (1) Subject to clauses (4), (5) and (7), a law shall not make any provision that is discriminatory either of itself or in its effect.

    (2) Subject to clauses (6), (7) and (8), a person shall not be treated in a discriminatory manner by any person acting by virtue of any written law or in the performance of the functions of any public office or any public authority.

    (3) In this Article the expression "discriminatory" means affording different treatment to different persons attributable, wholly or mainly to their respective descriptions by race, tribe, sex, place of origin, marital status, political opinions, colour or creed whereby persons of one such description are subjected to disabilities or restrictions to which persons of another such description are not made subject or are accorded privileges or advantages which are not accorded to persons of another such description.

    (4) Clause (1) shall not apply to any law so far as that law makes provision-
    - (a) for the appropriation of the general revenues of the Republic;
    - (b) with respect to persons who are not citizens of Zambia;
    - (c) with respect to adoption, marriage, divorce, burial, devolution of property on death or other matters of personal law;
    - (d) for the application in the case of members of a particular race or tribe, of customary law with respect to any matter to the exclusion of any law with respect to that matter which is applicable in the case of other persons; or
    - (e) whereby persons of any such description as is mentioned in clause (3) may be subjected to any disability or restriction or may be accorded any privilege or advantage which, having regard to its nature and to special circumstances pertaining to those persons or to persons of any other such description is reasonably justifiable in a democratic society.

    (5) Nothing contained in any law shall be held to be inconsistent with or in contravention of clause (1) to the exent that it is shown that it makes reasonable provision with respect to qualifications for service as a public officer or as a member of a disciplined force or for the service of a local government authority or a body corporate established directly by any law.

(6)   Clause (2) shall not apply to anything which is expressly or by necessary implication authorised to be done by any such provision or law as is referred to in clause (4) or (5).

(7)   Nothing contained in or done under the authority of any law shall be held to be inconsistent with or in contravention of this Article to the extent that it is shown that the law in question makes provision whereby persons of any such description as is mentioned in clause (3) may be subjected to any restriction on the rights and freedoms guaranteed by Articles 17, 19, 20, 21 and 22, being such a restriction as is authorised by clause (2) of Article 17, clause (5) of Article 19, clause (2) of Article 20, clause (2) of Article 21 or clause (3) of Article 22, as the case may be.

(8)   Nothing in clause (2) shall affect any discretion relating to the institution, conduct or discontinuance of civil or criminal proceedings in any court that is vested in any person by or under this Constitution or any other law.

Protection of young persons from exploitation

24.   (1)   A young person shall not be employed and shall in no case be caused or permitted to engage in any occupation or employment which would prejudice his health or education or interfere with his physical, mental or moral development:

           Provided that an Act of Parliament may provide for the employment of a young person for a wage under certain conditions.

     (2)   All young persons shall be protected against physical or mental ill-treatment, all forms of neglect, cruelty or exploitation.

     (3)   A young person shall not be the subject of traffic in any form.

     (4)   In this Article "young person" means any person under the age of fifteen years.

Derogation from fundamental rights and detention

25.   Nothing contained in or done under the authority of any law shall be held to be inconsistent with or in contravention of Articles 13, 16, 17, 19, 20, 21, 22, 23 or 24 to the extent that it is shown that the law in question authorises the taking, during any period when the Republic is at war or when a declaration under Article 30 is in force, of measures for the purpose of dealing with any situation existing or arising during that period; and nothing done by any person under the authority of any such law shall be held to be in contravention of any of the said provisions if it is shown that the measures taken were, having due regard to the circumstances prevailing at the time, reasonably required for the purpose of dealing with the situation in question.

Provisions relating to restriction and detention

26.   (1)   Where a person's freedom of movement is restricted, or he is detained, under the authority of any such law as is referred to in Article 22 or 25, as the case may be, the following provisions shall apply-

         (a)   he shall, as soon as reasonably practicable and in any case not more than fourteen days after the commencement of his detention or restriction, be furnished with a statement in writing in a language that he understands specifying in detail the grounds upon which he is restricted or detained;

         (b)   not more than fourteen days after the commencement of his restriction or detention a notification shall be published in the Gazette stating that he has been restricted or detained and giving particulars of the place of detention and the provision of law under which his restriction or detention is authorised;

         (c)   if he so requests at any time during the period of such restriction or detention not earlier than three months after the commencement thereof or after he last made such a request during that period, as the case may be, his case shall be reviewed by an independent and impartial tribunal established by law and presided over by a person, appointed by the Chief Justice who is or is qualified to be a judge of the High Court;

         (d)   he shall be afforded reasonable facilities to consult a legal representative of his own choice who shall be permitted to make representations to the authority by which the restriction or detention was ordered or to any tribunal established for the review of his case; and

         (e)   at the hearing of his case by such tribunal he shall be permitted to appear in person or by a legal representive of his own choice.

(2) On any review by a tribunal under this Article the tribunal shall advise the authority by which it was ordered on the necessity or expediency of continuing his restriction or detention and that authority shall be obliged to act in accordance with any such advice.

(3) The President may at any time refer to the tribunal the case of any person who has been or is being restricted or detained pursuant to any restriction or detention order.

(4) Nothing contained in paragraph (d) or (e) of clause (1) shall be construed as entitling a person to legal representation at the public expense.

(5) Parliament may make or provide for the making of rules to regulate the proceedings of any such tribunal including, but without derogating from the generality of the foregoing, rules as to evidence and the admissibility thereof, the receipt of evidence including written reports in the absence of the restricted or detained person and his legal representative, and the exclusion of the public from the whole or any portion of the proceedings.

(6) Clauses (11) and (12) of Article 18 shall be read and construed subject to the provisions of this Article.

Reference of certain matters to special tribunal

27. (1) Whenever-
　　(a) a request is made in accordance with clause (2) for a report on a bill or statutory instrument; or
　　(b) the Chief Justice considers it necessary for the purpose of determining claims for legal aid in respect of proceedings under Article 30 or 31;
　　the Chief Justice shall appoint a tribunal which shall consist of two persons selected by him from amongst persons who hold or have held the office of a judge of the Supreme Court or the High Court.

(2) A request for a report on a bill or a statutory instrument may be made by not less than thirty members of the National Assembly by notice in writing delivered-
　　(a) in the case of a bill, to the Speaker within three days after the final reading of the bill in the Assembly;
　　(b) in the case of a statutory instrument, to the authority having power to make the instrument within fourteen days of the publication of the instrument in the Gazette.

(3) Where a tribunal is appointed under this Article for the purpose of reporting on a bill or a statutory instrument, the tribunal shall, within the prescribed period, submit a report to the President and to the Speaker of the National Assembly stating-
　　(a) in the case of a bill, whether or not in the opinion of the tribunal any, and if so which, provisions of the bill are inconsistent with this Constitution;
　　(b) in the case of a statutory instrument, whether or not in the opinion of the tribunal any, and if so which, provisions of the instrument are inconsistent with this Constitution;
　　and, if the tribunal reports that any provision would be or is inconsistent with this Constitution, the grounds upon which the tribunal has reached that conclusion:
　　Provided that if the tribunal considers that the request for a report on a bill or statutory instrument is merely frivolous or vexatious, it may so report to the President without entering further upon the question whether the bill or statutory instrument would be or is inconsistent with this Constitution.

(4) In determining any claim for legal aid as referred to in clause (2), the tribunal may grant to any person who satisfies it that-
　　(a) he intends to bring or is an applicant in proceedings under clause (1) or (4) of Article 28;
　　(b) he has reasonable grounds for bringing the application; and
　　(c) he cannot afford to pay for the cost of the application;
　　a certificate that the application is a proper case to be determined at the public expense:
　　Provided that paragraph (c) shall not apply in any case where the application relates to the validity or a provision in respect of which the tribunal has reported that it would be or is inconsistent with this Constitution or where it appears to the tribunal that issues are or will be raised in the application which are of general public importance.

(5) Where a certificate is granted to any person by the tribunal in pursuance of clause (4), there shall be paid to that person out of the general revenues of the Republic such amount as the tribunal,

when hearing the application, may assess as the costs incurred by that person in connection with the application; and the sums required for making such payment shall be a charge on the general revenues of the Republic.

(6)   For the purposes of clause(5)-

    (a)   the costs incurred in an application shall include the cost of obtaining the advice of a legal representative and, if necessary, the cost of representation by a legal representative in any court in steps preliminary or incidental to the application;

    (b)   in assessing the costs reasonably incurred by a person in an application, regard shall be had to costs awarded against that person or recovered by him in those proceedings.

(7)   In this Article, "prescribed period" means-

    (a)   in relation to a bill, the period commencing from the appointment of the tribunal to report upon the bill and ending thirty days thereafter or if the Speaker, on the application of the tribunal considers that owing to the length or complexity of the bill thirty days is insufficient for consideration of the bill, ending on such later day as the Speaker may determine;

    (b)   in relation to a statutory instrument, the period of forty days commencing with the day on which the instrument is published in the Gazette.

(8)   Nothing in clause (1), (2) or (3) shall apply to a bill for the appropriation of the general revenues of the Republic or a bill containing only proposals for expressly altering this Constitution or the Constitution of Zambia Act.

Enforcement of protective provisions

28.   (1)   Subject to clause (5), if any person alleges that any of the provisions of Articles 11 to 26 inclusive has been, is being or is likely to be contravened in relation to him, then, without prejudice to any other action with respect to the same matter which is lawfully available, that person may apply for redress to the High Court which shall-

    (a)   hear and determine any such application;

    (b)   determine any question arising in the case of any person which is referred to it in pursuance of clause(2);

    and which may, make such order, issue such writs and give such directions as it may consider appropriate for the purpose of enforcing, or securing the enforcement of, any of the provisions of Articles 11 to 26 inclusive.

(2)   (a)   If in any proceedings in any subordinate court any question arises as to the contravention of any of the provisions of Articles 11 to 26 inclusive, the person presiding in that court may, and shall if any party to the proceedings so requests, refer the question to the High Court unless, in his opinion the raising of the question is merely frivolous or vexatious.

    (b)   Any person aggrieved by any determination of the High Court under this Article may appeal therefrom to the Supreme Court:

    Provided that an appeal shall not lie from a determination of the High Court dismissing an application on the ground that it is frivolous and vexatious.

(3)   An application shall not be brought under clause (1) on the grounds that the provisions of Articles 11 to 26 (inclusive) are likely to be contravened by reason of proposals contained in any bill which, at the date of the application, has not become a law.

(4)   Parliament may confer upon the Supreme Court or High Court such jurisdiction or powers in addition to those conferred by this Article as may appear to be necessary or desirable for the purpose of enabling that Court more effectively to exercise the jurisdiction conferred upon it by this Article or of enabling any application for redress to be more speedily determined.

Declaration of war

29.   (1)   The President may, in consultation with Cabinet, at any time, by Proclamation published in the Gazette declare war.

(2)   A declaration made under clause (1) shall continue in force until the cessation of hostilities.

(3)   An Act of Parliament shall provide for the conditions and circumstances under which a declaration may be made under clause (1).

30.   (1)   The President may, in consultation with Cabinet, at any time, by Proclamation published in the Gazette declare that a State of public emergency exists. Declaration of public emergency

(2)   A declaration made under clause (1) of this Article shall cease to have effect on the expiration of a period of seven days commencing with the day on which the declaration is made unless, before the expiration of such period, it has been approved by a resolution of the National Assembly supported by a majority of all the members thereof not counting the Speaker.

(3)   In reckoning any period of seven days for the purposes of clause (2) account shall not be taken of any time during which Parliament is dissolved.

(4)   A declaration made under clause (1) may, at any time before it has been approved by a resolution of the National Assembly, be revoked by the President by Proclamation published in the Gazette.

(5)   Subject to clause (6) a resolution of the National Assembly under clause (2) will continue in force until the expiration of a period of three months commencing with the date of its being approved or until revoked at such earlier date of its being so approved or until such earlier date as may be specified in the resolution:

Provided that the National Assembly may, by majority of all the members thereof, not counting the Speaker extend the approval of the declaration for periods of not more than three months at a time.

(6)   The National Assembly may, by resolution, at any time revoke a resolution made by it under this Article.

(7)   Whenever an election to the office of President results in a change of the holder of that office, any declaration made under this Article and in force immediately before the day on which the President assumes office shall cease to have effect on the expiration of seven days commencing with that da

(8)   The expiration or revocation of any declaration or resolution made under this Article shall not affect the validity or anything previously done in reliance on such declaration.

Declaration of war

31. (1)   The President may at any time by Proclamation published in the Gazette declare that a situation exists which, if is allowed to continue may lead to a state of public emergency.

(2)   A declaration made under clause (1) of this Article shall cease to have effect on the expiration of a period of seven days commencing with the day on which the declaration is made unless, before the expiration of such period, it has been approved by a resolution of the National Assembly supported by a majority of all the members thereof not counting the Speaker.

(3)   In reckoning any period of seven days for the purposes of clause (2) account shall not be taken of any time during which Parliament is dissolved.

(4)   A declaration made under clause (1) may, at any time before it has been approved by a resolution of the National Assembly, be revoked by the President by Proclamation published in the Gazette.

(5)   Subject to clause (6) a resolution of the National Assembly under clause (2) will continue in force until the expiration of a period of three months commencing with the date of its being approved or until revoked on an earlier date of its being so approved or until such earlier date as may be specified in the resolution.

(6)   The National Assembly may by resolution, at any time revoke a resolution made by it under this Article.

(7)   Whenever an election to the office of President results in a change of the holder of that office, any declaration made under this Article and in force immediately before the day on which the President assumes office, shall cease to have effect on the expiration of seven days commencing with that day.

(8)   The expiration or revocation of any declaration or resolution made under this Article shall not affect the validity or anything previously done in reliance on such declaration.

Interpretation and savings

32. (1)   In this Part, unless the context otherwise requires-

"contravention", in relation to any requirement, includes a failure to comply with that requirement and cognate expressions shall be construed accordingly;

"court" means any court of law having jurisdiction in Zambia, other than a court established by a disciplinary law; and in Articles 12 and 14 includes a court established by a disciplinary law;

"disciplinary law" means a law regulating the disciplined force;

"disciplined force" means-

      (a)   a naval, military or air force;

      (b)   the Zambia Police Force; or

      (c)   any other force established by or under an Act of Parliament;

"legal representative" means a person entitled to practice in Zambia as an advocate; and "member", in relation to a disciplined force, includes any person who, under the law regulating the discipline of that force is subject to that discipline.

(2)   In relation to any person who is a member of a disciplined force raised under the law of Zambia, nothing contained in or done under the authority of the disciplinary law of that force shall be held to be inconsistent with or in contravention of any of the provisions of this Part other than Articles 12, 14 and 15.

(3)   In relation to any person who is a member of a disciplined force raised otherwise than as aforesaid and lawfully present in Zambia, nothing contained in or done under the authority of the disciplinary law of that force shall be held to be inconsistent with or in contravention of any of the provisions of this Part.

THE INTERPRETATION AND GENERAL PROVISIONS ACT
CHAPTER 2 OF THE LAWS OF ZAMBIA

ARRANGEMENT OF SECTIONS

PART I PRELIMINARY

PART II GENERAL PROVISIONS OF INTERPRETATION

PART III GENERAL PROVISIONS REGARDING WRITTEN LAWS

PART IV STATUTORY INSTRUMENTS

CHAPTER 2

INTERPRETATION AND GENERAL PROVISIONS

An Act to amend and consolidate the law relating to the construction, application and interpretation of written law; to provide for the exercise of statutory powers and duties; and to provide for matters incidental to or connected with the foregoing.

PART I
PRELIMINARY

Short title

1. This Act may be cited as the Interpretation and General Provisions Act.

Application

2. (1) The provisions of this Act shall apply to every written law passed or made before or after the commencement, unless a contrary intention appears in this Act or in the written law concerned.

(2)   The provisions of this Act shall apply to this Act as they apply to an Act passed after the commencement.

PART II
GENERAL PROVISIONS OF INTERPRETATION

Interpretation

3.   The following words and expressions shall have the meanings hereinafter assigned to them respectively, that is to say:

"Act" and "Act of Parliament" mean an enactment of Parliament;

"act", used with reference to an offence or civil wrong, includes a series of acts, and words which refer to acts done extend to illegal omissions;

"this Act" includes any statutory instrument made and in force under the Act in which the expression appears;

"Administrative Officer" means, a District Secretary and an Assistant District Secretary;

"Appeal Judge" means a Judge of the supreme court or a High Court judge when exercising appellate jurisdiction.

"Applied Act" means an enactment of the Legislature of the former Federation of Rhodesia and Nyasaland in force in the Republic by virtue of the provisions of the Federation of Rhodesia and Nyasaland (Dissolution) Order in Council, 1963; App. 2

"area"- in relation to a City Council, Municipal Council, Town Council or District Council, has the meaning assigned thereto by section two of the Local Government Act; Cap. 281

"Assistant District Secretary" means a public officer appointed as such and, in relation to any District, means an Assistant District Secretary for the time being exercising and performing his functions in that District;

"Attorney-General" means the Attorney-General of Zambia;

"Auditor-General" means the Auditor-General for Zambia;

"British Act" means an Act of the Parliament of the United Kingdom extended or applied to the Republic;

"Cabinet" means the Cabinet established by the Constitution;

"Chief Justice" means the Chief Justice of Zambia;

"Christian name" means any name prefixed to the surname whether received in Christian baptism or not;

"coin" means any coin legally current in Zambia;

"commencement", used in or with reference to any written law, means the date on which the same came or comes into operation;

"commissioner for oaths" means a person appointed as a commissioner for oaths by or under the Commissioners for Oaths Act;

"Common Law" means the Common Law of England;

"Constitution" means the Constitution of Zambia as by law established;

"contravene", in relation to any requirement or condition prescribed in any written law or in any grant, permit, lease, licence or authority granted under any written law, includes a failure to comply with that requirement or condition;

"coroner" means a person empowered or appointed to hold inquests under the Inquests Act;

"council" means a City council, Municipal council, Town council or District council;

"court" means a court of competent jurisdiction for Zambia;

"customs officer" means an officer as defined in section two of the Customs and Excise Act;

"definition" means the interpretation given by any written law to any word or expression;

"Deputy Speaker" means the Deputy Speaker of the National Assembly;

"District" means any one of the administrative districts into which Zambia is divided by the President in exercise of powers conferred on him in that behalf under any written law;

"District Executive Secretary" in relation to a District Council means the chief Executive of a Council, and includes any person for the time being discharging the functions of the Chief Executive

"document" includes any publication and any matter written, expressed or described upon any substance by means of letters, figures or marks, or by more than one of those means, which is intended to be used or may be used for the purpose of recording that matter;

"export" means to take or cause to be taken out of Zambia;

"financial year" means the period of twelve months ending on the 31st December in any year;

"functions" includes powers and duties;

"Gazette" means the official Gazette of the Government and includes any supplement to the Gazette and any matter referred in the Gazette as being published with the Gazette;

"Government" means the Government of Zambia;

"Government Printer" means the Government Printer of Zambia and any other printer authorised by or on behalf of the Government to print any written law or any other document of the Government;

"High Court" means the High Court for Zambia;

"immigration officer" means an immigration officer as defined in section two of the Immigration and Deportation Act;

"import" means to bring or cause to be brought into Zambia;

"Judge" means a Judge of the High Court;

"Junior Minister" means a Deputy Minister;

"land" includes anything attached to the earth or permanently fastened to anything which is attached to the earth, but shall not include any mineral right in or under or in respect of any land;

"legal practitioner" means a person who has been admitted to practice as a barrister and solicitor under the Legal Practitioners Act and whose name is duly entered on the Roll kept in pursuance of the provisions of the said Act;

"magistrate" means any person empowered to preside over a subordinate court established under the Subordinate Courts Act;

"Minister", in relation to the functions conferred or imposed by any written law or any provision in a written law, means the member of the Cabinet or other person for the time being vested with such functions;

"month" means a calendar month;

"municipal council" has the meaning assigned thereto by section two of the Local Government Act;

"municipality" has the meaning assigned thereto by section two of the Local Government Act;

"National Assembly" means the National Assembly of Zambia;

"oath", "swear" or "affidavit" includes and applies to the affirmation or declaration of any person by law allowed to make an affirmation or declaration in lieu of oath;

"occupy" includes use, inhabit, to be in possession of or enjoy the premises in respect whereof the word is used, otherwise than as a mere servant or for the mere purpose of the care, custody or charge thereof;

"offence" means any crime, felony, misdemeanour, contravention or other breach of, or failure to comply with, any written law, for which a penalty is provided;

"Officer" in relation to a council, has the meaning assigned thereto by section two of the Local Government Act;

"Ordinance" means a statute enacted by the Legislature of Northern Rhodesia before the 24th October, 1964;

"Parliament" means the Parliament of Zambia;

"Part", "regulation", "rule", "Schedule" and "section" denote respectively a Part, regulation, rule and section of, and a Schedule to, the written law in which the word occurs; and a "paragraph" and "subsection" denote respectively a paragraph of the regulation, rule, section or subsection, and a subsection of the section, in which the word occurs;

"Permanent Secretary" means a public officer appointed as such and, in relation to any Ministry or Province means the Permanent Secretary for the time being exercising and performing his functions in that Ministry or Province;

"person" includes any company or association or body or persons, corporate or unincorporate;

"personal property", "personalty" or "goods" includes money, bonds, bills, notes, deeds, chattels real, mining rights in or under or in respect of any land and corporeal property of every description other than real property;

"police officer" means a member of the Zambia Police Force;

"prescribed" means prescribed by or under the written law in which the word occurs;

"President" means the President of Zambia;

"Province" means any one of the Provinces into which Zambia is divided by the President in exercise of powers conferred on him in that behalf under any written law;

"publication" includes all written and printed matter and any record, tape, wire, perforated roll, cinematograph film or other contrivance by means of which any words or ideas may be mechanically or electrically produced, reproduced, represented or conveyed, and everything whether of a nature similar to the foregoing or not, containing any visible representation, or by its form, shape or in any manner capable of producing, reproducing, representing or conveying words or ideas, and every copy and reproduction of any publication;

"public holiday" means any day which is a public holiday by virtue of the provisions of the Public Holidays Act;

"public office", "public officer" and "the public service" have the same meaning as in the Constitution;

"Public Seal" means the Public Seal of the Republic;

"public place" or "public premises" includes any public way and any building, place or conveyance to which, for the time being, the public are entitled or permitted to have access, either without any condition or upon condition of making any payment, and any building or place which is for the time being used for any public or religious meetings, or assembly or as an open court;

"registered", used with reference to a document or the title to any real property or personal property, means registered under the provisions of any written law for the time being applicable to the registration of such document or title;

"the Republic" means the sovereign Republic of Zambia;

"repeal" includes revoke, rescind or cancel;

"sell" includes barter, exchange and offer to sell or expose for sale;

"Speaker" means the Speaker of the National Assembly;

"statutory corporation" means anybody directly incorporated by an Act, Applied Act or Ordinance;

"statutory declaration", if made-

    (a) in Zambia, means a declaration made under the British Act known as the Statutory Declarations Act, 1835, or under any Act providing for statutory declarations;

    (b) in the Commonwealth, elsewhere than in Zambia, means a declaration made before a notary public, commissioner for oaths or other person having authority therein under any law for the time being in force to take or receive a declaration;

    (c) in any other place, means a declaration made before a British consul or vice-consul, or before any person having authority under any Act of Parliament of the United Kingdom for the time being in force to take or receive a declaration;

"statutory instrument" means any proclamation, regulation, order, rule, notice or other instrument (not being an Act of Parliament) of a legislative, as distinct from an executive, character;

"statutory notice" means a notice made by statutory instrument;

"statutory order" means an order made by statutory instrument;

"statutory proclamation" means a proclamation made by statutory instrument;

"street" or "road" includes any highway, street, road, bridge, square, court, alley, lane, footway, parade, thoroughfare, passage or open space to which the public are entitled or permitted to have access, whether on payment or otherwise;

"Supreme Court" means the Supreme for Zambia;

"vessel". includes any ship or boat or other floating craft used for transport by water;

    "veterinary surgeon" means a person registered as a veterinary surgeon under the Veterinary Surgeons Act;

"Vice-President" means the Vice-President of Zambia;

"will" includes a codicil and every writing making a voluntary posthumous disposition of property;

"writing" and expressions referring to writing include printing, photography, lithography, typewriting and any other modes of representing or reproducing words in visible form;

"written law" means an Act, an Applied Act, an Ordinance and a statutory instrument.

(As amended by Nos. 29, 39, 58 and 69 of 1965, No. 40 of 1967, No. 9 of 1968, Nos. 43 and 51 of 1970 and No. 20 of 1971)

Grammatical variations, gender and number

4.   (1)   Where any word or expression is defined in a written law, the definition shall extend to the grammatical variations of the word or expression so defined.

      (2)   Words and expressions in a written law importing the masculine gender include females.

      (3)   Words and expressions in a written law in the singular include the plural and words and expressions in the plural include the singular.

      (4)   Where the words "or", "other" and "otherwise" are used in any written law they shall be construed disjunctively and not as implying similarity, unless the word "similar" or some other word of like meaning is added.

Service by post

5.   Where any written law authorises or requires any document to be served by post, the service shall be deemed to be effected by properly addressing, prepaying and posting by registered post a letter containing the document and, unless the contrary is proved, to have been effected at the time at which the letter would be delivered in the ordinary course of the post.

Names of Provinces, Districts, etc.

5A. Whenever in any written law any Province, District or other area is referred to by name, the provision in question shall be read and construed as a reference to such Province, District or other area by the name currently assigned thereto by any written law.
    (No. 47 of 1970)

PART III
GENERAL PROVISIONS REGARDING WRITTEN LAWS

Acts, Applied Acts and Ordinances to be public Acts or Ordinances

6.   (1)   Every Act, Applied Act or British Act shall be a public Act and shall be judicially noticed as such.

      (2)   Every Ordinance shall be a public Ordinance and shall be judicially noticed as such.

Citation

7.   (1)   Where any written law is referred to, it shall be sufficient for all purposes to cite such written law either by the short title or citation, if any, by which it is made citable.

      (2)   An Ordinance or an Act contained in any revised edition or Ordinances and Acts issued under any written law providing for the revised edition of such Ordinances and Acts may be cited by its short title or its chapter number in the revised edition.

      (3)   An Applied Act contained in any revised edition of Applied Acts issued under any written law providing for the revised edition of such Applied Acts may be cited by its short title or its chapter number in the revised edition.

      (4)   Any citation as aforesaid of a written law shall be construed as a reference to such written law as amended from time to time by any other written law or other instrument.

Citation of Acts of the Parliament of the United Kingdom

8.   A British Act may be cited by its short title or citation, if any, or by reference to the regnal or calendar year in which it was passed and by its chapter or number.

Schedules and tables to be part of written laws

9.   Every Schedule to or table in any written law, together with notes thereto, shall be construed and have effect as part of such written law.

Subdivision of written laws

10. When a written law is divided into Parts, titles or other subdivisions, the fact and particulars of such divisions and subdivisions shall, with or without express mention thereof in such written law, be taken notice of in all courts and for all purposes whatsoever.

Repealed written law not revived

11.   Where any written law repealing in whole or in part any former written law is itself repealed, such last repeal shall not revive the written law or provisions before repealed unless words be added reviving such written law or provisions.

Repeal of amended law to include amendments

12.   Where any written law which has been amended by any other written law is itself repealed, such repeal shall include the repeal of all those provisions of other written laws by which such first-mentioned written law has been amended.

Repeal and substitution

13.   Where a written law repeals wholly or partially any former written law and substitutes provisions for the written law repealed, the repealed written law shall remain in force until the substituted provisions come into operation.

14.   (1)   Where in any written law a reference is made to another written law or the Constitution, such reference shall be deemed to include a reference to such last-mentioned written law or the Constitution as the same may from time to time be amended.   Provisions with respect to amended written law and effect of repealing written law

      (2)   Where a written law repeals and re-enacts, with or without modification, any provision of a former written law or the Constitution, references in any other written law to the provisions so repealed shall be construed as references to the provisions so re-enacted.

      (3)   Where a written law repeals in whole or in part any other written law, the repeal shall not-

          (a)   revive anything not in force or existing at the time at which the repeal takes effect; or

          (b)   affect the previous operation of any written law so repealed or anything duly done or suffered under any written law so repealed; or

          (c)   affect any right, privilege, obligation or liability acquired, accrued or incurred under any written law so repealed; or

          (d)   affect any penalty, forfeiture, or punishment incurred in respect of any offence committed against any written law so repealed; or

          (e)   affect any investigation, legal proceeding, or remedy in respect of any such right, privilege, obligation, liability, penalty, forfeiture or punishment as aforesaid, and any such investigation, legal proceedings, or remedy may be instituted, continued or enforced, and any such penalty, forfeiture or punishment may be imposed, as if the repealing written law had not been made.
(As amended by No. 43 of 1970)

Effect of repeal of written law on statutory instrument made under it

15.   Where any Act, Applied Act or Ordinance or part thereof is repealed, any statutory instrument issued under or made in virtue thereof shall remain in force, so far as it is not inconsistent with the repealing written law, until it has been repealed by a statutory instrument issued or made under the provisions of such repealing written law, and shall be deemed for all purposes to have been made thereunder.

Construction

16.   Where one written law amends another written law, the amending written law shall, so far as it is consistent with the tenor thereof, be construed as one with the amended written law. of amending written law with amended written law

Effect of expiry of written law

17.   Upon the expiry of any written law, the provisions of subsection (3) of section fourteen shall apply as if such written law had been repealed.

PART IV
STATUTORY INSTRUMENTS

Publication of statutory instruments

18.   Every statutory instrument shall be published in the Gazette and shall be judicially noticed.

Commencement of statutory instruments

19.   (1)   Subject to the provisions of this section-

(a)   the date of commencement of a statutory instrument shall be the date of its publication in the Gazette or, where a later date is specified therein, such later date; and

(b)   every statutory instrument shall be deemed to come into force immediately on the expiration of the day next preceding the date of its commencement.

(2)   A statutory instrument made and published on the date of commencement of the written law under which the instrument is made shall be deemed to come into force simultaneously with that written law.

(3)   References in this section to the date of commencement of the written law under which a statutory instrument is made shall, where different provisions of that written law come into force on different dates, be construed as references to the date of commencement of the particular provision under which the instrument is made.

(4)   The provisions of this section shall be without prejudice to the operation of section twenty-three.

General provisions relating to statutory instruments

20.   (1)   Any reference in a statutory instrument to "the Act" or "the Ordinance" shall be construed as a reference to the Act or Ordinance, as the case may be, under which the instrument was made.

(2)   Terms and expressions used in a statutory instrument shall have the same meaning as in the written law under which the instrument was made.

(3)   A statutory instrument may at any time be amended or repealed by the authority by which it was made or, if that authority has been lawfully replaced by another authority, by that other authority.

(4)   Any provision of a statutory instrument which is inconsistent with any provision of an Act, Applied Act or Ordinance shall be void to the extent of the inconsistency.

(5)   A statutory instrument may provide in respect of any contravention of any provision of that statutory instrument:

(a)   that the offender shall be liable-

(i)   to any fine not exceeding two thousand five hundred penalty units or any term of imprisonment not exceeding two years or both;

(ii)   in the case of a continuing offence, to an additional penalty not exceeding a fine of twenty-five penalty units in respect of each day on which the offence continues;

(iii)   in respect of a second or subsequent contravention, to a higher penalty not exceeding either of the limits prescribed in sub-paragraph (i);

(b)   that the court convicting the offender may or shall as the case may be, order the forfeiture to the State of anything with which the contravention was done or which was used in, or for the purpose of, or in relation to or in connection with, the commission of the contravention;

(c)   for the punishment of any director or other principal officer of a body of persons or other person purporting to act in any such capacity, where a contravention committed by, or in connection with, the affairs of a body of persons, was done with the consent or connivance of, or was attributable to the neglect of, any such director, principal officer or other person.

(6)   Any act done under or by virtue of or in pursuance of a statutory instrument shall be deemed to be done under or by virtue of or in pursuance of the written law conferring power to make the instrument.

(7)   Every statutory instrument shall be deemed to be made under all powers thereunto enabling, whether or not it purports to be made in exercise of a particular power or particular powers.

(8)   Where a written law confers power on any authority to make a statutory instrument for any general purpose, and also for any special purposes, the enumeration of the special purposes shall not be deemed to derogate from the generality of the powers conferred with reference to the general purpose.
(As amended by Act No. 4 of 1989 and Act No. 13 of 1994)

Reference to written law to include statutory instruments

21.   Any reference to a written law in any other written law shall include a reference to any statutory instrument made under the written law to which reference is made.

Rules to be laid before the National Assembly

22.   (1)   All rules, regulations and by-laws shall be laid before the National Assembly as soon as may be after they are made, and, if a resolution is passed within the next subsequent twenty-one days on which the National Assembly has sat after any such rule, regulation or by-law is laid before it that the rule, regulation or by-law be annulled, it shall thence-forth be void but without prejudice to the validity of anything previously done thereunder, or to the making of any new rule, regulation or by-law.

(2)   The reference to rules in subsection (1) shall not include a reference to rules of court.

PART V
POWERS AND DUTIES

Exercise of power between publication and commencement of Act

23.   Where by an Act which is not to come into force immediately on the publication thereof there is conferred-
(a)   a power to make or a power exercisable by making statutory instruments; or
(b)   a power to make appointments; or
(c)   a power to do any other thing for the purposes of the Act;
that power may be exercised at any time on or after the date of publication of the Act in the Gazette:
Provided that no instrument, appointment or thing made or done under that power shall, unless it is necessary to bring the Act into force, have any effect until the commencement of the Act.

Time for exercise of power

24.   Where any written law confers any power or imposes any duty, the power may be exercised and the duty shall be performed from time to time as occasion requires.

Implied power

25.   Where any written law confers a power on any person to do or enforce the doing of an act or thing, all such powers shall be understood to be also given as are reasonably necessary to enable the person to do or enforce the doing of the act or thing.

Power to appoint includes power to remove

26.   Where by any written law a power to make any appointment is conferred, the authority having power to make the appointment shall also have power (subject to any limitations or qualifications which affect the power of appointment) to remove, suspend, reappoint or reinstate any person appointed in the exercise of the power.

Power to appoint alternate or temporary members

27. Where by or under any written law any board, commission, committee, council or similar body, whether corporate or unincorporate, is established, any person who is by such written law empowered to appoint any or all of the members thereof may-
    (a) appoint one or more duly qualified persons to be alternate members of the same, and any one such alternate member may attend any meeting of the same when a substantive member is temporarily unable to attend;
    (b) appoint a duly qualified person to be a temporary member of the same in the place of any substantive member who is precluded by illness, absence from Zambia or other cause from exercising his functions as such;
    and when attending any meeting of such board, commission, committee, council or similar body, whether corporate or unincorporate, such alternate or temporary member shall be deemed for all purposes to be a member of the same.

Power to appoint chairman, etc.

28. Where by any written law a power is conferred on any authority to appoint the members of any board, commission, committee, council or similar body, that authority may appoint a chairman, a vice-chairman and a secretary of the same.

Appointment by name or office

29. Where by any written law any authority is empowered to appoint a person-
    (a) to exercise any power or perform any duty; or
    (b) to be a member of any board, commission, committee, council or similar body, whether corporate or unincorporate; or
    (c) to be or do any other thing;
    that authority may make the appointment either by appointing a person by name or by appointing the holder of an office by the terms designating his office; and any such appointment of the holder of an office shall be construed as the appointment of the person for the time being lawfully holding, acting in or performing the functions of the office.

Reference to holder of office includes a person discharging functions of office

30. Any reference in a written law to the holder of an office by the term designating his office shall be construed as a reference to the person for the time being lawfully holding, acting in or performing the functions of the office.
    (As amended by No. 13 of 1965)

Power of majority

31. Where by any written law any act or thing may or is required to be done by more than two persons, a majority of them may do it.

Law officers

32. Any power conferred or duty imposed on the Attorney-General by any written law may be exercised or performed by the Solicitor-General-
    (a) in the case where the Attorney-General is unable to act owing to illness or absence; and
    (b) in any case or class of cases where the Attorney-General has authorised the Solicitor-General to do so.

Powers of board, etc., not affected by vacancy, etc.

33. Where by or under any written law any board, commission, committee, council or similar body, whether corporate or unincorporate, is established, the powers of such board, commission, committee, council or similar body shall not be affected by-
    (a) any vacancy in the membership thereof; or
    (b) any defect afterwards discovered in the appointment or qualification of a person purporting to be a member thereof.

Affixing of common seal

34. Where by or under any written law any board, commission, committee, council or similar body is constituted to be a body corporate having perpetual succession and a common seal, and any document is required to be sealed with such common seal, then, in the absence of express provision to the contrary, such common seal shall be affixed by the chairman of such board, commission, committee, council or similar body and shall be authenticated by his signature and by the signature of one other member of such board, commission, committee, council or similar body.

PART VI
GENERAL PROVISIONS REGARDING TIME AND DISTANCE

Computation of time

35. In computing time for the purposes of any written law-
   (a) a period of days from the happening of an event or the doing of any act or thing shall be deemed to be exclusive of the day on which the event happens or the act or thing is done;
   (b) if the last day of the period is Sunday or a public holiday (which days are in this section referred to as "excluded days") the period shall include the next following day, not being an excluded day;
   (c) where any act or proceeding is directed or allowed to be done or taken on a certain day, then, if that day happens to be an excluded day, the act or proceeding shall be considered as done or taken in due time if it is done or taken on the next day afterwards, not being an excluded day;
   (d) where an act or proceeding is directed or allowed to be done or taken within any time not exceeding six days, excluded days shall not be reckoned in the computation of the time.

Provisions where no time prescribed

36. Where no time is prescribed, or allowed within which anything shall be done, such thing shall be done without unreasonable delay, and as often as due occasion arises.

Construction of power to extend time

37. Where in any written law a time is prescribed for doing any act or taking any proceeding and power is given to a court or other authority to extend such time, then, unless a contrary intention appears, such power may be exercised by the court or other authority although the application for the same is not made until after the expiration of the time prescribed.

Measurement of distance

38. In the determination of any distance for the purpose of any written law, the measured distance shall be reduced to that distance which would be recorded if the distance were measured in a straight line on a horizontal plane.

PART VII
GENERAL PROVISIONS REGARDING LEGAL PROCEEDINGS

Ex-officio proceedings not to abate on death, etc.

39. Any civil or criminal proceedings taken by or against any person in virtue of his office shall not be discontinued or abated by his death, resignation, or absence or removal from office, but may be carried on by or against, as the case may be, the person for the time being holding that office.

Imposition of a penalty no bar to civil action

40. The imposition of a penalty or fine by or under the authority of any written law shall not, in the absence of express provision to the contrary, relieve any person from liability to answer for damages to any person injured.

Provisions as to offences under two or more laws

41. (1) Where an act or omission constitutes an offence against any two or more statutory enactments or both under a statutory enactment and the Common Law or any customary law, the offender shall be liable to be prosecuted and punished under either or any of such statutory enactments or at Common Law or under customary law, but shall not be liable to be punished twice for the same offence.

    (2) For the purpose of this section, "statutory enactment" means any order in Council, British Act or written law.

Amendment of penalty

42. Where an act or omission constitutes an offence and the penalty for such offence is amended between the time of the commission of such offence and the conviction therefor, the offender shall, in the absence of express provision to the contrary, be liable to the penalty prescribed at the time of the commission of such offence.

Penalties prescribed may be maximum penalties, but may be cumulative

43. (1) Where in any written law a penalty is prescribed for an offence against that written law, such provision shall mean that the offence shall be punishable by a penalty not exceeding the penalty prescribed.

    (2) Where in any written law more than one penalty is prescribed for an offence, the use of the word "and" shall mean that the penalties may be inflicted alternatively or cumulatively.

Disposal of forfeits

44. (1) Where under the provisions of any written law any animal or any thing is adjudged by any court or other authority to be forfeited, it shall, in the absence of express provision to the contrary, be forfeited to the Republic and the net proceeds thereof, if it is ordered by a competent authority to be sold, shall be paid into the general revenues of the Republic, unless other provision is made.

    (2) Nothing in this section shall affect any provision in any written law whereby any portion of any fine or forfeit or of the proceeds of any forfeit is expressed to be recoverable by any person or may be granted by any authority to any person.

Disposal of fines and penalties

45. Any fine or penalty imposed by or under the authority of any written law shall, in the absence of express provision to the contrary, be paid into the general revenues of the Republic

Evidence of signature of Attorney-General or Director of Public Prosecutions

46. (1) Where under any written law the consent or authority of the Attorney-General or the Director of Public Prosecutions is necessary before any action or prosection is commenced, any document purporting to be the consent or authority of the Attorney-General or the Director of Public Prosecutions shall be received as prima facie evidence in any proceedings without proof being given that the signature to such consent or authority is that of the Attorney-General or the Director of Public Prosecutions, as the case may be.

    (2) Where under section thirty-two the Solicitor-General is exercising the powers of the Attorney-General, the provisions of this section shall apply to the Solicitor-General as they apply to the Attorney-General.

PART VIII
GENERAL MISCELLANEOUS PROVISIONS

Deviation from forms

47. Save as is otherwise expressly provided, whenever any form is prescribed by any written law, an instrument or document, which purports to be in such form, shall not be void by reason of any deviation therefrom which does not affect the substance of such instrument or document, or which is not calculated to mislead.

Gazette, etc., to be prima facie evidence

48. The production of a copy of the Gazette containing any written law, Order in Council, or any notice, or of any copy of any written law, Order in Council, or any notice, purporting to be printed by the Government Printer, shall be prima facie evidence in all courts and for all other purposes whatsoever of the due making and tenor of such written law, Order in Council or notice.

Evidence of Applied Acts

49. (1) For the purpose of ascertaining the content of any Applied Act or any statutory instrument made thereunder, published in or with the Federal Gazette, a reference may be made to the Federal Gazette, containing such Applied Act or statutory instrument, or to a copy thereof, purporting to be printed by or on the authority of the Government Printer, and either such copy shall be prima facie evidence for all purposes whatsoever of the Applied Act or statutory instrument so printed.

(2) Where in any Applied Act it is stated that such Act has been "Reprinted in terms of section 3 of the Amendments Incorporation Act, 1955" such Applied Act shall, for all purposes, be prima facie evidence of the Applied Act so reprinted.

(3) In this section-

"Federal Gazette" means the Government Gazette of the former Federation of Rhodesia and Nyasaland;

"Government Printer" means the Government Printer of the former Federation of Rhodesia and Nyasaland.

Provision in statutory instruments relating to fees

50. (1) Where any written law confers power on any person to make any statutory instrument and provision may be made by such statutory instrument in respect of fees or other charges, such statutory instrument may provide for all or any of the following matters:

(a) specific fees or charges;

(b) maximum or minimum fees or charges;

(c) maximum and minimum fees or charges;

(d) ad valorem fees or charges;

(e) the payment of fees or charges either generally or under specified conditions or in specified circumstances; and

(f) the reduction, waiver or refund, in whole or in part, of any such fees or charges, either upon the happening of a certain event or in the discretion of a specified person.

(2) Where any reduction, waiver or refund, in whole or in part, of any fee or charge is provided for, such reduction, waiver or refund may be expressed to apply or to be applicable either generally or specifically-

(a) in respect of certain matters or transactions or classes of matters or transactions;

(b) in respect of certain documents or classes of documents;

(c) when any event happens or ceases to happen;

(d) in respect of certain persons or classes of persons; or

(e) in respect of any combination of such matters, transactions, documents, events or persons;

and may be expressed to apply or to be applicable subject to such conditions as may be specified in the statutory instrument or in the discretion of any person specified therein.

Savings of rights of the Republic

51. (1) No written law shall in any manner whatsoever affect the rights of the Republic unless it is therein expressly provided or unless it appears by necessary implication that the Republic is bound thereby.

(2) Where any British Act binds the Crown, then that Act mutatis mutandis shall, to the like extent and subject to the same limitations, bind the Republic.

(As amended by No. 27 of 1965)

This Act to bind the Republic

52.   This Act shall bind the Republic.

THE OFFICIAL OATHS ACT CHAPTER 5 OF THE LAWS OF ZAMBIA

THE OFFICIAL OATHS ACT

ARRANGEMENT OF SECTIONS

Section

CHAPTER 5

OFFICIAL OATHS
An Act to repeal and replace the Official Oaths Act; to revise the oaths to be taken and subscribed by various office holders, and to provide for matters connected with or incidental to the foregoing.
[11th May, 1990 Act No 4 of 1990]
Statutory Instrument 127 of 1991

Short title

1.   This Act may be cited as the Official Oaths Act.

Interpretation

2.   (1)   In this Act, unless the context otherwise requires-
                "Oath" includes affirmation;
                "Vice-President" means the Vice-President of the Republic of Zambia;
      (2)   In this Act, unless the context otherwise requires, a reference to the holder of an office by the term designating his office shall be construed as including a reference to any person for the time being lawfully acting in or performing the functions of that office.

Oath of President

3.   A person assuming the Office of President shall take and subscribe the Oath of President as set out in the First Schedule, and the oath shall be administered by and subscribed before the Chief Justice.

Oath of Vice-President Speaker, Minister and Deputy Minister

4.   A person assuming the Office of Vice-President, Speaker of the National Assembly, Minister or Deputy Minister shall not perform the duties of his office unless he has taken and subscribed the Oath of Allegiance as set out in the Sixth Schedule and the Oath of his office as set out in the Second, Third, Fourth and Seventh Schedules, respectively.
(As amended by S.I. No. 127 of 1991)

Judicial Oath

5.   (1)   The Chief Justice, the Deputy Chief Justice, a judge of the Supreme Court, a puisne judge or a Commissioner of the High Court shall not enter upon the duties of his office unless he has taken and subscribed the Oath of Allegiance as set out in the Sixth Schedule and the Judicial Oath as set out in the Fifth Schedule, and both oaths shall be administered by and subscribed before the President.

(2)   A judicial officer appointed to an office under Article 91(1)(c) of the Constitution or a person lawfully appointed to act in or perform the functions of that office, shall not enter upon the duties of his office unless he has taken and subscribed the Oath of Allegiance as set out in the Sixth Schedule and the Judicial Oath as set out in the Fifth Schedule, and both oaths shall be administered by and subscribed before the Chief Justice.   Cap. 1

Oath of Office[1]

6.   The Oath of Office shall be in the form set out in the Seventh Schedule.

Affirmation

7.   A person required to take an oath under this Act or any other written law who expresses any objection to taking an oath or who expresses a desire to make an affirmation instead, without being questioned as to the grounds of his objection or desire or otherwise, may make a solemn affirmation in the form of the oath, substituting the words "solemnly and sincerely declared and affirm" for the word "swear" and omitting the words "So help me God" and his subscription of the affirmation shall be accordingly amended.

Unnecessary repetition of Oaths

8.   Where any person who has taken an oath by reason of the provisions of this Act is appointed to, or to act in, some other office whereby he is required to take the Oath of Allegiance, the Judicial Oath or the Oath of Office, or to be in attendance on the Cabinet he shall not be required to take any oath by reason of such appointment unless the oath required to be taken thereon is different from or in addition to any oath already taken by him and duly recorded in respect of any previous appointment:
Provided that nothing in this section shall apply to a person on assuming the office of President, Vice-President or Judge.

Failure to take Oath

9.   Any act done by any person in the execution or purported execution of his official duties shall not be rendered invalid by reason only of the omission of that person to take or subscribe an oath required by law to be taken or subscribed.

Custody of Oaths

10.   (1)   Every oath subscribed, and a record of every oath taken and subscribed, under this Act or any other written law shall be forwarded to the proper officer, and any oath or record produced from the custody of the proper officer shall be evidence for all purposes that the oath was duly and properly taken or subscribed under the provisions of this Act or the relevant written law, as the case may be.

(2)   For the purpose of this section, "proper officer" means:
(a)   in respect of oaths taken or subscribed before the National Assembly or the House of Chiefs, the Clerk of the National Assembly or the Clerk of the House of Chiefs, as the case may be;

---

[1] See Article 260 of the Constitution as amended by Act No 2 of 2016.

(b) in respect of oaths taken or subscribed under provision of section eight, the Registrar of the High Court;

(c) in respect of any other oaths, the Secretary to the Cabinet:

Provided that the Secretary to the Cabinet, by notice published in the Gazette may appoint any person to be the proper officer in respect of any oath or class of oaths to which this paragraph applies.

Powers of the President

11. (1) The President may by statutory instrument-

(a) specify any office to which a person appointed, elected or nominated, shall not act or perform duties of that office unless he has taken and subscribed the Oath of Office as set out in the Seventh Schedule;

(b) require any person, before performing the duties of any other office, to take and subscribe, any oath prescribed in this Act before the official specified in the instrument.

(2) Notwithstanding the provisions of section eight the President may require any person attending directly or indirectly on the President or engaged in any work for the Republic to take and to subscribe, any oath prescribed in this Act before any official the President may designate.

Repeal and savings

12. (1) The Official Oaths Act is hereby repealed. Cap. 436 (of the revised edition of 1972)

(2) Notwithstanding the provisions of subsection (1), any oath which was lawfully taken and subscribed prior to the commencement of this Act shall be deemed to have been properly taken and subscribed under this Act.

FIRST SCHEDULE

(Section 3)

OATH OF PRESIDENT

I ...., having been constitutionally elected/ re-elected to the Office of President of the Republic of Zambia, do swear/affirm that I will faithfully and diligently discharge my duties and perform my functions in this high office; that I will uphold and maintain the Constitution and Laws of Zambia and that I will dedicate my abilities to the service and welfare of the people of Zambia without fear, favour, or ill will.

SO HELP ME GOD.

....
President

Sworn at .... this .... day of ....
......................., 19.......
Before me,

....
Chief Justice

SECOND SCHEDULE

(Section 4)

OATH OF VICE-PRESIDENT

I ...., Vice-President do swear/affirm that I will well and diligently discharge my duties, and perform my functions under the Constitution of Zambia, that I will not directly or indirectly reveal or transmit any such information or matter as shall be brought under my consideraton, or shall be made known to me, by reason of my office except as may be required in the discharge of my duties as such or with the authority of the President; and that I will, to the best of my ability at all times when so required, give my counsel and advice to the President for the good management of the public affairs of the Republic of Zambia.

SO HELP ME GOD.

....
(Signature)
Sworn at .... this .... day of ....
...................., 19.......
Before me,

....
President

THIRD SCHEDULE

(Section 4)

OATH OF SPEAKER

(Sworn before the National Assembly)
I ...., having been appointed Speaker of the National Assembly do swear/affirm that I will and diligently discharge my duties and perform my functions in the office of the Speaker of the National Assembly; that I will not directly or indirectly reveal or transmit any such information or matter as shall be brought under my consideration, or shall be made known to me, by reason of my office except as may be required in the discharge of my duties as such or with the authority of the President.

SO HELP ME GOD.

FOURTH SCHEDULE

(Section 4)

OATH OF MINISTER OR JUNIOR MINISTER

I ...., having been appointed .... in the Government of the Republic of Zambia, do swear/affirm that I will in this office well and truly serve the Republic and the President of Zambia; and I will not directly or indirectly reveal or transmit any such information or matter as shall be brought under my consideration, or shall be made known to me, by reason of my office except as may be required in the discharge of my duties as such or with the authority of the President.

SO HELP ME GOD.

....
(Signature)
Sworn at .... this .... day of ....
...................., 19.......
Before me,

....
President

FIFTH SCHEDULE

(Section 5)

JUDICIAL OATH

I ...., having been appointed ....
.... do swear/affirm that I will well and truly serve the Republic and the President of Zambia, that I shall not directly or indirectly reveal or transmit any such information or matter as shall be brought under my consideration, or shall be made known to me, by reason of my office except as may be required in the discharge of my duties as such or with the authority of the President; and that I will do justice in accordance with the Constitution of Zambia as by law established, and in accordance with the Laws of Zambia, without fear, favour, or ill will.

SO HELP ME GOD.

....
(Signature)
Sworn at .... this .... day of ....
...................., 19.......
Before me,

....
President

SIXTH SCHEDULE

(Sections 4 and 5)

OATH OF ALLEGIANCE

I ...., do swear/affirm that I will be faithful and bear allegiance to the President of the Republic of Zambia, and that I will preserve, protect and defend the Constitution of Zambia, as by law established.

SO HELP ME GOD.

....
(Signature)
Sworn at .... this .... day of ....
...................., 19.......
Before me,

....
President

SEVENTH SCHEDULE

(Section 11)

OATH OF OFFICE

I ...., having been appointed/elected/
nominated..do swear/affirm that I will well and truly serve the Republic and the President of Zambia; that I will be faithful and bear true allegiance to the President and the Republic of Zambia, that I will preserve, protect and defend the Constitution of Zambia, as by law established; and that

190

I will not directly or indirectly reveal or transmit any such information or matter as shall be brought under my consideration, or shall be made known to me by reason of my office except as may be required in the discharge of my duties as such or with the authority of the President.

SO HELP ME GOD.

....
(Signature)
Sworn at .... this .... day of ....
...................., 19.......
Before me,

....
President

THE HIGH COURT ACT CHAPTER 27 OF THE LAWS OF ZAMBIA

PART VII
EVIDENCE

Summoning and compelling attendance of witnesses

27. (1) In any suit or matter, and at any stage thereof, the Court, either of its own motion or on the application of any party, may summon any person within the jurisdiction to give evidence, or to produce any document in his possession or power, and may examine such person as a witness and require him to produce any document in his possession or power, subject to just exceptions.

    (2) If any person summoned as in subsection (1) provided, having reasonable notice of the time and place at which he is required to attend and after tender of his reasonable travelling expenses to and from the Court, fails to attend accordingly and does not excuse his failure to the satisfaction of the Court, he shall, independently of any other liability, be guilty of a contempt of court, and may be punished therefor, and may be proceeded against by warrant to compel his attendance.

    (3) Nothing in this section contained shall be construed so as to make it lawful in any criminal proceeding for any person to refuse or fail to attend as a witness or to give evidence on the ground that his expenses have not first been paid or provided for.

Refusal to be sworn or to give evidence

28. If, in any suit or matter, any person, whether appearing in obedience to a summons or brought up under warrant, being required to give evidence, refuses to take an oath or make an affirmation in lieu thereof, or to answer any question lawfully put to him, or to produce any document in his possession or power, and does not excuse his refusal to the satisfaction of the Court, he shall independently of any other liability, be guilty of a contempt of court, and the Court may, by warrant, commit him to prison, there to remain until he consents to take the oath or make an affirmation, or to answer duly, or to produce any such document, as the case may be.

Evidence of bystander

29. Any person present in court, whether a party or not in a cause or matter, may be compelled by the Court to give evidence or to produce any document in his possession or power, in the same manner and subject to the same rules as if he had been duly summoned to attend and give evidence or to produce such document, and may be dealt with under the provisions of section twenty-eight for any refusal to obey the order of the Court.

Evidence of prisoners

30.   A Judge may issue a warrant under his hand to bring up any person confined as a prisoner under any sentence or otherwise, to be examined as a witness in any cause or matter depending in the Court, and the gaoler or person in whose charge such prisoner may be shall obey such warrant by bringing up such prisoner in custody and delivering him to an officer of the Court:

Provided that this section shall not apply in any case to which section sixty-four of the Prisons Act applies.

Allowances to witnesses

31.   (1)   It shall be lawful for the Court, in civil as well as criminal proceedings, to order and to allow to all persons required to attend or be examined as witnesses such sum of money as the Chief Justice may, by rule made with the concurrence of the Minister responsible for finance, prescribe, as well for defraying the reasonable expenses of such persons as for allowing them a reasonable compensation for their trouble and loss of time.

   (2)   All sums of money allowed under the provisions of this section shall be payable, in civil proceedings, by the party on whose behalf the witness is called, and shall be recoverable as ordinary costs of suit unless the Court shall otherwise order, and in criminal proceedings they shall, where not ordered to be paid by the person convicted or the prosecutor, be paid out of the general revenues of the Republic.

Commissioners of the Court

32.   (1)   A Judge may, in respect of any proceedings in the Court, appoint any person or persons to be a Commissioner or Commissioners for taking affidavits and declarations and receiving production of documents, or for taking and receiving the evidence of witnesses on interrogatories or otherwise.

   (2)   Any order of the Court or of a Judge for the attendance and examination of witnesses or the production of documents before any Commissioner appointed under the provisions of this section and within the jurisdiction of the Court shall be enforced in the same manner as an order to attend and be examined or produce documents before the Court.

Inspection

33.   In any cause or matter, the Court may make such order for inspection by the Court, the parties or witnesses of any real or personal property the inspection of which may be material to the determination of the matter in dispute, and may give such directions with regard to such inspection as to the Court may seem fit.

34.   (1)   The Court may, in any cause or matter in which questions of African customary law may be material to the issue- Evidence of African customary law and assessors thereof

   (a)   call as witnesses thereto chiefs or other persons whom the Court considers to have special knowledge of African customary law;

   (b)   call any such chiefs or persons to its assistance as assessors of African customary law;

   (c)   consult, if it shall think fit and, to such extent as to it seems proper, give effect to any book or publication which the Court shall consider to be an authority on African customary law.

   (2)   It shall be the duty of assessors called under the provisions of subsection (1) to advise the Court on all matters of African customary law which may arise in the cause or matter concerned, and to tender their opinions to the Court on such cause or matter generally, but in reaching its decision the Court shall not be bound to conform to such opinions.

   (3)   Assessors called under the provisions of subsection (1) shall be paid such fees and allowances as the Chief Justice may, by rule made with the concurrence of the Minister responsible for finance, determine, and such fees and allowances shall be paid out of the general revenues of the Republic unless the Court, in any particular civil cause or matter, orders that they shall be costs in the proceedings concerned.

Record of evidence, etc.

35. (1) Save as hereinafter in this section provided, no person shall be entitled as of right at any time or for any purpose to inspection or a copy of a record of evidence given in any case before the Court, or to a copy of the notes of the Court, save as may be expressly provided by rules of court.

    (2) Any party to any cause or matter before the Court shall, on payment of such fee as may be prescribed by rules of court, be entitled to a copy of the record of evidence given in such cause or matter.

    (3) The Director of Public Prosecutions shall, without payment of fee, be entitled to the record of evidence given in any criminal proceedings before the Court.
    (As amended by S.I. No. 63 of 1964)

Oaths, etc.

36. (1) Whenever an oath is required to be taken under the provisions of this or any other law, or in order to comply with any such law, the following provisions shall apply:

    (a) The person taking the oath shall hold, if a Christian, a copy of the Gospels of the Four Evangelists or of the New Testament, or, if a Jew, a copy of the Old Testament, in his uplifted right hand, or, if he be physically incapable of so doing, he may hold such copy otherwise, or, if necessary such copy may be held before him by the officer administering the oath, and shall say or repeat after such officer the words "I swear by Almighty God that . . ." followed by the words of the oath prescribed by law or by the practice of the court, as the case may be:
    Provided that if any person desires to take the oath in the form and manner in which an oath is usually administered in Scotland, he shall be permitted to do so.

    (b) If the person taking the oath is neither a Christian nor a Jew, he may take the oath in any manner which he declares to be, or accepts as, binding on his conscience or which is lawful according to any law, and in particular he may do so by raising his right hand and saying or repeating after the officer administering the oath the words "I swear by Almighty God that . . ." followed by the words of the oath prescribed by law or by the practice of the court, as the case may be:
    Provided that if the person taking the oath is physically incapable of raising his right hand, he may say or repeat the words of the oath without raising his right hand.

    (c) If any person shall express any objection to taking an oath or desires to make an affirmation in lieu thereof, he may make such affirmation without being further questioned as to the grounds of such objection or desire, or otherwise, and in such case there shall be substituted for the words "I swear by Almighty God" aforesaid the words "I do solemnly and sincerely affirm" and such consequential variations of form as may be necessary shall thereupon be made.

    (2) Notwithstanding any other provision contained in this section, any person may be required to make an affirmation in the form specified in paragraph (c) of subsection (1) if it is not reasonably practicable to administer an oath to him in the manner appropriate to his religious belief, and for the purposes of this subsection "reasonably practicable" means reasonably practicable without inconvenience or delay.

    (3) Where any oath has been duly administered and taken, the fact that the person to whom such oath was administered had, at the time of taking such oath, no religious belief, or had a religious belief other than that to which the oath taken normally applies, shall not for any purpose affect the validity of such oath.

    (4) For the purposes of this section, "officer" means any person duly authorised by law to administer oaths, and shall include any Assistant Registrar, Deputy Assistant Registrar and official interpreter administering an oath in the presence of a Judge or the Registrar or other person authorised by any law to administer oaths.
    (As amended by No. 43 of 1961)

Recording o proceedings

37. The proceedings in any cause or matter before the Court shall be taken down and recorded in such manner as may be prescribed by rules of court.
    (As amended by No. 43 of 1961)

Perjury

38. (1)   The Court, if it appears to it that a person has been guilty of perjury in any proceeding before it, may, after calling upon such person to show cause why he should not be punished as for a contempt of court, commit him to prison for any term not exceeding six months, with or without hard labour, or fine him any sum not exceeding one hundred penalty units, or impose both such penalties upon him, in each such case as for a contempt of court.

    (2)   Any penalty imposed under this section shall be a bar to any other criminal proceedings in respect of the same offence.
    (As amended by Act No. 13 of 1994)

ORDER V
EVIDENCE

I-Exclusion of Witnesses

Ordering witnesses out of court

1.   On the application of either party, or on its own motion, the Court may order witnesses on both sides to be kept out of court; but this rule does not extend to the parties themselves or to their professional representatives, although intended to be called as witnesses.

Preventing communication with witnesses

2.   The Court may, during any trial, take such means as it considers necessary and proper for preventing communication with witnesses who are within the Court House or its precincts awaiting examination.

II-Documentary Evidence

Entries in books of account

3.   Entries in books of account, kept in the course of business with such a reasonable degree of regularity as shall be satisfactory to the Court or a Judge, shall be admissible in evidence whenever they refer to a matter into which the Court or a Judge has to inquire, but shall not alone be sufficient evidence to charge any person with liability.

Government Gazettes

4.   The Government Gazette in Zambia and any Government Gazette of any Commonwealth Country may be proved by the bare production of the Government Gazette.
(As amended by SI No 63 of 1964 and SI No 71 of 1997)

Proof of Proclamations, etc.

5.   All Proclamations, Acts of State, whether legislative or executive, nominations, appointments, and other official communications of the Government, appearing in any Gazette referred to in the last preceding rule may be proved by the production of such Gazette, and shall be prima facie proof of any fact of a public nature which they were intended to notify.

Books of science, maps, charts, etc.

6.   On matters of public history, literature, science or art, the Court or a Judge may refer, if it or he shall think fit, for the purposes of evidence, to such published books, maps or charts as the Court or a Judge shall consider to be of authority on the subject to which they relate.

Foreign law

7.   Books printed or published under the authority of the government of a foreign country and purporting to contain the statutes, code or other written law of such country, and also printed and published books of reports of the decisions of the courts of such country, and books proved to be commonly admitted in such courts as evidence of the law of such country, shall be admissible as evidence of the law of such country.

Public maps

8. All maps made under the authority of any government or of any public municipal body, and not made for the purpose of any litigated question, shall prima facie be deemed to be correct, and shall be admitted in evidence without further proof.

Examined or certified copies of documents admissible in evidence

9. Whenever any book or other document is of such a public nature as to be admissible in evidence on its mere production from the proper custody, and no Act or statute exists which renders its contents provable by means of a copy, any copy thereof or extract therefrom shall be admissible in evidence, if it purports to be signed and certified as a true copy or extract by the officer to whose custody the original is entrusted.

Production of documents without giving evidence

10. Any person, whether a party or not, in a cause or matter may be summoned to produce a document, without being summoned to give evidence; and, if he cause such document to be produced, the Court or a Judge may dispense with his personal attendance.

III-Affidavits

Affidavits to be filed

11. Before an affidavit is used in any proceeding for any purpose, the original shall be filed in the Court, and the original or an office copy shall alone be recognised for any purpose by the Court or a Judge.

Not to be sworn before certain persons

12. An affidavit shall not be admitted which is proved to have been sworn before a person on whose behalf the same is offered, or before his Advocate, or before a partner or clerk of his Advocate.

Defective in form

13. The Court or a Judge may permit an affidavit to be used notwithstanding it is defective in form according to these Rules, if the Court or a Judge is satisfied that it has been sworn before a person duly authorised.
14. A defective or erroneous affidavit may be amended and re-sworn, by leave of the Court or a Judge, on such terms as to time, costs or otherwise as seem reasonable. Amendment and re-swearing

No extraneous matter

15. An affidavit shall not contain extraneous matter by way of objection or prayer or legal argument or conclusion.

Contents of affidavits

16. Every affidavit shall contain only a statement of facts and circumstances to which the witness deposes, either of his own personal knowledge or from information which he believes to be true.

Grounds of belief to be stated

17. When a witness deposes to his belief in any matter of fact, and his belief is derived from any source other than his own personal knowledge, he shall set forth explicitly the facts and circumstances forming the ground of his belief.

Informant to be named

18. When the belief of a witness is derived from information received from another person, the name of his informant shall be stated, and reasonable particulars shall be given respecting the informant, and the time, place and circumstances of the information.

Copies of exhibits

19. Where any document referred to in an affidavit and exhibited thereto is a handwritten document other than a statement of account, book of account or extract therefrom, there shall also be exhibited therewith a typewritten or printed copy thereof certified in such affidavit to be a true and correct copy of the original. (No. 106 of 1959)

Rules in taking affidavits

20. The following rules shall be observed by Commissioners and others before whom affidavits are taken:

To be properly entitled

(a) Every affidavit taken in a cause or matter shall be headed in the Court and in the cause or matter.

Description of witness

(b) It shall state the full name, trade or profession, residence and nationality of the witness.

In first person

(c) It shall be in the first person and divided into convenient paragraphs, numbered consecutively.

Erasures, etc., to be attested

(d) Any erasure, interlineation or alteration made before the affidavit is sworn shall be attested by the Commissioner, who shall affix his signature or initials in the margin immediately opposite to the interlineation, alteration or erasure.

If improperly written

(e) Where an affidavit proposed to be sworn is illegible or difficult to read, or is, in the judgment of the Commissioner, so written as to facilitate fraudulent alteration, he may refuse to swear the witness, and require the affidavit to be re-written in an unobjectionable manner.

Witness to sign

(f) The affidavit shall be signed by the witness (or, if he cannot write, marked by him with his mark in the presence of the Commissioner).

Form of jurat

(g) The jurat shall be written, without interlineation, alteration or erasure (unless the same be initialed by the Commissioner), immediately at the foot of the affidavit, and towards the left side of the paper, and shall be signed by the Commissioner.

Date and place

It shall state the date of the swearing and the place where it is sworn.
It shall state that the affidavit was sworn before the Commissioner or other officer taking the same. In presence of Commissioner

Illiterate or blind witness

Where the witness is illiterate or blind, it shall state the fact, and that the affidavit was read over (or translated into his own language in the case of a witness not having sufficient knowledge of English), and that the witness appeared to understand it.

Marksmen

Where the witness makes a mark instead of signing, the jurat shall state that fact, and that the mark was made in the presence of the Commissioner.

Joint affidavit

Where two or more persons join in making an affidavit, their several names shall be written in the jurat, and it shall appear by the jurat that each of them has been sworn to the truth of the several matters stated by him in the affidavit.

If affidavit altered, to be re-sworn

(h)   The Commissioner shall not allow an affidavit, when sworn, to be altered in any manner without being re-sworn.

New jurat

(i)   If the jurat has been added and signed, the Commissioner shall add a new jurat on the affidavit being re-sworn; and, in the new jurat, he shall mention the alteration.

New affidavit

(j)   The Commissioner may refuse to allow the affidavit to be re-sworn, and may require a fresh affidavit.

Declarations without oath

(k)   The Commissioner may take, without oath, the declaration of any person affirming that the taking of any oath whatsoever is, according to his religious belief, unlawful, or who, by reason of immature age or want of religious belief, ought not, in the opinion of the Commissioner, to be admitted to make a sworn affidavit. The Commissioner shall record in the attestation the reason of such declaration being taken without oath.

Certificate on exhibit

(l)   Every certificate on an exhibit referred to in an affidavit signed by the Commissioner before whom the affidavit is sworn shall be marked with the short title of the cause or matter.
(As amended by No 106 of 1959)

IV-Objections to Evidence

When to be made

21.   In every case, and at every stage thereof, any objection to the reception of evidence by a party affected thereby shall be made at the time the evidence is offered:
Provided that the Court may, in its discretion, on appeal, entertain any objection to evidence received in a subordinate court, though not objected to at the time it was offered.
(As amended by No 218 of 1944)

Where question objected to

22.   Where a question proposed to be put to a witness is objected to, the Court or a Judge, unless the objection appears frivolous, shall, if required by either party, take a note of the question and objection, and mention on the notes whether the question was allowed to be put or not and, if put, the answer to it.

V-Taking of Evidence

Marking of rejected documents

23.   Where a document is produced and tendered in evidence and rejected by the Court or a Judge, the document shall be marked as having been so tendered and rejected.

Evidence of witnesses, how taken

24.   In the absence of any agreement between the parties, and subject to these Rules, the witnesses at the trial or any suit shall be examined viva voce and in open court; but the Court may at any time, for sufficient reason, order that any particular fact or facts may be proved by affidavit, or that the affidavit of any

witness may be read at the hearing or trial, on such conditions as the Court may think reasonable; or that any witness whose attendance in court ought, for some sufficient cause, to be dispensed with be examined by interrogatories or otherwise before an officer of the Court or other person:

Provided that, where it appears to the Court that the other party bona fide desires the production of a witness for cross-examination, and that such witness can be produced, an order shall not be made authorising the evidence of such witness to be given by affidavit.

Admission of affidavits

25.   In any suit, the Court may, in its discretion, if the interests of justice appear absolutely so to require (for reasons to be recorded in the minutes of the proceedings), admit an affidavit in evidence, although it is shown that the party against whom the affidavit is offered in evidence has had no opportunity of cross-examining the person making the affidavit.

Evidence on commission

26.   The Court or a Judge may, in any suite where it shall appear necessary for the purpose of justice, make any order for the examination, before any officer of the Court or other person, and at any place, of any witness or person, and may order any deposition so taken to be filed in the Court, and may empower any party to any such suit to give such deposition in evidence therein on such terms, if any, as the Court or a Judge may direct.

How to be taken

27.   Evidence on commission, when not directed to be taken upon interrogatories previously settled, shall be taken, as nearly as may be, as evidence at the hearing of a suit, and then the notes of the evidence shall be read over to the witness and be signed by him. If the witness refuses, the officer of the Court or other person shall add a note of his refusal, and the statement may be used as if he had signed it.

28.   Evidence may be taken in like manner, on the application of any person, before suit instituted, where it is shown to the satisfaction of the Court or a Judge on oath that the person applying has good reason to apprehend that a suit will be instituted against him in the Court, and that some person within the jurisdiction at the time of the application can give material evidence respecting the subject of the apprehended suit, but that he is about to leave the jurisdiction, or that, from some other cause, the person applying will lose the benefit of his evidence if it be not at once taken; and the evidence so taken may be used at the hearing, subject to just exceptions: Evidence before suit instituted.

Provided always that the Court or a Judge may impose any terms or conditions with reference to the examination of such witness, and the admission of his evidence, as to the Court or a Judge may seem reasonable.

Facilities for proving deed, etc.

29.   Any party desiring to give in evidence any deed or other instrument which shows upon the face of it that it has been duly executed may deliver to the opposite party, not less than four clear days before the return day, a notice in writing specifying the date and nature of and the parties to such deed or instrument, and requiring the opposite party to admit that the same was executed as it purports to have been, saving all just exceptions as to its admissibility, validity and contents; and if, at or before the hearing of the suit, the party so notified shall neglect or refuse to give such admission, the Court or a Judge may adjourn the hearing in order to enable the party tendering such deed or instrument to obtain proof of the due execution thereof, and, upon production of such proof, the Court or a Judge may order the costs of such proof to be paid by the party so neglecting or refusing, whether he be the successful party or not.

Commission or letter of request

30.   Where the Court or a Judge to which or to whom application is made for the issue of a commission for the examination of a person residing at a place not within Zambia is satisfied that the evidence of such person is necessary, the Court may issue such commission or a letter of request.

Not to issue until sum deposited in court to cover cost thereof

31.   The Court shall not issue any commission or letter of request abroad for the taking of evidence, unless and until the person applying for the issue of such commission or letter of request shall have paid into court by way of deposit, or shall have given approved security for, such sum as the Court or a Judge shall consider sufficient to cover the expenses incurred, or likely to be incurred, in connection with and in consequence of the grant of any such application.

THE SUBORDINATE COURTS ACT CHAPTER 28 OF THE LAWS OF ZAMBIA

PART VIII
EVIDENCE

Summoning witnesses

41.   In any suit or matter, and at any stage thereof, a Subordinate Court, either of its own motion or on the application of any party, may summon any person within Zambia to attend to give evidence, or to produce any document in his possession or power, and may examine such person as a witness, and require him to produce any document in his possession or power, subject to just exceptions.

Compelling attendance-Penalty on non-attendance

42.   If the person summoned as in the last preceding section provided, having reasonable notice of the time and place at which he is required to attend, after tender of his reasonable travelling expenses to and from the Subordinate Court, fails to attend accordingly, and does not excuse his failure to the satisfaction of the court, he shall, independently of any other liability, be guilty of a contempt of court, and may be proceeded against by warrant to compel his attendance.

Refusal to be sworn or to give evidence

43.   If, in any suit or matter, any person, whether appearing in obedience to a summons or brought up under warrant, being required to give evidence, refuses to take an oath, or to answer any question lawfully put to him, or to produce any document in his possession or power, and does not excuse his refusal to the satisfaction of a Subordinate Court, he shall, independently of any other liability, be guilty of a contempt of court, and the court may, by warrant, commit him to prison, without hard labour, there to remain for not more than one month, unless he, in the meantime, consents to take an oath, or to answer duly, or to produce any such document, as the case may be; and he shall also be liable to a fine not exceeding seven hundred and fifty penalty units.
(As amended by Act No. 13 of 1994)

Bystander may be required to give evidence

44.   Any person present in court, whether a party or not in a cause or matter, may be compelled by a Subordinate Court to give evidence, or produce any document in his possession or in his power, in the same manner and subject to the same rules as if he had been summoned to attend and give evidence, or to produce such document, and may be punished in like manner for any refusal to obey the order of the court.

Prisoner may be brought up by warrant to give evidence

45.   A magistrate may issue a warrant under his hand to bring up any person confined as a prisoner under any sentence or otherwise, to be examined as a witness in any suit or matter depending in any Subordinate Court, and the gaoler, or person in whose custody such prisoner shall be, shall obey such warrant, by bringing such prisoner in custody and delivering him to an officer of the court.

Allowances to witnesses

46. It shall be lawful for the presiding magistrate, in civil as well as criminal proceedings, to order and allow to all persons required to attend, or examined, as witnesses, such sum or sums of money as shall seem fit, as well as for defraying the reasonable expenses of such witnesses as for allowing them a reasonable compensation for their trouble and loss of time. But it shall not be lawful, in any criminal proceeding, for any person to refuse to attend as a witness or to give evidence, when so required by process of the court, on the ground that his expenses have not been first paid or provided for.

How defrayed

47. All sums of money allowed under the provisions of the last preceding section shall be paid, in civil proceedings, by the party on whose behalf the witness is called, and shall be recoverable as ordinary costs of suit, if a Subordinate Court shall so order, and, in criminal proceedings, they shall, where not ordered to be paid by the party convicted or the prosecution, be paid out of the general revenues of the Republic.

Inspection

48. In any cause or matter, a Subordinate Court may make such order for the inspection by the court, the parties or witnesses of any real or personal property, the inspection of which may be material to the determination of the matter in dispute, and may give such directions with regard to such inspection as to the court may seem fit.

Witnesses as to African customary law

49. A Subordinate Court may, in any cause or matter in which questions of African customary law may be material to the issue, call as witnesses thereto chiefs or other persons whom the court considers to have special knowledge of African customary law.

A person not entitled to inspection or copy of record of evidence

50. A person shall not be entitled, as of right, at any time or for any purpose, to inspection or a copy of the record of evidence given in any case before any Subordinate Court, or to a copy of the notes of such court, save as may be expressly provided by any rules of court.

Evidence before Subordinate Courts, recording of

51. (1) In every case heard before a Subordinate Court, and at every stage thereof, the presiding magistrate shall, save as hereinafter provided, take down in writing the oral evidence given before the court:
    Provided that, should the presiding magistrate, in any case, find himself temporarily incapacitated from taking down such evidence, it shall be lawful for the magistrate to direct that such evidence shall be taken down by the clerk of the court or officer performing his duties in court.
    (2) Before any clerk of the court or other officer shall take down in writing any oral evidence as aforesaid, an oath shall be tendered to and taken by such clerk of the court or officer for the accurate and faithful recording of such oral evidence, according to the true purport and meaning thereof; and such oath shall be in such terms as to such presiding magistrate may seem apt and sufficient:
    Provided always that a clerk of the court or officer performing his duties in court, who shall once have duly taken such oath, shall not again be required to take such oath in respect of the same or of any subsequent case.
    (3) After taking such oath as aforesaid, the clerk of the court or other officer shall take down in writing such oral evidence in manner as aforesaid, under the supervision and control of the presiding magistrate, who may, at any time before appending his signature to such writing, amend anything therein which he may consider requires to be amended; and, before so appending his signature, such magistrate shall peruse and examine such writing, and satisfy himself that it is, in substance, an accurate and faithful record of the oral evidence given.
    (4) Notwithstanding the foregoing provisions of this section, the Chief Justice may authorise that the oral evidence given before a specified Subordinate Court, either generally or in a particular case, may be recorded in shorthand or by any other system of verbatim reporting and afterwards

transcribed into longhand. Any such authority given by the Chief Justice shall be subject to the following conditions:

(a) no person shall be employed for the purpose of so recording or transcribing unless the magistrate is satisfied that such person is competent, reliable and suitable for the purpose;

(b) before any person so records and transcribes, or so records or transcribes, he shall take an oath for the faithful and accurate recording and transcription, or recording or transcription, according to the true purport and meaning of the evidence. Such oath shall be in such terms as the Chief Justice may direct.

(As amended by No. 24 of 1952)

Perjury

52. (1) A Subordinate Court of the first or second class, if it appears to it that a person has been guilty of perjury in any proceeding before it, may-

(a) after calling upon such person to show cause why he should not be punished as for a contempt of court, commit him to prison for any term not exceeding six months, with or without hard labour, or fine him any sum not exceeding one thousand five hundred penalty units, or impose both such penalties upon him, in each such case as for a contempt of court; or

(b) after preliminary inquiry, commit him for trial upon information for perjury, and bind any person by recognizance to give evidence at such trial.

(2) On imposing any penalty as for a contempt of court under this section, a Subordinate Court shall, forthwith, send a copy of the proceedings to the High Court. The High Court may, thereupon, without hearing any argument, vary or set aside the order of the Subordinate Court.

(3) Except where the order of the Subordinate Court is set aside by the High Court, any penalty imposed under this section shall be a bar to any other criminal proceedings in respect of the same offence.

(As amended by Act No. 13 of 1994)

ORDER V
EVIDENCE

I-Exclusion of Witnesses

Ordering witnesses out of court

1. On the application of either party, or on its own motion, the court may order witnesses on both sides to be kept out of court; but this rule does not extend to the parties themselves or to their professional representatives, although intended to be called as witnesses.

2. The court may, during any trial, take such means as it considers necessary and proper for preventing communication with witnesses who are within the Court House or its precincts awaiting examination.

II-Documentary Evidence Preventing communication with witnesses

Entries in books of account

3. Entries in books of account, kept in the course of business with such a reasonable degree of regularity as shall be satisfactory to the court, shall be admissible in evidence whenever they refer to a matter into which the court has to inquire, but shall not alone be sufficient evidence to charge any person with liability.

4. Any Government Gazette of any British Dominion, colony or protectorate or any territory in respect of which Her Britannic Majesty has accepted a mandate may be proved by the bare production thereof before the court.

(As amended by S.I. No. 63 of 1964) Government Gazettes)

Proof of Proclamations, etc.

5. All Proclamations, Acts of State, whether legislative or executive, nominations, appointments, and other official communications of the Government, appearing in any Gazette referred to in the last preceding rule, may be proved by the production of such Gazette, and shall be prima facie proof of any fact of a public nature which they were intended to notify.

Books of science, maps, charts, etc.

6.   On matters of public history, literature, science or art, the court may refer, if it shall think fit, for the purposes of evidence, to such published books, maps or charts as the court shall consider to be of authority on the subject to which they relate.

Foreign law

7.   Books printed or published under the authority of the government of a foreign country and purporting to contain the statutes, code or other written law of such country, and also printed and published books of reports of the decisions of the courts of such country, and books proved to be commonly admitted in such courts as evidence of the law of such country, shall be admissible as evidence of the law of such country.

Public maps

8.   All maps made under the authority of any government or of any public municipal body, and not made for the purpose of any litigated question, shall prima facie be deemed to be correct, and shall be admitted in evidence without further proof.

Examined or certified copies of documents admissible in evidence

9.   Whenever any book or other document is of such a public nature as to be admissible in evidence on its mere production from the proper custody, and no Act or statute exists which renders its contents provable by means of a copy, any copy thereof or extract therefrom shall be admissible in evidence if it purports to be signed and certified as a true copy or extract by the officer to whose custody the original is entrusted.

10. Any person, whether a party or not in a cause or matter, may be summoned to produce a document without being summoned to give evidence; and, if he cause such document to be produced in court, the court may dispense with his personal attendance.

III-Affidavits Production of documents without giving evidence

Affidavits to be filed

11. Before an affidavit is used in the court for any purpose, the original shall be filed in the court, and the original or an office copy shall alone be recognised for any purpose in the court.

Not to be sworn before certain persons

12. An affidavit shall not be admitted which is proved to have been sworn before a person on whose behalf the same is offered, or before his solicitor, or before a partner or clerk of his solicitor.

Defective in form

13. The court may permit an affidavit to be used, notwithstanding it is defective in form according to these Rules, if the court is satisfied that it has been sworn before a person duly authorised.

Amendment and reswearing

14. A defective or erroneous affidavit may be amended and re-sworn, by leave of the court, on such terms as to time, costs or otherwise as seem reasonable.

No extraneous matter

15. An affidavit shall not contain extraneous matter by way of objection or prayer or legal argument or conclusion.

Contents of affidavits

16. Every affidavit used in the court shall contain only a statement of facts and circumstances to which the witness deposes, either of his own personal knowledge or from information which he believes to be true.

Grounds of belief to be stated

17. When a witness deposes to his belief in any matter of fact, and his belief is derived from any source other than his own personal knowledge, he shall set forth explicitly the facts and circumstances forming the ground of his belief.

Informant to be named

18. When the belief of a witness is derived from information received from another person, the name of his informant shall be stated, and reasonable particulars shall be given respecting the informant, and the time, place and circumstances of the information.

Copies of exhibits

19. Where any document referred to in an affidavit and exhibited thereto is a hand-written document, other than a statement of account, book of account or extract therefrom, there shall also be exhibited therewith a typewritten or printed copy thereof certified in such affidavit to be a true and correct copy of the original.
(No. 135 of 1959)

Erasures, etc., to be attested

20. The following rules shall be observed by Commissioners and others before whom affidavits are taken:

Rules in taking affidavits

(a) Every affidavit taken in a cause or matter shall be headed in the court and in the cause or matter. T   o be properly entitled

(b) It shall state the full name, trade or profession, residence and nationality of the witness. Description of witness

(c) It shall be in the first person and divided into convenient paragraphs, numbered consecutively. I   n first person

(d) Any erasure, interlineation or alteration made before the affidavit is sworn shall be attested by the Commissioner, who shall affix his signature or initials in the margin immediately opposite to the interlineation, alteration or erasure.

If improperly written

(e) Where an affidavit proposed to be sworn is illegible or difficult to read, or is, in the judgment of the Commissioner, so written as to facilitate fraudulent alteration, he may refuse to swear the witness and require the affidavit to be re-written in an unobjectionable manner.

Witness to sign

(f) The affidavit shall be signed by the witness (or, if he cannot write, marked by him with his mark) in the presence of the Commissioner.

Form of jurat

(g) The jurat shall be written, without interlineation, alteration or erasure (unless the same be initialed by the Commissioner), immediately at the foot of the affidavit, and towards the left side of the paper, and shall be signed by the Commissioner.

Date and place

It shall state the date of the swearing and the place where it is sworn.

In presence of Commissioner

It shall state that the affidavit was sworn before the Commissioner or other officer taking the same.

Illiterate or blind witness

Where the witness is illiterate or blind, it shall state the fact, and that the affidavit was read over (or translated into his own language in the case of a witness not having sufficient knowledge of English), and that the witness appeared to understand it.

Marksmen

Where the witness makes a mark instead of signing, the jurat shall state that fact, and that the mark was made in the presence of the Commissioner.

Joint affidavit

Where two or more persons join in making an affidavit, their several names shall be written in the jurat, and it shall appear by the jurat that each of them has been sworn to the truth of the several matters stated by him in the affidavit.

If affidavit altered, to be re-sworn

(h) The Commissioner shall not allow an affidavit, when sworn, to be altered in any manner without being re-sworn.

New jurat

(i) If the jurat has been added and signed, the Commissioner shall add a new jurat on the affidavit being re-sworn; and, in the new jurat, he shall mention the alteration.

New affidavit

(j) The Commissioner may refuse to allow the affidavit to be re-sworn, and may require a fresh affidavit.

Declarations without oath

(k) The Commissioner may take, without oath, the declaration of any person affirming that the taking of any oath whatsoever is, according to his religious belief, unlawful, or who, by reason of immature age or want of religious belief, ought not, in the opinion of the Commissioner, to be admitted to make a sworn statement. The Commissioner shall record in the attestation the reason of such declaration being taken without oath.

Certificate on exhibit

(l) Every certificate on an exhibit referred to in an affidavit signed by the Commissioner before whom the affidavit is sworn shall be marked with the short title of the cause or matter.
(As amended by No 135 of 1959)

IV-Objections to Evidence

When to be made

21. In every cause or matter, and at every stage thereof, any objection to the reception of evidence by a party affected thereby shall be made at the time the evidence is offered:
Provided that an appellate court may, in its discretion, entertain any objection to evidence received in the court below, though not objected to at the time it was offered.

Where question objected to

22. Where a question proposed to be put to a witness is objected to, the court, unless the objection appears frivolous, shall, if required by either party, take note of the question and objection, and mention on the notes whether the question was allowed to be put or not and, if put, the answer to it.

Marking of rejected documents

23. Where a document is produced and tendered in evidence and rejected by the court, the document shall be marked as having been so tendered and rejected.

V-Taking of Evidence

Evidence of witnesses, how taken

24. In the absence of any agreement between the parties, and subject to these Rules, the witnesses at the trial of any suit shall be examined viva voce and in open court; but the court may, at any time, for sufficient reason, order that any particular fact or facts may be proved by affidavit, or that the affidavit of any witness may be read at the hearing or trial, on such conditions as the court may think reasonable, or that any witness whose attendance in court ought, for some sufficient cause, to be dispensed with be examined by interrogatories or otherwise before an officer of the court or other person:

    Provided that, where it appears to the court that the other party bona fide desires the production of a witness for cross-examination, and that such witness can be produced, an order shall not be made authorising the evidence of such witness to be given by affidavit.

Admission of affidavits

25. In any suit, the court may, in its discretion, if the interests of justice appear so to require (for reasons to be recorded in the minutes of the proceedings), admit an affidavit in evidence, although it is shown that the party against whom the affidavit is offered in evidence has had no opportunity of cross-examining the person making the affidavit.

Evidence on commission

26. The court may, in any suit where it shall appear necessary for the purpose of justice, make any order for the examination, before any officer of the court or other person, and at any place, of any witness or person, and may order any deposition so taken to be filed in the court, and may empower any party to any such suit to give such deposition in evidence therein on such terms, if any, as the court may direct.

How to be taken

27. Evidence on commission, when not directed to be taken upon interrogatories previously settled, shall be taken, as nearly as may be, as evidence at the hearing of a suit, and then the notes of the evidence shall be read over to the witness and be signed by him. If the witness refuses to sign the notes of evidence, the officer of the court or other person shall add a note of his refusal, and the statement may be used as if he had signed it.

Evidence before suit instituted

28. Evidence may be taken in like manner, on the application of any person, before suit instituted, where it is shown to the satisfaction of the court on oath that the person applying has good reason to apprehend that a suit will be instituted against him in the court, and that some person within the jurisdiction at the time of the application can give material evidence respecting the subject of the apprehended suit, but that he is about to leave the jurisdiction, or that, from some other cause, the person applying will lose the benefit of his evidence if it be not at once taken; and the evidence so taken may be used at the hearing, subject to just exceptions:

    Provided always that the court may impose any terms or conditions with reference to the examination of such witness, and the admission of his evidence, as to the court may seem reasonable.

Facilities for proving deed, etc.

29. Any party desiring to give in evidence any deed or other instrument which shows upon the face of it that it has been duly executed may deliver to the opposite party, not less than four clear days before the return date, a notice in writing specifying the date and nature of and the parties to such deed or instrument, and requiring the opposite party to admit that the same was executed as it purports to have been, saving all just exceptions as to its admissibility, validity and contents; and if, at or before the hearing of the suit, the party so notified shall neglect or refuse to give such admission, the court may adjourn the hearing in order to enable the party tendering such deed or instrument to obtain proof of the due execution thereof, and, upon production of such proof, the court may order the costs of such proof to be paid by the party so neglecting or refusing, whether he be the successful party or not.

INQUESTS ACT CHAPTER 36 OF THE LAWS OF ZAMBIA

Commenced on 6 January 1939
[This is the version of this document at 31 December 1996.]

An Act relating to inquests.

PART I – PRELIMINARY

1.   Short title

This Act may be cited as the Inquests Act.

2.   Interpretation

In this Act, unless the context otherwise requires—"building operation" has the meaning assigned to that expression by section three of the Factories Act; [Cap. 441]"coroner" means any person empowered or appointed to hold inquests under this Act;"factory" has the meaning assigned thereto by section two of the Factories Act; [Cap. 441]"medical practitioner"* means any person registered or licensed as a medical practitioner under the Medical and Allied Professions Act; [Cap. 297]² mine" has the meaning assigned thereto by section two of the Mines and Minerals Act;[Cap. 213]"work of engineering construction" has the meaning assigned to that expression by section three of the Factories Act.[Cap. 441][As amended by No. 14 of 1957 and G.N. No. 303 of 1964]

PART II – POWERS AND DUTIES OF CORONERS

3.   Who may hold inquests

(1)   Every magistrate having authority under the provisions of the Subordinate Courts Act to hold a subordinate court of the first, second or third class may hold inquests under this Act.
(2)   The Judicial Service Commission may, by *Gazette* notice, appoint any other fit person to hold inquests under this Act within any area specified in such notice.
(3)   A coroner shall have jurisdiction—
    (a)   if he is a senior resident magistrate or resident magistrate, throughout Zambia;
    (b)   if, not being a senior resident magistrate or a resident magistrate, he is empowered to hold inquests in terms of subsection (1), within the limits of his magisterial jurisdiction;
    (c)   if he is appointed to hold inquests in terms of subsection (2), within such area as is specified in the notice referred to in that subsection.
(4)   Any inquest commenced by a coroner may be continued, resumed or reopened in the manner provided by this Act by such coroner or, if such coroner is absent or ill, by any other coroner having jurisdiction as provided by section nine.[As amended by No. 24 of 1939, No. 40 of 1959, No. 3 of 1963 and G.N. Nos. 303 and 493 of 1964][Cap. 28]

4.   When inquest to be held

Whenever a coroner is credibly informed that the body of a deceased person is lying within his jurisdiction, and that there is reasonable cause to suspect that such person has died either a violent or an unnatural death, or in prison or in police custody, or in any place or circumstances which, in the opinion of the coroner, makes the holding of an inquest necessary or desirable, such coroner shall, except as otherwise provided in this Act, hold an inquest on such body as soon as is practicable.

5.   Power to dispense with inquest in certain cases

Whenever it shall appear to the coroner, either from the report of a medical practitioner rendered under section fifteen or otherwise, that the death is due to natural causes, and that the body shows no appearance of death being attributable to or of having been accelerated by violence or by any culpable or negligent conduct either on the part of the deceased or of any other person, it shall thereupon be lawful for the coroner at his discretion (except in the cases specified in section eight) to dispense with the holding of an inquest.

---

1 *See section 56 of the Medical and Allied Professions Act (Cap. 245)"*.

6. Postponement and adjournment of inquests in certain cases

(1) Whenever the coroner is informed that some person has been or is about to be brought before a magistrate on a charge of the murder, manslaughter or infanticide of the deceased, or of causing the death of the deceased by the reckless or dangerous driving of a motor vehicle, or of complicity in the death of the deceased under section eight of the Suicide Act, in the absence of reason to the contrary, the inquest shall not be commenced, or if commenced shall not be continued or resumed, until after the conclusion of the criminal proceedings.

(2) After the conclusion of the criminal proceedings, the coroner may, subject as hereinafter provided, hold an inquest or resume the adjourned inquest if he is of opinion that public benefit is likely to result from his so doing; but, if he is of opinion that no public benefit is likely to result from his so doing, he shall certify his opinion to that effect and transmit such opinion to the Director of Public Prosecutions together with a certified copy of the inquest proceedings if the inquest has been commenced: Provided that, if in the course of the criminal proceedings any person has been charged upon information, then upon the resumed inquest no inquisition shall contain any finding that sufficient grounds have been disclosed for charging that person with any offence of which he could have been convicted on such information or any finding which is inconsistent with the determination of any matter by the result of those proceedings.

(3) Notwithstanding the provisions of subsection (2), where an inquest is postponed or adjourned in pursuance of subsection (1) and it is ascertained that a person to be charged cannot be found, the coroner shall commence or resume the inquest, as the case may be, and conclude it.

(4) For the purposes of this section, the expression "the criminal proceedings" means the proceedings before the magistrate and before the High Court, if the accused person is committed for trial by such court, or before any court to which the accused person may appeal from any conviction, and criminal proceedings shall not be deemed to be concluded until no appeal can be made in the course thereof without special leave. [As amended by No 14 of 1960, SI No 72 of 1964 and No 1 of 1967] [Cap. 89]

7. Power to order exhumation

Notwithstanding any law or custom to the contrary enacted or obtaining, whenever it shall appear to any coroner that the body of any person, who has died in circumstances requiring the holding of an inquest thereon, has been buried without being viewed or without such inquest having been held, or where such inquest, although held, has been quashed or reopened, it shall be lawful for such coroner by his warrant in Form 1 in the Schedule to order the exhumation of such body; and he shall, after such exhumation, proceed to hold an inquest on such body and thereupon direct the reinterment thereof; and the expenses of such exhumation and reinterment shall be paid, upon the coroner's order, from the general revenues of the Republic: Provided that such exhumation shall not be ordered in any case where, in the opinion of the coroner, it would be injurious to public health, or where there is no reasonable probability of a satisfactory result being obtained thereby.[As amended by S.I. No. 72 of 1964]

PART III
HOLDING OF INQUESTS

8. Inquest on persons in prison or custody

Notwithstanding anything contained in this Act, where—
    (a) a prisoner; or
    (b) a person in the custody of a police officer or detained in custody under a detention order; dies from any cause whatsoever, it shall be the duty of the prison officer having charge of such prisoner or the police officer or other person having charge of such person, as the case may be, to give notice of the death of such prisoner or person to a coroner within whose jurisdiction such death occurred and that coroner shall hold an inquest. [No. 43 of 1966]

9. Inquest to be held by coroner of place where body lying

A coroner only within whose jurisdiction the body of any person, upon whose death an inquest ought to be held, is lying shall hold the inquest, notwithstanding that the cause of death arose elsewhere; and if any body is found in any river or in any inland waters, the inquest shall be held by the coroner within whose jurisdiction the body is first brought to land: Provided that where it appears to a coroner by whom an inquest has been commenced that, owing to special circumstances to be entered upon the record of the inquest, it is expedient for the inquest to be continued by another coroner, he shall, after viewing the body (if such view is necessary in accordance with the provisions of subsection (1) of section seventeen) and making such entry upon the record as is required to be made under the provisions of subsection (4) of section seventeen, refer the record to such other coroner; and such other coroner shall thereupon, whether or not the body is lying within his jurisdiction and subject to any directions in that behalf which may be given by the High Court and which the High Court is hereby empowered to give, continue the inquest and conclude the same in accordance with the provisions of this Act. [As amended by No. 3 of 1963]

10. Inquest where body destroyed or irrecoverable

When a coroner has reason to believe that a death has occurred in the area within which he has jurisdiction in such circumstances that an inquest ought to be held, and that owing to the destruction of the body by fire or otherwise or to the fact that the body is lying in a place from which it cannot be recovered, an inquest cannot be held except by virtue of the provisions of this section, he may, if he considers it desirable so to do, hold an inquest touching the death, and the law relating to inquests shall apply with such modifications as may be necessary in consequence of the inquest being held otherwise than on or after view of a body lying within the coroner's jurisdiction.[As amended by No. 3 of 1963]

11. Coroner may postpone burial or cremation till after inquest

A coroner may prohibit the burial or cremation of any body lying within his jurisdiction until an inquest shall have been held.

12. Notice of death

When any body is found or a person has died in such circumstances as to make the holding of an inquest under this Act necessary or desirable, it shall be the duty of any person finding the body or becoming aware of the death forthwith to inform either a coroner having jurisdiction or a police officer or a chief or headman or district messenger, and upon receiving any such information such chief or headman or district messenger or police officer shall notify a coroner having jurisdiction to hold an inquest. Any person who fails without good cause to inform the chief or headman or district messenger or police officer as required by this section shall be guilty of an offence and shall be liable to a fine not exceeding seven hundred and fifty penalty units. [As amended by Act No. 13 of 1994]

13. Coroner may call for statements recorded by police officers

(1) Where a death has occurred in such circumstances that an inquest is required or ought to be held under the provisions of this Act, the coroner having jurisdiction may direct any police officer having charge of or concerned in an investigation into the death to produce to the coroner, prior to the holding of the inquest, any statement made to, and recorded in writing by, such police officer by any person having knowledge of the circumstances, the cause of the death or the identity of the deceased, as the case may be, and the coroner may postpone the holding of the inquest for such time as may be necessary to enable him to obtain and peruse any such statement.

(2) A coroner to whom a statement is produced under subsection (1) shall, before holding the inquest, return the statement to the police officer by whom it is so produced and may, at the same time, notify him of the name of any person whose attendance at the inquest will not be required unless otherwise ordered: Provided that nothing in this section shall be construed as to prohibit the attendance at the inquest of any such person if he desires to attend.[No. 43 of 1966]

PART IV – POST-MORTEM EXAMINATION

14. Coroner may direct post-mortem examination

(1) If any coroner considers it necessary with a view to investigating the circumstances of the death of any person, to obtain a medical report on the appearance of the body of such person, and as to the conclusions to be drawn therefrom, he may, by written order in Form 2 in the Schedule, require any Government Medical Officer within or without his jurisdiction or any other medical practitioner within his jurisdiction to make an examination of the body and to report thereon:
Provided that—
    (i) a coroner shall not make any order as aforesaid if he is of opinion—
        (a) that the body cannot be brought to a medical officer or practitioner for examination; and
        (b) that a medical officer or practitioner cannot make an examination at the place where the

body is; and

    (c)   that the body cannot be brought to some specified place at which a medical officer or practitioner could make an examination; so that the examination can be made within such time as would enable it to be of practical value;(ii)the coroner shall not make any order as aforesaid if he is of opinion that, by reason of the distance which a medical officer or practitioner would be obliged to travel in order to make an examination and the time which would be occupied in the journey, it would not be in the public interest that such an order should be made.

(2)   In any case of emergency where it would be impracticable to secure a coroner's order, any police officer of or above the rank of Sub Inspector may exercise the authority conferred on a coroner under subsection (1).[As amended by No. 45 of 1940, No. 3 of 1963, G.N. No. 224 of 1964 and No. 24 of 1977]

15. Medical practitioner to make an examination and report

Every medical practitioner upon the receipt of such order shall, unless he procures the services of some other medical practitioner to perform the duty, immediately make an examination of the body, with a view to determining therefrom the cause of death, and to ascertaining the circumstances connected therewith, and shall make a report in writing to the coroner describing the appearance of the body, and the conclusions which he draws therefrom touching the death of such person. The examination shall extend, when the medical practitioner considers it necessary but not otherwise, to such dissection of the body as he may think requisite. The report shall be in Form 3 in the Schedule, and shall state the cause of death, and shall be signed and dated by the medical practitioner. Such report, on being read at the inquest by the coroner, shall be *prima facie* evidence of the facts therein stated without further proof, unless it is proved that the medical practitioner purporting to sign the report did not in fact sign it: Provided that the coroner may, if he shall consider it necessary or desirable, call such medical practitioner to give evidence at the inquest.

PART V
PROCEDURE AT INQUEST

16. Evidence at inquest

The coroner shall at the inquest examine on oath in regard to the death all persons who tender their evidence respecting the facts and all persons having knowledge of the facts whom he thinks it expedient to examine.

17. Provisions regarding the viewing of body

(1)   At or before the first sitting of an inquest on a body, the coroner shall view the body or shall satisfy himself that the body has been viewed by a police officer, medical practitioner, chief, headman, district messenger or other trustworthy person:
Provided that, when an inquest on the body has been previously opened, it shall not be necessary upon a resumed, continued, or subsequent inquest for the body to be viewed a second time.

(2)   An order authorising the burial of a body upon which it has been decided to hold an inquest may be issued at any time after the body has been viewed.

(3)   If the body has been buried and has not been viewed in the manner provided in subsection (1), the coroner shall order the exhumation of the body for the purpose of a view in the manner provided by section seven unless he certifies that, in his opinion, such exhumation would be injurious to the public health or that no satisfactory result would be obtained thereby.

(4)   In any case in which the coroner himself has viewed the body, he shall certify the fact upon the record of the inquest and in other cases he shall record evidence (if any) of the view of the body by a police officer, medical practitioner, chief, headman, district messenger or other trustworthy person.

18. Coroner may summon witnesses

(1)   A coroner holding an inquest shall have and may exercise all the powers conferred upon a court by the Criminal Procedure Code with regard to summoning and compelling the attendance of witnesses and requiring them to give evidence, and with regard to the production of any document or thing at such inquest.

(2)   Every summons and warrant of arrest and summons to produce shall be in writing signed by the coroner.

(3)   Where the inquest concerns the death of a person executed in pursuance of a death warrant, the medical practitioner who was present at the execution shall be an essential witness at such inquest.

(4) The provisions of the Criminal Procedure Code shall, as far as may be, apply to summonses to produce issued by a coroner.[Cap. 88]

19. Coroner not bound by rules of evidence

A coroner holding an inquest shall not be bound by any rules of evidence which may pertain to civil or criminal proceedings, but if any witness objects to answer any question on the ground that it will tend to incriminate him, he shall not be required to answer the question nor be liable to any penalty for refusing so to answer.

20. Evidence: how recorded

The coroner shall take down or cause to be taken down in his presence the evidence of every witness and such evidence shall be read over

---

THE EVIDENCE ACT CHAPTER 43 OF THE LAWS OF ZAMBIA

ARRANGEMENTS OF SECTIONS

Section

1. Short title
2. Interpretation
3. Admissibility of documentary evidence as to facts in issue
4. Admissibility of certain trade or business or professional records in criminal proceedings
5. Weight to be attached to evidence
6. Proof of instrument to validity of which attestation is necessary
7. Presumptions as to documents twenty years old
8. Rules of court
9. Savings

CHAPTER 43
EVIDENCE
8 of 1967
3 of 1968
An Act to amend the law of evidence.
[27th January, 1967]

Short title

1. This Act may be cited as the Evidence Act.

Interpretation

2. In this Act, unless the context otherwise requires-
    "business" includes any public transport, public utility or similar undertaking carried on by a local authority and the activities of the General Post Office;
    "document" includes any device by means of which information is recorded or stored, and books, maps, plans and drawings;
    "proceedings" includes arbitration and references, and "court" shall be construed accordingly;
    "statement" includes any representation of fact, whether made in words or otherwise.
    (As amended by No. 3 of 1968)

Admissibility of documentary evidence as to facts in issue

3. (1) In any civil proceedings where direct oral evidence of a fact would be admissible, any statement made by a person in a document and tending to establish that fact shall, on production of the original document, be admissible as evidence of that fact if the following conditions are satisfied, that is to say: Admissibility of documentary evidence as to facts in issue

(a) if the maker of the statement either-
  (i) had personal knowledge of the matters dealt with by the statement; or
  (ii) where the document in question is or forms part of a record purporting to be a continuous record, made the statement (in so far as the matters dealt thereby are not within his personal knowledge) in the performance of a duty to record information supplied to him by a person who had, or might reasonably be supposed to have, personal know-ledge of those matters; and

(b) if the maker of the statement is called as a witness in the proceedings:
Provided that the condition that the maker of the statement shall be called as a witness need not be satisfied if he is dead, or unfit by reason of his bodily or mental condition to attend as a witness, or if he is outside Zambia and it is not reasonably practicable to secure his attendance, or if all reasonable efforts to find him have been made without success.

(2) In any civil proceedings, the court may, at any stage of the proceedings, if having regard to all the circumstances of the case it is satisfied that undue delay or expense would otherwise be caused, order that such a statement as is mentioned in subsection (1) shall be admissible as evidence or may, without any such order having been made, admit such a statement in evidence-

(a) notwithstanding that the maker of the statement is available but is not called as a witness

(b) notwithstanding that the original document is not produced, if in lieu thereof there is produced a copy of the original document or of the material part thereof certified to be a true copy in such manner as may be specified in the order or as the court may approve, as the case may be.

(3) For the purposes of this section, a statement in a document shall not be deemed to have been made by a person unless the document or the material part thereof was written, made or produced by him with his own hand, or was signed or initialed by him or otherwise recognised by him in writing as one for the accuracy of which he is responsible.

(4) For the purposes of deciding whether or not a statement is admissible as evidence by virtue of the foregoing provisions, the court may draw any reasonable inference from the form or contents of the documents in which the statement is contained, or from any other circumstances, and may, in deciding whether or not a person is fit to attend as a witness, act on a certificate purporting to be the certificate of a medical practitioner, and, where the proceedings are with the aid of assessors, the court may in its discretion reject the statement notwithstanding that the requirements of this section are satisfied with respect thereto, if for any reason it appears to it to be inexpedient in the interests of justice that the statement should be admitted.

Admissibility of certain trade or business or professional records in criminal proceedings

4. (1) In any criminal proceedings where direct oral evidence of a fact would be admissible, any statement contained in a document and tending to establish that fact shall, on production of the document, be admissible as evidence of that fact if-

(a) the document is, or forms part of, a record relating to any trade or business or profession and compiled, in the course of that trade or business or profession, from information supplied (whether directly or indirectly) by persons who have, or may reasonably be supposed to have, personal knowledge of the matters dealt with in the information they supply; and

(b) the person who supplied the information recorded in the statement in question is dead, or outside of Zambia, or unfit by reason of his bodily or mental condition to attend as a witness, or cannot with reasonable diligence be identified or found, or cannot reasonably be expected (having regard to the time which has elapsed since he supplied the information and to all the circumstances) to have any recollection of the matters dealt with in the information he supplied.

(2) For the purpose of deciding whether or not a statement is admissible as evidence by virtue of this section, the court may draw any reasonable inference from the form or content of the document in which the statement is contained, and may, in deciding whether or not a person is fit to attend as a witness, act on a certificate purporting to be a certificate of a fully registered medical practitioner.
(No 3 of 1968)

Weight to be attached to evidence

5. (1) In estimating the weight, if any, to be attached to a statement admissible as evidence by virtue of this Act, regard shall be had to all the circumstances from which any inference can reasonably be drawn as to the accuracy or otherwise of the statement, and in particular to the question whether or not the person who supplied the information contained or recorded in the statement did so contemporaneously with the occurrence or existence of the facts stated, and to the question whether or not that person, or any person concerned with making or keeping the record containing the statement, had any incentive to conceal or misrepresent the facts.

(2) For the purpose of any rule of law or practice requiring evidence to be corroborated or regulating the manner in which uncorroborated evidence is to be treated, a statement rendered admissible as evidence by this Act shall not be treated as corroboration of evidence given by the maker of the statement. (As amended by No. 3 of 1968)

Proof of instrument to validity of which attestation is necessary

6. Subject as hereinafter provided, in any proceedings, whether civil or criminal, an instrument to the validity of which attestation is requisite may, instead of being proved by an attesting witness, be proved in the manner in which it might be proved if no attesting witness were alive:

Provided that nothing in this section shall apply to the proof of wills or other testamentary documents.

Presumptions as to documents twenty years old

7. In any proceedings, whether civil or criminal, there shall, in the case of a document proved, or purporting, to be not less than twenty years old, be made any presumption which immediately before the commencement of this Act would have been made in the case of a document of like character proved, or purporting, to be not less than thirty years old.

Rules of court

8. It is hereby declared that section forty-four of the High Court Act and section fifty-seven of the Subordinate Courts Act authorise the making of rules of court providing for orders being made at any stage of any proceedings directing that specified facts may be proved at the trial by affidavit with or without the attendance of the deponent for cross-examination, notwithstanding that a party desires his attendance for cross-examination and that he can be produced for that purpose.

Savings

9. Nothing in this Act shall-
    (a) prejudice the admissibility of any evidence which would apart from the provisions of this Act be admissible; or
    (b) enable documentary evidence to be given to any declaration relating to a matter of pedigree, if that declaration would not have been admissible as evidence if this Act had not been passed.

THE EVIDENCE (BANKERS' BOOKS) ACT CHAPTER 44 OF THE LAWS OF ZAMBIA

ARRANGEMENT OF SECTIONS

CHAPTER 44
EVIDENCE (BANKERS' BOOKS)

An Act to amend the law of evidence with respect to bankers' books; and to provide for matters incidental thereto.

Short title

1. This Act may be cited as the Evidence (Bankers' Books) Act.

Interpretation

2. In this Act, unless the context otherwise requires-
    "bank" or "banker" means any person carrying on the business of banking in Zambia under the provisions of the Banking and Financial Services Act [Act No 7 of 2017]
    "banker' book" includes ledgers, day books, cash books, account books and all other records used in the ordinary business of the bank, whether such records are in form or in microfilm, magnetic tape or any other form of mechanical or electronic data retrieval mechanism
    (As amended by Act No. 12 of 1980)
    "building society" means a building society incorporated in Zambia under the law for the time being in force relating to building societies;
    "court" means the court, Judge, arbitrator or person or persons before whom a legal proceeding is held or taken;
    "Judge" means a Judge of the Supreme Court or a Judge of the High Court;
    "legal proceeding" means any civil or criminal proceeding or inquiry (including an arbitration) in which evidence is or may be given, in Zambia.
    (As amended by Act No. 12 of 1980)

Mode of proof of entries in banker's books

3. Subject to the provisions of this Act, a copy of any entry in a banker's book shall in all legal proceedings be received as prima facie evidence of such entry, and of the matters, transactions and accounts therein recorded.

Proof that book is a banker's book

4. (1)   A copy of an entry in a banker's book shall not be received in evidence under this Act unless it be first proved that the book was at the time of the making of the entry one of the ordinary books of the bank, and that the entry was made in the usual and ordinary course of business, and that the book is in the custody or control of the bank.

    (2)   Such proof may be given by a partner or officer of the bank, and may be given orally or by an affidavit sworn before any commissioner for oaths or person authorised to take affidavits.

Verification of copy

5. (1)   A copy of an entry in a banker's book shall not be received in evidence under this Act unless it be further proved that the copy has been examined with the original entry and is correct.

    (2)   Such proof shall be given by some person who has examined the copy with the original entry, and may be given either orally or by an affidavit sworn before any commissioner for oaths or person authorised to take affidavits.

Case in which banker, etc., not compellable to produce book, etc.

6. A banker or officer of a bank shall not, in any legal proceedings to which the bank is not a party, be compellable to produce any banker's book the contents of which can be proved under this Act, or to appear as a witness to prove the matters, transactions and accounts therein recorded, unless by order of a Judge made for special cause.

Court may order inspection, etc.

7. (1)   On the application of any party to a legal proceeding a court may order that such party be at liberty to inspect and take copies of any entries in a banker's book for any of the purposes of such proceedings.

(2)   An order under this section may be made either with or without summoning the bank or any other party, and shall be served on the bank three clear days before the same is to be obeyed, unless the court otherwise directs.

Warrant to investigate Costs

8. (1)   Where it is proved on oath to a Judge or a magistrate that in fact, or according to reasonable suspicion, the inspection of any banker's book is necessary or desirable for the purpose of any investigation into the commission of an offence, the Judge or magistrate may by warrant authorise a police officer or other person named therein to investigate the account of any specified person in any banker's book, and such warrant shall be sufficient authority for the production of any such banker's book as may be required for scrutiny by the officer or person named in the warrant, and such officer or person may take copies of any relevant entry or matter in such banker's book.

(2)   Any person who fails to produce any such banker's book to the police officer or other person executing a warrant issued under this section or to permit such police officer or other person to scrutinise the same or to take copies of any relevant entry or matter therein shall be guilty of an offence and liable to a fine not exceeding two thousand penalty units or to imprisonment for a term not exceeding one year, or to both. (As amended by Act No. 13 of 1994)

Savings

9. (1)   The costs of any application to a court under or for the purposes of this Act, and the costs of anything done or to be done under an order of a court made under or for the purposes of this Act, shall be in the discretion of the court, which may order the same or any part thereof to be paid to any party by the bank where the same have been occasioned by any default or delay on the part of the bank.

(2)   Any such order against a bank may be enforced as if the bank was a party to the proceedings.

THE STATE PROCEEDINGS ACT CHAPTER 71 OF THE LAWS OF ZAMBIA

Commenced on 4 June 1965

[This is the version of this document at 31 December 1996.]

[27 of 1965; 38 of 1970; 22 of 1974]

An Act to provide for civil proceedings by and against the State and the civil liabilities and rights of the State and its servants; and for purposes connected with the aforesaid matters.

PART I – PRELIMINARY

1.   Short title

This Act may be cited as the State Proceedings Act.

2.   Interpretation

(1)   In this Act, unless the context otherwise requires—

"**agent**", when used in relation to the State, includes an independent contractor employed by the State;"

civil proceedings" includes proceedings in the High Court or a subordinate court for the recovery of fines or penalties;

"**Defence Force**" means the Defence Force of Zambia maintained in accordance with the provisions of section four of the Defence Act;*[Cap. 106]*

"**prescribed**" means prescribed by any written law;

"**proceedings against the State**" includes a claim by way of set-off or counter-claim raised in proceedings by the State;

"**public officer**" means a person holding or acting in or performing the functions of an office in the civil service of the Government and includes the President, the Vice-President, a Minister, a Junior Minister, the Secretary to the Cabinet, the Attorney-General, the Solicitor-General, the Auditor-General and members of the Zambia Police Force;

"**rules of court**" means, when used in relation to the Supreme Court, the High Court or a subordinate court, rules made under the Supreme Court of Zambia Act, the High Court Act and the Subordinate Courts Act respectively;*[Cap. 25; Cap. 27; Cap. 28]*

"**State**" means the sovereign Republic of Zambia;

"**statutory duty**" means a duty imposed by or under any written law;

"**subordinate court**" means a court constituted under section three of the Subordinate Courts Act; *[Cap. 28]*

"**written law**" means the Constitution, an Order in Council, an Act, an Applied Act, a British Act, an Ordinance and a statutory instrument.

(2) Any reference in this Act to the provisions of this Act shall, unless the context otherwise requires, include a reference to rules of court made for the purposes of this Act.

(3) Any reference in Part IV or V to civil proceedings by or against the State, or to civil proceedings to which the State is a party, shall be construed as including a reference to civil proceedings to which the Attorney-General, or any Government department, or any public officer as such, is a party:Provided that the State shall not, for the purposes of Part IV or V, be deemed to be a party to any proceedings by reason only that they are brought by the Attorney-General upon the relation of some other person.*[As amended by No. 38 of 1970]*

PART II
SUBSTANTIVE LAW

3. Liability of State in contract

Subject to the provisions of this Act, the State shall be subject to those liabilities in contract to which, if it were a private person of full age and capacity, it would be subject and any claim arising therefrom may be enforced as of right against the State in accordance with the provisions of this Act.

4. Liability of State in tort

(1) Subject to the provisions of this Act, the State shall be subject to all those liabilities in tort to which, if it were a private person of full age and capacity, it would be subject—

    (a) in respect of torts committed by its servants or agents;

    (b) in respect of any breach of those duties which a person owes to his servants or agents at common law by reason of being their employers; and(c)in respect of any breach of the duties attaching at common law to the ownership, occupation, possession or control of property: Provided that no proceedings shall lie against the State by virtue of paragraph

    (a) in respect of any act or omission of a servant or agent of the State unless the act or omission would apart from the provisions of this Act have given rise to a cause of action in tort against that servant or agent or his estate.

(2) Where the State is bound by a statutory duty which is binding also upon persons other than the State and its officers, then, subject to the provisions of this Act, the State shall, in respect of a failure to comply with that duty, be subject to all those liabilities in tort (if any) to which it would be so subject if it were a private person of full age and capacity.(3)Where any functions are conferred or imposed upon a public officer as such either by any rule of the common law or by any written law, and that officer commits a tort while performing or purporting to perform those functions, the liabilities of the State in respect of the tort shall be such as they would have been if those functions had been conferred or imposed solely by virtue of instructions lawfully given by the State.(4)Any written law which negatives or limits the amount of the liability of any Government department or public officer in respect of any tort committed by that department or officer shall, in the case of proceedings against the State under this section in respect of a tort committed by that department or officer, apply in relation to the State as it would have applied in relation to that department or officer, if the proceedings against the State had been proceedings against that department or officer.(5)No proceedings shall lie against the State by virtue of this section in respect of anything done or omitted to be done by any person while discharging or purporting to discharge any responsibilities of a judicial nature vested in him, or any responsibilities which he has in connection with the execution of judicial process.

4A. Restriction on court orders against State

Notwithstanding the provisions of this Act, no court of law shall make an order for damages or compensation against the State in respect of anything done under or in the execution of any restriction or detention order signed by the President:

Provided that nothing in this section shall apply to a claim for damages or compensation arising from—

(i) physical or mental ill-treatment;

(ii) any error in the identity of the person restricted or detained. *[As amended by Act No. 22 of 1974]*

5. Provisions as to industrial property

(1) Where after the commencement of this Act any servant or agent of the State infringes a patent, or infringes a registered trade mark, or infringes any copyright (including any copyright in a design subsisting under the Registered Designs Act), and the infringement is committed with the authority of the State, then, subject to the provisions of this Act, civil proceedings in respect of the infringement shall lie against the State.

(2) Nothing in subsection (1) or in any other provision of this Act shall affect the rights of any Government department under the Patents Act or the Registered Designs Act.*[Cap. 400; Cap. 402]*

(3) Save as expressly provided by this section, no proceedings shall lie against the State by virtue of this Act in respect of the infringement of a patent, in respect of the infringement of a registered trade mark, or in respect of the infringement of any such copyright as is mentioned in subsection (1).*[Cap. 402]*

6. Application of law as to indemnity, contribution, joint and several tortfeasors and contributory negligence

(1) Where the State is subject to any liability by virtue of this Part, the law relating to indemnity and contribution shall be enforceable by or against the State in respect of the liability to which it is so subject as if the State were a private person of full age and capacity.

(2) *[1]* Without prejudice to the generality of subsection (1), Part V of the Law Reform (Miscellaneous Provisions) Act shall bind the State.*[Cap. 74][*These subsections are deemed to have come into force on 14th April, 1967.]*

(3) *[2]* Without prejudice to the general effect of section three, Part VI of the Law Reform (Miscellaneous Provisions) Act shall bind the State.*[Cap. 74][*These subsections are deemed to have come into force on 14th April, 1967][As amended by No. 38 of 1970]*

7. Provisions relating to Defence Force

(1) Nothing done or omitted to be done by a member of the Defence Force while on duty as such shall subject either him or the State to liability in tort for causing the death of another person, in so far as the death or personal injury is due to anything suffered by that other person while he is a member of the Defence Force if—

(a) at the time that thing is suffered by that other person, he is either on duty as a member of the Defence Force or is, though not on duty as such, on any land, premises, ship, aircraft or vehicle for the time being used for the purposes of the Defence Force; and

(b) the Minister responsible for finance certifies that his suffering that thing has been or will be treated as attributable to service for the purposes of entitlement to a gratuity or pension under any written law relating to the disablement or death of members of the Defence Force:

Provided that this subsection shall not exempt a member of the Defence Force from liability in tort in any case in which the court is satisfied that the act or omission was not connected with the execution of his duties as a member of the Defence Force.

(2) No proceedings in tort shall lie against the State for death or personal injury due to anything suffered by a member of the Defence Force if—

(a) that thing is suffered by him in consequence of the nature or condition of any such land, premises, ship, aircraft or vehicle as aforesaid, or in consequence of the nature or condition of any equipment or supplies used for the purposes of the Defence Force; and*[*These subsections are deemed to have come into force on 14th April, 1967.]*

(b) the Minister responsible for finance certified as mentioned in paragraph (b) of subsection (1);nor shall any act or omission of a public officer subject him to liability in tort for death or personal injury in so far as the death or personal injury is due to anything suffered by a member of the Defence Force being a thing as to which the conditions aforesaid are satisfied.

(3) The President or a Minister authorised by him if satisfied that it is the fact—

    (a) that a person was or was not on any particular occasion on duty as a member of the Defence Force; or

    (b) that at any particular time any land, premises, ship, aircraft, vehicle, equipment or supplies was or was not, or were or were not, used for the purpose of the Defence Force; may issue a certificate certifying that to be the fact, and any such certificate shall, for the purposes of this section, be conclusive as to the fact which it certifies.

8. Saving in respect of acts done under prerogative and written laws

(1) Nothing in this Part shall extinguish or abridge any powers or authorities which, if this Act had not been passed, would have been exercisable by virtue of the provisions of section 18 of the Zambia Independence Order, 1964, or any powers or authorities conferred on the State by any written law, and, in particular, nothing in this Part shall extinguish or abridge powers or authorities exercisable by the State, whether in time of peace or war, for the purposes of the defence of Zambia or of training, or maintaining the efficiency of the Defence Force.

(2) Where in any proceedings under this Act it is material to determine whether anything was properly done or omitted to be done for any of the purposes of subsection (1), the President or a Minister authorised by him may, if satisfied that the act or omission was necessary for any such purpose, issue a certificate to the effect that the act or omission was necessary for that purpose; and the certificate shall, in those proceedings, be conclusive as to the matter so certified.

PART III
JURISDICTION AND PROCEDURE

9. Civil proceedings in High Court

Subject to the provisions of this Act, all civil proceedings by or against the State in the High Court shall be instituted and proceeded with in accordance with rules of court and not otherwise.

10. Civil proceedings in subordinate courts

(1) Subject to the provisions of this Act, and to any written law limiting the jurisdiction of a subordinate court (whether by reference to the subject-matter of the proceedings to be brought or the amount sought to be recovered in the proceedings or otherwise), any civil proceedings against the State may be instituted in a subordinate court.

(2) Any proceedings by or against the State in a subordinate court shall be instituted and proceeded with in accordance with rules of court and not otherwise.

11. Interpleader

The State may obtain relief by way of interpleader proceedings, and may be made a party to such proceedings, in the same manner in which a subject may obtain relief by way of such proceedings or be made a party thereto, and may be made a party to such proceedings notwithstanding that the application for relief is made by a sheriff or other like officer; and all rules of court relating to interpleader proceedings shall, subject to the provisions of this Act, have effect accordingly.

12. Parties to proceedings

(1) Subject to the provisions of any other written law, civil proceedings by or against the State shall be instituted by or against the Attorney-General as the case may be.

(2) No proceedings instituted in accordance with this Part by or against the Attorney-General shall abate or be affected by any change in the person holding the office of Attorney-General.

13. Service of documents

All documents required to be served on the State for the purpose of or in connection with any civil proceedings by or against the State shall be served on the officer of the Attorney-General's Chambers having the conduct of such proceedings, or, if a legal practitioner in private practice is acting for the State in such proceedings, on such legal practitioner.

14. Venue and related matters

(1) In any case in which civil proceedings against the State in the High Court are instituted by the issue of a plaint out of a District Registry, the State may enter an appearance either in the District Registry or in the Principal Registry, and, if an appearance is entered in the Principal Registry, all steps in relation to proceedings up to the trial shall be taken in Lusaka.

(2) The trial of any civil proceedings by or against the State in the High Court shall be held at the High Court in Lusaka unless the court, with the consent of the State, otherwise directs.

(3) Where the State refuses its consent to a direction under subsection (2), the court may take account of the refusal in exercising its power in regard to costs.

(4) In this section—"District Registry" means a District Registry directed to be established under the High Court Act;"Principal Registry" means the office of the Registrar of the High Court at Lusaka.*[Cap. 27]*

15. Removal and transfer of proceedings

(1) If, in a case where proceedings are instituted against the State in a subordinate court, an application in that behalf is made by the State to the High Court, and there is produced to the court a certificate of the Attorney-General to the effect that the proceedings may involve an important question of law, or may be decisive of other cases arising out of the same matter, or are for other reasons more fit to be tried in the High Court, the proceedings shall be removed into the High Court.

(2) Where any proceedings have been removed into the High Court on the production of such a certificate as is mentioned in subsection (1), and it appears to the court by whom the proceedings are tried that the removal has occasioned additional expense to the person by whom the proceedings are brought, the court may take account of the additional expense so occasioned in exercising its powers in regard to the award of costs.

(3) Without prejudice to the right of the State under the preceding provisions of this section, the provisions of any written law relating to the removal or transfer of proceedings from a subordinate court to the High Court or the transfer of proceedings from the High Court to a subordinate court shall apply in relation to proceedings against the State:

Provided that an order for the transfer to a subordinate court of any proceedings against the State in the High Court shall not be made without the consent of the State.

16. Nature of relief

(1) In any civil proceedings by or against the State the court shall, subject to the provisions of this Act, have power to make all such orders as it has power to make in proceedings between subjects, and otherwise to give such appropriate relief as the case may require: Provided that—

    (i) where in any proceedings against the State any such relief is sought as might in proceedings between subjects be granted by way of injunction or specific performance, the court shall not grant an injunction or make an order for specific performance, but may in lieu thereof make an order declaratory of the rights of the parties; and

    (ii) in any proceedings against the State for the recovery of land or other property, the court shall not make an order for the recovery of the land or the delivery of the property, but may in lieu thereof make an order declaring that the plaintiff is entitled as against the State to the land or property or to the possession thereof.

(2) The court shall not in any civil proceedings grant any injunction or make any order against a public officer if the effect of granting the injunction or making the order would be to give any relief against the State which could not have been obtained in proceedings against the State.

17. Costs in civil proceedings to which State is a party

In any civil proceedings or arbitration to which the State is a party, the costs of and incidental to the proceedings shall be awarded in the same manner and on the same principles as in cases between subjects, and the court or arbitrator shall have power to make an order for the payment of costs by or to the State accordingly: Provided that—

    (i) in the case of proceedings to which by reason of any written law or otherwise the Attorney-General, or any other public officer as such is authorised to be made a party, the court or arbitrator shall have regard to the nature of the proceedings and the character and circumstances in which the Attorney-General or public officer appears, and may in the exercise of its or his discretion order any other party to the proceedings to pay the costs of the Attorney-General or officer, whatever may be the result of the proceedings; and

(ii) nothing in this section shall affect the power of the court or arbitrator to order, or any written law providing for, the payment of costs out of any particular fund or property, or any written law expressly relieving any Government department or public officer of the liability to pay costs.

18. Appeals and stay of execution

Subject to the provisions of this Act, all written laws relating to appeals and stay of execution shall, with any necessary modifications, apply to civil proceedings by or against the State as they apply to proceedings between subjects.

19. Scope of Part III

(1) Subject to the provisions of this section, any reference in this Part to civil proceedings by the State shall be construed as a reference to the following proceedings only:
   (a) proceedings for the enforcement or vindication of any right or the obtaining of any relief which, if this Act had not been passed, might have been enforced or vindicated or obtained by an action at the suit of any Government department or any public officer as such;
   (b) all such proceedings as the State is entitled to bring by virtue of this Act; and the expression "civil proceedings by or against the State" shall be construed accordingly.
(2) Subject to the provisions of this section, any reference in this Part to civil proceedings against the State shall be construed as a reference to the following proceedings only:
   (a) proceedings for the enforcement or vindication of any right or the obtaining of any relief which, if this Act had not been passed, might have been enforced or vindicated or obtained by an action against the Attorney-General or any public officer as such; and(b)all such proceedings as any person is entitled to bring against the State by virtue of this Act; and the expression "civil proceedings by or against the State" shall be construed accordingly.
(3) Notwithstanding anything in the preceding provisions of this section, the provisions of this Part shall not have effect with respect to any of the following proceedings, that is to say:
   (a) proceedings brought by the Attorney-General on the relation of some other person;(b) proceedings relating to charitable trusts by or against the Attorney-General.

PART IV
JUDGMENTS AND EXECUTION

20. Interest

The Minister responsible for finance may allow and cause to be paid out of the general revenues of the Republic to any person entitled by a judgment under this Act to any money or costs, interest thereon at a rate not exceeding six *per centum* from the date of the judgment until the money or costs are paid.

21. Satisfaction of orders against State

(1) Where in any civil proceedings by or against the State, or in any proceedings in connection with any arbitration to which the State is a party, any order (including an order for costs) is made by any court in favour of any person against the State or against a public officer as such, the proper officer of the court shall, on an application in that behalf made by or on behalf of that person at any time after the expiration of twenty-one days from the date of the order or, in case the order provides for the payment of costs and the costs require to be taxed, at any time after the costs have been taxed, whichever is the later, issue to that person a certificate in the prescribed form containing particulars of the order: Provided that, if the court so directs, a separate certificate shall be issued with respect to the costs (if any) ordered to be paid to the applicant.
(2) A copy of any certificate issued under this section may be served by the person in whose favour the order is made upon the Attorney-General.(3)If the order provides for the payment of any money by way of damages or otherwise, or of any costs, the certificate shall state the amount so payable, and the Permanent Secretary, Ministry of Finance, shall, subject as hereinafter provided, pay to the person entitled or to the legal practitioner acting for such person in the proceedings to which the order relates the amount appearing by the certificate to be due to him together with the interest, if any, allowed under section twenty: Provided that the court by which any such order as aforesaid is made, or any court to which an appeal against the order lies, may direct that, pending an appeal or otherwise, payment of the whole of any amount so payable, or any part thereof, shall be suspended and, if the certificate has not been issued, may order any such directions to be inserted therein.

(4) Save as aforesaid, no execution or attachment or process in the nature thereof shall be issued out of any court for enforcing payment by the State of any such money or costs as aforesaid, and no person shall be individually liable under any order for the payment by the State, or any public officer as such, of any such money or costs.

(5) This section shall apply both in relation to proceedings pending at the commencement of this Act and in relation to proceedings instituted thereafter.

22. No judgment by default without leave

In any proceedings against the State under this Act, judgment shall not be entered against the State in default of appearance or pleading without the leave of the court to be obtained on application of which at least fourteen clear days' notice has been given to the Attorney-General, or, if a legal practitioner in private practice is acting for the State in the proceedings, to such legal practitioner.

23. Execution by State

Subject to the provisions of this Act, any order made in favour of the State against any person in any civil proceedings to which the State is a party may be enforced in the same manner as an order made in an action between subjects and not otherwise.

24. Attachment of moneys payable by State

(1) Where any money is payable by the State to some person who, under any order of any court, is liable to pay any money to any other person, and that other person would, if the money so payable by the State were money payable by a subject, be entitled under rules of court to obtain an order for attachment thereof as a debt due or accruing due, or an order for the appointment of a sequestrator or receiver to receive the money on his behalf, the High Court may, subject to the provisions of this Act and in accordance with rules of court, make an order restraining the first-mentioned person from receiving that money and directing payment thereof to that person or to the sequestrator or receiver: Provided that no such order shall be made in respect of—
    (i) any wages or salary payable to any public officer as such;
    (ii) any money which is subject to the provisions of any written law prohibiting or restricting assignment or charging or taking in execution; or(iii)any money payable by the State to any person on account of a deposit in the Post Office Savings Bank.
(2) The provisions of subsection (1) shall, so far as they relate to forms of relief falling within the jurisdiction of a subordinate court, have effect in relation to subordinate courts as they have effect in relation to the High Court.

PART V
MISCELLANEOUS AND SUPPLEMENTAL

25. Discovery

(1) Subject to and in accordance with rules of court—
    (a) in any civil proceedings in the High Court or a subordinate court to which the State is a party, the State may be required by the court to make discovery of documents and produce documents for inspection; and
    (b) in any such proceedings as aforesaid, the State may be required by the court to answer interrogatories: Provided that this section shall be without prejudice to any rule of law which authorises or requires the withholding of any document or the refusal to answer any question on the ground that the disclosure of the document or the answering of the question would be injurious to the public interest.
(2) Any order of the court made under the powers conferred by paragraph (b) of subsection (1) shall direct by what public officer the interrogatories are to be answered.
(3) Without prejudice to the proviso to subsection (1), any rules made for the purposes of this section shall be such as to secure that the existence of a document will not be disclosed if, in the opinion of a Minister, it would be injurious to the public interest to disclose the existence thereof.

26. Exclusion of proceedings *in rem* against State

(1) Nothing in this Act shall authorise proceedings *in rem* in respect of any claim against the State, or the arrest, detention or sale of any ship or aircraft, or of any cargo or other property belonging to the State, or give to any person any lien on any such ship, aircraft, cargo or other property.

(2) Where proceedings *in rem* have been instituted in the High Court or in a subordinate court against any such ship, aircraft, cargo or other property, the court may, if satisfied, either on an application by the plaintiff for an order under this subsection or an application by the State to set aside the proceedings, that the proceedings were so instituted by the plaintiff in the reasonable belief that the ship, aircraft, cargo or other property did not belong to the State, order that the proceedings shall be treated as if they were in *personam* duly instituted against the State in accordance with the provisions of this Act or duly instituted against any other person whom the court regards as the proper person to be sued in the circumstances, and that the proceedings shall continue accordingly.

(3) Any order made in accordance with the provisions of subsection (2) may be made upon such terms, if any, as the court thinks just; and where the court makes any such order it may make such consequential orders as it thinks expedient.

27. Limitation of actions

Nothing in this Act shall prejudice the right of the State to rely upon any written law relating to the limitation of time for bringing proceedings against public authorities.

28. Application to State of certain statutory provisions

This Act shall not prejudice the right of the State to take advantage of the provisions of any written law although not named therein; and it is hereby declared that in any civil proceedings against the State the provisions of any written law which could, if the proceedings were between subjects, be relied upon by the defendant as a defence to the proceedings, whether in whole or in part, or otherwise, may, subject to any express provisions to the contrary, be so relied upon by the State.

29. Rules of court

(1) Any power to make rules of court shall include power to make rules for the purpose of giving effect to the provisions of this Act, and any such rules may contain provisions to have effect in relation to any proceedings by or against the State in substitution for or by way of addition to any of the provisions of the rules applying to proceedings between subjects.

(2) Provision shall be made by rules of court with respect to the following matters:

  (a) for providing for service of process, or notice thereof, in the case of proceedings by the State against persons, whether citizens of Zambia or not, who are not resident in Zambia;

  (b) for securing that where any civil proceedings are brought against the State in accordance with the provisions of this Act the plaintiff shall, before the State is required to take any step in the proceedings, provide the State with such information as the State may reasonably require as to the circumstances in which it is alleged that the liability of the State has arisen and as to the Government departments and public officers concerned;

  (c) for excepting proceedings brought against the State from the operation of any rule of court providing for summary judgment without trial, and for enabling any such proceedings to be put, in proper cases, into any special list which may be kept for the trial of short causes in which leave to defend is given under any such rule of court as aforesaid;

  (d) for enabling evidence to be taken on commission in proceedings by or against the State;(e)for providing—

  (i) that a person shall not be entitled to avail himself of any set-off or counter-claim in any proceedings by the State for the recovery of taxes, duties or penalties, or to avail himself in proceedings of any other nature by the State of any set-off or counter-claim arising out of a right or claim to repayment in respect of any taxes, duties or penalties;

  (ii) that a person shall not be entitled without the leave of the court to avail himself of any set-off or counter-claim in any proceedings by the State; and(iii)that the State shall not be entitled to avail itself of any set-off or counter-claim without the leave of the court.

(3) Provisions may be made by rules of court for regulating any appeals to the High Court or to the Supreme Court and whether by way of case stated or otherwise, under any written law relating to the revenue, and any rules made under this subsection may revoke any written law or rules in force immediately before the commencement of this Act so far as they regulate any such appeals and may make provision for any matters for which provision was made by any written law or rules so in force.

30. Repeal and transitional provisions

The Crown Proceedings Act, Chapter 242 of the 1953 Edition of the Laws, is hereby repealed:
Provided that any proceedings under the said Act pending before any court at the commencement of this Act shall be continued and concluded, and any judgment given may be enforced, in every respect as if the said Act had remained in force.

31. Savings

(1) Except as therein otherwise expressly provided, nothing in this Act shall—

    (a) subject the State to any greater liabilities in respect of the acts or omissions of any independent contractor employed by the State than those to which the State would be subject in respect of such acts or omissions if it were a private person; or

    (b) affect any rules of evidence or any presumption relating to the extent to which the State is bound by any written law; or

    (c) affect any right of the State to demand a trial at bar or to control or otherwise intervene in proceedings affecting its rights, property or profits.

(2) Nothing in this Act shall authorise a public officer as such to take proceedings against the State under or in accordance with this Act which he as such a public officer could not have taken if this Act had not been passed.

(3) Where any property vests in the State by virtue of any rule of law which operated independently of the acts or the intentions of the State, the State shall not by virtue of this Act be subject to any liabilities in tort by reason only of the property being so vested; but the provisions of this subsection shall be without prejudice to the liabilities of the State under this Act in respect of any period after the State or any person acting for the State has in fact taken possession or control of any such property, or entered into occupation thereof.

(4) This Act shall not operate to limit the discretion of the court to grant relief by way of *mandamus* in cases in which such relief might have been granted before the commencement of this Act, notwithstanding that by reason of the provisions of this Act some other further remedy is available.

(5) Save as is provided in the Postal Services Act, no proceedings shall lie against the State or its servants or agents—

    (a) by reason of anything done or omitted to be done or any damage or loss, whether negligent or otherwise, in relation to or in respect of any postal packet or telegram;

    (b) in respect of the amount of a money order;

    (c) in respect of the *bona fide* payment of any sum of money under that Act; or

    (d) by reason of anything lawfully done under that Act or any other written law.*[Cap. 470]*

(6) In subsection (5), the expressions "money order", "postal article" and "telegram" have the meanings respectively assigned to them in the Postal Services Act.*[Cap. 470]*

THE AUTHENTICATION OF DOCUMENTS ACT CHAPTER 75 OF THE LAWS OF ZAMBIA

ARRANGEMENT OF SECTIONS

CHAPTER 75
AUTHENTICATION OF DOCUMENTS

An Act to provide for the authentication of documents; and to provide for matters incidental to or connected with the foregoing.

Short title

1. This Act may be cited as the Authentication of Documents Act.

Interpretation

2. In this Act, unless the context otherwise requires-
   "authentication", when applied to a document, means the verification of any signature thereon;
   "document" means any deed, contract, power of attorney, affidavit, or other writing, but does not include an affidavit sworn before a Commissioner of the High Court.
   (As amended by S.I. No. 72 of 1964)

How documents executed outside Zambia are to be authenticated

3. Any document executed outside Zambia shall be deemed to be sufficiently authenticated for the purpose of use in Zambia if-
   (a) in the case of a document executed in Great Britain or Ireland it be duly authenticated by a notary public under his signature and seal of office;
   (b) in the case of a document executed in any part of Her Britannic Majesty's dominions outside the United Kingdom it be duly authenticated by the signature and seal of office of the mayor of any town or of a notary public or of the permanent head of any Government Department in any such part of Her Britannic Majesty's dominions;
   (c) in the case of document executed in any of Her Britannic Majesty's territories or protectorates in Africa it be duly authenticated by the signature and seal of office of any notary, magistrate, permanent head of a Government Department, Resident Commissioner or Assistant Commissioner in or of any such territory or protectorate;
   (d) in the case of a document executed in any place outside Her Britannic Majesty's dominions (hereinafter referred to as a "foreign place") it be duly authenticated by the signature and seal of office-   How documents executed outside Zambia are to be authenticated
      (i) of a British Consul-General, Consul or Vice-Consul in such foreign place; or
      (ii) of any Secretary of State, Under-Secretary of State, Governor, Colonial Secretary, or of any other person in such foreign place who shall be shown by the certificate of a Consul or Vice-Consul of such foreign place in Zambia to be duly authorised under the law of such foreign place to authenticate such document.

(As amended by No 42 of 1957, GN No 222 of 1964 and SI No 72 of 1964)

Authentication by magistrate in Her Britannic Majesty's dominions

4. Notwithstanding anything in the last preceding section contained, it shall be sufficient authentication of a document executed in any part of Her Britannic Majesty's dominions for use in Zambia which affects or relates to property not exceeding in value or amount four hundred kwacha if there be appended to or endorsed on such document a statement signed by a magistrate of the part of Her Britannic Majesty's dominions in which such document is executed-
   (a) that the person executing such document is a person known to him; or
   (b) that two other persons known to him have severally testified before him that the person executing such document is a person known to each of them.

(As amended by SI No 72 of 1964)

Saving as to affidavit sworn before a Commissioner of the High Court

5. An affidavit sworn before and attested by a Commissioner of the High Court beyond the confines of Zambia shall require no further authentication and may be used in all cases and matters in which affidavits are admissible as freely as if it had been duly made and sworn to within Zambia.

(As amended by SI No 72 of 1964)

THE CRIMINAL PROCEDURE CODE ACT CHAPTER 88 OF THE LAWS OF ZAMBIA

ARRANGEMENT OF SECTIONS

PART I PRELIMINARYPART I
PRELIMINARY

227

PART V MODE OF TAKING AND RECORDING EVIDENCE IN INQUIRIES AND TRIALSPART V MODE OF TAKING AND RECORDING EVIDENCE IN INQUIRIES AND TRIALS

PART VI PROCEDURE IN TRIALS BEFORE SUBORDINATE COURTSPART VI PROCEDURE IN TRIALS BEFORE SUBORDINATE COURTS

PART X SENTENCES AND THEIR EXECUTION PART X
SENTENCES AND THEIR EXECUTION

---

[3] Sections 303-306 have now been repealed following the enactment of s 6 of Act No 22 of 2022.

CHAPTER 88
CRIMINAL PROCEDURE CODE

An Act to make provision for the procedure to be followed in criminal cases
[1st April, 1934]   23 of 1933

[....]

PART I PRELIMINARYPART I
PRELIMINARY

Short title

1.   This Act may be cited as the Criminal Procedure Code Act Cap. 88

Interpretation

2.   In this Code, unless the context otherwise requires-
      "Christian marriage" means a marriage which is recognised, by the law of the place where it is contracted, as the voluntary union for life of one man and one woman to the exclusion of all others;
      "cognizable offence" means an offence for which a police officer may, in accordance with the First Schedule or under any written law for the time being in force, arrest without warrant;
      "complaint" means an allegation that some person known or unknown has committed or is guilty of an offence;
      "Court" means the High Court or any subordinate court as defined in this Code;
      "district" means the district assigned to a subordinate court as the district within which it is to exercise jurisdiction;
      "husband" and "wife" mean a husband and wife of a Christian marriage;
      "non-cognizable offence" means an offence for which a police officer may not arrest without warrant;
      "officer in charge of a police station" includes, when the officer in charge of the police station is absent from the station-house or unable, from illness or other cause, to perform his duties, the police officer present at the station-house who is next in rank to such officer, or any other police officer so present;

"police station" means a post or place appointed by the Inspector-General of Police to be a police station and includes any local area policed from such station;

"preliminary inquiry" means an inquiry into a criminal charge held by a subordinate court with a view to the committal of the accused person for trial before the High Court;

"public prosecutor" means any person appointed under the provisions of section eighty-six and includes the Attorney-General, the Solicitor-General, the Director of Public Prosecutions, a State Advocate and any practitioner as defined in the Legal Practitioners Act appearing on behalf of the People in any criminal proceedings;   Cap. 30

"Registrar" means the Registrar of the High Court and includes a Deputy Registrar and an Assistant Registrar;

"Session" has the meaning assigned to it by section two of the High Court Act;   Cap. 27

"subordinate court" means a subordinate court as constituted under the Subordinate Courts Act; Cap. 28

"summary trial" means a trial held by a subordinate court under Part VI.

(As amended by No. 28 of 1940, No. 23 of 1960, No. 5 of 1962, No. 27 of 1964 and S.I. No. 63 of 1964 and No. 13 of 2000)

Trial of offences under Penal Code

3.　(1)　All offences under the Penal Code shall be inquired into, tried and otherwise dealt with accordance to the provisions hereinafter contained.

Trial of offences under other written laws

(2)　All offences under any other written law shall be inquired into, tried and otherwise dealt with according to the same provisions, subject, however, to any enactment for the time being in force regulating the manner or place of inquiring into, trying or otherwise dealing with such offences.

PART II POWERS OF COURTSPART II
POWERS OF COURTS

Offences under Penal Code

4.　Subject to the other provisions of this Code, any offence under the Penal Code may be tried by the High Court.

Offences under other written laws

5.　(1)　Any offence under any written law, other than the Penal Code, may, when any court is mentioned in that behalf in such law, be tried by such court or by the High Court.

　　(2)　When no court is so mentioned, such offence may, subject to the other provisions of this Code, be tried by the High Court or by any subordinate court.

Sentences which High Court may pass

6.　The High Court may pass any sentence or make any order authorised by law.

Powers of subordinate courts

7.　Subject to the other provisions of this Code, a subordinate court of the first, second or third class may try any offence under the Penal Code or any other written law, and may pass any sentence or make any other order authorised by the Penal Code or any other written law:
Provided that-
　　(i)　a subordinate court presided over by a senior resident magistrate shall not impose any sentence of imprisonment exceeding a term of nine years;
　　(ii)　a subordinate court presided over by a resident magistrate shall not impose any sentence of imprisonment exceeding a term of seven years;
　　(iii)　a subordinate court presided over by a magistrate of the first class shall not impose any sentence of imprisonment exceeding a term of five years;
　　(iv)　a subordinate court other than a court presided over by a senior resident magistrate, a resident magistrate or a magistrate of the first class, shall not impose any sentence of imprisonment exceeding a term of three years.

(As amended by No. 23 of 1939, No. 26 of 1956, No. 28 of 1965 and No. 6 of 1972)

Reconciliation

8. In criminal cases, a subordinate court may promote reconciliation, and encourage and facilitate the settlement in an amicable way, of proceedings for assault, or for any other offence of a personal or private nature, not amounting to felony and not aggravated in degree, in terms of payment of compensation or other terms approved by such court and may, thereupon, order the proceedings to be stayed.

(No. 5 of 1962)

Sentences requiring confirmation

9. (1) No sentence imposed by a subordinate court presided over by a magistrate of the first class (other than a Senior Resident Magistrate or a Resident Magistrate) exceeding two years' imprisonment with or without hard labour shall be carried into effect in respect of the excess, until the record of the case or a certified copy thereof has been transmitted to and the sentence has been confirmed by the High Court.

   (2) Whenever a subordinate court of the first class (other than a court presided over by a Senior Resident Magistrate or a Resident Magistrate) imposes a fine exceeding three thousand penalty units, or imprisonment in default thereof, it shall be lawful for such court to levy the whole amount of such fine or to commit the convicted person to prison, in default of payment or distress, for the whole term of such imprisonment, without confirmation by the High Court; but such court shall immediately transmit the record of the case or a certified copy thereof to the High Court, which may, thereupon, exercise all the powers conferred upon it by subsection (3) of section thirteen:
   Provided always that such court may, in its discretion, in lieu of levying such fine in excess of three thousand penalty units or of committing the convicted person to prison, take security by deposit or by bond with two sureties, to be approved by the court, in such sum as it may think fit, pending any order of the High Court, for the performance of such order.

   (3) No sentence imposed by a subordinate court of the second class, exceeding one year's imprisonment with or without hard labour, shall be carried into effect in respect of the excess, until the record of the case or a certified copy thereof has been transmitted to and the sentence has been confirmed by the High Court.

   (4) Whenever a subordinate court of the second class imposes a fine exceeding one thousand and five hundred penalty units, or imprisonment in default thereof, it shall be lawful for such court to levy the whole amount of such fine or to commit the convicted person to prison, in default of payment or distress, for the whole term of such imprisonment, without confirmation by the High Court; but such court shall immediately transmit the record of the case or a certified copy thereof to the High Court, which may, thereupon, exercise all the powers conferred upon it by subsection (3) of section thirteen:
   Provided always that such court may, in its discretion, in lieu of levying such fine in excess of one thousand and five hundred penalty units or of committing the convicted person to prison, take security by deposit or by bond with two sureties, to be approved by the court, in such sum as it may think fit, pending any order of the High Court, for the performance of such order.

   (5) No sentence imposed by a subordinate court of the third class, exceeding six months' imprisonment with or without hard labour, shall be carried into effect in respect of the excess, and no fine exceeding seven hundred and fifty penalty units shall be levied in respect of the excess, until the record of the case or a certified copy thereof has been transmitted to and the sentence confirmed by the High Court. And no caning in excess of twelve strokes shall be administered until the record of the case or a certified copy thereof has been transmitted to and the order has been confirmed by the High Court.

   (6) Whenever a subordinate court passes sentence of death,[4] such court shall immediately transmit the record of the case or a certified copy thereof to the High Court, which may, thereupon, exercise all the powers conferred upon it by subsection (3) of section thirteen.

   (7) Any sentence passed by a subordinate court which requires confirmation by the High Court shall be deemed to have been so confirmed if on a first appeal to the Supreme Court or the High Court, as the case may be, the sentence is maintained by the appellate court.

(As amended by No. 23 of 1939, No. 30 of 1952, No. 26 of 1956, G.N. No. 493 of 1964, No. 28 of 1965, No. 23 of 1971, No. 6 of 1972 and Act No. 13 of 1994)

---

[4] In terms of s 2 of Act No 22 of 2022, '[s]ection 9(6) of the principal Act [has been] amended by the deletion of the word "death" and the substitution therefor of the words "life imprisonment".

Power of High Court to order preliminary inquiry

10.   The High Court may, by special order, direct that in the case of any particular charge brought against any person in a subordinate court, such court shall not try such charge but shall hold a preliminary inquiry under the provisions of Part VII.
(No. 26 of 1956)

Cases to be tried only by High Court

11.   (1)   The Chief Justice may, by statutory notice, order that any class of offence specified in such notice shall be tried by the High Court or be tried or committed to the High Court for trial by a subordinate court presided over by a senior resident magistrate only.

      (2)   No case of treason or murder or of any offence of a class specified in a notice issued under the provisions of subsection (1) shall be tried by a subordinate court unless special authority has been given by the High Court for such trial.
(No. 26 of 1956 as amended by No. 16 of 1959 and No. 28 of 1965)

Combination of sentences or orders

12.   Any court may pass any lawful sentence or make any lawful order combining any of the sentences or orders which it is authorised by law to pass or make.

Release on bail pending confirmation or other order

13.   (1)   Whenever a subordinate court shall pass a sentence which requires confirmation, the court imposing such sentence may, in its discretion, release the person sentenced on bail, pending confirmation or such order as the confirming court may make.

      (2)   If the person sentenced is so released on bail as aforesaid, the term of imprisonment shall run from the date upon which such person begins to serve his sentence after confirmation or other order of the confirming court:
Provided, however, that the person sentenced may, pending confirmation or other order, elect to serve his sentence from the date upon which he is sentenced by the subordinate court, in which case the term of imprisonment shall run from such date.

      (3)   The confirming court may exercise the same powers in confirmation as are conferred upon it in revision by Part XI.

14.   Repealed By Act No. 9 of 2003

Sentences in case of conviction for several offences at one trial

15.   (1)   When a person is convicted at one trial of two or more distinct offences, the court may sentence him, for such offences, to the several punishments prescribed therefor which such court is competent to impose; such punishments, when consisting of imprisonment, to commence the one after the expiration of the other, in such order as the court may direct, unless the court directs that such punishments shall run concurrently.

      (2)   For the purposes of confirmation, the aggregate of consecutive sentences imposed under this section, in case of convictions for several offences at one trial, shall be deemed to be a single sentence.

Power of courts to suspend sentence

16.   (1)   Whenever a person is convicted before any court for any offence other than an offence specified in the Fifth Schedule, the court may, in its discretion, pass sentence but order the operation of the whole or any part of the sentence to be suspended for a period not exceeding three years on such conditions, relating to compensation to be made by the offender for damage or pecuniary loss, or to good conduct, or to any other matter whatsoever, as the court may specify in the order.

      (2)   Where the operation of a sentence has been suspended under subsection (1) and the offender has, during the period of the suspension, observed all the conditions specified in the order, the sentence shall not be enforced.

      (3)   If the conditions of any order made under subsection (1) are not fulfilled, the offender may, upon the order of a magistrate or Judge, be arrested without warrant and brought before the court which suspended the operation of his sentence, and the court may direct that the sentence, or

part thereof, shall be executed forthwith or, in the case of a sentence of imprisonment, after the expiration of any other sentence of imprisonment which such offender is liable to serve:

Provided that the court that suspended the operation of the sentence may, in its discretion, if it be proved to its satisfaction by the offender that he has been unable through circumstances beyond his control to perform any condition of such suspension, grant an order further suspending the operation of the sentence subject to such conditions as might have been imposed at the time of the passing of the sentence.

(4)   In the alternative, where a court is satisfied that any person convicted before it of an offence has, by reason of such conviction, failed to fulfil the conditions of an order made under subsection (1), the court may direct that the sentence suspended by reason of the said order be either executed forthwith or, in the case of a sentence of imprisonment, after the expiration of any other sentence of imprisonment which such person is liable to serve.

(5)   For the purposes of any appeal therefrom, a direction by a court made under subsection (3) or (4) shall be deemed to be a conviction.

(No. 16 of 1959 as amended by No. 27 of 1964,
No. 76 of 1965 and No. 46 of 1967)

Medical examination of accused persons

17. (1)   A court may, at any stage in a trial or inquiry, order that an accused person be medically examined for the purpose of ascertaining any matter which is or may be, in the opinion of the court, material to the proceedings before the court.

(2)   Where an accused person is examined on the order of a court made under subsection (1), a document purporting to be the certificate of the medical officer who carried out the examination shall be receivable in evidence to prove the matters stated therein:

Provided that the court may summon such medical officer to give evidence orally.

(No. 11 of 1963)

PART III GENERAL PROVISIONSPART III
GENERAL PROVISIONS

Arrest, Escape and Retaking Arrest Generally

Arrest, how made

18. (1)   In making an arrest, the police officer or other person making the same shall actually touch or confine the body of the person to be arrested, unless there be a submission to the custody by word or action.

(2)   If such person forcibly resists the endeavour to arrest him, or attempts to evade the arrest, such police officer or other person may use all means reasonably necessary to effect the arrest.

(As amended by No. 28 of 1940)

Search of place entered by person sought to be arrested

19. (1)   If any person acting under a warrant of arrest, or any police officer having authority to arrest, has reason to believe that the person to be arrested has entered into or is within any place, the person residing in or being in charge of such place shall, on demand of such person acting as aforesaid or such police officer, allow him free ingress thereto and afford all reasonable facilities for a search therein.

(2)   If ingress to such place cannot be obtained under subsection (1), it shall be lawful, in any case, for a person acting under a warrant, and, in any case in which a warrant may issue, but cannot be obtained without affording the person to be arrested an opportunity to escape, for a police officer to enter such place and search therein, and, in order to effect an entrance into such place, to break open any outer or inner door or window of any house or place, whether that of the person to be arrested or of any other person, or otherwise effect entry into such house or place, if, after notification of his authority and purpose, and demand of admittance duly made, he cannot otherwise obtain admittance.

Power to break out of any house for purposes of liberation

20.   Any police officer or other person authorised to make an arrest may break out of any house or place in order to liberate himself or any other person who, having lawfully entered for the purpose of making an arrest, is detained therein.

No unnecessary restraint

21. The person arrested shall not be subjected to more restraint than is necessary to prevent his escape.

Search of arrested persons

22. Whenever a person is arrested-
    (a) by a police officer under a warrant which does not provide for the taking of bail or under a warrant which provides for the taking of bail and the person arrested cannot furnish bail; or
    (b) without warrant, or by a private person under a warrant, and the person arrested cannot legally be admitted to bail or is unable to furnish bail;
    the police officer making the arrest or, when the arrest is made by a private person, the police officer to whom he makes over the person arrested may search such person and place in safe custody all articles, other than necessary wearing apparel, found upon him.

Power of police officer to detain and search vehicles and persons in certain circumstances

23. Any police officer may stop, search and detain any vessel, aircraft or vehicle in or upon which there shall be reason to suspect that anything stolen or unlawfully obtained may be found and also any person who may be reasonably suspected of having in his possession or conveying in any manner anything stolen or unlawfully obtained, and may seize any such thing.
(No. 28 of 1940)

Mode of searching women

24. Whenever it is necessary to cause a woman to be searched, the search shall be made by another woman with strict regard to decency.

Arrest without Warrant Power to seize offensive weapons

25. The police officer or other person making any arrest may take from the person arrested any offensive weapons which he has about his person and shall deliver all weapons so taken to the court or officer before which or whom the officer or person making the arrest is required by law to produce the person arrested.

Arrest by police officer without warrant

26. Any police officer may, without an order from a magistrate and without a warrant, arrest-
    (a) any person whom he suspects, upon reasonable grounds, of having committed a cognizable offence;
    (b) any person who commits a breach of the peace in his presence;
    (c) any person who obstructs a police officer while in the execution of his duty, or who has escaped or attempts to escape from lawful custody;
    (d) any person in whose possession anything is found which may reasonably be suspected to be stolen property, or who may reasonably be suspected of having committed an offence with reference to such thing;
    (e) any person whom he suspects, upon reasonable grounds, of being a deserter from the Defence Force;
    (f) any person whom he finds in any highway, yard or other place during the night, and whom he suspects, upon reasonable grounds of having committed or being about to commit a felony;
    (g) any person whom he suspects, upon reasonable grounds, of having been concerned in any act committed at any place out of Zambia which, if committed in Zambia, would have been punishable as an offence, and for which he is, under the Extradition Act, or otherwise, liable to be apprehended and detained in Zambia;
    (h) any person having in his possession, without lawful excuse, the burden of proving which excuse shall lie on such person, any implement of housebreaking;
    (i) any released convict committing a breach of any provision prescribed by section three hundred and eighteen or of any rule made thereunder;
    (j) any person for whom he has reasonable cause to believe a warrant of arrest has been issued.
(As amended by No. 23 of 1937 and S.I. No. 63 of 1964)
Cap. 94

Arrest of vagabonds, habitual robbers, etc.

27. Any officer in charge of a police station may, in like manner, arrest or cause to be arrested-
    (a) any person found taking precautions to conceal his presence within the limits of such station, under circumstances which afford reason to believe that he is taking such precautions with a view to committing a cognizable offence;
    (b) any person, within the limits of such station, who has no ostensible means of subsistence, or who cannot give a satisfactory account of himself;
    (c) any person who is, by repute, a habitual robber, housebreaker or thief, or a habitual receiver of stolen property, knowing it to be stolen, or who, by repute, habitually commits extortion, or, in order to commit extortion, habitually puts or attempts to put persons in fear of injury.

Procedure when police officer deputes subordinate to arrest without warrant

28. When any officer in charge of a police station requires any officer subordinate to him to arrest without a warrant (otherwise than in such officer's presence) any person who may lawfully be arrested without a warrant, he shall deliver to the officer required to make the arrest an order in writing, specifying the person to be arrested and the offence or other cause for which the arrest is to be made.

Refusal to give name and residence

29. (1) When any person who, in the presence of a police officer, has committed or has been accused of committing a non-cognizable offence refuses, on the demand of such officer, to give his name and residence, or gives a name or residence which such officer has reason to believe to be false, he may be arrested by such officer, in order that his name or residence may be ascertained.
    (2) When the true name and residence of such person have been ascertained, he shall be released on his executing a bond, with or without sureties, to appear before a magistrate, if so required:
    Provided that, if such person is not resident in Zambia, the bond shall be secured by a surety or sureties resident in Zambia.
    (3) Should the true name and residence of such person not be ascertained within twenty-four hours from the time of arrest, or should he fail to execute the bond, or, if so required, to furnish sufficient sureties, he shall forthwith be taken before the nearest magistrate having jurisdiction.
    (4) Any police officer may arrest without a warrant any person who in his presence has committed a non-cognizable offence, if reasonable grounds exist for believing that, except by the arrest of the person offending, he could not be found or made answerable to justice.
(As amended by No. 4 of 1945)

Disposal of persons arrested by police officer

30. A police officer making an arrest without a warrant shall, without unnecessary delay and subject to the provisions herein contained as to bail, take or send the person arrested before a magistrate having jurisdiction in the case or before an officer in charge of a police station.

Arrest by private persons

31. (1) Any private person may arrest any person who, in his presence, commits a cognizable offence, or whom he reasonably suspects of having committed a felony.
    (2) Persons found committing any offence involving injury to property may be arrested without a warrant by the owner of the property or his servants or persons authorised by him.

Disposal of persons arrested by private person

32. (1) Any private person arresting any other person without a warrant shall, without unnecessary delay, make over the person so arrested to a police officer, or, in the absence of a police officer, shall take such person to the nearest police station.
    (2) If there is reason to believe that such person comes under the provisions of section twenty-six, a police officer shall re-arrest him.
    (3) If there is reason to believe that he has committed a non-cognizable offence, and he refuses, on the demand of a police officer, to give his name and residence, or gives a name or residence which such officer has reason to believe to be false, he shall be dealt with under the provisions of section twenty-nine. If there is no sufficient reason to believe that he has committed any offence, he shall be at once released.

Detention of persons arrested without warrant

33. (1) When any person has been taken into custody without a warrant for an offence other than an offence punishable with [life imprisonment],[5] the officer in charge of the police station to which such person shall be brought may, in any case, and shall, if it does not appear practicable to bring such person before an appropriate competent court within twenty-four hours after he was so taken into custody, inquire into the case, and, unless the offence appears to the officer to be of a serious nature, release the person, on his executing a bond, with or without sureties, for a reasonable amount, to appear before a competent court at a time and place to be named in the bond: but, where any person is retained in custody, he shall be brought before a competent court as soon as practicable. Notwithstanding anything contained in this section, an officer in charge of a police station may release a person arrested on suspicion on a charge of committing any offence, when, after due police inquiry, insufficient evidence is, in his opinion, disclosed on which to proceed with the charge.

   (2) In this section, "competent court" means any court having jurisdiction to try or hold a preliminary inquiry into the offence for which the person has been taken into custody.

(As amended by No. 28 of 1940 and No. 2 of 1960)

Police to report apprehensions

34. Officers in charge of police stations shall report to the nearest magistrate the cases of all persons arrested without warrant within the limits of their respective stations, whether such persons have been admitted to bail or not.

Offence committed in magistrate's presence

35. When any offence is committed in the presence of a magistrate within the local limits of his jurisdiction, he may himself arrest or order any person to arrest the offender, and may, thereupon, subject to the provisions herein contained as to bail, commit the offender to custody.

Escape and Retaking, Arrest by magistrate

36. Any magistrate may, at any time, arrest or direct the arrest, in his presence, within the local limits of his jurisdiction, of any person for whose arrest he is competent, at the time and in the circumstances, to issue a warrant.

Recapture of person escaping

37. If a person in lawful custody escapes or is rescued, the person from whose custody he escapes or is rescued may immediately pursue and arrest him in any place in Zambia.

Provisions of sections 19 and 20 to apply to arrests under section 37

38. The provisions of sections nineteen and twenty shall apply to arrests under the last preceding section, although the person making any such arrest is not acting under a warrant, and is not a police officer having authority to arrest.

Security for Keeping the Peace and for Good Behaviour, Duty to assist magistrate, Prevention of Offences etc.

39. Every person is bound to assist a magistrate or police officer reasonably demanding his aid-
   (a) in the taking or preventing the escape of any other person whom such magistrate or police officer is authorised to arrest;
   (b) in the prevention or suppression of a breach of the peace, or in the prevention of any injury attempted to be committed to any railway, canal, telegraph or public property.

Power of magistrate of subordinate court of the first or second class

40. (1) Whenever a magistrate empowered to hold a subordinate court of the first or second class is informed on oath that any person is likely to commit a breach of the peace or disturb the public tranquility, or to do any wrongful act that may probably occasion a breach of the peace or disturb the public tranquillity, the magistrate may, in manner hereinafter provided, require such person

---

[5] In terms of s 3 of Act No 22 of 2022, '[s]ection 33 (1) of the principal Act is amended by the deletion of the word "death" and the substitution therefor of the words "life imprisonment".'

to show cause why he should not be ordered to execute a bond, with or without sureties, for keeping the peace for such period, not exceeding one year, as the magistrate thinks fit.

(2)   Proceedings shall not be taken under this section, unless either the person informed against, or the place where the breach of the peace or disturbance is apprehended, is within the local limits of such magistrate's jurisdiction.

Security for good behaviour from persons disseminating seditious matters

41.   Whenever a magistrate empowered to hold a subordinate court of the first class is informed on oath that a person is within the limits of his jurisdiction and that such person, within or without such limits, either orally or in writing, or in any other manner, is disseminating, or attempting to disseminate, or in any wise abetting the dissemination of-

(a)   any seditious matter, that is to say, any matter the publication of which is punishable under section fifty-seven of the Penal Code; or

(b)   any matter concerning a Judge which amounts to libel under the Penal Code:
such magistrate may (in manner provided in this Code) require such person to show cause why he should not be ordered to execute a bond, with or without sureties, for his good behaviour for such period, not exceeding one year, as the magistrate thinks fit to fix.

(No. 28 of 1940)
Cap. 87

Powers of other magistrates

42.   (1)   When any magistrate not empowered to proceed under section forty has reason to believe that any person is likely to commit a breach of the peace or disturb the public tranquillity, or to do any wrongful act that may probably occasion a breach of the peace or disturb the public tranquillity, and that such breach of the peace or disturbance cannot be prevented otherwise than by detaining such person in custody, such magistrate may, after recording his reasons, issue a warrant for his arrest (if he is not already in custody or before the court), and may send him before a magistrate empowered to deal with the case, with a copy of his reasons.

(2)   A magistrate before whom a person is sent under this section may, in his discretion, detain such person in custody until the completion of the inquiry hereinafter prescribed.

Security for good behaviour from suspected persons

43.   Whenever a magistrate empowered to hold a subordinate court of the first or second class is informed on oath that any person is taking precautions to conceal his presence within the local limits of such magistrate's jurisdiction, and that there is reason to believe that such person is taking such precautions with a view to committing any offence, such magistrate may, in manner hereinafter provided, require such person to show cause why he should not be ordered to execute a bond, with sureties, for his good behaviour for such period, not exceeding one year, as the magistrate thinks fit.

Security for good behaviour from habitual offenders

44.   Whenever a magistrate empowered to hold a subordinate court of the first or second class is informed on oath that any person within the local limits of his jurisdiction-

(a)   is, by habit, a robber, housebreaker or thief; or

(b)   is, by habit, a receiver of stolen property, knowing the same to have been stolen; or

(c)   habitually protects or harbours thieves, or aids in the concealment or disposal of stolen property; or

(d)   habitually commits or attempts to commit, or aids or abets in the commission of, any offence punishable under Chapter XXX, XXXIV or XXXVII of the Penal Code; or

(e)   habitually commits or attempts to commit, or aids or abets in the commission of, offences involving a breach of the peace; or

(f)   is so desperate and dangerous as to render his being at large without security hazardous to the community;
such magistrate may, in manner hereinafter provided, require such person to show cause why he should not be ordered to execute a bond, with sureties, for his good behaviour for such period, not exceeding three years, as the magistrate thinks fit.

Cap. 87

Order to be made

45. When a magistrate acting under section forty, forty-three or forty-four deems it necessary to require any person to show cause under any such section, he shall make an order in writing setting forth-
    (a) the substance of the information received;
    (b) the amount of the bond to be executed;
    (c) the term for which it is to be in force; and
    (d) the number, character and class of sureties, if any, required.

Procedure in respect of person present in court

46. If the person in respect of whom an order under the last preceding section is made is present in court, it shall be read over to him, or, if he so desires, the substance thereof shall be explained to him.

Summons or warrant in case of person not so present

47. If the person referred to in the last preceding section is not present in court, the magistrate shall issue a summons requiring him to appear, or, when such person is in custody, a warrant directing the officer in whose custody he is to bring him before the court.
    Provided that, whenever it appears to such magistrate, upon the report of a police officer or upon other information (the substance of which report or information shall be recorded by the magistrate), that there is reason to fear the commission of a breach of the peace, and that such breach of the peace cannot be prevented otherwise than by the immediate arrest of such person, the magistrate may, at any time, issue a warrant for his arrest.

Copy of order under section 45 to accompany summons or warrant

48. Every summons or warrant issued under the last preceding section shall be accompanied by a copy of the order made under section forty-five, and such copy shall be delivered by the officer serving or executing such summons or warrant to the person served with or arrested under the same.

Power to dispense with personal attendance

49. The magistrate may, if he sees sufficient cause, dispense with the personal attendance of any person called upon to show cause why he should not be ordered to execute a bond for keeping the peace, and may permit him to appear by an advocate.

Inquiry as to truth of information

50. (1) When an order under section forty-five has been read or explained under section forty-six to a person present in court, or when any person appears or is brought before a magistrate in compliance with or in execution of a summons or warrant issued under section forty-seven, the magistrate shall proceed to inquire into the truth of the information upon which the action has been taken, and to take such further evidence as may appear necessary.
    (2) Such inquiry shall be made, as nearly as may be practicable, in the manner hereinafter prescribed for conducting trials and recording evidence in trials before subordinate courts.
    (3) For the purposes of this section, the fact that a person comes within the provisions of section forty-four may be proved by evidence of general repute or otherwise.
    (4) Where two or more persons have been associated together in the matter under inquiry, they may be dealt with in the same or separate inquiries, as the magistrate thinks just.

Order to give security

51. (1) If, upon such inquiry, it is proved that it is necessary for keeping the peace or maintaining good behaviour, as the case may be, that the person in respect of whom the inquiry is made should execute a bond, with or without sureties, the magistrate shall make an order accordingly:
    Provided that-
    (i) no person shall be ordered to give security of a nature different from, or of an amount larger than, or for a period longer than, that specified in the order made under section forty-five;
    (ii) the amount of every bond shall be fixed with due regard to the circumstances of the case and shall not be excessive;

241

(iii) when the person in respect of whom the inquiry is made is a minor, the bond shall be executed only by his sureties.

(2) Any person ordered to give security for good behaviour under this section may appeal to the High Court, and the provisions of Part XI (relating to appeals) shall apply to every such appeal.

Proceedings in all Cases Subsequent to Order to Furnish Security, Discharge of person informed against

52. If, on an inquiry under section fifty, it is not proved that it is necessary for keeping the peace or maintaining good behaviour, as the case may be, that the person in respect of whom the inquiry is made should execute a bond, the magistrate shall make an entry on the record to that effect, and, if such person is in custody only for the purposes of the inquiry, shall release him, or, if such person is not in custody, shall discharge him.

Commencement of period for which security is required

53. (1) If any person in respect of whom an order requiring security is made under section forty-five or fifty-one is, at the time such order is made, sentenced to or undergoing a sentence of imprisonment, the period for which such security is required shall commence on the expiration of such sentence.

(2) In other cases, such period shall commence on the date of such order, unless the magistrate, for sufficient reason, fixes a later date.

Contents of bond

54. The bond to be executed by any such person shall bind him to keep the peace or to be of good behaviour, as the case may be, and, in the latter case, the commission or attempt to commit, or the aiding, abetting, counselling or procuring the commission of any offence punishable with imprisonment, wherever it may be committed, shall be a breach of the bond.

Power to reject sureties

55. A magistrate may refuse to accept any surety offered under any of the preceding sections, on the ground that, for reasons to be recorded by the magistrate, such surety is an unfit person.

Procedure on failure of person to give security

56. (1) If any person ordered to give security as aforesaid does not give such security on or before the date on which the period for which such security is to be given commences, he shall, except in the case mentioned in subsection (2), be committed to prison, or, if he is already in prison, be detained in prison until such period expires, or until, within such period, he gives the security to the court or magistrate which or who made the order requiring it.

(2) When such person has been ordered by a magistrate to give security for a period exceeding one year, such magistrate shall, if such person does not give such security as aforesaid, issue a warrant directing him to be detained in prison pending the orders of the High Court, and the proceedings shall be laid, as soon as conveniently may be, before such Court.

(3) The High Court, after examining such proceedings and requiring from the magistrate any further information or evidence which it thinks necessary, may make such order in the case as it thinks fit.

(4) The period, if any, for which any person is imprisoned for failure to give security shall not exceed three years.

(5) If the security is tendered to the officer in charge of the prison, he shall forthwith refer the matter to the court or magistrate which or who made the order, and shall await the orders of such court or magistrate.

(6) Imprisonment for failure to give security for keeping the peace shall be without hard labour.

(7) Imprisonment for failure to give security for good behaviour may be with or without hard labour, as the court or magistrate, in each case, directs.

Power to release persons imprisoned for failure to give security

57. Whenever a magistrate empowered to hold a subordinate court of the first or second class is of opinion that any person imprisoned for failing to give security may be released without hazard to the community, such magistrate shall make an immediate report of the case for the orders of the High Court, and such Court may, if it thinks fit, order such person to be discharged.

Power of High Court to cancel bond

58. The High Court may, at any time, for sufficient reasons to be recorded in writing, cancel any bond for keeping the peace or for good behaviour executed under any of the preceding sections by order of any court or magistrate.

Discharge of sureties

59. (1) Any surety for the peaceable conduct or good behaviour of another person may, at any time, apply to a magistrate empowered to hold a subordinate court of the first or second class to cancel any bond executed under any of the preceding sections within the local limits of his jurisdiction.
(2) On such application being made, the magistrate shall issue his summons or warrant, as he thinks fit, requiring the person for whom such surety is bound to appear or to be brought before him.
(3) When such person appears or is brought before the magistrate, such magistrate shall cancel the bond and shall order such person to give, for the unexpired portion of the term of such bond, fresh security of the same description as the original security. Every such order shall, for the purposes of sections fifty-four, fifty-five, fifty-six and fifty-seven, be deemed to be an order made under section fifty-one.

Forfeiture

60. (1) If the conditions of any bond be not complied with, the court may endorse such bond and declare the same to be forfeited.
(2) On any forfeiture, the court may issue its warrant of distress for the amount mentioned in such bond, or for the imprisonment of the principal and his surety or sureties for a term not exceeding six months, unless the amount be sooner paid or levied.
(3) A warrant of distress under this section may be executed within the local limits of the jurisdiction of the court which issued it, and it shall authorise the distress and sale of any property belonging to such person and his surety or sureties without such limits, when endorsed by a magistrate holding a subordinate court of the first or second class within the local limits of whose jurisdiction such property is found.

Preventive Action of the Police

Police to prevent cognizable offences

61. Every police officer may interpose for the purpose of preventing, and shall, to the best of his ability, prevent the commission of any cognizable offence.

Information of design to commit such offences

62. Every police officer receiving information of a design to commit any cognizable offence shall communicate such information to the police officer to whom he is subordinate, and to any other officer whose duty it is to prevent or take cognizance of the commission of any such offence.

Arrest to prevent such offences

63. A police officer knowing of a design to commit any cognizable offence may arrest, without orders from a magistrate and without a warrant, the person so designing, if it appears to such officer that the commission of the offence cannot otherwise be prevented.

Prevention of injury to public property

64. A police officer may, of his own authority, interpose to prevent any injury attempted to be committed, in his presence, to any public property, movable or immovable, or the removal of or injury to any public landmark, or buoy, or other mark used for navigation.

PART IV
PROVISIONS RELATING TO ALL CRIMINAL INVESTIGATIONS

Place of Inquiry or Trial

General authority of courts of Zambia

65. Every court has authority to cause to be brought before it any person who is within the local limits of its jurisdiction, and is charged with an offence committed within Zambia, or which, according to law, may be dealt with as if it has been committed within Zambia, and to deal with the accused person according to its jurisdiction.

Accused person to be sent ot district where offence committed

66. Where a person accused of having committed an offence within Zambia has escaped or removed from the district within which the offence was committed, and is found within another district, the court within whose jurisdiction he is found shall cause him to be brought before it, and shall, unless authorised to proceed in the case, send him in custody to the court within whose jurisdiction the offence is alleged to have been committed, or require him to give security for his surrender to that court there to answer the charge and to be dealt with according to law.

Removal of accused person under warrant

67. Where any person is to be sent in custody in pursuance of the last preceding section, a warrant shall be issued by the court within whose jurisdiction he is found, and that warrant shall be sufficient authority to any person to whom it is directed to receive and detain the person therein named, and to carry him and deliver him up to the court within whose district the offence was committed or may be tried.

Mode of trial before High Court

68. (1) The High Court may inquire of and try any offence subject to its jurisdiction, at any place where it has power to hold sittings.
   (2) Criminal cases in the High Court shall, subject to the provisions of subsection (3), be tried upon information signed in accordance with the provisions of this Code.
   (3) The Chief Justice may, by statutory order, direct that any offences or class of offences, other than offences against sections one hundred and ninety-nine, two hundred, two hundred and fifteen, two hundred and sixteen and two hundred and nineteen of the Penal Code, may be tried by the High Court without a preliminary inquiry as if it were a court of summary jurisdiction.   Cap. 87
   (4) When an order has been made under subsection (3), the trial shall be conducted in accordance with the provisions of Part VI and the provisions of Part IX shall not apply to any such trial.
(No. 11 of 1946)

Ordinary place of inquiry and trial

69. Subject to the provisions of section sixty-eight and to the powers of transfer conferred by sections seventy-eight and eighty, every offence shall be inquired into or tried, as the case may be, by a court within the local limits of whose jurisdiction it was committed or within the local limits of whose jurisdiction the accused was apprehended, or is in custody on a charge for the offence, or has appeared in answer to a summons lawfully issued charging him with the offence.
(No. 28 of 1940)

Trial at place where act done or where consequence of offence ensues

70. When a person is accused of the commission of any offence, by reason of anything which has been done, or omitted to be done, or of any consequence which has ensued, such offence may be inquired into or

tried by a court within the local limits of whose jurisdiction any such thing has been done, or omitted to be done, or any such consequence has ensued.

Trial where offence is connected with another offence

71.   When an act or ommission is an offence by reason of its relation to any other act or omission which is also an offence, or which would be an offence if the doer were capable of committing an offence, a charge of the first-mentioned offence may be inquired into or tried by a court within the local limits of whose jurisdiction either act was done.

Trial where place of offence is uncertain

72.   When-
   (a)   it is uncertain in which of several districts an offence was committed; or
   (b)   an offence is committed partly in one district and partly in another; or
   (c)   an offence is a continuing one, and continues to be committed in more districts than one; or
   (d)   an offence consists of several acts or omissions done in different districts;
such offence may be inquired into or tried by a court having jurisdiction in any of such districts.

Offence near boundary of district

73.   (1)   When an offence is committed on or near the boundary or boundaries of two or more districts, or within a distance of ten miles from any such boundary or boundaries, it may be inquired into or tried by a court having jurisdiction in any of the said districts, in the same manner as if it had been wholly committed therein.
      (2)   When an offence is committed on any person or in respect of any property on any railroad, or within a distance of ten miles from any line of railway on either side thereof, such offence may be inquired into or tried by a court having jurisdiction in any district in or through any part whereof, or within such distance from the boundaries whereof, such line of railway passes, in the same manner as if such offence had been wholly committed within such district. Offence on or near railway

Offence committed on a journey

74.   An offence committed whilst the offender is in the course of performing a journey or voyage may be inquired into or tried by a court through or into the local limits of whose jurisdiction the offender, or the person against whom, or the thing in respect of which, the offence was committed passed in the course of that journey or voyage.

High Court to decide in cases of doubt

75.   Whenever any doubt arises as to the court by which any offence should be inquired into or tried, the High Court may decide by which court the offence shall be inquired into or tried.

Court to be open

76.   The place in which any court is held, for the purpose of inquiring into or trying any offence shall, unless the contrary is expressly provided by any Act for the time being in force, be deemed an open court to which the public generally may have access, so far as the same can conveniently contain them:
Provided that the presiding Judge or magistrate may, if he considers it necessary or expedient-
   (a)   in interlocutory proceedings; or
   (b)   in circumstances where publicity would be prejudicial to the interest of-
   (i)   justice, defence, public safety, public order or public morality; or
   (ii)   the welfare of persons under the age of eighteen years or the protection of the private lives of persons concerned in the proceedings;
order, at any stage of the inquiry into or trial of any particular case, that persons generally or any particular person other than the parties thereto or their legal representatives shall not have access to or be or remain in the room or building used by the court.
(As amended by No. 20 of 1953 and No. 54 of 1968)

Transfer of Cases

Transfer of case where offence committed outside jurisdiction

77. (1)   If, upon the hearing of any complaint, it appears that the cause of complaint arose out of the limits of the jurisdiction of the court before which such complaint has been brought, the court may, on being satisfied that it has no jurisdiction, direct the case to be transferred to the court having jurisdiction where the cause of complaint arose.

(2)   If the accused person is in custody, and the court directing such transfer thinks it expedient that such custody should be continued, or, if he is not in custody, that he should be placed in such custody, the court shall direct the offender to be taken by a police officer before the court having jurisdiction where the cause of complaint arose, and shall give a warrant for that purpose to such officer, and shall deliver to him the complaint and recognizances, if any, taken by the court directing such transfer, to be delivered to the court before whom the accused person is to be taken; and such complaint and recognizances, if any, shall be treated, for all purposes as if they had been taken by such last-mentioned court.

(3)   If the accused person is not continued or placed in custody as aforesaid, the court shall inform him that it has directed the transfer of the case as aforesaid, and, thereupon, the provisions of subsection (2) respecting the transmission and validity of the documents in the case shall apply.

Transfer of cases between magistrates

78.   Any magistrate holding a subordinate court of the first class-
   (a)   may transfer any case of which he has taken cognizance for inquiry or trial to any subordinate court empowered to inquire into or try such case within the local limits of such first class subordinate court's jurisdiction; and
   (b)   may direct or empower any subordinate court of the second or third class within the local limits of his jurisdiction which has taken cognizance of any case, whether evidence has been taken in such case or not, to transfer it for inquiry or trial to himself or to any other specified court within the local limits of his jurisdiction, which is competent to try the accused or commit him for trial, and such court may dispose of the case accordingly.

(As amended by No. 16 of 1959)

Procedure when, after commencement of inquiry or trial, magistrate finds case should be transferred to another magistrate

79. (1)   If, in the course of any inquiry or trial before a magistrate, the evidence appears to warrant a presumption that the case is one which should be tried or committed for trial by some other magistrate, he shall stay proceedings and submit the case, with a brief report thereon, to a magistrate holding a subordinate court of the first class and empowered to direct the transfer of the case under the last preceding section.

(2)   The provisions of this section and of section seventy-eight shall be without prejudice to the powers conferred upon a Judge of the High Court under section twenty-three of the High Court Act.

(As amended by No. 16 of 1959) Cap. 27

Power of High Court to change venue

80. (1)   Whenever it is made to appear to the High Court-
   (a)   that a fair and impartial inquiry or trial cannot be had in any court subordinate thereto; or
   (b)   that some question of law of unusual difficulty is likely to arise; or
   (c)   that a view of the place in or near which any offence has been committed may be required for the satisfactory inquiry into or trial of the same; or
   (d)   that an order under this section will tend to the general convenience of the parties or witnesses; or
   (e)   that such an order is expedient for the ends of justice or is required by any provision of this Code;
      it may order-
         (i)   that any offence be inquired into or tried by any court not empowered under the preceding sections of this Part but, in other respects, competent to inquire into or try such offence;

         (ii) that any particular criminal case or class of cases be transferred from a court subordinate to its authority to any other such court of equal or superior jurisdiction;

         (iii) that an accused person be committed for trial before itself.

(2) The High Court may act either on the report of the lower court, or on the application of a party interested, or on its own initiative.

(3) Every application for the exercise of the power conferred by this section shall be made by motion, which shall, except when the applicant is the Director of Public Prosecutions, be supported by affidavit.

(4) Every accused person making any such application shall give to the Director of Public Prosecutions notice in writing of the application, together with a copy of the grounds on which it is made; and no order shall be made on the merits of the application, unless at least twenty-four hours have elapsed between the giving of such notice and the hearing of the application.

(5) When an accused person makes any such application, the High Court may direct him to execute a bond, with or without sureties, conditioned that he will, if convicted, pay the costs of the prosecutor.

(As amended by S.I. No. 152 of 1965)

Criminal Proceedings

Power of Director of Public Prosecutions to enter nolle prosequi

81. (1) In any criminal case and at any stage thereof before verdict or judgment, as the case may be, the Director of Public Prosecutions may enter a nolle prosequi, either by stating in court, or by informing the court in writing, that the People intend that the proceedings shall not continue, and, thereupon, the accused shall stand discharged in respect of the charge for which the nolle prosequi is entered, and, if he has been committed to prison, shall be released, or, if he is on bail, his recognizances shall be treated as being discharged; but such discharge of an accused person shall not operate as a bar to any subsequent proceedings against him on account of the same facts.

    (2) If the accused shall not be before the court when such nolle prosequi is entered, the Registrar or clerk of such court shall forthwith cause notice in writing of the entry of such nolle prosequi to be given to the keeper of the prison in which such accused may be detained, and also, if the accused person has been committed for trial, to the subordinate court by which he was so committed, and such subordinate court shall forthwith cause a similar notice in writing to be given to any witnesses bound over to prosecute and give evidence and to their sureties (if any), and also to the accused and his sureties, in case he shall have been admitted to bail.

(As amended by No. 28 of 1940, No. 5 of 1962, S.I. No. 63 of 1964 and S.I. No. 152 of 1965)

Delegation of powers by Director of Public Prosecutions

82. The Director of Public Prosecutions may order in writing that all or any of the powers vested in him by the last preceding section, by section eighty-eight and by Parts VII and VIII, may be exercised also by the Solicitor-General, the Parliamentary Draftsmen and State Advocates and the exercise of these powers by the Solicitor-General, the Parliamentary Draftsmen and State Advocates shall then operate as if they had been exercised by the Director of Public Prosecutions:

Provided that the Director of Public Prosecutions may in writing revoke any order made by him under this section.

(No. 47 of 1955 as amended by No. 50 of 1957, No. 23 of 1960, No. 27 of 1964 and S.I. No. 63 of 1964)

Criminal informations by Director of Public Prosecutions

83. (1) Notwithstanding anything in this Code contained, the Director of Public Prosecutions may exhibit on behalf of the People in the High Court against persons subject to the jurisdiction of the High Court, informations for all purposes for which Her Britannic Majesty's Attorney-General for England may exhibit informations on behalf of the Crown in the High Court of Justice in England.

    (2) Such proceedings may be taken upon every such information as may lawfully be taken in the case of similar informations filed by Her Britannic Majesty's Attorney-General for England, so far as the circumstances of the case and the practice and procedure of the High Court will admit.

(3)   The Chief Justice may, by statutory instrument, make rules for carrying into effect the provisions of this section.

(As amended by No. 2 of 1960 and S.I. No. 63 of 1964)

Signature of Director of Public Prosecutions to be evidence

84.   Where, by any written law, the sanction, fiat or written consent of the Director of Public Prosecutions is necessary for the commencement or continuance of the prosecution of any offence, a document purporting to give such sanction, fiat or consent placed before the court by the prosecutor and purporting to be signed by the person for the time being exercising the powers and performing the duties of the Director of Public Prosecutions shall be prima facie evidence that such sanction, fiat or consent has been given.

(No. 50 of 1957 as amended by S.I. No. 63 of 1964)

Arrest of persons for offences requiring the consent of the Director of Public Prosecutions for commencement of prosecution

85. (1)   Where any written law provides that no prosecution shall be instituted against any person for an offence without the sanction, fiat or written consent of the Director of Public Prosecutions, such person may be arrested or a warrant for such arrest may be issued and executed and such person may be remanded in custody or on bail, notwithstanding that such sanction, fiat or written consent has not been first obtained, but no further proceedings shall be taken until such sanction, fiat or written consent has been obtained and produced to the court.

     (2)   The provisions of subsection (1) shall be subject to the other provisions of this Code relating to arrest, remand and the granting of bail.

(No. 5 of 1962 as amended by S.I. No. 152 of 1965)

Appointment of Public Prosecutors and Conduct of Prosecutions

Power to appoint public prosecutors

86. (1)   The Director of Public Prosecutions may appoint generally, or in any case, or for any specified class of cases, in any district, one or more officers to be called public prosecutors.

     (2)   The Director of Public Prosecutions may appoint any person employed in the public service to be a public prosecutor for the purposes of any proceedings instituted on behalf of the People.

     (3)   Every public prosecutor shall be subject to the express directions of the Director of Public Prosecutions.

(As amended by No. 28 of 1940, No. 16 of 1959, No. 23 of 1960, S.I. No. 63 of 1964 and S.I. No. 152 of 1965)

Powers of public prosecutors

87.   A public prosecutor may appear and plead without any written authority before any court in which any case of which he has charge is under inquiry, trial or appeal; and, if any private person instructs an advocate to prosecute in any such case, the public prosecutor may conduct the prosecution, and the advocate so instructed shall act therein under his directions.

Withdrawal from prosecution in trials before subordinate courts

88.   In any trial before a subordinate court, any public prosecutor may, with the consent of the court or on the instructions of the Director of Public Prosecutions, at any time before judgment is pronounced, withdraw from the prosecution of any person; and upon such withdrawal-

     (a)   if it is made before the accused person is called upon to make his defence, he shall be discharged, but such discharge of an accused person shall not operate as a bar to subsequent proceedings against him on account of the same facts;

     (b)   if it is made after the accused person is called upon to make his defence, he shall be acquitted.

(As amended by S.I. No. 63 of 1964)

Permission to conduct prosecution

89. (1)   Any magistrate inquiring into or trying any case may permit the prosecution to be conducted by any person, but no person, other than a public prosecutor or other officer generally or specially

authorised by the Director of Public Prosecutions in this behalf, shall be entitled to do so without permission.

(2)   Any such person or officer shall have the like power of withdrawing from the prosecution as is provided by the last preceding section, and the provisions of that section shall apply to any withdrawal by such person or officer.

(3)   Any person conducting the prosecution may do so personally or by an advocate.

(As amended by G.N. No. 303 of 1964 and S.I. No. 63 of 1964)

Institution of Proceedings Making of Complaint

Institution of proceedings

90.   (1)   Proceedings may be instituted either by the making of a complaint or by the bringing before a magistrate of a person who has been arrested without warrant.

(2)   Any person who believes from a reasonable and probable cause that an offence has been committed by any person may make a complaint thereof to a magistrate having jurisdiction.

(3)   A complaint may be made orally or in writing, but if made orally shall be reduced to writing and in either case shall be signed by the complainant.

(4)   The magistrate, upon receiving any such complaint, shall-
   (a)   himself draw up and sign; or
   (b)   direct that a public prosecutor or legal practitioner representing the complainant shall draw up and sign; or
   (c)   permit the complainant to draw up and sign;
        a formal charge containing a statement of the offence with which the accused is charged, and until such charge has been drawn up and signed no summons or warrant shall issue and no further step shall be taken in the proceedings.

(5)   When an accused person who has been arrested without a warrant is brought before a magistrate, a formal charge containing a statement of the offence with which the accused is charged shall be signed and presented to the magistrate by the police officer preferring the charge.

(6)   When the magistrate is of opinion that any complaint or formal charge made or presented under this section does not disclose any offence, the magistrate shall make an order refusing to admit such complaint or formal charge and shall record his reasons for such order.

(7)   Any person aggrieved by an order made by a magistrate under subsection (6) may appeal to the High Court within fourteen days of the date of such order and the High Court may, if satisfied that the formal charge or complaint, in respect of which the order was made, disclose an offence, direct the magistrate to admit the formal charge or complaint, or may dismiss the appeal.

(No. 28 of 1940 as amended by No. 5 of 1962)

Processes to Compel the Appearance of Accused Persons Summons

91.   (1)   Where a charge has been drawn up and signed in accordance with subsection (4) of the last preceding section, the magistrate may, in his discretion, issue either a summons or a warrant to compel the attendance of the accused person before a court having jurisdiction to inquire into or try the offence alleged to have been committed: Issue of summons or warrant
        Provided that a warrant shall not be issued in the first instance unless the complaint has been made upon oath before the magistrate, either by the complainant or by a witness or witnesses.

(2)   Any summons or warrant may be issued on a Sunday.

(No. 28 of 1940 as amended No. 5 of 1962)

Form and contents of summons

92.   (1)   Every summons issued by a court under this Code shall be in writing, in duplicate, and signed by the presiding officer of such court or by such other officer as the Chief Justice may, from time to time, by rule, direct.

(2)   Every summons shall be directed to the person summoned, and shall require him to appear, at a time and place to be therein appointed, before a court having jurisdiction to inquire into and deal with the complaint or charge. It shall state shortly the offence with which the person against whom it is issued is charged.

(As amended by No. 2 of 1960)

Services of summons

93. (1) Every summons shall be served by a police officer, or by an officer of the court issuing it, or other public servant, and shall, if practicable, be served personally on the person summoned, by delivering or tendering to him one of the duplicates of the summons.

    (2) Every person on whom a summons is so served shall, if so required by the serving officer, sign a receipt therefor on the back of the other duplicate.

Service when person summoned cannot be found

94. Where the person summoned cannot, by the exercise of due diligence, be found, the summons may be served by leaving one of the duplicates for him with some adult male member of his family, or with his servant residing with him; and the person with whom the summons is so left shall, if so required by the serving officer, sign a receipt therefor on the back of the other duplicate.

Procedure when service cannot be effected as before provided

95. If service, in the manner provided by the two last preceding sections, cannot, by the exercise of due diligence, be effected, the serving officer shall affix one of the duplicates of the summons to some conspicuous part of the house or homestead in which the person summoned ordinarily resides, and, thereupon, the summons shall be deemed to have been duly served.

Service on company

96. Service of a summons on an incorporated company or other body corporate may be effected by serving it on the secretary, local manager or other principal officer of the corporation, at the registered office of such company or body corporate, or by registered letter addressed to the chief officer of the corporation in Zambia. In the latter case, service shall be deemed to have been effected when the letter would arrive in ordinary course of post.

Service outside local limits of jurisdiction

97. When a court desires that a summons issued by it shall be served at any place outside the local limits of its jurisdiction, it shall send such summons in duplicate to a magistrate within the local limits of whose jurisdiction the person summoned resides or is, to be there served.

Proof of service when serving officer not present

98. (1) Where the officer who has served a summons is not present at the hearing of the case, and in any case where a summons issued by a court has been served outside the local limits of its jurisdiction, an affidavit, purporting to be made before a magistrate, that such summons has been served, and a duplicate of the summons, purporting to be endorsed, in the manner hereinbefore provided, by the person to whom it was delivered or tendered or with whom it was left, shall be admissible in evidence, and the statements made therein shall be deemed to be correct, unless and until the contrary is proved.

    (2) The affidavit mentioned in this section may be attached to the duplicate of the summons and returned to the court.

Power to dispense with personal attendance of accused

99. (1) Whenever a summons is issued in respect of any offence other than a felony, a magistrate may, if he sees reason to do so, and shall, when the offence with which the accused is charged is punishable only by fine or only by fine and/or imprisonment not exceeding three months, dispense with the personal attendance of the accused, if he pleads guilty in writing or appears by an advocate.

    (2) The magistrate inquiring into or trying any case may, in his discretion, at any subsequent stage of the proceedings, direct the personal attendance of the accused, and, if necessary, enforce such attendance in manner hereinafter provided.

    (3) If a magistrate imposes a fine on an accused person whose personal attendance has been dispensed with under this section, and such fine is not paid within the time prescribed for such payment, the magistrate may forthwith issue a summons calling upon such accused person to show cause why he should not be committed to prison, for such term as the magistrate may

then prescribe. If such accused person does not attend upon the return of such summons, the magistrate may forthwith issue a warrant, and commit such person to prison for such term as the magistrate may then fix.

(4) If, in any case in which, under this section, the attendance of an accused person is dispensed with, previous convictions are alleged against such person and are not admitted in writing or through such person's advocate, the magistrate may adjourn the proceedings and direct the personal attendance of the accused, and, if necessary, enforce such attendance in manner hereinafter provided.

(5) Whenever the attendance of an accused person has been so dispensed with, and his attendance is subsequently required, the cost of any adjournment for such purpose shall be borne, in any event, by the accused.

Warrant of Arrest

Warrant after issue of summons

100. Notwithstanding the issue of a summons, a warrant may be issued at any time before or after the time appointed in the summons for the appearance of the accused. But no such warrant shall be issued unless a complaint or charge has been made upon oath.

Summons disobeyed

101. If the accused does not appear at the time and place appointed in and by the summons, and his personal attendance has not been dispensed with under section ninety-nine, the court may issue a warrant to apprehend him and cause him to be brought before such court. But no such warrant shall be issued unless a complaint or charge has been made upon oath.

Form, contents and duration of warrant of arrest

102. (1) Every warrant of arrest shall be under the hand of the Judge or magistrate issuing the same.

(2) Every warrant shall state shortly the offence with which the person against whom it is issued is charged, and shall name or otherwise describe such person, and it shall order the person or persons to whom it is directed to apprehend the person against whom it is issued, and bring him before the court issuing the warrant or before some other court having jurisdiction in the case, to answer to the charge therein mentioned and to be further dealt with according to law.

(3) Every such warrant shall remain in force until it is executed, or until it is cancelled by the court which issued it.

Court may direct security to be taken

103. (1) Any court issuing a warrant for the arrest of any person, in respect of any offence other than murder or treason, may, in its discretion, direct by endorsement on the warrant that, if such person executes a bond with sufficient sureties for his attendance before the court at a specified time and thereafter until otherwise directed by the court, the officer to whom the warrant is directed shall take such security and shall release such person from custody.

(2) The endorsement shall state-
    (a) the number of sureties;
    (b) the amount in which they and the person for whose arrest the warrant is issued are to be respectively bound; and
    (c) the time at which he is to attend before the court.

(3) Whenever security is taken under this section, the officer to whom the warrant is directed shall forward the bond to the court.

Warrants to whom directed

104. (1) A warrant of arrest may be directed to one or more police officers, or to one police officer and to all other police officers of the area within which the court has jurisdiction, or generally to all police officers of such area. But any court issuing such a warrant may, if its immediate execution is necessary, and no police officer is immediately available, direct it to any other person or persons, and such person or persons shall execute the same.

(2)   When a warrant is directed to more officers or persons than one, it may be executed by all or by any one or more of them.

Order for assistance directed to land-holder

105. (1)   A magistrate empowered to hold a subordinate court of the first or second class may order any land-holder, farmer or manager of land, within the local limits of his jurisdiction, to assist in the arrest of any escaped convict, or person who has been accused of a cognizable offence and has eluded pursuit.

(2)   Such land-holder, farmer or manager shall, thereupon, comply with such order, if the person for whose arrest it was issued is in or enters on his land or farm or the land under his charge.

(3)   When such person is arrested, he shall be made over with the order to the nearest police officer, who shall cause him to be taken before a magistrate having jurisdiction, unless security is taken under section one hundred and three.

(4)   No land-holder, farmer or manager of land to whom such order is directed shall be liable at the suit of the person so arrested for anything done by him under the provisions of this section.

(5)   If any land-holder, farmer or manager of land to whom such order is directed fails to comply therewith, he shall be liable, on conviction, to a fine not exceeding seven hundred and fifty penalty units or, in default of payment, to imprisonment with or without hard labour for a period not exceeding six months.

(As amended by Act No. 13 of 1994)

Execution of warrant directed to police officer

106. A warrant directed to any police officer may also be executed by any other police officer whose name is endorsed upon the warrant by the officer to whom it is directed or endorsed.

Notification of substance of warrant

107. The police officer or other person executing a warrant of arrest shall notify the substance thereof to the person to be arrested, and, if so required, shall show him the warrant.

Person arrested to be brought before court without delay

108. The police officer or other person executing a warrant of arrest shall (subject to the provisions of section one hundred and three as to security), without unnecessary delay, bring the person arrested before the court before which he is required by law to produce such person.

Where warrant of arrest may be executed

109. A warrant of arrest may be executed at any place in Zambia.

Forwarding of warrants for execution outside jurisdiction

110. (1)   When a warrant of arrest is to be executed outside the local limits of the jurisdiction of the court issuing the same, such court may, instead of directing such warrant to a police officer, forward the same, by post or otherwise, to any magistrate within the local limits of whose jurisdiction it is to be executed.

(2)   The magistrate to whom such warrant is so forwarded shall endorse his name thereon, and, if practicable, cause it to be executed in the manner hereinbefore provided within the local limits of his jurisdiction.

Procedure in case of warrant directed to police officer for execution outside jurisdiction

111. (1)   When a warrant of arrest directed to a police officer is to be executed outside the local limits of the jurisdiction of the court issuing the same, he shall take it for endorsement to a magistrate within the local limits of whose jurisdiction it is to be executed.

(2)   Such magistrate shall endorse his name thereon, and such endorsement shall be sufficient authority to the police officer to whom the warrant is directed to execute the same within such limits, and the local police officer shall, if so required, assist such officer in executing such warrant.

(3) Whenever there is reason to believe that the delay occasioned by obtaining the endorsement of the magistrate within the local limits of whose jurisdiction the warrant is to be executed will prevent such execution, the police officer to whom it is directed may execute the same without such endorsement, in any place outside the local limits of the jurisdiction of the court which issued it.

Procedure on arrest of person outside jurisdiction

112. (1) When a warrant of arrest is executed outside the local limits of the jurisdiction of the court by which it was issued, the person arrested shall, unless the court which issued the warrant is within twenty miles of the place of arrest, or is nearer than the magistrate within the local limits of whose jurisdiction the arrest was made, or unless security is taken under section one hundred and three, be taken before the magistrate within the local limits of whose jurisdiction the arrest was made.

(2) Such magistrate shall, if the person arrested appears to be the person intended by the court which issued the warrant, direct his removal in custody to such court:

Provided that, if such person has been arrested for an offence other than murder or treason, and he is ready and willing to give bail to the satisfaction of such magistrate, or if a direction has been endorsed under section one hundred and three on the warrant, and such person is ready and willing to give the security required by such direction, the magistrate may take such bail or shall take such security, as the case may be, and shall forward the bond to the court which issued the warrant.

(3) Nothing in this section shall be deemed to prevent a police officer from taking security under section one hundred and three.

Miscellaneous Provisions Regarding Processes Irregularities in warrant

113. Any irregularity or defect in the substance or form of a warrant, and any variance between it and the written complaint or information, or between either and the evidence produced on the part of the prosecution at any inquiry or trial, shall not affect the validity of any proceedings at or subsequent to the hearing of the case, but, if any such variance appears to the court to be such that the accused has been thereby deceived or misled, such court may, at the request of the accused, adjourn the hearing of the case to some future date, and, in the meantime, remand the accused or admit him to bail.

Power to take bond for appearance

114. Where any person for whose appearance or arrest the magistrate presiding in any court is empowered to issue a summons or warrant is present in such court, such magistrate may require such person to execute a bond, with or without sureties, for his appearance in such court.

Arrest for breach of bond for appearance

115. When any person who is bound by any bond taken under this Code to appear before a court does not so appear, the magistrate presiding in such court may issue a warrant directing that such person be arrested and produced before him.

Power of court to order prisoner to be brought before it

116. (1) Where any person for whose appearance or arrest a court is empowered to issue a summons or warrant is confined in any prison within Zambia, the court may issue an order to the officer in charge of such prison requiring him to bring such prisoner in proper custody, at a time to be named in the order, before such court.

(2) The officer so in charge, on receipt of such order, shall act in accordance therewith, and shall provide for the safe custody of the prisoner during his absence from the prison for the purpose aforesaid.

(3) Notwithstanding anything to the contrary contained in this Code or in any written law, it is declared for the avoidance of doubt that upon a person being convicted or sentenced by a subordinate court and before the entering of an appeal by such person against the conviction or sentence or both, the subordinate court which convicted or sentenced such person or the High Court has and shall have no power to release that person on bail with or without securities.

(As amended by Act No. 6 of 1972)

Search Warrants

Provisions of this Part generally applicable to summonses and warrants

117. The provisions contained in this Part relating to a summons and warrant, and their issue, service and execution, shall so far as may be apply to every summons and every warrant of arrest issued under this Code.

Power to issue search warrant

118. Where it is proved on oath to a magistrate that, in fact or according to reasonable suspicion, anything upon, by or in respect of which an offence has been committed or anything which is necessary to the conduct of an investigation into any offence is in any building, vessel, carriage, box, receptacle or place, the magistrate may, by warrant (called a search warrant), authorise a police officer or other person therein named to search the building, vessel, carriage, box, receptable or place (which shall be named or described in the warrant) for any such thing, and, if anything searched for be found, to seize it and carry it before the court of the magistrate issuing the warrant or some other court, to be dealt with according to law.
(As amended by No. 28 of 1940)

Execution of search warrant

119. Every search warrant may be issued and executed on a Sunday, and shall be executed between the hours of sunrise and sunset, but a magistrate may, by the warrant, in his discretion, authorise the police officer or other person to whom it is addressed to execute it at any hour.

Persons in charge of closed place to allow ingress thereto and egress therefrom

120. (1) Whenever any building or other place liable to search is closed, any person residing in or being in charge of such building or place shall, on demand of the police officer or other person executing the search warrant, and on production of the warrant, allow him free ingress thereto and egress therefrom, and afford all reasonable facilities for a search therein.
    (2) If ingress to or egress from such building or other place cannot be so obtained, the police officer or other person executing the search warrant may proceed in the manner prescribed by section nineteen or twenty.
    (3) Where any person in or about such building or place is reasonably suspected of concealing about his person any article for which search should be made, such person may be searched. If such person is a woman, the provisions of section twenty-four shall be observed.

Detention of property seized

121. (1) When any article is seized and brought before a court, it may be detained until the conclusion of the case or the investigation, reasonable care being taken for its preservation.
    (2) If any appeal is made, or if any person is committed for trial, the court may order the article to be further detained for the purpose of the appeal or the trial.
    (3) If no appeal is made, or if no person is committed for trail, the court shall direct such thing to be restored to the person from whom it was taken, unless the court sees fit or is authorised or required by law to dispose of it otherwise.

Provisions as to Bail

Provisions applicable to search warrants

122. The provisions of section one hundred and two (1) and (3), one hundred and four, one hundred and six, one hundred and nine, one hundred and ten and one hundred and eleven shall, so far as may be, apply to all search warrants issued under section one hundred and eighteen.

Bail

123. (1) When any person is arrested or detained, or appears before or is brought before a subordinate court, the High Court or Supreme Court he may, at any time while he is in custody, or at any

stage of the proceedings before such court, be admitted to bail upon providing a surety or sureties sufficient, in the opinion of the police officer concerned or court, to secure his appearance, or be released upon his own recognizance if such officer or court thinks fit:

Provided that any person charged with-

    (i)   murder, treason or any other offence carrying a possible or mandatory capital penalty;

    (ii) misprision of treason or treason-felony; or

    (iii) aggravated robbery;

    (iv) theft of motor vehicle, if such person has previously been convicted of theft of motor vehicle.

shall not be granted bail by either a subordinate court, the High Court or Supreme Court or be released by any Police Officer.

(As amended by Act No. 35 of 1993, Act No. 9 of 2005)

(2)   Subject to the provisions of section one hundred and twenty-six, before any person is admitted to bail or released on his own recognizance, a bond (hereinafter referred to as a bail bond), for such sum as the court or officer, as the case may be, thinks sufficient, shall be executed by such person and by the surety or sureties, or by such person alone, as the case may be, conditioned that such person shall attend at the time and place mentioned in such bond and at every time and place to which during the course of the proceedings the hearing may from time to time be adjourned.

(3)   The High Court may, at any time, on the application of an accused person, order him, whether or not he has been committed for trial, to be admitted to bail or released on his own recognizance, and the bail bond in any such case may, if the order so directs, be executed before any magistrate.

(4)   Notwithstanding anything in this section contained, no person charged with an offence under the State Security Act shall be admitted to bail, either pending trial or pending appeal, if the Director of Public Prosecutions certifies that it is likely that the safety or interests of the Republic would thereby be prejudiced.   Cap. 111

(5)   Notwithstanding anything to the contrary contained in this Code or in any written law, it is declared for the avoidance of doubt that upon a person being convicted or sentenced by a subordinate court and before the entering of an appeal by such person against the conviction or sentence or both, the subordinate court which convicted or sentenced such person or the High Court has and shall have no power to release that person on bail with or without securities.

(No. 50 of 1957 as amended by No. 36 of 1969,
No. 59 of 1970, No. 6 of 1972 and Act No. 35 of 1993)

Additional conditions of bail bond

124. In addition to the condition mentioned in subsection (2) of section one hundred and twenty-three, the court or officer before whom a bail bond is executed may impose such further conditions upon such bond as may seem reasonable and necessary in any particular case.

(No. 50 of 1957)

Release from custody

125. (1)   As soon as a bail bond has been executed, the person for whose appearance it has been executed shall be released, and, when he is in prison, the court admitting him to bail shall issue an order of release to the officer in charge of the prison, and such officer, on receipt of the order, shall release him.

(2)   Nothing in this section or in section one hundred and twenty-three shall be deemed to require the release of any person liable to be detained for some matter other than that in respect of which a bail bond was executed.

(As amended by No. 50 of 1957)

Amount of bail, and deposits

126. (1)   The amount of bail shall, in every case, be fixed with due regard to the circumstances of the case, but shall not be excessive.

(2)   The court or police officer admitting a person to bail or releasing him on his own recognizance may, in lieu of a bail bond, accept a deposit of money, or a deposit of property, from any

person who would otherwise have had to execute a bail bond under the provisions of section one hundred and twenty-three, and may attach to such deposit such conditions as might have been attached to a bail bond, and on any breach of any such condition such deposit shall be forfeited.

(3)   The High Court may, in any case, direct that the bail or deposit required by a subordinate court or by a police officer be reduced, or may vary or add to any conditions imposed under the provisions of section one hundred and twenty-four.

(No. 50 of 1957 as amended by No. 27 of 1964)

Power to order sufficient bail when that first taken is insufficient

127. If, through mistake, fraud or otherwise, insufficient sureties have been accepted, or if they afterwards become insufficient, the court may issue a warrant of arrest directing that the person released on bail be brought before it, and may order him to find sufficient sureties, and, on his failing so to do, may commit him to prison.

Discharge of sureties

128. (1)   All or any of the sureties for the appearance and attendance of a person released on bail may, at any time, apply to a magistrate to discharge the bail bond either wholly or so far as it relates to the applicant or applicants.

(2)   On such application being made, the magistrate shall issue his warrant of arrest directing that the person so released be brought before him.

(3)   On the appearance of such person pursuant to the warrant, or on his voluntary surrender, the magistrate shall direct the bail bond to be discharged either wholly or so far as it relates to the applicant or applicants, and shall call upon such person to find other sufficient sureties, and, if he fails to do so, may commit him to prison.

(As amended by No. 50 of 1957)

Death of surety

129. Where a surety to a bail bond dies before the bond is forfeited, his estate shall be discharged from all liability in respect of the bond, but the party who gave the bond may be required to find a new surety.

(As amended by No. 50 of 1957)

Persons bound by recognizance absconding may be committed

130. If it is made to appear to any court, by information on oath, that any person bound by recognizance is about to leave Zambia, the court may cause him to be arrested, and may commit him to prison until the trial, unless the court shall see fit to admit him to bail upon further recognizance.

Forfeiture of recognizance

131. (1)   Whenever any person shall not appear at the time and place mentioned in any recognizance entered into by him, the court may, by order, endorse such recognizance and declare the same to be forfeited.

(2)   On the forfeiture of any recognizance, the court may issue its warrant of distress for the amount mentioned in such recognizance, or for the imprisonment of such person and his surety or sureties, for any term not exceeding six months, unless the amount mentioned in such recognizance be sooner paid or levied.

(3)   A warrant of distress under this section may be executed within the local limits of the jurisdiction of the court which issued it, and it shall authorise the distress and sale of any property belonging to such person and his surety or sureties, without such limits, when endorsed by a magistrate holding a subordinate court of the first or second class within the local limits of whose jurisdiction such property is found.

Appeal from and revision of orders

132. All orders passed under the last preceding section by any magistrate shall be appealable to and may be revised by the High Court.

Power to direct levy of amount due on recognizance

133. The High Court may direct any magistrate to levy the amount due on a recognizance to appear and attend at the High Court.

Charges and Informations

Offence to be specified in charge or information with necessary particulars

134. Every charge or information shall contain, and shall be sufficient if it contains, a statement of the specific offence or offences with which the accused person is charged, together with such particulars as may be necessary for giving reasonable information as to the nature of the offence charged.

(No. 28 of 1940)

Joinder of counts in a charge or information

135. (1) Any offences, whether felonies or misdemeanours, may be charged together in the same charge of or information if the offences charged are founded on the same facts or form, or are a part of, a series of offences of the same or a similar character.

(2) Where more than one offence is charged in a charge or information, a description of each offence so charged shall be set out in a separate paragraph of the charge or information called a count.

(3) Where, before trial, or at any stage of a trial, the court is of opinion that a person accused may be embarrassed in his defence by reason of being charged with more than one offence in the same charge or information, or that for any other reason it is desirable to direct that any person should be tried separately for any one or more offences charged in a charge or information, the court may order a separate trial of any count or counts of such charge or information.

(No. 28 of 1940)

Joinder of two or more accused in one charge or information

136. The following persons may be joined in one charge or information and may be tried together, namely:
   (a) persons accused of the same offence committed in the course of the same transaction;
   (b) persons accused of an offence and persons accused of abetment, or of an attempt to commit such offence;
   (c) persons accused of different offences committed in the course of the same transaction;
   (d) persons accused of any offence under Chapters XXVI to XXX of the Penal Code and persons accused of receiving or retaining property, possession of which is alleged to have been transferred by any such offence committed by the first-named persons, or of abetment of or attempting to commit either of such last-named offences;
   (e) persons accused of any offence relating to counterfeit coin under Chapter XXXVII of the Penal Code, and persons accused of any other offence under the said Chapter relating to the same coin, or of abetment of or attempting to commit any such offence.

(No. 28 of 1940)

Cap. 87

Mode in which offences are to be charged

137. The following provisions shall apply to all charges and informations and, notwithstanding any rule of law or practice, a charge or an information shall, subject to the provisions of this Code, not be open to objection in respect of its form or contents if it is framed in accordance with the provisions of this Code:
   (a) (i) A count of a charge or an information shall commence with a statement of the offence charged, called the statement of offence;
      (ii) the statement of offence shall describe the offence shortly in ordinary language avoiding as far as possible the use of technical terms, and without necessarily stating all the essential elements of the offence and, if the offence charged is one created by enactment, shall contain a reference to the section of the enactment creating the offence;
      (iii) after the statement of the offence, particulars of such offence shall be set out in ordinary language, in which the use of technical terms shall not be necessary:

Provided that, where any rule of law or any Act limits the particulars of an offence which are required to be given in a charge or an information, nothing in this paragraph shall require any more particulars to be given than those so required;

(iv) the forms set out in the Second Schedule or forms conforming thereto as nearly as may be shall be used in cases to which they are applicable; and in other cases forms to the like effect or conforming thereto as nearly as may be shall be used, the statement of offence and the particulars of offence being varied according to the circumstances in each case;

(v) where a charge or an information contains more than one count, the counts shall be numbered consecutively.

(b) (i) Where an enactment constituting an offence states the offence to be the doing or the omission to do any one of any different acts in the alternative, or the doing or the omission to do any act in any one of any different capacities, or with any one of different intentions, or states any part of the offence in the alternative, the acts, omissions, capacities or intentions, or other matters stated in the alternative in the enactment, may be stated in the alternative in the court charging the offence;

(ii) it shall not be necessary, in any count charging an offence constituted by an enactment, to negative any exception or exemption from, or qualification to, the operation of the enactment creating the offence.

(c) (i) The description of property in a charge or an information shall be in ordinary language, and such as to indicate with reasonable clearness the property referred to, and, if the property is so described, it shall not be necessary (except when required for the purpose of describing an offence depending on any special ownership of property or special value of property) to name the person to whom the property belongs or the value of the property;

(ii) where property is vested in more than one person, and the owners of the property are referred to in a charge or an information, it shall be sufficient to describe the property as owned by one of those persons by name with the others, and if the persons owning the property are a body of persons with a collective name, such as a joint stock company or "Inhabitants", "Trustees", "Commissioners" or "Club" or other such name, it shall be sufficient to use the collective name without naming any individual;

(iii) property belonging to, or provided for, the use of any public establishment, service or department may be described as the property of the Republic;

(iv) coin and bank notes may be described as money; and any allegation as to money, so far as regards the description of the property, shall be sustained by proof of any amount of coin or any bank or currency note (although the particular species of coin of which such amount was composed, or the particular nature of the bank or currency note, shall not be proved); and in cases of stealing and defrauding by false pretences, by proof that the accused person dishonestly appropriated or obtained any coin or any bank or currency note, or any portion of the value thereof, although such coin or bank or currency note may have been delivered to him in order that some part of the value thereof should be returned to the party delivering the same or to any other person and such part shall have been returned accordingly.

(d) The description or designation in a charge or an information of the accused person, or of any other person to whom reference is made therein, shall be such as is reasonably sufficient to identify him, without necessarily stating his correct name, or his abode, style, degree or occupation, and if, owing to the name of the person not being known or for any other reason, it is impracticable to give such a description or designation, such description or designation shall be given as is reasonably practicable in the circumstances, or such person may be described as "a person unknown"

(e) Where it is necessary to refer to any document or instrument in a charge or an information, it shall be sufficient to describe it by any name or designation by which it is usually known, or by the purport thereof, without setting out any copy thereof.

(f) Subject to any other provisions of this section, it shall be sufficient to describe any place, time, thing, matter, act or omission whatsoever to which it is necessary to refer in any charge or information in ordinary language in such a manner as to indicate with reasonable clearness the place, time, thing, matter, act or omission referred to.

(g) It shall not be necessary in stating any intent to defraud, deceive or injure to state an intent to defraud, deceive or injure any particular person, where the enactment creating the offence does not make an intent to defraud, deceive or injure a particular person an essential ingredient of the offence.

(h) Where a previous conviction of an offence is charged in a charge or an information, it shall be charged at the end of the charge or information by means of a statement that the accused person has been previously convicted of that offence at a certain time and place without stating the particulars of the offence.

(i) Figures and abbreviations may be used for expressing anything which is commonly expressed thereby.

(No. 28 of 1940 as amended by No. 11 of 1963
and S.I. No. 63 of 1964)

Previous Conviction or Acquittal

Persons convicted or acquitted not to be tried again for same offence

138. A person who has been once tried by a court of competent jurisdiction for an offence, and convicted or acquitted of such offence, shall, while such conviction or acquittal remains in force, not be liable to be tried again on the same facts for the same offence.

Person may be tried again for separate offence

139. A person convicted or acquitted of any offence may be afterwards tried for any other offence with which he might have been charged on the former trial under subsection (1) of section one hundred and thirty-five.
(No. 28 of 1940)

Consequences supervening or not known at time of former trial

140. A person convicted or acquitted of any act causing consequences which, together with such act, constitute a different offence from that for which such person was convicted or acquitted, may be afterwards tried for such different offence, if the consequences had not happened, or were not known to the court to have happened, at the time when he was acquitted or convicted.

Where original court was not competent to try subsequent charge

141. A person convicted or acquitted of any offence constituted by any acts may, notwithstanding such conviction or acquittal, be subsequently charged with and tried for any other offence constituted by the same acts which he may have committed, if the court by which he was first tried was not competent to try the offence with which he is subsequently charged.

Previous conviction, how proved

142. (1) In any inquiry, trial or other proceeding under this Code, a previous conviction may be proved, in addition to any other mode provided by any law for the time being in force-

(a) by an extract certified, under the hand of the officer having the custody of the records of the court in which such conviction was had, to be a copy of the sentence or order; or

(b) by a certificate signed by the officer in charge of the prison in which the punishment or any part thereof was suffered, or by production of the warrant of commitment under which the punishment was suffered;

together with, in each of such cases, evidence as to the identity of the accused person with the person so convicted.

(2) A certificate in the form prescribed given under the hand of an officer authorised by the *President in that behalf, who shall have compared the fingerprints of an accused person with the fingerprints of a person previously convicted, shall be sufficient evidence of all facts therein set forth provided it is produced by the person who took the fingerprints of the accused.
*Officer in Charge, Fingerprint Department, authorised by Gazette Notice No. 5 of 1964.

(3) A previous conviction in any place outside Zambia may be proved by the production of a certificate purporting to be given under the hand of a police officer in the country where the conviction was had, containing a copy of the sentence or order, and the fingerprints, or photographs of the fingerprints of the person so convicted, together with evidence that the fingerprints of the person so convicted are those of the accused person; such a certificate shall be sufficient evidence of all facts therein set forth without proof that the officer purporting to sign it did in fact sign it and was empowered so to do.

(4) Where a person is convicted by a subordinate court, other than a juvenile court, and it is proved to the satisfaction of the court on oath or in the manner prescribed that, not less than seven days

previously, a notice was served on the accused in the prescribed form and manner specifying any alleged previous conviction of the accused of an offence proposed to be brought to the notice of the court in the event of his conviction of the offence charged, and the accused is not present in person before the court, the court may take account of any such previous conviction so specified as if the accused had appeared and admitted it.

(5)   In this section, "prescribed" means prescribed by rules made by the Chief Justice.

(As amended by No. 4 of 1944, No. 2 of 1960,
No. 5 of 1962 and G.N. No.303 of 1964)

Compelling Attendance of Witnesses

Summons for witness

143. If it is made to appear that material evidence can be given by, or is in the possession of, any person, it shall be lawful for a court having cognizance of any criminal cause or matter to issue a summons to such person requiring his attendance before such court, or requiring him to bring and produce to such court, for the purpose of evidence, all documents and writings in his possession or power, which may be specified or otherwise sufficiently described in the summons.

(As amended by No. 28 of 1940)

Warrant for witness who disobeys summons

144. If, without sufficient excuse, a witness does not appear in obedience to the summons, the court, on proof of the proper service of the summons a reasonable time before, may issue a warrant to bring him before the court at such time and place as shall be therein specified.

Warrant for witness in first instance

145. If the court is satisfied that any person will not attend as a witness unless compelled to do so, it may at once issue a warrant for the arrest and production of such person before the court at a time and place to be therein specified.

Mode of dealing with witness arrested under warrant

146. When any witness is arrested under a warrant, the court may, on his furnishing security by recognizance, to the satisfaction of the court, for his appearance at the hearing of the case, order him to be released from custody, or shall, on his failing to furnish such security, order him to be detained for production at such hearing.

Power of court to order prisoner to be brought up for examination

147. (1)   Any court, desirous of examining as a witness, in any case pending before it, any person confined in any prison within Zambia, may issue an order to the officer in charge of such prison requiring him to bring such prisoner in proper custody, at a time to be named in the order, before the court for examination.

(2)   The officer so in charge, on receipt of such order, shall act in accordance therewith, and shall provide for the safe custody of the prisoner during his absence from the prison for the purpose aforesaid.

Penalty for non-attendance of witness

148. (1)   Any person summoned to attend as a witness who, without lawful excuse, fails to attend as required by the summons, or who, having attended, departs without having obtained the permission of the court, or fails to attend after adjournment of the court, after being ordered to attend, shall be liable, by order of the court, to a fine not exceeding six hundred penalty units.

(2)   Such fine shall be levied by attachment and sale of any movable property belonging to such witness within the local limits of the jurisdiction of such court.

(3)   In default of recovery of the fine by attachment and sale, the witness may, by order of the court, be imprisoned for a term of fifteen days, unless such fine is paid before the end of the said term.

(4)   For good cause shown, the High Court may remit or reduce any fine imposed under this section by a subordinate court.
(As amended by Act No. 13 of 1994)

Examination of Witnesses

Procedure where person charged is called for defence

149. Where the person charged is called by the defence as a witness to the facts of the case or to make a statement without being sworn he shall be heard immediately after the close of the evidence for the prosecution.
(As amended by Act No. 6 of 1972)

Refractory witnesses

150. (1)   Whenever any person, appearing either in obedience to a summons or by virtue of a warrant, or being present in court and being verbally required by the court to give evidence-
    (a)   refuses to be sworn; or
    (b)   having been sworn, refuses to answer any question put to him; or
    (c)   refuses or neglects to produce any document or thing which he is required to produce; or
    (d)   refuses to sign his deposition;
without, in any such case, offering any sufficient excuse for such refusal or neglect, the court may adjourn the case for any period not exceeding eight days and may, in the meantime, commit such person to prison, unless he sooner consents to do what is required of him.

(2)   If such person, upon being brought before the court at or before such adjourned hearing, again refuses to do what is required of him, the court may, if it sees fit, again adjourn the case and commit him for the like period, and so again, from time to time, until such person consents to do what is so required of him.

(3)   Nothing herein contained shall affect the liability of any such person to any other punishment or proceeding for refusing or neglecting to do what is so required of him, or shall prevent the court from disposing of the case in the meantime, according to any other sufficient evidence taken before it.

Cases where wife or husband may be called without consent of accused

151. (1)   In any inquiry or trial, the wife or husband of the person charged shall be a competent witness for the prosecution or defence without the consent of such person-
    (a)   in any case where the wife or husband of a person charged may, under any law in force for the time being, be called as a witness without the consent of such person;
    (b)   in any case where such person is charged with an offence under Chapter XV of the Penal Code or with bigamy;   Cap. 87
    (c)   in any case where such person is charged in respect of an act or omission affecting the person or property of the wife or husband of such person or the children of either of them.

(2)   For the purposes of this section-
    (a)   "wife" and "husband" include the parties to a customary marriage:
    (b)   "customary marriage" includes a union which is regarded as marriage by the community in which the parties live.
(As amended by No. 20 of 1969)

Commissions for the Examination of Witnesses

Issue of commission for examination of witness

152. (1)   Whenever, in the course of any inquiry, trial or other proceeding under this Code, the High Court is satisfied that the examination of a witness is necessary for the ends of justice, and that the attendance of such witness cannot be procured without an amount of delay, expense or inconvenience which, in the circumstances of the case, would be unreasonable, the court may issue a commission to any magistrate, within the local limits of whose jurisdiction such witness resides, to take the evidence of such witness.

(2)   The magistrate to whom the commission is issued shall proceed to the place where the witness is, or shall summon the witness before him, and shall take down his evidence in the same manner and may, for this purpose, exercise the same powers as in the case of a trial.

Parties may examine witness

153. (1)   The parties to any proceeding under this Code in which a commission is issued may respectively forward any interrogatories in writing which the court directing the commission may think relevant to the issue, and the magistrate to whom the commission is directed shall examine the witness upon such interrogatories.

(2)   Any such party may appear before such magistrate by advocate, or, if not in custody, in person, and may examine, cross-examine and re-examine (as the case may be) the said witness.

Power of magistrate to apply for issue of commission

154.   Whenever, in the course of any inquiry, trial or other proceeding under this Code before any magistrate, it appears that a commission ought to be issued for the examination of a witness whose evidence is necessary for the ends of justice, and that the attendance of such witness cannot be procured without an amount of delay, expense or inconvenience which, in the circumstances of the case, would be unreasonable, such magistrate shall apply to the High Court, stating the reasons for the application; and the High Court may either issue a commission, in the manner hereinbefore provided, or reject the application.

Return of commission

155.   After any commission issued under section one hundred and fifty-two or one hundred and fifty-four has been duly executed, it shall be returned, together with the deposition of the witness examined thereunder, to the court in which the case is depending, and the commission, the return thereto, and the deposition shall be open, at all reasonable times, to inspection by the parties, and may, subject to all just exceptions, be read in evidence in the case by either party, and shall form part of the record.

Evidence for Defence

Adjournment of inquiry or trial

156.   In every case in which a commission is issued under section one hundred and fifty-two or one hundred and fifty-four, the inquiry, trial or other proceeding may be adjourned for a specified time reasonably sufficient for the execution and return of the commission.

Competency of accused and husband or wife as witnesses

157.   Every person charged with an offence, and the wife or husband, as the case may be, of the person so charged, shall be a competent witness for the defence at every stage of the proceedings, whether the person so charged is charged solely or jointly with any other person:
Provided that-

Own application

(i)   a person so charged shall not be called as a witness in pursuance of this section, except upon his own application;

No comment if not called as witness

(ii)   the failure of any person charged with an offence or of the wife or husband, as the case may be, of the person so charged, to give evidence shall not be made the subject of any comment by the prosecution;

Spouses

(iii)   the wife or husband of the person charged shall not, save as hereinbefore mentioned, be called as a witness except upon the application of the person so charged;

Communications during marriage

(iv) nothing in this section shall make a husband compellable to disclose any communication made to him by his wife during the marriage, or a wife compellable to disclose any communication made to her by her husband during the marriage;

Cross-examination

(v) a person charged and being a witness in pursuance of this section may be asked any question in cross-examination, notwithstanding that it would tend to criminate him as to the offence charged;

No question to show commission of offence not charged

(vi) a person charged and called as a witness, in pursuance of this section, shall not be asked, and, if asked, shall not be required to answer, any question tending to show that he has committed or been convicted of, or been charged with any offence other than that wherewith he is then charged, or is of bad character, unless-
    (a) the proof that he has committed or been convicted of such other offence is admissible evidence to show that he is guilty of the offence wherewith he is then charged; or
    (b) he has, personally or by his advocate, asked questions of the witnesses for the prosecution with a view to establishing his own good character, or has given evidence of his own good character, or the nature or conduct of the defence is such as to involve imputations on the character of the complainant or the witnesses for the prosecution; or

Exceptions

(c) he has given evidence against any other person charged with the same offence;

Evidence from box

(vii) every person called as a witness in pursuance of this section shall, unless otherwise ordered by the court, give his evidence from the witness box or other place from which the other witnesses have given their evidence;

Statement by person charged

(viii) nothing in this section shall affect the provisions of section two hundred and twenty-eight or any right of the person charged to make a statement without being sworn.

Procedure where person charged is called for defence

158. Where the person charged is called by the defence as a witness to the facts of the case or to make a statement without being sworn, he shall be heard immediately after the close of the evidence for the prosecution.
(No. 6 of 1972)

Completion of proceedings

158A. (1) Where the presiding Judge or Magistrate is, on account of illness, death, relinquishment or cesser of jurisdiction or any other similar cause, unable to deliver a judgment already prepared by him, then the Chief Justice may direct-
    (a) that another Judge of the High Court shall deliver in open court the judgment prepared by the presiding Judge; and
    (b) that another Magistrate of co-ordinate jurisdiction shall deliver in open court the judgment prepared by the presiding Magistrate, in the manner prescribed in subsection (1) of section one hundred and fifty-seven of this Code:
    Provided that in either case the judgment shall be dated and signed by the Judge or Magistrate at the time of delivering it.
    (2) After delivering the judgment under subsection (1), the Judge or the Magistrate, as the case may be, shall complete the proceedings of the case as if he had himself heard and determined the case.

(3)   In any case where a Judge has been appointed whether before or after the commencement of the Criminal Procedure Code (Amendment) Act, 1972, to be or to act as a Justice of Appeal or where a Magistrate has been appointed to be a Magistrate of a higher class or to be or to act as a Judge, he shall complete any proceedings already commenced before him, and for this purpose he shall be deemed to retain the position and powers which he held immediately before his being so appointed.

(4)   Where a Magistrate is transferred to another District he shall complete any proceedings already commenced before him.

(As amended by No. 6 of 1972)

Right of reply

159. In cases where the right of reply depends upon the question whether evidence has been called for the defence the fact that the person charged has been called as a witness shall not of itself confer on the prosecution the right of reply:

Provided that the Director of Public Prosecutions or Solicitor-General, when appearing personally as advocate for the prosecution, shall, in all cases, have the right of reply.

(As amended by S.I. No. 63 of 1964)

Procedure in Case of the Insanity or Other Incapacity of an Accused Person

Question whether accused capable of making his defence

160.   Where on the trial of a person charged with an offence punishable by[6] imprisonment the question arises, at the instance of the defence or otherwise, whether the accused is, by reason of unsoundness of mind or of any other disability, incapable of making a proper defence, the court shall inquire into and determine such question as soon as it arises.

(No. 76 of 1965 as amended by No. 18 of 1966)

Procedure where accused unfit to make his defence

161. (1)   Where a court, in accordance with the provisions of section one hundred and sixty, finds an accused incapable of making a proper defence, it shall enter a plea of "not guilty" if it has not already done so and, to the extent that it has not already done so, shall hear the evidence for the prosecution and (if any) for the defence.

(2)   At the close of such evidence as is mentioned in subsection (1), the court, if it finds that the evidence as it stands-

(a)   would not justify a conviction or a special finding under section one hundred and sixty-seven, shall acquit and discharge the accused; or

(b)   would, in the absence of further evidence to the contrary, justify a conviction, or a special finding under section one hundred and sixty-seven, shall order the accused to be detained during the President's pleasure.

(3)   An acquittal and discharge under subsection (2) shall be without prejudice to any implementation of the provisions of the Mental Disorders Act, and the High Court may, if it considers in any case that an inquiry under the provisions of section nine of that Act is desirable, direct that the person acquitted and discharged be detained and taken before a magistrate for the purpose of such inquiry.

(No. 76 of 1965)   Cap. 305

Procedure following order of detention during President's pleasure

162. (1)   Where an order for the detention of an accused during the President's pleasure is made by a subordinate court-

(a)   the court shall transmit the record or a certified copy thereof to the High Court for confirmation of such order;

(b)   the High Court may, and at the request of the prosecution or defence made within fourteen days of the order of the subordinate court shall, admit additional evidence or hear the prosecution and defence in relation to the disability of the accused; and

(c)   the High Court in dealing with the confirmation of such an order may exercise all or any of the powers which are conferred upon it under Part XI for the purposes of revision.

---

[6] In terms of s 4 of Act No 22 of 2022, [s]ection 160 of the principal Act is amended by the deletion of the words "death or" immediately after the words "punishable by".

(2) Where an order for the detention of an accused during the President's pleasure is made or confirmed by the High Court, the Judge concerned shall submit a written report to the President containing any recommendations or observations on the case which he may think fit to make, together with a certified copy of the record.

(No. 76 of 1965)

Detention during President's pleasure

163. (1) Where under this Code any person is ordered to be detained during the President's pleasure, the order shall be sufficient authority for his detention, until otherwise dealt with under this Code, in any mental institution, prison or other place where facilities exist for the detention of persons, and for his conveyance to that place.

(2) A person ordered under this Code to be detained during the President's pleasure shall be liable to be detained in such place and under such conditions as the President may by order direct, and while so detained shall be in lawful custody.

(3) The officer in charge of the place in which any person is detained during the President's pleasure under this Code shall, at intervals not exceeding six months, submit a report to the President containing the prescribed information in relation to every person so detained in his custody.

(No. 76 of 1965)

Discharge of persons detained during President's pleasure

164. (1) The President may at any time by order discharge from detention any person detained during the President's pleasure and such discharge may be absolute or subject to conditions, and if absolute the order under which he has been detained shall cease to be of effect accordingly.

(2) The President may at any time by order revoke an order of conditional discharge made under subsection (1) and thereupon the person concerned shall be detained during the President's pleasure as though he had never been discharged from detention.

(No. 76 of 1965)

Resumption of trial

165. (1) If on the advice of a medical officer the President, having regard to the requirements of the Constitution, considers that the question of the capacity to make a proper defence of any person detained following an order under section one hundred and sixty-one should be re-examined, he shall by order direct that such person be taken before a court and the court shall inquire into and determine that question.

Cap 1

(2) Where a court, after inquiry under subsection (1), finds the accused capable of making a proper defence, any order under which the accused has been detained during the President's pleasure shall thereupon cease to have effect and the accused shall be called upon to plead to the charge or information and the trial shall commence de novo.

(3) Where a court, after inquiry under subsection (1), finds the accused to be still incapable of making a proper defence, the order under which the accused has been detained during the President's pleasure shall continue to be of force and effect.

(4) For the purposes of an inquiry under subsection (1), a report concerning the capacity of the accused to conduct his defence by the medical officer in charge of the asylum or other place in which the accused has been detained may be read as evidence but without prejudice to the right of the court to summon and examine such medical officer.

(No. 76 of 1965)

Preliminary inquiries

166. The question whether-

(a) while before the subordinate court an accused person is by reason of unsoundness of mind or of any other disability incapable of making a proper defence; or

(b) at the time of the act or omission in respect of which an accused person is charged, such person was by reason of unsoundness of mind incapable of understanding what he was doing, or of knowing that he ought not to do the act or make the omission;

shall not be determined in any preliminary inquiry held under Part VII and, for the purposes of any decision whether an accused should be committed for trial, the accused shall be deemed to have been at all material times free from any such disability.
(No. 76 of 1965)

Defence of insanity at the time of the offence

167. (1) Where an act or omission is charged against any person as an offence, and it is given in evidence on the trial of such person for that offence that he was insane so as not to be responsible for his actions at the time when the act was done or omission made, then, if it appears to the court before which such person is tried that he did the act or made the omission charged but was insane as aforesaid at the time when he did or made the same, the court shall make a special finding to the effect that the accused was not guilty by reason of insanity.

   (2) For the purposes of appeal, whether to the High Court or to the Court of Appeal, a special finding made under subsection (1) shall be deemed to be a conviction.

   (3) Where a special finding is made under subsection (1), the court so finding shall order the person to whom such finding relates to be detained during the President's pleasure.

(No. 76 of 1965)

167A. The provisions of sections one hundred and sixty-three, one hundred and sixty-four, one hundred and sixty-five, one hundred and sixty-six and one hundred and sixty-seven shall apply mutatis mutandis to any person detained during the President's pleasure in terms of an order made under section one hundred and fifty-one of Chapter 7 of the 1965 Edition of the Laws before the *commencement of Act No. 76 of 1965.

* *7th January, 1966. Application to persons detained in terms of orders made under former provisions
(No. 24 of 1970)

Judgment

Mode of delivering judgment

168. (1) The judgment in every trial in a subordinate court shall be pronounced, or the substance of such judgment shall be explained, in open court, either immediately after the termination of the trial or, without undue delay, at some subsequent time, of which notice shall be given to the parties and their advocates, if any:
   Provided that the whole judgment shall be read out by the presiding magistrate, if he is requested so to do, either by the prosecution or the defence.

   (2) The accused person shall, if in custody, be brought up, or, if not in custody, be required by the court to attend, to hear judgment delivered, except where his personal attendance during the trial has been dispensed with, and the sentence is one of fine only, or he is acquitted.

   (3) No judgment delivered by any court shall be deemed to be invalid by reason only of the absence of any party or his advocate on the day or from the place notified for the delivery thereof, or of any omission to serve, or defect in serving, on the parties or their advocates, or any of them, the notice of such day and place.

   (4) Nothing in this section shall be construed to limit, in any way, the provisions of section three hundred and fifty-three.

Contents of judgment

169. (1) The judgment in every trial in any court shall, except as otherwise expressly provided by this Code, be prepared by the presiding officer of the court and shall contain the point or points for determination, the decision thereon and the reasons for the decision, and shall be dated and signed by the presiding officer in open court at the time of pronouncing it.

   (2) In the case of a conviction, the judgment shall specify the offence of which and the section of the Penal Code or other written law under which the accused person is convicted, and the punishment to which he is sentenced.

*7th January, 1966.

(3)   In the case of an acquittal, the judgment shall state the offence of which the accused person is acquitted and shall direct that he be set at liberty.

(No. 28 of 1940 as amended by No. 17 of 1945, No. 5 of 1962 and No. 11 of 1963)

Completion of proceedings

169A. (1) Where the presiding Judge or Magistrate is, on account of illness, death, relinquishment or cesser of jurisdiction or any other similar cause, unable to deliver a judgment already prepared by him, then the Chief Justice may direct-

(a) that another Judge of the High Court shall deliver in open court the judgment prepared by the presiding Judge; and

(b) that another magistrate of co-ordinate jurisdiction shall deliver in open court the judgment prepared by the presiding magistrate, in the manner prescribed in subsection (1) of section one hundred and sixty-eight;

Provided that in either case the judgment shall be dated and signed by the Judge or magistrate at the time of delivering it.

(2) After delivering the judgment under subsection (1), the Judge or magistrate, as the case may be, shall complete the proceedings of the case as if he had himself heard and determined the case.

(3) In any case where a Judge has been appointed, whether before or after the commencement of Act No. 6 of 1972, to be or to act as a Justice of Appeal or where a magistrate has been appointed to be a magistrate of a higher class or to be or to act as a Judge, he shall complete any proceedings already commenced before him, and for this purpose he shall be deemed to retain the position and powers which he held immediately before his being so appointed.

(4) Where a magistrate is transferred to another District, he shall complete any proceedings already commenced before him.

Copy of judgment, etc., to be given to accused on application

170. On the application of the accused person, a copy of the judgment, or, when he so desires, a translation in his own language, if practicable, shall be given to him without delay. Such copy or translation shall be given free of cost.

Entry of judgment where public officer convicted of offence

171. (1) The court before which any person employed in the public service is convicted of a prescribed offence shall enter judgment, and civil jurisdiction is hereby conferred upon it for that purpose, for the amount of the value of the property in respect of which the offence was committed-

(a) in favour of the Attorney-General where such property is the property of the or of any corporation, body or board, including any institutions of higher learning, in which the Government has a majority or controlling interest

(2) No appeal shall lie against a statutory judgment but if, on an appeal against conviction, the appeal is allowed or a conviction for an offence which is not a prescribed offence is substituted, the statutory judgment shall be deemed to have been set aside, but without prejudice to any other right of recovery by way of civil proceedings.

(3) The entering of an appeal against conviction shall not operate as a stay of execution under a statutory judgment, unless the court otherwise orders.

(4) Execution may be levied under a statutory judgment against all or any persons employed in the Public Service jointly charged with and convicted of a prescribed offence, but the total amount levied shall not exceed the amount for which the statutory judgment was entered.

(5) Where a person employed in the public service is convicted of an offence and such person asks the court to take another offence, which is a prescribed offence, into account for the purposes of sentence and the court does so, such person shall, for the purposes of this section, be deemed to have been convicted of such prescribed offence and the court shall enter judgment accordingly as provided in subsection (1).;

(6) In this section, unless the context otherwise requires-

"prescribed offence" means an offence under Chapter XXVI, XXVII, XXX, XXXI or XXXIII of the Penal Code where the property in respect of which the offence is committed is the property of the Government or any corporation, body or board including an institution of learning, in which the Government has a majority or controlling interest or a local authority or is property which comes into the possession of the person employed in the public service by virtue of his employment;

"person employed in the public service" means a person who, at the time of commission of the prescribed offence, was a person employed in the public service as defined in section four of the Penal Code;

"statutory judgment" means a judgment entered in pursuance of the provisions of subsection (1).

(As amended by Act No. 54 of 1968, 12 of 1973, 34 of 1973 and 32 of 1974) Cap. 87

Costs, Compensation and Damages

172. (1)   It shall be lawful for a Judge or a magistrate to order any person convicted before him of an offence to pay such reasonable costs, as to such Judge or magistrate may seem fit, in addition to any other penalty imposed and such costs shall be paid, where the prosecution was in the charge of a public prosecutor, into the general revenues of the Republic, and in any other case to the person by or on behalf of whom the prosecution was instituted. Costs against accused or prosecution

(2)   It shall be lawful for a Judge or a magistrate who acquits or discharges a person accused of an offence to order that such reasonable costs, as to such Judge or magistrate may seem fit, be paid to such person and such costs shall be paid, where the prosecution was in the charge of a public prosecutor, from the general revenues of the Republic, and in any other case by the person by or on behalf of whom the prosecution was instituted:

Provided that no such order shall be made if the Judge or magistrate shall consider that there were reasonable grounds for making the complaint.

(3)   The costs awarded under this section may be awarded in addition to any compensation awarded under section one hundred and seventy-four.

(As amended by No. 5 of 1962 and S.I. No. 63 of 1964)

Order to pay costs appealable

173. An appeal shall lie from any order of a subordinate court awarding costs, under the last preceding section, to the High Court. The appellate court shall have power to give such costs of the appeal as it shall deem reasonable.

Compensation in case of frivolous or vexatious charge

174. If, on the dismissal of any case, any court shall be of opinion that the charge was frivolous or vexatious, such court may order the complainant to pay to the accused person a reasonable sum, as compensation for the trouble and expense to which such person may have been put by reason of such charge, in addition to his costs.

Power of court to order accused to pay compensation

175. (1)   When an accused person is convicted by any court of any offence not punishable with [life imprisonment][7] and it appears from the evidence that some other person, whether or not he is the prosecutor or a witness in the case, has suffered material loss or personal injury in consequence of the offence committed and that substantial compensation is, in the opinion of the court, recoverable by that person by civil suit, such court may, in its discretion and in addition to any other lawful punishment, order the convicted person to pay to that other person such compensation, in kind or in money, as the court deems fair and reasonable:

Provided that in no case shall the amount or value of the compensation awarded exceed fifty kwacha.

(2)   When any person is convicted of any offence under Chapters XXVI to XXXI, both inclusive, of the Penal Code, the power conferred by subsection (1) shall be deemed to include a power to award compensation to any bona fide purchaser of any property in relation to which the offence was committed for the loss of such property if the same is restored to the possession of the person entitled thereto.

(3)   Any order for compensation under this section shall be subject to appeal and no payment of compensation shall be made before the period allowed for presenting the appeal has elapsed or, if an appeal be presented, before the decision of the appeal.

(No. 28 of 1940)

---

[7] As amended by s 5 of Act No 22 of 2022.

Costs and compensation to be specified in order; how recoverable

176. The sums allowed for costs or compensation shall, in all cases, be specified in the conviction or order, and the same shall be recoverable in like manner as any penalty may be recovered under this Code; and, in default of payment of such costs or compensation or of distress as hereinafter provided, the person in default shall be liable to imprisonment with or without hard labour for a term not exceeding three months, unless such costs or compensation shall be sooner paid.

Power of court to award expenses or compensation out of fine

177. (1) Whenever any court imposes a fine, or confirms on appeal, revision or otherwise a sentence of fine, or a sentence of which a fine forms part, the court may, when passing judgment, order the whole or any part of the fine recovered to be applied-
    (a) in defraying expenses properly incurred in the prosecution;
    (b) in the payment to any person of compensation for any loss or injury caused by the offence, when substantial compensation is, in the opinion of the court, recoverable by civil suit.

Compensation recovered to be taken into account in subsequent civil suit

(2) At the time of awarding any compensation in any subsequent civil suit relating to the same matter, the court hearing the civil suit shall take into account any compensation paid or recovered under section one hundred and seventy-five or this section.
(As amended by No. 28 of 1940)

Restitution of Property Wrongful conversion and detention of property

Any damages awarded shall be recoverable as a penalty

178. Where, in a charge of stealing, dishonest receiving or fraudulent conversion, the court shall be of opinion that the evidence is insufficient to support the charge, but that it establishes wrongful conversion or detention of property, such court may order that such property be restored, and may also award damages.

Property found on accused person

179. Where, upon the apprehension of a person charged with an offence, any property is taken from him, the court before which he is charged may order-
    (a) that the property or a part thereof be restored to the person who appears to the court to be entitled thereto, and, if he be the person charged, that it be restored either to him or to such other person as he may direct; or
    (b) that the property or a part thereof be applied to the payment of any fine or any costs or compensation directed to be paid by the person charged.

Stolen property

180. (1) If any person guilty of any offence as is mentioned in Chapters XXVI to XXXI, both inclusive, of the Penal Code, in stealing, taking, extorting, obtaining, converting or disposing of, or in knowingly receiving, any property, is prosecuted to conviction by or on behalf of the owner of such property, the property shall be restored to the owner or his representative.
    Cap. 87
(2) In every case in this section referred to, the court before whom such offender is convicted shall have the power to award, from time to time, writs of restitution for the said property or to order the restitution thereof in a summary manner:
    Provided that nothing in this section shall apply to-
    (i) any valuable security which has been bona fide paid or discharged by any person liable to pay or discharge the same; or
    (ii) any negotiable instrument which shall have been bona fide received by transfer or delivery by any person for a just and valuable consideration without notice, or without reasonable cause to suspect that it has been stolen or dishonestly obtained.
(3) On the restitution of any stolen property, if it appears to the court by the evidence that the offender has sold the stolen property to any person, that such person has had no knowledge that the same was stolen, and that any moneys have been taken from the offender on his apprehension,

the court may, on the application of such purchaser, order that out of such moneys a sum not exceeding the amount of the proceeds of such sale be delivered to the said purchaser.

(4)   The operation of any order under this section shall (unless the court before which the conviction takes place directs to the contrary in any case in which the title to the property is not in dispute) be suspended-

        (a) in any case until the time for appeal has elapsed; and

        (b) in any case where an appeal is lodged, until the final determination of such appeal;

        and in cases where the operation of any such order is suspended until the determination of the appeal, the order shall not take effect as to the property in question if the conviction is quashed on appeal.

(5)   In this section, unless the context otherwise requires, "property" means not only such property as has been originally in the possession or under the control of any person but also any property into or for which the same has been converted or exchanged, and anything which has been acquired by such conversion or exchange, whether immediately or otherwise.

(No. 50 of 1957)

Miscellaneous Provisions

When offence proved is included in offence charged

181. (1)   When a person is charged with an offence consisting of several particulars, a combination of some only of which constitutes a complete minor offence, and such combination is proved but the remaining particulars are not proved, he may be convicted of the minor offence although he was not charged with it.

(2)   When a person is charged with an offence and facts are proved which reduce it to a minor offence, he may be convicted of the minor offence although he was not charged with it.

(No. 28 of 1940)

Person charged with any offence may be convicted of attempt

182. When a person is charged with an offence, he may be convicted of having attempted to commit that offence, although he was not charged with the attempt.

(No. 28 of 1940)

Person charged with treason may be convicted of treason-felony and person charged with treason or treason-felony may be convicted of sedition

183. (1)   Where a person is charged with treason and the facts proved in evidence authorise a conviction for treason-felony and not for treason, he may be convicted of treason-felony although he was not charged with that offence.

(2)   Where a person is charged with treason or treason-felony and the facts proved in evidence authorise a conviction for sedition and not for treason or treason-felony, as the case may be, he may be convicted of sedition although he was not charged with that offence.

(No. 6 of 1965)

Alternative verdicts in various offences involving the homicide of children

184. (1)   When a woman is charged with the murder of her child, being a child under the age of twelve months, and the court is of opinion that she, by any wilful act or omission, caused its death but at the time of the act or omission she had not fully recovered from the effect of giving birth to such child and that by reason thereof or by reason of the effect of lactation consequent upon the birth of the child the balance of her mind was then disturbed, she may, notwithstanding that the circumstances were such that but for the provisions of section two hundred and three of the Penal Code she might be convicted of murder, be convicted of the offence of infanticide although she was not charged with it.   Cap. 87

(2)   When a person is charged with the murder or manslaughter of any child or with infanticide, or with an offence under section one hundred and fifty-one or one hundred and fifty-two of the Penal Code (relating to the procuring of abortion), and the court is of opinion that he is not guilty of murder, manslaughter or infanticide or of an offence under section one hundred and fifty-one or one hundred and fifty-two of the Penal Code but that he is guilty of the offence of child destruction, he may be convicted of that offence although he was not charged with it. Cap. 87

(3)   When a person is charged with the offence of child destruction and the court is of opinion that he is not guilty of that offence but that he is guilty of an offence under either section one hundred and fifty-one or one hundred and fifty-two of the Penal Code, he may be convicted of that offence although he was not charged with it.   Cap. 87

(4)   When a person is charged with the murder or infanticide of any child or with child destruction and the court is of opinion that he is not guilty of any of the said offences but that he is guilty of the offence of concealment of birth, he may be convicted of the offence of concealment of birth although he was not charged with it.

(No. 28 of 1940)

Person charged with manslaughter in connection with the driving of a motor vehicle may be convicted of reckless or dangerous driving

185. When a person is charged with manslaughter in connection with the driving of a motor vehicle by him and the court is of the opinion that he is not guilty of that offence, but that he is guilty of an offence under [section one hundred and fifty-four and one hundred and fifty-five of the Road Traffic Act] (relating to reckless or dangerous driving), or under any written law in substitution therefor, he may be convicted of that offence although he was not charged with it.

(No. 28 of 1940)   [Act No 11 of 2002]

Alternative verdicts in charges of rape and kindred offences.

186. (1)   When a person is charged with rape and the court is of opinion that he is not guilty of that offence but that he is guilty of an offence under one of sections one hundred and thirty-seven, one hundred and thirty-eight, one hundred and forty-one and one hundred and fifty-nine of the Penal Code, he may be convicted of that offence although he was not charged with it. Cap. 87

(2)   When a person is charged with an offence under section one hundred and fifty-nine of the Penal Code and the court is of opinion that he is not guilty of that offence but that he is guilty of an offence under one of the sections one hundred and thirty-eight and one hundred and thirty-nine of the Penal Code, he may be convicted of that offence although he was not charged with it. Cap. 87

(3)   When a person is charged with the defilement of a girl under the age of sixteen years and the court is of opinion that he is not guilty of that offence but that he is guilty of an offence under subsection (1) or (3) of section one hundred and thirty-seven of the Penal Code, he may be convicted of that offence although he was not charged with it.

(No. 28 of 1940) Cap. 87

Person charged with burglary, etc., may be convicted of kindred offence.

187. When a person is charged with an offence under one of sections three hundred and one to three hundred and five of the Penal Code and the court is of opinion that he is not guilty of that offence but that he is guilty of any other offence under another of the said sections, he may be convicted of that other offence although he was not charged with it: Cap. 87

Provided that, in such case, the punishment imposed shall not exceed the maximum punishment which may be imposed for the offence with which the accused was charged.

(No. 28 of 1940)

Alternative verdicts in charges of stealing and kindred offences.

188. (1)   When a person is charged with stealing anything and-

    (a)   the facts proved amount to an offence under subsection (1) of section three hundred and eighteen of the Penal Code, he may be convicted of the offence under that section although he was not charged with it; Cap. 87

    (b)   it is proved that he obtained the thing in any such manner as would amount, under the provisions of the Penal Code, to obtaining it by false pretences with intent to defraud, he may be convicted of the offence of obtaining it by false pretences although he was not charged with it;

    (c)   the facts proved amount to an offence under section three hundred and nineteen of the Penal Code, he may be convicted of the offence under that section although he was not charged with it. Cap. 87

(2)   When a person is charged with obtaining anything capable of being stolen by false pretences with intent to defraud, and it is proved that he stole the thing, he may be convicted of the offence of stealing although he was not charged with it.

(No. 28 of 1940 as amended by No. 47 of 1955)

Construction of sections 181 to 188

189. The provisions of sections one hundred and eighty-one to one hundred and eighty-eight shall be construed as in addition to, and not in derogation of, the provisions of any other Act and the other provisions of this Code, and the provisions of sections one hundred and eighty-two to one hundred and eighty-eight shall be construed as being without prejudice to the generality of the provisions of section one hundred and eighty-one. (No. 28 of 1940)

Person charged with misdemeanour not to be acquitted if felony proved

190. If, on any trial for misdemeanour, the facts proved in evidence amount to a felony, the accused shall not be therefore entitled to be acquitted of such misdemeanour; and no person tried for such misdemeanour shall be liable afterwards to be prosecuted for felony on the same facts, unless the court before which such trial may be had shall think fit, in its discretion, to discharge such person in respect of the misdemeanour and to direct such person to be prosecuted for felony, whereupon such person may be dealt with as if not previously put on trial for misdemeanour.

PART V
MODE OF TAKING AND RECORDING EVIDENCE IN INQUIRIES AND TRIALS

Evidence to be taken in presence of accused

191. Except as otherwise expressly provided, all evidence taken in any inquiry or trial under this Code shall be taken in the presence of the accused, or, when his personal attendance has been dispensed with, in the presence of his advocate (if any).

(No. 33 of 1972)

Reports by medical officers in public service

191A. (1) The contents of any document purporting to be a report under the hand of a medical officer employed in the public service upon any matter relevant to the issue in any criminal proceedings shall be admitted in evidence in such proceedings to prove the matters stated therein:
Provided that-
(i)   the court in which any such report is adduced in evidence may, in its discretion, cause the medical officer to be summoned to give oral evidence in such proceedings or may cause written interrogatories approved by the court to be submitted to him for reply, and such interrogatories and any reply thereto purporting to be a reply from such person shall likewise be admissible in evidence in such proceedings;
(ii)   at the request of the accused, made not less than seven days before the trial, such witness shall be summoned to give oral evidence.

(2)   The court may presume that the signature on any such report is genuine and that the person signing it held the office and qualifications which he professed to hold as appearing in the report at the time when he signed it.

(3)   Nothing in this section contained shall be deemed to affect any provision of any written law under which any certificate or other document is made admissible in evidence, and the provisions of this section shall be deemed to be additional to, and not in substitution of, any such provision.

(4)   For the purposes of this section, the expression "medical officer" shall mean a medical practitioner registered as such under the Medical and Allied Professions Act.

(No. 33 of 1972) Cap. 297

Evidence of analyst

192. (1) Whenever any fact ascertained by any examination or process requiring chemical or bacteriological skill is or may become relevant to the issue in any criminal proceedings, a document purporting to be an affidavit relating to any such examination or process shall, if purporting to have been

made by any person qualified to carry out such examination or process, who has ascertained any such fact by means of any such examination or process, be admissible in evidence in such proceedings to prove the matters stated therein:

Provided that-

    (i)   the court in which any such document is adduced in evidence may, in its discretion, cause such person to be summoned to give oral evidence in such proceedings or may cause written interrogatories to be submitted to him for reply, and such interrogatories and any reply thereto purporting to be a reply from such person shall likewise be admissible in evidence in such proceedings;

    (ii)   at the request of the accused, made not less than seven days before the trial, such witness shall be summoned to give oral evidence.

(2)   Nothing in this section contained shall be deemed to affect any provision of any written law under which any certificate or other document is made admissible in evidence, and the provisions of this section shall be deemed to be additional to, and not in substitution of, any such provision.

(No. 1 of 1936 as amended by No. 11 of 1963)

Evidence of photographic process

193. Where any photograph is or may become relevant to the issue in any criminal proceedings, a document purporting to be an affidavit made by the person who processed such photograph shall be admissible in evidence in any such proceedings as proof of such processing:

Provided that the court in which any such document is produced may, if it thinks fit, summon such person to give evidence orally.

(No. 50 of 1957)

Evidence of plans, theft of postal matters and goods in transit on railways

194. (1)   In any criminal proceedings, a certificate purporting to be signed by a police officer or any other person authorised under rules made in that behalf by the Chief Justice, by statutory instrument, and certifying that a plan or drawing exhibited thereto is a plan or drawing made by him of the place or object specified in the certificate and that the plan or drawing is correctly drawn to a scale so specified and clearly indicates, where applicable, the direction of North in relation to the places or objects depicted thereon, shall be evidence of the relative positions of the things shown on the plan or drawing.

(2)   In any proceedings for an offence consisting of the stealing of goods in the possession of the Zambia Railways, or receiving or retaining goods so stolen knowing them to have been stolen, or for the theft of postal matter under the Penal Code, or for an offence under the Postal Services Act, a statutory declaration made by any person- Cap. 470

    (a)   that he despatched or received or failed to receive any goods or postal packet or that any goods or postal packet when despatched or received by him were in a particular state or condition; or

    (b)   that a vessel, vehicle or aircraft was at any time employed by or under the Postmaster-General for the transmission of postal packets under contract;

    shall be admissible as evidence of the facts stated in the declaration.

(3)   Nothing in this section shall be deemed to make a certificate or statutory declaration admissible as evidence in proceedings for an offence except in a case where and to the extent to which oral evidence to the like effect would have been admissible in those proceedings.

(4)   Nothing in this section shall be deemed to make a certificate or any plan or drawings exhibited thereto or a statutory declaration admissible as evidence in proceedings for any offence-

    (a)   unless a copy thereof has, not less than seven days before the hearing or trial, been served on the person charged with the offence; or

    (b)   if that person, not later than three days before the hearing or trial or within such further time as the court may in special circumstances allow, serves notice in writing on the prosecutor requiring the attendance at the trial of the person who signed the certificate or the person by whom the declaration was made, as the case may be; or

    (c)   if the court before whom the said proceedings are brought requires the attendance at the trial of the person who signed the certificate or the person by whom the declaration was made, as the case may be.

(No. 16 of 1959)

Interpretation of evidence to accused or his advocate

195. (1) Whenever any evidence is given in a language not understood by the accused, and he is present in person, it shall be interpreted to him in open court in a language understood by him.

(2) If he appears by advocate, and the evidence is given in a language other than the English language, and not understood by the advocate, it shall be interpreted to such advocate in the English language.

(3) When documents are put in for the purpose of formal proof, it shall be in the discretion of the court to cause to be interpreted as much thereof as appears necessary.

Remarks respecting demeanour of witness

196. A magistrate shall record the sex and approximate age of each witness, and may also record such remarks (if any) as he thinks material respecting the demeanour of any witness whilst under examination.

PART VI
PROCEDURE IN TRIALS BEFORE SUBORDINATE COURTS

Provisions Relating to the Hearing and Determination of Cases

Trials in subordinate courts

197. (1) All trials in subordinate courts shall be held before a magistrate sitting alone, or before a magistrate sitting with the aid of assessors (if the presiding magistrate so decides), the number of whom shall be two or more, as the court thinks fit:
Provided always that every trial on a charge of treason or murder in a subordinate court shall be held with the aid of assessors, if assessors are procurable therefor.

(2) Where an accused person has been committed for trial before the High Court, and the case has been transferred by the High Court for trial before a subordinate court, such of the provisions of Parts VII and IX as are applicable shall, with all necessary modifications and alterations, apply to such trial before such subordinate court:
Provided that-
(i) no provisions relating to the inclusion of a count charging a previous conviction in an information shall be deemed applicable to such trial before such subordinate court;
(ii) the recognizances of witnesses bound to appear and give evidence at such trial before the High Court shall be deemed, for all purposes, to have been executed as if the obligations to attend the High Court had included attendance at any court to which the case might be transferred.

Trials with assessors

198. If a trial is held in a subordinate court with the aid of assessors, all the provisions in this Code contained as to a trial with assessors in the High Court shall apply, so far as the same are applicable, to a trial held with assessors in a subordinate court.

Non-appearance of complainant at hearing

199. If, in any case which a subordinate court has jurisdiction to hear and determine, the accused person appears in obedience to the summons served upon him at the time and place appointed in the summons for the hearing of the case or is brought before court under arrest, then, if the complainant, having had notice of the time and place appointed for the hearing of the charge, does not appear, the court shall dismiss the charge, unless, for some reason, it shall think it proper to adjourn the hearing of the case until some other date, upon such terms as it shall think fit, in which event it may, pending such adjourned hearing, either admit the accused to bail or remand him to prison, or take such security for his appearance as the court shall think fit.
(As amended by No. 28 of 1940)

Appearance of both parties

200. If, at the time appointed for the hearing of the case, both the complainant and the accused person appear before the court which is to hear and determine the charge, or if the complainant appears and the personal attendance of the accused person has been dispensed with under section ninety-nine, the court shall proceed to hear the case.

Withdrawal of complaint

201. If a complainant, at any time before a final order is passed in any case under this Part, satisfies the court that there are sufficient grounds for permitting him to withdraw his complaint, the court may permit him to withdraw the same, and shall, thereupon, acquit the accused.

Adjournment

202. Before or during the hearing of any case, it shall be lawful for the court, in its discretion, to adjourn the hearing to a certain time and place, to be then appointed and stated in the presence and hearing of the party or parties or their respective advocates then present, and, in the meantime, the court may suffer the accused person to go at large, or may commit him to prison, or may release him, upon his entering into a recognizance, with or without sureties, at the discretion of the court, conditioned for his appearance at the time and place to which such hearing or further hearing shall be adjourned:

Provided that no such adjournment shall be for more than thirty clear days, or, if the accused person has been committed to prison, for more than fifteen clear days, the day following that on which the adjournment is made being counted as the first day.

(As amended by No. 5 of 1962)

Non-appearance of parties after adjournment

203. (1) If, at the time or place to which the hearing or further hearing shall be adjourned, the accused person shall not appear before the court which shall have made the order of adjournment, it shall be lawful for such court, unless the accused person is charged with felony, to proceed with the hearing or further hearing, as if the accused were present, and, if the complainant shall not appear, the court may dismiss the charge, with or without costs, as the court shall think fit.

(2) If the court convicts the accused person in his absence, it may set aside such conviction, upon being satisfied that the cause of his absence was reasonable, and that he had a reasonable defence on the merits.

(3) Any sentence passed under subsection (1) shall be deemed to commence from the date of apprehension subsequent to judgment, and the person effecting such apprehension shall endorse the date thereof on the back of the warrant of commitment.

(4) If the accused person who has not appeared as aforesaid is charged with felony, or if the court, in its discretion, refrains from convicting the accused in his absence, the court shall issue a warrant for the apprehension of the accused person and cause him to be brought before the court.

Accused to be called upon to plead

204. (1) The substance of the charge or complaint shall be stated to the accused person by the court, and he shall be asked whether he admits or denies the truth of the charge:

Provided that where the charge or complaint contains a count charging the accused person with having been previously convicted of any offence, the procedure prescribed by section two hundred and seventy-five shall, mutatis mutandis, be applied.

(2) If the accused person admits the truth of the charge, his admission shall be recorded, as nearly as possible, in the words used by him, and the court shall convict him and pass sentence upon or make an order against him, unless there shall appear to it sufficient cause to the contrary.

(3) If the accused person does not admit the truth of the charge, the court shall proceed to hear the case as hereinafter provided.

(4) If the accused person refuses to plead, the court shall order a plea of "not guilty" to be entered for him.

(As amended by No. 50 of 1957)

Procedure on plea of "not guilty"

205. (1) If the accused person does not admit the truth of the charge, the court shall proceed to hear the complainant and his witnesses and other evidence, if any.

(2)   The accused person or his advocate may put questions to each witness produced against him.

(3)   If the accused person does not employ an advocate, the court shall, at the close of the examination of each witness for the prosecution, ask the accused person whether he wishes to put any questions to that witness, and shall record his answer.

Acquittal

206. If, at the close of the evidence in support of the charge, it appears to the court that a case is not made out against the accused person sufficiently to require him to make a defence, the court shall dismiss the case, and shall forthwith acquit him.

(As amended by No. 2 of 1960)

The defence

207. (1)   At the close of the evidence in support of the charge, if it appears to the court that a case is made out against the accused person sufficiently to require him to make a defence, the court shall again explain the substance of the charge to the accused and shall inform him that he has the right to give evidence on his own behalf and that, if he does so, he will be liable to cross-examination, or to make a statement not on oath from the dock, and shall ask him whether he has any witnesses to examine or other evidence to adduce in his defence, and the court shall then hear the accused and his witnesses and other evidence, if any.

(2)   If the accused person states that he has witnesses to call, but that they are not present in court, and the court is satisfied that the absence of such witnesses is not due to any fault or neglect of the accused person, and that there is likelihood that they could, if present, give material evidence on behalf of the accused person, the court may adjourn the trial and issue process, or take other steps, to compel the attendance of such witnesses.

(As amended by No. 28 of 1940 and No. 5 of 1962)

Defence

208. Unless the only witness to the facts of the case called by the defence is the accused, the accused person or his advocate may then open his case, stating the facts or law on which he intends to rely, and making such comments as he thinks necessary on the evidence for the prosecution. If an accused person wishes to give evidence or to make an unsworn statement on his own behalf, he shall do so first, and thereafter he or his advocate may examine his witnesses, and, after their cross-examination and re-examination, if any, may sum up his case.

(No. 16 of 1959 as amended by No. 6 of 1972)

Procedure where defence calls no witnesses other than accused

209. (1)   If the only witness to the facts of the case called by the defence is the accused, or if the accused elects to make an unsworn statement without calling any witnesses, the accused shall forthwith give his evidence or make his unsworn statement, as the case may be.

(2)   At the conclusion of such evidence or unsworn statement, the prosecutor shall then have the right to sum up the case against the accused.

(3)   The court shall then call on the accused person personally or by his advocate to address the court on his behalf.

(No. 16 of 1959)

Evidence reply

210. If the accused person adduces evidence in his defence introducing new matter which the advocate for the prosecution could not by the exercise of reasonable diligence have foreseen, the court may allow the advocate for the prosecution to adduce evidence in reply to contradict the said matter.

(No. 16 of 1959)

Prosecutor's reply

211. If the accused person, or any one of several accused persons, adduces any evidence through any witness other than himself, the prosecutor shall be entitled to reply.

(No. 16 of 1959)

Where the accused person does not give evidence or make unsworn statement

212. If the accused person says that he does not mean to give or adduce evidence or make an unsworn statement, and the court considers that there is evidence that he committed the offence, the advocate for the prosecution may then sum up the case against the accused person, and the court shall then call upon the accused person personally or by his advocate to address the court on his own behalf.
(No. 16 of 1959)

Variance between charge and evidence and amendment of charge

213. (1) Where, at any stage of a trial before the accused is required to make his defence, it appears to the court that the charge is defective either in substance or in form, the court may, save as in section two hundred and six otherwise provided, make such order for the alteration of the charge, either by way of amendment of the charge or by the substitution or addition of a new charge, as the court thinks necessary to meet the circumstances of the case:
Provided that, where a charge is altered under this subsection-
    (i) the court shall thereupon call upon the accused person to plead to the altered charge;
    (ii) the accused may demand that the witnesses, or any of them, be recalled and give their evidence afresh or be further cross-examined by the accused or his advocate and, in such last-mentioned event, the prosecution shall have the right to re-examine any such witness on matters arising out of such further cross-examination.

    (2) Variance between the charge and the evidence adduced in support of it with respect to the time at which the alleged offence was committed is not material and the charge need not be amended for such variance if it is proved that the proceedings were in fact instituted within the time (if any) limited by law for the institution thereof.

    (3) Where an alteration of a charge is made under subsection (1) or there is a variance between the charge and the evidence as described in subsection (2), the court shall, if it is of the opinion that the accused has been thereby misled or deceived, adjourn the trial for such period as may be reasonably necessary.
(No. 28 of 1940 as amended by No. 76 of 1965)

The decision

214. The court, having heard both the complainant and the accused person and their witnesses and evidence, shall either convict the accused and pass sentence upon or make an order against him, according to law, or shall acquit him.
(As amended by No. 28 of 1940)

Drawing up of conviction or order

215. The conviction or order may, if required, be afterwards drawn up, and shall be signed by the court making the conviction or order, or by the clerk or other officer of the court.

Order of acquittal bar to further proceedings

216. The production of a copy of an order of acquittal, certified by the clerk or other officer of the court, shall, unless the acquittal has been set aside by a competent court, without other proof, be a bar to any subsequent information or complaint for the same matter against the same accused person.
(As amended by No. 2 of 1960)

Committal to High Court for sentence

217. (1) Where, on the trial by a subordinate court of an offence, a person who is of not less than the apparent age of seventeen years is convicted of the offence, and the court is of opinion that his character and antecedents are such that greater punishment should be inflicted for the offence than that court has power to inflict, or if it appears to the court that the offence is one in respect whereof a mandatory minimum punishment is provided by law which is greater than that court has power to inflict, it may, after recording its reasons in writing on the record of the case, commit such person to the High Court for sentence, instead of dealing with him in any other manner in which it has power to deal with him.

(2) For the purposes of this section, the aggregate of consecutive sentences which might be imposed by the subordinate court upon any person in respect of convictions for other offences joined in the charge of the offence referred to in subsection (1) shall be deemed to be the sentence which could be imposed for such last-mentioned offence.

(No. 26 of 1956 as amended by No. 2 of 1960, 12 of 1973 and 28 of 1979)

Procedure on committal for sentence

218. (1) In any case where a subordinate court commits a person for sentence under the provisions of section two hundred and seventeen, the subordinate court shall forthwith send a copy of the record of the case to the High Court.

(2) Any person committed to the High Court for sentence shall be brought before the High Court at the first convenient opportunity.

(3) When any person is brought before the High Court in accordance with the provisions of subsection (2), the High Court shall proceed as if he had been convicted on trial by the High Court.

(As amended by no 26 of 1956, 16 of 1959, 2 of 1960, 5 of 1962 and Act 12 of 1973)

Limitations and Exceptions Relating to Trials before

Subordinate Courts

Limitation of time for summary trials in certain cases

219. Except where a longer time is specially allowed by law, no offence, the maximum punishment for which does not exceed imprisonment for six months and/or a fine of one thousand and five hundred penalty units, shall be triable by a subordinate court, unless the charge or complaint relating to it is laid within twelve months from the time when the matter of such charge or complaint arose.

(As amended by Act No. 13 of 1994)

Procedure in case of offence unsuitable for summary trial

220. (1) If, before or during the course of a trial before a subordinate court, it appears to the magistrate that the case is one which ought to be tried by the High Court or if, before the commencement of the trial, an application in that behalf is made by a public prosecutor acting on the instructions of the Director of Public Prosecutions that it shall be so tried, the magistrate shall not proceed with the trial but in lieu thereof he shall hold a preliminary inquiry in accordance with the provisions hereinafter contained, and in such case the provisions of section two hundred and thirty-two shall not apply.

(2) Where, in the course of a trial, the magistrate has stopped the proceedings under the provisions of subsection (1), it shall, in the case of any witness whose statement has already been taken, be sufficient compliance with the provisions of section two hundred and twenty-four if the statement is read over to the witness and is signed by him and by the magistrate:

Provided that the accused person shall, if he so wishes, be entitled to a further opportunity for cross-examining such witness.

(No. 2 of 1960 as amended by S.I. No. 63 of 1964)

Payment by accused persons of fines which may be imposed for minor offences without appearing in court

221. (1) When any person is summoned to appear before a subordinate court or is arrested or informed by a police officer that proceedings will be instituted against him, then-

(a) if the offence in respect of which the summons is issued, the arrest made or the proceedings are to be instituted is punishable by-

(i) a fine not exceeding one thousand and five hundred penalty units or imprisonment in default of payment of such fine; or

(ii) a fine not exceeding one thousand and five hundred penalty units or imprisonment not exceeding six months; or

(iii) a fine not exceeding one thousand and five hundred penalty units or imprisonment not exceeding six months, or both;

or is an offence specified by the Chief Justice, by statutory notice, has been an offence to which the provisions of this section shall apply; and

(b) if such person has been served with a concise statement, in such form as may be prescribed by the Chief Justice, of the facts constituting and relating to the offence in respect of which the summons is issued, the arrest made or the proceedings are to be instituted;

such person may, before appearing in court to answer the charge against him, sign and deliver to the prescribed officer a document, in such form as may be prescribed by the Chief Justice (in this section called an "Admission of Guilt Form") admitting that he is guilty of the offence charged; and

(c) if such person forthwith-

    (i) deposits with the prescribed officer the maximum amount of the fine which may be imposed by the court or such lesser sum as may be fixed by such officer; or

    (ii) furnishes to the prescribed officer such security, by way of deposit of property, as may be approved by such officer for the payment within one month of any fine which may be imposed by the court;

such person shall not be required to appear in court to answer the charge made against him unless the court, for reasons to be recorded in writing, shall otherwise order. The appearance in court of such person may be enforced by summons, or if necessary, by warrant.

(2) A copy of the aforesaid concise statement of facts and the Admission of Guilt Form signed and delivered as aforesaid shall forthwith be transmitted by the prescribed officer to the court before which such person would otherwise have been required to appear and may be entered by the court in the court records.

(3) A person who has signed and delivered an Admission of Guilt Form may, at any time before the fixed day, transmit to the clerk of the court-

(a) an intimation in writing purporting to be given by him or on his behalf that he wishes to withdraw the Admission of Guilt Form aforesaid; or

(b) in writing, any submission which he wishes to be brought to the attention of the court with a view to mitigation of sentence.

(4) On receipt of an intimation of withdrawal transmitted under the provisions of subsection (3), the clerk of the court shall forthwith inform the prosecutor thereof.

(5) On the fixed day the court may adjourn the hearing in accordance with the provisions of this Code or may proceed to hear and dispose of the case in open court in accordance with such one of the following procedures as is appropriate:

(a) If the accused person has not withdrawn the Admission of Guilt Form aforesaid, the court shall cause the charge as stated therein and the statement of facts aforesaid and any written submission in mitigation received in accordance with the provisions of subsection (3) to be read out in court and shall then proceed to judgment in accordance with law as if such person had appeared and pleaded guilty:

Provided that the accused person, or his advocate, if no submission in mitigation as aforesaid has been received by the clerk of court, shall be entitled to address the court in mitigation before sentence is passed on him.

(b) If the accused person has withdrawn the admission of guilt and appears in court, the court shall immediately, or after any such adjournment as the court may think fit, try the offence alleged to have been committed, in accordance with the provisions of this Code as if this section had not been passed.

(c) If the accused person has withdrawn his admission of guilt and does not appear in court, the court shall thereupon issue a summons commanding the attendance of the accused person before the court, which shall, on the date stated on the summons, inquire into and try the offence alleged to have been committed, in accordance with the provisions of this Code as if this section had not been passed.

(6) On the trial of an accused person who has withdrawn his admission of guilt, the court shall not permit any evidence to be led or any cross-examination of such accused person in any way relating to his Admission of Guilt Form.

(7) (a) If payment of the fine imposed has not been made in accordance with the terms of the security given under paragraph (c) (ii) of subsection (1), the property so deposited may be sold and the fine paid out of the proceeds of such sale.

(b) If the sum of money deposited under paragraph (c) (i) of subsection (1) or the proceeds of a sale of property effected under paragraph (a) of this subsection be not sufficient to pay the fine imposed the balance of the fine remaining due shall be recovered from the convicted person in the manner provided by section three hundred and eight.

(c) Any balance remaining of the sum of money deposited under paragraph (c) (i) of subsection (1) or of the proceeds of a sale of property effected under paragraph (a) of this subsection after the deduction of the amount of any fine imposed shall be paid over to the accused person, and, in any case where no fine is imposed, the whole of such sum shall be paid over or the property deposited shall be returned to the accused person.

(d) Where an accused person in respect of whom a summons has been issued in accordance with paragraph (c) of subsection (5) is not found and is not served with the summons as aforesaid within twenty-eight days from the date of issue of the summons, the court shall, upon the application of the person having custody of the money or security deposited, order the sum of money deposited under paragraph (c) (i) of subsection (1) or the property deposited by way of security under paragraph (c) (ii) of subsection (1) to be forfeited and, in the case of property deposited as aforesaid, to be sold.

(8) For the purposes of this section, the "prescribed officer" shall be any police officer of or above the rank of Sub-Inspector and "fixed day" means the day stated in the Admission of Guilt Form for the appearance of the accused before the court.

(9) (a) Subject to the provisions of paragraph (b), no punishment other than a fine shall be imposed on any person convicted under this section.

(b) Where an accused person is, under the provisions of this section, convicted of an offence under [the Roads Traffic Act], the court may, in addition to any fine imposed, exercise the powers of suspension, cancellation, disqualifying and endorsement conferred upon courts by the said Act. [Act No 11 of 2002]

(c) Any fee paid into court, under paragraph (b), as a fine, in respect of a road traffic offence under the Roads Traffic Act, shall be paid into the general revenues of the Republic. [Act No 11 of 2002]

(10) The provisions of this section shall not apply-

(a) where the accused person is a juvenile within the meaning of the Juveniles Act; or Cap. 53

(b) in respect of such offences or classes of offence as the Chief Justice may specify by statutory notice.

(No. 16 of 1959 as amended by No. 2 of 1960, No. 27 of 1964, No. 6 of 1972, Act No. 13 of 1994 and Act No. 5 of 1997)

PART VII
PROVISIONS RELATING TO THE COMMITTAL OF ACCUSED PERSONS FOR TRIAL BEFORE THE HIGH COUR

Preliminary Inquiry by Subordinate Courts

Power to commit for trial

222. Any magistrate empowered to hold a subordinate court of the first, second or third class may commit any person for trial to the High Court.

Court to hold preliminary inquiry

223. (1) Whenever any charge has been brought against any person of an offence not triable by a subordinate court, or as to which the High Court has given an order or direction under section ten or eleven, or as to which the subordinate court is of opinion that it is not suitable to be disposed of upon summary trial, a preliminary inquiry shall be held, according to the provisions hereinafter contained, by a subordinate court, locally and otherwise competent.

(2) Notwithstanding anything to the contrary contained in this Code or any other written law, any person who could have been joined in one charge under section one hundred and twenty-seven B with a person who has been committed to the High Court for trial, but was not so joined, may be joined in an information by the Director of Public Prosecutions-

        (a)   if such person could not be found before the completion of the preliminary inquiry held under this Part; or

        (b)   it is discovered after the completion of the preliminary inquiry that such person could have been joined in the charge brought against the person so committed.

(3)   A copy of the information referred to in subsection (3) signed by the Director of Public Prosecutions shall be sufficient authority for any subordinate court before which such other person or persons appear or have appeared to discontinue any proceedings in respect of such person and to either admit them to bail or send them to prison for safe-keeping until the trial before the High Court.

(4)   Where any person has been joined in an information under subsection (3) the prosecution shall, not less than twenty-one clear days before the date fixed for trial of the case, furnish to him or to his legal practitioner-

        (a)   if his co-accused was committed under section two hundred and nine, a copy of the depositions taken in respect of his co-accused together with a copy of the statements of any additional evidence which it is intended to adduce at the trial whether from witnesses who appeared at the preliminary inquiry or from further witnesses;

        (b)   if his co-accused was committed under section two hundred and thirty-one C, a list of the persons whom it is intended to call as witnesses for the prosecution at the trial and a statement of the evidence of each witness which it is intended to adduce at the trial;

        (c)   in either of the cases mentioned in paragraph (a) or (b), and if so requested, a translation of the depositions or statements in a language which such person appears to understand: Provided that the Court may, upon such conditions as it may determine, permit the prosecution to call a witness, whose name does not appear as a deponent or witness, to give evidence.

(As amended by Act No. 6 of 1972)

Depositions

224. (1)   When the accused person charged with an offence referred to in the last preceding section comes before a subordinate court, on summons or warrant or otherwise, the court shall cause the charge to be read over to the accused person, and shall, in his presence, take down in writing, or cause to be so taken down, the statements on oath of those who know the facts and circumstances of the case. Statements of witnesses so taken down in writing are termed depositions.

     (2)   The accused person may put questions to each witness produced against him, and the answer of the witness thereto shall form part of such witness's depositions.

     (3)   If the accused person does not employ an advocate, the court shall, at the close of the examination of each witness for the prosecution, as the accused person whether he wishes to put any questions to that witness.

     (4)   The deposition of each witness shall be read over to such witness, and shall be signed by him and by the magistrate holding the inquiry.

How certain documents proved

225. At any preliminary inquiry under this Part, any document, purporting to be a report under the hand of a medical officer or a Government analyst upon any examination or analysis carried out by him, shall, if it bears his signature, be admitted in evidence, unless the court shall have reason to doubt the genuineness of such signature.

Variance between evidence and charge

226. No objection to a charge, summons or warrant for defect in substance or in form, or for variance between it and the evidence of the prosecution, shall be allowed; but, if any variance appears to the court to be such that the accused person has been thereby deceived or misled, the court may, on the application of the accused person, adjourn the inquiry, and allow any witness to be recalled, and such questions to be put to him as, by reason of the terms of the charge, may have been omitted.

Remand

227. (1)   If, from the absence of witnesses or any other reasonable cause, to be recorded in the proceedings, the court considers it necessary or advisable to adjourn the inquiry, the court may, from time to time, by warrant, remand the accused for a reasonable time, not exceeding fifteen days at any

one time, to some prison or other place of security. Or, if the remand is for not more than three days, the court may, by word of mouth, order the officer or person in whose custody the accused person is, or any other fit officer or person, to continue to keep the accused in his custody, and to bring him up at the time appointed for the commencement or continuance of the inquiry.

(2) During a remand the court may, at any time, order the accused to be brought before it.

(3) The court may, on a remand, admit the accused to bail.

Provisions as to taking statement or evidence of accused person

228. (1) If, after examination of the witnesses called on behalf of the prosecution, the court considers that, on the evidence as it stands, there are sufficient grounds for committing the accused for trial, the magistrate shall frame a charge under his hand declaring with what offence or offences the accused is charged and shall read the charge to the accused person and explain the nature thereof to him in simple language and address to him the following words or words to the like effect:
"This is not your trial. You will be tried later on in another court and before another Judge, where all the witnesses you have heard here will be produced and you will be allowed to question them. You will then be able to make any statement you may wish or to give evidence on oath and to call any witnesses on your own behalf. Unless you wish to reserve your defence, which you are at liberty to do, you may now either make a statement not on oath or give evidence on oath, and may call witnesses on your behalf. If you give evidence on oath you will be liable to cross-examination. Anything you may say whether on oath or not will be taken down and may be used in evidence at your trial."

(2) Before the accused person makes any statement in answer to the charge, or gives evidence, as the case may be, the magistrate shall state to him and give him clearly to understand that he has nothing to hope from any promise of favour and nothing to fear from any threat which may have been held out to him to induce him to make any admission or confession of his guilt, but that whatsoever he then says may be given in evidence on his trial notwithstanding the promise or threat.

(3) Everything which the accused person says, either by way of statement or evidence, shall be recorded in full and shall be shown or read over to him, and he shall be at liberty to explain or add to anything contained in the record thereof.

(4) When the whole is made conformable to what he declares is the truth, the record thereof shall be attested by the magistrate, who shall certify that such statement or evidence was taken in his presence and hearing and contains accurately the whole statement made, or evidence given, as the case may be, by the accused person. The accused person shall sign or attest by his mark such record. If he refuses, the court shall add a note of his refusal, and the record may be used as if he had signed or attested it.

(No. 28 of 1940)

Evidence and address in defence

229. (1) Immediately after complying with the requirements of the preceding section relating to the statement or evidence of the accused person, and whether the accused person has or has not made a statement or given evidence, the court shall ask him whether he desires to call witnesses on his own behalf.

(2) The court shall take the evidence of any witnesses called by the accused person in like manner as in the case of the witnesses for the prosecution, and every such witness, not being merely a witness to the character of the accused person, shall, if the court be of opinion that his evidence is in any way material to the case, be bound by recognizance to appear and give evidence at the trial of such accused person.

(3) If the accused person states that he has witnesses to call, but that they are not present in court, and the court is satisfied that the absence of such witnesses is not due to any fault or neglect of the accused person, and that there is a likelihood that they could, if present, give material evidence on behalf of the accused person, the court may adjourn the inquiry and issue process, or take other steps, to compel the attendance of such witnesses and, on their attendance, shall take their depositions and bind them by recognizance in the same manner as witnesses under subsection (2).

(4) (a) In any preliminary inquiry under this Part the accused person or his advocate shall be at liberty to address the court-

(i) after the examination of the witnesses called on behalf of the prosecution;

(ii) if no witnesses for the defence are to be called, immediately after the statement or evidence of the accused person;

(iii) if the accused person elects-

    A. to give evidence or to make a statement and witnesses for the defence are to be called; or

    B. not to give evidence or to make a statement, but to call witnesses;

    immediately after the evidence of such witnesses.

(b) If the accused person or his advocate addresses the court in accordance with the provisions of sub-paragraph (i) or (iii) of paragraph (a), the prosecution shall have the right of reply.

(5) Where the accused person reserves his defence, or at the conclusion of any statement in answer to the charge, or evidence in defence, as the case may be, the court shall ask him whether he intends to call witnesses at the trial, other than those, if any, whose evidence has been taken under the provisions of this section, and, if so, whether he desires to give their names and addresses so that they may be summoned. The court shall thereupon record the names and addresses of any such witnesses whom he may mention.

(No. 28 of 1940)

Discharge of accused person

230. If, at the close of the case for the prosecution or after hearing any evidence in defence, the court considers that the evidence against the accused person is not sufficient to put him on his trial, the court shall forthwith order him to be discharged as to the particular charge under inquiry; but such discharge shall not be a bar to any subsequent charge in respect of the same facts:

Provided always that nothing contained in this section shall prevent the court from either forthwith, or after such adjournment of the inquiry as may seem expedient in the interests of justice, proceeding to investigate any other charge upon which the accused person may have been summoned or otherwise brought before it, or which, in the course of the charge so dismissed as aforesaid, it may appear that the accused person has committed.

(No. 28 of 1940)

Committal for trial

231. (1) If the court considers the evidence sufficient to put the accused person on his trial, the court shall commit him for trial to the High Court and, except in the case of a corporation, shall, until the trial, either admit him to bail or send him to prison for safe-keeping. The warrant of such first-named court shall be sufficient authority to the officer in charge of any prison appointed for the custody of prisoners committed for trial, although out of the jurisdiction of such court.

(2) The order of committal shall state that such person is committed for trial to a Sessions of the High Court to be held in the Province in which such subordinate court is situate.

(As amended by No. 76 of 1965 and No. 38 of 1969)

Summary adjudication

232. If, at the close of or during the inquiry, it shall appear to the subordinate court that the offence is of such a nature that it may suitably be dealt with under the powers possessed by the court, the court may, subject to the provisions of Part VI, hear and finally determine the matter, and either convict the accused person or dismiss the charge:

Provided that, in every such case, the accused shall be entitled to have recalled for cross-examination all witnesses for the prosecution whom he has not already cross-examined.

Complainant and witnesses to be bound over

233. (1) A subordinate court conducting a preliminary inquiry shall bind by recognizance, with or without surety or sureties, as it may deem requisite, the complainant and every witness, to appear in the event of the accused person being committed for trial before the High Court, at such trial to give evidence, and also to appear, if required, at any further examination concerning the charge which may be held by direction of the Director of Public Prosecutions.

(2) A recognizance under this section shall not be estreated unless the High Court is satisfied that the person bound has been informed of the date of the Sessions in which the accused person comes before the High Court for trial.

(No. 5 of 1962 as amended by S.I. No. 63 of 1964 and No. 38 of 1969)

Refusal to be bound over

234. If a person refuses to enter into the recognizance referred to in the last preceding section, the court may commit him to prison or into the custody of any officer of the court there to remain until after the trial, unless, in the meantime, he enters into a recognizance. But, if afterwards, from want of sufficient evidence or other cause, the accused is discharged, the court shall order that the person imprisoned for so refusing be also discharged.

Accused person entitled to copy of depositions

235. A person who has been committed for trial before the High Court shall be entitled, at any time before the trial, to have a copy of the depositions, on payment of a reasonable sum, not exceeding five ngwee for every hundred words, or, if the court thinks fit, without payment. The court shall, at the time of committing him for trial, inform the accused person of the effect of this provision.

Binding over of witnesses conditionally

236. (1) Where any person, charged before a subordinate court with an offence triable upon information before the High Court, is committed for trial, and it appears to such subordinate court, after taking into account anything which may be said with reference thereto by the accused or the prosecutor, that the attendance at the trial of any witness who has been examined before it is unnecessary, by reason of anything contained in any statement by the accused person, or of the evidence of the witness being merely of a formal nature, the subordinate court shall, if the witness has not already been bound over, bind him over to attend the trial conditionally upon notice given to him and not otherwise, or shall, if the witness has already been bound over, direct that he shall be treated as having been bound over to attend only conditionally as aforesaid, and shall transmit to the High Court a statement in writing of the names, addresses and occupations of the witnesses who are, or who are to be treated as having been, bound over to attend the trial conditionally.

(2) Where a witness has been, or is to be treated as having been, bound over conditionally to attend the trial, the Director of Public Prosecutions or the person committed for trial may give notice, at any time before the opening of the Sessions of the High Court, to the committing subordinate court, and, at any time thereafter, to the Registrar, that he desires the witness to attend at the trial, and any such court or Registrar to whom any such notice is given shall forthwith notify the witness that he is required so to attend in pursuance of his recognizance. The subordinate court shall, on committing the accused person for trial, inform him of his right to require the attendance at the trial of any such witness as aforesaid, and of the steps which he must take for the purpose of enforcing such attendance.

(3) Any documents or articles produced in evidence before the subordinate court by any witness whose attendance at the trial is stated to be unnecessary, in accordance with the provisions of this section, and marked as exhibits shall, unless, in any particular case, the subordinate court otherwise orders, be retained by the subordinate court and forwarded with the depositions to the Registrar.

(As amended by No. 28 of 1940 and S.I. No. 63 of 1964)

Preservation of Testimony in Certain Cases

Taking the depositions of persons dangerously ill

237. Whenever it appears to any magistrate that any person dangerously ill or hurt and not likely to recover is able and willing to give material evidence relating to any offence triable by the High Court, and it shall not be practicable to take the deposition, in accordance with the provisions of this Code, of the person so ill or hurt, such magistrate may take in and shall subscribe the same, and certify that it contains accurately the whole of the statement made by such person, and shall add a statement of his reason for taking the same, and of the date and place when and where the same was taken, and shall preserve such statement and file it for record.

Notice to be given

238. If the statement relates or is expected to relate to an offence for which any person is under a charge or committal for trial, reasonable notice of the intention to take the same shall be given to the prosecutor

and the accused person, and, if the accused person is in custody, he may, and shall, if he so requests, be brought by the person in whose charge he is, under an order in writing of the magistrate, to the place where the statement is to be taken.
(As amended by No. 24 of 1950)

Transmission of statement

239. If the statement relates to an offence for which any person is then or subsequently committed for trial, it shall be transmitted to the Registrar, and a copy thereof shall be transmitted to the Director of Public Prosecutions
(As amended by S.I. No. 63 of 1964)

Use of statement in evidence

240. Such statement, so taken, may afterwards be used in evidence on the trial of any person accused of an offence to which the same relates, if the person who made the statement be dead, or if the court is satisfied that, for any sufficient cause, his attendance cannot be procured, and if reasonable notice of the intention to take such statement was given to the person (whether prosecutor or accused person) against whom it is proposed to be read in evidence, and he had or might have had, if he had chosen to be present, full opportunity of cross-examining the person making the same.
(As amended by No.24 of 1950)

Proceedings after Committal for Trial

Transmission of records to High Court and Director of Public Prosecutions

241. In the event of a committal for trial, the written charge, the depositions, the statement of the accused person, the recognizances of the complainant and of the witnesses, the recognizances of bail (if any) and all documents or things which have been tendered or put in evidence shall be transmitted without delay by the committing court to the Registrar, and an authenticated copy of the depositions and statement aforesaid shall be also transmitted to the Director of Public Prosecutions.
(As amended by S.I. No. 63 of 1964)

Power of Director of Public Prosecutions to direct further investigation

242. If, after receipt of the authenticated copy of the depositions and statement provided for by the last preceding section, and before the trial before the High Court, the Director of Public Prosecutions shall be of opinion that further investigation is required before such trial, it shall be lawful for the Director of Public Prosecutions to direct that the original depositions be remitted to the court which committed the accused person for trial, and such court may, thereupon, reopen the case and deal with it, in all respects, as if such person had not been committed for trial as aforesaid; and, if the case be one which may suitably be dealt with under the powers possessed by such court, it may, if thought expedient by the court, or if the Director of Public Prosecutions so directs, be so tried and determined accordingly.
(As amended by S.I. No. 63 of 1964)

Powers of Director of Public Prosecutions as to additional witnesses

243. If, after receipt of the authenticated copy of the depositions and statement as aforesaid and before the trial before the High Court, the Director of Public Prosecutions shall be of opinion that there is, in any case committed for trial, any material or necessary witness for the prosecution or the defence who has not been bound over to give evidence on the trial of the case, the Director of Public Prosecutions may require the subordinate court which committed the accused person for trial to take the depositions of such witness and compel his attendance either by summons or by warrant as herein before provided.
(No. 28 of 1940 as amended by S.I. No. 63 of 1964.)

Return of depositions with a view to summary trial

244. (1) If, before the trial before the High Court, the Director of Public Prosecutions is of opinion, upon the record of the committal proceedings received by him, that the case is one which may suitably be tried by a subordinate court, he may cause the depositions to be returned to the court which committed the accused, and thereupon the case shall be tried and determined in the same manner as if such person had not been committed for trial.

(2) Where depositions are returned under the provisions of subsection (1), the Director of Public Prosecutions may direct that the person concerned shall be tried on the charge in respect of which he was committed, if such charge is within the competence of the subordinate court concerned, or upon such other charge within such competence as the Director of Public Prosecutions may specify.

(No. 28 of 1940 as amended by No. 23 of 1960 and S.I. No. 63 of 1964)

Filing of information

245. (1) If, after the receipt of the authenticated copy of the depositions as aforesaid, the Director of Public Prosecutions shall be of the opinion that the case is one which should be tried upon information before the High Court, an information shall be drawn up in accordance with the provisions of this Code, and, when signed by the Director of Public Prosecutions, shall be filed in the registry of the High Court.

(2) In such information the Director of Public Prosecutions may charge the accused person with any offences which, in his opinion, are disclosed by the depositions either in addition to, or in substitution for, the offences upon which the accused person has been committed for trial.

(3) Notwithstanding anything to the contrary contained in this Code or any other written law, any person who could have been joined in one charge under section one hundred and thirty-six with a person who has been committed to the High Court for trial, but was not so joined, may be joined in an information by the Director of Public Prosecutions-

(a) if such person could not be found before the completion of the preliminary inquiry held under this Part; or

(b) if it is discovered after the completion of the preliminary inquiry that such person could have been joined in the charge brought against the person so committed.

(4) A copy of the information referred to in subsection (3) signed by the Director of Public Prosecutions shall be sufficient authority for any subordinate court before which such other person or persons appear or have appeared to discontinue any proceedings in respect of such persons and either to admit them to bail or send them to prison for safe-keeping until the trial before the High Court.

(5) Where any person has been joined in an information under subsection (3) the prosecution shall, not less than twenty-one clear days before the date fixed for trial of the case, furnish to him or to his legal practitioner-

(a) if his co-accused was committed under section two hundred and thirty-one, a copy of the depositions taken in respect of his co-accused together with a copy of the statements of any additional evidence which it is intended to adduce at the trial, whether from witnesses who appeared at the preliminary inquiry or from further witnesses;

(b) if his co-accused was committed under section two hundred and fifty-five, a list of the persons whom it is intended to call as witnesses for the prosecution at the trial and a statement of the evidence of each witness which it is intended to adduce at the trial;

(c) in either of the cases mentioned in paragraph (a) or (b), and if so requested, a translation of the depositions or statements in a language which such person appears to understand: Provided that the High Court may, upon such conditions as it may determine, permit the prosecution to call a witness, whose name does not appear as a deponent or witness, to give evidence.

(As amended by No. 28 of 1940, S.I. No. 63 of 1964 and No. 6 of 1972)

Time in which information to be filed

246. (1) The period within which the Director of Public Prosecutions may file an information under the provisions of this Code shall be one month from the date of receipt by him of the authenticated copy of the depositions and other documents referred to in section two hundred and forty-one.

(2) The Director of Public Prosecutions shall inform the High Court and the person committed of the date of receipt aforesaid.

(3) If the Director of Public Prosecutions has not within the period of one month aforesaid exercised his powers under section two hundred and forty-two or two hundred and forty-four or filed an information, the High Court may of its own motion, and shall upon the application of the person committed, discharge such person unless the High Court sees fit to extend the time for filing an information.

(4) Where the High Court has extended the period for filing an information and the Director of Public Prosecutions does not file an information within the period so extended, the High Court may of its own motion, and shall upon the application of the person committed, discharge such person.

(No. 38 of 1969)

Notice of trial

247. The Registrar or the Clerk of Sessions appointed under subsection (3) of section nineteen of the High Court Act shall endorse on or annex to every information filed as aforesaid, and to every copy thereof delivered to the officer of the court or police officer for service thereof, a notice of trial, which notice shall specify the particular Sessions of the High Court at which the accused person is to be tried on the said information, and shall be in the following form, or as near thereto as may be: Cap. 27

"A.B.

Take notice that you will be tried on the information whereof this is a true copy at the Sessions of the High Court to be held at .... on the .... day of .... [20] ....."

(As amended by No. 5 of 1962)

Copy of information and notice of trial to be served

248. The Registrar shall deliver or cause to be delivered to the officer of the court or police officer serving the information a copy thereof with the notice of trial endorsed on the same or annexed thereto, and, if there are more accused persons committed for trial than one, then as many copies as there are such accused persons; and the officer of the court or police officer aforesaid shall, as soon as may be after having received the copy or copies of the information and notice or notices of trial, and three days at least before the day specified therein for trial, by himself or his deputy or other officer, deliver to the accused person or persons committed for trial the said copy or copies of the information and notice or notices, and explain to him or them the nature and exigency thereof; and, when any accused person shall have been admitted to bail and cannot readily be found, he shall leave a copy of the said information and notice of trial with someone of his household for him at his dwelling-house, or with someone of his bail for him, and, if none such can be found, shall affix the said copy and notice to the outer or principal door of the dwellinghouse or dwelling-houses of the accused person or of any of his bail:

Provided always that nothing herein contained shall prevent any person committed for trial, and in custody at the opening of or during any Sessions of the High Court, from being tried thereat, if he shall express his assent to be so tried and no special objection be made thereto on the part of the Director of Public Prosecutions. (As amended by S.I. No. 63 of 1964)

Return of service

249. The officer serving the copy or copies of the information and notice or notices of trial shall forthwith make to the Registrar a return of the mode of service thereof.

Postponement of trial

250. (1) It shall be lawful for the High Court, upon the application of the prosecutor or the accused person if it considers that there is sufficient cause for the delay, to postpone the trial of any accused person to the next Sessions of the court held in the district, or at some other convenient place, or to a subsequent Sessions, and to respite the recognizances of the complainant and witnesses, in which case the respited recognizances shall have the same force and effect as fresh recognizances to prosecute and give evidence at such subsequent Sessions would have had.

(2) The High Court may give such directions for the amendment of the information and the service of any notices which the court may deem necessary in consequence of any order made under subsection (1).

(As amended by No. 28 of 1940)

Rules as to Informations by the Director of Public Prosecutions

Informations by Director of Public Prosecutions

251. All informations drawn up in pursuance of section two hundred and forty-five shall be in the name of and (subject to the provisions of section eighty-two) signed by the Director of Public Prosecutions.

(As amended by S.I. No. 63 of 1964)

Form of information

252. Every information shall bear date of the day when the same is signed, and, with such modifications as shall be necessary to adapt it to the circumstances of each case, may commence in the following form:

In the High Court for Zambia

The   day of   19

At the Sessions holden at   on the day of   , 19   , the Court is informed by the Director of Public Prosecutions on behalf of the People that A.B. is charged with the following offence (or offences).

(As amended by S.I. No. 63 of 1964)

PART VIII SUMMARY COMMITTAL PROCEDURE FOR TRIAL OF ACCUSED PERSON BEFORE THE HIGH COURTPART VIII

(No. 27 of 1964)

SUMMARY COMMITTAL PROCEDURE FOR TRIAL OF ACCUSED PERSON BEFORE THE HIGH COURT

Interpretation

253. In this Part, unless the context otherwise requires-

"summary procedure case" means any case certified under the provisions of this Part as a proper case for trial before the High Court after summary committal procedure.

Certifying of case as a summary procedure case

254. Notwithstanding anything contained in Part VII, in any case where a person is charged with an offence not triable by a subordinate court, the Director of Public Prosecutions may issue a certificate in writing that the case is a proper one for trial by the High Court as a summary procedure case and such case shall, upon production to a subordinate court of such certificate, be dealt with by the subordinate court in accordance with the provisions of this Part. (As amended by S.I. No. 63 of 1964)

No preliminary inquiry in summary procedure case

255. No such preliminary inquiry as is referred to in Part VII shall be held in respect of any case in which the Director of Public Prosecutions has issued and the prosecutor has produced to a subordinate court a certificate issued under the provisions of section two hundred and fifty-four, but the subordinate court before whom the accused person is brought shall, upon production of such certificate, and whether or not a preliminary inquiry has already been commenced, forthwith commit the accused person for trial before the High Court upon such charge or charges as may be designated in the certificate. (As amended by S.I. No. 63 of 1964)

Record to be forwarded

256. Upon the committal of the accused person for trial in a summary procedure case, the record of the proceedings, including, in any case where a preliminary inquiry has been commenced, any depositions taken and any exhibits produced, shall be transmitted without delay by the committing court to the Registrar, and an authenticated copy of the record shall also be transmitted to the Director of Public Prosecutions. (As amended by S.I. No. 63 of 1964)

Filing of an information

257. (1) The Director of Public Prosecutions may, after receipt of the authenticated copy of the record in a summary procedure case as aforesaid, draw up and sign an information in accordance with the provisions of this Code, which shall be filed in the Registry of the High Court.

   (2) In such information the Director of Public Prosecutions may alter or redraft the charge or charges against the accused person or frame an additional charge or charges against him.

   (3) The provisions of sections two hundred and forty-seven to two hundred and fifty-two inclusive, shall apply mutatis mutandis to an information filed under the provisions of this section as they do to an information filed under the provisions of section two hundred and forty-five.

(As amended by S.I. No. 63 of 1964)

288

Statements, etc., to be supplied to the accused

258. In every summary procedure case in which an information has been filed under the provisions of section two hundred and fifty-seven, the prosecution shall, not less than fourteen clear days before the date fixed for the trial of the case, furnish to the accused person or his legal practitioner, if any, and to the Registrar a list of the persons whom it is intended to call as witnesses for the prosecution at the trial and a statement of the evidence of each witness which it is intended to adduce at the trial:
Provided that the Court may, upon such conditions as it may determine, permit the prosecution to call a witness whose name does not appear on the said list, to give evidence.
(As amended by Act 30 of 1976)

Affidavit of medical witness may be read as evidence

259. (1) The affidavit of a medical officer or other medical witness, attested before a magistrate, may be read as evidence although the deponent is not called as a witness.

(2) The Court may, if it thinks fit, summon and examine such deponent as to the subject-matter of his affidavit.

PART IX
PROCEDURE IN TRIALS BEFORE THE HIGH COURT

Practice and Mode of Trial

Practice of High Court in its criminal jurisdiction

260. The practice of the High Court, in its criminal jurisdiction, shall be assimilated, as nearly as circumstances will admit, to the practice of Her Britannic Majesty's High Court of Justice in its criminal jurisdiction and of Courts of Oyer and Terminer and General Gaol Delivery in England.
(As amended by S.I. No. 63 of 1964)

Trials before High Court

List of Assessors

261. All trials before the High Court shall be held before a Judge sitting alone, or before a Judge with the aid of assessors (if the presiding Judge so decides), the number of whom shall be two or more as the court thinks fit.

Preparation of list of assessors

262. Magistrates shall, before the 1st March in each year, and subject to such rules as the Chief Justice may, from time to time, prescribe, prepare lists of suitable persons in their districts liable to serve as assessors. (As amended by No. 2 of 1960 and S.I. No. 63 of 1964)

Liability to serve

263. Subject to the exemptions in the next succeeding section contained, all male persons between the ages of twenty-one and sixty shall be liable to serve as assessors:
Provided that the Chief Justice may, from time to time, make rules regulating the area within which a person may be summoned to serve. (As amended by No. 2 of 1960)

Exemptions

264. The following persons are exempt from liability to serve as assessors, save with their own consent, namely:
    (a) all Government officers;
    (b) Members of the National Assembly;
    (c) persons actively discharging the duties of priests or ministers of their respective religions;
    (d) physicians, surgeons, dentists and apothecaries in actual practice;
    (e) legal practitioners in actual practice;
    (f) officers and others in the Defence Force on full pay;
    (g) persons disabled by mental or bodily infirmity;
    (h) persons exempted by the High Court.
(As amended by G.N. No. 303 of 1964 and S.I. No. 63 of 1964)

Gates on Evidence: Zambian Theory and Practice

Publication of list

265. (1) When the lists aforesaid have been prepared, extracts therefrom containing the names of the persons liable to serve as assessors, residing in each district, shall be posted for public inspection at the Court House of such district.

(2) To every such extract shall be subjoined a notice stating that objections to the list will be heard and determined by a magistrate of the district, at a time and place to be mentioned in such notice.

Revision of list

266. (1) Every magistrate shall, at the time and place mentioned in the notice relating to his district, revise the list and hear the objections (if any) of persons interested in the amendment thereof, and shall strike out the name of any person not suitable, in his judgment, to serve as an assessor, or who may establish his right to any exemption from service given by section two hundred and sixty-four, and insert the name of any person omitted from the list whom he deems qualified for such service.

(2) A copy of the revised list shall be signed by the magistrate and sent to the Registrar.

(3) Any order of the magistrate as aforesaid, in preparing and revising the list, shall be final.

(4) Any exemption not claimed under this section shall be deemed to be waived, until the list is next revised.

(5) The list, so prepared and revised, shall be again revised once in every year.

(6) If any person suitable to serve as an assessor shall be found in any district after the list has been settled, his name may be added to the list by a magistrate of that district, and he shall be liable to serve.

Attendance of Assessors

Summoning assessors

267. (1) The Registrar shall ordinarily, seven days at least before the day which from time to time may be fixed for holding a Sessions of the High Court, send a letter to a magistrate of the district in which such Sessions are to be held, requesting him to summon as many persons as seem to the Judge who is to preside at the Sessions to be needed at the said Sessions.

(2) The magistrate shall, thereupon, summon such number of assessors, excluding those who have served within six months, unless the number cannot be made up without them.

Form of summons

268. Every summons to an assessor shall be in writing, and shall require his attendance at a time and place to be therein specified.

Excuses

269. The High Court may, for reasonable cause, excuse any assessor from attendance at any particular Sessions, and may, if it shall think fit, at the conclusion of any trial, direct that the assessors who have served at such trial shall not be summoned to serve again for a period of twelve months.

List of assessors attending

270. (1) At each Sessions, the Registrar shall cause to be made a list of the names of those who have attended as assessors at such Sessions, and such list shall be kept with the list of the assessors as revised under section two hundred and sixty-six.

(2) A reference shall be made, in the margin of the said revised list, to each of the names which are mentioned in the list prepared under this section.

(As amended by No. 5 of 1962)

Penalty for non-attendance of assessor

Arraignment

271. (1) Any person summoned to attend as an assessor who, without lawful excuse, fails to attend as required by the summons, or who, having attended, departs without having obtained the permission of the High Court, or fails to attend after adjournment of the court, after being ordered to attend, shall be liable, by order of the High Court, to a fine not exceeding fifty kwacha.

(2) Such punishment may be inflicted summarily, on an order to that effect, by the High Court, and any fine imposed shall be recoverable by distress and sale of the real and personal property of the person fined, by warrant of distress to be signed by the Registrar; and such warrant shall be issued by the Registrar, without further order of the High Court, if the fine is not paid within six days of its having come to the knowledge of the person fined, by notice or otherwise, that the fine has been imposed:

Provided that it shall be lawful for the High Court, if it shall see fit, to remit any fine, or any portion of such fine, so imposed.

(3) The Registrar shall send notice of the imposition of such fine to any person so fined in his absence, requiring him to pay the fine or to show cause before the High Court, within four days, for not paying the same.

(4) In default of recovery of the fine by distress and sale, the person fined may, by order of the High Court, be imprisoned for a term of twenty-one days, if the fine be not sooner paid.

Pleading to information

272. The accused person to be tried before the High Court, upon an information, shall be placed at the bar unfettered, unless the court shall see cause otherwise to order, and the information shall be read over to him by the Registrar or other officer of the court, and explained, if need be, by that officer, or interpreted by the interpreter of the court, and such accused person shall be required to plead instantly thereto, unless, where the accused person is entitled to service of a copy of the information, he shall object to the want of such service, and the court shall find that he has not been duly served therewith.

Orders for amendment of information, separate trial, and postponement of trial

273. (1) Every objection to any information, for any formal defect on the face thereof, shall be taken immediately after the information has been read over to the accused person, and not later.

(2) Where, before a trial upon information or at any stage of such trial, it appears to the court that the information is defective, the court shall make such order for the amendment of the information as the court thinks necessary to meet the circumstances of the case, unless, having regard to the merits of the case, the required amendments cannot be made without injustice. All such amendments shall be made upon such terms as to the court shall seem just.

(3) Where an information is so amended, a note of the order for amendment shall be endorsed on the information, and the information shall be treated, for the purposes of all proceedings in connection therewith, as having been filed in the amended form.

(4) Where, before a trial upon information or at any stage of such trial, the court is of opinion that the accused may be prejudiced or embarrassed in his defence, by reason of being charged with more than one offence in the same information, or that, for any other reason, it is desirable to direct that the accused should be tried separately for any one or more offences charged in an information, the court may order a separate trial of any count or counts of such information.

(5) Where, before a trial upon information or at any stage of such trial, the court is of opinion that the postponement of the trial of the accused is expedient, as a consequence of the exercise of any power of the court under this Code, the court shall make such order as to the postponement of the trial as appears necessary.

(6) Where an order of the court is made under this section for a separate trial or for postponement of a trial-

(a) the court may order that the assessors are to be discharged from giving opinions on the count or counts, the trial of which is postponed, or on the information, as the case may be; and

(b) the procedure on the separate trial of a count shall be the same, in all respects, as if the count had been found in a separate information, and the procedure on the postponed trial shall be the same, in all respects (if the assessors, if any, have been discharged), as if the trial had not commenced; and

(c) the court may make such order as to admitting the accused to bail, and as to the enlargement of recognizances and otherwise, as the court thinks fit

(7) Any power of the court under this section shall be in addition to, and not in derogation of, any other power of the court for the same or similar purposes.

Quashing of information

274. If an information does not state, and cannot, by any amendment authorised by the last preceding section, be made to state, any offence of which the accused has had notice, it shall be quashed, either on a motion made before the accused pleads, or on a motion made in arrest of judgment. A written statement of every such motion shall be delivered to the Registrar or other officer of the court by or on behalf of the accused, and shall be entered upon the record.

Procedure in case of previous convictions

275. Where an information contains a count charging an accused person with having been previously convicted of any offence, the procedure shall be as follows:
- (a) The part of the information stating the previous conviction shall not be read out in court, nor shall the accused be asked whether he has been previously convicted as alleged in the information, unless and until he has either pleaded guilty to or been convicted of the subsequent offence;
- (b) If he pleads guilty to or is convicted of the subsequent offence, he shall then be asked whether he has been previously convicted as alleged in the information;
- (c) If he answers that he has been so previously convicted, the Judge may proceed to pass sentence on him accordingly; but, if he denies that he has been so previously convicted, or refuses to or does not answer such question, the court shall then hear evidence concerning such previous conviction:

    Provided, however, that if, upon the trial of any person for any such subsequent offence, such person shall give evidence of his own good character, it shall be lawful for the advocate for the prosecution, in answer thereto, to give evidence of the conviction of such person for the previous offence or offences before he is convicted of such subsequent offence, and the court shall inquire concerning such previous conviction or convictions at the same time that it inquires concerning such subsequent offence.

Plea of "not guilty"

276. Every accused person, upon being arraigned upon any information, by pleading generally thereto the plea of "not guilty", shall, without further form, be deemed to have put himself upon his trial.

Plea of autrefois acquit and autrefois convict

277. (1) Any accused person against whom an information is filed may plead-
- (a) that he has been previously convicted or acquitted, as the case may be, of the same offence; or
- (b) that he has been granted a pardon for his offence.

(2) If either of such pleas are pleaded in any case and denied to be true in fact, the court shall try whether such plea is true in fact or not.

(3) If the court holds that the facts alleged by the accused do not prove the plea, or if it finds that it is false in fact, the accused shall be required to plead to the information.

(As amended by G.N. No. 303 of 1964)

Refusal to plead

278. If an accused person, being arraigned upon any information, stands mute of malice, the court, if it thinks fit, shall order the Registrar or other officer of the court to enter a plea of "not guilty" on behalf of such accused person, and the plea so entered shall have the same force and effect as if such accused person had actually pleaded the same.

(No. 11 of 1963)

Plea of "guilty"

279. If the accused pleads "guilty", the plea shall be recorded and he may be convicted thereon.

Proceedings after plea of "not guilty"

280. If the accused pleads "not guilty", or if a plea of "not guilty" is entered in accordance with the provisions of section two hundred and seventy-eight, the court shall proceed to choose assessors, as hereinafter directed (if the trial is to be held with assessors), and to try the case:

Provided that the same assessors may aid in the trial of as many accused persons successively, as the court thinks fit.

Power to postpone or adjourn proceedings

281. (1)   If, from the absence of witnesses or any other reasonable cause, to be recorded in the proceedings, the court considers it necessary or advisable to postpone the commencement of or to adjourn any trial, the court may, from time to time, postpone or adjourn the same, on such terms as it thinks fit, for such time as it considers reasonable, and may, by warrant, remand the accused to some prison or other place of security.

(2)   During a remand the court may, at any time, order the accused to be brought before it.

(3)   The court may, on a remand, admit the accused to bail.

Selection of Assessors

Selection of assessors

282. When a trial is to be held with the aid of assessors, the court shall select two or more from the list of those summoned to serve as assessors at the Sessions, as it deems fit.

Absence of an assessor

283. (1)   If, in the course of a trial with the aid of assessors, at any time before the finding, any assessor is, from any sufficient cause, prevented from attending throughout the trial, or absents himself, and it is not practicable immediately to enforce his attendance, the trial shall proceed with the aid of the other assessor or assessors.

(2)   If two or more of the assessors are prevented from attending, or absent themselves, the proceedings shall be stayed and a new trial shall be held with the aid of fresh assessors.

Case for the Prosecution

Assessors to attend at adjourned sittings

284. If the trial is adjourned, the assessors shall be required to attend at the adjourned sitting, and at any subsequent sitting, until the conclusion of the trial.

Opening of case for prosecution

285. When the assessors have been chosen (if the trial is before a Judge with the aid of assessors), the advocate for the prosecution shall open the case against the accused person, and shall call witnesses and adduce evidence in support of the charge.

Additional witnesses for prosecution

286. No witness who has not given evidence at the preliminary inquiry shall be called by the prosecution at any trial, unless the accused person has received reasonable notice in writing of the intention to call such witness. The notice must state the witness's name and address and the substance of the evidence which he intends to give. The court shall determine what notice is reasonable, regard being had to the time when and the circumstances under which the prosecution became acquainted with the nature of the witness's evidence and determined to call him as a witness. No such notice need be given if the prosecution first became aware of the evidence which the witness could give on the day on which he is called.

Cross-examination of witnesses for prosecution

287. The witnesses called for the prosecution shall be subject to cross-examination by the accused person or his advocate, and to re-examination by the advocate for the prosecution.

Depositions may be read as evidence in certain cases

288. (1)   Where any person has been committed for trial for any offence, the deposition of any person taken before the committing subordinate court may, if the conditions set out in subsection (2) are satisfied, without further proof, be read as evidence on the trial of that person, whether for that

offence or for any other offence arising out of the same transaction or set of circumstances as that offence.

(2) The conditions referred to in subsection (1) are the following:

    (a)   (i)   The deposition must be the deposition either on a witness whose attendance at the trial is stated to be unnecessary in accordance with the provisions of section two hundred and thirty-six, of a witness who is proved at the trial by oath of a credible witness to be absent from Zambia, or dead or insane, or so ill as not to be able to travel, or to be kept out of the way by means of the procurement of the accused or on his behalf; or

          (ii)   the deposition must be the deposition of a witness who cannot be found or is incapable of giving evidence, or of a witness whose presence cannot be obtained without an amount of delay or expense which, in the circumstances of the case, the court considers unreasonable:

              Provided that, before any such deposition as is referred to in this sub-paragraph is read, the court shall satisfy itself that the reading of such deposition will not unduly prejudice the accused.

    (b)   It must be proved at the trial, either by a certificate purporting to be signed by the magistrate of the subordinate court before whom the deposition purports to have been taken, or by the clerk to such court, or by the oath of a credible witness, that the deposition was taken in the presence of the accused, and that the accused or his advocate had full opportunity of cross-examining the witness.

    (c)   The deposition must purport to be signed by the magistrate of the subordinate court before whom it purports to have been taken:

        Provided that the provisions of this subsection shall not have effect in any case in which it is proved-

          (i)   that the deposition, or, where the proof required by paragraph (b) is given by means of a certificate, that the certificate was not in fact signed by the magistrate by whom it purports to have been signed; or   (ii)   where the deposition is that of a witness whose attendance at the trial is stated to be unnecessary as aforesaid, that the witness has been duly notified that he is required to attend the trial.

(As amended by No. 28 of 1940)

Deposition of medical witness may be read as evidence

289. (1) The deposition of a medical officer or other medical witness, taken and attested by a magistrate in the presence of the accused person, may be read as evidence, although the deponent is not called as a witness.

    (2) The court may, if it thinks fit, summon and examine such deponent as to the subject-matter of his deposition.

(No. 28 of 1940)

Statement or evidence of accused

290. Any statement or evidence of the accused person duly certified by the committing magistrate in the manner provided by subsection (4) of section two hundred and twenty-eight may, whether signed by the accused person or not, be given in evidence without further proof thereof, unless it is proved that the magistrate purporting to certify the same did not in fact certify it.

(No. 28 of 1940)

Close of case for prosecution

291. (1) When the evidence of the witnesses for the prosecution has been concluded, and the statement or evidence (if any) of the accused person before the committing court has been given in evidence, the court, if it considers that there is no evidence that the accused or any one of several accused committed the offence shall, after hearing, if necessary, any arguments which the advocate for the prosecution or the defence may desire to submit, record a finding.

    (2) When the evidence of the witnesses for the prosecution has been concluded, and the statement or evidence (if any) of the accused person before the committing court has been given in evidence, the court, if it considers that there is evidence that the accused person or any one or more of

several accused persons committed the offence, shall inform each such accused person, who is not represented by an advocate, of his right to address the court, either personally or by his advocate (if any), to give evidence on his own behalf, or to make an unsworn statement, and to call witnesses in his defence, and in all cases shall require him or his advocate (if any) to state whether it is intended to call any witnesses as to fact other than the accused person himself. Upon being informed thereof, the court shall record the same. If such accused person says that he does not mean to give evidence or make an unsworn statement, or to adduce evidence, then the advocate for the prosecution may sum up the case against such accused person. If such accused person says that he means to give evidence or make an unsworn statement, or to adduce evidence, the court shall call upon such accused person to enter upon his defence.

(No. 28 of 1940 as amended by No. 50 of 1957)

Case for the Defence

The defence

292. Unless the only witness to the facts of the case called by the defence is the accused, the accused person or his advocate may then open his case, stating the facts or law on which he intends to rely, and making such comments as he thinks necessary on the evidence for the prosecution. The accused person may then give evidence on his own behalf, and he or his advocate may examine his witnesses, and, after their cross-examination and re-examination (if any), may sum up his case.

Additional witnesses for defence

293. The accused person shall be allowed to examine any witness not previously bound over to give evidence at the trial, if such witness is in attendance, but he shall not be entitled, as of right, to have any witness summoned, other than the witnesses whom he named to the subordinate court committing him for trial, as witnesses whom he desired to be summoned.

Evidence in reply

294. If the accused person adduces evidence in his defence introducing new matter which the advocate for the prosecution could not by the exercise of reasonable diligence have foreseen, the court may allow the advocate for the prosecution to adduce evidence in reply to contradict the said matter.

(No. 28 of 1940)

Prosecutor's reply

295. If the accused person, or any one of several accused persons, adduces any evidence through any witness other than himself, the prosecutor shall be entitled to reply.

(As amended by No. 16 of 1959)

Where accused person does not give evidence

296. If the accused person says that he does not mean to give or adduce evidence, and the court considers that there is evidence that he committed the offence, the advocate for the prosecution may then sum up the case against the accused person, and the court shall then call on the accused person personally or by his advocate to address the court on his own behalf.

(As amended by No. 50 of 1957)

Close of Hearing

Delivery of opinions by assessors

297. (1) When the case on both sides is closed, the Judge may sum up the evidence for the prosecution and the defence, and shall (if the trial is being held with the aid of assessors) then require each of the assessors to state orally his opinion whether the accused is guilty or not, and shall record such opinion.

(2) The Judge shall then give judgment, but, in so doing, shall not be bound to conform to the opinions of the assessors.

(3) If the accused person is convicted, the Judge shall pass sentence on him according to law.

(4)   Nothing in this section shall be read as prohibiting the assessors, or any of them, from retiring to consider their opinions if they so wish or, during any such retirement or at any time during the trial, from consultation with one another.

(As amended by No. 28 of 1940)

Passing Sentence

Motion in arrest of judgment

298. (1)   The accused person may, at any time before sentence, whether on his plea of guilty or otherwise, move in arrest of judgment, on the ground that the information does not, after any amendment which the court is willing and has power to make, state any offence which the court has power to try.

(2)   The court may, in its discretion, either hear and determine the matter during the same sitting, or adjourn the hearing thereof to a future time to be fixed for that purpose.

(3)   If the court decides in favour of the accused, he shall be discharged from that information.

Sentence

299. If no motion in arrest of judgment is made, or if the court decides against the accused person upon such motion, the court may sentence the accused person at any time during the Sessions.

Power to reserve decision on question raised at trial

300. The court before which any person is tried for an offence may reserve the giving of its final decision on questions raised at the trial, and its decision, whenever given, shall be considered as given at the time of trial.

Objections cured by judgment

301. No judgment shall be stayed or reversed on the ground of any objection which, if stated after the information was read over to the accused person, or during the progress of the trial, might have been amended by the court, nor for any informality in swearing the witnesses or any of them.

Evidence for arriving at proper sentence

302. The court may, before passing sentence, receive such evidence as it thinks fit, in order to inform itself as to the sentence proper to be passed.

PART X
SENTENCES AND THEIR EXECUTION[8]

Sentence of Death

303. When any person is sentenced to death, the sentence shall direct that he shall be hanged by the neck till he is dead.

Authority for detention

304. A certificate, under the hand of the Registrar or the clerk of the court, as the case may be, that sentence of death has been passed, and naming the person condemned, shall be sufficient authority for the detention of such person.

Record and report to be sent to President

305. (1)   As soon as conveniently may be after sentence of death has been pronounced by the High Court, if no appeal from the sentence is preferred, or if such appeal is preferred and dismissed, then as soon as conveniently may be thereafter, the presiding Judge shall forward to the President a copy of the notes of evidence taken on the trial, with a report in writing signed by him containing any recommendation or observations on the case he may think fit to make.

---

[8] Sections 303, 304, 305 and 306 have now been repealed by s 6 of Act No 22 of 2022.

(2)   In any case where a sentence of death passed by a subordinate court shall be confirmed by the High Court, such subordinate court shall, on receipt of the confirmation of such sentence, inform the convicted person that he may appeal to the Court of Appeal as if he had been convicted on a trial before the High Court, and, if he wishes to appeal, inform him that his appeal must be preferred within fourteen days from the date on which he is given such information; and where no appeal from such confirmation is preferred or, if preferred, is dismissed by the Court of Appeal, then as soon as conveniently may be after the expiration of the period of fourteen days as aforesaid or after the receipt of the order of the Court of Appeal dismissing the appeal, as the case may be, the Judge confirming the sentence shall transmit the record of the case or a certified copy thereof to the President with a report in writing signed by him containing any recommendation or observations on the case he may think fit to make.

(3)   After receiving the advice of the Advisory Committee on the Prerogative of Mercy on the case, in accordance with the provisions of the Constitution, the President shall communicate to the said Judge, or his successor in office, the terms of any decision to which he may come thereon, and such Judge shall cause the tenor and substance thereof to be entered in the records of the court.
Cap. 1

(4)   The President shall issue a death warrant, or an order for the sentence of death to be commuted, or a pardon, under his hand and the seal of the Republic, to give effect to the said decision. If the sentence of death is to be carried out, the warrant shall state the place where and the time when execution is to be had, and shall give directions as to the place of burial of the body of the person executed. If the sentence is commuted for any other punishment, the order shall specify that punishment. If the person sentenced is pardoned, the pardon shall state whether it is free, or to what conditions (if any) it is subject:

Provided that the warrant may direct that the execution shall take place at such time and at such place, and that the body of the person executed shall be buried or cremated at such place, as shall be appointed by some officer specified in the warrant.

(5)   The warrant or order or pardon of the President shall be sufficient authority in law to all persons to whom the same is directed to execute the sentence of death or other punishment awarded, and to carry out the directions therein given in accordance with the terms thereof.

(As amended by No. 14 of 1938, G.N. No. 303 of 1964 and S.I. No. 63 of 1964)

Procedure where woman convicted of capital offence alleges she is pregnant

306. (1)   Where a woman convicted of an offence punishable with death alleges that she is pregnant, or where the court before which a woman is so convicted thinks fit so to order, the question whether or not the woman is pregnant shall, before sentence is passed on her, be determined by the court.

(2)   The question whether such woman is pregnant or not shall be determined by the court on such evidence as may be laid before it either on the part of the woman or on the part of the prosecution, and the court shall find that the woman is not pregnant unless it is proved affirmatively to its satisfaction that she is pregnant.

(3)   Where, on proceedings under this section, a subordinate court finds that the woman in question is not pregnant, the woman may appeal to the High Court, and the High Court, if satisfied that for any reason the finding should be set aside, shall quash the sentence passed on her and, in lieu thereof, pass on her a sentence of imprisonment for life.

(As amended by No. 28 of 1940)

Other Sentences

306A. (1) A court may make an order for the community service where in the case of an adult, the offence is misdemeanour and is punishable with imprisonment.

(2)   Before making an order for community service, the court shall consider the report submitted by a superior police officer or other person or institution as the court may consider appropriate as regards the character, antecedents, home surroundings, health or mental condition of the offender, or to the nature of the offence, or to any extenuating circumstances in which the offence was committed.

(3)   Before making an order for community service, the court shall explain to the offender in the language the offender understands, the effect of the order and shall obtain the consent of the offender to perform community service and explain that where the offender fails to comply with the order the offender shall be liable to the term of imprisonment the court has imposed in respect of that offence.

306B. 1. An order for community service shall specify-
    (a) the number of hours to be worked;
    (b) the days on which the work is to be performed;
    (c) the period of community service;
    (d) the place where the offender is to perform community service;
    (e) that the offender shall, during the period of the community service, be under the supervision of an authorised officer; and
    (f) any other special terms and conditions of the order.

(2) For the purposes of section three hundred and six A, this section and of section three hundred and six C-
"authorised police officer" has the meaning assigned to it in the Prison act; and
"superior police officer" has the meaning assigned to it in the Zambia Police Act.

306C. Upon making an order for community service, the court shall order is made to report forthwith to an authorised officer in the area community service will be performed.

306D. (1) If at any one time during the community service period it appears to the court that the offender has failed to comply with the requirements of the community service order, the court may issue summons requiring the offender to appear at the place and time specified therein or may issue a warrant of arrest.

(2) A summons or warrant shall direct the offender to appear or to be brought before the court by which the community service order was made.

(3) If it is proved to the satisfaction of the court that the offender has failed to comply with any of the requirements of the community service order, the court may-
    (a) vary the order to suit the circumstances of the case;
    (b) impose on the offender a fine not exceeding three hundred penalty units; or
    (c) cancel the order and send the offender is liable, subject nevertheless to a reduction of the number of days, if any, for which community service has already been performed.

306E. Where an offender has been ordered to undergo community service on conviction by an original court but has been sentenced to imprisonment by a subsequent court for another offence committed during the period of community service, the following shall apply:
    (a) the subsequent court may add to the sentence imposed a further term of imprisonment which might have been passed by the original court and cancel the order of community service;
    (b) in making the sentence the subsequent court may take into account the period of community service served in reduction of the additional imprisonment;
    (c) where the original court was the High Court and the subsequent court is the subordinate court, the subordinate court shall send the copy of the proceedings to the High Court and on receipt, the High Court shall proceed under paragraphs (a) and (b) of this section;
    (d) where the original court was a subordinate court, and the subsequent court is the High Court dealing with the matter at first instance or an appeal or otherwise, the High Court shall proceed under paragraphs (a) and (b) of this section;
    (e) where both the original court and the subsequent court are subordinate courts, the subsequent court shall proceed under paragraphs (a) and (b) of this section;
    (f) where a subsequent court has convicted the offender of an offence, that court may pass the sentence other than imprisonment and order the offender to continue undergoing community service.

Offender to report to an authorised officer
Failure of offender to comply with community service order

Commission of further offence

Warrant in case of sentence of imprisonment

307. A warrant under the hand of the Judge or magistrate by whom any person shall be sentenced to imprisonment, ordering that the sentence shall be carried out in any prison within Zambia, shall be issued by the sentencing Judge or magistrate, and shall be full authority to the officer in charge of such prison and to all other persons for carrying into effect the sentence described in such warrant.[9]
(As amended by No. 28 of 1940 and No. 16 of 1959)

---

[9] As amended by s 7 of Act No 22 of 2022.

Warrant for levy of fine, etc.

308. (1) When a court orders money to be paid by an accused person or by a prosecutor or complainant for fine, penalty, compensation, costs, expenses, or otherwise, the money may be levied on the movable and immovable property of the person ordered to pay the same, by distress and sale under warrant. If he shows sufficient movable property to satisfy the order, his immovable property shall not be sold.

(2) Such person may pay or tender to the officer having the execution of the warrant the sum therein mentioned, together with the amount of the expenses of the distress up to the time of payment or tender, and, thereupon, the officer shall cease to execute the same.

(3) A warrant under this section may be executed within the local limits of the jurisdiction of the court issuing the same, and it shall authorise the distress and sale of any property belonging to such person without such limits, when endorsed by a magistrate holding a subordinate court of the first or second class within the local limits of whose jurisdiction such property was found.

Objections to attachment

309. (1) Any person claiming to be entitled to have a legal or equitable interest in the whole or part of any property attached in execution of a warrant issued under section three hundred and eight may, at any time prior to the receipt by the court of the proceeds of sale of such property, give notice in writing to the court of his objection to the attachment of such property. Such notice shall set out shortly the nature of the claim which such person (hereinafter in this section called "the objector") makes to the whole or part of the property attached, and shall certify the value of the property claimed by him. Such value shall be deposed to an affidavit which shall be filed with the notice.

(2) Upon receipt of a valid notice given under subsection (1), the court shall, by an order in writing addressed to the officer having the execution of the warrant, direct a stay of the execution proceedings.

(3) Upon the issue of an order under subsection (2), the court shall, by notice in writing, direct the objector to appear before such court and establish his claim upon a date to be specified in the notice.

(4) A notice shall be served upon the person whose property was, by the warrant issued under section three hundred and eight, directed to be attached and, unless the property is to be applied to the payment of a fine, upon the person entitled to the proceeds of the sale of such property. Such notice shall specify the time and place fixed for the appearance of the objector and shall direct the person upon whom the notice is served to appear before the court at the same time and place if he wishes to be heard upon the hearing of the objection.

(5) Upon the date fixed for the hearing of the objection, the court shall investigate the claim and, for such purpose, may hear any evidence which the objector may give or adduce and any evidence given or adduced by any person served with a notice in accordance with subsection (4).

(6) If, upon investigation of the claim, the court is satisfied that the property attached was not, when attached, in the possession of the person ordered to pay the money or of some person in trust for him, or in the occupancy of a tenant or other person paying rent to him, or that, being in the possession of the person ordered to pay the money at such time, it was so in his possession not on his own account or as his own property but on account of or in trust for some other person, or partly on his own account and partly on account of some other person, the court shall make an order releasing the property, wholly or to such extent as it thinks fit, from attachment.

(7) If, upon the date fixed for his appearance, the objector fails to appear, or if, upon investigation of the claim in accordance with subsection (5), the court is of opinion that the objector has failed to establish his claim, the court shall order the attachment and execution to proceed and shall make such order as to costs as it deems proper.

(8) Nothing in this section shall be deemed to deprive a person who has failed to comply with the requirements of subsection (1) of the right to take any other proceedings which, apart from the provisions of this section, may lawfully be taken by a person claiming an interest in property attached under a warrant.

(No. 28 of 1940)

Suspension of execution of sentence of imprisonment in default of fine

310. (1) When a convicted person has been sentenced to a fine only and to imprisonment in default of payment of that fine, and whether or not a warrant of distress has been issued under section three hundred and eight, the court may, if it is satisfied that such fine cannot be immediately paid, allow the convicted person time to pay such fine.

    (2) When a court allows a convicted person time to pay a fine under this section, it shall make a note to that effect on the record of the case.

    (3) Where a convicted person is allowed time to pay a fine under this section, no warrant of commitment to prison in respect of the non-payment of such fine shall be issued until after the expiration of the time allowed for such payment.

(No. 5 of 1962)

Commitment for want of distress

311. If the officer having the execution of a warrant of distress reports that he could find no property, or not sufficient property, whereon to levy the money mentioned in the warrant with expenses, the court may, by the same or a subsequent warrant, commit the person ordered to pay to prison, for a time specified in the warrant, unless the money and all expenses of the distress, commitment and conveyance to prison, to be specified in the warrant, are sooner paid.

Commitment in lieu of distress

312. When it appears to the court that distress and sale of property would be ruinous to the person ordered to pay the money or to his family, or (by his confession or otherwise) that he has no property whereon the distress may be levied, or other sufficient reason appears to the court, the court may, if it thinks fit, instead of or after issuing a warrant of distress, commit him to prison for a time specified in the warrant, unless the money and all expenses of the commitment and conveyance to prison, to be specified in the warrant, are sooner paid.

Payment in full after commitment

313. Any person committed for non-payment may pay the sum mentioned in the warrant, with the amount of expenses therein authorised (if any), to the person in whose custody he is, and that person shall, thereupon, discharge him, if he is in custody for no other matter.

Part payment after commitment

314. (1) If any person committed to prison for non-payment shall pay any sum in part satisfaction of the sum adjudged to be paid, the term of his imprisonment shall be reduced by a number of days bearing, as nearly as possible, the same proportion to the total number of days for which such person is committed, as the sum so paid bears to the sum for which he is liable.

    (2) If any person committed to prison for default of sufficient distress shall pay any sum in part satisfaction thereof, or if any part of the fine is levied by process of law, whether before or subsequent to his commitment to prison, the term of his imprisonment shall be reduced as in subsection (1) provided.

    (3) The officer in charge of a prison in which a person is confined who is desirous of taking advantage of the provisions of the preceding subsections shall, on application being made to him by such prisoner, at once take him before a court, and such court shall certify the amount by which the term of imprisonment originally awarded is reduced by such payment in part satisfaction, and shall make such order as is required in the circumstances.

Who may issue warrant

315. Every warrant for the execution of any sentence may be issued either by the Judge or magistrate who passed the sentence, or by his successor in office.

Limitation of imprisonment

Previously Convicted Offenders

316. No commitment for non-payment shall be for a longer period than nine months, unless the written law under which the conviction has taken place enjoins or allows a longer period.

Person twice convicted may be subjected to police supervision

317. (1)   When any person, having been convicted of any offence punishable with imprisonment for a term of three years or more, is again convicted of any offence punishable with imprisonment for a term of three years or more, the court may, if it thinks fit, at the time of passing sentence of imprisonment on such person, also order that he shall be subject to police supervision, as hereinafter provided, for a term not exceeding five years from the date of his release from prison.

     (2)   If such conviction is set aside on appeal or otherwise, such order shall become void.

     (3)   An order under this section may be made by the High Court when exercising its powers of revision.

     (4)   Every such order shall be stated in the warrant of commitment.

(As amended by No. 5 of 1962)

Requirements from persons subject to police supervision

318. (1)   Every person subject to police supervision shall, on discharge from prison, be furnished by the prescribed officer with an identity book in the prescribed form, and, while at large in Zambia, shall-

        (a)   report himself personally at such intervals of time, at such place and to such person, as shall be endorsed on his book; and

        (b)   notify his residential address, any intention to change his residential address and any change thereof, in such manner and to such person as may be prescribed by rules under this section.

     (2)   The President may, by statutory instrument, make rules for carrying out the provisions of this section.

(As amended by No. 5 of 1962 and G.N. No. 303 of 1964)

Defects in Order or Warrant

Failure to comply with requirements under section 318

319.   If any person subject to police supervision who is at large in Zambia refuses or neglects to comply with any requirement prescribed by the last preceding section or by any rule made thereunder, such person shall, unless he proves to the satisfaction of the court before which he is tried that he did his best to act in conformity with the law, be guilty of an offence and liable to imprisonment for a term not exceeding six months.

Errors and omissions in orders and warrants

320.   The court may, at any time, amend any defect in substance or in form in any order or warrant, and no omission or error as to time or place, and no defect in form in any order or warrant given under this Code, shall be held to render void or unlawful any act done or intended to be done by virtue of such order or warrant, provided that it is therein mentioned, or may be inferred therefrom, that it is founded on a conviction or judgment, and there is a valid conviction or judgment to sustain the same.

PART XI
APPEALS

Appeals

321. (1)   Any person convicted by a subordinate court may appeal to the High Court- Cap. 27

        (a)   against his conviction on any ground of appeal which involves a question of law alone; or

        (b)   against his conviction on any ground of appeal which involves a question of fact alone, or a question of mixed law and fact; or

        (c)   against the sentence passed on his conviction, unless the sentence is one fixed by law; and shall be so informed by the magistrate at the time when sentence is passed.

     (2)   For the purposes of this Part "sentence" includes any order made on conviction not being-

        (a)   a probation order or an order for conditional discharge;

        (b)   an order under any enactment which enables the court to order the destruction of an animal; or

301

(c) an order made in pursuance of any enactment under which the court has no discretion as to the making of the order or its terms.

Appeals by Director of Public Prosecutions

321A. (1) If the Director of Public Prosecutions is dissatisfied with a judgment of a subordinate court as being erroneous in point of law, or as being in excess of jurisdiction, he may appeal against any such judgment to the High Court within fourteen days of the decision of the subordinate court.

(2) On an appeal under this section the High Court may-
   (a) reverse, affirm or amend any such judgment;
   (b) find the person in relation to whom such judgment was given guilty of the offence of which he was charged in the subordinate court or of any other offence of which he could have been convicted by the subordinate court and may convict and sentence him for such or such other offence;

(G.N. No. 493 of 1964 as amended by No. 23 of 1971 and 30 of 1976)

322. No appeal shall be heard unless entered-
   (a) in the case of an appeal against sentence, within fourteen days of the date of such sentence;
   (b) in the case of an appeal against conviction, within fourteen days of the date of sentence imposed in respect of such conviction:
   (c) remit the matter to the subordinate court for rehearing and determination, with such directions as it may deem necessary; or
   (d) make such other order including an order as to costs, as it may deem fit.Limitation

(3) The provisions of sections three hundred and twenty-three, three hundred and twenty-four, three hundred and twenty-five, three hundred and twenty-eight, three hundred and twenty-nine, three hundred and thirty-three and three hundred and thirty-four shall apply mutatis mutandis to appeals under this section as they apply to appeals under the provisions of section three hundred and twenty-one.   (4) The provisions of section three hundred and forty-eight shall apply mutatis mutandis in relation to the decision of the High Court in any appeal under this section, as they apply in relation to a decision given on a case stated under section three hundred and forty-one.

(5) In this section, "judgment" includes conviction, acquittal, sentence, order and decision.
Provided that the appellate court may at its discretion hear an appeal in respect of which an application has been made in accordance with the provisions of section three hundred and twenty-four.

(No. 5 of 1962 as amended by No. 76 of 1965 and Act 12 of 1973)

Procedure preliminary to appeal

323. (1) An appeal shall be entered-
   (a) by filing with the court below a notice of appeal in the form prescribed; or
   (b) if the appellant is in prison, by handing such notice to the officer in charge of the prison in which he is lodged.

(2) The officer in charge of any prison shall, on receipt of a notice of appeal, endorse upon such notice the date it was handed to him and shall transmit the notice to the court below.

(3) The court below shall transmit to the appellate court a notice of appeal filed with or transmitted to it under this section together with the record of the case and the judgment or order therein. (No. 76 of 1965)

Procedure for application to appeal out of time

324. (1) Where the period has expired within which, under section three hundred and twenty-two, an appeal shall be entered, an appellant may nevertheless make application in the prescribed form for his appeal to be heard and shall in support of any such application enter an appeal, and the form of application shall be attached to the notice of appeal when that notice is filed with or transmitted to the court below and the appellate court.

(2) In any case where an appellate court refuses an application made under subsection (1), the appeal entered in support of the application shall be deemed never to have been entered. (No. 76 of 1965)

Procedure on appeal

325. Every appellant shall be entitled, if he so desires, to be present at the hearing of his appeal, and to be heard, either personally or by his advocate. If he does not desire to be present or to be heard, either personally or by his advocate, then the appellate court shall decide the appeal summarily, without hearing argument, unless it sees fit to direct otherwise, on the documents forwarded to it as in section three hundred and twenty-three provided.

Notice of time and place of hearing

326. If the appellate court does not determine the appeal summarily, it shall cause notice to be given to the appellant or his advocate, and to the public or private prosecutor at the place where the appeal is to be heard, of the time and place at which such appeal will be heard, and shall furnish such prosecutor with a copy of the documents prescribed by section three hundred and twenty-three.

Powers of appellate court

327. (1) The appellate court, after perusing the documents forwarded to it, if the appeal is being heard summarily, or after hearing the appellant or his advocate, if he appears, and the prosecutor, if he appears, may, if it considers that there is no sufficient ground for interfering, dismiss the appeal, or may-

   (a) on an appeal from a conviction-
      (i)   reverse the finding and sentence, and acquit or discharge the accused, or order him to be retried by a subordinate court of competent jurisdiction or by the High Court; or
      (ii) alter the finding, maintaining the sentence, or, with or without altering the finding, reduce or increase the sentence; or
      (iii) with or without such reduction or increase, and with or without altering the finding, alter the nature of the sentence;

   (b) on an appeal against sentence, quash the sentence passed at the trial, and pass such other sentence warranted in law (whether more or less severe) in substitution therefor as it thinks ought to have been passed, and, in any other case, dismiss the appeal;

   (c) on an appeal from any other order, alter or reverse such order;
   and, in any case, may make any amendment or any consequential or incidental order that may appear just and proper.

(2) Where the High Court has directed that an appellant shall be retried by the High Court under the provisions of paragraph (a) of subsection (1), the trial shall be conducted without a preliminary inquiry in accordance with the provisions of subsection (4) of section sixty-eight.

(As amended by No. 2 of 1960 and G.N. No. 493 of 1964)

Pronouncement of decision of the High Court sitting as an appellate court

328. (1) The High Court sitting as an appellate court may, at the close of an appeal, pronounce its decision on the appeal and give its reasons for the decision.

(2) Where the High Court pronounces its decision at the close of an appeal under subsection (1), the judgment of the court shall be pronounced in such manner as the court may direct:
   Provided that, where an appeal is heard by more than one Judge, any such Judge may give directions as to the manner in which the judgment shall be pronounced, and the judgment may be so pronounced whether or not the other Judge or Judges who heard the appeal are present.

(No. 11 of 1963 as amended by No. 23 of 1971)

Order of appellate court to be certified

329. The appellate court shall certify its judgment or order to the court below, which shall, thereupon, make such orders as are conformable to the judgment or order of the appellate court, and, if necessary, the records shall be amended in accordance therewith.

330.   I(As amended by No. 14 of 1938, No. 11 of 1963 and Repealed by Act No. 9 of 2003)

Suspension of orders on conviction

331. The operation of any order for the restitution of any property to any person made on a conviction, and the operation, in the case of any conviction, of any rule of law as to the revesting of the property

in stolen goods on conviction, as also the operation of any order of compensation to an injured party, shall be suspended-

(a) in any case, until the expiration of fourteen days after the date of the conviction; and

(b) in cases where an appeal has been entered, until the determination of the appeal.

(As amended by No. 28 of 1940)

Admission to bail or suspension of sentence pending appeal

332. (1) After the entering of an appeal by a person entitled to appeal, the appellate court, or the subordinate court which convicted or sentenced such person, may, for reasons to be recorded by it in writing, order that he be released on bail with or without sureties, or if such person is not released on bail shall, at the request of such person, order that the execution of the sentence or order appealed against shall be suspended pending the hearing of his appeal.

(2) If the appeal is ultimately dismissed and the original sentence confirmed, or some other sentence of imprisonment substituted therefor, the time during which the appellant has been released on bail, or during which the sentence has been suspended, shall, unless the court shall otherwise order, be excluded in computing the term of imprisonment to which he is finally sentenced. (No 28 of 1940 as amended by No. 1959)

Further evidence

333. (1) In dealing with an appeal from a court below, the appellate court, if it thinks additional evidence is necessary, shall record its reasons, and may either take such evidence itself or direct it to be taken by the court below.

(2) When the additional evidence is taken by the court below, such court shall certify such evidence to the appellate court, which shall, thereupon, proceed to dispose of the appeal.

(3) Unless the appellate court otherwise directs, the accused or his advocate shall be present when the additional evidence is taken.

(4) Evidence taken in pursuance of this section shall be taken as if it were evidence taken at a trial before a subordinate court.

Appeals to be heard by one Judge unless the Chief Justice otherwise directs

334. (1) Appeals from subordinate courts to the High Court shall be heard by one Judge except where the Chief Justice shall direct that the appeal be heard by more than one Judge.

(2) Where an appeal is heard by more than one Judge and such Judges are divided equally in opinion, the appeal shall be dismissed. (No. 11 of 1963)

Abatement of appeals

335. Every appeal from a subordinate court (except an appeal from a sentence of fine) shall finally abate on the death of the appellant.

Bail in cases of appeals to Supreme Court

336. (1) The High Court may, if it deems fit, on the application of an appellant from a judgment of that Court and pending the determination of his appeal or application for leave to appeal to the Supreme Court in a criminal matte-

(a) admit the appellant to bail, or if it does not so admit him, direct him to be treated as an unconvicted prisoner pending the determination of his appeal or of his application for leave to appeal, as the case may be; and

(b) postpone the payment of any fine imposed upon him.

(2) The time during which an appellant, pending the determination of his appeal, is admitted to bail, and, subject to any directions which the Supreme Court may give to the contrary in any appeal, the time during which the appellant, if in custody, is treated as an unconvicted prisoner under this section, shall not count as part of any term of imprisonment under his sentence. Any imprisonment under the sentence of the appellant, whether it is the sentence passed by the court of trial or by the High Court in its appellate jurisdiction or the sentence passed by the Supreme Court, shall, subject to any directions which the Supreme Court may give to the contrary, be deemed to be resumed or to begin to run, as the case requires-

(a) if the appellant is in custody, as from the day on which the appeal is determined;

(b) if the appellant is not in custody, as from the day on which he is received into gaol under the sentence. (No. 47 of 1955 as amended by G.N. No. 303 of 1964, No. 23 of 1971 and 30 of 1976)

Revision

Power of High Court to call for records

337. The High Court may call for and examine the record of any criminal proceedings before any subordinate court, for the purpose of satisfying itself as to the correctness, legality or propriety of any finding, sentence or order recorded or passed; and as to the regularity of any proceedings of any such subordinate court.

338. (1) In the case of any proceedings in a subordinate court, the record of which has been called for, or which otherwise comes to its knowledge, the High Court may-

Powers of High Court on revision

(a) in the case of a conviction-

(i) confirm, vary or reverse the decision of the subordinate court, or order that the person convicted be retried by a subordinate court of competent jurisdiction or by the High Court, or make such other order in the matter as to it may seem just, and may by such order exercise any power which the subordinate court might have exercised;

(ii) if it thinks a different sentence should have been passed, quash the sentence passed by the subordinate court and pass such other sentence warranted in law, whether more or less severe, in substitution therefor as it thinks ought to have been passed;

(iii) if it thinks additional evidence is necessary, either take such additional evidence itself or direct that it be taken by the subordinate court;

(iv) direct the subordinate court to impose such sentence or make such order as may be specified;

(b) in the case of any other order, other than an order of acquittal, alter or reverse such order.

(2) No order under this section shall be made to the prejudice of an accused person unless he has had an opportunity of making representations in writing on his own behalf.

(3) The High Court shall not exercise any powers under this section in respect of any convicted person who has appealed, unless such appeal is withdrawn, or who has made application for a case to be stated, unless the subordinate court concerned refuses to state a case under the provisions of section three hundred and forty-three.

(4) Nothing in this section shall be to the prejudice of the exercise of any right of appeal given under this Code or under any other law.

(5) The provisions of subsections (2), (3) and (4) of section three hundred and thirty-three shall apply, mutatis mutandis, in respect of any additional evidence.

(6) When the High Court gives a direction under subparagraph (iv) of paragraph (a) of subsection (1), the record of the proceedings shall be returned to the subordinate court and that court shall comply with the said direction.

(As amended by No. 16 of 1959 and No. 11 of 1963)

Discretion of High Court as to hearing parties

339. No party has any right to be heard, either personally or by advocate, before the High Court when exercising its powers of revision:
Provided that the High Court may, if it thinks fit, when exercising such powers, hear any party either personally or by advocate.
(As amended by G.N. No. 493 of 1964)

Order to be certified to lower court

340. When a case is revised by the High Court, the Court shall certify its decision or order to the court by which the sentence or order, so revised, was recorded or passed, and the court to which the decision or order is so certified shall, thereupon, make such orders as are conformable to the decision so certified, and, if necessary, the record shall be amended in accordance therewith.
(As amended by G.N. No. 493 of 1964)

Case Stated

Case stated by subordinate court

341. After the hearing and determination by any subordinate court of any summons, charge, information or complaint, either party to the proceedings before the said subordinate court may, if dissatisfied with the said determination, as being erroneous in point of law, or as being in excess of jurisdiction, apply in writing, within fourteen days after the said determination, to the said subordinate court to state and sign a case setting forth the facts and the grounds of such determination, for the opinion thereon of the High Court, and such party (hereinafter called "the appellant") shall-

    (a) within fourteen days after receiving the case transmit the same to the High Court; and

    (b) within thirty days after receiving the case serve a copy of the case so stated and signed on the other party to the proceedings in which the determination was given (hereinafter called "the respondent").

(No. 28 of 1940)

Recognizance to be taken and fees paid

342. The appellant, at the time of making such application, and before the case shall be stated and delivered to him by the subordinate court, shall, in every instance, enter into a recognizance before such subordinate court, with or without surety or sureties, and in such sum not exceeding one hundred kwacha as to the subordinate court shall seem meet, conditioned to prosecute without delay such appeal, and to submit to the judgment of the High Court, and to pay such costs as may be awarded by the same; and, before he shall be entitled to have the case delivered to him, he shall pay to the clerk of such subordinate court his fees for and in respect of the case and recognizance, which fees shall be in accordance with the Third Schedule. The appellant, if then in custody, shall be liberated upon the recognizance being further conditioned for his appearance before the same subordinate court, or, if that is impracticable, before some other subordinate court exercising the same jurisdiction, within fourteen days after the judgment of the High Court shall have been given, to abide such judgment, unless the determination appealed against be reversed:

Provided that nothing in this section shall apply to an application for a case stated by or under the direction of the Director of Public Prosecutions.

(As amended by S.I. No. 152 of 1965)

Subordinate court may refuse case when it thinks application frivolous

343. If the subordinate court be of opinion that the application is merely frivolous, but not otherwise, it may refuse to state a case, and shall, on the request of the appellant, and on payment of the fee set out in the Third Schedule, sign and deliver to him a certificate of such refusal:

Provided that the subordinate court shall not refuse to state a case when the application for that purpose is made to it by or under the direction of the Director of Public Prosecutions, who may require a case to be stated with reference to proceedings to which he was not a party.

(As amended by S.I. No. 63 of 1964)

Procedure on refusal of subordinate court to state case

344. Where a subordinate court refuses to state a case, the High Court may, on the application of the person who applied for the case to be stated, make an order of mandamus requiring the subordinate court to state a case.

Constitution of court hearing case stated

345. A case stated for the opinion of the High Court shall be heard by one Judge of the Court except when, in any particular case, the Chief Justice shall direct that it shall be heard by two Judges. Such direction may be given before the hearing or at any time before judgment is delivered. If, on the hearing, the Court is equally divided in opinion, the decision of the subordinate court shall be affirmed.

(No. 2 of 1960)

High Court to determine questions on case

346. The High Court shall (subject to the provisions of the next succeeding section) hear and determine the question or questions of law arising on the case stated, and shall, thereupon, reverse, affirm or amend

306

the determination in respect of which the case has been stated, or remit the matter to the subordinate court with the opinion of the High Court thereon, or may make such other order in relation to the matter, and may make such order as to costs, as to the Court may seem fit, and all such orders shall be final and conclusive on all parties:

Provided that-

(i) no magistrate who shall state and deliver a case in pursuance of this Part, or bona fide refuse to state one, shall be liable to any costs in respect or by reason of such appeal against his determination or refusal;

(ii) no costs shall be awarded against the People, except where the People are the appellant.

(As amended by S.I. No. 63 of 1964)

Case may be sent back for amendment or rehearing

347.   The High Court shall have power, if it thinks fit-

(a) to cause the case to be sent back for amendment or restatement, and, thereupon, the same shall be amended or restated accordingly, and judgment shall be delivered after it has been so amended or restated;

(b) to remit the case to the subordinate court for rehearing and determination, with such directions as it may deem necessary.

Powers of subordinate court after decision of High Court

348. After the decision of the High Court has been given on a case stated, the subordinate court in relation to whose determination the case has been stated, or any other subordinate court exercising the same jurisdiction, shall have the same authority to enforce any conviction or order which may have been affirmed, amended or made by the High Court as the subordinate court which originally decided the case would have had to enforce its determination, if the same had not been appealed against; and no action or proceeding whatsoever shall be commenced or had against the magistrate holding such subordinate court for enforcing such conviction or order, by reason of any defect in the same respectively.

Appellant may not proceed both by case stated and by appeal

349. No person who has appealed under section three hundred and twenty-one shall be entitled to have a case stated, and no person who has applied to have a case stated shall be entitled to appeal under section three hundred and twenty-one.

Contents of case stated

350.   A case stated by a subordinate court shall set out-

(a) the charge, summons, information or complaint;

(b) the facts found by the subordinate court to be proved;

(c) any submission of law made by or on behalf of the complainant during the trial or inquiry;

(d) any submission of law made by or on behalf of the accused during the trial or inquiry;

(e) the finding and, in case of conviction, the sentence of the subordinate court;

(f) any question or questions of law which the subordinate court or any of the parties may desire to be submitted for the opinion of the High Court;

(g) any question of law which the Director of Public Prosecutions may require to be submitted for the opinion of the High Court.

(As amended by S.I. No. 63 of 1964)

High Court may enlarge time

351. The High Court may, if it deems fit, enlarge any period of time prescribed by section three hundred and forty-one or three hundred and forty-two.

(As amended by No. 5 of 1962)

Interpretation

351A.   In this Part, "appellate court" means the High Court.

(No. 23 of 1971)

PART XII
SUPPLEMENTARY PROVISIONS

Irregular Proceedings

Proceedings in wrong place

352. No finding, sentence or order of any court shall be set aside merely on the ground that the inquiry, trial or other proceeding in the course of which it was arrived at or passed took place in a wrong district, unless it appears that such error has in fact occasioned a substantial miscarriage of justice.
(As amended by No. 16 of 1959)

Finding or sentence when not reversible

353. Subject to the provisions hereinbefore contained, no finding, sentence or order passed by a court of competent jurisdiction shall be reversed or altered on appeal or revision on any ground whatsoever unless any matter raised in such ground has, in the opinion of the appellate court, in fact occasioned a substantial miscarriage of justice:
Provided that, in determining whether any such matter has occasioned a substantial miscarriage of justice, the court shall have regard to the question whether the objection could and should have been raised at an earlier stage in the proceeding.
(No. 16 of 1959)

Miscellaneous Distress not illegal nor distrainer a trespasser for defect or want of form in proceedings

354. No distress made under this Code shall be deemed unlawful, nor shall any person making the same be deemed a trespasser, on account of any defect or want of form in the summons, conviction, warrant of distress or other proceedings relating thereto.

Disposal of exhibits

355. (1) Where anything which has been tendered or put in evidence in any criminal proceedings before any court has not been claimed by any person who appears to the court to be entitled thereto within a period of twelve months after the final disposal of such proceedings or of any appeal entered in respect thereof, such thing may be sold, destroyed or otherwise disposed of in such manner as the court may by order direct, and the proceeds of any such sale shall be paid into the general revenues of the Republic.

(2) If anything which has been tendered or put in evidence in any criminal proceedings before any court is subject to speedy and natural decay the court may, at any stage of the proceedings or at any time after the final disposal of such proceedings, order that it be sold or otherwise disposed of but shall hold the proceeds of any such sale and, if unclaimed at the expiration of a period of twelve months after the final disposal of such proceedings or of any appeal entered in respect thereof, shall pay such proceeds into the general revenues of the Republic.

(3) Notwithstanding the provisions of subsection (1), the court may, if it is satisfied that it would be just and equitable so to do, order that anything tendered or put in evidence in criminal proceedings before it should be returned at any stage of the proceedings or at any time after the final disposal of such proceedings to the person who appears to be entitled thereto, subject to such conditions as the court may see fit to impose.

(4) Any order of a court made under the provisions of subsection (1) or (2) shall be final and shall operate as a bar to any claim by or on behalf of any person claiming ownership of or any interest in such thing by virtue of any title arising prior to the date of such order.
(No. 11 of 1963)

Corporations

356. (1) Where a corporation is charged with an offence before a court, the provisions of this section shall have effect.

(2) A representative may, on behalf of the corporation, make a statement before the court in answer to the charge.

(3) Where a representative appears, any requirement of this Code that anything shall be done in the presence of the accused, or shall be read or said to the accused, shall be construed as a

requirement that that thing shall be done in the presence of the representative or read or said to the representative.

(4) Where a representative does not appear, any requirement referred to in subsection (3) shall not apply.

(5) A subordinate court may, after holding an inquiry in accordance with the provisions of Part VII, make an order certifying that it considers the evidence against an accused corporation sufficient to put that corporation on its trial and the corporation shall thereupon be deemed to have been committed for trial to the High Court.

(6) Where, at the trial of a corporation, a representative does not appear at the time appointed in and by the summons or information or such representative having appeared fails to enter any plea, the court shall order a plea of "not guilty" to be entered and the trial shall proceed as though the corporation had duly entered a plea of "not guilty".

(7) Subject to the provisions of subsections (2) to (6), both inclusive, the provisions of this Code relating to the inquiry into and to the trial by any court of offences shall apply to a corporation as they apply to an individual over the age of twenty-one years.

(8) In this section, "representative" means a person duly appointed in accordance with subsection (9) by the corporation to represent it for the purpose of doing any act or thing which the representative of a corporation is by this section authorised to do, but a person so appointed shall not, by virtue only of being so appointed, be qualified to act on behalf of the corporation before any court for any other purpose.

(9) A representative for the purposes of this section need not be appointed under the seal of the corporation, and a statement in writing purporting to be signed by a managing director of the corporation, or by any person (by whatever name called) having, or being one of the persons having, the management of the affairs of the corporation, to the effect that the person named in the statement has been appointed as the representative of the corporation for the purposes of this section, shall be admissible without further proof as prima facie evidence that that person has been so appointed.

(No. 76 of 1965)

Prescribed fees

357. In addition to or in substitution for the fees set forth in the Third Schedule, the Chief Justice may prescribe the fees to be paid for any proceedings in the High Court and in subordinate courts. Such fees shall be paid by the party prosecuting, and may be charged as part of the costs, if so ordered. The payment of fees may, on account of the poverty of any person or for other good reason, be dispensed with by the court of trial.

(As amended by No. 2 of 1960)

Prescribed forms

358. (1) The Chief Justice may by rule prescribe forms for the purposes of this Code, and such forms, with such variations as the circumstances of each case may require, may be used and, if used, shall be sufficient for the respective purposes therein mentioned.

(2) The forms in the Fourth Schedule shall be deemed to have been prescribed by the Chief Justice under the provisions of this section.

(No. 2 of 1960)

Rules

359. (1) The Chief Justice may, by statutory instrument, make rules for the better administration of this Code.

(2) In particular and without prejudice to the generality of the foregoing, such rules may-
    (a) prescribe anything which by this Code may or is to be prescribed;
    (b) prescribe the allowances and expenses of witnesses and assessors;
    (c) make provisions for the procedure to be followed in relation to appeals under this Code;
    (d) amend the Second Schedule by varying or annulling forms contained therein or by adding new forms thereto.

(No. 11 of 1963)

Non-application of British Act

Non-application

360.   The Criminal Evidence Act, 1898, of the United Kingdom, shall not apply to the Republic.

FIRST SCHEDULE[10]

(Section 2)

OFFENCES UNDER THE PENAL CODE

Explanatory Note.-The entries in the second and fourth columns of this Schedule, headed respectively "Offence" and "Punishment under the Penal Code", are not intended as definitions of the offences and punishments described in the several corresponding sections of the Penal Code or even as abstracts of those sections, but merely as references to the subject of the section, the number of which is given in the first column.

Chapter V-Parties to Offences

1	2	3	4
Section	Offence	Whether the police may arrest without warrant (N.B.-Vide also sections 26 and 38, Penal Code.)	Punishment under the Penal Code. (or not)
21.	Aiding, abetting, counselling or procuring the commission of an offence aided, abetted, counselled or procured.	May arrest without warrant for the offence aided, abetted, counselled or procured.	Same punishment as counselling or procuring-warrant,if arrest for the offence aided, abetted, counselled or offence. may be made without warrant, but not otherwise.

DIVISION I-OFFENCES AGAINST PUBLIC ORDER

Chapter VII-Treason and other offences
Chapter VII-Treason and other offences

43.	Treason.	May arrest without warrant	[imprisonment for life][11]
44.	Misprision of treason.	Ditto.	Imprisonment for life.
45.	Treason-felony.	May arrest without warrant	Imprisonment for twenty years.
46.	Promoting tribal war.	Ditto.	Imprisonment for life.
48.	Inciting to mutiny.	Ditto.	Ditto.
49.	Aiding in acts of mutiny	Shall not arrest without warrant.	Imprisonment for two years.
50.	Inducing desertion.	Ditto.	Imprisonment for six months.
51 (a)	Aiding prisoner of war to escape.	May arrest without warrant.	Imprisonment for life.
51 (b)	Permitting prisoner of war to escape.	Shall not arrest without warrant.	Imprisonment for two years.
54. (1)	Offences in respect of prohibited publication.	May arrest without warrant.	Imprisonment for two years or fine of three thousand penalty units or both for first offence. Imprisonment for three years for subsequent offence.
54. (2)	Possession of prohibited publication	Ditto.	Imprisonment for one year or fine of one thousand five hundred penalty units or both for first offence. Imprisonment for two years for subsequent offence.

---

[10] This schedule has been variously amended by s 8 of Act No 22 of 2022, which Act is reproduced below for ease of reference.

[11] As asmended by s 8(a) of Act No 22 of 2022.

No.	Offence	Arrest	Penalty
55.	Failure to deliver possession of prohibited publication.	May arrest without warrant.	Imprisonment for one year or fine of one thousand five hundred penalty units or both.
57. (1)	Offences in respect of seditious practices.	Ditto.	Imprisonment for seven years or fine of six thousand penalty units or both for first offence.
57. (2)	Possession seditious publication.	Ditto.	Imprisonment for two years or fine of three thousand penalty units or both for first offence. Imprisonment for five years for subsequent offence.
58D.	Insulting National Anthem	May arrest without warrant	Imprisonment for two years
58E.[12]			
58.F.	Expressing or showing hatred, ridicule or contempt for persons because of race, tribe, place of origin or colour	Ditto	Imprisonment for two years.
63.	Administering or taking - oath to commit capital offence.	Ditto.	Imprisonment for life.
64.	Administering or taking - other unlawful oaths.	Ditto.	Imprisonment for seven years.
66. (1)	Unlawful drilling. Ditto.	Ditto.	
66. (2)	Being unlawfully drilled.	Ditto.	Imprisonment for two years.
67	False information with certain intents.	Ditto.	Imprisonment for three years.
68.	Insulting national anthem.	Ditto.	Imprisonment for two years.
69.[13]			
70.	Expressing or showing hatred, ridicule or contempt for persons because of race, tribe, place of origin or colour. (As amended by Act 9 of 1968)	Ditto.	Imprisonment for two years.

Chapter VIII-Offences affecting Relations with Foreign States and External Tranquillity

No.	Offence	Arrest	Penalty
71.[14]			
72.	Foreign enlistment. Ditto.	Ditto.	
72A. (1)	Possession of firearms and other offensive weapons	Ditto	Imprisonment for seven years.
72A. (2)	Consorting with persons in possession of firearms and other offensive weapons	Ditto	Imprisonment for five years.
72A. (3)	Delivery of firearms to persons for purposes prejudicial to public order	Ditto	Imprisonment for five years.
72A. (4)	Possession of offensive weapons in public	Ditto	Imprisonment for one year.

---

[12] As asmended by s 8(a) of Act No 22 of 2022.

[13] See s 8(c) of Act No 22 of 2022.

[14] See s 8(d) of Act No 22 of 2022.

73.	Piracy.	May arrest without warrant.	Punishment prescribed by law of England.

Chapter IX-Unlawful Assemblies, Riots and other Offences against Public Tranquility

1	2	3	4
Section	Offence	Whether the police may arrest without warrant or not	Punishment under the Penal Code. (N.B.-Vide also sections 26 and 38, Penal Code.)
75.	Unlawful assembly.	May arrest without warrant.	Imprisonment for five years.
76.	Riot.	Ditto.	Imprisonment for seven years.
79.	Rioting after proclamation.	Ditto.	Imprisonment for ten years.
80.	Obstructing proclamation.	Ditto.	Ditto.
81.	Rioters destroying buildings.	Ditto.	Imprisonment for life.
82.	Rioters injuring buildings.	Ditto.	Imprisonment for seven years.
83.	Riotously interfering with railway, etc.	Ditto.	Imprisonment for two years.
84.	Going armed in public.	Ditto.	Ditto.
85. (1)	Possession of offensive weapons or materials.	Ditto.	Imprisonment for seven years.
86.	Forcible entry.	Ditto.	Imprisonment for two years.
87.	Forcible detainer.	Ditto.	Ditto.
88.	Committing affray.	Ditto.	Imprisonment for six months or fine of seven hundred and fifty penalty units.
89.	Challenging to fight a duel.	Shall not arrest without warrant.	Imprisonment for two years.
90.	Threatening violence.	May arrest without warrant.	Imprisonment for five years.
91.	Proposing violence.	Ditto.	Imprisonment for seven years.
92.	Wrongfully inducing boycott.	Ditto.	Imprisonment for six months.
93.	Assembling for purpose of smuggling.	Ditto.	Imprisonment for six months or fine of three thousand penalty units.

DIVISION II-OFFENCES AGAINST THE ADMINISTRATION OF LAWFUL AUTHORITY
Chapter X-Corruption and Abuse of Office

98.	False claims by officials.	Ditto.	Imprisonment for two years.
99.	Abuse of office.	Ditto.	Ditto.
	Ditto (if for purposes of gain).	Ditto.	Imprisonment for three years.
100.	False certificates by public officers.	Ditto.	Imprisonment for two years.
101.	False assumption of authority.	Ditto.	Ditto.
102.	Personating public officers.	May arrest without warrant.	Imprisonment for three years.

103.	Threat of injury to persons employed in public service.	Shall not arrest without warrant.	Imprisonment for two years.

Chapter XI-Offences Relating to the Administration of Justice

105.	False statements by interpreters.	Shall not arrest without warrant.	Same punishment as for perjury.
106.	Perjury or subornation of perjury.	Ditto.	Imprisonment for seven years.
108.	Fabricating evidence.	Ditto.	Ditto.
109.	False swearing.	Ditto.	Imprisonment for two years.
110.	Deceiving witnesses.	Ditto.	Ditto.
111.	Destroying evidence.	Ditto.	Ditto.
112.	Conspiracy to defeat justice, and interference with witnesses.	Ditto.	Ditto.
113.	Compounding felonies.	Ditto.	Ditto.
114.	Compounding penal actions.	Ditto.	Ditto.
115.	Advertising for stolen property.	Ditto.	Ditto.
116. (1)	Contempt of court.	Ditto.	Imprisonment for six months or fine of seven hundred and fifty penalty units.
116. (2)	Contempt of court (if committed in view of court).	May arrest without warrant.	Fine of six hundred penalty units-in default of payment imprisonment for one month.
117.	Prohibition on taking photographs, etc., in court.	Ditto.	Fine of one thousand five hundred penalty units for each offence.

Chapter XII-Rescues, Escapes and Obstructing Officers of Court of Law

118. (1)	Rescue-		
	(a) if person rescued is under sentence of imprisonment for life or charged with offence punishable with imprisonment for life[15]	May arrest without	Imprisonment for life.
	(b) If person rescued is imprisoned on a charge or under sentence for any other offence;	Ditto.	Imprisonment for seven years.
	(c) In any other case.	Ditto.	Imprisonment for two years.
119.	Escape.	Ditto.	Ditto.
120.	Aiding prisoners to escape.	Ditto.	Imprisonment for seven years.
121.	Removal, etc., of property under lawful seizure.	Ditto.	Imprisonment for three years.
122.	Obstructing court officers.	Ditto.	Imprisonment for one year.

---

[15] See s 8(e) of Act No 22 of 2022.

Chapter XIII-Miscellaneous Offences against Public Authority

1	2	3	4
Section	Offence	Whether the police may arrest without warrant or not	Punishment under the Penal Code. (N.B.-Vide also sections 26 and 38, Penal Code.)
123.	Frauds and breaches of trust by public officers.	Shall not arrest without warrant.	Imprisonment for two years.
125.	False information to public officer.	Ditto.	Imprisonment for six months or fine of one thousand five hundred penalty units or both.
126.	Disobedience of statutory duty.	Ditto.	Imprisonment for two years.
127.	Disobedience of lawful orders.	Ditto.	Ditto.

DIVISION III-OFFENCES INJURIOUS TO THE PUBLIC IN GENERAL

Chapter XIV-Offences Relating to Religion

128.	Insult to religion of any class.	May arrest without warrant.	Imprisonment for two years.
129.	Disturbing religious assemblies.	Ditto.	Ditto.
130.	Trespassing on burial places.	May arrest without warrant.	Imprisonment for two years.
131.	Uttering words with intent to wound religious feelings.	Shall not arrest without warrant.	Imprisonment for one year.

Chapter XV-Offences Against Morality

133.	Rape.	May arrest without warrant.	Imprisonment for life.
134.	Attempted rape.	Ditto.	Ditto.
135.	Abduction.	Ditto.	Imprisonment for seven years.
136.	Abduction of girl under sixteen.	Ditto.	Imprisonment for two years.
137. (1)	Indecent assault on females.	Ditto.	Imprisonment for fourteen years.
137. (3)	Indecently insulting or annoying females.	Ditto.	Imprisonment for one year.
138. (1)	Defilement of girl under sixteen.	Ditto.	Imprisonment for life.
138. (2)	Attempted defilement of girl under sixteen.	Ditto.	Imprisonment for fourteen years.
139.	Defilement of an idiot or imbecile.	Ditto.	Ditto.
140.	Procuration.	Ditto.	Imprisonment for two years.
141.	Procuring defilement by threats or fraud or administering drugs.	Ditto.	Ditto.
142.	Householder permitting defilement of girl under twelve on his premises.	Ditto.	Imprisonment for five years.
143.	Householder permitting defilement of girl under sixteen on his premises.	Ditto.	Imprisonment for two years.

144.	Detention with unlawful intent or in brothel.		Ditto.	Ditto.

Chapter XV-Offences Against Morality-Continued

1	2	3	4
Section	Offence	Whether the police may arrest without warrant or not	Punishment under the Penal Code. (N.B.-Vide also sections 26 and 38, Penal Code.)
146.	Male person living on earnings of prostitution or persistently soliciting.	Ditto.	Ditto.
147.	Woman aiding, etc., for gain prostitution of another woman.	Ditto.	Ditto.
149.	Keeping a brothel.	Ditto.	Ditto.
150.	Conspiracy to defile.	Ditto.	Imprisonment for three years.
151.	Attempt to procure abortion.	Ditto.	Imprisonment for fourteen years.
152.	Woman attempting to procure her own abortion.	May arrest without warrant.	Imprisonment for seven years.
153.	Supplying drugs or instruments to procure abortion.	Ditto.	Imprisonment for three years.
155.	Unnatural offences.	Ditto.	Imprisonment for fourteen years.
156.	Attempt to commit unnatural offence.	Ditto.	Imprisonment for seven years.
157.	Indecent assault on boys under fourteen years.	Ditto.	Ditto.
158.	Indecent practices between males.	Ditto.	Imprisonment for five years.
159.(1)	Incest by males.	Ditto.	Ditto.
	If female person is under the age of twelve years.	Ditto.	Imprisonment for life.
159.(3)	Attempt to commit incest	Ditto.	Imprisonment for two years.
161.	Incest by females.	Ditto.	Imprisonment for five years.

Chapter XVI-Offences Relating to Marriage and Domestic Obligations

165.	Fraudulent pretence of marriage.	May arrest without warrant.	Imprisonment for ten years.
166.	Bigamy.	Ditto.	Imprisonment for five years.
167.	Dishonestly or fraudulently - going through ceremony of marriage.	Ditto.	Ditto.
168.	Desertion of children.	Shall not arrest without warrant.	Imprisonment for two years.
169.	Neglecting to provide food, etc., for children.	Ditto.	Ditto.
170.	Master not providing for servants or apprentices.	Ditto.	Ditto.
171.	Child stealing.	May arrest without warrant.	Imprisonment for seven years.

Chapter XVII-Nuisances and Offences Against Health and Convenience

1	2	3	4
Section	Offence	Whether the police may arrest without warrant or not	Punishment under the Penal Code. (N.B.-Vide also sections 26 and 38, Penal Code.)
172.	Committing common nuisance.	Shall not arrest without warrant.	Imprisonment for one year.
173.	Watching and besetting.	May arrest without warrant.	Fine of three thousand penalty units or imprisonment for six months or both.
174. (3)	Keeping common gaming house.	Shall not arrest without warrant.	Imprisonment for two years.
174. (4)	Being found in common gaming house	Ditto.	Fine of one hundred and fifty penalty units for first offence, and for each subsequent offence a fine of six hundred penalty units or imprisonment for three months or both.
175.	Keeping or permitting the keeping of a common betting house.	Ditto.	Imprisonment for one year.
177.	Trafficking in obscene publications.	May arrest without warrant.	Imprisonment for two years or fine of three thousand penalty units.
178.	Being an idle or disorderly person	Ditto.	Imprisonment for one month or fine of sixty penalty units or both.
179.	Use of insulting language.	Ditto.	Fine of four hundred and fifty penalty units or imprisonment for three months or both.
181.	Being a rogue or vagabond.	Ditto.	Imprisonment for three months for first offence, and for each subsequent offence imprisonment for one year.
182. (1)	Wearing uniform without authority.	Ditto.	Imprisonment for one month or fine of three hundred penalty units.
182. (2)	Bringing contempt on uniform.	Ditto.	Imprisonment for three months or fine of six hundred penalty units.
182. (3)	Importing or selling uniform without authority.	Ditto.	Imprisonment for six months or fine of three thousand penalty units.
182. (5)	Unauthorised wearing of medals, etc.	Ditto.	Imprisonment for three months or fine of three hundred penalty units.
183.	Doing any act likely to spread infection of dangerous disease.	Ditto.	Imprisonment for two years.
184.	Adulteration of food or drink intended for sale.	Shall not arrest without warrant.	Ditto.
185.	Selling, or offering or exposing for sale, noxious food or drink.	Ditto.	Ditto.

186.	Adulteration of drugs intended for sale.	Shall not arrest without warrant.	Imprisonment for two years.
187.	Selling adulterated drugs.	Ditto.	Ditto.

Chapter XVII-Nuisances and Offences Against Health and Convenience-Continued

1	2	3	4
Section	Offence	Whether the police may arrest without warrant or not	Punishment under the Penal Code. (N.B.-Vide also sections 26 and 38, Penal Code.)
188.	Fouling water of public spring or reservoir.	May arrest without warrant.	Ditto.
189.	Making the atmosphere noxious to health.	Shall not arrest without warrant.	Ditto.
190.	Carrying on offensive trade.	Ditto.	Imprisonment for one year.

Chapter XVIII-Defamation

191.	Libel.	Shall not arrest without warrant.	Imprisonment for two years.

DIVISION IV-OFFENCES AGAINST THE PERSON

Chapter XIX-Murder and Manslaughter

201.	Murder.	May arrest without warrant.	[imprisonment for life].[16]
202.	Manslaughter.	Ditto.	Imprisonment for life.
203.	Infanticide.	Ditto.	Ditto.

Chapter XXI-Offences Connected with Murder

215.	Attempted murder.	May arrest without warrant.	Imprisonment for life.
216.	Attempted murder by convict.	Ditto.	Ditto.
217.	Being accessory after the fact to murder.	Ditto.	Imprisonment for seven years.
218.	Sending written threat to murder.	Ditto.	Ditto.
219.	Conspiracy to murder.	Ditto.	Imprisonment for fourteen years.
220.	Concealing the birth of a child.	Ditto.	Imprisonment for two years.
221.	Child destruction.	Ditto.	Imprisonment for life.

Chapter XXII-Offences Endangering Life or Health

222.	Disabling in order to commit felony or misdemeanour.	May arrest without warrant.	Imprisonment for life.
223.	Stupefying in order to commit felony or misdemeanour.	Ditto.	Ditto.
224.	Acts intended to cause grievous harm or prevent arrest.	Ditto.	Ditto.
225.	Preventing escape from wreck.	May arrest without warrant.	Imprisonment for life.

---

[16] See s 8(f) of Act No 22 of 2022.

226.	Intentionally endangering safety of persons travelling by railway.	Ditto.	Ditto.
227. (1)	Trespass on railway.	Ditto.	Fine of three thousand penalty units or imprisonment for two years or both.
227. (2)	Trespass on railway while in possession of articles or implements.	Ditto.	Imprisonment for fourteen years.
228.	Acts endangering the safety of persons travelling in motor vehicles.	Ditto.	Imprisonment for life.
229.	Doing grievous harm.	Ditto.	Imprisonment for seven years.
230.	Attempting to injure by explosive substances.	Ditto.	Imprisonment for fourteen years.
231.	Administering poison with intent to harm.	Ditto.	Ditto.
232.	Wounding and similar acts.	Ditto.	Imprisonment for three years.
233.	Failing to provide necessaries of life.	Ditto.	Ditto.

Chapter XXIII-Criminal Recklessness and Negligence

237.	Rash and negligent acts.	May arrest without warrant.	Imprisonment for two years.
238.	Other negligent acts causing harm.	Ditto.	Imprisonment for six months.
239.	Dealing with poisonous substances in negligent manner.	Shall not arrest without warrant.	Imprisonment for six months or fine of three thousand penalty units.
240.	Endangering safety of persons travelling by railway.	May arrest without warrant.	Imprisonment for two years.
241.	Exhibiting false light, mark or buoy.	Ditto.	Imprisonment for seven years.
242.	Conveying person by water for hire in unsafe or overloaded vessel.	Ditto.	Imprisonment for two years.
243.	Obstruction of waterways.	Ditto.	Imprisonment for three years.
244.	Causing danger or obstruction in public way or line of navigation.	Shall not arrest without warrant.	Fine.
245.	Trespass on aerodrome.	May arrest without warrant.	Fine of seven hundred and fifty penalty units or imprisonment for one month or both.
246.	Obstruction of roads or runways.	Ditto.	Imprisonment for three years.

Chapter XXIV -Assaults

247.	Common assault.	Shall not arrest without warrant.	Imprisonment for one year.
248.	Assault occasioning actual bodily harm.	May arrest without warrant.	Imprisonment for five years.
249.	Assaulting person protecting wreck.	Ditto.	Imprisonment for seven years.

250.	Various assaults.	Ditto.	Imprisonment for five years.

Chapter XXV-Offences Against Liberty

1	2	3	4
Section	Offence	Whether the police may arrest without warrant or not	Punishment under the Penal Code. (N.B.-Vide also sections 26 and 38, Penal Code.)
254.	Kidnapping.	May arrest without warrant	Imprisonment for seven years.
255.	Kidnapping or abducting in order to murder.	Ditto.	Imprisonment for ten years.
256.	Kidnapping or abducting with intent to confine a person.	Ditto.	Imprisonment for seven years.
257.	Kidnapping or abducting in order to subject person to grievous harm, slavery, etc.	Ditto.	Imprisonment for ten years.
258.	Wrongfully concealing or keeping in confinement a kidnapped or abducted person.	Ditto.	Same punishment as for kidnapping or abduction.
259.	Kidnapping or abducting child under fourteen with intent to steal from its person.	Ditto.	Imprisonment for seven years.
260.	Wrongful confinement.	Ditto.	Imprisonment for one year or fine of six thousand penalty units.
261.	Buying or disposing of any person as a slave.	Ditto.	Imprisonment for seven years.
262.	Habitually dealing in slaves.	Ditto.	Imprisonment for ten years.
263.	Unlawful compulsory labour.	Ditto.	Imprisonment for two years.

DIVISION V-OFFENCES RELATING TO PROPERTY

Chapter XXVI-Theft

272.	Theft.	May arrest without warrant.	Imprisonment for three years.
273.	Stealing wills.	Ditto.	Imprisonment for ten years.
274.	Stealing postal matter, etc.	Ditto.	Ditto
275.	Stealing cattle, etc.	Ditto.	Imprisonment for seven to fifteen years.
276.	Stealing from the person, in a dwelling-house, in transit, etc.	Ditto.	Imprisonment for seven years.
277.	Stealing by person in the public service.	Ditto.	Ditto.
278.	Stealing by clerks and servants.	Ditto.	Ditto.
279.	Stealing by directors or officers of companies.	Ditto.	Ditto.
280.	Stealing by agents, etc.	Ditto.	Ditto.

281.	Stealing by tenants or lodgers.	Ditto.	Ditto.
282.	Stealing after previous conviction.	Ditto.	Ditto.

Chapter XXVII-Offences Allied to Stealing

283.	Concealing registers.	May arrest without warrant.	Imprisonment for ten years.
284.	Concealing wills.	Ditto.	Ditto.
285.	Concealing deeds.	Ditto.	Imprisonment for three years.
286.	Killing animals with intent to steal.	Ditto.	Same punishment as if the animal had been stolen.
287.	Severing with intent to steal.	Ditto.	Same punishment as if the thing had been stolen.
288.	Fraudulent disposition of mortgaged goods.	Ditto.	Imprisonment for two years.
289.	Fraudulently dealing with ore or minerals in mines.	Ditto.	Imprisonment for five years.
290.	Fraudulent appropriation of mechanical or electrical power.	Ditto.	Ditto.
291.	Conversion not amounting to theft.	Ditto.	Imprisonment for six months or fine of one thousand five hundred penalty units or both.

Chapter XXVII-Robbery and Extortion

292.	Robbery.	May arrest without warrant.	Imprisonment for fourteen years.
293.	Assault with intent to steal.	Ditto.	Imprisonment for seven years.
294.	Aggravated robbery.	Ditto.	Imprisonment for life; with a minimum of fifteen years.
295.	Aggravated assault with intent to steal.	Ditto.	Imprisonment for ten to twenty years.
296.	Demanding property by written threats.	Ditto.	Imprisonment for fourteen years.
297.	Threatening with intent to extort-		
	in certain specified cases;	Ditto.	Ditto.
	in any other case.	Ditto.	Imprisonment for three years.
298.	Procuring execution of deeds, etc., by threats.	Ditto.	Imprisonment for fourteen years.
299.	Demanding property with menaces with intent to steal.	Ditto.	Imprisonment for five years.

Chapter XXIX-Burglary, Housebreaking and Similar Offences

301.	Housebreaking.	May arrest without warrant.	Imprisonment for seven years.
301.	Burglary.	Ditto.	Imprisonment for ten years.

302.	Entering dwelling-house with intent to commit felony.	Ditto.	Imprisonment for five years.
	If offence is committed in the night.	Ditto.	Imprisonment for seven years.
303.	Breaking into building and committing felony.	Ditto.	Ditto.
304.	Breaking into building with intent to commit felony.	Ditto.	Imprisonment for five years.
305.	Being found armed, etc., with intent to commit felony.	Ditto.	Imprisonment for three years.
	If offender has been previously convicted of a felony relating to property.	Ditto.	Imprisonment for seven years.
306.	Criminal trespass.	Ditto.	Imprisonment for three months.
	If property upon which offence committed is building used as human dwelling or as place of worship or place for custody of property.	Ditto.	Imprisonment for one year.
309.	Obtaining property by false pretence.	May arrest without warrant.	Imprisonment for three years.
310.	Obtaining execution of a security by false pretence.	Ditto.	Ditto.
311.	Cheating.	Ditto.	Ditto.
312.	Obtaining credit, etc., by false pretences.	Ditto.	Imprisonment for one year.
313.	Conspiracy to defraud.	Ditto.	Imprisonment for three years.
314.	Frauds on sale or mortgage of property.	Ditto.	Imprisonment for two years.
315.	Pretending to tell fortunes.	Ditto.	Ditto.
316.	Obtaining registration, etc., by false pretence.	Ditto.	Imprisonment for one year.
317.	False declaration for passport.	Ditto.	Imprisonment for two years.

Chapter XXXI-Receiving Property Stolen or Unlawfully Obtained and Like Offences

318. (1)	Receiving or retaining stolen property.	May arrest without warrant.	Imprisonment for seven years.
318. (2)	Receiving property unlawfully obtained, converted or disposed of.	Ditto.	Same punishment as for offender by whom the property was unlawfully obtained, converted or disposed of.
319.	Failing to account for possession of property suspected to be stolen or unlawfully obtained.	Ditto.	Imprisonment for two years.
320.	Receiving goods stolen outside Zambia	Ditto.	Imprisonment for seven years.

Chapter XXXIII-Frauds by Trustees and Persons in a Position of Trust, and False Accounting

323.	Fraudulently disposing of trust property.	May arrest without warrant.	Imprisonment for seven years.
324.	Directors and officers of corporations fraudulently appropriating property, or keeping fraudulent accounts, or falsifying books or accounts.	Ditto.	Ditto.
325.	False statements by officials of corporations.	May arrest without warrant.	Imprisonment for seven years.
326.	Fraudulent false accounting by clerk or servant.	Ditto.	Ditto.
327.	False accounting by public officer.	Ditto.	Imprisonment for two years.

DIVISION VI-MALICIOUS INJURIES TO PROPERTY

Chapter XXXIV-Offences Causing Injury to Property

328.	Arson.	May arrest without warrant.	Imprisonment for life.
329.	Attempt to commit arson.	Ditto.	Imprisonment for fourteen years.
330.	Setting fire to crops or growing plants.	Ditto.	Ditto.
331.	Attempting to set fire to crops or growing plants.	Ditto.	Imprisonment for seven years
332.	Casting away a vessel.	Ditto.	Imprisonment for life.
333.	Attempt to cast away a vessel.	Ditto.	Imprisonment for fourteen years.
334.	Injuring animals-		
	In certain specified cases;	Ditto.	Imprisonment for seven years.
	In any other case.	Ditto.	Imprisonment for two years.
335. (1)	Destroying or damaging property in general.	Ditto.	Ditto.
335. (2)	Destroying or damaging an inhabited house or a vessel with explosives.	Ditto.	Imprisonment for life.
335. (3)	Destroying or damaging river bank or wall, or navigation works or bridges.	Ditto.	Ditto.
335. (4)	Destroying or damaging wills or registers.	Ditto.	Imprisonment for fourteen years.
335. (5)	Destroying or damaging wrecks.	Ditto.	Imprisonment for seven years.
335. (6)	Destroying or damaging railways.	Ditto.	Imprisonment for fourteen years.

1	2	3	4
Section	Offence	Whether the police may arrest without warrant or not	Punishment under the Penal Code. (N.B.-Vide also sections 26 and 38, Penal Code.)
335. (7)	Destroying or damaging property of special value.	Ditto.	Imprisonment for seven years.

Section	Offence	Whether the police may arrest without warrant or not	Punishment under the Penal Code. (N.B.-Vide also sections 26 and 38, Penal Code.)
335. (8)	Destroying or damaging deeds or records.	Ditto.	Ditto.
336.	Attempt to destroy or damage property by use of explosives.	May arrest without warrant.	Imprisonment for fourteen years.
337.	Communicating infectious disease to animals.	Ditto.	Imprisonment for seven years.
338.	Removing boundary marks with intent to defraud.	Ditto.	Imprisonment for three years.
339.	Removing or injuring survey or boundary marks.	Ditto.	Imprisonment for three months or fine or six hundred penalty units.
340.	Injuring or obstructing railway works, etc.,	Ditto.	Ditto.
341.	Threatening to burn any building, etc., or to kill or wound any cattle.	Ditto.	Imprisonment for ten years.

DIVISION VII-FORGERY, COINING, COUNTERFEITING AND SIMILAR OFFENCES

Chapter XXXVI-Forgery

Section	Offence	Whether the police may arrest without warrant or not	Punishment under the Penal Code. (N.B.-Vide also sections 26 and 38, Penal Code.)
347.	Forgery (where no special punishment is provided).	May arrest without warrant.	Imprisonment for three years.
348.	Forgery of a will, document of title, security, cheque, etc.	Ditto.	Imprisonment for life.
349.	Forgery of judicial or official document.	Ditto.	Imprisonment for seven years.
350.	Forgery, etc., of stamps.	Ditto.	Ditto.
351.	Making of instruments, etc., for forgery.	Ditto.	Ditto.
352.	Uttering false document.	Ditto.	Same punishment as for forgery of document.
353.	Uttering cancelled or exhausted document.	Ditto.	Ditto.
354.	Procuring execution of document by false pretences.	Ditto.	Ditto.
355.	Obliterating or altering the crossing on a cheque.	Ditto.	Imprisonment for seven years.
356.	Making or executing document without authority.	Ditto.	Ditto.
357.	Demanding property upon forged testamentary instrument.	Ditto.	Same punishment as for forgery of instrument.
358.	Purchasing or receiving forged bank note.	May arrest without warrant.	Imprisonment for seven years.
359.	Falsifying warrant for money payable under public authority.	Ditto.	Ditto.
360.	Permitting falsification of register or record.	Ditto.	Ditto.

1	2	3	4
Section	Offence	Whether the police may arrest without warrant or not	Punishment under the Penal Code. (N.B.-Vide also sections 26 and 38, Penal Code.)

361.	Sending false certificate of marriage to registrar.	Ditto.	Ditto.
362.	Making false statement for insertion in register of births, deaths or marriages.	Ditto.	Imprisonment for three years.

Chapter XXXVII-Offences Relating to Coin

364.	Counterfeiting coin.	May arrest without warrant.	Imprisonment for life.
365.	Making preparations for coining.	Ditto.	Ditto.
366.	Clipping current coin.	Ditto.	Imprisonment for seven years.
367.	Melting down of currency.	Ditto.	Imprisonment for six months or fine of three thousand penalty units or both.
368.	Being in possession of clippings.	Ditto.	Imprisonment for seven years.
369.	Uttering counterfeit coin.	Ditto.	Imprisonment for two years.
370.	Repeated uttering of counterfeit coin.	Ditto.	Imprisonment for three years.
371.	Uttering foreign coin or metal as current coin.	Ditto.	Imprisonment for one year.
372.	Exporting counterfeit coin.	Ditto.	Imprisonment for fourteen years.

Chapter XXXVIII-Counterfeit Stamps

374.	Being in possession etc., of, die or paper used for purpose of making revenue stamps.	May arrest without warrant.	Imprisonment for seven years.
375.	Being in possession, etc., of die or paper used for postage stamps.	Ditto.	Imprisonment for one year or fine of one thousand five hundred penalty units.

Chapter XXXIX-Counterfeiting Trade Marks

377.	Counterfeiting, etc., trade mark.	Shall not arrest without warrant.	Imprisonment for two years.

Chapter XL-Personation

378.	Personation in general.	May arrest without warrant.	Imprisonment for two years.
	If representation that the offender is a person entitled by will or operation of law to any specific property and he commits the offence to obtain such property.	Ditto.	Imprisonment for seven years.
379.	Falsely acknowledging deeds, recognizances, etc.	Ditto.	Imprisonment for two years.
380.	Personation of a person named in a certificate.	Ditto.	Same punishment as for forgery of certificate.
381.	Lending, etc., certificate for purposes of personation.	Ditto.	Imprisonment for two years.

382.	Personation of person named in a testimonial of character.	Ditto.	Imprisonment for one year.
383.	Lending, etc., testimonial of character for purposes of personation.	Ditto.	Imprisonment for two years.

DIVISION IX-ATTEMPTS AND CONSPIRACIES TO COMMIT CRIMES, AND ACCESSORIES AFTER THE FACT

Chapter XLII-Attempts

390.	Attempt to commit a felony or misdemeanour.	According as to whether or not the offence is one for which the police may arrest without a warrant.	Imprisonment for two years, unless otherwise stated.
391.	Attempt to commit a felony punishable with [life imprisonment][17] or imprisonment for fourteen years or upwards.	May arrest without warrant.	Imprisonment for seven years.
392.	Attempts to procure commission of criminal acts in Zambia or elsewhere.	May arrest without warrant if arrest for offence attempted to be procured may be made without warrant, but not otherwise.	Same punishment as for an attempt to commit the act attempted to be procured.
393.	Neglecting to prevent commission or completion of a felony.	Shall not arrest without warrant.	Imprisonment for two years.

Chapter XLIII-Conspiracies

394.	Conspiracy to commit a felony.	May arrest without warrant.	Imprisonment for seven years.
395.	Conspiracy to commit a misdemeanour.	According as to whether or not the misdemeanour is one for which the police may arrest without warrant.	Imprisonment for two years.
396.	Conspiracy to effect certain specified purposes.	Shall not arrest without warrant.	Ditto.

Chapter XLIV-Accessories after the Fact

398.	Being an accessory after the fact to a felony.	May arrest without warrant.	Imprisonment for three years.
399.	Being an accessory after the fact to a misdemeanour.	Shall not arrest without warrant.	Imprisonment for two years.

(As amended by No. 28 of 1940, No. 5 of 1962, Nos. 11 and 18 of 1963, No. 1 of 1967, No. 9 of 1968 and No. 40 of 1969)

SECOND SCHEDULE

(Section 137)

(As amended by G.N. No. 55 of 1939 and Act No. 11 of 1963)

FORMS OF STATING OFFENCES IN INFORMATIONS

1-MURDER

Murder, contrary to section 200 of the Penal Code.

---

[17] See s 8(g) of Act No 22 of 2022.

Particulars of Offence
A.B., on the   day of   , in the   District of
the Province of Zambia, murdered J.S.
2-ACCESSORY AFTER THE FACT TO MURDER
   Accessory after the fact to murder, contrary to section 217 of the Penal Code.

Particulars of Offence
   A.B., well knowing that one, H.C., did on the   day of   ,
in the   District of the   Province of Zambia,
murder C.C., did on the   day of   , in the   District
of the   Province of Zambia, and on other days thereafter,
receive, comfort, harbour, assist and maintain the said H.C.
3-MANSLAUGHTER
   Manslaughter, contrary to section 199 of the Penal Code.

Particulars of Offence
   A.B., on the   day of   , in the   District of
the   Province of Zambia, unlawfully killed J.S.
4-RAPE
   Rape, contrary to section 132 of the Penal Code.

Particulars of Offence
   A.B., on the   day of   , in the   District of
the Province of Zambia, had carnal knowledge of E.F., without her consent.
5-WOUNDING

First Count
   Wounding with intent, contrary to section 224 of the Penal Code.

Particulars of Offence
   A.B., on the   day of   , in the   District of
the Province of Zambia, wounded C.D., with intent to maim, disfigure or disable, or to do some
grievous harm, or to resist the lawful arrest of him the said A.B. (as the case may be).

Second Count
   Wounding, contrary to section 232 of the Penal Code.

Particulars of Offence
   A.B., on the   day of   , in the   District
of the   Province of Zambia, unlawfully wounded C.D.
6-THEFT

First Count
   Theft, contrary to section 272 of the Penal Code.

Particulars of Offence
   A.B., on the   day of   , in the   District of
the Province of Zambia, stole a bag, the property of C.D.

Second Count
   Receiving stolen goods, contrary to section 318 of the Penal Code.

Particulars of Offence
   A.B., on the   day of   , in the   District of
the   Province of Zambia, did receive a bag, the property of
C.D., knowing the same to have been stolen.

7-THEFT BY CLERK
Theft by clerk or servant, contrary to section 272 and section 278 of the Penal Code.

Particulars of Offence

A.B., on the   day of   , in the   District of the   Province of Zambia, being clerk or servant to M.N., stole from the said M.N. ten yards of cloth.

8-ROBBERY
Robbery with violence, contrary to section 292 of the Penal Code.

Particulars of Offence

A.B., on the   day of   , in the   District of the   Province of Zambia, robbed C.D. of a watch, and at or immediately before or immediately after the time of such robbery did use personal violence to the said C.D.

9-BURGLARY
Burglary, contrary to section 301 of the Penal Code.

Particulars of Offence

A.B., in the night of the   day of   , in the   District of the   Province of Zambia, did break and enter the dwelling-house of C.D., with intent to commit a felony therein.

10-BURGLARY AND THEFT
Burglary and theft, contrary to section 301 and section 272 of the Penal Code.

Particulars of Offence

A.B., in the night of the   day of   , in the   District of the   Province of Zambia, did break and enter the dwelling-house of C.D. with intent to steal therein, and did steal therein one watch, the property of S.T., the said watch being of the value of twenty kwacha.

11-THREATS
Demanding property by written threats, contrary to section 296 of the Penal Code.

Particulars of Offence

A.B., on the   day of   , in the   District of the   Province of Zambia, with intent to extort money from C.D., caused the said C.D. to receive a letter containing threats of injury or detriment to be caused to E.F.

12-ATTEMPTS TO EXTORT
Attempt to extort by threats, contrary to section 297 of the Penal Code.

Particulars of Offence

A.B., on the   day of   , in the   District of the   Province of Zambia, with intent to extort money from C.D., accused or threatened to accuse the said C.D. of an unnatural offence.

13-FALSE PRETENCES
Obtaining goods by false pretences, contrary to section 309 of the Penal Code.

Particulars of Offence

A.B., on the   day of   , in the   District of the   Province of Zambia, with intent to defraud, obtained from S.P. five yards of cloth by falsely pretending that the said A.B. was a servant to J.S., and that he, the said A.B., had then been sent by the said J.S. to S.P., for the said cloth, and that he, the said A.B., was then authorised by the said J.S. to receive the said cloth on behalf of the said J.S.

14-CONSPIRACY TO DEFRAUD
Conspiracy to defraud, contrary to section 313 of the Penal Code.

Particulars of Offence

A.B., and C.D., on the   day of   , and on divers days between that day and the day of   , in the District of the Province of Zambia, conspired together with intent to defraud by means of an advertisement inserted by them, the said A.B. and C.D., in the H.S. newspaper, falsely representing that A.B. and C.D. were then carrying on a genuine business as jewellers at   , in the Province of   , and that they were then able to supply certain articles of jewellery to whomsoever would remit to them the sum of four kwacha.

15-ARSON

Arson, contrary to section 328 of the Penal Code.

Particulars of Offence

A.B., on the   day of   ,in the   District of the   Province of Zambia, wilfully and unlawfully set fire to a house.

16-ARSON AND ACCESSORY BEFORE THE FACT

A.B., arson, contrary to section 328 of the Penal Code.
C.D., accessory before the fact to same offence.

Particulars of Offence

A.B., on the   day of   , in the   District of the   Province of Zambia, wilfully and unlawfully set fire to a house.
C.D., on the same day, in the   District of the
Province of Zambia, did counsel or procure the said A.B. to commit the said offence.

17-DAMAGE

Damaging trees, contrary to section 335 of the Penal Code.

Particulars of Offence

A.B., on the   day of   , in the   District of the   Province of Zambia, wilfully and unlawfully damaged a cocoa tree there growing.

18-FORGERY

First Count

Forgery, contrary to section 348 of the Penal Code.

Particulars of Offence

A.B., on the   day of   , in the   District of the   Province of Zambia, forged a certain will purporting to be the will of C.D.

Second Count

Uttering a false document, contrary to section 352 of the Penal Code.

Particulars of Offence

A.B., on the   day of   , in the   District of the   Province of Zambia, knowingly and fraudulently uttered a certain forged will purporting to be the will of C.D.

19-COUNTERFEIT COIN

Uttering counterfeit coin, contrary to section 369 of the Penal Code.

Particulars of Offence

A.B., on the   day of   , at   market in the   District of the Province of Zambia, uttered a counterfeit ngwee, knowing the same to be counterfeit.

20-PERJURY

Perjury, contrary to section 104 of the Penal Code.

Particulars of Offence

A.B., on the   day of   ,in the   District of
the   Province of Zambia, being a witness upon
the trial of an action in the High Court for Zambia at Lusaka, in which one was plaintiff,
and one   was defendant, knowingly gave false testimony that he saw one M.W.
in the street called   on the day of

21-DEFAMATORY LIBEL

Publishing defamatory matter, contrary to section 191 of the Penal Code.

Particulars of Offence

A.B., on the   day of   , in the   District of
the   Province of Zambia, published defamatory matter affecting E.F., in the form of
a letter (book, pamphlet, picture, or as the case may be).

(Innuendo should be stated where necessary.)

22-FALSE ACCOUNTING

First Count

Fraudulent false accounting, contrary to section 326 of the Penal Code.

Particulars of Offence

A.B., on the   day of   , in the   District of
the   Province of Zambia, being clerk or servant to C.D.,
with intent to defraud, made or was privy to making a false entry in a cash book belonging to
the said C.D., his employer, purporting to show that on the said day two hundred kwacha had
been paid to L.M.

Second Count

Same as first count.

Particulars of Offence

A.B., on the   day of   ,in the   District of
the   Province of Zambia, being clerk or servant to C.D.,
with intent to defraud, omitted or was privy to omitting from a cash book belonging to the said
C.D., his employer, a material particular, that is to say, the receipt of the said day of one hundred
kwacha from H.S.

23-THEFT BY AGENT

First Count

Theft by agent, contrary to section 272 and section 280 of the Penal Code.

Particulars of Offence

A.B., on the   day of   , in the   District of
the   Province of Zambia, stole two hundred kwacha which
had been entrusted to him by H.S., for him, the said A.B., to retain in safe custody.

Second Count

Theft by agent, contrary to section 272 and section 280 of the Penal Code.

Particulars of Offence

A.B., on the   day of   , in the   District of
the   Province of Zambia, stole two hundred kwacha which
had been received by him, for an on account of L.M.

24-PREVIOUS CONVICTION

Prior to the commission of the said offence, the said A.B. had been previously convicted
of   on the   day of   at the
held at

THIRD SCHEDULE
(Sections 342, 343 and 357)

PRESCRIBED FEES

A-FEES GENERALLY

	Units
On every summons or warrant	4
On certifying a copy of a document as an office copy	8
On copies of proceedings, for every 100 words or part of 100 words	2

B-FEES TO BE TAKEN BY MAGISTRATE UNDER SECTION 342
On drawing case and copy-
Units

	Units
when the case does not exceed 5 folios of 100 words each	15
when the case exceeds 5 folios, then for every additional folio	2
On recognizance	8
On every enlargement or renewal thereof	

4

On certificate of refusal of case	

3

(As amended by Act No. 13 of 1994)

FOURTH SCHEDULE

(Section 358)

PRESCRIBED FORMS

1. Charge.
2. Summons to accused.
3. Proof of previous convictions.
4. Warrant to arrest accused.
5. Warrant to bring a prisoner before the court.
6. Information to ground search warrant.
7. Search warrant for stolen goods.
8. Summons to a witness.
8a. Summons to a Witness.
9. Warrant where witness has not obeyed summons.
10. Warrant for witness in first instance.
11. Warrant for prisoner to give evidence.
12. Deposition of witnesses on investigation before commitment.
13. Statement of accused on investigation before commitment.
14. Warrant of commitment on remand.
15. Warrant of commitment on remand.
16. Commitment of witness for refusing to enter into recognizance.
17. Recognizance to surrender for trial.
18. Recognizance to surrender after remand or adjournment.
19. Recognizance of witness under arrest, to give evidence.
20. Recognizance of witness to give evidence.
21. Recognizance of witness to give evidence.
22. Recognizance to keep the peace or be of good behaviour.
23. Recognizance of person sentenced, pending confirmation of sentence.
24. Recognizance of appellant to prosecute appeal and submit to judgment.
25. Notice to witness bound over that he is to be treated as having been bound over conditionally.
26. Notice directing witness to appear at a Sessions of the High Court other than that specified in his recognizance.
27. Notice requiring attendance of witness bound over or treated as bound over conditionally.
28. Certificate and order to be endorsed on recognizance on non-performance.

29. Conviction for a penalty to be levied by distress, and, in default of sufficient distress, imprisonment.
30. Warrant of distress.
31. Warrant of commitment (on default of distress or of payment).
32. Warrant of commitment to undergo sentence of imprisonment (where no alternative punishment).
33. Notice of appeal against conviction and/or sentence.
34. Case stated.
35. Summons to assessor.
36. Notification of acquittal.
37. Certificate of previous convictions.

1-CHARGE

In the Subordinate Court of
    A.B., of , being first duly sworn, charges that (state the
offence with time and place where committed).
(Complainant)
Taken and sworn at this   day of   , 19   ,
before me:
(Magistrate)

2-SUMMONS TO ACCUSED

In the Subordinate Court of   .
To A.B., of   .
    Whereas your attendance is necessary to answer to a complaint of (state shortly the offence complained
of with time and place).
    You are hereby commanded in the name of the President to appear (in person), before this Court at
on the   day of   , 19   ,
and on every adjournment of the Court until the case be disposed of.
Issued at   the   day of   , 19   .
(Magistrate)
(As amended by S.I. No. 152 of 1965)

3-PROOF OF PREVIOUS CONVICTIONS

PART I

NOTICE OF INTENTION TO CITE PREVIOUS CONVICTIONS (Section 142 (3))
    In the Subordinate Court (Class ....) of the
holden at ....

THE PEOPLE

v.

    You   are hereby given notice that
if, but only if, you are convicted of (any of) the offence(s) of

in respect of which you are required to appear, or are entitled, having signed an Admission of Guilt, under
the provisions of section 221 of the Criminal Procedure Code, to appear before the above-mentioned
Subordinate Court on the   19 .....
the undermentioned convictions which are recorded against you will be brought to the notice of the Court;
and if you are not present in person before the Court, the Court may take account of any such previous
conviction as if you had appeared and admitted it.

Item No.	Date of conviction	Court	Offence	Sentence

(Signed)
for Officer in Charge

If you do not intend to appear in person at the hearing and you dispute any of the above convictions, or any of the details in connection with them, you should immediately notify the officer in charge of the Police*
at   so that further inquiries can be made.

Nothing in this notice limits in any way your right to appear in person on the date fixed for the hearing and to dispute any conviction alleged against you.

NOTE.-This form and the provisions of sections 142 (3) and 221, Criminal Procedure Code, have no application to charges against juveniles.

*Insert "Station" or "Traffic Section" or otherwise as appropriate

PART II

NOTICE THAT RECORD OF PREVIOUS CONVICTIONS IS DISPUTED

(To be completed by the person served with the notice in Part I above, then detached and handed to the police officer who served Part I or to the addressee.)

To Officer in Charge,
          (Insert designation of police formation.)

1. I,   ., acknowledge receipt of a notice of intention to cite previous convictions in the event of my being convicted of the charge(s) to be made against me in the Subordinate Court (Class   )
at   . on the .... day of .... 19 ......

2. I dispute the accuracy of the statement of previous convictions contained in the said notice in respect of the following particulars:

(i)   I deny the following convictions:

Item No.	Date of conviction	Court	Offence	Sentence

(Here insert particulars of convictions recorded in the notice in Part I which are not admitted.)

(ii)   I say that the particulars of the conviction shown in item(s) No(s)...........are incorrect and should be as stated below:

Item No.	Date of conviction	Court	Offence	Sentence

(Here insert against the appropriate date the particulars of the court, offence and sentence which are admitted .)

Witness
               (Signature or thumbprint)

(G.N. No. 1 of 1961)

4-WARRANT TO ARREST ACCUSED

In the Subordinate Court of   .
To X.Y., Police Officer, and other Officers.

Whereas   of   is accused of the offence of (state the offence with time and place.).

You are hereby commanded in the name of the President forthwith to apprehend the said and produce him before the Court at   .

Issued at   the   day of   , 19   .
(Magistrate)

If the said   shall give bail himself in the sum of   with one surety in the sum of   (or two sureties each in the sum of to attend before the Court at on the   day of   and to continue so to attend until otherwise directed by the Court, he shall be released.

Issued at   the   day of   ,19   .
(Magistrate)

(As amended by S.I. No. 152 of 1965 and S.I. No. 177 of 1968)

5-WARRANT TO BRING A PRISONER BEFORE THE COURT

In the Subordinate Court of   .
To the Officer in charge of the Prison at
    Whereas A.B., a prisoner under your custody, is accused of the offence of (state offence).
    You are hereby commanded to produce the said A.B. before the Court at
on   the   day of   , 19   .
    Issued at   the   day of   , 19   .
(Magistrate)

6-INFORMATION TO GROUND SEARCH WARRANT

In the Subordinate Court of   .
    A.B., of , being first duly sworn, complains that on the
          day of   the following goods (here describe the goods) were stolen and unlawfully
carried away from and out of   at
and that he has reasonable cause to suspect, and does suspect that these goods, or some of them, are
concealed in the dwelling-house or premises (or as the case may be) of C.D., situate at , for he, the said A.B.,
deposes and says that (state shortly the grounds on which the warrant is applied for).
(Signature of the person applying for warrant)
    Taken and sworn at this   day of   ,19
,
before me:
(Magistrate)

7-SEARCH WARRANT FOR STOLEN GOODS

In the Subordinate Court of   .
To X.Y., Police Officer, and other Officers.
    A.B.,   of has this day made information on oath that (copy
No. 6 from "the following" down to "for he").
    You are hereby authorised and commanded in the name of the President with proper assistance, to enter
the
of C.D. aforesaid (in the daytime), and there diligently search for the said goods, and if the same or any
thereof are found on search, to bring the goods so found, and also the said C.D., before this Court to be dealt
with according to law.
    Issued at   the   day   of   , 19   .
(Magistrate)
(As amended by S.I. No. 152 of 1965)

8-SUMMONS TO A WITNESS

In the Subordinate Court of   .

A.B.

v.

C.D.
To
    You are hereby commanded in the name of the President to attend in person before this Court at
on the day of   and so from day to day till the above cause be tried,
to testify all that you know in the said cause.
    You are summoned at the instance of
    Issued at the   day of   19   .
(Clerk of the Court)
(G.N. No. 470 of 1964 as amended by S.I. No. 152 of 1965)
APPENDIX (Paragraph 2 (b))

8A-SUMMONS TO A WITNESS

In the High Court for Zambia
....holden at
THE PEOPLE
versus

To   of ....
You are hereby commanded in the name of the President to attend in person before this Court at
on the .... day of   19.......... and so
from day to day till the above cause be tried, to testify all that you know in the said cause.
You are summoned at the instance of the STATE.
Issued at   the ....day of .... ,
19.............
(Clerk of Sessions)
(As Amended by S.I. No. 224 of 1979)

9-WARRANT WHERE WITNESS HAS NOT OBEYED SUMMONS

In the Subordinate Court of   .

A.B.

v.

C.D.
To X.Y., Police Officer, and other Officers.
E.F. was commanded to appear before this Court at   on the
day of   ,19   , and subsequent days, to testify what he
knew in the above cause; but he has not appeared according to the said summons and has not excused his
failure.
Therefore you are hereby commanded in the name of the President to apprehend and to bring and have
the said E.F. before this Court at on the   day of   , 19   .
Issued   at   the   day of   , 19   .
(Magistrate)
(As amended by S.I. No. 152 of 1965)

10-WARRANT FOR WITNESS IN FIRST INSTANCE

In the Subordinate Court of   .
A.B.

v.

C.D.
To X.Y., Police Officer, and other Officers.
It appears to the Court that E.F. is likely to give material evidence concerning the above cause, and will not
probably attend unless compelled to do so.
Therefore you are hereby commanded in the name of the President to apprehend and to bring and have
the said E.F. before this Court at on the   day of   , 19   .
Issued   at   the   day of   , 19   .
(Magistrate)
(As Amended by S.I. No. 152 of 1965)

11-WARRANT FOR PRISONER TO GIVE EVIDENCE

In the Subordinate Court of   .

A.B.

v.

C.D.

To the Officer in charge of the Prison at

You are hereby commanded to have E.F., a prisoner under your custody, before the Court at   on the   day of   next, to give evidence in the above-named cause, and immediately after he has there and then given his evidence to return.

Issued at   the   day of   ,19   .

(Magistrate)

12-DEPOSITION OF WITNESSES ON INVESTIGATION BEFORE COMMITMENT

In the Subordinate Court of   .

A.B., of   , stands charged before the Court for that he (state offence as in summons or warrant) and (in the presence and hearing of the said A.B.) C.D., E.F., etc., depose on oath as follows:

First. The said C.D., being sworn, says as follows: (state the deposition of the witness in the precise words he uses, or as nearly as possible. when his deposition is complete it shall be read to the witness and he shall sign it. The Magistrate shall also sign it).

Secondly. The said E.F., being sworn, etc. (record successively, in like manner as the first, the deposition of all the witnesses for the prosecution and for the defence, distinguishing the latter by placing the words " called for defendant", or to the like effect, after their names. Where the witness deposes in any language but English, the language shall be stated, with the name and description of the interpreter, who also shall sign the deposition).

The above depositions of C.D., E.F., etc., were taken before me at the   day of   , 19   .(a)

(Magistrate)

(Interpreter)

(a) If the depositions have been taken on more days than one, the date of each is to be stated.

13-STATEMENT OF ACCUSED ON INVESTIGATION BEFORE COMMITMENT

In the Subordinate Court of   .

A.B., of , stands accused before the Court for that he (state offence as in the summons or warrant), and C.D., E.F., etc., the witnesses for the prosecution, having been severally examined in his presence and hearing, these questions are now put to the said A.B. by the Court, and the answer noted after each question are returned thereto by the said A.B., namely:

(a)   Do you wish to say anything in answer to the charge? You are not obliged to say anything unless you desire to do so, but whatever you say will be taken down in writing and may be given in evidence upon your trial.

(b)   Do you wish to call any witnesses before this Court?

(c)   Do you wish to call any witnesses at your trial? If so, do you wish to give their names, so that they may be summoned?

(Each question, with its answer, is to be noted before putting the subsequent question. Where the statement of the accused is made through an interpreter, it is to be so stated, with the name and description of the interpreter, who shall also sign.)

And I certify that the foregoing was taken at on the   day of   , 19   , in my presence and hearing, and contains accurately the whole of the statement of the said A.B.

Taken at   the   day of   , 19   .

(Accused)

(Magistrate)

(Interpreter)

14-WARRANT OF COMMITMENT ON REMAND (Sections 202 and 227)

In the Subordinate Court (Class   ) of the
         holden at

Case No.   /19   .

To each and all Police Officers of Zambia and to the Superintendent/Officer in Charge of the Government Prison at

WHEREAS   (hereinafter called

the accused) appeared this day before this Court charged with*

AND the hearing being adjourned, and the accused remanded in custody:

YOU, the said Police Officers, are hereby commanded to convey the accused to the said prison and there deliver the accused to the Superintendent/Officer in Charge thereof, together with this warrant; and you, the Superintendent/Officer in Charge of the said prison to receive him/her into your custody and, unless he/she shall have been bailed in the meantime, to keep him/her until the   day of   19 , †and on that day to convey him/her at the hour of   o'clock in the   noon before this Court to be further dealt with according to law, unless you, the said Superintendent/Officer in Charge, shall be otherwise ordered in the meantime.

Dated at the   day of   , 19   .

(Magistrate)

*State the offence.

† No adjournment shall be for more than fifteen clear days.

NOTE.-For endorsement for bail, see back.

ENDORSEMENT

(To be completed only where bail is allowed)

The Court hereby certifies that the accused may be bailed by recognizance, himself/herself in the sum of
     , with

surety/ies in the sum of   (each), to appear before this Court on the   day of   , 19   , at the hour of   o'clock in the   .   noon (and at every time and place to which during the course of the proceedings against the accused the hearing may be from time to time adjourned), and that the accused has (not) entered into his/her recognizance.

(G.N. No. 366 of 1962)

15-WARRANT OF COMMITMENT IN CUSTODY FOR TRIAL (Section 231)

In the Subordinate Court (Class   ) of the
holden at

Case No.   /19   .

To each and all Police Officers of Zambia and to the Superintendent/Officer in Charge of the Government Prison at

and to any Prison Officer into whose hands this warrant shall come.

WHEREAS   (hereinafter

called the accused) appeared this day before this Court charged with*

AND WHEREAS the said Court, after due inquiry, committed the accused for trial at the next sessions of the High Court for the

Province and remanded him in custody,

NOW THEREFORE YOU, the said Police Officers, are hereby commanded to convey the accused to the said prison and there deliver the accused to the Superintendent/Officer in Charge thereof, together with this warrant; and you the Superintendent/Officer in Charge of the said prison are hereby commanded to receive the accused into your custody and to keep the accused until delivered in due course of law.

Dated at   the   day of   19   .

(Magistrate)

(G.N. No. 366 of 1962)

*State the offence.

16-COMMITMENT OF WITNESS FOR REFUSING TO ENTER INTO RECOGNIZANCE

In the Subordinate Court of   .
To X.Y., Police Officer, and other Officers.
    A.B., of , has been charged before this Court with the offence
of (state the offence).
    And E.F., of   , having been now examined before this Court
concerning the said charge, and being required, refuses to enter into a recognizance to give evidence
concerning the said charge.
Therefore you are hereby commanded in the name of the President to lodge the said E.F. in the prison
at
, there to be imprisoned by the officer in charge of the said prison until after the trial of the said A.B. for
the said offence, unless the said E.F. in the meantime consents to enter into such recognizance as aforesaid.
        Dated   at   the   day of   , 19   .
        (Magistrate)

17-RECOGNIZANCE TO SURRENDER FOR TRIAL (Section 231)

In the Subordinate Court of   .
    Whereas (state cause of complaint with time and place).
    The undersigned principal party to this recognizance hereby binds himself to perform the following
obligation:
    To attend the Sessions at   on the   day
of   , 19   , and there to surrender himself, and
plead to any information filed against him for the said offence, and so from day to day, and take his trial
for the same and not depart the Court without leave, and also to attend at any investigation or proceeding
concerning the said charge, before the trial, when and where he may be required.
    And the said principal party, together with the undersigned sureties, hereby severally acknowledge
themselves bound to forfeit the sums following, viz.:
    The said principal party the sum of   kwacha, and
the said sureties the sum of   kwacha each, in case the said
principal party fails to perform the above obligation or any part thereof.
    (Signed)   Principal Party.
    (Signed)
    (Signed)   } Sureties.
    Taken before me at the   day of   , 19   .
(Magistrate)
(G.N. No. 128 of 1961 as amended by S.I. No. 152 of 1965)

18-RECOGNIZANCE TO SURRENDER AFTER REMAND OR ADJOURNMENT (Section 123 or 227)

In the Subordinate Court of   .
    Whereas   (hereinafter called "the principal
party") stands charged with   (state cause of
complaint with time and place) contra section   of   .
    The undersigned principal party to this recognizance hereby binds himself to perform the following
obligations:
    To appear before the Court at   . on   and
on any other prior or subsequent day when required by the Court to answer the said charge and to be dealt
with according to law.
    And the said principal party, together with the undersigned sureties, hereby severally acknowledge
themselves bound to forfeit the sums following viz.:
    The said principal party the sum of   kwacha and the said sureties the
sum of   kwacha each, in case the said principal party fails to
perform the above obligation or any part thereof.
    (Signed)   Principal Party.
    (Signed)
    (Signed)   } Sureties.

337

Taken before me at   the   day of   , 19   .
(Magistrate)
(G.N. No. 128 of 1961 as amended by S.I. No. 152 of 1965)

19-RECOGNIZANCE OF WITNESS UNDER ARREST, TO GIVE EVIDENCE (Section 146)
In the Subordinate Court of   .
   Whereas   stands charged before this Court for
that he   (state cause of
complaint with time and place).
   The undersigned principal party to this recognizance hereby binds himself to perform the following obligation:
   To attend the Court at   on the   day of
           , 19   , and on any other prior or subsequent
day when required by the Court, and there to give evidence touching and concerning the said charge.
   And the said principal party, together with the undersigned sureties, hereby severally acknowledge themselves bound to forfeit the sums following, viz.:

The said principal party the sum of   kwacha and the said sureties the
sum of   kwacha each. in case the said principal party fails to
perform the above obligation or any part thereof.
   (Signed)   Principal Party.
   (Signed)
   (Signed)   } Sureties.
Taken before me at   the   day of   , 19   .
(Magistrate)
(G.N. No. 128 of 1961 as amended by S.I. No. 152 of 1965)

20-RECOGNIZANCE OF WITNESS TO GIVE EVIDENCE (Section 233)

(This form is to be used where the next Sessions of the High Court for the Province or District in which the subordinate court is situate are due to be held more than fourteen days from the date of the committal.)

In the Subordinate Court of   .
   Whereas   stands charged before this Court for
that he (state cause of complaint with time and place).
   The undersigned principal party to this recognizance hereby binds himself to perform the following obligation (see note below):
   To attend the Sessions of the High Court to be held at   on
the   day of   , 19   , or such other Sessions of
which the principal party may be notified in writing, and there to give evidence touching and concerning the said charge, and also to attend and give evidence at any further examination, investigation or proceeding concerning the said charge, before the trial, when and where he may be required by notice in writing.
And the said principal party, together with the undersigned sureties, hereby severally acknowledge themselves bound to forfeit the sums following, viz.:
   The said principal party the sum of   kwacha and the said sureties the
sum of   kwacha each, in case the said principal party fails to
perform the above obligation or any part thereof.
   (Signed)   Principal Party.
   (Signed)
   (Signed)   } Sureties.
Taken before me at   the   day of   , 19   .
(Magistrate)
NOTE.-In the case of a conditional recognizance made under section 236, Criminal Procedure Code here insert: "conditionally upon receipt of a notice in that behalf".
(G.N. No. 128 of 1961 as amended by S.I. No. 152 of 1965)

21-RECOGNIZANCE OF WITNESS TO GIVE EVIDENCE (Section 233)

(This form is to be used where the next Sessions of the High Court for the Province or District in which the subordinate court is situate are due to be held within fourteen days or less from the date of committal.)
In the Subordinate Court of   .
    Whereas   stands charged before this Court
for that he   (state cause of complaint with time
and place).
    The undersigned principal party to this recognizance hereby binds himself to perform the following obligation (see note below):
    To attend the Sessions of the High Court of which the principal party shall be notified in writing, and there to give evidence touching and concerning the said charge, and also to attend and give evidence at any further examination, investigation or proceeding concerning the said charge, before the trial, when and where he may be required by notice in writing.
    And the said principal party, together with the undersigned sureties, hereby severally acknowledge themselves bound to forfeit the sums following, viz.:
    The said principal party the sum of   kwacha and the said sureties the
sum of   kwacha each, in case the said principal party fails to
perform the above obligation or any part thereof.
    (Signed)   Principal Party.
    (Signed)
    (Signed)   }Sureties.
    Taken before me at   the   day of   , 19   .
(Magistrate)
NOTE.-In the case of a conditional recognizance made under section 236, Criminal Procedure Code, here insert: "conditionally upon receipt of a notice in that behalf".
(G.N. No. 128 of 1961 as amended by S.I. No. 152 of 1965)

22-RECOGNIZANCE TO KEEP THE PEACE OR BE OF GOOD BEHAVIOUR (Section 51, Criminal Procedure Code, or Section 31, Penal Code)

In the Subordinate Court of   .
    Whereas   (state cause of complaint with time and place).
    The undersigned principal party to this recognizance hereby binds himself to perform the following obligation:
    To keep the peace (or be of good behaviour) towards all persons within Zambia, and particularly
    towards   of   for
    the space of months.
    And the said principal party, together with the undersigned sureties, hereby severally acknowledge themselves bound to forfeit the sums following, viz.:
    The said principal party the sum of   kwacha and the said sureties the
sum of   kwacha each, in case the said principal party fails to
perform the above obligation or any part thereof.
    (Signed)   Principal Party.
    (Signed)
    (Signed)   }Sureties.

    Taken before me at   the   day of   , 19   .
(Magistrate)
(G.N. No. 128 of 1961 as amended by S.I. No. 152 of 1965)

23-RECOGNIZANCE OF PERSON SENTENCED, PENDING CONFIRMATION OF SENTENCE (Section13 (1))

In the Subordinate Court of   .
    Whereas the undersigned principal party was convicted by this Court on the
day of   , 19   , for the offence of (state offence with particulars
of law contravened and date and place of offence) and was sentenced or ordered to (state sentence or order).
    And whereas the said sentence requires to be confirmed by the High Court. The principal party to this

recognizance hereby binds himself to perform the following obligation:
Unless the said sentence or order shall not be confirmed and no other sentence or order substituted by the High Court, to appear before this Court at within ten days after the principal party shall be notified of the decision of the High Court with regard to the said conviction or order.

And the said principal party, together with the undersigned sureties, hereby severally acknowledge themselves bound to forfeit the sums following, viz.:

The said principal party the sum of kwacha and the said sureties the sum of kwacha each, in case the said principal party fails to perform the above obligation or any part thereof.

(Signed) Principal Party.
(Signed)
(Signed) } Sureties.
Taken before me at the day of , 19 .
(Magistrate)
(G.N. No. 128 of 1961 as amended by G.N. No. 493 of 1964 and S.I. No. 152 of 1965)

24-RECOGNIZANCE OF APPELLANT TO PROSECUTE APPEAL AND SUBMIT TO JUDGMENT (Section 332)

In the Subordinate Court of .

Whereas the undersigned principal party was convicted by this Court on the day of , 19 , for the offence of (state offence with particulars of law contravened and date and place of offence) and was sentenced or ordered to (state sentence or order).

And whereas the principal party desires to appeal to the High Court against the said conviction and/or sentence.

The principal party to this recognizance hereby binds himself to perform the following obligation:

To prosecute without delay his appeal to the High Court against the said conviction and/or sentence, to submit to the judgment of the High Court and pay such costs as may be awarded by such Court and, unless the determination appealed against is reversed, to appear before this Court at within ten days after the said judgment is given.

And the said principal party, together with the undersigned sureties, hereby severally acknowledge themselves bound to forfeit the sums following, viz.:

The said principal party the sum of kwacha and the said sureties the sum of kwacha each, in case the said principal party fails to perform the above obligation or any part thereof.

(Signed) Principal Party.
(Signed)
(Signed) } Sureties.
Taken before me at the day of , 19 .
(Magistrate)
(G.N. No. 128 of 1961 as amended by G.N. No. 493 of 1964
and S.I. No. 152 of 1965)

25-NOTICE TO WITNESS BOUND OVER THAT HE IS TO BE TREATED AS HAVING BEEN BOUND OVER CONDITIONALLY (SECTION 236 (1))

In the Subordinate Court of .

To (insert name of witness).

Whereas you, , of , were on the day of , 19 , bound by a recognizance in the sum of to attend the Sessions of the High Court to be held at on the day of , 19 , or such other Sessions of which you may be notified in writing and there to give evidence on the trial of :

And whereas the subordinate court has (since committed the said for trial at the next Sessions of the High Court for the Province of to be held at , and has) directed that you are to be treated as having been bound over to attend the trial conditionally upon notice being given to you:

THIS IS TO GIVE YOU NOTICE that you are NOT required to attend the said Sessions of the High Court for the purpose aforesaid unless you subsequently receive notice directing you to appear thereat.

Dated   the   day of   , 19   .
(Magistrate)
(G.N. No. 128 of 1961)

26-NOTICE DIRECTING WITNESS TO APPEAR AT A SESSIONS OF THE HIGH COURT OTHER THAN THAT SPECIFIED IN HIS RECOGNIZANCE Section 233 (2))

In the Subordinate Court of   .
   To (insert name of witness).
   Whereas you,   of   , were on the
day of   , 19   , bound by a recognizance in the sum of to attend the
Sessions of the High Court to be held at on the   day of ,
19 , or such other Sessions of which you may be notified in writing and there to give evidence on the trial
of   :
   THIS IS TO GIVE YOU NOTICE that you are no longer required to attend the Sessions of the High Court
as aforesaid, but you are hereby DIRECTED AND REQUIRED to attend at the next Sessions of the High
Court, to be held at
on the   day of   19   .
   And unless you so attend and give evidence, the said recognizance entered into by you will be forthwith
enforced against you.
   Dated the   day of   , 19   .
(Magistrate)
(G.N. No. 128 of 1961)

27-NOTICE REQUIRING ATTENDANCE OF WITNESS BOUND OVER OR TREATED AS BOUND OVER CONDITIONALLY (Section 236 (2))

In the High Court for Zambia
or in the Subordinate Court of   .
   To (insert name of witness).
   Whereas you   , of   , were on the
day   of   19   , bound over by a recognizance in
the sum of to attend *upon notice being given to you at the Sessions of the High Court specified in such
notice and there to give evidence on the trial of :
(Or (Where witness has been treated as bound over conditionally and served with a notice in Form 25, insert
instead after asterisk*) at the next Sessions of the High Court to be held at on the   day of   ,
19   , or
such other Sessions of the High Court of which you may be notified, to give evidence on the trial of
; and whereas notice was subsequently given
to you that you would not be required to attend the said Sessions for the said purpose unless you received
notice:)
   THIS IS TO GIVE YOU NOTICE that you ARE required to attend at the next Sessions of the High Court to
be held at on the day of   , 19   , and there to give evidence accordingly, and that unless you do so
the said recognizance will be forthwith enforced against you.
   Dated this   day of   , 19   .
(Registrar/Senior/Resident Magistrate/ Magistrate Class)
(G.N. No. 128 of 1961)

28-CERTIFICATE AND ORDER TO BE ENDORSED ON RECOGNIZANCE ON NON-PERFORMANCE

   I certify that the within   has not performed the foregoing
obligation.
   Dated at   the   day of   , 19   .
(Magistrate)
   I order that the sum of   be levied off the goods of the said
                    and the sum of   off the goods of each of the
said   and
   Dated at   the   day of   , 19   .
(Magistrate)
(G.N. No. 128 of 1961)

29-CONVICTION FOR A PENALTY TO BE LEVIED BY DISTRESS, AND, IN DEFAULT OF SUFFICIENT DISTRESS, IMPRISONMENT

In the Subordinate Court of   .
    The   day of   19   .
    C.D., of   , is this day convicted before this Court for that (state
offence and time and place when and where committed).
    And this Court adjudges the said C.D., for his said offence, to pay a fine of (state the penalty, compensation, if any, to the party aggrieved, and costs according to the order made).
    And if the said sums be not paid forthwith (or on or before
next), then this Court orders that the same be levied by distress and sale of the property of the said C.D.
    And, in default of such distress, this Court adjudges the said C.D. to be imprisoned (with hard labour) for the space of   unless the said sums
and all costs of the said distress be sooner paid.
(Magistrate)

30-WARRANT OF DISTRESS

In the Subordinate Court of   .
To and other Officers of this Court.
    Whereas C.D., of   , was on the   day of   ordered
by this Court forthwith (or on or before the   ) to pay (state the penalty,
compensation or costs according to the order made), which he has not paid.
    This is to command you to levy the said sum of by distress of the
property of the said C.D.
    And, if within   days next after the distress, the said sum
of K   together with the costs of distress shall not be paid, that you do
sell the property of the said C.D. and that you do pay the money so levied to .
    This warrant is to be returned in   days.
    Issued at   the   day of   , 19   .
(Magistrate)

Officer's Return, if no Sufficient Distress, to be endorsed on Warrant
    I,   , Officer of the Court, do hereby certify to the Court that
by virtue of the above written warrant, I have made diligent search for the property of the within named C.D.
and that I can find no sufficient property of the said C.D. whereon the said sums can be levied.
(Officer)

31-WARRANT OF COMMITMENT (ON DEFAULT OF DISTRESS OR OF PAYMENT)

In the Subordinate Court of   .
    To   and other Officers of this Court.
    Whereas C.D., of   , was on the   day
of   convicted before this Court of the offence of (state offence) and
was ordered to pay forthwith (or on or before the   ) (state penalty,
compensation or costs according to the order), and the said order has not been satisfied.

    This is to command you to lodge the said C.D. in the prison of
together with this warrant, in which prison the said C.D. shall be imprisoned (with hard labour) for the
space of
unless the said sums (with K   for costs of distress) be sooner paid.
    Dated at   the   day of   , 19
(Magistrate)

32-WARRANT OF COMMITMENT TO UNDERGO SENTENCE OF IMPRISONMENT (WHERE NO ALTERNATIVE PUNISHMENT) (SECTION 307)

In the Subordinate Court (Class   ).
To
    Whereas   of   was convicted before this
Court of the offence of (state offence with place and date), and was sentenced to (state the punishment fully and distinctly. If it is intended to backdate the sentence by virtue of section 37 of the Penal Code care should be taken ascertain whether the prisoner is already serving a sentence or not).
    You are required to lodge the said   in
the prison of   together with this warrant, in which prison
the aforesaid sentence shall be carried into execution according to law and for this the present warrant shall be a sufficient authority to all whom it may concern.
    Dated at   the   day of   , 19   .
(Magistrate)
(G.N. No. 168 of 1961)

33-NOTICE OF APPEAL AGAINST CONVICTION AND/OR SENTENCE (Sections 321-323)
In the High Court for Zambia.
H .... A .... /19 ....
    Name of appellant

    Convicted on the day of .... 19........
in the (1) Subordinate Court of the   class for the ....
District, holden at   (Case No. .... of 19.......)
(2) of the offence(s) of

and on the .... day of   19...... , committed to the High
Court for sentence/sentenced* to

To the Clerk of the above Court:
    I, the above-named appellant, hereby give notice that I desire to appeal to the High Court against my conviction and/or* sentence on the grounds set forth overleaf.
    The following legal practitioner is acting for me

of   (address).
    I desire/do not desire* to be present when the court considers the appeal.
    Dated this .... day of   , 19 ....
            (1) Details of Subordinate Court and Case No. (2) Statement of Offence(s) *Delete as appropriate
            (Witness)   (Appellant (3))

        (Address of witness)   (Prison or full address if
                                                         not in custody)

The above notice was handed to me   The above notice was filed ....
this .... day of ....   day of .... 19.....
.... 19 ....

        Officer in Charge   Clerk of the Court
        Prison   (3) This notice MUST be signed by the appellant. If he cannot write he must affix his mark in the presence of a witness. The name and address of such attesting witness must be given

NOTES-(1) This notice must be submitted in triplicate and within fourteen days of-
(a)   the date of sentence, if the Subordinate Court has sentenced the appellant;
(b) the date of conviction, if the Subordinate Court has committed the appellant to the High Court for

343

sentence.

(2) If the fourteen-day period has expired and if it is desired to appeal out of time, the appellant should also complete the attached Application to Appeal out of Time.

(3) The Clerk of the Court will forward to the appropriate Assistant Registrar of the High Court the three copies of this notice together with the original record and copies thereof.

GROUNDS OF APPEAL (4)

(4)The Appellant MUST here set out the grounds or reasons he alleges why his conviction should be quashed or his sentence reduced. The Appellant can also, if he wishes, set out, in addition to his above reasons, his case and argument fully

APPLICATION TO APPEAL OUT OF TIME

(Section 324)

I, the above-named appellant, apply to the High Court for my appeal to be heard although entered out of time. The reasons for the delay in entering the appeal and the grounds on which I submit that the court should hear the appeal are as follows:

(Applicant)
DECISION BY JUDGE

(Judge)
(Date). .... 19..........
(S.I. No. 312 of 1967)

34-CASE STATED

In the Subordinate Court of   .

A.B.

v.

C.D.

1. On the   day of   , before   , Magistrate presiding over the Subordinate Court of , C.D. was charged with
the following offence: (here set out charge in full).

2. At the hearing the following facts were proved: (here set out in order all relevant facts proved).

3. The following submissions of law were made during the trial: (here set out the submissions made by the complainant and by the accused).

4. The Court, being of opinion that (state the grounds of the decision) did adjudicate and determine as follows:

5. The questions on which the opinion of the High Court is desired are: (here set out the questions desired to be submitted by the Court or any of the parties or the Director of Public Prosecutions).
(Magistrate)

35-SUMMONS TO ASSESSOR

In the Subordinate Court of   .
To   , of   .
You are hereby required to attend on the   day of ,
19   , at the hour of   o'clock in the   noon at the Subordinate Court at to serve as an assessor, and to continue in attendance until duly discharged by the said Court from further attendance.
Dated at the day of , 19 .
(Magistrate)

Appendix

36-NOTIFICATION OF ACQUITTAL

*In the High Court for Zambia.
at ....
*In the Subordinate Court (Class ....) of the
holden at ....
To: The Officer in Charge   prison.
    WHEREAS on the............... day of   , 19.......
1 stood charged before this Court for that he
on the .... day of   , at
.... did 2 .

    I hereby notify you that he has been found not guilty of the said charge and has been acquitted.
Dated at   this......................... day
of .... 19.......

                    (Deputy Assistant Registrar or Clerk
                        of the Court)

* Delete where inapplicable.
1 Here insert name of accused.
2 Here insert brief details of charge including section and Act alleged to have been contravened.
(G.N. No. 212 of 1962)

37-CERTIFICATE OF PREVIOUS CONVICTIONS (Section 142 (2))

Criminal Investigation Department,
P.O. Box RW.104,
Lusaka.
.... , 19....
F.P.R. No.
To

    I   (name and rank)
being an officer authorised by the President in that behalf certify that-
(a)   I have compared the fingerprints shown on the attached Form ZP.83 with those of   C.R.O.
No. CB/CP   in the Criminal
Record Office and find that they are identical; and
(b)   that the previous convictions of the said convict recorded in that office are as set forth overleaf.
I have, for better identification, signed and dated the said Form ZP.83.

NOTES-(1) One copy to be handed in to Court.
    (2) Duplicate to be attached to Warrant of Commitment for information of prison.
    (3) Triplicate to be returned to the Criminal Record Office, together with fingerprints, or Form ZP.84,
certified with conviction and sentence on present charge IMMEDIATELY after completion of case.
    (4) If charge is withdrawn, or the accused is acquitted or discharged, one copy of this form will be endorsed
appropriately and returned to the Criminal Record Office.

Name   C.R.O.
No.   F.P.Class

Place and C.C.R.B. No.   Date of
Sentence
Sentence
Offence
Name convicted under
Remarks

(G.N. No. 484 of 1964)

FIFTH SCHEDULE

(Section 16)

OFFENCES FOR WHICH COURTS MAY NOT SUSPEND SENTENCE

[Any offence punishable with imprisonment for life][18]
Any offence against section 226 of the Penal Code.
Arson.
Robbery.
Any offence in respect of which any written law imposes a minimum punishment.
Any conspiracy, incitement or attempt to commit any of the above-mentioned offences.
(No. 16 of 1959 as amended by No. 2 of 1960)

SUBSIDIARY LEGISLATION

SECTION 11-THE OFFENCES TO BE TRIED BY THE HIGH COURT ORDER, 1973

Order by the Chief Justice

1.   This Order may be cited as the Offences to be Tried by the High Court Order. Title

2.   The classes of offences specified in the Schedule hereto shall be tried by the High Court:Offences to be tried by the High Court

Provided-
(i)   that where the accused is a juvenile, and the case is required to be disposed of in accordance with the provisions of section sixty-five of the Juvenile Act, this Order shall not apply; and
(ii)   that this Order shall not apply in respect of offences committed prior to the 23rd day of March, 1973.   Cap. 99

SCHEDULE

(Paragraph 2)

Offence							Section of the State Security Act Contravened	
Espionage	..	..	..	..	..	..	..	3
Communication of certain information	..	..	..	..	..	4		
Protection of classified information	..	..	..	..	..			5
Unauthorised use of uniforms, passes, etc.		..	..	..	..			6
Interfering with persons on guard at protected places			..	..	..			7
Harbouring	..	..	..	..	..	..	..	8
Attempted espionage	..	..	..	..	..	..		9

(As amended by S.I. No. 186 of 1973)   Cap. 88

CRIMINAL PROCEDURE CODE
SECTION 11-CLASS OF OFFENCE FOR TRIAL BY HIGH COURT
Order by the Chief Justice   Government Notices
5 of 1962
172 of 1962
135 of 1963
Statutory Instrument
277 of 1965

It is hereby ordered that the classes of offences specified in the Schedule shall be tried by the High Court:

Provided that where the accused is a juvenile and the case is required to be disposed of in accordance with

---

[18] See s 9 of Act No 22 of 2022.

the provisions of subsection (1) of section sixty-four of the Juveniles Act, this Order shall not apply.　Cap. 53

SCHEDULE

Section of

Penal Code

Offence

contravened

Offence	Section of Penal Code contravened
Concealment of treason	44
Treason-felony	45
Piracy	73
Attempt by any person to procure abortion of a woman	151
Attempt by woman with child to procure her own abortion	152
Bigamy	166
Manslaughter	199
Infanticide	203
Attempted murder	215
Attempted murder by a convict	216
Accessory after the fact to murder	217
Conspiracy to murder	219
Child destruction	221
Disabling in order to commit felony or misdemeanour	222
Stupefying in order to commit felony or misdemeanour	223
Any prescribed act intended to maim, disfigure, disable or do grievous harm to any person, or done in resistance to, or prevention of the lawful arrest or detention of any person	224
Preventing escape from wreck	225
Intentionally endangering safety of persons travelling by railway	226
Attempting to injure by explosive substances	230
Maliciously administering poison with intent to harm	231
Aggravated robbery	294
Aggravated assault with intent to steal	295
Demanding property by written threats	296
Attempted extortion by threats or accusations	297
Procuring execution, etc., of deeds, or valuable securities by threats, violence, restraint or accusation	298
False statements by company officials	325
Casting away vessels, etc.	332
Attempts to cast away vessels	333
Malicious injuries	335 (2), 335 (3) (a), 335 (3) (b), 335 (3) (c), 335 (6), 335 (7) (e), 335 (7) (h)
Attempt to destroy property by explosives	336
Sending, etc., written threats to burn or destroy any building, agricultural produce or vessel, or to kill, maim or wound any cattle	364
Making counterfeit coins	364
Preparations for coining	365
Attempts to commit any of the foregoing offences, if not already specified	390, 391
Conspiracy to commit any of the foregoing offences, if not already specified	394
Conspiracy to commit any of the foregoing misdemeanours, if not already specified	395

Section of

Roads and		Road
Traffic		Act

contravened

Causing death by reckless or dangerous driving of motor vehicles   . .   199

SECTIONS 194 AND 358-THE CRIMINAL PROCEDURE
(EVIDENCE OF PLANS BY CERTIFICATE) RULES   Government Notice
262 of 1960

Rules by the Chief Justice

1.   These Rules may be cited as the Criminal Procedure (Evidence of Plans by Certificate) Rules.
     Title

2.   Any one of the following persons is hereby authorised to give a certificate for the purposes of section
     one hundred and ninety-four of the Criminal Procedure Code, that is to say-
     (a)   any person licensed as a land surveyor under the provisions of the Land Survey Act; and
     (b)   any person registered as an architect or quantity surveyor under the provisions of the Architects
           and Quantity Surveyors Act.   Persons authorised to sign certificates
Cap. 188
Cap. 438

3.   A certificate given for the purposes of subsection (1) of section one hundred and ninety-four of the
     Criminal Procedure Code shall be endorsed on the plan or drawing, as the case may be, and shall be in
     the following form:
          "I hereby certify that the plan (or drawing) exhibited hereon was made by me of (here specify
     the place or object) ....; that it was correctly drawn to the scale of (here specify the scale) ....; and (where
     applicable) that the direction of North in relation to the places or objects depicted hereon is clearly indicated.
                              ....(Signature)
                    ... .(Qualification)
                              ....(No. of Gazette
          notice notifying signatory's licensing or registration, as the case may be)"   Form of certificate

SECTION 221-FORMS PRESCRIBED FOR ADMISSION OF GUILT PROCEDURE   Government
Notices
252 of 1959
497 of 1964

REPUBLIC OF ZAMBIA

The Criminal Procedure Code

FORM 1
(Section 221 (1) (b))

NOTICE TO DEFENDANT AND STATEMENT OF FACTS

In the Subordinate Court (Class   ) of
To:
          Name
          Address   Tribe
                         Village
                         Chief
          Occupation   District

1. You are charged with the offence(s) of

at (place) .... on (date)
at (time)   particulars whereof are set forth in the
Statement of Facts written on the back of this form.Charge

2. Proceedings in respect of this charge (these charges) will be instituted before the magistrate at the above-mentioned court on (date)....... (hereinafter called the Fixed Day).   Fixed Day

3. If you admit the offence(s) referred to above and do not wish to appear before the court you may be relieved of the obligation of personal attendance under the following conditions:
   - (a) that you sign an Admission of Guilt form and deliver it to the Police at .... Police Station; and
   - (b) that you deposit with the Police either-
     - (i) the sum of K .... or
     - (ii) property of such value as may be required by the Police to secure the payment within one

   month of such fine as may be imposed by the court in respect of such charge(s).
   Notwithstanding that you have complied with these conditions, the magistrate may, in his discretion and for reasons stated, order your attendance before the court. You would be informed of such an order and there would be no need for you to attend unless notified provided you have complied with the above conditions.   Conditions for admission of guilt

4. If you deposit the sum of money referred to in paragraph 3 it will be used to defray whatever fine may be imposed by the court. If the amount deposited is insufficient to meet the fine you will be called upon to pay the balance and if you fail to pay this on demand, sufficient of your property may be seized and sold to pay the balance. If the fine imposed is less than the sum deposited the surplus will be returned to you if you will call at the   Police Station
not less than one day after the Fixed Day.   Disposal of money deposited

5. If you deposit property as stated in paragraph 3 (b) (ii) above it will be held for up to one month after the Fixed Day. If before the expiry of that month you pay the fine imposed by the court your property will be returned to you upon your applying at the   Police Station. If you fail to pay the fine before
the expiry of the month the property you deposit will be sold and the proceeds of sale will be used to defray the fine. If the proceeds of sale are insufficient to meet the fine you will be called on to pay the balance and if you fail to pay such balance on demand more of your property may be seized and sold as required to meet the balance. If the proceeds of the sale of the property you deposit are more than sufficient to meet the fine the surplus will be returned to you if you will call at the .... Police Station not less than two months after the Fixed Day.   Disposal of property deposited

6. If you sign an Admission of Guilt and make a deposit in accordance with paragraph 3 above you will nevertheless have the following rights:
   - (a) You may by written notice addressed to the above-mentioned court withdraw the Admission of Guilt. Such notice of withdrawal must be delivered to the Clerk of the Court before the Fixed Day. In that case you must attend at the above court on the Fixed Day to answer the charge. The court may then proceed with the trial of the charge immediately or may adjourn the case for trial on another day. If you fail to attend at the court on the Fixed Day a summons may be issued against you and if such summons is not served on you within twenty-eight days thereafter the sum of money or the property you deposit, which will remain in the hands of the Police in the meantime, may be forfeited by court order. If you withdraw the Admission of Guilt and the charge is tried by the court the prosecution will not be permitted to prove that Admission against you or to cross-examine you about it.
   - (b) You may before the Fixed Day deliver to the Clerk of the above-mentioned court a written submission to the court setting out any facts which you may wish the court to take into account with a view to reducing the sentence. If you deliver a written submission in this way you will not be permitted by yourself or by your advocate to address the court further on the Fixed Day.
   - (c) You may attend the court by yourself or by your advocate on the Fixed Day and provided you have delivered no written submission under sub-paragraph (b) above you or your advocate may address the court in mitigation before sentence is passed.

NOTE 1-If you intend to consult a solicitor about the case you would be well advised to do so before the signing the Admission of Guilt or if you have done so, then before withdrawing the Admission or delivering a written submission in mitigation of sentence.

NOTE 2-If you are charged with an offence under the Roads and Road Traffic Act, you should note that the court may in addition to any fine imposed, whether after an Admission of Guilt or other disposal of the case, exercise the powers of suspension, cancellation, disqualifying and endorsement conferred upon courts by the Act.

NOTE 3-Deliver any letter or notice to -

> The Clerk of the Court,
> > Subordinate Court,
> (Street)
> (Town)

I,   , have fully understood the contents of the above notice (which has been interpreted to me).

> Signed .
> (or thumbprint)   Remaining rights where Admission of Guilt signed

INTERPRETER'S CERTIFICATE

(Where applicable)

I,   , certify that I have this day interpreted the above notice to   in the

>   language and, to the best of my knowledge and

belief, he has understood its meaning and signed (impressed his thumbprint) in my presence.

> Signed

(DATE STAMP)   Witness

> (to be signed by a prescribed officer)
> Rank

STATEMENT OF FACTS

(Section 221 (1) (b) Criminal Procedure Code)

   If you sign an Admission of Guilt in respect of the charge(s) specified at the head of the notice printed overleaf and the court proceeds to hear and dispose of the case in your absence under section 221 of the Criminal Procedure Code, the following Statement of Facts will be read out in open court before the court proceeds to judgment. If you do not withdraw the Admission of Guilt the court will not hear any other statements on behalf of the prosecution with respect to any facts relating to the charge unless an issue has been raised in any statement in mitigation which you may have delivered and which requires further investigation. In this event the case will be adjourned to enable you to appear and call evidence as to the facts in dispute.

STATEMENT OF FACTS

> Signed
> (Rank)
> On behalf of the Prosecutor

REPUBLIC OF ZAMBIA

THE CRIMINAL PROCEDURE CODE

FORM 2
(Section 221)

ADMISSION OF GUILT FORM

> THE PEOPLE versus
> WITH REFERENCE to the charge of

in answer to which I have been required to appear before the Subordinate Court
(Class)

on the   19 ..... I hereby admit that I am guilty of the offence charged and request that sentence may be passed in my absence. I deposit herewith-

(a)   the sum of   kwacha and .... ngwee being the maximum amount of the fine which may be imposed by the court (or, as the case may be, the amount fixed by the prescribed officer);

(b)   as security for the payment within one month, of any fine which may be imposed on me by the court.

I have received a Notice and Statement of Facts relating to the charge referred to above (which has been interpreted and explained to me).

        Signature
        (or Thumbprint)   Strike out (a) or
(b) whichever is inapplicable

INTERPRETER'S CERTIFICATE
(Where applicable)

I certify that I have interpreted the foregoing to the accused person whose signature appears above, and to the best of my knowledge he has understood its meaning.

        (Signed)

DEPOSIT RECEIPT
    RECEIVED:
(a) the sum of   kwacha and .... ngwee; or
(b) .... the above-mentioned security.
        (Signed)
(DATE STAMP)   (Prescribed officer)

        Witness

NOTES-(a) In no circumstances whatsoever is a member of the Zambia Police Force other than a prescribed officer to accept any sum of money the subject of this receipt.

        (b) A receipt for the sum deposited, or any portion thereof, which is subsequently refunded should be obtained wherever practicable on the reverse of the triplicate copy of this form.

SECTION 221-APPLICATION
Notices by the Chief Justice   Statutory Instruments
10 of 1967
343 of 1968

The offences set out in the First Schedule are hereby specified as offences to which the provisions of section two hundred and twenty-one of the Criminal Procedure Code shall apply, and the offences set out in the Second Schedule are hereby specified as offences to which the provisions of section two hundred and twenty-one of the Criminal Procedure Code shall not apply.

SCHEDULE

(Paragraph 2)

OFFENCES TO WHICH THE PROVISIONS OF SECTION 221 OF THE CRIMINAL PROCEDURE CODE SHALL APPLY

Offences-
    (a)   created by sections 23, 25(10), 77, 83, 98, 160, 161(2), 177(b), 192, 193, 195 (1), 214 and 215 of the Roads and Road Traffic Act;
    (b)   against the provisions of the Roads and Road Traffic Act in respect of which no penalty is provided other than by section 241 of the said Act;

(c) against the provisions of the Roads and Road Traffic (Public Service Vehicles, Licensing and Use) Regulations in respect of which no penalty is provided other than by regulation 26 of the said Regulations;

(d) against the provisions of the Roads and Road Traffic (Registration and Licensing) Regulations in respect of which no penalty is provided other than by regulation 28 of the said Regulations;

(e) created by the Roads and Road Traffic (International Circulation) Regulations;

(f) against the provisions of the Roads and Road Traffic (Construction Equipment and Use) Regulations in respect of which no penalty is provided other than by regulation 59 of the said Regulations;

(g) against the provisions of the Rules of the Road Regulations in respect of which no penalty is provided other than by regulation 19 of the said Regulations;

(h against the provisions of the Roads and Road Traffic (Bus and Taxicab Drivers Uniform) Regulation, 1982, in respect of which no penalty is provided other than by regulation 5 of the said Regulations;

(i) created by sections 7 (1) and 14 (1) (a), (b) and (c) of the Broadcasting Act;

(j) created by section 82 (1) (a) (iii) of the Posts and Telecommunications Corporation Act.

(As amended by S.I. No. 50 of 1986)

SECTION 318-THE CRIMINAL PROCEDURE CODE (POLICE SUPERVISION) RULES   Government Notices
397 of 1963
493 of 1964
497 of 1964

Rules by the President

1. These Rules may be cited as the Criminal Procedure Code (Police Supervision) Rules.   Title

2. Every person subject to police supervision under section three hundred and eighteen of the Criminal Procedure Code, hereinafter referred to as a police supervisee, shall before the date on which he is entitled to be released from prison inform a prison officer of his residential address after his release. Residential address to be notified

3. On his release from prison every such police supervisee shall be issued by a prison officer with an identity book in the form of the Schedule, in which shall be completed the several particulars respecting such police supervisee, and further, there shall be endorsed therein-
    (a) a certificate that the provisions concerning his supervision have been explained to the police supervisee in a language which he understands, which certificate shall be signed by a prison officer and interpreter, if used, or, in the absence of such interpreter, witnessed by a person who was present when such provisions were explained to the police supervisee and such explanation shall be acknowledged as understood by the police supervisee by impressing thereon his right thumbprint;
    (b) the name of the place at which and the officer in charge of the police station, or the Administrative Officer, to whom he shall report.   Identity book

4. Every police supervisee shall, on receiving such identity book as provided for in rule 3, report himself-
    (a) immediately on his release to a police officer at the police station or to an Administrative Officer at the administrative office at the place of release;
    (b) and then to a police officer at the police station or to an Administrative Officer at the administrative office specified in such identity book within seven days of his arrival at his residential address and shall declare to such officer his residential address.   Police supervisee to report

5. Every police supervisee shall report himself to a police officer at the police station or to an Administrative Officer at the administrative office specified in his identity book at such intervals of time as may be directed by such officer.   Time for reporting

6. Whenever any police supervisee intends to change his residential address to any other residential address, he shall notify a police officer at the police station or an Administrative Officer at the administrative office specified in his identity book not less than forty-eight hours before he so changes his residential address of the fact of such intention and of the address at which thereafter he intends to reside. Such officer shall amend the endorsement in the identity book of such police supervisee to accord with the change of residential address and shall, if necessary, specify therein the police station or administrative office to which he shall report. Every such police supervisee shall, within forty-eight hours of his change of residential address, report himself to a police officer at the police station or to an Administrative Officer at the administrative office specified in his identity book and shall notify to such

officer his residential address and thereafter shall continue to report himself at such intervals of time as may be directed by such officer. Change of residential address

7. Every notification of report required to be made by any police supervisee shall be made by him in person: Manner of reporting

Provided that if from illness (the proof of which shall lie upon him) any police supervisee is prevented from making in person any notification or report required by these Rules, he may do so in any one of the following ways:

    (i)   in person, to any Administrative Officer or to any police officer residing in the township or Government station nearest to the place of his residence; or

    (ii)   in person, to the village headman or a member of the local authority exercising jurisdiction in the area in which he resides; or

    (iii)   by oral communication sent by a messenger, and production of the identity book to a police officer at the police station or to an Administrative Officer at the administrative office specified in his identity book.

(As amended by No. 493 of 1964)

8. In any case where a notification or report has been made under the provisions of paragraph (i) or (ii) of the proviso contained in rule 7, it shall be incumbent on the person receiving such report to inform a police officer of the police station or an Administrative Officer of the administrative office at which such police supervisee should have reported, as soon as may be convenient, of the fact and date of such report. Officer mentioned in identity book to be informed of any report

9.   (1)   On the occasion of every notification or report required to be made under these Rules, the identity book issued to the police supervisee making such notification or report shall be produced. Identity book to be produced

    (2)   If any police supervisee loses his identity book, he shall forthwith report the loss to a police officer at the nearest police station or Administrative Officer in the district in which he resides and shall apply for a new identity book, which shall be issued to him with the necessary particulars entered therein.

10. At the end of the term of police supervision ordered by the court, the police supervisee shall surrender his identity book to the officer to whom he last reported, who shall forward the identity book to the officer in charge of the Criminal Investigation Department, Zambia Police. Surrender of identity books

11. A copy of these Rules shall be printed in each identity book issued to a police supervisee. Copy of Rules to be included in identity books

SCHEDULE

(Rule 3)

POLICE SUPERVISION-CRIMINAL PROCEDURE CODE

(Sections 317 to 319)
Name
Aliases
Tribe or Nationality   Village or Town
Chief or Local Authority   District
Criminal Records Office Reference
Order of police supervision made by
Court at   on .... for a
period of   years from date of his release from prison (see page 2)

(Page 1)

PHOTOGRAPHS

.... Government Prison No. ....

(Page 2)

(Rule 3 (a))

To be completed by prison officer at prison of release

Date of release .... from Government Prison

Order of police supervision will accordingly expire on

   I certify that I have explained the requirements of the Criminal Procedure Code (Police Supervision) Rules to Police supervisee (name)

in the   language which he understands and acknowledges

beneath. I have informed him that if he does not comply with them, he may be guilty of an offence and I have instructed him to report to a police/administrative officer (delete as applicable) at   (place) directly upon his release and thereafter as instructed.

Address and destination

Right thumbprint

PRISON

DATE STAMP

Signature of interpreter/witness

Signature and rank of prison officer issuing identity book

....

(Pages 3 and 4)

Police supervisee   is hereby required to

report himself in accordance with the Rules annexed hereto, to a police officer at the police station or an Administrative Officer at the administrative office shown, at such intervals of time specified.

	Signature and rank of police officer, or Admini-
Intervals of time	To strative Officer

(Pages 5 and 6)

CHANGE OF RESIDENTIAL ADDRESSES

(Rule 6)

Date   To

(Pages 7, 8, 9 and 10)

REPORTS

    Police supervisee   has reported at:

	Signature and rank of police officer, or Admini-
Place Date	strative Officer

(Pages 11, 12 and 13)

SUPERVISION RULES

SECTION 359-THE CRIMINAL PROCEDURE (WITNESSES' AND ASSESSORS' ALLOWANCES AND EXPENSES) RULES

Rules by the Chief Justice

        Government Notices

6 of 1963

497 of 1964

Statutory Instruments

63 of 1964

424 of 1968

1.   These Rules may be cited as the Criminal Procedure (Witnesses' and Assessors' Allowances and Expenses) Rules.   Title

2. For the purposes of these Rules-   Interpretation

"Registrar" means the Registrar of the High Court, a Deputy Registrar or District Registrar;

"witness" includes an interpreter who attends and interprets at any criminal proceedings.

3. These Rules shall apply to all criminal proceedings in the High Court and subordinate courts.
    Application

4. The following persons shall be entitled to allowances and expenses:
    (a) witnesses and assessors who have duly attended at or for the criminal proceedings at the instance of the People, unless the Judge or magistrate presiding at such proceedings shall, for sufficient reason, disallow the allowances or expenses of any such witness or assessor;
    (b) witnesses who have duly attended at or for the criminal proceedings at the instance of any party, other than the People, when a certificate for the payment of allowances and expenses is granted- Persons entitled
        (i) by the Judge or magistrate presiding at such proceedings; or
        (ii) if such Judge or magistrate is not available for any sufficient reason, by the Registrar, in respect of proceedings before the High Court, and in respect of proceedings in a subordinate court by the magistrate presiding over such court at the time of the application for any such certificate.

(As amended by S.I. No. 63 of 1964)

5. (1) The allowances for witnesses and assessors shall be as follows:
        Amounts

	Minimum sum payable per day	Maximum sum per day
Class of Person		
Professional persons, owners, directors or managers of businesses and expert witnesses	K250	K500
Clerks and artisans and per- sons of similar status:	K.150	K.350

Provided that the sum payable under class (b) shall not, unless otherwise ordered by the presiding Judge or magistrate, exceed the sum of K75 per day if the witness has lost no wages or earnings or other income by reason of attending the proceedings, or where the period during which he has been away from home or in respect of which he has lost wages, earnings or other income by reason of his attendance does not exceed four hours

    (2) The above-mentioned allowances will be paid during the time for which a witness or assessor is necessarily detained and for the time reasonably occupied in travelling.
    (3) No additional allowance will be paid merely because the witness or assessor attends in respect of more than one case on the same day.
    (4) If, in the opinion of the Registrar or magistrate to whom a claim has been submitted in terms of rule 7-
        (a) a strict adherence to the above scales in any particular case would result in hardship, he may at his discretion increase the amounts payable; or
        (b) a reduction in any of the allowances provided for by this rule is justified in any particular case, he may at his discretion reduce or disallow the amounts payable.

(As amended by S.I. No. 177 of 1990)

6. (1) In addition to any sum to which a witness or assessor may be entitled under rule 5, all witnesses and assessors provided for in rule 4 shall also be entitled to be reimbursed in respect of any expenses actually and reasonably incurred in travelling to and from the court, or for necessary accommodation and subsistence.   Travelling expenses

(2) If, in the opinion of the Registrar or magistrate to whom a claim has been submitted for the reimbursement of expenses, the sums expended and claimed exceed what is reasonable, he may in his discretion reduce or disallow the amounts payable.

(3) A witness or assessor who is entitled to claim travelling expenses under rule 6 (1) shall be paid-
  (a) thirty ngwee per kilometre where he uses his own motor car;
  (b) ten ngwee per kilometre where he uses his own motor cycle.
(As amended by S.I. No. 51 of 1981)

7. For the purpose of determining the amount payable to witnesses and assessors under these Rules, claims for payment of allowances and expenses shall be submitted to and dealt with by-
  (a) the Registrar, in respect of proceedings before the High Court:
    Provided that any person wishing to submit a claim for the minimum sum payable to him under the provisions of rule 5, may submit his claim, together with his claim, if any, for expenses payable under rule 6, to a Deputy Assistant Registrar who shall have full power to deal with such claims, including the powers vested in the Registrar by rule 6(2);
  (b) the magistrate who presided over the proceedings, in respect of proceedings in a subordinate court, or if he is not available for any sufficient reason then the magistrate who, at the time of the submission of the claim is presiding over the court in which the proceedings took place:
    Provided that any person wishing to submit a claim for the minimum sum payable to him under the provisions of rule 5, may submit his claim to the clerk of the court, who shall have full power to deal with such claim.
(As amended by No. 424 of 1968)   Submission of claims

8. No allowances or travelling expenses shall be paid to public officers under these Rules: Public officers

Provided that any public officer who has attended any criminal proceedings for the purpose of interpreting any African language not ordinarily spoken in Zambia or any other foreign language, shall be entitled to the same allowances as any other interpreter under these Rules.

INDEX TO CRIMINAL PROCEDURE CODE

THE PROBATION OF OFFENDERS ACT, CHAPTER 93 OF THE LAWS OF ZAMBIA

ARRANGEMENT OF SECTIONS

PROBATION OF OFFENDERS 15 of 1953

**An Act to provide for the probation
of offenders; and to provide for matters
incidental thereto.**

[4th December 1953]

Short title and application

1.   This Act may be cited as the Probation of Offenders Act. (As amended by G.N. No. 276 of 1964)

Interpretation

2.   In this Act, unless the context otherwise requires- Interpretation
      "probation officer" means a probation officer appointed under the provisions of section fifteen;
      "probation order" has the meaning assigned to it by section three;
      "probation period" means the period for which a probationer is placed under supervision by virtue of a probation order;
      "probationer" means a person placed under supervision by a probation order;
      "senior probation officer" means a senior probation officer appointed under the provisions of section fifteen. (As amended by No. 13 of 1961)

Power to make probation orders

3.   (1)   Where a court by or before which a person is convicted of an offence, not being an offence the sentence for which is fixed by law, is of the opinion that, having regard to the youth, character, antecedents, home surroundings, health or mental condition of the offender, or to the nature of the offence, or to any extenuating circumstances in which the offence was committed, it is expedient to do so, the court may, instead of sentencing him, make an order, hereinafter in this Act referred to as a "probation order", requiring him to be under the supervision of a probation officer for am period to be specified in the order of not less than one year nor more than three years.

376

(2)   Before making a probation order, the court shall satisfy itself that the offender understands the effects of the order, including any additional requirements proposed to be inserted therein under subsections (2) and (3) of section four, and that if he fails to comply therewith or commits another offence during the probation period he will be liable to be sentenced for the original offence; and if the offender is not less than nineteen years of age the court shall not make the order unless he expresses his willingness to comply with the requirements thereof.(As amended by No. 14 of 1963)

Contents of probation orders

4.   (1)   A probation order shall name the District in which the probationer resides or will reside, and the probationer shall notify the probation officer responsible for his supervision of any change of residence.

(2)   A probation order may require the probationer to comply during the whole or any part of the probation period with such requirements as the court, having regard to the circumstances of the case, considers necessary for securing the good conduct of the offender or for preventing a repetition by him of the same offence or the commission of other offences:
Provided that, without prejudice to the powers of the court to make an order for the payment of sums by way of costs, damages or compensation, the payment of such sums shall not be included among the requirements of a probation order.

(3)   Without prejudice to the generality of subsection (2), a probation order may include requirements relating to the residence of the probationer: Provided that-
(i)   before making an order containing any such requirements, the court shall consider the home surroundings of the offender; and
(ii)   where the order requires the probationer to reside in an institution, the name of the institution and the period for which he is so required to reside shall be specified in the order, and that period shall not extend beyond twelve months from the date of the order.

(4)   Where a probation order requires the probationer to reside in any institution, the court making the order shall forthwith give notice of the terms of the order to the Minister.

(5)   Where the District named in a probation order as the District in which the probationer resides or will reside is not the District in which the order is made, the court shall transmit to the court for the District named all documents and information relating to the case, and thereupon the last-mentioned court shall be deemed for all the purposes of this Act to be the court by which the probation order was made.(As amended by No. 13 of 1961)

Probation order may require probationer to submit to treatment of mental condition

5. (1)   Where the court is satisfied, on the evidence of a registered medical practitioner, appearing to the court to be experienced in the diagnosis of mental disorders, that the mental condition of an offender is such as requires and may be susceptible to treatment, but is not such as to justify his being adjudicated as a mentally disordered or defective person under the Mental Disorders Act, the court may, if it makes a probation order, include therein a requirement that the offender shall submit for such period, as may
be specified therein, not extending beyond twelve months from the date of the order, to treatment by or under the direction of a duly qualified medical practitioner with a view to the improvement of the offender's mental condition.

(2)   The treatment required by any such order shall be such one of the following kinds of treatment as may be specified in the order, that is to say:
(a)   treatment as a resident patient in such institution or place prescribed for the purpose of this section as may be specified in the order;
(b)   treatment as a non-resident patient at such institution or place as may be specified in the order;
(c)   treatment by or under the direction of such duly qualified medical practitioner as may be specified in the order; but, except as aforesaid, the nature of the treatment shall not be specified in the order.

(3)   A court shall not make a probation order containing such a requirement as aforesaid unless it is satisfied that arrangements have been or can be made for the treatment intended to be specified in the order, and, if the offender is to be treated as a resident patient as aforesaid, for his reception.

(4)   While the probationer is under treatment as a resident patient in pursuance of a requirement of the probation order, the probation officer responsible for his supervision shall carry out the supervision to such extent only as may be necessary for the purpose of the discharge or amendment of the order.

(5)   Where the medical practitioner by whom or under whose direction a probationer is being treated for his mental condition in pursuance of a probation order, is of the opinion that part of the treatment can be better or more conveniently given in or at an institution or place not specified in the order, being an institution or place in or at which the treatment of the probationer will be given by or under the direction of a duly qualified medical practitioner, he may, with the consent of the probationer, make arrangements for him to be treated accordingly, and to receive part of his treatment as a resident patient in an institution or place notwithstanding that the institution or place is not one which could have been specified in that behalf in the probation order.

Copies of orders

6.   The court by which a probation order is made or which makes an order amending or discharging a probation order shall furnish copies of the order to the probationer, the principal probation officer, the probation officer responsible for the supervision of the probationer, and to the person in charge of the institution, if any, in which the probationer is to reside or is residing.

(As amended by No. 13 of 1961 and No. 21 of 1964)

Failure of probationer to comply with probation order

7. (1)   If at any time during the probation period it appears to any Judge or magistrate that a probationer has failed to comply with any of the provisions of the probation order, he may issue a summons to the probationer requiring him to appear at the place and time specified therein or may issue a warrant for his arrest: Provided that a magistrate shall not issue such a summons or such a warrant except on information on oath.

  (2)   A summons or warrant under this section shall direct the probationer to appear or to be brought before the court by which the probation order was made.

  (3)   If it is proved to the satisfaction of the court by which the probation order was made that the probationer has failed to comply with any of the provisions of the probation order, then-

      (a)   without prejudice to the continuance in force of the probation order, the court may impose a fine not exceeding three hundred penalty units; or

      (b)   the court may pass any sentence in respect of the original offence in respect of which the probation order was made which it could pass if the probationer had just been convicted before the court of that offence:

               Provided that where a court has, under the provisions of paragraph (a), imposed a fine on the probationer, then, upon any subsequent sentence being passed upon the probationer under the provisions of this section or the next following section, the imposition of the said fine shall be taken into account in fixing the amount of the said sentence.

(As amended by Act No. 13 of 1994)

Commission of further offences by probationers

8. (1)   If it appears to any Judge or magistrate that a probationer has been convicted of an offence committed during the probation period, he may issue a summons requiring the probationer to appear at the place and time specified therein or may issue a warrant for his arrest: Provided that a magistrate shall not issue such a summons or such a warrant except on information on oath.

  (2)   A summons or warrant issued under subsection (1) shall direct the probationer to appear or to be brought before the court by which the probation order was made.

  (3)   Where a probationer is convicted by a magistrate of an offence committed during the probation period, the magistrate may commit the probationer to custody or release him on bail, with or without sureties, until he can be brought or appear before the court by which the probation order was made.

  (4)   Where it is proved to the satisfaction of the court by which the probation order was made that the probationer has been convicted of an offence committed during the probation period, such court may pass any sentence in respect of the original offence which it could pass if the probationer had just been convicted before that court of such offence.

(5)   Where a probationer is convicted before the High Court of an offence committed during the probation period, the High Court may pass any sentence which the court which made the probation order could pass if the probationer had just then been convicted before that court of the original offence.

Transmission of documents when case is remitted to another court

9.   Where a magistrate commits a probationer to custody, or releases him on bail, under the provisions of subsection (3) of section eight, the magistrate shall transmit to the court by which the probation order was made-
(a)   such particulars of the matter as he thinks fit; and
(b)   a signed certificate of the conviction for the offence committed during the probationary period; and, for the purposes of the proceedings in the court to which it is transmitted, such certificate, if purporting to be so signed, shall be admissible as evidence of the conviction.

No conviction in case where probation order made

10.   (1)   Subject as hereinafter provided, a conviction for an offence for which a probation order is made shall be deemed not to be a conviction for any purpose other than the purposes of the proceedings in which the order is made and of any subsequent proceedings which may be taken against the offender under the foregoing provisions of this Act.

Provided that where an offender, being not less than nineteen years of age at the time of his conviction for an offence for which he is placed on probation, is subsequently sentenced under this Act, the provisions of this subsection shall cease to apply to the conviction.
(2)   Without prejudice to the provisions of subsection (1), the conviction of an offender who is placed on probation shall, in any event, be disregarded for the purposes of any enactment which imposes any disqualification or disability upon convicted persons, or authorises or requires the imposition of any such disqualification or disability.
(3)   The foregoing provisions of this section shall not affect-
(a)   any right of such offender as aforesaid to appeal against his conviction, or to rely thereon in bar of any subsequent proceedings for the same offence;
(b)   the revesting or restoration of any property in consequence of the conviction of any such offender.
(As amended by No. 21 of 1964)

Amendment of probation orders

11.   (1)   Subject to the provisions of this section, where, on the application of a probationer or of the probation officer responsible for the supervision of the probationer, the court which made the probation order is satisfied that the provisions of the probation order should be varied, or that any provision should be inserted or cancelled, the court may by order amend the probation order accordingly:
Provided that no order shall be made under this section reducing the probation period, or extending that period beyond a period of three years from the date of the probation order.
(2)   An order under subsection (1) may require a probationer to reside in an institution for any period not extending beyond twelve months from the date of that order, if the total period or aggregate of the periods for which he is required to reside in any institution or institutions under the probation order does not exceed twelve months.
(3)   The court shall, if it is satisfied on the application of the probation officer responsible for the supervision of the probationer that the probationer has changed, or is about to change, his residence from the District named in the order to another District, by order vary the probation order by substituting for the reference to the District named therein a reference to the District where the probationer is residing or about to reside, and shall transmit to the court for the new District all documents and information relating to the case, and thereupon the last-mentioned court shall be deemed for all the purposes of this Act to be the court by which the probation order was made.
(4)   Where an application is made by the probation officer responsible for the supervision of the probationer under this section, the court shall summon the probationer to appear before the court; and if the probationer is not less than nineteen years of age, the court shall not amend a probation

order unless the probationer expresses his willingness to comply with the requirements of the order as amended:

Provided that this subsection shall not apply to an order cancelling a requirement of the probation order or reducing the period of any requirement or substituting a new District for the District named in the order.

(5)   Where an order is made under this section for the variation, insertion, or cancellation of a provision requiring a probationer to reside in an institution, the court shall forthwith give notice of the terms of the order to the Minister. (As amended by No. 13 of 1961 and No. 21 of 1964)

Discharge of probation orders

12. (1)   The court by which a probation order was made may, on the application of the probationer or the probation officer responsible for the supervision of the probationer, discharge the probation order, and, where the application is made by the probation officer responsible for the supervision of the probationer, the court may deal with it without summoning the probationer.

(2)   Where an offender in respect of whom a probation order has been made is subsequently sentenced for the offence in respect of which the probation order was made, the probation order shall cease to have effect. (As amended by No. 13 of 1961)

Selection of probation officers

13. (1)   The probation officer who is to be responsible for the supervision of any probationer shall be selected by a senior probation officer.

(2)   Where a woman or girl is placed under the supervision of a probation officer, the probation officer shall be a woman. (As amended by No. 13 of 1961)

Contribution towards probationers and institutions

14. Such contribution may be made towards the maintenance of probationers and the establishment or maintenance of institutions for the reception of probationers as Parliament may approve.

(As amended by No. 13 of 1961 and G.N. No. 276 of 1964)

Appointments

15. The Minister may appoint-
  (a)   a principal probation officer;
  (b)   such number of senior probation officers as he may deem necessary;
  (c)   a sufficient number of probation officers to perform such duties as may be prescribed.

(As amended by No. 13 of 1961)

Powers and duties and delegation

16. (1)   The principal probation officer may exercise or perform all the powers and duties of a senior probation officer or of a probation officer.

(2)   The principal probation officer may delegate all or any of his powers or duties in relation to any probationer to a senior probation officer, or to the probation officer who is responsible for the supervision of the probationer.

(3)   A senior probation officer may exercise or perform all or any of the powers and duties of a probation officer. (As amended by No. 13 of 1961)

Probation Committee

17. (1)   The Minister may, by Gazette notice, establish a Probation Committee which shall consist of such persons as the Minister may appoint.

(2)   The Probation Committee shall exercise and perform such powers and duties, incur such expenses and regulate its procedure in such manner as may be prescribed.

(As amended by No. 13 of 1961)

Regulations

18. (1) The Minister may, by statutory instrument, make regulations for carrying this Act into effect.

    (2) Without prejudice to the generality of the foregoing power, such regulations may prescribe-

        (a) the duties of the principal probation officer;

        (b) the duties of senior probation officers and of probation officers;

        (c) the constitution and duties of a probation committee or probation committees;

        (d) the form of records to be kept under this Act;

        (e) what shall be an institution for the purposes of this Act;

        (f) the remuneration of any person appointed to carry out any duties under this Act, and the fees and charges to be made for any act, matter or thing under this Act to be done or observed;

        (g) anything to be prescribed under this Act. (As amended by No. 13 of 1961)

SUBSIDIARY LEGISLATION
SECTION 18-THE PROBATION OF OFFENDERS (PRESCRIBED FORMS) REGULATIONS

Regulations by the Minister
Government Notices
143 of 1955
198 of 1961
Statutory Instrument
53 of 1965
Title

1. These Regulations may be cited as the Probation of Offenders (Prescribed Forms) Regulations.

Prescribed forms

2. The forms set out in the Schedule are hereby prescribed for use, with such variations as the circumstances of each case may require, in the cases to which they refer.

SCHEDULE
(Regulation 2)
PRESCRIBED FORMS

P.O. Form 1
(Section 3)
PROBATION ORDER
IN THE SUBORDINATE COURT (CLASS) of the .... holden at

....

THE PEOPLE v..

.... (hereinafter called the defendant) is this day convicted/found guilty for that he/she on the.................................. day of ...., 19........,
at.. did

.... and the Court is of opinion, having

regard to the nature of the offence, including any extenuating circumstances, and the character of the defendant, that it is

expedient to make a probation order;

And the Court has explained to the defendant the effect of this order, including the additional requirement specified

below, and that if he/she fails to comply therewith or commits another offence during the probation period, he/she will be

liable to be sentenced/have an order made against him/her, for the offence in respect of which he/she has now been

convicted/found guilty (and the defendant being not less than nineteen years of age has expressed his/her willingness to

comply with the requirements of this order);

It is therefore ordered that the defendant, who resides (or will reside) in the District of

....
....

be required for the period of .... years from the date of this order to be under the supervision of a probation

officer appointed for or assigned to that District: and it is further ordered that the defendant shall, during the said period,

notify forthwith to the said probation officer any change of his/her residence and comply with the following requirements:

*( ) That he/she shall notify forthwith to his/her supervising probation officer any change of employment.

*( ) That he/she shall keep in touch with his/her supervising probation officer in accordance with such instructions as

may from time to time be given by the probation officer and in particular that he/she will, if the probation officer so requires,

receive visits from the probation officer at his/her home.

(   )

....
....
....

(   )

....
....

(And it is ordered that the defendant do pay to...
....

.... the sum of ....
....

(as damages for injury or compensation for loss) and do further pay to ....
....

....the sum of ....
....

for costs, the same sums to be paid (by instalments of ....
....

....for every .... days/
months, the

first instalment to be paid) forthwith (or on the ....
....

day of ...., 19).)

Dated the .... day of ...., 19 .

....

Magistrate

Copy to: Probationer.

 Probation Officer.

 Principal Probation Officer.

 † Person in Charge ....

 † Minister of Labour and Social Services.

*These are specimens of additional requirements which are commonly inserted and are not part of the prescribed
form.

† In cases where institutional residence ordered by the Court.

(No. 198 of 1961 as amended by No. 53 of 1965)

P.O. FORM 2

(Section 7 (1))

INFORMATION FOR FAILURE TO COMPLY WITH PROBATION ORDER

IN THE SUBORDINATE COURT (CLASS) of the ....

holden at ....
....

THE PEOPLE v ....

THE INFORMATION of .... who

upon
oath states:

.... was on the .... day of

...., 19........, convicted by the Subordinate Court (Class

............)

of the .... holden at .... of *...

....

and on the said date the said Court made a probation order requiring the said ....

....

for the period of .... years then next ensuing to be under the supervision of a probation officer appointed

for or to the District of .... and further requiring the said.......................

*State offence

*...

....

....

And the said .... did on the ....

day of ...., 19........., fail to comply with the last-mentioned requirement inasmuch as he/ she did

*State required contravention

*..

....

....

....

Taken and sworn before me ....

....

Magistrate

(As amended by No. 53 of 1965)

*State particulars

of breach

P.O. FORM 3

(Section 7 (2))

SUMMONS FOR FAILURE TO COMPLY WITH PROBATION ORDER

IN THE SUBORDINATE COURT (CLASS ....) of the ....

....

holden at ....

....

THE PEOPLE v ....

INFORMATION on oath has been laid this day by ....

....

for that you on the .... day of ...., 19........., were

convicted by or before the Subordinate Court (Class...........) of the ....

....

holden at................ of *...

....

....

....

and that on the said date the said Court made a probation order requiring you for the period of ....

....

years then next ensuing to be under the supervision of a probation officer appointed for or assigned to the District

of...and further

requiring you

*State offence

to*..

....

....

....

and by the said information it is further alleged that you did on the................. day of ....,

19........., fail to
comply with the last-mentioned requirement of the said order.
You are therefore hereby summoned to appear on the .... day of .... 19........, at the
hour of .... in the ....noon, before the Court of the .... sitting at .... to
answer the said information.
Dated the .... day of ...., 19........

....
(Magistrate
(As amended by No. 53 of 1965)
*State requirement contravention

P.O. FORM 4
(Section 7 (2))
WARRANT OF ARREST FOR FAILURE TO COMPLY WITH PROBATION ORDER
IN THE SUBORDINATE COURT (CLASS...............) of the...
....
holden at ....
....
To:
 Commissioner of Police.
INFORMATION on oath has been laid this day (on the...
....
day of..............................., 19........,) by...................................that............................hereinafter called the defendant, was
on the...........................day of..............................., 19......., convicted by or before the Subordinate Court (Class..............)
of the .... holden at...................................... of *
....
....
and that on the said date the said Court made a probation order requiring the defendant for the period of.................years
then next ensuing to be under the supervision of a probation officer appointed for or assigned to the District of...........................and further requiring the defendant to *...
....
....
....
*State offence
And by the said information it is further alleged that the defendant did on the...........................day of..................................., 19......., fail to comply with the last-mentioned requirement of the said order.
You are therefore hereby commanded to bring the said defendant forthwith before the (said) Court of the...................................sitting at.................................... to answer the said information.
Dated the .... day of ...., 19........

....
(Magistrate
*State requirement contravened
ENDORSEMENT AS TO BAIL
It is directed that the defendant on arrest be released on bail on his/her entering into a
recognizance in the sum of........................with........................surety in the sum of.........................(each) for his/her
appearance before the Court last within mentioned, at the hour of ....in the ....noon on the
.... day of................., 19........

....
(Magistrate

P.O. FORM 5
(Section 7 (3))

ORDER ON FAILURE TO COMPLY WITH REQUIREMENTS OF PROBATION ORDER

IN THE SUBORDINATE COURT (CLASS...............) of the...

holden at...

....

THE PEOPLE v..

....(hereinafter called the defendant) was on the ....day

of..............................., 19........, convicted by or before the Court of the............................... holden

at...................................... of *...................................... and on the said date the said Court made a probation order

requiring him/her for the period of ......years then next ensuing to be under the supervision of a probation officer appointed

for or assigned to the District of .... and further requiring him/her*.........................

....

....

....

*State offence

And the said defendant has this day appeared (or been brought) before the (said) Court of

the...................................sitting at...and it has been proved to the satisfaction of the Court that

he/she had failed to comply with the last-mentioned requirement of the said order inasmuch as *.................

....

....

....

*State requirement contravention

It is adjudged that the defendant in respect of his/her failure to comply with the said requirement do forfeit and pay a

fine of............................((or, where defendant is dealt with for original offence) for the said offence in respect of which the

said order was made to *...

....

....

......).

*State particulars of breach

....

(Magistrate

(As amended by No. 53 of 1965)

*State judgment

P.O. FORM 6

(Section 7 (3))

WARRANT OF COMMITMENT FOR FAILURE TO COMPLY WITH PROBATION ORDER

IN THE SUBORDINATE COURT (CLASS..............) of the...

....

holden at ....

....

THE PEOPLE v..

To: Commissioner of Police.

Superintendent of the Government Prison at..

....

.... (hereinafter called the defendant) was on the

...................day

of..............................., 19......., convicted by or before the Court of the...

....

holden at...of *.......................................

....

....

....

and on the said date the said Court made a probation order requiring him/her for the period of ....

years then
next ensuing to be under the supervision of a probation officer appointed for or assigned to the District of
.... and further requiring him/her*...
....
*State
offence
And the defendant has this day appeared (or been brought) before the (said) Court of the.............................
..sitting
at...and it has been proved to the satisfaction of the Court that he/she has failed to
comply with the
last-mentioned requirement of the said order inasmuch as *...
....
....
....

*State requirement contravention

It is adjudged that the defendant in respect of his/her failure to comply with the said requirement do forfeit
and pay a
fine of............................((or, where defendant is dealt with for original offence) for the said offence in respect
of which the
said probation order was made *...
....
....
....

*State particulars of breach
You are required to lodge the defendant in the prison of....................................... together with this warrant,
in which
prison the aforesaid sentence shall be carried into execution according to law, and for this the present
warrant shall be a
sufficient authority to all whom it may concern.

....
(Magistrate
(As amended by No. 53 of 1965)
*State judgment

P.O. FORM 7
(Section 8 (1))
INFORMATION ON COMMISSION OF FURTHER OFFENCE DURING PROBATION PERIOD
IN THE SUBORDINATE COURT (CLASS..............) of the...
....
holden at...
....
THE PEOPLE v ....
The information of.. who upon oath states .... was
on the ....day of................................, 19......., convicted by or before the Court of the
.................................holden at................................of *..
.....
....
....
and on the said date the said Court made a probation order requiring him/her for the period of............................
years then
next ensuing to be under the supervision of a probation officer appointed for or assigned to the District
of...And the said .... was on the.............................
..day
of............................... 19......., convicted by or before the Court of the....................holden at ....
.......of the
following offence, namely, *...
....
....

....
* State offence committed by him/her during the said period, to wit, on the.................................day of ....
.........................., 19......., and
was sentenced to (or ordered to)...
....
Taken and sworn before me,
....
(Magistrate
(As amended by No. 53 of 1965)
*State shortly particulars of offence

P.O. FORM 8
(Section 8 (1))
SUMMONS ON COMMISSION OF FURTHER OFFENCE DURING PROBATION PERIOD
IN THE SUBORDINATE COURT (CLASS........) of the...
....
 holden at ....
....
THE PEOPLE v...................................
To ....
of ....
INFORMATION on oath has been laid this day by ....
for that you on the .... day of ...., 19......., were convicted
by or before the Court of the ....holden at ....
....
of * .... and that
on the
said date the said Court made a probation order requiring you for the period of .... years then next
ensuing to be under the supervision of a probation officer appointed for or assigned to the District '
of.......................................; and by the said information it is further alleged that you were on the
..............................day of
..........................., 19......, convicted by or before the Court of the .... holden at ....
....of the following offence, namely, *...
....
....
*State judgment
committed by you during the said period, to wit, on the..............................day of ....
............,
19........, and that you were sentenced (or ordered) to *...
....
*State shortly particulars of offence
You are therefore hereby summoned to appear on the ....day of ....,
19......., at the hour of............................in the ....noon, before the Court of the .... sitting at
.... to answer the said information.
Dated the............................day of...................................., 19......
....
(Magistrate
(As amended by No. 53 of 1965)
*State judgment

P.O. FORM 9
(Section 8 (1))
WARRANT OF ARREST ON COMMISSION OF FURTHER OFFENCE DURING PROBATION PERIOD
IN THE SUBORDINATE COURT (CLASS ....) of the..
....

holden at ....
....

THE PEOPLE v ....

To: The Commissioner of Police.

INFORMATION on oath has been laid this day (or on the ....
....

day of ...., 19.....) by .... that ....
....

(hereinafter called the defendant) was on the .... day of..
.................,

19......., convicted by or before the Court of ....
holden at

.... of * .... and that on the

said date

the said Court made a probation order requiring the defendant for the period of ....years then next
ensuing to be

under the supervision of a probation officer appointed for or assigned to the District of.............................
and by the said

information it is further alleged that the defendant was on the.............................. day of ....,
19.......,

convicted by or before the Court of the .... holden at ....of the following
offence,

namely, *...
....

*State offence

committed by him/her during the said period, to wit, on the .... day of ....,
19....., and was

sentenced (or ordered) to *..
....

....
....

*State shortly particulars of offence

You are therefore hereby commanded to bring the said defendant forthwith before the Court of the
................................sitting at .... to answer the said information.

Dated the................................. day of ...., 19.....

....

(Magistrate
*State
judgme

ENDORSEMENT AS TO BAIL

It is directed that the defendant on arrest be released on bail on his/her entering into a recognizance in the
sum of

.... with ....surety .... in the sum of ....
(each) for his/her appearance before the last-mentioned Court at the hour of .... in the
.... noon on

the .... day of ...., 19 ....

....

(Magistrate

(As amended by No. 53 of 1965)

P.O. FORM 10
(Section 8 (3))

ORDER FOR REMAND OF A PROBATIONER CONVICTED OF FRESH OFFENCE DURING PROBATION
PERIOD

IN THE SUBORDINATE COURT (CLASS...........) of the...
....

holden at ....
....

THE PEOPLE.v..

To: Commissioner of Police.

Superintendent of the Government Prison at ....
....

....(hereinafter called the defendant) has this day been brought before the Subordinate Court (Class.........) of the .... holden at ....charged with the

commission of a further offence during the currency of a probation order made in his/her case on the .... day of ...., 19......, by the Court of the .... holden at .... and sentenced (or ordered) to .... and it appears to the Court

that on the date when the said offence was committed, to wit, the .... day of ...., 19.......,

there was in force a probation order made in his/her case on the .... day of ...., 19......, by the

Court of ....holden at ....

And whereas it appears necessary to remand the defendant until he/she can be brought before the Court by which

the probation order is made.

You, the said Commissioner of Police, are hereby commanded to convey the defendant to the said prison, and there

to deliver him/her to the Superintendent thereof, together with this warrant; and you, the Superintendent of the said prison,

to receive him/her into your custody and keep him/her until the next Court of the .... holden at

.... and then convey him/her before the said Court at the hour of ....
. in the

.... noon to be further dealt with according to law.

Dated the .... day of ...., 19 ....

....

(Magistrate

ENDORSEMENT AS TO BAIL

The Court hereby certifies that defendant may be bailed by recognizance himself/herself in .... and .... surety .... in .... (each) to appear before the Court of the .... above mentioned holden at .... at the hour and on the day above mentioned, and that the defendant has

(not) entered into his/her recognizance.

....

(Magistrate

(As amended by No. 53 of 1965)

P.O. FORM 11

(Section 8 (4))

ORDER IN RESPECT OF ORIGINAL OFFENCE ON COMMISSION OF FURTHER OFFENCE DURING PROBATION PERIOD

IN THE SUBORDINATE COURT (CLASS............) of the ....
....

holden at ....
....

THE PEOPLE v ....

.... (hereinafter called the defendant) was on the .... day of ....
19 ......, convicted by or before the Court of the .... holden at ....

of *................................... and on the said date the said Court made a probation order requiring him/her for the period of

.... years then next ensuing to be under the supervision of a probation officer appointed for or assigned to the

District of ....

And the said defendant has this day appeared (or been brought) before the (said) Court of the

.................................sitting at .... and it has been proved to the satisfaction of the Court that the

defendant had on the .... day of ...., 19 ......, been convicted by or before the Court of the .... holden at .... of the following offence,
*State
offence
namely, *...................................committed by him/her during the said period, to wit, on the .... day of ...., 19......, and that he/she had been dealt with in respect of that offence.
It is adjudged that the defendant for the offence in respect of which such order was made *...........................
....
*State fresh offence

....
(Magistrate
(As amended by No. 53 of 1965)
*State judgment

P.O. FORM 12
(Section 8 (4))
ORDER IN RESPECT OF ORIGINAL OFFENCE ON COMMISSION OF FURTHER OFFENCE DURING PERIOD OF PROBATION ORDER
IN THE SUBORDINATE COURT (CLASS ....) of the ....
.... holden
at ....
THE PEOPLE v...................................
To: Commissioner of Police.
Superintendent of the Government Prison at ....
.... (hereinafter called the defendant) was on the ....
....
day of..........................., 19......., convicted by or before the Court of the ....
....
holden at................................of *.................................. and on the said date the said Court made a probation
order
requiring him/her for the period of .... years then next ensuing to be under the supervision of a probation officer
appointed for or assigned to the District of ....
And the defendant has this day appeared (or been brought) before the (said) Court of the ....
sitting
at ....and it was proved to the satisfaction of the Court that the defendant had on the ....
day
of....................., 19......., been convicted by or before the Court of the ....holden at........................
of the
following offence, namely, *...
....
*State offence committed by him/her during the said period, to wit, on the ....day of......................
....,
19......, and that he/she had been dealt with in respect of that offence; and it was adjudged that the defendant for the
offence in respect of which the said order was made*..
....
*State further offence
You are hereby required to lodge the defendant in the prison of .... together with this warrant, in
which prison the aforesaid sentence shall be carried into execution according to law and for this the present warrant shall
be a sufficient authority to all whom it may concern.
Dated the ....day of................................, 19.......
....
(Magistrate
(As amended by No. 53 of 1965)
*State judgment

P.O. FORM 13
(Section 11)
ORDER DISCHARGING OR AMENDING A PROBATION ORDER
IN THE SUBORDINATE COURT (CLASS) of the............... holden at
(District)...
THE PEOPLE v...................................
A probation order having on the ....day of...................., 19......., been made in the case of
....by the Subordinate Court (Class.......) of the .... holden at
.... requiring him/her to be under the supervision of a probation officer appointed for or assigned to the
District of............................ (and further requiring him/her to * ....
....
....).
Upon the application of the principal probation officer/probationer the Court hereby discharges (or amends) the said
probation order (as follows: *...
............).
*State
require
amend
Dated the...............................day of................................, 19.......
....
(Magistrate
NOTE.-If the amendment requires the probationer to reside in an institution, the name of the institution and the period for
which he/she is so required to reside must be stated, and a copy of the order must be sent to the Minister of Labour and
Social Services. See section 11 (5) of the Act.
(As amended by No. 53 of 1965)
*State details amend

P.O. FORM 14
(Section 11 (3))
ORDER AMENDING A PROBATION ORDER DUE TO CHANGE OF ADDRESS
IN THE SUBORDINATE COURT (CLASS.........) of the..
. holden at
(District) ....
A probation order having on the .... day of......................... 19....., been made in the case
of.................................... by the Subordinate Court (Class ....) of the............................. holden
at.................................requiring him/her to be under the supervision of a probation officer appointed for or assigned to the
District of .... and further requiring him/her to notify the probation officer of any change of residence.
Upon the application of the principal probation officer the Court hereby amends the said probation order by
substituting the District of............................... for the District of....................................
Dated the......................day of........................, 19........
....
(Magistrate

P.O. FORM 15
(Section 11 (4))
SUMMONS TO PROBATIONER AS REQUIRED UNDER THE ACT
IN THE SUBORDINATE COURT (CLASS........) of the..
. holden at
(District).......................................
THE PEOPLE v ....
To .... of ....
YOU are hereby summoned to appear before the Court of the .... sitting at ....
.........on

the........................day of.........................., 19......, at the hour of..........................in the..............noon on the hearing of an

application by the principal probation officer to amend in the following manner the probation order made in your case on

the......................day of.........................., 19......, by the Subordinate Court (Class.......)

of the.. for the District of ....

. holden

at...*..

....

Dated the..........................day of.............................., 19........

....

(Magistrate

(As amended by No. 53 of 1965)

*State proposed amendment of probation order

SECTION 18-THE PROBATION COMMITTEE REGULATIONS
Regulations by the Minister

Government Notices
271 of 1961
497 of 1964
Statutory Instrument
52 of 1964
1 of 1976
37 of 1985

Title

1.   These Regulations may be cited as the Probation Committee Regulations.

Interpretation

2.   In these Regulations, unless the context otherwise requires- "Committee" means the Probation Committee.

Duties of Committee

3.   It shall be the duty of the Committee to advise the Minister on all matters of policy affecting the probation of offenders and the development of the probation system in Zambia.

Chairman and Deputy Chairman

4.   The chairman of the Committee shall be the Commissioner for Social Development in his capacity as the Principal Probation Officer and the deputy chairman shall be the Deputy Commissioner for Social Development. (No. 52 of 1964 . As amended by S.I. No. 52 of 1964, No. 1 of 1976 and No. 37 of 1985)

Appointment of Secretary

5.   The Minister shall appoint a person to be secretary of the Committee.

Meetings of Committee

6.   (1)   The Committee shall hold a meeting within three months of the 30th June of each year, and may meet more frequently at the discretion of the chairman:
Provided the chairman may, at any time, and shall at the request in writing of not less than half the number of members, within twenty-eight days then next ensuing, call a meeting of the Committee.
     (2)   The Committee shall cause minutes of every Committee meeting to be kept.
     (3)   The Committee shall submit to the Minister a report of the activities of the Committee at the end of each calendar year.

Quorum and proceedings of Committee

7. (1) At all meetings of the Committee the chairman or in his absence the deputy chairman, or, in the absence of both, such member as the members present shall select, shall preside as chairman of the meeting.

    (2) At any meeting of the Committee one-third of the members of the Committee shall constitute a quorum for the transaction of business.

    (3) At a meeting of the Committee every question shall be determined by a majority of the members voting on that question and, if the votes are equally divided, the chairman of the meeting shall have a second or casting vote, in addition to a deliberative vote.

    (4) The proceedings of the Committee shall not be invalidated by any defect in the appointment or qualification of any member of the Committee so long as there is a quorum at any meeting.

    (5) The Committee may appoint any sub-committee for any purpose that it may deem expedient, and may co-opt any person willing to be a member of any sub-committee so appointed.

Allowances payable to members

8. Members of the Committee and persons co-opted to any sub-committee under the provisions of regulation 7 (5), other than public officers, shall be paid such subsistence and travelling allowances as the Minister may from time to time determine.

THE ZAMBIA POLICE ACT CHAPTER 107 OF THE LAWS OF ZAMBIA

[...]

PART IV
POWERS, DUTIES AND PRIVILEGES OF POLICE OFFICERSPART

Section
13. Police officers not to engage in other employment
14. General powers and duties of police officers
15. Search by police officers
16. Right of entry in case of fire
17. Power to take photographs, measurements, fingerprints, etc.
18. Power to lay information
19. No fee to be chargeable on bail bonds
20. Power to inspect licenses
21. Duty of the Force to keep order on public roads
22. Traffic barriers and cordons
23. Non-liability for act done under authority of a warrant
24. Power to use firearms
25. Power to seize weapons

PART IV
POWERS, DUTIES AND PRIVILEGES OF POLICE OFFICERS

13. No police officer shall, without the consent of the Minister, engage in any employment or office whatsoever, other than in accordance with his duties under this Act. Police officers not to engage in other
Employment

General powers and duties of police officers

14. (1) Every police officer shall exercise such powers and perform such duties as are by law conferred or imposed upon a police officer, and shall obey all lawful directions in respect of the execution of his office, which he may from time to time receive from police officers superior in rank to him.

(2) Every police officer shall be deemed to be on duty at all times and may at any time be detailed for duty in any part of Zambia.

(3) It shall be the duty of every police officer promptly to obey and execute all orders and warrants lawfully issued to him by any competent authority, to collect and communicate intelligence affecting the public peace, to prevent the commission of offences and public nuisances, to detect and bring offenders to justice, and to apprehend all persons whom he is legally authorised to apprehend and for whose apprehension sufficient grounds exist.

(4) It shall be lawful for any police officer, in the interests of public order or public morality, without a warrant to enter at any hour of the day or night any place in which he has reasonable grounds to suspect that illegal drinking or gambling is taking place or dissolute or disorderly characters are resorting.

(5) The provisions of this Act shall be in addition to and not in substitution for or in derogation of any of the powers, authorities, privileges and advantages nor in substitution for or in derogation of the duties and responsibilities of a constable at common law.

Search by police officers

15. (1) Whenever a police officer, of or above the rank of Sub-Inspector, has reasonable grounds for believing that anything necessary for the purpose of an investigation into any offence which he is authorised to investigate may be found in any place within the limits of the police station of which he is in charge, or to which he is attached, and that such thing cannot in his opinion be otherwise obtained without undue delay, that police officer may, after recording in writing the grounds of his belief and specifying therein so far as possible, the thing for which search is to be made, search or cause search to be made for such thing in any place within the limits of such station.

(2) A police officer proceeding under subsection (1) shall, if practicable, conduct the search in person.

(3) If a police officer proceeding under subsection (1) is unable to conduct the search in person and there is no other person competent to make the search present at that time, he may, after recording in writing his reasons for so doing, require any police officer subordinate to him to make the search, and he shall deliver to that police officer an order in writing specifying the place to be searched and so far as possible the thing for which search is to be made, and that police officer may thereupon search for the thing in the place so specified in the order.

(4) The provisions of the Criminal Procedure Code relating to search warrants shall, so far as may be, apply to a search made under this section.

(5) Copies of any record made under subsection (1) or (3) shall forthwith be sent to the nearest magistrate empowered to take cognizance of the offence and the owner or occupier of the place searched shall on application be furnished with a copy of the same by the magistrate.

(6) The occupant of the place searched, or some other person on his behalf, shall in every instance be permitted to attend during the search.

(7) Any police officer conducting a search of any private premises under the provisions of this section shall produce his police identity card to any person in or about the premises who may wish to confirm the authority of the police officer, and any officer required to make a search of private premises under the provisions of subsection (3) shall in addition carry with him upon such search the order in writing mentioned in the said subsection.

(8) A police officer who finds the thing for which search is made shall seize it and take it before the nearest magistrate empowered to take cognizance of the offence.

Right of entry in case of fire

16. Any police officer may break into and enter upon any premises being or appearing to be on fire, or any premises or land adjoining or adjacent thereto, without the consent of any person, and may do all acts or things as may be deemed necessary for extinguishing the fire on any premises or land, or for protecting the same or other property, or rescuing any person or property thereon from fire.

Power to take photographs, measurements, fingerprints, etc.

17. (1) Any police officer of or above the rank of Sergeant may on the prescribed form take or cause to be taken in his presence, for the purpose of record and identification, the measurements, photographs, fingerprints, handprints and footprints of any person in lawful custody.

(2) A police officer acting in accordance with subsection (1) shall certify on the form prescribed that

the fingerprints have been taken by him, or that he has caused them to be taken in his presence, in accordance with the directions contained on the form, and that the particulars entered on the form are, to the best of his knowledge and belief, accurate and true.

(3) All records of the measurements, photographs, fingerprints, handprints, and footprints and any negatives and copies of such photographs, or of photographs of such fingerprints, handprints and footprints, taken of a person under this section shall be forthwith destroyed or handed over to that person, if he is not charged with an offence or is discharged or acquitted by a court, and has not previously been convicted by a court.

(4) For the purposes of this section, "person in lawful custody" means any person in lawful custody otherwise than on account of non-payment of a civil debt or under an order, writ or judgment of a court made or given in civil proceedings or under an order for detention made under any law authorising the detention in custody of witnesses.

Power to lay information

18. It shall be lawful for any police officer to lay any information before a magistrate and to apply for a summons, warrant, search warrant, or such other legal process as may by law issue against any person.

No fee to be chargeable on bail bonds

19. Notwithstanding any other law for the time being in force, no fee or duty shall be chargeable upon bail bonds for criminal cases, recognizances to prosecute or give evidence or recognizances for personal appearance or otherwise issued or taken by a police officer.

Power to inspect licences

20. (1) It shall be lawful for any police officer to stop and question any person whom he sees doing any act for which a license is required under the provisions of any law for the time being in force, and to require that person to produce his license.

(2) Subject to the provisions of any written law, any person who fails to produce a licence when so required under subsection (1) by a police officer may be arrested without a warrant unless he gives his name and address or otherwise satisfies the police officer that he will duly answer any summons or other proceedings which may be taken against him.

(3) Any person who refuses to comply with any lawful requirement of a police officer in the performance of his duty under this section shall be guilty of an offence and shall be liable on conviction to a fine not exceeding four hundred penalty units or to imprisonment for a period not exceeding three months.

Duty of the Force to keep order on public roads

21. (1) It shall be the duty of the Force to regulate and control traffic; to divert all or any particular kind of traffic when, in the opinion of a divisional commander of police or officer in charge of police, it is in the public interest to do so; to close any street in the vicinity of the National Assembly or the High Court for the purposes of preventing the interruption of the proceedings of the National Assembly or High Court by the noise of street traffic; to keep order on public roads, streets, thoroughfares and landing places, and at other places of public resort or places to which the public have access; and to prevent obstructions on the occasions of assemblies and processions on the public roads and streets, or in the neighbourhood of places of public worship during the time of worship and in any case when any road, street, thoroughfare or landing place may be thronged or may be liable to be obstructed.

(2) Any person who opposes or disobeys any lawful order given by any police officer in the performance of his duty under this section shall be guilty of an offence and shall be liable on conviction to a fine not exceeding four hundred penalty units or to imprisonment for three months.

(3) Any person who opposes or disobeys any lawful order given by a police officer in the performance of his duty under this section may be arrested without a warrant unless he gives his name and address or otherwise satisfies the police officer that he will duly answer any summons or other proceedings which may be taken against him. (*As amended by Act No. 13 of 1994*)

Traffic barriers and cordons

22. (1) Notwithstanding the provisions of any other law, if any police officer of or above the rank of Sub-Inspector considers it necessary so to do for the maintenance and preservation of law and order or for the prevention and detection of crime, he may-
    (a) erect or place or cause to be erected or placed barriers or cause a cordon to be formed, in or across any road or street or any other public place in such manner as he may think fit;
    (b) cause a cordon to be placed in or across any public place or private property in such manner as he may think fit, and for that purpose it shall be lawful for the police officers forming the cordon, without the consent of any person, to enter any property and do any act or thing necessary for the effective formation of the cordon.
    (2) Where a barrier has been erected or placed or a cordon formed under the provisions of subsection (1), any police officer may take all reasonable steps to prevent any person passing or any vehicle being driven past the barrier or cordon.
    (3) The driver of any vehicle who fails to comply with any reasonable signal of a police officer requiring such driver to stop his vehicle before reaching any barrier erected or placed or cordon formed under the provisions of subsection (1), shall be guilty of an offence and shall be liable on conviction to a fine not exceeding one thousand penalty units or to imprisonment for a period not exceeding twelve months, or to both.
    (4) Any person who breaks through or attempts to break through any barrier erected or placed or cordon formed, under the provisions of subsection (1), shall be guilty of an offence and shall be liable on conviction to a fine not exceeding one thousand penalty units or to imprisonment for a period not exceeding twelve months, or to both.

(*As amended by Act No. 13 of 1994*)

Non-liability for act done under authority of a warrant

23. (1) When the defence to any suit instituted against a police officer is that the act complained of was done in obedience to a warrant purporting to be issued by a Judge, magistrate, or other competent authority, the court shall, upon production of the warrant containing the signature of the Judge or magistrate and upon proof that the act complained of was done in obedience to such warrant, enter judgment in favour of the police officer.
    (2) No proof of the signature of such Judge or magistrate as aforesaid shall be required unless the court has reason to doubt the genuineness thereof, and where it is proved that the signature is not genuine, any act done by the police officer under or in pursuance of the warrant shall nevertheless be lawful and judgment shall be given in favour of the police officer if it is proved that, at the time when the act complained of was committed, he believed on reasonable grounds that the signature was genuine.

Power to use firearms

24. (1) Any police officer may, subject to subsections (2) and (3), use any firearms which have been issued to him against-
    (a) any person in lawful custody charged with or convicted of a felony when such person is escaping or attempting to escape;
    (b) any person who by force rescues or attempts to rescue any other person from lawful custody;
    (c) any person who by force prevents or attempts to prevent the lawful arrest of himself or of any other person:
        Provided that a police officer shall not use any firearms-
        (i) as authorised under paragraph (a) unless the police officer has reasonable ground to believe that he cannot otherwise prevent the escape and unless he shall give a warning to such person that he is about to use firearms against him and the warning is unheeded;
        (ii) as authorised under paragraph (b) or (c) unless the police officer has reasonable ground to believe that he or any other person is in danger of grievous bodily harm and that he cannot otherwise effect such arrest or prevent such rescue.
    (2) A police officer shall not, in the presence of his superior officer, use a firearm against any person except under the orders of that superior officer.
    (3) The use of firearms under this section shall as far as possible be to disable and not to kill.

396

(4)   The authority vested in a police officer by subsection (1) shall be in addition to and not in substitution for any authority to use firearms vested in a police officer by any nother law.

Power to seize weapons

25.   (1)   Whenever any person goes armed with any weapon in public, without lawful excuse, in such manner as to cause or be likely to cause terror to any other person, any police officer may seize that weapon.

(2)   For the purposes of this section, "weapon" means any weapon which is calculated to or likely to cause harm to any person.

THE STATE SECURITY ACT CHAPTER 111 OF THE LAWS OF ZAMBIA

ARRANGEMENT OF SECTIONS

CHAPTER 111

STATE SECURITY

An Act to make better provision relating to State security; to deal with espionage, sabotage and other activities prejudicial to the interests of the State; and to provide for purposes incidental to or connected therewith.
[23rd October, 1969]
        36 of 1969
17 of 1973
27 of 1985

Short title

1.   This Act may be cited as the State Security Act.

Interpretation

2.   (1)   In this Act, unless the context otherwise requires-
        "authorised officer", in relation to any provision of this Act, means a person authorised

by the person responsible for the administration of this Act to exercise the powers or perform the duties conferred or imposed by such provision;

"classified matter" means any information or thing declared to be classified by an authorised officer;

"Defence Force" has the meaning assigned to it in section two of the Defence Act;

"Director" means the Director of Public Prosecutions;

"disaffected person" includes any person carrying on a seditious activity, that is to say, an activity constituting an offence under section fifty-seven of the Penal Code;

"foreign agent" includes any person who is or has been reasonably suspected of being or having been directly or indirectly employed by a state other than the Republic for the purpose of doing in the Republic or elsewhere any act prejudicial to the safety or interests of the Republic, or who has or is reasonably suspected of having done or attempted to do such an act in the Republic or elsewhere in the interests of a state other than the Republic;

"model" includes a design, pattern or specimen;

"munitions of war" means any article, material, or device, including military stores, or any part thereof, whether actual or proposed, intended or adapted for use in war or the defence of the Republic or capable of being adapted for such use, or any article used, or capable of being used or converted or adapted for use, in the production thereof;

"necessary service" includes-

   (a) any service relating to the generation, supply or distribution of electricity;
   (b) any fire brigade or fire service;
   (c) any sewerage, rubbish disposal or other sanitation service;
   (d) any health, hospital or ambulance service;
   (e) any service relating to the supply or distribution of water;
   (f) any service relating to the production, supply, delivery or distribution of food or fuel;
   (g) mining;
   (h) any communications service;
   (i) any transport service;
   (j) any road, railway, bridge, ferry, pontoon, airfield, harbour or dock; or
   (k) any other service or facility, whether or not of a kind similar to the foregoing, declared by the President to be a necessary service for the purposes of this Act;

"officer in charge of police" means the officer, not below the rank of Sub-Inspector, appointed by the Inspector-General of Police to be in charge of any police station, and includes, when the officer in charge of the police station is absent therefrom or unable, from illness or other cause, to perform his duties, the police officer present at the police station who is next in rank to such officer;

"official document" includes a passport, any pass of the Defence Force, any police or other official pass, permit, certificate, licence or other similar document;

"protected place" means-

   (a) any place or area declared by the President, by statutory instrument, to be a protected place for the purposes of this Act;
   (b) any premises declared to be a protected place under the provisions of section five of the Protected Places and Areas Act; or
   (c) any area declared to be a protected area under the provisions of section six of the Protected Places and Areas Act;

"sketch" includes any photographic or other copy or representation of any place or thing;

"telegram" means any communication transmitted or intended to be transmitted by telegraph or delivered or intended to be delivered from any post office or telegraph office as a communication transmitted either wholly or partially by telegraph, and includes a communication transmitted or intended to be transmitted by means of a radiocommunication service which is reduced to writing.

(2) For the purposes of this Act-

   (a) expressions referring to communicating or receiving include the communicating or receiving of part of the sketch, plan, model, note or other document, article or information, or of the substance, effect or description thereof;
   (b) expressions referring to obtaining or retaining any sketch, plan, model, note or other document or article include the copying or causing to be copied the whole or any part thereof; and

(c)   expressions referring to the communication of any sketch, plan, model, note or other document or article include the transfer or transmission thereof.

(As amended by Act No. 27 of 1985)

Espionage

3.   Any person who, for any purpose prejudicial to the safety or interests of the Republic-

(a)   approaches, inspects, passes over, is in the vicinity of or enters any protected place;

(b)   makes any sketch, plan, model or note or in any manner whatsoever makes a record of or relating to anything which might be or is intended to be directly or indirectly useful to a foreign power or disaffected person;

(c)   obtains, collects, records, publishes or communicates to any person any code, password, sketch, plan, model, note or other document, article or information which might be or is intended to be directly or indirectly useful to a foreign power or disaffected person; or

(d)   without lawful excuse damages, hinders or interferes with, or does any act which is likely to damage, hinder or interfere with, any necessary service or the carrying on thereof;
shall be guilty of an offence and liable on conviction to imprisonment for a period of not less than twenty years but not exceeding thirty years.

(As amended by Act No. 17 of 1973)

Communication of certain information

4.   (1)   Any person who has in his possession or under his control any code, password, sketch, plan, model, note or other document, article or information, which relates to or is used in a protected place or anything in such a place, or which has been made or obtained in contravention of this Act, or which has been entrusted in confidence to him by any person holding office under the Government, or which he has obtained or to which he has had access owing to his position as a person who holds or has held such office or as a person who is or was a party to a contract with the Government or a contract the performance of which in whole or in part is carried out in a protected place, or as a person who is or has been employed by or under a person who holds or has held such an office or is or was a party to such a contract, and who-

(a)   uses the same in any manner or for any purpose prejudicial to the safety or interests of the Republic;

(b)   communicates the same to any person other than a person to whom he is authorised to communicate it or to whom it is in the interests of the Republic his duty to communicate it;

(c)   fails to take proper care of, or so conducts himself as to endanger the safety of, the same; or

(d)   retains the sketch, plan, model, note, document or article in his possession or under his control when he has no right or when it is contrary to his duty so to do, or fails to comply with any lawful directions with regard to the return or disposal thereof;
shall be guilty of an offence and liable on conviction to imprisonment for a term of not less than fifteen years but not exceeding twenty-five years.

(2)   Any person who has in his possession or under his control any sketch, plan, model, note or other document, article or information, relating to munitions of war and who communicates it directly or indirectly to any person in any manner for any purpose prejudicial to the safety or interests of the Republic shall be guilty of an offence and liable on conviction to imprisonment for a term of not less than fifteen years but not exceeding twenty-five years.

(3)   Any person who receives any code, password, sketch, plan, model, note or other document, article or information, knowing or having reasonable grounds to believe at the time when he receives it that the same is communicated to him in contravention of the provisions of this Act, shall, unless he proves that the communication thereof to him was against his wish, be guilty of an offence and liable on conviction to the penalty prescribed in subsection (1).

(4)   Any person who communicates to any person, other than a person to whom he is authorised by an authorised officer to communicate it or to whom it is in the interests of the Republic his duty to communicate it, any information relating to the defence or security of the Republic shall be guilty of an offence and liable on conviction to imprisonment for a term of not less than fifteen years but not exceeding twenty-five years.

(5)   For the purposes of subsection (4), "information relating to the defence or security of the Republic" includes (but without derogating from the generality or the ordinary meaning of that

expression) information relating to the movements or locations of the Defence Force or the Police Force, the steps taken to protect any vital installations or protected places, and the acquisition or disposal of munitions of war.

(As amended by Act No. 17 of 1973)

Protection of classified information

5. (1) Any person who communicates any classified matter to any person other than a person to whom he is authorised to communicate it or to whom it is in the interests of the Republic his duty to communicate it shall be guilty of an offence and liable on conviction to imprisonment for a term of not less than fifteen years but not exceeding twenty-five years.

    (2) In a prosecution for a contravention of subsection (1) it shall be no defence for the accused person to prove that when he communicated the matter he did not know and could not reasonably have known that it was classified matter.

(As amended by Act No. 17 of 1973)

Unauthorised use of uniforms, passes, etc.

6. (1) Any person who, for the purpose of gaining or assisting any other person to gain admission to a protected place or for any other purpose prejudicial to the safety or interests of the Republic-

    (a) without lawful authority uses wears, has in his possession, imports or manufactures any uniform of the Defence Force or of the Police Force or any other official uniform of the Republic, or any uniform or dress so closely resembling the same as to be likely to deceive, or falsely represents himself to be a person who is or has been entitled to wear or use any such uniform;

    (b) without lawful authority uses any vehicle belonging to the Government or any branch thereof, or any vehicle which because of false number-plates or other reason so closely resembles such a vehicle as to be likely to deceive, or falsely represents himself to be a person who is entitled to use such a vehicle;

    (c) orally or in writing in any declaration or application or in any document signed by him or on his behalf, omits any material fact or makes any statement which in any particular he knows to be false or does not believe to be true;

    (d) forges, alters or tampers with any official document or uses or has in his possession any forged, altered or irregular official document;

    (e) personates or falsely represents himself to be a person holding, or in the employ of a person holding, office under the Government, or to be or not to be a person to whom an official document or a secret official code or password has been duly issued or communicated, or, with intent to obtain, whether for himself or for any other person, an official document or any secret official code or password, makes any statement which in any particular he knows to be false or does not believe to be true; or

    (f) without lawful authority uses or has in his possession or under his control any die, seal or stamp of or belonging to or used, made or provided by any Government department or by any diplomatic, naval, army or air force authority appointed by or acting under the authority of the Government, or any die, seal or stamp so closely resembling any such die, seal or stamp as aforesaid as to be likely to deceive, or counterfeits any such die, seal or stamp or uses or has in his possession or under his control any such counterfeit die, seal or stamp;

    shall be guilty of an offence and liable on conviction to imprisonment for a term of not less than fifteen years but not exceeding twenty-five years.

    (2) Any person who-

    (a) retains any official document, whether or not completed or issued for use, when he has no right or when it is contrary to his duty so to do, or fails to comply with any lawful directions with regard to the return or disposal thereof;

    (b) allows any other person to have possession of any official document issued for his use alone, or communicates to any person any secret official code or password so issued, or without lawful authority or excuse has in his possession any official document or secret official code or password issued for the use of some person other than himself, or, on obtaining possession of any official document, whether by finding or otherwise, neglects or fails to hand it over to the person or authority by whom or for whose use it was issued or to a police officer; or

(c) without lawful authority or excuse manufactures or sells, or has in his possession for sale, any such die, seal or stamp as aforesaid;

shall be guilty of an offence and liable on conviction to the penalties prescribed in subsection (1).

(As amended by No. 54 of 1970 and Act 17 of 1973)

Interfering with persons on guard at protected places

7.   Any person who, in the vicinity of any protected place, knowingly obstructs, misleads or otherwise interferes with any person engaged on guard, sentry, patrol or other similar duty in relation to the protected place shall be guilty of an offence and liable on conviction to imprisonment for a term of not less than fifteen years but not exceeding twenty five years.

(As amended by Act No. 17 of 1973)

Harbouring

8.   Any person who-
   (a) knowingly harbours or conceals any person whom he knows or has reasonable grounds for supposing to be a person who is about to commit or has committed an offence under this Act, or knowingly permits any such persons to meet or assemble in any premises in his occupation or under his control; or
   (b) having harboured or concealed any such person or permitted any such persons to meet or assemble in any premises in his occupation or under his control, wilfully omits or refuses to disclose to a police officer of or above the rank of Inspector any information that it is in his power to give in relation to any such person;

   shall be guilty of an offence and liable on conviction to imprisonment for a term of not less than fifteen years but not exceeding twenty-five years.

(As amended by Act No. 17 of 1973)

Attempts, etc

9.   Any person who attempts to commit any offence under this Act, or solicits or incites or endeavours to persuade another person to commit any such offence, or aids or abets or does any act preparatory to the commission of such an offence, shall be guilty of an offence and liable on conviction to the same penalties as if he had been convicted of that offence.

Presumptions

10. (1) If in any prosecution against any person for an offence under section three it is proved that he has been in communication with, or attempted to communicate with, a foreign agent in the Republic or elsewhere it shall, unless the contrary is proved, be presumed that he has, for a purpose prejudicial to the safety or interests of the Republic, obtained or attempted to obtain information which might be or is intended to be directly or indirectly useful to a foreign power.

   (2) For the purposes of subsection (1), but without derogating from the generality of that subsection, a person shall, unless he proves the contrary, be deemed to have been in communication with a foreign agent if-
      (a) he has, whether within or outside the Republic, visited or addressed any communication to the address of, or associated with, a foreign agent; or
      (b) whether within or outside the Republic, the name or address of, or any other information regarding, a foreign agent has been found in his possession or under his control, or has been supplied by him to any other person or has been obtained by him from any other person.

   (3) Any address, whether within or outside the Republic, reasonably suspected of being an address used for the receipt of communications intended for a foreign agent, or at which a foreign agent resides or to which he resorts or at which he carries on business, shall be deemed to be the address of a foreign agent.

   (4) If in a prosecution under this Act it is alleged that the accused acted for a purpose prejudicial to the safety or interests of the Republic he shall, unless the contrary is proved, be deemed so to have acted if, from the circumstances of the case or his character or general conduct as proved, it appears that he acted for such a purpose.

(5)   If in a prosecution under this Act it is alleged that the accused made, obtained, collected, recorded, published or communicated anything for a purpose prejudicial to the safety or interests of the Republic and it is proved that the making, obtaining, collecting, recording, publishing or communicating was by any person other than a person acting under lawful authority it shall, unless the contrary is proved, be presumed that the purpose of the act or conduct in question was a purpose prejudicial to the safety or interests of the Republic.

(6)   Where the lack of lawful authority or excuse is an ingredient of an offence under this Act, the burden of proving such authority or excuse shall lie on the accused and the burden shall not be on the prosecution to prove such lack.

Search warrants

11. (1)   If a magistrate is satisfied by information on oath that there is reasonable ground for suspecting that an offence under this Act has been or is about to be committed he may grant a search warrant in the form set out in the Schedule authorising any police officer named therein of or above the rank of Sub Inspector, together with such other police officers and other persons who may be authorised by such named police officer, at any time to enter any premises, place, aircraft, ship, boat, train or other vehicle, or receptacle, as the case may be, named or described in the warrant, if necessary by force, and to search the same and every person or vehicle found thereon or therein or in the vicinity thereof, and to seize anything which he may find in the course of such search which is or may be evidence of an offence under this Act having been or being about to be committed or with regard to or in connection with which he has reasonable grounds for suspecting that an offence has been or is about to be committed.

(2)   Where it appears to a police officer of or above the rank of Chief Inspector or to an officer in charge of police that the matter is one of such urgency that in the interests of the Republic immediate action is necessary, he may by written order under his hand give to any police officer of or above the rank of Sub Inspector the like authority as may be given by the warrant of a magistrate under this section.

(3)   Notwithstanding anything contained in any other law, it shall not be necessary for anything found in the course of any search conducted in terms of a warrant or authority issued or given under this section to be brought before any court.

(4)   If at the conclusion of any proceedings, including proceedings on appeal, before any court against any person for an offence under this Act application is made by the prosecution, on the ground that the return of such article would be prejudicial to the safety or interests of the Republic, that any article seized in the course of a search conducted in terms of a warrant or authority issued or given under this section shall become the property of the Republic, the court shall make an order to that effect.

Arrest without warrant

12. (1)   Any person who is found committing an offence under this Act or who is reasonably suspected of having committed or having attempted to commit or being about to commit such an offence may be arrested by any police officer and detained.

(2)   Any person arrested under the provisions of this section shall, whether or not the police inquiries are completed, be brought before a magistrate as soon as practicable.

Duty to give information as to commission of offences

13. (1)   Where the Attorney-General is satisfied that there is reasonable ground for suspecting that an offence under this Act has been or is about to be committed and for believing that some person is able to furnish information with regard thereto, he may by writing under his hand authorise a named police officer to require that person to give any information in his power relating to such suspected offence or anticipated offence and, if so required and on tender of his reasonable expenses, to attend at such reasonable time and place as may be specified by such police officer.

(2)   Any person who, having been required in terms of subsection (1) to give information or to attend at a specified time and place, wilfully fails to comply with such requirement or knowingly gives false information shall be guilty of an offence.

Authority of Director of Public Prosecutions required for prosecution

14. Where any person is brought before a court on a charge under this Act no further proceedings in respect thereof shall be taken against him without the authority in writing of the Director, save such as may be necessary by remand to secure the due appearance of the person charged.

Power to exclude public from court proceedings

15. (1) If in the course of any proceedings, including proceedings on appeal, before any court against any person for an offence under this Act application is made by the prosecution, on the ground that the publication of any evidence to be given or of any statement to be made in the course of such proceedings would be prejudicial to the interests of the Republic, that all or any portion of the public be excluded during the whole or any part of the hearing, the court shall make an order to that effect:

    Provided that the passing of sentence shall take place in public.

    (2) The powers of the court under this section shall be in addition to any other powers such court may have to exclude the public from any proceedings.

General penalty

16. Any person convicted of an offence under this Act for which no penalty is provided shall be liable on conviction to imprisonment for a term of not less than five years but not exceeding ten years.
(As amended by Act No. 17 of 1973)

Production of telegrams

17. (1) Where it appears to the President that it is expedient in the public interest so to do he may by warrant under his hand require any person who owns or controls any apparatus within the Republic used for the sending or receipt of telegrams to produce to the person named in the warrant the originals and transcripts of all telegrams or of telegrams of any specified class or description, or of telegrams sent from or addressed to any specified person or place, and all other papers relating to any such telegram.

    (2) Any person who, on being required to produce any such original or transcript or paper as aforesaid, refuses or neglects to do so shall be guilty of an offence.

Extra-territorial application of Act, and place of trial

18. (1) Any act, omission or other conduct constituting an offence under this Act shall constitute such offence wherever such conduct took place, whether within or outside the Republic.

    (2) An offence under this Act, for the purpose of determining the jurisdiction of a court to try the offence, shall be deemed to have been committed either at the place in which it was actually committed or at any place in the Republic in which the accused may be found.

Repeal and saving of Act No. 12 of 1967

19. The Official Secrets Act, 1967, is repealed:

    Provided that any person may after the commencement of this Act be prosecuted under the said Official Secrets Act in respect of any act, omission or other conduct taking place prior to the commencement of this Act as if this Act had not come into operation.

SCHEDULE

(Section 11)

REPUBLIC OF ZAMBIA

STATE SECURITY ACT

SEARCH WARRANT

IN THE SUBORDINATE COURT of the
class for the   District
holden at
To: Police Officer

WHEREAS

of

has this day made information on oath that there is reasonable ground for suspecting that an offence under the State Security Act has been or is about to be committed;

NOW THEREFORE you are hereby authorised and commanded in the name of the President to enter at any time, with such other police officers and other persons as may be authorised by you, and search the same and any person or vehicle found therein or thereon or in the vicinity thereof and to seize anything which may be found on such search which is or may be evidence of an offence under the said Act having been or being about to be committed or with regard to or in connection with which you have reasonable grounds for suspecting that an offence under the said Act has been or is about to be committed.

ISSUED AT   the

day of   19   .

....
Magistrate

THE PRESERVATION OF PUBLIC SECURITY ACT CHAPTER 112 OF THE LAWS OF ZAMBIA

ARRANGEMENT OF SECTIONS

Section
1.   Short title
2.   Interpretation
3.   Public security regulations
4.   Incidental and supplementary provisions in regulations
5.   Application and effect of regulations
6.   Proof of documents

CHAPTER 112

PRESERVATION OF PUBLIC SECURITY
An Act to make provision for the preservation of public security; and to provide for matters incidental thereto.
[…]

Short title

1.   This Act may be cited as the Preservation of Public Security Act.

Interpretation

2.   In this Act, the expression "public security" includes the securing of the safety of persons and property, the maintenance of supplies and services essential to the life of the community, the prevention and suppression of violence, intimidation, disorder and crime, the prevention and suppression of mutiny, rebellion and concerted defiance of, and disobedience to, the law and lawful authority, and the maintenance of the administration of justice.
(As amended by G.N. No. 229 of 1964 and S.I. No. 85 of 1964)

Public security regulations

3.   (1)   The provisions of this section shall have effect during any period when a declaration made under the Constitution has effect.   Cap. 1.
     (2)   The President may, for the preservation of public security, by regulation-
            (a)   make provision for the prohibition of the publication and dissemination of matter prejudicial to public security, and, to the extent necessary for that purpose, for the regulation and control of the production, publishing, sale, supply, distribution and possession of publications;
            (b)   make provision for the prohibition, restriction and control of assemblies;
            (c)   make provision for the prohibition, restriction and control of residence, movement and

404

transport of persons, the possession, acquisition, use and transport of movable property, and the entry to, egress from, occupation and use of immovable property;

  (d) make provision for the regulation, control and maintenance of supplies and services; or

  (e) make provision for, and authorise the doing of, such other things as appear to him to be strictly required by the exigencies of the situation in Zambia.

  (3) If the President is satisfied that the situation in Zambia is so grave that it is necessary so to do, he may, by statutory instrument, make regulations to provide for-

  (a) the detention of persons;

  (b) requiring persons to do work and render services.

(As amended by S.I. No. 85 of 1964)

Incidental and supplementary provisions in regulations

4. Regulations made under section three may-

  (a) make provision for the payment of compensation and remuneration to persons affected by the regulations;

  (b) make provision for the apprehension and trial of persons offending against the regulations and for such penalties as the President may think fit for offenders thereunder;

  (c) make provision for suspending the operation of any written law other than the Constitution; Cap. 1

  (d) make provision for empowering such authorities and persons as may be specified in the regulations to make orders and rules for any of the purposes for which such regulations may be made;

  (e) make provision for the delegation and transfer of powers and duties conferred and imposed by or under the regulations; and

  (f) contain such other incidental and supplementary provisions as appear to the President to be necessary or desirable for the purposes of such regulations:

  Provided that nothing in the foregoing provisions of this section or in the provisions of section three shall authorise the making of any regulations providing for the trial of persons by military courts.

(As amended by S.I. No. 85 of 1964)

Application and effect of regulations

5. (1) Any regulations made under this Act may be made to apply to Zambia or to any part thereof, and to any person or class of persons or to the public generally.

  (2) Subject to the provisions of section twenty-two of the Interpretation and General Provisions Act, any regulation made under this Act, and any order or rule made under any such regulation, shall have effect notwithstanding anything inconsistent therewith contained in any written law other than the Constitution and to the extent of any such inconsistency any such law as aforesaid shall have no effect so long as such regulation, order or rule shall remain in force. Cap. 2
  Cap. 1

  (3) Where any regulation made under this Act or any order or rule made under any regulation made under paragraph (d) of section four has not been laid before the National Assembly on a sitting day within three months of the date of making thereof, such regulation, order or rule shall, on the expiration of the said period of three months, cease to have effect, but without prejudice to the validity of anything previously done thereunder or to the making of any new regulation, order or rule.

(As amended by G.N. No. 229 of 1964 and S.I. No. 85 of 1964)

Proof of documents

6. Every document purporting to be an order, licence, permit, certificate, direction, authority, or other document made, granted or issued by the Governor of Northern Rhodesia prior to the 24th October, 1964, or thereafter by the President, or any other authority or person in pursuance of this Act or any regulation made under this Act or any order or rule made under any such regulation, and purporting to be signed by or on behalf of the Governor of Northern Rhodesia prior to the 24th October, 1964, or thereafter by the President, or such other authority or person, shall be received in evidence, and shall, until the contrary is proved, be deemed to have been made, granted or issued by the Governor of

Northern Rhodesia prior to the 24th October, 1964, or thereafter by the President, or that authority or person.
(As amended by S.I. No. 85 of 1964)

PROHIBITION AND PREVENTION OF MONEY LAUNDERING ACT NO 14 OF 2001

Assented to on 8 November 2001
Commenced on 9 November 2001
[This is the version of this document from 29 November 2010.]
[Amended by Prohibition and Prevention of Money Laundering (Amendment) Act, 2010 (Act 44 of 2010) on 29 November 2010]

An Act to provide for the prohibition and prevention of money laundering; the constitution of the Anti-money Laundering Authority and the Anti-Money Laundering Investigations Unit; to provide for the forfeiture of property of persons convicted of money laundering; to provide for international cooperation in investigations, prosecution and other legal processes of prohibiting and preventing money laundering; and to provide for matters connected with or incidental to the foregoing.[long title amended by section 2 of Act 44 of 2010]

Enactment

ENACTED by the Parliament of Zambia

Part I – Preliminary

1.   Short title and commencement

This Act may be cited as the Prohibition and Prevention of Money Laundering Act, 2001 and shall come into operation on such date as the minister may, by statutory instrument, appoint.

2.   Interpretation

In this Act, unless the context otherwise requires—

"**authorised officer**" means an officer authorised by the Commissioner to perform functions under this Act;"

Authority" means the Anti-Money Laundering Authority constituted under section three;

"**business transaction**" means any arrangement, including opening of a bank account, between two or more persons where the purpose of the arrangement is to facilitate a transaction between the two or more persons;

"**business transaction record**" in relation to a business transaction, includes—
   (a)   the identification record of all the persons party to that transaction;(b)a description of that transaction sufficient to identify its purpose and method of execution;(c)the details of any bank account used for that transaction, including bank, branch and sort code; and(d)the total value of that transaction;

"**Centre**" means the Financial Intelligence Centre established under the Financial Intelligence Centre Act, 2010; *[Act No. 46 of 2010][definition of "Centre" inserted by section 3(e) of Act 44 of 2010]*

"**Commissioner**" means the person appointed as Commissioner under the Narcotic Drugs and Psychotropic Substances Act; *[Cap. 96]*

"**Court**" means the Subordinate Court and the High Court;

"**crime**" means an act or omission which constitutes an offence under any written law in Zambia or any other country;*[definition of "crime" inserted by section 3(e) of Act 44 of 2010]*

"**financial institution**" shall have the meaning assigned to it under the Banking and Financial Services Act; *[Cap. 387]*

"**identification record**" means—
   (a)   where the person is a corporate body, the details of—(i)the certificate of incorporation;(ii)the

most recent annual return to the Supervisory Authority; or (b) in any other case, sufficient documentary evidence to prove to the satisfaction of a financial institution that the person is who that person claims to be; and for these purposes "person" shall include any person who is a nominee, agent, beneficiary or principal in relation to a business transaction;

"**illegal activity**" means any activity, whenever or wherever carried out which under any written law in the Republic amounts to a crime;

"**money laundering**" means where a reasonable inference may be drawn, having regard to the objective factual circumstances, any activity by a person —

    (a) who knows or has reason to believe that the property is the proceeds of a crime; or

    (b) without reasonable excuse, fails to take reasonable steps to ascertain whether or not the property is proceeds of a crime;where the person—

        (i) engages, directly or indirectly, in a transaction that involves proceeds of a crime; or

        (ii) acquires, receives, possesses, disguises, transfers, converts, exchanges, carries, disposes, uses, removes from or brings into Zambia proceeds of a crime; or(iii)conceals, disguises or impedes the establishment, of the true nature, origin, location, movement, disposition, title of, rights with respect to, or ownership of, proceeds of crime; *[definition of "money laundering" substituted by section 3(b) of Act 44 of 2010]*

"**proceeds of crime**" means property or benefit that is—

    (a) wholly or partly derived or realised directly or indirectly, by any person from the commission of a crime;

    (b) wholly or partly derived or realised from a disposal or other dealing with proceeds of a crime;

    (c) wholly or partly acquired proceeds of a crime;

    and includes, on a proportional basis, property into which any property derived or realised directly from the illegal activity is later converted, transformed or intermingled, and any income, capital or other economic gains derived or realised from the property at any time after the crime; or

    (d) any property that is derived or realised, directly or indirectly, by any person from any act or omission that occurred outside Zambia and would, if the act or omission had occurred in Zambia, have constituted a crime; *[definition of "proceeds of crime" substituted by section 3(c) of Act 44 of 2010]*

"**property**" includes any real or personal property, money, things in action or other intangible or incorporeal property, whether located in Zambia or elsewhere, and includes property of corresponding value in the absence of the original illegally acquired property whose value has been determined; *[definition of "property" substituted by section 3(d) of Act 44 of 2010]*

"**regulated institution**" *[definition of "regulated institution" deleted by section 3(a) of Act 44 of 2010]*

"**reporting entity**" has the meaning assigned to it in the Financial Intelligence Centre Act, 2010; *[Act No. 46 of 2010] [definition of "reporting entity" inserted by section 3(e) of Act 44 of 2010]*

"**Supervisory Authority**" *[definition of "Supervisory Authority" deleted by section 3(a) of Act 44 of 2010]*

"**Unit**" means the Anti-Money Laundering Investigations Unit Constituted under section five.

PART II
ANTI-MONEY LAUNDERING AUTHORITY

3.   Constitution of Anti-Money Laundering Authority

There is hereby constituted the Anti-Money Laundering Authority which Authority shall be composed of the following members appointed by the Minister—

    (a) the Attorney-General, who shall be the chairman;

    (b) the Inspector-General of the Zambia Police Force;

    (c) the Commissioner;

    (d) the Director-General of the Anti-Corruption Commission;

    (e) the Governor, Bank of Zambia;

    (f) the Commissioner-General, Zambia Revenue Authority; and

    (g) two other persons.

4.   Functions of Authority

The functions of the Anti-money Laundering Authority shall be—

    (a) to provide general or specific policy directives to the Commissioner and the Commissioner shall give effect to such directives; and

    (b) to advise the Minister on measures required to prevent and detect money laundering in the Republic.

PART III
ANTI-MONEY LAUNDERING INVESTIGATIONS UNIT

5. Anti-Money Laundering Investigations Unit

There shall be the Anti-Money Laundering Investigations Unit which shall comprise the Commissioner and such other officers as the Commissioner shall appoint.

6. Functions of Unit

(1) The functions of the Anti-Money Laundering Investigations Unit shall be—
   (a) to investigate financial and other business transactions suspected to be part of money laundering offences; *[paragraph (a) substituted by section 4(a) of Act 44 of 2010]*
   (b) to conduct investigations and prosecutions of money laundering offences;
   (c) to liase with other law enforcement agencies in the conduct of investigations and prosecutions of money laundering offences; and *[paragraph (c) amended by section 4(b) of Act 44 of 2010]*
   (d) to cooperate with law enforcement agencies and institutions in other jurisdictions responsible for investigations and prosecution of money laundering offences.*[paragraph (d), previously paragraph (f), renumbered by section 4(d) of Act 44 of 2010]*

(2) The Commissioner shall make periodic reports to the Authority concerning the activities of the Unit as the Authority may determine.

PART IV
MONEY LAUNDERING OFFENCES

7. Prohibition of money laundering

A person who, after the commencement of this Act, engages in money laundering, shall be guilty of an offence and shall be liable, upon conviction to a fine not exceeding one hundred and seventy thousand penalty units or to imprisonment for a term not exceeding ten years or to both.

8. Offences committed by body of persons

Where an offence under the provisions of this Act is committed by a body of person, whether corporate or unincorporated—
   (a) the body of persons shall be guilty of an offence and liable upon conviction to a fine not exceeding four hundred thousand penalty units; and
   (b) every person who, at the time of the offence, acted in an official capacity for or on behalf of such a body of persons, whether as a Director, Manager, Secretary or other similar capacity, or was purporting to act in such capacity and who was invoked in the commission of that offence, shall be guilty of that offence; and shall be liable, upon conviction to a fine not exceeding one hundred and seventy thousand penalty units or to imprisonment for a term not exceeding ten years, or to both.

9. Attempts, aiding and abetting or conspiring to commit offence

(1) Any person who attempts, aids, abets, counsels or procures the commission of the offence of money laundering shall be guilty of an offence and shall be liable, on conviction, to a fine not exceeding one hundred and thirty-nine thousand penalty units or to imprisonment for a term not exceeding five years, or to both.

(2) Any person who conspires with another to commit the offence of money laundering shall be guilty of an offence and shall be liable upon conviction to a fine not exceeding one hundred and thirty-nine thousand penalty units or to imprisonment for a term not exceeding five years or to both.

10. Falsification of documents

Any person who knows or suspects that an investigation into money laundering has been, is being or is about to be conducted, falsifies, conceals, destroys or otherwise disposes of, causes or permits the falsification of material which is or is likely to be relevant to the investigation of the offence, shall be guilty of an offence and shall be liable, upon conviction, to a fine not exceeding one hundred and thirty-nine thousand penalty units or to imprisonment for a term not exceeding five years or to both.

11. Divulging information to unauthorised person

Any person who knows or suspects that an investigation into money laundering has been, is being or is about to be conducted, without lawful authority, divulges that fact or information to another person, shall be guilty of an offence and shall be liable, upon conviction, to a fine not exceeding one hundred and thirty-nine thousand penalty units or to imprisonment for a term not exceeding five years or to both.

PART V
PREVENTION OF MONEY LAUNDERING
[Part V substituted by section 5 of Act 44 of 2010]

12. Prohibition of tipping off

(1) A person who knows or has reason to suspect that—
  (a) an authorised officer has commenced, or is about to commence, an investigation under this Act and unlawfully or recklessly discloses to any other person information or any other matter which is likely to prejudice that investigation or proposed investigation; or
  (b) a disclosure has been made to an authorised officer under this Act, and unlawfully discloses to any other person information or any other matter which is likely to prejudice an investigation or proposed investigation following the disclosure;

commits an offence and is liable, upon conviction, to a fine not exceeding five hundred thousand penalty units or to imprisonment for a period not exceeding five years, or to both.

(2) Notwithstanding subsection (1), a legal practitioner may make a disclosure in the course of the legal practitioner's professional duty—
  (a) to the legal practitioner's client or the client's representative in connection with the giving of advice to the client; or(b)to any person in contemplation of, or connection with and for the purpose of, any legal proceedings.

(3) Subsection (2) does not apply in relation to any information or other matter which is disclosed with a view to furthering any illegal purpose.

[section 12 substituted by section 5 of Act 44 of 2010]

13. Investigation of suspicious transaction reports from Centre

The Unit shall, where it receives a suspicious transaction report from the Centre in accordance with the Financial Intelligence Centre Act, 2010, cause an investigation to be conducted where it has reason to suspect that a person has committed or is about to commit an offence under Part IV.*[Act No. of 2010][section 13 substituted by section 5 of Act 44 of 2010]*

14. Protected disclosures

A disclosure made by a person in compliance with this Act shall be a protected disclosure for the purposes of the Public Interest Disclosure (Protection of Whistleblowers) Act, 2010.*[Act No. 4 of 2010][section 14 substituted by section 5 of Act 44 of 2010]*

PART VI
SEIZURE AND FORFEITURE OF PROPERTY IN RELATION TO MONEY LAUNDERING

15. Seizure of property

An authorised officer shall seize property which that officer has reasonable grounds to believe that the property is derived or acquired from money laundering.

16. Release of seized property

(1) Where property is seized under this Act, the authorised officer who effected the seizure may, at any time before it is forfeited under this Act, order the release of the property to the person from whom the property was seized if the officer is satisfied that the property is not liable to forfeiture under this Act and is not otherwise required for the purpose of any investigations or proceedings under this Act or for the purpose of any prosecution under any other written law.

(2) Where property is released under subsection (1)—
  (a) the officer effecting the seizure, or the State or any person acting on behalf of the State, shall not be liable to any civil proceedings by any person unless it is proved that the seizure and

the release had not been effected in good faith; and(b)a record in writing shall be made by the officer effecting the release, specifying in detail the circumstances of, and the reasons for, the release.

17. Forfeiture of property

(1) Any property—
    (a) Which has been seized under subsection (1) of section fifteen; and
    (b) which is in the possession or under the control of a person convicted of a money laundering offence and which property is derived or acquired from proceeds of the crime shall be liable to forfeiture by the court.

(2) Where the person whose property has been forfeited dies before or after the order under the subsection (1) is made, the order shall have effect against the estate of the deceased.

18. Forfeiture of property where no proceedings or claim

(1) Where any property has beeen seized under this Act and—
    (a) no prosecution for any offence under any written law is instituted with regard to the property;
    (b) no claim in writing is made by any person; and
    (c) no proceedings are commenced within six months from the date of seizure, for the forfeiture of property; the Commissioner shall apply to the Court upon the expiration of the period of six months for an order of forfeiture of that property.

(2) The Court shall not make an order of forfeiture under subsection (1) unless—
    (a) the Commissioner has given notice by publication in the *Gazette* and in one national newspaper to the effect that property which has been seized under this Act shall be liable to vest in the State if it is not claimed within three months; and(b)three months after the giving of the notice under paragraph (a) the property remains unclaimed.

(3) Where a claim in writing is made by any person that is lawfully entitled to the property seized under this Act that the property is not liable to forfeiture under this Act the Commissioner may order release of the property to the claimant if satisfied that there is no dispute as to ownership of the property and that it is not liable for forfeiture.

(4) Where a claim is made against property seized under this Act and the Commissioner finds that—
    (a) there is a dispute as to the ownership of the property;
    (b) there is insufficient evidence to determine the ownership of property;
    (c) the Commissioner is unable to ascertain whether the property is liable to forfeiture or not; the Commissioner shall refer the claim to High Court.

19. Property tracking and monitoring

(1) For the purpose of determining whether any property belongs to, or is in the possession or under the control of any person, the High Court may upon application by the Commissioner—
    (a) order that any document relevant to: (i) identifying, locating or quantifying property of that person; or(ii)identifying or locating any document necessary for the transfer of property of that person; be delivered to the Commissioner; and
    (b) order a regulated institution to produce to the Commissioner all information obtained by that institution about any business transaction conducted by or for that person with the institution before or after the date of the order as the court directs.

(2) Where the Commissioner is satisfied that the person is failing to comply with, is delaying or is otherwise obstructing an order made in accordance with subsection (1), an authorised officer may enter any premises of that person, search the premises and remove any material document or other thing therein for the purposes of executing such order.

20. Property to be forfeited to State

Where any property is forfeited under this Act, the property shall vest in the State.

21. Tampering with forfeited property

Any person who tampers with property seized or forfeited under this Act shall be guilty of an offence and shall be liable, upon conviction, to a fine not exceeding one hundred and forty thousand penalty units or to imprisonment for a term not exceeding five years or to both.

PART VII
INVESTIGATION, ARREST AND SEARCH

22. Power of arrest

(1) Every offence under this Act shall be a cognisable offence for the purposes of the Criminal Procedure Code.(2)Where a person arrested under this Act is serving a sentence of imprisonment, or is in lawful custody, that person shall, upon an order by magistrate, be produced before that magistrate at such place as may be specified in the order for the purpose of investigations into the matter in respect of which the person is liable to be arrested under this Act. *[Cap. 88]*

23. Power of entry, search and seizure

Whenever an authorised officer has reasons to believe that there is reasonable cause to suspect that in or on any premises there is concealed or deposited any property liable to seizure or forfeiture under this Act; or to which an offence under this Act is reasonably suspected to have been committed, or any book or document directly or indirectly relating to, or connected with, any dealing or intended dealing, whether within or outside Zambia, in respect of any property liable to seizure or forfeiture under this Act, or which would, if carried out, be an offence under this Act, the authorised officer may with a warrant issued by a court of competent jurisdiction—

    (a) enter the premises and search for, seize and detain any such property, book or document;

    (b) search any person who is suspected or connected with the offence, in or on the premises, and take that person into custody in order to facilitate the investigations;

    (c) arrest any person who is in or on the premises in whose possession any property liable seizure or forfeiture under this Act is found, or whom the officer reasonably believes to have concealed or deposited the property;

    (d) break, open, examine and search any premises, article, container or receptacle suspected or connected with the offence; or

    (e) stop, search and detain any conveyance.

PART VII
GENERAL

24. Sentence for previous offenders

Any person convicted on a second or subsequent offence under this Act shall be liable to imprisonment for a term of not less than five years or to two times the amount of the fine specified for the first offence or to both.

25. Extradition

An offence under this Act shall be deemed to be an extraditable offence under the provisions of the Extradition Act. *[Cap. 94]*

26. Obstruction of authorised officer

Any person who—

    (a) obstructs, assaults, hinders or delays any authorised officer in the lawful exercise of any powers conferred on the officer by or under this Act;

    (b) refuses to furnish to any authorised officer on request, any particulars or information to which the authorised officer is entitled to by or under this Act;

    (c) fails to comply with any lawful demand of an authorised officer under this Act;

    (d) willfuly or recklessly gives to any authorised officer any false or misleading particulars or information with respect to any fact or particulars to which the authorised officer is entitled to by or under this Act;

    (e) fails to produce, conceals or attempts to conceal any property, document or book in relating to which there is reasonable ground to suspect that an offence has been or is being committed under this Act, or which is liable to seizure under this Act, or

    (f) before or after any seizure, destroys anything to prevent the seizure or securing of that property or article; shall be guilty of an offence and shall be liable, upon conviction, to imprisonment for a term not exceeding five years without the option of a fine.

27. Failure or refusal to disclose information or produce anything

Any person who willfully fails or refuses to disclose any information or produce any accounts, documents or articles to an authorised officer during an investigation into an offence under this Act, shall be guilty of an offence and shall be liable, upon conviction, to a fine not exceeding two hundred penalty units or imprisonment for a term not exceeding five years or to both.

28. Application of Cap. 98

The Mutual Legal Assistance in Criminal Matters Act, applies to offences under this Act except where the provisions of that Act are inconsistent with this Act.

29. Jurisdiction

(1) This Act shall have effect within as well as outside Zambia and notwithstanding where any offence is committed by any person, that person may be dealt with in respect of such offence as if it has been committed within Zambia.

(2) Any proceedings against any person under this section which would be a bar to subsequent proceedings against such person for the same offence, if such offence had been committed in Zambia, shall be a bar to further proceedings against that person under any written law for the time being in force relating to the extradition of persons, in respect of the same offence outside Zambia. *[section 29 substituted by section 6 of Act 44 of 2010]*

30. General penalty

A person who commits an offence under this Act, for which no penalty is provided shall be guilty of an offence and shall be liable upon conviction to a fine not exceeding one hundred and forty thousand penalty units or to imprisonment for a term not exceeding four years or to both.

31. Repeal of section 22 of Cap 96

Section twenty-two of the Narcotic drugs and Psychotropic Substances Act is hereby repealed.

32. Regulations

The Minister may, by statutory instrument, make regulations prescribing matters necessary or convenient for the better carrying out or giving effect to, this Act.

THE PUBLIC INTEREST DISCLOSURE (PROTECTION OF WHISTLEBLOWERS) ACT NO 4 OF 2010

ARRANGEMENT OF SECTIONS

PART I
PRELIMINARY

PART II
PUBLIC INTEREST DISCLOSURES

GOVERNMENT OF ZAMBIA
ACT
No. 4 of 2010

Date of Assent: 12th April, 2010

An Act to provide for the disclosure of conduct adverse to the public interest in the public and private sectors; provide for a framework within which public interest disclosures shall be independently and rigorously dealt with; provide for procedures in terms of which employees in both the private and the public sectors may disclose information regarding unlawful or irregular conduct by their employers or other employees in the employ of their employers; safeguard the rights, including employment rights, of persons who make public interest disclosures; provide a framework within which persons who make a public interest disclosure shall be protected; and for matters connected with, or incidental to, the foregoing.

[16thApril, 2010

Enactment

ENACTED by the Parliament of Zambia. Enactment

PART I
PRELIMINARY

Short title and Commencement

1. This Act may be cited as the Public Interest Disclosure (Protection of Whistleblowers) Act, 2010, and shall come into operation on such date as the Minister may, by statutory instrument, appoint.

Interpretation

2   (1) In this Act, unless the context otherwise requires-
   " act " includes investigate;
   " conduct " includes an act or omission;
   " corrupt " has the meaning assigned to it under the Anti-Corruption Commission Act;
   " detriment " means —
       (a) injury, damage or loss;
       (b) intimidation or harassment; or

(c) discrimination, disadvantage or adverse treatment in relation to career, profession, employment, trade or business;

"disciplinary offence " means conduct that constitutes grounds for disciplinary action, in respect of a public officer, under the General Orders or the officer's contract of employment, or in relation to any other person, under the person's contract of employment or conditions of service;

" disclosable conduct " in relation to any person or a public officer, means—

(a) conduct of the person, whether or not a public officer, that adversely affects, or could adversely affect, either directly or indirectly, the honest or impartial performance of official functions by the person, public officer or agency;

(b) conduct of the public officer which amounts to the performance of any of the public officer's functions dishonestly or with partiality;

(c) conduct of the public officer, a former public officer or a government agency that amounts to a breach of public trust;

(d) conduct of the public officer, a former public officer or a government agency that amounts to the misuse of information or material acquired in the course of the performance of the public officer functions, whether for the benefit of that person or agency or otherwise;

(e) conduct of the public officer that amounts to maladministration which is action or inaction of a serious nature that is

(i) contrary to any law;

(ii) unreasonable, unjust, oppressive or discriminatory; or

(iii) based wholly or partly on improper motives;

(f) conduct of the person or public officer that would, if proven, constitute

(i) criminal offence;

(ii) a disciplinary offence;

(iii) serious and substantial public wastage or abuse of financial or other public resources or assets; or

(iv) reasonable grounds for dismissing or dispensing with, or otherwise terminating, the services of the person or public officer who is engaged in it; or

(g) a conspiracy or attempt to engage in conduct referred to in paragraphs *(a)* to *(e)* inclusive;

" disclosure " means any communication or release of information regarding any disclosable conduct of any person, a public officer or employer made by an employee or any person who has reason to believe that the information shows or tends to show one or more of the following:

(a) that a criminal offence has been committed, is being committed or is likely to be committed;

(b) that a person has failed, is failing or is likely to fail to comply with any obligation to which that person is subject;

(c) that a miscarriage of justice has occurred, is occurring or *is* likely to occur;

(d) that the health or safety of any person has been, is being or is likely to be endangered;

(e) that the environment has been, is being or is likely to be endangered; or

(f) that any matter referred to in paragraphs *(a)* to *(e)* has been, is being or is likely to be deliberately concealed;

" employee " means—

(a) any person, excluding an independent contractor, who works for another person, whether incorporated or not, or for a government agency, and who receives, or is entitled to receive, any remuneration; or

(b) any other person who in any manner assists in carrying on or conducting the business of an
employer;

"employer" means any person—

(a) who employs or provides work for another person and who remunerates or expressly or tacitly undertakes to remunerate that other person; or

(b) who permits any other person in any manner to assist in the carrying on or conducting of the person's business, including any person acting on behalf of or on the authority of such employer;

" exercise " in relation to a function includes, where the function is a duty, the performance of the duty;

" function " includes power, authority or duty;

" government agency " means —

    (a)   a Government department, Ministry or institution;

    (b)   a statutory body, local authority, organisation or agency established under any law;

    (c)   a body, organ or institution incorporated under any law or established by Government for any public purpose;

    (d)   a body, organ or institution owned by Government or in which Government has any interest or is under Government control; or

    (e)   any other functionary or institution:

        (i)   exercising a power or performing a duty in terms of the Constitution or any other law;
            or

        (ii)   exercising a public power or performing a public function in terms of any law;

" impropriety " means any conduct which falls within any of the categories referred to in paragraphs (a) to (g) of the definition of "disclosable conduct", irrespective of whether or not —

    (a)   the impropriety occurs or occurred in the Republic of Zambia or elsewhere; or

    (b)   the law applying to the impropriety is that of the Republic of Zambia or of another country;

" investigate " includes inquire or audit;

" investigation Act " means—

    (a)   in relation to the Auditor -General, the Constitution;

    (b)   in relation to the Investigator-General, the Commission for Investigations Act, Cap. 39;

    (c)   the Public Finance Act, 2004, Act No. 15 of 2004

    (d)   the Zambia Police Act, Cap. 107;

    (e)   the Narcotic Drugs and Psychotropic Substances Act [No. 35 of the Laws of Zambia];

    (f)   the Judicial Code of Conduct Act, 1999;

    (g)   the Anti-Corruption Commission Act; and

    (h)   the Prohibition and Prevention of Money Laundering Act, 2001;

" investigating authority " means—

    (a)   the Auditor-General;

    (b)   the Anti-Corruption Commission;

    (c)   the Drug Enforcement Commission;

    (d)   the Investigator-General;

    (e)   the Police Public Complaints Authority;

    (f)   the Judicial Complaints Authority; or

    (g)   any other person or body prescribed under this Act or any other law;

" legal practitioner " has the meaning assigned to it in the Legal Practitioners Act;

" local authority " means any municipal, district or city council established under the Local Government Act;

" maladministration " means any conduct that involves action or inaction of a serious nature that is —

    (a)   contrary to the law;

    (b)   unreasonable, unjust, oppressive or discriminatory; or

    (c)   based wholly or partly on improper motives;

" occupational detriment " in relation to the working environment of an employee, means the employee–

    (a)   being subjected to any disciplinary action;

    (b)   being dismissed, suspended, demoted, harassed or intimidated;

    (c)   being transferred against the employee's will;

    (d)   being refused transfer or promotion;

    (e)   being subjected to a term or condition of employment or retirement which is altered or kept altered to the employee's disadvantage;

    (f)   being refused a reference or being provided with an adverse reference, from the employer;

    (g)   being denied appointment to *any* employment, profession or office;

    (h)   being threatened with any of the actions referred to in paragraphs (a) to (g); or (*i*)   being otherwise adversely affected in respect of employment, profession or office, including employment opportunities and work security;

Parliament " means the Parliament of Zambia;

" protected disclosure " means a disclosure made to—

    (*a*)   a legal practitioner in accordance with section *thirtyseven;*

    (*b*)   an employer in accordance with section *thirty-eight;*

    (*c*)   a person or body in accordance with section *thirty-nine;*
       or

    (*d*)   any other person or body in accordance with Part III, but does not include a disclosure—

         (i)   in respect of which the employee making the disclosure commits an offence by making that disclosure; or

         (ii)   made by a legal practitioner to whom the information was disclosed in the course of obtaining legal advice in accordance with section *thirty-seven;*

" public interest disclosure " means a disclosure of information made by any person or an employee, regarding any conduct of any person or an employer, or an employee of that employer, that the person making the disclosure believes on reasonable grounds shows or tends to show one or more of the following:

    (*a*)   that a person has engaged, is engaging, or proposes to engage, in disclosable conduct;

    (*b*)   public wastage;

    (*c*)   conduct involving substantial risk or danger to the environment;

    (*d*)   that a person has engaged, is engaging, or proposes to engage, in an unlawful reprisal;

    (*e*)   that a public officer has engaged, is engaging, or proposes to engage, in conduct that amounts to a substantial and specific danger to the health or safety of the public;

    (*f*)   that a criminal offence has been committed, is being committed or is likely to be committed;

    (*g*)   that a person has failed, is failing or is likely to fail to comply with any legal obligation to which that person is subject;

    (*h*)   that a miscarriage of justice has occurred, is occurring or is likely to occur; or

    (*i*)   that any matter referred to in paragraphs (*a*) to (*h*) has been, is being or is likely to be deliberately concealed;

" public officer " means—

    (*a*)   an employee of a government agency, including an agency head;

    (*b*)   a person employed by, or on behalf of, a government agency or in the service of an investigating authority, whether under a contract of service or a contract for services, or a person who has ceased to perform those services; or

    (*c*)   a person otherwise authorised to perform functions on behalf of a government agency or an appropriate authority;

"public wastage" means conduct by a public officer that amounts to negligent, incompetent or inefficient

management within, or of, any government agency resulting, or likely to result, directly or indirectly, in a substantial waste of public funds or resources;

" serious and substantial waste " includes uneconomical, inefficient or ineffective use of public funds or resources, whether authorised or unauthorised, which results in a loss or wastage of public funds or resources, having regard to the nature and materiality of the wastage; and

"unlawful reprisal" means conduct that causes, or threatens to cause, detriment—

    (*a*)   to a person directly because a person has made, or may make, a public interest disclosure; or

    (*b*)   to a public officer directly because the public officer has resisted attempts by another public officer to involve the officer in the commission of an offence.

Application

2   (1)   This Act applies to any disclosure made after the date Application on which it comes into operation, irrespective of whether or not the impropriety occurred before or after that date.

(2)   For the avoidance of doubt, this Act applies to any government agency, any private or public company, institution, organisation, body or organ registered, established or incorporated under any law.

Void Contracts

2.   Any provision in a contract of employment or other agreement between an employer and an employee is void in so far contracts as it —

   (a)   purports to exclude any provision of this Act, including an agreement to refrain from instituting or continuing any proceedings under this Act or any proceedings for breach of contract; or

   (b)   purports to preclude the employee or has the effect of discouraging the employee, from making a protected disclosure.

Disclosures during proceedings

5.   If information that could amount to a public interest disclosure is disclosed in the course of any proceedings of a court or tribunal, the court or tribunal shall refer the information to an investigating authority.

Other protection preserved

6.   (1)   This Act does not limit the protection given by any other law to a person who makes a public interest disclosure or prejudice any other remedy available to the person under that law

   (2)   Nothing in this Act affects the rights and privileges of Parliament in relation to the freedom of speech, and debates and proceedings, in Parliament.

Liability of agent of State

7.   An agent of the State who commits an offence under this Act is liable for the penalty for the offence.

Legal professional privilege

8.   Nothing in this Act shall be taken to entitle a person to disclose information which would otherwise be the subject of legal professional privilege.

Relationship of Act with other Acts

9.   (1)   This Act prevails, to the extent of any inconsistency, over the provisions of any investigationAct.

   (2)   Notwithstanding subsection (1), nothing in this Act otherwise limits or affects the operation of any Act or the exercise of the functions conferred or imposed on an investigating authority or any other person or body under it.

   (3)   Nothing in this Act authorises an investigating authority to investigate any complaint that it is not authorised to investigate under the relevant investigation Act.

   (4)   Nothing in this Act affects the proper administration and management of an investigating authority or public authority, including action that may or is required to be taken in respect of the salary, wages and conditions of employment or discipline of a public officer, subject to the following:

   (a)   detrimental action is not to be taken against a person if to do so would be in contravention of this Act; and

   (b)   beneficial treatment is not to be given in favour of a person if the purpose, or one of the purposes for doing so is to influence the person to make, to refrain from making, or to withdraw a disclosure.

PART II
PUBLIC INTEREST DISCLOSURES

Employee not to be subjected to occupational detriment

10.   An employer shall not subject an employee to any Employee occupational detriment on account, or partly on account, of the not to be subjected to employee having made a protected disclosure or public interest occupational disclosure.

Making public interest disclosure

11. (1) Any person may make a public interest disclosure to Making an investigating authority.

   (2) Without limiting the generality of subsection (I), a person disclosure may make *a* public interest disclosure—

      (*a*) about conduct in which a person is engaged, or about matters arising before the commencement of this Act; and

      (*b*) whether or not the person is able to identify any person that the information disclosed concerns.

Anonymous Disclosures

12. (1) A person may make an anonymous disclosure in accordance with this section and the disclosure is protected by this Act.

   (2) An anonymous disclosure shall be made to any investigating authority where the disclosure does not relate to the investigating authority to whom the disclosure is made.

   (3) A person making an anonymous disclosure shall identify themselves to the head of an investigating authority and request that that person's identity be kept confidential by the investigating authority.

   (4) The head of an investigating authority shall personally consider an anonymous disclosure and make a preliminary assessment of the disclosure against the matters referred to under section *thirteen* before referring the matter without any identification of the person making the disclosure, to any relevant member of staff of the investigating authority for further and full investigation.

   (5) An investigating authority shall maintain confidentiality when examining a matter referred in accordance with this section.

   (6) An investigating authority shall subject any anonymous disclosure to the tests set out in section *thirteen*.

Frivolous, vexatious, etc., disclosures

13. (1) An investigating authority may decline to act on a public vexatious, interest disclosure received by it where the investigating authority etc. disclosures considers that—

      (*a*) the disclosure is malicious, frivolous, vexatious or made in bad faith;

      (*b*) the disclosure is misconceived or lacking in substance;

      (*c*) the disclosure is trivial;

      (*d*) there is a more appropriate method of dealing with the disclosure reasonably available;

      (*e*) the disclosure has already been dealt with adequately; or

      (*f*) the disclosure is made for pecuniary gain or other illegal purpose.

   (2) An investigating authority shall, where an issue raised in a public interest disclosure has been determined by a court or tribunal authorised to determine the issue at law, after consideration of the matters raised by the disclosure, decline to act on the disclosure to the extent that the disclosure attempts to re-open the issue.

   (3) A person who makes a public interest disclosure that falls within the meaning of paragraphs (*a*) and *a*) of subsection (1) commits an offence and is liable, upon conviction, to a fine not exceeding seven hundred thousand penalty units or to imprisonment for a period not exceeding seven years, or to both.

   (4) Where a public interest disclosure is made against any person and the person is suspended or any other administrative action is taken against that person by the employer pending investigation into the matter, and the investigating authority determines that the disclosure falls under subsection (1), the person shall be entitled to—

      (a) reinstatement by the employer;

      (b) compensation for any detriment suffered as a result of the disclosure made;

      (c) re-location to another position of equivalent level of salary and duties, in the employing agency; or

      (d) any other action to remedy to any detriment caused to the person by the disclosure.

   (5) Where a person is re-located in accordance with subsection (4), the employing agency of the person being relocated shall —

   meet all reasonable re-location expenses; and take all reasonable steps to ensure that the person is placed in a position of equivalent level of salary and duties.

Referral without investigation

14. Subject to section *seventeen*, if a public interest disclosure received by an investigating authority is not related to —

    (a) the conduct of the investigating authority or of a public officer in relation to the investigating authority; or

    (b) a matter, or the conduct of any person, that it has a function or power to investigate; the investigating authority shall refer the disclosure to another investigating authority that, because it has a function or power to deal with the conduct or matter the disclosure concerns, is a proper authority to receive the disclosure.

Investigation by authority

15. (1) An investigating authority shall investigate a public interest disclosure received by it if the disclosure relates to—

    (a) its own conduct or conduct of a public officer in relation to the investigating authority;

    (b) a matter, or the conduct of any person, that the investigating authority has a function or power to investigate; or

    (c) the conduct of a person, other than a public officer, performing services for or on behalf of the investigating authority

  (2) Where an investigating authority investigates a matter in accordance with subsection (1) and is unable to investigate the matter impartially or without a conflict of interest, the authority shall refer the matter to another investigating authority.

  (3) A disclosure may be referred before or after the matter has been investigated and whether or not any investigation of the matter is complete or any findings have been made by the investigating authority.

  (4) An investigating authority may communicate to another investigating authority to a public officer or public authority any information relevant for purposes of an investigating authority has obtained during the investigation of any matter under this Act.

  (5) An investigating authority may recommend what action should be taken by the other investigating authority, a public officer or public authority.

  (6) An investigating authority shall not refer the disclosure to another investigating authority, or to a public officer or public authority, except after taking into consideration the views of the investigating authority, public officer or public authority.

Referral with investigation

16. (1) Subject to subsection (2), if a public interest disclosure being investigated by an investigating authority relates to—

    (a) the conduct of another agency or the conduct of a public officer in relation to another agency; or

    (b) a matter, or the conduct of any person, that another agency has a function or power to investigate; the investigating authority shall refer the public interest disclosure to another investigating authority

  (2) Nothing in this section affects the duty of an investigating authority to act under section *fifteen*.

No referral

17. (1) An investigating authority shall not refer a public interest disclosure to another investigating authority under section *fourteen* or subsection (1) of section-sixteen K in the investigating authority's opinion—

    (a) there is a serious risk that a person would engage in an unlawful reprisal; or

    (b) the proper investigation of the disclosure would be prejudiced; as a result of the reference to the other investigating authority.

  (2) Where a non-referral of the type referred to in subsection (1) occurs, the matter shall be referred immediately to the Investigator-General who shall decide what action is to be taken in relation to the matter.

Action by investigating authority

18. Where after investigation, an investigating authority is of the opinion that a public interest disclosure has revealed—

(a) that a person has engaged, is engaging, or intends to engage, in disclosable conduct;
(b) public wastage;
(c) that a person has engaged, is engaging, or intends to engage, in an unlawful reprisal; or
(d) that a public officer has engaged, is engaging, or intends to engage, in conduct that amounts to a substantial and specific danger to the health or safety of the public; the investigating authority shall take such action as is necessary and reasonable —
  (i) to prevent the conduct or reprisal continuing or occurring in future;
  (ii) discipline any person responsible for the conduct or reprisal;
  (iii) bring an action in court or prosecute any person responsible for the conduct or reprisal, under this Act or relevant investigating Act; or
  (iv) confiscate or forfeit any property, benefit or other proceed obtained from or through the conduct or reprisal or acquired by any person through the commission of any offence under this Act or any investigating Act.

Progress report

19. (1) A person who makes a public interest disclosure, or a Progress investigating authority which refers a disclosure to another report investigating authority, may request the investigating authority to which the disclosure was made or referred to provide a progress report.
   (2) Where a request is made under subsection (1), the investigating authority to which the request is made shall provide a progress report to the person who, or investigating authority which requested it—
     (a) within fourteen days from the date of receipt of the request; and
     (b) if the investigating authority takes further action with respect to the disclosure after providing a progress report under paragraph (a)—
       (i) while the authority is taking action, at least once in every ninety day period commencing on the
       date of provision of the report under paragraph (a); and
       (ii) on completion of the action.
   (3) A progress report provided under subsection (2) shall contain the following particulars with respect to the investigating authority that provides the report:
     (a) where the investigating authority has declined to act on the public interest disclosure, that it has declined to act and the ground on which it so declined;
     (b) where the investigating authority has referred the public interest disclosure to another investigating authority, that it has referred the disclosure to another investigating authority and the name of the authority to which the disclosure has been referred;
     (c) where the investigating authority has accepted the public interest disclosure for investigation, the current status of the investigation; and
     (d) where the investigating authority has accepted the public interest disclosure for investigation and the investigation is complete, its findings and any action it has taken or proposes to take as a result of its findings.
   (4) Nothing in this section prevents any investigating authority from providing a progress report in accordance with subsection (3) to a person who may make a request under subsection (1).

Joint action

20. If more than one investigating authority is required by this Act to act on a public interest disclosure, the investigating authorities may enter into such arrangements with each other as are necessary and reasonable to—
   (a) avoid duplication of action;
   (b) allow the resources of the authorities to be efficiently and economically used to take action; and
   (c) achieve the most effective result.

PART III
PROTECTED DISCLOSURES

Effect of Part

21. A disclosure is protected by this Act if it satisfies the applicable requirements of this Part.

General

22. (1) A disclosure is a protected disclosure if —
    (a) it is made in good faith by an employee —
        (i) who reasonably believes that the information disclosed, and any allegation contained in it, are substantially true; and
        (ii) who does not make the disclosure for purposes of personal gain, excluding any reward payable in terms of any law;
    (b) one or more of the conditions specified in subsection (2) apply; and
    (c) in all the circumstances of the case, it is reasonable to make the disclosure.

    (2) The conditions referred to in paragraph (b) of subsection (1) are
    (a) that at the time of making a disclosure the employee who makes the disclosure has reason to believe that the employee shall be subjected to an occupational detriment if the employee makes a disclosure to the employer in accordance with section *thirty-eight;*

    (b) that, in a case where no person or body is prescribed for the purposes of section *thirty-nine* in relation to the relevant impropriety, the employee making the disclosure has reason to believe that it is likely that evidence relating to the impropriety shall be concealed or destroyed if the employee makes the disclosure to the employer;

    (c) that the employee making the disclosure has previously made a disclosure of substantially the same information to —
        (i) the employer; or
        (ii) a person or body referred to in section *thirty nine,* in respect of which no action was taken within a reasonable period after the disclosure;
        or
    (d) that the impropriety is of an exceptionally serious nature.

    (3) In determining for the purposes of paragraph (c) of subsection (1) whether it is reasonable for the employee to make the disclosure, consideration shall be given to —
    (a) the identity of the person to whom the disclosure is made;
    (b) the seriousness of the impropriety;
    (c) whether the impropriety is continuing or is likely to occur in the future; whether the disclosure is made in breach of a duty of confidentiality of the employer towards any other person;
    (e) in a case falling within paragraph (c) of subsection (2), any action which the employer or the person or body to whom the disclosure was made, has taken, or might reasonably be expected to have taken, as a result of the previous disclosure;
    (f) in a case falling within subparagraph (i) of paragraph (c) of subsection (2), whether in making the disclosure to the employer the employee complied with any procedure which was authorised by the employer; and
    (g) the public interest.

    (4) For the purposes of this section, a subsequent disclosure may be regarded as a disclosure of substantially the same information referred to in paragraph (c) of subsection (2) where the subsequent disclosure extends to information concerning an action taken or not taken by any person as a result of the previous disclosure.

Lodging of public interest disclosure

23. Any of the following may receive a public interest disclosure concerning a government agency's conduct or the conduct of a public officer in relation to a government agency, or a public interest disclosure that a person has engaged, is engaging, or intends to engage, in an unlawful reprisal:
    (a) the head of the government agency;
    (b) the Anti-Corruption Commission;
    (c) the Police Public Complaints Authority:

(d) the Judicial Complaints Authority;
(e) the Drug Enforcement Commission;
(f) the Investigator-General; and
(g) the Auditor-General.

Disclosures made by public officers

24. (1) A disclosure by a public officer shall be made to—
    (a) an investigating authority;
    (b) the principal officer of a government agency or investigating authority or other public officer of a government agency;
    (c) another officer of the government agency or investigating authority to which the public officer belongs; or
    (d) an officer of the government agency or investigating authority to which the disclosure relates; in accordance with any procedure established by the authority concerned for the reporting of allegations of corrupt conduct, maladministration or serious and substantial waste of public money by that authority or any of its officers.

    (2) A disclosure is protected by this Act even if it is made about conduct or activities engaged in, or about matters arising, before the commencement of this Act.

    (3) A disclosure made while a person was a public officer is protected by this Act even if the person who made it is no longer a public officer.

    (4) A disclosure made about the conduct of a person while the person was a public officer is protected by this Act even if the person is no longer a public officer.

Disclosures to be made voluntarily

25. (1) To be protected by this Act, a disclosure shall be made voluntarily

    (2) A disclosure is not made voluntarily for the purposes of this section if it is made by a public officer in the exercise of a duty imposed on the public officer by, or under, any law

    (3) A disclosure is made voluntarily for the purposes of this section if it is made by a public officer in accordance with a code of conduct, however described, adopted by an investigating authority or government agency and setting out rules or guidelines to be observed by public officers for reporting corrupt conduct, maladministration or serious and substantial waste of public money by investigating authorities, government agencies or public officers.

    (4) A disclosure made by a member of the Zambia Police Force is made voluntarily for the purposes of this section even if it relates to the same conduct as an allegation that the member of the Zambia Police Force has made in performance of a duty imposed on the member by, or under, the Zambia Police Act or any other law. Cap. 107

    (5) A disclosure made by a prison officer, within the meaning of the Prisons Act is made voluntarily for the purposes of this section even if it relates to the same conduct as an allegation that the prison officer has made in the performance of a duty imposed on the prison officer by, or under, that Act or any other law. Cap. 97

Disclosure concerning corrupt conduct

26. To be protected by this Act, a disclosure by a public officer to the Anti-Corruption Commission shall be made in accordance with the Anti-Corruption Commission Act and be a disclosure of information that shows or tends to show that a government agency or another public officer has engaged, is engaged or intends to engage in corrupt conduct.

Disclosure to Investigator-General concerning maladminishation

27. To be protected by this Act, a disclosure by a public officer to the Investigator-General shall—
    (a) be made in accordance with the Commission for Investigations Act; and
    (b) be a disclosure of information that shows or tends to show that, in the exercise of a function relating to a matter of administration conferred or imposed on a government agency or another public officer, the government agency or public officer has engaged, is engaged or intends to engage in conduct of a kind that amounts to maladministration.

Disclosure to Auditor-General concerning serious and substantial waste

28. To be protected by this Act, a disclosure by a public officer to the Auditor-General shall be a disclosure of information that shows or tends to show that an authority or officer of an authority has seriously and substantially wasted public money contrary to the provisions of the Public Finance Act, 2004.

Disclosure concerning police officer

29. To be protected by this Act, a disclosure by a public officer to the Police Public Complaints Authority shall —
    (a) be made in accordance with the Zambia Police Act [Act No. 15 of 2004]; and
    (b) be a disclosure that shows or tends to show corrupt conduct, maladministration or serious and substantial waste of public money by a police officer.

Disclosure concerning serious and substantial waste in local government

30. (1) To be protected by this Act, a disclosure by a public officer to the Minister responsible for local authority shall—
    (a) be made in accordance with the Local Government Act; and
    (b) be a disclosure of information that shows or tends to show serious and substantial waste of local authority money by any one or more of the following:
        (i) a local authority;
        (ii) a delegate of a local authority;
        (iii) a councillor, within the meaning of the Local Government Act [Cap. 281]; and
        (iv) a member of staff of a local authority.
    (2) In this section, "local authority money" includes all revenue, loans and other money collected, received or held by, for or on account of a local authority.

Disclosure about investigating authorities

31. (1) A disclosure by a public officer to the Anti-Corruption Commission that shows or tends to show that, in the exercise of a function relating to a matter of administration conferred or imposed on a head or officer of any investigating authority, the head or the officer of the investigating authority has engaged, is engaged or intends to engage in conduct that amounts to maladministration is protected by this Act.

    (2) The Anti-Corruption Commission may investigate, and Cap. 91 report, in accordance with the Anti-Corruption Commission Act on any matter raised by a disclosure made to it under subsection (1).

    (3) Notwithstanding section *eleven*, a disclosure by a public officer to the Investigator-General or Anti-Corruption Commission that shows or tends to show that the Auditor-General or a member of the staff of the Auditor-General has seriously and substantially wasted public money is protected by this Act.

    (4) The Anti-Corruption Commission may investigate, and Cap. 91 report, in accordance with the Anti-Corruption Commission Act on any matter raised by a disclosure made to it that is of a kind referred to in subsection (3).

    (5) For the purposes of any investigation under subsection (4), the Anti-Corruption Commission may engage consultants or other persons for the purpose of getting expert assistance.

    (6) Notwithstanding section *ten*, a disclosure by a public officer to the Anti-Corruption Commission that shows or tends to show that, in the exercise of a function relating to a matter of administration conferred or imposed on the Inspector-General or Commissioner of Police, the Inspector-General or Commissioner of Police has engaged or intends to engage in conduct that amounts to corrupt conduct or maladministration or has seriously and substantially wasted public money is protected by this Act.

    (7) The Anti-Corruption Commission may investigate, and Cap. 91 report, in accordance with the Anti-Corruption Commission Act on any matter raised by a disclosure made to it in subsection (6).

    (8) A disclosure referred to in this section is protected by this Act only if it satisfies all other applicable requirements of this Part.

Disclosures to public officers

32. (1) To be protected by this Act, a disclosure by a public officer to the principal officer, or other public officer, of a government agency shall be a disclosure of information that shows or tends to show corrupt conduct, maladministration or serious and substantial waste of public money by the government agency or any of its officers or by another government agency or any of its officers.

    (2) To be protected by this Act, a disclosure by a public officer to —

    (a) another officer of the government agency to which the public officer belongs; or

    (b) an officer of the government agency to which the disclosure relates;

    in accordance with any procedure established by the government agency for the reporting of allegations of corrupt conduct, maladministration or serious and substantial waste of public money by that government agency or any of its officers shall be a disclosure of information that shows or tends to show the corrupt conduct, maladministration or serious and substantial waste, whether by that government agency or any of its officers or by another government agency or any of its officers.

    (3) A public officer may refer any disclosure concerning an allegation of corrupt conduct, maladministration or serious and substantial waste made to the public officer to an investigating authority, or a principal officer or other public officer of a government agency considered by the public officer to be appropriate in the circumstances, for investigation or other action.

    (4) If the public officer to whom the disclosure referred to in subsection (1) is made does not belong to the investigating authority to which the disclosure relates, the public officer shall refer the disclosure to the principal officer or other public officer of a government agency, for investigation or other action.

    (5) A public officer may communicate to an investigating authority or principal officer or other public officer of a government agency to whom a matter is referred under subsection (4), any information the public officer has obtained during the investigation of the matter.

    (6) In this section, " government agency " includes an investigating authority.

Referred disclosures protected

33. (1) A disclosure is protected by this Act if it is made by a public officer to an investigating authority and is referred, whether because it is not authorised to investigate the matter under the relevant investigation Act or otherwise, by the investigating authority to another investigating authority or to a public officer or government agency.

    (2) A disclosure is protected by this Act if it is made by a public officer to another public officer in accordance with paragraph *(b)* or *(c)* of section *twenty-four* and is referred under Part II by the other public officer to an investigating authority or to another public officer or government agency.

Disclosures made on frivolous or other grounds

34. (1) An investigating authority, a principal officer or other public officer of a government agency, may decline to investigate or may discontinue the investigation of any matter raised by a disclosure made to the authority or public officer of a kind referred to in this Part if the investigating authority or officer is of the opinion that the disclosure was made maliciously, frivolously, vexatiously, in bad faith, for pecuniary gain or for an illegal purpose.

    (2) A disclosure referred to in subsection (1) is not, despite any other provision of this Part, protected by this Act if an investigating authority or officer declines to investigate or discontinues the investigation of a matter under this section.

Disclosures concerning merits of government policy

35. (1) A disclosure made by a public officer that principally involves questioning the merits of government policy is not, despite any other provision of this Part, protected by this Act.

    (2) In this section, "government policy" includes the policy of a local authority.

Disclosures motivated by object of avoiding disciplinary action

36. A disclosure that is made solely or substantially with the motive of avoiding dismissal or other disciplinary action, not being disciplinary action taken in reprisal for the making of a protected disclosure, is not, notwithstanding any other provision of this Part, a protected disclosure.

Protected disclosure to legal practitioner

37. Any disclosure made to a legal practitioner with the object of, and in the course of, obtaining legal advice, is a protected disclosure.

Protected disclosure to employer

38. (1) Any disclosure made in good faith—

    (a) and substantially in accordance with any procedure prescribed, or authorised by the employee's employer for reporting or otherwise remedying the impropriety; or

    (b) to the employer of the employee, where there is no procedure as contemplated in paragraph (a); is a protected disclosure.

  (2) Any employee who, in accordance with a procedure authorised by the employer, makes a disclosure to a person other than the employer, is deemed, for the purposes of this Act, to be making the disclosure to the employer.

Protected disclosure to certain persons or bodies

39. (1) Any disclosure made in good faith to a person or body prescribed for purposes of this Act and in respect of which an employee reasonably believes that —

    (a) the relevant impropriety falls within any description of matters which, in the ordinary course are dealt with by the person or body; and

    (b) the information disclosed, and any allegation contained in it, are substantially true; is a protected disclosure.

  (2) A person or body referred to in, or prescribed in terms of, subsection (1) who is of the opinion that the matter would be more appropriately dealt with by another person or body referred to in, or prescribed in terms of, that subsection, shall render such assistance to the employee as is necessary to enable that employee to comply with this section.

PART IV
PROVISIONS RELATING TO INVESTIGATING AUTHORITIES

Procedures by investigating authorities on public interest disclosures

40. (1) An investigating authority shall, within twelve months after the commencement of this Act, establish procedures —

    (a) to facilitate the making of public interest disclosures; and

    (b) to deal with public interest disclosures that it is the proper authority to receive.

  (2) The procedures to be established under subsection (1) shall include procedures dealing with the following:

    (a) making public interest disclosures;

    (b) assisting and providing information to a person who is considering making or who makes a public interest disclosure;

    (c) protecting a person who makes a public interest disclosure from unlawful reprisals, including unlawful reprisals taken by public officers in relation to the government agency; and

    (d) acting on public interest disclosures.

Report on disclosures

41. An investigating authority that is required by an Act to prepare an annual report of its activities during a year for tabling before Parliament shall include in the report a description of the procedures established by it under section *forty* and such other information as may be prescribed.

PART V
PROTECTION AGAINST REPRISALS

Protection against reprisals

42. (1) A person who takes any detrimental action that is in reprisal for a person who makes a protected disclosure commits an offence, and is liable, upon conviction, to a fine not exceeding two hundred thousand penalty units or to imprisonment for a period not exceeding two years, or to both.

    (2) A civil proceeding in respect of a detrimental action under this section may be instituted at any time within three years after the detrimental action is alleged to have been committed.

    (3) In this section, "detrimental action" means action causing, comprising or involving any of the following:
        (a) injury, damage or loss;
        (b) intimidation or harassment;
        (c) discrimination, disadvantage or adverse treatment in relation to employment;
        (d) dismissal from, or prejudice in, employment; or
        (e) disciplinary proceeding.

Protection against actions

43. (1) A person is not subject to any liability for making a protected disclosure in good faith and no action, claim or demand shall be taken or made of or against the person for making the disclosure.

    (2) Subject to the State Security Act, this section has effect despite any duty of secrecy or confidentiality or any other restriction on disclosure, whether or not imposed by an Act, applicable to a person.

Non-disclosure of person's identity

44. An investigating authority, an officer of an investigating authority or public officer to whom a protected disclosure is made or referred shall not disclose information that might identify or tend to identify a person who has made any protected disclosure unless-
        (a) the person consents in writing to the disclosure of that information;
        (b) it is essential, having regard to the principles of natural justice, that the identifying information be disclosed to a person whom the information provided by the disclosure may concern; or
        (c) the investigating authority, public authority or public officer is of the opinion that disclosure of the identifying information is necessary to investigate the matter effectively or it is otherwise in the public interest to do so.

PART VI
UNLAWFUL REPRISALS

Employer to protect its officers against reprisals

45. Within six months of the commencement of this Act, an protect its employer shall establish procedures to protect its employees from officers' reprisals that are, or may be, taken against them.

Prohibition of unlawful reprisals

46. (1) A person shall not engage, or attempt or conspire to of unlawful engage, in an unlawful reprisal. reprisal

    (2) Any person who contravenes subsection (1) commits an offence and is liable, upon conviction, if the offender is a natural person, to a fine not exceeding two hundred thousand penalty units or to imprisonment for a period not exceeding two years, or to both, or if the offender is a body corporate, to a fine not exceeding seven hundred thousand penalty units.

Relocation powers

47. (1) Where an employee applies in writing to the employer for relocation and the employer considers—

(a) that there is a danger that a person will engage in an unlawful reprisal in relation to the employee if the employee continues to hold the employee's current position; and

(b) that the only practical means of removing or substantially removing the danger is relocation of the employee to another position in an employing agency;

the employer shall, as far as practicable, make arrangements for relocation of the employee to another position in the employing agency.

(2) Where an employee is relocated in accordance with this section, the employing agency of the employee being relocated shall—

(a) meet all reasonable relocation expenses; and

(b) take all reasonable steps to ensure that the employee is placed in a position of equivalent level of salary and duties.

Consent to relocation

48. Section *forty-seven* does not authorise the relocation of an employee in relation to an employer to another position in the employing agency without the consent of the employee.

PART VII
REMEDIES

Remedies

49. (1) Any employee who has been subjected, is subject or Remedies may be subjected, to any occupational detriment in breach of section *ten, may*—

(a) apply to any court having jurisdiction, including the Industrial and Labour Relations Court for appropriate relief; or

(b) pursue any other process allowed or prescribed by any law.

(2) For the purposes of the Industrial and Labour Relations Act, including the consideration of any matter emanating from this Act by the Industrial and Labour Relations Court—

(a) any dismissal in breach of section *ten* is deemed to be an unfair dismissal; and

(b) any other occupational detriment in breach of section *ten* is deemed to be an unfair labour practice.

(3) Any employee who has made a protected disclosure and who reasonably believes that the employee may be adversely affected on account of having made that disclosure, shall, at that employee's request and if reasonably possible or practicable, be transferred from the post or position occupied by that employee at the time of the disclosure, to another post or position in the same division or another division of the employer or, where the person making the disclosure is employed by a government agency to another government agency.

(4) The terms and conditions of employment of a person transferred in terms of subsection (3) shall not, without the person's written consent, be less favourable than the terms and conditions applicable to that person immediately before the person's transfer.

Liability in damages

50 (1) A person who engages in an unlawful reprisal is liable in damages to any person who suffers detriment as a result of the unlawful reprisal.

(2) The damages referred to under subsection (1) may be recovered in an action in any court of competent jurisdiction.

Application for injunction or order

51. Subject to the State Proceedings Act, an application to a court for an injunction or order under section fifty-two may be made—

(a) by a person claiming that the person is suffering or may suffer detriment from an unlawful reprisal; or

(b) by the Investigator-General on behalf of a person referred to in paragraph (a).

Injunction or order to take action

52. (1) If, on receipt of an application under section fifty-one, a court is satisfied that a person has engaged, or is proposing to engage, in—

    (a) an unlawful reprisal; or

    (b) conduct that amounts to or would amount to aiding, abetting, counselling or procuring a person to engage in an unlawful reprisal; inducing or attempting to induce, whether by threats, promises or otherwise, a person to engage in an unlawful reprisal; or

    (c) being in any way, directly or indirectly, knowingly concerned in, or party to, an unlawful reprisal; the court may—

        (a) order the person to take specified action to remedy any detriment caused by the unlawful reprisal; or

        (b) grant an injunction in terms the court considers appropriate.

  (2) A court may, pending the final determination of an application under section fifty-one, make an interim order or grant an interim injunction.

  (3) A court may grant an injunction or an interim injunction under this section whether or not the person has previously engaged in conduct of that kind.

  (4) A court may make an order or an interim order under this section requiring a person to take specified action, whether or not the person has previously refused or failed to take that action.

Undertakings as to damages and costs

53. (1) If the Investigator-General applies under section fifty-one for an injunction or order, no undertaking as to damages or costs is required.

  (2) The Investigator-General may give an undertaking as to damages or costs on behalf of a person applying under section fifty-*one* and, in that event, no further undertaking is required.

PART VIII
GENERAL PROVISIONS

Prohibition of disclosure of information

54. (1) A public officer shall not, without reasonable excuse, make a record of, or wilfully disclose to another person, confidential information gained through the public officer's involvement in the administration of this Act.

  (2) Any person who contravenes subsection (1) commits an offence and is liable, upon conviction, to a fine not exceeding two hundred thousand penalty units or to imprisonment for a period not exceeding two years, or to both.

  (3) Subsection (1) shall not apply to a public officer who makes a record of, or discloses, confidential information—

    (a) to another person for the purposes of this Act; to another person, if expressly authorised under any other law; or for the purposes of a proceeding in a court or tribunal.

  (4) In this section, " confidential information " means—

    (a) information about the identity, occupation or whereabouts of a person who has made a public interest disclosure or against whom a public interest disclosure has been made;

    (b) information contained in a public interest disclosure;

    (c) information concerning an individual's personal affairs; or

    (d) information that, if disclosed, may cause detriment to a person.

False or misleading information

55. (1) A person shall not knowingly or recklessly make a misleading false or misleading statement, orally or in writing, to any investigating information authority with the intention that it be acted on as a public interest disclosure.

  (2) Any person who contravenes subsection (1) commits an offence and is liable, upon conviction, if the offender is a natural person, to a fine not exceeding seven hundred thousand penalty units or to imprisonment for a period not exceeding seven years, or to both, or if the offender is a body corporate, to a fine not exceeding one million penalty units.

Limitation of of liability

56. (1) A person is not subject to any liability for making a liability public interest disclosure in good faith or providing any further information in relation to the disclosure to an investigating authority investigating it, and no action, claim or demand shall be taken or made of or against the person for making the disclosure or providing the further information.

(2) Without limiting subsection (1), in proceedings for defamation, a person has a defence of absolute privilege in respect of the making of a public interest disclosure, or the provision of further information in relation to a public interest disclosure, to an investigating authority.

(3) The defence of absolute privilege is not available where the making of a public interest disclosure is frivolous, vexatious or otherwise meets the conditions specified in section *thirteen*.

Liability of person disclosing

57. A person's liability for the person's own conduct is not affected by the person's disclosure of that conduct in a public interest disclosure.

Notification to person making disclosure

An investigating authority or principal officer, or other public officer, of a government agency to whom a disclosure is made under this Act or, if the disclosure is referred, the investigating authority or principal officer, or other public officer, of a government agency, to whom the disclosure is referred, shall notify the person who made the disclosure, within six months of the disclosure being made, of the action taken or proposed to be taken in respect of the

Regulation

59. The Minister may, by statutory instrument, make Regulations for the better carrying out of the provisions of this Act.

FORFEITURE OF PROCEEDS OF CRIME ACT NO 19 OF 2010

Assented to on 13 April 2010
Commencement date unknown
[This is the version of this document from 16 April 2010.]

An Act to provide for the confiscation of the proceeds of crime; provide for the deprivation of any person of any proceed, benefit or property derived from the commission of any serious offence; facilitate the tracing of any proceed, benefit and property derived from the commission of any serious offence; provide for the domestication of the United Nations Convention against Corruption; and provide for matters connected with, or incidental to, the foregoing.

Enactment

ENACTED by the Parliament of Zambia.

PART I
PRELIMINARY

1. **Short title and commencement**

This Act may be cited as the Forfeiture of Proceeds of Crime Act, 2010, and shall come into operation on such date as the Minister may, by statutory instrument, appoint.

2. **Interpretation**

In this Act, unless the context otherwise requires—

"**account**" means any facility or arrangement through which a financial institution accepts deposits or allows withdrawals or fund transfers or a facility or arrangement for a fixed term deposit or a safety deposit box;

"**administrator**" means the person appointed as such under section thirty-nine;

"**Attorney-General**" means the person appointed as such under the Constitution; [Cap. 1]

"**bank**" means the Bank of Zambia or an institution providing any financial service within the meaning of the Banking and Financial Services Act; [Cap. 387]

"**benefit**" includes any property, service or advantage, whether direct or indirect;

"**building society**" means a body registered or incorporated as a co-operative, housing society or similar society under any law;

"**casual gift**" has the meaning assigned to it in the Anti-Corruption Commission Act; [Cap. 91]

"**confiscation order**" means an order made by the court under subsection (1) of section nineteen;

"**court**" means a High Court or a subordinate court;

"**credit union**" means a union or society carrying on credit business under any law;

"**Director of Public Prosecutions**" means the person appointed as such under the Constitution; [Cap. 1]

"**document**" means any one or more of the following:

(a) anything on which there is writing;

(b) a map, a photograph, plan, graph or drawing;

(c) anything on which there are marks, figures, symbols or perforations having meaning for persons to interpret;

(d) a disk, tape, sound track or other device in which sound or other data not being visual images, are embodied so as to be capable, with or without the aid of some other equipment, of being reproduced therefrom; or

(e) a film, negative, tape or other device in which one or more visual images are embodied so as to be capable of being reproduced therefrom;

"**encumbrance**" in relation to a property, includes any interest, mortgage, charge, right, claim or demand made on the property;

"**facsimile copy**" means a copy obtained by facsimile transmission;

"**film**" includes a microfilm or microfiche;

"**financial institution**" has the meaning assigned to it in the Banking and Financial Services Act;

"**fixed term deposit**" means an interest bearing deposit lodged for a fixed period;

"**foreign confiscation order**" means a confiscation order made in relation to a foreign serious offence;

"**foreign forfeiture order**" means a forfeiture order made in relation to a foreign serious offence;

"**foreign restraining order**" means a restraining order made in relation to a foreign serious offence;

"**foreign serious offence**" means a serious offence against the law of a foreign country;

"**forfeiture order**" means an order made by a court under subsection (1) of section ten;

"**Fund**" means the Forfeited Assets Fund established under section seventy-five;

"**interest**" in relation to property, means—

(a) a legal or equitable estate or interest in the property; or(b)a right, power or privilege in connection with the property;

"**police officer**" means a member of the Zambia Police Force, and includes an officer from the Anti-Corruption Commission, Drug Enforcement Commission and any other investigative institution of the State;

"**premises**" includes vessel, aircraft, vehicle or any place, whether built upon or not;

"**proceeds**" in relation to an offence, means any property that is derived or realised, directly or indirectly, by any person from the commission of the offence in or outside Zambia;

"**proceeds of crime**" in relation to a serious offence or a foreign serious offence, means property or benefit that is—

(a) wholly or partly derived or realised directly or indirectly, by any person from the commission of a serious offence or a foreign serious offence;

(b) wholly or partly derived or realised from a disposal or other dealing with proceeds of a serious offence or a foreign serious offence;

(c) wholly or partly acquired proceeds of a serious offence or a foreign serious offence;
and includes, on a proportional basis, property into which any property derived or realised directly from the serious offence or foreign serious offence is later converted, transformed or intermingled, and any income, capital or other economic gains derived or realised from the property at any time after the offence; or

(d) any property that is derived or realised, directly or indirectly, by any person from any act or omission that occurred outside Zambia and would, if the act or omission had occurred in Zambia, have constituted a serious offence;

431

"**production order**" means an order made by the court under section fifty-seven;

"**property**" includes any real or personal property, money, things in action or other intangible or incorporeal property, whether located in Zambia or elsewhere and includes property of corresponding value in the absence of the original illegally acquired property whose value has been determined;

"**property-tracking document**" in relation to an offence, means—

    (a) a document relevant to—

        (i) identifying, locating or quantifying the property of a person who committed the offence; or(ii)identifying or locating any document necessary for the transfer of property of person who committed the offence; or

    (b) a document relevant to—

        (i) identifying, locating or quantifying tainted property in relation to the offence; or(ii) identifying or locating any document necessary for the transfer of tainted property in relation to the offence;

"**public prosecutor**" has the meaning assigned to it in the Criminal Procedure Code; *[Cap. 88]*

"**realisable property**" means, subject to subsections (3) and (4) of section three—

    (a) any property held or controlled by a person who has been convicted of, or charged with, a serious offence;(b)any property held by a person in respect of which a confiscation or forfeiture order may be made; and(c)any property held by any other person to whom the person so convicted or charged has directly or indirectly made a casual gift within the meaning of this Act;

"**relevant application period**", in relation to a person's conviction of a serious offence, means the period of twelve months after—

    (a) where the person is to be taken to have been convicted of the offence by reason of paragraph

    (a) of the definition of "proceeds of crime" the day on which the person was convicted of the offence;(b)where the person is to be taken to have been convicted of the offence by reason of paragraph (b) the definition of "proceeds of crime" the day on which the person was discharged without conviction; or

    (c) where the person is to be taken to have been convicted of the offence by reason of paragraph (c) of the definition of "proceeds of crime" the day on which the court took the offence into account in passing sentence for the other offence referred to in that paragraph;

"**relevant offence**" in relation to tainted property, means—

    (a) an offence by reason of the commission of which the property is tainted property; or(b)any other offence that is prescribed by regulation as a serious offence for the purposes of this definition or is of a class of offences that is so prescribed;

"**restraining order**" means an order made by the court under subsection (1) of section forty-two;

"**serious offence**" means an offence for which the maximum penalty prescribed by law is [life imprisonment],[19] or imprisonment for not less than twelve months;

"**tainted property**" in relation to a serious offence or a foreign serious offence, means—

    (a) any property used in, or in connection with, the commission of the offence;

    (b) property intended to be used in, or in connection with, the commission of the offence; or(c) proceeds of the offence; and when used without reference to a particular offence means tainted property in relation to a serious offence; and

"**unlawful activity**" means an act or omission that constitutes an offence under any law in force in Zambia or a foreign country.

3.   Definition of certain terms

(1)   In this Act, a reference to a benefit derived or obtained by, or otherwise accruing to, a person includes a reference to a benefit derived or obtained by, or otherwise accruing to, another person at the request or direction of the person.

(2)   For the purposes of this Act, a person is taken to be convicted of a serious offence where—

    (a) the person is convicted, whether summarily or on indictment, of the offence;

    (b) the person is charged with, and found guilty of, the offence but is discharged upon conviction; or

    (c) a court, with the consent of the person, takes the offence, of which the person has not been found guilty, into account in passing sentence on the person for another offence.

---

[19] See Act No 23 of 2022.

(3) Property is not realisable property if—
    (a) there is in force, in respect of that property, a forfeiture order under this Act or under any other law; or
    (b) a forfeiture order is proposed to be made against that property under this Act or any other law.

(4) For the purposes of sections twenty-one and twenty-two, the amount that may be realised at the time a confiscation order is made against a person is the total of the value at that time of all the realisable property held by the person less the total amounts payable under an obligation, where there is an obligation having priority at that time, together with the total of the value at that time of all casual gifts falling within the meaning of this Act.

(5) For the purposes of subsection (4), an obligation has priority at any time where it is an obligation of the person to—
    (a) pay an amount due in respect of a fine, or other order of a court, imposed or made on conviction of an offence, where the fine was imposed or the order was made before the confiscation order;
    (b) pay an amount due in respect of any tax, rate, duty or other impost payable under any law; or(c) pay any other civil obligation as may be determined by the court.

(6) Subject to subsections (7) and (8), for the purposes of this Act, the value of property, other than cash, in relation to a person holding the property, is—
    (a) where any other person holds an interest in the property, the market value of the first-mentioned person's beneficial interest in the property, less the amount required to discharge any encumbrance on that interest; or
    (b) in any other case, its market value.

(7) References in this Act to the value at any time, referred to in subsection (8) as "the material time" of the transfer of any property, are references to—
    (a) the value of the property to the recipient when the recipient receives it, adjusted to take account of subsequent changes in the value of money; or
    (b) where subsection (8) applies, the value mentioned in that subsection; whichever is the greater.

(8) Where at the material time a recipient holds—
    (a) any property which the recipient received, not being cash; or
    (b) any property which, in whole or in part, directly or indirectly represents in the recipient's hands the property which the recipient received;
    the value referred to under paragraph (b) of subsection (6) is the value to the recipient at the material time of the property referred to in paragraph (a) or, as the case may be, of the property mentioned in paragraph (b), so far as it represents the property which the recipient received.

(9) Subject to subsection (13), a reference to the value at any time, referred to in subsection (10) as "the material time", of a casual gift is a reference to—
    (a) the value of the casual gift to the recipient when the recipient received it, adjusted to take account of subsequent changes in the value of money; or(b)where subsection (10) applies, the value mentioned in that subsection; whichever is the greater.

(10) Subject to subsection (13), where at the material time a person holds—
    (a) property which the person received, not being cash; or
    (b) property which, in whole or in part, directly or indirectly represents in the person's hands, the property which the person received;
    (c) the value referred to under paragraph (b) of subsection (9) is the value to the person at the material time of the property mentioned in paragraph (a) or the value of the property mentioned in paragraph (b) so far as it so represents the property which the person received.

(11) A gift, including a casual gift made before the commencement of this Act, falls under this Act where—
    (a) it was made by the person convicted or charged at a time after the commission of the offence or, if more than one, the earliest of the offences to which the proceedings for the time being relate, and the court considers it appropriate in all the circumstances to take the casual gift into account;
    (b) it was made by the person convicted or charged at any time and was a casual gift of property— (i)received by the person in connection with the commission of a serious offence committed by the person or by another person; or (ii)which in whole or in part directly or indirectly represented in the person's hands, property received by the person in that connection.(12)Any reference in subsection (11) to " an offence to which the proceedings for the time being relate " includes, where the proceedings have resulted in the conviction of a person, a reference to any offence which the court takes into consideration when determining sentence.

Gates on Evidence: Zambian Theory and Practice

(13) For the purposes of this Act—

    (a) the circumstances in which a person must be treated as making a casual gift include those where the person transfers property to another person directly or indirectly for a consideration the value of which is significantly less than the value of the consideration provided or the property transferred by the person; or

    (b) in the circumstances referred to under paragraph (a), subsections (9), (10) and (11) shall apply as if the person had made a casual gift of such share in the property as bears to the whole property the same proportion as the difference between the value referred to in paragraph (a) bears to the value of the consideration provided or the property transferred by the person.

PART II
FORFEITURE ORDERS, CONFISCATION ORDERS AND RELATED MATTERS

Division 1 - Application for forfeiture or confiscation order

4. Application for forfeiture order or confiscation order on conviction

(1) Subject to subsection (2), where a person is convicted of a serious offence committed after the coming into force of this Act, a public prosecutor may apply to the court for one or both of the following orders: (a) a forfeiture order against property that is tainted property in respect of the offence; (b)a confiscation order against the person in respect of benefits derived by the person from the commission of the offence.

(2) A public prosecutor shall not make an application after the end of the relevant application period in relation to the conviction unless the public prosecutor has reasonable grounds for doing so.

(3) An application under this section may be made in respect of one or more than one serious offence.

(4) Where an application under this section is finally determined, no further application for a forfeiture order or a confiscation order may be made in respect of the offence for which the person was convicted unless the court grants leave for the making of a new application on being satisfied—

    (a) that the property or benefit to which the new application relates was identified after the previous application was determined;

    (b) that necessary evidence became available only after the previous application was determined; or

    (c) that it is in the interests of justice that the new application be made.

(5) Any application under subsection (2) shall be made *ex parte* and shall be in writing and be accompanied by an affidavit.

5. Jurisdiction of court

The court has jurisdiction to make a forfeiture order irrespective of the value of the property.

6. Notice of application

(1) Where a public prosecutor applies for a forfeiture order against property in respect of a person's conviction of an offence—

    (a) the public prosecutor shall give written notice of the application to the person and any other person who the public prosecutor has reason to believe may have an interest in the property;

    (b) the person, and any other person, who claims an interest in the property, may appear and adduce evidence at the hearing of the application; and(c)the court may, at any time before the final determination of the application, direct the public prosecutor—

        (i) to give notice of the application to any person who, in the opinion of the court, appears to have an interest in the property; or

        (ii) to publish in the *Gazette* and in a daily newspaper of general circulation in Zambia, notice of the application, in the manner and containing such particulars and within the time that the court considers appropriate.

(2) Where a public prosecutor applies for a confiscation order against a person—

    (a) the public prosecutor shall give the person written notice of the application; and

    (b) the person may appear and adduce evidence at the hearing of the application.

7. Amendment of application

(1) The court hearing an application under subsection (1) of section four may, before final determination of the application, and on the application of a public prosecutor, amend the application to include any

other property or benefit, as the case may be, upon being satisfied that—

    (a)   the property or benefit was not reasonably capable of identification when the application was originally made;

    (b)   necessary evidence became available only after the application was originally made; or

    (c)   the property or benefit was acquired after the application was originally made.

(2)   Where a public prosecutor applies to amend an application for a forfeiture order and the amendment would have the effect of including property in the application for the forfeiture order, the public prosecutor shall give written notice of the application to amend to any person who the public prosecutor has reason to believe may have an interest in property to be included in the application for the forfeiture order.

(3)   Any person who claims an interest in the property to be included in the application for the forfeiture order may appear and adduce evidence at the hearing of the application to amend.

(4)   Where a public prosecutor applies to amend an application for a confiscation order against a person and the effect of the amendment would be to include an additional benefit in the application for the confiscation order the public prosecutor shall give the person written notice of the application to amend.

(5)   Section nine shall apply for the purposes of written notice in subsection (4) where the person required to be notified has absconded.

8. Procedure on application

(1)   Where an application is made to the court for a forfeiture order or a confiscation order in respect of a person's conviction of an offence, the court may, in determining the application, have regard to the transcript of any proceedings against the person for the offence.

(2)   Where an application is made for a forfeiture order or a confiscation order to the court before which the person was convicted, and the court has not, when the application is made, passed sentence on the person for the offence, the court may, if it is satisfied that it is reasonable to do so in the circumstances, defer passing sentence until it has determined the application for the order.

9. Application for forfeiture order where person has absconded

(1)   Where a person absconds in connection with a serious offence committed after the coming into force of this Act, a public prosecutor may, within a period of six months after the person so absconds, apply to the court for a forfeiture order under section seventeen in respect of any tainted property.(2)For the purposes of this section, a person shall be deemed to have absconded in connection with an offence where— (a)an information has been laid alleging the commission of the offence by the person;(b)a warrant for the arrest of the person is issued in relation to that information;(c)reasonable attempts to arrest the person pursuant to the warrant have been unsuccessful during a period of six months commencing on the day the warrant was issued; or (d)the person dies after the warrant is issued or an investigation into the offence has commenced.

(3)   A person is deemed to have absconded on the last day of the period of six months or where the person has died, on the date of death.

(4)   Where a public prosecutor applies under this section for a forfeiture order against any tainted property the court shall, before hearing the application—

    (a)   require notice of the application to be given to any person who, in the opinion of the court, appears to have an interest in the property; or

    (b)   direct notice of the application to be published in the *Gazette* and in a newspaper of general circulation in Zambia, of such particulars and for so long as the court may require.

Division 2 - Forfeiture orders

10. Forfeiture order on conviction

(1)   Where a public prosecutor applies to the court for an order under this Part against any property and the court is satisfied that the property is tainted property, the court may order that the property, or such of the property as is specified by the court in the order, be forfeited to the State.(2)In determining whether property is tainted property the court may infer—

(a) where the evidence establishes that the property was in the person's possession at the time of, or immediately after, the commission of the offence of which the person was convicted, that the property was used in, or in connection with, the commission of the offence;

(b) where the evidence establishes that the property, and in particular money, was found in the person's possession or under the person's control in a building, vehicle, receptacle or place during the course of investigations conducted by the police before or after the arrest and charge of the person for the offence of which the person was convicted, that the property was derived, obtained or realised as a result of the commission by the person of the offence of which the person was convicted;

(c) where the evidence establishes that the value, after the commission of the offence, of all ascertainable property of a person convicted of the offence exceeds the value of all ascertainable property of that person prior to the commission of that offence, and the court is satisfied that the income of that person from sources unrelated to criminal activity of that person cannot reasonably account for the increase in value, that the value of the increase represents property which was derived, obtained or realised by the person directly or indirectly from the commission of the offence of which the person was convicted; and

(d) where the evidence establishes that the property was under the effective control of the person at the time of, or immediately after, the commission of the offence of which the person was convicted, that the property was derived, obtained or realised as a result of the commission by the person of the offence of which the person was convicted, and for purposes of this paragraph effective control has the same meaning as in section twenty-four of this Act.

(3) Where the court orders that property, other than money, be forfeited to the State, the court shall specify in the order the amount that it considers to be the value of the property at the time when the order is made.

(4) In considering whether a forfeiture order should be made under subsection (1), the court may have regard to—

(a) the rights or interests, if any, of third parties in the property;
(b) the gravity of the offence concerned;
(c) any hardship that may reasonably be expected to be caused to any person by the operation of the order; and
(d) the use that is ordinarily made of the property, or the use to which the property was intended to be put.

(5) Where the court makes a forfeiture order, the court may give directions necessary or convenient to give effect to the order.

11. Effect of forfeiture order

(1) Subject to subsection (2), where the court makes a forfeiture order against any property, the property vests absolutely in the State by virtue of the order.

(2) Where a forfeiture order is made against registrable property—

(a) the property vests in the State in equity but does not vest in the State at law until the applicable registration requirements have been complied with;
(b) the State is entitled to be registered as owner of the property; and
(c) the Attorney-General has power on behalf of the State to do, or authorise the doing of, anything necessary or convenient to obtain the registration of the State as owner, including the execution of any instrument required to be executed by a person transferring an interest in property of that kind.

(3) If a forfeiture order has been made against registrable property—

(a) a public prosecutor has the power on behalf of the State to do anything necessary or convenient to give notice of, or otherwise protect, the equitable interest of the State in the property; and
(b) any action by, or on behalf of, the State is not a dealing for the purpose of paragraph
(a) of subsection (4).

(4) Where the court makes a forfeiture order against property—

(a) the property shall not, except with the leave of the court and in accordance with any directions of the court, be disposed of, or otherwise dealt with, by or on behalf of the State, before the relevant appeal date; and
(b) if, after the relevant appeal date, the order has not been discharged, the property may be disposed of, and the proceeds applied or otherwise dealt with, in accordance with the direction of the Attorney-General.

(5) Without limiting the generality of paragraph (b) of subsection (4), the directions that may be given pursuant to that paragraph include a direction that property is to be disposed of in accordance with the provisions of any law specified in the direction.

(6) Money forfeited to the State under a forfeiture order shall be paid into the Fund.

(7) In this section—"registrable property" means property the title to which is passed by registration on a register; and "relevant appeal date" in relation to a forfeiture order made in consequence of a person's conviction of a serious offence, means—

    (a) the date on which the period allowed by the rules of court for the lodging of an appeal against a person's conviction, or for the lodging of an appeal against the making of a forfeiture order, expires without an appeal having been lodged, whichever is the later; or

    (b) where an appeal against a person's conviction or against the making of a forfeiture order is lodged, the date on which the appeal, or the later appeal, lapses in accordance with the rules of court or is finally determined.

12. Protection of third parties

(1) Where an application is made for a forfeiture order against any property, a person who claims an interest in the property may apply to the court, before the forfeiture order is made, for an order under subsection (2).

(2) Where a person applies to the court for an order under this subsection in respect of the person's interest in any property and the court is satisfied that—

    (a) the applicant has an interest in the property;

    (b) the applicant was not in any way involved in the commission of the offence in respect of which the forfeiture of the property is sought, or the forfeiture order against the property was made; and

    (c) the applicant—

        (i) had the interest before the serious offence occurred;

        (ii) acquired the interest during or after the commission of the offence, *bona fide* and for fair value, and did not know or could not reasonably have known at the time of the acquisition that the property was tainted property; the court may make an order declaring the nature, extent and value, as at the time when the order is made, of the applicant's interest.

(3) Subject to subsection (4), where a forfeiture order has already been made directing the forfeiture of any property, a person who claims an interest in the property may, before the end of the period of six months commencing on the day on which the forfeiture order is made, apply under this subsection to the court for an order under subsection (2).

(4) A person who had knowledge of an application for the forfeiture order before the order was made, or appeared at the hearing of the application, shall not be permitted to make an application under subsection (3), except with the leave of the court.

(5) A person who makes an application under subsection (1) or (3) shall give notice of the application to the Director of Public Prosecutions, who shall be a party to any proceedings in the application.

(6) An applicant or a public prosecutor may, in accordance with the rules of court, appeal against an order made under subsection (2).

(7) The Attorney-General shall, on application by any person who has obtained an order under subsection (2), and where the period allowed by the rules of court for appeal has expired or any appeal from that order has been determined—

    (a) direct that the property, or the part thereof to which the interest of the applicant relates, be returned to the applicant; or

    (b) direct that an amount equal to the value of the interest of the applicant, as declared in the order, be paid to the applicant.

(8) For the purposes of an application under subsection (1), where the person who claims an interest in the property is a minor, an application may be made on behalf of the minor by a guardian *ad litem* appointed by the court.

13. Discharge of forfeiture order on appeal and quashing of conviction

(1) Where the court makes a forfeiture order against property in reliance on a person's conviction of an offence and the conviction is subsequently quashed, the quashing of the conviction discharges the order: Provided that the discharge shall not take effect until the date on which the period allowed by

the rules of court for the lodging of an appeal expires without an appeal having been lodged, or the appeal has been finally determined in accordance with the rules of court.

(2) Where a forfeiture order against property is discharged as provided by subsection (1) or by the court hearing an appeal against the making of the order, any person who claims to have had an interest in the property immediately before the making of the forfeiture order may apply to the Attorney-General in writing, for the transfer of the interest to the person.

(3) The Attorney-General shall, on receipt of an application under subsection (2) from a person who had an interest in the property—

    (a) where the interest is vested in the State, give directions that the property or part thereof to which the interest of the applicant relates be transferred to the person; or

    (b) in any other case, direct that there be payable to the person an amount equal to the value of the interest as at the time the order is made.

(4) In the exercise of powers under this section and section twelve, the Attorney-General shall have the power to do, or authorise the doing of, anything necessary or convenient to effect the transfer or return of property, including the execution of any instrument and the making of an application for the registration of an interest in the property on any appropriate register.

14. Effect of discharge of forfeiture order

(1) If a forfeiture order is discharged, a person who claims to be the person in whom the property was vested immediately before the making of the forfeiture order may—

    (a) where the property is still vested in the State institution in which it was vested under the forfeiture order, by application in writing to the Attorney-General, request the return of the property; or

    (b) where the property is no longer vested in the State, apply to the court which made the forfeiture order for an order declaring the value, as at the time of making the order under this paragraph, of the property.

(2) On receipt of an application under paragraph (a) of subsection (1), the Attorney-General shall, subject to subsection (3), arrange for the property to be transferred to the applicant or other person or body as the Attorney-General determines and, for this purpose, the Attorney-General shall do, or authorise the doing of, anything necessary to carry out the transfer.

(3) On an application under paragraph (b) of subsection (1), the court may make an order declaring the value, as at the time of making the order, of the property.

(4) After an order is made under subsection (3), the applicant for the order may, by application in writing to the Attorney-General, request the payment of the amount declared by the order.

(5) On receipt of an application under subsection (4), the Attorney-General shall direct the State institution concerned to pay to the applicant or to such other person or body as the Attorney-General determines the amount declared by the order made under subsection (3) less the total amount paid by the State institution in respect of the property under any order.

15. Payment instead of forfeiture order

Where the court is satisfied that a forfeiture order should be made in respect of property of a person pursuant to section ten or seventeen but that the property or any part thereof or interest therein cannot be made subject to such an order and, in particular—

    (a) cannot, on the exercise of due diligence, be located;

    (b) has been transferred to a third party in circumstances that do not give rise to a reasonable inference that the title or interest was transferred for the purpose of avoiding the forfeiture of the property;

    (c) is located outside Zambia;

    (d) has been mixed with other property that cannot be divided without difficulty; or

    (e) has been transferred to a *bona fide* third-party purchaser for fair value without notice;

    the court may, instead of ordering the property or part thereof or interest therein to be forfeited, order the person to pay to the State an amount equal to the value of the property, part or interest.

16. Enforcement of order for payment instead of forfeiture

(1) An amount payable by a person to the State under section fifteen is a debt due to the State and shall be summarily recoverable as a civil debt.

(2) An order made under section fifteen may be enforced as if it were an order made in civil proceedings instituted by the State against the person to recover a debt due by the person to the State and the debt arising from the order shall be taken to be a judgment debt.

17. Forfeiture order where person has absconded

(1) Subject to subsection (3) of section nine, where an application is made to the court under subsection (1) of section ten for a forfeiture order against any tainted property because a person has absconded in connection with a serious offence and the court is satisfied that—
    (a) the property is tainted property in respect of the offence;(b)proceedings in respect of a serious offence committed in relation to that property were commenced; and(c)the accused charged with the offence referred to in paragraph (b) has absconded;
    the court may order that the property, or such of the property as is specified by the court in the order, be forfeited to the State.

(2) Subsections (2), (3), (4) and (5) of section ten and sections eleven and twelve shall apply with such modifications as are necessary to give effect to this section.

18. Registered foreign forfeiture orders

If a foreign forfeiture order is registered in the court under the Mutual Legal Assistance in Criminal Matters Act, this Division applies in relation to the order as if—*[Cap. 98]*

    (a) any reference to an appeal against the making of an order and to the relevant appeal date were omitted; and

    (b) a period of six weeks were substituted for the period of six months provided in subsection (3) of section twelve.

Division 3 - Confiscation orders

19. Confiscation order on conviction

(1) Subject to subsections (1) and (2) of section twenty, where a public prosecutor applies to the court for a confiscation order against a person in respect of that person's conviction of a serious offence, the court may, if it is satisfied that the person has benefited from that offence, order the person to pay into court an amount equal to the value of the person's benefits from the offence or such lesser amount as the court certifies in accordance with section twenty-two to be the amount that might be realised at the time the confiscation order is made.

(2) The court shall assess the value of the benefits derived by a person from the commission of an offence in accordance with sections twenty to twenty-three.

(3) The court shall not make a confiscation order under this section—
    (a) until the period allowed by the rules of court for the lodging of an appeal against conviction has expired without the appeal having been lodged; or
    (b) where an appeal against conviction has been lodged, until the appeal lapses in accordance with the rules of court or is finally determined.

20. Rules for determining benefit and assessing value

(1) Where a person obtains property as a result of, or in connection with the commission of, a serious offence, the person's benefit is the value of the property so obtained.

(2) Where a person derives an advantage as a result of, or in connection with the commission of, a serious offence, the person's advantage is deemed to be a sum of money equal to the value of the advantage so derived.

(3) The court, in determining whether a person has benefited from the commission of a serious offence or from that offence taken together with other serious offences and, if so, in assessing the value of the benefit, shall, unless the contrary is proved, deem—
    (a) all property appearing to the court to be held by the person on the day on which the application is made and all property appearing to the court to be held by the person at any time—
        (i) within the period between the day the offence, or the earliest offence, was committed and the day on which the application is made; or
        (ii) within the period of five years immediately before the day on which the application is made, whichever is the shorter; to be property that came into the possession or under the control of the person by reason of the commission of that offence or offences;
    (b) any expenditure by the person since the beginning of that period to be expenditure met out of payments received by the person as a result of, or in connection with, the commission of that offence or offences; or(c)any property received or is deemed to have been received by the person at any time as a result of, or in connection with, the commission by the person of that offence, or offences, to be property received by the person free of any interests therein.

(4) Where a confiscation order has previously been made against a person, in assessing the value of any benefit derived by the person from the commission of the serious offence in respect of which the order was made, the court shall leave out of account any of the person's benefits that are shown to the court to have been taken into account in determining the amount to be recovered under that order.

(5) If evidence is given at the hearing of the application that the value of the person's property at any time after the commission of the serious offence exceeded the value of the person's property before the commission of the offence, the court shall, subject to subsection (6), treat the value of the benefits derived by the person from the commission of the offence as being not less than the amount of the excess.

(6) If, after evidence of the kind referred to in subsection (5) is given, the person satisfies the court that the whole or part of the excess was due to causes unrelated to the commission of the offence, subsection (5) does not apply to the excess or, as the case may be, that part.

21. Statements relating to benefits from commission of serious offences

(1) Where—

    (a) a person has been convicted of a serious offence and the Director of Public Prosecutions tenders to the court a statement as to any matters relevant—

    (i) to determining whether the person has benefited from the offence or from any other serious offence of which the person is convicted in the same proceedings or which is taken into account in determining that person's sentences; or(ii)to an assessment of the value of the person's benefit from the offence or any other serious offence of which the person is so convicted in the same proceedings or which is so taken into account; and(b)a person accepts to any extent an allegation in the statement tendered under paragraph (a),

    the court may, for the purposes of so determining or making that assessment, treat the person's acceptance as conclusive of the matters to which it relates.

(2) Where a statement is tendered under paragraph (a) of subsection (1) and the court is satisfied that a copy of that statement has been served on any person, the court may require the person to indicate to what extent the person accepts each allegation in the statement and, so far as the person does not accept any allegation, to indicate any matter the person proposes to rely on.(3)Where any person fails in any respect to comply with a requirement under subsection (2), the person may be treated for the purposes of this section as having accepted every allegation in the statement, other than—

    (a) an allegation in respect of which the person has complied with the requirement; and(b)an allegation that the person has benefited from any serious offence or that any property or advantage was obtained by the person as a result of, or in connection with, the commission of the offence.(4)Where—

    (a)any person tenders to the court a statement as to any matters relevant to determining the amount that might be realised at the time the confiscation order is made; and(b)a public prosecutor accepts to any extent any allegation in a tendered statement;

    the court may, for the purposes of the determination, treat the acceptance of the public prosecutor as conclusive of the matters to which it relates.

(5) An allegation may be accepted or matter indicated for the purposes of this section either orally before the court or in writing in accordance with rules of court.(6)An acceptance by a person under this section that the person received any benefit from the commission of a serious offence is admissible in any proceedings for any offence.

22. Amount to be recovered under confiscation order

(1) Subject to subsection (2), the amount to be recovered in a person's case under a confiscation order shall be the amount which the court assesses to be the value of the person's benefit from the offence or, if more than one, all the offences in respect of which the order may be made.

(2) Where the court is satisfied as to any matter relevant to determining the amount which might be realised at the time the confiscation order is made, whether by an acceptance under section twenty-one or otherwise, the court may issue a certificate giving the court's opinion as to the matters concerned, and shall do so if satisfied that the amount that might be realised at the time the confiscation order is made is less than the amount that the court assesses to be the value of the person's benefit from the offence, or if more than one, all the offences in respect of which the confiscation order may be made.

23. Variation of confiscation orders

(1) Where—

    (a) the court makes a confiscation order in relation to an offence;(b)in calculating the amount of the confiscation order, the court took into account a forfeiture of property, a proposed forfeiture of property or a proposed forfeiture order in respect of property; and(c)an appeal against any forfeiture or forfeiture order is allowed or the proceedings for the proposed forfeiture order terminate without the proposed forfeiture order being made;

a public prosecutor may apply to the court for a variation of the confiscation order to increase the amount of the order by the value of the property and the court may, if it considers it appropriate to do so, vary the order accordingly.

(2) Where—

    (a) the court makes a confiscation order against a person in relation to an offence;(b)in calculating the amount of the confiscation order, the court took into account, in accordance with subsections (4) and (5) of section three, an amount of tax paid by the person; and(c)an amount is repaid or refunded to the person in respect of any tax;

a public prosecutor may apply to the court for a variation of the confiscation order to increase the amount of the order by the amount repaid or refunded and the court may, if it considers it appropriate to do so, vary the order accordingly.

24. Court may lift corporate veil

(1) In assessing the value of benefits derived by a person from the commission of an offence or offences, the court may treat as property of the person any property that, in the opinion of the court, is subject to the effective control of the person whether or not the person has—

    (a) any legal or equitable interest in the property; or(b)any right, power or privilege in connection with the property.

(2) Without limiting the generality of subsection (1), the court may have regard to—

    (a) shareholdings in, debentures over or directorships of a company that has an interest, whether direct or indirect, in the property, and for this purpose the court may order the investigation and inspection of the books of a named company;(b)a trust that has a relationship to the property; and(c)any relationship whatsoever between persons having an interest in the property, or in companies referred to in paragraph (a) or trusts referred to in paragraph (b), and other persons

(3) Where the court, for the purposes of making a confiscation order against a person, treats particular property as the person's property pursuant to subsection (1), the court may, on application by a public prosecutor, make an order declaring that the property is available to satisfy the order.(4) Where the court declares that a property is available to satisfy a confiscation order—

    (a) the order may be enforced against the property as if the property were property of the person against whom the order is made; and(b)a restraining order may be made in respect of the property as if the property were property of the person against whom the order is made. (5)Where a public prosecutor makes an application for an order under subsection (3) that any property is available to satisfy a confiscation order against a person—

    (a) the public prosecutor shall give written notice of the application to the person and to any other person who the public prosecutor has reason to believe may have an interest in the property; and(b)the person and that other person who claims an interest in the property may appear and adduce evidence at the hearing of the application.

25. Enforcement of confiscation orders

(1) An amount payable by a person to the State under a confiscation order is a debt due to the State and shall be summarily recoverable as a civil debt.

(2) A confiscation order against a person may be enforced as if it were an order made in civil proceedings instituted by the State against the person to recover a debt due by the person to the State and the debt arising from the order shall be taken to be a judgment debt.

26. Amounts paid in respect of registered foreign confiscation orders

Where a foreign confiscation order is registered in the court under the Mutual Legal Assistance in Criminal Matters Act, any amount paid, whether in Zambia or elsewhere, in satisfaction of the foreign confiscation order shall be taken to have been paid in satisfaction of the debt that arises by reason of the registration of the foreign confiscation order in the court.[Cap. 98]

Division 4 - Civil forfeiture orders

27. Application for restraining order for tainted property

(1) Where there are reasonable grounds to suspect that any property is property in respect of which a forfeiture order may be made under section thirty-one, a public prosecutor may apply to the court for a restraining order under subsection (2) against that property.

(2) An application for a restraining order may be made *ex parte* and shall be in writing and be accompanied by an affidavit stating—

    (a) a description of the property in respect of which the restraining order is sought;

    (b) the location of the property; and

    (c) the grounds for the belief that the property is tainted property for which a forfeiture order may be made under section thirty-one.

28. Prohibition from disposal, etc of tainted property

(1) Where a public prosecutor applies to the court for a restraining order against property and the court is satisfied that there are reasonable grounds for suspecting that the property is tainted property for which a forfeiture order may be made under section thirty-one, the court may make an order—

    (a) prohibiting any person from disposing of, or dealing with, the property or any part thereof or interest except in the manner specified in the order; and

    (b) at the request of the public prosecutor, where the court is satisfied that the circumstances so require, that the Attorney-General take custody of the property or any part thereof and manage or otherwise deal with all or any part of the property in accordance with the directions of the court.

(2) For the avoidance of doubt, the court may make an order under subsection (1) in respect of money or other property located in Zambia or elsewhere.

(3) Where the court gives the Attorney-General a direction under paragraph (b) of subsection (1), the Attorney-General may do anything that is reasonably necessary for preserving the property and for this purpose may exercise any power that the owner of the property could exercise and do so to the exclusion of the owner.

(4) Where a public prosecutor applies to the court for an order under subsection (1), a witness shall not be required to answer a question or to produce a document where the court is satisfied that answering the question or producing the document may prejudice the investigation of, or prosecution of a person for, an offence.

29. Application for non-conviction based forfeiture order for tainted property

A public prosecutor may apply to a court for an order forfeiting to the State all or any property that is tainted property.

30. Notice of application

Where a public prosecutor applies under section twenty-nine for a forfeiture order—

    (a) the public prosecutor shall give not less than thirty days written notice of the application to any person who is known to have an interest in the tainted property in respect of which the application is being made;

    (b) any person who claims an interest in the property in respect of which the application is made may appear and produce evidence at the hearing of the application; and

    (c) the court may, at any time before the final determination of the application, direct the public prosecutor to—

        (i) give notice of the application to any person who, in the opinion of the court, appears to have an interest in the property; and

        (ii) publish in the *Gazette* or a daily newspaper of general circulation in Zambia, a notice of the application.

31. Non-conviction based forfeiture order for tainted property

(1) Subject to subsection (2), where a public prosecutor applies to the court for an order under this section and the court is satisfied on a balance of probabilities that the property is tainted property, the court may

order that the property, or such of the property as is specified by the court in the order, be forfeited to the State.

(2) Where a person claiming an interest in property to which an application relates satisfies the court that the person—

   (a) has an interest in the property; and(b)did not acquire the interest in the property as a result of any serious offence carried out by the person and—

      (i) had the interest before any serious offence occurred; or(ii)acquired the interest for fair value after the serious offence occurred and did not know or could not reasonably have known at the time of the acquisition that the property was tainted property;

the court shall order that the interest shall not be affected by the forfeiture order, and the court shall declare the nature and extent of the interest in question.

(3) The court may, where it makes a forfeiture order or at any time thereafter, make any other orders that it considers appropriate, including orders for and with respect to facilitating the transfer of property.

(4) The validity of an order under subsection (1) is not affected by the outcome of criminal proceedings, or of an investigation with a view to institute such proceedings, in respect of an offence with which the property concerned is in some way associated.

(5) Sections six and seven, subsections (2), (3), (4) and (5) of section ten and sections eleven, twelve, fifteen, and sixteen shall apply with the appropriate modifications as are necessary to an application for a forfeiture order under this section.

Division 5 – General

32. Voiding of contract

A court may, before making a forfeiture order or confiscation order, set aside any conveyance or transfer of money or other property or interest therein that occurred in circumstances that give rise to a reasonable inference that the money, property or interest was conveyed or transferred for the purpose of avoiding the forfeiture order or confiscation order unless the conveyance or transfer was to a third party acting in good faith and without notice.

33. Proceedings civil, not criminal

(1) Any proceeding on an application for a restraining order, forfeiture order or confiscation order is not a criminal proceeding.

(2) Except in relation to an offence under this Act—

   (a) the rules of construction applicable only in relation to criminal law do not apply in the interpretation of this Act; and

   (b) the rules of evidence applicable in civil proceedings apply, and those applicable only in criminal proceedings do not apply, to proceedings under this Act.

34. Onus of proof

The applicant in any proceedings under this Act bears the onus of proving the matters necessary to establish the grounds for making the order applied for.

PART III
PROVISIONS FOR FACILITATING POLICE INVESTIGATIONS AND PRESERVING PROPERTY LIABLE TO FORFEITURE AND CONFISCATION ORDER

Division 1 - Powers of search and seizure

35. Warrant to search premises, etc. for tainted property

(1) A police officer may apply to a magistrate for a warrant to search premises for tainted property in the same way as a police officer may apply for the issue of a search warrant under the Criminal Procedure Code.[Cap. 88]

(2) Where an application is made under subsection (1), the magistrate may, subject to conditions, issue a search warrant under the Criminal Procedure Code and, subject to this Division, the warrant may be executed in the same manner as if it had been issued under the Criminal Procedure Code.[Cap. 88]

36. Defects in warrants

A search warrant is not invalidated by any defect, other than a defect which affects the substance of the warrant in a material particular.

37. Police may seize other tainted property

In the course of a search under a warrant issued under section thirty-five, a police officer may seize—
  (a) any property that the police officer believes, on reasonable grounds, to be tainted property in relation to any serious offence; or
  (b) any thing that the police officer believes, on reasonable grounds, will afford evidence as to the commission of a criminal offence;
  where the police officer believes, on reasonable grounds, that it is necessary to seize that property or thing in order to prevent its concealment, loss or destruction, or its use in committing, continuing or repeating the offence or any other offence.

38. Return of seized property

(1) Where any property has been seized under this Division, otherwise than because it may afford evidence of the commission of an offence, a person who claims an interest in the property may apply to the court for an order that the property be returned to the person.(2)Where a person makes an application under subsection (1) and the court is satisfied that—
  (a) the person is entitled to possession of the property;
  (b) the property is not tainted property in relation to the relevant offence; and
  (c) the person in respect of whose conviction, charging or proposed charging the seizure of the property was made has no interest in the property;
  the court shall order the police officer to return the property to the person and the police officer shall arrange for the property to be returned.
(3) Where—
  (a) any property has been seized under this Division, otherwise than because it may afford evidence as to the commission of an offence;

  (b) at the time when the property was seized, information had not been laid in respect of a relevant offence; and
  (c) at the end of a period of forty-eight hours after the time when the property was seized, information has not been laid in respect of a relevant offence;
  a police officer shall, subject to subsections (5) and (6), arrange for the property to be returned to the person from whose possession it was seized as soon as practicable after the end of that period.
(4) Where—
  (a) any property has been seized under this Division, otherwise than because it may afford evidence as to the commission of an offence; and(b)no forfeiture order has been made against the property within a period of fourteen days after the property was seized and the property is in the possession of a police officer at the end of that period;
  the police officer shall, subject to subsections (5) and (6), arrange for the property to be returned to the person from whose possession it was seized as soon as practicable after the end of that period.
(5) Where—
  (a) any property has been seized under this Division, otherwise than because it may afford evidence as to the commission of an offence;
  (b) but for this subsection, a police officer would be required to arrange for the property to be returned to a person as soon as practicable after the end of a particular period; and(c)before the end of that period, a restraining order is made in relation to the property; the police officer shall—
      (i) if the restraining order directs the Attorney-General to take custody and control of the property, arrange for the property to be given to the Attorney-General in accordance with the restraining order; or
      (ii) if the court that made the restraining order has made an order under subsection (6) in relation to the property, arrange for the property to be kept until it is dealt with under another provision of this Act.

444

(6) Where—

    (a) any property has been seized under this Division, otherwise than because it may afford evidence as to the commission of an offence;

    (b) a restraining order is made in relation to the property; and

    (c) at the time when the restraining order is made, the property is in the possession of a police officer;

the police officer may apply to the court that made the restraining order for an order that the police officer retain possession of the property and the court may, if satisfied that there are reasonable grounds for believing that the property may afford evidence as to the commission of a relevant offence or any other offence, make an order that the police officer is to retain the property for so long as the property is so required as evidence as to the commission of that offence.

(7) Where the police officer applies to the court for an order under subsection (6), a witness shall not be required to answer a question or to produce a document if the court is satisfied that the answering of the question or the production of the document may prejudice the investigation of, or the prosecution of a person for, an offence.

(8) Where any property has been seized under this Division and while the property is in the possession of the police officer, a forfeiture order is made in respect of the property, the police officer shall deal with a property as required by the order.

39. Appointment of administrator

The Attorney-General may appoint an administrator to administer property forfeited or subject to any order made or to be enforced under this Act.

40. Search for and seizure of tainted property in relation to foreign offences

(1) Where a police officer is authorised, under the Mutual Legal Assistance in Criminal Matters Act, to apply to a magistrate for a search warrant under this Act in relation to tainted property in respect of a foreign serious offence, the police officer may apply for the warrant accordingly and this Division applies to the application and to any warrant issued as a result of the application as if—*[Cap. 98]*

    (a) references in this Division to tainted property were references to tainted property in relation to a foreign serious offence;

    (b) references in this Division to a relevant offence were references to a relevant foreign serious offence;

    (c) references in this Division to seizure of property under this Division were references to seizure of property under a warrant issued under section thirty-five in respect of a foreign serious offence;

    (d) the reference in paragraph (c) of subsection (2) of section thirty-eight to the person in respect of whose conviction, charging or proposed charging the seizure of the property was made were a reference to the person who is believed or alleged to have committed the relevant foreign serious offence;

    (e) the reference in subsection (4) of section thirty-eight to a period of fourteen days were a reference to a period of thirty days;

    (f) the references in subsections (5) and (6) of section thirty-eight to the making of a restraining order in relation to seized property were references to—

        (i) the registration in the court under the Mutual Legal Assistance in Criminal Matters Act, of a foreign restraining order in relation to the seized property; or *[Cap. 98]*(ii)the making by the court under this Act of a restraining order in respect of the seized property in relation to the foreign serious offence;

    (g) the reference in subsection (8) of section thirty-eight to the making of a forfeiture order were a reference to the registration in the court under the Mutual Legal Assistance in Criminal Matters Act of a foreign forfeiture order; and*[Cap. 98]*(h)section thirty-seven and subsection (3) of section thirty-eight were omitted.

(2) If, in the course of searching under a warrant issued under section thirty-five, for tainted property in relation to a foreign serious offence, a police officer finds—

    (a) property that the police officer believes, on reasonable grounds, to be tainted property in relation to any foreign serious offence in respect of which a search warrant under section thirty-five is in force; or

(b) anything that the police officer believes, on reasonable grounds —

    (i) to be relevant to a criminal proceeding in the foreign country in respect of the foreign serious offence;
or

    (ii) will afford evidence as to the commission of a criminal offence; and the police officer believes, on reasonable grounds, that it is necessary to seize that property or thing in order to prevent its concealment, loss or destruction, or its use in committing, continuing or repeating the offence, the warrant shall be deemed to authorise the police officer to seize that property or thing.

Division 2 - Restraining orders

41. Application for restraining order

(1) Where there are reasonable grounds to suspect that any property is property in respect of which a forfeiture order may be made under sections ten or eighteen, a public prosecutor may apply to the court for a restraining order under subsection (3) against that property.

(2) Where there are reasonable grounds to suspect that a confiscation order may be issued under section nineteen, a public prosecutor may apply to the court for a restraining order under subsection (5) against any realisable property held by a person.

(3) An application for a restraining order may be made *ex parte* and shall be in writing.(4)An application under subsection (1) shall be accompanied by an affidavit stating—

  (a) a description of the property in respect of which the restraining order is sought;(b)the location of the property; and

  (c) the grounds for the belief that the property is tainted property for which a forfeiture order may be made under section ten or eighteen.

(5) An application under subsection (2) shall be accompanied by an affidavit stating—

  (a) a description of the property in respect of which the restraining order is sought;

  (b) the location of the property;(c)the grounds for the belief that the person who is suspected of having committed a serious offence has obtained a benefit directly or indirectly from the commission of the offence; and

  (d) where the application seeks a restraining order against property of a person other than the person who is suspected of having committed a serious offence, the grounds for the belief that the property is subject to the effective control of that person.

42. Restraining order

(1) Where a public prosecutor applies to the court for a restraining order against property under subsection (1) of section forty-one and the court is satisfied that there are reasonable grounds for suspecting that the property is tainted property, the court may make an order under subsection (3).

(2) Where a public prosecutor applies to the court for a restraining order against property under subsection (2) of section forty-one and the court is satisfied that—

  (a) there are reasonable grounds for suspecting that the person suspected of having committed a serious offence has derived a benefit directly or indirectly from the commission of the offence;(b)the property is the realisable property of the person; the court may make an order under subsection (3).

(3) Where satisfied under subsection (1) or (2), the court may make an order—

  (a) prohibiting the defendant or any person from disposing of, or dealing with, the property or any part thereof or interest except in the manner specified in the order; and

  (b) at the request of a public prosecutor, where the court is satisfied that the circumstances so require that the Attorney-General take custody of the property or any part thereof and manage or otherwise deal with all or any part of the property in accordance with the directions of the court.

(4) For the avoidance of doubt, the court may make an order under subsection (3) in respect of money or property located in Zambia or elsewhere.

(5) An order under subsection (1) may be made subject to conditions as the court thinks fit and, without limiting the generality of this section, may make provision for meeting, out of the property or a specified part of the property—

  (a) the person's reasonable living expenses, including the reasonable living expenses of the person's dependants and reasonable business expenses;

  (b) the person's reasonable expenses in defending a criminal charge and any proceedings under this Act; or(c)other specified debt incurred by the person in good faith;

(6) The court shall not make any provision under subsection (2) unless it is satisfied that the person cannot meet the expenses or debt concerned out of property that is not subject to a restraining order.

(7) In determining whether there are reasonable grounds for believing that property is subject to the effective control of the defendant, the court may have regard to the matters referred to in subsection (2) of section twenty-four.

(8) Where the Attorney-General is given a direction under paragraph (f) of subsection (1), the Attorney-General may do anything that is reasonably necessary for preserving the property and for this purpose may exercise any power that the owner of the property could exercise and do so to the exclusion of the owner.

(9) Where a public prosecutor applies to the court for an order under subsection (1), a witness shall not be required to answer a question or to produce a document if the court is satisfied that answering the question or producing the document may prejudice the investigation of, or prosecution of a person for, an offence.

(10) The court may make a restraining order whether or not there are reasonable grounds for believing that there is an immediate risk of the property being disposed of or otherwise dealt with.

(11) The court hearing an application for an order under subsection (1) may, before final determination of the application, and on the application of a public prosecutor, amend the application to include any other property upon being satisfied that the property was acquired after the application was originally made.

43. Undertaking by Attorney-General

(1) Before making an order under section forty-two, the court may require the Attorney-General to give an undertaking as to damages or costs, or both, in relation to the making and execution of the order.

(2) For the purposes of this section, the Director of Public Prosecutions may, after consultation with the Attorney-General, give to the court an undertaking with respect to the payment of damages or costs, or both, as

44. Notice of application for restraining order

(1) Subject to subsection (2), before making a restraining order, the court shall require notice to be given to, and may hear, any person who, in the opinion of the court, may have an interest in the property.

(2) Where the Director of Public Prosecutions so requests, the court shall consider an application without requiring notice to be given under subsection (1).

(3) A restraining order in accordance with subsection (2) ceases to have effect after fourteen days or such lesser period as the court specifies in the order.

(4) The court may, on application by the Director of Public Prosecutions, extend the period of operation of a restraining order made under subsection (2) and shall not consider the application without requiring notice to be given under subsection (1).

45. Service of restraining order

(1) Subject to subsection (2), a copy of a restraining order shall be served on a person affected by the order in such manner as the court directs or as prescribed by rules of court.

(2) Where the court is satisfied that it is in the public interest to do so it may order that service under subsection (1) be delayed for a specified period.

46. Further orders

(1) Where the court makes, or has made, a restraining order, the court may, on application by the Director of Public Prosecutions, a person whose property is the subject of the restraining order, in this section called "the owner", or the Attorney-General, if the restraining order directs the Attorney-General to take custody and control of property or, with the leave of the court, any other person, make any ancillary orders it considers appropriate.

(2) Without limiting the generality of subsection (1), an ancillary order may —
    (a) vary the property to which a restraining order relates;
    (b) vary any condition to which a restraining order is subject;
    (c) order the examination on oath before the court, of any person about the affairs of the owner or the defendant;
    (d) provide for the carrying out of any undertaking with respect to the payment of damages or costs given by the State in connection with the making of the restraining order;

    (e)   direct the owner or the defendant to give a specified person a statement on oath setting out the particulars of the property, or dealings with the property, as the Court thinks fit; or

    (f)   where the restraining order directs the Attorney-General to take custody and control of property—

        (i)   regulate the performance or exercise, of the Attorney-General's functions, duties or powers under the restraining order;

        (ii)   determine any question relating to the property;

        (iii)   direct a person to do any act or thing to enable the Attorney-General to take custody and control of the property;

        (iv)   where the restraining order provides that a person's reasonable expenses in defending a criminal charge be met out of the property, direct that the expenses be taxed as provided in the order before being met; or

        (v)   make provision for the payment to the Attorney-General out of the property of the costs, charges and expenses incurred in connection with the performance or exercise by the Attorney-General of functions, duties or powers under the restraining order.

(3)   Where a person who has an interest in property in respect of which a restraining order was made applies to the court for a variation of the order to exclude the person's interest from the order, the court shall grant the application if the court is satisfied—

    (a)   that the interest is not tainted property and that it cannot be required to satisfy a confiscation order; or

    (b)   that the applicant was not in any way involved in the commission of the offence in respect of which the restraining order was made and, where the applicant acquired the interest at the time of or after the commission, or alleged commission of, the offence, that the applicant acquired the interest—

        (i)   for sufficient consideration; and

        (ii)   without knowing, and in a circumstance such as not to arouse a reasonable suspicion, that the property was tainted property or that the property was a benefit obtained from or in connection with the commission of a serious offence; or

    (c)   in any case it is in the public interest to do so having regard to all the circumstances, including any financial hardship or other consequence of the interest remaining subject to the order.

(4)   An application under subsection (1) shall not be heard by the court unless the applicant has given to the other person who is entitled to make an application under subsection (1) in relation to the restraining order, notice in writing of the application.

(5)   The court may, require notice of the application to be given to, and hear, any person who, in the opinion of the court, appears to have an interest in the property.

(6)   Where a person is required, in accordance with an order under paragraphs (c) or (e) of subsection (2), to make or give a statement on oath, the person is not excused from making or giving the statement on the ground that the statement, or part of the statement, might tend to incriminate the person or make the person liable to forfeiture or a penalty but the statement, and any information, document or thing obtained as a direct or indirect consequence of the statement, is not admissible against the person in any criminal proceedings except a proceeding in respect of the falsity of the statement.

47. Attorney-General to satisfy confiscation order

(1)   Where—

    (a)   a confiscation order is made against a defendant's conviction of an offence; and

    (b)   a restraining order is made against any property of the defendant, or property of another person in relation to which an order under subsection (3) of section twenty-four is in force, in reliance on the defendant's conviction, or alleged commission, of the offence;

        the court may, upon the making of the later of the orders or, on application by a public prosecutor, while the restraining order remains in force, direct the Attorney-General to satisfy the confiscation order by a payment out of the property to the Fund.

(2)   The court may, for the purposes of enabling the Attorney-General to comply with a direction under subsection (1)—

    (a)   direct the Attorney-General to sell or otherwise dispose of the property or any part of the property as the court specifies; and

    (b)   order that the Attorney-General may execute, and do anything necessary to give validity and operation to, any deed or instrument in the name of a person who owns or has an interest in the property.

(3) Where the court makes an order under subsection (2), the execution of the deed or instrument by the Attorney-General has the same force and validity as if the deed or instrument had been executed by the person.

(4) The Attorney-General shall refrain from taking any action to sell any property pursuant to a direction under subsection (1) until the relevant appeal date.

(5) In this section "relevant appeal date", used in relation to a confiscation order made in consequence of a person's conviction of a serious offence, means—

(a) the date on which the period allowed by the rules of court for the lodging of an appeal against a person's conviction, or for the lodging of an appeal against the making of a confiscation order, expires without an appeal having been lodged, whichever is the later; or

(b) where an appeal against a person's conviction or against the making of a confiscation order is lodged, the date on which the appeal, or the later appeal, lapses in accordance with the rules of court or is finally determined.

48. Registration of restraining order

Where a restraining order applies to property of a particular kind and the provisions of any law provide for the registration of title to, or charges over, property of that kind, the authority responsible for administering that law may, on application by a public prosecutor, record on the register kept pursuant to those provisions the particulars of the restraining order and, if those particulars are so recorded, a person who subsequently deals with the property, for the purposes of section forty-nine, is deemed to have notice of the restraining order at the time of the dealing.

49. Contravention of restraining orders

(1) A person who knowingly contravenes a restraining order by disposing of, or dealing with, property that is subject to the restraining order commits a cognizable offence and is liable, upon conviction, to—

(a) in the case of a natural person, a fine not exceeding five hundred thousand penalty units or imprisonment for a period not exceeding five years, or to both; or

(b) in the case of a body corporate a fine not exceeding seven hundred thousand penalty units.

(2) Where a restraining order is made against any property and the property is disposed of, or dealt with, in contravention of the restraining order, and the disposition or dealing was either not for sufficient consideration or not in favour of a person who acted in good faith, a public prosecutor may apply to the court that made the restraining order for an order that the disposition or dealing be set aside.(3) The court may, where a public prosecutor makes an application under subsection (2) in relation to a disposition or dealing —

(a) set aside the disposition or dealing as from the day on which the disposition or dealing took place; or

(b) set aside the disposition or dealing as from the day of the order under this subsection; and declare the respective rights of any person who acquired interests in the property on or after the day on which the disposition or dealing took place and before the day of the order under this subsection.

50. Court may revoke restraining orders

(1) The court may, where the court has made a restraining order against a person's property, on application by the person, revoke the order if the applicant—

(a) where the applicant is a defendant, gives security satisfactory to the court for the satisfaction of any confiscation order that may be made against the person under this Act; or

(b) gives undertakings satisfactory to the court concerning the person's property.

(2) An applicant under subsection (1) shall give written notice of the application to a public prosecutor and, if the restraining order directed the Attorney-General to take control of the property, the Attorney-General.

51. When restraining order ceases to be in force

(1) Subject to subsection (2), a restraining order made in reliance on a person's conviction, or alleged commission, of a serious offence ceases to be in force, in whole or in part—

(a) where the order is made in reliance on the proposed charging of the person with the offence and the person is not so charged within a period of forty-eight hours after the making of the order, at the end of that period;

(b)   when the charge against the person is withdrawn or the person is acquitted of the charge;

(c)   when property subject to the order is used to satisfy a confiscation order which was made in reliance on the person's conviction of the offence;

(d)   when the court refuses an application for a confiscation order in reliance on the person's conviction of the offence; or

(e)   when property subject to the order is forfeited under section eleven or seventeen.

(2)   Notwithstanding subsection (1), a restraining order ceases to be in force at the end of six months from the date of the restraining order.

(3)   The court may, within the period referred to under subsection (1), on application by a public prosecutor, order that a restraining order shall continue in force until a specified time or event, where the court is satisfied that a forfeiture order may still be made in respect of the property or the property may be required to satisfy a confiscation order which has not yet been made.

(4)   A public prosecutor shall give a person written notice of an application under subsection (3) in relation to a restraining order in respect of any property of the person.

52.   Interim restraining order in respect of foreign serious offence

(1)   Notwithstanding the Mutual Legal Assistance in Criminal Matters Act, the Director of Public Prosecutions shall apply for a restraining order under this Act against any property of a person in respect of a foreign serious offence, and this Division applies to the application and to any restraining order made as a result of the application as if—*[Cap. 98]*

(a)   a reference in this Division to a serious offence were a reference to the foreign serious offence;

(b)   a reference in this Division to a person charged or about to be charged with a serious offence were a reference to a person against whom a criminal proceeding in respect of a foreign serious offence has commenced, or is reasonably believed to be about to commence, in a foreign country;

(c)   there were substituted for the words of paragraph (a) of subsection (1) of section forty-two the following words:" the defendant has been convicted of a foreign serious offence, or a criminal proceeding in respect of a foreign serious offence has commenced, or is reasonably believed to be about to commence, against the defendant in a foreign country";

(d)   there were substituted for the words of paragraph (b) of subsection (1) of section forty-two the following words:" where the defendant has not been convicted of a foreign serious offence, the offence which the defendant is believed to have committed and the grounds for that belief";

(e)   the reference in paragraph (b) of subsection (2) of section forty-two to a person's reasonable expenses in defending a criminal charge included a reference to the person's reasonable expenses in being represented in a criminal proceeding in a foreign country; and

(f)   paragraphs (c) and (f) of subsection (1) of section forty-two, paragraph (a) of subsection (3) of section forty-six and sections forty-seven, fifty and fifty-one were omitted.

(2)   Subject to subsections (3) and (4), a restraining order made in respect of a foreign serious offence ceases to have effect at the end of the period of thirty days commencing on the day on which the order is made.

(3)   Where the court makes a restraining order in respect of a foreign serious offence, it may, on application made by a public prosecutor before the end of the period referred to in subsection (2), extend the period of operation of the restraining order.

(4)   Where—

(a)   a restraining order against property is made in respect of a foreign serious offence; and

(b)   before the end of the period referred to in subsection (2), including that period as extended under subsection (3), a foreign restraining order against the property is registered in the court under the Mutual Legal Assistance in Criminal Matters Act; the restraining order referred to in paragraph (a) ceases to have effect upon the registration of the foreign restraining order referred to in paragraph (b).*[Cap. 98]*

53.   General provision on registered foreign restraining order

Where a foreign restraining order is registered in the court under the Mutual Legal Assistance in Criminal Matters Act, this Division applies to the order as if—

(a)   section forty-six, subsections (3) and (4) of section forty-seven and sections fifty and fifty-one were omitted;

(b)   a reference in sections forty-five, forty-seven, forty-eight or forty-nine to a restraining order included a reference to an order under section fifty-four; and

(c)   the reference in subsection (1) of section forty-seven to the making of a restraining order were a reference to the registration by the court of a foreign restraining order under the Mutual Legal Assistance in Criminal Matters Act and the making of an order under section fifty-four.

[Cap. 98]

54. Court may direct Attorney-General to take custody, etc of property

(1) Where a foreign restraining order against any property is registered in the court under the Mutual Legal Assistance in Criminal Matters Act, the court may, upon application by the Director of Public Prosecutions, order the Attorney-General to take custody and control of the property or part thereof as is specified in the court's order and to manage or deal with all or any part of the property in accordance with the directions of the court.*[Cap. 98]*

(2) Before making an order under subsection (1), the court shall require notice to be given to, and may hear, any person who, in the opinion of the court, has an interest in the property.

(3) Where the Attorney-General is given an order under subsection (1) in relation to any property, the Attorney-General may do anything that is reasonably necessary for preserving the property and for this purpose may exercise any power that the owner of the property could exercise and do so to the exclusion of the owner.

(4) Where an order is made under subsection (1) in respect of property of a person, in this subsection called the "respondent", the court may, at the time when it makes the order or any later time, order —

    (a) the respondent to give the Attorney-General a statement on oath setting out such particulars of the property, or dealings with the property, as the court thinks proper;

    (b) the performance or exercise of the Attorney-General's functions, duties or powers under the restraining order;(c)the determination of any question relating to the property;(d)where a registered foreign restraining order provides that a person's reasonable expenses in defending a criminal charge be met out of the property, that expenses be taxed as provided in the order before being met; or(e)the payment to the Attorney-General out of the property of the costs, charges and expenses incurred in connection with the performance or exercise by the Attorney-General of functions, duties or powers under the restraining order.

55. Undertakings relating to registered foreign restraining orders

Where —

    (a) a foreign restraining order against any property is registered in the court under the Mutual Legal Assistance in Criminal Matters Act; or*[Cap. 98]*

    (b) the court makes an order under section fifty-four in respect of any property;

    (c) the court may, upon application by a person claiming an interest in the property, make an order as to the giving, or carrying out, of an undertaking by the Attorney-General on behalf of the State, with respect to the payment of damages or costs in relation to the registration, making or operation of the order.

56. Time when registered foreign restraining order ceases to be in force

A foreign restraining order registered in the court under the Mutual Legal Assistance in Criminal Matters Act ceases to be in force when the registration is cancelled in accordance with that Act or any other law.

[Cap. 98]

Division 3 - Production orders and other powers

57. Production and inspection orders

(1) Where a police officer has reasonable grounds for suspecting that a person has possession or control of a property-tracking document, the police officer may apply to the court in Chambers in accordance with subsection (2) for an order under subsection (5) against the person suspected of having possession or control of the document.

(2) An application under subsection (1) shall be made *ex parte* and shall be in writing and be accompanied by an affidavit.

(3) Where a police officer applies for an order under subsection (5) and includes in the affidavit a statement to the effect that the officer has reasonable grounds to believe that —

    (a) the person who, was convicted of the offence, or is believed to have committed the offence, derived a benefit, directly or indirectly, from the commission of the offence; and(b) property specified in the affidavit is subject to the effective control of the person referred to in paragraph (a);

the court may treat any document relevant to identifying, locating or quantifying that property as a property-tracking document in relation to the offence for the purposes of this section.

(4) In determining whether to treat a document, under subsection (3), as a property-tracking document in relation to an offence, the court may have regard to the matters referred to in subsection (2) of section twenty-four.

(5) Notwithstanding any law which prohibits disclosure of information of a particular type, where an application is made under subsection (1) the court may, if satisfied that there are reasonable grounds for doing so, order the person to—

(a) produce to a police officer, at a specified time and place, any documents of the kind referred to in subsection (1) that are in the person's possession or control; or

(b) make available to a police officer for inspection, at a specified time or times, any documents that are in the person's possession or control.

58. Scope of police powers under production order, etc.

(1) Where a document is produced to a police officer, or made available to a police officer for inspection, pursuant to an order under section fifty-seven, the police officer may—

(a) inspect the document;

(b) take extracts from the document;

(c) make copies of the document; or

(d) in the case of an order under paragraph (a) of subsection (5) of section fifty-seven, retain the document if, and for so long as, retention of the document is reasonably necessary for the purposes of this Act.

(2) Where a police officer retains a document pursuant to an order under section fifty-seven, the police officer shall—

(a) give the person to whom the order was addressed a copy of the document certified by the police officer in writing to be a true copy of the document retained; and

(b) unless the person has received a copy of the document under paragraph (a), permit the person to—

(i) inspect the document;

(ii) take extracts from the document; or

(iii) make copies of the document.

59. Evidential value of information

(1) Where a person produces or makes available a document pursuant to an order under section fifty-seven, the production or making available of the document, or any information, document or thing obtained as a direct or indirect consequence of the production or making available of the document, is not admissible against the person in any criminal proceedings except a proceeding for an offence under section sixty-one.

(2) For the purposes of subsection (1), proceedings on an application for a restraining order, a forfeiture order or a confiscation order are not criminal proceedings.

(3) A person is not excused from producing or making available a document when required to do so by an order under section fifty-seven on the ground that—

(a) the production or making available of the document might tend to incriminate the person or make the person liable to a penalty; or

(b) the production or making available of the document would be in breach of an obligation, whether imposed by any law or otherwise, of the person not to disclose the existence or contents of the document.

60. Variation of production order

Where a court makes a production order requiring a person to produce a document to a police officer, the person may apply to the court for a variation of the order and if the court hearing the application is satisfied that the document is essential to the business activities of the person, the court may vary the production order so that it requires the person to make the document available to a police officer for inspection.

61. Failure to comply with production order

(1) Where a person is required by a production order to produce a document to a police officer or make a document available to a police officer for inspection, the person commits an offence if the person—

(a) contravenes the order without reasonable excuse; or

(b) in purported compliance with the order produces or makes available a document known to the person to be false or misleading in a material particular without—

    (i) indicating to the police officer to whom the document is produced or made available that the document is false or misleading and the respect in which the document is false or misleading; and

    (ii) providing correct information to the police officer if the person is in possession of, or can reasonably acquire, the correct information.

(2) A person who contravenes subsection (1) commits an offence and is liable, upon conviction, to—

(a) if the offender is a natural person, a fine not exceeding five hundred thousand penalty units or imprisonment for a term not exceeding five years, or to both; or

(b) if the offender is a body corporate, a fine not exceeding seven hundred thousand penalty units.

62. Search warrant to facilitate investigation

(1) Where—

(a) a person is convicted of a serious offence and a police officer has reasonable grounds for suspecting that there is in any premises a property-tracking document in relation to the offence; or(b)a police officer has reasonable grounds for suspecting that a person has committed a serious offence and there is in any premises a property-tracking document in relation to the offence;

the police officer may apply to a court for a warrant under subsection (4) to search the premises for the document.

(2) Where a police officer applies for a warrant under subsection (4) in respect of an offence and includes in the affidavit a statement to the effect that the officer has reasonable grounds to believe that—

(a) the person who was convicted of the offence, or who is believed to have committed the offence, derived a benefit, directly or indirectly, from the commission of the offence; and

(b) property specified in the affidavit is subject to the effective control of the person referred to in paragraph (a);

the court may treat any document relevant to identifying, locating or quantifying that property as a property-tracking document in relation to the offence for the purposes of this section.

(3) In determining whether to treat a document, under subsection (2), as a property-tracking document in relation to an offence, the court may have regard to the matters referred to in subsection (2) of section twenty-four.

(4) Subject to subsection (5), and notwithstanding any law which prohibits disclosure of information of a particular type, where an application is made under subsection (1) for a warrant to search premises for a property-tracking document, the court may, issue a warrant of the kind and in the same manner, and subject to the same conditions, under the Criminal Procedure Code and, subject to this Division, the warrant may be executed in the same manner as if it had been issued under the Criminal Procedure Code.*[Cap. 88]*

(5) A court shall not issue a search warrant under subsection (4) unless the court is satisfied that—

(a) it would not be appropriate to make a production order in respect of the document; or

(b) the investigation for the purposes of which the search warrant is being sought might be seriously prejudiced if the police officer does not gain immediate access to the document without notice to any person.

(6) Where a police officer enters premises in execution of a warrant issued under this section, the police officer may seize and retain—

(a) any document which the officer has reasonable grounds to believe is relevant to the investigation for the purpose of which the warrant was issued; or

(b) anything that the police officer believes, on reasonable grounds, will afford evidence as to the commission of a criminal offence.

63. Production orders and search warrants in relation to foreign offences

(1) Where under the Mutual Legal Assistance in Criminal Matters Act—*[Cap. 98]*

(a) a police officer is authorised to apply to a court for a search warrant under this Act in relation to a property-tracking document in respect of a foreign serious offence, the police officer may apply for the warrant accordingly; and

(b) the Attorney-General may apply to a court for a production order under this Act in respect of a foreign serious offence, the Attorney-General may apply for the order accordingly;

(c)   and this Division applies to the application and to any order or warrant issued as a result of the application as if a reference in this Division to a serious offence were a reference to a foreign serious offence.

(2)   Where a police officer takes possession of a document under a warrant issued, or the Director of Public Prosecutions takes possession of a document under a production order made in respect of a foreign serious offence, the police officer or the Director of Public Prosecutions may retain the document for a period not exceeding one month pending a written direction from the Attorney-General as to the manner in which the document is to be dealt with, which may include a direction that the document is to be sent to an authority of the foreign country that requested the issue of the warrant.

Division 4 - Monitoring orders

64.   Monitoring orders

(1)   The Director of Public Prosecutions may apply to a court in chambers under subsection (2) for a monitoring order directing a financial institution to give information to a police officer.

(2)   An application under subsection (1) shall be made *ex parte* and shall be in writing and be accompanied by an affidavit.

(3)   A monitoring order shall direct a financial institution to give information obtained by the financial institution about transactions conducted through an account held by a particular person with the financial institution.

(4)   A monitoring order shall apply in relation to transactions conducted during the period specified in the order, being a period commencing not earlier than the day on which notice of the order is given to the financial institution and ending not later than three months after the date of the order.

(5)   A court shall not make a monitoring order unless the court is satisfied that there are reasonable grounds for suspecting that—
   (a)   the person in respect of whose account the information is sought—
      (i)   has committed, or is about to commit, a serious offence or a foreign serious offence;(ii)   was involved in the commission, or is about to be involved in the commission, of a serious offence or a foreign serious offence; or
      (iii)   has benefited directly or indirectly, or is about to benefit directly or indirectly, from the commission of a serious offence or a foreign serious offence; or
   (b)   the account is related to or is being used for the purposes of the commission of a serious offence or a foreign serious offence.

(6)   A monitoring order shall specify—
   (a)   the name or names in which the account is believed to be held;
   (b)   the class of information that the financial institution is required to give; and
   (c)   the name of the police officer to whom the information is to be given, and the manner in which the information is to be given.

(7)   Where a financial institution that has been given notice of a monitoring order knowingly—
   (a)   contravenes the order; or
   (b)   provides false or misleading information in purported compliance with the order;
      the financial institution commits an offence and is liable, upon conviction, to a fine not exceeding seven hundred thousand penalty units.

(8)   A reference in this section to a transaction conducted through an account includes a reference to—
   (a)   the making of a fixed term deposit;
   (b)   in relation to a fixed term deposit, the transfer of the amount deposited, or any part of it, at the end of the term; and
   (c)   the opening, existence or use of a deposit box held by the financial institution.

65.   Monitoring orders not to be disclosed

(1)   A financial institution that is, or has been, subject to a monitoring order shall not disclose the existence or the operation of the order to any person except—
   (a)   the Commissioner of Police or a police officer authorised in writing by the Commissioner of Police to receive the information;
   (b)   an officer or agent of the financial institution, for the purpose of ensuring that the order is complied with; or
   (c)   a legal practitioner, for the purpose of obtaining legal advice or representation in relation to the order.

(2) A person referred to in paragraph (a), (b) or (c) of subsection (1) to whom a disclosure of the existence or operation of a monitoring order has been made, whether in accordance with subsection (1) or a previous application of this subsection or otherwise, shall not —

   (a) disclose the existence or operation of the order except to another person referred to in paragraphs (a), (b) or (c) of subsection (1) for the purposes of—

   (i) if the disclosure is made by a police officer, the performance of that person's duties;

   (ii) if the disclosure is made by an officer or agent of the financial institution, ensuring that the order is complied with or obtaining legal advice or representation in relation to the order; or

   (iii) if the disclosure is made by a legal practitioner, giving legal advice or making representations in relation to the order; or

   (b) where the person is no longer a person referred to in paragraphs (a), (b) or (c) of subsection (1), make a record of, or disclose, the existence or the operation of the order in any circumstances.

(3) Nothing in subsection (2) prevents the disclosure by a person referred to in paragraph (a) of subsection (1) of the existence or operation of a monitoring order—

   (a) for the purposes of, or in connection with, legal proceedings; or

   (b) in the course of proceedings before a court.

(4) A person referred to in paragraph (a) of subsection (1) shall not be required to disclose to any court the existence or operation of a monitoring order.

(5) A person who contravenes subsection (1) or (2) commits an offence and is liable, upon conviction, to—

   (a) if the person is a natural person, a fine not exceeding five hundred thousand penalty units or imprisonment for a term not exceeding five years, or to both; or

   (b) if the person is a body corporate, a fine not exceeding seven hundred thousand penalty units.

(6) A reference in this section to disclosing the existence or operation of a monitoring order to a person includes a reference to disclosing information to the person from which the person could reasonably be expected to infer the existence or operation of the monitoring order.

Division 5 - Obligations of financial institutions

66. Register of original documents

(1) Where a financial institution is required by law to release an original of a document before the end of the minimum retention period applicable to the document, the financial institution shall retain a complete copy of the document until the period has ended or the original document is returned, whichever occurs first.

(2) A financial institution shall maintain a register of documents released under subsection (1).

(3) A financial institution that contravenes subsection (1) or (2) commits an offence and is liable, upon conviction, to a fine not exceeding seven hundred thousand penalty units.

Division 6 - Disclosure of information held by Government departments

67. Direction to disclose information

(1) Notwithstanding any provision in any other law, the Attorney-General may direct the person in charge of any Government department or statutory body to disclose a document or information which is in the possession or under the control of that person or to which that person may reasonably have access, not being a document readily available to the public, if the Attorney-General is satisfied that the information is relevant to—

   (a) establishing whether a serious offence has been, or is being, committed; or

   (b) the making, or proposed or possible making, of an order under Part II or III of this Act.

(2) Where the Attorney-General directs disclosure of information under subsection (1), the person shall disclose the document or information to the Director of Public Prosecutions or a police officer authorised by the Director of Public Prosecutions.

68. Further disclosure of information and documents

(1) A person to whom information has been disclosed under section sixty-seven shall not further disclose the information except and for the purpose of—

   (a) the investigation, prosecution, or proposed or possible prosecution, of a person for a serious offence; or(b)an investigation relating to proceedings, or proposed or possible proceedings, for the making of an order under this Act or an investigation relating to the making, or proposed or possible making, of such an order.

(2) A person to whom information has been disclosed under subsection (1) or this subsection, shall not disclose the information to another person except for the purpose referred to in paragraphs (a) and (b) of subsection (1).

(3) Where information is communicated to a person under section sixty-seven, or subsection (1) or (2), the person shall not—

    (a) voluntarily give the information in evidence in a proceeding before the court other than a proceeding referred to in paragraph (a) or (b) of subsection (1); and(b)be required to communicate the information to the court.

(4) A person who contravenes this section commits an offence and is liable, upon conviction, to a fine not exceeding two hundred thousand penalty units or imprisonment for a term not exceeding two years, or to both.

69. Evidential value of copies

Where any document is examined or provided under section sixty-seven, the person by whom it is examined or to whom it is provided, or any officer or person authorised for the purpose by the person in charge of the relevant Government department or statutory body, may make or cause to be made one or more copies thereof and any copy purporting to be certified by the person in charge of the relevant Government department or statutory body to be a copy made pursuant to this section is evidence of the nature and content of the original document and has the same probative value as the original document would have had if it had been proved in the ordinary way.

PART IV
DISPOSAL ORDERS

70. Disposal orders

(1) Where an application is made to a court under subsection (1) of section nineteen for an order in respect of a particular property, the court may order that the property be forfeited to the State and destroyed or disposed of in such manner as it thinks fit.

(2) A Court may give directions that are necessary to give effect to a disposal order made by it.

PART V
OFFENCES

71. Possession of property suspected of being proceeds of crime

(1) A person who, after the commencement of this Act, receives, possesses, conceals, disposes of or brings into Zambia any money, or other property, that may reasonably be suspected of being proceeds of crime commits an offence and is liable upon conviction to—

    (a) if the offender is a natural person, imprisonment for a period not exceeding five years; or(b)if the offender is a body corporate, a fine not exceeding seven hundred thousand penalty units.

(2) It is a defence under this section, if a person satisfies the court that the person had no reasonable grounds for suspecting that the property referred to in the charge was derived or realised, directly or indirectly, from any unlawful activity.

(3) The offence under subsection (1) is not predicated on proof of the commission of a serious offence or foreign serious offence.

72. Conduct by directors, servants or agents

(1) Where it is necessary, for the purposes of this Act, to establish the state of mind of a body corporate in respect of conduct engaged in, or deemed by subsection (2) to have been engaged in, by the body corporate, it is sufficient to show that a director, servant or agent by whom the conduct was engaged in within the scope of the director's, servant's or agent's actual or apparent authority, had that state of mind.

(2) Any conduct engaged in on behalf of a body corporate—

    (a) by a director, servant or agent of the body corporate within the scope of the director's, servant's or agent's actual or apparent authority; or

(b) by any other person at the direction or with the consent or agreement, whether express or implied of a director, servant or agent of the body corporate, where the giving of the direction, consent or agreement is within the scope of the actual or apparent authority of the director, servant or agent;
is deemed, for the purposes of this Act, to have been engaged in by the body corporate.

(3) Where it is necessary, for the purposes of this Act, to establish the state of mind of a person in relation to conduct deemed by subsection (4) to have been engaged in by the person, it is sufficient to show that a servant or agent of the person, being a servant or agent by whom the conduct was engaged in within the scope of the actual or apparent authority of the servant or agent, had that state of mind.

(4) Conduct engaged in on behalf of a person other than a body corporate—
(a) by a servant or agent of the person within the scope of the servant's or agent's actual or apparent authority; or
(b) by any other person at the direction or with the consent or agreement, whether express or implied, of a servant or agent, of the person, where the giving of the direction, consent or agreement is within the scope of the actual or apparent authority of the servant or agent; is deemed, for the purposes of this Act, to have been engaged in by the person.

(5) A reference in this section to the state of mind of a person includes a reference to the knowledge, intention or purpose of the person and the person's reasons for the person's intention or purpose.

PART VI
FORFEITED ASSESTS FUND

73. Establishment of Forfeited Assets Fund

(1) There is hereby established the Forfeited Assets Fund for the purposes of receiving credits from the proceeds of convictions of serious offences and payments made or debts recovered under this Act.

(2) The Minister may, by statutory instrument, provide for the administration, management and operation of the Fund.

74. Credits to Fund

There shall be credited to the Fund amounts equal to—
(a) proceeds of forfeiture orders;
(b) proceeds of confiscation orders;
(c) money paid under section fifteen;
(d) money paid to the Republic of Zambia by a foreign country, under a treaty or arrangement or otherwise, for providing mutual assistance in criminal matters; and
(e) money, other than money referred to in paragraph (d), paid to the Republic of Zambia by a foreign country in connection with assistance provided by the Republic of Zambia in relation to the recovery by that country of the proceeds of unlawful activity or the investigation or prosecution of unlawful activity.

75. Shared confiscated property with foreign countries to be credited to Fund

(1) The Attorney-General may enter into an arrangement with the competent authorities of a foreign country for the reciprocal sharing with that country of such part of any property realised—
(a) in the foreign country, as a result of action taken by the Attorney-General pursuant to a forfeiture or confiscation order; or
(b) in Zambia, as a result of action taken in Zambia pursuant to a forfeiture or confiscation order.

(2) Any proceeds or benefits of crime—
(a) forfeited or confiscated in a foreign country pursuant to a request by Zambia; or
(b) forfeited or confiscated in Zambia pursuant to a request by a foreign country; to the extent available under any sharing of confiscated property arrangement or otherwise, shall be credited to the Fund.

76. Payments from Fund

(1) The purposes of the Fund are to—
(a) make such payments to foreign countries as the Minister, with the approval of the Minister responsible for finance, considers appropriate under an approved programme;

(b) make payments under a programme approved by the Minister under section seventy-seven and approved by the Minister responsible for finance;

(c) make such payments as the Minister considers necessary to satisfy Zambia's obligation in respect of

(i) a registered foreign forfeiture order; or

(ii) a registered foreign confiscation order; with the approval of the Minister responsible for finance;

(d) make payments, as directed, under section fourteen; and

(e) make payments for the purposes of the administration of the Fund.

(2) Any payment out of the Fund is deemed to be an appropriation by law.

77. Programmes for expenditure on enforcement, etc

(1) The Minister may, with the approval of the Minister responsible for finance, in writing, approve a programme for the expenditure in a particular financial year of money standing to the credit of the Fund.

(2) The expenditure under subsection (1) shall be approved for one or more of the following purposes: (a)measures for the enforcement of this Act, and the Mutual Legal Assistance in Criminal Matters Act;[Cap. 98]

(b) assets and the provision of services to strengthen law enforcement measures relevant to the Acts referred to in paragraph (a) and related crime prevention measures; and

(c) any priority health, education or development programmes approved with the relevant responsible minister.

PART VII
GENERAL PROVISIONS

78. Standard of proof

Save as otherwise provided in this Act, any question of fact to be decided by the court in proceedings under this Act is to be decided on the balance of probabilities.

79. Costs

(1) Where—

(a) a person brings, or appears at, a proceeding under this Act before a court in order—

(i) to prevent a forfeiture, confiscation or restraining order from being made against property of the person; or

(ii) to have property of the person excluded from a forfeiture, confiscation or restraining order;

(b) the person is successful in any of the proceedings referred to under paragraph (a), and(c) the court is satisfied that the person was not involved in any way in the commission of the offence in respect of which the forfeiture, confiscation or restraining order was sought or made; the court may order the State to pay all costs reasonably incurred by the person in connection with the proceedings or such part of those costs as is determined by the court.

(2) If upon the determination of a proceeding under this Act, the court is of the opinion that the charge was frivolous or vexatious, the court may order the person to pay the costs reasonably incurred by the State in connection with the proceedings or such part of those costs as is determined by the court.

80. Operation of other laws not affected

Nothing in this Act prejudices, limits or restricts—

(a) the operation of any other law which provides for the forfeiture of property or the imposition of penalties or fines;

(b) the remedies available to the State apart from this Act, for the enforcement of its rights and the protection of its interests; or

(c) any power of search or any power to seize or to detain property which is exercisable by a police officer apart from this Act.

81. Appeals

A person aggrieved by a decision made under this Act, may appeal against such decision.

82. No criminal or civil liability for compliance

(1) It shall not be a breach of professional confidentiality for a legal practitioner or any other person to comply with any order or direction of the court made under this Act.

(2) No proceedings for breach of professional confidentiality may be instituted against a legal practitioner or any other person who in good faith complies with an order or direction of the court in accordance with this Act.

83. Rules

The Chief Justice may, by statutory instrument, make rules of court for the better carrying into effect of the provisions of this Act and in particular prescribing anything which by any of those provisions is to be prescribed.

84. Regulations

The Minister may, by statutory instrument, make regulations to give effect to the provisions of this Act.

THE PLEA NEGOTIATIONS AND AGREEMENT ACT NO 20 OF 2010

ARRANGMENT OF SECTIONS

PART I

PRELIMINARY

PART II
PLEA NEGOTIATIONS

PART III
PLEA AGREEMENTS

PART IV
GENERAL PROVISIONS

Gates on Evidence: Zambian Theory and Practice

SCHEDULE

GOVERNMENT OF ZAMBIA

Date of Assent: 13th April, 2010

An Act to provide for the introduction and implementation of plea negotiations and plea agreements in the criminal justice system and for matters connected with, or incidental to, the foregoing.

Enactment

ENACTED by the Parliament of Zambia.

PART I
PRELIMINARY

Short title and commencement

1. This Act may be cited as the Plea Negotiations and Agreements Act, 2010, and shall come into operation on such date as the Minister may, by statutory instrument, appoint.

Interpretation

2. In this Act, unless the context otherwise requires-
    "court" means a High Court or a subordinate court;
    "legal practitioner" has the meaning assigned to it in the Legal Practitioners Act;
    "plea agreement" means an agreement made pursuant to section four;
    "plea negotiation" means any negotiation carried out between an accused person or the accused person's legal representative, and a public prosecutor in relation to the accused person pleading guilty to a lesser offence than the offence charged or to one of multiple charges in return for any concession or benefit in relation to which charges are to be proceeded with;
    "public prosecutor" has the meaning assigned to it in the Criminal Procedure Code; and
    "victim" in relation to an offence, means a person who has suffered actual physical bodily harm, loss of any kind, mental illness or mental shock as a direct result of an act or omission involved in the offence;

Declaration of certain existing rights

3. (1) Nothing in this Act affects the right of an accused person to plead guilty to a charge without entering into any plea negotiation or a plea agreement.
    (2) Except as expressly agreed by a public prosecutor in a plea agreement, nothing in this Act affects the powers conferred upon the public prosecutor under the Constitution or any other written law.

PART II
PLEA NEGOTIATIONS

Plea negotiation

4. (1) Subject to section six, where a public prosecutor considers it desirable in any case, or where the circumstances of the case so warrant, the public prosecutor may, at any time before judgment and in accordance with the provisions of this Act, enter into a plea negotiation with the accused person for the purpose of reaching an agreement in accordance with the provisions of subsection (3), for the disposition of any charge against the accused person.
    (2) An accused person may, at any time before judgment and in accordance with the provisions of this Act, enter into a plea negotiation with a public prosecutor for the purpose of reaching an agreement in accordance with the provisions of subsection (3), for the disposition of any charge against the accused person.

(3)   An agreement under subsection (1) shall require that-
   (a)   the accused person undertakes to-
       (i)   make a guilty plea to an offence which is disclosed on the facts on which the charge against the accused person is based; and
       (ii)   fulfil the accused person's other obligations specified in the agreement; and
   (b)   a public prosecutor, having regard to the accused person's undertaking under paragraph (a) agrees to-
       (i)   take a course of action consistent with the exercise of the powers specified in section five; and
       (ii)   fulfil the other obligations of the State specified in the agreement.

Exercise by public prosecutor of certain powers

5.   The powers of a public prosecutor referred to in subparagraph (i) of paragraph (b) of subsection (3) of section four are to-
   (a)   withdraw or discontinue the original charge against the accused person; or
   (b)   accept the plea of the accused person to a lesser offence, whether originally included or not, than that charged.

Legal representation

6.   (1)   Notwithstanding any other provision to the contrary in any other law, a public prosecutor shall, before commencing any plea negotiation, inform the accused person of the accused person's right to representation by a legal practitioner of the accused person's choice and of the right to apply for legal aid in respect of the negotiations.
   (2)   Plea negotiations shall be held by a public prosecutor with the accused person only through the accused person's legal representative.

PART III
PLEA AGREEMENTS

Plea agreement

7.   A plea agreement that is brought before a court shall-
   (a)   be in writing;
   (b)   contain the information set out in the Schedule; and
   (c)   be signed by a public prosecutor, the accused person and the accused person's legal representative in each other's presence.

Victim to be informed of plea agreement

8.   (1)   Subject to section seventeen, where a plea agreement is concluded, a public prosecutor shall, where applicable, and unless otherwise required by compelling reasons in the interest of justice, as soon as is reasonable practicable, inform the victim-
       (a)   of the substance of, and reasons for, the plea agreement; and
       (b)   that the victim is entitled to be present when the court considers the plea agreement.
   (2)   Where the victim has died or is incapacitated, a public prosecutor shall communicate with a member of the victim's immediate family or authorized representative in respect of the matters set out in subsection (1).

Public prosecutor to notify court of existence of plea agreement

9.   (1)   A prosecutor shall in open court or on showing of good cause in chambers-
       (a)   before the accused person is required to plead; or
       (b)   at any time after arraignment;
       inform the court, as the case may be, of the existence of a plea agreement.
   (2)   The court may, where the circumstances appear to so require, question the accused person in order to conform the accused person's knowledge of the existence of a plea agreement.

Court not bound by plea agreement

10. A court shall not be bound to accept any plea agreement of justice and public interest.

Matters for consideration of court before accepting plea agreement

11. A court shall, before accepting a plea agreement, make a determination in open court that-
    (a) no inducement was offered to the accused person to encourage the accused person to enter into the plea agreement;
    (b) the accused person understands the nature, substance and consequence of the plea agreement;
    (c) there is a factual basis upon which the plea agreement has been made; and
    (d) acceptance of the plea agreement would not be contrary to the interests of justice and public interest.

Refusal by court to accept plea agreement

12. (1) Subsection (2) shall apply where, upon a determination of the matters referred to in section eleven, the court decides that-

    (a) acceptance of the plea agreement would be contrary to the interests of justice and public interest;
    (b) the offence for which the accused person is charged is not disclosed on the facts; or
    (c) there is no confirmation by the accused person of the agreement or the admission contained in the agreement.
    (2) The court shall, in the circumstances described in subsection (1)-
    (a) refuse to accept the plea agreement;
    (b) inform the public prosecutor of the decision and the reasons therefore.
    (3) The rejection of a plea agreement by a court shall not operate as a bar to the conduct of any subsequent plea negotiation and the conclusion of a subsequent plea agreement in respect of the same case.
    (4) The court shall, where it rejects a plea agreement under subsection (2), proceed to try the accused person on the original charge.

Effect of accepting plea agreement

13. Where a plea agreement is accepted by a court, the accused person shall be requested to plead to the new charge.

Accepted plea agreement to form part of record

14. Subject to section seventeen, where a plea agreement has been accepted by the court, the contents thereof shall be entered on the record.

Withdrawal from plea agreement

15. (1) The court may on its own motion, or upon application by an accused person who entered into a plea agreement, allow the accused person to withdraw from that agreement before sentence, or to appeal against a conviction based on the agreement, if-
    (a) the accused person entered into the agreement as a result of an improper inducement;
    (b) the court determines that the public prosecutor has breached the terms of the plea agreement; or
    (c) the accused person entered into the agreement as a result of a misrepresentation or misapprehension as to the substance or consequences of the plea agreement.
    (2) A public prosecutor may withdraw from a plea agreement before sentence where the public prosecutor subsequently discovers-
    (a) that a public prosecutor was in the course of plea negotiations misled by the accused person or by the accused person's legal representative in some material respect; or
    (b) that the accused person was induced to conclude the plea agreement.

Admissibility of plea agreement

16. Evidence of the following matters is not, in any civil or criminal proceedings, admissible against an accused person who entered into an agreement or is a party to any plea negotiations:

(a) a plea of guilty which was later withdrawn or nay statement made in the course of any proceedings under this Act regarding the plea of guilty; or

(b) any statement made in the course of plea negotiations with the public prosecutor which does not result in a plea of guilty or which result in a plea of guilty that is later withdrawn.

Sealing of records of plea negotiations

17. The court may, upon application, order that the records of any plea negotiation or a plea agreement be sealed, where the court is satisfied that the sealing of the records is in the interests of the effective administration of justice.

Obligation for secrecy

18. (1) A person exercising any function under this Act shall treat as secret and confidential, all information relating to a plea agreement before it is presented to the court or consequent upon the records thereof being sealed by the court.

   (2) Any person referred to in subsection (1) having possession of, or control over, any document, information or record, who communicates or attempts to communicate anything contained in the document or record or any such information to any person otherwise than in accordance with this Act or pursuant to a court order, commits an offence and is liable, upon conviction, to a fine not exceeding one hundred thousand penalty units or to imprisonment for a period not exceeding twelve months, or to both.

   (3) Any person to whom information is communicated in accordance with this Act shall regard and deal with the information as secret and confidential.

   (4) A person referred to in subsection (3) who at any time communicates or attempts to communicate any information referred to in that subsection to any person otherwise than for the purposes of this Act, commits an offence and is liable, upon conviction, to a fine not exceeding one hundred thousand penalty units or to imprisonment for a period not exceeding twelve months, or to both.

Grant of legal aid

19. Legal aid may be granted to-

   (a) any person who is detained at a police station or in a lock up, correctional institution or other similar place; or

   (b) an accused person in respect of the conduct of any plea negotiation under section four.

PART IV
GENERAL PROVISIONS

Regulations

20. (1) The Minister may, by statutory instrument, make regulations generally for the purpose of giving effect to the provisions of this Act.

   (2) The Minster may, by statutory instrument, amend the Schedule.

SCHEDULE
(Section 7)
CONTENTS OF PLEA AGREEMENT

1. The name and jurisdiction of the court in which the matter is held or to be held.

2. The case number and file number

3. The name, position, business address, business telephone and facsimile numbers of the public prosecutor.

4. The name, position, business address, business telephone and facsimile numbers of the defence counsel.

5. The proper name and alias, if any, and the last known address of the accused person.

6. The original information or indictment shall be attached to the Agreement.

7. The draft information or indictment shall be attached to the Agreement.

8.   The elements of the various offences to which the accused person is pleading shall be set out.

9.   A statement of facts may be attached and incorporated by reference. Any document containing any promise, agreement, understanding or inducement which forms part of the Agreement shall be attached to the Agreement.

10.   A statement that the accused person was informed of, and has waived, the following rights:

   (a)   the right not to be compelled to give self-incriminating evidence;

   (b)   the right to confront and cross-examine any witness against the accused person; and

   (c)   the right to pursue pre-trial motions and appeal preliminary points.

11.   A statement that the provisions of the Agreement are not binding on the court.

12.   A statement of the rights of the accused person under the Agreement, including the right to persist in a plea of not guilty.

13.   The obligations of the accused person under the Agreement.

14.   The obligations of the State under the Agreement

15.   A Statement that the State is free to prosecute the accused person for any other unlawful past conduct which is not the subject of the Agreement or for which the accused person has not been acquitted or convicted, or any unlawful conduct that occurs after the date of the Agreement.

16.   A statement that the Director of Public Prosecutions may, in any case where the Director of Public Prosecutions consider it desirable so to do, discontinue at any stage before judgment is delivered any criminal proceedings instituted or undertaken by the Director of Public Prosecutions or any other person or authority.

17.   The grounds upon which an accused person may withdraw from the Agreement.

18.   Consequences of any breach of the Agreement.

19.   Provisions relating to a right of appeal.

20.   A statement that the Agreement applies only to an offence committed by the accused person with which the accused person is charged and has no effect on any proceedings against the accused person not expressly mentioned therein.

21.   The date on which the Agreement was concluded.

22.   That the Agreement becomes effective upon signature by the accused person, the accused person's legal counsel and the public prosecutor, before a court.

23.   The following statement by the accused person:

"I have read this Agreement and carefully discussed each paragraph with my legal counsel. I understand the terms of this Agreement and agree to it without reservation. I voluntarily and of my free will agree to these terms. I am pleading guilty to the following charge (s):

   *(a)...

   (b)...

My legal representative has advised me of my rights, of possible defence, of the penalties and the consequences of entering into this Agreement. No promises, agreements, understanding or inducements have been made to me other than those contained in this Agreement. No one has threatened or forced me in any way to enter into this Agreement. I have had sufficient time to confer with my legal counsel concerning this Plea Agreement. I am satisfied with the representation of my legal representative in this matter.

*State as applicable

Signature of accused person

....
Name of accused person   Date

24. The following statement by the legal practitioner representing the accused person:

"I am the legal representative for

....
Name of accused person

I have read this Agreement and carefully discussed each paragraph of this Agreement with my client. Further, I have fully advised my client of my client's rights, of possible defences, of the penalties, and of the

consequences of entering into this Agreement. To the best of my knowledge and belief, my client's decision to enter into this Agreement is an informed and voluntary one.

....
Signature of legal practitioner
representing the accused person

....
Name of legal practitioner   Date

25. A statement whether the accused person communicated with a prosecutor through an interpreter. If the accused communicated through an interpreter, a certificate by the interpreter as to the accuracy of the interpretation during the negotiations and in respect of the contents of the agreement shall be appended to the Agreement.

26. Such other provision as the Director of Public Prosecutions considers necessary or desirable.

THE ANTI-GENDER-BASED VIOLENCE ACT NO 1 OF 2011

ARRANGEMENT OF SECTIONS

PART I
PRELIMINARY

1. Short title
2. Application of relevant Acts
3. Interpretation

PART II
FILING OF, AND DEALING WITH, COMPLIANTS OF GENDER-BASED-VIOLENCE

4. Number of acts amounting to gender-based violence
5. Duty to assist or inform complainant of rights, etc.
6. Filing of complaint to police
7. Police to respond promptly
8. Police assistance after receipt of complaint
9. Arrest by police

An Act to provide for the protection of victims of gender-based violence; constitute the Anti-Gender-Based Violence Committee; establish the Anti-Gender-Based Violence Fund; and provide for matters connected with, or incidental to, the foregoing.

Enactment

ENACTED by the Parliament of Zambia.

PART I
PRELIMINARY

Interpretation

1. This Act may be cited as the Anti-Gender-Based Violence Act, 2010.

Short title

2. (1) An act of gender-based violence shall be inquired into, tried, and otherwise dealt with in accordance with the Criminal Procedure Code, the Penal Code and any other written law.

    (2) Subject to the Constitution, where there is any inconsistency between the provisions of this Act and the provisions of any other written law the provisions of this Act shall prevail to the extent of the inconsistency.

Application of relevant Acts

3. (1) In this Act, unless the context otherwise requires—

    " abuse " means conduct that harms or is likely to cause harm to the safety, health or wellbeing of a person;

    " aggravated " in relation to gender-based violence, means any act of gender-based violence which—

      (a) causes the victim to suffer wounding or grievous bodily harm; or

      (b) the court otherwise considers to be so serious as to be aggravated, taking into account—

        (i) whether a weapon was used;

        (ii) evidence of pre-meditation;

        (iii) whether the victim is particularly vulnerable;

        (iv) any failure, by the police, the court or any official body, to respond to previous warnings; and

        (v) any other consideration the court considers appropriate;

    " applicant " means a victim who applies for a protection order, or on whose behalf an application for a protection order is made, under this Act;

    " associated respondent " means a person associated with a person against whom an application for a protection order is made;

    " care institution " includes an educational institution;

    " child " means a person below sixteen years;

    " court " means a subordinate court;

    " domestic relationship " means a relationship, between a victim and a respondent in any of the following ways:

      (a) the victim and the respondent are or were married to each other, under any law, custom or religion;

      (b) the victim cohabits with the respondent in a relationship in the nature of a marriage notwithstanding that they are not married, were not married to each other or could not or cannot be married to each other;

      (c) the victim is engaged to the respondent, courting the respondent or in an actual or perceived romantic, intimate, cordial or sexual relationship of any duration;

      (d) the victim and the respondent are parents of a child, are expecting a child together or are foster parents to a child;

      (e) the victim and the respondent are family members related by consanguinity, affinity or adoption, or would be so related if they are married either customarily or under any law or religion, or are able to be married, or if they are living together as spouses although they are not married;

      (f) the victim and the respondent, share or shared the same residence or are co-tenants;

      (g) the victim is a house-help in the household of the respondent;

      (h) the victim lives in or attends a public or private care institution and is under the care and control of the respondent; or

      (i) the victim is in a relationship with the respondent determined by the court to be a domestic relationship;

" economic abuse " means—

    (a)   the unreasonable deprivation of any economic or financial resources to which a victim, or a family member or dependent of the victim is entitled under any law, requires out of necessity or has a reasonable expectation of use, including household necessities, medical expenses or school fees and mortgage bond repayments or rent payments in respect of a shared household;

    (b)   denying a person the right to seek employment or to engage in an income-generating activity;

    (c)   unreasonably depriving a victim, a family member or dependent of the victim, of property in which the victim, family member or dependent of the victim has an interest or a reasonable expectation of use, or unreasonably disposing of such property; or

    (d)   intentionally destroying or damaging property in which the victim of gender-based violence, a family member or a dependent of the victim of gender-based violence has an interest or a reasonable expectation of use;

" emergency monetary relief " means compensation for monetary loss suffered by a victim of gender-based violence at the time of the issue of a protection order as a result of the gender-based violence, including, as appropriate—

    (a)   loss of earnings;

    (b)   medical and dental expenses;

    (c)   relocation and accommodation expenses; and

    (d)   household necessities;

" emotional, verbal and psychological abuse " means a pattern of degrading or humiliating conduct towards a person, including—

    (a)   insults, ridicule or name-calling;

    (b)   threats to cause emotional pain or distress;

    (c)   the exhibition of obsessive possessiveness which is such as to constitute a serious invasion of the person's privacy, liberty, integrity or security; or

    (d)   any act, omission or behaviour constituting gender-based violence which, when committed in the presence of minor members of the family, is likely to cause them mental injury;

" gender " means female or male and the role individuals play in society as a result of their sex and status;

" gender-based violence " means any physical, mental, social or economic abuse against a person because of that person's gender, and includes—

    (a)   violence that results in, or is likely to result in, physical, sexual or psychological harm or suffering to the person, including threats of such acts, coercion or arbitrary deprivation of liberty, whether occurring in public or private life; and

    (b)   actual or threatened physical, mental, social or economic abuse that occurs in a domestic relationship;

" harassment " means engaging in a pattern of conduct that induces in a person the fear of imminent harm or feelings of annoyance and aggravation, including—

    (a)   sexual contact without the consent of the person with whom the contact is made and making unwanted sexual advances;

    (b)   following, pursuing or accosting a person or making persistent, unwelcome communication with a person and includes—

        (i)   watching, loitering outside or near a building where the harassed person resides, works, carries on business, studies or happens to be;

        (ii)   repeatedly making phone calls or using a third party to make phone calls to the harassed person, whether or not conversation ensues;

        (iii)   repeatedly sending, delivering or causing the delivery of offensive or abusive letters, telegrams, packages, facsimiles, electronic mail or other offensive objects or messages to the harassed person; or

        (iv)   engaging in any other menacing behaviour;

" HIV " means human immunodeficiency virus;

" household chattels " include jewellery, clothes, books, furniture and furnishings, refrigerator, television, radiogram, other electrical and electronic appliances, kitchen and laundry equipment, simple agricultural equipment, hunting equipment, motor vehicles, other than vehicles used wholly

for commercial purposes, and household livestock;

" imminent harm " in relation to an applicant, includes harm that the applicant fears is likely to happen taking into consideration the history of the respondent's violent behaviour towards the complainant or other relevant factors;

" interim protection order " means an order made by the court under subsection (6) of section *twelve* pending the final determination of an application;

" intimidation " means intentionally inducing fear of imminent harm in a person whether by words or actions and whether by oneself or by the use of a third party by—

    (a)   threatening to abuse that person or a third party;

    (b)   threatening to damage, destroy or dispose of property in which that person or a third party has a material interest; or

    (c)   exhibiting a weapon before that person;

" marriage " includes marriage under any law, custom or religion;

" next friend " means a person who intervenes to assist a victim who is a child or who has a mental disability to bring a legal action;

" order " means a protection order or other order that the court may make under this Act;

" physical abuse " means physical assault or use of physical force against another person, including the forcible confinement or detention of another person and the deprivation of another person of access to adequate food, water, clothing, shelter, rest, or subjecting another person to torture or other cruel, inhuman or degrading treatment or punishment;

" physical, mental, social or economic abuse " means any act, omission or behaviour or threat of any such act, omission or behaviour which results in death or is likely to result in the direct infliction of physical, sexual or mental injury to any person, and includes—

    (a)   physical abuse;

    (b)   sexual abuse;

    (c)   emotional, verbal or psychological abuse, including any conduct that makes another person feel constantly unhappy, humiliated, ridiculed, afraid or depressed or to feel inadequate or worthless;

    (d)   economic abuse;

    (e)   intimidation;

    (f)   harassment;

    (g)   stalking;

    (h)   controlling behaviour such as isolating a person from the person's family and friends, monitoring the person's movement and restricting the person's access to information or assistance;

    (i)   malicious damage to property;

    (j)   forcible entry into a person's residence, where the parties do not share the same residence;

    (k)   depriving a person of, or hindering a person from access to or a reasonable share of the use of the facilities associated with the person's residence or forcible entry into a person's room or into a room occupied by a person, where the parties share the same residence;

    (l)   the unreasonable disposal of household effects or other property in which a person has interest;

    (m)   abuse delivered from the following cultural or customary rites or practices:

        (i)   forced virginity testing;

        (ii)   female genital mutilation;

        (iii)   pledging of a person for purposes of appeasing spirits;

        (iv)   forced marriage;

        (v)   sexual cleansing;

        (vi)   child marriage;

        (vii)   forced spouse inheritance; or

        (viii)   sexual intercourse between persons within the prohibited relations of affinity or consanguinity;

    (n)   abuse perpetrated on a person by virtue of the person's age, physical or mental incapacity, disability or illness;

    (o)   conduct that in any way harms or may harm another person, including any omission that results in harm and either—

        (i)   endangers the safety, health or wellbeing of another person;

        (ii)   undermines another person's privacy, integrity or security; or

(iii) detracts or is likely to detract from another person's dignity or worth as a human being; and

    (p) trafficking in persons;

" place of safety " means premises where the welfare of a victim of gender-based violence is assured;

" protection order " means an order made by the court under sections *thirteen, fourteen, fifteen* and *seventeen* on the final determination of an application;

" respondent " means a person against whom an application for a protection order is made or against whom a protection order has been granted;

" sexual abuse " includes the engagement of another person in sexual contact, whether married or not, which includes sexual conduct that abuses, humiliates or degrades the other person or otherwise violates another person's sexual integrity, or sexual contact by a person aware of being infected with HIV or any other sexually transmitted infection with another person without that other person being given prior information of the infection;

" stalking " includes following, pursuing or accosting a person; and

" victim " means a person against whom an act of gender-based violence has been, is being or is likely to be committed.

(2) A court shall, in determining whether a person is in a domestic relationship, have regard to—
    (a) the place where the person's time is ordinarily spent;
    (b) the manner in which the person's time is spent; and
    (c) the duration of the relationship.

(3) Without prejudice to subsection (1), a person is in a domestic relationship where the person—
    (a) is providing refuge to a victim whom a respondent seeks to attack; or
    (b) is acting as an agent of the respondent or encouraging the respondent to commit an act of gender-based violence.

PART II
FILING OF, AND DEALING WITH, COMPLAINTS OF GENDER-BASED VIOLENCE

Number of acts amounting to gender-based violence

4. A single act may amount to gender-based violence.

Duty to assist or inform complainant of rights, etc.

5. A police officer, labour inspector, social worker, counsellor, medical practitioner, legal practitioner, nurse, religious leader, traditional leader, teacher, employer or other person or institution with information concerning the commission of an act of gender-based violence shall—
    (a) inform a victim of the victim's rights and any basic support which may be available to assist the victim;
    (b) obtain for the victim, or advise the victim how to obtain shelter, medical treatment, legal services, counselling or other service that may be required in the circumstances; and
    (c) advise the victim of the victim's right to lodge a complaint against the respondent including remedies available to the victim under this Act.

Filing of complaint to police

6. (1) A victim of gender-based violence may file a complaint about the gender-based violence.
    (2) A child or a person with a mental disability may be assisted by a next friend to file a complaint of gender-based violence.
    (3) Notwithstanding subsection (1), a complaint of gender-based violence may be filed by any other person or institution with information about the gender-based violence where the intervention is in the interest of the victim.
    (4) A complaint of gender-based violence shall be filed with the police at the place—
        (a) where the offender resides;
        (b) where the victim resides;
        (c) where the gender-based violence occurred or is occurring or is likely to occur;
        (d) if the victim has left the victim's usual place of abode, where the victim is residing temporarily; or
        (e) that is convenient for the person filing the complaint.

Police to respond promptly

7.   A police officer shall respond promptly to a request by any person for assistance from gender-based violence and shall offer such protection as the circumstances of the case or the person who made the report requires even when the person reporting is not the victim of the gender-based violence.

Police assistance after receipt of complaint

8.   (1)   Where a police officer receives a complaint under subsection (4) of section *six*, the police officer shall—
   (a)   interview the parties and witnesses to the gender-based violence;
   (b)   record the complaint in detail and provide the victim with an extract of the complaint, upon request, in a language the victim understands;
   (c)   assist the victim to obtain medical treatment, where necessary;
   (d)   assist the victim to a place of safety as the circumstances of the case or as the victim requires where the victim expresses concern about safety;
   (e)   protect the victim to enable the victim retrieve personal belongings, where applicable; and
   (f)   assist and advise the victim to preserve evidence.

   (2)   Where one of the parties or witnesses to an act of gender-based violence, a complaint of which has been made under subsection (4) of section *six*, is a child, a police officer who receives the complaint shall interview the child in the presence of —
   (a)   the parent or guardian of the child; or
   (b)   a next friend, where the parent or guardian is the respondent.

   (3)   Police assistance to a victim under paragraph (c) of subsection (1) consists of issuing a medical form to the victim and, where necessary, sending the victim to a health facility.

   (4)   A victim of gender-based violence who is assisted by the police to obtain medical treatment under paragraph (c) of subsection (1), shall be entitled to free medical treatment at a public health facility and a free medical report within a reasonable period of time.

   (5)   Family mediation or intervention shall not be a bar to the investigation or prosecution of a complaint of gender-based violence.

   (6)   For the purposes of this section, "health facility" has the meaning assigned to it in the Health Professions Act, 2009.

Arrest by police

9.   A police officer may, without a warrant, arrest a person where the police officer has reasonable grounds to believe that the person—
(a) is committing, or has committed, an offence under this Act;
   (b)   is about to commit an offence under this Act and there is no other way to prevent the commission of the offence;
   (c)   unless arrested, will—
      (i)   escape or cause an unreasonable delay, trouble or expense in being made answerable to justice;
      (ii)   interfere with the witnesses; or
      (iii)   tamper with, or destroy, relevant evidence or material;
(d) is willfully obstructing the police officer in the execution of police duties; or
(e) has contravened or is contravening an order issued under this Act.

PART III
PROTECTION ORDERS

Application for protection order

10.   (1)   A victim may, in the prescribed manner, apply to a court for a protection order to prevent—
   (a)   a respondent;
   (b)   an associated respondent; or
   (c)   both a respondent and an associated respondent; from carrying out a threat of gender-based violence against the victim or to prevent the respondent, an associated respondent, or both, from further committing acts which constitute gender-based violence against the victim.

(2) If the victim is not represented by a legal representative, the clerk of court shall inform the applicant—

    (a) of the remedies available to the victim in terms of this Act; and

    (b) of the procedure for lodging an application for a protection order.

(3) Notwithstanding subsection (1) and any other law, and subject to subsections (4) and (5), where a victim is for any reason unable to apply for a protection order personally, any other person with information about the gender-based violence may assist the victim to apply for a protection order.

(4) Where the gender-based violence involves a child or a person with a mental disability the application shall be made by—

    (a) a person with whom the child or person with a mental disability normally resides or resides on a regular basis;

    (b) a parent or guardian of the child with a mental disability;

    (c) a social worker;

    (d) a police officer or probation officer;

    (e) a medical officer;

    (f) a representative of a non-governmental organisation; or

    (g) an institution with information about the gender-based violence.

(5) A person who assists a victim to make an application shall—

    (a) obtain the victim's consent, in writing, except where the victim—

        (i) is a child;

        (ii) has a mental disability ;

        (iii) is unconscious; or

        (iv) is a person whom the court is satisfied is unable to provide the required consent; and

    (b) seek the leave of the court to make an application without the consent of the victim.

(6) The application may be filed in a court situated where—

    (a) the victim resides, carries on business or is employed;

    (b) the respondent resides, carries on business or is employed;

    (c) the act of gender-based violence occurred or is occurring or is likely to occur; or

    (d) the victim is residing temporarily, if the victim has left the victim's usual place of abode.

(7) An application or action shall be commenced in the prescribed manner and form.

(8) A court before which criminal proceedings in relation to gender-based violence are pending may, on its own motion, considering the circumstances of the case, or on an application by the victim, issue a protection order in respect of the victim.

Conduct of proceedings

11. (1) Notwithstanding any other law, proceedings for a protection order shall be held in chambers in the presence of the parties, their legal representatives and any other person permitted by the court to be present.

(2) Notwithstanding subsection (1), where the court is of the opinion that the presence of the respondent is likely to have a serious adverse effect on the victim or a witness, the court may take such steps as it considers necessary to separate the respondent from the victim or the witness.

(3) Subject to subsection (3) of section *ten*, the court shall consider an application for a protection order within a period of fourteen days of the filing of the application, and may, for such purpose—

    (a) enquire whether an interim protection order or protection order has at any time been issued to either of the parties;

    (b) call for any evidence whether oral or by affidavit, as it considers necessary including medical evidence supported by a police report forming the basis on which a victim's examination was conducted; or

    (c) examine any witness before the court.

(4) Where a respondent is not represented by a legal representative, the respondent shall not address the applicant directly but shall address the applicant through the court.

(5) A person who utters a false statement in an affidavit knowing the statement to be false commits an offence and is liable, upon conviction, to imprisonment for a term not exceeding three years.

(6) The court may request a report on any of the parties to the proceedings and the report shall be prepared and submitted to the court by a social worker, probation officer or other person appointed by the court, as appropriate.

(7) The report shall contain details of the circumstances of the gender-based violence, an assessment of the effect of the violence and any other information considered expedient by the social worker, probation officer or other person appointed by the court.

Interim protection order

12. (1) Where an application is made *exparte* to the court for a protection order, the court shall issue an interim protection order if it considers the order to be in the best interest of the applicant.

(2) In determining whether it is in the best interest of the applicant to issue an interim protection order, the court shall take into account—

   (a) whether there is a risk of harm to the applicant or a relation or friend of the applicant if the order is not made immediately;

   (b) whether it is likely that the applicant will be deterred or prevented from pursuing the application if an order is not made immediately; and

   (c) whether there is reason to believe that the respondent is deliberately evading service of notice of the proceedings and the applicant, or any person in a domestic relationship with the respondent, will be prejudiced by the delay involved in effecting service.

(3) An interim protection order shall be for a period of three months and the court may, where it thinks fit, extend it for a period not exceeding three months.

(4) The court shall, when making an interim protection order where the respondent is not already before the court, summon the respondent to appear within the period of three months referred to in subsection (3) to show cause why the interim order should not be made final.

(5) If the respondent fails to appear before the court in accordance with subsection (4), the order shall become final.

(6) Where an application is made on notice to the court for a protection order and the court is of the opinion that—

   (a) the respondent is committing, has committed or is likely to commit an act of gender-based violence; and

   (b) the applicant will suffer significant harm if a protection order is not issued; the court may issue an interim protection order pending the consideration of the order applied for.

(7) Where the court grants an interim protection order, it shall apply the provisions of section *thirteen* and subsection (1) of section *fifteen* and may apply any of the provisions contained in section *fourteen*.

Issuance of protection order

13. The court may issue a protection order to prohibit a respondent from committing or threatening to commit an act of gender-based violence personally or otherwise, against an applicant or a relation or associate of the applicant.

Effect of protection order

14. A protection order may prohibit the respondent or an associated respondent, or both, from—

   (a) physically assaulting or using physical force against the applicant or any relation, friend, a legal representative or any other person associated with the applicant;

   (b) forcibly confining or detaining the applicant or any relation or friend of the applicant;

   (c) depriving the applicant access to adequate food, water, clothing, shelter or rest;

   (d) forcing the applicant to engage in any sexual contact, whether married or not;

   (e) engaging in any sexual conduct that abuses, humiliates or degrades the complainant or otherwise violates the applicant's integrity, whether married or not;

   (f) depriving or threatening to deprive the applicant of —

      (i) economic or financial resources to which the applicant is entitled by law, including house mortgage repayments or rent payments or any other payments; and

      (ii) household chattels required by the applicant as a matter of necessity;

   (g) contacting the applicant at work or other places frequented by the applicant;

   (h) contacting the applicant by telephone or any other form of communication;

   (i) disposing of, or threatening to dispose of, movable or immovable property in which the applicant has an interest;

(j) destroying or damaging, or threatening to destroy or damage, property in which the applicant has an interest;

(k) hiding or hindering the use of property in which the applicant has an interest;

(l) threatening to abuse the applicant;

(m) harassing the applicant;

(n) entering the applicant's residence without consent, where the parties do not share the same residence;

(o) emotionally, verbally or psychologically abusing the applicant;

(p) coming within one hundred metres of the applicant;

(q) enlisting the assistance of another person to commit an act of gender-based violence against the applicant; or

(r) doing any act which the court considers not in the best interest of the applicant.

Conditions of protection order

15. (1) A protection order may, at the request of the applicant or on the court's own motion, include any or all of the following:

 (a) a provision which—
   (i) binds the respondent to be of good behaviour;
   (ii) directs the respondent to seek counselling or other rehabilitative service; or
   (iii) forbids the respondent to be, except under conditions specified in the order, at or near places frequented by the applicant or by any child or other person in the care of the applicant;

 (b) a provision directing the respondent to surrender any firearm or other specified weapon in the possession of the respondent to the police, which may also include, if appropriate—
   (i) a provision suspending any firearm licence in the name of the respondent for the duration of the protection order; or
   (ii) a provision authorising the police to search for and seize any weapon at any specified place where there is probable cause to believe that the weapon may be located;

 (c) a provision restraining the applicant or respondent, or both, from taking, converting, damaging, or otherwise dealing in property in which the other party may have an interest or a reasonable expectation of use;

 (d) a provision temporarily directing the respondent to make periodic payments in respect of the maintenance of the applicant, and of any child of the applicant, if the respondent is legally liable to support the applicant or the child, as an emergency measure where no such maintenance order is already in force, together with such other emergency monetary relief as is appropriate;

 (e) a provision granting temporary sole custody—
   (i) of a child of the applicant to any appropriate custodian other than the respondent; or
   (ii) of any child of the applicant or any child in the care of the applicant to the applicant or to another appropriate custodian if the court is satisfied that that is necessary for the safety of the child in question;

 (f) a provision temporarily—
   (i) forbidding contact between the respondent and any child of the applicant;
   (ii) specifying that contact between the respondent and a child of the applicant, must take place only in the presence and under the supervision of a social worker or a family member designated by the court for that purpose; or
   (iii) allowing such contact only under specified conditions designed to ensure the safety of the applicant, any child who may be affected, and any other family members; if the court is satisfied that that is reasonably necessary for the safety of the child in question;

 (g) a provision ordering the relocation of the applicant to a shelter to be provided by the Minister responsible for social welfare, or other place of safety, and compelling the respondent to pay rent for the period the applicant resides in such other place of safety if the court is satisfied that that is reasonably necessary for the safety of the applicant or any child or person in the care of the applicant; and

(h) any other provisions that the court considers necessary to ensure the safety of the applicant or any child or other person who is affected.

(2) A court shall not refuse to issue a protection order or impose any other condition solely on the ground that other legal remedies are available to the applicant.

Modification of protection order

16. An applicant or respondent may apply to the court which granted an order, for the modification or cancellation of the order.

Duration of final protection order

17. A final protection order issued by the court shall not exceed twelve months in the first instance but may, for good cause shown, be extended, modified or rescinded by the court on application by the applicant in the original proceedings.

Extension of protection order to other persons

18. (1) A court may extend a protection order to any person specified in the order other than the applicant if the court is satisfied that—

   (a) the respondent is engaging in or has engaged in conduct, which, if the person specified in the order, were or had been in a domestic relationship with the respondent, the conduct would amount to gender-based violence against the specified person;

   (b) the respondent's conduct towards the specified person is due, in whole or in part to the applicant's relationship with the specified person; or

   (c) the extension of the protection order is necessary for the protection of the specified person.

Grant of protection order not to exclude criminal liability

19. The grant of a protection order under subsection (8) of section *ten* does not exclude a person's criminal liability under the Penal Code or any other law.

Occupation order

20. (1) Subject to subsections (2) and (3), where the court, in issuing a protection order, considers it expedient to issue an occupation order, the court may issue an order requiring a respondent to vacate the matrimonial home or other home which the respondent shares with the applicant and to continue to pay rent, mortgage payment and maintenance to the applicant.

   (2) The court shall issue an occupation order after it considers a social enquiry report, prepared by a social worker, a probation officer or other person appointed by the court, as appropriate.

   (3) Where the applicant and the respondent are in a marital relationship, the court shall consider the effect of the order or omission of the order on the health, education and development of the family.

   (4) A landlord shall not evict an applicant solely on the basis that the applicant is not a party to a lease, where a residence is rented by a respondent but exclusive occupation is given to the applicant by the court.

   (5) A landlord shall, in furtherance of subsection (4), provide the details of the lease to the applicant on request.

Appeals

21. A person who is aggrieved by a decision of court may appeal to the High Court.

Power to discharge protection order

22. (1) A court may discharge an order on an application by an applicant or a respondent in the prescribed manner and form, where the court is satisfied that the circumstances that led to the grant of the order have ceased to exist.

   (2) The discharge of the order may occur even though the order—

   (a) applies for the benefit of a specified person in the order other than the applicant; or

   (b) applies against an associated respondent.

(3)   Where an order is discharged under subsection (2), the order shall cease to have effect for the benefit of any specified person or associated respondent as if the specified person or associated respondent had applied for or been granted a discharge of the order.

(4)   Where a discharge order applies for the benefit of a specified person or against an associated respondent, the specified person or associated respondent may apply for the order to be discharged in so far as it applies to them.

(5)   An application may be made under this section for the discharge of an interim order.

(6)   Where an application is made under subsection (5) the court shall, within thirty days of the filing of the application, fix a hearing date.

Contravention of protection order

23. (1)   A person who contravenes an order commits an offence and is liable, upon conviction, to imprisonment for a period not exceeding two years.

(2)   An applicant who, with intent to induce a police officer or a judicial officer to perform any act or exercise any power provided in this Act in relation to a contravention of a protection order, intentionally gives false information to the police officer or judicial officer or fails to provide information to the police officer or judicial officer in order to induce the police officer to do any act or exercise any power under this Act, commits an offence and is liable, upon conviction, to a fine not exceeding one thousand five hundred penalty units or to imprisonment for a period not exceeding one year, or to both.

PART IV
SHELTERS FOR VICTIMS

Establishment of shelters for victims

24. The Minister responsible for social welfare shall—
(a)   from money appropriated by Parliament for that purpose, establish and operate shelters for victims; and
(b)   ensure an appropriate spread of such shelters throughout Zambia.

Minimum norms and standards of shelters

25. A shelter for victims shall comply with the norms and standards as the Minister may, by statutory instrument, prescribe.

Inspectors of shelters

26. (1)   The Minister may appoint suitably qualified persons as inspectors to ensure compliance with the norms and standards prescribed pursuant to section *twenty-four*.

(2)   An inspector shall be provided with a certificate of appointment which shall be produced by the inspector when any person requires it to be produced.

(3)   An inspector may, during an inspection—
(a)   examine and make copies of any book, records or other documents containing information relevant to the administration or enforcement of this Act;
(b)   examine any computer and retrieve any information relevant to the administration or enforcement of this Act;
(c)   open and inspect any package or container;
(d)   inspect any shelter or facility relevant for the purposes of this Act; and
(e)   examine or inspect anything relevant to the administration or enforcement of this Act.

(4)   An inspector may, at any reasonable time, for the purposes of performing that inspector's functions under this Act, without warrant, enter into any shelter or other premises which the inspector reasonably believes is being used as a shelter in contravention of this Act.

(5)   A person who—
(a)   delays or obstructs an inspector in the performance of the inspector's functions;
(b)   refuses to give an inspector such reasonable assistance as the inspector may require for the purpose of exercising the inspector's functions or powers;

(c)   gives an inspector false or misleading information in answer to any query made by the inspector; or

(d)   impersonates or falsely presents oneself to be an inspector; commits an offence and is liable, upon conviction, to a fine not exceeding two hundred thousand penalty units or to imprisonment for a period not exceeding two years, or to both.

Shelters for child victims

27.   A shelter for child victims—

     (a)   shall secure the physical safety of a child victim;

     (b)   shall provide temporary basic material support for the care of a child victim;

     (c)   shall offer a programme for—

         (i)   the provision of counselling to child victims; and

         (ii)   the provision of rehabilitation services to child victims; and

     (d)   shall, in cooperation with the Ministry responsible for education, offer a programme aimed at the provision of education to child victims.

Shelters for adult victims

28.   A shelter for adult victims—

     (a)   shall secure the safety of adult victims;

     (b)   shall offer a programme aimed at—

     (i)   the provision of counselling to adult victims;

     (ii)   the provision of rehabilitation services to adult victims; and

     (iii)   the reintegration of adult victims into their families and communities;

     (c)   may, in cooperation with the Ministry responsible for education, offer a programme aimed at the provision of education to adult victims; and

     (d)   may, in cooperation with the Ministry responsible for vocational training, offer a programme aimed at the provision of skills development training to adult victims.

(2)   A shelter for adult victims that provides accommodation to an adult victim who has a child in the victim's care shall offer a programme aimed at the reception, care and development of such a child.

(3)   Subject to subsection (4), a child referred to in subsection

(2)   may be cared for at any other premises only with the explicit consent of the adult victim.

(4)   A child referred to in subsection (2) shall be referred to a designated social worker for investigation to determine whether the child is in need of care and protection.

Assessment of victim

29.   Upon admission of a victim to a shelter, an assessment shall be made by a social worker to determine—

     (a)   the risks to the safety and life of the victim;

     (b)   the immediate needs of the victim; and

     (c)   the long term needs of the victim.

Rehabilitation of victim

30.   (1)   The Ministry responsible for social welfare shall provide mechanisms and programs for the rehabilitation of victims.

     (2)   Victims may receive financial assistance from the Fund under this Act.

     (3)   The best interest of the child shall be paramount in any assistance given to rescue, rehabilitate or reintegrate the child.

PART V
ANTI-GENDER-BASED VIOLENCE COMMITTEE

Anti-Gender-Based Violence Committee

31.   (1)   There is hereby established the Anti-Gender-Based Violence Committee.

     (2)   The provisions of the Schedule apply in respect to the Committee.

     (3)   The Committee shall—

         (a)   monitor the activities of all the relevant institutions on matters connected with gender-based violence;

    (b) make recommendations for a national plan of action against gender-based violence;

    (c) monitor and report on the progress of the national plan of action;

    (d) advise the Minister on policy matters connected with gender-based violence;

    (e) propose and promote strategies to prevent and combat gender-based violence;

    (f) recommend guidelines for disbursements from the Fund; and

    (g) deal with any matter relating to gender-based violence.

PART VI
ANTI-GENDER-BASED VIOLENCE FUND

Establishment of Fund

32. (1) There is hereby established the Anti-Gender-Based Violence Fund.

    (2) The Fund shall consist of—

        (a) voluntary contributions to the Fund from any person;

        (b) such monies as Parliament may approve for purposes of the Fund; and

        (c) any grants from any source within or outside Zambia with approval of the Minister.

    (3) The monies of the Fund shall be applied for—

        (a) the basic material support of victims; and

        (b) any other matter connected with the counselling and rehabilitation of victims in their best interest.

Administration and management of Fund

33. (1) The Fund shall be vested in the Minister responsible for finance and shall be managed and administered by the Minister responsible for social welfare.

    (2) The Committee shall develop guidelines for the disbursements from the Fund.

Accounts and audit

34. (1) The Ministers referred to in section *thirty-three* shall cause to be prepared proper books of account in relation to the Fund.

    (2) The accounts of the Fund for each financial year shall be audited by the Auditor-General and, for that purpose, the Auditor-General and any officer authorised by the Auditor-General shall have access to all books and other records relating to the accounts of the Fund.

    (3) The Auditor-General shall, not later than twelve months after the end of each financial year, submit a report on the accounts of the Fund for that financial year to the Minister.

    (4) The Ministers referred to in subsection (1) of section *thirty three* shall, not later than seven days after the first sitting of the National Assembly next after the receipt of the report, lay it before the National Assembly.

PART VII
GENERAL PROVISIONS

Service of process

35. (1) Subject to subsections (2) and (3), the provisions of the Subordinate Courts Act apply with respect to service of process of any document issued pursuant to this Act and for which service is required.

    (2) Service of process shall be made by the Clerk of court or such other person as the court may order.

    (3) The court shall not direct a complainant to serve any document.

Settlement of matter out court

36. (1) Where in a criminal trial in respect of gender-based violence which is not aggravated—

        (a) the complainant expresses the desire to have the matter settled out of court, the court shall refer the case for settlement by any alternative dispute resolution method; or

        (b) the court is of the opinion that the case can be amicably settled, it may, with the consent of the complainant refer the case for settlement by any alternative dispute resolution method.

(2) Where any case is referred for settlement under subsection (1), the court shall, in addition—

    (a) refer the complainant and the offender for counselling;

    (b) where necessary, require the offender to receive psychiatric help; or

    (c) after consultation with the Ministry responsible for home affairs, appoint a probation officer to observe and report on the subsequent conduct of the offender to the court.

(3) Where a probation officer reports that the offender has engaged in any act of gender-based violence after the settlement, the offender shall be brought before the court and shall, subject to section *two*, be prosecuted.

(4) In any criminal trial in respect of gender-based violence which is aggravated, the court shall not consider or approve any settlement of the matter out of court, whether in accordance with subsections (1), (2) and (3), or not.

Proceedings in camera

37. Proceedings under this Act may be held in camera.

Publication of proceedings prohibited

38. (1) A person shall not publish a report of proceedings under this Act, other than criminal proceedings, except with the leave of court.

(2) Where a person reports proceedings under subsection (1), the person shall protect the identity of the complainant and any witness to the proceedings.

(3) A person who contravenes subsection (1) or (2) commits an offence and is liable, upon conviction, to a fine not exceeding two hundred thousand penalty units or to imprisonment for a period not exceeding two years, or to both.

Public education

39. The Minister responsible for gender shall, for the purpose of this Act, provide for public education on gender-based violence and the contents of this Act.

Rules of court

40. The Chief Justice may, by rules of court, make provision with respect to the procedure on applications to any court under this Act, and in particular as to—

    (a) the manner and form for the commencement of an action under this Act;

    (b) the giving of notice to persons affected by an application under this Act;

    (c) the joinder of the persons referred to in paragraph (b) as parties to the proceedings;

    (d) the discharge of an order issued pursuant to this Act; and

    (e) the forms necessary for the purposes of this Act.

Regulations

41. (1) The Minister may, by statutory instrument, make regulations for the better carrying out of the provisions of this Act.

(2) Without limiting the generality of subsection (1), regulations made under that subsection may provide for—

    (a) the training of the police and court officials on gender-based violence;

    (b) the education and counseling of victims and perpetrators of gender-based violence;

    (c) places of shelter for victims;

    (d) enhancement of social welfare services for victims;

    (e) the modalities for the provision of free medical treatment for victims; and

    (f) any matter for the effective implementation of this Act.

SCHEDULE
ANTI-GENDER-BASED VIOLENCE COMMITTEE

1. (1) The Committee shall consist of the following part-time members:

    (a) one representative each from the Ministries responsible for—

        (i) social services;

        (ii) gender;

(iii) children and youth;

(iv) health; and

(v) education;

    (b) a representative of the Attorney-General;

    (c) a representative from the Human Rights Commission;

    (d) a representative of the House of Chiefs;

    (e) a representative of the Law Association of Zambia;

    (f) a representative of the Zambia Police Force;

    (g) a representative of a non-governmental organisation dealing with matters concerning gender-based violence; and

    (h) two other persons.

(2) The members shall be nominated by their institutions and appointed by the Minister.

(3) The Chairperson and the Vice-Chairperson shall be appointed by the Minister from amongst the members.

2. (1) Subject to the other provisions of this Act, a member shall hold office for a period of three years from the date of appointment and may be re-appointed for a further like period.

(2) The office of a member shall become vacant if—

    (a) the member has been absent without reasonable excuse from three consecutive meetings of the Committee of which the member has had notice;

    (b) the member dies;

    (c) the member is adjudged bankrupt;

    (d) the member is removed by the Minister;

    (e) the member becomes mentally or physically incapable of performing the duties of a member of the Committee;

    or

    (f) the member is convicted of an offence under any other written law and sentenced therefor to imprisonment for a term exceeding six months.

3. (1) Subject to the other provisions of this Act, the Committee may regulate its own procedure.

(2) The Committee shall meet for the transaction of business at least once in every three months at such places and at such times as the Chairperson may determine.

(3) Upon giving notice of not less than fourteen days, a meeting of the Committee may be called by the Chairperson and shall be called if not less than one-third of the members so request in writing:

Provided that if the urgency of any particular matter does not permit the giving of such notice, a special meeting may be called upon giving a shorter notice.

(4) The quorum at any meeting of the Committee shall be one-half of the members.

(5) There shall preside at any meeting of the Committee—

    (a) the Chairperson;

    (b) in the absence of the Chairperson, the Vice-Chairperson; or

    (c) in the absence of the Chairperson and the Vice-Chairperson, such member as the members present may elect from amongst themselves for the purpose of that meeting.

(6) A decision of the Committee on any question shall be by a majority of the members present and voting at the meeting and, in the event of an equality of votes, the person presiding at the meeting shall have a casting vote in addition to the deliberative vote.

(7) Where a member is for any reason unable to attend any meeting of the Committee, the member may, in writing, nominate another person from the same organisation to attend such meeting in that member's stead and such person shall be considered to be a member for the purpose of such meeting.

(8) The Committee may invite any person whose presence is in its opinion desirable to attend and to participate in the deliberations of a meeting of the Committee but such person shall have no vote.

(9) The validity of any proceedings, act or decision of the Committee shall not be affected by any vacancy in the membership of the Committee or by any defect in the appointment of any member or by reason that any person not entitled so to do, took part in the proceedings.

(10) The Committee shall cause minutes to be kept of the proceedings of every meeting of the Committee and of any subcommittee established by the Committee.

4. (1) The Committee may, for the purpose of performing its functions under this Act, constitute any sub-committee and may delegate to any such sub-committee such of its functions as it thinks fit.

(2) The Committee may appoint as members of the subcommittees constituted under subparagraph

(1), persons who are or are not members of the Committee and such persons shall hold office for such period as the Committee may determine.

5. There shall be paid to the members of the Committee or any sub-committee of the Committee such allowances as the Committee may, with the approval of the Minister, determine.

6. (1) If a member is present at a meeting of the Committee or any sub-committee of the Committee at which any matter in which the member or the member's spouse is directly or indirectly interested in a private capacity, is the subject of consideration, the member shall, as soon as is practicable after the commencement of the meeting, disclose such interest, and shall not, unless the Committee or the sub-committee otherwise directs, take part in any consideration or discussion of or vote on any question relating to that matter.

   (2) A disclosure of interest made under this section shall be recorded in the minutes of the meeting at which it is made.

7. No action or other proceedings shall lie or be instituted against any member or any member of a sub-committee for, or in respect of, any act or thing done or omitted to be done in good faith in the exercise or purported exercise of the member's functions under this Act.

8. (1) A person shall not, without the consent in writing given by, or on behalf of, the Committee, publish or disclose to any other person, otherwise than in the course of the person's duties, thecontents of any document, communication or information whatsoever, which relates to, and which has come to the person's knowledge in the course of that person's duties under this Act.

   (2) Any person who contravenes subsection (1) commits an offence and is liable, upon conviction, to a fine not exceeding two hundred thousand penalty units or to imprisonment for a period not exceeding two years, or to both.

   (3) A person who, having information which to that person's knowledge has been published or disclosed in contravention of subsection (1), unlawfully publishes or communicates the information to any other person, commits an offence and is liable, upon conviction, to a fine not exceeding two hundred thousand penalty units or to imprisonment for a period not exceeding two years, or to both.

9. (1) The Minister shall appoint a Secretariat of the Committee comprising such staff as the Minister may determine.

   (2) The Secretariat of the Committee shall be based at the Ministry.

ANTI-CORRUPTION ACT NO 3 OF 2012

Published in Government Gazette on 16 April 2012
Assented to on 12 April 2012
Commenced on 16 April 2012
[This is the version of this document from 16 April 2012.]

An Act to continue the existence of the Anti-Corruption Commission and provide for its powers and functions; provide for the prevention, detection, investigation, prosecution and punishment of corrupt practices and related offences based on the rule of law, integrity, transparency, accountability and management of public affairs and property; provide for the development, implementation and maintenance of coordinated anti-corruption strategies through the promotion of public participation; provide for the protection of witnesses, experts, victims and other persons assisting the Commission; provide for nullification of corrupt transactions; provide for payment of compensation for damage arising out of corrupt activities; provide for the domestication of the United Nations Convention Against Corruption, the African Union Convention on Preventing and Combating Corruption, the Southern African Development Community Protocol Against Corruption and other regional and international instruments on corruption to which Zambia is a party; repeal and replace the Anti-Corruption Act, 2010; and provide for matters connected with, or incidental to, the foregoing.

Enactment

ENACTED by the Parliament of Zambia.

PART I
PRELIMINARY

1. Short title

This Act may be cited as the Anti-Corruption Act, 2012.

2. Application

All offences under this Act shall be enquired into, tried and otherwise dealt with in accordance with the Criminal Procedure Code and any other written law. *[Cap. 88]*

3. Interpretation

In this Act, unless the context otherwise requires—

"**agent**" means a person employed by, or acting for, another and includes an officer of a public body or private body who acts for, or on behalf of, a public body or a private body or any other person, a trustee, an executor or an administrator of an estate of a deceased person;"

appropriate authority" means a person or institution to whom a recommendation is made under section *eight*;

"**associate**", in relation to a person, means—

    (a) a person who is a nominee or an employee of that person;

    (b) a person who manages the affairs of that person;

    (c) a former spouse or conjugal partner of that person;(

    d) a firm of which that person, or that person's nominee, is a partner or a person in charge or in control of its business or affairs;

    (e) a company in which that person or that person's nominee, is a director or is in charge or in control of its business or affairs, or in which that person, alone or together with that person's nominee, holds a controlling interest or shares amounting to more than thirty percent of the total share capital; or

    (f) the trustee of a trust, where—

        (i) the trust has been created by that person; or(ii)the total value of the assets contributed by that person before or after the creation of the trust, amounts, at any time, to not less than twenty percent of the total value of the assets of the trust;

"**Board**" means the Board of the Commission constituted under paragraph 2 of the Schedule;

"**casual gift**" means any conventional hospitality, on a modest scale or unsolicited gift of modest value, offered to a person in recognition or appreciation of that person's services, or as a gesture of goodwill towards that person, and includes any inexpensive seasonal gift offered to staff or associates by a public or private body or a private individual on festive or other Special occasions, which is not in any way connected with the performance of a person's official duty so as to constitute an offence under Part III;"

Chairperson" means the person appointed as Chairperson under paragraph 2 of the Schedule;"

Commission" means the Anti-Corruption Commission referred to in section *four*;

"**Commissioner**" means a person appointed as Commissioner under paragraph 2 of the Schedule;

"**corrupt**" means the soliciting, accepting, obtaining, giving, promising or offering of a gratification by way of a bribe or other personal temptation or inducement, or the misuse or abuse of a public office for advantage or benefit for oneself or another person, and " corruption " shall be construed accordingly;

" **Deputy Director-General**" means a person appointed as Deputy Director-General under section *twelve*;

"**Director-General**" means the person appointed as such under section *nine*;

"**Director of Public Prosecutions**" means the person appointed as such under the Constitution;*[Cap. 1]*

"**document**" means any device by means of which information is recorded or stored, and includes—

    (a) anything on which there is writing;

    (b) anything in which there are marks, figures, symbols or perforations having meaning for persons qualified to interpret them;

    (c) anything from which sounds, images or writing can be produced, with or without the aid of anything else; or

(d) any of the things referred to in paragraphs (a) to (c) kept or maintained in electronic form;

"foreign public official" means—

(a) a person holding any executive, legislative, administrative or judicial office at any level of the government of a foreign State;

(b) any person performing public functions for a foreign State, or any board, commission, corporation or other body or authority performing a duty or function on behalf of the foreign State; or

(c) an official or agent of a public international organisation formed by two or more States or two or more public international organisations;

"foreign State" means any country other than Zambia;"

"Government" includes any Ministry, department, Service or undertaking of the Government;

"gratification" includes—

(a) money, any gift, loan, fee, reward, commission, valuable security, property, or interest in property of any description, whether movable or immovable;

(b) any employment or contract of employment or services and any promise to give employment or render services in any capacity;

(c) any payment, release, discharge or liquidation of any loan, obligation or other liability, whether in whole or in part;

(d) any service, favour or advantage of any description, such as protection from any penalty or from any action or proceedings of a disciplinary or penal nature, and including the exercise or the omission from the exercise of any right of any official power or duty;

(e) any valuable consideration or benefit of any kind, discount, commission, rebate, bonus deduction or percentage;

(f) any right or privilege; and

(g) any aid, vote, consent or influence;

"head of public institution" means a Chairperson, manager, chief executive or person in charge of a public body;

"illegal activity" means an activity carried out which, under any written law in the Republic, amounts to an offence;

"local authority" has the meaning assigned to it in the Local Government Act;*[Cap. 281]*

"officer" means a person appointed under section *thirteen*;

"official emoluments" includes an honorarium, a pension, gratuity or other terminal benefits;

"parastatal" means any company, association, statutory corporation, body or board or any institution of learning, in which the State has a financial interest;

"police officer" means a member of the Zambia Police Force;

"principal" includes an employer, beneficiary under a trust, and a trust estate as though it were a person, and any person beneficially interested in the estate of a deceased person as though the estate were a person, and, in relation to a public officer, the authority or body of persons in which the public office is held;

"private body" means a voluntary organisation, non-governmental organisation, political party, charitable institution, company, partnership, club or any other person or organisation which is not a public body;

"property" includes any real or personal property, money, things in action or other intangible or incorporeal property, whether located in Zambia or elsewhere, and property of corresponding value in the absence of the original illegally acquired property whose value has been determined;

"public body" means the Government, any Ministry or department of the Government, the National Assembly, the Judicature, a local authority, parastatal, board, council, authority, commission or other body appointed by the Government, or established by, or under, any written law;

"public funds" has the meaning assigned to it in the Public Finance Act, 2004;*[Act No. 15 of 2004]*

"public officer" means any person who is a member of, holds office in, is employed in the service of, or performs a function for or provides a public service for, a public body, whether such membership, office, service, function or employment is permanent or temporary, appointed or elected, full-time or part time, or paid or unpaid, and "public office" shall be construed accordingly;

"public property" means property belonging to or under the control of, or consigned or due to, a public body;

"relative", in relation to a person, means—

(a) a parent, son, daughter, brother, sister, nephew, niece, uncle, aunt, grandparent or cousin of that person or that person's spouse; and

(b) a spouse of that person;

"**repealed Act**" means the Anti-Corruption Act, 2010;*[Act No. 38 of 2010]*

"**Secretary**" means the person appointed Secretary under section *thirteen*;

"**seizure**" means temporarily prohibiting the transfer, conversion, disposition or movement of any property or temporarily assuming the custody or control of property on the basis of an order issued by a court or a notice by the Director-General;

"**sporting event**" means an event or contest in any sport, between individuals or teams, or in which an animal competes, and which is usually attended by the public and is governed by rules of any sporting body or regulatory body;

"**staff**" means the staff of the Commission appointed under section *thirteen*;

"**unexplained property**" means property in respect of which the value is disproportionate to a person's known sources of income at or around the time of the commission of the offence and for which there is no satisfactory explanation;

"**valuable security**" means any document—

(a) creating, transferring, surrendering or releasing any right to, in or over property;

(b) authorising the payment of money or delivery of any property; or

(c) evidencing the creation, transfer, surrender or release of any right, the payment of money or delivery of any property or the satisfaction of any obligation; and

"**victim**" means a person who suffers damage as a result of an act of corruption.

PART II
THE ANTI-CORRUPTION COMMISSION

4. Continuation of Commission

(1) The Anti-Corruption Commission continued under the repealed Act shall continue to exist as if established under this Act, and shall be a body corporate with perpetual succession and a common seal, capable of suing and of being sued in its corporate name and with power, subject to this Act, to do all such acts and things as a body corporate may, by law, do or perform.*[Act No. 38 of 2010]*

(2) The provisions of the State Proceedings Act shall apply to civil proceedings by, or against, the Commission as if, for a reference to the State there were substituted a reference to the Commission. *[Cap. 71]*

(3) The provisions of the Schedule apply to the Commission.

5. Autonomy of Commission

Subject to the Constitution, the Commission shall not, in the performance of its functions, be subject to the direction or control of any person or authority. *[Cap. 1]*

6. Functions of Commission

(1) The functions of the Commission are to—

(a) prevent and take necessary and effective measures for the prevention of corruption in public and private bodies, including, in particular, measures for—

(i) examining the practices and procedures of public and private bodies in order to facilitate the discovery of opportunities of corrupt practices and secure the revision of methods of work or procedures which in the opinion of the Commission, may be prone or conducive to corrupt practices;

(ii) advising public bodies and private bodies on ways and means of preventing corrupt practices, and on changes in methods of work or procedures of such public bodies and private bodies compatible with the effective performance of their duties, which the Commission considers necessary to reduce the likelihood of the occurrence of corrupt practices;

(iii) disseminating information on the evil and dangerous effects of corrupt practices on society;

(iv) creation of committees in institutions for monitoring corruption in the institution; and(v)enlisting and fostering public confidence and support against corrupt practices;

(b) initiate, receive and investigate complaints of alleged or suspected corrupt practices, and, subject to the directions of the Director of Public Prosecutions, prosecute—

(i) offences under this Act; and

(ii) such other offence under any other written law as may have come to the notice of the Commission during the investigation of an offence under this Act:

Provided that nothing in this paragraph shall be considered as precluding any public prosecutor from prosecuting, subject to the directions of the Director of Public Prosecutions, any offence under this Act which has come to the notice of the police during investigation of an offence under any written law;

(c) investigate any conduct of any public officer which, the Commission has reasonable grounds to believe may be connected with, or conducive to, corrupt practices;

(d) be the lead agency in matters of corruption;

(e) co-ordinate or co-operate, as applicable, with other institutions authorised to investigate, prosecute, prevent and combat corrupt practices so as to implement an integrated approach to the eradication of corruption;

(f) consult, co-operate and exchange information with appropriate bodies of other countries that are authorised to conduct inquiries or investigations in relation to corrupt practices;

(g) adopt and strengthen mechanisms for educating the public to respect the public good and public interest and, in particular—

(i) create awareness in the fight against corruption and related offences;

(ii) develop educational and other programmes for the sensitisation of the media;

(iii) promote an environment for the respect of ethics; and

(iv) disseminate information and sensitise the public on the negative effects of corruption and related offences; and(h)do all such things as are incidental or conducive to the attainment of its functions.

(2) The Commission may establish specialised units to investigate and deal with such matters as the Commission considers appropriate.

7. Instructions by Commission

(1) The Commission may instruct a public body on practices and procedures that are necessary to prevent, reduce or eliminate the occurrence of corrupt practices.

(2) A public body shall, not later than ninety days from the receipt of the instructions from the Commission pursuant to subsection (1), effect the necessary changes in its practices and procedures.

(3) A public body which considers that the changes in practices and procedures contained in the instructions from the Commission shall be impracticable or otherwise disadvantageous to the effective discharge of its functions shall, within thirty days of the receipt of the instructions, make representations to the Director-General in writing.

(4) The Commission may, after considering the representations of a public body made under subsection (3), confirm, vary or cancel the instruction given to the public body.

(5) The head of a public body which, without any reasonable explanation, fails to comply with the instructions of the Commission commits an offence and is liable, upon conviction, to a fine not exceeding one hundred thousand penalty units or to imprisonment for a period not exceeding one year, or to both.

(6) In addition to the penalty prescribed in subsection (5), the head of the public body which fails to comply with the instructions of the Commission shall be subject to disciplinary action, including dismissal from office by the relevant authority.

8. Reports and recommendation by Commission

(1) The Commission may, after an investigation into an offence under this Act, depending on the findings made, make such recommendation as it considers necessary to an appropriate authority.

(2) An appropriate authority shall, within thirty days from the date of receipt of the recommendation of the Commission under subsection (1), make a report to the Commission on the action taken by the appropriate authority.

(3) The head of a public body which, without reasonable excuse, fails to comply with sub-section (2), commits an offence and is liable, upon conviction, to a fine not exceeding one hundred thousand penalty units or to imprisonment for a period not exceeding one year, or to both.

9. Director-General

(1) There shall be a Director-General of the Commission who shall be the chief executive officer of the Commission.

(2) The Director-General shall be appointed by the President, subject to ratification by the National Assembly, on such terms and conditions as the President may determine.

(3) A person is not qualified to be appointed as Director-General unless the person is qualified to be appointed judge of the High Court.

(4) The Director-General shall be responsible for—

    (a) the control, direction, management and administration of the Commission; and

    (b) the implementation of any policy matters referred to the Director-General by the Board.

(5) The Director-General may, subject to any specific or general direction of the Board, make standing orders providing for—

    (a) the control, direction and administration of the Commission;

    (b) the discipline, training, classification and promotion of officers of the Commission;

    (c) the duties of officers of the Commission; and

    (d) such other matters as the Director-General may consider necessary or expedient for preventing the abuse of power or neglect of duty by officers or other staff.

(6) The Director-General shall not, while holding the office of Director-General, discharge the duties of any other office of emolument in the Republic.

(7) The Director-General shall, before taking office, take an oath or affirmation before the President in the prescribed manner and form.

10. Tenure of office of Director-General

(1) Subject to subsection (2), a person appointed Director-General shall vacate that office on attaining the age of sixty-five years: Provided that the President may permit a person who has attained that age to continue in office for such period as may be necessary to enable that person to do anything in relation to proceedings that were commenced before the person attained that age.

(2) A person appointed Director-General may be removed from office for inability to perform the functions of office, whether arising from infirmity of body or mind or from any other cause, or for misconduct, and shall not be removed except by, or in accordance with, a resolution passed by the National Assembly pursuant to subsection (3).

(3) If the National Assembly, by resolution supported by a simple majority, resolves that the question of removing the Director-General ought to be investigated, the Speaker of the National Assembly shall send a copy of such resolution to the Chief Justice who shall appoint a tribunal consisting of a chairperson and two other persons to inquire into the matter.

(4) The Chairperson and one other member of the tribunal shall be persons who hold or have held high judicial office.

(5) The tribunal shall inquire into the matter and send a report on the facts of that matter to the President and a copy to the National Assembly.

(6) Where a tribunal appointed under subsection (3) advises the President that the Director-General ought to be removed from office for inability as aforesaid or for misconduct, the President shall remove the Director-General from office.

(7) If the question of removing the Director-General from office has been referred to a tribunal under subsection (2), the President may suspend the Director-General from performing the functions of office, and any such suspension shall cease to have effect if the tribunal advises the President that the Director-General ought to be removed from office.

(8) The Director-General may resign by giving three months' notice, in writing, to the President, of the Director-General's intention to resign.

11. Powers of Director-General

(1) The Director-General may, for the performance of the Commission's functions under this Act—(a) authorise, in writing, any officer of the Commission to conduct an inquiry or investigation into alleged or suspected offences under this Act;

    (b) require the head, of any public body, to produce or furnish within such time as may be specified by the Director-General, any document or a certified true copy of any document which is in that person's possession or under that person's control and which the Director-General considers necessary for the conduct of an investigation into alleged or suspected offences under this Act: Provided that if the document is classified or falls under the State Security Act, the Commission may apply to a judge in chambers to determine whether the document is likely to—

        (i)   prejudice the security, defence or international relations of the Republic; or(ii)involve the disclosure of any matter or deliberations of a secret or confidential nature of the Government; or *[Cap. 111]*

    (c)   require any person to answer, to the best of that person's knowledge and belief, questions with respect to the whereabouts or existence of any documents or records that may be relevant to an investigation.

(2)   In determining an application under paragraph (b) of subsection (1), the court may—

    (a)   order the release of the document; or

    (b)   confirm that the release of the document will prejudice the security, defence or international relations of the Republic or involve the disclosure of a confidential matter of Government.

(3)   Notwithstanding any written law to the contrary, the Director-General may, where the Director-General has reasonable grounds to believe that a person who is the subject of an investigation in respect of an offence under this Act is likely to leave Zambia, require such person to surrender their travel document or any other document in that person's possession.

(4)   The Commission shall, where a person surrenders that person's travel document pursuant to subsection (1), return the document after the investigation of the offence is completed, and if no criminal proceedings are to be instituted.

(5)   A person who is aggrieved with the decision of the Director-General made pursuant to subsection (1) may apply to the High Court.

(6)   The High Court may, upon hearing an application made under subsection (3), reverse, vary or dismiss the application or make such other order as the court considers appropriate.

12. Deputy Director-General

(1)   The Commission shall appoint a Deputy Director-General on such terms and conditions as it may determine.

(2)   The Deputy Director-General shall assist the Director-General in performing the Director-General's duties under this Act.

(3)   A person shall not qualify for appointment as Deputy Director-General unless the person is qualified to be appointed judge of the High Court.

(4)   If the office of the Director-General is vacant or the Director-General is absent from duty or unable for any other reason to perform the functions of that office, the Deputy Director-General shall, save where the Commission otherwise directs, act as Director-General.

(5)   If both the Director-General and the Deputy Director-General are absent from office or unable for any other reason to perform the functions of their offices, the President shall appoint another person to act as Director-General.

(6)   The Deputy Director-General may resign by giving three months' notice, in writing, to the Chairperson, of the Deputy Director-General's intention to resign.

(7)   The Deputy Director-General shall, on appointment, take an oath or affirmation before the President in the prescribed manner and form.

13. Directors, Secretary, investigating officers and other staff of Commission

(1)   The Commission may appoint Directors, the Secretary, investigating officers, and such other staff of the Commission, on such terms and conditions as it may determine, to assist the Director-General in the performance of the Director-General's functions under this Act.

(2)   The Secretary shall be in charge of the general administration and shall keep the records of the Commission.

(3)   An officer shall have such powers, functions and duties as provided for, or as delegated to the officer by the Director-General, under this Act.

(4)   The Director-General may, if satisfied that it is in the best interest of the Commission, terminate the appointment of any officer of the Commission and shall assign the reasons therefor, subject to any directions by the Commission.

(5)   A person aggrieved with the decision of the Director-General to terminate that person's employment pursuant to subsection (3) may appeal against that decision to the Board.

(6)   The Commission may, in the exercise of its functions, engage the services of such advisors and experts as it considers necessary.

(7)   The Directors, Secretary, advisors, experts and other members of staff of the Commission shall, on appointment, take an oath or affirmation before the Director-General in the prescribed manner and form.

14. Declaration of assets

The Director-General, Deputy Director-General, officers and Secretary shall, before taking office under this Act and every five years thereafter—

(a) in the case of the Director-General, Deputy Director-General and Secretary, submit to the Chief Justice a written declaration, in the prescribed form, of all the assets they own or liabilities owed to them; and

(b) in the case of the other staff of the Commission, submit to a magistrate a written declaration, in the prescribed form, of all the assets they own or liabilities owed to them.

15. Identity card

(1) The Director-General shall issue to an officer of the Commission an identity card which shall be *prima facie* evidence of the officer's appointment as such.

(2) An officer shall, in performing any function under this Act—

(a) be in possession of the identity card referred to in subsection (1); and

(b) show the identity card to any person who requests to see it or is subject to an investigation under this Act.

16. Prohibition of disclosure of information to unauthorised persons

(1) A person shall not, without the consent in writing given by, or on behalf of, the Commission, publish or disclose to any person otherwise than in the course of such person's duties, the contents of any document, communication or information which relates to, or which has come to that person's knowledge in the course of that person's duties under this Act.

(2) A person who contravenes subsection (1) commits an offence and is liable, upon conviction, to a fine not exceeding two hundred thousand penalty units or to imprisonment for a period not exceeding two years, or to both.

(3) A person who, having information which to that person's knowledge has been published or disclosed in contravention of subsection (1), unlawfully publishes or communicates such information to any other person, commits an offence and is liable, upon conviction, to a fine not exceeding two hundred thousand penalty units or to imprisonment for a period not exceeding two years, or to both.

17. Immunity of staff

(1) No proceedings, civil or criminal, shall lie against the Director-General, Deputy Director-General, Directors, Secretary, an officer or member of staff of the Commission for anything done in good faith in the exercise of the officer's or member of staff's functions under this Act.

(2) Subject to the provisions of this Act, the Director-General, Deputy Director-General, an officer or member of staff of the Commission shall not be called to give evidence before any court or tribunal in respect of anything coming to such person's knowledge in the exercise of such person's functions under this Act.

18. Impersonation and procurement of officer

A person who pretends to—

(a) be an officer of the Commission or to have any of the powers of an officer under this Act, or under any authorisation or warrant issued under this Act; or

(b) be able to procure an officer of the Commission to do or refrain from doing anything in connection with the duties of such officer; commits an offence and is liable, upon conviction, to imprisonment for a period of not less than two years.

PART III
CORRUPT PRACTICES

19. Corrupt practices by, or with, public officers

(1) A public officer who, by oneself, or by or in conjunction with, any other person, corruptly solicits, accepts or obtains, or agrees to accept or attempts to receive or obtain, from any person for oneself or for any other person, any gratification as an inducement or reward for doing or forbearing to do, or for having done or forborne to do, anything in relation to any matter or transaction, actual or proposed, with which any public body is or may be concerned, commits an offence.

(2)   A person who, by oneself, or by, or in conjunction with, any other person, corruptly gives, promises or offers any gratification to any public officer, whether for the benefit of that public officer or of any other public officer, as an inducement or reward for doing or forbearing to do, anything in relation to any matter or transaction, actual or proposed, with which any public body is or may be concerned, commits an offence.

20.   Corrupt transactions by, or with, private bodies

(1)   A person who, by oneself, or by, or in conjunction with, any other person, corruptly solicits, accepts or obtains, or agrees to accept or attempts to receive or obtain, from any person for oneself or for any other person, any gratification as an inducement or reward for doing or forbearing to do, or for and having done or forborne to do, anything in relation to any matter or transaction actual or proposed, with which any private body is or may be concerned, commits an offence.

(2)   A person who, by oneself, or by, or in conjunction with, any other person, corruptly gives, promises or offers any gratification to any person, whether for the benefit of that person or of any other person, as an inducement or reward for doing or forbearing to do, or for having done or forborne to do, anything in relation to any matter or transaction, actual or proposed, with which any private body is or may be concerned, commits an offence.

21.   Abuse of authority of office

(1)   A public officer commits an offence who—
    (a)   does, or directs to be done, in abuse of the public officer's position, office or authority any arbitrary act prejudicial to the rights or interests of the Government or any other person;
    (b)   uses that public officer's position, office or authority or any information that the public officer obtains as a result of, or in the course of, the performance of that public officer's functions to obtain property, profit, an advantage or benefit, directly or indirectly, for oneself or another person;
    (c)   uses the public officer's position, office or information to obtain, promise, offer, or give an undue advantage to oneself or another person, directly or indirectly, in order for the public officer to perform or refrain from performing the public officer's duties; or
    (d)   solicits or accepts directly or indirectly an undue advantage or benefit for oneself or for another person in order for the public officer to perform or refrain from performing the public officer's duties.

(2)   For the purposes of subsection (1), a public officer shall be presumed, until the contrary is proved, to have used that public officer's position, office or information for an advantage or benefit where the public officer takes any decision or action in relation to any matter in which the public officer or a relative or associate of that public officer, has a direct or indirect interest.

(3)   A public officer who, being concerned with any matter or transaction falling within, or connected with, that public officer's jurisdiction, powers, duties or functions, corruptly solicits, accepts or obtains, or agrees to accept or attempts to receive or obtain for oneself or for any other person any gratification in relation to such matter or transaction, commits an offence.

(4)   A person who, being concerned with any matter or transaction falling within the scope of authority, or connected with the jurisdiction, powers, duties or functions of any public officer, by oneself, or by, or in conjunction with, any other person, corruptly gives, promises or offers any gratification, whether directly or indirectly, to such public officer either for oneself or for any other person, commits an offence.

(5)   A public officer who unreasonably delays, refuses, neglects or omits to perform that public officer's duties or functions in order to procure or induce a person to offer or give gratification to that public officer, commits an offence.

22.   Possession of unexplained property

(1)   Subject to the Constitution, any public officer who—
    (a)   maintains a standard of living above which is commensurate with the public officer's present or past official emoluments or other income;
    (b)   is in control or possession of pecuniary resources or property disproportionate to the public officer's present or past official emoluments; or
    (c)   is in receipt of the benefit of any services which the public officer may reasonably be suspected of having received corruptly or in circumstances which amount to an offence under this Act;shall,

unless the contrary is proved, be liable for the offence of having, or having had under the public officer's control or in the public officer's possession pecuniary resources or property reasonably suspected of having been corruptly acquired, or having misused or abused the public officer's office, as the case may be.

(2) Where a court is satisfied in proceedings for an offence under subsection (1) that, having regard to the closeness of the public officer's relationship to the accused and to other relevant circumstances, there is reason to believe that any person was holding pecuniary resources or property in trust for or otherwise on behalf of the accused, or acquired such pecuniary resources or property as a gift, or loan without adequate consideration, from the accused, such pecuniary resources or property shall, unless the contrary is proved, be deemed to have been under the control or in the possession of the accused.

23. Corrupt transactions by, or with, agents

(1) An agent who, with or without the principal's knowledge or concurrence, corruptly solicits, accepts or obtains, or agrees to accept or attempts to receive or obtain, from any person for oneself or for any other person, any gratification as an inducement or reward for doing or forbearing to do, or for having done or forborne to do, anything in relation to the principal's affairs or business, or for showing or having shown favour or disfavour to any person in relation to the principal's affairs or business, commits an offence.

(2) A person who corruptly gives, promises or offers any gratification to an agent as an inducement or reward for doing or forbearing to do, or for having done or forborne to do, anything in relation to the principal's affairs or business, or for showing or having shown favour or disfavour to any person in relation to the principal's affairs or business, commits an offence.

(3) A person who gives to an agent, or any agent who, with intent to deceive the principal, uses any receipt, account or other document in respect of which the principal is interested or which relates to the principal's affairs or business and which contains any statement which is false or erroneous or defective in any material particular, and which to the agent's knowledge or belief is intended to mislead the principal, commits an offence.

24. Corruption of members of public or private bodies with regard to meetings

(1) A person who being a member of any public or private body by oneself, or by, or in conjunction with, any other person, corruptly solicits, accepts or obtains, or agrees to accept or attempts to receive or obtain, from any person for oneself or for any other person, any gratification as an inducement or reward for—(a)that person's voting or abstaining from voting at any meeting of such public or private body in favour of, or against, any measure, matter, resolution or question submitted to such public or private body;

    (b) that person's performing or abstaining from performing, or for that person's aid in procuring, expediting, delaying, hindering or preventing the performance of, any official act by such public or private body; or

    (c) that person's aid in procuring or preventing the passing of any vote or the granting of any contract or advantage in favour of any person; commits an offence.

(2) A person who, by oneself or by, or in conjunction with, any other person, corruptly gives, promises or offers any gratification to a member of any public or private body in any circumstance referred to in subsection (1), commits an offence.

25. Corruption of witness

(1) A person who, directly or indirectly, corrupts a witness so as to induce false testimony, an advantage or benefit for oneself or another person from the witness in a trial, hearing or other proceeding before any court, tribunal, judicial officer, committee, commission or any officer authorised by law to hear evidence or take testimony commits an offence and is liable, upon conviction, to imprisonment for a period not exceeding seven years.

(2) A person who, by oneself, or by, or in conjunction with, any other person, corruptly promises, offers or gives any gratification to any witness whether for the benefit of that witness or any other person, with intent to influence the witness to be absent from trial, to give false testimony or withhold testimony, commits an offence and is liable, upon conviction, to imprisonment for a period not exceeding seven years.

(3) A witness who, by oneself or by, or in conjunction with, any other person, corruptly solicits, accepts or receives, or agrees to accept or attempts to receive or obtain, from any person for oneself or another

person, any gratification as an inducement or reward whether for the witness's benefit or any other person, in order for the witness to be absent from trial or to give false testimony or withhold testimony, commits an offence and is liable, upon conviction, to imprisonment for a period not exceeding seven years.

26. Corrupt practices by, or with, foreign public official

(1) A person who, by oneself or by, or in conjunction with, any other person, corruptly promises, offers or gives any gratification to any foreign public official, whether for the benefit of that foreign public official or any other person, as an inducement or reward for doing or forbearing to do, or for having done or forborne to do, anything in relation to any matter or transaction, actual or proposed, with which any foreign public body is or may be concerned, commits an offence.

(2) A foreign public official who, by oneself or by, or in conjunction with, any other person corruptly solicits, accepts or obtains, or agrees to accept or attempts to receive or obtain, from any person for oneself or for any other person, any gratification as an inducement or reward for doing or forbearing to do, or for having done or forbone to do, anything in relation to any matter or transaction, actual or proposed, with which any foreign public body is or may be concerned, commits an offence.

(3) A person who unlawfully promises, offers, or gives to a foreign public official, directly or indirectly, an undue advantage, for the benefit of the foreign public official or another person, in order that the public official may do or forbear to do, in the exercise of the official duties, in order to obtain or retain business or other undue advantage in relation to the conduct of international affairs or business, commits an offence.

(4) A foreign public official who solicits or accepts, directly or indirectly, an undue advantage, for the benefit of the foreign public official or another person, in order that the foreign public official may act or refrain from acting in the exercise of official duties, commits an offence.

27. Corruption in relation to sporting events

A person who, directly or indirectly, corruptly—
    (a) solicits or accepts or agrees to accept any gratification, whether for the benefit of that person or any other person, as an inducement or reward for a person influencing or having influenced the run of play or the outcome of any sporting event; or
    (b) offers or gives or agrees to give to any other person any gratification as an inducement to influence or as a reward for influencing or having influenced the run of play or the outcome of a sporting event;commits an offence.

28. Conflict of interest

(1) Where a public body in which a public officer is a member, director, employee or is otherwise engaged proposes to deal with any person or company, partnership or other undertaking in which that public officer has a direct or indirect private or personal interest, that public officer shall forthwith disclose, in writing to that public body, the nature of such interest and shall not take part in any proceedings or process of that public body relating to such decision.

(2) Where a public officer or a relative or associate of such public officer has a personal interest in a decision to be taken by a public body, that public officer shall forthwith disclose, in writing to that public body, the nature of such interest and shall not vote or take part in any proceedings or process of that public body relating to such decision.

(3) A public officer who contravenes subsection (1) or (2) commits an offence.

29. Gratification for giving assistance, etc., with regard to contracts

(1) A public officer who, directly or indirectly, by oneself, or by, or in conjunction with, any other person, corruptly solicits, accepts or obtains, or agrees to accept or attempts to receive or obtain, from any person for oneself or for any other person, any gratification as an inducement or reward for or otherwise on account of, that public officer giving assistance or using influence in, or having given assistance or used influence in—
    (a) the promotion, execution or procurement of—
        (i) any contract with a public body or private body for the performance of any work, the provision of any service, the doing of anything or the supplying of any article, material or substance; or

(ii) any sub-contract to perform any work, provide any service, do anything or supply any article, material or substance required to be performed, provided, done or supplied under any contract with a public body or private body; or

(b) the payment of the price, consideration or other moneys stipulated or otherwise provided for in any contract or sub-contract; commits an offence.

(2) A person who corruptly gives, promises or offers any gratification to any public officer as an inducement or reward for, or otherwise on account of, such public officer giving assistance or using influence in, or having given assistance or used influence in—

(a) the promotion, execution or procurement of; or (b)the payment of the price, consideration or other moneys stipulated or otherwise provided for in; any contract or sub-contract commits an offence.

30. Gratification for procuring withdrawal of tender

(1) A person who, directly or indirectly, by oneself, or by, or in conjunction with, any other person, corruptly solicits, accepts or obtains, or agrees to accept or attempts to receive or obtain from any person for oneself or for any other person, any gratification as an inducement or reward for, or otherwise on account of, the withdrawal of a tender, or the refraining from the making of a tender for any contract with a public body or private body for the performance of any work, the provision of any service, the doing of anything or the supplying of any article, material or substance, commits an offence.

(2) A person who corruptly gives, promises or offers any gratification to any other person as an inducement or reward for, or otherwise on account of, the withdrawal of a tender, or the refraining from making of a tender for a contract, commits an offence.

31. Obstruction of justice

(1) A person who, by use of corrupt means or with intent to pervert the course of justice, interferes with the exercise of official duties by a judge, magistrate, judicial officer or any other arbiter or law enforcement officer, commits an offence and is liable, upon conviction, to imprisonment for a period not exceeding seven years.

(2) A person who accepts or obtains, agrees to accept or attempts to obtain, or offers or gives, a gratification for oneself or for any other person in consideration of that person—

(a) concealing an offence;(b) shielding any other person from legal proceedings for an offence;

(c) not proceeding against any other person in relation to an alleged offence; or

(d) abandoning or withdrawing, or obtaining or endeavouring to obtain the withdrawal of, a prosecution against any other person; commits an offence and is liable, upon conviction, to imprisonment for a period not exceeding seven years.

32. Gratification with regard to bidding at auction sale

(1) A person who, directly or indirectly by oneself, or by, or in conjunction with, any other person, corruptly solicits, accepts or obtains, or agrees to accept or attempts to receive or obtain, from any person for oneself or for any other person, any gratification as an inducement or reward for, or otherwise on account of, that person refraining or having refrained from bidding at any sale by auction conducted by, or on behalf of, any public body or private body, commits an offence.

(2) A person who corruptly gives, promises or offers any gratification to any other person as an inducement or reward for, or otherwise on account of, that other person's refraining or having refrained from bidding at an auction commits an offence.

33. Coercion of investor

A public officer who—

(a) performs or abstains from performing any act in that public officer's capacity as a public officer;

(b) expedites, delays, hinders or prevents the performance of any act; or

(c) assists, favours, hinders or delays any person in the transaction of any business with a public body;in order that an investor or potential investor is coerced, compelled or induced to abandon the investment or induced to abandon the investment to the advantage of another person, commits an offence and is liable, upon conviction, to a fine not exceeding two hundred thousand penalty units or to imprisonment for a period not exceeding two years, or to both.

34. Corrupt acquisition of public property and revenue

(1) A person who, by oneself or with or through another person, fraudulently or unlawfully — (a) acquires public funds or property or a public service or benefit for that person's or another person's benefit;

    (b) diverts any public property for purposes other than for what it is intended, for that person's or another person's benefit;

    (c) mortgages, charges or disposes of any public property for that person's or another person's benefit; or(d)obtains any exemption, remission, reduction or abatement from payment of any tax, fee, levy or charge required to be paid under any law; commits an offence.

(2) A person whose functions concern the administration, custody, management, receipt or use of any public revenue or public property or in whom any public revenue or public property is vested by virtue of that person's position or office, commits an offence if that person—

    (a) fraudulently facilitates or makes payment from the public revenue for—

        (i) sub-standard or defective goods;

        (ii) goods not supplied or not supplied in full; or

        (iii) services not rendered or not adequately rendered; or

    (b) willfully fails to comply with any law or applicable procedure or guideline relating to the procurement, allocation, sale or disposal of property, tendering of contracts, management of funds or incurring of public expenditure.

(3) A person who administers, keeps, manages, receives or uses any private funds or property, who fraudulently or unlawfully—

    (a) acquires private funds or property for that person's or another person's benefit; or

    (b) misappropriates the private funds or property; commits an offence.

35. Electoral corruption

(1) The Commission has jurisdiction to investigate and prosecute any offence of bribery prescribed under section *seventy-nine* of the Electoral Act, 2006.*[Act No. 12 of 2006]*(2)A person who uses any funds acquired through illegal or corrupt practices to fund a political party or for any purpose related to an election commits an offence.

36. Concealment of property

A person who—

    (a) converts, transfers or disposes of property, knowing that such property is the proceeds of corruption or related offences for the purpose of concealing or disguising the illicit origin of the property or of helping any other person who is involved in the commission of the offence to evade the consequences of that person's action;

    (b) conceals or disguises the true nature, source, location, disposition, movement or ownership of, or rights with respect to, property which is from the proceeds of corruption or related offences; or

    (c) acquires, possesses or uses any property with the knowledge at the time of receipt, that such property is from the proceeds of corruption or related offences; commits an offence and is liable, upon conviction, to imprisonment for a period not exceeding two years.

37. Dealing with, using and concealing gratification

(1) A person who, directly or indirectly, whether on that person's behalf or any other person, knowingly —

    (a) enters into, or causes to be entered into, any dealing in relation to any proceeds of crime; or

    (b) uses or causes to be used, or receives, holds, controls or conceals any property or any part thereof, which was obtained as gratification, or derived from the proceeds of crime obtained in the commission of an offence under this Part; commits an offence.

(2) For purposes of subsection (1), " dealing " includes—

    (a) any purchase, sale, loan, charge, mortgage, lien, pledge, transfer, delivery, assignment, subrogation, transmission, gift, trust, settlement, deposit, withdrawal, transfer between accounts or extension of credit;

    (b) any agency or grant of power of attorney; or

    (c) any act which results in any right, interest, title or privilege, whether present or future or whether vested or contingent, in the whole or in part of any property being conferred on any person.

38. Concealment of offence

A person commits an offence who, with intent to defraud or to conceal the commission of an offence under this Part, or to obstruct an officer in the investigation of any offence—

    (a) destroys, alters, mutilates or falsifies any book, document, valuable security, account, computer system, disk, computer printout or other electronic device which belongs to, or is in the possession of, or has been received by that person or that person's employer, or any entry in such book, document, account or electronic device, or is privy to any such act;

    (b) makes or is privy to the making of any false entry in any book, document, account or electronic device; or

    (c) omits or is privy to the omission of any information from any book, document, account or electronic device.

39. Public officer's duty to report

(1) A public officer to whom any gratification is corruptly given, promised or offered shall make a full report of the circumstances of the case to an officer of the Commission or a police officer within twenty-four hours of the occurrence of the event, and if the public officer fails to do so without reasonable cause, the public officer commits an offence and is liable, upon conviction, to a fine not exceeding two hundred thousand penalty units or to imprisonment for a period not exceeding two years, or to both.

(2) An officer of the Commission or a police officer may arrest without warrant any person in respect of whom a report is made under subsection (1),(3)An officer of the Commission or a police officer may search any person arrested for an offence under this Act and take possession of all the articles found upon that person which the police officer or officer of the Commission believes upon reasonable grounds to constitute evidence of the commission of an offence by that person under this Part: Provided that a person shall not be searched except by a police officer, or officer of the Commission or by any person authorised in that behalf by a police officer or officer of the Commission, of the same sex.

40. Attempts and conspiracies

(1) A person who aids, abets or counsels or conspires with any person to commit an offence under this Part, commits an offence and is liable, upon conviction, to a sentence as if that person committed the offence.

(2) A person who attempts to commit an offence under this Act commits an offence and is liable, upon conviction, to a sentence as if that person committed the offence.

41. General penalty

A person who is convicted of an offence under this Part, for which no penalty is provided, is liable—(a)upon first conviction, to imprisonment for a period not exceeding fourteen years;

    (b) upon a second or subsequent conviction, to imprisonment for a term of not less than five years but not exceeding fourteen year; and

    (c) in addition to any other penalty imposed under this Act, to forfeiture to the State of any pecuniary resource, property, advantage, profit or gratification received in the commission of an offence under this Act.

42. Restitution

Where a person is convicted of an offence under this Part, the court may, in addition to the sentence that it may impose under section *forty-one*, order the convicted person to pay to the rightful owner the amount or value, as determined by the court, of any gratification actually received by that person, and such order shall be deemed to form part of the sentence: Provided that where, after reasonable inquiry, the rightful owner cannot be ascertained or traced, or where the rightful owner is implicated in the giving of the gratification, the court shall order that the amount or value thereof be paid into the general revenues of the Republic.

43. Recovery of gratification by distress, etc.

Any fine imposed under the provisions of this Part and the amount or value of any gratification ordered to be paid under section *forty-two* may be recovered in accordance with the provisions of sections *three hundred* and *eight* and *three hundred* and *nine* of the Criminal Procedure Code by distress and sale of the movable and immovable property of the person sentenced.*[Cap. 88]*

44. Recovery of gratification corruptly received by agent

(1) Where a person gives gratification to, or for, or on account of, an agent in contravention of any provision of this Act, the principal may recover, as a civil debt, the amount or value of such gratification from the agent, and the acquittal of the agent or such person in respect of an offence under this Part shall not operate as a bar to any proceedings for such recovery.

(2) Nothing in subsection (1) shall be deemed to prejudice or affect any right which any principal may have under any written law or rule to recover from the agent any money or property.

45. Certificate of Government valuation officer or other specialist valuer

In any proceedings under this Act, a certificate by a Government valuation officer or other specialist valuer with respect to the value of any gratification or of any movable or immovable property shall be sufficient proof of such value, unless the contrary is proved.

46. Certain matters not to constitute defence

(1) If in any proceedings for an offence under any section of this Part, it is proved that the accused person accepted any gratification believing or suspecting or having reasonable grounds to believe or suspect that the gratification was given as an inducement or reward for, or otherwise on account of, the accused person's doing or forbearing to do, or having done or forborne to do, any act referred to in that section, it shall not be a defence that—
   (a) the accused person did not actually have the power, right or opportunity to do so or forbear;
   (b) the accused person accepted the gratification without intending to do so or forbear; or
   (c) the accused person did not in fact do so or forbear.

(2) If, in any proceedings for an offence under any section of this Part it is proved that the accused person offered any gratification to any other person as an inducement or reward for, or otherwise on account of, that other person's doing or forbearing to do, or having done or forborne to do, any act referred to in that section, believing or suspecting or having reasonable grounds to believe or suspect that such other person had the power, right or opportunity to do so or forbear, it shall not be a defence that such other person did not have such power, right or opportunity.

47. Suspension of public officer charged with corruption

(1) Subject to the applicable legal and administrative procedures relating to the right to justice and a fair hearing applicable to public officers under their conditions of service, a public officer who is charged with corruption shall be suspended, at half pay, with effect from the date of the charge.

(2) A public officer ceases to be suspended if the proceedings against the public officer are discontinued or if the public officer is acquitted.

(3) This section does not derogate from any administrative power, disciplinary code, regulation, law or any other inherent powers of an employer under which the public officer may be suspended without pay or dismissed.

(4) This section does not apply with respect to an office in respect of which the Constitution limits or provides for the grounds upon which a holder of the office may be removed or the circumstances in which the office shall be vacated.*[Cap. 1]*

48. Suspension of public officer convicted of corruption

(1) A public officer who is convicted of an offence shall be suspended without pay with effect from the date of the conviction pending the outcome of any appeal.

(2) A public officer ceases to be suspended if a conviction is overturned on appeal.(3)A public officer shall be dismissed if—
   (a) the time period for appealing against the conviction expires without the conviction being appealed; or
   (b) the conviction is upheld on appeal.

49. Effect of conviction

(1) A person convicted of an offence under this Part shall, by reason of such conviction, be disqualified for a period of five years from the date of such conviction, from being elected or appointed to, or from holding or continuing to hold, any office or position in any public body.

(2) Notwithstanding subsection (1), the State shall endeavour to ensure the implementation of effective measures for the reintegration into society, of a person convicted of an offence under this Act.

(3) A court may, where it convicts a person of an offence under this Act, set aside any transaction that occurred in circumstances that gave rise to the conviction, unless the transaction was with a third party acting in good faith and without notice.

(4) A transaction set aside under subsection (3) shall be void *ab initio* and shall not give rise to a claim for damages.

50. Offences by body corporate or unincorporate body

Where an offence under this Act is committed by a body corporate or unincorporate body, every director or manager of the body corporate or unincorporate body shall be liable, upon conviction, as if the director or manager had personally committed the offence, unless the director or manager proves to the satisfaction of the court that the act constituting the offence was done without the knowledge, consent or connivance of the director or manager or that the director or manager took reasonable steps to prevent the commission of the offence.

PART IV
INVESTIGATION OF CORRUPT PRACTICES

51. Lodging of complaint

(1) A person who alleges that another person has engaged or is about to engage in a corrupt practice may lodge a complaint with the Commission in the prescribed manner and form.

(2) The Commission may investigate a matter under this Act on receipt of a complaint or on its own initiative.

(3) The Commission may refer any offence that comes to its notice in the course of an investigation under subsection (2) to any other appropriate investigation authority or agency.

52. Consideration of complaint

(1) The Director-General shall, upon receipt of a complaint under section *fifty-one*, examine each alleged corrupt practice and decide whether or not an investigation in relation to the allegation is warranted.

(2) The Director-General may, in deciding whether to investigate an alleged corrupt practice, consider—(a) the seriousness of the conduct or involvement to which the allegation relates;
    (b) whether or not the allegation is frivolous or vexatious;
    (c) whether or not the conduct or involvement to which the allegation relates is or has been the subject of an investigation or other action by any other appropriate authority under any other written law; and(d)whether or not, in all the circumstances, the carrying out of an investigation for the purpose of this Act in relation to the allegation will disclose the commission or likelihood of the commission of an offence under this Act.

(3) The Director-General shall, where the Director-General determines that an investigation into an allegation is warranted, decide whether the Commission shall carry out the investigation or whether the allegation should be referred to another appropriate authority for investigation or action.

(4) The Director-General may, for purposes of performing the functions under this section—
    (a) make such preliminary inquiry as the Director-General considers necessary; and
    (b) consult any other appropriate authority.

(5) The Director-General shall inform the complainant, in writing, of the decision of the Commission in relation to the allegation.

(6) A person who, in bad faith, makes a frivolous or vexatious complaint to the Commission commits an offence and is liable, upon conviction, to a fine not exceeding seven hundred thousand penalty units or to imprisonment for a period not exceeding seven years, or to both.

53. Power to require attendance before Director-General

(1) The Director-General may, by notice, in writing, require any person whose affairs are being investigated or any other person who the Director-General has reason to believe may have information or documents relevant to an investigation to—
    (a) attend before the Director-General as may be specified in the notice;
    (b) answer questions with respect to any matter or supply any information that may be relevant to the investigation; or
    (c) produce for inspection any documents which are specified in the notice.

(2) Subsection (1) shall apply without prejudice to a person's rights under any other law relating to privilege.

54. Search without warrant

(1) An officer may, where the officer reasonably suspects that an offence is being, has been or is about to be committed under this Act, without a warrant, enter and search any premises, other than a private dwelling except if the private dwelling is used for business purposes, for the purpose of attaching and removing, if necessary, any record, return, report, document or article, if the owner, occupier of the premises or other person in control of the premises consents to the entry, search, seizure and removal of the record, return, book, document or article.
(2) An officer exercising any power under this section shall, before entering and searching any premises, ensure that the owner, occupier or person in control of the premises is present.

55. Search with warrant

(1) The Director-General, the Deputy Director-General or an officer of the Commission, in the performance of their duties, may apply for a warrant to a judge or a magistrate.
(2) A judge or magistrate to whom an application for a warrant is made under subsection (1) may issue the warrant where—
    (a) there are reasonable grounds to believe that—
        (i) a person has failed to produce the documents required for purposes of this Act;
        (ii) a person has failed to answer any questions asked for purposes of an investigation or that any answer given to any question is false or misleading in a material particular or is incomplete;
        (iii) it is not practicable to serve a notice on a person by reason of the fact that the person cannot be located or is absent from Zambia, or that the service of a notice might prejudice an investigation; or
    (b) there are reasonable grounds to believe that any document or other thing relevant to an investigation or that may be evidence of an offence under this Act is placed, deposited or concealed in the premises to which the warrant relates.
(3) A warrant issued under subsection (2) shall confer on the Director-General, the Deputy Director-General or an officer of the Commission power to—
    (a) access all the books, records, returns, reports and other documents relating to the work of any public or private body;
    (b) enter and search, at any time, the premises of any public or private body or any vessel, boat, aircraft or other conveyance, where the Director-General, Deputy Director-General or officer has reasonable grounds to believe that any property or thing corruptly acquired has been placed, deposited or concealed therein;
    (c) search for and remove any document or other thing that may be relevant to an investigation or may be evidence of an offence;
    (d) where necessary, take copies of any document or extracts from documents that the person executing the warrant believes on reasonable grounds may be relevant to an investigation; and
    (e) where necessary, to require any person to reproduce, or to assist to reproduce, in usable form, any information recorded or stored in any documents.
(4) In the exercise of powers of entry and search conferred under paragraph (b) of subsection (3), the Director-General, the Deputy Director-General or other officer of the Commission, may use such reasonable force as is necessary and justifiable in the circumstances, and may be accompanied or assisted by such other persons as they consider necessary to assist them to enter into, or upon, any premises, or upon any vessel, boat, aircraft or other conveyance, as the case may be.
(5) A person who accompanies or assists the Director-General, the Deputy Director-General or other officer of the Commission to enter into or upon any premises or upon any vessel, boat, aircraft or other conveyance, as the case may be, shall, during the period of such accompaniment or assistance, enjoy the same immunity as is conferred under section *seventeen* upon an officer of the Commission.

56. Inspection of banker's books

(1) The Director-General, Deputy Director-General or an officer may, with a court order, investigate any bank account, share account, purchase account, expense account or any other account or safe deposit box in any bank.

(2) An order made under subsection (1) shall be sufficient for the disclosure or production by any person of all or any information, account, document or article that may be required by an officer of the Commission so authorised.

57. Power of arrest

(1) The Director-General, the Deputy Director-General or an officer of the Commission authorised in that behalf by the Director-General may arrest a person,, without warrant, if the officer has reasonable grounds to believe that such person has committed or is about to commit an offence under this Act.

(2) Where a person is arrested without warrant under subsection (1), such person may, at any time before appearing in court, while the person is in custody, be released on bond upon providing surety or sureties sufficient, in the opinion of the Director-General, Deputy Director-General or an officer authorised in that behalf by the Director-General, to secure that person's appearance before court, or the person may be released upon that person's own recognizance on such conditions as the officer thinks fit.

(3) A bond issued under this section shall be dealt with in accordance with the provisions of the Criminal Procedure Code. *[Cap. 88]*

58. Seizure of property

(1) Where in the course of an investigation into an offence under this Act, an officer has reasonable grounds to suspect that any movable or immovable property is derived or acquired from corrupt practices, is the subject matter of an offence or is evidence relating to an offence, the officer shall, with a warrant, seize the property.

(2) An officer who seizes any property pursuant to subsection (1) shall prepare and sign a list of all the movable or immovable property seized under that subsection and of the places in which the property is found.

(3) An officer shall serve a copy of the list referred to in subsection (2) on the owner of the property or on the person from whom the property was seized, not later than thirty days from the date of seizure.

(4) For the purpose of this section, "property" means real or personal property of any description, and includes money and any interest in the real or personal property.

59. Custody and release of seized property

(1) An officer shall effect a seizure by removing the movable property from the custody or control of the person from whom it is seized and placing it under the custody of such other person or authority and at such place as the officer may determine.

(2) An officer shall, where it is not practicable or otherwise not desirable to effect the removal of any property under subsection (1), leave it at the premises in which it is seized under the custody of such person as the officer may determine.

(3) An officer shall, where property is seized under subsection (2), make a record in writing specifying in detail the circumstances of, and the reason for, the seizure of the property and subsequent leaving of the property at the premises.

60. Restriction on disposal of property

(1) The Director-General may, by written notice to a person who is the subject of an investigation in respect of an offence alleged or suspected to have been committed under this Act, or against whom a prosecution for an offence has been instituted, direct that such person shall not dispose of, or otherwise deal with, any property specified in such notice without the consent of the Director-General.

(2) A notice issued under subsection (1) may be served by delivering it personally to the person to whom it is addressed or may, where the Director-General is satisfied that that person cannot be found, or is not in the Republic, be served on or brought to the knowledge of that person in such other manner as the Director-General may direct.

(3) A notice issued under subsection (1) shall—
   (a) in respect of an investigation within the jurisdiction, have effect from the time of service and shall' continue in force for a period of nine months or until cancelled by the Director-General, whichever is earlier; and
   (b) in respect of an investigation outside the jurisdiction, have effect from the time of service and shall continue in force for a period of twelve months or until cancelled by the Director-General, whichever is earlier: Provided that the Director-General may issue a fresh notice upon the expiry of the previous one for a further final term of six months to facilitate the conclusion of an investigation.

(4) A person who, having been served with, or having knowledge of a notice issued under subsection (1), disposes of or otherwise deals with, any property specified in the notice other than in accordance with the consent of the Director-General, commits an offence, and is liable, upon conviction, to imprisonment for a term not exceeding five years.

(5) A person aggrieved with the directive of the Director-General issued under subsection (1) may apply to the High Court for an order to reverse or vary the directive.

(6) An application made under subsection (5) shall give notice to the Director-General of the day appointed for the hearing of the application as a judge of the High Court may order.

(7) The High Court may, on the hearing of an application under subsection (5)(a) confirm the directive;
    (b) reverse the directive and consent to the disposal of, or other dealing with, any property specified in the notice, subject to such terms and conditions as it thinks fit; or
    (c) vary the directive as it thinks fit.

61. Restriction on disposal of property by third party

(1) The Commission may, where it has reasonable grounds to believe that a third party is holding any property, including money in a bank account for, or on behalf of, or to the order of a person who is under investigation, by notice, in writing, under the hand of the Director-General, serve a notice on the third party directing that the third party shall not dispose of, or otherwise deal with, any property specified in the notice.

(2) A notice issued under subsection (1) shall be served on the third party to whom it is directed and on the person being investigated.

(3) The Commission may, in issuing a notice under this section impose such conditions as it may determine.

(4) A notice issued under subsection (1) shall—
    (a) in respect of an investigation within the jurisdiction, have effect from the time of service upon the person and shall continue in force for a period of nine months or until cancelled by the Director-General, whichever is earlier; and
    (b) in respect of an investigation outside the jurisdiction, have effect from the time of-service upon the person and shall continue in force for a period of twelve months or until cancelled by the Director-General, whichever is earlier: Provided that the Director-General may issue a fresh notice upon the expiry of the previous one for a further final term of six months to facilitate the conclusion of an investigation.

(5) A third party on whom a notice is served under subsection (1) who disposes of, or deals with, the property specified in the notice without the consent of the Director-General commits an offence and is liable, upon conviction, to imprisonment for a period not exceeding five years.

(6) A third party on whom a notice is served under this section shall not dispose of, or otherwise deal with, the property specified in the notice except in accordance with the terms of the notice.

(7) Subsections (5), (6) and (7) of section *sixty* apply to this section.

62. Forfeiture of unexplained property

The Commission may commence proceedings for forfeiture of unexplained property under this section against a person where—
    (a) after due investigation, the Commission is satisfied that the person has unexplained assets; and
    (b) the person has, in the course of the exercise by the Commission of its powers of investigation or otherwise, been afforded a reasonable opportunity to explain the disproportion between the assets concerned and the person's known legitimate sources of income and the Commission is not satisfied that an adequate explanation of that disproportion has been given.

63. General offences

A person who—
    (a) knowingly makes, or causes to be made, to the Commission, false testimony or a false report in any material particular on any offence or matter under investigation;
    (b) knowingly misleads the Director-General, the Deputy Director-General or any other officer of the Commission by giving any false information or statement or making a false allegation;
    (c) obstructs, assaults, hinders or delays an officer of the Commission in the lawful exercise of the powers conferred on the officer under this Act;
    (d) refuses or fails, without reasonable cause, to give to the Director-General or an officer of the Commission on request, any document or information required for purposes of this Act;

(e) fails to comply with any lawful demand of the Director-General, Deputy Director-General or an officer of the Commission under this Act; or

(f) destroys anything to prevent the seizure of any property or document or securing of the property or documents; commits an offence and is liable, upon conviction, to imprisonment for a period not exceeding two years.

PART V
POWERS OF THE DIRECTOR OF PUBLIC PROSECUTIONS

64. Consent of Director of Public Prosecutions

(1) A prosecution for an offence under Part III shall not be instituted except by, or with, the consent of the Director of Public Prosecutions.

(2) Notwithstanding subsection (1), a person may be charged with an offence under Part III and may be arrested, or a warrant for that person's arrest may be issued and executed, and the person may be remanded by the court in custody or on bail notwithstanding that the written consent of the Director of Public Prosecutions to the institution of a prosecution for the offence with which that person is charged has not been obtained.

(3) Where a person is brought before a court before the written consent of the Director of Public Prosecutions to the institution of a prosecution against that person is obtained, the charge shall be explained to the accused person but the accused person shall not be called upon to plead.

65. Bail where suspect or accused person about to leave Zambia

If any person, against whom investigations or proceedings for an offence under Part III are pending, is preparing or about to leave Zambia, whether temporarily or permanently, the Director of Public Prosecutions or any officer authorised in that behalf, may apply to any court for an order requiring such person to furnish bail in any sum, or, if already admitted to bail, in such greater sum and on such additional conditions, as the case may be, with or without sureties, and in any such application the court may make such order as it considers appropriate.

PART VI
EVIDENCE, PRESUMPTIONS AND OTHER MATTERS

66. Presumption of corrupt intent

(1) Where, in any proceedings for an offence under this Act, it is proved that the accused person offered or accepted gratification, the gratification shall, unless the contrary is proved, be presumed to have been offered or accepted as an inducement or reward, as is alleged in the particulars of the offence.

(2) The presumption of corrupt intent shall, in relation to an offence under this Act, include—
   (a) misuse of position, office or authority; and
   (b) breach of procurement procedure or wilful failure to comply with applicable procedures or guidelines relating to the management of funds or incurring of public expenditure.

(3) Where, in any proceedings for an offence under this Act, it is proved that a person offered, gave, solicited, accepted or obtained or agreed to accept or attempted to receive or obtain, a payment in any of the circumstances set out in the relevant section under which the person is charged, such payment shall, in the absence of evidence to the contrary, be presumed to have been offered, given, solicited, accepted, obtained or agreed to be accepted, received or obtained corruptly.

(4) For the purposes of subsection (3), "payment" means any corrupt payment, whether cash or in kind, in respect of an offence under this Act.

(5) Where, in any proceeding under this Act, it is proved that any gratification has been offered, given, accepted or received by any person with the knowledge and acquiescence or consent of the accused person, and the court is satisfied, having regard to that person's relationship to the accused person or to any other circumstances that such person has offered, given, accepted or received the gratification for, or on behalf of, the accused person, or otherwise on account of, or in connection with, the office or duties of the accused person, or otherwise on account of, or in connection with, the office or duties of the accused person, the gratification, in the absence of evidence to the contrary, shall be presumed to have been offered, given, accepted or received by the accused person.

67. Corroborative evidence of pecuniary resources or property

(1) The fact that an accused person cannot reasonably account for any pecuniary resources or property of which the accused person is in possession disproportionate to the accused person's official emoluments or other income may be taken by the court—

    (a) as corroborating the testimony of any witness giving evidence in such proceedings that the accused person accepted or solicited any pecuniary resources or property; and

    (b) as showing that such possession of pecuniary resources or property was accepted or solicited as an inducement or reward.

(2) For the purposes of subsection (1), an accused person shall be deemed to be in possession of pecuniary resources or property if—

    (a) held by the accused person's relative or associate and the accused person, relative or associate is unable to reasonably account as to how such ownership, possession, custody or control came about; or

    (b) the accused person entered into any dealing for the acquisition of any property and the accused person is unable to reasonably account for the consideration used to acquire such property.

68. Grant of indemnity by Director of Public Prosecutions

(1) Subject to the Plea Negotiations and Agreements Act, 2010, the Director of Public Prosecutions may, at any time, with a view to obtaining at a trial the evidence of any person directly or indirectly concerned with or privy to an offence under Part III, tender indemnity to such person on condition that the person makes a full and true disclosure of all facts or circumstances within that person's knowledge relating to the offence and to every other person involved in the commission thereof, whether as principal or in any other capacity, together with the delivery up of any document or thing constituting evidence or corroboration of the commission of the offence by the person to be charged or the accused person, as the case may be.*[Act No. 20 of 2010]*

(2) The court shall record in the manner prescribed by the Criminal Procedure Code the evidence on oath of every person accepting indemnity under subsection (1) and shall transmit the record of such evidence to the Director of Public Prosecutions.*[Cap. 88]*

(3) A person accepting indemnity under this section shall be examined as a witness at the trial.

(4) Where a person who has accepted indemnity under this section has, either by wilfully concealing anything material to the case, or by giving false evidence, not complied with the condition on which the indemnity was made, that person may be prosecuted for the offence in respect of which the indemnity was tendered or for any other offence which the person appears to have committed in connection with the same matter.

(5) A person to whom indemnity has been made under subsection (1), who in the opinion of the court, has made a true and full disclosure of all things as to which that person is lawfully examined, shall be entitled to receive a certificate of indemnity under the hand of the Director of Public Prosecutions stating that the person has made a true and full disclosure of all things as to which the person was examined, and such certificate shall be a bar to all legal proceedings against that person in respect of all such things as aforesaid.

69. Protection of whistleblowers, victims, experts, etc.

(1) The provisions of the Public Interest Disclosure (Protection of Whistleblowers) Act, 2010, shall apply in relation to the protection of whistleblowers and other related matters.*[Act No. 4 of 2010]*

(2) Notwithstanding subsection (1), where it appears to the Director-General that as a result of assisting the Commission or the court, the safety of a witness, expert, victim or other person may be prejudiced or the witness, expert, victim or other person may be subject to threats, intimidation or harassment, the Director- General shall make such arrangements as are necessary to protect—

    (a) the safety of such witness, expert or victim; or (b)any other person from threats, intimidation or harassment.

(3) For the purposes of subsection (2), "assisting the Commission or court" includes—(a)appearance or impending appearance before the Commission or the court to give evidence or produce a document or other thing;

    (b) production or proposed production of a document or other thing to the Commission or the court under this Act; or (c)assisting or having assisted the Commission or the court in some other manner in accordance with the provisions of this Act.

(4)   The Director-General may, in providing the arrangements referred to in subsection (2), collaborate with other law enforcement agencies and authorities.

(5)   The law enforcement agencies and authorities shall, as far as reasonably possible, assist the Director-General in the provision of arrangements for the protection of the persons referred to in subsection (2).

(6)   Subject to subsection (1), in any trial for an offence under this Act, a witness shall not be obliged to—(a) disclose the identity or address of an informer or person assisting or who assisted the Commission in an investigation into an alleged or suspected offence under this Act; or(b)state any matter which may disclose the identity or address of an informer or person referred to in paragraph (a).

(7)   Where any document which is in evidence or liable to inspection in any civil or criminal proceeding under this Act contains any entry or passage in which an informer is named or described or which might lead to the person's discovery, the court before which the proceedings is held-shall cause such entry or passage to be concealed from view or to be obliterated in such a manner as, in the opinion of the court, shall not disclose the identity of the informer.

(8)   An action or proceeding, including disciplinary action, shall not be instituted or maintained against a witness, expert, victim or other person in respect of—

(a)   assistance given by the witness, expert, victim or other person to the Commission or the court; or

(b)   a disclosure of information made by the witness, expert, victim or outer person to the Commission or the court.

(9)   A person who contravenes this section commits an offence and is liable, upon conviction, to a fine not exceeding two hundred thousand penalty units or to imprisonment for a period not exceeding two years, or to both.

70.   Evidence of custom inadmissible

(1)   In any proceeding for an offence under Part III, it shall not be a defence that any gratification solicited, accepted or obtained or agreed to be accepted, given, offered or promised, is customary in any profession, business, trade, vocation or calling.

(2)   Notwithstanding subsection (1), no entertainment or casual gift offered or accepted under such conditions as may be prescribed shall constitute an offence under Part III.

71.   Absence of power, authority or opportunity, no defence

Where a public officer has corruptly solicited, accepted, obtained or agreed to accept or attempted to receive or obtain any gratification, it shall not be a defence in any trial in respect of an offence under Part III that—

(a)   the appointment, nomination or election of such person or any other person as a public officer was invalid or void;

(b)   the public officer or any other public officer did not have the power, authority or opportunity of doing, or of forbearing from doing, the act, favour or disfavour to which the gratification related; or

(c)   the public officer did not actually do any act, favour or disfavour to induce the gratification, or never had the intention of doing so.

72.   Corrupt practices coming to notice of commission, body or tribunal

Where any commission, body or tribunal established by or under the Constitution, or appointed under the Inquiries Act, in the course, or upon conclusion, of any proceedings before it, is of the opinion that the conduct of any person appears to constitute an offence under this Act and ought to be inquired into for the purposes of this Act, the commission, body or tribunal concerned shall, subject to any prohibition, restriction or restraint imposed upon it by, or under, the Constitution or any other written law, communicate its opinion to the Director-General, together with the particulars of the person concerned and such other facts of the case as the commission, body or tribunal may consider necessary. [Cap. 1], [Cap. 41]

73.   Affidavit evidence

For the purposes of any proceedings in respect of an offence under this Act, the court may, at any stage of the proceedings, direct that any specified fact may be proved at the trial: Provided that the deponent may be summoned for cross-examination.

74.   False, frivolous or groundless complaints or allegations

(1)   Where, at the conclusion of the trial of a person charged with an offence under Part III, the court is of the opinion that any person has wilfully, and with intent to harm or injure the accused person in any

manner made a false, frivolous or groundless complaint or allegation against the accused person, the court shall find the person liable for an offence under section *thirty-one* and shall convict the person accordingly.

(2) Any person who, in the opinion of the court certified under subsection (1), has made a false, frivolous or groundless complaint or allegation to the effect that any person has committed or attempted to commit, or aided, abetted or counselled the commission of, or conspired with any other person to commit, any offence under Part III, commits an offence and is liable, upon conviction, to a fine not exceeding three hundred thousand penalty units or to imprisonment for a period not exceeding seven years or to both.

75. Forfeiture of proceeds or property corruptly acquired

The provisions of the Forfeiture of Proceeds of Crime Act, 2010, shall apply in relation to the seizure and forfeiture of any proceeds or property corruptly acquired by any person and any other related matters. *[Act No. 19 of 2010]*

76. Tampering with seized and forfeited property

A person who tampers with any property that is seized or forfeited under this Act commits an offence and is liable, upon conviction, to imprisonment for a period not exceeding three years.

77. Alternative conviction of accused person

(1) If, on the trial of a person who has committed an offence under Part III, it is not proved that the accused person committed the offence charged but it is proved that the accused person committed some other offence under this Act, the accused person may, notwithstanding the absence of the written consent of the Director of Public Prosecutions in respect of such other offence, be convicted of such other offence, and be liable to be dealt with accordingly.

(2) If, on the trial of any person for any offence under Part III, there is any material variance between the particulars of the offence charged and the evidence adduced in support thereof, such variance shall not, of itself, entitle the accused person to an acquittal of the offence charged if, in the opinion of the court, there is *prima facie* evidence of the commission of that offence.

(3) Subject to subsection (2), notwithstanding the absence of the written consent of the Director of Public Prosecutions in respect of the particulars supported by the evidence adduced, the court may make the necessary amendment to the particulars and shall thereupon read and explain the same to the accused person and the accused person shall be called to plead to the amended particulars and the parties shall be allowed to recall and examine, on matters relevant to such amendment, any witness who may have been examined and to call any further witness.

(4) If an amendment is made under subsection (3) after the prosecution's case is closed, no further witness shall be called by the prosecution other than a witness on such matters only as it would, apart from the provisions of this subsection, be permissible to call and put in evidence in rebuttal.

78. Disapplication of secrecy obligations

The provisions of this Act shall have effect notwithstanding any obligation as to secrecy or other restriction on the disclosure of information imposed under any written law or otherwise.

79. Compensation for damage

(1) A person who does anything that constitutes corruption is liable to any person or victim who suffers loss or damage as a result, for the amount that constitutes full compensation for the loss or damage suffered by the person or victim.

(2) The compensation payable under subsection (1) shall be recoverable as a civil debt.

(3) The court may, on its own motion or upon an application by a person who suffers damage, in addition to any punishment which it may impose in respect of any offence under this Act, order the person convicted of such offence to pay appropriate compensation to any person for damage suffered as a result of an act of corruption.

(4) The Commission shall, where it has reasonable grounds to believe that a person has been a party to any corruption and has benefitted from it, institute civil proceedings for damages in respect of the corruption.

(5) Where a court determines that compensation payable under this section is payable to the State, the amount of compensation shall be paid into the Forfeited Assets Fund established under section seventy-three of the Forfeiture of Proceeds of Crime Act, 2010, and shall be expended in accordance with section *seventy-seven* of that Act.*[Act No. 19 of 2010]*

80. Out of court settlement

(1) In any matter where the Commission is mandated by this Act or any other law to institute civil proceeding or applications, it shall be lawful for the Commission to issue a notice or letter of demand to the person intended to be sued, and may, in such notice or letter, inform the person about the claim against that person and further inform the person that that person could settle the claim within a specified time before the filing of court proceedings.

(2) The Commission may negotiate and enter a settlement with any person against whom the Commission intends to bring, or has actually brought, a civil claim or application in court.

(3) The Commission may tender an undertaking, in writing, not to institute criminal proceedings against a person who—

  (a) has given a full and true disclosure of all material facts relating to past corrupt conduct and an illegal activity by that person or others; and

  (b) has voluntarily paid, deposited or refunded all property the person acquired through corruption or illegal activity.

(4) A settlement or undertaking under this section shall be registered in court.

PART VII
PUBLIC PARTICIPATION AND ACCESS TO INFORMATION

81. Public participation

(1) The Commission shall ensure that public participation in the prevention and eradication of corruption is undertaken on the principle that public participation—

  (a) is based on the belief that those who are affected by a problem have a right to be involved in finding a solution;

  (b) includes the promise that the people's contribution will effect change;

  (c) promotes sustainable decision by recognising and communicating the needs and interests of all participants, including decision makers;

  (d) seeks input from participants in designing how they participate;

  (e) provides participants with information they need to participate in a meaningful way; and

  (f) communicates to participants how their input affects decisions,(2)The Commission shall put in place measures to facilitate the participation of individuals and groups—

  (a) in the prevention of, and the fight against corruption and the raising of public awareness regarding the existence, causes and gravity of and threat caused by corruption;

  (b) in as far as is reasonably practicable, in the decision-making process;

  (c) in free exchange of opinions and ideas and respecting, promoting and protecting the freedom to seek, receive, publish and disseminate information concerning corruption; and

  (d) self mobilisation awareness raising initiatives and programmes.

(3) The Commission shall inform the public of the various authorities involved in combating corruption and the services available to the public and how the public may assist and otherwise participate in ensuring the effective functioning of the authorities.

(4) The Commission and the appropriate authorities shall establish mechanisms to collect and respond to public comments, concerns and questions relating to the fight against corruption including public debates and hearings.

82. Analysis and dissemination of information

(1) The Commission shall—

  (a) maintain information on the harmful effects of corruption on society for dissemination to the general public;

  (b) subject to any other written law, provide access to any data collected on corruption for use by members of the public;

  (c) analyse information relating to corruption and disseminate information on patterns and trends of corruption;

  (d) subject to any other written law, disseminate information on practices and procedures of public and private bodies on prevention and eradication of corruption;

  (e) commission studies on corruption and trends impacting on corruption prevention, eradication and general ethical issues;

  (f) carry out public information and education campaigns;

  (g) advise the President on existing information gaps and needs in the fight against corruption;

and(h)establish, in consultation with public and private bodies, guidelines and principles for the gathering, processing and dissemination of anti-corruption information.

(2) The Commission shall publish information on the prevention, eradication and effects of corruption as it considers necessary for public education and awareness on the existence, causes and gravity of corruption.

(3) The Commission shall annually cause the names of all persons convicted of offences or who have admitted guilt under this Act in a particular year to be published in the *Gazette*.

83. Anti-corruption education and awareness

The Commission shall, in consultation with the relevant authorities and civil society organisations—

(a) take measures for the integration of anti-corruption practices and strategies in schools, colleges and institutions of higher learning; and

(b) undertake public information activities that contribute to non-tolerance of corruption and transparency and accountability in the mobilisation and utilisation of public resources and management of public affairs.

84. Maintenance of information

The Commission shall maintain information for the use of the general public on the laws, international anti-corruption agreements to which Zambia is a party, and any policies, plans, guidelines, studies, reports, decisions, recommendations and other publications relating to corruption published by the Commission.

85. Guidelines on public participation

The Commission may make guidelines relating to public participation and information for purposes of this Act.

PART VIII
GENERAL PROVISIONS

86. Procedure for commencement of application

Except where otherwise specifically provided for, all applications under this Act shall be commenced by way of originating summons.

87. Register of gifts

(1) A public body shall keep a register of gifts which shall be administered by the controlling officer or chief executive officer of the public body, as the case may be.

(2) The Commission may, by statutory instrument, make rules relating to the management of the register of gifts.

88. Mutual legal assistance

The Mutual Legal Assistance in Criminal Matters Act applies to offences under this Act, except where the provisions of that Act are inconsistent with this Act. *[Cap. 98]*

89. Supremacy of Act

Subject to the Constitution, where there is any inconsistency between the provisions of this Act and those of any other written law relating to corrupt practices, the provisions of this Act shall prevail to the extent of the inconsistency. *[Cap. 1]*

90. Defence

In any proceedings for an offence under this Act it shall be a valid defence that the gratification offered or accepted is an entertainment or a casual gift.

91. Offences committed outside Zambia

(1) This Act shall have effect within as well as outside Zambia and notwithstanding where any offence is committed by any person, that person may be dealt with in respect of such offence as if it has been committed within Zambia.

(2) Any proceedings against any person under this section which would be a bar to subsequent proceedings against such person for the same offence, if such offence had been committed in Zambia, shall be a bar to further proceedings against that person under any written law for the time being in force relating to the extradition of persons, in respect of the same offence outside Zambia.

(3) Subject to subsection (2), the court may, in relation to an offence committed outside Zambia take into account the previous conviction or criminal record of a person as may be necessary in the application of this Act.

92. Extraditable offences

An offence under this Act shall be deemed to be an extraditable offence under the provisions of the Extradition Act. *[Cap. 94]*

93. Rules

The Commission may, by statutory instrument, make rules for the—
(a) appointment, including the power to confirm appointments of persons, to any office in respect of which the Commission is charged with the responsibility under this Act;
(b) disciplinary control of persons holding or acting in any office;
(c) termination of appointments and the removal of persons from office; and
(d) practice and procedure of the Commission in the exercise of its functions under this Act.

94. Regulations

(1) The Commission may make regulations for the better carrying out of the provisions of this Act.
(2) Without prejudice to the generality of subsection (1), the regulations made under that subsection may provide for—
(a) the prevention of corruption generally;
(b) the disclosure by public officers of interest in contracts or proposed contracts;
(c) the control and maintenance of the register of gifts;
(d) protection of informers, witnesses, whistleblowers, complainants and other persons for purposes of this Act;
(e) the procedure for lodging and dealing with complaints;
(f) the procedure for declaring of interest and assets by officers of the Commission;
(g) the disposal of recovered gratification;
(h) anti-corruption strategies in private and public bodies;
(i) the form of oaths to be declared under this Act;
(j) the establishment, composition, tenure, procedure and any other matters in respect of committees; and
(k) generally the carrying into effect of the purposes of this Act.

95. Repeal of Act No 38 of 2010

(1) The Anti-Corruption Act, 2010, is hereby repealed.
(2) Notwithstanding subsection (1), all the investigations, prosecutions and other legal proceedings, instituted or commenced under the repealed Act, and pending immediately before the commencement of this Act by or against the Commission, may be continued by or against it.
(3) Notwithstanding subsection (1), all the property, assets, rights, liabilities and obligations of the Commission existing immediately before the commencement of this Act, shall vest and continue to vest in, and subsist against the Commission, together with the rights, liabilities and obligations arising out of any contract or otherwise, as if this Act had not come into force.
(4) Subject to the other provisions of this Act, a person who, immediately before the commencement of this Act, held office as a Commissioner of the Commission shall continue to hold such office as a Commissioner until the expiry of the term.

96. Staff of Commission

A person who was an officer or member of staff of the Commission before the commencement of this Act shall continue to be an officer or member of the Commission, as the case may be, as if appointed or employed under this Act.

SCHEDULE (SECTION 4 (3))

ADMINISTRATION OF COMMISSION

PART I – THE BOARD OF THE COMMISSION

1. Seal of Commission

(1) The seal of the Commission shall be such device as may be determined by the Board and shall be kept by the Secretary.

(2) The affixing of the seal shall be authenticated by the Chairperson or any other person authorised in that behalf by a resolution of the Board.

(3) Any document purporting to be under the seal of the Commission or issued on behalf of the Commission shall be received in evidence and shall be deemed to be so executed or issued, as the case may be, without further proof, unless the contrary is proved.

2. Board of Commission

(1) There is hereby constituted a Board of Commissioners which shall be the governing body of the Commission.

(2) The Board shall consist of the following Commissioners:
   (a) the Chairperson, who shall be a person who has held, or is qualified to hold, high judicial office;
   (b) the Vice-Chairperson; and
   (c) three other persons.

(3) The Commissioners shall be appointed by the President, subject to ratification by the National Assembly.

(4) A person is eligible to be appointed as a Commissioner if that person—
   (a) is a citizen of Zambia;
   (b) is permanently resident in Zambia;
   (c) is of high integrity; and
   (d) has served with distinction at a senior level in a Government office or a registered profession or vocation.

(5) A person shall not be appointed as a Commissioner if that person—
   (a) holds office in, or is an employee of, any political party; or
   (b) has been convicted of an offence involving fraud or dishonesty, or any other offence under this Act or any other written law and sentenced therefor to a term of imprisonment of six months or more without the option of a fine.

3. Tenure of office of Commissioner

(1) A Commissioner shall, subject to the other provisions of this Schedule, hold office for a period of three years and may be appointed for a further period of three years:
Provided that a Commissioner shall only hold office for two terms.

(2) A Commissioner may resign upon giving one month's notice, in writing, to the President.

(3) The office of a Commissioner shall become vacant—
   (a) if the Commissioner is absent, without reasonable excuse, from three consecutive meetings of the Commission of which the Commissioner has had notice;
   (b) if the Commissioner is adjudged bankrupt;
   (c) if the Commissioner is convicted of an offence under this Act or any other written law and sentenced therefor to imprisonment for a term of six months or more, without the option of a fine;
   (d) if the Commissioner is declared to be of unsound mind; or
   (e) upon the Commissioner's death.

4. Declaration of assets: A Commissioner shall not take up office unless the Commissioner furnishes a declaration of assets and liabilities to the Chief Justice in the prescribed form.

5. Proceedings of Board

(1) Subject to the other provisions of this Act, the Board may regulate its own procedures.

(2) The Board shall meet for the transaction of business at least once in every three months at such places and times as the Board may determine.

(3) A meeting of the Board maybe called by the Chairperson upon giving notice of not less than fourteen days, and shall be called by the Chairperson if not less than one third of the members so request in

writing: Provided that if the urgency of any particular matter does not permit the giving of such notice, a special meeting may be called upon a shorter notice given by three members of the Board.

(4)   The Chairperson with two other Commissioners shall constitute a quorum at any meeting of the Board.

(5)   There shall preside at any meeting of the Board—

     (a)   the Chairperson;

     (b)   in the absence of the Chairperson, the Vice-Chairperson; or

     (c)   in the absence of both the Chairperson and the ViceChairperson, such other Commissioner as the Commissioners present may elect for the purpose of that meeting.

(6)   A decision of the Board on any question shall be by a majority of the Commissioners present and voting at the meeting and in the event of an equality of votes, the person presiding at the meeting shall have a casting vote, in addition to that person's deliberative vote.

(7)   The Board may invite any person, whose presence is in its opinion desirable, to attend and to participate in the deliberations of a meeting of the Board, but such person shall have no vote.

(8)   The validity of any proceedings, acts or decisions of the Board shall not be affected by any vacancy in the membership of the Board or by any defect in the appointment of any Commissioner or by reason that any person not entitled to do so, took part in the proceedings.

6.   Committees of Board

(1)   The Board may, for the purpose of performing its functions under this Act, establish such committees as it considers necessary and delegate to any of those committees such of its functions as it considers fit.

(2)   Subject to sub-paragraph (1), the Board may appoint as members of a committee persons who are, or are not, Commissioners, except that at least one member of a committee shall be a Commissioner.

(3)   A person serving as a member of a committee shall hold office for such period as the Board may determine.

(4)   Subject to any specific or general direction of the Board, a committee may regulate its own procedure.

7.   Remuneration and allowances of Commissioners

There shall be paid to a Commissioner or a member of a committee such remuneration and allowances or honorarium as the Board may determine with the approval of the President.

8.   Disclosure of interest

(1)   If any person is present at a meeting of the Board or any committee at which any matter is the subject of consideration, and in which matter that person or that person's spouse, relative, friend or associate is directly or indirectly interested in a private capacity, that person shall, as soon as is practicable after the commencement of the meeting, declare such interest and shall not, unless the Board or the committee otherwise directs, take part in any consideration or discussion of, or vote on, any question relating to that matter.

(2)   A disclosure of interest made under sub-paragraph (1) shall be recorded in the minutes of the meeting at which it is made.

9.   Prohibition of publication of, or disclosure of, information to unauthorised persons

(1)   A person shall not, without the consent in writing given by, or on behalf of, the Commission, publish or disclose to any unauthorised person, otherwise than in the course of duties of that person, the contents of any document, communication or information whatsoever, which relates to or which has come to the knowledge of that person in the course of that person's duties under this Act.

(2)   A person who contravenes sub-paragraph (1) commits an offence and is liable, upon conviction, to a fine not exceeding two hundred thousand penalty units or to imprisonment for a period not exceeding two years, or to both.

(3)   A person who, having any information which to the knowledge of that person has been published or disclosed in contravention of sub-paragraph (1), unlawfully publishes or communicates the information to any other person, commits an offence and is liable, upon conviction, to a fine not exceeding two hundred thousand penalty units or to imprisonment for a period not exceeding two years, or to both.

10.   ImmunityAn action or other proceeding shall not lie or be instituted against a Commissioner or a member of a committee of the Commission for, or in respect of, any act or thing done or omitted to be done in good faith in the exercise of or performance, or purported exercise or performance of any of the powers, functions or duties conferred under this Act.

PART II
FINANCIAL PROVISIONS

11. Funds of Commission

(1) The funds of the Commission shall consist of such monies as may—
    (a) be appropriated to the Commission by Parliament for the purposes of the Commission;
    (b) be paid to the Commission by way of grants or donations; and
    (c) otherwise vest in or accrue to the Commission.
(2) The Commission may, subject to the approval of the President—
    (a) accept monies by way of grants or donations from any source within or outside Zambia; and
    (b) raise by way of loans or otherwise, such monies as it may require for the discharge of its functions.
(3) There shall be paid from the funds of the Commission—
    (a) the salaries, allowances, pensions and loans of the members of staff of the Commission;
    (b) such reasonable travelling and other allowances for the Commissioners and the members of any committee when engaged on the business of the Commission, at such rates as the Board may determine; and
    (c) any other expenses incurred by the Commission in the performance of its functions under this Act.

12. Financial year

The financial year of the Commission shall be a period of twelve months ending on 31st December in each year.

13. Accounts

(1) The Commission shall cause to be kept proper books of account and other records relating to its accounts.
(2) The accounts of the Commission shall be audited annually by the Auditor-General or an auditor appointed by the Auditor-General.

14. Annual report

(1) As soon as practicable, but not later than ninety days after the end of the financial year, the Commission shall submit to the President a report concerning its activities during the financial year.
(2) The report referred to in sub-paragraph (1) shall include information on the financial affairs of the Commission and there shall be appended to the report—
    (a) an audited balance sheet;
    (b) an audited statement of income and expenditure; and
    (c) such other information as the President may require.
(3) The President shall, not later than seven days after the first sitting of the National Assembly next after receipt of the report referred to in subparagraph (1), lay the report before the National Assembly.

THE ELECTORAL PROCESS ACT NO 35 OF 2016

ARRANGEMNET OF SECTIONS

PART I
PRELIMINARY

510

PART VII
OBSERVERS, MONITORS AND VOTER EDUCATION

PART VII
CORRUPT AND ILLEGAL PRACTICES AND OTHER ELECTION OFFENCES

SCHEDULE
GOVERNMENT OF ZAMBIA
ACT
No. 35 of 2016
Date of Assent: 6th June, 2016

An Act to provide for a comprehensive process for a general election; provide for the conduct of elections by the Electoral Commission of Zambia and empower the Commission to make regulations in matters relating to elections; provide for the registration of voters and the keeping of voters registers; prescribe the procedures for nominations for elections; provide for the role of presiding officers, election officers and conflict management officers; prescribe the procedure for voting during an election; provide for the accreditation and roles of observers and monitors; criminalise corrupt practices and other illegal practices related to elections and provide for penalties in connection with an election; provide for election petitions and the hearing and determination of applications relating to a general election; provide for voter education; prescribe the electoral code of conduct; repeal and replace the Electoral Act, 2006; and provide for matters connected with, or incidental to, the foregoing.

[7th June, 2016]

Enactment

ENACTED by the Parliament of Zambia.

PART I
PRELIMINARY PROVISIONS

Short title

1. This Act may be cited as the Electoral Process Act, 2016.

Interpretation

2. In this Act, unless the context otherwise requires—

"area" has the meaning assigned to it in section two of the Local Government Act; [Cap. 281]

"ballot box" means a box prescribed by the Commission for the purpose of an election;

"ballot paper" means the document prescribed by the Commission in respect of an election;

"ballot paper account" means a document prescribed by the Commission for purposes of recording the ballot papers issued to a returning officer and completed by a presiding officer at the close of a poll;

"by-election" has the meaning assigned to it in the Constitution;

"campaign material" means party or candidate manifestos, advertisements, billboards, posters, tshirts, cloth or other material depicting colours regarding symbols, and other designs of a party or pictural images of a candidate;

"campaign period" means a period of three months before the holding of an election;

"candidate" means a person contesting a presidential, parliamentary or local government election;

"caricature" means the exaggerated imitation of a cartoon, effigy, picture, drawing or sketch of a person or literary style for comic or satirical effect;

"casual vacancy" means a vacancy in the office of councillor as specified in the Local Government Act;

"Chief Electoral Officer" has the meaning assigned to it in the Electoral Commission of Zambia Act, 2016;

"Code" means the Electoral Code of Conduct set out in the Schedule;

"Commission" means the Electoral Commission of Zambia established by the Constitution;

"conflict management officer" means an officer appointed as a conflict management officer in accordance with section one hundred and thirteen;

"constituency" has the meaning assigned to it in the Constitution;

"Constitutional Court" has the meaning assigned to it in the Constitution;

"corrupt practice" means any conduct which is declared to be a corrupt practice in accordance with section eighty-one;

"costs"includes charges and expenses;

"council"has the meaning assigned to it in the Constitution;

"council chairperson" has the meaning assigned to it in the Constitution;

"councillor" has the meaning assigned to it in the Constitution;

"designated person" means a person or officer appointed by the Chief Justice for the purpose of receiving election petitions filed before a tribunal and attending to such other matters regarding petitions before a tribunal as are assigned to the Registrar under this Act;

"election" has the meaning assigned to it in the Constitution;

"election agent" means a person appointed as an agent of a candidate for the purpose of an election and who is specified in the candidate's nomination paper;

"election officer" means a person appointed by the Commission as—

(a) a registration officer;

(b) an assistant registration officer;

(c) a district electoral officer;

(d) a returning officer;

(e) a presiding officer;

(f) an assistant presiding officer; or

(g) a polling assistant;

and includes a person appointed to assist the Chief Electoral Officer in the performance of the functions of the Chief Electoral Officer as specified in this Act;

513

"election petition" means an election petition related to a presidential, parliamentary or local government election as specified in the Constitution;

"election timetable" means a timetable for an election published by the Commission in accordance with section twenty-eight;

"employee" has the meaning assigned to it in section two of the Local Government Act;

"general election" has the meaning assigned to it in the Constitution;

"illegal practice" means an offence which is declared under this Act to be an illegal practice;

"interim period" means the period commencing at the commencement of this Act and expiring on such date as the President may prescribe by statutory order;

"media" includes publicly or privately operated print and electronic media;

"Member of Parliament" has the meaning assigned to it in the Constitution;

"monitor" means a person accredited as such by the Commission;

"national registration card" means a national registration card issued under and in terms of the National Registration Act;

"national registration number" means the serial number inserted on a national registration card issued in accordance with the National Registration Act;

"nomination day" means the day appointed by the Commission as the day on which a candidate files that candidate's nomination paper with the Commission;

"nomination centre" means a place prescribed by the Commission as a nominating office;

"nomination paper" means a document prescribed by the Commission for the purpose of a candidate registering that candidate's intention to contest an election under this Act;

"observer" means a person accredited as such by the Commission;

"petitioner" in relation to an election petition, means a person who signs and presents an election petition under section ninety-eight, and includes a person substituted for a petitioner;

"political party" has the meaning assigned to it in the Constitution;

"polling agent" means an agent appointed by a candidate in respect of a polling station;

"polling assistant" means a person appointed as polling assistant by the Commission;

"polling day" means—

(a)   in relation to a general election, the day specified in accordance with the Constitution for the taking of the poll in a general election; and

(b)   in relation to a by-election, a day appointed by the Commission for the taking of the poll in a by-election;

"polling district" means a district established by the Commission as a polling district under section twenty-one;

"polling station" means a place established as a polling station by the Commission under section twenty-four;

"public officer" has the meaning assigned to it in the Constitution;

"presidential election" has the meaning assigned to it in the Constitution;

"presiding officer" means a person appointed as a presiding officer by the Commission under section thirty-seven;

"Register of Voters" means the Register of Voters prepared and certified by the Commission under section fourteen;

"registration officer" means a person appointed as a registration officer by the Commission;

"Registrar" means the Chief Registrar of the High Court, and includes the Deputy Registrar, District Registrar and Assistant Registrar;

"respondent" means a person against whom an election petition is filed in accordance with section ninety-eight;

"Returning Officer" has the meaning assigned to it in the Constitution;

"returning officer" has the meaning assigned to it in the Constitution;

"traditional leader" means a paramount chief, senior chief, chief or village headman;

"tribunal" means a local government elections tribunal established in accordance with Article 159 of the Constitution;

"voter" means a person who is registered as a voter and whose name appears in the Register of Voters;

"voter's card" means a voter's card prescribed and issued by the Commission; and

"ward" means any of the divisions into which a council area is divided under section twenty-five.

Principles of electoral system and process

3.   Subject to the Constitution, the principles applied in the electoral system and process shall ensure the following:
   (a)   equal and universal suffrage;
   (b)   no discrimination based on gender or disability when providing electoral services;
   (c)   transparent and credible electoral process;
   (d)   no special privileges accorded to a political party or social group, except for persons with special needs;
   (e)   no impediments to lawful inclusion in the electoral register;
   (f)   impartial voter-education programmes;
   (g)   access to polling stations for representatives of political parties, accredited local or international election monitors, observers and the media;
   (h)   secrecy of the vote;
   (i)   design of the ballot paper that promotes easy use;
   (j)   transparent and secure ballot boxes;
   (k)   impartial assistance to voters at the polling station;
   (l)   transparent, accurate and reliable vote counting procedure;
   (m)   proper management of invalid ballot papers;
   (n)   precautionary measures for transporting of election materials;
   (o)   impartial protection of polling stations;
   (p)   established procedures for lodging and dealing with complaints;
   (q)   impartial handling of election complaints;
   (r)   impartial delimitation of electoral boundaries; and
   (s)   timely resolution of electoral disputes.

Administration, enforcement and prosecution

4.   (1)   This Act shall be administered and enforced by the Commission and the Commission shall not be subject to the direction or control of any person or authority in the exercise of its functions under the Constitution and this Act.
   (2)   The Commission shall, in order to ensure compliance with the provisions of this Act, appoint such number of officers as it may consider necessary for purposes of this Act.
   (3)   An officer appointed pursuant to subsection (2) shall be provided with a letter of appointment which shall be prima facie evidence of that person's appointment.
   (4)   An officer shall, on demand by a person affected by the exercise of the powers of that officer under this Act, produce for inspection the letter referred to in subsection (3).
   (5)   The Anti-Corruption Commission shall investigate and prosecute any corrupt practice committed under this Act in accordance with the Anti-Corruption Act, 2012.
   (6)   The Zambia Police Service shall enforce law and order at polling stations and undertake any criminal proceedings, subject to subsection (2), in respect of an offence committed by any person in contravention of this Act.

Delegation of powers and duties by Commission

5.   (1)   The Commission may—
      (a)   delegate any of its powers under this Act to a member, employee or officer of the Commission excluding the power to prescribe anything under this Act or make an appointment under this Act or any other written law; and
      (b)   instruct a member, employee or officer of the Commission to perform any of its duties under this Act or any other written law.
   (2)   A delegation or instruction made under subsection (1)—
      (a)   shall be subject to any limitations and conditions that the Commission may impose; and
      (b)   does not prevent the Commission from exercising or performing the assigned power or duty.
   (3)   The Commission may, by statutory order, confer powers or impose duties on an officer or authority of the Government or council for the purpose of discharging its functions under this Act.

Delegation of powers and duties by Chief Electoral Officer

6. (1) The Chief Electoral Officer may —

    (a) delegate any of the powers of the Chief Electoral Officer under this Act or any other law to an employee or officer of the Commission; or

    (b) instruct an employee or officer of the Commission to perform any of the duties of the Chief Electoral Officer under this Act or any other written law.

    (2) Subsection (2) of section five with the necessary modification, shall apply to a delegation or instruction of the Chief Electoral Officer under subsection (1).

PART II
REGISTRATION OF VOTERS AND REGISTERS

Continuous voter registration

7. The Commission shall conduct a continuous registration of voters.

Qualification for registration as voters

8. (1) A person qualifies for registration as a voter if that person —

    (a) is a citizen of Zambia;

    (b) has attained the age of eighteen years; and

    (c) is in possession of a national registration card.

    (2) The Commission shall register a person as a voter as prescribed.

    (3) A person who has been registered in the Register of Voters shall be issued with a voter's card.

    (4) A person shall not register as a voter in more than one constituency.

Disqualification from registration as voter

9. (1) The Commission shall not register a person as a voter if that person

    (a) is not a citizen of Zambia;

    (b) is not in possession of a national registration card;

    (c) suffers from a mental disability which makes the person unable to exercise their right to vote;

    (d) is detained under the Criminal Procedure Code during the pleasure of the President;

    (e) is disqualified from voting under section forty-seven;

    (f) is under a sentence of death imposed by a competent court, or a sentence of imprisonment imposed by a court or substituted by a competent authority for some other sentence imposed by that court; or

    (g) does not qualify to be registered as a voter as may be prescribed;

    (2) In this section, the reference to a sentence of imprisonment shall not be construed as including a sentence of imprisonment the execution of which is suspended or a sentence of imprisonment imposed in default of payment of a fine.

De-registration of Voter

10. A registration officer shall de-register a voter if the registration officer is satisfied that the voter —

    (a) does not qualify to be registered as a voter;

    (b) no longer meets the qualifications for registration as specified in section eight;

    (c) has been fraudulently registered; or

    (d) obtained the registration through submission of false information or making of a misleading statement.

Notification by registration officer

11. (1) A registration officer shall notify a person —

    (a) whose registration as a voter has been refused;

    (b) whose application to have a change of name or ordinary place of residence recorded has been refused;

    (c) who has been disqualified from registration as a voter under section ten; or

    (d) whose registration details have been changed.

(2)   A notification given under subsection (1) shall give reasons for the refusal or action taken.

Suspension of registration of voters

12. (1)   The Commission may suspend the registration of voters whenever an election is due for the purposes of the conduct of the election.

(2)   The Commission shall, where it prescribes the polling day for a byelection, immediately suspend the registration of voters in the district in which the byelection is to take place until the byelection is concluded.

Provisional Register of Voters

13. (1)   The Commission shall establish a Provisional Register of Voters as prescribed.

(2)   The Provisional Register of Voters shall include the details of persons entitled to vote in an election or referendum under this Act or the Referendum Act.

Register of voters

14. (1)   The Commission shall compile and maintain the Register of Voters as prescribed.

(2)   The Register of Voters shall include the details of persons entitled to vote in an election or referendum under this Act or the Referendum Act.

(3)   The Register of Voters shall not preclude any person from voting in a referendum in accordance with the Constitution.

Application to change registration details

15. A voter whose name or ordinary place of residence has changed may apply, in the prescribed manner, to have that change recorded in the Register of Voters, except that a person shall not apply when a change of name is due to change in marital status.

Amendments to Register of Voters

16. (1)   A registration officer shall—

(a)   change the registration details of a voter if the registration officer is satisfied that the details of a voter as reflected in the Register of Voters are incorrect or have changed;

(b)   add the name and other particulars of a voter resulting from a new registration, as prescribed; or

(c)   delete the name of a voter who is deceased.

(2)   A registration officer shall record, in the Register of Voters, a change in a polling district for which a person is registered as a voter if that person's place of ordinary residence after a change in the boundaries of the polling district falls in another polling district.

Objections concerning details in provisional register of voters

17. (1)   A person whose name appears in the Provisional Register of Voters may object to an error or omission regarding the person's details, in the prescribed manner, within ninety days' of the publication of the Provisional Register of Voters.

(2)   A person may object to an error or omission to the exclusion or regarding the registration details of another person.

(3)   A person who objects to another person's registration details shall serve notice of the objection on that person.

(4)   The Commission shall consider an objection to the Provisional Register of Voters within fourteen days from the date the objection was made and shall notify the person who made the objection and the registration officer.

(5)   A registration officer shall give effect to a decision of the Commission, made under this section, within three days of the decision.

Publication of register of Voters

18. (1)   A copy of the Register of Voters, as it exists at any time, shall be available for inspection during office hours at the Commission's head office.

(2) A person who requires a copy or extract of the Register of Voters may, upon payment of a prescribed fee, obtain the copy or extract which shall be certified by the Chief Electoral Officer.

(3) A document purporting to be a copy or extract of the Register of Voters, which is duly certified by the Chief Electoral Officer, shall be received in evidence in any legal proceedings as to the matters stated in the Register of Voters.

Inspection of register of Voters

19. (1) The Register of Voters or the segments of the Register of Voters that shall be used for an election shall be the register certified for the purposes of that election.

(2) The Chief Electoral Officer shall certify the Register of Voters, or segments of the Register of Voters, and publish the Register of Voters or the segments of the Register of Voters and make the Register of Voters or the segments of the Register of Voters available for inspection at the following venues:

    (a) at the Commission's head office;

    (b) at the polling station in each polling district; and

    (c) at the office of each council.

Cut off dates for registration of Voters and Register of Voters

20. (1) The Commission may prescribe cut-off dates with respect to the registration of voters and the compilation of the Register of Voters, including the date by which—

    (a) a person may apply to be registered as a voter or change the person's registration details;

    (b) a registration officer shall give notice of the venue and dates on which the Provisional Register of Voters may be inspected;

    (c) the Commission shall consider an objection made under section seventeen and notify the objector and the registration officer and a person other than the objector whose name or registration details are involved; and

    (d) a registration officer shall complete the compilation of the Register of Voters and publish it.

PART III
POLLING DISTRICTS AND BOUNDARIES

Establishment of polling districts

21. (1) The Commission shall—

    (a) establish polling districts for the whole of the territory of the Republic;

    (b) determine the boundaries of each polling district in accordance with the criteria provided in section twenty-two; and

    (c) keep a map of each district.

(2) The polling districts for an election shall be those polling districts which, on the date on which an election is called, are within the area in which the election is called.

Criteria for determining polling district boundaries

22. The Commission shall determine the boundaries of a polling district by taking into account any factor within the proposed polling districts that could affect the free, fair and orderly conduct of elections, including—

    (a) the availability of a suitable venue for a polling station;

    (b) the number and distribution of eligible voters;

    (c) the accessibility of a polling station to voters given—

        (i) the radius of the proposed polling district;

        (ii) the availability of transport;

        (iii) telecommunications facilities; and

        (iv) any geographical or physical feature that may impede access to the polling station;

    (d) district and provincial boundaries; and

    (e) cultural diversity.

Inspection and copies of maps of polling district

23. (1) As soon as practicable after the polling districts have been established, the Chief Electoral Officer shall give notice that copies of the map of each polling district are available for inspection.

(2) The notice referred to in subsection (1) shall be published in the Gazette and publicised in the media so as to ensure wide publicity of the maps.

(3) The notice shall state, and the Chief Electoral Officer shall ensure, that copies of—
   (a) the maps are available for inspection at the Commission's head office; and
   (b) the maps of the polling districts are available for inspection at the office of the person administering the district.

(4) A person may inspect a copy of a map provided for in subsection (1).

(5) The Chief Electoral Officer shall provide a certified copy of a map of a polling district to any person who pays the prescribed fee for that purpose.

Establishment of polling station

24. (1) The Commission shall establish a polling station for an election, in each polling district, as the Commission may prescribe.

(2) The Commission shall, when determining the location of a polling station, take into account any factor that could affect the free, fair and orderly conduct of elections, including—
   (a) the number and distribution of eligible voters in the polling districts;
   (b) the availability of suitable venues for polling stations;
   (c) the distance to be travelled to reach the polling station;
   (d) access routes to the polling station;
   (e) the availability of transport to the polling station;
   (f) traffic density at or near the polling station;
   (g) telecommunications facilities at the polling station;
   (h) general facilities at the polling station;
   (i) the safety and convenience of voters;
   (j) any geographical or physical feature that may impede access to or at the polling station; and
   (k) the accessibility of the polling station.

(3) The Commission may, before determining the location of a polling station, consult on the proposed location of that polling station with the council for the area in which that polling station shall fall.

(4) The Chief Electoral Officer shall, not later than the date stated in the election timetable, publicise a list containing the addresses of the established polling stations available for inspection.

(5) Section twenty-three shall apply, with the necessary modifications, to the inspection and obtaining of copies of the established polling stations.

Division of area of councils into wards

25. (1) The Commission shall, after consultation with every council, by statutory order, divide the area of each council into wards, defining the boundaries of the wards by reference to polling districts, and assigning names to the wards and polling districts.

(2) The number of wards into which the area of a council is divided shall be equal to the number of elected councillors prescribed in respect of that council by the Minister under the Local Government Act.

(3) The Commission shall exercise its powers under this section so that each ward comprises one or more complete polling districts.

(4) Whenever the Minister alters the area of a council or the number of councillors of a council, the Commission shall, after consultation with such council, by statutory order, make such alterations to the boundaries of the wards of such council or to the division of the area of such council into wards as may be necessary to give effect to the provisions of this section.

(5) Whenever the Commission is satisfied that there has been a material alteration in the number of registered voters in the area of a council or of any of the wards into which such area is divided, the Commission may, after consultation with the council concerned, exercise in respect of the area of that council or any part of the council the powers conferred by this section.

Election in newly created Council

26. (1) The Commission may, by statutory order, whenever—
    (a) a new council is established; or
    (b) an alteration is made in the division of the area of an existing council into wards or in the definition of the boundaries of any ward; direct that an ordinary election of councillors in every ward or in any particular ward of that council shall be held on such date as may be appointed by the statutory order.
    (2) A statutory order made under this section shall specify the day or days on which, and the hours within which, returning officers may receive nominations of candidates for election in any ward to which such order relates.

Relocation of polling station in emergencies

27. (1) Despite section twenty, the Commission may relocate a polling station if it is necessary to do so for the conduct of a free and fair election.
    (2) The Chief Electoral Officer shall publicise the relocation of a polling station among voters in the polling district concerned.

PART IV
NOMINATIONS FOR ELECTIONS

Election timetable

28. (1) Subject to the Constitution, the Commission shall, before the polling day—
    (a) compile an election timetable for each election to provide for the following:
        (i) the closing date of the registration of voters;
        (ii) the dates for inspection of the Provisional Register of Voters;
        (iii) the date and method for the submission of nominations;
        (iv) the date and method for the acceptance of nominations;
        (v) the opening and closing dates of the campaign period;
        (vi) the date of the election and voting hours for the election;
        (vii) any cut-off time for any act to be performed; and
        (viii) any other relevant information; and
    (b) publish the election timetable in the Gazette.
    (2) The Commission may amend the election timetable by notice in the Gazette if—
    (a) it considers it necessary for a free and fair election; or
    (b) the polling day is postponed under section fifty-six.
    (3) The campaign period shall commence and close on such date as the Commission may determine.

Electoral campaign

29. (1) A public officer and public entity shall give equal treatment to candidates.
    (2) A candidate and political party has the right to have the content of the candidate's or political party's campaign message reported in public media in a fair and balanced manner.
    (3) A candidate or political party may, during an electoral campaign, publish or distribute campaign materials of such a nature and in such a manner as may be prescribed by the Commission.
    (4) For the purposes of this section "campaign messages" means an activity, statement or any other form of expression aimed at promoting particular political ideas, policies and strategies for purposes of obtaining votes for a candidate or political party contesting an election.

Nomination of Presidential and Vice-Presidential candidates

30. (1) A candidate for election as President or Vice-President shall deliver to the Returning Officer—
    (a) the candidate's nomination paper;
    (b) the prescribed election fee, except that a candidate for election as a Vice-President shall not pay the prescribed fee;
    (c) the prescribed statutory declaration of the candidate's assets and liabilities; and
    (d) an affidavit attesting that the person is qualified for election as President or Vice-President, as the case may be.

(2) A person who swears or affirms falsely under this section commits an offence and is liable, upon conviction, to imprisonment for a term of seven years without the option of a fine.

(3) A candidate delivering a nomination paper, referred to in subsection (1), to the Returning Officer shall be supported by one hundred supporters from each Province who are registered voters in that Province.

Nomination for election in constituency

31. (1) A person who applies to be a candidate for election in any, constituency shall lodge with the returning officer for that constituency that person's nomination paper and an affidavit in the prescribed manner and form.

(2) A nomination submitted under subsection (1) may be withdrawn at any time, before the expiry of the period appointed for lodging nomination papers in respect of the constituency concerned, if the candidate delivers to the returning officer a written notice to that effect.

Conduct of local government elections

32. Subject to the other provisions of this Act, the Commission shall conduct local government elections.

Nomination of candidates in district or ward

33. (1) Subject to subsection (2), a candidate for election in a district or ward of a council shall be nominated by means of a nomination paper in such form as may be prescribed and such nomination paper shall be subscribed, in the presence of the returning officer for that council, by a proposer and a seconder and not less than seven other persons, each of whom shall be a voter registered in a polling district in such ward.

(2) A person appearing before a returning officer for the purpose of subscribing a nomination paper under subsection (1) shall produce a voter's card and a national registration card to the returning officer for inspection as proof of identity.

(3) A person qualifies to be a mayor or council chairperson if that person—
   (a) possesses the same qualifications as those specified for a Member of Parliament in Article 70 of the Constitution;
   (b) is not a Member of Parliament; and
   (c) has a certificate of clearance showing the payment of council taxes, where applicable.

Restriction on nomination papers

34. (1) In an election, a person shall lodge nomination papers in only one constituency, district or ward.

(2) Where, upon the expiry of the period for lodging nomination papers in any constituency, district or ward a person is found to have lodged, and not withdrawn, nomination papers in more than one constituency, district or ward then every one of those nominations shall be invalid.

Appointment of election agents and polling agents

35. (1) A candidate may appoint—
   (a) two polling agents for each polling station; and
   (b) two election agents for each venue where counting of the votes will take place.

(2) An election or polling agent—
   (a) shall be a Zambian citizen or resident permit holder; and
   (b) shall not be a candidate in an election.

(3) The appointment and revocation of appointment of a person as an election or polling agent shall be effected in the prescribed manner.

Powers and duties of election or polling agents

36. (1) An election or polling agent may observe the proceedings during—
   (a) voting;
   (b) the counting of votes; and
   (c) the announcement and declaration of the result of an election.

(2) The absence of an election or polling agent from a gazetted or prescribed place where an electoral proceeding is being conducted shall not invalidate those proceedings.

521

(3)   An election or polling agent shall, while at a polling station or venue where the proceedings are taking place—

    (a)   wear the prescribed identification indicating—

        (i)   that the person is an election or polling agent; and

        (ii)   the candidate represented by that election or polling agent; and

    (b)   comply with any lawful order issued by—

        (i)   an election officer; or

        (ii)   a police officer acting on the instructions of an election officer.

PART V
ELECTION OFFICERS

Appointment of presiding officer

37.   The Commission shall, after prescribing a date for an election, appoint a presiding officer for each polling station at which the election is conducted.

Powers and duties of presiding officer

38.   (l)   A presiding officer shall coordinate and supervise the voting at a polling station so as to ensure that the election at the polling station is free and fair.

    (2)   A presiding officer—

    (a)   shall exercise the powers and perform the duties assigned to a presiding officer by or under this Act;

    (b)   shall ensure orderly conduct at a polling station; and

    (c)   may order a police officer to assist in ensuring orderly conduct at that polling station and the police officer shall comply with the order.

    (3)   A presiding officer for a polling station or venue for the counting of votes shall coordinate and supervise the counting of votes and announcement of the result of the election at the polling station or venue.

    (4)   A presiding officer shall exclude from the area within the boundary of a polling station any person other than—

    (a)   a member, employee or officer of the Commission;

    (b)   an election or polling agent who is entitled under this Act to be present at a polling station;

    (c)   a candidate in that election;

    (d)   an accredited observer or monitor;

    (e)   a voter present for the purpose of casting a vote; and

    (f)   a person or category of persons authorised by the Commission to be present at the polling station.

    (5)   Despite subsection (4), a presiding officer may order a person referred to in paragraphs (b) to (f) of subsection (4), to leave the area within the boundary of the polling station if that person's conduct is not conducive to a free and fair election at that polling station and shall give that person the reasons for making the order.

    (6)   If a person refuses to comply with an order under subsection (5), a presiding officer may direct a police officer to forcibly remove that person, and the police officer shall comply with that order.

Appointment of polling assistant

39.   The Commission shall appoint for each polling station as many polling assistants as it considers necessary to conduct an election.

Powers and duties of polling assistant

40.   A polling assistant shall—

    (a)   assist the presiding officer in the exercise of the presiding officer's powers and the performance of the presiding officer's duties; and

    (b)   exercise the powers and perform the duties assigned to a polling assistant by or under this Act.

Appointment of additional persons as election officers

41. (1) The Commission may appoint as many additional persons as election officers as may be necessary to enable the Commission to exercise its powers and perform its duties effectively during an election.

    (2) A person appointed by the Commission under this section shall exercise any power and perform any duty assigned to an election officer by or under this Act.

    (3) An appeal shall not be brought against a decision by the Commission to appoint a person as an election officer or to dismiss an election officer.

    (4) Despite subsection (3), a person may object to the appointment of an election officer under this section if the person appointed is disqualified under section 42 (3).

General provisions concerning appointment of election officer

42. (1) The Commission shall determine, in writing, the terms and conditions of appointment of an election officer.

    (2) The assignment of a power or duty to an election officer shall not prevent the Chief Electoral Officer from exercising that power or performing that duty.

    (3) A person shall not be appointed as an election officer or remain in that office if that person—

        (a) is a candidate contesting an election;

        (b) is an election or polling agent in an election;

        (c) holds political office in a registered party or is affiliated to a political party; or

        (d) was convicted of an offence or reported of any corrupt practice or illegal practice, under this Act, within a period of five years preceding an election.

    (4) A person shall not be appointed as an election officer unless that person signs a prescribed undertaking which shall include an undertaking to be bound by—

        (a) the Code; and

        (b) a declaration of secrecy.

    (5) An election officer shall exercise the powers and perform the duties assigned to that election officer subject to the direction, control and discipline of the Commission.

    (6) An election officer shall not place in jeopardy that officer's independence or harm the credibility, impartiality, independence or integrity of the Commission by any membership, association, statement or conduct.

    (7) An appointment as an election officer does not constitute an employment relationship.

    (8) The Commission may dismiss an election officer for—

        (a) misconduct, incompetence or incapacity;

        (b) absence from duty without leave of the Chief Electoral Officer;

        (c) a material contravention of this section;

        (e) a material contravention of the declaration of secrecy; or

        (f) any other consideration related to a free and fair election.

Immunity of election officer

43. An election officer shall not be liable for any loss suffered by a person as a result of an act performed or omitted in good faith in the exercise of a power or the performance of a duty under this Act.

PART VI
VOTING

Qualifications for voting

44. A voter is entitled to vote at an election held in a district, constituency or ward.

Identification of voter

45. A voter shall produce identification documents to a presiding officer as may be prescribed.

One vote and secrecy

46. (1) A voter shall not be entitled to vote more than once in the same election.

    (2) A poll shall be taken by means of a secret ballot in accordance with the Constitution, this Act and as may be prescribed.

Disqualification from voting

47. A person shall not be entitled to vote at an election if, at the date of the election, that person is in lawful custody or the person's freedom of movement is restricted under any written law.

Special vote

48. (1) The Commission may allow a person to apply for a special vote if that person cannot vote at a polling station in the polling district in which the person is registered as a voter due to that person's—
    (a) physical infirmity or disability;
    (b) pregnancy;
    (c) absence from that polling district while serving as an election officer in the election concerned; or
    (d) while on duty as a member of the security services in connection with the election.

    (2) The Commission shall prescribe the procedure and conditions under which a voter who is unable to vote in the polling district in which that voter is registered may apply for a special vote.

Election officers at polling stations

49. On polling day each polling station shall be staffed by the—
    (a) presiding officer appointed for that polling station;
    (b) polling assistants appointed for that polling station; and
    (c) other officers appointed by the Commission.

Hours of voting

50. (1) The Commission shall prescribe the voting hours for an election.
    (2) The Commission may, where it is necessary to do so, prescribe different voting hours for different polling stations.
    (3) The Commission shall publish the prescribed voting hours in the media.
    (4) A polling station shall—
        (a) open for voting at the prescribed time; and
        (b) subject to subsection (7)(b), remain open for voting until the prescribed time or such later time as the Commission may determine under subsection (7)(a).
    (5) A person shall not be admitted to a polling station for the purpose of voting after the polling station has closed for voting.
    (6) Voting at a polling station shall continue until every voter who had reported at a polling station to vote at the time prescribed for voting hours has voted.
    (7) The Commission—
        (a) may extend voting hours at a polling station after the voting day or prescribed time; and
        (b) may temporarily close a polling station for part of a polling day if it is temporarily impossible to conduct an election at that voting station.

Ballot paper

51. Subject to the other provisions of this Act and section fiftytwo, the Commission shall prescribe the form and design of a ballot paper and the manner in which ballot papers issued shall be accounted for.

Design of ballot paper

52. (1) Despite section fifty-one, a ballot paper shall be designed in a way that prevents fraudulent voting.
    (2) A ballot paper shall include—
        (a) a portrait of the candidate nominated for elections to the office of President, Member of Parliament, mayor, council chairperson and councillor; and
        (b) the symbol of a political party registered with the Commission under which a candidate shall stand for elections and where the candidate is an independent candidate, the symbol the Commission shall allocate to the independent candidate.
    (3) A ballot paper shall be colour coded so as to differentiate the ballot paper for use in a presidential, parliamentary or local government elections.

Ballot boxes

53. (1)   The Commission shall use in an election transparent ballot boxes capable of being securely closed.

(2)   The Commission shall prescribe the manner in which ballot boxes shall be—
   (a)   numbered and labelled; and
   (b)   closed, secured, opened, sealed and unsealed.

Voting compartments

54. (1)   Subject to subsection (2), the Commission shall prescribe the design and material of voting compartments to be used in an election.

(2)   A voting compartment shall, while screening a voter from observation by other persons when marking a ballot paper, be designed and placed in such a manner as to ensure that a clear view of the voters' back can be observed from the outside.

Conduct of general election

55.   A general election shall be held in accordance with the Constitution, this Act and as may be prescribed.

Postponement of voting at polling station

56. (1)   If it is not possible to conduct a free and fair election at a polling station on a prescribed polling day, the Commission may, at any time before voting at the polling station has commenced, postpone voting at that polling station.

(2)   A postponement under subsection (1) shall be—
   (a)   effected in the prescribed manner;
   (b)   to a day that would fall within the period referred to in section twenty-eight; and
   (c)   publicised in the media so as to ensure wide publicity of the postponement of the polling day at the polling station.

Postponement of by-election

57.   The Commission may postpone the polling day of a by-election if it is satisfied that—
   (a)   the postponement is necessary for ensuring a free and fair election; and
   (b)   the polling day for the election shall fall within the period required by the Constitution.

Voting materials

58. (1)   The Commission shall supply, before voting opens at a polling station, the voting materials necessary for the election at that station including—
   (a)   ballot papers;
   (b)   ballot boxes;
   (c)   voting compartments;
   (d)   a certified register of voters for the polling district concerned; and
   (e)   a document to be signed by the presiding officer detailing the voting materials entrusted to that presiding officer.

(2)   A presiding officer shall be responsible for the safe-keeping of all the voting materials supplied to that presiding officer.

Initial procedures

59.   A presiding officer shall, immediately before opening a polling station for voting—
   (a)   show all accredited observers, monitors, election and polling agents present, that each ballot box to be used at that polling station is empty; and
   (b)   in the presence of the accredited observers, monitors, election and polling agents, close, seal and secure the ballot boxes in the prescribed manner.

Voting procedure

60. (1)   Subject to section forty-eight, a voter shall only vote at the polling station in the polling district for which that voter is registered.

(2)   A voter is entitled to vote at a polling station—
- (a) on production of that voter's national registration card and voter's card to the presiding officer or election officer at the polling station; and
- (b) if that voter's details are in the certified segment of the Register of Voters for the polling district concerned.

(3)   When a voter produces a national registration card to the presiding officer or election officer as required by subsection (2), the presiding officer or election officer shall examine the identity document and determine whether—
- (a) the voter is the person described in that national registration card;
- (b) the voter's details are in the certified segment of the Register of Voters for the polling district concerned; and
- (c) the voter has not already voted in the election.

(4)   For the purposes of subsection (3) (c), the presiding officer or election officer shall examine the voter's hands to ensure that the voter does not possess the mark indicating that the voter has already voted.

(5)   If the presiding officer or election officer is satisfied in respect of all the matters referred to in subsection (3), the presiding officer shall—
- (a) record that the voter is treated as having voted in the election;
- (b) mark the hand of the voter in the prescribed manner;
- (c) mark the back of a ballot paper for that election; and
- (d) hand the ballot paper to the voter.

(6)   A voter shall, once the voter has received a ballot paper marked under subsection (5)(c) —
- (a) enter an empty voting compartment;
- (b) mark the ballot paper in a way that indicates the candidate the voter wishes to vote for;
- (c) fold the ballot paper to conceal the voter's vote;
- (d) cast the ballot paper in the ballot box; and
- (f) without delay leave the voting station.

Assistance to voters with disabilities

61. (1)   A person may assist a voter to vote where—
- (a) the voter requires assistance due to a physical disability;
- (b) the voter has requested to be assisted by that person; and
- (c) the presiding officer is satisfied that the person assisting the voter has attained the age of eighteen years.

(2)   In the absence of a person referred to in subsection (1), the presiding officer or another election officer, at the request of a voter who is unable to read, shall assist that voter to vote.

(3)   Subject to subsection (2), the presiding officer or election officer shall assist voters in the presence of—
- (a) a person appointed by the presiding officer or an accredited observer or monitor, if available; or
- (b) two election agents of different candidates, if available.

(4)   A presiding officer shall record in a copy of the Register of Voters, by means of a mark placed next to the name of the voter concerned, that the presiding officer or another person has assisted the voter as provided under this section and give the reasons for doing so.

(5)   A person assisting another person under subsection (2) shall maintain the secrecy of the vote cast by the person being assisted.

Issuance of new ballot paper

62. (1)   If a voter accidentally marks a ballot paper in a way that does not indicate for whom the voter wishes to vote and the ballot has not yet been placed in the ballot box—
- (a) the voter may return that ballot paper to the presiding officer or a polling assistant;
- (b) the presiding officer or polling assistant shall deal with the ballot paper in accordance with subsection (2), and shall give the voter a new ballot paper in accordance with this section; and
- (c) the voter may vote in accordance with section sixty.

(2)   Upon receiving a ballot paper from a voter under subsection (1), the presiding officer or a polling assistant shall mark "cancelled" on the back of the ballot paper and file it separately to be dealt with in accordance with section sixty-three.

Spoilt ballot papers

63. Where a voter inadvertently deals with a ballot paper in such manner that it cannot be used as a valid ballot paper, the voter shall deliver that ballot paper to the presiding officer and, if the presiding officer is satisfied that the ballot paper has been spoilt inadvertently, the presiding officer shall issue another ballot paper to the voter, and shall cancel the spoilt ballot paper and the counterfoil to which it relates.

Objections concerning voting

64. (1) A person may, at any time before a voter is handed a ballot paper, object to that voter being entitled to vote or to vote at the polling station concerned.

   (2) A person may object to a voter's vote where the voter—
   (a) has already voted;
   (b) is not the owner of the voter's card;
   (c) is not registered at the polling station;
   (d) is not a citizen; or
   (e) is disqualified from voting.

   (3) An election agent or a voter may object to any conduct of an election officer or any other person present at a polling station.

   (4) An objection under this section shall be made to the presiding officer in the prescribed manner.

   (5) A presiding officer shall make a decision on the objection and notify the objector and any other parties involved in the objection of the presiding officer's decision in the prescribed manner.

   (6) An appeal against the decision of a presiding officer may be made to a returning officer in the prescribed manner.

   (7) A presiding officer or returning officer shall keep a written record of each objection and decision made under this section in the prescribed manner.

Sealing of full ballot boxes

65. (1) As soon as a ballot box is full, a presiding officer, in the presence of an accredited observer, monitor or polling agent, shall seal the ballot box and allow the agents to affix their seals to the ballot box.

   (2) Immediately after the last vote has been cast, every remaining used ballot box shall be similarly dealt with.

   (3) A sealed ballot box shall remain—
   (a) sealed until opened for the counting of votes; and
   (b) in the polling station until the commencement of the counting of the votes.

Completion of ballot paper account form and sealing of voting materials

66. (1) A presiding officer shall, at the close of a polling station, in the presence of an accredited observer, monitor or election agent
   (a) complete a ballot paper account form reflecting the number of—
       (i) ballot boxes entrusted to that presiding officer;
       (ii) used ballot boxes;
       (iii) unused ballot boxes;
       (iv) ballot papers entrusted to that presiding officer;
       (v) issued ballot papers;
       (vi) unissued ballot papers; and
       (vii) cancelled ballot papers;
   (b) seal each unused ballot box entrusted to that presiding officer; and
   (c) seal in separate ballot boxes
       (i) the certified segment of the Register of Voters for that polling district;
       (ii) the unused ballot papers entrusted to that presiding officer;
       (iii) the spoilt ballot papers; and
       (iv) the written record of any objections concerning voting.

Place and time of counting of votes

67. (1) Votes shall be counted at the polling station at which those votes were cast.
   (2) A presiding officer shall ensure that the procedures set out in this Part relating to the counting of votes commences immediately after the polling station is closed for voting and continue the counting of votes until completion.

527

(3)   The procedures provided for in this Part relating to the counting of votes may be suspended only with the approval of the Commission and, if they are suspended, the presiding officer shall ensure the safekeeping of all the voting materials entrusted to the presiding officer until the counting of votes has been completed.

Counting of votes and announcement of provisional results

68. (1)   A presiding officer shall open the ballot boxes and—
    (a)   cause the ballot papers to be sorted on the basis of the ballot papers for each election, if more than one election was held at a polling station on the same day;
    (b)   cause the ballot papers for each election to be sorted and compare them with the number of ballot papers issued in the prescribed manner;
    (c)   cause the votes cast in each election to be counted in the prescribed manner; and
    (d)   announce and publish the result of each count at that polling station in both figures and words in the prescribed manner.

(2)   A presiding officer shall reject a ballot paper—
    (a)   that indicates the identity of the voter;
    (b)   on which a vote is cast for more than one candidate;
    (c)   that is unmarked;
    (d)   that is marked in such a way that it is not reasonably possible to determine the voter's choice;
    (e)   that does not bear the official mark required in terms of section sixty (5) (c); or
    (f)   that is not an official ballot paper.

(3)   The presiding officer shall mark A for rejection on the back of each rejected ballot paper and file the rejected ballot paper separately.

Objections concerning sorting of ballot papers

69. (1)   An election or polling agent may object to any alleged irregularity in the sorting of the ballot papers.

(2)   An objection under subsection (1) shall be made to a presiding officer, in the prescribed form, at any stage before the presiding officer has commenced the count.

(3)   Section sixty-four, with the necessary modifications, applies to an objection under this section.

Objections concerning counting of votes and announcement of provisional result

70. (l)   An election or polling agent may object to an alleged inaccuracy in the counting of the votes or the announcement of a result under section seventy-one.

(2)   An objection under subsection (l) shall be made to a presiding officer, in the prescribed form, at any stage before the presiding officer has announced the result.

(3)   A presiding officer shall determine the objection and decide whether to order a recount.

(4)   A presiding officer shall notify the objector and any other party involved in the objection, of the decision made under subsection (3).

(5)   If a presiding officer orders a recount, the presiding officer shall announce the result afresh.

(6)   An appeal against the decision of a presiding officer may be made to the returning officer in the prescribed form.

(7)   A presiding officer shall keep a written record, in the prescribed form, of each objection under subsection (l) and each decision under this section.

Procedure concerning provisional results and voting materials

71. (1)   After announcing the result at a polling station, a presiding officer shall complete a form, as may be prescribed, reflecting—
    (a)   the number of ballot papers supplied to the polling station;
    (b)   the result at the polling station;
    (c)   the number of rejected ballot papers;
    (d)   the number of spoilt ballot papers; and
    (e)   the number of unused ballot papers.

(2)   When a presiding officer has complied with subsection (1), the presiding officer shall publicly announce the result of the count at the polling station to members of the public, the accredited observers, monitors, election and polling agents present at the polling station.

(3) When the presiding officer has complied with subsection (2), the presiding officer shall inform the returning officer of the result of that count at the polling station.

(4) When the presiding officer has complied with subsection (3), the presiding officer shall—

(a) seal in separate ballot boxes each of the items mentioned in subsection (l) and the written record of any objections; and

(b) deliver the form, completed in terms of subsection (l), and the sealed ballot boxes to the returning officer.

Announcement and declaration of results by returning officer

72. (1) Upon receipt of the items mentioned in section seventy-one, a returning officer shall tally the results of the votes received from the polling station in the constituency, district and ward and shall—

(a) announce the results of the votes for the presidential and mayoral or council chairperson elections; and

(b) declare the results for the National Assembly and Ward election.

(2) The returning officer shall submit the results referred to in subsection (1) (a) and (b) to the Commission.

Announcement and declaration of results in Presidential election

73. (1) The Returning Officer shall tally, announce and declare the result of a presidential election as soon as they are received.

(2) The Returning Officer shall announce and declare the result of a presidential election without having received the results of all polling stations if—

(a) to wait for the receipt of the result from every polling station would unduly and unreasonably delay the determination and declaration of the result of that election; and

(b) the outstanding results are not likely to materially influence the overall result of that election.

Electronic transmission of results

74. The Commission may use electronic means to transmit results from polling stations.

Re-voting at polling station

75. (1) If ballot papers used in an election at a polling station are lost, destroyed or unlawfully removed before the votes cast at the polling station have been counted and announced, the Commission shall allow a revote at that polling station.

(2) A revote at a polling station shall be—

(a) conducted on a date that would fall within the period referred to in section twenty-eight;

(b) publicised in the media so as to ensure wide publicity of the date determined for the revote; and

(c) conducted in accordance with a procedure prescribed by the Commission.

Correction of mistakes

76. The Commission may correct a mistake committed by an electoral officer in the tabulation of results within seven days after the declaration of the results.

PART VII
OBSERVERS, MONITORS AND VOTER EDUCATION

Accreditation of observers and monitors

77. (1) A juristic person may apply to the Commission, in the prescribed manner, for accreditation to observe or monitor an election.

(2) The Commission may require any information it may consider necessary in support of an application under subsection (1).

(3) The Commission shall, where it decides to accredit an applicant—

(a) issue the applicant with a certificate of accreditation in the applicant's name, stating the period and other conditions of accreditation; and

(b) enter the applicant's name in the register of persons accredited as observers and monitors.

(4) The Commission may accredit an applicant, without the payment of a fee, to observe or monitor an election after considering the application and any other information provided by the applicant, and whether—

(a) the accreditation of the applicant shall promote conditions conducive to a free and fair election; and

(b) the persons appointed by the applicant shall—

(i) observe the election impartially and independently of any registered party or candidate contesting that election;

(ii) be competent and professional in observing the election; and

(iii) subscribe to a code governing observers and monitors issued by the Commission under this Act.

(5) The Commission shall, where it decides not to accredit the applicant, inform the applicant accordingly, in writing, and give the reasons for its decision.

(6) If a person accredited as an observer or monitor fails to comply, to a material extent, with the conditions of the accreditation, the Commission may cancel that accreditation and, in writing, notify the person concerned of the cancellation and state the reasons for such cancellation.

(7) Any person may inspect the register and copies of the certificates of persons accredited as observers and monitors.

(8) The register and copies of the certificate shall be kept at the Commission's head office.

(9) The Chief Elections Officer shall provide a certified copy of, or extract from, the register or a certificate to any person upon payment of the prescribed fee.

(10) A person representing an accredited observer or monitor shall abide by the Code.

(11) A person representing an accredited observer or monitor who is found guilty of violating any election law shall be disqualified from observing or monitoring an election.

(12) A register of juristic persons and institutions accredited as observers or monitors and copies of the certificates of the observers and monitors shall be kept at the Commission's head office.

(13) In this section "juristic person" includes an institution and organisation registered under the Non-Governmental Organisations Act, 2009.

Powers and duties of accredited observers and monitors

78. (1) An accredited observer or monitor may, in relation to an election for which that observer or monitor is accredited, observe the proceedings concerning voting, the counting of votes and the announcement and declaration of the election results.

(2) Whilst observing an election, a person appointed by an accredited observer or monitor shall wear the prescribed identification indicating that the person is representing an accredited observer or monitor.

(3) A person appointed by an accredited observer or monitor shall comply with any order issued by an election officer or a police officer acting on the instructions of an election officer.

Provision of voter education generally

79. (1) Any natural or juristic person may provide voter education for an election.

(2) Any natural or juristic person providing voter education shall do so in a manner that—

(a) is impartial and independent of any registered party or candidate contesting an election; and

(b) shall promote conditions conducive to free and fair elections.

Voter education

80. Despite section eight, the Commission shall provide voter education for an election.

PART VIII
Bribery

81. (1) A person shall not, either directly or indirectly, by oneself or with any other person corruptly—

(a) give, lend, procure, offer, promise or agree to give, lend, procure or offer, any money to a voter or to any other person on behalf of a voter or for the benefit of a voter in order to induce that voter to vote or refrain from voting or corruptly do any such act as aforesaid on account of such voter having voted or refrained from voting at any election;

(b) give, lend or procure, offer, promise or agree to give, lend, procure, offer or promise, any money to a voter or for the benefit of a voter or to any other person or on behalf of that person on behalf of any voter or to or for any other person for acting or joining in any procession or demonstration before, during or after any election;

(c) make any gift, loan, offer, promise, procurement or agreement to or for the benefit of any person in order to induce the person to procure or to endeavour to procure the return of any candidate at any election or the vote of any voter at any election;

(d) upon or in consequence of any gift, loan, offer, promise, procurement or agreement, procure or engage, promise or endeavour to procure, the return of any candidate at any election or the vote of any voter at any election;

(e) advance or pay or cause to be advanced or paid any money to or for the use of any other person with the intent that such money or any part thereof shall be expended in bribery at any election, or knowingly pay or cause to be paid any money to any person in discharge or repayment of any money wholly or partially expended in bribery at any election;

(f) before or during any election, receive or contract for any money or loan for oneself or for any other person for voting or agreeing to vote or for refraining or agreeing to refrain from voting at any election;

(g) after any election, receive any money on account of any person having voted or refrained from voting or having induced any other person to vote or refrain from voting at any election; or

(h) convey or transfer or be concerned with the conveyance or transfer of any property, or pay or be concerned with the payment of any money, to any person for the purpose of enabling that person to be registered as a voter, thereby to influence that person's vote at any future election, or pay to or be concerned with the payment of any money on account of any voter for the purpose of inducing that person to vote or refrain from voting.

(2) A person who contravenes any provision of subsection (1) commits an offence.

(3) Nothing in this Act shall be construed as applying to any money paid or agreed to be paid for, or on account of, any expenditure bona fide and lawfully incurred in respect of the conduct or management of an election.

Impersonation

82. (1) A person shall not—

(a) at any election, apply for a ballot paper in the name of some other person, living or dead, or of a fictitious person;

(b) having voted once at any election, apply again at the same election for a ballot paper;

(c) vote at any election knowing that the person is not entitled to vote at that election or induce or procure any person to vote at any election knowing that person is not entitled to vote at that election;

(d) apply to be registered as a voter in the name of any other person, whether living, dead or fictitious; or

(e) impersonate—

(i) a representative of a registered political party;

(ii) a candidate in an election;

(iii) a member, employee or officer of the Commission; or

(iv) a person appointed by an accredited observer, or monitor.

(2) A person who contravenes any provision of subsection (1) commits an offence.

Undue influence

83. (1) A person shall not directly or indirectly, by oneself or through any other person—

(a) make use of or threaten to make use of any force, violence or restraint upon any other person;

(b) inflict or threaten to inflict by oneself or by any other person, or by any supernatural or non-natural means, or pretended supernatural or non-natural means, any physical, psychological, mental or spiritual injury, damage, harm or loss upon or against any person;

531

    (c)   do or threaten to do anything to the disadvantage of any person in order to induce or compel any person—
        (i)   to register or not to register as a voter;
        (ii) to vote or not to vote;
        (iii) to vote or not to vote for any registered political party or candidate;
        (iv) to support or not to support any political registered party or candidate; or
        (v) to attend and participate in, or not to attend and participate in, any political meeting, march, demonstration or other political event;

    (d) interfere with the independence or impartiality of the Commission, any member, employee or officer of the Commission;

    (e) prejudice any person because of any past, present or anticipated performance of a function under this Act;

    (f) advantage, or promise to advantage, a person in exchange for that person not performing a function under this Act; or

    (g) unlawfully prevent the holding of any political meeting, march, demonstration or other political event.

(2)   Subject to the other provisions of this Act, a person shall not prevent another person from exercising a right conferred by this Act.

(3)   A person, knowing that another person is not entitled to be registered as a voter, shall not—
    (a) persuade that other person that, that other person is entitled to be registered as a voter; or
    (b) represent to anyone else that the person is entitled to be registered as a voter.

(4)   A person, knowing that another person is not entitled to vote shall not—
    (a) assist, compel or persuade that other person to vote; or
    (b) represent to anyone else that the other person is entitled to vote.

(5)   A person who contravenes any of the provisions of subsections (l) to (4) commits an offence.

(6)   A person who, by abduction, duress or any fraudulent device or contrivance, impedes or prevents the free exercise of the vote of any voter or thereby compels, induces or prevails upon any voter either to give or to refrain from giving the person's vote at any election, commits an offence.

Illegal practice of publishing false statements in respect of candidates

84. (1)   A person shall not, before or during an election, publish a false statement of the illness, death or withdrawal from election of a candidate at that election for the purpose of promoting or procuring the election of another candidate, knowing that statement to be false or not believing it to be true.

     (2)   A person who, contravenes subsection (1) commits an illegal practice, unless that person had reasonable grounds for believing, and did believe, the statement to be true.

Illegal practice in respect of nomination of candidates

85. (1)   A person shall not—
    (a) forge or fraudulently destroy any written authority of a candidate or nomination paper; or
    (b) deliver to a returning officer any written authority of a candidate or nomination paper or affidavit knowing the same to be forged.

     (2)   A person who knowingly makes a false statement relating to that person's nomination in that person's nomination paper or affidavit commits an offence.

Illegal practices in respect of public meetings

86. A person shall not, at a lawful public meeting held in connection with the election of any person between the day of the publication of a notice appointing a nomination day and the day on which the result of the election is published, act or incite others to act in a disorderly manner for the purpose of preventing the transaction of the business for which the meeting is called.

Illegal practices relating to the poll

87. (1)   A person shall not—
    (a) forge, counterfeit or fraudulently deface or fraudulently destroy any ballot paper or the official mark on any ballot paper;

(b) without authority supply any ballot paper to any person;

(c) without authority put into any ballot box any ballot paper which that person is not authorised by law to put in;

(d) sell or offer to sell any ballot paper or voter's card to any person or purchase or offer to purchase any ballot paper or voter's card from any person;

(e) not being a person entitled under this Act to be in possession of a ballot paper or voter's card, have any such ballot paper or voter's card in that person's possession;

(f) without authority destroy, take, open or otherwise interfere with any ballot box or packet of ballot papers in use or intended to be used for the purpose of an election;

(g) without authority print or make any ballot paper or what purports to be or is capable of being used as a ballot paper or any identity document at an election;

(h) manufacture, construct, have in that person's possession, supply, or use for the purpose of an election, or cause to be manufactured constructed, supplied or used for the purposes of any election any appliance, device or mechanism by which a ballot paper may be extracted or manipulated after having been deposited in a ballot box in the course of polling at any polling station; or

(i) at an election obstruct a voter either at the polling station or on that voter's way thereto or therefrom.

Penalty for illegal practices

88. A person who engages in an illegal practice commits an offence and is liable, upon conviction, to a fine not exceeding five hundred thousand penalty units or to imprisonment for a period not exceeding five years, or to both.

Other election offences

89. (1) A person shall not—

(a) within a period prescribed for the receipt of nominations, under this Act, loiter in any public place within four hundred metres from the entrance to a nomination centre;

(b) having been required to leave a nomination office, fail to leave such nomination office or the precincts thereof;

(c) put into any ballot box anything other than the ballot paper which that person is authorised by law to put therein;

(d) without due authority take out of the polling station any ballot paper or be found in possession of any ballot paper outside a polling station;

(e) on any polling day, at the entrance to or within a polling station, or in any public place or in any private place within four hundred metres from the entrance to such polling station

(i) canvass for votes;

(ii) solicit the vote of any person;

(iii) induce any person not to vote; or

(iv) induce any person not to vote for a particular candidate;

(f) on any polling day loiter in any public place within four hundred metres from the entrance to any polling station;

(g) on any polling day exhibit in any public or private place within one hundred metres from the entrance to any polling station any notice or sign, other than an official notice or sign authorised by an election officer under this Act, relating to the election;

(h) not being a presiding officer, an election officer, candidate, an election agent or a polling agent in the course of their functions within a polling station, make any record showing that any particular person has voted in an election;

(i) without lawful authority, destroy, mutilate, deface or remove any notice which is exhibited in accordance with this Act or under any regulations issued under this Act, or any document made available for inspection under this Act and any such regulations;

(j) wilfully obstruct or interfere with a returning officer, presiding officer, or election officer in the execution of their duties;

(k) make a false answer to any question put to that person by a presiding officer or an election officer under this Act;

(l) have any communication with a voter while such voter is in the precincts of a polling station for the purpose of voting;

(m) fail to comply with any requirement or direction to leave a polling station or the precincts thereof; or

(n) being a candidate use a symbol in the course of an election other than the symbol registered with the Chief Electoral Officer in accordance with this Act and any regulations thereunder or, in the case of any other person, associate any candidate with, any symbol in the course of an election other than the candidate's registered symbol.

(2) A person who contravenes any of the provisions of subsection (1) commits an offence and is liable, upon conviction, to a fine not exceeding two hundred thousand penalty units or to imprisonment for a period not exceeding two years, or to both.

Property in certain election material

90. In a prosecution for an offence in relation to a nomination paper, ballot box or ballot paper, the property in such nomination paper, ballot box, as well as the property in the counterfoil of any ballot paper, shall be vested in the Commission at that election.

Secrecy and penalty for breach of secrecy

91. (1) A person in attendance at a polling station shall maintain, and aid in maintaining, the secrecy of the voting at such station and shall not communicate, except for some purpose authorised by law, to any person, any information as to the name or number on the Register of Voters of any voter who has or has not applied for a ballot paper or voted at such polling station, or as to the official mark or official seal at such polling station.

(2) A person other than a presiding officer or polling assistant in exercise of the presiding officer or polling assistants' functions under this Act shall not, obtain or attempt to obtain in a polling station information as to the candidate for whom any person in such polling station is about to vote or has voted or communicate at any time, to any person, any information obtained in a polling station as to the candidate for whom any person in such polling station is about to vote or has voted, or as to the number on the ballot paper issued to any person at such polling station.

(3) A person in attendance at the counting of the votes shall maintain, and aid in maintaining, the secrecy of the voting and shall not ascertain at the counting the number on any ballot paper or communicate any information obtained at the counting as to the manner in which any vote is given by any particular ballot paper.

(4) A person who contravenes any of the provisions of this section commits an offence and is liable, upon conviction, to a fine not exceeding two hundred thousand penalty units or to imprisonment for a term not exceeding two years, or to both.

Offences by election officers

92. An election officer who wilfully fails to perform the functions of that office under this Act commits an offence and is liable, upon conviction, to a fine not exceeding two hundred thousand penalty units or to imprisonment for a term not exceeding two years, or to both.

Offences by printers and publishers

93. (1) A bill, placard, poster, pamphlet, circular or other printed matter having reference to an election shall bear upon the face thereof the name and address of the printer and of the publisher.

(2) A person who prints, publishes or posts, or causes to be printed, published or posted any matter referred to in subsection (1), which does not bear upon the face thereof such name and address of the printer or publisher commits an offence.

(3) The proprietor and publisher of every newspaper shall cause the word advertisement to be printed as a headline to each article or paragraph appearing in that person's newspaper containing electoral matter, the insertion of which is or is to be paid for, and any proprietor or publisher who fails to comply with this provision commits an offence.

(4) For the purposes of this section—

(a) any process for producing copies of a document, other than by copying it by hand, shall be deemed to be printing, and the expression "printed" shall be construed accordingly; and

(b) "electoral matter" shall be deemed to include all matters which, on the face of them, are intended or calculated to affect the result of an election.

Obstruction of officer

94. (1)   A person shall not—
    (a)   wilfully delay or obstruct an officer in the carrying out of that officer's duties and powers under this Act; or
    (b)   assault an officer in the lawful exercise of that officers duties and power under this Act.

(2)   A person who contravenes a provision of subsection (1), commits an offence and is liable, upon conviction, to a fine not exceeding fifty thousand penalty units or to imprisonment for a term not exceeding six months, or to both.

Attempts to commit offence

95.   A person who attempts to commit an offence under this Part commits an offence and is liable upon conviction to the penalty specified for that offence.

PART IX
ELECTION PETITIONS

Application to members and officers of Parliament

96. (1)   A question which may arise as to whether—
    (a)   a person has been validly appointed or nominated as a Member of Parliament;
    (b)   the seat of an elected or nominated Member of Parliament, mayor, council chairperson or councillor, has become vacant, other than a question arising from the election of a candidate as a Member of the Parliament; or
    (c)   a petition may be heard and determined by the High Court or tribunal upon application made by—
        (i)   any person to whom the question relates; or
        (ii)   the Attorney-General; may be determined by the High Court or a tribunal, as the case may be.

(2)   A person who makes an application to the High Court or a tribunal under subsection (1), has the right to appear and be represented before the High Court or tribunal.

(3)   Subject to any rules of court or tribunal, the powers, practice and procedure of the High Court or a tribunal in respect of the trial of an election petition under this Part shall apply, with the necessary modifications, to the hearing and determination of such applications.

Avoidance of election

97. (1)   An election of a candidate as a Member of Parliament, mayor, council chairperson or councillor shall not be questioned except by an election petition presented under this Part.

(2)   The election of a candidate as a Member of Parliament, mayor, council chairperson or councillor shall be void if, on the trial of an election petition, it is proved to the satisfaction of the High Court or a tribunal, as the case may be, that—
    (a)   a corrupt practice, illegal practice or other misconduct has been committed in connection with the election—
        (i)   by a candidate; or
        (ii)   with the knowledge and consent or approval of a candidate or of that candidate's election agent or polling agent; and the majority of voters in a constituency, district or ward were or may have been prevented from electing the candidate in that constituency, district or ward whom they preferred;
    (b)   subject to the provisions of subsection (4), there has been non-compliance with the provisions of this Act relating to the conduct of elections, and it appears to the High Court or tribunal that the election was not conducted in accordance with the principles laid down in such provision and that such non-compliance affected the result of the election; or
    (c)   the candidate was at the time of the election a person not qualified or a person disqualified for election.

(3)   Despite the provisions of subsection (2), where, upon the trial of an election petition, the High Court or a tribunal finds that a corrupt practice or illegal practice has been committed by, or with the knowledge and consent or approval of, any agent of the candidate whose election is the subject of such election petition, and the High Court or a tribunal further finds that such candidate has proved that—

- (a) a corrupt practice or illegal practice was not committed by the candidate personally or by that candidate's election agent, or with the knowledge and consent or approval of such candidate or that candidate's election agent;
- (b) such candidate and that candidate's election agent took all reasonable means to prevent the commission of a corrupt practice or illegal practice at the election; and
- (c) in all other respects the election was free from any corrupt practice or illegal practice on the part of the candidate or that candidate's election agent; the High Court or a tribunal shall not, by reason only of such corrupt practice or illegal practice, declare that election of the candidate void.

(4) An election shall not be declared void by reason of any act or omission by an election officer in breach of that officer's official duty in connection with an election if it appears to the High Court or a tribunal that the election was so conducted as to be substantially in accordance with the provisions of this Act, and that such act or omission did not affect the result of that election.

Presentation of election petition

98. An election petition may be presented to the High Court or a tribunal by one or more of the following persons:
- (a) a person who lawfully voted or had a right to vote at the election to which the election petition relates;
- (b) a person claiming to have had a right to be nominated as a candidate or elected at the election to which the election petition relates;
- (c) a person claiming to have been a candidate at the election to which the election petition relates; and
- (d) the Attorney-General.

Relief which may be claimed in election petition

99. Any of the following reliefs may be claimed in an election petition:
- (a) a declaration that the election was void; or
- (b) a declaration that any candidate was duly elected.

Form and procedure for presentation of election petition

100. (1) An election petition shall be in such form as the Chief Justice may by rules prescribe.

(2) An election petition shall be presented —
- (a) in the case of an election of a candidate as a Member of Parliament, to the Principal Registry or District Registry of the High Court by lodging it with the Registrar in accordance with this Act; or
- (b) in the case of an election of a candidate as a mayor, council chairperson or councillor, to the appropriate, tribunal by lodging it with the designated person.

(3) An election petition shall be signed by the petitioner or by all the petitioners, if more than one, and shall be presented not later than fourteen days after the date on which the result of the election to which it relates is duly declared.

(4) Where an election petition is presented under this section —
- (a) in the case of an election petition presented in respect of an election of a candidate as a Member of Parliament, the Registrar shall, in writing, inform the Speaker of the National Assembly and the Commission of such presentation; and
- (b) in the case of an election petition presented in respect of the election of a candidate as a mayor, council chairperson or councillor, the designated person shall, in writing, inform the Commission of the presentation.

Duty of Registrar and designated person to make out list of election petition

101. (1) Subject to the provisions of subsection (2), the Registrar and the designated person shall make out a list of all election petitions presented under this Act, placing them on such list in the order in which they are presented, and the Registrar or the designated person, as the case may be, shall keep at the Registrars office or the designated person's office a copy of the list which shall be open for inspection by any person making application for inspection thereof.

(2) An election petition shall, unless the High Court or a tribunal orders otherwise, be tried in the order in which it stands on the list made out by the Registrar or designated person under subsection (1), but where more election petitions than one are presented in respect of the same

election, the election petitions shall be bracketed together and shall be dealt with as one petition, standing, unless the High Court or a tribunal orders otherwise, in the list in the place where the last of the election petitions would have stood if it had been the only election petition presented in respect of that election.

Rules of practice and procedure, security for costs etc

102. (1)   Subject to the other provisions of this Act, the Chief Justice may make rules regulating generally the practice and procedure of the High Court and tribunals with respect to the presentation and trial of election petitions, including rules as to the time within which any requirement of the rules is to be complied with and as to the costs of and incidental to the presentation and trial of the election petitions and as to the fees to be charged in respect of proceedings therein, and generally as regard to any other matter relating thereto as the Chief Justice may consider necessary or desirable.

(2)   After the presentation of an election petition, a petitioner to it shall give such security for costs, not exceeding in amount the sum of eight thousand fee units, as the High Court or a tribunal may order, and such security shall be given within the time and in the manner and form as the Chief Justice may prescribe by rules under this section or, in the absence of the rules, as the High Court or a tribunal may order.

(3)   Where, after the presentation of an election petition, no security for costs is given as required by or under this section, no further proceedings shall be heard on that election petition.

Withdrawal of election petition

103. (1)   A petitioner shall not withdraw an election petition without the leave of the High Court or a tribunal.

(2)   An application for leave to withdraw an election petition shall not be made until notice of intention to withdraw the election petition has been given in such manner as the Chief Justice may prescribe.

(3)   Where an election petition is presented by two or more petitioners, an application to withdraw the election petition shall not be made except with the consent of all the petitioners to it.

(4)   The High Court or a tribunal may, upon an application for leave to withdraw an election petition, make such order as to costs as it may consider just.

Substitution of new petitioners

104. (1)   Upon the hearing of an application under section one hundred and three for leave to withdraw an election petition, any person who might have been a petitioner in respect of the election to which that election petition relates may, despite the provisions of section one hundred, apply to the High Court or tribunal to be substituted for the petitioner applying to withdraw, and the High Court or a tribunal may, if it grants leave to the petitioner to withdraw, order that person (hereinafter referred to as "the substituted petitioner") to be substituted for the petitioner.

(2)   Subject to the other provisions of this section, the substituted petitioner shall, as nearly as may be, stand in the same position, and be subject to the same liabilities, under this Act as the petitioner for whom a substitution was made (hereinafter referred to as "the original petitioner").

(3)   Where the High Court or a tribunal makes an order under subsection (1), it may direct that the security for costs given by the original petitioner shall remain as security for any costs caused thereafter by the substituted petitioner upon the trial of the election petition, and may direct that, to the extent of the amount of the security, the original petitioner shall be liable to pay the costs of the substituted petitioner.

(4)   Unless the High Court or tribunal gives directions as in subsection (3), section one hundred and three (1) and (2) shall apply to the substituted petitioner as they apply in relation to a petitioner presenting an election petition.

Abatement of election petition

105. (1)   If a sole petitioner or the survivor of several petitioners dies, then subject to the provisions of this section, no further proceedings shall be heard upon the election petition.

(2)   The death of a petitioner shall not affect that petitioner's liability for the payment of costs previously incurred.

(3)   On the abatement of an election petition under subsection (1), any person who might have been a petitioner in respect of the election to which that election petition relates may, despite section one hundred and one apply to the High Court or tribunal to be substituted as a petitioner in place of the deceased petitioner and the High Court or a tribunal may, if it thinks fit, order that such person be substituted accordingly.

(4)   Where the High Court or a tribunal makes an order under this section for the substitution of a person in place of a deceased petitioner such person shall, as nearly as may be, stand in the same position, and be subject to the same liabilities, under this Act as the deceased petitioner would have been but for the death, and section one hundred and three (1) and (2) shall apply to the person as they apply in relation to a petitioner presenting an election petition.

Trial of election petitions

106. (1)   An election petition shall be tried and determined by the High Court or a tribunal in open court—
    (a)   in the case of the election of a candidate as a Mayor, council chairperson or Councillor, within thirty days from the date of filing an election petition; and
    (b)   in the case of the election of a candidate as a Member of Parliament, within ninety days from the date of filing an election petition.

(2)   Where an election petition is not tried and determined within the period specified in subsection (1) due to a failure by the petitioner to actively prosecute the petition, the High Court or a tribunal shall dismiss the petition for want of prosecution.

(3)   The High Court or a tribunal may adjourn the trial of an election petition from time to time and from place to place.

(4)   Subject to the provisions of this Act, the High Court may in respect of the trial of an election petition, exercise such powers within its civil jurisdiction as it may deem appropriate.

(5)   On the trial of an election petition, a verbatim record of all evidence given orally in the trial shall be taken and transcripts of the record shall, at the conclusion of the proceedings, be delivered to the Commission by the Registrar or designated person, as the case may be.

Witnesses

107. (1)   On the trial of an election petition, the High Court or a tribunal may—
    (a)   order a person who appears to the High Court or a tribunal to have been concerned in the election to attend as a witness at the trial; and
    (b)   examine any witness or any person who is present at the trial although such witness or person is not called as a witness by any party to the proceedings, except that after the examination by the High Court or a tribunal of a witness or person, the witness or person may be cross examined by or on behalf of the petitioner or the respondent.

(2)   A person who is called as a witness at the trial of an election petition shall not be excused from answering any question relating to any offence connected with an election on the ground that the answer thereto may tend to incriminate that person, or on the ground of privilege.

(3)   Despite subsection (2), a witness who answers to the satisfaction of the High Court or a tribunal every question which is required to be answered under subsection (2), and the answers to which may tend to incriminate that witness, shall not be liable to prosecution for any offence committed by that witness in connection with the election and in respect of which that witness is examined and the witness shall be entitled to receive a certificate of indemnity under the hand of the Registrar or designated person as the case may be, stating that the witness is freed and discharged from liability to prosecution for that offence.

(4)   Despite subsection (2), an answer by a witness to a question before the High Court or tribunal under subsection (2) shall not, except in the case of any criminal proceedings for giving false evidence in respect of the evidence, be admissible in any proceedings, civil or criminal, in evidence against that witness.

(5)   Where a person has received a certificate of indemnity under subsection (3), and any legal proceedings are at any time brought against that person for any offence to which the certificate relates, the court having conduct of the case shall, on proof of the certificate of indemnity, stay the proceedings and may award to that person such costs as that person may have been put to in the proceedings.

(6)   All reasonable expenses incurred by any person in attending at or appearing before the High Court or a tribunal to give evidence as a witness at the trial of an election petition shall be allowed to that person according to the scale of allowances and expenses appropriate in civil proceedings before the High Court.

Conclusion of trial of election petition

108. (1)   At the conclusion of the trial of an election petition, the High Court or a tribunal shall determine whether the respondent, or any other, and which, person, was duly elected, or whether the election to which the election petition relates was void, and the Registrar or designated person shall, as soon as is practicable, submit a copy of such determination to—

    (a)   in the case of an election petition in the High Court, the Speaker of the National Assembly and the Commission; and

    (b)   in the case of an election petition in a tribunal, the Commission.

(2)   Where the High Court or a tribunal determines that the respondent was duly elected, the election shall be and remain valid.

(3)   Where the High Court or a tribunal determines that the respondent was not duly elected but that some other person was duly elected, that other person shall be deemed to have been elected accordingly.

(4)   Where the High Court or a tribunal determines that the respondent was not duly elected, and that no other person was duly elected, at the election concerned, the vacancy in the membership of the National Assembly or a Council in respect of which that election was held shall be deemed to continue until duly filled.

(5)   Where a determination under subsection (1) alters the results of an election as previously declared, the Commission shall publish the results as so altered in the Gazette.

(6)   Where it appears to the High Court or a tribunal upon the trial of an election petition that any corrupt practice or illegal practice has been committed by any person in connection with the election to which the election petition relates, the High Court or tribunal shall, at the conclusion of the proceedings, prepare a report stating:

    (a)   the evidence given in the proceedings in respect of the corrupt practice or illegal practice;

    (b)   the names and particulars of any person by whom the corrupt practice or illegal practice was, in the opinion of the High Court or a tribunal, committed;

    (c)   in the event that there is an appeal, the Constitutional Court shall prepare the report, except that the Court shall not state the name of any person under this paragraph unless the person has been given an opportunity of appearing before the Court and of showing cause why that person's name should not be so stated.

(7)   The Registrar or designated person shall deliver a copy of every report prepared by the High Court or a tribunal under subsection (6) to—

    (a)   the Commission; and

    (b)   the Director of Public Prosecutions.

(8)   The Commission shall, as soon as it receives the report under subsection (7), recommend the prosecution of the person stated in the report by the Director of Public Prosecutions.

Costs

109. (1)   Subject to the provisions of this section, costs, charges and expenses of, and incidental to, the presentation and trial of an election petition shall be borne in such manner and in such proportions as the High Court or a tribunal may order and in particular, any costs which in the opinion of the High Court or a tribunal have been caused by any vexatious conduct or by any frivolous or vexatious allegations or objections on the part of the petitioner or of the respondent, may be ordered to be paid by the party by whom such costs have been caused.

(2)   Where, on the trial of an election petition, the High Court or a tribunal determines that the respondent was not duly elected and is of the opinion, having regard to the circumstances, that it would be just and reasonable to relieve any party to the election petition from all or a portion of the costs thereof, then—

    (a)   if the High Court or a tribunal finds that the election of the respondent was due to a mistake or improper performance or failure or performance of any function bona fide made by any election officer, it may, after sufficient notice to the Attorney-General to show cause to the contrary, make such order as to the payment by the State of the costs of the proceedings or a portion thereof, as it may deem proper;

    (b)   if the High Court or a tribunal finds that the election of the respondent was due to a mistake or improper performance, or failure of performance of any function mala fide made by any election officer, it may, after sufficient notice to such officer to show cause to the contrary, make such order as to the payment by such election officer of the costs of the proceedings or a portion thereof, as it may consider proper.

(3)   The High Court or a tribunal may, on application made by any person to whom any costs, charges or expenses are payable under this Act, order the same to be paid out of any deposit made to secure the same, or by any surety who gave a recognizance to secure the same.

(4)   The notice of an application made pursuant to subsection (3) shall be given, in such manner as may be prescribed by rules of the High Court or a tribunal, to the party by or on whose behalf the deposit was made or for whom the surety gave a recognizance, requiring the party, or the surety and the party, as the case may be, to state, within the time and in the manner as prescribed, whether that party resists the application.

(5)   Where, on the trial of an election petition, any person appears to the High Court or a tribunal to have been guilty of any corrupt practice or illegal practice relating to the election which is the subject of the election petition, the High Court or a tribunal may, after giving that person an opportunity of making a statement to show cause why the order should not be made, order the whole or a portion of the costs of, or incidental to, the trial of the election petition to be paid by that person to such person or persons as the High Court or a tribunal may determine.

(6)   Execution may be levied under any order for payment made by the High Court or a tribunal under this section in the same manner and to the same extent as execution may be levied under a judgement of the High Court or tribunal for the payment of money.

(7)   Money deposited as security shall, when no longer needed as security for costs, be returned to the person in whose name it is deposited or to any person entitled to received the same by order of the High Court or a tribunal which may be upon motion after notice and proof that all just claims have been satisfied or otherwise sufficiently provided for as the High Court or a local government elections tribunal may require.

PART X
GENERAL PROVISIONS

Code of conduct

110. (1)   The Commission shall enforce the Code of Conduct specified in the Schedule.
    (2)   The Commission may disqualify a political party or candidate in breach of the Code.

Appeal against decision of registration officer

111. (1)   A person aggrieved by a decision or action taken by a registration officer may appeal to the Commission in the prescribed manner.
    (2)   The Commission shall notify the appellant of its decision within thirty days from the date of receipt of the appeal.

Powers to decide objections and appeals

112. (1)   Whenever the Commission, is required under this Act to decide an objection, dispute, complaint or an appeal, the Commission may resolve the issue, that is the subject of the objection, dispute, complaint or appeal, through conciliation or mediation where applicable.
    (2)   The Commission shall prescribe the manner for handling any objection, dispute, complaint or appeal under this Act.

Constitution of conflict management committees

113. (1)   The Commission shall, for purposes of resolving electoral disputes, constitute such number of conflict management committees as the Commission may determine.
    (2)   A conflict management committee shall comprise, as members, such number of conflict management officers appointed by the Commission, as the Commission shall determine.
    (3)   The Chairperson of the committee shall be appointed by the Commission and the Vice-Chairperson shall be elected by the members from amongst themselves.
    (4)   Subject to subsection (5), a member of a committee shall hold office for such period as the Commission shall determine.
    (5)   A member shall be paid such allowances as the Emoluments Commission may, on the recommendation of the Commission, determine.
    (6)   A committee shall meet for the transaction of business at such places and times as the Chairperson of the Committee may determine.

(7)   The quorum at any meeting of a committee shall be one half of the members of the committee.

(8)   There shall preside at any meeting of a committee—

    (a)   the Chairperson;

    (b)   in the absence of the Chairperson, the Vice-Chairperson; or

    (c)   in the absence of both the Chairperson and the Vice-Chairperson, such member as the members present may elect from their number for the purposes of that meeting.

(9)   The determination of any matter before a committee shall be according to the votes of the majority of the members present and considering the matter.

(10)   A committee may invite any person whose presence in its opinion is desirable to attend and to participate in the deliberations of a meeting of the committee but such person shall have no vote.

(11)   A committee shall cause minutes to be kept of the proceedings of every meeting of a committee.

(12)   The Commission shall assign persons employed in the Commission to perform such secretarial and administrative functions in connection with a committee as may be necessary for the performance of its functions.

Printing, manufacture, use, removal etc., of election materials

114. The Commission may authorise—

    (a)   the printing, manufacture or supply of any voting or election material;

    (b)   the use of the register of voters or any voting or election material for a purpose other than an election purpose; or

    (c)   the removal or destruction of any voting or election material.

Ownership of voting and election material and disposal

115. (1)   The Commission shall own all voting and election materials used for, or provided by it in, an election.

    (2)   Unless the Constitutional Court, the High Court or a tribunal orders otherwise, the Commission may dispose of the voting and election materials used in a particular election six months after the date on which the final result of the election was declared, in the manner directed by the Commission.

Effect of certain irregularities

116. A mistake in the certified segment of the register of voters under this Act shall not invalidate that register of voters.

Inspection and copying of documents

117. Where this Act requires that documents be publicised, or made available for inspection or copying, the Commission shall endeavour to also publicise or make available those documents in electronic form.

When incapacity may be removed

118. Whenever a person has become subject to any incapacity under this Act by reason of a conviction or by reason of any declaration or report of any court, and any witness who gave evidence against such person upon the proceeding for such conviction, declaration or report is convicted of perjury in respect of that evidence, such person may apply to the High Court or a tribunal which, if satisfied that the conviction, declaration or report, so far as it concerns that person, was based upon perjured evidence, may order that, that person's incapacity shall from that time cease, and the same shall cease accordingly.

Person not required to state how person voted

119. A person who has voted at an election shall not in any proceedings, whether brought under this Act or otherwise, be required, to state for whom the person voted.

Evidence as to holding of election

120. Upon any charge of a corrupt practice or an illegal practice, or any other offence against this Act, alleged to have been committed at or in connection with an election, the certificate of a returning officer that the election mentioned therein was being or had been held shall be sufficient evidence of the fact that such election was being or had been held.

Validation of certain documents

121. A misnomer or inaccurate description of a person or place in a register, nomination paper, notice or other document required for the purposes of this Act shall not affect the full operation of the document with respect to that person or place in any case where the description of the person or place is such as to be commonly understood.

Powers of officer

122. (1) An officer may, during the campaign period and on polling day, enter any area, place and premises in which the officer reasonably believes there is being, or had been carried on, an activity
that is an offence under this Act, except that an officer shall not enter into a private dwelling without the consent of the occupant or the authority of a court warrant.

(2) An officer may request any information from any person who appears to have custody or control of any material or thing which the officer reasonably believes is being used, or was intended to be used or is likely to be used, to commit an offence under this Act.

(3) An officer may seize or detain any material or thing where the officer has reasonable ground to believe that the material or thing is being used, was intended to be used or is likely to be used, to commit an offence under this Act.

Power of arrest

123. (1) A police officer may, without warrant, arrest a person and keep that person in custody where—
    (a) the person is found committing an offence or is reasonably suspected of having committed an offence under this Act; or
    (b) upon being requested by the police officer, the person wilfully, fails or refuses to furnish that person's name, address or other relevant information to the satisfaction of the police officer; and
    (c) the police officer has reasonable grounds to believe that unless arrested, the person shall—
        (i) escape or cause unreasonable delay to or trouble during or for, the election;
        (ii) interfere with witnesses; or
        (iii) tamper with or destroy relevant evidence or material.

(2) Any person arrested under subsection (1), shall be taken before a court within forty-eight hours, and shall not be detained for longer than is reasonably necessary for the purpose.

General penalty

124. A person who is convicted of an offence under this Act for which a penalty is not prescribed is liable, upon conviction—
    (a) for a first offence, to a fine not exceeding five hundred thousand penalty units or to a term of imprisonment not exceeding five years, or to both;
    (b) for a second or subsequent offence, to a fine not exceeding seven hundred thousand penalty units or to a term of imprisonment not exceeding seven years, or to both.

Regulations

125. (1) Subject to the provisions of the Constitution and this Act, the Commission may, by statutory instrument, make regulations providing for the registration of voters for the purposes of elections and for the procedure and manner of conducting elections.

(2) Without prejudice to the generality of subsection (1), the Commission may, by statutory instrument, make regulations providing for all or any of the following matters:
    (a) the registration of voters;
    (b) the preparation of, and the form of, registers to be used in the registration of voters;
    (c) the manner of ascertaining whether persons applying for registration as voters are qualified for registrations or for their inclusion in a register for a particular constituency;
    (d) the making and determination of appeals, claims and objections with respect to the registration of voters;
    (e) voter education;
    (f) the correction, amendment and certification of registers of voters;

542

(g) the manner in which the name of any person may be deleted from a register of voters, the transfer of the names of persons from the register of voters of one polling district to that of another polling district and the restoration of the name of a registered voter;

(h) the manner and form for nomination of candidates for any election that a candidate at a direct election for the National Assembly is the authorised candidate of a political party;

(i) the publication of the names of candidates whose nominations are accepted;

(j) the payment of election fees by candidates, and the circumstances in which such fees are to be returned.

(k) the use of symbols at an election;

(l) the manner and procedure of voting at an election;

(m) the manner of ascertaining the identity of persons wishing to vote at elections and whether such persons are qualified to vote;

(n) the administering of oaths by election officers in respect of such matters as may be prescribed;

(o) the procedure to be followed at the conclusion of a poll in an election;

(p) for the purpose of declaring any candidate duly elected, the procedure to be followed where there is an equality of votes between candidates in an election for members of the National Assembly or Council;

(q) the procedure to be followed where only one person is duly nominated for election to the office of President, in a constituency for election to the National Assembly or in an election to a Council;

(r) the declaration, notification and publication of the results of an election;

(s) the custody and disposal of nomination papers, ballot papers, records, documents or other things relating to the registration of voters and the conduct of elections;

(t) election expenses and the return of election expenses;

(u) the notification and publication of any casual vacancy in the elected membership of the National Assembly or a Council and the fixing of a date of an election to fill such vacancy;

(v) the forms and records to be used for any of the purposes of this Act;

(w) the delimitation of provinces, constituencies, wards and polling districts; and

(x) any matter to be prescribed by or under this Act.

(3) Separate regulations may be made in respect of each category of elections.

(4) Regulations under this section may provide in respect of any contravention thereof that the offender shall be liable to a fine not exceeding two hundred thousand penalty units or to a term of imprisonment not exceeding two years, or to both.

(5) A prosecution for an offence against this Act shall not be commenced after the lapse of one year from the date on which the offence is alleged to have been committed.

Repeal of Act No 12 of 2006

126. The Electoral Act, 2006, is repealed.

SCHEDULE
(Section 107)
CODE OF CONDUCT

Enforcement of Code

1. (1) A person has, subject to paragraph (2), the right to—
    (a) express political opinions;
    (b) debate the policies and programmes of political parties;
    (c) canvas freely for membership and support from voters;
    (d) distribute election literature and campaign materials;
    (e) publish and distribute notices and advertisements;
    (f) erect banners, placards and posters;
    (g) campaign freely;
    (h) participate freely in partisan political activities; and
    (i) seek the protection of the law from harm as a result of that person's political opinion or affiliation.

543

(2)   A public officer shall not engage in any active partisan political activity referred to in subparagraph (1) whilst in the public service.

Promotion of free and fair elections

2.   A person shall, during an election campaign or election, promote conditions conducive to the conduct of free and fair elections and be bound by this Code.

Duty of Commission

3.   (1)   The Commission shall, where reasonable and practicable to do so—
     (a)   meet political party representatives on a regular basis to discuss matters of concern related to on election campaign and election itself;
     (b)   ensure that political parties do not use State resources to campaign for the benefit of any political party or candidate;
     (c)   avail political parties with the election timetable and election notices in accordance with the Act;
     (d)   censure acts done by leaders of political parties, candidates, supporters, and Government and its organs, which are aimed at jeopardising elections or done in contravention of this Code;
     (e)   declare election results expeditiously from the close of the election day;
     (f)   ensure that a campaign rally or meeting which is legally organised by a political party is not disrupted or arbitrarily prohibited;
     (g)   ensure that an election officer, police officer, monitor, observer or media person is not victimised in the course of their election duties;
     (h)   ensure that police officers act professionally and impartially during the electoral process;
     (i)   ensure that traditional leaders do not exert undue influence on their subjects to support a particular political party or candidate;
     (j)   ensure that equal opportunity is given to all stakeholders, particularly political parties and independent candidates to participate in and conduct their political activities in accordance with the law; and
     (k)   condemn acts of media organisations and personnel aimed at victimisation, punishment or intimidation of media practitioners implementing any of the provisions of this Code.
   (2)   A member of the Commission may attend political rallies to monitor compliance with this Code.

Obligation of Political Party and candidate during election

4.   (1)   A political party and candidate shall—
     (a)   establish and maintain effective lines of communication with the Commission and with other registered political parties and candidates, at national, political and local level, including the provision of names and the contact details and addresses of or a candidate's party election agents and of other relevant office bearers and representatives;
     (b)   accept and respect decisions of the Commission in respect of election results announced by returning officers and the Commission in accordance with the law;
     (c)   issue directives to their members and supporters to observe this Code and take any necessary steps to ensure compliance;
     (d)   hold public meetings in compliance with the law;
     (e)   adhere to the election timetable issued by the Commission in conducting election campaigns in accordance with this Act;
     (f)   take appropriate measures to ensure environmental protection and cleanliness in the course of posting or distributing electoral campaign material;
     (g)   remove campaign materials within fourteen days of the declaration of election results;
     (h)   take necessary measures to ensure public safety in the course of posting or distributing electoral campaign material; and
     (i)   carry out campaign meetings and rallies peacefully.
   (2)   A member or supporter of a political party or a candidate shall not—
     (a)   use language which incites hatred or violence in any form against any person;
     (b)   issue any pamphlet, newsletter, poster or other propaganda which contains materials that incite people to violence or rebellion;
     (c)   deface, remove or destroy campaign materials of another political party or publications of the Commission;

(d) disrupt another political party's rally, meeting, march or demonstration or seek to obstruct another person from attending a political rally of another political party;

(e) continuously remain at a polling station during the campaign period or elections; and

(f) wear any campaign materials within four hundred metres of the polling station on the polling day.

(3) Without prejudice to any other written law, any person who contravenes subparagraph (2) commits an offence and shall be liable upon conviction to a fine not exceeding one hundred thousand penalty units or to imprisonment not exceeding one year, or to both.

Duty of election agent or polling agent during election

5. (1) An election agent or polling agent shall, subject to this Code, have the following duties during an election:

(a) observe the opening and closing of a polling station assigned to them on polling day;

(b) witness the voting process;

(c) witness the count of ballot papers for candidates;

(d) witness the announcement of results; and

(e) witness the declaration of results, where applicable.

(2) An election agent or polling agent shall counter sign the election results duly announced or declared by a presiding officer or returning officer, as the case may be, except that failure to countersign the election results by such election agent or polling agent shall not render the results invalid.

Duties of Zambia Police

6. The Zambia Police Service shall—

(a) enforce law and order at campaign meetings and processions in order to maintain peace and order;

(b) ensure that police officers do not abuse their authority or Government resources to campaign for the benefit of any political party or candidate;

(c) refrain from disrupting any campaign, rally or meeting which is legally convened by any political party; and

(d) ensure that police officers do not use their office to oppress any political party, candidate or supporter.

Duties of media

7. (1) Print and electronic media shall—

(a) provide fair and balanced reporting of the campaigns, policies, meetings, rallies and press conferences of all registered political parties and candidates during the campaign period;

(b) provide news of the electoral process up to the declaration of results;

(c) abide by regional codes of conduct in the coverage of elections provided that such guidelines are not in conflict with this Code;

(d) be bound by the provisions of this Code during elections; and

(e) in liaison with the Commission, recognise a representative media body authorised to receive complaints and provide advice regarding fair coverage of elections.

(2) A media organisation shall endeavour to—

(a) undertake capacity building of media personnel in their respective organisations;

(b) report election news in an accurate manner and not make any abusive editorial comment, incite violence or advocate hatred based on race, ethnicity, tribe, gender, sex, political or religious conviction; and

(c) identify any editorial comment it intends to make and separate it from the factual reporting of the news.

(3) The heads, senior management and staff of public and private media organisations shall not intimidate media practitioners and shall allow them to exercise professional judgment without undue influence.

(4) Public and private media personnel shall—

(a) conduct interviews with candidates with fairness both in the style of the interview and in the amount of the time given;

     (b) refrain from broadcasting their own political opinions, commentary or assessment, and where they do so, clearly identify the opinion, commentary or assessment as their own and carefully balance it in order to avoid bias; and

     (c) be duly accredited by the Commission to enter a nomination centre, polling centre or totalling centre.

Allocation of air time

8. (1) A public television, radio and electronic media shall allocate public air time equally to all political parties and candidates for their political broadcasts.

   (2) The Commission shall prescribe the amount of air time in any given language on public television or radio to be allocated to a political party or candidate.

   (3) On polling day, media shall not broadcast any campaign interviews for political parties or independent candidates or predict election results.

   (4) Broadcasters shall inform the public on the source of any public opinion poll and shall indicate the margin of error.

Election results programme

9. (1) Media shall disclose accurate election results and provide updates on the progress of the vote counting process and shall not speculate election results but shall broadcast confirmed election results as they are announced and published by presiding officers.

   (2) Television and radio stations shall—

     (a) maintain full records of all radio and television news bulletins and recordings of all other programmes related to the election, including party political broadcasts and shall institute a close and meticulous monitoring system to ensure balance throughout the campaign and up to the close of poll; and

     (b) provide the Commission, at any reasonable time, with such records, information and recordings as the Commission may require to fulfill its monitoring role.

   (3) The Commission shall require newspapers to make available archived copies of newspapers for inspection in the event of a complaint.

   (4) A candidate or political party who alleges that the candidate or political party has been unfairly treated or covered by any media organisation in the course of the election campaign, may lodge a complaint against the media organisation, in writing, to the Commission.

   (5) Where a complaint made under subparagraph (4) requires any media organisation to rectify an error, the candidate or political party making the complaint shall send the complaint to that media organisation and a copy of the complaint to the Commission and the media organisation shall respond to the complaint.

   (6) Where a right of reply, a retraction or the correction of a matter of significance is necessary, it shall be made in a like manner and with equal prominence as the original report or publication.

Monitors and observers

10. (1) A person shall not act as a monitor or observer, during an election campaign or election unless the person is duly accredited by the Commission.

   (2) A monitor shall be nominated by the organisation to which the monitor belongs and shall undergo training and assessment by that organisation.

   (3) A monitor or observer shall be provided with necessary identification by the Commission and the monitor's or observer's organisations.

   (4) A monitor or observer shall discharge monitors or observer's functions in accordance with this Code and any other written law or such lawful directives as may be given by the Commission or any person acting on its behalf.

   (5) A monitor or observer shall—

     (a) bring to the attention of the presiding officer or returning officer or member of the Commission any observed electoral malpractice;

     (b) be impartial in the conduct of the monitor's or observer's duty and shall, at no time, publicly indicate or express any bias or preference with reference to any political party or candidate;

     (c) be in a sufficient number at each polling station and shall ensure that their presence is widely known and recognised by the electorate;

(d) not interfere with the duties of the election officials in any way and shall immediately report any violation to the proper authority;

(e) ensure that any material information or report which the monitor or observer receives or any event, occurrence or statement of which the monitor or observer has been notified or which indicates the commission of an offence or contravention of the Act or this Code are brought to the attention of the monitor's or observer's organisations, the police, the Commission, conflict management committees and other parties concerned;

(f) not by themselves or through the monitor's or observer's organisation, forecast, declare or disclose the result of any election before the declaration by the Commission;

(g) when so requested, immediately identify themselves to any election officer or police officer and shall, during the conduct of the monitor's or observer's activities, at all times carry, wear or otherwise prominently display the identification issued by the Commission;

(h) not display allegiance to any political party at any time and shall refrain from carrying, wearing and displaying electoral material or any article of clothing, colours, badges or other items denoting support for or opposition to any political party or candidates or any of the issues in contention in the elections;

(i) not be involved in corrupt practices or accept any favours, so as to make statements in favour of or against any candidate or political party; and

(j) not carry or display arms or other dangerous weapons during the conduct of the monitor's or observer's activities or while wearing the identification issued by the Commission.

(6) Monitors and observers and their sponsoring organisations shall, whenever requested by the Commission, attend such briefings, training workshops and other meetings convened in order to coordinate their activities.

(7) After the declaration of results of the elections, monitors and observers shall hand over to the Commission any identification received from it.

(8) The Commission may revoke the accreditation of any monitor or observer who contravenes the provisions of this Code.

Powers of Commission

11. (1) The Commission may—
    (a) reprimand a political party, candidate or stakeholder for any conduct in violation of this Code;
    (b) report a breach of this Code to the Zambia Police Service, Anti-Corruption Commission and Drug Enforcement Commission or any other relevant law enforcement agency;
    (c) revoke the accreditation of election agents, polling agents, monitors observers or the media where it is necessary in the interest of public safety and security to do so; and
    (d) impose any administrative measures on any person, candidate or political party for persistent breach of this code.

    (2) The Commission may where practicable to do so, summon any person contravening this Code and any voter, candidate or political party alleging a breach to appear before it.

Complaints

12. (1) The following persons may lodge a complaint to the Commission in relation to an election:
    (a) a voter or candidate in a constituency where a breach of this Code has been committed; or
    (b) from a political party participating in an election.

    (2) Complaints arising during election campaigns and elections may be made to an election officer or to a conflict management committee at the place where the conduct complained against occurred.

    (3) The Commission may refer and report any violation of the Code to the Zambia Police Service, Anti-Corruption Commission or any other appropriate law enforcement agency for investigation and prosecution where appropriate.

Conflict management committee

13. (1) Conflict management committees established by the Commission pursuant to section one hundred and eight may resolve electoral disputes.

(2)   The conflict management committees shall take into account the provisions of this Code in resolving electoral disputes.

(3)   Conflict management committees shall mediate in electoral disputes and shall encourage amicable settlement of electoral disputes within twenty-four hours of receipt of a formal complaint.

Prohibition on coercion and intimidation

14.   A person or a member of a law enforcement agency, civil society, a Church, faith-based organisation, traditional leader, political party or media shall not, by means of threats, violence or sanction, coerce or intimidate another person during campaigns, public debates or elections.

General offence

15.   (1)   A person shall not—

(a)   cause violence or use any language or engage in any conduct which leads or is likely to lead to violence or intimidation during an election campaign or election;

(b)   carry or display arms or weapons, traditional or otherwise, of any kind at a political meeting or in the course of any march, demonstration or other public gathering of a political nature;

(c)   make false, defamatory or inflammatory allegations concerning any person or political party in connection with an election;

(d)   arrange a public meeting, demonstration, rally or march at the same time and venue as another similar political event organised by another political party or candidate;

(e)   prevent the reasonable access to voters of any candidate or political party in any manner for the purposes of conducting voter education, fund raising, canvassing membership or soliciting support;

(f)   plagiarise the symbols, colours or acronyms of candidates or other political parties;

(g)   deface, remove or destroy any political campaign materials of any person or political party or publications of the Commission;

(h)   offer any inducement, reward or bribe to any person in consideration of such person—

(i)   joining or not joining any political party;

(ii)   attending or not attending any political event;

(iii)   voting or not voting;

(iv)   accepting, refusing or withdrawing that person's domination as a candidate in an election;

(v)   surrendering that person's voter's card, or national registration card or both; or

(vi)   offering to surrender a voter's card or national registration card, or both;

(i)   abuse or attempt to abuse a position of power, privilege or influence, including parental, patriarchal or traditional authority for political purposes including any offer of a reward or for the issuance of a threat;

(j)   any opinion or action which is prejudicial to—

(i)   the sovereignty, integrity or security of the country;

(ii)   the maintenance of public order; or

(iii)   the independence of any institution;

(k)   use Government or parastatal transportation or facilities for campaign purposes, except that this paragraph shall not apply to the President and the Vice President in connection with their respective offices;

(l)   use Government transportation or resources or facilities to transport voters to polling stations;

(m)   discriminate against any person on grounds of race, ethnicity, class, disability, gender, sex, religion or in any other manner in connection with an election or political activity;

(n)   carry any statue, caricature or anything which tends to ridicule, revile or scandalise any political party or its leader, a candidate or the Government, at any public political gathering, meeting or procession; and

(o)   be in possession of a voter's card or national registration card belonging to another person during the campaign period.

(2)   A person who contravenes subparagraph (1) commits an offence and is liable, upon conviction, to a fine not exceeding two hundred thousand penalty units or to imprisonment for a term not exceeding two years, or to both.

General Penalty

16. A person who contravenes any provision of this Code for which no specific penalty is provided commits an offence and is liable, upon conviction, to a fine not exceeding two hundred thousand penalty units or to imprisonment for a period not exceeding two years, or to both.

Revocation of SI No 90 of 2006

17. The Electoral (Code of Conduct) Regulations, 2006, are revoked.

THE CYBER SECURITY AND CYBER CRIMES ACT NO 2 OF 2021

ARRANGEMENT OF SECTIONS

PART I
PRELIMINARY PROVISIONS

> **An Act to provide for cyber security in the Republic; provide for the constitution of the Zambia Computer Incidence Response Team and provide for its functions; provide for the constitution of the National Cyber Security Advisory and Coordinating Council and provide for its functions; provide for the continuation of the Central Monitoring and Co-ordination Centre; provide for the protection of persons against cybercrime; provide for child online protection; facilitate identification, declaration and protection of critical information infrastructure; provide for the collection of and preservation of evidence of computer and network related crime; provide for the admission; in criminal matters, of electronic evidence; provide for registration of cyber security service providers; and provide for matters connected with, or incidental to, the foregoing.**

Enactment

ENACTED by the Parliament of Zambia.

PART I
PRELIMINARY PROVISIONS

Short title and commencement

1. This Act may be cited as the Cyber Security and Cyber Crimes Act, 2021, and shall come into operation on the date appointed by the Minister by statutory instrument.

Interpretation

2. In this Act, unless the context otherwise requires—
    "access" has the meaning assigned to the word in the Electronic Communications and Transactions Act, 2021;
    "advanced electronic signature" has the meaning assigned to the words in the Electronic Communications and Transactions Act, 2021;
    "article" means any data computer program, computer data storage medium or computer system which—
        (a) is concerned with, connected with or is, on reasonable grounds, believed to be concerned with or connected with the commission of a crime or suspected commission of a crime;

(b) may afford evidence of the commission or suspected commission of a crime; and

(c) is intended to be used or is, on reasonable grounds, believed to be intended to be used in the commission of a crime;

"Authority" has the meaning assigned to the word in the Information and Communications Technologies Act, 2009;

"cache" means the storing of data in a transmission system in order to speed up data transmission or processing";

"caching" has the meaning assigned to the word in the Electronic Communications and Transactions Act, 2021;

"child" has the meaning assigned to the word in the Constitution;

"child pornography" means pornography in audio, visual, text or other digital format that depicts or represents a child engaged in sexually explicit conduct;

"child solicitation" means persuading, luring, or attempting to persuade or lure a child into sexual activity through the use of a computer system or device, regardless of the outcome;

"computer" has the meaning assigned to the word in the Electronic Communications and Transactions Act, 2021;

"computer data" means a representation of facts, concepts or information in a form suitable for processing in a computer system, including a program suitable to cause a computer system to perform a function;

"computer data storage medium" means an apparatus or object from which electronic information is capable of being reproduced, with or without the aid of an article or device;

"computer system" means a set of integrated devices that input, output, process, and store data and information including internet;

"controller" means a person, either alone or in common with other persons, who controls and is responsible for critical information infrastructure;

"Council" means the National Cyber Security Advisory and Coordinating Council constituted under section 7;

"critical information" means information that is declared by the Minister to be critical for the purposes of national security or the economic and social wellbeing of the Republic;

"critical information infrastructure" means the cyber infrastructure that is essential to vital services for public safety, economic stability, national security, international stability and for the sustainability and restoration of critical cyberspace;

"cyber" means the—

(a) computer simulated environment; or

(b) state of connection or association with electronic communications systems or networks including the internet;

"cyber crime" means a crime committed in, by or with the assistance of the simulated environment or state of connection or association with electronic communications or networks including the internet;

"cyber ecosystem" means the interconnected information infrastructure of interactions among persons, processes, data, and information and communication technologies, along with the environment and the conditions that influence those interactions;

"cyber inspector" means a person appointed as cyber inspector under section 8;

"cyber security" means tools, policies, security concepts, security safeguards, guidelines, risk management approaches, actions, training, best practices, assurances and technologies that can be used to protect the cyber environment, organisation and user assets;

"cyber security incident" means an act or activity on or through a computer or computer system, that jeopardises or adversely impacts, without lawful authority, the security, availability or integrity of a computer or computer system, or the availability, confidentiality or integrity of information stored on, processed by, or transiting a computer or computer system;

"damage" means the impairment to the integrity or availability of data, a program, a system or information;

"device" includes—

(a) components of computer systems such as graphic cards, memory chips and processors;

(b) storage components such as hard drives, memory cards, compact discs and tapes;

(c) input devices such as keyboards, mouse, trackpad, scanner and digital cameras;

(d) output devices such as printer and screens; and

(e) an apparatus which can be used to intercept a wire, oral or electronic communications;

"denial of service" means rendering a computer system incapable of providing a normal service to its legitimate user;

"digital forensics" means the application of scientific investigatory techniques to cyber crimes by collecting, identifying and validating the digital information for purposes of reconstructing past events;

"digital forensic tool" means hardware or software used for conducting digital forensics;

"Director-General" means a person appointed as Director-General under the Information and Communication, Technologies Act, 2009;

"electronic communications" has the meaning assigned to the words in the Electronics Communications and Transactions Act, 2021;

"electronic communications service" means any service which provides the ability to send, receive, process or store electronic communications;

"electronic signature" has the meaning assigned to the words in the Electronic Communications and Transactions Act, 2021;

"explicit sexual conduct" includes sexual intercourse, or other sexual conduct whether between persons or between a person and an animal, masturbation, sexual sadistic or masochistic abuse, or the lascivious exhibition of the genitals or pubic area of any person;

"Genocide" has the meaning assigned to the word in theUnited Nations Convention on the Prevention and Punishment of the Crime of Genocide;

"hate speech and conduct" means verbal or non-verbal communication, action, material whether video, audio, streaming or written, that involves hostility or segregation directed towards an individual or particular social groups on grounds of race, ethnicity, antisemitism, tribalism, sex, age, disability, colour, marital status, pregnancy, health status and economic status, culture, religion, belief, conscience, origin;

"hosting" has the meaning assigned to the word in the Electronic Communications and Transactions Act, 2021;

"hyperlink" means a clickable electronic reference or link of a data message that contains information about another source and when clicked points to and causes to display another data message;

"interception" means an act, by a person who is not a party to a conversation, of wiretapping subscribers or aural or other acquisition of conversation of any wire, electronic or oral communication through the use of an electronic, mechanical or other device;

"internet connection record" shall include—

(a) connections which are made automatically by a person, browser or device;

(b) a customer account reference such as an account number or identifier of the customer's device or internet connection;

(c) the time stamp of the session log;

(d) the source and destination IP addresses and their associated identity information;

(e) the volume of data transferred in either, or both, directions;

(f) the name of the internet service or server connected to;

(g) those elements of a URL which constitutes communications data; or

(h) any other related meta data.

"information infrastructure" means the communication networks and associated software that support interaction among people and organisations;

"Information Technology Auditor" means a person who possesses the expertise to examine and evaluate an information security management system as it relates to information technology infrastructure;

"Judge" means a Judge of the High Court;

"law enforcement officer" means—

(a) a police officer above the rank of sub inspector;

(b) an officer of the Anti-Corruption Commission;

(c) an officer of the Drug Enforcement Commission;

(d) an officer of the Zambia Security Intelligence Service; and

(e) any other person appointed as such by the Minister for purposes of this Act;

"malicious software" means a computer program written to allow access to a computer system, whether with or without user intervention for purposes of negatively affecting normal computer system usage or modifying data or transmitting data to another computer system;

"meta data" means data that describes other data;

"multiple electronic mail message" means a mail message including email and instant messaging sent more than once to a recipient;

"penetration testing service" means a service for assessing, testing or evaluating the cyber security of a computer or computer system and the integrity of any information stored in or processed

553

by the computer or computer system, by searching for vulnerabilities in, and compromising, the cyber

security defences of the computer or computer system with express permission of the system owner;

"pornography" means audio or visual material that depicts images of a person engaged in explicit sexual conduct;

"premises" includes a computer and data messages;

"racist and xenophobic material" includes any image, video, audio recording or any other representation of ideas or theories, which advocates, promotes or incites hatred, discrimination or violence, against any individual or group of individuals, based on race, colour, descent or national or ethnic origin;

"service provider" means a public or private entity authorised to—

    (a)   provide or offer an electronic communication system;

    (b)   process or store computer data on behalf of a communication service or user of such service; or

    (c)   own an electronic communication system to provide or offer an electronic communication service;

"traffic data" means digital data that—

    (a)   relates to a communication by means of a computer system;

    (b)   is generated by a computer system that is part of the chain of communication; and

    (c)   shows the communication's origin, destination, route, time, date, size, duration or the type of underlying services;

"Uniform Resource Locator (URL)" means the unique address of the world wide web page; and

"Zambia Computer Incidence Response Team" means the Zambia Computer Incidence Response Team constituted under section 6.

Supremacy of Act

3.   Subject to the Constitution, where there is an inconsistency between the provisions of this Act and the provisions of any other written law relating to the regulation of cyber security, cybercrimes and digital forensics, the provisions of this Act shall prevail to the extent of the inconsistency.

PART II
REGULATION OF CYBER SECURITY SERVICES

Supremacy of Act

3.   Subject to the Constitution, where there is an inconsistency between the provisions of this Act and the provisions of any other written law relating to the regulation of cyber security, cyber crimes and digital forensics, the provisions of this Act shall prevail to the extent of the inconsistency.

Cyber security regulator

4.   The Authority is responsible for the implementation of this Act.

Functions of Authority

5.   (1)   The functions of the Authority are to—

    (a)   co-ordinate and oversee activities relating to cyber security and the combatting of cyber crime;

    (b)   provide quarterly reports to the Council;

    (c)   assess the work of the incident response teams within the public and private sectors;

    (d)   disseminate information on emerging cyber threats and vulnerabilities as presented;

    (e)   develop and promote an all-inclusive secure cyber ecosystem;

    (f)   create a safe cyber space in critical information infrastructure;

    (g)   issue guidelines, cyber security codes of practice and standards of performance for implementation by owners of critical information infrastructure;

    (h)   promote, develop, maintain and improve competencies, expertise and professional standards in the cyber security community;

    (i)   promote research and development in the use of new and appropriate technologies and techniques in cybercrimes;

    (j)   promote education and awareness of the need for and importance of cyber security;

> *(k)* establish international cooperation with foreign states and cyber security entities and strengthen partnerships in combatting cyber crime;
>
> *(l)* undertake information security audits and penetration testing services on all critical information infrastructure.
>
> *(m)* maintain a register of cyber security service providers;
>
> *(n)* coordinate with law enforcement agencies to ensure safe cyber space and investigations of cyber incidences; and
>
> *(o)* issue guidelines relating to digital forensics.

(2) The Authority shall in performing its functions, collaborate with the Ministry responsible for security, defence, and other relevant agencies on matters relating to cyber security.

Constitution of Zambia Computer Incidence Response Team

6. (1) The Authority shall constitute the Zambia Computer Incidence Response Team which shall —

> *(a)* be the first point of contact with reference to the handling of cyber incidents and communication between local, regional and international cyber security emergency response teams or cyber security incident response teams;
>
> *(b)* provide incident response and management services in a coordinated manner through established industry standard policies and procedures to manage threats associated with cyber incidents;
>
> *(c)* provide alerts and warnings on the latest cyber threats and vulnerabilities which may impact the national community;
>
> *(d)* assess and analyse the impact of incidents such as network security breaches, website hackings, virus and network attacks;
>
> *(e)* assess and coordinate the work of sectorial cyber incidence response teams within the public and private sector;
>
> *(f)* participate in information sharing and disseminate information with international cyber security incidence response teams and computer emergency response teams on the emerging threats to critical information infrastructure and internet resources;
>
> *(g)* participate in and be a member of regional and international computer emergency response team groups; and
>
> *(h)* perform any other functions conferred on it by the Authority for purposes of this Act.

(2) The Authority shall determine the composition, tenure and procedures of the Zambia Computer Incidence Response Team.

Constitution of National Cyber Security, Advisory and Co-ordinating Council

7. (1) The Minister shall constitute the National Cyber Security Advisory Coordinating Council which shall consist of part-time members who are experts in cyber security and cyber crime and in matters related to the Act.

(2) The Council constituted under subsection (1) shall—

> *(a)* coordinate and strengthen collaboration between security wings on matters to do with cyber security;
>
> *(b)* oversee the implementation of cyber security related functions of the Authority;
>
> *(c)* monitor and evaluate the performance of the Authority in relation to cyber security;
>
> *(d)* provide periodic reports to the Minister on cyber security matters;
>
> *(e)* provide advice to the Minister and the Authority on matters relating to cyber security;
>
> *(f)* provide guidance in the issuance of cyber security linked advisories affecting the Republic; and
>
> *(g)* any other functions as the Minister may delegate.

(3) Subject to any specific or general directive of the Minister, the Council may regulate its own procedure.

(4) The members of the Council shall elect a Chairperson and Vice-Chairperson from among themselves.

(5) The Minister may, by statutory instrument, make regulations to provide for the composition and tenure of the Council.

(6) There shall be paid to the members of the Council allowances that the Emoluments Commission may, on the recommendation of the Minister, determine.

PART III
INSPECTORATE

Appointment of cyber inspector

8. (1) The Authority may appoint a suitably qualified person as a cyber inspector for the purposes of ensuring compliance with this Act.

    (2) The Authority shall, issue a certificate of appointment to a person appointed as a cyber inspector.

    (3) The certificate of appointment referred to in subsection (2), shall be in a prescribed form and shall be *prima facie* evidence of the cyber inspector's appointment.

    (4) A cyber inspector shall in performing any function under this part—
        (a) be in possession of a certificate of appointment referred to in subsection (2); and
        (b) show the certificate of appointment to a person who requests to see the certificate.

    (5) A person commits an offence if that person falsely holds oneself out as a cyber inspector.

    (6) A person convicted of an offence under subsection (5) is liable, on conviction, to a fine not exceeding two hundred thousand penalty units or to imprisonment for a term not exceeding two years, or to both.

Power to inspect and monitor

9. A cyber inspector may in the performance of the inspector's functions, with a warrant—
    (a) monitor and inspect a computer system or activity on an information system, where such activity or information is not in public domain or is not accessible to the public;
    (b) enter and inspect the premises of a cyber security service provider if there is reasonable ground to believe that the licensee has contravened the provisions of this Act; and
    (c) audit critical information infrastructure.

Data retention notice

10. (1) Where a data retention notice is issued requiring an electronic communications service provider to retain internet connection records the specific data that the electronic communications service provider may be required to retain shall be specified in the retention notice.

    (2) An electronic communication service provider shall not be required to retain data as part of an internet connection record.

Power to access, search and seize

11. (1) A cyber inspector may, in the performance of the cyber inspector's functions, with a warrant, at any reasonable time and without prior notice, enter any premises or access an information system and—
        (a) search the premises or that information system;
        (b) search any person on the premises if there are reasonable grounds to believe that the person has possession of an article, document or record that has a bearing on an investigation;
        (c) take extracts from, or make copies of any book, document or record that is on or in the premises or in the information system and that has a bearing on an investigation;
        (d) demand the production of, and inspect, relevant licences and registration certificates;
        (e) inspect any facilities on the premises which are linked or associated with the information system;
        (f) access and inspect the operation of any computer or equipment forming part of an information system and any associated apparatus or material which the cyber inspector has reasonable cause to believe is, or has been used in, connection with any offence;
        (g) use or cause to be used any information system or part thereof to search any data contained in or available to such information system;
        (h) require the person by whom, or on whose behalf, the cyber inspector has reasonable cause to suspect the computer or information system is or has been used, or require any person in control of, or otherwise involved with the operation of the computer or information system, to provide the cyber inspector with such reasonable technical and other assistance as the cyber inspector may require for the purposes of this Part; or
        (i) make such inquiries as may be necessary to ascertain whether the provisions of this Act or any other law on which an investigation is based, have been complied with.

    (2) A person shall be searched with decency by a designated person of the same sex.

Obstruction of cyber inspector

12. (1) A person commits an offence if that person obstructs a cyber inspector from conducting a lawful search or seizure under This Act.

    (2) A person convicted of an offence under subsection (1) is liable, on conviction, to a fine not exceeding two hundred thousand penalty units or to imprisonment for a period not exceeding two years, or to both.

Appointment of cyber security technical expert

13. (1) The Director-General may, appoint in a prescribed manner and form, any person as a cyber security technical expert for a specified period to assist a cyber inspector in the cyber inspector's exercise of any powers under this Act.

    (2) The Director-General shall issue an identification card, which shall be carried at all times by the cyber security technical expert when performing the functions of a cyber security technical expert under in this Act.

Emergency cyber security measures and requirements

14. (1) The Minister may, in consultation with other relevant agencies, issue regulations authorising or directing a person or organisation specified in the regulations to take such measures or comply with such requirements, where the Minister considers it necessary for the purposes of preventing, detecting or countering a threat to—

    (a) the essential services;
    (b) national security and defence;
    (c) foreign relations;
    (d) economy;
    (e) public health and public safety;
    (f) public order of the Republic; or
    (g) an electronic communication system, computer system and information system.

    (2) A person who fails to take any measure or comply with any requirement directed by the Minister under subsection (1) commits an offence and is liable on conviction to a fine not exceeding one hundred thousand penalty units or to imprisonment for a term not exceeding three months or to both.

PART IV
INVESTIGATION OF CYBER SECURITY INCIDENTS

Power to investigate

15. (1) Where the Authority receives information regarding an alleged cyber security threat or an alleged cyber security incident a cyber inspector appointed under section 8 may, having regard to the impact or potential impact of the alleged cyber security threat or alleged cyber security incident—

    (a) require, by written notice, a person to attend at such reasonable time and place as may be specified in the notice to answer any question or to provide a signed statement inwriting concerning the alleged cyber security incident or alleged cyber security threat;
    (b) require, by written notice, a person to produce a physical or electronic record, document or copy thereof in the possession of that person;
    (c) require, by written notice, a person to provide the cyber inspector with information, which the cyber inspector considers to be relevant to the investigation;
    (d) copy or take extracts from any physical or electronic record or document; or
    (e) examine orally a person who appears to be acquainted with the facts and circumstances relating to the alleged cyber security incident or cyber security threat and to reduce to writing a statement made by the person so examined.

    (2) The cyber inspector may specify in the notice mentioned in subsection (1)(b)—

    (a) the time and place at which any record or document is to be produced or any information is to be provided; and
    (b) the manner and form in which it is or be produced or provided.

    (3) A person examined under this section who, in good faith, discloses any information to a cyber inspector shall not be treated as being in breach of any restriction on the disclosure of information imposed by law, contract or rules of professional conduct.

(4)   A person commits an offence if that person—

     (a) willfully gives false information or without lawful excuse refuses to give any information or produce any record, document or copy thereof required of that person by a cyber inspector under subsection (1); or

     (b) refuses to cooperate with or hinders a cyber inspector from conducting a lawful search or seizure.

(5)   A person convicted of an offence under subsection (4) is liable to a fine not exceeding two hundred thousand penalty units or to imprisonment for a term not exceeding two years or to both.

PART V
PROTECTION OF CRITICAL INFORMATION AND INFRASCTRUCTURE

Scope of protecting critical information infrastructure

16. The provisions of this Part apply to a critical information infrastructure or parts thereof and to the controllers of critical information infrastructure.

Declaration of critical information

17. (1) The Minister may by statutory instrument declare information which is of importance to the protection of national security, economic or social wellbeing of the Republic, to be critical information for the purposes of this part.

(2) Infrastructure containing critical information shall be declared critical information infrastructure.

Localisation of critical information

18. (1) A controller of critical information shall store all critical information on a server or data center located within the Republic.

(2) Despite subsection (1), the Minister may authorise a controller of critical information to externalise the critical information outside the Republic as prescribed.

(3) In an event where the purpose for which critical information collected expires or the data controller ceases to exist, such critical information shall be surrendered to the Authority.

Registration of critical information infrastructure

19. (1) The Minister may by statutory instrument prescribe—

     (a) the requirements for the registration of critical information infrastructure with the Authority;

     (b) the procedure to be followed for the registration of critical information infrastructure; and

     (c) any other matter relating to the registration of critical information infrastructure.

Change in ownership of critical information infrastructure

20. (1) A person who owns a critical information infrastructure and intends to change ownership of the critical information infrastructure shall apply to the Authority in the prescribed manner and form on payment of the prescribed fee.

(2) A person who contravenes subsection (1), commits an offence.

Register of critical information infrastructure

21. The Authority shall maintain a register of critical information infrastructure which shall contain such information as may be prescribed.

Auditing of critical information infrastructure to ensure compliance

22. (1) A controller of a critical information infrastructure shall, annually appoint an information technology auditor to audit the critical information infrastructure as prescribed.

(2) Despite subsection (1), the Authority may at any time require a controller of a critical information infrastructure to perform an audit.

(3) A controller of a critical information infrastructure who contravenes subsection (2) commits an offence and is liable on conviction to a fine not exceeding five hundred thousand penalty units or to imprisonment for a term not exceeding one year or to both.

Duty to report cyber security incident in respect of critical information infrastructure

23. (1) A controller of a critical information infrastructure shall report to the Authority on or after the occurrence of any of the following events:

(a) a cyber security incident in respect of the critical information infrastructure;

(b) a cyber security incident in respect of any computer or computer system under the controller's control that is interconnected with or communicates with the critical information infrastructure; and

(c) any other type of cyber security incident in respect of the critical information infrastructure that the Authority may specify by written direction.

(2) A report under subsection (1) shall be in the prescribed manner and form.

(3) The controller of critical information infrastructure shall submit a monthly cyber security incident and threat report to the Authority.

(4) A controller of a critical information infrastructure shall Establish mechanisms and processes, in accordance with information security standards published in the *Gazette*, as may be necessary for the detection of a cyber security threat in respect of its critical information infrastructure.

(5) A controller of a critical information infrastructure who contravenes subsection (1) commits an offence and is liable on conviction to a fine not exceeding five hundred thousand penalty units or to imprisonment for a term not exceeding five years or to both.

National cyber security exercises

24. (1) The Authority shall conduct cyber security exercises for the purposes of testing the state of readiness of owners of different critical information infrastructure in responding to significant cyber security incidents at the national level.

(2) A controller of a critical information infrastructure shall participate in a national cyber security exercise as directed inwriting by the Authority.

(3) A person who fails to comply with a written direction issued under subsection (2) commits an offence and is liable on conviction—

(a) to a fine not exceeding one hundred thousand penalty units or to imprisonment for a term not exceeding one year or to both; and

(b) in the case of a continuing offence, a further fine not exceeding one hundred thousand penalty units for every day and part thereof during which the offence continues.

Non-compliance with Part V

25. (1) The Authority shall, where an audit reveals that a controller of a critical information infrastructure has contravened a provision of this Part, notify the said controller in writing, stating the—

(a) finding of the audit report;

(b) action required to remedy the noncompliance; and

(c) period within which the controller shall take the remedial action.

(2) A controller that fails to take any remedial action within the period stipulated under subsection (1) commits an offence and is liable, on conviction, to a fine not exceeding five hundred thousand penalty units or to imprisonment for a term not exceeding five years, or to both.

PART VI
INTERCEPTION OF COMMUNICATIONS

Prohibition of interception of communications

26. (1) A person commits an offence, if that person—

(a) intercepts, attempts to intercept or procures another person to intercept or attempt to intercept any communication; or

(b) use, attempt to use or procure another person to use or attempt to use any electronic, software, mechanical or other device to intercept any communication.

(2)   A person who contravenes subsection (1) commits an offence and is liable, on conviction, to a fine not exceeding one million penalty units or to imprisonment for a term not exceeding ten years or to both.

Central Monitoring and Co-ordination Centre

27. (1)   There is established the Central Monitoring and Co-ordination Centre.

(2)   The Central Monitoring and Co-ordination Centre is the sole facility through which authorised interceptions in terms of this Act shall be effected and all the intercepted communication and call related information of any particular interception target forwarded.

(3)   The Central Monitoring and Co-ordination Centre shall be managed, controlled and operated by the department responsible for Government communications in liaison with the Authority.

Lawful interception

28. (1) Subject to subsection (2), a law enforcement officer may, where the law enforcement officer has reasonable grounds to believe that an offence has been committed, is likely to be committed or is being committed and for the purpose of obtaining evidence of the commission of an offence under this Act, apply, *ex-parte*, to a Judge, for an interception of communications order.

(2)   A law enforcement officer shall, apply for a written consent of the Attorney-General in a prescribed manner and form, before making an application under subsection (1).

(3)   A Judge to whom an application is made under subsection (1) may make an order—

(a)   requiring a service provider to intercept and retain a specified communication or communications of a specified description received or transmitted, or about to be received or transmitted by that service provider;

(b)   authorising the law enforcement officer to enter specified premises with a warrant and to install on such premises any device for the interception and retention of a specified communication or communications of a specified description and to remove and retain such device;

(c)   requiring any person to furnish the law enforcement officer with such information, facilities and assistance as the Judge considers necessary for the purpose of the installation of the interception device; or

(d)   imposing the terms and conditions for the protection of the interests of the persons specified in the order or any third parties or to facilitate any investigation.

(4)   A Judge may grant an order under subsection (3) where the Judge is satisfied that—

(a)   the written consent of the Attorney General has been obtained as required by subsection (2); and

(b)   there are reasonable grounds to believe that material information relating to the—

(i)   commission of an offence under this Act or any other law; or

(ii)   whereabouts of the person suspected by the law enforcement officer to have committed the offence; is contained in that communication or communications of that description.

(5)   Any information contained in a communication—

(a)   intercepted and retained pursuant to an order under subsection (3); or

(b)   intercepted and retained in a foreign State in accordance with the law of that foreign State and certified by a Judge of that foreign State to have been so intercepted and retained, shall be admissible in proceedings for an offence under this Act, as evidence of the truth of its contents despite the fact that it contains hearsay.

(6)   An interception of communications order referred to in this section shall be valid for a period of three months and may, on application by a law enforcement officer, be renewed for such period as the Judge may determine.

(7)   An action does not lie in any court against a service provider, any officer, employee or agent of the service provider or other specified person, for providing information, facilities or assistance in accordance with the terms of a court order under this Act or any other law.

Interception of communication to prevent bodily harm, loss of life or damage to property

29. (1)   A law enforcement officer may, intercept any communication and orally request a service provider to route duplicate signals of indirect communications specified in that request to the Central Monitoring and Coordination Centre where the law enforcement officer has reasonable grounds to believe that—

(a) a person who is a part of any communication—
- (i) has caused, or may cause, the infliction of bodily harm to another person;
- (ii) threatens, or has threatened, to cause the infliction of bodily harm to another person;
- (iii) threatens, or has threatened, to kill oneself or another person, or to perform an act which would or may endanger that party's own life or that of another person, would or may cause the infliction of bodily harm to that party or another person;
- (iv) has caused or may cause damage to property; or
- (v) has caused or may cause financial loss to banks, financial institutions, account holders or beneficiaries of funds being remitted or received by such account holders or beneficiaries;

(b) it is not reasonable or practical to make an application under section 28 for an interception of communication order because the delay to intercept a specified communication would result in the actual infliction of bodily harm, the death of another person or damage to property; or

(c) the sole purpose of the interception is to prevent bodily harm to, or loss of life of, any person or damage to property.

(2) An electronic communication service provider shall, on receipt of a request made under subsection (1) by a law enforcement officer, route the duplicate signals of the indirect communication to the Central Monitoring and Coordination Centre.

(3) A law enforcement officer who makes a request to a service provider under subsection (1) shall, immediately after making that request, furnish the service provider with a written confirmation of the request setting out the information given by that law enforcement officer to that service provider in connection with the request.

(4) A law enforcement officer who intercepts any communication under this section, shall immediately after the interception of the communication, submit to a Judge—
- (a) a copy of the written confirmation referred to in subsection (3);
- (b) an affidavit setting out the results and information obtained from that interception; and
- (c) a recording of the communication that has been obtained by means of that interception, a full or partial transcript of the recording of the communication and any notes made by the law enforcement officer.

(5) An electronic communications service provider who, in accordance with subsection (2), routes duplicate signals of indirect communications to the Central Monitoring and Coordination Centre shall, as soon as practicable thereafter, submit an affidavit to a Judge setting out the steps taken by that service provider in giving effect to the request and the results obtained from such steps.

(6) A Judge shall cause to be kept all written confirmations and affidavits, recording, transcripts or notes submitted under this section for a period of at least five years.

(7) Where a Judge, on receipt of a written confirmation and affidavit under this section, determines that the interception was effected or used for purposes contrary to, or in contravention of the provisions of this Act or any other law, the Judge may make an order as the Judge considers appropriate in relation to the service provider, or the person whose communication has been intercepted or law enforcement officer.

Interception of communication for purposes of determining location

30. (1) Where a person is a party to a communication and that person, as a result of information received from another party to the communication, in this section referred to as the "sender", has reasonable grounds to believe that an emergency exists by reason of the fact that—
- (a) theft of finances from a bank or a financial institution is likely to occur;
- (b) the life of another person, whether or not the sender, is being endangered;
- (c) a person is dying, or is being or has been injured;
- (d) a person's life is likely to be endangered;
- (e) a person is likely to die or to be injured; or
- (f) property is likely to be damaged, is being damaged or has been damaged.

(2) The location of the sender is unknown to the person, that person may, if that person is—
- (a) a law enforcement officer, and has reasonable grounds to believe that determining the location of the sender is likely to be of assistance in dealing with the emergency, orally request, or cause another law enforcement officer to orally request, an electronic communications service provider to—

(i) intercept any communication to or from the sender, for purposes of determining the sender's location; or

(ii) determine the location of the sender; or

(b) not a law enforcement officer, inform or cause another person to inform, any law enforcement officer of the matter referred to in subsection (1)(a), (b), (c), (d) and (e).

(3) A law enforcement officer who receives information under subsection (1) may, orally request, or cause another law enforcement officer to orally request, an electronic communication service provider to determine the location of the sender, where the law enforcement officer has reasonable grounds to believe that determining the location of the sender is likely to be of assistance in dealing with an emergency.

(4) An electronic communication service provider shall, on receipt of a request made under subsections (1) or (2)—

(a) intercept any communication to, or from, the sender for purposes of determining the sender's location; or

(b) use its best efforts to determine the location of the sender in any other manner which the service provider considers appropriate.

(5) Where the location of the sender has been determined, the electronic communication service provider shall, immediately after determining that location, provide the law enforcement officer who made the request with the location of the sender and any other information obtained which is likely to assist in the investigation.

(6) A law enforcement officer who makes a request to an electronic communication service provider under subsections (1) or (2) shall—

(a) immediately after making that request, furnish—(i) the electronic communication service provider with a written confirmation and affidavit of the request setting out the information given by that law enforcement officer to that electronic communications service provider in connection with the request; and

(ii) a judge with a copy of the written confirmation; and

(b) where the location of the sender and any other information has been provided to the law enforcement officer under subsection (3), immediately after receipt thereof, submit to a judge an affidavit setting out the results and information obtained from that interception.

(7) An electronic communication service provider who has taken any of the steps referred to in subsection (3), shall, immediately submit to a judge—

(a) an affidavit setting out the steps taken by the electronic communication service provider in giving effect to the request of a law enforcement officer and the results and information obtained from such steps; and

(b) where the steps included the interception of an indirect communication, any recording of that indirect communication obtained by means of the interception, a full or partial transcript of the recording and any notes made by that service provider of the indirect communication.

(8) A judge shall keep written confirmation and affidavit and any recordings, transcripts or notes submitted under subsections (6) and (7) or cause it to be kept, for a period of at least five years.

(9) Where a judge, on receipt of any written confirmation and affidavits under this section, determines that the interception was effected or used for purposes contrary to, or in contravention of the provisions of this Act or any other written law, the Judge may make an order that the judge considers appropriate in relation to the electronic communications service provider, the person whose communication has been intercepted or the law enforcement officer.

Prohibition of disclosure of intercepted communication

31. (1) Subject to section 32, a law enforcement officer who intercepts any communication pursuant to an interception of communication order shall not disclose the communication or use the communication in any manner other than in accordance with the provisions of this Act.

(2) A person commits an offence if that person without authorisation—

(a) accesses, discloses or attempts to disclose to another person, the contents of any intercepted communication; or

(b) uses or attempts to use, the contents of any intercepted communication.

(3) A person who contravenes subsection (2), commits an offence and is liable, on conviction, to a fine not exceeding one million penalty units or to imprisonment not exceeding ten years, or to both.

Disclosure of intercepted communication by law enforcement officer

32. (1) A law enforcement officer who intercepts a communication pursuant to an interception of communication order may disclose the information to another law enforcement officer where the disclosure is necessary for the determination of the commission of an offence or the whereabouts of a person suspected to have committed an offence.

(2) Where a law enforcement officer, in the performance of any functions under this Act, intercepts a communication relating to the commission of an offence under any other law, the law enforcement officer shall disclose or use the communication in accordance with the provisions of this Act or that other law.

Privileged communication to retain privileged character

33. A privileged communication, oral or electronic communication intercepted in accordance with the provisions of this Act does not lose its privileged character.

Prohibition of random monitoring

34. (1) An electronic communication service provider shall not utilise the service for observing or random monitoring except for mechanical or service quality control checks.

(2) An electronic communications service provider who contravenes subsection (1) commits an offence and is liable, on conviction, to a fine not exceeding five hundred thousand penalty units, or to imprisonment for a period not exceeding five years, or to both.

(3) In this section "monitoring" includes listening to or recording communication by means of a monitoring device; and "monitoring device" means any electronic, software, mechanical or other instrument, device, equipment or apparatus which is used or can be used, whether by itself or in combination with any other instrument, device, equipment or apparatus, to listen to or record any communication.

Protection of user from fraudulent or other unlawful use of service

35. (1) An electronic communication service provider shall record that a wire or electronic communication was initiated or completed in order to protect the service provider, another service provider giving a service for the completion of a wire or electronic communication or a user of the service, from fraudulent, unlawful or abusive use of the service.

(2) An electronic communication service provider who records an electronic communication under subsection (1) shall immediately inform a law enforcement officer.

(3) An electronic communication service provider may disclose the contents of a communication referred to under subsection (1)—

(a) with the consent of the originator, to the addressee or intended recipient of the communication;

(b) to a person employed or authorised, or whose facilities are used, to forward the communication to its destination; or

(c) to a law enforcement officer, where the information relates to the commission of an offence.

(4) A person who contravenes subsection (1) commits an offence and is liable, on conviction, to a fine not exceeding five hundred thousand penalty units or to imprisonment for a period not exceeding five years, or to both.

Interception of satellite transmission

36. (1) An interception of satellite transmission that is not encrypted or scrambled and that is transmitted to a broadcasting station for purposes of transmission to the public or as an audio subcarrier intended for redistribution to facilities open to the public is not an offence under this section unless the interception is for the purpose of a direct or indirect commercial advantage or private financial gain.

(2) Subsection (1) does not apply to any data transmission or a telephone call.

Prohibition of use of interception device

37. (1) Subject to subsection (3), a person shall not use an interception device or system software or hardware or other instrument, equipment or apparatus whether electronic or mechanical.

(2) A person who contravenes subsection (1) commits an offence and is liable, on conviction, to a fine not exceeding three million penalty units or to imprisonment for a term not exceeding twenty-five years, or to both.

(3) Subsection (1) does not apply to the use of an interception device by an electronic communication service provider or law enforcement officer as the case may be—

   (a) for the operation, maintenance and testing of a communication service;

   (b) to protect the rights or property of the electronic communication service provider or the users of the service from abuse of service or any other unlawful use of the service;

   (c) to record that the communication was initiated or completed in order to protect the electronic communications service provider or another electronic communication service provider in the completion of the communication, or a user of the service from fraudulent, unlawful or abusive use of the service; or

   (d) where the consent of the user of the service has been obtained.

Assistance by service provider

38. (1) An electronic communication service provider shall ensure that the electronic communication service provider—

   (a) uses an electronic communication system that is technically capable of supporting lawful interceptions in accordance with this Act;

   (b) installs hardware and software facilities and devices to enable the interception of communications when so required by a law enforcement officer or under a court order;

   (c) provides services that are capable of rendering real time and fulltime monitoring facilities for the interception of communications;

   (d) provides all call-related information in real time or as soon as possible upon call termination;

   (e) provides one or more interfaces from which any intercepted communication shall be transmitted to the Central Monitoring and Coordination Centre;

   (f) transmits intercepted communication to the Central Monitoring and Coordination Centre through fixed or switched connections, as the case may be; and

   (g) provides access to all intercepted subjects operating temporarily or permanently within the service provider's communications systems, and where the interception subject is using features to divert calls to other service providers or terminal equipment, access to such other providers or equipment.

(2) An electronic communication service provider who contravenes subsection (1) commits an offence and is liable, on conviction, to a fine not exceeding five hundred thousand penalty units or to imprisonment for a period not exceeding five years, or to both.

Duties of service provider in relation to customers

39. (1) An electronic communication service provider shall, before entering into a contract with a person for the provision of any service, obtain—

   (a) the person's full name, residential address and identity number contained in the person's identity document;

   (b) in the case of a corporate body, its business name and address and the manner in which it is incorporated or registered; and

   (c) any other information which the electronic communication service provider considers necessary for the purpose of enabling it to comply with the requirements of this Act.

(2) An electronic communication service provider shall ensure that proper records are kept of the information referred to in subsection (1) and any change in that information.

Interception capability of service provider

40. (1) Despite any other written law, an electronic communication service provider shall—

   (a) provide a service which has the capability to be intercepted; and

   (b) store call-related information in accordance with the provisions of this Act.

(2) The Minister may, in consultation with the Authority, by statutory instrument, make regulations to provide for the—

   (a) manner in which effect is to be given to subsection (1)(a) by every service provider;

   (b) security, technical and functional features of the facilities and devices to be acquired by every service provider to enable the—

(i) interception of communication under this Act; and

(ii) storing of call-related information; and

(c) period within which the requirements shall be complied with.

(3) The Regulation made under subsection (2) shall specify—

(a) the capacity and technical features of the devices or systems to be used for interception purposes;

(b) the connectivity of the devices or systems to be used for interception purposes with the Central Monitoring and Coordination Centre;

(c) the manner of routing intercepted information to the Central Monitoring and Coordination Centre; and

(d) any other matter which is necessary to give effect to the provisions of this Part.

(4) An electronic communication service provider shall, at the provider's own expense, acquire the facilities and devices specified in the regulations made under subsection (2).

(5) Subject to this Act a cost incurred by a service provider for the purpose of—

(a) enabling—

(i) any electronic communication to be intercepted; and

(ii) call-related information to be stored; and

(b) complying with this Part; shall be borne by the electronic communications service provider.

PART VII
LICENSING OF CYBER SECURITY SERVICE PROVIDERS

Prohibition from providing cyber security service without licence

41. (1) A person shall not, without a licence—

(a) engage in the business of providing, for reward or otherwise, cyber security service to other persons; or

(b) advertise, or in any way hold out, that the person is in the business of providing a licensable cyber security service, provides for reward or otherwise, or is willing to provide for reward or otherwise, the licensable cyber security service, except under and in accordance with a cyber security service provider's license granted under this Act.

(2) A person who contravenes subsection (1) commits an offence and is liable on conviction to a fine not exceeding one hundred thousand penalty units or to imprisonment for a term not exceeding one year or to both.

(3) This section does not apply to a person employed under a contract of service by another person to carry out a cyber security service for a computer or computer system belonging to that other person.

Application for licence

42. (1) A person who intends to engage in a cyber security service shall apply to the Authority in a prescribed form and manner on payment of a prescribed fee.

(2) The Authority shall within thirty days of receipt of an application, grant or reject the application on terms and conditions the Authority may determine.

(3) Where the Authority fails to make a decision within the period referred to under subsection (2), except as otherwise provided, the application shall be deemed to have been granted.

(4) The Authority shall, where it rejects an application for a licence, inform the applicant and give the reasons for the rejection.

(5) The Authority may request for further particulars or information in respect of an application under this section in a prescribed manner and form.

(6) Where the Authority requests for further particulars, the Period under subsection (2), shall stop running.

Renewal of licence

43. (1) A person may apply for the renewal of a licence to the Authority in a prescribed manner and form on payment of a prescribed fee.

(2) The Authority may on receipt of an application under subsection (1), within thirty days—

(a) renew the licence applied for, with or without conditions; or

(b) reject the application.

Refusal to grant or renew licence

44. (1)   The Authority may refuse to grant or to renew a licence where the Authority determines that—

          (a)   in the case of an individual, that individual is not a fit or proper person to hold or to continue to hold the licence;

          (b)   in the case of a business entity, an officer of the business entity is not a fit or proper person;

          (c)   it is not in the public interest to grant or renew the licence, or the grant or renewal of the licence may pose a threat to national security; or

          (d)   the applicant has not met the prescribed criteria.

     (2)   A person commits an offence if that person, in making an application for a licence—

          (a)   makes any statement or furnishes any particulars, information or document which the person knows to be false or does not believe to be true; or

          (b)   intentionally suppresses any material fact, or furnishes any information which is misleading in a material particular.

     (3)   A person convicted of an offence under subsection (3) is liable to a fine not exceeding one hundred thousand penalty units or to imprisonment for a term not exceeding one year or to both.

     (4)   The Authority may consider any of the following matters as applicable in deciding for the purposes of this section whether a person or an officer of a business entity or the business entity is a fit and proper person:

          (a)   that the person or officer associates with a person in a way that indicates involvement in an unlawful activity;

          (b)   that in dealings in which the person or officer has been involved, the person or officer has shown dishonesty or lack of integrity;

          (c)   that the person or officer is or was suffering from amental disorder;

          (d)   that the person or officer is an undischarged bankrupt or has entered into a composition with the creditor of the person or officer;

          (e)   that the person or officer has had a license revoked by the Authority previously;

          (f)   any other criteria prescribed by the Authority.

     (5)   Subsection (4) does not limit the circumstances in which a person or an officer of a business entity may be considered by the Authority not to be a fit and proper person.

Validity of licence

45.   A licence is valid for the period prescribed by statutory instrument.

Revocation or suspension of licence

46. (1)   Subject to subsection (3), the Authority may by order revoke any license if the Authority is satisfied that—

          (a)   the licensee has failed to comply with any condition imposed by the Authority on the license;

          (b)   the license had been obtained by fraud or misrepresentation;

          (c)   a circumstance which the Authority becomes aware of would have required or permitted the Authority to refuse to grant or renew the licensee's license, had the Authority been aware of the circumstance immediately before the license was granted or renewed;

          (d)   the licensee has ceased to carry on in the Republic the business or activity for which the licensee is licensed;

          (e)   the licensee has been declared bankrupt or has gone into compulsory or voluntary liquidation other than for the purpose of amalgamation or reconstruction;

          (f)   the licensee has been convicted of an offence under this Act, or an offence involving dishonesty;

          (g)   where the licensee is an individual the licensee is no longer a fit and proper person to continue to hold the license;

          (h)   where the licensee is a business entity an officer of the business entity or the business is no longer a fit and proper person; or

          (i)   it is in the public interest to do so.

     (2)   Subject to subsection (3), the Authority may, in any case in which the Authority considers that no cause of sufficient gravity for revoking any license exists, by order—

(a) suspend the license for a period not exceeding six months;

(b) censure the licensee concerned; or

(c) impose such other directions or restrictions as the Authority considers appropriate.

(3) The Authority shall not exercise its powers under subsections (1) or (2) except where an opportunity to be heard whether in person or by a representative and whether in writing or otherwise, had been given to the licensee against whom the Authority intends to exercise the licensing officer's powers, being a period of not more than fourteen days after the Authority informs the licensee of such intention.

(4) Where the Authority has by order revoked a licence under subsection (1) or made any order under subsection (2) in respect of a licensee, the Authority shall serve on the licensee concerned a notice of the order made under those subsections.

(5) Despite subsection (3), where a licensee has been charged with or convicted of a prescribed offence, being an offence, which would make it undesirable in the public interest for the licensee to continue to carry out the functions of a licensee—

(a) the Authority may serve on the licensee a notice of immediate suspension of the licence; and

(b) the licensee shall, upon a notice being served under paragraph (a) but subject to subsection (7), immediately cease to carry out any function of a licensee to which the licence refers.

(6) A licensee whose licence has been suspended under subsection (5) may, within fourteen days after the Authority has served the notice of suspension, apply to the Authority for review of the Authority's decision.

(7) The Authority may, on review of its decision, by order—

(a) revoke the licence in question;

(b) suspend that licence for a period not exceeding six months starting from the date of immediate suspension of that licence; or

(c) rescind the immediate suspension of that licence.

(8) Where the Authority has by order revoked or suspended a licence under subsection (7), the Authority shall serve on the licensee concerned a copy of the order.

(9) An order under this section shall not take effect until the expiration of fourteen days after the order has been served on the licensee.

PART VIII
INTERNATIONAL COOPERATION IN MAINTAINING CYBER SECURITY

Identifying areas of cooperation

47. The Authority shall identify and ensure that it cooperates with private, international organisations and other government entities involved in cyber security matters at international level.

Entering into agreement

48. The Republic may enter into any agreement with any foreign State and international body regarding—

(a) the provision of mutual assistance and cooperation relating to the investigation and prosecution of—

(i) an offence committed under this Act;

(ii) any other offence in terms of the laws of the Republic which is or was committed by means or facilitated by the use of an article; or

(iii) any other offence substantially similar to an offence recognised in the Republic which is or was committed by means of, or facilitated by the use of an article, in that foreign State.

PART IX
CYBER CRIME

Unauthorised access to, interception of or interference with computer system or data

49. (1) A person who intentionally accesses or intercepts any data without authority or permission to do so or who exceeds the authorised access, commits an offence and is liable, on conviction, to a fine not exceeding five hundred thousand penalty units or to imprisonment not exceeding five years, or to both.

(2) A person who intentionally and without authority to do so, interferes with or deviates data in a way which causes such data to be modified, destroyed or otherwise rendered ineffective, commits an offence and is liable, on conviction to a fine not exceeding five hundred thousand penalty units or, to imprisonment for a period not exceeding five years, or to both.

(3) Where an offence under this section is committed in relation to data that is in a critical information infrastructure or that is concerned with national security or the provision of an essential service, the penalty is a fine not exceeding two million five hundred thousand penalty units or to imprisonment not exceeding twenty-five years, or to both.

(4) A person commits an offence if that person—

    (a) without authority to do so, communicates, discloses or transmits any data, information, program, access code or command to any person not entitled or authorised to access the data, information, program, code or command;

    (b) without authority to do so, introduces or spreads a software code that damages a computer, computer system or network;

    (c) accesses or destroys any files, information, computer System or device without authorisation, or for purposes of concealing information necessary for an investigation into the commission, or otherwise, of an offence; or

    (d) damages, deletes, alters or suppresses any communication or data without authorisation.

(5) A person who commits an offence under subsection (4) is liable, on conviction, to a fine not exceeding two hundred thousand penalty units or to imprisonment for a period not exceeding two years, or to both.

(6) Subject to the Public Interest Disclosure (Protection of Whistleblowers) Act, 2010 or any other relevant law, a person who knowingly possesses unauthorised data, commits an offence and is liable, on conviction, to a fine not exceeding two hundred thousand penalty units or to imprisonment for a term not exceeding two years, or to both.

Illegal devices and software

50. (1) A person commits an offence if that person—

    (a) unlawfully produces, sells, procures for use, imports, exports, distributes or otherwise makes available—

        (i) a device, including a computer program, that is designed or adapted for the purpose of committing an offence under this Part; or

        (ii) a computer password, access code or similar data by which the whole or any part of a computer system is capable of being accessed; or

        (iii) introduces or spreads a software code that damages a computer or computer system with the intent that it be used by any person for the purpose of committing an offence defined by other provisions under this Part; or

    (b) knowingly has an item mentioned in subparagraph (a)(i) or (ii) in that person's possession with the intent that it be used by any person for the purpose of committing any offence under this Part.

(2) A person convicted of an offence under subsection (1), is liable to a fine not exceeding five hundred thousand penalty units or to imprisonment for a period not exceeding five years, or to both.

(3) This provision shall not be interpreted as imposing criminal liability where the production, sale, procurement for use, import, distribution or otherwise making available or possession referred to in subsection (1)(a) is not for the purpose of committing an offence established in accordance with other provisions of this Part, such as for the authorised testing or protection of a computer system.

Computer related misrepresentation

51. (1) A person who knowingly, without lawful excuse, inputs, alters, deletes, or suppresses computer data, resulting in unauthentic data with the intent that it be considered or acted on as if it were authentic, regardless whether or not the data is directly readable and intelligible commits an offence and is liable, on conviction, to a fine not exceeding seven hundred thousand penalty units or to imprisonment for a period not exceeding seven years or to both.

(2) Where the offence in subsection (1) is committed by sending out multiple electronic mail messages from or through computer systems, the penalty is one million five hundred thousand penalty units or imprisonment for a period not exceeding fifteen years, or to both.

Cyber extortion

52. (1) A person commits an offence if that person, through a computer system with intent to extort or gain anything from any person—

  (a) accuses or threatens to accuse any person of committing a crime or offering or making any solicitation or threat to any person as an inducement to commit or permit the commission of a crime;

  (b) threatens that any person shall be accused by any other person of commission of an offence;

  (c) knowing the contents of the writing, causes any person to receive any writing containing such accusation or threat;

  (d) knowingly transmits any communication containing any threat to cause damage to a computer system with the intent to extort from any person any money or other thing of value;

  (e) obtains any advantage from another person; or

  (f) compels another person to perform or to abstain from performing any act.

  (2) A person convicted of an offence under subsection (1), is liable to a fine not exceeding seven hundred thousand penalty units or imprisonment for a period not exceeding seven years, or to both.

Identity related crimes

53. A person who, knowingly without lawful excuse by using a computer system transfers, possesses, or uses, a means of identification of another person, commits an offence and is liable, on conviction, to a fine not exceeding one million penalty units or to imprisonment for a term not exceeding ten years, or to both.

Publication of information

54. A person who, with intent to compromise the safety and security of any other person, publishes information or data presented in a picture, image, text, symbol, voice or any other form in a computer system commits an offence and is liable, on conviction, to a fine of not less than five hundred thousand penalty units or to imprisonment for a term exceeding five years or to both.

Aiding, abetting, counselling etc.

55. (1) A person who aids, abets, counsels, procures, incites or solicits another person to commit or conspires to commit any offence under this Act, commits an offence and is liable, on conviction, to the penalty specified for that offence.

  (2) A person who attempts to commit any of the offences under this Act, commits an offence and is liable, on conviction, to the penalty specified for that offence.

Prohibition of pornography

56. (1) A person shall not produce or participate in the production of pornography using a computer system.

  (2) A person convicted of an offence under subsection (1) is liable, to a fine not exceeding five hundred thousand penalty units or to imprisonment for a period not exceeding five years, or both.

  (3) A person who knowingly—

  (a) produces pornography for the purpose of its distribution for profit through a computer system commits an offence and is liable on conviction to a fine not exceeding one million penalty units or to imprisonment for a period not exceeding ten years, or to both; or

  (b) offers, circulates or makes available, pornography through a computer system commits an offence and is liable on conviction, to a fine not exceeding five hundred thousand penalty units or to imprisonment for a period not exceeding five years, or to both.

Child pornography

57. (1) A person commits an offence if that person knowingly—

  (a) produces child pornography for the purpose of its distribution through a computer system;

569

        (b)   sells or makes available any pornography to a child through a computer system;

        (c)   compels, invites or allows a child to view pornography through a computer system intended to corrupt a child's morals;

        (d)   offers or makes available child pornography through a computer system;

        (e)   distributes or transmits child pornography through a computer system;

        (f)   procures and obtains child pornography through a computer system for oneself or for another person;

        (g)   possesses child pornography in a computer system or on a computer data storage medium; or

        (h)   obtains access, through information and communication technologies, to child pornography.

(2)   A person convicted of an offence under subsection (1) is liable to imprisonment for a period not less than fifteen years.

(3)   Subsections (1)*(d)* to *(h)* do not apply to a person performing a *bona fide* law enforcement function.

Child solicitation

58.   (1)   A person commits an offence if that person—

        (a)   uses computer system to meet a child for the purpose of committing a sexual related crime;

        (b)   communicates with a child through a computer system for the purpose of making it easier to procure the child to engage in sexual activity with that person;

        (c)   attracts a child for the purpose of making it easier to procure the child to engage in sexual activity with that person;

        (d)   attracts a child for the purpose of making it easier to procure the child to engage in sexual activity with another person; or

        (e)   recruits a child to participate in pornographic performances that is intended to be produced or recorded with or without the intent to distribute such material through a computer system or computer network;

(2)   A person convicted of an offence under subsection (1) is liable to imprisonment for a period not exceeding fifteen years.

Obscene matters or things

59.   (1)   A person commits an offence under subsection (1) is liable to imprisonment for a period not exceeding fifteen years—

        (a)   makes, produces or has in the persons possession any one or more obscene, drawings, paintings, pictures, images, posters, emblems, photographs, videos or any other object tending to corrupt morals; or

        (b)   imports, conveys or exports, or causes to be imported conveyed or exported, any such matters or things, or in any manner whatsoever puts any of them in circulation; or

        (c)   carries on or takes part in any business, whether public or private, concerned with any such matters or things, or deals in any such matters or things in any manner whatsoever, or distributes any of them, or exhibits any of them publicly, or makes a business of lending any of them;

        (d)   advertises or makes known by any means whatsoever with a view to assisting the circulation of, or traffic in, any such matters or things, that a person is engaged in any of the acts referred to in this section, or advertises or makes known how, or from whom, any such matters or things can be procured either directly or indirectly through a computer system; or

        (e)   publicly exhibits any indecent show or performance or any show or performance tending to corrupt morals through a computer system.

(2)   A person convicted of an offence under subsection (1) is liable to a fine not exceeding ten thousand penalty units.

(3)   A prosecution for an offence under this section shall not be instituted without the written consent of the Director of Public Prosecutions.

Introduction of malicious software into computer system

60.   A person who intentionally introduces or spreads malicious software into a computer system commits an offence and is liable, on conviction, to a fine not exceeding five hundred thousand penalty units or to imprisonment for a period not exceeding five years, or to both.

Denial of service attacks

61. A person who intentionally renders a computer system incapable of providing normal services to its legitimate users commits an offence and is liable, on conviction, to a fine not exceeding one million penalty units or to imprisonment for a term not exceeding ten years, or to both.

Unsolicited electronic messages

62. (1) A person commits an offence if that person, knowingly and without lawful excuse or justification—

    (a) initiates the transmission of multiple electronic communications from or through a computer system;

    (b) uses a computer system to relay or retransmit multiple electronic communications, with the intent to deceive or mislead users, or any electronic mail of licensee, as to the origin of such messages, or

    (c) materially falsifies header information in multiple electronic communications and intentionally initiates the transmission of such messages.

(2) A person convicted of an offence under subsection (1), is liable, on conviction, to imprisonment for a period not exceeding two years, or a fine not exceeding two hundred thousand penalty units, or to both.

(3) Despite subsection (1), it shall not be an offence under this Act where—

    (a) the transmission of multiple electronic communications from or through such computer system is done within customer, business or any other relationships where a person would reasonably be expected to transmit multiple electronic mail messages;

    (b) the recipient of such electronic communications has not opted out of the business, customer or other relationship; and

    (c) the transmission is by public institutions and is for purposes of raising awareness or collecting information with regard to education, health, security, safety outages and emergencies.

Prohibition of use of computer system for offences

63. (1) person shall not use a computer system for any activity which constitutes an offence under any written law which is not provided under this Act.

(2) A person who contravenes subsection (1) commits an offence and is liable, on conviction, to the penalty specified for that offence in the applicable written law.

Application of offences under this Act

64. (1) Subject to subsection (2), this Act has effect in relation to a person, whatever the person's nationality or citizenship, outside as well as within the Republic, and where an offence under this Act is committed by a person in a place outside the Republic, the person shall be dealt with as if the offence had been committed within the Republic.

(2) For the purposes of subsection (1), this Act shall apply if, for the offence in question—

    (a) the accused was in the Republic at the material time;

    (b) the computer, program or data was in the Republic at the material time; or

    (c) the damage occurred within the Republic whether or not paragraph *(a)* or *(b)* applies.

Hate speech

65. A person who, using a computer system, knowingly without lawful excuse, uses hate speech commits an offence and is liable, on conviction, to a fine not exceeding five hundred thousand penalty units or to imprisonment for a period not exceeding two years, or to both.

Minimisation etc., of genocide and crimes against humanity

66. A person who, knowingly without lawful excuse distributes or otherwise makes available, through a computer system to the public or another person, material which denies, grossly minimises, approves or justifies acts constituting genocide or crimes against humanity commits an offence and is liable, on conviction, to a fine not exceeding two million penalty units, or to imprisonment for a period not exceeding twenty years, or to both.

Unlawful disclosure of details of investigation

67. (1)   A person commits an offence if that person receives an order related to a criminal investigation and without lawful excuse discloses—
     (a)   the fact that an order has been made;
     (b)   anything done under the order; or
     (c)   any data collected or recorded under the order.

     (2)   A person convicted of an offence under subsection (1) is liable to a fine not exceeding five hundred thousand penalty units or to imprisonment for a period not exceeding five years, or to both.

Obstruction of law enforcement officer or cyber inspection officer

68. A person who obstructs or hinders a law enforcement officer, cyber inspector or any person in the exercise of any powers under this Act or who neglects or fails to comply with an order commits an offence and is liable, on conviction, to a fine not exceeding two hundred thousand penalty units or to imprisonment for a period not exceeding two years, or to both.

Harassment utilising means of electronic communication

69. A person who using a computer system intentionally initiates any electronic communication, with the intent to coerce, intimidate, harass, or cause emotional distress to a person commits an offence and is liable, on conviction, to a fine not exceeding five hundred thousand penalty units or to imprisonment for a period not exceeding five years, or to both.

Cyber terrorism

70. (1)   A person who uses or causes to be used a computer system for the purposes of cyber terrorism commits an offence and is liable on conviction to life imprisonment.

     (2)   In this section "cyber terrorism" means the unlawful use of computers and information technology to unlawfully attack or threaten to attack computers, networks and the information stored therein done to intimidate or coerce a government or its people in furtherance of political or social objectives and to cause severe disruption or widespread fear in society.

Cyber attack

71. A person who carries out a cyber attack commits an offence and is liable, on conviction, to a fine not exceeding five hundred thousand penalty units or to imprisonment for a period not exceeding five years, or to both.

Cognizable offence

72. An offence under this Act shall be deemed to be a cognizable offence for the purposes of the Criminal Procedure Code.

PART X
ELECTRONIC EVIDENCE

Admissibility of electronic evidence

73. (1)   In any legal proceedings, the rules of evidence shall not be applied so as to deny the admissibility of a data message in evidence—
     (a)   on the mere grounds that it is constituted by a data message; or
     (b)   if it is the best evidence that the person adducing it could reasonably be expected to obtain, on the grounds that it is not in its original form.

     (2)   Information in the form of a data message shall be given due evidential weight.

     (3)   In assessing the evidential weight of a data message, regard shall be had to—
     (a)   the reliability of the manner in which the integrity of the data message was generated, stored or communicated;
     (b)   the reliability of the manner in which the integrity of the data message was maintained;
     (c)   the manner in which its originator was identified; and
     (d)   any other relevant factor.

PART XI
GENERAL PROVISIONS

Appeals

74. (1)   A person aggrieved by a decision made by the Authority may appeal to the Minister.

(2)   A person aggrieved by the decision made by the Minister may appeal to the High Court.

Search and seizure

75. (1)   The provisions of the Criminal Procedure Code relating to warrants shall apply to this Part.

(2)   A law enforcement officer may with warrant, where the law enforcement officer or an authorised officer has reasonable grounds to believe that there may be in a specified computer system or part of it—

(a)   material as evidence in proving an offence; or

(b)   material that has been acquired by a person as a result of an offence, enter the place where the computer system is to search and seize the computer system including search or similarly access—

(i)   a computer system or part of it; and

(ii)   a computer data storage medium in which computer data may be stored within or outside the Republic.

(3)   A law enforcement officer that is undertaking a search under this Act may, where the law enforcement officer has reasonable grounds to believe that the data sought is stored in another device or computer system or part of it in its territory, and such data is lawfully accessible from or available to the initial device or system, extend the search or similar accessing to the other device or system.

(4)   A law enforcement officer or an authorised officer that is undertaking a search is empowered to seize or similarly secure computer data accessed according to subsections (1) or (2).

Prohibition of disclosure of information to unauthorised persons

76. (1)   A person shall not without the consent in writing given by, or on behalf of the Authority, publish or disclose to any person otherwise than in the cause of such person's duties, the contents of any documents, communication, or information which relates to, and which has come to that person's knowledge in the course of that person's duties under this Act.

(2)   A person who contravenes subsection (1), commits an offence and is liable, on conviction, to a fine not exceeding three hundred thousand penalty units or to imprisonment for a term not exceeding three years, or to both.

Assistance

77. (1)   A person, who is not a suspect of a crime or otherwise excluded from an obligation to follow such order, but who has knowledge about the functioning of the computer system or measures applied to protect the computer data therein that is the subject of a search under this Act shall permit, and assist if reasonably required and requested by the person authorised to make the search by—

(a)   providing information that enables the undertaking of necessary measures in the circumstances;

(b)   accessing and using a computer system or computer data storage medium to search any computer data available to or in the system;

(c)   obtaining and copying such computer data; or

(d)   obtaining an intelligible output from a computer systemin such a format that is admissible for the purpose of legal proceedings.

Production order

78.   Where a judge is satisfied on the basis of an *ex-parte* application by a law enforcement officer that specified computer data, or a printout or other information, is reasonably required for the purpose of a criminal investigation or criminal proceedings, the Judge may order that—

(a)   a person in control of a computer system produce from the system specified computer data or a printout or other intelligible output of that data; or

(b) an electronic communications service provider in the Republic to produce information about persons who subscribe to or otherwise use the service.

Expedited preservation

79. (1) A law enforcement officer may, where the law enforcement officer has grounds to believe that computer data that is reasonably required for the purposes of a criminal investigation is particularly vulnerable to loss or modification, by written notice given to a person in control of the computer data, require the person to ensure that the data specified in the notice be preserved for a period of up to seven days as specified in the notice.

(2) The law enforcement officer may apply to a Judge for the extension of the period referred to under subsection (1).

Partial disclosure of traffic data

80. A law enforcement officer may, where the law enforcement officer is satisfied computer data is reasonably required for the purposes of a criminal investigation, by written notice given to a person in control of the computer system, require the person to disclose relevant traffic data about a specified communication to identify—

(a) the electronic communications service providers; or

(b) the path through which a communication was transmitted.

Collection of traffic data

81. (1) Where a judge is satisfied on the basis of an *ex-parte* application by a law enforcement officer, supported by affidavit that there are reasonable grounds to suspect or believe that traffic data associated with a specified communication is reasonably required for the purposes of a criminal investigation, the Judge may order a person in control of such data to—

(a) collect or record traffic data associated with a specified communication during a specified period; or

(b) permit and assist a specified law enforcement officer to collect or record that data.

(2) If the Judge is satisfied on the basis of an application by a law enforcement officer, supported by affidavit that there are reasonable grounds to suspect or believe that traffic data is reasonably required for the purposes of a criminal investigation, the Judge may authorise a law enforcement officer to collect or record traffic data associated with a specified communication during a specified period through application of technical means.

No monitoring obligation

82. (1) An electronic communication service provider shall not have a general obligation to monitor the data which it transmits or stores; or actively seek facts or circumstances indicating an unlawful activity.

(2) The Minister may, subject to the provisions of any other law, prescribe procedures for service providers to—

(a) inform the competent public authorities of alleged illegal activities undertaken or information provided by recipients of their service; and

(b) to communicate to the competent authorities, at their request, information enabling the identification of recipients of their service.

Limitation of liability

83. An electronic communications service provider shall not be criminally liable for providing access and transmitting information on condition that it meets the limitation of liability criteria stipulated in the Electronic Communications and Transactions Act, 2021.

Extradition

84. An offence under the provisions of this Act is an extraditable offence for the purposes of the Extradition Act.

Evidence obtained by unlawful interception not admissible in criminal proceedings

85. Despite any other law, evidence which is obtained by means of any interception effected in contravention of this Act, shall not be admissible in any criminal proceedings except with the leave of the court, and in granting or refusing such leave, the court shall have regard, among other things, to the circumstances in which it was obtained, the potential effect of its admission or exclusion on issues of national security and the unfairness to the accused person that may be occasioned by its admission or exclusion.

General penalty

86. A person who commits an offence under this Act for which no penalty is provided is liable, on conviction—
    (a) in the case of an individual, to a penalty not exceeding five hundred thousand penalty units or to imprisonment for a period not exceeding five years, or to both; or
    (b) in the case of a body corporate or unincorporate body to a penalty not exceeding one million penalty units.

Power of court to order cancellation of licence, forfeiture etc.

87. (1) The court may on conviction of a person of an offence under this Act order—
        (a) forfeiture of any—
            (i) property constituting proceeds of such offence; or
            (ii) device or property used or intended to be used to commit or facilitate the commission of the offence; or
        (b) the cancellation of a licence issued under this Act.
    (2) The Forfeiture of Proceeds of Crime Act, 2010 applies in relation to an order of forfeiture made by the court under subsection (1).

Guidelines

88. (1) The Authority may issue guidelines as are necessary for the better carrying out of the provisions of this Act.
    (2) The guidelines issued by the Authority under this Act shall bind all persons regulated under this Act.
    (3) The Authority shall publish the guidelines on the website, in a daily newspaper of general circulation in the Republic or the *Gazette*.

Exemptions

89. (1) The Authority may, by declaration, exempt a person or class of persons, for a limited or unlimited period of time, from the requirement to abide by the provisions of this Act.
    (2) The Authority may, where it issues a declaration under subsection (1), reverse its decision where it considers necessary.
    (3) The Authority shall, where it reverses its decision under subsection (2), notify by declaration, the affected persons.

Regulations

90. (1) The Minister may, on the recommendation of the Authority, by statutory instrument, make regulations for the better carrying out of the provisions of this Act.
    (2) Despite the generality of subsection (1), the regulations may make provisions for—
        (a) the form and manner of making applications for registration, licences duration of licences and the fees payable on that application; and
        (b) fees payable under this Act.

THE ELECTRONIC COMMUNICATIONS AND TRANSACTIONS ACT NO 4 2021 OF THE LAWS OF ZAMBIA

> **An Act to provide a safe and effective environment for electronic transactions; promote secure electronic signatures; facilitate electronic filing of documents by public authorities; provide for the use, security, facilitation and regulation of electronic communications and transactions; promote legal certainty and confidence, and encourage investment and innovation in relation to electronic transactions; regulate the National Public Key Infrastructure; repeal and replace the Electronic Communications and Transactions Act, 2009; and provide for matters connected with, or incidental, to the foregoing.**
> **[24th March, 2021**

Enactment

ENACTED by the Parliament of Zambia.

PART I
PRELIMINARY
Short title and commencement

1. This Act may be cited as the Electronic Communications and Transactions Act, 2021, and shall come into operation on the date appointed by the Minister by statutory instrument.

2. **Interpretation**

2. In this Act, unless the context otherwise requires—
   "access" in relation to a computer system or electronic communication system, means the right to use or open the whole or any part of the computer system or electronic communication system, or to see, open, use, get or enter information in a computer system;

"advanced electronic signature" means a digital signature that is based on a certificate, that is unique to the user, capable of verification, under the sole control of the person using it and linked to the data in a manner that if the data is changed, the signature is invalidated;

"addressee" means a person who is intended by the originator to receive the electronic communication, but excludes a person acting as an intermediary in respect of that electronic communication;

"authenticity" means the assurance that a message, transaction or other exchange of information is from the author or service it purports to be from;

"Authority" has the meaning assigned to the word in the Information and Communications Technology Act, 2009;

"automated transaction" means an electronic transaction conducted or performed, in whole or in part, by means of electronic communications in which the conduct or electronic communication of one or both parties are not reviewed by a natural person in the ordinary course of that natural person's business or employment;

"automated message system" means a preprogrammed system, or other automated system, used to initiate an action, respond to electronic communications or generate other performances in whole or in part without review or intervention by a party each time an action is initiated or a response is generated by the system;

"asymmetric crypto system" means a system capable of generating a secure key pair, consisting of a private key for creating a digital signature, and a public key to verify the digital signature;

"caching" means the storage of data in an information system in order to speed up data transmission or processing;

"ccTLD" means a country code domain at the top level of the internet's main system signed according to the two letter codes in the International Standard ISO 3166 or any other standards as may be prescribed by the Minister;

"certificate" means a digital record issued by a certification authority for the purpose of supporting digital signatures which purports to confirm the identity or other significant characteristics of the person who holds a particular key pair;

"certificate holder" means a natural person in the case of a digital signature, and either a natural or a legal person in the case of a digital seal, to whose data the public key contained in the certificate is linked in the same certificate to whom a certificate is issued under this Act;

"certification authority" means an entity licensed under section 28 to manage and issue certificates and public keys;

"certification practice statement" means a statement issued by a certification authority specifying the practices that the certification authority employs in issuing a certificate;

"certificate revocation list" means a list of certificates that have been revoked by the issuing certification authority before their scheduled expiration date and are no longer trusted certificates;

"certification service" means a service of—

(a) issuing certificates necessary for giving digital signatures or digital seals to users;

(b) enabling the verification of digital signatures or digital seals given on the basis of certificates;

(c) implementing procedures for suspension, termination of suspension and revocation of certificates;

(d) checking the revocation status of the certificate and advising the relying party; or

(e) issuing cross-pair certificates;

"commerce business entity" means an entity that provides ecommerce services;

"communication" means oral, written, wire or electronic communication;

"Competition and Consumer Protection Commission" means the Competition and Consumer Protection Commission established by the Competition and Consumer Protection Act, 2010;

"computer" means equipment or any part thereof, that perform predetermined arithmetic, logical, routing, processing or storage operations in accordance with set instructions and includes input devices, output devices, processing devices, computer data storage mediums and other equipment and
devices related to, or connected with the computer system;

"computer network" means the interconnection of one or more computers or an information system through—

> (a) the use of satellite, microwave, terrestrial line or other communication media; or
>
> (b) terminals or a complex consisting of two or more interconnected computers whether or not the interconnection is continuously maintained;

"consumer" means a person who enters or intends to enter into an electronic transaction with a supplier as the end user of goods or services offered by the supplier;

"correspond" in relation to public key infrastructure or encryption keys, means to belong to the same key pair;

"cryptography" means the method of protecting information by transforming the information into unreadable format;

"cryptography product" means a product that makes use of cryptographic techniques in respect of data for the purpose of ensuring—

> (a) that the data can be accessed only by a relevant person;
>
> (b) the authenticity of the data;
>
> (c) the integrity of the data; and
>
> (d) that the source of the data can be correctly ascertained;

"cryptography provider" means any person who provides a cryptography service or product in the Republic;

"cryptography service" means a service which is provided to a seller or a recipient of a data message, or anyone storing a data message, and which is designed to facilitate the use of cryptographic techniques for the purpose of ensuring—

> (a) that the data or data message can be accessed, or can be put into an intelligible form only by a certain person;
>
> (b) that the authenticity and integrity of that data or data message is capable of being ascertained; and
>
> (c) the integrity of the data or data message or that the source of the data or data message can be correctly ascertained.

"data" means an electronic representation of information in any form;

"data message" means data generated, sent, received or stored by electronic, optical or similar means and includes, but is not limited to electronic data interchange (EDI), voice, stored record, electronic mail, mobile communications audio and video recordings;

"digital seal" means a digital signature for use by a person authorised to use a seal under any law and may be used by more than one person or system under that person's authorisation;

"digital signature" means an electronic signature consisting of a

transformation of an electronic record using an asymmetric

cryptosystem and a hash function such that a person having the initial untransformed electronic record and the signer's public key can accurately determine whether the—

> (a) transformation was created using the private key that corresponds to the signer's public key; and
>
> (b) initial electronic record has been altered since the transformation was made;

"domain name" means the alphanumeric designation that is registered or assigned in respect of an electronic address or other resource on the internet;

"domain name system" means a system to translate domain names into IP addresses or other resources;

"ecommerce" means a system which allows a commercial transaction to be conducted electronically on the internet or any other network using electronic, optical or similar media for information exchange;

"electronic" in relation to technology, means having electrical, digital, magnetic, wireless, optical, electromagnetic or similar capabilities;

"electronic agent" means a computer program or an electronic or other automated means used independently to initiate an action or respond to electronic records or performances in whole or in part without review or action by an individual at the time of the action or response;

"electronic communication" means a transfer of signs, signals, writings, images, sounds, data or intelligence of any nature transmitted in whole or in part by radio, electromagnetic, photo-electronic or photo-optic system, but does not include—

> (a) direct oral communication; or
>
> (b) any communication made through a tone only paging device;

"electronic communications system" means a radio, electromagnetic, photooptical or photoelectronic facility for the transmission of electronic communications, and any computer facility or related electronic equipment, for electronic storage of those communications;

"electronic signature" means—
  (a) sound;
  (b) symbol;
  (c) process; or
  (d) other data created or adopted by a person with the intent to sign a data message;
"electronic transaction" means a transaction, action or set of transactions of a commercial or non-commercial nature, that takes place electronically;
"hash function" means an algorithm mapping data of arbitrary size to fixed size values such that—
  (a) a record yields the same hash result every time the algorithm is executed using the same record as input;
  (b) it is computationally infeasible that a record can be derived or reconstituted from the hash result produced by the algorithm; and
  (c) it is computationally infeasible that two or more records can be found that produce the same hash result using the algorithm;
"hosting" means the service of storage of data or providing storage of computing resources for one self or others;
"information system" means a system for generating, sending, receiving, storing, displaying or otherwise processing a data message;
"information system service" includes providing a connection, operating facilities for information systems, providing access to information systems, transmitting or routing of data messages between or among points specified by a user and the processing and storage of data, at the request of the recipient of the service;
"key pair" in an asymmetric cryptosystem, means a private key and its mathematically related public key, having a property that allows the public key to verify a digital signature that the private key creates;
"National Public Key Infrastructure" means a Government deployed public key infrastructure whose root certification authority is established as the highest level certification authority of Zambia and is managed by the National Root Certification Authority as a regulatory function;
"National Root Certification Authority" means the National Root Certification Authority referred to under section 25;
"operational period" in relation to a certificate, means a period beginning on the date and time the certificate is issued by a certification authority, or a later date and time specified in the certificate and ending on the date and time the certificate expires or as stated in the certificate, unless earlier revoked or suspended;
"private certification authority" means a certification authority registered by the National Root Certification Authority to provide certification services to institutions whose information infrastructure is not critical;
"private key" means the key of a key pair used to create a digital signature;
"public key" means the key of a key pair used to verify a digital signature;
"public key infrastructure" means a system comprising hardware, software, policies, processes, and procedures required to create, manage, distribute, use, store, and revoke digital certificates and public keys;
"recovery agent" means a person or entity who provides recovery information for storage services;
"recovery information" means a parameter that may be used with an algorithm, other data or hardware, to decrypt data or communications;
"registrar" means a person who is given authority to populate a .zm domain registry;
"Registry" means a database of domain names registered under .zm;
"registrant" means the person or organisation whose application of a domain name is successful;
"registration authority" means a person or entity that is entrusted by the certification authority to register or vouch for the identity of users of a certification authority, but does not sign certificates;
"repository" means a system for storing and retrieving certificates or other information relevant to a certificate;
"secure signature creation device" means an adapted piece of software or hardware, and includes a microchip card equipped with a security chip, which is used for the storage and application of a private key;
"subscriber" means a person who is the subject named or identified in a certificate issued to that person and who holds a private key that corresponds to a public key listed in that certificate;

"timestamp" means a data unit created using a system of technical and organisational means which certifies the existence of electronic data at a given time;

"time stamping service" is the issue of a time stamp necessary to prove the official time and temporary order of a digital signature and digital seal and the creation of conditions for verification of the issued time stamp; and

"trustworthy system" means computer hardware, software and procedures that—

    (a)   are reasonably secure from intrusion and misuse;

    (b)   provide a reasonable level of availability, reliability and correct operation;

    (c)   are reasonably suited to perform their intended function; and

    (d)   adhere to generally accepted security procedures.

Application

3.   (1)   This Act applies to electronic transactions, electronic communications and electronic records used in the context of commercial and noncommercial activitiesthat include domestic and international transactions, arrangements, agreements and exchanges and storage of information and other related transactions.

    (2)   Except as otherwise specified, this Act shall not be construed as—

        (a)   requiring any person to generate, communicate, produce, process, send, receive, record, retain, store or display any information, document or signature by, or in electronic form; or

        (b)   prohibiting a person from establishing requirements in respect of the manner in which that person will accept data messages.

    (3)   Except as otherwise specified, this Act does not limit the operation of any written law that authorises electronic payments, electronic money and value transaction services, prohibits or regulates the use of data messages, including any requirement by, or under, any law for information to be posted or displayed in a specified manner, or for any information or document to be transmitted, stored or retained by a specified method.

PART II
LEGAL REQUIREMENTS FOR DATA MESSAGES

Legal requirements for data message

4.   (1)   Data has legal force and effect if that data—

        (a)   is wholly or partly in the form of a data message; and

        (b)   is not contained in the data message purporting to give legal effect, but is merely referred to in that data message.

    (2)   Information incorporated into an agreement and that is not in the public domain shall be treated as having been incorporated into a data message if that information is—

        (a)   referred to in a way in which a reasonable person would have noticed the reference to and the incorporation of the information; or

        (b)   accessible in a form in which it may be read, stored and retrieved by the other party, whether electronically or as a computer printout as long as the information is reasonably capable of being reduced to electronic form by the party incorporating it.

Writing

5.   A requirement in law that a document or information shall be in writing is met if the document or information is—

    (a)   in the form of a data message; and

    (b)   accessible and capable of being retained in a manner usable for subsequent reference.

Use of advanced electronic signature

6. (1)   Where the signature of a person is required by law and that law does not specify the type of signature, that requirement in relation to a data message is met if an advanced electronic signature is used.

    (2)   Subject to subsection (1), an electronic signature is not without legal force and effect merely on the grounds that it is in electronic form.

Use of electronic signature

7.   (1)   Where an electronic signature is required by the parties to an electronic transaction and the parties have not agreed on the type of electronic signature to be used, that requirement is met in relation to a data message if—

         (a) a method is used to identify the person and to indicate the person's approval of the information communicated; and

         (b) having regard to the relevant circumstances at the time the method was used, the method was reliable and appropriate for the purposes for which the information was communicated.

      (2)   Where an electronic signature is not required by the parties to an electronic transaction, an expression of intent or other statement shall not be without legal effect merely on the grounds that—

         (a) it is in the form of a data message; or

         (b) it is not evidenced by an electronic signature but is evidenced by other means from which that person's intent or other statement may be inferred.

      (3)   Where an advanced electronic signature is used as a valid signature, that signature shall be treated as a valid electronic signature and to have been applied properly, unless the contrary is proved.

Determination of originality of data message

8.   (1)   Where a law requires information to be presented or retained in its original form, that requirement is met by a data message if—

         (a) the integrity of the information from the time when it was first generated in its final form as a data message, or otherwise, has passed the assessment specified under subsection (2); and

         (b) that information is capable of being displayed or produced to the person to whom it is to be presented.

      (2)   For the purposes of subsection (1)(a), the integrity of any information is assessed—

         (a) by considering whether the information has remained complete and unaltered, except for the addition of any endorsement and any change which arises in the normal course of communication, storage and display;

         (b) in the light of the purpose for which the information was generated; and

         (c) by having regard to other relevant circumstances.

Admissibility and evidential weight of data message

9.   (1)   In any legal proceedings, the rules of evidence shall not be applied so as to deny the admissibility of a data message in evidence —

         (a) on the mere grounds that it is constituted by a data message; or

         (b) if it is the best evidence that the person adducing it could reasonably be expected to obtain, on the grounds that it is not in its original format provided the substance is the same.

      (2)   Information in the form of a data message shall be given due evidential weight.

      (3)   In any legal proceedings, when assessing the evidential weight of a data message, regard shall be had to—

         (a) the reliability of the manner in which the data message was generated, stored or communicated;

         (b) the reliability of the manner in which the integrity of the data message was maintained;

         (c) the manner in which its originator was identified; and

         (d) any other relevant factor.

      (4)   A data message made by a person in the ordinary course of business, or a copy or printout of, or an extract from, the data message certified to be correct by an officer in the service of that person, shall on its mere production in any civil, criminal, administrative or disciplinary proceedings under a written law, be admissible in evidence against a person and rebuttable proof of the facts contained in a record, copy, printout or extract.

Retention of information in data message

10. (1) Where a law requires information to be retained, that requirement is met by retaining the information in the form of a data message if—

    (a) the information contained in the data message is accessible and usable for subsequent reference;

    (b) the data message is in the form or format in which it was generated, sent or received, or in a format which can be demonstrated to represent accurately the information generated, sent or received; and

    (c) the origin and destination of that data message, and the date and time it was sent or received, may be determined.

  (2) The obligation to retain information under subsection (1) does not extend to any information whose sole purpose is to enable the message to be sent or received.

Production of document or information

11. (1) Subject to section 24, where a law requires a person to produce a document or information, that requirement is met if the person produces, by means of a data message, an electronic form of that document or information and if—

    (a) considering all the relevant circumstances at the time that the data message was sent, the method of generating the electronic form of that document provided a reliable means of assuring the maintenance of the integrity of the information contained in that document; and

    (b) at the time the data message was sent, it was reasonable to expect that the information contained therein would be readily accessible and usable for subsequent reference.

  (2) For the purposes of subsection (1), the integrity of the information contained in a document is maintained if that information has remained complete and unaltered, except for—

    (a) the addition of any endorsement; or

    (b) any immaterial change, which arises in the normal course of communication, storage or display.

Notarisation, acknowledgment and certification

12. (1) Where a law requires a signature, statement or document to be notarised, acknowledged, verified or made under oath, that requirement shall be met if the advanced electronic signature of the person authorised to perform those acts is attached to, incorporated in or logically associated with the data message containing that notarisation, acknowledgment or verification.

  (2) Where a law requires or permits a person to provide a certified copy of a document and the document exists in electronic form, that requirement shall be met if the person provides a printout certified to be a true reproduction of the document or information.

  (3) Where a law requires or permits a person to provide a certified copy of a document and the document exists in paper or other physical form, that requirement is met if an electronic copy of the document is certified to be a true copy thereof and the certification is confirmed by the use of an advanced electronic signature.

Other legal requirement

13. (1) A requirement in a law for multiple copies of a document to be submitted to a single addressee at the same time is satisfied by the submission of a single data message that is capable of being reproduced by that addressee.

  (2) An expression in a law, whether used as a noun or verb, including the words "document", "record", "file", "submit", "lodge", "deliver", "issue", "publish", "write in", "print" or words or expressions of similar effect, shall be interpreted to include or permit that form, format or action in relation to a data message unless otherwise provided for in this Act.

  (3) Where a seal is required by a written law to be affixed to a document and that written law does not prescribe the method or form by which that document may be sealed by electronic means, that requirement is met if the document indicates that it is required to be under seal and it includes the advanced electronic signature of the person by whom it is required to be sealed.

  (4) Where any law requires or permits a person to send a document or information by registered or certified post or similar service, that requirement shall be met if an electronic copy of the document or information is sent to the office of a courier service provider, is registered and sent by that courier service provider to the electronic address provided by the sender.

Automated transaction

14. In an automated transaction—
    (a) an agreement may be formed where an electronic agent performs an action required by law for purposes of an agreement;
    (b) an agreement may be formed where the parties to a transaction or either one of them uses an electronic agent;
    (c) a party using an electronic agent to form an agreement shall, subject to paragraph (d), be presumed to be bound by the terms of that agreement irrespective of whether that person reviewed the actions of the electronic agent or the terms of the agreement;
    (d) a party interacting with an electronic agent to form an agreement is not bound by the terms of the agreement unless those terms are capable of being reviewed by a natural person representing that party prior to agreement formation;
    (e) an agreement shall not be formed where a natural person interacted directly with the electronic agent of another person and made a material error during the creation of a data message and—
        (i) the electronic agent did not provide that natural person with an opportunity to prevent or correct the error;
        (ii) that natural person notified the other person of the error as soon as practicable after that person learnt of it;
        (iii) that natural person takes reasonable steps, including steps that conform to the other person's instructions to return any performance received, or, if instructed to do so, to destroy that performance; and
        (iv) that natural person has not used or received any material benefit or value from any performance received from the other person.

Dispatch of electronic record

15. Unless otherwise agreed between the originator and the addressee, the dispatch of an electronic record occurs when it enters an information system outside the control of the originator or the agent of the originator.

Receipt of electronic record

16. The time of receipt of an electronic record shall be determined as follows:
    (a) where the addressee designates an information system for the purpose of receiving electronic records, receipt occurs at the time when the electronic record enters the designated information system; or
    (b) where the addressee does not designate an information system, receipt occurs when the electronic record enters an information system of the addressee through which the addressee retrieves the electronic record.

Expression of intent or other statement

17. An expression of intent or other electronic representation of an electronic record between the originator and the addressee of an electronic record is admissible in circumstances where the intent or other electronic representation is relevant at law.

Attribution of electronic records to originator

18. (1) An electronic record is considered to be that of the originator if it was sent by—
        (a) the originator personally;
        (b) a person who has authority to act on behalf of the originator in respect of that electronic record; or
        (c) an information system programmed by or on behalf of the originator to operate automatically, unless it is proved that the information system did not properly execute the programme.
    (2) An addressee is entitled to regard an electronic record as being that of the originator and to act on that assumption, if—
        (a) the addressee properly applied a procedure previously agreed with the originator in order to ascertain whether the electronic record was that of the originator; or

(b) the electronic record received by the addressee resulted from the actions of a person whose relationship with the originator or with an agent of the originator enabled that person to gain access to a method used by the originator to identify an electronic record as the originator's own.

(3) Where a procedure has not been agreed to by both parties to ascertain the originator, the person who appears to be the originator shall be presumed to be the originator.

(4) The presumption under subsection (3) does not apply where

(a) the addressee has received notice from the originator that the electronic record was issued without the knowledge or consent of the originator;

(b) the addressee knew or should reasonably have known, or used any agreed procedure to know that the electronic record was not that of the originator and that the person who sent the electronic record did not have the authority of the originator to issue or send the electronic record; or

(c) the addressee knew or should reasonably have known, that the transmission resulted in an error in the electronic record as received.

Acknowledgment of receipt of electronic record

19. (1) An acknowledgment of receipt may be given through

(a) a communication by the addressee, whether automated or otherwise; or

(b) any conduct of the addressee to indicate to the originator that the electronic record has been received.

(2) An acknowledgment of receipt is not required to give legal effect to a message unless otherwise agreed by the parties.

PART III
COMMUNICATION OF DATA MESSAGES

Application of Part

20. This Part applies if the parties involved in the generation, sending, receipt, storage or other processing of data message have not reached an agreement on the issues provided for in the data message.

Formation and validity of agreement

21. (1) An agreement shall not be without legal effect merely because it was concluded partly or in whole by means of a data message.

(2) An agreement concluded between parties by means of a data message shall be concluded at the time when, and place where, the acceptance of the offer was received by the offeror.

Expression of intent or other statement

22. An expression of intent or other statement as between the originator and the addressee of a data message shall not be without legal effect merely on the grounds that it is—

(a) in the form of a data message; or

(b) not evidenced by an electronic signature, but by other means from which that person's intent or other statement may be inferred.

Acceptance of electronic filing and issuing of document

23. A public body that, subject to any written law, accepts the filing of documents, or requires that a document be created or retained, issues any permit, licence or approval or provides for a manner of payment, may, despite anything to the contrary in that law—

(a) accept the filing of the document, or the creation or retention of the document in the form of a data message;

(b) issue the permit, licence or approval in the form of a data message; or

(c) make or receive payment in an electronic form or by electronic means.

Requirements for electronic filing and issuing of document

24. A public body may, where that public body performs any of the functions under section 23, specify, in the Gazette, a daily newspaper of general circulation in the Republic or any other form of the public body's electronic platform—

(a) the manner and format in which a data message shall be filed, created, retained or issued;
(b) in cases where a data message has to be signed, the type of electronic signature required;
(c) the manner and format in which an electronic signature shall be attached to, incorporated in or otherwise associated with, a data message;
(d) the identity of, or criteria that shall be met by a designated certification authority used by the person filing a data message;
(e) the appropriate control processes and procedures to ensure adequate integrity, security and confidentiality of data messages or payments; and
(f) any other requirements for data messages or payments.

PART IV
NATIONAL PUBLIC KEY INFRASTRUCTURE

National Root Certification Authority

1.   For the purposes of this Part, the Authority shall perform the functions of the National Root Certification Authority.

Functions of National Root Certification Authority

26. (1)   The National Root Certification Authority shall regulate the national public key infrastructure.
     (2)   Without limiting the generality of subsection (1), the functions of the National Root Certification Authority are to—
           (a) licence certification authorities and time stamping service providers;
           (b) register cryptography service providers;
           (c) monitor the conduct, systems and operations of certification authorities, time stamping service providers and cryptography service providers to ensure compliance with this Act;
           (d) appoint an independent auditing firm to conduct periodic audits of a certification authority to ensure compliance with the provisions of this Act;
           (e) verify the accuracy of results of the information systems audit submitted to the National Root Certification Authority;
           (f) conduct inspections and audits;
           (g) maintain a certificate revocation list and any other repositories;
           (h) conduct research and development with regard to certification and cryptography services;
           (i) issue guidelines relating to national public key infrastructure; and
           (j) regulate the provision of secure signature creation devices.

Prohibition of providing certification service or time-stamping service without licence

27. (1)   A person shall not provide a certification service or a timestamping service to an institution with critical information infrastructure without a licence issued under this Act.
     (2)   A person who contravenes subsection (1) commits an offence and is liable, on conviction, to a fine not exceeding one million penalty units or to imprisonment for a term not exceeding ten years, or to both.
     (3)   A private certification authority shall not provide a certification service under this Act without notifying the Authority in the prescribed manner and form.

Licence

28. (1)   A person who intends to provide a certification service or a time stamping service to an institution with critical information infrastructure, shall apply to the National Root Certification Authority for a licence in the prescribed manner and form on payment of the prescribed fee.
     (2)   The National Root Certification Authority shall, within sixty days of receipt of an application, under subsection (1), grant or reject the application.
     (3)   The National Root Certification Authority shall, in considering an application for a licence made under subsection (1) have regard to the—

(a) financial and technical capability of the applicant;
(b) the ability of an electronic signature to—
   (i) uniquely be linked to the user;
   (ii) identify the user;
   (iii) be maintained under the sole control of the user;
   (iv) be linked to the data or data message to which it relates in a manner that any subsequent change of the data or data message is detectable; and
   (v) enable face to face identification of the user;
(c) the quality of the hardware and software systems;
(d) the procedures for the processing of products or services;
(e) the availability of information to third parties relying on the certification service;
(f) the regularity and extent of audits by an independent body;
(g) the applicant's ability to comply with the latest version of Request for Comments 3161 standard issued by the Internet Engineering Task Force; and
(h) any other relevant factor that may be prescribed.

(4) The National Root Certification Authority shall, where it rejects an application for a licence, inform the applicant, in writing, giving reasons for the decision.

(5) Where the National Root Certification Authority fails to make a decision within the period specified under subsection (2), the application is considered to have been granted.

(6) The National Root Certification Authority may request for further particulars in respect of an application.

(7) Where the National Root Certification Authority requests for particulars referred to in subsection (6), the period referred to in subsection (2) shall stop running.

Certification authority

29. (1) The following entities may apply to be licensed as a certification authority under the national public key infrastructure:
   (a) public companies;
   (b) private limited companies; or
   (c) statutory bodies.

(2) The following entities shall form part of the national public key infrastructure:
   (a) Government entities; and
   (b) entities providing certification services to entities whose information infrastructure has been declared as critical under the applicable written law.

Variation of licence

30. (1) A licensee may, at any time during the validity of the licence, apply to the Authority for variation of the terms and conditions of the licence or any matter relating to the licence.

(2) The National Root Certification Authority shall consider the application under subsection (1) and may grant or reject the application.

(3) The National Root Certification Authority may, on its own motion, vary the terms and conditions of a licence where—
   (a) the variation is necessary in the public interest; or
   (b) the variation is necessary to address the concerns of the members of the public or subscribers.

(4) The National Root Certification Authority shall, before making any variation of the terms and conditions of a licence under this section, notify the licensee—
   (a) of its intention to vary the licence in the manner specified in the notice; and
   (b) specifying the period, not being less than thirty days from the date of service of the notice on the licensee, within which a written representation in respect of the proposed variation may be made to the National Root Certification Authority by the licensee.

(5) Where a licence is varied under subsection (1), the National Root Certification Authority shall not refund any fees paid for with respect to the licence.

Surrender of licence

31. (1) A licensee shall, where a licensee decides not to continue providing the services relating to the licence, notify the National Root Certification Authority in writing and shall agree with the

National Root Certification Authority on the terms and conditions of the surrender of the licence, with particular reference to anything done or any benefit obtained under the licence.

(2)   Where a licence is surrendered under sub- section (1)—

    (a) the licence shall lapse and the licensee shall cease to be entitled to any benefits arising from the licence;

    (b) the licensee shall not be refunded the licence fees.

(3)   Where a licence is surrendered under subsection (1), the licensee is not entitled to a refund of any fees paid with respect to the licence.

Transfer cede or assignment of licence

32. (1)   A licensee shall not cede, pledge, encumber or otherwise dispose of a licence.

    (2)   A licensee may transfer or assign a licence with the prior approval of the National Root Certification Authority.

    (3)   An application for approval to transfer or assign a licence shall be made to the National Root Certification Authority in a prescribed manner and form and the Authority may, within thirty days of receipt of the application—

    (a) approve the application on terms and conditions that it may determine; or

    (c) reject the application in accordance with this Act.

Suspension or cancellation of licence

33. (1)   Subject to this Act, the National Root Certification Authority may suspend or cancel a licence if the holder—

    (a) obtained the licence by fraud or submission of false information or statements;

    (b) contravenes this Act, any other written law relating to the licence or any terms and conditions of the licence;

    (c) fails to comply with a decision or guidelines issued by the National Root Certification Authority;

    (d) enters into receivership or liquidation or takes an action for voluntary winding up or dissolution;

    (e) enters into any scheme of arrangement, other than for the purpose of reconstruction or amalgamation, on terms and within a period that may previously have been approved in writing by the National Root Certification Authority;

    (f) is the subject of any order that is made by a court or tribunal for its compulsory winding up or dissolution;

    (g) has ceased to fulfil the eligibility requirements under this Act; or

    (h) the suspension or cancellation is in the public interest.

    (2)   The National Root Certification Authority shall before suspending or cancelling the licence, give written notice to the holder thereof of its intention to suspend or cancel the licence and shall—

    (a) give the reasons for the intended suspension or cancellation;

    (b) require the holder to show cause, within a period of not more than thirty days, why the licence should not be suspended or cancelled.

    (3)   The National Root Certification Authority shall not suspend or cancel a licence under this section where the licensee takes remedial measures to the satisfaction of the National Root Certification Authority within the period specified under subsection (2).

    (4)   The National Root Certification Authority shall, in making its final determination on the suspension or cancellation of the licence consider submissions made by the licensee under subsection (2).

    (5)   The National Root Certification Authority may suspend or cancel a licence where the holder, after being notified under subsection (2) fails to show cause or does not take remedial measures, to the satisfaction of the Authority within the time specified in the notice.

    (6)   The National Root Certification Authority shall, where it suspends or cancels a licence under this section, enter the suspension or revocation in the Register.

Registration of cryptography service provider

34. (1)   A person who intends to provide cryptography services shall apply for registration to the National Root Certification Authority in the prescribed manner and form on payment of a prescribed fee.

    (2)   A person shall not provide a cryptography service without registration.

(3)   A person who contravenes subsection (1), commits an offence and is liable, on conviction, to a fine not exceeding five hundred thousand penalty units or to imprisonment for a term not exceeding five years or to both.

Recognition of foreign certification authority

35. (1)   The National Root Certification Authority may, by notice in the Gazette and subject to the conditions that the National Root Certification Authority may determine, recognise a licence, accreditation or recognition granted to a foreign certification authority by a foreign country.

(2)   A foreign certification authority that falsely holds out any products or services as recognised by the National Root Certification Authority under subsection (1), commits an offence and is liable, on conviction, to a fine not exceeding two hundred thousand penalty units or to imprisonment for a term not exceeding two years, or to both.

Issue of certificate to subscriber

36. A certification authority may issue a certificate to a subscriber where—

(a)   the certification authority has received an application from the subscriber;

(b)   the certification authority has complied with its certification practice statement, including procedures regarding identification of the subscriber;

(c)   the prospective subscriber is the person to be listed in the certificate to be issued;

(d)   in the case of a subscriber acting through an agent, the certification authority has verified that the subscriber has authorised the agent to have custody of the subscriber's private key and to request issuance of a certificate listing the corresponding public key;

(e)   the information in the certificate to be issued is accurate;

(f)   the subscriber rightfully holds the private key corresponding to the public key to be listed in the certificate;

(g)   the subscriber holds a private key capable of creating a digital signature; and

(h)   the public key to be listed in the certificate can be used to verify a digital signature affixed by the private key held by that subscriber.

Details of certificate

37. A certificate shall set out—

(a)   the number of the certificate;

(b)   the name of the certificate holder;

(c)   the personal identification code or registry code of the certificate holder;

(d)   the public key of the certificate holder;

(e)   the period of validity of the certificate;

(f)   the issuer and registry code of the issuer; and

(g)   a description of the limitations on the scope of use of the certificate.

PART V
CERTIFICATION AUTHORITY

Trustworthy system

38. A certification authority shall utilise a trustworthy system in performing its services.

Disclosure and compliance with certification practice statement

39. (1)   A certification authority shall disclose—

(a)   its certificate that contains the public key corresponding to the private key used by that certification authority to digitally sign another certificate;

(b)   a certification practice statement as prescribed;

(c)   notice of the revocation or suspension of certificate; and

(d)   any other fact that materially and adversely affects either the reliability of a certificate that the authority has issued or the authority's ability to carry out its obligations.

(2)   In the event of an occurrence that materially and adversely affects a certification authority's trustworthy system or its certificate, the certification authority shall—

     (a)   use reasonable efforts to notify any person who is known or likely to be affected by that occurence.

     (b)   act in accordance with procedures governing such an occurrence as specified in its certification practice statement.

Audit services

40. (1)   A certification authority shall conduct an information system audit annually and submit the audit report to the National Root Certification Authority.

     (2)   Despite subsection (1), the National Root Certification Authority may require a certification authority to conduct an information system audit as and when the Authority considers it necessary at the cost of the certification authority.

Publication of certificate revocation list

41. (1)   A certification authority shall maintain a certificate revocation list.

     (2)   A certification authority that contravenes subsection(1) commits an offence and is liable, on conviction, to a fine not exceeding five hundred thousand penalty units.

Prohibition of publication of certificate

42. A person shall not publish a certificate or otherwise make it available to another person if—

     (a)   that person is not the certification authority listed in that certificate;

     (b)   the subscriber listed in that certificate has not accepted it; or

     (c)   the certificate has been suspended or revoked, unless that publication is for the purpose of verifying a digital signature created prior to that suspension or revocation.

Representations on issuance of certificate

43. A certification authority by issuing a certificate, represents to any person who reasonably relies on the certificate, that—

     (a)   the certification authority has issued the certificate in accordance with the applicable certification practice statement incorporated by reference in the certificate, or of which the relying party has notice;

     (b)   the certification authority has complied with requirements under this Act for issuing of certificate, and that the subscriber listed in the certificate has accepted it;

     (c)   the subscriber identified in the certificate holds the private key corresponding to the public key listed in the certificate;

     (d)   the subscriber's public key and private key constitute a functioning key pair;

     (e)   information in the certificate is accurate, unless the certification authority has stated in the certificate or incorporated by reference in the certificate a statement that the accuracy of specified information is not confirmed; and

     (f)   the certification authority has no knowledge of any material fact which if included in the certificate would adversely affect the reliability of the representations in paragaphs (a) to (d).

Recommended reliance limits

44. (1)   A certification authority shall, in issuing a certificate to a subscriber, specify a recommended reliance limit in the certificate.

     (2)   The certification authority may specify different reliance limits in different certificates as it considers fit.

Liability limits for certification authority

45. Subject to an agreement between a certification authority and a subscriber, a certification authority is not liable—

     (a)   for any loss caused by reliance on a false or forged digital signature of a subscriber, if, with respect to the false or forged digital signature, the certification authority complied with the requirements of this act; or

     (b)   in excess of the amount specified in the certificate as its recommended reliance limit for either

> (i) a loss caused by reliance on a misrepresentation in the certificate of any fact that the certification authority is required to confirm; or
>
> (ii) failure to comply with requirements for issuance of the certificate and representations on issuance of the certificate.

Suspension of certification authority certificate

46. A certification authority may suspend a certificate—

    (a) on request by the subscriber listed in the certificate or a person duly authorised by that subscriber;

    (b) by court order; or

    (c) if there are reasonable grounds to believe that incorrect data has been entered in the certificate or that it is possible to use the private key corresponding to the public key contained in the certificate without the consent of the holder.

Notice of suspension

47. A certification authority shall, after the suspension of a certificate under section 46 publish a signed notice of the suspension in the repository.

Revocation of certificate

48. A certification authority shall revoke a certificate—

    (a) on receiving a request for revocation by the subscriber listed in the certificate and confirming that the person requesting the revocation is the subscriber, or is an agent of the subscriber with authority to request the revocation;

    (b) on receiving a certified copy of the subscriber's death certificate, or on confirming by other evidence that the subscriber is dead; or

    (c) on presentation of documents effecting a dissolution of the subscriber, or on confirming by other evidence that the subscriber has been dissolved or ceases to exist.

Revocation without subscriber's consent

49. (1) A certification authority shall revoke a certificate, regardless of whether the subscriber listed in the certificate consents, where the certification authority confirms that—

    (a) a material fact represented in the certificate is false;

    (b) a requirement for issuance of the certificate was not satisfied;

    (c) the certification authority's private key or trustworthy system was compromised in a manner materially affecting the certificate's reliability;

    (d) an individual subscriber is dead; or

    (e) a subscriber has been dissolved, wound up or otherwise ceases to exist.

    (2) The certification authority shall, where the certification authority revokes the certificate under subsection (1), immediately notify the subscriber listed in the revoked certificate.

Notice of revocation

50. (1) A certification authority shall, publish a signed notice of the revocation under section 48 in a repository specified in the certificate.

    (2) The certification authority shall, where one or more repositories are specified, publish a signed notice of the revocation in all those repositories.

Appointment of registration authority

51. The certification authority may appoint any person as a registration authority as prescribed.

52. Appeals under this Part

52. A person aggrieved with the decision of a certification authority may appeal to the Authority within fourteen days of receiving the move of suspension or revocation.

PART VI
DUTIES OF SUBSCRIBERS

Generating key pair

53. (1)   A subscriber shall, where the subscriber generates a key pair whose public key is to be listed in a certificate and accepted by the subscriber, generate that key pair using a trustworthy system.

(2)   This section shall not apply to a subscriber who generates the key pair using a system approved by a certification authority.

Obtaining certificate

54.   A subscriber shall ensure that all material representation to a certification authority for purposes of obtaining a certificate, including all information known to the subscriber and represented in the certificate, shall be accurate and complete to the best of the subscriber's knowledge and belief, regardless of whether such representations are confirmed by the certification authority.

Acceptance of certificate

55. (1)   A subscriber is deemed to have accepted a certificate if the subscriber—
    (a)   publishes or authorises the publication of the certificate
        (i)   to one or more persons; or
        (ii)   in a repository; or
    (b)   otherwise demonstrates approval of the certificate while knowing or having notice of its contents.

(2)   A subscriber who accepts a certificate issued by a certification authority, shall certify that—
    (a)   the subscriber rightfully holds the private key corresponding to the public key listed in the certificate;
    (b)   a representation made by the subscriber to the certification authority to the information listed in the certificate is true; and
    (c)   information in the certificate that is within the knowledge of the subscriber is true.

Control of private key

56. (1)   A subscriber identified in the certificate who accepts a certificate issued by a certification authority, shall exercise reasonable care in retaining control of the private key corresponding to the public key listed in that certificate and prevent its disclosure to a person not authorised to create that subscriber's digital signature.

(2)   A subscriber shall continue to perform the duty under subsection (1) during the operational period of the certificate and during any period of suspension of the certificate.

Suspension or revocation of compromised certificate

57.   A subscriber who has accepted a certificate from a certification authority shall, where the private key corresponding to the public key listed in the certificate has been compromised, request the issuing certification authority as soon as possible to suspend or revoke the certificate.

PART VII
TIME STAMPING SERVICE PROVIDERS

Timestamping service

58. (1)   A person who intends to provide a timestamping service shall ensure that the timestamp is linked to data in a manner that precludes the possibility of changing the data undetectably after obtaining the time-stamp.

(2)   A timestamping service provider shall confirm the time stamps issued by that provider when required.

(3)   A timestamping service provider shall ensure that it is impossible for that timestamping service provider's systems to issue identical time stamps for a time earlier or later than the relevant point in time to which the time-stamping service is applied.

Timestamping service provider

59. The following entities may provide a time stamping service:
     (a) public company;
     (b) private limited company; or
     (c) State body.

Requirements for timestamping service provider

60. (1) A timestamping service provider shall comply with the requirements established by this Act and be capable of ensuring a reliable timestamping service in accordance with this Act.

     (2) A timestamping service provider shall annually conduct an information systems audit and submit the results to the Authority.

     (3) Despite subsection (2), the Authority may require a timestamping service provider to conduct an information system audit as and when the Authority determines and at the cost of the time stamping service provider.

     (4) A timestamping service provider shall procure insurance relating to the provider's licensed services up to a prescribed amount and in the manner prescribed.

Duties of timestamping service provider

61. A timestamping service provider shall—
     (a) make correct indications of time in time stamps pursuant to the descriptions provided in guidelines issued by the Authority;
     (b) maintain records of issued time- stamps;
     (c) preserve documentation in order to verify issued time stamps;
     (d) ensure that it is possible to obtain and verify time stamps in the data communication network as and when required;
     (e) conduct an annual information systems audit and submit the results of the audit to the authorised processor of the register of certification;
     (f) publicise the conditions of compulsory insurance contracts in a data communication network where applicable; and
     (g) inform the authorised processor of the register of certification of any changes to a public key used in the provision of a timestamping service.

PART VIII
CONSUMER PROTECTION

Scope of application

62. This Part is without prejudice to any other written law in force on consumer protection in relation to electronic transactions.

Information to be provided by supplier

63. (1) A supplier offering goods or services for sale, hire or exchange by way of an electronic transaction shall, where applicable, make the following information available to consumers on the website, application or other electronic media platform, where the goods or services are offered:
     (a) the supplier's full name and legal status;
     (b) the supplier's physical address and telephone number;
     (c) the supplier's website address and email address;
     (d) membership to any self-regulatory or accreditation body to which that supplier belongs or subscribes and the contact details of that body;
     (e) any code of conduct to which that supplier subscribes and how that code of conduct may be accessed electronically by the consumer;
     (f) in the case of a legal person, its registration number, the names of its office bearers and its place of registration;
     (g) the physical address where that supplier will receive legal service of documents;
     (h) a description of the main characteristics of the goods or services offered by that supplier to enable a consumer make an informed decision on the proposed electronic transaction;

        (i)   the full price of the goods or services, including transport costs, taxes and any other fees or costs;

        (j)   the manner of payment for the goods or services;

        (k)   any terms of agreement, including any guarantees, that will apply to the transaction and how those terms may be accessed, stored and reproduced electronically by consumers;

        (l)   the time within which the goods will be dispatched or delivered or within which the services will be rendered;

        (m) the manner and period within which consumers can access and maintain a full record of the transaction;

        (n)   the return, exchange and refund policy of that supplier;

        (o)   any alternative dispute resolution code to which that supplier subscribes and how the wording of that code may be accessed electronically by the consumer;

        (p)   the security procedures and privacy policy of that supplier in respect of payment, payment information and personal information;

        (q)   where appropriate, the minimum duration of the agreement in the case of an agreement for the supply of products or services to be performed on an ongoing basis or recurrently;

        (r)   the rights of consumers in terms of section 65 where applicable;

        (s)   health and safety information; and

        (t)   any other information as maybe prescribed.

(2)   A supplier shall provide a consumer with an opportunity to—

        (a)   review the entire electronic transaction;

        (b)   correct any mistakes; and

        (c)   withdraw from the transaction, before finally placing any order.

(3)   Despite subsection (2), if a supplier fails to comply with the provisions of subsection (1) or (2), the consumer may cancel the transaction within fourteen days of receiving the goods or services under the transaction.

(4)   If a transaction is cancelled under subsection (3)—

        (a)   the consumer shall return the goods to the supplier or, where applicable, cease using the services performed;

        (b)   the supplier shall refund all payments made by the consumer for goods or services where applicable minus the direct cost of returning the goods; and

        (c)   the consumer shall return the goods to the supplier in a condition as may be prescribed by the Minister.

(5)   A supplier shall utilise a payment system that is sufficiently secure in accordance with accepted technological standards at the time of the transaction and the type of transaction concerned.

(6)   A supplier is liable for any damage suffered by a consumer due to a failure by the supplier to comply with subsection (5).

(7)   A person who contravenes provisions of subsection (1) commits an offence.

(8)   A supplier referred to under subsection (1) shall register with the Authority in the prescribed manner and form.

Online market

64. (1)   A person may market a product or service by means of electronic communication.

     (2)   A person marketing by means of electronic communication shall provide the addressee with

        (a)   the person's identity and contact details including its registered office and place of business, email, contact and customer service number;

        (b)   a valid and operational optout facility from receiving similar communications in future;

        (c)   the identifying particulars of the source from which the originator obtained the addressee's personal information; and

        (d)   applicable privacy and other user policies.

Unsolicited goods, services or communications

65. (1)   A person may send one unsolicited commercial communication to a consumer.

     (2)   A person shall only send a commercial communications to an address where the optin requirement is met.

     (3)   The optin requirement is met where the addressee consents to the receipt of commercial communication and where—

(a) the addressee's email address, phone number and other personal information was collected by the originator of the message in the course of a sale or negotiations for a sale;

(b) the originator only sends promotional messages relating to its "similar products and services" to the addressee;

(c) the personal information and address was collected by the originator, the originator offered the addressee the opportunity to optout, free of charge except for the cost of transmission, and the addressee declined to opt out; and

(d) the opportunity to optout is provided by the originator to the addressee with every subsequent message.

(4) A person shall not send a commercial communication on goods or services unless—

(a) the consumer consents to the communication;

(b) at the beginning of the communication, the sender discloses the identity of the sender and its purpose; and

(c) that communication gives an optout option to reject further communication.

(4) A contract is not formed where an addressee does not respond to commercial communication.

(5) An originator who fails to provide the recipient with an operational optout facility under subsections (2)(c) and (d) commits and offence.

(6) An originator who sends unsolicited commercial communications to an addressee who has opted-out from receiving any further electronic communications from the originator through the originator's optout facility, commits an offence.

(7) A person who advertises or who knowingly has goods or services advertised in contravention of this section commits an offence.

(8) A person convicted of an offence under this section is liable on conviction to a fine not exceeding five thousand penalty units or imprisonment for a term not exceeding five years, or to both.

Cooling-off period

66. (1) A consumer may cancel, without giving any reason and without incurring any penalty, a transaction and a related credit agreement for the supply of

(a) goods within seven days after the date of the receipt of the goods; or

(b) services within seven days after the date of the conclusion of the agreement.

(2) Where a consumer cancels a transaction under subsection (1), the only charge that may be levied on the consumer is the direct cost of returning the goods.

(3) If payment for the goods or services has been effected prior to a consumer exercising the right under subsection (1), the supplier shall give the consumer a full refund of the payment, which refund shall be made within thirty days of the date of cancellation.

(4) This section shall not be construed as prejudicing the rights of a consumer provided for in any other written law.

(5) Subsection (1) does not apply to an electronic transaction—

(a) for a financial service, including an investment service, insurance and reinsurance operation, banking service or operation relating to dealings in securities;

(b) by way of an auction;

(c) for the supply of food stuffs, beverages or other goods intended for everyday consumption supplied to a home, residence or workplace of a consumer;

(d) for services which have been performed in full with the consumer's consent before the end of the sevenday period specified under subsection (1);

(e) where the price for the supply of goods or services is dependent on fluctuations in the financial markets and which cannot be controlled by the supplier;

(f) where the goods—

(i) are made to the consumer's specifications;

(ii) are clearly personalised;

(iii) by reason of their nature, cannot be returned; or

(iv) are likely to deteriorate or expire rapidly;

(g) where audio or video recordings or computer software were unsealed, streamed or downloaded by the consumer;

(h) for the sale of newspapers, periodicals, magazines and books;

(i) for the provision of gaming and lottery services; or

(j) any other goods or services as the Minister may prescribe.

Performance

67. (1) A supplier shall execute an order within thirty days from the date on which the supplier received the order, unless the parties have agreed otherwise.

(2) Where a supplier fails to execute an order within thirty days or within the agreed period, the consumer may cancel the agreement on giving seven days' written notice.

(3) Where a supplier is unable to perform under the agreement on the grounds that the goods or services ordered are unavailable, the supplier shall immediately notify the consumer of this fact and refund any payments immediately.

Application of foreign law

68. The protection provided to consumers in this Part applies irrespective of the legal system applicable to the agreement in question.

Non-exclusion

69. A provision in an agreement which excludes a right provided for in this Part is void to the extent of the exclusion.

Complaints to Authority

70. (1) A consumer may lodge a complaint with the Authority in respect of any non-compliance with the provisions of this Part by a supplier.

(2) The Authority may investigate and determine any complaint in accordance with this Act and any other applicable written law.

(3) The Authority shall, in managing consumer complaints, have the power to—

(a) carry out market surveys to determine consumer demand and consumption trends;

(b) conduct quality of experience survey;

(c) monitor the information and communications technology sector for possible infringements of consumer rights not being reported to the Authority;

(d) hear a complaint and make a determination including the award of compensation in relation to the complaint;

(e) refer any complaints to a suitable body with appropriate recommendations; and

(f) implement mitigating strategies in instances where, there is a reoccurrence of similar complaints.

Directives, code of conduct and guidelines

71. (1) The Authority may issue—

(a) directives to address special circumstances, for children and vulnerable consumers;

(b) a code of conduct for licensees on consumer related matters; or

(c) guidelines on consumer related matters.

(2) The Authority shall collaborate with the Competition and Consumer Protection Commission on matters related to unfair trading.

PART IX
DOMAIN NAME REGULATION

Regulation of domain name

72. (1) The Authority shall—

(a) administer and manage the .zm domain name space;

(b) comply with international best practice in the administration of the .zm domain name space;

(c) licence and regulate registrars; and

(d) publish guidelines on–

(i) the general administration and management of the .zm domain name space; and

(ii) the requirements and procedures for domain name registration.

(2) The Authority shall enhance public awareness on the economic and commercial benefits of domain name registration.

(3) The Authority, in relation to domain name regulation—

    (a) may conduct investigations that it may consider necessary;

    (b) shall conduct research into, and keep abreast of, developments in the Republic and elsewhere on the domain name system; and

    (c) shall continually survey and evaluate the extent to which the .zm domain name space meets the needs of the citizens of the Republic.

(4) The Authority may, and shall when so requested by the Minister, make recommendations to the Minister in relation to policy on any matter relating to the .zm domain name space.

(5) The Authority shall continually evaluate the effectiveness and the management of the .zm domain name space.

(6) The Authority may—

    (a) liaise, consult and cooperate with any person or other authority; and

    (b) appoint experts and other consultants on conditions that the Authority may determine.

(7) The Authority may delegate any of its functions under this Part to a person or institution that the Authority may determine.

(8) The Authority shall, in relation to the .zm domain name space existing prior to the commencement of this Act, uphold the vested rights and interests of parties involved in the management and administration of the .zm domain name space at the date of its establishment.

(9) Despite subsection (8)—

    (a) the parties shall be granted a period of six months during which they may continue to operate in respect of their existing delegated sub domains; and

    (b) after the expiry of the sixmonth period, the parties shall apply to be licensed registrars and registries as provided for in this Part.

Licensing of registers and registries

73. (1) A person shall not update a registry or administer a licensing of second level domain unless the person is licensed to do so by the Authority.

    (2) A person who intends to update a registry or administer a licensing of a second level domain as a registrar or registry shall apply to the Authority in the prescribed manner on payment of the prescribed fee.

    (3) A person who contravenes subsection (1), commits an offence and is liable, on conviction, to a fine not exceeding five hundred thousand penalty units or to imprisonment for a term not exceeding five years, or to both.

Regulations regarding registrars, etc.

74. The Minister may, in consultation with the Authority, by statutory instrument, make regulations to provide for—

    (a) the requirements which registrars shall meet in order to be licensed, including standards relating to operational accuracy, stability, robustness and efficiency;

    (b) the circumstances and manner in which registrations may be assigned, transferred, registered, renewed, refused, or revoked by the registry;

    (c) the pricing policy;

    (d) the provisions for the restoration of a domain name registration and penalties for late payments;

    (e) the terms of the domain name registration agreement which registrars shall adopt and use in registering domain names, including issues in respect of privacy, consumer protection and alternative dispute resolution;

    (f) the processes and procedures to avoid unfair and anticompetitive practices, including bias to, or preferential treatment of actual or prospective registrants, registries or registrars, protocols or products;

    (g) the requirements to ensure that each domain name contains an administrative and technical contact;

    (h) the creation of new subdomains;

    (i) licensing fees;

    (j) the procedures for ensuring the monitoring of compliance with the provisions of this Act, including regular .zm domain name space technical audits; and

    (k) any other matter relating to the .zm domain name space as may be necessary to achieve the objectives of this Part.

PART X
LIMITATION OF LIABILITY OF SERVICE PROVIDER

Definition

75. In this Part, "service provider" means a person providing an information system service.

No liability for mere conduit

76. (1) A service provider is not liable for providing access to, or for operating facilities for, information systems or transmitting, routing or storage of data messages through an information system under the service provider's control, as long as the service provider
    (a) does not initiate the transmission;
    (b) does not select the addressee;
    (c) performs the functions in an automatic, technical manner without selection of the data; and
    (d) does not modify the data contained in the transmission.
    (2) The acts of transmission, routing and provision of access under subsection (1), include the automatic, intermediate and transient storage of the information transmitted in so far as this takes place
    (a) for the sole purpose of carrying out the transmission in the information system;
    (b) in a manner that makes it inaccessible to any person other than anticipated recipients; and
    (c) for a period no longer than is reasonably necessary for the transmission.

Caching

77. A service provider that transmits data provided by a recipient of the service through an information system under the service provider's control shall not be liable for the automatic, intermediate and temporary storage of that data, where the purpose of storing that data is to make the onward transmission of the data more efficient to other recipients of the service upon their request, as long as the service provider—
    (a) does not modify the data;
    (b) complies with conditions on access to the data; and
    (c) removes or disables access to the data stored on receiving a takedown notice under section 81.
    (2) Despite this section, a court may order a service provider to terminate or prevent any unlawful activities under this Act or any other law.

Hyperlink provider

78. An internet service provider who enables the access to information provided by a third person by providing an electronic hyperlink shall not be liable for the information where—
    (a) the internet service provider expeditiously removes or disables access to the information after receiving an order from any court to remove the link; or
    (b) the internet service provider, on obtaining knowledge or awareness about specific illegal information stored by other ways than an order from a public authority, expeditiously informs the relevant authority to enable them to evaluate the nature of the information and if necessary issue an order to remove the content.

Hosting

79. (1) A service provider that provides a hosting service , is not liable for damages arising from data stored at the request of the recipient of the service, as long as the service provider—
    (a) does not have actual knowledge that the data message, or an activity relating to the data message, is infringing the rights of the recipient or a third party;
    (b) is not aware of facts or circumstances from which the infringing activity or the infringing nature of the data message is apparent; and
    (c) on receipt of a takedown notification referred to in section 99, acts expeditiously to remove or to disable access to the data.
    (2) The limitations on liability established by this section do not apply to a service provider unless the service provider has designated an agent to receive notifications of infringement and has

provided through the service provider's services, including the websites in locations accessible to the public, the name, address, phone number and email address of the agent.

(3) Subsection (1) does not apply where the recipient of the service is acting under the authority or the control of the service provider.

Order by court to terminate illegal activity

80. Despite other provisions of this Act, a court may order a service provider to terminate or prevent any unlawful activities under this Act or any other written law.

Use of information location tools by service provider

81. (1) A service provider is not liable for any damage incurred by a person if the service provider refers or links users to a web page containing an infringing data message or infringing activity, by using information location tools, including a directory, index, reference, pointer, or hyperlink, and where the service provider—

(a) does not have actual knowledge that the data message or an activity relating to the data message is infringing the rights of that person;

(b) is not aware of facts or circumstances from which the infringing activity or the infringing nature of the data message is apparent;

(c) does not receive a financial benefit directly attributable to the infringing activity; and

(d) removes, or disables access to, the reference or link to the data message or activity within a reasonable time after being informed that the data message or the activity relating to that data message, infringes the rights of a person.

Take-down notification

82. (1) A recipient of a service or any person whose rights have been affected may, through a take-down notification, in writing, notify the service provider of—

(a) any data or activity infringing the rights of the recipient or of a third party;

(b) any unlawful material or activity; or

(c) any other matter conducted or provided contrary to the provisions of this Act.

(2) Where a service provider receives a takedown notification under subsection (1), the service provider shall, as soon as practicable, take down the infringing data, activity or material.

(3) A dispute regarding a takedown notification may be referred to the Authority for determination.

(4) A takedown notification to a service provider or that service provider's designated agent shall include—

(a) the full names and address of the complainant;

(b) a signature of the complainant;

(c) the right that has allegedly been infringed;

(d) an identification of the material or activity that is claimed to be the subject of unlawful activity;

(e) the remedial action required to be taken by the service provider in respect of the complaint;

(f) the telephonic and electronic contact details, if any, of the complainant;

(g) a statement that the complainant is acting in good faith; and

(h) a statement by the complainant that the information in the take down notification is, based on the complainant's knowledge, true and correct.

(5) A person who lodges a false takedown notification with a service provider commits an offence and is liable, on conviction, to a fine not exceeding two hundred thousand penalty units or to imprisonment for a term not exceeding two years, or to both.

83. No general obligation on service provider to monitor unlawful activities

83. (1) Subject to the other provisions of this Part, a service provider is not under any obligation to—

(a) monitor the data which the service provider transmits or stores; or

(b) actively seek facts or circumstances indicating an unlawful activity.

(2) The Minister may, on the advice of the Authority, by statutory instrument, prescribe procedures for service providers to—

(a) inform the competent public authorities of alleged illegal activities undertaken, or information provided, by recipients of their service; and

(b) communicate to the competent authorities, at their request, information enabling the identification of recipients of their service.

Savings

84. This Part does not affect—
    (a) the obligation of a service provider acting under a licensing or other regulatory system established by, or under, any written law;
    (b) any obligation imposed by any written law or by a court, to remove, block or deny access to any data message; or
    (c) any right to limitation of liability based on the Constitution.

PART XI
ENCRYPTING COMMUNICATION

Use of encrypted communication

85. A person providing an encryption service shall use an encryption, regardless of encryption algorithm selected, encryption key length chosen, or implementation technique or medium used, in the manner provided for under this Act.

No limitation on encryption function

86. Nothing in this Act shall be construed as requiring the use by a person of any form of encryption that—
    (a) limits or affects the ability of the person to use encryption without a key escrow function; or
    (b) limits or affects the ability of the person who uses encryption with a key escrow function not to use a key holder.

Prohibition of unauthorised decryption or release of decryption key

87. (1) Unless otherwise provided in this Act, a person shall not release a decryption key or decrypt any data without authorisation.
    (2) A person who contravenes subsection (1), commits an offence and is liable, on conviction, in the case of—
        (a) an advanced electronic signature private key, to imprisonment for a minimum term of ten years and a maximum period not exceeding twentyfive years without the option of a fine;
        (b) any other electronic signature, to imprisonment for a term not exceeding ten years without the option of a fine.
    (3) A key holder may release a decryption key or decrypt any data or communication—
        (a) with the approval of the person whose key is held or managed by the key holder or the owner of the data or communication;
        (b) where the release of the decryption key or decryption of the data or communication is necessary or incidental to the provision of encryption services or to the holding or management of the key by the key holder; or
        (c) to assist a law enforcement officer pursuant to an interception order issued by a court to access transactional records or stored data.
    (4) A law enforcement officer to whom a key is released under subsection (3) shall use the key in the manner and for the purpose and duration provided for under an interception and communications court order authorising the release and use and shall not exceed the duration of the electronic surveillance for which the key is released.
    (5) A law enforcement officer to whom a decryption key is released shall, on or before the completion of the authorised release period, destroy the decryption key.

Prohibition of disclosure of record or other information by key holder

88. (1) A key holder shall not disclose a record or any other personal information relating to an owner of a key held or managed by the key holder except—
        (a) with the consent of the owner; or
        (b) to a law enforcement officer pursuant to a court order.

(2)   A recovery agent shall not disclose to any person the use of any stored recovery information, any decrypted data or communication or other assistance provided to a law enforcement officer in the performance of functions under this Act.

(3)   A person who contravenes subsection (1) or (2) commits an offence and is liable, on conviction, to imprisonment for a term of not less than fifteen years but not exceeding twentyfive years without an option of a fine.

(4)   A recovery agent may decrypt any data or communication in the recovery agent's possession, custody or control, where the applicable law otherwise requires the recovery agent to provide the data or communication to a law enforcement officer in plain text or other form readily understood by the law enforcement officer—

(a)   using or disclosing plain text in the recovery agent's possession, custody or control;

(b)   using or disclosing recovery information that is not stored recovery information held by the recovery agent under the circumstances described in this Act; or

(c)   using stored recovery information in the recovery agent's possession, custody or control.

Obstruction of law enforcement officer

89.   A person who uses an encryption to obstruct or impede a law enforcement officer or in any manner interferes with the performance by the law enforcement officer of any functions under this Act commits an offence and is liable, on conviction, to a fine not exceeding two hundred thousand penalty units or to imprisonment for a term not exceeding two years, or to both.

Prohibition of disclosure or use of stored recovery information

90.   (1)   A recovery agent shall implement technical and organisational measures to comply with the Data Protection Act, 2020 and shall not—

(a)   disclose stored recovery information; or

(b)   use stored recovery information to decrypt any data or communication.

(2)   A person shall not access any stored recovery information from a recovery agent without authorisation.

(3)   A recovery agent may disclose stored recovery information or use stored recovery information to decrypt any data or communication with the consent of the person who stored the recovery information or the agent of that person or pursuant to a court order.

Immunity of recovery agents

91.   A cause of action shall not lie in any court against a recovery agent for providing information, facilities or assistance to a law enforcement officer in accordance with the terms of a court order.

PART XII
GENERAL PROVISIONS

Appeals

92.   (1)   A person aggrieved by a decision of the Authority may, within thirty days of the decision, appeal to the Minister.

(2)   The Minister may, in considering an appeal, set aside, vary or uphold the Authority's decision and shall, in writing, communicate the decision to the appellant.

(3)   A person aggrieved by a decision of the Minister may, appeal to the High Court.

(4)   A licensee or service provider aggrieved with a decision of the Authority may within, thirty days of the decision, appeal to the Tribunal established under the Information and Communications Technologies Act, 2009.

(5)   A licensee or service provider aggrieved with a decision of the Tribunal shall appeal to the High Court.

Register

93.   (1)   The Authority shall establish and maintain a Register under this Act in which the Authority shall enter names and other details relating to—

(a)   licensed and private certification authorities;

(b)   timestamping service providers;

(c) cryptography service providers;

(d) applications rejected by the Authority and the reasons thereof; and

(e) any other information that the Authority considers necessary for purposes of this Act.

(2) The Register under subsection (1), shall be kept at a place that the Authority may determine, and shall be open for inspection by the public during normal working hours.

Offence by body corporate or unincorporate body

94. Where an offence under this Act is committed by a body corporate or unincorporated body, with the knowledge, consent or connivance of the director, manager, shareholder or partner, that director, manager, shareholder or partner of the body corporate or unincorporated body commits an offence and is liable, on conviction, to the penalty specified for that offence.

General penalty

95. A person who commits an offence under this Act for which no penalty is provided is liable, on conviction—

(a) in the case of an individual, to a penalty not exceeding five hundred thousand penalty units or to imprisonment for a term not exceeding five years, or to both; or

(b) in the case of a body corporate or un incorporate body to a penalty not exceeding one million penalty units.

Evidence obtained by unlawful interception not admissible in criminal proceedings

96. Despite any other written law, evidence which is obtained by means of an interception effected in contravention of this Act, is not admissible in any criminal proceedings except with the leave of the court, and in granting or refusing such leave, the court shall have regard, among other things, to the circumstances in which it was obtained, the potential effect of its admission or exclusion on issues of national security and the unfairness to the accused person that may be occasioned by its admission or exclusion.

Guidelines

97. (1) The Authority shall issue guidelines and publish electronic platforms, in a daily newspaper of general circulation in the Republic and in the Gazette, and the guidelines shall not take effect until they are so published.

(2) The guidelines issued by the authority under this Act shall bind all persons regulated under this act.

(3) A person who contravenes or fails to comply with a provision of a guideline or decision issued by the authority under this Act, commits an offence and is liable, on conviction, for each such breach, to a fine not exceeding fifty thousand penalty unit or to imprisonment for a period not exceeding six months, or to both, and forty thousand penalty units for each day of continued default.

Supervision of compliance with Act

98. The Authority shall supervise the compliance with the provisions of this Act.

Regulations

99. The Minister may, on the recommendation of the Authority, by statutory instrument, make regulations prescribing matters which by this Act are required or permitted to be prescribed.

Extraterritorial application of offences

100. (1) Subject to subsection (2), this Act shall have effect in relation to any person, whatever the person's nationality or citizenship, outside as well as within the Republic, where an offence under this Act is committed by a person in any place outside the Republic, the person shall be dealt with as if the offence had been committed within the Republic.

(2) For purposes of subsection (1), this Act shall apply to the offence where the—

(a) accused was in the Republic at the material time;

(b) computer, program or data was in the Republic at the material time; or

(c) damage occurred within the Republic whether or not paragraph (a) or (b) applies.

Act to bind Republic

101. This Act binds the Republic.

Repeal of Act No 21 of 2009

102. (1)   The Electronic Communications and Transactions Act, 2009 is repealed.

   (2)   Despite subsection (1), any legal proceedings commenced or pending under the repealed Act shall continue as if instituted under this Act.

THE NARCOTIC DRUGS AND PSYCHOTROPIC SUBSTANCES ACT NO 35 OF 2021

ARRANGEMENT OF SECTIONS

PART I
PRELIMINARY PROVISIONS

Section

An Act to provide for the functions of the Drug Enforcement Commission; revise and consolidate the law relating to drugs and precursor chemicals; provide for special measures relating to the prevention, treatment and rehabilitation of victims of drug abuse; domesticate the Convention on Psychotropic Substances 1971, the United Nations Convention against Illicit Traffic in Nacortic Drugs and Psychotropic Substances, 1988 and the United Nations Convention against Transnational Organised Crime, 2003 repeal and replace the Nacortic Drugs and Psychotropic Substances Act, 1993, and provide for matters connected with, or incidental to, the foregoing.

[20th May, 2021]

Enactment

ENACTED by the Parliament of Zambia.

PART I
PRELIMINARY PROVISIONS

Short title

1. This Act may be cited as the Narcotic Drugs and Psychotropic Substances Act, 2021.

Interpretation

2. In this Act, unless the context otherwise requires—
    "administer" has the meaning assigned to the word in the Medicines and Allied Substances Act, 2013;
    "analogue" means a substance not listed in the Schedules to this Act whose chemical structure is substantially similar to a drug of abuse that stimulates psychoactive effects;
    "appropriate authority" means a relevant public body, statutory body or person, having powers or regulatory functions under any other written law designated by the Minister;
    "associate" has the meaning assigned to the word in the Anti-Corruption Act, 2012, and includes a friend;
    "authorised prescriber" has the meaning assigned to the words in the Medicines and Allied Substances Act, 2013;
    "authorisation" means an approval issued by the Authority or Committee to cultivate, manufacture, produce, distribute import, export, trade, package, re-package, transit, remove, divert, possess, consume, administer or deal with a drug;

"Authority" means the Zambia Medicines Regulatory Authority established under the Medicines and Allied Substances Act, 2013;

"bank" has the meaning assigned to the word in the Banking and Financial Services Act; 2017;

"child" has the meaning assigned to the word in the Constitution;

"Commission" means the Drug Enforcement Commission established under the Constitution;

"Commission on Narcotic Drugs" means a Commission on Narcotic Drugs under the United Nations responsible for making drug policies and supervising the application of

International Drug Treaties;

"Committee" means the National Cannabis Coordinating Committee established under the Cannabis Act, 2021;

"consume" means to inject into one's body, sniff, chew, drink, smoke or administer a narcotic drug or psychotropic substance, and "consumption" shall be construed accordingly;

"controlled delivery" means the technique of allowing illicit or suspect consignments of drugs or substances substituted for them, to pass out of, through or into the territory of one or more countries with the knowledge and under the supervision of their competent authorities, with a view to identifying persons involved in the commission of offences;

"conviction" includes a conviction by a court outside the Republic and a conviction whether a conditional or unconditional discharge is ordered;

"Conventions" means the—

    (a) Convention on Psychotropic Substances which entered into force on 16th August, 1976, and was acceded to by Zambia on 28th May, 1993;

    (b) United Nations Convention Against Illicit Traffic in Narcotic Drugs and Psychotropic Substances which entered into force on 11th November, 1990, and was ratified by Zambia on 28th May, 1993; and

    (c) United Nations Convention against Transnational Organised Crime which entered into force on 29th September, 2003, and was acceded to by Zambia on 24th April, 2005;

"Council" means the Health Professions Council of Zambia established under the Health Professions Act, 2009;

"court" means a court of competent jurisdiction or as otherwise specified in the Act;

"cultivation" means the growing of a plant which can be used or consumed as a narcotic drug or psychotropic substance or from which a narcotic drug or psychotropic substance can be extracted and the word "cultivate" shall be construed accordingly;

"Deputy Director-General" means a person appointed as a Deputy Director-General under section 9;

"Director-General" means a person appointed as Director General under section 7;

"Director of Public Prosecutions" means the person appointed as Director of Public Prosecutions under the Constitution;

"document" has the meaning assigned to the word in the Statistics Act, 2018;

"drug" means a narcotic drug or psychotropic substance;

"drug abuser" means a person who uses a drug or analogue—

    (a) without a medical prescription; or

    (b) for a purpose other than medical, scientific or research;

"drug dependant person" means a person who —

    (a) as a result of repeated administration of a drug to that person, demonstrates impaired control in

relation to the use of that drug;

    (b) exhibits drug seeking behaviour that suggests impaired control; or

    (c) when the administration of the drug ceases, suffers or is likely to suffer mental or physical distress or disorder;

"educational institution" has the meaning assigned to the words in the Education Act, 2011;

"Emoluments Commission" means the Emoluments Commission established under the Constitution;

"health facility" has the meaning assigned to the words in the Health Professions Act, 2009;

"health practitioner" has the meaning assigned to the words in the Health Professions Act, 2009;

"health professional" has the meaning assigned to the words in the Health Professions Act, 2009;

"industrial hemp" has the meaning assigned to the words in the Industrial Hemp Act, 2021;

"learner" has the meaning assigned to the word in the Education Act, 2011;

"local authority" has the meaning assigned to the words in the Constitution;

"manufacture" in relation to drugs, includes all processes by which the drugs, may be obtained, refined, transformed or prepared;

"medical doctor" means a person registered as a medical doctor under the Health Professions Act, 2009;

"mental patient" has the meaning assigned to the words in the Mental Health Act, 2019;

"narcotic drug" means a natural or synthetic substance set out in the Second Schedule to this Act;

"oath" has the meaning assigned to the word in the Constitution;

"precursor chemical" means a substance that is requisite in the manufacture of a narcotic drug or psychotropic substance as set out in the Fifth Schedule to this Act;

"prescription" has the meaning assigned to the word in the Medicine and Allied Substances Act, 2013;

"private body" means a voluntary organisation, nongovernmental organisation, political party, charitable institution, company, partnership, club or any other person or organisation which is not a public body;

"property" has the meaning assigned to the word in the Forfeiture of Proceeds of Crime Act, 2010;

"psychotropic substance" means a natural or synthetic substance set out in the Third Schedule to this Act;

"public officer" has the meaning assigned to the words in the Constitution;

"relative" has the meaning assigned to the word in the Anti-Corruption Act, 2012;

"repealed Act" means the Narcotic Drugs and Psychotropic Substances Act;

"securities" has the meaning assigned to the word in the Securities Act, 2016;

"State institution" has the meaning assigned to the words in the Constitution;

"Staff Board" means the Staff Board of the Commission constituted under section 5;

"tainted property" has the meaning assigned to the words in the Forfeiture of Proceeds of Crime Act, 2010;

"trafficking" means—

(a) being involved directly or indirectly in the unlawful buying or selling of narcotic drugs or psychotropic substances and includes the commission of an offence under this Act in circumstances suggesting that the offence was being committed in connection with buying or selling; or

(b) being found in possession of narcotic drugs or psychotropic substances in amounts or quantities that the Minister may, by statutory instrument, declare to be trafficking;

"treatment order" means an order made under section 79;

"treatment and rehabilitation centre" means a health facility registered under the Health Professions Act, 2009, used for the treatment or rehabilitation of a drug abuser or drug dependent person;

"youth" has the meaning assigned to the word in the Constitution; and

"Zambia Qualifications Authority" means the Zambia Qualifications Authority established under the Zambia Qualifications Authority Act, 2011.

PART II
THE DRUG ENFORCEMENT COMMISSION

Establishment of Commission

3. (1) The Commission established under the Constitution is responsible for the administration of this Act.

(2) The First Schedule applies to the Commission.

Functions of Commission

4. (1) The functions of the Commission are to—

(a) prevent, investigate and control the supply and demand of a drug and precursor chemicals;

(b) prevent and investigate money laundering and related offences;

(c) provide counselling and rehabilitation services to drug addicts in consultation with the ministry responsible for health;

(d) develop strategies for the prevention of abuse of drugs and ensure the treatment and rehabilitation of victims of drug abuse with particular emphasis on special measures for children and youths;

(e) co-operate with other institutions in investigating, prosecuting, preventing and combating drug trafficking and prohibited activities relating to drugs or precursor chemicals so as to implement an integrated approach to the eradication of drug trafficking and prohibited activities relating to drugs or precursor chemicals;

(f)   consult, co-operate and exchange information with appropriate bodies regionally or internationally that are authorised to conduct inquiries or investigate cases of drug trafficking and other transnational crimes;

(g)   promote and coordinate policies for the control of drug trafficking, drug abuse and money laundering; and

(j)   maintain a national database on drug trafficking, abuse, money laundering and other related information.

(2)   The Commission may, in implementing its functions—

(a)   examine the practices and procedures of State institutions and private bodies in order to facilitate the discovery of opportunities of drug trafficking and prohibited activities relating to drugs;

(b)   advise State institutions and private bodies on methods of preventing drug trafficking and prohibited activities relating to drugs, and on changes in methods of work or procedures of the State institutions and private bodies compatible with the effective performance of their duties, which the Commission considers necessary to reduce the occurrence of drug trafficking and prohibited activities relating to drugs;

(c)   disseminate information on the dangerous effects of drug trafficking and prohibited activities relating to drugs on society; and

(d)   enlist and foster public confidence and support against drug trafficking and prohibited activities relating to drugs.

(3)   The Commission may establish specialised units to investigate and deal with matters that the Commission considers appropriate for purposes of this Act.

Constitution of Staff Board

5.   (1)   There is constituted a Staff Board for the Commission which consists of seven members from the Commission appointed by the Minister.

    (2)   The Minister shall appoint the Chairperson and the Vice Chairperson of the Staff Board.

    (3)   The Director responsible for legal services shall be the Secretary of the Staff Board.

    (4)   The First Schedule applies to the Staff Board.

Functions of Staff Board

6.   (1)   The functions of the Staff Board are to—

(a)   advise the Director-General on matters relating to recruitment, appointment and termination of appointment, promotion, resignation, transfer, discipline and welfare of an officer in the Commission.

(b)   advise the Director-General on the proper usage of financial and material resources of the Commission;

(c)   examine the security of the officers of the Commission and recommend appropriate security measures for consideration and implementation by the Commission; and

(d)   consider any matter that may be referred to the Staff Board by the Director-General.

    (2)   The Director-General may on the recommendation of the Staff Board, vary a decision, in the interest of the Commission.

Director-General

7.   (1)   The President shall appoint, as a public officer, the Director-General who shall be the chief executive officer responsible, subject to the general and specific directions of the President, for the day-to-day administration of the Commission.

    (2)   A person qualifies to be appointed as Director-General if that person—

(a)   holds a bachelor's degree or an equivalent qualification in economics, finance, accounting, banking, law or other field relevant to the Act which is accredited or recognised and validated by the Zambia Qualifications Authority; and

(b)   has a minimum of ten years' experience at a senior management level in law enforcement

    (3)   The Director-General may resign on giving three months' notice, in writing, to the President.

Powers of Director-General

8.   (1)   The Director-General may, in the performance of the Commission's functions under this Act—

(a)   authorise an officer of the Commission to conduct an inquiry or investigation into alleged or suspected offences under this Act;

(b) require the chief executive officer, controlling officer or controlling body of a State institution to produce or furnish, within a time that may be specified by the Director-General or an investigating officer, a document or certified true copy of a document which is in that person's possession or under that person's control and which the Director-General considers necessary for the conduct of an investigation into alleged or suspected offences under this Act; or

(c) require a person to produce or furnish any documentation or a certified true copy of a document, where applicable, or to answer, to the best of that person's knowledge and belief, questions with respect to the whereabouts or existence of a document or record that may be relevant to an investigation.

(2) Despite any written law to the contrary, the Director General may, where the Director-General has reasonable grounds to believe that a person who is the subject of an investigation in respect of an offence under this Act is likely to leave the Republic, require the person to surrender that person's travel document or any other document in that person's possession.

(3) The Commission shall, where a person surrenders that person's travel document under subsection (2), return the document to the person after the investigation of the offence is completed, or if no criminal proceedings are to be instituted.

(4) A person who fails to comply with the request of the Director-General under subsection (1) commits an offence and is liable, on conviction, to a fine not exceeding two hundred thousand penalty units, or to imprisonment for a term not exceeding two years.

Deputy Director-General

9. (1) The President shall appoint, as a public officer, a Deputy Director-General of the Commission.
   (2) A person qualifies to be appointed as Deputy Director General if that person—
      (a) holds a bachelor's degree or an equivalent qualification in economics, finance, accounting, banking, law or other field relevant to the Act which is accredited or recognized and validated by the Zambia Qualifications Authority; and
      (b) has a minimum of ten years' experience at a senior management level in law enforcement.
   (3) The Deputy Director-General shall assist the Director General in performing the Director-General's functions under this Act.
   (4) Whenever the office of the Director-General is vacant or the Director-General is absent from duty or unable for any other reason to perform the functions of that office, the Deputy Director General shall, except where the President otherwise directs, act as Director-General.
   (5) The Deputy Director-General may resign on giving three months' notice, in writing, to the President.

Investigating officers and other staff

10. (1) The Director-General may appoint, as public officers, Directors, investigating officers and other staff of the Commission that may be necessary for the performance of the functions under this Act.
    (2) An investigating officer has powers of a police officer.
    (3) The Commission may, in the exercise of its functions, engage the services of advisors and experts that it considers necessary.

Identity card

11. (1) The Director-General shall issue to an investigating officer of the Commission an identity card which shall be evidence of that investigating officer's appointment.
    (2) An investigating officer shall, in performing any function under this Act—
       (a) be in possession of the identity card under subsection (1); and
       (b) show the identity card to a person who requests to see it or is subject to an investigation under this Act.

Oath and declaration of assets on appointment

12. (1) The Director-General, Deputy Director-General, Directors, investigation officers and other staff of the Commission shall, on appointment, take an oath in accordance with the Official Oaths Act.
    (2) The Director-General, Deputy Director-General, Directors, investigating officers and other staff of the Commission shall before taking office under this Act and after every five years thereafter—

(a) in the case of the Director-General and Deputy Director General, submit to the Chief Justice a written declaration in the prescribed form of all the assets they own or liabilities owed to them and;

(b) in the case of investigating officers and other staff of the Commission, submit to a Magistrate a written declaration in the prescribed form of all the assets they own or liabilities owed to them.

Guidance by Commission

13. (1) The Commission may guide a State institution or private body on practices and procedures that are necessary to prevent, reduce or eliminate the occurrence of drug trafficking and prohibited activities relating to drugs and the implementation of special measures with regard to children or youth.

(2) A State institution or private body shall, not later than ninety days from the date of receipt of the guidance from the Commission under subsection (1), effect the necessary changes in its practices and procedures.

(3) A State institution or private body that considers that the changes in practices and procedures contained in the guidance from the Commission are impracticable or disadvantage the effective discharge of the State institution or private body functions shall, within thirty days of the receipt of the instructions, make representations to the Director-General, in writing.

(4) The Commission may, after considering the representations of a State institution or private body made under subsection (3), confirm, vary or cancel the guidance given to the State institution or private body.

(5) A State institution or private body may, appeal to the Minister against a decision of the Commission made under subsection (4).

Report and recommendations by Commission

14. (1) The Commission may, after an investigation into an alleged offence under this Act, make recommendations that the Commission considers necessary to an appropriate authority.

(2) An appropriate authority shall, within thirty days of the date of receipt of the recommendation of the Commission under subsection (1), make a report to the Commission on the action taken by the appropriate authority.

PART III
OFFENCES AND PENALTIES

Prohibition of trafficking in drug or precursor chemical

15. (1) A person shall not engage in the trafficking of a drug or precursor chemical.

(2) A person who contravenes subsection (1) commits an offence and is liable, on conviction, to imprisonment for a term not less than one year but not exceeding twenty five years.

Prohibition of import or export of drugs or precursor chemical

16. (1) A person shall not, without lawful authority, import or export a drug or precursor chemical set out in the Second, Third and Fifth Schedules.

(2) A person who contravenes subsection (1) commits an offence and is liable, on conviction, to imprisonment for a term not exceeding twenty years.

Prohibition of trade in drug or precursor chemical

17. (1) A person shall not trade in a drug or a precursor chemical without lawful authority.

(2) A person who contravenes subsection (1) commits an offence and is liable, on conviction, to imprisonment for a term not exceeding twenty-five years without the option of a fine.

Prohibition of possession of drug or precursor chemical

18. (1) A person shall not, without lawful authority, have in that person's possession or under that person's control a drug or precursor chemical.

(2)   A person who contravenes subsection (1) commits an offence and is liable, on conviction, to imprisonment for a term not exceeding fifteen years.

(3)   Despite subsection (2), where a drug is cannabis or catha edulis commonly referred to as khat or miraa, a person is liable, on admission, to a fine not exceeding one thousand two hundred penalty units.

(4)   The admission of guilt procedure under subsection (3) shall be as provided in the Criminal Procedure Code.

Prohibition of cultivation of plant for drug purposes

19. (1)   A person shall not, without lawful authority, cultivate a plant which can be used or consumed as a drug.

(2)   A person who contravenes subsection (1), commits an offence and is liable, on conviction, to a fine not exceeding one million penalty units or to imprisonment for a term not exceeding ten years, or to both.

Prohibition of unlawful manufacture of drug or precursor chemical

20. (1)   A person shall not unlawfully manufacture or carry out a process for the manufacture of a drug or precursor chemical.

(2)   A person who contravenes subsection (1), commits an offence and is liable, on conviction, to imprisonment for a term not less than two years but not exceeding twenty five years, without the option of a fine.

Prohibition of possession, manufacture, etc. of drug precursor chemical, equipment or material

21. (1)   A person shall not without lawful authority, produce, manufacture, import, export, transport, offer, sell, distribute, deliver, consign, dispatch, offer to purchase or possess a drug, precursor chemical, equipment or material for the cultivation, production or manufacture of a drug.

(2)   A person who contravenes subsection (1), commits an offence and is liable, on conviction, to imprisonment for a term not less than one year but not exceeding fifteen years, without the option of a fine.

Prohibition of consumption or administration of drug

22. (1)   A person shall not, without lawful authority, consume or administer on another person a drug or precursor chemical.

(2)   A person who contravenes subsection (1) commits an offence and is liable, on conviction, to a fine not exceeding two hundred thousand penalty units or to imprisonment for a period not exceeding two years.

Prohibition of inducing person to take drug

23. (1)   A person shall not, by force, deceit or any other means, induce another person to take a drug.

(2)   A person who contravenes subsection (1) commits an offence and is liable, on conviction, to imprisonment for a term not exceeding ten years.

Prohibition of double doctoring

24. (1)   A person shall not, with intent to deceive, obtain a drug or a prescription for a drug from an authorised prescriber without disclosing to that authorised prescriber the particulars of the drug or prescription for the drug issued to the person by a different authorised prescriber within the preceding thirty days.

(2)   A person who contravenes subsection (1) commits an offence and is liable, on conviction, to a fine not exceeding one hundred thousand penalty units or to imprisonment for a term not exceeding one year, or to both.

Prohibition of unlawful possession of instrument or utensil for administering drug

25. (1)   A person shall not, without lawful authority, have in the person's possession or control an instrument or utensil used in administering a drug.

(2)   A person who contravenes subsection (1) commits an offence and is liable, on conviction, to imprisonment for a term not exceeding ten years.

Prohibition of use of premises for unlawful administration etc. of drug or precursor chemical

26. (1)   A person who occupies or controls premises shall not use or permit those premises to be used for the illicit consumption, administration, preparation, set out in the Fourth Schedule, manufacture or trade in drugs or precursor chemicals.

      (2)   A person who contravenes subsection (1) commits an offence and is liable, on conviction, to imprisonment for a term not exceeding five years.

Prohibition of unlawful supply, etc., of drug or precursor chemical

27. (1)   A person shall not, without lawful authority, supply to or procure for another person a drug or precursor chemical or advertise for sale a drug or precursor chemical.

      (2)   A person who contravenes subsection (1) commits an offence and is liable, on conviction, to imprisonment for a term not exceeding five years.

Prohibition of financing of offence under Act

28. (1)   A person shall not—

          (a)   invite another person to provide or make available money or property for an illegal activity; or

          (b)   provide or make available to another person money or property knowing that the money or property shall be used for an illegal activity.

      (2)   A person who contravenes this section commits an offence and is liable, on conviction, to imprisonment for a term not exceeding fifteen years.

Prohibition of unlawful use of property for commission of offence

29. (1)   A person shall not, directly or indirectly, deal in or use any property within or outside the Republic for the purpose of committing an offence under this Act.

      (2)   A person who contravenes subsection (1) commits an offence and is liable, on conviction, to imprisonment for a term not exceeding ten years.

Prohibition of possession of tainted property

30. (1)   A person shall not knowingly acquire or have in the person's possession or control tainted property.

      (2)   A person shall not, directly or indirectly, whether on that person's behalf or on behalf of another person, knowingly use or cause to be used, or receive any tainted property.

      (3)   A person who contravenes this section commits an offence and is liable, on conviction, to imprisonment for a term not exceeding ten years.

Concealment of tainted property

31. (1)   A person shall not—

          (a)   convert, transfer or dispose of any property knowing that the property is tainted property or conceal or disguise the illicit origin of the property for the purpose of or of helping any other person who is involved in the commission of an offence to evade the consequences of that person's action; or

          (b)   conceal or disguise the true nature, source, location, disposition, movement or ownership of or rights with respect to tainted property.

      (2)   A person who contravenes subsection (1) commits an offence and is liable, on conviction, to imprisonment for a period not exceeding ten years.

Concealment of offence

32. (1)   A person commits an offence if that person, with intent to defraud or to conceal the commission of an offence under this Part or to obstruct an investigating officer in the investigation of an offence—

(a) destroys, alters, mutilates or falsifies a book, document, valuable security, account, computer system, disk, computer printout or other electronic device which belongs to, or is in the possession of, or is received by that person or that person's employer, or an entry in the book, document, account or electronic device, or is privy to that act;

(b) makes or is privy to the making of any false entry in any book, document, account or electronic device; or

(c) omits or is privy to the omission of any information from any book, document, account or electronic device.

(2) A person convicted of an offence under subsection (1) is liable, to imprisonment for a term not exceeding two years.

Impersonation and procurement of officer

33. (1) A person shall not—

(a) impersonate an officer of the Commission or pretend to have any of the powers of an officer under this Act or under any authorisation or warrant issued under this Act; or

(b) pretend to procure an officer of the Commission to do or refrain from doing anything in connection with the duties of that officer.

(2) A person who contravenes subsection (1) commits an offence and is liable, on conviction, to a fine not exceeding two hundred thousand penalty units or to imprisonment for a term not exceeding two years, or to both.

General penalty

34. A person who is convicted of an offence under this Part for which no penalty is provided is liable—

(a) on conviction, to imprisonment for a term not exceeding ten years or to a fine not exceeding one million penalty units, or to both;

(b) on a second or subsequent conviction, to imprisonment for a term of not less than ten years but not exceeding fifteen years; and

(c) in addition to any other penalty imposed under this Act, to forfeiture to the State of any pecuniary resource, property, advantage or profit received in the commission of an offence under this Act.

Effect of conviction

35. A person convicted of an offence under this Part shall, by reason of the conviction, be disqualified for a period of five years from the date of the conviction, from being elected or appointed to, or from holding or continuing to hold, an office or position in a State institution.

Offence by body corporate or unincorporate body

36. Where an offence under this Act is committed by a body corporate or unincorporate body, with the knowledge, consent or connivance of the director, manager shareholder or partner, that director, manager, shareholder or partner of the body corporate or unincorporate body commits an offence and is liable, on conviction, to the penalty specified for that offence.

Grounds for aggravation

37. (1) A court shall, in determining the nature and extent of a penalty to be ordered in relation to a person convicted of an offence under this Part, take into account whether—

(a) the convict—

(i) belonged to an organised criminal syndicate;

(ii) participated in other illegal activities facilitated by the offence;

(iii) used violence or a firearm;

(iv) committed the offence in the exercise of a public office or duty;

(v) added any drug or precursor chemical which aggravated the danger of the drug or psychotropic substance to a user;

(vi) made use or took advantage of a child or person with a physical or mental disability in committing the offence; or

(vii) has a previous conviction relating to the offence;

(b) the offence was committed—
    (i) by an officer or a law enforcement officer;
    (ii) by a health professional or person responsible for combating drug abuse or trafficking in drugs;
    (iii) in an educational institution, a health facility, a social service facility or in any other establishment where learners or students resort for educational, sports or social activities, or in the immediate vicinity of the institution, facility or establishment; or
    (iv) in a penal institution or a military establishment;
(c) the narcotic drug or psychotropic substance was supplied or offered to a child or a person with a physical disability or a mental patient undergoing treatment; or
(d) the drug supplied caused death or seriously impaired the health of a person.

(2) For the purposes of subsection (1) —
"law enforcement officer" means an officer of—
(a) the Zambia Police Service, established under the Constitution;
(b) the Anti-Corruption Commission established under the Constitution;
(c) the Drug Enforcement Commission; and
(d) any other investigative institution that the Minister may, by statutory instrument, designate; and
"organised criminal syndicate" means a structured group of three or more persons existing for a period of time in concert with the aim of committing an offence under this Act or any other law, in order to obtain, directly or indirectly, a financial or other material benefit.

Alternative sentence

38. (1) A court may, where a person is convicted of an offence under this Part, order the restriction of the movement of that person within the Republic for a prescribed term.
(2) A court may, where a person is convicted of an offence under this Part, and it appears to the court that it would be appropriate, in the interest of justice and not contrary to the broader public interest to do so—
(a) order the surrender and suspension of the convict's passport, and in the case of a non-citizen, withdraw the convict's visa, deport or prohibit the convict's re-entry into the Republic;
(b) order —
    (i) the disqualification, cancellation or suspension of any right in the Republic to operate a vehicle, vessel or aircraft used by the convict in connection with the commission of the offence; or
    (ii) the disqualification to hold public office in the Republic by the convict;
(c) order the suspension of any licence or registration entitling the convict to carry on any trade or business carried on by the convict in connection with the commission of the offence; or
(d) recommend to the appropriate professional body the suspension or disqualification of the convict's right to practice any profession practiced by the convict in connection with the commission of the offence, for a term that the court may consider appropriate.
(3) Where a non-citizen is convicted of an offence under this Part, the court may, in addition to ordering the penalty provided for the offence or alternative sentence in this section, order the withdrawal of the person's visa, deportation or prohibit the person's re-entry into the Republic.

Suspension and revocation of suspended sentence

39. (1) A court may order suspension of the whole or any part of the penalties imposed on a person, on such terms and conditions considered necessary to ensure that the person does not commit a similar offence, except that it is in the interest of justice and not contrary to the broader public interest to make an order, where a person convicted of an offence under this Part is—
(a) below the age of eighteen years;
(b) a first offender;
(c) a drug abuser; or
(d) a drug dependent person.
(2) A court may, where a person fails, without reasonable excuse, to abide by the terms and conditions of a suspension order under subsection (1), revoke the order.

PART IV
DIVISION

Application for authorisation

40. (1) A person who intends to cultivate, manufacture, produce, distribute, import, export, trade, package, repackage, transit, remove, divert, posses, consume, administer, research on, or otherwise deal with a drug or precursor chemical shall apply to the Authority or Committee where applicable for authorisation in accordance with this Act and the Medicines and Allied Substances Act, 2013, Dangerous Drugs Act and the Cannabis Act, 2021.

(2) The Authority or Committee shall, where it grants an authorisation, notify the Commission of the grant of authorisation.

Drug or precursor chemical in transit

41. (1) A person may bring a drug or precursor chemical into the Republic in transit if the drug or precursor chemical is in transit from a country from which it may lawfully be exported to a country into which it may lawfully be imported.

(2) Despite subsection (1), where the drug or precursor chemical comes from a country which is not party to the Convention, it shall be accompanied by the documents authorising the export or diversion.

(3) An investigating officer may seize and detain a drug or precursor chemical in transit—

(a) where there are reasonable grounds to believe that the document authorising export or diversion accompanying the drug or precursor chemical is false, or that it has been obtained by fraud or wilful misrepresentation of a material particular;

(b) where the drug or precursor chemical is not accompanied by a document authorising an export or diversion by reason of the fact that the drug comes from a country not party to the Convention; or

(c) where there are reasonable grounds to believe that the drug or precursor chemical is being conveyed in an unlawful manner or for an unlawful purpose or is in transit for the purpose of being imported into another country in contravention of the laws of that country.

(4) This section shall not apply to—

(a) a drug or precursor chemical in transit by post or air if the aircraft passes over the Republic without landing; or

(b) to quantities of a drug or precursor chemical that may reasonably form part of the medical stores of any ship or aircraft.

Release of seized or detained drug or precursor chemical

42. The Director-General, Deputy Director-General or an investigating officer authorised by the Director-General in that behalf, may release a drug or precursor chemical seized or detained under section 41 where the Director-General or investigating officer determines that—

(a) the document authorising the export or diversion is valid and was not obtained by fraud or wilful misrepresentation; or

(b) the drug or precursor chemical is being conveyed in a lawful manner or for a lawful purpose.

Removal permit

43. (1) A person shall not, except under, and in accordance with an authorisation issued by the Authority—

(a) remove a drug or precursor chemical in transit from the conveyance by which it is brought into the Republic; or

(b) move or transfer into any part of the Republic any drug or precursor chemical after its removal from a conveyance.

(2) A person who contravenes subsection (1) commits an offence and is liable, on conviction, to a fine not exceeding five hundred thousand penalty units or to imprisonment for a term not exceeding five years, or to both.

(3) Despite subsection (1), the Authority may, authorise the temporary removal for safe custody of quantities of drugs or precursor chemical that the Authority may determine from an aircraft or ship which is in transit in the Republic.

616

Prohibition of altering nature of, or tampering with drug or precursor chemical in transit

44. (1) A person shall not subject or cause a drug or precursor chemical in transit to be subjected to any process which may alter its nature, or wilfully open or break or otherwise tamper with any package containing a drug, or precursor chemical, except under and in accordance with an authorisation issued by the Authority.

(2) A person who contravenes subsection (1) commits an offence and is liable, on conviction, to a fine not exceeding five hundred thousand penalty units or to imprisonment for a term not exceeding five years, or to both.

Prohibition of diversion of drug, or precursor chemical

45. (1) A person shall not, without authorisation, cause or procure a drug or precursor chemical in transit through the Republic to be diverted to a destination other than that to which it was originally consigned.

(2) In the case of a drug in transit accompanied by a document authorising the export or the diversion, of that drug to the country to which the drug or precursor chemical was originally consigned shall be the country of destination.

(3) A person who contravenes subsection (1) commits an offence and is liable, on conviction, to a fine not exceeding five hundred thousand penalty units or to imprisonment for a term not exceeding five years, or to both.

Application for diversion certificate

46. A person who intends to divert a drug or precursor chemical in transit to a destination other than that to which it was originally consigned may, with the authorisation of the Authority and in consultation with the Commission, divert a drug or precursor chemical.

Exemption of medicinal preparation in possession of traveller

47. (1) Subject to subsection (2), this Part does not apply to a drug or precursor chemical in the form of a medicinal preparation—
    (a) in the possession of a person who arrives in the Republic by land, air or water from any place outside the Republic as is reasonably required for the use by the person; and
    (b) which is bona fide supplied to the person by or on the prescription of a medical doctor residing outside the Republic in accordance with the law of the country in which the medicinal preparation was supplied.

(2) A person in possession of a drug or precursor chemical in the form of a medicinal preparation under subsection (1) shall, as soon as practicable on arrival, declare the person's possession of the medicinal preparation to an officer and shall submit to a medical examination that may be required of that person.

Application, grant, modification etc. of authorisation, permit or certificate

48. The Minister responsible for health may, on recommendation from the Authority and the Commission, prescribe, by statutory instrument, in relation to an authorisation, issued under this Part—
    (a) the criteria and procedure for applying for an authorisation and the grant, variation, renewal, transfer and revocation of the authorisation;
    (b) the terms and conditions attaching to an authorisation and the grant, variation, refusal, renewal, transfer or revocation of an authorisation; and
    (c) any other matters that are necessary or incidental to the effective regulation of authorisations.

PART V
INVESTIGATIONS

Investigations

49. (1) A person who has information or reasonable grounds to believe that another person has engaged or is engaging in trafficking or a prohibited activity involving a drug or precursor chemical shall inform the Director-General.

(2) The Director-General may investigate a matter under this Act on receipt of information or on the Director-General's own initiative.

(3) The Director-General may refer an offence that comes to its notice in the course of an investigation under subsection (2) to any other appropriate authority.

(4) A person who provides information under subsection (1) is entitled to protection as a whistle blower in accordance with section 71.

Examination of information

50. (1) The Director-General shall, on receipt of information under section 49, examine it and decide whether or not an investigation in relation to the allegation contained in the information is warranted.

(2) The Director-General may, in deciding whether or not to investigate the allegation, determine if—

    (a) the conduct to which the allegation relates constitutes an offence under this Act; or

    (b) the allegation is frivolous or vexatious.

(3) The Director-General shall, where the Director-General determines that an investigation into an allegation is warranted, carry out the investigation.

(4) The Director-General may, for purposes of performing the functions under this section—

    (a) make a preliminary inquiry that the Director-General considers necessary; and

    (b) consult any other appropriate authority.

(5) The Director-General shall inform a person under section

Power to require attendance before Director-General

49(1), in writing, of the decision of the Commission in relation to the allegation.

Power of entry, search and seizure

51. (1) The Director-General may, by notice, in writing, require a person under investigation or any other person who the Director General has reason to believe may have information or documents relevant to an investigation to—

    (a) attend before the Director-General as may be specified in the notice;

    (b) answer questions with respect to any matter or supply any information that may be relevant to the investigation; or

    (c) produce for inspection any documents which are specified in the notice.

(2) Subsection (1) shall not affect a person's rights under any other written law relating to privilege.

Search, seizure and inspection

52. (1) Where the Director-General has reasonable grounds to suspect that in, or on, any premises there is concealed or deposited any property liable to forfeiture under this Act, or as to which an offence under this Act is reasonably suspected to have been committed, or any book or document directly or indirectly relating to, or connected with, any dealing or intended dealing, whether within or outside the Republic, in respect of any property liable to seizure or forfeiture under this Act, or which would, if carried out, be an offence under this Act, the Director-General may, by order in writing, authorise an investigating officer or police officer to—

    (a) enter the premises and search for, seize and detain the property, book or document;

    (b) search any person who is in, or on, the premises, and detain that person or remove the person to any place in order to facilitate the search;

    (c) arrest any person who is in, or on, the premises in whose possession or control of any suspected drug or precursor chemical or any property liable to seizure or forfeiture under this Act is found, whom the officer reasonably believes to have concealed or deposited the property;

    (d) break open, examine and search any article, container or receptacle; and

    (e) stop, search and detain any conveyance.

(2) An investigating officer under subsection (1) may, if it is necessary to do so—

    (a) break open any outer or inner door or window of any premises;

    (b) forcibly enter the premises or any part of it;

    (c) remove by force any obstruction to entry, search, seizure and removal; or

    (d) detain any person found in, or on, the premises until the premises is searched.

(3)   A drug or precursor chemical seized under subsection (1) shall be presented to a public analyst for analytical and scientific examination.

Power to intercept communication

53. (1)   An investigating officer may, with a warrant, at any time—
    (a)   enter and search any premises or any other premises, including a private dwelling, where information or documents which may be relevant to an investigation may be kept;
    (b)   search any person on the premises if there are reasonable grounds for believing that the person has personal possession of any document or article that has a bearing on the investigation, except that a person shall only be searched by a person of the same sex;
    (c)   examine any document or article found on the premises that has a bearing on the investigation;
    (d)   require information to be given about any document or article by—
        (i)   the owner of the premises;
        (ii)   the person in control of the premises;
        (iii) any person who has control of the document or article; or
        (iv)   any other person who may have the information;
    (e)   take extracts from, or make copies of, any book or document found on the premises that has a bearing on the investigation;
    (f)   use any computer system on the premises, or require assistance of any person on the premises to use that computer system to—
        (i)   search any data contained in, or available from, the computer system;
        (ii)   reproduce any record from the data; or
        (iii) seize any output from the computer for examination and copying; or
    (g)   attach and, if necessary, remove from the premises for examination and safeguarding any document or article that appears to have a bearing on the investigation.
    (2)   An investigating officer who removes any document or article from any premises in accordance with subsection (4)(g) shall—
    (a)   issue a notice of seizure for the document or article to the owner of, or person in control of, the premises; and
    (b)   return the document or article as soon as practicable after achieving the purpose for which it was removed.
    (3)   A person shall not—
    (a)   delay or obstruct an investigating officer, in the performance of the investigating officer's functions;
    (b)   refuse to give an investigating officer any reasonable assistance that the investigating officer may require for the purpose of exercising that investigating officer's powers; or
    (c)   give an investigating officer false or misleading information in answer to an inquiry made by the investigating officer.
    (4)   A person who contravenes subsection (3) commits an offence and is liable, on conviction, to a fine not exceeding two hundred thousand penalty units or to a term of imprisonment not exceeding two years, or to both.
    (5)   An investigating officer shall furnish the Director-General with a written report and any other information relating to an inspection that the Director-General may require.
    (6)   Nothing in this section requires a person to disclose or produce information or a document if the person would in an action in a court be entitled to refuse to disclose or produce the information or document.

Undercover and controlled delivery operations

54.   An investigating officer may intercept any communication or postal article reasonably suspected to contain any information or substance which is likely to be relevant for the purpose of an investigation into an offence under this Act, in accordance with the

Power of arrest

55. (1)   Where the Director-General suspects on reasonable grounds that a person has committed, or is about to commit, an offence under this Act, the Director-General may give approval, in writing, for—

(a)   a controlled delivery to be carried out; and

(b)   specified persons or classes of persons to carry out or participate in the controlled delivery.

(2)   Despite any other written law, the activities which may be undertaken in the course and purposes of a controlled delivery include —

(a)   allowing any vehicle, vessel, aircraft or other means of transport to enter or leave the Republic;

(b)   allowing any—

(i)   drug, analogue, precursor chemical, equipment or material or other items in or on the vehicle, vessel, aircraft or other means of transport; or

(ii)   tainted property to enter or leave the Republic or be delivered or collected in the Republic;

(c)   using force that may be reasonable in the circumstances to enter and search the vehicle, vessel, aircraft or other means of transport;

(d)   placing a tracking device on board the vehicle, vessel, aircraft or other means of transport; and

(e)   allowing any person who has possession or custody of the drug, analogue, precursor chemical, equipment or material or other thing to enter or leave the Republic.

(3)   Where the Director-General suspects on reasonable grounds that a person has committed, or is about to commit, an offence under this Act, the Director-General, may give approval, in writing, for—

(a)   undercover operations to be carried out for a specified period; and

(b)   specified persons or classes of persons to carry out or participate in the undercover operations for purposes of gathering evidence relating to the commission of the offence.

(4)   The Director-General may renew the approval given under subsection (3) for a period not exceeding three months.

(5)   A drug, analogue, precursor chemical, equipment, material or other item imported into the Republic in the course of an approved undercover operation or controlled delivery shall, when no longer required for the purposes of the enforcement of this Act, be disposed of.

(6)   Despite any other written law, an authorised participant in an undercover operation or a controlled delivery incurs no criminal liability by taking part in it in accordance with the terms of approval.

Power to use firearm

56.   The Director-General or an investigating officer authorised in that behalf by the Director-General may arrest a person, without a warrant, if the Director-General or an investigating officer has reasonable grounds to believe that the person has committed or is about to commit an offence under this Act.

Seizure of property

57.   (1)   An investigating officer may, subject to subsections (2) and (3), use a firearm issued to that investigating officer against —

(a)   a person in lawful custody charged with or convicted of an offence under this Act if that person is escaping or attempting to escape;

(b)   a person who, by force, rescues or attempts to rescue another person from lawful custody;

(c)   any person who, by force, prevents or attempts to prevent the lawful arrest of the person or of another person, except that the investigating officer shall not use a firearm—

(i)   as authorised under paragraph (a), unless the investigating officer has reasonable grounds to believe that the investigating officer cannot otherwise prevent the escape and unless the investigating officer gives a warning to the person that the investigating officer is about to use the firearm against that person and that person does not heed the warning; or

(ii)   as authorised under paragraph (b) or (c), unless the investigating officer has reasonable grounds to believe that the person or any other person is in danger of grievous bodily harm and that the investigating officer cannot otherwise effect the arrest or prevent the rescue.

(2)   An investigating officer shall not, in the presence of the investigating officer's superior, use a firearm against any person except under the orders of that superior.

(3)   The use of a firearm under this section shall, as far as possible, be to disable and not to kill.

(4)   Authority vested in an investigating officer under subsection (1) shall be in addition to and not in substitution for any authority to use a firearm vested in the investigating officer by any other written law.

Custody and release of seized property

58. (1)   Where, in the course of an investigation into an offence under this Act, an investigating officer has reasonable grounds to suspect that any movable or immovable property is derived or acquired from trafficking or from an illegal activity, is the subject matter of an offence or is evidence relating to an offence, the investigating officer shall, with a warrant, seize the property.

     (2)   An investigating officer who seizes any property pursuant to subsection (1) shall prepare and sign a list of all the movable or immovable property seized under that subsection and of the places in which the property is found.

     (3)   An investigating officer shall serve a copy of the list under subsection (2) on the owner of the property or on the person from whom the property was seized, not later than thirty days from the date of seizure.

Restriction on disposal of property

59. (1)   An investigating officer shall effect a seizure by removing the movable property from the custody or control of the person from whom it is seized and placing it under the custody of another person or authority and at a place as the officer may determine.

     (2)   An investigating officer shall, where it is not practicable or otherwise not desirable to effect the removal of any property under subsection (1), leave it at the premises in which it is seized under the custody of that person that the investigating officer may determine.

     (3)   An investigating officer shall, where property is seized under subsection (1), make a record in writing specifying in detail the circumstances of, and the reason for, the seizure of the property and subsequent leaving of the property at the premises.

Restriction on disposal of property

60. (1)   The Director-General may, by written notice to a person who is the subject of an investigation in respect of an offence alleged or suspected to have been committed under this Act, or against whom a prosecution for an offence is instituted, direct that the person shall not dispose of, or otherwise deal with, any property specified in the notice without the consent of the Director-General.

     (2)   A notice issued under subsection (1) may be served by delivering it personally to the person to whom it is addressed or may, where the Director-General is satisfied that the person cannot be found, or is not in the Republic, be served on or brought to the knowledge of that person in a manner that the Director-General may direct.

     (3)   A notice issued under subsection (1) shall have effect from the time of service and shall continue in force for a period of nine months or until cancelled by the Director-General, whichever is earlier, except that the Director-General may issue a fresh notice on the expiry of the previous one for a further and final term of six months to facilitate the conclusion of an investigation.

     (4)   A person who, having been served with or having knowledge of a notice issued under subsection (1), disposes of or otherwise deals with any property specified in the notice other than in accordance with the consent of the Director-General commits an offence and is liable, on conviction, to imprisonment for a term not exceeding five years.

     (5)   A person aggrieved with the directive of the Director General issued under subsection (1) may, within thirty days from the date of receipt of the notice, appeal to the High Court.

Restriction on disposal of property by third party

61. (1)   The Director-General may, where the Director-General has reasonable grounds to believe that a third party is holding any property, including money in a bank account for or on behalf of, or to the order of, a person who is under investigation, serve a notice on the third party directing that the third party shall not dispose of, or otherwise deal with, any property specified in the notice without the consent of the Director-General.

     (2)   A notice issued under subsection (1) shall be served on the third party to whom it is directed and on the person being investigated.

(3)   The Director-General may, in issuing a notice under this section, impose conditions that the Director-General may determine.

(4)   A notice issued under subsection (1) shall have effect from the time of service on the person to whom it is addressed and shall continue in force for a period of nine months unless cancelled by the Director-General, whichever is earlier, except that the Director General may issue a fresh notice on the expiry of the previous one for a further final term of six months to facilitate the conclusion of an investigation.

(5)   A third party on whom a notice is served under subsection (1) who disposes of, or deals with, the property specified in the notice without the consent of the Director-General commits an offence and is liable, on conviction, to imprisonment for a term not exceeding five years.

(6)   A third party on whom a notice is served under this section shall not dispose of, or otherwise deal with, the property specified in the notice except in accordance with the terms of the notice.

(7)   A person aggrieved with the directive of the Director General issued under subsection (1) may appeal to the High Court.

Disposal of recovered, seized and forfeited drug or precursor chemical

62.   The disposal of recovered, seized and forfeited drugs or precursor chemicals shall be in a manner and in accordance with any relevant written law.

Delegation of powers

63.   The powers of the Director-General under this Part may be exercised by the Director-General in person or by a member of staff of the Commission that may be specified by the Director General acting in accordance with the Director-General's special or general instructions.

General offences

64. (1)   A person shall not—
        (a)   knowingly make, or cause to be made, to the Commission, false testimony or a false report in any material particular on any offence or matter under investigation;
        (b)   destroy, alter, conceal or remove any book, document, record or evidence that the person believes may be relevant to an investigation or proceeding under this Act;
        (c)   destroy, alter, mutilate or falsify any valuable security, account, computer system, disk, computer printout or other electronic device or any entry in any book, document, account or electronic device;
        (d)   knowingly mislead the Director-General, the Deputy Director-General or any investigating officer or other staff of the Commission by giving any false information or statement or making a false allegation;
        (e)   obstruct, insult, assault, hinder or delay an investigating officer in the lawful exercise of the powers conferred on that investigating officer under this Act;
        (f)   refuse or fail, without reasonable cause, to give to the Director-General or an investigating officer on request, any document or information required for purposes of this Act;
        (g)   fail to comply with any lawful demand of the Director General, Deputy Director-General or an investigating officer under this Act;
        (h)   fail to produce, conceal or attempt to conceal any document or book in relation to which there are reasonable grounds to believe is used to commit an offence;
        (i)   destroy anything to prevent the seizure of any property or document or securing of the property or document; or
        (j)   without lawful authority or reasonable excuse, disclose to another person who is the subject of an investigation under this Act that the person is under investigation or the details of any investigation;
        (k)   while at any Drug Enforcement Commission premises, conduct oneself in a riotous, indecent, disorderly or insulting manner.
     (2)   A person who contravenes subsection (1) commits an offence and is liable, on conviction, to a fine not exceeding two hundred thousand penalty units or imprisonment for a term not exceeding two years, or to both.

PART VI
EVIDENCE, PRESUMPTIONS AND OTHER MATTERS

Factual presumptions relating to possession of drugs or precursor chemical, etc.

65. Where in the prosecution of a person for an offence under this Act it is proved that the following was found on a child, any animal, vehicle, vessel or aircraft and that the accused person was at the time on or in charge of the animal, vehicle, vessel or aircraft or in any place under the control or supervision of the accused person, or on the accused person, it shall be presumed, until the contrary is proved, that the accused person was found in possession of the drug, plant, instrument, utensil, precursor chemical, equipment, material or analogue:

   (a) a drug;

   (b) a plant which can be used or consumed as a drug or from which a drug can be extracted;

   (c) a precursor chemical, equipment or material for the unlawful cultivation, production or manufacture of a drug;

   (d) an instrument or utensil used in administering a drug; or

   (e) any other thing used for the commission of an offence under this Act.

Factual presumptions relating to samples

66. Where in the prosecution of an offence under this Act, it is proved that a sample which was taken from any drug or precursor chemical possess particular properties, it shall be presumed, until the contrary is proved, that the drug or precursor chemical possesses the same properties as the sample.

Factual presumptions relating to purpose of supply of drug or precursor chemical

67. (1) Where in the prosecution of a person for an offence under section 18 it is proved that the accused person was found in unlawful possession of a drug or precursor chemical, it shall be presumed, until the contrary is proved, that the possession was for the purpose of trafficking.

   (2) For the purposes of this Act, where a person has in the person's possession whether for the purpose of importing into or exporting from the Republic or not; or imports into or exports from the Republic a prescribed quantity of a drug or precursor chemical, it shall be presumed until the contrary is proved, that the possession, import, export, intended import or intended export, is for the purpose of trafficking.

Factual presumption relating to weight of a drug or precursor chemical

68. Where a substance is mixed with a drug or precursor chemical, the weight of the substance after measuring shall be the total weight of the drug or precursor chemical unless the contrary is proven.

Proof of prohibited import or export of drug, precursor chemical, equipment, material instrument or utensil

69. A certificate purporting to be issued by, or on behalf of, a foreign state to the effect that the import or export of a drug, precursor chemical, equipment, material, instrument or utensil is prohibited by the law of that State shall, for the purpose of any proceedings under this Act, be prima facie evidence of the matters stated therein.

Grant of indemnity by Director of Public Prosecutions

70. (1) Subject to the Plea Negotiations and Agreements Act, 2010, the Director of Public Prosecutions may, at any time, with a view to obtaining at a trial the evidence of any person directly or indirectly concerned with or privy to an offence under Part IV, tender indemnity to that person on condition that the person makes a full and true disclosure of all facts or circumstances within that person's knowledge relating to the offence and to every other person involved in the commission of the offence, whether as principal or in any other capacity, together with the delivery up of any document or thing constituting evidence or corroboration of the commission of the offence by the person to be charged or the accused person.

   (2) A court shall record in the manner prescribed by the Criminal Procedure Code the evidence on oath of a person accepting indemnity under subsection (1) and shall transmit the record of the evidence to the Director of Public Prosecutions.

(3)   A person accepting indemnity under this section shall be examined as a witness at the trial.

(4)   Where a person who has accepted indemnity under this section has, either by wilfully concealing anything material to the case, or by giving false evidence, not complied with the condition on which the indemnity was made, that person may be prosecuted for the offence in respect of which the indemnity was tendered or for any other offence of which the person appears to be guilty of in connection with the same matter.

(5)   A person to whom indemnity is made under subsection (1) who, in the opinion of the court has made a true and full disclosure of all things as to which that person is lawfully examined shall be entitled to receive a certificate of indemnity under the hand of the Director of Public Prosecutions stating that the person has made a true and full disclosure of all things as to which the person was examined, and the certificate shall be a bar to any legal proceedings against the person in respect of all those things.

Protection of whistle blowers

71. (1)   The Public Interest Disclosure (Protection of Whistle blowers) Act, 2010, shall apply in relation to the protection of whistle blowers and other related matters.

(2)   Despite subsection (1), where it appears to the Director General that as a result of assisting the Commission or the court, the safety of a witness, expert, victim or other person may be prejudiced or the witness, expert, victim or other person may be subject to threats, intimidation or harassment, the Director-General shall make arrangements that are necessary to protect—

   (a)   the safety of such witness, expert or victim; or

   (b)   any other person from threats, intimidation or harassment.

(3)   For the purposes of subsection (2), "assisting the Commission or court" includes—

   (a)   appearance or impending appearance before the Commission or the court to give evidence or produce a document or other thing;

   (b)   production or proposed production of a document or other thing to the Commission or the court under this Act; or

   (c)   assisting or having assisted the Commission or the court in some other manner in accordance with the provisions of this Act.

(4)   The Director-General may, in providing the arrangements under subsection (2), collaborate with other law enforcement agencies and authorities.

(5)   The law enforcement agencies and authorities shall, as far as reasonably possible, assist the Director-General in the provision of arrangements for the protection of the persons under subsection (2).

(6)   Subject to subsection (1), in any trial for an offence under this Act, a witness shall not be obliged to—

   (a)   disclose the identity or address of an informer or person assisting or who assisted the Commission in an investigation into an alleged or suspected offence under this Act; or

   (b)   state any matter which may disclose the identity or address of an informer or person referred to in paragraph (a).

(7)   Where any document which is in evidence or liable to inspection in any civil or criminal proceeding under this Act contains any entry or passage in which an informer is named or described or which might lead to the person's discovery, the court before which the proceedings is held shall cause that entry or passage to be concealed from view or to be obliterated in a manner that, in the opinion of the court, shall not disclose the identity of the informer.

(8)   An action or proceeding, including disciplinary action, shall not be instituted or maintained against a witness, expert, victim or other person who, in good faith, assists, or discloses information to, the Commission or the court.

(9)   A person who contravenes this section commits an offence and is liable, on conviction, to a fine not exceeding two hundred thousand penalty units or to imprisonment for a term not exceeding two years, or to both.

Forfeiture of proceeds of illegal activity

72. (1)   The Forfeiture of Proceeds of Crime Act, 2010, shall apply in relation to the seizure and forfeiture of any proceeds or property acquired through drug trafficking or prohibited activities involving drugs or precursor chemical by any person and any other related matters.

(2)   Any property which is forfeited to the State in terms of subsection (1) may be disposed of by the Commission in accordance with the Public Finance Management Act, 2018.

Affidavit evidence

73. For the purposes of any proceedings in respect of an offence under this Act, the court may admit affidavit evidence, at any stage of the proceedings and the same shall be prima facie evidence, except that the deponent may be summoned for cross-examination.

Tampering with seized or forfeited property, substance or sample

74. (1) A person shall not, without lawful authority, use, take or dispose of any property drug or precursor chemical or any sample thereof which is seized or forfeited under this Act.

    (2) A person shall not tamper with, or falsify the results of, any analysis with the intention of interfering with the proper course of justice.

    (3) A person who contravenes subsection (1) or (2) commits an offence and is liable, on conviction, to imprisonment for a term not exceeding three years.

PART VII
DRUG ABUSE PREVENTION, TREATMENT AND REHABILITATION

National awareness campaign

75. The Commission shall, in consultation with an appropriate authority, develop and implement strategies for carrying out national campaigns to educate the public on the dangers relating to abuse of drugs or precursor chemicals and other substances.

Prohibition of operation of drug treatment or rehabilitation centre without authority

76. A person shall not operate a drug treatment and rehabilitation centre without authority from the Council.

Eligibility for treatment and rehabilitation

77. A person is eligible to undergo treatment at a treatment and rehabilitation centre or health facility if—
    (a) the person is charged with an offence, under this Act or any other written law;
    (b) the person walks in voluntarily;
    (c) the person is brought in by another person;
    (d) the person's drug dependency contributed to the commission of an offence;
    (e) the facts alleged in connection with the offence, combined with any previous criminal record of the person and any other relevant information available to the court, indicate that it is likely that the person shall be sentenced to imprisonment for a minimum term of one year;
    (f) the person is a child in conflict with the law who is drug dependent; or
    (g) the person satisfied any other criteria as may be prescribed under this Act.

Referral to health facility for treatment and rehabilitation

78. The Commission may refer a person to a health facility to undergo treatment and rehabilitation if the person is a drug dependent person.

Treatment order

79. (1) A court may, where it convicts a person for an offence under this Act and it is satisfied that the person is addicted to a drug order that the person be sent to a treatment and rehabilitation centre.

    (2) A person who is sent to a treatment and rehabilitation centre under subsection (1) shall have the time spent at the treatment and rehabilitation centre taken into account for the purposes of remission of a sentence imposed by the court.

Imposition of final sentence

80. (1) As soon as may be reasonably practicable after the termination of a treatment programme of a person, the person shall be brought before the court to be dealt with in accordance with this section.

    (2) A court shall, where it terminates a treatment programme of a person, reconsider the person's initial sentence, taking into consideration—
        (a) the nature of the person's participation in the treatment programme; and

      (b) any sanctions that are imposed on the person during the treatment programme.

(3)   A court shall, after considering a person's initial sentence, determine the person's final sentence—

      (a) by making an order setting aside the initial sentence and discharging the person, either unconditionally or conditionally, on conditions that the court may impose;

      (b) by making an order setting aside the initial sentence deferring the passing of sentence and releasing the person conditionally on conditions that the court may impose;

      (c) by making an order setting aside the initial sentence and imposing instead any sentence that it could have been imposed for the offence to which the initial sentence related; or

      (d) by making an order confirming the initial sentence.

(4)   Where a person is discharged unconditionally under subsection (3)(a), the conviction in respect of the offence concerned shall not form part of the person's criminal record.

(5)   The final sentence determined for a person in relation to an offence is not to be greater than the initial sentence imposed on the person in relation to that offence.

PART VIII
GENERAL PROVISIONS

Bail

81.   A court shall not grant bail in respect of an offence under section 15, 16 or 17.

Disposal of abandoned and perishable goods

82. (1)   Where property which is seized under this Act is subject to speedy and natural decay, and it is proved on oath to a magistrate that in fact or according to reasonable suspicion, the property was used in, or in connection with, the commission of an offence by or in respect of which an offence is committed, the court may order that the property be sold or otherwise disposed of but shall order the proceeds of that sale to be paid into the general revenues of the Republic.

(2)   Where it is proved on oath or on reasonable suspicion to a magistrate that any abandoned property was used in, or in connection with, the commission of an offence by or in respect of which an offence was or has been committed or was about to be committed remains unclaimed for a period of six months or more, the court may order that the property be sold or otherwise be disposed of and shall order that the proceeds of that sale be paid into the general revenues of the Republic.

Forfeiture of property where no proceedings or claim

83. (1)   Where any property is seized under this Act, the property shall become forfeited immediately on the expiration of the period of six months if—

      (a) no prosecution for any offence under any written law is instituted with regard to the property;

      (b) no claim in writing is made by any person that the person is lawfully entitled to the property or that it is not liable to forfeiture under this Act; or

      (c) no proceedings are commenced by the Commission, within six months from seizure, for the forfeiture of the property.

(2)   The Director-General may, where within six months from the date of the seizure of any property under this Act, a claim in writing is made by any person in terms of subsection (1)(b)—

      (a) may order the release of the property to the claimant if the Director-General is satisfied that there is no dispute as to the ownership of the property and that it is not liable to forfeiture; or

      (b) if the Director-General is satisfied that there is a dispute as to the ownership of the property or is doubtful as to the person who owns it, or whether it is liable to forfeiture, the Director-General shall, within fourteen days after the expiry of the period of six months, refer the claim to the High Court for its decision.

(3)   This section shall be without prejudice to the power of an officer or police officer to release from seizure any property under section 52.

Disposal and destruction of seized substances

84. (1)   Unless the conservation of the drug or precursor chemical is essential for the proceedings, a court shall order the immediate destruction of the drug or precursor chemical.

(2)   Drugs or precursor chemicals that are usable in the pharmaceutical industry or another industry, depending on the nature of the substance may be disposed of by their supply to a public or private body authorised to utilise or export them.

(3)   If the conservation of a drug or precursor chemicals is deemed essential for the proceedings, their disposal or destruction shall be carried out as soon as the decision ordering their confiscation becomes final.

(4)   Any cases of disposal and destruction shall be certified by a report stating precisely which sealed containers have been disposed of or destroyed and the labels on the containers or the particulars entered on their wrappings, if any, shall be annexed to the report, which shall be signed by all the persons who took part in, or were present at, the disposal or destruction.

Mutual legal assistance

85.   The Mutual Legal Assistance in Criminal Matters Act applies to offences under this Act, except where the provisions of that Act are inconsistent with this Act.

Sentence for previous offenders

86.   A person convicted on a second or subsequent offence for trafficking is liable to imprisonment for a term of not less than ten years.

Extraditable offences

87.   An offence under this Act shall be deemed to be an extraditable offence for the purposes of the Extradition Act.

Rules

88.   The Commission may, by statutory instrument, make Rules for the —
    (a)   appointment and termination of appointment of staff of the Commission;
    (b)   disciplinary control of persons holding or acting in any office; and
    (c)   practice and procedure of the Commission in the exercise of its functions under this Act.

Regulations

89.   (1)   The Minister may, on the recommendation of the Commission, make Regulations for the better carrying out of the provisions of this Act.
    (2)   Despite the generality of subsection (1), the Regulations made under subsection (2) may provide for—
        (a)   the prevention of the commission of offences under this Act;
        (b)   the amendment of the Schedules;
        (c)   the procedure for lodging and dealing with complaints;
        (d)   the procedure for declaration of interest and assets by the Director-General, Deputy Director-General and officers of the Commission;
        (e)   anti-trafficking strategies in private and public bodies and special measures for children and youths;
        (f)   the form of oaths to be declared under this Act;
        (g)   the establishment, composition, tenure, procedure and any other matters in respect of committees;
        (h)   the establishment and management of treatment and rehabilitation centres; and
        (i)   generally, the carrying into effect of the purposes of this Act.

Repeal of Cap 96

90.   The Narcotic Drugs and Psychotropic Substances Act, 1993, is repealed.

Savings and transitional provisions

91.   (1)   The Director-General under the repealed Act shall continue to be an officer or employee of the Commission, as if appointed or employed under this Act.
    (2)   The service of members of staff of the Commission under the repealed Act shall be treated as continuous service.

(3)   Nothing in this Act affects the rights and liabilities of any person employed or appointed by the Commission before the commencement date.

SCHEDULES

FIRST SCHEDULE
(Sections 3 (2) and 5 (4))

ADMINISTRATION OF COMMISSION AND STAFF BOARD

PART I
STAFF BOARD OF COMMISSION

Tenure of office of member Committees

1.   A member of the Staff Board shall hold office for a term of two years and may be reappointed for a further term of two years.

Committees

2.   (1)   The Staff Board may, for the purpose of performing its functions under this Act, establish committees as it considers necessary and delegate to any of those committees' functions that the Staff Board considers fit.

      (2)   Subject to any specific or general direction of the Board, a committee may regulate its own procedure.

Disclosure of interest

3.   (1)   A person who is present at a meeting of the Staff Board or any committee at which any matter is the subject of consideration, and in which matter that person or that person's relative or associate is directly or indirectly interested in a private capacity shall, as soon as is practicable after the commencement of the meeting, declare such interest and shall not, unless the Staff Board or the committee otherwise directs, take part in any consideration or discussion of, or vote on any question relating to that matter.

      (2)   A disclosure of interest made under subparagraph (1) shall be recorded in the minutes of the meeting at which it is made.

Prohibition of publication or disclosure of information to unauthorised persons

4.   (1)   A person shall not, without the consent, in writing, given by or on behalf of the Committee, otherwise than in the course of the duties of that person, publish or disclose to any other person, the contents of any document, communication or information, which relates to, or which has come to the knowledge of that person in the course of that person's duties under this Act.

      (2)   A person who contravenes subsection (1) commits an offence and is liable, on conviction, to a fine not exceeding two hundred thousand penalty units or to imprisonment for a term not exceeding two years, or to both.

Immunity

5.   An action or other proceeding shall not lie or be instituted against a member of the Staff Board, a member of a committee of the Staff Board or a member of staff of the Staff Board for or in respect of an act or thing done or omitted to be done in good faith in the exercise or performance of any of the powers, functions or duties conferred under this Act.

PART II
FINANCIAL PROVISIONS

Funds of Commission

6. (1) The funds of the Commission consists of monies as may —
        (a) be appropriated to the Commission by Parliament;
        (b) be paid to the Commission by way of grants or donations; and
        (c) otherwise vest in or accrue to the Commission.
    (2) The Commission may, subject to the approval of the Minister responsible for finance —
        (a) accept monies by way of grants or donations from any source within or outside Zambia; and
        (b) raise by way of loans or otherwise, such monies as it may require for the performance of the Commission's functions.
    (3) There shall be paid from the funds of the Commission —
        (a) the emoluments of the staff of the Commission;
        (b) such reasonable travelling and other allowances for the members of the staff at rates that the Emoluments Commission may, on the recommendation of the Minister, determine; and
        (c) any other expenses incurred by the Commission in the performance of its functions under this Act.
    (4) The Commission may, subject to the approval of the Minister, invest in a manner that it considers appropriate funds of the Commission which it does not immediately require for the discharge of its functions.

Financial year

7. The financial year of the Commission shall be a period of twelve months ending on 31st December in each year.

Accounts and audit

8. (1) The Commission shall cause to be kept proper books of account and other records relating to its accounts.
    (2) The accounts of the Commission shall be audited annually by the Auditor-General or an auditor appointed by the Auditor General.
    (3) The Auditor-General's fees shall be paid by the Commission.

Annual report

9. (1) As soon as practicable, but not later than ninety days after the end of the financial year, the Commission shall submit to the Minister a report concerning its activities during that financial year.
    (2) The report referred to in subparagraph (1) shall include information on the financial affairs of the Commission and there shall be appended to that report —
        (a) an audited statement of financial position;
        (b) an audited statement of comprehensive income; and
        (c) such other information as the President may require.
    (3) The Minister shall, not later than seven days after the first sitting of the National Assembly next after receipt of the report referred to in subparagraph (1), lay the report before the National Assembly.

SECOND SCHEDULE
(Section 2 and 16)

Narcotic Drugs
- Acetorphine
- Acetyl alpha methyl fentanyl
- Alphacetylmethadol

- Alpha methylfentanyl
- Acetyldihydrocodeine
- Acetylmethadol
- Alfentanil
- Allylprodine
- Alphameprodine
- Alphamethadol
- Alphamethylthiofentanyl
- Alphaprodine
- Anileridine
- Beta hydroxyfentanyl
- Beta hydroxy methyl 3 fentantayl
- Benzethidine
- Benzylmorphine
- Betacetylmethadol
- Betameprodine
- Betamethadol
- Betaprodine
- Bezitramide
- Coca (leaf)
- Cocaine
- Clonitazene
- Codeine
- Codoxime
- Concentrate of poppy straw
- Desomorphine
- Dextromoramide
- Dextropropoxyphene
- Diampromide
- Diethylthiambutene
- Difenoxin
- Dihydrocodeine
- Dihydroetorphine
- Dihydromorphine
- Dimenoxadol
- Dimepheptanol
- Dimethylthiambutene
- Dioxaphetyl butyrate
- Diphenoxylate
- Dipipanone
- Drotebanol
- Ecgonine, its esters and derivatives
- Ethylmethylthiambutene
- Ethylmorphine
- Etonitazene
- Etorphine
- Etoxeridine
- Fentanyl
- Furethidine
- Heroin
- Hydrocodone
- Hydromorphinol
- Hydromorphone
- Hydroxypethidine
- Isomethadone
- Ketobemidone
- Levomethorphan
- Levomoramide
- Levophenacylmorphan

- Levorphanol
- Metazocine
- Methadone
- Methadone intermediate (4 cyano 2 dimethylamino 4, 4 diphenylbutane)
- Methyldesorphine
- Methyldihydromorphine
- Methyl 3 fentanyl
- Methyl 3 thio fentanyl
- Metopon
- Moramide
- Morpheridine
- Morphine
- Morphine methobromide
- MPPP
- Para fluorofentanyl
- PEPAP
- Thiofentanyl and
- Other pentavalent nitrogen morphine Derivatives
- Morphine N oxide
- Myrophine
- Nicocodine
- Nicodicodine
- Nicomorphine
- Norcodeine
- Noracymethadol
- Norlevorphanol
- Normethadone
- Normorphine
- Norpipanone
- Opium
- Oripavine
- Oxycodone
- Oxymorphone
- Pethidine
- Pethidine intermediate A (4 cyano 1 methyl 4 phenyl piperidine)
- Pethidine intermediate B (4 phenylpiperidine 4 carboxylic acid ethyl ester)
- Pethidine intermediate C (1 methyl 4 phenylpiperidine-4 carboxylic acid)
- Phenadoxone
- Phenampromide
- Phenazocine
- Phenomorphan
- Phenoperidine
- Pholcodine
- Piminodine
- Piritramide
- Proheptazine
- Properidine
- Propiram
- Racemethorphan
- Racemoramide
- Racemorphan
- Remifentanil
- Sufentanil
- Thebacon
- Thebaine
- Tilidine
- Trimeperidine

THIRD SCHEDULE
(Section 2 and 16)

Psychotropic Substances
 - Allobarbital
 - Alprazolam
 - Aminorex
 - Amobarbital
 - Amphetamine
 - Amphepramone
 - Barbital
 - Benzphetamine
 - Brolamphetamine
 - Bromazepam
 - Brotizolam
 - Buprenorphine
 - Butalbital
 - Butobarbital
 - Camazepam
 - Cathine
 - Cathinone
 - Chlordiazepoxide
 - Clobazam
 - Clonazepam
 - Clorazepate
 - Clotiazepam
 - Cloxazolam
 - Cyclobarbital
 - Delorazepam
- DET
- DMA
- DMHP
- DMT
 - Dexamphetamine
 - Diazepam
- DOET
Substances
 - Estazolam
 - Etizolam
 - Ethchlorvynol
 - Ethinamate
 - Etilamphetamine
 - Eticyclidine
 - Ethyl loflazepate
 - Etryptamine
 - Fencamfamine
 - Fenetylline
 - Fenproporex
 - Flualprazolam
 - Fludiazepam
 - Flurazepam
 - Flunitrazepam
 - Glutethimide
 - Halazepam
 - Haloxazolam
 - Ketazolam
 - Levamphetamine
 - Loprazolam
 - Lorazepam
 - Lormetazepam

- (+)-Lysergide
- Mazindol
- Mecloqualone
- Medazepam
- MDA
- MDMA
- Mefenorex
- MMDA
- Meprobamate
- Mescaline
- Methyl-4-aminorex
- Mesocarb
- Methcathinone
- Methamphetamine
- Methamphetamine racemate
- Methaqualone

350 No. 35 of 2021] Narcotic Drugs and Psychotropic
Substances

- Methylphenidate
- Methylpheno barbital
- Methylprylon
- Midazolam
- N-ethyl MDA
- N-hydroxy MDA
- Nimetazepam
- Nitrazepam
- Nordazepam
- Oxazepam
- Oxazolam
- Parahexyl
- Pemoline
- PMA
- Pentazocine
- Pentobarbital
- phenazepam
- Phencyclidine
- Phendimetrazine
- Phenmetrazine
- Phenobarbital or Phenobarbitone
- Phentermine
- Pinazepam
- Pipradrol
- Prazepam
- Products of Cannabis containing more than 0.3 percent Delta-9-
Tetrahydrocannabino, (THC)
(i) Herbal products known as Marijuana;
(ii) Cannabis resins or hashish cake;
(iii) Cannabis oil or hashish oil; and
(iv) any other cannabis products
- Psilocine, psilotsin
- Psilocybine
- Pyrovalerone
- Rolicyclidine
- Secobarbital
- STP, DOM
- Temazepam
- TMA

Narcotic Drugs and Psychotropic [No. 35 of 2021 351
Substances

- Tenamphetamine
- Tenocyclidine
- Tetrahydrocannabinol
- Tetrazepam
- Triazolam
- Vinylbital
- Zipeprol
- The isomers, unless specifically excepted, of the drugs in these
Schedules whenever the existence of such isomers is possible within
the specific chemical designation;
- The esters and ethers, of the drugs in these Schedules whenever the
existence of such esters or ethers is possible.
The salts of the drugs listed in these Schedules, including the salts of
esters, ethers and isomers as provided above whenever the existence
of such salts is.

FOURTH SCHEDULE
(Section 26(1))
PREPARATIONS

Any compound, mixture, or preparation containing any of the following limited quantities of narcotic drugs, which shall include one or more non-narcotic active medicinal ingredients in sufficient proportion to confer on the compound, mixture, or preparation valuable medicinal qualities other than those possessed by the narcotic drug alone:

(1) Not more than 200 milligrams of codeine per 100 milliliters or per 100 grams.
(2) Not more than 100 milligrams of dihydrocodeine per 100 milliliters or per 100 grams.
(3 Not more than 100 milligrams of ethylmorphine per 100 milliliters or per 100 grams.
(4) Not more than 2.5 milligrams of diphenoxylate and not less than 25 micrograms of atropine sulfate per dosage unit.
(5) Not more than 100 milligrams of opium per 100 milliliters or per 100 grams.

FIFTH SCHEDULE
(Section 2 and 16)
PRECURSOR CHEMICALS

- The following substances, designated by their international nonproprietary names used in the international conventions in force;
- The salts of these substances, whenever the existence of such salts is possible, with the exception of sulphuric acid and hydrochloric acid.

DIVISION I
(Table I of the 1988 Convention)

Ephedrine N-acetylanthranilic acid
Ergometrine Isosafrole
Ergotamine 3, 4 methylenedioxyphenyl
Lysergic acid 2 propanone
1-phenyl-2-propanone Piperonal
Pseudoephedrine Safrole

DIVISION II

(Table II of the 1988 Convention)
Acetic anhydride Hydrochloric acid
Acetone Methyl ethyl ketone
Anthranilic acid Potassium Permanganate
Ethyl ether Sulphuric acid
Phenylacetic acid Toluene
Piperidine

GOVERNMENT OF ZAMBIA
ACT
No. 12 of 2022
Date of Assent: 9th August, 2022

An Act to reform and consolidate the law relating to children; provide for parental responsibility, custody, maintenance, guardianship, foster care, adoption, care and protection of children; provide for the grant of legal aid to, and establish procedures for the treatment of, children in conflict with the law; provide for the making of social welfare reports in respect of a child in conflict with the law; establish diversion and alternative correctional programmes and promote the rehabilitation of a child in conflict with the law through programmes to facilitate restorative justice and compliance with laws; provide for the protection of a child victim and child witness in investigative and judicial processes; provide for the probation of a child in conflict with the law and provision of probation services; provide for the development of treatment programmes, early intervention services and programmes to combat crime and prevent further offending; limit the negative effects of confinement by minimising the impact of a finding of guilty on the family of a child in conflict with the law and facilitate the reintegration of the child in conflict with the law into society; provide for the establishment of child approved centres and child reformatory centres; provide for the regulation of child care facilities; provide for child safeguarding; domesticate the Convention on the Rights of the Child, the African Charter on the Rights and Welfare of the Child, the Convention on Protection of Children and Cooperation in Respect of Inter-Country Adoption and the Convention on the Civil Aspects of International Child Abduction; repeal the Legitimacy Act, 1929, the Adoption Act, 1956, the Juveniles Act,1956 and the Affiliation and Maintenance of Children Act, 1995 and provide for matters connected with, or incidental to, the foregoing.

[11th August, 2022]

Enactment

ENACTED by the Parliament of Zambia.

PART I
PRELIMINARY PROVISIONS

This Act may be cited as the Children's Code Act, 2022.

Age of criminal responsibility of child

45.   A child is not criminally liable for an act or omission except as provided under the Penal Code.

Rights of child during apprehension

46.   (1)   A child has a right to privacy and protection of the child's identity from exposure by the media —
      (a)   during an apprehension or arrest;
      (b)   during an investigation of an offence or court proceedings;
      (c)   while serving an order of the court; and
      (d)   whilst in custody.

(2)   A child has the right to remain silent during an apprehension, arrest, an investigation of an offence or court proceedings, or whilst in custody and shall be informed of the right to remain silent when apprehended or arrested.

(3)   A person shall not release any information for publication that is likely to lead to the identification of a child in the course of an apprehension or arrest while in custody, during an investigation of an offence or court proceedings, and while serving an order of the court.

(4)   A person who contravenes subsection (3) commits an offence and is liable, on conviction, to a fine not exceeding three hundred thousand penalty units or to imprisonment for a term not exceeding three years, or to both.

Apprehension of child

47. (1)   A law enforcement officer or other person shall, in apprehending a child, touch or confine the child to be apprehended if the child does not submit to the apprehension by word or action.

(2)   A law enforcement officer shall not be in uniform or carry a firearm when apprehending a child at that child's dwelling home.

(3)   Despite subsection (2), a law enforcement officer shall—

(a)   wear a uniform and carry a firearm where—

(i)   the child or a person at a child's dwelling home posses a danger to the law enforcement officer, the child or any other person at the child's dwelling home; or

(ii)   the law enforcement officer is aware that there is an imminent threat at the child's dwelling home and the wearing of a uniform and the possession of a firearm is necessary for the protection and safety of persons within the vicinity of the child's dwelling home; and

(b)   on request by a child, parent, guardian or person having parental responsibility for the child, provide an identification and which shall be prima facie evidence that the person is a law enforcement officer.

(4)   A law enforcement officer or other person may, where a child forcibly resists a apprehension or attempts to evade the apprehension, use reasonable means to effect the apprehension.

Apprehension by person

48. (1)   Subject to section 45 and the Criminal Procedure Code, a person may, without warrant, apprehend a child who, in the presence of that person, commits an offence or the child is reasonably suspected to have committed an offence.

(2)   A person who apprehends a child shall immediately hand over the child to the nearest police station.

Apprehension and arrest by law enforcement officer

49. (1)   A law enforcement officer may apprehend a child with or without a warrant.

(2)   A law enforcement officer may apprehend a child, without a warrant, if the law enforcement officer has reasonable grounds to suspect that the child—

(a)   has committed an offence;

(b)   is about to commit an offence where—

(i)   there is no other way of preventing the commission of the offence; or

(ii)   the surroundings indicate that an offence is likely to be committed.

(c)   commits an offence in the presence of the law enforcement officer;

(d)   obstructs the law enforcement officer in the execution of law enforcement duties;

(e)   escapes or attempts to escape from lawful custody; or

(f)   is in possession of an implement adapted or intended to be used for the unlawful entry into a building without reasonable explanation for the possession of that implement.

(3)   An arrest of a child by a law enforcement officer shall be made with due regard to the dignity and well-being of the child and in the presence of a parent, guardian, close relative of the child, person having parental responsibility for the child or a child welfare inspector.

Information of arrest of child

50. (1)   A child welfare inspector shall, within forty-eight hours, where an arrest of a child is made in the presence of a child welfare inspector as provided under section 49 (3) and the child's parent, guardian, close relative of the child or person having parental responsibility for the child cannot be found, trace the parent, guardian or close relative of the child or the person having parental responsibility for the child.

(2)   A child welfare inspector shall, where a child welfare inspector cannot trace the parent, guardian, close relative of the child or the person having parental responsibility for the child, take responsibility of the child and place the child in a place of safety.

Issuance of warrant of arrest

51. A warrant for the arrest of a child shall be issued in accordance with the Criminal Procedure Code.

Notification of reason for arrest or substance of warrant

52. (1) A law enforcement officer effecting an arrest of a child shall, having regard to the age and maturity of the child, inform the child of the reason for the arrest.

(2) A law enforcement officer acting under the authority of the warrant shall, where an arrest is made under warrant and having regard to the age and maturity of the child, notify the child of the content of the warrant and exhibit a copy of the warrant to the child.

Search of arrested child

53. (1) A child may, where a child is arrested under section 48, be searched by a law enforcement officer in the presence of a child welfare inspector.

(2) A child shall be searched by a law enforcement officer of the same sex, and where a law enforcement officer of the same sex is not available, an adult of the same sex authorised by the law enforcement officer shall conduct the search.

(3) A law enforcement officer to whom the child is handed over to may take the articles of the child, other than clothing into safe custody.

(4) A search of a child shall be made with decency.

(5) The right to search shall not include the right to examine the private parts of the child, except where the circumstances of the offence warrant the examination of the private parts of the child, and that examination shall be carried out by a health practitioner.

(6) The examination referred to under subsection (5) shall be carried out in the presence of the child's parents, guardian or close relative, a person having parental responsibility for the child or a child welfare inspector, unless the child decides otherwise.

(7) Where a child is released on recognisance or on police bond, a law enforcement officer shall search the child or any suspected premises if the law enforcement officer has reasonable grounds to believe that the child is in possession of—

(a) stolen articles;

(b) instruments of violence;

(c) tools connected with the kind of offence the child is alleged to have committed and is charged with; or

(d) other articles which may provide evidence against the child with regard to the offence that the child is alleged to have committed.

Caution by law enforcement officer

54. (1) A law enforcement officer may, where it is in the best interests of the child, give an informal caution for a minor offence instead of arresting a child.

(2) An informal caution shall be a verbal warning of which no record shall be required to be kept.

(3) A law enforcement officer may give a formal caution to a child, with or without conditions, on the recommendation of a child welfare inspector.

(4) A formal caution to a child shall be given in private in the presence of a parent, guardian, close relative of the child or person having parental responsibility for the child.

(5) A law enforcement officer shall give a formal caution to a child in the presence of a child welfare inspector if the parent, guardian, close relative of the child or the person having parental responsibility for the child is absent or cannot be found by the law enforcement officer.

(6) A law enforcement agency shall cause a record of formal cautions to be kept in a register for the purpose of that law enforcement agency.

(7) A register of formal cautions referred to in subsection (6) shall be made available to a child welfare inspector for the purposes of this Act.

(8) A record of a formal caution shall be expunged after a period of five years from the date on which the caution was entered in the register.

Interview of child

55. (1) A child shall only be questioned or interviewed by a law enforcement officer in relation to an alleged offence if a parent, guardian, child welfare inspector, legal representative, close relative of the child or the person having parental responsibility for the child is present at the questioning or interview.

    (2) A law enforcement officer shall, if the law enforcement officer fails to contact a child's parent, guardian, legal representative, close relative of the child or the person having parental responsibility for the child to be present at the questioning or interview of the child, request the presence of a child welfare inspector.

    (3) Despite subsection (1), where the law enforcement officer considers that it is not in the best interests of a child for the child's parent, guardian, legal representative, close relative of the child or the person having parental responsibility for the child to be present, the law enforcement officer shall arrange for a child welfare inspector to be present at the interview.

Recognisance

56. (1) A child under arrest shall be released by a law enforcement officer on the child's own recognisance or a recognisance entered into by the child's parent, guardian, close relative of the child or the person having parental responsibility for the child, unless the offence which the child is accused of is a serious offence.

    (2) A law enforcement officer shall, where a child is not released on recognisance, seek an order from a court to place the child in a place of safety.

    (3) A court shall make an order to place a child in a place of safety within forty-eight hours after the arrest of the child.

Custody of child

57. (1) A child shall not be taken into custody —
        (a) except as a measure of last resort; or
        (b) for a period of more than forty-eight hours.

    (2) A child in custody at a police station has a right to—
        (a) food;
        (b) medical attention, if required;
        (c) reasonable visits from the child's parent, guardian, legal representative, close relative of the child or the person having parental responsibility for the child; and
        (d) any other condition reasonably required for the welfare of the child.

    (3) A law enforcement officer shall, where a child is not released on recognisance under section 56 or within forty-eight hours after the child is arrested, make arrangements to place the child in custody in a part of a police station designated for children or in a part of a police station which is separate from the area where adults are detained.

    (4) A child shall not be allowed to associate with a person other than the child's parent, guardian, close relative of the child, child welfare inspector, legal representative, the person having parental responsibility for the child or a police officer while in custody at a police station or while being transported to a child transit centre or place of safety.

    (5) A child shall be under the care of an adult of the same sex while in custody in a police station or while being transported to a child transit centre or place of safety.

    (6) Male children in custody shall be held separately from female children.

PART VII
COURT PROCEEDINGS

Constitution of juvenile court

65. A subordinate court sitting for the purposes of hearing a charge against a child or for any other purpose relating to a child shall constitute itself as a juvenile court.

Jurisdiction of juvenile court

66. (1) A juvenile court shall —
        (a) conduct civil proceedings on matters set out under Parts IV, VI, IX, X, XI and XII;

        (b) hear any charge against a child, other than a charge—
            (i) of murder or treason;
            (ii) of a class of offences specified under the Criminal Procedure Code to be tried by the High Court; or
            (iii) in which the child is charged together with an adult; and
        (c) exercise any other jurisdiction conferred by this Act or any other written law.

(2) A juvenile court shall, where on the trial of a person the question of age of the accused person arises, at the instance of the defence or otherwise, inquire into and determine the question as soon as it arises.

(3) An appeal against the decision of a juvenile court shall lie with the Children's Court.

Jurisdiction of Children's Court

67. (1) A Children's Court shall—
        (a) hear a charge against a child—
            (i) of murder or treason;
            (ii) of a class of offences specified under the Criminal Procedure Code to be tried by the High Court;
            (iii) in which the child is charged together with an adult;
        (b) hear an appeal against a decision of a juvenile court;
        (c) conduct civil proceedings on matters set out under Parts XIII and XIV; and
        (d) exercise any other jurisdiction conferred by this Act or any other written law.

(2) A charge against a child for an offence which if committed by an adult would be punishable by [imprisonmemnt for life][20] shall be heard by a Children's Court.

(3) An appeal against the decision of the Children's Court shall lie with the Court of Appeal.

(4) Where any conviction or sentence made or passed by a court, other than a juvenile court, is appealed against or is brought before a Children's Court for confirmation or revision and it appears that the person convicted was at the time of the commission of the offence a child, the Children's Court may substitute for the conviction, a finding of guilty and substitute for the sentence, an order.

Sittings of juvenile court or Children's Court

68. (1) A juvenile court or Children's Court shall sit in a different building or room from that in which sittings of other courts are held, or at different times or dates from those on which sittings of other courts are held.

(2) A person shall not be present at a sitting of a juvenile court or Children's Court, except—
        (a) a member or officer of the juvenile court or Children's Court;
        (b) a party to the case before the juvenile court or Children's Court;
        (c) a party's legal representative;
        (d) a witness;
        (e) a parent, guardian or person having parental responsibility for the child;
        (f) a person that the juvenile court or Children's Court may authorise to be present; and
        (g) any other person directly concerned with the case.

(3) Subject to section 78 (4) (d), the juvenile court or Children's Court may, where in any proceedings in relation to an offence against or by a child, or any conduct contrary to decency or morality, a person who, in the opinion of a juvenile court or Children's Court, is a child and is called as a witness, direct that all or any persons, who are not members or officers of the juvenile court or Children's Court, or parties to the case or the parties lega representatives, be excluded from the juvenile court or Children's Court.

(4) Proceedings in a juvenile court or Children's Court shall be informal and a law enforcement officer shall not be in uniform or carry a firearm.

(5) A restraint shall only be used on a child if there are exceptional circumstances which warrant the use of the restraint for the safety of any person.

Prohibition of other courts hearing charge or matter against child

69. (1) A court, other than a juvenile court or Children's Court, shall not hear any charge against a child or dispose of any matter which affects a person who appears to the court to be a child if it determines that—

---

[20] See Acts No 22 & 23 of 2022.

        (a)   the charge or matter is one in which jurisdiction is conferred on the juvenile court or Children's Court; or

        (b)   a juvenile court or Children's Court is constituted for the place, district or area concerned.

(2)   A court shall, where the court makes a determination under subsection (1), make an order transferring the charge or matter to a juvenile court or Children's court.

(3)   Despite subsection (1), where a juvenile court or Children's Court is not constituted for a place, district or area concerned, a court of competent jurisdiction may deal with an application for bail concerning a child if it is in the best interests of the child to do so.

(4)   A court shall, where it refuses to grant bail, record the reasons for the refusal and inform the applicant of the right to apply for bail to—

        (a)   the Children's Court where bail is denied in a juvenile court; or

        (b)   the Court of Appeal where bail is denied in the Children's Court.

(5)   A court shall, where the court, other than a juvenile court or Children's Court, hears a charge against a child, apply the provisions of this Act relating to the safeguards to be accorded to a child in conflict with the law.

Remission of child to Children's Court

70. (1)   Where a child appears before a court of competent jurisdiction, other than the Children's Court, on a charge made jointly against the child and an adult, that court shall remit the case to the Children's Court for hearing and determination.

(2)   A court by which an order remitting a case to the Children's Court is made under this section—

        (a)   may give direction that the court considers necessary with respect to the custody of the child or for the release of the child on bail until the child can be brought before the Children's Court; and

        (b)   shall cause to be transmitted to the registrar of the Children's Court a certificate setting out the nature of the offence.

Presumption and determination of age

71. (1)   Where a person, whether charged with an offence or not, is brought before a court and it appears to the court that the person is a child or the person alleges that the person is a child, the court shall make an inquiry as to the age of that person.

(2)   In the absence of a birth certificate or an affidavit sworn for the purpose of certifying a person's date of birth, a certificate signed by a health practitioner as to the age of a person below nineteen years of age shall be evidence of that age before a court without proof of signature, unless the court directs otherwise.

(3)   An order of a court shall not be invalidated by any subsequent proof that the age of the child has not been correctly stated to the court and the age presumed or declared by the court to be the age of the child shall be deemed to be the true age for the purpose of any proceeding under this Act.

(4)   Despite subsections (3), a court may vary its order under this section on subsequent proof that the age of the child has not been correctly stated to the court.

Guarantees to child in conflict with the law

72. (1)   A child in conflict with the law shall—

        (a)   be informed promptly and directly of the charges against that child;

        (b)   have the matter determined without delay;

        (c)   not be compelled to give testimony or to confess guilt;

        (d)   have free assistance of an interpreter if the child cannot understand or speak the language used;

        (e)   if a finding of guilty is made, have the decision and any measures imposed in consequence thereof reviewed by a higher court;

        (f)   have the child's privacy fully respected at all stages of the proceedings; and

        (g)   if that child has a disability, be given special care and be treated with the same dignity as a child without disability.

(2)   A child in conflict with the law before a court is entitled to legal representation.

(3)   The Legal Aid Board shall provide legal aid services where a child cannot afford legal representation of choice.

(4)   A court may, where a child is brought before the court in proceedings under this Act or any other written law and the child is not represented, cause the issuance of a certificate of legal aid or cause the child to be assisted by a child welfare inspector.

(5)   Any expenses incurred in relation to the legal representation of a child under subsection (3) shall be defrayed out of monies appropriated by Parliament.

Appearance of child in a juvenile court or children's Court and bail

73. (1)   A juvenile court or Children's Court shall, at the commencement of proceedings in a juvenile court or Children's Court inform the child in a language that the child understands of the following rights:

       (a)   the right to have the child's parent, guardian, probation officer or child welfare inspector or the person having parental responsibility for the child present at the proceedings;

       (b)   the right to legal representation; and

       (c)   the right to legal aid.

(2)   Where a child appears before a juvenile court or Children's Court charged with an offence, the court shall enquire into the case and, unless there is a serious danger to the child or the community, release the child on bail.

(3)   A child granted bail shall be released from custody after giving security or accepting specified conditions.

(4)   A juvenile court or Children's Court may grant bail on the child's own undertaking or with sureties from the child's parent, guardian or person having parental responsibility for the child.

(5)   The amount of the bail shall be fixed with due regard to the circumstances of the case and shall not be unreasonable or excessive.

Procedure in court

74. (1)   A charge sheet or information shall be translated in a language that a child in conflict with the law understands.

(2)   A juvenile court or Children's Court shall request a child in conflict with the law to indicate to the juvenile court or Children's Court whether or not the child admits the offence in the charge sheet or information.

(3)   A charge may be withdrawn at any stage of the proceedings and—

       (a)   if the charge is withdrawn before the child is put on defence, the child shall be discharged; or

       (b)   if the charge is withdrawn after the child has made a defence, that child shall be acquitted.

(4)   The discharge of a child under subsection (3)(a) shall not be a bar to subsequent proceedings against the child on the same facts.

(5)   If it appears to the court that a prima facie case is established, the evidence of any witness for the defence shall be heard and the child shall have a right to remain silent or be allowed to give evidence or make a statement.

(6)   A child shall, where a court is satisfied that the offence is proven against a child, request the child to say anything in mitigation of the penalty or otherwise before sentencing.

(7)   Subject to subsection (6), a court shall before deciding on how to deal with the child, where practicable, obtain information in relation to the child's general conduct, home surroundings, school record, and medical history that may assist the court to deal with the case in the best interests of the child, and the court may ask the child any question arising out of the information obtained.

Remand of apprehended child during trial

75. (1)   A juvenile court or Children's Court may, where a child is not released on bail, make an order to remand the child to a child transit centre situated within a reasonable distance from a juvenile court or Children's Court.

(2)   An order for remand made under subsection (1) shall be delivered with the child to the person who is vested with the care of the child and shall be sufficient authority for the detention of the child by that person.

(3)   A child under a remand order shall be deemed to be in legal custody while on remand and while being conveyed to or from the child transit centre, and if the child escapes, the child may be apprehended without warrant.

(4)   The maximum period of a remand warrant shall be seven days, and the remand warrant shall not be renewed without the appearance of the child at the hearing.

(5)   The total period of remand of a child shall not exceed ninety days except in the case of an offence punishable by death, where the period of remand shall not exceed one hundred and eighty days.

(6)   A child shall not be placed on remand in an adult prison or correctional centre.

(7)   A female child shall not be remanded in the same child transit centre at the same time with a male child.

(8)   A child on remand shall be supervised only by a person of the same sex as the child.

(9)   A child on remand who is ill, or who complains of illness, shall be examined and treated promptly by a health practitioner.

(10) A police officer or probation officer shall be responsible for transporting a child between a juvenile court or Children's Court and the child transit centre, and that police officer or probation officer shall be of the same sex as the child.

Social welfare report of child

76. (1)   A juvenile court or Children's Court shall, where a child is charged with an offence, order a child welfare inspector to submit a social welfare report to the juvenile court or Children's Court and that juvenile court or Children's Court shall take the social welfare report into account in the making of an order.

(2)   A child welfare inspector shall, in preparing the social welfare report under subsection (1), visit the home of the child.

(3)   A social welfare report shall include particulars on the background of the child, the present circumstances of the child, the conditions under which the offence was committed and recommendations for an order.

(4)   A social welfare report may include a recommendation that the matter before a juvenile court or Children's Court be dealt with under the diversion procedures under Part VI.

(5)   The social welfare report referred to in this section is confidential and shall not be accessed by any other person except an officer of the juvenile court or Children's Court.

(6)   A juvenile court or Children's Court shall—

(a)   inform the child in relation to whom a social welfare report is made about the contents of the social welfare report; and

(b)   avail a copy of the social welfare report to the child in respect of whom it is made or the child's legal representative.

(7)   A juvenile court or Children's Court may request an oral report from a child welfare inspector in addition to a social welfare report.

(8)   A juvenile court or Children's Court shall, where it rejects the recommendations given in a social welfare report, give written reasons for the rejection and make an alternative order as the uvenile court or Children's Court considers necessary in the best interests of the child.

Parent, guardian to give security

77. (1)   A juvenile court or Children's Court may, where a child is charged with an offence, order the child's parent, guardian or the person having parental responsibility for the child to give security to the juvenile court or Children's Court for the good behaviour of the child.

(2)   Where a juvenile court or Children's Court determines that a charge against a child is proved, it may make an order against the child's parent, guardian or person having parental responsibility for the child for the payment of damages or costs, or require the parent, guardian or person having parental responsibility for the child to give security for good behaviour, without proceeding to make an order against the child.

(3)   A juvenile court or Children's Court may make an order under subsection (2) against a child's parent, guardian or person having parental responsibility for the child who has been asked to attend the juvenile court or Children's Court but has failed to do so, but shall not make the order without giving the parent, guardian or person having parental responsibility for the child an opportunity to be heard.

(4)   Any sums imposed and ordered to be paid under this section by the parent, guardian or person having parental responsibility for the child may be recovered by distress.

(5)   A juvenile court or Children's Court shall not exercise the powers conferred under this section in a discriminatory manner.

(6)   A parent, guardian or person having parental responsibility for the child may appeal against an order made under this section.

Evidence of child

78. (1)   Where, in any criminal or civil proceedings against a person, a child is called as a witness, the juvenile court or Children's Court shall receive the evidence, on oath, of the child if, in the opinion

of the juvenile court or Children's Court, the child possesses sufficient intelligence to justify the reception of the child's evidence, on oath, and understands the duty of speaking the truth.

(2)   If, in the opinion of the juvenile court or Children's Court, the child does not possess sufficient intelligence to justify the reception of the child's evidence, on oath, and does not understand the duty of speaking the truth, the child may give —

    (a)   unsworn evidence that may be received as evidence in a juvenile court or Children's Court; or

    (b)   evidence through a child welfare inspector responsible for the child's case.

(3)   A child required to give evidence in a juvenile court or Children's Court shall be prepared to testify by a child welfare inspector or any other authorised officer.

(4)   A child that is giving evidence in a court shall —

    (a)   be questioned in an environment that is child friendly;

    (b)   be questioned in camera;

    (c)   be questioned in a manner that is proportional to the child's age and maturity of the child;

    (d)   not interact or be in the same room with a person the child is testifying against; and

    (e)   not be questioned more than twice.

(5)   Subject to subsection (4) (d), a person the child is testifying against or that person's legal practitioner shall cross examine a child witness through —

    (a)   a child welfare inspector, an authorised officer or a child's next friend, acting as an intermediary; or

    (b)   the use of a video link.

(6)   The juvenile court or Children's Court shall —

    (a)   permit recorded pre-trial interviews with a child to be presented as evidence in lieu of a live testimony by a child; or

    (b)   request a report from a child welfare inspector or other authorised officer who has interviewed a child to be used as evidence.

(7)   Information about the previous sexual history of a child witness or child victim, or a delay between the alleged commission of the offence and the reporting of the offence shall not be presented as evidence before a juvenile court or Children's Court.

(8)   A child witness shall be protected from threats, intimidation, reprisal or any other form of victimisation prior to and when giving evidence before a juvenile court or Children's Court.

(9)   A juvenile court or Children's Court may, having regard to the nature and circumstances of the offence in question, require evidence presented before the juvenile court or Children's Court to be corroborated by some other material evidence.

Methods of dealing with child in conflict with law

79.   (1)   A juvenile court or Children's Court may deal with a child in one or more of the following ways:

    (a)   dismiss the case against the child or discharge the child;

    (b)   make a probation order in respect of the child;

    (c)   send the child to a child approved centre or child reformatory centre;

    (d)   commit the child to the care of a fit person or child care facility;

    (e)   in the case of a child who is a young person, order the young person to pay a fine, damages or costs;

    (f)   order the child's parent, guardian or person having parental responsibility for the child to pay a fine, damages or cost;

    (g)   order the child's parent, guardian or person having parental responsibility for the child to give security for the good behaviour of the child;

    (h)   make a restorative justice order in accordance with programmes established under section 84; or

    (i)   in any other manner that the juvenile court or Children's Court determines in the administration of justice.

(2)   A juvenile court or Children's Court shall, in making an order under subsection (1), take into consideration the ability of the young person, child's parent, guardian or a person having parental responsibility for the child to pay the fine, damages or costs before the order is made.

(3)   A child below the age of sixteen shall not be given a custodial order by a court.

(4)   A child who is aged sixteen to eighteen shall not be given a custodial order if the child can be suitably dealt with in any other manner.

(5)   A juvenile court or Children's Court shall not pronounce or record an order of death against a child.

(6)   A juvenile court or Children's Court shall not use the words "conviction" and "sentence" in relation to a child before the court and a reference in any written law to "conviction" and "sentence" shall not apply but the words "finding of guilty" or "order" shall be used.

(7)   A juvenile court or Children's Court shall expeditiously deal with the case of a child and if the case is not completed within six months of the child's first appearance before the court, the juvenile court or Children's Court may discharge the child immediately.

(8)   Nothing in this section shall be construed as restricting the power of a juvenile court or Children's Court to pass any order or a combination of orders which it is empowered to pass under this Act or any other written law in relation to a child.

Payment of fine by parent, guardian or person having parental responsibility

80. (1)   A juvenile court or Children's Court may, when dealing with a child on whom a fine, damages or costs may be imposed, order that the fine, damages or costs awarded be paid by the child's parent or guardian or person having parental responsibility for the child instead of the child, unless the juvenile court or Children's Court is satisfied that the child's parent or guardian or person having parental responsibility for the child —
    (a)   cannot be found; or
    (b)   has not contributed to the commission of the offence by neglecting to exercise due care for the child.

(2)   A juvenile court or Children's Court may exercise the power conferred under subsection (1) without imposing any other punishment.

General principles with regard to proceedings in a juvenile court or Children's Court

81. (1)   Subject to section 4, where a juvenile court or Children's Court is considering whether or not to make one or more orders under this Act with respect to a child, the juvenile court or the Children's Court shall only make the order or orders if it considers that doing so would be more beneficial to the welfare of the child than not making an order at all.

(2)   A juvenile court or Children's Court shall, in any proceedings in which the issue of the upbringing of a child arises, have regard to the general principle that any delay in determining the question is likely to be prejudicial to the welfare of the child.

(3)   A juvenile court or Children's Court shall, in considering whether or not to make an order with regard to a child, have regard to the best interests of a child referred to under section 3.

(4)   A juvenile court or Children's Court may, if it considers necessary for the determination of any matter in issue before it, of its own motion or on application, call any expert witness that it considers appropriate to provide assistance to the juvenile court or Children's Court, and the expense of that expert witness shall be determined by the juvenile court or Children's Court and shall be defrayed out of moneys appropriated by Parliament.

(5)   In any proceedings concerning a child, whether instituted under this Act or any other written law, a child's name, identity, home, last place of residence, school or the particulars of the child's parents, photograph, depiction or caricature of the child shall not be published or revealed in any publication, report or otherwise.

(6)   In this section, "report" includes a law report.

(7)   A person who contravenes subsection (5) commits an offence and is liable, on conviction, to a fine not exceeding fifty thousand penalty units or to imprisonment for a term not exceeding six months, or to both.

Presence of child welfare inspector or authorised officer

82. A juvenile court or Children's Court shall ensure that a child welfare inspector or any other authorised officer is present at all stages of the proceedings in a juvenile court or Children's Court to safe guard the interests of the child.

Reports

83. (1)   A juvenile court or Children's Court may, in considering a question with respect to a child under this Act, require a report to be presented to it, either oral or written as the juvenile court or the Children's Court may direct, by a person designated by that juvenile court or Children's Court on matters relating to the child that the juvenile court or Children's Court considers necessary.

(2)   A juvenile court or Children's Court may, in considering a report under this section, take into account–

(a) any statement contained in the report, or

(b) any evidence given in respect of the matters referred to in the report which is relevant to the question before the juvenile court or Children's Court.

PART X
AFFILIATION, STATUS OF CHILD, MAINTENCE AND CUSTODY

Division 1 - Affiliation Orders

Application by child's mother

116. A court may make an affiliation order on the application of a child's mother at any time after giving birth to a child, or on proof that the biological or putative father of the child has paid money for the child's maintenance.

Application by party to void marriage

117. A court may, on the application of a child's mother who has given birth to a child, make an affiliation order on proof that before the birth, the child's mother was a party to a marriage which would have been valid except for the fact that the child's mother or the other party were under the age at which either party might have legally contracted a marriage.

Application by child

118. A court may, on the application of a child, made through the child's next friend, make an affiliation order, subject to the limitations contained in this Act.

Corroboration of evidence

119. (1) A court shall, on the hearing of an application for an affiliation order, hear—
    (a) the evidence of the mother; and
    (b) any evidence tendered by or on behalf of the biological or putative father.

(2) A court shall not make an affiliation order unless the evidence of the mother or any other party is corroborated in some material particular by other evidence.

Order of unfitness for custody

120. Where a court makes an affiliation order, it may include in the order that either party to the proceedings is unfit to have the custody of a child.

(2) Where an order is made under this section and the party to whom the order relates is a parent of a child, that party shall not, on the death of the other parent, be entitled as of right to the custody or the guardianship of that child, except with the leave of the court.

(3) A court may vary or discharge an order made under this section or suspend any provision of the order temporarily and revive the operation of any provision so suspended.

GOVERNMENT OF ZAMBIA
ACT
No 13 of 2022
Date of Assent: 9th August, 2022
An Act to amend the Penal Code
[11th August, 2022

Enactment

ENACTED by the Parliament of Zambia.

1. This Act may be cited as the Penal Code (Amendment) Act, 2022, and shall be read as one with the Penal Code Act, in this Act referred to as the principal Act.
2. The principal Act is amended by the repeal of section 14 and the substitution therefor of the following:
14. A child under the age of twelve years is not criminally responsible for an act or omission.

GOVERNMENT OF ZAMBIA
ACT
No 22 of 2022
Date of Assent: 23rd December, 2022
An Act to amend the Criminal Procedure Code.
[27th December, 2022

Enactment

ENACTED by the Parliament of Zambia.

Short title

1.   This Act may be cited as the Criminal Procedure Code (Amendment) Act, 2022 and shall be read as one with the Criminal Procedure Code, in this Act referred to as the principal Act.

Amendment of section 9

2.   Section 9 (6) of the principal Act is amended by the deletion of the word "death" and the substitution therefor of the words "life imprisonment".

Amendment of section 33

3.   Section 33 (1) of the principal Act is amended by the deletion of the word "death" and the substitution therefor of the words "life imprisonment".

Amendment of section 160

4.   Section 160 of the principal Act is amended by the deletion of the words "death or" immediately after the words "punishable by".

Amendment of section 175

5.   Section 175 (1) of the principal Act is amended by the deletion of the word "death" and the substitution therefor of the words "life imprisonment".

Repeal of sections 303, 304, 305 and 306

6.   The principal Act is amended by the repeal of sections 303, 304, 305 and 306.

Amendment of section 307

7.   Section 307 of the principal Act is amended by the deletion of the words "not being a sentence of death".

Amendment of First Schedule

8.   The First Schedule to the principal Act is amended—
   (a)   under Division I relating to section 43, in the fourth column, by the deletion of the word "death" and the substitution therefor of the words "imprisonment for life";
   (b)   under Division I relating to section 58E, in the second, third and fourth column, by the deletion of the words "Defamation of President", "Ditto" and "Imprisonment for three years";
   (c)   under Division I relating to section 69, in the second, third and fourth column, by the deletion of the words "Defamation of President", "Ditto" and "Imprisonment for two years";
   (d)   under Division I relating to section 71, in the second, third and fourth column, by the deletion of the words "Defamation of foreign princes" "shall not arrest without warrant" and "Imprisonment for two years";
   (e)   under Division II relating to section 118 (1), in the first column, by the deletion of paragraph (a) and the substitution therefor of the following:
   (a)   if person rescued is under sentence of imprisonment for life or charged with offence punishable with imprisonment for life;
   (f)   under Division IV relating to section 201, in the fourth column, by the deletion of the word "death" and the substitution therefor of the words "imprisonment for life"; and

(g) under Division IX relating to section 391, in the first column, by the deletion of the word "death" and the substitution therefor of the words "life imprisonment".

Amendment of Fifth Schedule

9. The Fifth Schedule to the principal Act is amended by the deletion of the words "Any offence punishable by death" and the substitution therefor of the words "Any offence punishable with imprisonment for life".

GOVERNMENT OF ZAMBIA
ACT
No 23 of 2022
Date of Assent: 23rd December, 2022
An Act to amend the Penal Code.
[27th December, 2022]

Enactment

ENACTED by the Parliament of Zambia.

Short Title

1. This Act may be cited as the Penal Code (Amendment) Act, 2022.

Amendment of section 4

2. Section 4 of the principal Act is amended by the deletion of the definition of "felony" and the substitution therefor of the following:
    "felony" means an offence which is declared by this Act or any other written law to be a felony or, if not declared to be a misdemeanor, is punishable, without proof of previous conviction with life imprisonment or imprisonment with hard labour for three years or more or with life imprisonment;.

Amendment of section 24

3. Section 24 of the principal Act is amended by the —
    (a) deletion of paragraph (a); and
    (b) renumbering of paragraphs (b), (c), (d), (e), (f), (g), (h) and (i) as paragraphs (a), (b), (c), (d), (e), (f), (g) and (h), respectively.

Repeal of section 25

4. The principal Act is amended by the repeal of section 25.

Amendment of section 31

5. Section 31 of the principal Act is amended by the deletion of the words "not punishable with death" and the substitution therefor of the words "not punishable with life imprisonment".

Amendment of section 39

6. Section 39 (1) of the principal Act is amended by the deletion of the words "sentence of death" and the substitution therefor of the words "sentence of life imprisonment".

Amendment of section 40

7. Section 40 (1) of the principal Act is amended by the deletion of the words "if of death, fine" and the substitution therefor of the words "if of fine".

Amendment of section 43

8. Section 43 (1) of the principal Act is amended by the deletion of the words "suffer death" and the substitution therefor of the words "life imprisonment".

Amendment of section 63

9. Section 63 (a) of the principal Act is amended by the deletion of the word "death" and the substitution therefor of the words "life imprisonment".

Amendment of section 64

10. Section 64 (a) of the principal Act is amended by the—
    (a) deletion of subparagraph (ii);
    (b) renumbering of subparagraphs (iii), (iv), (v), (vi) and (vii) as subparagraphs (ii), (iii), (iv), (v), and (vi), respectively; and
    (c) insertion of the following new subparagraph immediately after subparagraph (vi): (vii) to commit any other offence; or.

Repeal of section 69

11. The principal Act is amended by the repeal of section 69.

Repeal of section 71

12. The principal Act is amended by the repeal of section 71.

Amendment of section 118

13. Section 118 (1) of the principal Act is amended by the deletion of paragraph (a) and the substitution therefor of the following:
    (a) is, if such last-named person is under sentence of imprisonment for life or charged with an offence punishable with imprisonment for life, guilty of a felony and is liable, on conviction, to imprisonment for life;.

Amendment of section 201

14. Section 201 of the principal Act is amended by the—
    (a) deletion of subsection (1) and the substitution therefor of the following:
    (1) A person convicted of murder shall be sentenced to life imprisonment or, where there are extenuating circumstances, a sentence other than life imprisonment.;
    (b) insertion of the following new subsection immediately after subsection (1):
    (2) An extenuating circumstance referred to under subsection (1) shall not apply to murder committed in the course of aggravated robbery with a firearm under section 294.; and
    (c) renumbering of subsection (2) as subsection (3).

Amendment of section 294

15. Section 294 (2) of the principal Act is amended by the deletion of the word "death" and the substitution therefor of the words "life imprisonment".

Amendment of section 297

16. Section 297 (1)(c)(i) of the principal Act is amended by the deletion of the words "death or".

Amendment of section 391

17. Section 391 of the principal Act is amended by the deletion of the words "death or" and the substitution therefor of the words "life imprisonment".

GOVERNMENT OF ZAMBIA

STATUTORY INSTRUMENT NO. [....] OF 2022

The High Court Act
(Cap 27, Volume 3, Laws of Zambia)

The [Proposed] High Court (Amendment) Rules, 2022

IN EXERCISE of the powers contained in sections forty-four and forty-five of the High Court Act, the following rules are hereby made:

Title
Cap 27

These Rules may be cited as the High Court (Amendment) Rules, 2022, and shall be read as one with High Court Rules, in these Rules referred to as the principal Rules.

Amendment
Of Order V

1.   The Principal Rules are amended in Order V by the insertion, immediately after rule 31 of the following new rules

VI- Expert Evidence

Party expert
Witness 32

1,   In this rule, the term "party expert witness" means a person called to testify under this rule\
(2)   A party may call a party expert witness to give evidence on a specific issue.
(3)   The parties may agree to jointly instruct a single party expert witness.
(4)   A party intending to call a party expert witness shall file a witness statement, which shall refer to the report submitted by the party expert witness under rule 34.
(5)   An expert report shall be contained in the bundle of documents filed by the party at whose instance the party expert witness is called.
(6)   A party expert witness shall assist the Court by giving an unbiased analysis of an issue in respect of which the witness has been called to testify.
(7)   The duty of a party expert witness under sub-rule (6) overrides any duty which the witness may have to a party or to a person by whom the witness' fees or expenses are payable.

Court Expert 33

(1)   In this rule, the term "court expert" means a person appointed as an independent expert witness under this rule.
(2)   Subject to this rule, the Court may, on the Court's own motion or on application by a party, appoint a court expert to inquire into and report on an issue other than an issue relating to a question of law or of construction of the law.
(3)   An order of appointment of a court expert under these Rules shall be in Form 23B set out in Appendix 1.
(4)   The Court may, on the Court's own motion, appoint a court expert -
       (a)   agreed on by the parties; or
       (b)   if the parties fail to agree, from among persons named by the parties.
(5)   In deciding whether to appoint a court expert, the Court shall consider -
       (a)   the complexity of the issue in relation to which the appointment is required;
       (b)   the impact of the appointment on the cost of the proceedings;
       (c)   the likelihood of the appointment expediting or delaying the trial of the case;
       (d)   the interests of justice; and
       (e)   any other factor which the court considers appropriate.

Submission of question to court expert 34

(1) Subject to sub-rule (2), the parties shall agree on the question to be submitted to the court expert for the court expert's opinion

(2) Where the parties fail to agree on the question to be submitted to the court expert, the Court shall settle the question.

(3) A court expert shall, not less than twenty-one days before the date of hearing, or within such period as the Court may order, submit to the Registrar, such number of copies of the court expert's report as the court may direct.

(4) The Registrar shall, within seven days of receiving a report by the court expert under this rule, cause to be served a copy of the report on each party.

(5) Where a court expert considers that an examination, measurement, test or experiment is necessary for making a report, the court expert shall inform the parties accordingly and advise them as to —
   (a) the persons to attend the examination; measurement, test or experiment;
   (b) the expenses involved; and
   (c) any other relevant matters.

Remuneration of court expert 35

(1) The remuneration pf a court expert shall be fixed by the Court and include-
   (a) a fee for the expert report; and
   (b) a sum for each day during which the court expert attends court

(2) The Court shall determine the remuneration of a court expert in accordance with the fees set out in the Third Schedule.

(3) The court may, by the order appointing a court expert, direct that the remuneration of the court expert be paid by one or more of the parties in proportions which the Court considers just.

Conference of expert witnesses 36

(1) The court may, on its own motion or on application of a party, direct expert witnesses to -
   (a) confer on specified matters;
   (b) confer in the absence of the parties' advocates;
   (c) prepare and sign a joint witness statement stating the matters on which the expert witnesses agree and the matters on which they do not agree, including the reasons for their disagreement; or
   (d) prepare a joint witness statement without the assistance of the parties' advocates.

(2) A joint witness statement prepared by expert witnesses shall —
   (a) be served on each party by the parties at whose instance the expert witnesses have been engaged;
   (b) be produced in evidence by an expert witness who signed the statement; and
   (c) where the parties agree, be produced in evidence without the need to call any of the expert witnesses who signed the statement.

Form and content of expert report 37

(1) An expert's report shall-
   (a) be in the English language or , if originally expressed in a language other than English, translated into English;
   (b) contain a statement regarding the expert witness' present and past relationship, if any, with a party or the party's advocate;
   (c) state the academic and professional qualifications, and experience by which the expert witness making the report has acquired specialized knowledge;
   (d) state the questions which the expert witness has been asked to address;
   (e) give details of literature or other materials, if any, which have been relied on in making the report;
   (f) separately set out each factual finding or assumption on which the opinion of the expert witness is based;
   (g) clearly state the facts which are within the expert witness' personal knowledge;
   (h) state the name and qualifications of the person who carried out any examination, measurement, test or experiment which the expert witness has used to make the report, and whether or not the examination, measurement, test or experiment was carried out under the witness' supervision;

(i) contain reasons for the expert witness' opinion;
(j) contain a summary of the conclusions reached, including a description of the methods, used in arriving at the conclusions;
(k) contain a declaration that the expert witness who made the report understands that witness' overriding duty to the court, and has complied with that duty;
(l) be signed by the expert witness who made the report; and
(m) such other information as the expert witness considers necessary.

Amendment of Order VI

3. Order VI rule 1 (3) of the principal Rules is amended by the insertion, immediately after the word "support", of the words "and skeleton arguments".

Amendment of Order X

4. Order X of the Principal Rules is amended by the deletion of rule 22 and the renumbering of rule 23 and 24 as rule 22 and 23.

Amendment of Order XI

5. Order XI rule I of the principal Rules is amended by the insertion immediately after sub-rule (3) of the following new sub-rules:
(4) A defendant served with a writ of summons under these Rules may enter conditional appearance, accompanied by summons to set aside the writ, affidavit in support skeleton arguments and list of authorities.
(5) A conditional memorandum of appearance filed under sub-rule (4) shall be in Form 18A set out in the First Schedule.
(6) A conditional memorandum of appearance filed under this rule shall —
(a) be effective from the date on which it is filed; and
(b) not require endorsement by the Registrar.

Repeal and replacement of Order XIX

6. The principal Rules are amended by the deletion of replacement Order XIX and the substitution therefor of the following:

ORDER XIX
PRE-TRIAL DIRECTIONS AND CONFERENCES
Application

1. This order applies to an action commenced by writ of summons
2. (1) A judge shall, within thirty days of the filing of a memorandum of appearance, defence and counterclaim if any, and accompanying documents, summon the parties to a scheduling conference.
   (2) A judge shall, at the scheduling conference, give directions with respect to any of the following:
       (a) filing of a reply and defence to counterclaim, if any;
       (b) discovery and inspection of documents;
       (c) filing and exchanging bundles of documents;
       (d) filing and exchanging witness statements, skeleton arguments and lists of authorities;
       (e) admissions;
       (f) interrogatories;
       (g) planning of the trial time;
       (h) setting of a date for trial; and
       (i) setting of a date for status conference
   (3) At the scheduling conference, a Judge shall, in addition to giving directions referred to in sub-rule (2)
       (a) identify contested and uncontested issues;
       (b) explore methods to resolve contested issues;
       (c) where possible, secure agreement of the parties on —
           a specific schedule of events in the proc0eedings; or

(d)   the use of technology in the conduct of proceedings; narrow or resolve outstanding issues; and

(e)   create a timetable for the proceedings.

(4)   At the scheduling conference, a Judge may, in addition to directions given under sub-rule (3) –

    (a)   refer a matter wrongly filed in the Registry to the correct division of the High Court;

    (b)   consolidate actions where appropriate;

    (c)   refer the matter to mediation, in accordance with Order XXXI;

    (d)   refer the parties to arbitration, in accordance with the Arbitration Act: **Act No 19 of 2000**

    (e)   give further directions for the expeditious disposal of the case or any outstanding issue;

    (f)   encourage the parties to cooperate with each other in the conduct of the proceedings;

    (g)   encourage the parties to settle the whole or part of the case;

    (h)   deal with as many aspects of the case as possible on the same occasion; and

        (i)   make orders which the Judge considers appropriate, including striking off the action or defence;

        (ii)   expunging a document or part of the document; or making an award for costs.

(5)   A witness statement referred to in sub-rule (2) shall-

    (a)   be expressed in the first person, stating

        (i)   the full name of the person making the statement; the place of residence of the person making the statement, or if making the statement in a professional, business or other occupational capacity, the address of the place of business, the position and the name of the firm or employer;

        (iii)   the occupation of the person making the statement or if none, the description;

        (iv)   the capacity in which the person making the statement is doing so; the chronological sequence of events or matters dealt with, divided into consecutively numbered paragraphs; and where applicable, dates, sums or other numbers expressed in figures and not in words;

    (b)   be in a clear narrative form;

    (c)   contain all the facts relevant to the claim, defense or counter-claim, as the case may be;

    (d)   make reference to the documents relied upon in the bundle of documents;

    (e)   contain a statement by the person making the statement that the contents are true to the best of that person's knowledge and belief; and

    (t)   be treated, upon production, as the evidence-in-chief of the witness by whom the statement is made.

(6)   A party filing a witness statement under this rule shall not be required to have the witness' signature authenticated under the Authentication of Documents Act. Cap 75

(7)   A party filing a witness statement shall, at the same time, file skeleton arguments and a list of authorities to be relied upon by that party.

(8)   A party may amend a witness statement in accordance with Order XVIII.

Scheduling Conference Order

3.   A Judge shall, on conclusion of the scheduling conference, issue a scheduling conference order in Form 23A set out in the First Schedule.

Status Conference

4.   (1)   A Judge shall, after the scheduling conference, convene a status conference to –

    (a)   confirm the date for trial;

    (b)   determine any outstanding issues, and

    (c)   consider the length of trial

(2)   Each party or the party's advocate shall provide the Judge with information that the Judge require, in accordance with this Order, for purposes f considering the length of time that may be required for the hearing of the case.

(3)   A Judge shall order, costs against a party or advocate who fails to comply with pre-trial directions unless, for reasons to be recorded, the Judge considers that it would not be just to make such an order.

Non-attendance

5.   (1)   A Judge shall dismiss an action if the plaintiff fails to attend the scheduling conference or status conference on two occasions without justifiable cause

     (2)   Where the defendant fails to attend the scheduling conference or status conference, a judge may-
         (a)   in the case of a scheduling conference proceed to issue directions; or
         (b)   in the case of a status conference, proceed to review the progress made in the proceedings and confirm the date of trial.

Dismissal on lapse of sixty days

6.   A Judge may dismiss an action if, after the filing of an action, sixty days elapse and the plaintiff has not taken further steps to prosecute the matter

Amendment of Order XXX

7.   Order XXX rule 6A (1) of the principal rules is amended by the insertion of the words "of the ruling" after the words "the date of delivery".

Amendment of Order XXXV

8.   Order XXXV of the principal Rules is amended by the deletion of rule 6 and the substitution therefor of the following new rule;

Restoration after striking off

6.   (1)   A party whose action or application has been struck off for non-attendance may apply to restore the action or application to the active cause list within fourteen days from the date it is struck off, failing which the Court shall dismiss that action or application

     (2)   After hearing an application for restoration of an action, or application to the active cause list the Court may, as a condition for the restoration, order the payment of a hearing fee of two thousand five hundred fee units.

     (3)   The Court may dismiss an action or, application if the party at whose instance the action or application is restored fails to-
         (a)   attend the next hearing without justification cause; or
         (b)   pay a hearing fee as ordered under this rule.

     (4)   The Court shall not restore an action or application which has twice been struck and restored to the active cause list.

Repeal and replacement of Order L111

9.   The principal Rules are amended by the deletion of Order LIII and the substitution of the following;

ORDER LIII
COMMERCIAL ACTIONS

Interpretation

In this Order, unless the context otherwise requires-
    "commercial action" means an action of a business nature or any other matter or question of fact or law which is suitable for determination by a Judge of the Commercial Court Division, and includes a cause arising out of a transaction relating to-
Commerce, trade and industry
Partnership and shareholder agreements
Corporate insolvency;
Insurance;
Banking and finance;
Carriage of goods;
Operation of capital markets and exchanges both domestic and international;
Construction and performance of mercantile contracts;
Law and practice of arbitration and questions connected with or arising from commercial arbitration
loans from licensed money lenders, excluding debts between unlicensed individuals;

disputes arising from investments agreements;
joint ventures
(m)commercial lease financing; and
(n) intellectual property rights and patents

"Commercial Court Division" means a division of the High Court that deals with commercial actions;
"Court" means-
a judge of the High Court assigned to the Commercial Court Division and designated by the Chief Justice under rule 3; or
the Registrar;
"Registrar" means the person designated as Registrar of the Commercial Court and includes the Deputy Registrar, a District Registrar and any other person acting in that capacity
"Registry" means the Commercial Court Division Registry established under rule 2.

Registry

(1)   There shall be a Registry at Lusaka and at any other place the Chief Justice may determine.
(2)   The Registrar shall administer the day-to-day affairs of the Registry and superintend over the Deputy Registrar, District Registrar, Senior Assistant Registrar and Assistant Registrar

Designation of judges to Commercial Court Division

The Chief Justice shall designate a Judge-in-Charge of the Commercial Court Division and other judges as the Chief Justice mat determine.

Conduct of actions

(1)   A commercial action shall be-commenced and filed in the Registry; and persecuted in accordance with this Order
(2)   Where there is an inconsistence between this Order and any other rules in relation to commercial actions, this order shall, to the extent of the inconsistency, prevail.

Pleadings

5.   (1)   A statement of claim or counter-claim shall-
             (a)   state in clear terms the material facts upon which a party relies, and
             (b)   show a clear cause of action
      (2)   Where a statement of claim or counter-claim fails to meet the requirements of sub-rule (1), a judge may subject to a party's right to apply for leave to amend-
             (a)   strike off or set aside the statement of claim or counter-claim, as the case may be; or
             (b)   on applications by a party or on the judge's own motion, dismiss the action.
      (3)   A defence shall specifically traverse every allegation of fact made in a statement of claim, or counter-claim as the case may be.
      (4)   Where a defence does not satisfy sub-rule (3) or makes a general or bare denial of a fact alleged, or a general statement of non-admission of a fact alleged, subject to the defendant's right to apply for leave to amend the defence-
             (a)   that defence shall be deemed to have admitted the fact alleged; and
             (b)   the judge may, on the judge's own motion of application by the plaintiff or defendant, as the case may be enter judgment on admission.

Service of process

6.   (1)   A party shall, after filing process, serve the process on the other party and file an affidavit of service
      (2)   Where it is established that a party filing process has failed to serve the process on the other party without justifiable cause, and the default results in an adjournment, the Court shall order the party that occasioned the default to pay a hearing fee or higher hearing fee specified in the Second Schedule
7.   (1)   A judge shall, within fourteen days of the filing of a memorandum of appearance, defence , and counter-claim if any, and accompanying documents, summon the parties to a scheduling conference;

    (2)   A judge shall, at the scheduling conference, give directions with respect to any of the following;

- (a) filing of a reply and defence to counter-claim, if any;
- (b) discovery and inspection of documents;
- (c) filing and exchanging bundles of documents;
- (d) filing and exchanging witness statements, skeleton arguments and list of documents;
- (e) admissions;
- (f) interrogations;
- (g) planning of the trial time;
- (h) setting of a date for trial; and
- (i) setting of a date for status conference

    (3)   At the scheduling conference a judge shall , in addition to giving directions for trial-

- (a) identity contested and uncontested issues;
- (b) explore methods to resolve contested issues;
- (c) where possible, secure an agreement of the parties on a specific schedule of events to the proceedings;
- (d) narrow or resolve outstanding issues;
- (e) create a timetable for the proceedings;
- (f) deal with the case in a way which is proportionate to the complexity of the issues; and
- (g) ensure that the matter is dealt with expeditiously and fairly.

    (4)   at the scheduling conference, a judge may, in addition to directions given under sub-rule (3)-

- (a) refer to a matter wrongly filed in the Registry to the correct division of the High Court;
- (b) consolidate actions where appropriate;
- (c) refer to the matter to mediation, in accordance with Order XXX1;

Act No 19 of 2000

- (d) refer the parties to arbitration in accordance with the Arbitration Act;
- (e) give suitable directions to facilitate expeditious disposal of the case or any outstanding issue;
- (f) encourage the parties to cooperate with each other in the conduct of the proceedings
- (g) encourage the parties to settle the whole or part of the case;
- (h) deal with the case justly, so far as practicable, by considering whether the likely benefits of taking a particular step justify the cost of taking that step;
- (i) deal with as many aspects of the case as possible on the same occasion; and
- (j) make orders which the Court considers appropriate, including-
  - (i) striking off the action or defence;
  - (ii) expunging a document or part of a document;
  - (iii) making an award for costs, or
  - (iv) entering judgment on admission.

    (5)   A judge shall dismiss an action if the plaintiff or applicant fails, without justifiable cause, to attend a scheduling conference on two occasions.

    (6)   A witness statement referred to under sub-rule (2) shall-

- (a) be expressed on the first person, stating-
  - (i) the full name of the witness
  - (ii) place of residence, or if making the statement in a professional, business or other occupational capacity, the address of the place of business, the position and the name of the firm or employer,
  - (iii) the witness' occupation or description of occupation;
  - (iv) the capacity of the person making the statement;
  - (v) the chronological sequence of events or matter dealt with dvided into consecutively numbered paragraphs;
  - (vi) be in a clear narrative form; and
  - (vii) where applicable, dates, sums or other numbers expressed in figures and not in words;
- (b) contain all the facts relevant to the claim, defence or counter-claim, as the case may be;
- (c) make reference to the documents relied upon to the bundle of documents, by page number;
- (d) contain a statement by the witness that the contents are true to the best of that witness' knowledge and belief and
- (e) be treated, upon production, as the evidence-in-chief of the witness by whom the statement is made

Cap 75

(7) a party filing a witness' statement under this rule shall not be required to have the witness' signature authenticated under the Authentication of Documents Act

(8) A party filing a witness statement shall, at the same time, the skeleton arguments and a list of authorities to be relied upon by the party.

(9) A party may amend a witness statement in accordance with Order XVIII, subject to the time limit specified in these Rules.

Status conference

8. (1) A Judge shall, after the scheduling conference, convene a status conference to –

    (a) consider the parties' compliance with the direction given at the scheduling conference

    (b) confirm the date for trial set at the scheduling conference;

    (c) where necessary, enlarge the time for compliance with the scheduling conference order, subject to costs; and

    (d) determine any outstanding issues.

  (2) A judge shall dismiss an action if the plaintiff or applicant fails, without justifiable cause, to attend a status conference on two occasions.

Failure of mediation

9. (1) Where a matter referred to mediation by judge is not settled or mediated within forty-five day from the date of the referral-

    (a) the mediator shall send the matter back to the judge for trial clearly stating the reasons for the failure of the mediator and

    (b) the judge shall, within fourteen days of the matter being sent back as provided in paragraph (a), summon the parties to a status conference and issue directions in accordance with rule 8

  (2) The Court shall order a party who, without reasonable cause, failed to attend mediation and the non-attendance caused the mediation proceedings to fail, to bear all the costs of the litigation from the point of failure of the mediation regardless of the final outcome.

Out-of-court settlement

10.(1) Where the parties request to attempt an out-of-court settlement, the Court shall give directions-

(a) and, subject to sub-rule (2), give the parties fourteen days within which to settled out of court, and

(b) as to the steps to be taken by the parties in the event that they fail to reach an out-of-court settlement within the period specified by the Court under this rule

(2) The Court may, for sufficient reason, attend the time allowed for an out-of-court settlement by a period not exceeding 7 days.

11. (1) The Court shall not allow an adjournment of a trial or interlocutory application except in compelling and exceptional circumstances.

  (2) A party may, not less than ten days before the date set for hearing of the matter, apply for an adjournment by filing-

    (a) notice to vary the date of hearing

    (b) an affidavit in support;

    (c) skeleton arguments; and

    (d) list of authorities.

  (3) Where the Court allows an adjournment under this rule, the Court may, apart from exercising discretion to award costs, order the party that has caused the adjournment to pay a hearing fee or a higher hearing fee specified in the Second Schedule.

  (4) A hearing fee or a higher hearing fee shall be paid to the Court before the date of the next hearing

  (5) Where a party ordered to pay a hearing fee fails or neglects to pay the fee as provided in sub-rule (4), the Court shall-

    (a) proceed to hear the plaintiff if the defaulting party is the defendant; and

    (b) dismiss the action of application if the defaulting party is the plaintiff or applicant.

Interlocutory applications

12. (1)   In this Rule, "interlocutory application" includes and application-
    (a)   for judgement in default of appearance and defence'
    (b)   for assessment; and
    (c)   made to the judge at chambers before trial

    (2)   An interlocutory application, other than an application for assessment, shall be made to a judge at chambers.

    (3)   An interlocutory application shall be made by filing-
    (a)   summons or notice, accompanied by an affidavit in support;
    (b)   skeleton arguments; and
    (c)   list and copies of authorities relied upon by the applicant.

    (4)   Sub-rule (3)(b) and (c) shall apply to a respondent filing an affidavit in opposition.

    (5)   Subject to this rule, a party shall not file, and a judge shall not consider an interlocutory application filed fourteen days before the date set for trial.

    (6)   A judge may, in the judge's discretion, the exercise of which shall not be subject of an appeal, entertain an interlocutory application-
    (a)   which, with reasonable diligence, could not have been made before the time specified in sub-rule (5); or
    (b)   if the applicant shows justifiable cause for the delay in making the application.

    (7)   The Court shall, apart from exercising its discretion to award costs against a party making an interlocutory application-
    (a)   strike a balance between the prejudice which may be occasioned to the applicant if the application were not granted and the prejudice to the Court, the respondent or other court user if the application were granted; and
    (b)   consider the following:
        (i)   the seriousness or significance of the failure by the applicant to comply with a rule, direction or order of the Court;
        (ii)   the reason for failure referred to in sub-paragraph (i);
        (iii) the need for litigation to be conducted efficiently and at proportionate cost;
        (iv)   the need to enforce compliance with rules, directions and orders of the Court; and
        (v)   all the circumstances of the case so as to enable the Court to deal justly with the matter.

    (8)   An application that arises in the course of proceedings before a taxing officer shall be made to the taxing officer.

Restoration after striking off

13. (1)   A party whose action or application has been struck off for non-attendance may apply to restore the action or application to the active cause list within fourteen days from the date it is struck off, failing which the Court shall dismiss that action or application.

    (2)   After hearing an application for restoration of am action or application to the active cause list, the Court may, as a condition for the restoration, order the payment of a hearing fee or higher hearing fee specified in Appendix 2.

    (3)   The Court may dismiss an action or application if the party at whose instance the action or application is restored fails to-
    (a)   attend the next hearing without justifiable cause, or
    (b)   pay a hearing fee of higher hearing fee as ordered under this rule

    (4)   The Court shall not restore an action or application which has twice been struck off and restored to the active cause list.

Dismissal for want of prosecution

14.   A judge may, on application by a party to an action, or on the judge's own motion, dismiss the action if, after the filing of that action, forty days elapse without the plaintiff or applicant taking further steps to prosecute the action.

Transfer of action

15. (1)   A party to an action may, at or before the scheduling conference, apply to a Judge for the action to be transferred out of the Commercial Court Division.

    (2)   A Judge shall, on application for transfer of an action under this rule or, subject to sub-rule (3), on the Judge's own motion, determine whether the cause of action or issues of fact or las likely to arise, or the procedures to be followed in the action, make that action suitable for transfer out of the Commercial Court Division

    (3)   A Judge shall not, on the Judge's own motion, make a determination referred to in sub-rule (2) without giving the parties an opportunity to be heard in relation to the motion.

    (4)   Where an action is transferred into the Commercial Court Division, the party filing the action shall pay the difference between the filing fees applicable in the Commercial Court Division and the filing fees paid by that party before the transfer

Users Committee

16. (1)   The Commercial Court Users Committee constituted under the High Court (Amendment) Rules, 2012 shall continue to exist as if constituted under this Order and shall consist of the following: [S.I No. 27 of 2012]

        (a)   the Judge-in-charge of the Commercial Court Division, as Chairperson;

        (b)   all judges of the Commercial Court Division;

        (c)   two representatives of the Law Association of Zambia;

        (d)   One representative of the Zambia Association of Chamber of Commerce and Industry;

        (e)   one representative of the Bankers Association of Zambia;

        (f)   the Chief Administration of the Judiciary;

        (g)   two members of the public appointed by the Chief Justice; and

        (h)   the Registrar, as Secretary.

    (2)   A Users Committee meeting shall in the absence of the Judge-in-charge, be chaired by the senior most Judge of the Commercial Court Division

    (3)   The quorum at a Users Committee meeting shall be formed by two thirds of the membership.

17. (1)   Subject to this rule, a member of the Users Committee, other than a Judge, the Chief Administrator and the Registrar, shall hold office for a period of three years which may be extended for a further three years.

    (2)   The office of a member shall become vacant-

        (a)   upon the member's death;

        (b)   if the member is absent without reasonable excuse from three consecutive meetings of which the member has had notice;

        (c)   on ceasing to be a representative of the organization which nominated the member, and

        (d)   if the member becomes mentally or physically incapable of performing the duties of a member of the Users Committee,

    (3)   A member may resign from the office by giving three month's notice in writing, to the Judge-in-charge of the Commercial Court Division

Functions of Users Committee

18.   The Commercial Court Users Committee shall be a forum for-

        (a)   exchange of ideas or views relating to the operations of the Commercial Court Division' and

        (b)   making recommendations to improve the operations of the Commercial Court Division.

Transitional Provision

19.   This Order shall not effect the jurisdiction of the Court over a matter which was pending before the Court prior to the commencement of the Order.

Amendment of First Schedule

20.   The principal Rules are amended in the First Schedule by-

        (a)   the insertion, after Form 18 of Form 18A; and

        (b)   the deletion of Form 23A and Form 23B, and the substitution therefore, of the Forms set out in Appendix 1.

Amendment of Second Schedule

21. The principal Rules are amended by the deletion of the Second Schedule and substitution therefore of the Schedule set out in Appendix 2

APPENDIX I

Form 18A

Order X! rule 7

REPUBLIC OF ZAMBIA

CONDITIONAL MEMORANDUM OF APPEARANCE

(Genera Title)

"conditional upon the defendant filing an application to set aside the writ or dismiss the action for irregularity"

Enter an appearance for (full names) in this action.

Dated at the   day of   20   .

PART A

(This Part is only for use where a defendant desires to appear without an Advocate.)

(signed).....................................

My residential address is

My postal address is

Defendant in person

        *As my residential address is more than ten kilometres from the Registry concerned, I give the following as a postal address within ten kilometres thereof to which documents may be posted to me:

PART B

(This Part is only for use where a defendant appears by Advocate)

      (Signed)

        Advocate for

Business address

Postal address

whose address for service is*

whose postal address for service is*

Agents for   of

*Delete if inapplicable

DIRECTIONS FOR THE GUIDANCE OF DEFENDANTS IN PERSON WHO

DESIRE TO ENTER APPEARANCE   Sch. 1

Section X below should be followed where a defendant intends to attend himself at the Registry

Section Y below should be followed where a defendant wishes to appear by post

Section X Personal Appearance by a Defendant

The Conditional Memorandum of Appearance must be completed in duplicate. (O.XI,r.1.)

Fill in the full title and number of the action by copying the heading from the writ served on you.

Insert your full names in the blank space provided after the words "Enter an appearance for". Observe that if a defendant is sued in the firm name, e.g. Smith and Co., appearance must be in the name of the partner or partners so appearing, as an appearance in the name of a firm cannot be accepted. Further, a limited company can only appear by Advocate.

Date the forms

Complete the information required in and sign Part a. Delete Part B.

Attend in person at the Registry or District Registry in which the action is proceeding and deliver both copies to the Registry Officer.

On the same day as appearance is entered, deliver or send by post to the plaintiff's Advocate, or the plaintiff if he is suing in person, the duplicate memorandum returned to you by the Registry officer. (The address at or to which to deliver or send the memorandum is on the writ) (O.XI, r.3 (1)),

The appearance should be entered within the time stated for so doing on the writ and if not so entered the plaintiff will be entitled to proceed by default and judgment may be given without further notice to you.

Section Y. Personal Appearance by Post

The Memorandum of Appearance must be completed in triplicate. (O.XI, r,2,)

Fill in the full title and number of the action by copying the heading from the writ served on you.

Insert your full name in the blank space provided after the words 'Enter an appearance for". Observe that if a defendant is sued in the firm name, e.g., Smith and Co., appearance must be in the name of the partner or partners so appearing, as an appearance in the name of a firm cannot be accepted. Further, a limited company can only appear by Advocate.

Date the forms.

Complete the information required in and sign Part A. Delete Part B.

Send all three copies, when completed, without fee by prepaid registered post to the address stated in Note 3 on the front page of the writ (Note 2 in the case of an originating summons), at the same time enclosing two stamped addressed envelopes, one to the plaintiffs Advocates, or to the plaintiff if he sues in person, at the postal address shown on the document served on you and the other to yourself at your postal address for service. (O. XI, r. 2.)

The forms must be posted so as to be delivered at the Registry or District Registry concerned before the time allowed for appearance (as shown on the first page of the writ) has expired. If the forms are not so delivered, the plaintiff will be entitled to proceed by default and judgment may be given without further notice to you. If the forms, when received, are incorrect or incomplete, then appearance cannot be entered and the action may proceed as in 7 above. The time for appearance cannot be extended.

If you do not employ a Advocate you are advised to refer to Order XI of the High Court Rules for all requirements relating to the entry of appearance.

FORM 23A

(Order XIX rule 3)

REPUBLIC OF ZAMBIA

IN THE HIGH COURT OF ZAMBIA AT..........

CAUSE NO:...

BETWEEN

PLAINTIFF/APPPLICANT

AND

DEFENDANT/RESPONDENT

SCHEDULING CONFERENCE ORDER

UPON HEARING THE PARTIES in Chambers on the .... day of .... 20 at ....hours, and by consent of the parties, the following PRE-TRIAL DIRECTIONS are given:

(a) The Plaintiff/Applicant shall file a reply, if any, on or before...........

(b) The parties shall conduct discovery and inspection on or before...........

(c) The parties shall file and exchange bundles of documents on or before...........

(d) The Plaintiff/Applicant shall call witnesses;

(e) The Defendant/ Respondent shall call ...... witnesses;

(f) The estimated time of trial is ....hours;

(g) The parties shall file and exchange witness statements on or before ....;

(h) The Plaintiff/Applicant shall file Skeleton Arguments and List of Authorities, if any, on or before ....

(i) The Defendant/ Respondent shall file Skeleton Arguments and List of Authorities, if any, on or before...........

(j) The Plaintiff/ Applicant shall file Skeleton Arguments in Reply, if any, on or before...........

(k) Status Conference shall be held on...........

(l) The costs of scheduling shall be in the cause.

Dated this   day of   20

JUDGE

FORM 23B
(Order V rule 33(2))
REPUBLIC OF ZAMBIA
IN THE HIGH COURT OF ZAMBIA AT ·········
CAUSE NO:···
BETWEEN
································ PLAINTIFF/APPLICANT
AND
································ DEFENDANT/RESPON

ORDER OF APPOINTMENT OF COURT EXPERT

IT IS ORDERED that -
(a)...BE AND IS HEREBY
APPOINTED as a Court expert on the issue of··································; and

(b)   the remuneration of the Court expert be paid by

....

....

....

Dated this   ....day of..20.........

HIGH COURT JUDGE

APPENDIX 2
SECOND SCHEDULE
(Rules 11 and 13)

FEES

		Fee Units
Hearing fee		3,333.33
Higher Hearing fee	not less than 6,666.66	
		but not exceeding

APPENDIX 3
THIRD SCHEDULE
(Rule 35)
REMUNERATION OF COURT EXPERT
Fee
1 .
2.

GOVERNMENT OF ZAMBIA
STATUTORY INSTRUMENT NO 58 of 2020
THE HIGH COURT ACT
(Laws, Volume 3, Cap 27)

The High Court (Amendment) Rules, 2020

The High Court (Amendment) Rules, 2020

In exercise of the powers contained in sections 44 and 45 of the High Court Act, the following rules are made (Title cap 27) 1 These rules may be cited as the High Court (Amendment) Rules, 2020, and shall be read as one with the High Court Rules, in these Rules referred to as the principal rules.

(Amendment order II) 2 Order II of the principal Rules is amended by the deletion of the words "the Court or" wherever they appear.

(Amendment order III) 3 Subject to sub-rules (2) and (3), the registrar may transact any business and exercise authority and jurisdiction as a judge at chambers may transact or execute under the Act or any the written law.

(2)   An interlocutory application shall be made to and heard by the registrar.

(3)   The Registrar shall, not transact business or exercise the authority or jurisdiction in respect of-

      (a)   Matters relating to criminal proceeding or to the liberty of a person;

      (b)   Appeals from District Registrars

      (c)   Injunctions: and

      (d)   Reviewing taxation of costs, save as provided in Order XL rules 3 and 4

(Amendment of Order VI) 4 Order VI of the principal Rules is amended by the deletion of rule 1 and the substitution of the following:

(Commencement of proceedings) 1. (1) except as otherwise provided by any written law or these Rules, an action in the High Court shall be commenced, in writing or electronically by writ of summons endorsed and accompanied by_

      (a)   a statement of claim;

      (b)   list and description of document to relied on at trial:

      (c)   list of witnesses to be called by the plaintiff at trial; and

      (d)   letter of demand whose receipt shall be acknowledged by the defendant or an affidavit of service attesting to the service of the letter of demand, which shall set out the claim and circumstances surrounding the claim in detail.

(2)   writ of summons which is not accompanied by the documents under sub-rule (1) shall not be accepted.

(3)   A matter which, under any written law or these rules, may be disposed of in chambers shall be commenced by an originating summons accompanied by an affidavit in support.

(4)   The proper officer shall-

      (a)   seal, with the official seal, the writ of summons and statement of claim where that statement f claim is on a separate sheet;

      (b)   stamp the accompanying documents with the official stamp; and

      (c)   and return the copies of the writ of summons, statement of claim and accompanying document to the person commencing the action.

(Amendment of Order XI) 5. Order XI of the principal rules is amended by the deletion of Rule 1 and the substitution of therefore of the following;

(Mode of entering appearance) 1. (1) a defendant shall enter appearance to a writ of summons by delivering to the proper officer, in writing or electronically sufficient copies of the: -

      (a)   memorandum of appearance dated on the day of delivery stating as the case may be-

            (i)   the name of the defendant's advocate; or

            (ii)   that the defendant is defending in person; and

      (b)   defence and the counterclaim, if any, together with the list of-

            (i)   description of documents to be relied on by the defendant at trial; and

            (ii)   list of witnesses to be called by the defendant at trial.

(2)   The proper officer shall-.

      (a)   seal the memorandum of appearance and defence;

      (b)   stamp the accompanying document with the official stamp: and

     (c)   return the copies of the memorandum of appearance, defence and accompanying documents to person filing them for service on the plaintiff

(3)   The court shall not accept an appearance after the entry of a judgment in default of appearance, unless the judgment in default of appearance is set aside.

(Amendment of Order XII) 6. Order XII of the principal Rules is amended by the deletion of the words 'Deputy or District Registrar' and the substitution therefore of the word 'Judge'.

(Amendment of Order XV) 7. Order XV of the principal Rules is amended by the deletion of the words 'the court or', wherever the words appear.

(Amendment of Order XVI) 8. Order XVI of the principal Rules is amended by the deletion of the words 'the Court or' wherever the words appear.

(Repeal and replacement of Order XIX) 9. The principal rules are amended by the deletion of Order XIX and the substitution therefore of the following;

ORDER XIX
PRE-TRIAL DIRETIONS AND CONFERENCES

(Application) 1. This Order applies to an action commenced by writ of summons.

(Orders for directions) 2. (1) A Judge shall, within thirty days after the filing of the defence under rule 1 of Order XI, give orders for directions with respect to the following matters:

    (a)   reply and defence to counter claim, if any;
    (b)   inspection of documents
    (c)   exchange of bundle of documents and witness statements;
    (d)   admissions;
    (e)   interrogatories; and
    (f)   date for scheduling conference.

(2)   The parties shall, not less than seven days before the scheduling conference, prepare a scheduling conference brief and exchange their briefs which shall include-

    (a)   a concise summary of the facts, including he agreed facts and admissions;
    (b)   a concise summary of the issues and the law to be relied on by each party, including the rights and interests of the party
    (c)   witness statement which shall contain all the facts relevant to the claim, as the case may be and shall make reference to the document relied upon in the bundle of documents; and
    (d)   expert reports, if any and the relevant portions of documents relied on by the parties subject to the applicable Rules of the Supreme Court Practice 1999 Edition.

(Scheduling Conference) 3. (1) A judge shall, at the scheduling conference-

    (a)   Considers a party's Compliance with orders for directions
    (b)   Plan the trial time
    (c)   Set a date for status conference;
    (d)   Set a date for trial;
    (e)   Identify contested and uncontested issues;
    (f)   Explore methods to resolve contested issues
    (g)   Where possible, secure an agreement of the parties on a specific schedule of events in the proceedings;
    (h)   Narrow or resolve outstanding issues
    (i)   Create a timetable for proceedings
    (j)   refer any matter filed wrongly in the principal registry to the correct division of the court
    (k)   consider consolidation of action; and
    (l)   provide the parties and the parties advocates an opportunity to settle the case or narrow down the issues.

(2)   A Judge may, in addition to any other general power, exercise the following powers at a scheduling conference:

    (a)   deal with any interlocutory applications for the expeditious disposal of these applications
    (b)   order the filing and service of necessary further and better particulars within a period that the Court may specify:
    (c)   order the giving of evidence on the basis of affidavit evidence or give order for discovery production, inspection pr interrogatories that may be appropriate to the case:
    (d)   order the examination of a witness outside jurisdiction in accordance with Order V rule 30 and admit evidence of that examination in Court
    (e)   Make any procedural Order

    (f)   by consent of the parties, or where appropriate on the courts own motion, make an order for interlocutory relief;

    (g)   make a referral order on its own motion or on the application of a party for-
        (i)   mediation, in accordance with rule 4 of Order XXXI; or
        (ii) arbitration, in accordance with Arbitration Act. 2000

    (h)   convene hearing

    (i)   give suitable directions to facilitate expeditious disposal of the case or any outstanding issue;

    (j)   encourage the parties to cooperate with each other in the conduct of proceedings

    (k)   encourage the parties to settle the whole or part of the case

    (l)   consider whether the likely benefits of taking a particular step justify the cost of taking that step;

    (m) deal with as many aspects of the case as possible on the same occasion: and

    (m) make orders which the Court considers appropriate including-
        (i)   striking out the action or defence;
        (ii)   striking out a document or part of a document
        (iii) making an award for costs; or
        (iv) creating or amending a case timetable.

(3)   A party shall not lodge; and a judge shall not consider any interlocutory application fourteen days before commencement of trial.

(4)   Subject to sub-rule (3), a Judge may in the judge's discretion, which decision shall not be subject of an interlocutory appeal, entertain an interlocutory application which with reasonable diligence, could not have been don made before the time specified under sub-rule (3).

(Scheduling Conference Order) 4. A judge shall on conclusion of the scheduling conference, issue a scheduling conference order in Form 23A set out in the appendix.

(Status Conference) 5. (1) A judge shall, not less than thirty-one days before the date of hearing of the case, convene a status conference for purpose of

    (a)   Confirming the dates for trial;

    (b)   Determining any outstanding issues, and;

    (c)   Considering the length of trial.

(2)   Each party or the party's advocates shall provide the judge with information that the judge may require, in accordance with this Order, for purposes of considering the length of time that may be required for the hearing of the case.

(3)   A judge shall consider costs against a party or advocate who fails to comply with this Order unless, for reasons to be recorded, the judge considers that it would not be just to make that order.

(Dismissal of action for non-attendance of parties) 7. A judge shall dismiss an action if the parties fail to attend a scheduling conference or status conference on two occasions without justifiable cause.

(Dismissal of action for lapse of sixty days) 8. A judge may dismiss an action if sixty days after the filing there is no progress.

(Amendment of order XII) 10. Order XXII of the principal rules is amended by the

    (a)   deletion of rule 1; and

    (b)   renumbering of rules 2,3 and 4, as rule 1,2 and 3

(Amendment of Order XXVI) 11. Order XXVI of the principal rules is amended in-

    (a)   in rule 1, by the deletion of the word 'five hundred thousand' and the substitution therefor of the words 'five hundred'; and

    (b)   by the deletion of the words "the Court or' wherever they appear.

(Amendment of Order XXX) 12. Order XXX of the principal rules is amended-

    (a)   in rule 1, by the insertion, immediately after the word summons of the words 'to be supported by an affidavit';

    (b)   in rule 3, by the deletion of the word 'two' and the substitution therefor of the word 'four';

    (c)   by the insertion, immediately after rule 3, of the following new rule:

(Skeleton Arguments and list of Authorities) 3A. (1) At the time of the filing of the summons, the applicant shall file skeleton arguments of their case and list of authorities

(2)   the skeleton arguments shall be set out as concisely as possible the-

    (a)   issue arising in the application

    (b)   brief argument that will form the basis of the case by the party filing it and authorities in support; and

    (c)   reasons for or against the application.

(3) On receipt of the affidavit in support of the application, skeleton arguments and List of authorities, the respondent shall file an affidavit in opposition with skeleton arguments and list of authorities.

(4) The skeleton arguments to be file by the respondent shall meet the requirement set out under sub rule (2); and

(d) the insertion immediately after rule 6 of the following new rule:

(Relying on documentary evidence) 6A. (1) Where the court is satisfied that the application can be disposed of on the basis of the documents before it, the court may determine the matter without the attendance of the parties or their advocates and shall issue a notice of the date delivery.

(2) This rule shall apply to-

    (a) an interlocutory application:

    (b) an application under Rule 11 (a):

    (c) an application for determination of questions of law or construction of documents; or

    (d) any other applications as maybe directed by the court.

(Amendment of Order XXXI) 13. Order XXXI of the principal rules is amended by the deletion of rule 3 and the substitution therefor of the following:

(Lodging of documents) 3. (1) Each of the bundles under Order XIX shall-

    (a) be bound up in book form in chronological order

    (b) have the pages thereof serially numbered

    (c) contain a complete index of the contents thereof;

    (d) bear the receipt number of the fees paid on filing; and

    (e) be endorsed on a back sheet thereon the title of the action, together with the names, physical address, email address, and telephone numbers of the advocates for the parties, or in the case of a party who has no advocate, of that party.

(2) the documents shall be clear and legible

(3) a bundle which does not comply with the provisions of sub-rule (1) shall not be accepted for filing

(Amendment of Order XXXIII) 14. The principal rules are amended by the deletion of Order XXXIII and the substitution therefor of the following;

ORDER XXXIII
ADJOURMENTS

(Adjournments on exceptional circumstances) 1. A judge shall mot grant an application for an adjournment except in compelling and exceptional circumstances.

(Notice of intention to seek adjournment) 2. A party intending to apply for adjournment of a hearing shall not less than ten days before the date set for the hearing file a notice of that intention.

(Amendment of Order XXXV) 15. Order XXXV of the principal rules is amended by the deletion and the substitution therefor the following:

(Restoration to active cause list) 6. (1) A party whose application is struck out for nonattendance may apply to restore the application within thirty days from the date the application was struck out, failing which the applications stands dismissed.

(2) the judge may on the hearing of an application for the restoration of an application struck out for nonattendance by the applicant, where appropriate, order the payment of a hearing fee as a condition for the restoration.

(Amendment of Order XXXVI) 16. Order XXXVI of the principal rules is amended by the-

    (a) deletion of rule 2 and the substitution therefor of the following:

(Time frame for delivery of judgment) 2. (1) A court may, on conclusion of a hearing-

    (a) pronounce its judgment or ruling at once:

    (b) subject to sub-rule 2, reserve its judgment or ruling.

(2) Where the court reserves its judgment or ruling, the court shall-

    (a) give the parties, or the advocates of the parties, notice indicating the date on which the court shall deliver the judgment or ruling;

    (b) in the case of a judgment, deliver the judgment within one hundred and eighty days from the date set for filing of the final submissions; and

    (c) in the case of a ruling, deliver it within ninety days after the conclusion of the hearing.

(3) Where the court fails to deliver its judgment or ruling within the period of specified in sub-rule (2) the court shall-

    (a) record the reasons for the failure:

    (b) forward to the chief justice a copy of the reasons in accordance with paragraph (a); and

(c)   immediately give the parties, or the advocates of the parties, notice of the new date on which the Court shall deliver the judgment or ruling; and

(b)   Insertion of the following new rule immediately after rule 2:

(Contents of Judgment) 2A. Where-

(a)   an action is defended, the judgment shall contain a concise statement of the case, the points for determination, the decision on the case, and the reasons for that decision; and

(b)   issues in an action have been framed, the Court shall stat, in the relation to each issue, the Courts finding or decision and the reasons for that finding or decision.

(Amendment of the first schedule) 17. The principal rules are amended in the first schedule by the insertion of the forms set out in the Appendix immediately after Form 23.

GOVERNMENT OF ZAMBIA
STATUTORY INSTRUMENT NO 72 OF 2018
THE HIGH COURT ACT
(Laws, Volume 3, Cap 27)

The High Court (Amendment) Rules, 2018

In exercise of the powers contained in sections 44 and 45 of the High Court Act, the following rules are made:

(Title cap 27) 1 These rules may be cited as the High Court (Amendment) Rules, 2018, and shall be read as one with the High Court Rules, in these Rules referred to as the principal rules.

(Amendment order XXX I) 2 Order XXXI of the principal Rules is amended-

a.   By the deletion of rule 4 and the substitution therefore of the following:

4   (1)   A trial judge shall at the scheduling, conference and before setting an action down for trial, refer the action for mediation, except for a case involving a constitutional issue, the issue, the liberty of an individual, an injunction or where the trial judge considers the case to be unsuitable for referral.

(2)   The referral order under sub-rule (1) shall be in form 28A set out in the first schedule.

(3)   The Judge shall, where mediation fails inform the parties of a trial date for hearing of the matter by way of notice of hearing.

(4)   The following interlocutory matter shall be referred to mediation in matrimonial causes:

(a)   Maintenance of spouse, children or both and property settlement; and

(b)   Application for the custody of children by a party

(b)   By the deletion of rule 5 and the substitution therefore of the following

(List of Mediators) 5 (1) The mediation officer shall keep a list of trained and certified mediators.

(2)   A mediator shall only act in the capacity of the field of specialisation or experience in respect of which that mediator is listed

(3)   A mediator shall only be listed if that mediator has five or more years of work experience in that mediator's field.

(4)   The parties to proceedings that have been referred to mediation shall be accorded an opportunity to select a mediator from the list of mediators within five days of the date of referral.

(c)   By the deletion of rules 6 and 7, and the substitution therefore of the following:
(Collection of copies of record by mediator) 6 the mediation officer or court shall provide a mediator with copies of the record of proceedings and pleadings, except that the original record and pleadings shall remain in the court registry.

7   (1)   the mediator shall, within forty-five days from the date of receiving copies of record of proceedings and pleadings mediate and conclude the matter between the parties.

(2)   The mediator shall at least five days before the intended date of mediation, inform the parties of a date, time and venue for mediation by way of a notice of mediation.

(3) the mediators shall, where the parties fail to settle the matter through mediation, refer the matter back to the referral court for the adjudication trough the mediation officer, with a brief report stating that the mediation was unsuccessful;

    (d) by the insertion, immediately after rule 7 of the following new rule:

      (Extension of time for mediation)7A. where the court considers that a mediator should be given an extension of time within which to mediate, or where the parties themselves request for an extension of time to mediate, the court shall impose a reasonable time within the matter shall be concluded.

    (e) By the deletion of rule and the substitution therefore of the following:

      (Appearance before mediator) 8. (1) the parties shall attend mediation either in person or with a legal representative.

(2) Where the party is a body corporate, state institution or entity other than an individual, a director or a senior officer of that body corporate, partnership, state institution or entity shall attend the mediation.

(3) The court shall, where the party has received notice of mediation in accordance with rule 7 fails to attend without reasonable cause, make an order as to costs from the day of the referral of the proceedings to mediation in favor of the party in attendance, despite the defaulting party being successful in the action

    (f) By the deletion of rules 10 and 11 and the substitution therefore of the following:

10. (1) A mediator, whether court appointed or appointed by the parties to the mediation, shall return the copies of the record f proceedings and the report within five days of the conclusion of the mediation to the mediation officer and shall inform the parties of such return.

    (2) A mediator shall not communicate with any trial judge about the mediation.

    (3) Statements made during mediation are confidential and privileged, and shall not be used as evidence any matter.

    (4) The record of mediation, statements made at any mediation session and any information obtained during the mediation shall not be admissible as evidence in any subsequent proceedings.

    (Filings of mediation report with mediation officer and referral of matter back to court) 11. (1) the mediator shall not more than five as after the close of the mediation proceedings, if the mediations fails, forward copies of the record to the mediation officer with a report in form 28C set out in the first schedule.

(13) Sub-rule 10 shall not affect the right of a party to make use of that party's own documents and information, except that the reference shall not be made to the mediation in connection with or related to such documents and information.

GOVERNMENT OF ZAMBIA
STATUTORY INSTRUMENT NO 28 OF 2012
THE HIGH COURT ACT
(Laws, Volume 3, Cap 27)

The High Court (Amendment) Rules, 2012

ARRANGEMENT OF RULES

Rule

PART I PRELIMINARY

1. Title
2. Interpretation

PART II ELECTRONIC FILING

3. Documents not permitted to be e-filed
4. General e-filing guidelines
5. E-filing implementation
6. Format of e-filing

7. Accepted file formats
8. Hyperlinks, bookmarks and other navigational aids
9. User ID and electronic signatures
10. File transmission, confirmation, acceptance and rejections
11. Responsibilities for filing
12. Original documents to be maintained by filing party

PART III SERVICE

13. Electronic service to other parties
14. Proof of service

PART IV GENERAL PROVISIONS

15. Public access
16. Lodged documents
17. Printing of e-filed documents
18. Certified copies
19. Payment of filing fees
20. Interruption in service
21. Court orders and judgements
22. Special instructions where rules not complied with
23. Judicial transfers outside an e-filing court
24. Fees

In exercise of the powers contained in section forty-four of the High Court Act, the following Rules are hereby made:

PART I
PRELIMINARY

1. These Rules may be cited as the High Court (Electronic Filing) Rules, 2012.
2. In these Rules, unless the context otherwise requires—

"case management system" means the system used by the Registrar and the Court to calendar, assign and track cases;

"conventionally file" means the act of filing or serving of paper documents;

"document management system" means the electronic document storage and imaging system maintained by the Registrar;

"e-filing" means electronic transmission of an original document to the Court;

"electronic service" means electronic transmission of a document to parties as required by a written law and rules of a court and as designated by the filing party;

"electronic document" means an original document filed with the Registrar in electronic format;

"filing" means the act of submitting documents, electronically or in paper form, to the Registrar for filing;

"hyperlink" means an electronic connection or reference to another place in a document, such that when selected, the user is taken to the portion of the document to which the hyperlink refers;

"ID" means a unique user identification;

"parties" means the parties related to a case, including a plaintiff and defendant or an advocate representing a plaintiff or defendant;

"PDF" means portable document format, a file format that preserves all fonts, formatting colours and graphics of any source document, regardless of the application platform used;

"Registrar" means a Registrar or Deputy Registrar appointed under section seven of the act;

"TIFF" means a Tag Image File Format, a standardized file format used to store imaged documents;

"scanned document" means an electronic image created by scanning a paper document; and

"source document" means the document as originally submitted to the Registrar for filing

PART II
ELECTRONIC FILING

3. Notwithstanding any other rules of court, the following types of documents shall be filed conventionally, unless expressly required to be filed electronically by the Court:

      (a)   any document required to be filed under the Criminal Procedure Code Act;

      (b)   documents filed under seal;

      (c)   audio recordings not expressly authorized by the Court, in writing, for filing electronically; and

      (d)   affidavits of service for conventionally served or filed documents.

4.   (1)   Where a matter requires the filing of a document, that document may be filed electronically.

     (2)   Any case participant with standing to file conventionally with the Court may file electronically in accordance with these Rules and all applicable laws and rules of Court.

     (3)   A party appearing in person may file documents using e-filing or conventional filing.

5.   All pleadings, motions, memoranda, orders and other documents electronically filed in a matter shall be maintained in electronic format by the Registrar and shall be maintained as the original and official record of the Court.

6.   (1)   A filing party shall ensure that an electronically filed document is formatted in accordance with the applicable rules governing formatting of paper documents, rules of procedure and such other formats as the Court may require:

             Provided that those formats shall not cause participants to a matter to invest significant resources in making changes to the document.

     (2)   The Registrar shall not reject a document solely for the reason that it is not in substantial conformity with a specific rule of procedure or written law.

7.   (1)   A participant may electronically transmit a document in Microsoft Word, Microsoft Works, Microsoft Excel, Rich Text Format, WordPerfect, Portable Document Format and any standard nonproprietary graphic formats.

     (2)   All documents electronically filed shall, upon acceptance and filing by the Registrar, be converted to Portable Document Format in compliance with the requirements set out in these Rules

     (3)   The Court may require a participant to produce the original of a scanned exhibit that has been filed electronically by the participant.

     (4)   Parties and other case participants shall ensure that all proposed forms of order are submitted electronically in a Microsoft Word file format.

8.   (1)   An electronically filed document may include hyperlinks, bookmarks and other electronic navigational aids for the convenience of the Court.

     (2)   A hyperlink shall not form part of the filed document.

     (3)   Each hyperlink shall contain a text reference to the target of the link.

     (4)   Notwithstanding anything contained in these Rules, a hyperlink shall not form part of the official court record and shall not be preserved in electronically filed documents submitted and stored on the Registrar's electronic document management system.

9.   (1)   The Registrar shall register every party and practitioner and provide each with a personally selected user name (ID) and password.

     (2)   The user name referred to in sub-rule (1) shall, when used in conjunction with the personally selected password, constitute a signature of the registered participant on documents submitted to the Court or by the Court.

     (3)   Notwithstanding sub-rule (2), a participant may apply an electronic signature to a document to be submitted to the Court.

     (4)   In order to ensure the intent of the filing participant, the signature line on an electronically filed document shall bear the printed name of the filing participant preceded by the symbol "/s/".

     (5)   An electronic document may be signed by the Registrar through the use of a printed signature preceded by the "/s/" symbol or through the use of the Court's e-filing Manager (EFM) application judicial signature stamp.

     (6)   The e-filing Manager (EFM) application judicial signature stamp shall be merged with the electronic document and shall be visible when the document is printed and viewed electronically.

     (7)   A document requiring the signature of a party or participant or other identifying indicators shall be filed with the court in paper format and scanned and maintained consistent with applicable record retention schedules and archival rules.

10. (1)   The Registrar shall, upon completion of the transmission of an electronic document for filing, immediately scan the document for viruses.

     (2)   Where the document transmitted under sub-rule (1) is free from infection, the document shall be deemed submitted and the Registrar shall send an acknowledgement of receipt of the document to the filing participant.

     (3)   A document which has been successfully received shall be reviewed for compliance with all standard filing practices and, if it complies with the standards, shall be accepted and deemed filed as of the date and time it was received by the Registrar's e-filing system.

(4)   Where a document is infected, the Registrar shall discard and send the document with a notice to the filing participant that the document was infected and has not been filed.

(5)   A notice under sub-rule (4) shall be sent to a filing participant or any authorized third-party facilitating entity and shall set forth the grounds for rejection.

(6)   A party whose document has been rejected may re-submit any rejected document with appropriate corrections.

(7)   A document received under sub-rule (4) shall be received subject to such review, payment of applicable fees and acceptance by the Registrar.

(8)   The Registrar shall, upon completion of the electronic filing review process, send notification of the filing's status and, if accepted, the official file date and time of the filing.

(9)   A document accepted for filing by the Registrar shall be electronically file stamped with the time and date of filing and the name of the Registrar accepting the filing, and the words "ELECTRONICALLY FILED."(10) The file stamp referred to in sub-rule (9) shall be merged with the electronic document and shall be visible when the document is printed and viewed online.

(11)   An electronically filed document that foes not bear an electronic file stamp shall be deemed to be incomplete.

(12)   An e-filing file stamped in accordance with these Rules shall have the same force and effect as documents filed in the conventional manner.

11. A participant who files a document electronically shall have the same responsibility as a person filing a document in paper format for ensuring that the document is properly filed, complete and legible and that the appropriate copies have been provided to other parties in the case.

12. (1)   Notwithstanding any other rules of court, a party who files any document electronically with the Registrar shall not submit a courtesy paper copy of the document to the Court unless ordered by the Court to do so.

(2)   Where the Act requires a pleading or affidavit to be attested or sworn to, the original signed affidavit or pleading shall be maintained by the advocate or self-represented litigant and produced in its original form within five days at the demand of another party or the Court: Provided that the original hard copy shall be maintained by the filing party.

(3)   An affidavit may be e-filed but the filing party shall maintain the signed original.

PART III
SERVICE

13. (1)   Where electronic service is available through the provided e-filing system, electronic service shall comply with all applicable court rules.

(2)   Where the e-filing system does not provide a means for electronic service, the filing party shall serve other parties with any filed process or document as would be done when filing a document conventionally.

14. (1)   Where a document has been served electronically, the document shall be deemed to have been received when it has arrived at the server for incoming communications in connection with which the user ID or signature is associated.

(2)   Where a document has been served electronically, the burden of disproving the service shall be with the served party.

PART IV
GENERAL PROVISIONS

15. (1)   The Registrar shall make electronically filed and scanned documents available to case participants, the Court and the public.

(2)   The public may access electronically filed and scanned documents of public record in the manner stipulated by the Registrar.

(3)   The Registrar shall cause to be maintained, for the purpose of facilitating retrieval of electronically maintained documents by the public, access to an electronic document management system.

16. A document required to be lodged with the Court and any draft order shall be transmitted electronically to the Court and other parties through the provided electronic filing system.

17. An electronically filed document shall be maintained in a printable format with the same content and formatting as if printed from its authoring program.

18. A certified copy of an electronically filed document shall not be obtained electronically and be issued in the conventional manner by the Registrar.

19. Where an e-filing requires a filing fee, the Registrar shall, prior to accepting an e-filed document, assess the fee and notify the filing party to make the appropriate payment.

20. (1)   The Court and Registrar shall not be liable for any malfunction or error occurring in electronic transmission or receipt of electronically filed documents.

   (2)   Notwithstanding any other Rule, where an e-filing is not filed with the Registrar by reason of an error in the transmission of the document that was unknown to the sending participant or a failure to process an electronic filing after receipt, the Court may enter an order permitting the document to be filed retrospectively to the date it was sent electronically.

21. (1)   Subject to the provisions of these Rules, the Court may issue, file and serve notices, orders and other documents electronically in an e-file case.

   (2)   Where a Registrar is required to endorse a document, the typed name of the Registrar shall be deemed to be the Registrar's signature on an electronic document.

22. (1)   The Court or the Registrar may determine, if necessary, special instructions connected with e-filing cases in the Court and shall notify the parties involved in the case through an electronic entry of any special circumstances surrounding their case.

   (2)   The Registrar or the Court shall determine if any filing deadlines may be extended as a result of the rejection of the e-filed documents.

   (3)   The Registrar may order the filing party to electronically refile any document that is not in compliance with these rules or may order the document to be filed conventionally.

23. Where a Court transfers a case previously assigned to a Court participating in e-filing to a Court that is not participating in e-filing, filing parties shall no longer be required to electronically file documents and shall file the document conventionally.

24. (1)   The filing fees applicable to a conventionally document shall apply to an electronic document.

   (2)   A document that has been electronically filed which requires to be accompanied by a fee may be rejected within two days from the date of submission of the document if payment has not been rendered.

                                                                          E. L. Sakala
Lusaka   Chief Justice
27th April, 2012

GOVERNMENT OF ZAMBIA
STATUTORY INSTRUMENT NO 69 OF 1998
The High Court Act
(Laws, Volume 3, Cap. 27)

_____

The High Court (Amendment) Rules, 2005

In exercise of the powers contained in sections 44 and 45 of the High Court Act, the following rules are made

(Title cap 27) 1 These rules may be cited as the High Court (Amendment) Rules, 1998, and shall be read as one with the High Court Rules, in these Rules referred to as the principal rules.

(Amendment Order VI) 2 Order VI of the principal Rules is amended in Rule 1 by the deletion of sub-rules (1) and (2) and the substitution of therefor of the following-

   (1)   Except as otherwise provided by any written law or these rules every action in the High court shall be commenced by Writ of Summons endorsed and accompanied by a full statement of claim.

   (2)   (2) Any matter which under any written law or these rules may be disposed of in chambers shall be commenced by an Originating Summons.

(Amendment of Order X) 3. Order X of the principal rules is amended in rule 11 by the deletion of sub-rule 3.

(Amendment of Order XI) 4 Order XI of the principal rules is amended in rule 1-
- *(a)* by the deletion of the proviso to sub-rule (1) and the substitution therefo of the following:
    Provided no appearance shall be accepted after entry of judgment in default of appearance;
- *(b)* By the insertion after sub-rule (3) of the following new sub-rule:
(4) any person served with a writ under Order VI of these rules may enter conditional appearance and apply by summons to the Court to set aside the writ on grounds that the writ is irregular or that the Court has no jurisdiction.

5. Order XII of the principal Rules is amended –

   (a) by the deletion of sub-rules (1) and (3) and the substitution therefor of the following:

      (1) where the Writ of Summons is endorsed for a liquidated demand and the defendant fails or all the defendants if more than one fail to appear, the plaintiff may enter final judgment for any sum not exceeding the sum endorsed on the writ together with interest and costs, upon an affidavit or certificate as the case may be, of due service being filed.

      (3) Where the writ is endorsed with a claim for pecuniary damages and the defendant fails, or all the defendants if more than one, fail to appear, the plaintiff may enter interlocutory Judgment and a notice of assessment shall issue to assess the /value of goods and the damages, or damages only as the case may be, in respect of the causes of action. disclosed by the statement of claim:
      Provided that the Court or a Judge may order particulars to be filed before any assessment of damages

   (b) by the insertion after sub-rule (9) of the following new sub-rule:

(10) Where the claim is endorsed with a claim for possession of any chattel and the defendant fails, or all the defendants if more than one fail to appear, the plaintiff may sign Judgment against the defendant or defendants so failing to appear for possession of the chattel.

(Revocation and replacement of Order XIX) 6 The principal Rule are amended by the revocation of Order XIX and the substitution therefore of the following:

ORDER XIX
ORDERS FOR DIRECTION

(Order for direction) (1) The Court or trial Judge shall not later than twenty-one days after appearance and defence have been filed, give directions with respect to the following matters:
- *(a)* reply and defence to counter claim, if any;
- *(b)* discovery of documents;
- *(c)* inspection of documents;
- *(d)* admissions:
- *(e)* interrogatories; and
- *(f)* place and mode of trial;
Provided that the period for doing any of these acts shall not exceed fourteen days.

(Extension of time) 2. Notwithstanding rule 1, the Court may, for sufficient reason, Extension of extend the period within which to do any of the acts specified in time rule I.

(Revocation and replacement of Order XXII) 7. The principal rules are amended by the revocation of Order XXII and the substitution therefor of the following:

ORDER XXII
SETTLEMENT OF ISSUES

(At or before hearing) 1. (1) at any time before or at the hearing, the court or a judge may if it thinks fit, proceed to ascertain and determine what are the material questions in controversy between the parties and may reduce such question into writing and settle them in the form of issue, which issues, when settled, may state questions of law on admitted facts or questions of disputed fact, or questions partly of the one kind and partly of the other

(2) The Court or a Judge may, if it or he thinks fit, direct the parties to prepare issues, and the same shall be settled by the Court or a Judge.

(3) The issues may be settled, without any previous notice, at any stage of the proceedings at which all the parties are actually present, or at the hearing. If otherwise, notice shall be given to the parties to attend at the settlement of the issue.

(4) At any time before the decision of the case, if it shall appear to the Court necessary for the purpose of determining the real question or controversy between the parties, the Court may amend the issues of frame additional issues, on such terms as it shall determine.

(Amendment of Order XXVI) 8 Order XXVI of the principal rules is amended in rule 1 by the deletion of 'fifty thousand kwacha' and the substitution therefor of 'five hundred thousand kwacha'.

(Amendment of Order XXVI) 9 Order XXVI of the principal rules is amended-.

(a) In rule 3 by the deletion of sub-rule (1) and the substitution therefor of the following.

(Mediation fee) 13. There shall be paid to the mediator in equal proportion by parties to a suit, a mediation fee in accordance with the scale that may be presented by Chief Justice.

SUPREME COURT PRACTICE DIRECTION NO 1

Reference to Authorities in Proceedings before the Supreme Court

1. The Supreme Court Rules, 1975 (S.I. No. 70 of 1975) make provision for Heads of Argument in all proceedings before the Supreme Court; in civil proceedings these are mandatory (Rule 70) and in criminal proceedings they are discretionary (Rule 35).

2. Civil Appeals, and Criminal Appeals in which the Court has called for Heads of Argument

    (i) The authorities on which the parties intend to rely having been set out in the various paragraphs of the Heads of Argument no separate list of authorities should be lodged.

    (ii) In civil cases the Heads of Argument must be lodged and copies delivered to each of the other parties to the appeal within the times set out in Rule 70. In criminal cases the periods will be specified at the time the parties are notified by the Master of the court's decision to call for Heads of Argument.

3. Criminal cases other than those dealt with under 2 above

    (i) List of authorities must be lodged in quintuplicate not less than two full working days before the time fixed for the hearing of the appeals thus, if an appeal is set down for hearing at 09:00 hours on a Tuesday the lists of authorities must be lodged with the court by no later than 09:00 hours on the previous Friday.
    (ii) Where it is desired to refer to an authority other than the All England Law Reports the list lodged shall set out the passages to which reference is intended to be made. There must be lodged also in triplicate photostatic or other suitably produced copies of the passages in question. This last requirement is to be regarded as essential.

4. The directions concerning copies of passages from authorities contained in paragraphs 3 (ii) above apply also to authorities referred to in Heads of Argument.

5.   Practice Direction No. 6 of 1972 (8th September, 1972) is hereby revoked.

BY ORDER OF THE CHIEF JUSTICE OF ZAMBIA

A.S JENGAJENGA,

MASTER OF THE SUPREME COURT OF ZAMBIA

PRACTICE DIRECTION (PD 1)

A. Taxation of Costs

In accordance with long standing practice every bill of costs for taxation by a Taxing Master should, after the general title of the section, state -

- (a)   The party whose bill is to be taxed;
- (b)   The basis of the taxation;
- (c)   Brief details of the Order directing taxation.

For example:

'Bill of Costs of the Plaintiff to be taxed as between party and party pursuant to order of dated the 19....

Plaintiff's Costs of action commenced by writ.'

Failure to comply with this rule of practice may result in an appointment being refused.

B.   Ancillary Relief in Matrimonial Causes

When an application for ancillary relief (e.g., alimony pending suit, maintenance for a wife and for children of the family) has been duly made to the Court, the following is the appropriate procedure in order to have such application heard by the Registrar:

When the pleadings (i.e., the affidavits of means of the parties) are completed, or the time for delivering them has expired, an appointment with the Registrar is applied for (unless the matter has been, or is being dealt with by the judge at the hearing) see rules 68 to 85 of the Matrimonial Causes Rules, 1973. A form for obtaining an appointment can be obtained from the Civil Registry.

When an appointment has been obtained, notice of the date and time of that appointment must be given forthwith by the party obtaining the same to the other party or parties to be heard.

On this appointment (or after any adjournment) the order is made either by consent or after investigation.

If no answering affidavit has been filed, the wife's solicitor must bring affidavit evidence as to the means of both the husband and the wife, and if no appearance has been entered, the completed form of acknowledgement of service, or if none, an affidavit of service of the notice of application for ancillary relief, or of the petition, if the claim for alimony was included therein, will be required.

By direction of the Chief Justice.

26th September, 1960
Deputy Registrar

PRACTICE DIRECTION (PD 2)

Petitions for Winding up of Companies

The attention of Practitioners is drawn to the following practice procedure to be adopted when presenting a petition for the winding up of a company:

1. The petition shall include in the prayer a request for the appointment of a named person as an official liquidator or provisional liquidator and for a determination by the Court as to whether and if so what security he should give.

2. An affidavit of fitness of the proposed liquidator and his written consent to act as liquidator should either be filed when the petition is presented or produced in Court.

Dated at Lusaka this 11th day of October, 1960.

BY ORDER OF THE CHIEF JUSTICE.
Deputy Registrar

PRACTICE DIRECTION (PD 3)

Application to Review a Taxing Master's Decision

The attention of all practitioners is drawn to the following practice and procedure to be adopted with effect from the 22nd December, 1960, when applying to a judge to review a taxing master's decision:

1. Every application under Order XXXIV, Rule 2.C.[21] of the High Court Rules to review a taxing master's decision in respect of the taxation of a bill of costs shall be made to a Judge by summons to be served within three days after issue and returnable on a day to be appointed by the Judge.

2. Every summons must contain full particulars of the item or items or the amount allowed in respect of which the application to review is made.

3. After the issue of the summons the party applying shall forthwith give notice thereof to the taxing master and on receipt of such notice the taxing master shall lodge with the Deputy Assistant Registrar attached to the Judge the bill of costs, and the objections and answers made and given by the parties respectively at the review of the taxation of the bill of costs by the taxing master.

4. Each party shall within four days after service of the summons lodge with the said Deputy Assistant Registrar the documents produced in evidence by that party at the hearing before the taxing master relating to the matter under review; and the Deputy Assistant Registrar shall then deliver these documents and the summons, objections and answers mentioned in paragraph (3 to the Judge.

5. The Judge shall appoint a day for the hearing of the summons and the Deputy Assistant Registrar shall give to each of the parties notice of the day appointed by the Judge for the hearing of the summons.

Dated at Lusaka this 28th day of November, 1960

BY ORDER OF THE CHIEF JUSTICE.
Deputy Registrar

---

[21] It is to be noted that while the PD as formulated made reference to Order XXXIV (34) Rule 2C, HCR., the law has since been amended and presently, provision for review of the Taxing Masters decision is made under Order XL (40) HCR.

PRACTICE NOTE (PD 4)

Probate, Divorce and Admiralty Division

Ancillary Relief: Discharge of Magistrates' Orders

Where there is in force a matrimonial order or an interim Order of a Magistrates' court for maintenance of the wife and/or the children, and application is made to the Divorce Division of the High Court for an order for maintenance of the wife and/or the children, a copy of the order of the magistrates' court should be lodged in the Registry by the applicant prior to the hearing of the application.

KENNETH MOORE,

Senior Registrar

1st December, 1961

Principal Probate Registry

PRACTICE DIRECTION (PD 5)

Amendment of Documents - Civil Causes or matters
Including Divorce

The Chief Justice has requested that the attention of all practitioners is drawn to Direction 15 of the Masters' Practice Directions (paragraph 916 of the 1976 Edition of the Supreme Court Practice, Volume 2) which is to be strictly adhered to in future and which will apply to all documents requiring amendment.

It should be noted that where any lengthy clause is required to be deleted from a document an exact copy of the document should be filed showing the words neatly ruled through in ink of the required colour. This document should be endorsed with the words 'Re-issued on amendments this day of 19   '. If leave to amend has been obtained the following words should also be added 'pursuant to order of the

Dated the   day of 19   '.

Deputy Registrar

PRACTICE DIRECTION (PD 6)

Summons for Direction

On the hearing of a Summons for Directions under Order XVII, Rule 1 of the High Court Rules, Registrars will, in future, give all necessary directions in respect of all proceedings to be taken in the action including the fixing of the mode and place of trial.[22]

It will be noted that it is a mandatory requirement of Order XXVIII, Rule 3 (1), that every order, made in an action commenced by Summons and which provides for the mode of trial, must fix the period within which

---

[22] This rule no longer applies because Summons for Directions are presently issued pursuant to Order 25 of the RSC. Further, SI 58 of 2020 captured above, amends Order 19 of the HCR such that the Judge (not the Registrar) will call for a scheduling conference within 30 days after filing of the Defence wherein an order for directions will be issued (in the case of the general list); In terms of procedure in Civil matters that come before the Commercial Division of the High Court, Order 53 Rule 7 HCR provides, as regards this point, that the judge (not the Registrar) will call for Scheduling Conference wherein an Order for Directions will be issued in consultation with the parties.

the action is to be set down for trial. Registrars will therefore include in such orders a direction that the action be set down within six weeks of the close of pleadings.

In order to comply with the provisions of Order XXVIII, Rule 3 (3), practitioners will be required on the hearing of the Summons for Direction to give a rough estimation of the length of trial. This will then be included in the order made on the summons.

BY ORDER OF THE CHIEF JUSTICE.

Deputy Registrar

5th February, 1963

PRACTICE DIRECTION (PD 7)

Decree Absolute - Expedition

Wherever it is possible, there should be an application to expedite a hearing of the suit in preference to an application at or after the trial to expedite the decree absolute.

Where nevertheless an application to expedite a decree absolute is necessary, it should normally be made to the Trial Judge, at the hearing of the suit. The practitioner (or respondent as the case may be) should then have available all such evidence (including where appropriate a medical certificate as to the expected date of birth of a child) as is necessary to enable the Judge to rule whether the decree absolute should be expedited. If some matter arises after the decree nisi making it desirable that the decree absolute should be expedited, a party may apply to a Judge in Chambers for an order to that effect or for directions. The practice of referring cases to the Queen's Proctor will not in future be followed, unless the Judge specifically directs.

Registrar,

November, 1964

Probate, Divorce and Admiralty Division

PRACTICE DIRECTION (PD 8)

Payment Out of Funds Held in Court on Trust

The attention of all practitioners is drawn to the informal procedure available in the High Court whereby an application for the withdrawal of funds held in trust by the High Court for the benefits of an infant beneficiary, for the payment of education fees, clothing expenses, etc., may be made by letter addressed by the parent or guardian of the infant to the Registrar setting out the requirements. If the application is approved, the Registrar will then seal and sign an order by the High Court authorising the payment out of court applied for. The order will be filed on the case record.

1. In certain cases, where the Registrar requires information on oath as to the needs of the parent or guardian, it may be necessary for the application to be accompanied by an affidavit of means, but the Registrar will normally advise the applicant on the type of affidavit required.

2. Whenever an infant beneficiary attains full age and wishes to withdraw the trust funds, application therefore must be made by affidavit and the Registrar will again advise on the appropriate form of affidavit to be used.

3. The procedure set out above, which is in accordance with the practice in England (see 1965 Annual Practice, page 1950-Practice-Infants and Widows') will be followed in every case in which it is applicable. *

BY ORDER OF THE CHIEF JUSTICE

Deputy Registrar

*Now appearing on page 1147 of the 1970 Edition of the Supreme Court Practice, Volume 1 (O.80/12/6).

10th August, 1965

PRACTICE DIRECTION (PD 9)

Order XIII: Summonses in the Michaelmas
Christmas Vacation

Some doubt appears to exist as to whether or not Order XIII Summonses can be issued and heard in the Michaelmas and Christmas Vacations.

The High Court Rules make no specific provision either way, but Order XIII Rule 3, dealing with cases under Order XIII where conditional or unconditional leave is given to defend, specifically empowers the court or a judge to give orders for directions for the further conduct of the action, and to order the action to be forthwith set down for trial; and by Order XLIX, Rule 3 (3), it is provided that where the court or a judge dealing with an application under Order XIII, Rule 3, is satisfied that there is urgent need for the trial of the action during the next Michaelmas or Christmas Vacation, an order may be made that the trial shall take place in the vacation. By inference, and a fortiori, an Order XIII Summons may be issued in the Michaelmas or Christmas Vacations, and if leave to defend is not given the court or a Judge may make an order empowering the Plaintiff to enter judgment in accordance with Order XIII, Rule 1.

Orders XIII and XLIX are modelled on the provisions of the Rules of the Supreme Court, Orders 14 and 63 respectively. Reference to the notes to *R.S.C., O.63, r. 4, appearing at page 1812 of the 1966 Annual Practice, makes it clear that in England a Summons for judgment under Order 14 may be issued in the Long Vacation.

This Practice Direction may be cited as authority for the issue and disposal of H.C.R., O.XIII Summonses under Rule 1 of that Order during the Michaelmas and Christmas Vacations.

Dated at Lusaka this 24th day of September, 1966.

BY DIRECTION OF THE CHIEF JUSTICE.

Registrar

*Now appearing on page 1052 of the 1976 Edition of the Supreme Court Practice, Volume 1 (O.64/4).

PRACTICE DIRECTION (PD 10)

High Court Summons and Application

To simplify procedure, to save time, and in particular to avoid any inordinate delay, as is sometimes occasioned by heavy Registrar's Chamber hearings, the Chief Justice has approved the institution of 'Consent Summons'.

In future when there is no opposition to a Summons, or Application, of any nature, which is normally dealt with at Chambers by a Judge, Registrar or Assistant Registrar, the following practice will be observed:

1. The Summons, or Application, will be drawn and filed as normal, duly franked with the appropriate Court Fee, or Fees, and will accompanied by any necessary documents in support, also suitably franked

2. A 'Consent Order' will also be drawn and filed, but such Order must be endorsed-upon all copies filed-with the written, signed and dated consent of the opposing party. Such consent, when filed, must be franked with the appropriate Court Fee or Fees.

3. The return day of the Summons, or Application, will be left blank, or deleted, as the case may be.

4. The matter will be placed before a Judge, Registrar or Assistant Registrar, empowered to deal with the Summons, or application, who will signify his assent to the Order and same will be issued.

5. If a Judge, Registrar or Assistant Registrar, as the case may be, refuses to give his assent to the 'Consent Order', the Summons, or Application, will be given a return date for hearing.

The foregoing may be extended to Bills for taxation where the opposing party does not dispute any of the items therein. In such cases the 'Consent' must be endorsed-as in 2 above-at the foot of the last folio of the bill, and after the bill has been totalled, etc.

Practice Direction dated 8th December, 1966, is hereby revoked.

Dated at Lusaka this 12th day of January, 1968.

BY ORDER OF THE CHIEF JUSTICE.

Acting Registrar of the High Court

PRACTICE DIRECTION (PD 11)[23]

Ex Parte Applications

The attention of practitioners is invited to the following practice and procedure to be adopted when issuing ex parte applications:

1. All Ex Parte applications which would, if made in England, be made to be the Queen' Bench Division, shall be made in accordance with the practice and procedure at present in force in England (see Supreme Court Practice, 1967, Volume 1-Order 32, Rules 1-6)*.

2. The affidavit of facts, etc., supporting the application (be it to a Judge at Chambers or to a Registrar), shall be left with the Assistant Registrar (Civil), or in his absence with the Officer in Charge of the Principal Civil or District Registry in which the action is proceeding. There will be no need for the applicant to attend unless a Judge or Registrar otherwise directs.

3. The Judge's or Registrar's, decision will be endorsed on the affidavit and the applicant shall draw up the requisite Order, unless a formal Order is not required.

4. Where circumstances require it to be so, the Judge, or Registrar, may direct that a Summons be Issued.

Practice Direction dated 14th November, 1960 and appearing at page 73 of the Selected Judgments of Northern Rhodesia, 1960, is hereby revoked.

Dated at Lusaka this 12th day of January, 1968.

BY ORDER OF THE CHIEF JUSTICE.

Acting Registrar of the High Court

---

[23] 1968. It must be noted that Supreme Court directions mentioned in this PD have been repealed and replaced by relevant parts of the RSC, 1965, (White-Book) 1999 edition.

*Now Supreme Court Practice, 1976, Volume 1. Page 500-505.

PRACTICE DIRECTION (PD 12)[24]

Setting Down for Trial

To avoid the necessity for the attendance of Legal Practitioners in Court merely to fix the date of trial of any cause, or matter, the following practice will take effect from the first day of Hilary Sittings 1969, and will be strictly enforced by the Court.

A legal Practitioner when filing the Pleadings in accordance with Order 28, Rule 4 of the High Court Rules will also file a certificate, signed by the Legal Practitioners for all the parties, certifying that certain stated dates are suitable to the parties involved for the trial of the action. The certificate will also indicate an appropriate estimate of the expected length of the trial.

The Court will then allocate a date, or dates, for the trial, and notify the parties by the issue of a Notice of Hearing.

In the event of the Legal Practitioners not being able to agree upon a date or dates, the Court must be so notified and the Court will then allocate a date, or dates, for the trial and the parties will be notified as aforementioned.

If it becomes necessary for a date, or dates, as allocated by the Court to be varied the Legal Practitioner so requiring the variation must apply, to the Judge seized of the action, by way of a Notice of Motion.

Practice Direction dated 17th September, 1966, appearing on page 48 of the Legal Directory and Legal Calendar 1979, is revoked.

Practice Direction dated 25th February, 1963, appearing on page 35 of the Legal Directory and Legal Calendar 1968, is amended by the deletion of the final sentence on paragraph 3*.

Dated at Lusaka this 2nd day of January, 1969.

BY ORDER OF THE CHIEF JUSTICE

Registrar of the High Court

*Now appearing on page 48 of this Edition.

PRACTICE DIRECTION (PD 13)

Writs of *Fieri Facias*

The attention of practitioners is invited to the following practice and procedure to be applied when issuing execution.

1.   Warrants on Writs of Fieri Facias are no longer necessary.

2.   The Under Sheriff has power to act upon the Writ of Fieri Facias alone.

Dated at Lusaka this 3rd day of September, 1968.

---

[24] 1969. This practice direction is now conducted in line with the Scheduling Conference provisions: See O19 R 3(1) and O5 (1) of SI No 58 of 2020.

BY ORDER OF THE CHIEF JUSTICE.

Deputy Registrar

PRACTICE DIRECTION (PD 14)[25]

List of Authorities to be Referred to

In High Court Proceedings, either in Court or in Chambers, practitioners should, in all cases, furnish the Judge, Deputy Registrar or District Registrar who will hear the proceedings, with lists of the authorities to which they propose to refer.

Such lists should clearly specify any passage or passages to which reference will be made at the hearing.

Such lists must be delivered to the Judge's Marshal, or the Secretary to the Deputy Registrar or District Registrar, not later than two clear days before the date set down for the hearing of the proceeding.

Practitioners are reminded that failure to lodge lists within the time specified may possibly serve to protract proceedings.

Practice Direction No 1 of 1970 dated the 17th day of March, 1970, is hereby revoked.

Dated at Lusaka this 12th day May, 1971.

BY ORDER OF THE CHIEF JUSTICE.

B.P. CULLINAN,

Registrar of the High Court

PRACTICE DIRECTION No OF 1975 (PD 15)

Right of Audience of Unqualified Persons in the High Court and Subordinate Courts

It is hereby notified for the information and guidance of practitioners that the right of audience of unqualified persons other than litigants in person, shall be as follows:

(a)   Registrars and Magistrates in Chambers

Such unqualified persons, whose names have been sent to the Court by a practitioner in accordance with section 54 © of the Legal Practitioners Act (No 22 of 1973), as the Chief Justice, after such consultation with the Law Association of Zambia (hereinafter called the Law Association) as he may deem necessary, may approve, to appear before the Registrar, the Deputy Registrar, a District Registrar, or an Assistant Registrar, and all Magistrates in Chambers.

(b)   Judges of the High Court in Chambers

Such unqualified persons who are lawyers as described in Section 11B (a) of the Legal Practitioners Act, or who are qualified persons within the definition contained in Section 3 (4) (b) of the Legal Practitioners Act, as the Chief Justice, after such consultation with the Law Association as he may deem necessary, may approve.

Intending applicants under (a) and/or (b) must be members of the Law Association, and should in the first instance address their application by way of informal letter (giving details of educational qualifications and

---

[25] 1970. Suffice it to say that SI 58 of 2020 somewhat repeals and replaces this PD: See O30 R 3a(1).

professional experience) to the Deputy Registrar for onward transmission to the Chief Justice.

Dated at Lusaka this 13th day of August, 1975.

BY ORDER OF THE CHIEF JUSTICE.

MWAMBA

Registrar

PRACTICE DIRECTION No 2 OF 1975 (PD 16)

Matrimonial Causes Act, 1973

1.   Attention is drawn to subsections (1) and (4) of section 41 of the above Act in relation to Orders of the Court.

2.   Subsection (1) reads:

'The Court shall not make absolute a decree of divorce or of nullity of marriage, or make a decree of judicial separation, unless the court, by order, has declared that it is satisfied-

   (a)   That for the purposes of this section there are no children of the family to whom this section applies; or

   (b)   That the only children who are or may be children of the family to whom this section applies are the children named in the order and that-

      (i)   Arrangements for the welfare of every child so named have been made and are satisfactory or are the best that can be devised in the circumstances; or

      (ii)   It is impracticable for the party or parties appearing before the court to make any such arrangements; or

   (c)   That there are circumstances making it desirable that the decree should be made absolute or should be made, as the case may be without delay notwithstanding that there are or may be children of the family to whom this section applies and that the court is unable to make a declaration in accordance with paragraph (b) above.

The Court must by Order make the particular declaration accordingly whether there are children of the family or not.

3.   The Order must be drawn up in the usual way in terms of Rule 51 of the Matrimonial Causes Rules, 1973. If the judge has made the necessary declaration at the hearing in open court, then such declaration should be included in the decree nisi. If, on the other hand, the matters falling within the ambit of section 41 of the Matrimonial Causes Act, 1973, have been adjourned to Chambers, then the order made by the Judges in Chambers must be the subject of a separate order formally drawn up in the usual way,

4.   Without such formal order, either included in the decree nisi or as a separate order, the decree cannot be made absolute.

Practice Direction No. 1 of 1973 dated and 18th day of June, 1973, is revoked.

Dated at Lusaka this 4th day of December, 1975.

BY ORDER OF THE CHIEF JUSTICE

KENNETH MOORE,

Acting Registrar of the High Court

PRACTICE DIRECTION No 3 OF 1975 (PD 17)

Applications for Transfer of Causes or Matters under the Provisions
of Section 24 of the High Court Act, Cap. 50

The attention of practitioners is drawn to the following procedure to be adopted when desiring to make an ex parte application for the transfer of a cause or matter in accordance with the provisions of section 24 of the High Court Act, Cap. 50.

Ex Parte Applications

1. An affidavit in support of the application must be filed in accordance with the provisions of the Practice Direction PD. 11 dated the 12th day of January, 1968, and the procedure set out therein is to be followed in respect of applications the subject of this practice direction.

2. The affidavit in support of such application shall, in addition to complying with Order V, Part III of the High Court Rules state:

   (i) The reason why the transfer is required;
   (ii) The present address of the defendant
   (iii) The Court to which it is desired that the Cause or Matter be transferred;
   (iv) The reason why it is alleged that the particular Court to which it is desired to transfer the cause or matter is a suitable Court.

3. Nothing contained in this practice direction shall affect the practice procedure set out in the Practice Direction PD. 11dated the 12th day of January, 1968, referred to in paragraph 1 hereof, except with regard to an application for transfer made under section 24 of the High Court Act, Cap. 50.

Applications on Summons

4. Any affidavit filed in support of an application under S. 24 not made ex parte, shall comply with paragraph 2 above.

Practice Direction PD. 3 dated the 15th day of November, 1960, is revoked.

Dated at Lusaka this 4th day of December, 1975.

BY ORDER OF THE CHIEF JUSTICE

Acting Deputy Registrar of the High Court

PRACTICE DIRECTION No 2 OF 1977 (PD 18)

Right of Audience of Unqualified Persons in the High Court and
Subordinate Courts

It is hereby notified for the information and guidance of practitioners and other interested persons that the right of audience of unqualified persons other than litigants in person, shall be as follows:

(a) Registrar of the High Court and Magistrates in Chambers

Such unqualified persons, whose names have been sent to the Court by practitioner in accordance with section 54 of the Legal Practitioners Act (No 22 of 1973), as the Chief Justice may approve after such consultation with the Law Association of Zambia (hereinafter called the Law Association) as he may deem necessary.

The term 'Registrar' shall include the Deputy Registrar, a District Registrar or an Assistant Registrar.

(b) Judges of the High Court in Chambers

Such unqualified persons who are qualified lawyers in terms of section 11B (a) of the Legal Practitioners Act (No 22 of 1973), as the Chief Justice may approve after such consultation with the Law Association as he may deem necessary.

Any unqualified person who has been granted the right of audience under paragraph (b) above will automatically have the right of audience under paragraph (a).

The words 'unqualified person' in this direction shall have the same meaning as in the Legal Practitioners Act (No 22 of 1973).

Intending applicants must be members of the Law Association and should in the first instance address their application by way of informal letter (giving details of educational qualifications and professional experience) to the Deputy Registrar for transmission to the Chief Justice.

Practice Direction No 1 of 1975 is hereby revoked

Dated at Lusaka this 15th day of June, 1977.

BY ORDER OF THE CHIEF JUSTICE

WIJESEKERA,

Acting Deputy Registrar of the High Court

PRACTICE DIRECTION No 3 of 1977 (PD 19)

Court Dress in the Supreme Court, High Court and Subordinate
Court

The Honourable the Acting Chief Justice has directed that Court dress for Advocates in the Supreme Court, High Court and Subordinate Courts shall be as follows:

(a) The Supreme Court and High Court

(i) Female Advocates

A black gown, white, blue-striped or red-striped long sleeved collarless blouse, a stiff white wing collar and white bands, black, navy blue or dark grey skirt with a matching coat when desired

With the exception of State Counsel it shall not be compulsory to wear wigs.

(ii) Male Advocates

A black gown, dark or dark-striped long trousers and jacket, a white, blue-striped or red-striped collarless shirt, a stiff white wing collar and white bands.

With the exception of State Counsel it shall not be compulsory to wear wigs.

(b) The Subordinate Courts

(i)   Female Advocates

Any neat costume of decent and reasonable length.

(ii) Male Advocates

A suit or jacket and long trousers worn with a shirt and tie or a safari suit with cravat.

(c)   In either (a) or (b) above the attire should be smart.

(d)   Practice Direction No. 1 of 1977 dated 28th March, 1977, is hereby revoked.

By direction of the Acting Chief Justice.

Dated at Lusaka at this 18th day of August, 1977.

J. N. KAKAD

Acting Registrar of the High Court

PRACTICE DIRECTION NO 4 OF 1977 (PD 20)

Times within which appearance must be entered on Court Writs

It is hereby notified for the information and guidance of practitioners, the Registrar, District Registrar and Assistant Registrars that the time within which appearance must be entered on Court Writs shall be as follows:-

1.   Where a Writ is to be served at a place less than 100 kilometers from the issuing Registry, the time within which an appearance must be entered shall be fourteen days.

2.   Where a Writ is to be served at a place which is 100 kilometers or more from the issuing Registry but less than 500 kilometers, the time within which an appearance must be entered shall be twenty-one days.

3.   Where a Writ is to be served at a place which is 500 kilometers or more from the issuing Registry, the time within which an appearance must be entered shall be thirty days.

4.   Where a Writ or notice of such Writ is to be served out of the jurisdiction pursuant to Order X, rule 15, of the High Court Rules, Cap. 50, the time within which an appearance must be entered shall be forty-two days.

5.   The Registrar, or District Registrar may, for good cause shown, extend any of the above periods in cases where particular hardship is likely to be caused to a defendant by strict adherence to the period,

6.   The foregoing provisions shall not affect the rights of the State under section 22 of the State Proceedings Act, Cap. 92.

Dated at Lusaka this 15th day of November, 1977.

Gates on Evidence: Zambian Theory and Practice

BY ORDER OF THE CHIEF JUSTICE.

Deputy Registrar

PRACTICE DIRECTION NO 1 OF 1979 (PD 21)

RE: Appeals from assessment of damages by a Registrar
Or Deputy Registrar

IT IS HEREBY NOTIFIED that all appeals from assessments of damages by Registrar or Deputy Registrar shall lie direct to the Supreme Court.

Dated at Lusaka this 3rd day May, 1979.

BY ORDER OF THE CHIEF JUSTICE

SIMUZIYA,

Acting Registrar of the High Court

SUPREME COURT PRACTICE DIRECTION NO 1 OF 1984

Record of Proceedings - Criminal Cases

1. When preparing records for submission to the High Court as a result of an appeal from a Subordinate Court Judgment or order, or after a committal by a Subordinate Court for sentence (sections 217, 218 and 323 of the Criminal Procedure Code), such records are to be typed upon stencils. The requisite number of copies of the record required by the High Court must then be duplicated, bound and forwarded to the High Court with the stencils. Copies must also be supplied to the appellants (Judicial Circular No. 8 of 1966) and to the Director of Public Prosecutions or Senior State Advocate at Ndola.

2. The attention of Subordinate Courts typing staff is to be drawn to the Supreme Court of Zambia Rules, 1975, rules 10 and 31 (3) (a). The records must be typed and prepared as far as is possible in conformity with those Rules.

3. In the event of an appeal from the High Court to the Supreme Court arising from the hearing before the High Court the only additional stencils to be typed, i.e., additional to those typed by the Subordinate Court and forwarded to the High Court, will be of the proceedings and judgment of the High Court and such forms etc. required under the Supreme Court of Zambia Rules, 1975. The High Court is to undertake the typing of those additional stencils. The index to the record will also need to be amended.

4. Subordinate Courts should therefore take immediate steps to obtain an adequate stock of stencils and duplicating paper to implement this direction resorting to local purchase if necessary.

5. In the event of the Subordinate Court not having facilities available for duplicating, the stencils, after checking and certification, must be forwarded to the High Court which will undertake the task of duplicating for its own use and the distribution as set out in paragraph (1) above. A copy must be returned to the Subordinate Court for their records.

Civil Cases

6. (i) The record of appeal shall be prepared by the appellant, or by his legal presentative if he has one.

(ii) If the appellant is not represented, the Registrar of the High Court upon request by such appellant shall prepare the record and distribute a copy thereof to every party to the appeal (Rule 58 (6).

7. (i) The record shall be prepared in conformity with Rules 10 and 58 (4)

(a) of the Supreme Court of Zambia Rules.

(ii) The master may reject a record at the time of lodging the appeal if the record does not conform to the requirements of the Rules. It is therefore, advisable for the appellant to lodge five copies of the record at least three days before the expiry of the time allowed within which to lodge the appeal, to enable the Master to check the record.

8. Practice Direction No. 2 of 1975 dated the 31st July, 1975 is hereby revoked.

Dated at Lusaka this 23rd day of February, 1984.
BY ORDER OF THE CHIEF JUSTICE OF ZAMBIA,

SIMPUTE

Acting Master of the Supreme Court of Zambia

PRACTICE DIRECTION (1963-1964) Z AND NRLR 23

Petitions on matrimonial causes

Flynote

Practice - applications for ancillary relief - Applications for maintenance of children agreements between the parties - Matrimonial Causes Act, 1963, section 4 (2) and (3) - Matrimonial Causes (Amendment No. 2) Rules, 1963.

Headnote

The Practice Direction dated 7th August, 1963 (which dealt with applications for ancillary relief and for maintenance of children) was based upon Hodge v Hodge [1963] 1 All ER 358 and Bancroft v Bancroft [1963] 1 All ER 367. These decisions are no longer good law, by virtue of subsections (2) and (3) of section 4 of the Matrimonial Causes Act, 1963. That Practice Direction is therefore revoked, although any orders for ancillary relief made between the date of those decisions and the amendment of the Act are preserved in force.

2. The attention of practitioners is also drawn to the provisions of the Matrimonial Causes (Amendment No. 2) Rules, 1963, dealing with applications to the court to take into consideration an agreement or arrangement, made or proposed to be made, between the parties in relation to the proceedings and to give such directions in the matter as the court thinks fit. Under the rules the application is to be made to a judge and must, if made before the presentation of the petition, be made by originating summons. An application made before the institution of the proceedings must be disclosed in the petition.

Dated at Lusaka this 22nd day of January, 1964.

By Order of the Chief Justice.

F. MALLON
Deputy Registrar

PRACTICE DIRECTION (1963-1964) Z AND NRLR 71

Practice in matrimonial causes

Flynote

Practice - collusion a discretionary bar only - Matrimonial Causes Act, 1950, section 4 (2) as amended by the Matrimonial Clauses Act, 1963, section 4 (1) - principles on which court will exercise discretion - role of counsel.

Headnote

The attention of practitioners is drawn to the decision in the case of Head (formerly Cox) v Cox (Smith cited) [1964] 2. Weekly Law Reports, page 358.

2. This is the first case in England under section 4 (2) of the Matrimonial Causes Act, 1950, as amended by section 4 (1) of the Matrimonial Causes Act, 1963, the effect of which is that collusion has been removed from the category of absolute bars to the jurisdiction of the court to grant a decree for the dissolution of marriage, and placed in the category of discretionary bars.

3. The above decision sets out the principles upon which the court will exercise its discretion, and indicates the practice which should be followed. In particular, it will be noted that counsel immediately informed the court of the terms of the collusive agreement at the commencement of the hearing.

Dated at Lusaka this 2nd day of April, 1964.

By order of the Chief Justice.

F. MALLON
Acting Registrar

PRACTICE DIRECTION (1963-1964) Z AND NRLR 13 (HC)

Right of audience of unqualified persons in the high court

Flynote

Unqualified persons - appearance before judge in chambers - appearance before registrars - section 34A (c) of the Legal Practitioners Ordinance, Cap. [30].

Headnote

It is hereby notified for the information and guidance of practitioners that the right of audience of unqualified persons, other than litigants in person, in the High Court shall be as follows:
  (a) No unqualified person may appear before a judge in chambers.
  (b) Such unqualified persons, whose names have been sent to the Court by a practitioner in accordance with section 34A (c) of the Legal Practitioners Ordinance, as the Chief Justice, having consulted the Law Society, may approve, to appear before the registrar, the deputy registrar, a district registrar or an assistant registrar.

Dated at Lusaka this 30th day of December, 1963.
                    By Order of the Chief Justice.
                    F. MALON
                    Deputy Registrar

INDEX

Made in the USA
Columbia, SC
23 October 2024

44592410R00393